COMPLETE HOCKEY BOOK

1990-91 EDITION

Editor
LARRY WIGGE

Compiled by
FRANK POLNASZEK, BARRY SIEGEL

Contributing Editors
**CRAIG CARTER, TOM DIENHART
DAVE SLOAN, RON SMITH
STEVE ZESCH**

President-Chief Executive Officer
THOMAS G. OSENTON

Director, Specialized Publications
GARY LEVY

Published by

The Sporting News

1212 North Lindbergh Boulevard
P.O. Box 56 — St. Louis, MO 63166

Copyright © 1990
The Sporting News Publishing Company

 A Times Mirror
Company

ISBN 0-89204-367-9   ISSN 0278-4955

TABLE OF CONTENTS

NATIONAL HOCKEY LEAGUE

(Organized November 22, 1917)

Montreal Office
Sun Life Building
1155 Metcalfe Street, Suite 960
Montreal, Que., Canada H3B 2W2
Phone—(514) 871-9220
FAX—(514) 871-1663

New York Office
650 Fifth Avenue
33rd Floor
New York, NY 10019
Phone—(212) 398-1100
FAX—(212) 245-8221

Toronto Office
Central Scouting & Officiating
Suite 200, 1 Greensboro Drive
Rexdale, Ont. M9W 1C8
Phone—(416) 245-2926

Chairman of the Board
WILLIAM W. WIRTZ
President
JOHN A. ZIEGLER, JR.
Vice-Chairman
RONALD COREY

Secretary
ROBERT O. SWADOS
Executive Vice-President
BRIAN F. O'NEILL
Vice-President and General Counsel
GILBERT STEIN

John A. Ziegler, Jr.

Vice-President, Project Development
IAN "SCOTTY" MORRISON
Vice-President, Finance
KENNETH G. SAWYER
Vice-President, Hockey Operations
JIM GREGORY

Vice-President, Broadcasting
JOEL NIXON
Vice-President, Marketing-Public Relations
STEVE RYAN

Special Assistant to the President
Darcy Rota
Director of Central Scouting
Frank Bonello
Director of Central Registry
Garry Lovegrove
Director of Officiating
Bryan Lewis
Assistant Director of Officiating
Wally Harris
Executive Director of Communications
Gary Meagher (Montreal)
Director of Public Relations
Gerry Helper (New York)
Director of Broadcasting and Publishing
Stu Hackel
Supervisors of Officials
John Ashley, Matt Pavelich, Jim Christison,
John D'Amico
Coordinator of Development
Will Norris
Director of Administration
Phil Scheuer
Director of Security
Frank Torpey
Assistant Director of Security
Al Wiseman

1990-91

CAMPBELL CONFERENCE		PRINCE OF WALES CONFERENCE	
Smythe Division	**Norris Division**	**Patrick Division**	**Adams Division**
Calgary Flames	Chicago Blackhawks	New Jersey Devils	Boston Bruins
Edmonton Oilers	Detroit Red Wings	New York Islanders	Buffalo Sabres
Los Angeles Kings	Minnesota North Stars	New York Rangers	Hartford Whalers
Vancouver Canucks	St. Louis Blues	Philadelphia Flyers	Montreal Canadiens
Winnipeg Jets	Toronto Maple Leafs	Pittsburgh Penguins	Quebec Nordiques
		Washington Capitals	

BOARD OF GOVERNORS

Boston
Jeremy M. Jacobs

Buffalo
Seymour H. Knox. III

Calgary
Cliff Fletcher

Chicago
William W. Wirtz

Detroit
Michael Ilitch

Edmonton
Peter Pocklington

Hartford
Richard H. Gordon

Los Angeles
Bruce McNall

Minnesota
Norman N. Green

Montreal
Ronald Corey

New Jersey
John J. McMullen

N.Y. Islanders
John O. Pickett, Jr.

N.Y. Rangers
Richard H. Evans

Philadelphia
Jay T. Snider

Pittsburgh
Marie Denise DeBartolo York

Quebec
Marcel Aubut

St. Louis
Michael F. Shanahan

Toronto
Donald P. Giffin

Vancouver
Arthur R. Griffiths

Washington
Abe Pollin

Winnipeg
Barry L. Shenkarow

Cam Neely scored 55 goals in 1989-90 to become only the second Boston player in 15 years to score at least 50 goals in a season.

Andy Moog has a lower goals against average in play-off competition (2.87) than he does during regular-season play (3.44).

Ray Bourque has won the Norris Trophy as the NHL's best defenseman three times in the last four years.

Glen Wesley scored nine goals in 1989-90 for Boston but four of them were game-winners.

BOSTON BRUINS

CLUB DIRECTORY

Owner and Governor
Jeremy M. Jacobs
Alternative Governor
Louis Jacobs
Alternate Governor, President and General Manager
Harry Sinden
Vice President
Tom Johnson
Assistant to the President
Nate Greenberg
Director of Administration
Dale Hamilton
Assistant General Manager and Coach
Mike Milbury
Assistant Coaches
Gordie Clark, Ted Sator
Goaltending Coach
Joe Bertagna
Coordinator of Minor League Player Personnel/Scouting
Bob Tindall
Director of Player Evaluation
Bart Bradley

Scouting Staff
Jim Morrison, Andre Lachapelle, Joe Lyons, Don Saatzer, Lars Waldner, Marcel Pelletier, Jean Ratelle
Controller
John J. Dionne
Trainer
Jim Narrigan
Equipment Manager
Ken Fleger
Director of Media Relations
Heidi Holland
Home Ice
Boston Garden
Address
150 Causeway Street, Boston, Mass. 02114
Seating Capacity
14,448
Club Colors
Gold, Black and White
Phone
(617) 227-3206
FAX
(617) 523-7184

YEAR-BY-YEAR RESULTS

Season	W.	L.	T.	Pts.	Position	Season	W.	L.	T.	Pts.	Position
1924-25	6	24	0	12	Sixth	1958-59	32	29	9	73	Second—b
1925-26	17	15	4	38	Fourth	1959-60	28	34	8	64	Fifth—*
1926-27	21	20	3	45	Second—c	1960-61	15	42	13	43	Sixth—*
1927-28	20	13	11	51	First—b	1961-62	15	47	8	38	Sixth—*
1928-29	26	13	5	57	First—xx	1962-63	14	39	17	45	Sixth—*
1929-30	38	5	1	77	First—c	1963-64	18	40	12	48	Sixth—*
1930-31	28	10	6	62	First—b	1964-65	21	43	6	48	Sixth—*
1931-32	15	21	12	42	Fourth—*	1965-66	21	43	6	48	Fifth—*
1932-33	25	15	8	58	First—b	1966-67	17	43	10	44	Sixth—*
1933-34	18	25	5	41	Fourth—*	1967-68	37	27	10	84	Third—a
1934-35	26	16	6	58	First—b	1968-69	42	18	16	100	Second—b
1935-36	22	20	6	50	Second—a	1969-70	40	17	19	99	Second—xx
1936-37	23	18	7	53	Second—a	1970-71	57	14	7	121	First—a
1937-38	30	11	7	67	First—b	1971-72	54	13	11	119	First—xx
1938-39	36	10	2	74	First—xx	1972-73	51	22	5	107	Second—a
1939-40	31	12	5	67	First—b	1973-74	52	17	9	113	First—c
1940-41	27	8	13	67	First—xx	1974-75	40	26	14	94	Second—†
1941-42	25	17	6	56	Third—b	1975-76	48	15	17	113	First—b
1942-43	24	17	9	57	Second—c	1976-77	49	23	8	106	First—c
1943-44	19	26	5	43	Fifth—*	1977-78	51	18	11	113	First—c
1944-45	16	30	4	36	Fourth—b	1978-79	43	23	14	100	First—b
1945-46	24	18	8	56	Second—c	1979-80	46	21	13	105	Second—a
1946-47	26	23	11	63	Third—b	1980-81	37	30	13	87	Second—†
1947-48	23	24	13	59	Third—b	1981-82	43	27	10	96	Second—a
1948-49	29	23	8	66	Second—b	1982-83	50	20	10	110	First—b
1949-50	22	32	16	60	Fifth—*	1983-84	49	25	6	104	First—†
1950-51	22	30	18	62	Fourth—b	1984-85	36	34	10	82	Fourth—†
1951-52	25	29	16	66	Fourth—b	1985-86	37	31	12	86	Third—†
1952-53	28	29	13	69	Third—c	1986-87	39	34	7	85	Third—†
1953-54	32	28	10	74	Fourth—b	1987-88	44	30	6	94	Second—c
1954-55	23	26	21	67	Fourth—b	1988-89	37	29	14	88	Second—a
1955-56	23	34	13	59	Fifth—*	1989-90	46	25	9	101	First—c
1956-57	34	24	12	80	Third—c	Totals	2040	1593	639	4719	
1957-58	27	28	15	69	Fourth—c						

From 1917-18 through the 1925-26 season, National Hockey League champions played against the Pacific Coast Hockey League for the Stanley Cup. So, only Stanley Cup championships are designated in the following club records for that period.

Key to standings: *—Missed playoffs. †—Eliminated in first round of new playoff format (1974-75). a—Eliminated in quarterfinal round. b—Eliminated in semifinal round. c—Eliminated in final round. xx—Stanley Cup champion.

—DID YOU KNOW—

That despite winning two of its last three playoff series with Montreal, Boston's playoff series record against the Canadiens since 1946 is 2-19?

1990-91 SCHEDULE

▨ Home games shaded.
* At Chicago Stadium.

OCTOBER

Sun	Mon	Tue	Wed	Thu	Fri	Sat
	1	2	3	4 PHI	5	6 QUE
7 QUE	8	9	10 WIN	11 MIN	12	13 LA
14	15	16	17 VAN	18	19 EDM	20 CAL
21	22	23	24	25 VAN	26	27 CHI
28	29	30	31 BUF			

NOVEMBER

Sun	Mon	Tue	Wed	Thu	Fri	Sat
				1 STL	2	3 BUF
4	5 NYR	6	7 MON	8	9	10 PIT
11 WAS	12	13	14 HAR	15 QUE	16	17 MON
18	19 TOR	20	21	22	23 HAR	24 HAR
25	26	27	28	29 EDM	30	

DECEMBER

Sun	Mon	Tue	Wed	Thu	Fri	Sat
						1 NYR
2	3	4 DET	5	6 MON	7	8 MON
9 BUF	10	11	12 HAR	13 HAR	14	15 NJ
16	17	18 NJ	19	20 BUF	21	22 MIN
23 NYR	24	25 BUF	26 WIN	27	28 MIN	29
30	31					

JANUARY

Sun	Mon	Tue	Wed	Thu	Fri	Sat
		1	2	3 VAN	4	5 WAS
6	7 WIN	8 QUE	9	10 QUE	11	12 PHI
13	14 DET	15 NYI	16	17 LA	18	19 ALL-STAR GAME*
20	21	22 BUF	23	24 HAR	25	26 CAL
27 MON	28	29	30	31 MON		

FEBRUARY

Sun	Mon	Tue	Wed	Thu	Fri	Sat
					1	2 PIT
3 PIT	4	5 EDM	6	7 CAL	8	9 CHI
10 QUE	11	12	13 MON	14	15	16 LA
17	18	19	20	21 CHI	22	23 STL
24	25	26	27	28 NYI		

MARCH

Sun	Mon	Tue	Wed	Thu	Fri	Sat
					1	2 BUF
3 NJ	4	5 TOR	6	7 STL	8	9 TOR
10	11	12	13	14 MON	15	16 DET
17 PHI	18	19 HAR	20	21 QUE	22	23 BUF
24 WAS	25	26 QUE	27	28	29	30 NYI
31 HAR						

5

1989-90 RESULTS

Oct.	5—Pittsburgh	W	5-4
	7—At Quebec	L	1-4
	9—Montreal	W	2-0
	11—At Montreal	L	2-4
	13—At Edmonton	T	3-3 (OT)
	15—At Vancouver	L	6-7
	17—At Los Angeles	W	3-2
	20—At Edmonton	W	3-0
	21—At Calgary	L	2-5
	26—Quebec	W	4-2
	28—Hartford	L	0-1
	29—At Buffalo	L	3-4
Nov.	2—Los Angeles	W	5-4 (OT)
	4—Buffalo	T	3-3 (OT)
	9—Edmonton	W	6-2
	10—At Washington	W	5-3
	15—At Hartford	W	5-2
	16—Montreal	W	3-2
	18—New Jersey	W	6-4
	21—At Detroit	W	2-1 (OT)
	23—Toronto	W	6-0
	25—At Montreal	L	3-5
	28—At St. Louis	W	5-1
	30—Buffalo	W	5-1
Dec.	2—St. Louis	L	1-2
	3—At Philadelphia	W	2-1
	5—At Quebec	T	3-3 (OT)
	7—Hartford	L	3-4
	9—Washington	L	3-7
	12—At Pittsburgh	L	5-7
	13—At Buffalo	W	4-2
	16—Buffalo	L	1-3
	17—At New Jersey	L	1-3
	20—At Hartford	L	3-4
	21—Minnesota	W	4-2
	23—Detroit	W	6-5
	26—Toronto	W	6-4
	29—At Buffalo	W	4-3 (OT)
	30—At Toronto	L	6-7 (OT)
Jan.	2—At Pittsburgh	W	5-2
	4—Winnipeg	W	4-2
	6—Washington	W	5-3
	7—At Buffalo	W	2-1
	11—Quebec	W	3-1
	13—N.Y. Rangers	L	2-3
	15—Hartford	W	4-1
	17—At Hartford	T	5-5 (OT)
	18—Calgary	T	2-2 (OT)
	23—At Quebec	W	9-2
	25—N.Y. Islanders	W	5-2
	27—Philadelphia	W	2-1
	29—At Montreal	W	2-1
Feb.	1—Montreal	L	2-4
	3—N.Y. Rangers	L	1-2
	4—At Quebec	W	3-2
	6—At Detroit	W	2-0
	8—Quebec	W	5-1
	10—N.Y. Islanders	L	3-4 (OT)
	11—At Vancouver	L	2-4
	14—At Winnipeg	L	2-3
	18—At Vancouver	W	7-2
	20—At Calgary	W	5-3
	22—At Chicago	W	6-3
	24—At Minnesota	W	3-2
	26—At N.Y. Rangers	L	1-6
Mar.	1—Montreal	W	5-3
	3—Chicago	W	4-3
	4—At Chicago	W	4-1
	6—At Philadelphia	W	2-1
	8—Buffalo	L	4-10
	10—At N.Y. Islanders	T	3-3 (OT)
	11—At Hartford	W	4-3
	15—Winnipeg	T	3-3 (OT)
	17—Los Angeles	L	4-5
	22—Quebec	W	7-3
	24—Minnesota	L	6-7
	27—At St. Louis	W	3-0
	29—Hartford	W	3-2
	31—At Montreal	T	2-2 (OT)
Apr.	1—New Jersey	T	3-3 (OT)

1990-91 ROSTER

No.	FORWARDS	Hgt./Wt.	Place of Birth	Age	NHL exp.	1989-90 club (league)	G.	A.	Pts.
25	Andy Brickley	5-11/200	Melrose, Mass.	29	7	Boston (NHL)	12	28	40
12	Randy Burridge	5-09/180	Fort Erie, Ont.	24	5	Boston (NHL)	17	15	32
	John Byce	6-01/180	Madison, Wis.	23	0	Univ. of Wisconsin (WCHA)	27	44	71
34	Lyndon Byers	6-01/200	Nipawin, Sask.	26	7	Boston (NHL)	4	4	8
11	Bobby Carpenter	6-00/190	Beverly, Mass.	27	10	Boston (NHL)	25	31	56
31	John Carter	5-10/175	Winchester, Mass.	27	5	Maine (AHL)	2	2	4
						Boston (NHL)	17	22	39
27	Dave Christian	6-00/175	Warroad, Minn.	31	11	Washington (NHL)	3	8	11
						Boston (NHL)	12	17	29
14	Robert Cimetta	6-00/190	Toronto, Ont.	20	2	Maine (AHL)	3	2	5
						Boston (NHL)	8	9	17
16	Peter Douris	6-01/195	Toronto, Ont.	24	4	Maine (AHL)	17	20	37
						Boston (NHL)	5	6	11
18	Bobby Gould	6-00/195	Petrolia, Ont.	33	11	Boston (NHL)	8	17	25
	Ken Hodge	6-02/190	Windsor, Ont.	24	1	Kalamazoo (IHL)	33	53	86
44	Ron Hoover	6-01/185	Oakville, Ont.	23	1	Maine (AHL)	28	26	54
						Boston (NHL)	0	0	0
23	Craig Janney	6-01/190	Hartford, Conn.	23	3	Boston (NHL)	24	38	62
29	Jarmo Kekalainen	6-00/190	Tampere, Finland	24	0	Boston (NHL)	2	2	4
						Maine (AHL)	5	11	16
17	Nevin Markwart	5-10/180	Toronto, Ont.	25	6	Boston (NHL)	1	2	3
8	Cam Neely	6-01/210	Comox, B.C.	25	7	Boston (NHL)	55	37	92
	Chris Nilan	6-00/205	Boston, Mass.	32	11	N.Y. Rangers (NHL)	1	2	3
19	Dave Poulin	5-11/190	Timmins, Ont.	32	8	Philadelphia (NHL)	9	8	17
						Boston (NHL)	6	19	25
	Shayne Stevenson	6-01/190	Newmarket, Ont.	19	0	Kitchener (OHL)	28	62	90
20	Bob Sweeney	6-03/200	Concord, Mass.	26	4	Boston (NHL)	22	24	46
	Wes Walz	5-10/180	Calgary, Alta.	20	1	Lethbridge (WHL)	54	86	140
						Boston (NHL)	1	1	2
	DEFENSEMEN								
43	Bob Beers	6-02/200	Pittsburgh, Pa.	23	1	Maine (AHL)	7	36	43
						Boston (NHL)	0	1	1
33	John Blum	6-03/205	Detroit, Mich.	31	8	Maine (AHL)	1	20	21
						Boston (NHL)	0	0	0
77	Ray Bourque	5-11/210	Montreal, Que.	29	11	Boston (NHL)	19	65	84
28	Garry Galley	5-11/190	Ottawa, Ont.	27	6	Boston (NHL)	8	27	35
6	Gord Kluzak	6-03/214	Climax, Sask.	26	8	Boston (NHL)	0	2	2
41	Allen Pedersen	6-03/210	Edmonton, Alta.	25	4	Boston (NHL)	1	2	3
21	Stephane Quintal	6-03/215	Boucherville, Que.	21	2	Boston (NHL)	2	2	4
						Maine (AHL)	4	16	20
40	Bruce Shoebottom	6-02/200	Windsor, Ont.	25	3	Maine (AHL)	3	11	14
						Boston (NHL)	0	0	0
32	Don Sweeney	5-11/170	St. Stephen, N.B.	24	2	Maine (AHL)	0	8	8
						Boston (NHL)	3	5	8
22	Michael Thelven	5-11/185	Stockholm, Sweden	29	5	Boston (NHL)	0	2	2
26	Glen Wesley	6-01/195	Red Deer, Alta.	22	3	Boston (NHL)	9	27	36
30	Jim Wiemer	6-04/197	Sudbury, Ont.	29	7	Maine (AHL)	3	4	7
						Boston (NHL)	5	14	19

	GOALTENDERS						Ga.	SO	Avg.
	Norm Foster	5-09/175	Vancouver, B.C.	25	0	Maine (AHL)	64	3	3.55
1	Reggie Lemelin	5-11/170	Quebec City, Que.	35	12	Boston (NHL)	43	2	2.81
35	Andy Moog	5-08/170	Penticton, B.C.	30	10	Boston (NHL)	46	3	2.89
	Mike Parson	6-00/170	Listowel, Ont.	20	0	Owen Sound (OHL)	49	1	4.39

1989-90 RECORDS

1989-90 regular-season records: 46-25-9 (.631, 101 points, 1st in Adams Division); 23-13-4 at home; 23-12-5 on road; 3-2-9 in overtime; 18-10-4 vs. Adams (4-3-1 vs. Sabres; 4-3-1 vs. Whalers; 4-3-1 vs. Canadiens; 6-1-1 vs. Nordiques); 9-7-2 vs. Patrick; 12-3-0 vs. Norris; 7-5-3 vs. Smythe.

MISCELLANEOUS DATA

1989-90 team rankings: Shorthanded goals for, 5 (20th in NHL); shorthanded goals against, 3 (1st); power play, 23.6% (T2nd); penalty killing, 83.2% (2nd); penalty minutes/game, 18.2.

TEAM HAT TRICKS, CAREER, ACTIVE

Ray Bourque (1)	Craig Janney (1)
Andy Brickley (2)	Brian Lawton (2)
Randy Burridge (2)	Cam Neely (6)
Bobby Carpenter (3)	Ray Neufeld (3)
Dave Christian (2)	Dave Poulin (5)
Bob Gould (1)	Bob Sweeney (1)

MINOR LEAGUE AFFILIATIONS

Maine (AHL)

Reggie Lemelin

1990 DRAFT SELECTIONS

Rnd.	Player	Hgt.	Wgt.	Overall	(Pos.)	1989-90 Club	(League)
1—	Bryan Smolinski	6:00	185	21	(C)	Michigan State University	
3—	Cameron Stewart	5:10	188	63	(C)	Elmira (Ont.) Jr. B	
4—	Jerome Buckley	6:02	200	84	(RW)	Northwood Prep (N.Y.)	
5—	Mike Bales	6:01	180	105	(G)	Ohio State University	
6—	Mark Woolf	5:11	200	126	(RW)	Spokane (WHL)	
7—	Jim Mackey	6:04	220	147	(D)	Hotchkiss H.S. (Ct.)	
8—	John Gruden	6:00	180	168	(D)	Waterloo (Ia.) Jr. A	
9—	Darren Wetherill	6:00	180	189	(D)	Minot (N.D.) T-II	
10—	Dean Capuano	6:01	177	210	(D)	Mount St. Charles (R.I.)	
11—	Andy Bezeau	5:09	161	231	(LW)	Niagara Falls (OHL)	
12—	Ted Miskolczi	6:03	182	252	(RW)	Belleville (OHL)	

FIRST-ROUND ENTRY DRAFT SELECTIONS

Year	Name	Overall	Last Amateur Team	(League)	Years in NHL
1969—	Don Tannahill	3	Niagara Falls (OHL)		2
	Frank Spring	4	Edmonton (WCHL)		5
	Ivan Boldirev	11	Oshawa (OHL)		15
1970—	Reggie Leach	3	Flin Flon (WCHL)		13
	Rick MacLeish	4	Peterborough (OHL)		14
	Ron Plumb	9	Peterborough (OHL)		1
	Bob Stewart	13	Oshawa (OHL)		0
1971—	Ron Jones	6	Edmonton (WCHL)		5
	Terry O'Reilly	14	Oshawa (OHL)		14
1972—	Mike Bloom	16	St. Catharines (OHL)		3
1973—	Andre Savard	6	Quebec (QMJHL)		12
1974—	Don Larway	18	Swift Current (WCHL)		0
1975—	Doug Halward	14	Peterborough (OHL)		14
1976—	Clayton Pachal	16	New Westminster (WCHL)		3
1977—	Dwight Foster	16	Kitchener (OHL)		10
1978—	Al Secord	16	Hamilton (OHL)		12
1979—	Ray Bourque	8	Verdun (QMJHL)		11
	Brad McCrimmon	15	Brandon (WHL)		11
1980—	Barry Pederson	18	Victoria (WHL)		10
1981—	Norm Leveille	14	Chicoutimi (QMJHL)		2
1982—	*Gord Kluzak	1	Billings (WHL)		6
1983—	Nevin Markwart	21	Regina (WHL)		6
1984—	Dave Pasin	19	Prince Albert (WHL)		2
1985—	No first round selection				
1986—	Craig Janney	13	Boston College		3
1987—	Glen Wesley	3	Portland (WHL)		3
	Stephane Quintal	14	Granby (QMJHL)		2
1988—	Robert Cimetta	18	Toronto (OHL)		2
1989—	Shayne Stevenson	17	Kitchener (OHL)		0
1990—	Bryan Smolinski	21	Michigan State University		0

*Designates first player chosen in draft.

Terry O'Reilly

COACHING HISTORY

Arthur H. Ross, 1924-25 to 1927-28
Cy Denneny, 1928-29
Arthur H. Ross, 1929-30 to 1933-34
Frank Patrick, 1934-35 to 1935-36
Arthur H. Ross, 1936-37 to 1938-39
Ralph (Cooney) Weiland, 1939-40 to 1940-41
Arthur H. Ross, 1941-42 to 1944-45
Aubrey (Dit) Clapper, 1945-46 to 1948-49
George Boucher, 1949-50
Lynn Patrick, 1950-51 to 1953-54
Lynn Patrick and Milt Schmidt, 1954-55
Milt Schmidt, 1955-56 to 1960-61
Phil Watson, 1961-62
Phil Watson and Milt Schmidt, 1962-63

Milt Schmidt, 1963-64 to 1965-66
Harry Sinden, 1966-67 to 1969-70
Tom Johnson, 1970-71 to 1971-72
Tom Johnson and Bep Guidolin, 1972-73
Bep Guidolin, 1973-74
Don Cherry, 1974-75 to 1978-79
Fred Creighton and Harry Sinden, 1979-80
Gerry Cheevers, 1980-81 to 1983-84
Gerry Cheevers and Harry Sinden, 1984-85
Butch Goring, 1985-86
Butch Goring and Terry O'Reilly, 1986-87
Terry O'Reilly, 1987-88 to 1988-89
Mike Milbury since 1989-90

FRANCHISE LEADERS

Current players in bold type
(1924-25 through 1989-90)

Games
1. 1436—John Bucyk
2. 1027—Wayne Cashman
3. 891—Terry O'Reilly
4. 881—Rick Middleton
5. 868—Don Marcotte
6. 861—Dallas Smith
7. 830—Dit Clapper
8. **794—Ray Bourque**
9. 776—Milt Schmidt
10. 771—Woody Dumart

Goals
1. 545—John Bucyk
2. 459—Phil Esposito
3. 402—Rick Middleton
4. 289—Ken Hodge
5. 277—Wayne Cashman
6. 264—Bobby Orr
7. 263—Peter McNab
8. **230—Ray Bourque**
   230—Don Marcotte
10. 229—Milt Schmidt

Assists
1. 794—John Bucyk
2. 624—Bobby Orr
3. **610—Ray Bourque**
4. 553—Phil Esposito
5. 516—Wayne Cashman
6. 496—Rick Middleton
7. 402—Terry O'Reilly
8. 385—Ken Hodge
9. 346—Bill Cowley
   346—Milt Schmidt

Points
1. 1339—John Bucyk
2. 1012—Phil Esposito
3. 898—Rick Middleton
4. 888—Bobby Orr
5. **840—Ray Bourque**
6. 793—Wayne Cashman
7. 674—Ken Hodge
8. 606—Terry O'Reilly
9. 587—Peter McNab
10. 575—Milt Schmidt

Penalty Minutes
1. 2095—Terry O'Reilly
2. 1552—Mike Milbury
3. 1261—Keith Crowder
4. 1041—Wayne Cashman
5. 1038—Eddie Shore
6. 1029—Ted Green

Goaltenders
Games
1. 468—Cecil Thompson
2. 444—Frankie Brimsek
3. 443—Eddie Johnston
4. 416—Gerry Cheevers
5. 277—Gilles Gilbert
6. 236—Jim Henry

Shutouts
1. 74—Cecil Thompson
2. 35—Frankie Brimsek
3. 27—Eddie Johnston
4. 26—Gerry Cheevers
5. 24—Jim Henry
6. 19—Hal Winkler
7. 16—Gilles Gilbert
8. 15—Don Simmons

Goals Against Average
(2400 minutes minimum)
1. 1.56—Hal Winkler
2. 1.99—Cecil Thompson
3. 2.46—Charles Stewart
4. 2.52—John Henderson
5. 2.57—Terry Sawchuk
6. 2.58—Frankie Brimsek
   2.58—Jim Henry

Wins
1. 252—Cecil Thompson
2. 230—Frankie Brimsek
3. 229—Gerry Cheevers
4. 182—Eddie Johnston
5. 155—Gilles Gilbert

Pierre Turgeon's 40 goals and 66 assists last season were the exact totals compiled by Buffalo Hall of Famer Gil Perreault in 1979-80.

Daren Puppa's 31 victories in 1989-90 tied the Buffalo team record for the second most wins by a goaltender in one season. Don Edwards won 38 games for the Sabres in 1977-78.

Dave Andreychuk scored 20 goals and 22 assists at home last season and had 20 goals and 20 assists in games on the road.

Newcomer Dale Hawerchuk was the Winnipeg Jets' leading scorer in each of the last nine seasons.

BUFFALO SABRES

CLUB DIRECTORY

Chairman of the Board and President
Seymour H. Knox, III
Vice-Chairman of the Board and Counsel
Robert O. Swados
Vice-Chairman of the Board
Robert E. Rich, Jr.
Treasurer
Joseph T. J. Stewart
Assistant to the President
Seymour H. Knox IV
Senior Vice-President, Administration
Mitchell Owen
Senior Vice-President, Finance
Robert W. Pickel
General Manager
Gerry Meehan
Coach
Rick Dudley
Assistant Coaches
John Tortorella, John Van Boxmeer
Assistant to the General Manager
Craig Ramsay
Director of Player Personnel
Don Luce
Director of Scouting
Rudy Migay
Coordinator of Minor League Professional Development
Joe Crozier

Scouting Staff
Don Barrie, Jack Bowman, Larry Carriere, Dennis McIvor, Paul Merritt, Mike Racicot, Frank Zywiec
Director of Communications
Paul Wieland
Director of Public Relations
John Gurtler
Director of Information
Budd Bailey
Trainer
Jim Pizzutelli
Assistant Trainer
Rip Simonick
Equipment Supervisor
John Allaway
Home Ice
Memorial Auditorium
Address
Memorial Auditorium, Buffalo, N.Y. 14202
Seating Capacity
16,433 (including standees)
Club Colors
Blue, White and Gold
Phone
(716) 856-7300 or (800) 333-7825
Public Relations FAX
(716) 856-2104

YEAR-BY-YEAR RESULTS

Season	W.	L.	T.	Pts.	Position	Season	W.	L.	T.	Pts.	Position
1970-71	24	39	15	63	Fifth—*	1981-82	39	26	15	93	Third—†
1971-72	16	43	19	51	Sixth—*	1982-83	38	29	13	89	Third—a
1972-73	37	27	14	88	Fourth—a	1983-84	48	25	7	103	Second—†
1973-74	32	34	12	76	Fifth—*	1984-85	38	28	14	90	Third—†
1974-75	49	16	15	113	First—c	1985-86	37	37	6	80	Fifth—*
1975-76	46	21	13	105	Second—a	1986-87	28	44	8	64	Fifth—*
1976-77	48	24	8	104	Second—a	1987-88	37	32	11	85	Third—†
1977-78	44	19	17	105	Second—a	1988-89	38	35	7	83	Third—†
1978-79	36	28	16	88	Second—†	1989-90	45	27	8	98	Second—†
1979-80	47	17	16	110	First—b	**Totals**	**766**	**571**	**255**	**1787**	
1980-81	39	20	21	99	First—a						

Key to standings: *—Missed playoffs. †—Eliminated in first round of new playoff format (1974-75). a—Eliminated in quarterfinal round. b—Eliminated in semifinal round. c—Eliminated in final round. xx—Stanley Cup champion.

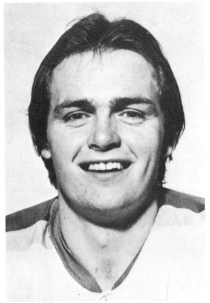

Danny Gare

Jim Schoenfeld

1990-91 SCHEDULE

▨ Home games shaded.

* At Chicago Stadium.

OCTOBER

Sun	Mon	Tue	Wed	Thu	Fri	Sat
	1	2	3	4 MON	5	6 MON
7	8	9	10 HAR	11	12 QUE	13 QUE
14	15	16	17 MON	18	19 PIT	20 NYI
21	22	23	24	25 NJ	26	27 TOR
28 HAR	29	30	31 BOS			

NOVEMBER

Sun	Mon	Tue	Wed	Thu	Fri	Sat
				1	2	3 BOS
4 CAL	5	6	7 NYR	8	9 VAN	10 WAS
11	12	13	14 LA	15	16 EDM	17 CAL
18	19	20	21 NYR	22	23 EDM	24
25 NYR	26	27	28 MON	29	30	

DECEMBER

Sun	Mon	Tue	Wed	Thu	Fri	Sat
						1 QUE
2 DET	3	4	5	6 PHI	7 HAR	8
9 BOS	10	11 DET	12	13	14 PIT	15
16 STL	17	18 HAR	19	20 BOS	21	22
23 QUE	24	25	26 BOS	27	28 CHI	29 NJ
30	31 PHI					

JANUARY

Sun	Mon	Tue	Wed	Thu	Fri	Sat
		1	2 NYI	3	4 WIN	5
6	7	8 VAN	9	10 LA	11	12 MIN
13	14 TOR	15	16 DET	17	18	19 ALL-STAR GAME*
20	21	22 BOS	23	24 CHI	25	26 MON
27 CAL	28	29 STL	30	31 QUE		

FEBRUARY

Sun	Mon	Tue	Wed	Thu	Fri	Sat
					1	2
3 EDM	4	5	6 STL	7	8 LA	9
10 WIN	11	12 QUE	13 MIN	14	15 MON	16
17 TOR	18	19 PIT	20	21	22	23 HAR
24 HAR	25	26 NYI	27	28 QUE		

MARCH

Sun	Mon	Tue	Wed	Thu	Fri	Sat
					1	2 BOS
3	4	5	6 NJ	7	8 CHI	9
10 VAN	11	12 MIN	13 WIN	14	15	16 MON
17 HAR	18	19	20 MON	21	22	23 BOS
24 PHI	25	26 WAS	27	28 QUE	29	30 HAR
31 WAS						

1989-90 RESULTS

Oct.	5—Quebec	W	4-3
	7—At Montreal	L	1-5
	8—Minnesota	T	2-2 (OT)
	11—At Toronto	W	7-1
	13—Hartford	W	4-1
	14—At Detroit	L	2-6
	18—At Hartford	L	1-2
	20—Montreal	W	6-2
	21—At Pittsburgh	W	4-2
	25—At Minnesota	L	2-4
	27—Toronto	W	6-5 (OT)
	29—Boston	W	4-3
Nov.	2—At Montreal	W	4-3
	4—At Boston	T	3-3 (OT)
	5—Los Angeles	W	5-3
	8—At Hartford	W	6-3
	10—Vancouver	W	4-2
	12—Edmonton	W	6-5
	16—At Calgary	T	4-4 (OT)
	17—At Edmonton	L	0-3
	19—At Vancouver	T	2-2 (OT)
	22—New York Rangers	W	4-1
	25—At Quebec	W	3-2
	26—Hartford	W	4-2
	28—At Hartford	W	4-2
	30—At Boston	L	1-5
Dec.	1—New Jersey	W	6-4
	3—St. Louis	W	4-3
	5—At N.Y. Islanders	L	0-3
	7—At Philadelphia	L	3-4 (OT)
	10—Washington	W	4-3
	13—Boston	L	2-4
	16—At Boston	W	3-1
	17—Philadelphia	W	4-3
	20—At N.Y. Rangers	T	2-2 (OT)
	22—Montreal	T	2-2 (OT)
	23—At Quebec	W	6-5
	26—Detroit	W	6-3
	29—Boston	L	3-4 (OT)
	31—N.Y. Islanders	L	2-4
Jan.	2—At New Jersey	L	3-5
	6—At Montreal	L	3-6
	7—Boston	L	1-2
	11—At Calgary	L	3-5
	13—At Vancouver	W	5-3
	16—At Los Angeles	W	4-2
	19—Washington	L	3-6
	23—At Philadelphia	W	3-2
	24—At Chicago	W	3-2
	26—Chicago	L	2-4
	28—Pittsburgh	W	7-2
	30—At Quebec	W	5-2
	31—Quebec	W	6-3
Feb.	3—At Montreal	L	0-1
	4—N.Y. Islanders	L	0-1
	7—Montreal	W	3-1
	9—N.Y. Rangers	W	3-2
	11—At St. Louis	L	2-4
	13—At Chicago	L	1-4
	16—Montreal	W	5-3
	18—Hartford	L	4-6
	20—At Winnipeg	W	4-3 (OT)
	21—At Edmonton	L	3-7
	23—Hartford	W	7-3
	25—Winnipeg	W	3-1
	27—At St. Louis	L	1-4
Mar.	3—At Quebec	T	3-3 (OT)
	4—Quebec	W	5-3
	6—At Washington	T	1-1 (OT)
	8—At Boston	W	10-4
	10—At Hartford	W	5-0
	14—Los Angeles	L	5-6 (OT)
	16—Toronto	L	3-4
	18—Winnipeg	W	4-3 (OT)
	21—Calgary	W	5-4
	25—New Jersey	L	3-4
	27—At Detroit	W	6-5
	29—Minnesota	W	4-2
	31—At Pittsburgh	W	3-2 (OT)
Apr.	1—Quebec	W	5-2

1990-91 ROSTER

No.	FORWARDS	Hgt./Wt.	Place of Birth	Age	NHL exp.	1989-90 club (league)	G.	A.	Pts.
25	Dave Andreychuk	6-03/220	Hamilton, Ont.	27	8	Buffalo (NHL)	40	42	82
	Donald Audette	5-08/177	Laval, Que.	21	0	Rochester (AHL)	42	46	88
	Mike Donnelly	5-11/185	Detroit, Mich.	26	3	Rochester (AHL)	43	55	98
						Buffalo (NHL)	1	2	3
17	Mike Foligno	6-02/195	Sudbury, Ont.	31	11	Buffalo (NHL)	15	25	40
	Jody Gage	6-00/190	Toronto, Ont.	30	5	Rochester (AHL)	45	38	83
	Francois Guay	6-00/190	Gatineau, Que.	22	0	Rochester (AHL)	28	35	63
20	Mike Hartman	6-00/198	Detroit, Mich.	23	4	Buffalo (NHL)	11	10	21
	Dale Hawerchuk	5-11/170	Toronto, Ont.	27	9	Winnipeg (NHL)	26	55	81
33	Benoit Hogue	5-10/190	Repentigny, Que.	24	3	Buffalo (NHL)	11	7	18
	Jim Jackson	5-08/185	Oshawa, Ont.	30	4	Rochester (AHL)	16	37	53
89	Alexander Mogilny	5-11/195	Khabarovsk, USSR	21	1	Buffalo (NHL)	15	28	43
56	Ken Priestlay	5-10/190	Richmond, B.C.	23	4	Buffalo (NHL)	7	7	14
						Rochester (AHL)	19	39	58
32	Robert Ray	6-00/210	Stirling, Ont.	22	1	Rochester (AHL)	2	13	15
						Buffalo (NHL)	2	1	3
21	Christian Ruuttu	5-11/190	Lappeen, Finland	26	4	Buffalo (NHL)	19	41	60
	Joel Savage	5-11/205	Surrey, B.C.	20	0	Rochester (AHL)	6	7	13
16	Darrin Shannon	6-02/200	Barrie, Ont.	20	2	Rochester (AHL)	20	23	43
						Buffalo (NHL)	2	7	9
18	Dave Snuggerud	6-00/190	Minnetonka, Minn.	24	1	Buffalo (NHL)	14	16	30
77	Pierre Turgeon	6-01/203	Rouyn, Que.	21	3	Buffalo (NHL)	40	66	106
22	Rick Vaive	6-01/200	Ottawa, Ont.	31	11	Buffalo (NHL)	29	19	48
	DEFENSEMEN								
37	Shawn Anderson	6-01/200	Montreal, Que.	22	4	Buffalo (NHL)	1	3	4
						Rochester (AHL)	2	16	18
8	Doug Bodger	6-02/210	Chemainus, B.C.	24	6	Buffalo (NHL)	12	36	48
	Greg Brown	6-00/185	Hartford, Conn.	27	0	Boston College (H. E.)	5	35	40
	Kevin Haller	6-02/183	Trochu, Alta.	19	0	Regina (WHL)	16	37	53
						Buffalo (NHL)	0	0	0
	Jim Hofford	6-00/205	Sudbury, Ont.	26	3	Rochester (AHL)	1	9	10
26	Dean Kennedy	6-02/190	Redver, Sask.	27	7	Buffalo (NHL)	2	12	14
4	Uwe Krupp	6-06/235	Cologne, W. Germany	25	4	Buffalo (NHL)	3	20	23
55	Reed Larson	6-00/195	Minneapolis, Minn.	34	14	Alleghe (Italy)	24	50	74
						Buffalo (NHL)	0	0	0
3	Grant Ledyard	6-02/200	Winnipeg, Man.	28	6	Buffalo (NHL)	2	13	15
	Don McSween	5-11/195	Detroit, Mich.	26	1	Rochester (AHL)	16	43	59
						Buffalo (NHL)	0	0	0
	Brad Miller	6-04/220	Edmonton, Alta.	21	1	Rochester (AHL)	2	10	12
						Buffalo (NHL)	0	0	0
5	Mike Ramsey	6-03/195	Minneapolis, Minn.	29	11	Buffalo (NHL)	4	21	25
24	Jay Wells	6-01/210	Paris, Ont.	31	11	Philadelphia (NHL)	3	16	19
						Buffalo (NHL)	0	1	1

No.	GOALTENDERS	Hgt./Wt.	Place of Birth	Age	NHL exp.	1989-90 club (league)	Ga.	SO	Avg.
30	Clint Malarchuk	6-00/187	Grande, Alta.	29	8	Buffalo (NHL)	29	0	3.35
31	Daren Puppa	6-03/205	Kirkland Lake, Ont.	25	5	Buffalo (NHL)	56	1	2.89
	Darcy Wakaluk	5-11/180	Pincher Creek, Alta	24	1	Rochester (AHL)	56	2	3.35

1989-90 RECORDS

1989-90 regular-season records: 45-27-8 (.613, 98 points, 2nd in Adams Division); 27-11-2 at home; 18-16-6 on road; 4-3-8 in overtime; 20-9-3 vs. Adams (3-4-1 vs. Bruins; 6-2-0 vs. Whalers; 4-3-1 vs. Canadiens; 7-0-1 vs. Nordiques); 9-7-2 vs. Patrick; 7-7-1 vs. Norris; 9-4-2 vs. Smythe.

MISCELLANEOUS DATA

1989-90 team rankings: Shorthanded goals for, 7 (T17th in NHL); shorthanded goals against, 7 (T4th); power play, 22.1% (9th); penalty killing, 83.5% (1st); penalty minutes/game, 18.1.

TEAM HAT TRICKS, CAREER, ACTIVE

Dave Andreychuk (6) Mikko Makela (1)
Mike Foligno (8) John Tucker (1)
Dale Hawerchuk (11) Pierre Turgeon (1)
Steve Ludzik (1) Rick Vaive (13)

MINOR LEAGUE AFFILIATIONS

Rochester (AHL)

Alexander Mogilny

1990 DRAFT SELECTIONS

Rnd.	Player	Hgt.	Wgt.	Overall	(Pos.)	1989-90 Club	(League)
1—Brad May		6:00	200	14	(LW)	Niagara Falls (OHL)	
4—Brian McCarthy		6:02	190	82	(C)	Pingree H.S. (Mass.)	
5—Richard Smehlik		6:03	208	97	(D)	Vitkovice, Czech.	
5—Todd Bojcun		5:08	151	100	(G)	Peterborough (OHL)	
5—Brad Pascall		6:02	192	103	(D)	University of North Dakota	
7—Viktor Gordijuk		5:10	176	142	(RW)	Krylja Sovetov, USSR	
8—Milan Nedoma		5:10	176	166	(D)	Zetor Brno, Czech.	
9—Jason Winch		6:01	203	187	(LW)	Niagara Falls (OHL)	
10—Sylvain Naud		5:10	188	208	(RW)	Laval (QMJHL)	
11—Kenneth Martin		6:01	149	229	(LW)	Belmont Hill H.S. (Mass.)	
12—Brad Rubachuk		5:11	173	250	(C)	Lethbridge (WHL)	

FIRST-ROUND ENTRY DRAFT SELECTIONS

Year	Name	Overall	Last Amateur Team	(League)	Years in NHL
1970—	*Gilbert Perreault	1	Montreal (OHL)		17
1971—	Rick Martin	5	Montreal (OHL)		11
1972—	Jim Schoenfeld	5	Niagara Falls (OHL)		13
1973—	Morris Titanic	12	Sudbury (OHL)		2
1974—	Lee Fogolin	11	Oshawa (OHL)		13
1975—	Robert Sauve	17	Laval (QMJHL)		13
1976—	No first round selection				
1977—	Ric Seiling	14	St. Catherines (OHL)		10
1978—	Larry Playfair	13	Portland (WCHL)		12
1979—	Mike Ramsey	11	University of Minnesota		11
1980—	Steve Patrick	20	Brandon (WHL)		6
1981—	Jiri Dudacek	17	Kladno (Czechoslovakia)		0
1982—	Phil Housley	6	South St. Paul H.S. (Minn.)		8
	Paul Cyr	9	Victoria (WHL)		7
	Dave Andreychuk	16	Oshawa (OHL)		8
1983—	Tom Barrasso	5	Acton Boxboro H.S. (Mass.)		7
	Norm Lacombe	10	University of New Hampshire		6
	Adam Creighton	11	Ottawa (OHL)		7
1984—	Bo Andersson	18	Vastra Frolunda (Sweden)		5
1985—	Carl Johansson	14	Vastra Frolunda (Sweden)		3
1986—	Shawn Anderson	5	Team Canada		4
1987—	*Pierre Turgeon	1	Granby (QMJHL)		3
1988—	Joel Savage	13	Victoria (WHL)		0
1989—	Kevin Haller	14	Regina (WHL)		1
1990—	Brad May	14	Niagara Falls (OHL)		0

*Designates first player chosen in draft.

Gil Perreault

COACHING HISTORY

Punch Imlach, 1970-71
Punch Imlach and Joe Crozier, 1971-72
Joe Crozier, 1972-73 to 1973-74
Floyd Smith, 1974-75 to 1976-77
Marcel Pronovost, 1977-78
Marcel Pronovost and Bill Inglis, 1978-79
Scotty Bowman, 1979-80

Roger Neilson, 1980-81
Jim Roberts and Scotty Bowman, 1981-82
Scotty Bowman, 1982-83 to 1984-85
Jim Schoenfeld and Scotty Bowman, 1985-86
Scotty Bowman, Craig Ramsay and Ted Sator, 1986-87
Ted Sator, 1987-88 to 1988-89
Rick Dudley since 1989-90

FRANCHISE LEADERS

Current players in bold type
(1970-71 through 1989-90)

Games
1. 1191—Gil Perreault
2. 1070—Craig Ramsay
3. 854—Bill Hajt
4. 766—Don Luce
5. **741—Mike Ramsey**
6. 681—Rick Martin
7. 664—Ric Seiling
8. **631—Mike Foligno**
9. 608—Lindy Ruff
10. 584—Jim Schoenfeld

Goals
1. 512—Gil Perreault
2. 382—Rick Martin
3. 267—Danny Gare
4. 252—Craig Ramsay
5. **243—Mike Foligno**
6. **242—Dave Andreychuk**
7. 222—Rene Robert
8. 216—Don Luce
9. 178—Phil Housley
10. 176—Ric Seiling

Assists
1. 814—Gil Perreault
2. 420—Craig Ramsay
3. 380—Phil Housley
4. 330—Rene Robert
5. 313—Rick Martin
6. 310—Don Luce
7. **308—Dave Andreychuk**
8. **259—Mike Foligno**
9. 233—Danny Gare
10. 216—Jerry Korab

Points
1. 1326—Gil Perreault
2. 695—Rick Martin
3. 672—Craig Ramsay
4. 558—Phil Housley
5. 552—Rene Robert
6. **550—Dave Andreychuk**
7. 526—Don Luce
8. **502—Mike Foligno**
9. 500—Danny Gare
10. 376—Ric Seiling

Penalty Minutes
1. **1,405—Mike Foligno**
2. 1,390—Larry Playfair
3. 1,126—Lindy Ruff
4. 1,025—Jim Schoenfeld
5. 870—Jerry Korab

Goaltenders
Games
1. 307—Don Edwards
2. 266—Tom Barrasso
3. 246—Bob Sauve
4. 202—Roger Crozier
5. 144—Jacques Cloutier
6. 120—Dave Dryden
   120—Daren Puppa
8. 116—Gerry Desjardins

Shutouts
1. 14—Don Edwards
2. 13—Tom Barrasso
3. 10—Roger Crozier
4. 7—Bob Sauve

Goals Against Average (entire roster)
(2400 minutes minimum)
1. 2.81—Gerry Desjardins
2. 2.90—Don Edwards
3. 3.06—Dave Dryden
4. 3.20—Bob Sauve
5. 3.23—Roger Crozier
6. **3.25—Daren Puppa**
7. 3.28—Tom Barrasso
8. 3.70—Jacques Cloutier

Wins
1. 156—Don Edwards
2. 124—Tom Barrasso
3. 119—Bob Sauve
4. 74—Roger Crozier
5. 66—Gerry Desjardins
6. **59—Daren Puppa**

Joe Nieuwendyk has led the Flames in goals scored in each of the last three seasons.

Al MacInnis' playoff goal on a penalty shot against Los Angeles on April 4, 1990, was the first by a defenseman in NHL history.

Doug Gilmour (above) and Paul Ranheim set an NHL record by scoring shorthanded goals four seconds apart against Quebec on October 17, 1989.

Sergei Makarov in 1989-90 became the third Flames player in five years to capture NHL Rookie of the Year honors.

12

CALGARY FLAMES

CLUB DIRECTORY

Owners
Harley N. Hotchkiss, Norman L. Kwong, Sonia Scur-field, Byron J. Seaman, Daryl K. Seaman
President, General Manager and Governor
Cliff Fletcher
Vice-President, Business and Finance
Clare Rhyasen
Vice-President, Hockey Operations
Al MacNeil
Vice-President, Sales and Broadcasting
Leo Ornest
Vice-President, Corporate and Community Relations
Lanny McDonald
Director of Hockey Administration
Al Coates
Assistant General Manager/Coach
Doug Risebrough
Assistant Coaches
Guy Charron, Paul Baxter
Goaltending Consultant
Glenn Hall
Director of Public Relations
Rick Skaggs
Assistant Public Relations Director
Mike Burke
Director of Professional Development
Terry Crisp

Chief Scout
Gerry Blair
Coordinator of Scouting
Ian McKenzie
Scouts
Al Godfrey, Larry Popein, Ray Clearwater, Lou Rey-croft, Gerry McNamara
Scouting Staff
Garth Malarchuk, David Mayville, Lars Norrman, Tom Thompson, Pekka Rautakallio
Controller
Lynne Tosh
Trainer
Jim "Bearcat" Murray
Equipment Manager
Bobby Stewart
Home Ice
The Olympic Saddledome
Address
P.O. Box 1540, Station M, Calgary, Alta. T2P 3B9
Seating Capacity
20,130
Club Colors
Red, White and Gold
Phone
(403) 261-0475
FAX
(403) 261-0470

YEAR-BY-YEAR RESULTS

Season	W.	L.	T.	Pts.	Position
1972-73	25	38	15	65	Seventh—*
1973-74	30	34	14	74	Fourth—a
1974-75	34	31	15	83	Fourth—*
1975-76	35	33	12	82	Third—†
1976-77	34	34	12	80	Third—†
1977-78	34	27	19	87	Third—†
1978-79	41	31	8	90	Fourth—†
1979-80	35	32	13	83	Fourth—†
1980-81	39	27	14	92	Third—b
1981-82	29	34	17	75	Third—†

Season	W.	L.	T.	Pts.	Position
1982-83	32	34	14	78	Second—a
1983-84	34	32	14	82	Second—a
1984-85	41	27	12	94	Third—†
1985-86	40	31	9	89	Second—c
1986-87	46	31	3	95	Second—†
1987-88	48	23	9	105	First—a
1988-89	54	17	9	117	First—xx
1989-90	42	23	15	99	First—†
Totals	673	539	224	1570	

Key to standings: *—Missed playoffs. †—Eliminated in first round of new playoff format (1974-75). a—Eliminated in quarterfinal round. b—Eliminated in semifinal round. c—Eliminated in final round. xx—Stanley Cup champion.

Lanny McDonald

Kent Nilsson

1990-91 SCHEDULE

▨ Home games shaded.

* At Chicago Stadium.

OCTOBER

Sun	Mon	Tue	Wed	Thu	Fri	Sat
	1	2	3	4 VAN	5	6 TOR
7	8 WIN	9	10 DET	11	12	13 NJ
14 CHI	15	16	17	18 STL	19	20 BOS
21 EDM	22	23	24	25 EDM	26	27 WAS
28	29	30 NJ	31			

NOVEMBER

Sun	Mon	Tue	Wed	Thu	Fri	Sat
				1 WIN	2	3 TOR
4 BUF	5	6 PIT	7	8 PHI	9	10 NYI
11 NYR	12	13	14	15 NYI	16	17 BUF
18	19 VAN	20	21	22 LA	23	24 CHI
25	26	27	28 WIN	29	30	

DECEMBER

Sun	Mon	Tue	Wed	Thu	Fri	Sat
						1 MON
2 QUE	3	4	5 NYR	6	7 QUE	8
9 EDM	10	11 MIN	12	13 LA	14	15
16 VAN	17	18 VAN	19	20 LA	21	22 EDM
23	24	25	26	27 EDM	28	29 HAR
30	31 MON					

JANUARY

Sun	Mon	Tue	Wed	Thu	Fri	Sat
		1	2 WIN	3	4	5 DET
6	7	8 TOR	9	10 PIT	11 WAS	12
13 WIN	14	15 WIN	16	17	18	19 ALL-STAR GAME*
20	21	22 PHI	23 HAR	24	25	26 BOS
27 BUF	28	29	30 NYR	31		

FEBRUARY

Sun	Mon	Tue	Wed	Thu	Fri	Sat
					1	2 CHI
3	4	5 NJ	6	7 BOS	8	9 HAR
10	11	12 LA	13	14	15 WAS	16
17 STL	18	19 DET	20	21 VAN	22	23 QUE
24 VAN	25	26	27 EDM	28		

MARCH

Sun	Mon	Tue	Wed	Thu	Fri	Sat
					1 PIT	2 MIN
3	4 MON	5	6	7 PHI	8	9 STL
10 MIN	11	12 WIN	13	14 NYI	15	16 LA
17	18 WIN	19	20 VAN	21	22	23 LA
24	25	26 VAN	27	28 EDM	29 EDM	30
31 LA						

1989-90 RESULTS

Oct.	5—Detroit	W	10-7
	7—N.Y. Islanders	W	6-3
	10—At New Jersey	W	4-2
	11—At N.Y. Rangers	L	4-5
	14—At Washington	T	4-4 (OT)
	15—At Philadelphia	W	3-2
	17—At Quebec	T	8-8 (OT)
	18—At Montreal	L	1-2
	21—Boston	W	5-2
	23—Washington	T	3-3 (OT)
	25—At Los Angeles	W	5-0
	27—Vancouver	T	5-5 (OT)
	28—At Vancouver	L	3-4
Nov.	1—Winnipeg	W	5-3
	3—At Edmonton	L	2-5
	4—New Jersey	W	7-3
	6—Edmonton	W	5-1
	8—At Los Angeles	W	5-4
	11—At Minnesota	L	2-3 (OT)
	12—At Winnipeg	L	2-3
	14—Los Angeles	L	6-8
	16—Buffalo	T	4-4 (OT)
	18—Chicago	T	4-4 (OT)
	20—At Montreal	L	2-3
	21—At Quebec	T	4-4 (OT)
	24—At Detroit	L	2-3
	25—At St. Louis	T	3-3 (OT)
	30—Minnesota	W	5-2
Dec.	2—Toronto	W	7-4
	6—Winnipeg	L	3-4
	10—At Winnipeg	L	1-4
	11—At Edmonton	T	3-3 (OT)
	14—Quebec	W	8-2
	16—Pittsburgh	W	4-3
	19—At Vancouver	W	2-1 (OT)
	20—Vancouver	W	2-1
	23—At Edmonton	L	1-2
	27—At Los Angeles	T	5-5 (OT)
	29—Winnipeg	L	1-2 (OT)
	30—Montreal	W	5-3
Jan.	2—Philadelphia	T	4-4 (OT)
	5—Hartford	W	6-4
	7—At Edmonton	W	3-1
	9—Edmonton	L	2-3 (OT)
	11—Buffalo	W	5-3
	13—At Toronto	L	5-6
	14—At Chicago	W	6-5
	16—At St. Louis	W	5-2
	18—At Boston	T	2-2 (OT)
	19—At Hartford	T	3-3 (OT)
	25—N.Y. Rangers	W	8-5
	27—Minnesota	W	3-1
	30—At Vancouver	W	7-2
Feb.	1—Vancouver	W	4-3 (OT)
	3—At Los Angeles	L	3-4
	6—Los Angeles	L	3-5
	10—At Detroit	L	5-7
	11—At N.Y. Rangers	W	5-2
	13—At N.Y. Islanders	W	4-2
	15—At Chicago	W	4-1
	18—At Winnipeg	L	1-5
	20—Boston	L	3-5
	22—Toronto	W	12-2
	25—Edmonton	W	10-4
Mar.	1—Philadelphia	L	2-4
	3—Vancouver	W	5-1
	5—Los Angeles	W	5-0
	7—Pittsburgh	W	6-3
	9—At Vancouver	T	4-4 (OT)
	11—At Winnipeg	W	6-4
	12—Winnipeg	W	5-4 (OT)
	15—New Jersey	W	5-4
	17—Hartford	W	5-4
	19—St. Louis	W	5-2
	21—At Buffalo	L	4-5
	24—At Pittsburgh	T	3-3 (OT)
	25—At Washington	L	1-4
	27—At N.Y. Islanders	W	4-2
	30—Edmonton	W	6-2
Apr.	1—Los Angeles	W	8-4

1990-91 ROSTER

No.	FORWARDS	Hgt./Wt.	Place of Birth	Age	NHL exp.	1989-90 club (league)	G.	A.	Pts.
33	Marc Bureau	6-00/190	Trois-Rivieres, Que.	24	1	Salt Lake (IHL)	43	48	91
						Calgary (NHL)	0	0	0
14	Theo Fleury	5-06/160	Oxbow, Sask.	22	2	Calgary (NHL)	31	35	66
39	Doug Gilmour	5-11/170	Kingston, Ont.	27	7	Calgary (NHL)	24	67	91
35	Stu Grimson	6-05/220	Kamloops, B.C.	25	2	Salt Lake (IHL)	8	8	16
						Calgary (NHL)	0	0	0
17	Jiri Hrdina	6-00/195	Prague, Czech.	32	3	Calgary (NHL)	12	18	30
22	Mark Hunter	6-00/200	Petrolia, Ont.	27	9	Calgary (NHL)	2	3	5
19	Tim Hunter	6-02/202	Calgary, Alta.	30	9	Calgary (NHL)	2	3	5
26	Jim Korn	6-05/220	Hopkins, Minn.	33	11	New Jersey (NHL)	2	3	5
						Calgary (NHL)	0	2	2
27	Brian MacLellan	6-03/215	Guelph, Ont.	31	8	Calgary (NHL)	20	18	38
42	Sergei Makarov	5-11/185	Chelyabinsk, USSR	32	1	Calgary (NHL)	24	62	86
	Stephane Matteau	6-03/185	Rouyn, Que.	21	0	Salt Lake (NHL)	23	35	58
25	Joe Nieuwendyk	6-01/195	Oshawa, Ont.	24	4	Calgary (NHL)	45	50	95
29	Joel Otto	6-04/220	Elk River, Minn.	28	6	Calgary (NHL)	13	20	33
11	Colin Patterson	6-02/195	Rexdale, Ont.	30	7	Calgary (NHL)	5	3	8
16	Sergei Priakin	6-03/210	Moscow, Soviet Union	26	2	Calgary (NHL)	2	2	4
						Salt Lake (IHL)	1	0	1
28	Paul Ranheim	6-00/195	St. Louis, Mo.	24	2	Calgary (NHL)	26	28	54
	Robert Reichel	5-10/185	Litvinov, Czech.	19	0	Litvinov (Czech.)	49	34	83
10	Gary Roberts	6-01/190	North York, Ont.	24	4	Calgary (NHL)	39	33	72
	Martin Simard	6-03/215	Montreal, Que.	24	0	Salt Lake (IHL)	22	23	45
	Tim Sweeney	5-11/180	Boston, Mass.	23	0	Salt Lake (IHL)	46	51	97
	DEFENSEMEN								
32	Brian Glynn	6-04/215	Iserlohn, W. Germany	22	3	Salt Lake (IHL)	17	44	61
						Calgary (NHL)	0	0	0
	Kevin Grant	6-03/210	Toronto, Ont.	21	0	Salt Lake (IHL)	7	17	24
21	Roger Johansson	6-03/185	Ljungby, Sweden	23	1	Calgary (NHL)	0	5	5
2	Al MacInnis	6-02/196	Inverness, N.S.	27	9	Calgary (NHL)	28	62	90
34	Jamie Macoun	6-02/200	Newmarket, Ont.	29	7	Calgary (NHL)	8	27	35
5	Dana Murzyn	6-02/200	Calgary, Alta.	23	5	Calgary (NHL)	7	13	20
6	Ric Nattress	6-02/210	Hamilton, Ont.	28	8	Calgary (NHL)	1	14	15
55	Ken Sabourin	6-03/205	Scarborough, Ont.	24	2	Salt Lake (IHL)	5	19	24
						Calgary (NHL)	0	0	0
20	Gary Suter	6-00/190	Madison, Wis.	26	5	Calgary (NHL)	16	60	76

No.	GOALTENDERS	Hgt./Wt.	Place of Birth	Age	NHL exp.	1989-90 club (league)	Ga.	SO	Avg.
1	Steve Guenette	5-10/175	Gloucester, Ont.	24	4	Salt Lake (IHL)	47	0	3.45
						Calgary (NHL)	2	0	4.03
30	Mike Vernon	5-09/170	Calgary, Alta.	27	7	Calgary (NHL)	47	0	3.13
31	Rick Wamsley	5-11/185	Simcoe, Ont.	31	10	Calgary (NHL)	36	2	3.26

1989-90 RECORDS

1989-90 regular-season records: 42-23-15 (.619, 99 points, 1st in Smythe Division); 28-7-5 at home; 14-16-10 on road; 3-3-15 in overtime; 16-12-4 vs. Smythe (4-3-1 vs. Oilers; 4-3-1 vs. Kings; 5-1-2 vs. Canucks; 3-5-0 vs. Jets); 9-4-2 vs. Norris; 6-4-5 vs. Adams; 11-3-4 vs. Patrick.

MISCELLANEOUS DATA

1989-90 team rankings: Shorthanded goals for, 11 (T8th in NHL); shorthanded goals against, 6 (T2nd); power play, 27.7% (1st); penalty killing, 79.2% (13th); penalty minutes/game, 21.9.

TEAM HAT TRICKS, CAREER, ACTIVE

Doug Gilmour (2)	Dana Murzyn (1)
Jiri Hrdina (2)	Joe Nieuwendyk (7)
Mark Hunter (6)	Joel Otto (1)
Jim Korn (1)	Gary Roberts (1)
Brian MacLellan (4)	

MINOR LEAGUE AFFILIATIONS

Salt Lake (IHL)

Paul Ranheim

Mike Vernon

14

1990 DRAFT SELECTIONS

Rnd.	Player	Hgt.	Wgt.	Overall	(Pos.)	1989-90 Club	(League)
1	Trevor Kidd	6:02	176	11	(G)	Brandon	(WHL)
2	Nicolas Perreault	6:03	200	26	(D)	Hawkesbury Tier II	
2	Vesa Viitakoski	6:02	205	32	(LW)	Saipa, Finland	
2	Etienne Belzile	6:01	179	41	(D)	Cornell University	
3	Glen Mears	6:03	215	62	(D)	Rochester (Minn.) Jr. A	
4	Paul Kruse	6:00	202	83	(LW)	Kamloops	(WHL)
6	Chris Tschupp	6:02	180	125	(C)	Trinity Pawling H.S. (N.Y.)	
7	Dimitri Frolov	6:03	213	146	(D)	Dynamo Moscow	
8	Shawn Murray	5:09	160	167	(G)	Hill Murray H.S. (Minn.)	
9	Mike Murray	6:01	185	188	(RW)	Cushing Academy (Ct.)	
10	Rob Sumner	6:01	210	209	(D)	Victoria	(WHL)
11	Pick voided			230			
12	Leo Gudas	.....	....	251	(D)	Sparta Praha, Czech.	

FIRST-ROUND ENTRY DRAFT SELECTIONS

Year	Name	Overall	Last Amateur Team	(League)	Years in NHL
1972	Jacques Richard	2	Quebec	(QMJHL)	10
1973	Tom Lysiak	2	Medicine Hat	(WCHL)	13
	Vic Mercredi	16	New Westminster	(WCHL)	1
1974	No first round selection				
1975	Richard Mulhern	8	Sherbrooke	(QMJHL)	6
1976	Dave Shand	8	Peterborough	(OHL)	8
	Harold Phillipoff	10	New Westminster	(WCHL)	3
1977	No first round selection				
1978	Brad Marsh	11	London	(OHL)	12
1979	Paul Reinhart	12	Kitchener	(OHL)	11
1980	Denis Cyr	13	Montreal	(QMJHL)	6
1981	Al MacInnis	15	Kitchener	(OHL)	9
1982	No first round selection				
1983	Dan Quinn	13	Belleville	(OHL)	7
1984	Gary Roberts	12	Ottawa	(OHL)	4
1985	Chris Biotti	17	Belmont Hill H.S. (Mass.)		0
1986	George Pelawa	16	Bemidji H.S. (Minn.)		0
1987	Bryan Deasley	19	University of Michigan		0
1988	Jason Muzzatti	21	Michigan State University		0
1989	No first round selection				
1990	Trevor Kidd	11	Brandon	(WHL)	0

Paul Reinhart

COACHING HISTORY

Bernie Geoffrion, 1972-73 to 1973-74
Bernie Geoffrion and Fred Creighton, 1974-75
Fred Creighton, 1975-76 to 1978-79
Al MacNeil, 1979-80 to 1981-82

Bob Johnson, 1982-83 to 1986-87
Terry Crisp, 1987-88 to 1989-90
Doug Risebrough for 1990-91

FRANCHISE LEADERS

Current players in bold type
(1972-73 through 1989-90)

Games
1. 705—Jim Peplinski
2. 539—Eric Vail
3. **528—Al MacInnis**
4. 517—Paul Reinhart
5. 514—Guy Chouinard
6. 492—Lanny McDonald
7. **481—Tim Hunter**
8. **470—Jamie Macoun**
9. 468—Rey Comeau
10. 462—Ken Houston

Goals
1. 229—Kent Nilsson
2. 215—Lanny McDonald
3. 206—Eric Vail
4. 193—Guy Chouinard
   193—Hakan Loob
6. 190—Joe Mullen
7. 161—Jim Peplinski
8. 155—Tom Lysiak
9. **152—Joe Nieuwendyk**
10. 150—Willi Plett

Assists
1. **381—Al MacInnis**
2. 336—Guy Chouinard
3. 335—Paul Reinhart
4. 333—Kent Nilsson
5. 276—Tom Lysiak
6. **268—Gary Suter**
7. 262—Jim Peplinski
8. 246—Eric Vail
9. 236—Hakan Loob
10. 199—Joe Mullen

Points
1. 562—Kent Nilsson
2. 529—Guy Chouinard
3. **507—Al MacInnis**
4. 452—Eric Vail
5. 444—Paul Reinhart
6. 431—Tom Lysiak
7. 429—Hakan Loob
8. 423—Jim Peplinski
9. 406—Lanny McDonald
10. 389—Joe Mullen

Penalty Minutes
1. **2095—Tim Hunter**
2. 1456—Jim Peplinski
3. 1267—Willi Plett
4. **924—Joel Otto**
5. **839—Gary Roberts**
6. **623—Al MacInnis**
7. 606—Neil Sheehy

Goaltenders

Games
1. 398—Dan Bouchard
2. 324—Reggie Lemelin
3. **238—Mike Vernon**
4. 211—Phil Myre
5. 119—Pat Riggin
6. 114—Don Edwards
7. **73—Rick Wamsley**

Shutouts
1. 20—Dan Bouchard
2. 11—Phil Myre
3. 6—Reggie Lemelin
4. 4—Pat Riggin
   4—Rick Wamsley
6. **3—Mike Vernon**

Goals Against Average (entire roster)
(2400 minutes minimum)
1. 3.03—Dan Bouchard
2. **3.13—Rick Wamsley**
3. 3.21—Phil Myre
4. **3.30—Mike Vernon**
5. 3.67—Reggie Lemelin
6. 3.88—Pat Riggin
7. 4.06—Don Edwards

Wins
1. 170—Dan Bouchard
2. 144—Reggie Lemelin
3. **138—Mike Vernon**
4. 76—Phil Myre
5. 50—Pat Riggin
6. 40—Don Edwards

Steve Larmer has not missed a regular-season game in the last eight years.

Doug Wilson has led Chicago defensemen in scoring in each of the last nine seasons.

Three of Steve Thomas' seven playoff goals for Chicago last season were game-winners.

Wayne Presley scored nine goals in 19 playoff games last year after scoring just six in 49 regular-season games.

CHICAGO BLACKHAWKS

CLUB DIRECTORY

President
William W. Wirtz
Vice-President
Arthur M. Wirtz, Jr.
Vice-President and Assistant to the President
Thomas N. Ivan
Senior Vice-President
Bob Pulford
General Manager and Coach
Mike Keenan
Assistant General Manager and Director of Player Personnel
Jack Davison
Associate Coach
Darryl Sutter
Assistant Coach
E. J. McGuire
Scouts
Jimmy Walker, Dave Lucas, Kerry Davison, Michel

Dumas, Jim Pappin, Jan Spieczny, Duane Sutter, Steve Lyons, Brian DeBruyn
Public Relations
Jim DeMaria
Trainers
Mike Gapski, Lou Varga, Randy Lacey
Home Ice
Chicago Stadium
Address
1800 W. Madison Street, Chicago, Illinois 60612
Seating Capacity
17,317
Club Colors
Red, Black and White
Phone
(312) 733-5300

YEAR-BY-YEAR RESULTS

Season	W.	L.	T.	Pts.	Position	Season	W.	L.	T.	Pts.	Position
1926-27	19	22	3	41	Third—a	1959-60	28	29	13	69	Third—b
1927-28	7	34	3	17	Fifth—*	1960-61	29	24	17	75	Third—xx
1928-29	7	29	8	22	Fifth—*	1961-62	31	26	13	75	Third—c
1929-30	21	18	5	47	Second—a	1962-63	32	21	17	81	Second—b
1930-31	24	17	3	51	Second—c	1963-64	36	22	12	84	Second—b
1931-32	18	19	11	47	Second—a	1964-65	34	28	8	76	Third—c
1932-33	16	20	12	44	Fourth—*	1965-66	37	25	8	82	Second—b
1933-34	20	17	11	51	Second—xx	1966-67	41	17	12	94	First—b
1934-35	26	17	5	57	Second—a	1967-68	32	26	16	80	Fourth—b
1935-36	21	19	8	50	Third—a	1968-69	34	33	9	77	Sixth—*
1936-37	14	27	7	35	Fourth—*	1969-70	45	22	9	99	First—b
1937-38	14	25	9	37	Third—xx	1970-71	49	20	9	107	First—c
1938-39	12	28	8	32	Seventh—*	1971-72	46	17	15	107	First—b
1939-40	23	19	6	52	Fourth—a	1972-73	42	27	9	93	First—c
1940-41	16	25	7	39	Fifth—b	1973-74	41	14	23	105	Second—b
1941-42	22	23	3	47	Fourth—a	1974-75	37	35	8	82	Third—a
1942-43	17	18	15	49	Fifth—*	1975-76	32	30	18	82	First—a
1943-44	22	23	5	49	Fourth—c	1976-77	26	43	11	63	Third—†
1944-45	13	30	7	33	Fifth—*	1977-78	32	29	19	83	First—a
1945-46	23	20	7	53	Third—b	1978-79	29	36	15	73	First—a
1946-47	19	37	4	42	Sixth—*	1979-80	34	27	19	87	First—a
1947-48	20	34	6	46	Sixth—*	1980-81	31	33	16	78	Second—†
1948-49	21	31	8	50	Fifth—*	1981-82	30	38	12	72	Fourth—b
1949-50	22	38	10	54	Sixth—*	1982-83	47	23	10	104	First—b
1950-51	13	47	10	36	Sixth—*	1983-84	30	42	8	68	Fourth—†
1951-52	17	44	9	43	Sixth—*	1984-85	38	35	7	83	Second—b
1952-53	27	28	15	69	Fourth—b	1985-86	39	33	8	86	First—†
1953-54	12	51	7	31	Sixth—*	1986-87	29	37	14	72	Third—†
1954-55	13	40	17	43	Sixth—*	1987-88	30	41	9	69	Third—†
1955-56	19	39	12	50	Sixth—*	1988-89	27	41	12	66	Fourth—b
1956-57	16	39	15	47	Sixth—*	1989-90	41	33	6	88	First—b
1957-58	24	39	7	55	Fifth—*	**Totals**	**1695**	**1853**	**658**	**4048**	
1958-59	28	29	13	69	Third—b						

Key to standings: *—Missed playoffs. †—Eliminated in first round of new playoff format (1974-75). a—Eliminated in quarterfinal round. b—Eliminated in semifinal round. c—Eliminated in final round. xx—Stanley Cup champion.

—DID YOU KNOW—

That Chicago has missed the playoffs just once in the last 32 years?

That the Blackhawks' 22-point improvement in 1989-90 from the year before was the largest of any NHL team?

1990-91 SCHEDULE

☐ Home games shaded.

* At Chicago Stadium.

OCTOBER

Sun	Mon	Tue	Wed	Thu	Fri	Sat
	1	2	3	4 NYR	5	6 STL
7 NYI	8	9	10	11 PIT	12	13 MIN
14 CAL	15	16 DET	17	18 TOR	19	20 TOR
21 MIN	22	23	24	25 WAS	26	27 BOS
28 MON	29	30	31			

NOVEMBER

Sun	Mon	Tue	Wed	Thu	Fri	Sat
				1 QUE	2	3 PHI
4 LA	5	6 HAR	7	8 EDM	9	10 TOR
11 WIN	12	13	14 DET	15	16 WAS	17 QUE
18	19	20 EDM	21 VAN	22	23	24 CAL
25	26	27	28	29 DET	30	

DECEMBER

Sun	Mon	Tue	Wed	Thu	Fri	Sat
						1 DET
2 STL	3	4	5	6 NYI	7	8 TOR
9 PHI	10	11 PIT	12	13 WIN	14	15 MIN
16 MIN	17	18	19 WAS	20	21	22 STL
23 DET	24	25	26 STL	27	28 BUF	29 NYI
30	31 DET					

JANUARY

Sun	Mon	Tue	Wed	Thu	Fri	Sat
		1	2	3 NJ	4	5
6 LA	7	8	9	10 TOR	11 WIN	12
13 MIN	14	15	16 NJ	17 NYR	18	19 ALL-STAR GAME*
20	21	22	23	24 BUF	25	26 TOR
27	28 VAN	29	30	31		

FEBRUARY

Sun	Mon	Tue	Wed	Thu	Fri	Sat
					1 EDM	2 CAL
3	4	5	6 MON	7	8	9 BOS
10 HAR	11	12	13	14 QUE	15	16
17 DET	18 PHI	19	20	21 BOS	22	23 MIN
24 STL	25	26 STL	27	28 HAR		

MARCH

Sun	Mon	Tue	Wed	Thu	Fri	Sat
					1	2
3 VAN	4	5	6 MON	7	8 BUF	9
10 NYR	11	12	13	14 LA	15	16 STL
17 STL	18	19	20	21 NJ	22	23 PIT
24 MIN	25	26 TOR	27	28 MIN	29	30 MIN
31 DET						

1989-90 RESULTS

Oct.	5—St. Louis	L	3-8
	7—At Washington	W	3-2
	8—N.Y. Rangers	L	3-5
	12—Toronto	W	9-6
	14—At St. Louis	L	1-2
	15—Detroit	W	3-0
	17—At N.Y. Rangers	T	3-3 (OT)
	19—Quebec	L	3-6
	20—At Winnipeg	W	4-2
	22—Los Angeles	W	7-4
	24—At Detroit	W	5-3
	26—Montreal	W	5-3
	28—At New Jersey	L	2-3
	29—Washington	W	1-0
	31—At Quebec	W	5-3
Nov.	2—Minnesota	W	4-3 (OT)
	4—At Minnesota	L	0-3
	5—Winnipeg	W	4-3 (OT)
	9—Pittsburgh	W	4-3
	11—At N.Y. Islanders	W	5-3
	12—Hartford	W	4-2
	16—At Vancouver	L	3-4
	18—At Calgary	T	4-4 (OT)
	19—At Edmonton	L	4-5 (OT)
	22—At Los Angeles	L	3-6
	26—At Minnesota	L	3-5
	30—N.Y. Islanders	L	0-2
Dec.	3—Detroit	L	3-4
	6—Toronto	W	6-4
	9—At Pittsburgh	W	6-4
	10—Vancouver	W	7-1
	13—At Montreal	W	3-1
	15—At Detroit	L	4-8
	17—Edmonton	W	6-5
	20—St. Louis	W	9-6
	22—Toronto	L	3-5
	23—At Toronto	W	7-5
	26—At St. Louis	L	3-8
	28—Minnesota	T	1-1 (OT)
	30—Hartford	W	7-3
Jan.	3—Edmonton	W	3-2
	6—Philadelphia	W	8-5
	10—At N.Y. Rangers	T	2-2 (OT)
	11—At Philadelphia	W	5-4
	14—Calgary	L	5-6
	15—At Toronto	L	6-7
	17—Minnesota	W	3-1
	19—Vancouver	W	5-2
	24—Buffalo	L	2-3
	26—At Buffalo	W	4-2
	27—At Hartford	L	4-6
Feb.	1—At Los Angeles	W	7-4
	4—At Winnipeg	L	3-7
	8—At Detroit	W	8-6
	10—At Minnesota	L	4-6
	13—Buffalo	W	4-1
	15—Calgary	L	1-4
	17—At N.Y. Islanders	W	3-1
	18—Pittsburgh	W	6-4
	20—At St. Louis	W	8-3
	22—Boston	L	3-6
	24—At New Jersey	L	2-3
	25—Philadelphia	W	4-1
	27—At Washington	L	0-4
Mar.	1—St. Louis	L	4-6
	3—At Boston	L	3-4
	4—Boston	L	1-4
	7—At Minnesota	L	4-5
	10—At St. Louis	T	2-2 (OT)
	11—St. Louis	L	4-6
	13—Detroit	T	3-3 (OT)
	15—At Quebec	W	6-3
	17—At Montreal	L	2-3 (OT)
	19—At Toronto	W	3-2
	22—New Jersey	W	6-3
	24—At Detroit	L	3-5
	25—Detroit	W	3-2
	29—Toronto	W	4-2
	31—At Toronto	L	4-6
Apr.	1—Minnesota	W	4-1

1990-91 ROSTER

No.	FORWARDS	Hgt./Wt.	Place of Birth	Age	NHL exp.	1989-90 club (league)	G.	A.	Pts.
15	Bob Bassen	5-10/180	Calgary, Alta.	25	5	Indianapolis (IHL)	22	32	54
						Chicago (NHL)	1	1	2
22	Adam Creighton	6-05/214	Burlington, Ont.	25	8	Chicago (NHL)	34	36	70
11	Mike Eagles	5-10/180	Sussex, N.B.	27	6	Indianapolis (IHL)	11	13	24
						Chicago (NHL)	1	2	3
14	Greg Gilbert	6-01/192	Mississauga, Ont.	28	9	Chicago (NHL)	12	25	37
16	Michel Goulet	6-01/195	Peribonka, Que.	30	11	Quebec (NHL)	16	29	45
						Chicago (NHL)	4	1	5
33	Dirk Graham	5-11/190	Regina, Sask.	31	7	Chicago (NHL)	22	32	54
43	Mike Hudson	6-01/185	Guelph, Ont.	23	2	Chicago (NHL)	9	12	21
	Jim Johansson	6-02/200	Rochester, Minn.	26	0	Indianapolis (IHL)	22	41	63
28	Steve Larmer	5-10/189	Peterborough, Ont.	29	10	Chicago (NHL)	31	59	90
26	Jocelyn Lemieux	5-10/200	Mont-Laurier, Que.	22	4	Montreal (NHL)	4	2	6
						Chicago (NHL)	10	11	21
19	Troy Murray	6-01/195	Calgary, Alta.	28	9	Chicago (NHL)	17	38	55
10	Brian Noonan	6-01/180	Boston, Mass.	25	3	Indianapolis (IHL)	40	36	76
						Chicago (NHL)	0	2	2
17	Wayne Presley	5-11/172	Detroit, Mich.	25	6	Chicago (NHL)	6	7	13
27	Jeremy Roenick	5-11/170	Boston, Mass.	20	2	Chicago (NHL)	26	40	66
	Warren Rychel	6-00/190	Tecumseh, Ont.	23	1	Indianapolis (IHL)	23	16	39
32	Steve Thomas	5-10/185	Stockport, England	27	6	Chicago (NHL)	40	30	70
23	Wayne Van Dorp	6-04/225	Vancouver, B.C.	29	4	Chicago (NHL)	7	4	11
	DEFENSEMEN								
	Adam Bennett	6-04/206	Georgetown, Ont.	19	0	Sudbury (OHL)	18	43	61
4	Keith Brown	6-01/191	Cornerbrook, Nfld.	30	11	Chicago (NHL)	5	20	25
37	Bruce Cassidy	5-11/176	Ottawa, Ont.	25	6	Indianapolis (IHL)	11	46	57
						Chicago (NHL)	1	1	2
	Chris Chelios	6-01/192	Chicago, Ill.	28	7	Montreal (NHL)	9	22	31
5	Steve Konroyd	6-01/195	Scarborough, Ont.	29	10	Chicago (NHL)	3	14	17
	Rick Lanz	6-01/195	Karlouyvary, Czech.	29	9	Ambri (Switz.)	...	...	...
3	Dave Manson	6-02/190	Prince Albert, Sask.	23	4	Chicago (NHL)	5	23	28
25	Bob McGill	6-01/190	Edmonton, Alta.	28	9	Chicago (NHL)	2	10	12
	Ryan McGill	6-02/197	Sherwood Park, Alta.	21	0	Indianapolis (IHL)	11	17	28
26	Mike Peluso	6-04/225	Pengilly, Minn.	25	0	Indianapolis (IHL)	7	10	17
						Chicago (NHL)	0	0	0
52	Cam Russell	6-04/175	Halifax, Nova Scotia	21	1	Indianapolis (IHL)	3	15	18
						Chicago (NHL)	0	1	1
	Michael Speer	6-02/202	Toronto, Ont.	19	0	Owen Sound (OHL)	18	39	57
24	Doug Wilson	6-01/187	Ottawa, Ont.	33	13	Chicago (NHL)	23	50	73
8	Trent Yawney	6-03/183	Hudson Bay, Sask.	25	3	Chicago (NHL)	5	15	20

No.	GOALTENDERS	Hgt./Wt.	Place of Birth	Age	NHL exp.	1989-90 club (league)	Ga.	SO	Avg.
30	Ed Belfour	5-11/170	Carman, Man.	25	2	Canadian National Team	33	0	3.08
31	Jacques Cloutier	5-07/168	Noranda, Que.	30	8	Chicago (NHL)	43	2	3.09
	Dominik Hasek	5-11/165	Pardubice, Czech.	25	0	Dukla Jihlava	...	...	...
29	Greg Millen	5-09/175	Toronto, Ont.	33	12	St. Louis (NHL)	21	1	2.94
						Quebec (NHL)	18	6	5.28
						Chicago (NHL)	10	0	3.34
	Darren Pang	5-05/155	Medford, Ont.	26	3	Indianapolis (IHL)	7	1	2.54
	Jimmy Waite	6-00/163	Sherbrooke, Que.	21	2	Indianapolis (IHL)	54	5	2.53
						Chicago (NHL)	4	0	4.59

1989-90 RECORDS

1989-90 regular-season records: 41-33-6 (.550, 88 points, 1st in Norris Division); 25-13-2 at home; 16-20-4 on road; 2-2-6 in overtime; 14-15-3 vs. Norris (4-3-1 vs. Red Wings; 3-4-1 vs. North Stars; 2-5-1 vs. Blues; 5-3-0 vs. Maple Leafs); 8-6-1 vs. Smythe; 8-7-0 vs. Adams; 11-5-2 vs. Patrick.

MISCELLANEOUS DATA

1989-90 team rankings: Shorthanded goals for, 11 (T8th in NHL); shorthanded goals against, 9 (10th); power play, 22.9% (6th); penalty killing, 80.2% (12th); penalty minutes/game, 30.3.

TEAM HAT TRICKS, CAREER, ACTIVE

Adam Creighton (2)	Jocelyn Lemieux (1)
Greg Gilbert (2)	Troy Murray (4)
Michel Goulet (13)	Wayne Presley (1)
Dirk Graham (1)	Jeremy Roenick (1)
Steve Larmer (4)	Steve Thomas (3)

MINOR LEAGUE AFFILIATIONS

Indianapolis (IHL)

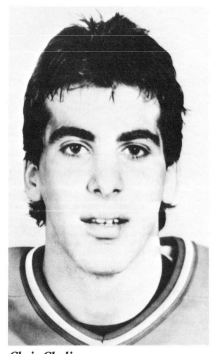

Chris Chelios

1990 DRAFT SELECTIONS

Rnd.	Player	Hgt.	Wgt.	Overall	(Pos.)	1989-90 Club	(League)
1	Karl Dykhuis	6:02	184	16	(D)	Hull	(QMJHL)
2	Ivan Droppa	6:02	209	37	(D)	L. Mikulas, Czech.	
4	Chris Tucker	5:11	183	79	(C)	Jefferson H.S.	(Minn.)
6	Brett Stickney	6:05	205	121	(C)	St. Paul's H.S.	(N.H.)
6	Derek Edgerly	6:01	190	124	(C)	Stoneham H.S.	(Mass.)
8	Hugo Belanger	6:01	190	163	(LW)	Clarkson University	
9	Owen Lessard	6:01	196	184	(LW)	Owen Sound	(OHL)
10	Erik Peterson	6:00	185	205	(C)	Brockton H.S.	(Mass.)
11	Steve Dubinsky	6:00	180	226	(C)	Clarkson University	
12	Dino Grossi	6:00	190	247	(RW)	Northeastern University	

FIRST-ROUND ENTRY DRAFT SELECTIONS

Year	Name	Overall	Last Amateur Team	(League)	Years in NHL
1969	J.P. Bordeleau	13	Montreal	(OHL)	9
1970	Dan Maloney	14	London	(OHL)	11
1971	Dan Spring	12	Edmonton	(WCHL)	0
1972	Phil Russell	13	Edmonton	(WCHL)	15
1973	Darcy Rota	13	Edmonton	(WCHL)	11
1974	Grant Mulvey	16	Calgary	(WCHL)	10
1975	Greg Vaydik	7	Medicine Hat	(WCHL)	1
1976	Real Cloutier	9	Quebec	(WHA)	6
1977	Doug Wilson	6	Ottawa	(OHL)	13
1978	Tim Higgins	10	Ottawa	(OHL)	11
1979	Keith Brown	7	Portland	(WHL)	11
1980	Denis Savard	3	Montreal	(QMJHL)	10
	Jerome Dupont	15	Toronto	(OHL)	6
1981	Tony Tanti	12	Oshawa	(OHL)	9
1982	Ken Yaremchuk	7	Portland	(WHL)	6
1983	Bruce Cassidy	18	Ottawa	(OHL)	6
1984	Ed Olczyk	3	U.S. Olympic Team		6
1985	Dave Manson	11	Prince Albert	(WHL)	4
1986	Everett Sanipass	14	Verdun	(QMJHL)	4
1987	Jimmy Waite	8	Chicoutimi	(QMJHL)	2
1988	Jeremy Roenick	8	Thayer Academy	(Mass.)	2
1989	Adam Bennett	6	Sudbury	(OHL)	0
1990	Karl Dykhuis	16	Hull	(QMJHL)	0

Phil Russell

COACHING HISTORY

Pete Muldoon, 1926-27
Barney Stanley and Hugh Lehman, 1927-28
Herb Gardiner, 1928-29
Tom Shaughnessy and Bill Tobin, 1929-30
Dick Irvin, 1930-31
Dick Irvin and Bill Tobin, 1931-32
Godfrey Matheson and Emil Iverson, 1932-33
Tom Gorman, 1933-34
Clem Loughlin, 1934-35 to 1936-37
Bill Stewart, 1937-38
Bill Stewart and Paul Thompson, 1938-39
Paul Thompson, 1939-40 to 1943-44
Paul Thompson and John Gottselig, 1944-45
John Gottselig, 1945-46 to 1946-47
John Gottselig and Charlie Conacher, 1947-48
Charlie Conacher, 1948-49 to 1949-50
Ebbie Goodfellow, 1950-51 to 1951-52

Sid Abel, 1952-53 to 1953-54
Frank Eddolls, 1954-55
Dick Irvin, 1955-56
Tommy Ivan, 1956-57
Tommy Ivan and Rudy Pilous, 1957-58
Rudy Pilous, 1958-59 to 1962-63
Billy Reay, 1963-64 to 1975-76
Billy Reay and Bill White, 1976-77
Bob Pulford, 1977-78 to 1978-79
Eddie Johnston, 1979-80
Keith Magnuson, 1980-81
Keith Magnuson and Bob Pulford, 1981-82
Orval Tessier, 1982-83 to 1983-84
Orval Tessier and Bob Pulford, 1984-85
Bob Pulford, 1985-86 to 1986-87
Bob Murdoch, 1987-88
Mike Keenan since 1988-90

FRANCHISE LEADERS

Current players in bold type
(1926-27 through 1989-90)

Goals
1. 604—Bobby Hull
2. 541—Stan Mikita
3. 351—Denis Savard
4. 298—Dennis Hull
   298—**Steve Larmer**
6. 258—Bill Mosienko
7. 252—Ken Wharram
8. 243—Pit Martin
9. 217—Doug Bentley
10. 216—Jim Pappin
11. 214—**Doug Wilson**
12. 213—Al Secord
13. 208—Cliff Koroll
14. 207—Eric Nesterenko
15. 182—**Troy Murray**
16. 176—John Gottselig
17. 161—Darryl Sutter
18. 153—Ed Litzenberger
    153—Harold March
20. 149—Chico Maki

Assists
1. 926—Stan Mikita
2. 662—Denis Savard
3. 549—Bobby Hull
4. 525—**Doug Wilson**
5. 400—Pierre Pilote
6. 384—Pit Martin
7. 382—Bob Murray
8. 380—**Steve Larmer**
9. 342—Dennis Hull
10. 313—Doug Bentley
11. 292—Chico Maki
12. 288—Bill Mosienko
    288—Eric Nesterenko
14. 286—Pat Stapleton
15. 283—Bill Hay
16. 281—Ken Wharram
17. 275—Tom Lysiak
18. 264—**Troy Murray**
19. 254—Cliff Koroll
20. 240—**Keith Brown**

Points
1. 1,467—Stan Mikita
2. 1,153—Bobby Hull
3. 1,013—Denis Savard
4. 739—**Doug Wilson**
5. 678—**Steve Larmer**
6. 640—Dennis Hull
7. 627—Pit Martin
8. 550—Bill Mosienko
9. 533—Ken Wharram
10. 531—Doug Bentley
11. 514—Bob Murray
12. 495—Eric Nesterenko
13. 477—Pierre Pilote
14. 462—Cliff Koroll
15. 446—**Troy Murray**
16. 444—Jim Pappin
17. 441—Chico Maki
18. 412—Tom Lysiak
19. 386—Bill Hay
20. 383—Harold March

Goaltenders

Shutouts
1. 74—Tony Esposito
2. 51—Glenn Hall
3. 42—Chuck Gardiner
4. 28—Mike Karakas
5. 17—Al Rollins
6. 13—Denis DeJordy
7. 8—Murray Bannerman
   8—Lorne Chabot
9. 6—Paul Goodman
   6—Hugh Lehman

Jimmy Carson has averaged 40 goals per season in his four-year NHL career. He missed 32 games last season, the first time in his career he has failed to play all 80 games.

Gerard Gallant (from 1986-87 through 1989-90) is only the second Detroit player to score 34 or more goals in four consecutive seasons. Gordie Howe did it from 1949-50 through 1952-53.

Steve Yzerman scored goals in more than 75 percent of Detroit's games last year. Yzerman scored at least one goal in 61 of the Red Wings' 80 games.

Joey Kocur set career highs in goals (16), assists (20) and points (36) during the 1989-90 season.

DETROIT RED WINGS

CLUB DIRECTORY

Owner and President
Michael Ilitch
Executive Vice-President
James Lites
Secretary/Treasurer
Marian Ilitch
General Counsel
Denise Ilitch-Lites
Senior Vice-President
Jim Devellano
General Manager and Coach
Bryan Murray
Assistant General Manager
Nick Polano
Assistant Coaches
Dave Lewis, Doug MacLean
Goaltenders Consultant
Phil Myre
Pro Scout
Dan Belisle
Director of Amateur Scouting
Ken Holland
USA College/High School Scouts
Billy Dea, Chris Coury
Eastern USA Scout
Jerry Moschella

Northern Ontario Scout
Dave Polano
Western Hockey League Scout
Wayne Meier
Director of Public Relations
Bill Jamieson
Director of Advertising Sales
Terry Murphy
Physical Therapist
Kirk Vickers
Trainer
Mark Brennan
Assistant Trainer
Larry Wasylon
Home Ice
Joe Louis Sports Arena
Address
600 Civic Center Drive, Detroit, Mich. 48226
Seating Capacity
19,275
Club Colors
Red and White
Phone
(313) 567-7333
FAX
(313) 567-0296

YEAR-BY-YEAR RESULTS

Season	W.	L.	T.	Pts.	Position	Season	W.	L.	T.	Pts.	Position
1926-27	12	28	4	28	Fifth—*	1959-60	26	29	15	67	Fourth—b
1927-28	19	19	6	44	Fourth—*	1960-61	25	29	16	66	Fourth—c
1928-29	19	16	9	47	Third—a	1961-62	23	33	14	60	Fifth—*
1929-30	14	24	6	34	Fourth—*	1962-63	32	25	13	77	Fourth—c
1930-31	16	21	7	39	Fourth—*	1963-64	30	29	11	71	Fourth—c
1931-32	18	20	10	46	Third—a	1964-65	40	23	7	87	First—b
1932-33	25	15	8	58	Second—b	1965-66	31	27	12	74	Fourth—c
1933-34	24	14	10	58	First—c	1966-67	27	39	4	58	Fifth—*
1934-35	19	22	7	45	Fourth—*	1967-68	27	35	12	66	Sixth—*
1935-36	24	16	8	56	First—xx	1968-69	33	31	12	78	Fifth—*
1936-37	25	14	9	59	First—xx	1969-70	40	21	15	95	Third—a
1937-38	12	25	11	35	Fourth—*	1970-71	22	45	11	55	Seventh—*
1938-39	18	24	6	42	Fifth—b	1971-72	33	35	10	76	Fifth—*
1939-40	16	26	6	38	Fifth—b	1972-73	37	29	12	86	Fifth—*
1940-41	21	16	11	53	Third—c	1973-74	29	39	10	68	Sixth—*
1941-42	19	25	4	42	Fifth—c	1974-75	23	45	12	58	Fourth—*
1942-43	25	14	11	61	First—xx	1975-76	26	44	10	62	Fourth—*
1943-44	26	18	6	58	Second—b	1976-77	16	55	9	41	Fifth—*
1944-45	31	14	5	67	Second—c	1977-78	32	34	14	78	Second—a
1945-46	20	20	10	50	Fourth—b	1978-79	23	41	16	62	Fifth—*
1946-47	22	27	11	55	Fourth—b	1979-80	26	43	11	63	Fifth—*
1947-48	30	18	12	72	Second—c	1980-81	19	43	18	56	Fifth—*
1948-49	34	19	7	75	First—c	1981-82	21	47	12	54	Sixth—*
1949-50	37	19	14	88	First—xx	1982-83	21	44	15	57	Fifth—*
1950-51	44	13	13	101	First—b	1983-84	31	42	7	69	Third—†
1951-52	44	14	12	100	First—xx	1984-85	27	41	12	66	Third—†
1952-53	36	16	18	90	First—b	1985-86	17	57	6	40	Fifth—*
1953-54	37	19	14	88	First—xx	1986-87	34	36	10	78	Second—b
1954-55	42	17	11	95	First—xx	1987-88	41	28	11	93	First—b
1955-56	30	24	16	76	Second—c	1988-89	34	34	12	80	First—†
1956-57	38	20	12	88	First—b	1989-90	28	38	14	70	Fifth—*
1957-58	29	29	12	70	Third—b	Totals	1725	1804	677	4127	
1958-59	25	37	8	58	Sixth—*						

Key to standings: *—Missed playoffs. †—Eliminated in first round of new playoff format (1974-75). a—Eliminated in quarterfinal round. b—Eliminated in semifinal round. c—Eliminated in final round. xx—Stanley Cup champion.

—DID YOU KNOW—

That Detroit has drawn more than 19,000 fans for all but two of its last 145 games at Joe Louis Arena? The building's seating capacity is 19,275.

1990-91 SCHEDULE

Home games shaded.

* At Chicago Stadium.

OCTOBER

Sun	Mon	Tue	Wed	Thu	Fri	Sat
	1	2	3	4 NJ	5	6 WAS
7 PHI	8	9	10 CAL	11	12 HAR	13 TOR
14	15	16 CHI	17	18 MON	19	20 QUE
21	22	23 VAN	24	25	26 MIN	27 MIN
28	29	30 STL	31			

NOVEMBER

Sun	Mon	Tue	Wed	Thu	Fri	Sat
				1 TOR	2	3 MON
4	5	6 VAN	7	8 LA	9	10 STL
11	12	13	14 CHI	15	16 TOR	17 TOR
18	19 WAS	20	21 MIN	22	23 STL	24
25	26	27 LA	28	29 CHI	30	

DECEMBER

Sun	Mon	Tue	Wed	Thu	Fri	Sat
						1 CHI
2 BUF	3	4 BOS	5	6	7 STL	8 STL
9	10	11 BUF	12	13 QUE	14	15 PHI
16 PIT	17	18 PHI	19	20 WIN	21	22 WIN
23 CHI	24	25	26	27	28 PIT	29
30	31 CHI					

JANUARY

Sun	Mon	Tue	Wed	Thu	Fri	Sat
		1 MIN	2	3	4 EDM	5 CAL
6	7	8 EDM	9	10	11 NYR	12 NYI
13	14 BOS	15	16 BUF	17	18	19 ALL-STAR GAME*
20	21	22 WAS	23	24	25 STL	26 STL
27	28 NJ	29	30 MIN	31		

FEBRUARY

Sun	Mon	Tue	Wed	Thu	Fri	Sat
					1 TOR	2 TOR
3	4 LA	5	6	7	8 NYI	9 MIN
10	11	12 WIN	13 HAR	14	15	16 MIN
17 CHI	18	19 CAL	20	21	22 EDM	23 VAN
24	25	26	27 MON	28		

MARCH

Sun	Mon	Tue	Wed	Thu	Fri	Sat
					1 NJ	2
3	4	5 QUE	6	7 NYI	8	9 MIN
10 STL	11	12	13 NYR	14 HAR	15	16 BOS
17	18	19	20	21	22 TOR	23 TOR
24	25	26	27 PIT	28	29	30 NYR
31 CHI						

1989-90 RESULTS

Oct.	5—At Calgary	L	7-10
	7—At Vancouver	L	3-5
	8—At Los Angeles	L	0-5
	12—Winnipeg	W	5-4
	14—Buffalo	W	6-2
	15—At Chicago	L	0-3
	18—Minnesota	W	4-3
	19—At St. Louis	W	4-3
	21—At Hartford	T	3-3 (OT)
	24—Chicago	L	3-5
	26—Pittsburgh	T	3-3 (OT)
	28—At Toronto	L	4-6
Nov.	1—Philadelphia	T	5-5 (OT)
	3—Hartford	L	3-4
	4—At N.Y. Islanders	L	2-3
	6—At N.Y. Rangers	L	1-6
	9—At Minnesota	L	1-5
	11—At Toronto	L	2-4
	14—Hartford	L	0-3
	16—St. Louis	L	2-7
	18—At Quebec	W	8-1
	21—Boston	L	1-2 (OT)
	24—Calgary	W	3-2
	27—Edmonton	L	2-6
	29—Washington	L	3-5
Dec.	1—At Winnipeg	T	3-3 (OT)
	3—At Chicago	W	4-3
	5—St. Louis	T	2-2 (OT)
	8—Minnesota	W	2-1
	9—At Minnesota	W	3-1
	13—Toronto	L	2-4
	15—Chicago	W	8-4
	16—At Montreal	L	1-3
	20—Toronto	W	4-2
	23—At Boston	L	5-6
	26—At Buffalo	L	3-6
	27—At Toronto	T	7-7 (OT)
	29—At Washington	L	1-2
	31—New Jersey	W	6-4
Jan.	2—Vancouver	W	4-1
	4—Quebec	W	4-1
	6—At Minnesota	L	3-4
	9—Minnesota	W	9-0
	12—At Winnipeg	L	5-7
	13—At Minnesota	L	4-6
	16—At Edmonton	W	6-4
	18—At Los Angeles	L	4-9
	23—St. Louis	L	3-6
	25—Pittsburgh	L	3-5
	27—At Quebec	W	8-6
	31—Edmonton	W	7-5
Feb.	2—Toronto	W	5-2
	3—At St. Louis	L	2-4
	6—Boston	L	0-2
	8—Chicago	L	6-8
	10—Calgary	W	7-5
	12—At New Jersey	T	1-1 (OT)
	14—Los Angeles	W	6-5
	16—Philadelphia	W	9-6
	17—At St. Louis	L	1-6
	19—Montreal	T	5-5 (OT)
	21—N.Y. Rangers	T	4-4 (OT)
	24—At N.Y. Islanders	T	3-3 (OT)
	25—At Washington	L	4-9
	28—N.Y. Islanders	W	4-3
Mar.	2—Toronto	W	3-2 (OT)
	3—At Toronto	W	5-2
	5—At N.Y. Rangers	L	2-3
	8—St. Louis	W	3-2
	10—At Montreal	T	3-3 (OT)
	13—At Chicago	T	3-3 (OT)
	15—At Pittsburgh	L	1-6
	17—At St. Louis	W	4-3 (OT)
	20—Vancouver	T	4-4 (OT)
	22—Minnesota	L	1-5
	24—Chicago	W	5-3
	25—At Chicago	L	2-3
	27—Buffalo	L	5-6
	31—At New Jersey	L	1-5
Apr.	1—At Philadelphia	T	3-3 (OT)

1990-91 ROSTER

No.	FORWARDS	Hgt./Wt.	Place of Birth	Age	NHL exp.	1989-90 club (league)	G.	A.	Pts.
22	Dave Barr	6-01/190	Toronto, Ont.	29	9	Detroit (NHL)	10	25	35
						Adirondack (AHL)	1	14	15
11	Shawn Burr	6-01/195	Sarnia, Ont.	24	6	Detroit (NHL)	24	32	56
						Adirondack (AHL)	4	2	6
10	Jimmy Carson	6-00/200	Southfield, Mich.	22	4	Edmonton (NHL)	1	2	3
						Detroit (NHL)	20	16	36
16	John Chabot	6-02/200	Summerside, P.E.I.	28	7	Detroit (NHL)	9	40	49
	Sergei Federov	6-01/191	Pskow, Russia	20	0	CSKA Moscow (USSR)	19	10	29
15	Brent Fedyk	6-00/195	Yorkton, Sask.	23	3	Adirondack (AHL)	14	15	29
						Detroit (NHL)	1	4	5
17	Gerard Gallant	5-10/185	Summerside, P.E.I.	27	6	Detroit (NHL)	36	44	80
	John Garpenlov	5-11/185	Stockholm, Sweden	22	0	Djurgarden (Sweden)	20	13	33
25	Marc Habscheid	6-00/185	Swift Current, Sask.	27	9	Detroit (NHL)	15	11	26
12	Sheldon Kennedy	5-10/170	Brandon, Man.	21	1	Adirondack (AHL)	11	15	26
						Detroit (NHL)	2	7	9
26	Joe Kocur	6-00/195	Calgary, Alta.	25	6	Detroit (NHL)	16	20	36
	Kory Kocur	5-11/188	Kelvington, Sask.	21	0	Adirondack (AHL)	18	37	55
18	Kevin McClelland	6-02/205	Oshawa, Ont.	28	9	Edmonton (NHL)	1	1	2
						Detroit (NHL)	4	5	9
29	Randy McKay	6-01/185	Montreal, Que.	23	2	Adirondack (AHL)	16	23	39
						Detroit (NHL)	3	6	9
5	Chris McRae	6-00/200	Beaverton, Ont.	25	3	Adirondack (AHL)	9	10	19
						Detroit (NHL)	1	0	1
	Keith Primeau	6-04/217	Toronto, Ont.	18	0	Niagara Falls (OHL)	57	70	127
24	Bob Probert	6-03/215	Windsor, Ont.	25	5	Detroit (NHL)	3	0	3
34	Daniel Shank	5-10/190	Montreal, Que.	23	1	Adirondack (AHL)	8	8	16
						Detroit (NHL)	11	13	24
	Mike Sillinger	5-10/191	Regina, Sask.	19	0	Regina (WHL)	57	72	129
19	Steve Yzerman	5-11/185	Cranbrook, B.C.	25	7	Detroit (NHL)	62	65	127

No.	DEFENSEMEN	Hgt./Wt.	Place of Birth	Age	NHL exp.	1989-90 club (league)	G.	A.	Pts.
3	Steve Chiasson	6-01/205	Barrie, Ont.	23	4	Detroit (NHL)	14	28	42
	Per Djoos	5-11/175	Mora, Sweden	22	0	Brynas (Sweden)	5	13	18
	Rick Green	6-03/220	Belleville, Ont.	34	13	Marano (Italy)	5	12	17
27	Doug Houda	6-02/200	Blairmore, Alta.	24	4	Detroit (NHL)	2	9	11
	Brad McCrimmon	5-11/197	Dodsland, Sask.	31	11	Calgary (NHL)	4	15	19
23	Lee Norwood	6-01/198	Oakland, Calif.	30	8	Detroit (NHL)	8	14	22
7	Robert Picard	6-02/207	Montreal, Que.	33	13	Quebec (NHL)	0	5	5
						Detroit (NHL)	0	3	3
33	Yves Racine	6-00/185	Matane, Que.	21	1	Adirondack (AHL)	8	27	35
						Detroit (NHL)	4	9	13
	Bob Wilkie	6-02/200	Calgary, Alta.	21	0	Adirondack (AHL)	5	33	38
4	Rick Zombo	6-01/195	Des Plaines, Ill.	27	6	Detroit (NHL)	5	20	25

No.	GOALTENDERS	Hgt./Wt.	Place of Birth	Age	NHL exp.	1989-90 club (league)	Ga.	SO	Avg.
32	Tim Cheveldae	5-10/175	Melville, Sask.	22	2	Adirondack (AHL)	31	0	3.77
						Detroit (NHL)	28	0	3.79
	Alain Chevrier	5-08/180	Cornwall, Ont.	29	5	Chicago (NHL)	39	0	4.18
						Pittsburgh (NHL)	3	0	5.06
	Dave Gagnon	6-00/185	Windsor, Ont.	22	0	Colgate (ECAC)	33	2	2.81
1	Glen Hanlon	6-00/185	Brandon, Man.	33	13	Detroit (NHL)	45	1	4.03
	Scott King	6-01/185	Thunder Bay, Ont.	23	0	U. of Maine (Hockey East)	29	1	2.63
30	Greg Stefan	5-11/180	Brantford, Ont.	29	9	Detroit (NHL)	7	0	4.01
						Adirondack (AHL)	3	0	3.28

1989-90 RECORDS

1989-90 regular-season records: 28-38-14 (.438, 70 points, 5th in Norris Division); 20-14-6 at home; 8-24-8 on road; 2-1-14 in overtime; 14-15-3 vs. Norris (3-4-1 vs. Blackhawks; 4-4-0 vs. North Stars; 3-4-1 vs. Blues; 4-3-1 vs. Maple Leafs); 7-6-2 vs. Smythe; 4-8-3 vs. Adams; 3-9-6 vs. Patrick.

MISCELLANEOUS DATA

1989-90 team rankings: Shorthanded goals for, 18 (2nd in NHL); shorthanded goals against, 13 (T14th); power play, 16.4% (20th); penalty killing, 75.3% (18th); penalty minutes/game, 26.8.

TEAM HAT TRICKS, CAREER, ACTIVE

Gregory C. Adams (1)
Dave Barr (2)
Shawn Burr (2)
Jimmy Carson (7)
John Chabot (1)

Gerard Gallant (4)
Bob Probert (1)
Torrie Robertson (1)
Steve Yzerman (9)

MINOR LEAGUE AFFILIATIONS

Adirondack (AHL)

Brad McCrimmon

1990 DRAFT SELECTIONS

Rnd.	Player	Hgt.	Wgt.	Overall	(Pos.)	1989-90 Club	(League)
1	Keith Primeau	6:04	217	3	(C)	Niagara Falls	(OHL)
3	Viacheslav Kozlov	5:10	172	45	(C)	Chimik, USSR	
4	Stewart Malgunas	5:11	190	66	(D)	Seattle	(WHL)
5	Tony Burns	6:01	195	87	(D)	Duluth-Denfeld H.S.	(Minn.)
6	Claude Barthe	6:02	197	108	(D)	Victoriaville	(QMJHL)
7	Jason York	6:01	192	129	(D)	Kitchener	(OHL)
8	Wes McCauley	6:00	175	150	(D)	Michigan State University	
9	Anthony Gruba	6:00	205	171	(RW)	Hill Murray H.S.	(Minn.)
10	Travis Tucker	6:04	205	192	(D)	Avon Old Farms H.S.	(Ct.)
11	Brett Larson	6:00	175	213	(D)	Duluth-Denfeld H.S.	(Minn.)
12	John Hendry	6:01	180	234	(LW)	Lake Superior State Univ.	

FIRST-ROUND ENTRY DRAFT SELECTIONS

Year	Name	Overall	Last Amateur Team	(League)	Years in NHL
1969	Jim Rutherford	10	Hamilton	(OHL)	13
1970	Serge Lajeunesse	12	Montreal	(OHL)	5
1971	Marcel Dionne	2	St. Catharines	(OHL)	18
1972	No first round selection				
1973	Terry Richardson	11	New Westminster	(WCHL)	0
1974	Bill Lochead	9	Oshawa	(OHL)	6
1975	Rick Lapointe	5	Victoria	(WCHL)	11
1976	Fred Williams	4	Saskatoon	(WCHL)	1
1977	*Dale McCourt	1	St. Catharines	(OHL)	7
1978	Willie Huber	9	Hamilton	(OHL)	10
	Brent Peterson	12	Portland	(WCHL)	11
1979	Mike Foligno	3	Sudbury	(OHL)	11
1980	Mike Blaisdell	11	Regina	(WHL)	9
1981	No first round selection				
1982	Murray Craven	17	Medicine Hat	(WHL)	8
1983	Steve Yzerman	4	Peterborough	(OHL)	7
1984	Shawn Burr	7	Kitchener	(OHL)	6
1985	Brent Fedyk	8	Regina	(WHL)	3
1986	*Joe Murphy	1	Michigan State University		4
1987	Yves Racine	11	Longueuil	(QMJHL)	1
1988	Kory Kocur	17	Saskatoon	(WHL)	0
1989	Mike Sillinger	11	Regina	(WHL)	0
1990	Keith Primeau	3	Niagara Falls	(OHL)	0

*Designates first player chosen in draft.

Jim Rutherford

COACHING HISTORY

Art Duncan and Duke Keats, 1926-27
Jack Adams, 1927-28 to 1946-47
Tommy Ivan, 1947-48 to 1953-54
Jimmy Skinner, 1954-55 to 1956-57
Jimmy Skinner and Sid Abel, 1957-58
Sid Abel, 1958-59 to 1967-68
Bill Gadsby, 1968-69
Bill Gadsby and Sid Abel, 1969-70
Ned Harkness and Doug Barkley, 1970-71
Doug Barkley and Johnny Wilson, 1971-72
Johnny Wilson, 1972-73
Ted Garvin and Alex Delvecchio, 1973-74

Alex Delvecchio, 1974-75
Doug Barkley and Alex Delvecchio, 1975-76
Alex Delvecchio and Larry Wilson, 1976-77
Bobby Kromm, 1977-78 to 1978-79
Bobby Kromm and Ted Lindsay, 1979-80
Ted Lindsay and Wayne Maxner, 1980-81
Wayne Maxner and Billy Dea, 1981-82
Nick Polano, 1982-83 to 1984-85
Harry Neale, Brad Park and Dan Belisle, 1985-86
Jacques Demers, 1986-87 to 1989-90
Bryan Murray for 1990-91

FRANCHISE LEADERS

Current players in bold type
(1926-27 through 1989-90)

Games
1. 1687—Gordie Howe
2. 1549—Alex Delvecchio
3. 983—Marcel Pronovost
4. 875—Norm Ullman
5. 862—Ted Lindsay
6. 861—Nick Libett
7. 846—Red Kelly
8. 793—Syd Howe
9. 708—Reed Larson
10. 706—Gary Bergman

Goals
1. 786—Gordie Howe
2. 456—Alex Delvecchio
3. 335—Ted Lindsay
4. 324—Norm Ullman
5. **291—Steve Yzerman**
6. 259—John Ogrodnick
7. 217—Nick Libett
8. 202—Syd Howe
9. 188—Reed Larson
10. 184—Sid Abel

Assists
1. 1023—Gordie Howe
2. 825—Alex Delvecchio
3. 434—Norm Ullman
4. **401—Steve Yzerman**
5. 393—Ted Lindsay
6. 382—Reed Larson
7. 297—Red Kelly
8. 279—Sid Abel
9. 275—John Ogrodnick
10. 250—Nick Libett

Points
1. 1809—Gordie Howe
2. 1281—Alex Delvecchio
3. 758—Norm Ullman
4. 728—Ted Lindsay
5. **692—Steve Yzerman**
6. 570—Reed Larson
7. 534—John Ogrodnick
8. 467—Nick Libett
9. 463—Sid Abel
10. 451—Red Kelly

Goaltenders
Games
1. 734—Terry Sawchuk
2. 324—Harry Lumley
3. 314—Jim Rutherford
4. 310—Roger Crozier
5. **299—Greg Stefan**
6. 221—Roy Edwards
7. 178—Norm Smith
8. **157—Glen Hanlon**
9. 152—John Mowers
10. 148—Glenn Hall

Shutouts
1. 85—Terry Sawchuk
2. 26—Harry Lumley
3. 20—Roger Crozier
4. 17—Clarence Dolson
   17—Glenn Hall
   17—Harry Holmes
   17—Norm Smith

Goals Against Average
(2400 minutes minimum)
1. 2.06—Clarence Dolson
2. 2.11—Harry Holmes
3. 2.14—Glenn Hall
4. 2.25—Alex Connell
5. 2.26—John Ross Roach
6. 2.34—Norm Smith
7. 2.46—Terry Sawchuk
8. 2.63—John Mowers
9. 2.65—Cecil Thompson
10. 2.73—Harry Lumley

Wins
1. 352—Terry Sawchuk
2. 163—Harry Lumley
3. 130—Roger Crozier
4. **115—Greg Stefan**
5. 97—Jim Rutherford
6. 95—Roy Edwards
7. 76—Norm Smith

Mark Messier holds the NHL record with 11 short-handed goals during playoff competition.

Goaltender Bill Ranford did not allow a goal during a span of 154:24 in last year's playoffs.

Randy Gregg led the Oilers with a plus 24 plus/minus rating in 1989-90. Nine Edmonton players finished with better ratings during the Oilers' 1986-87 Stanley Cup season.

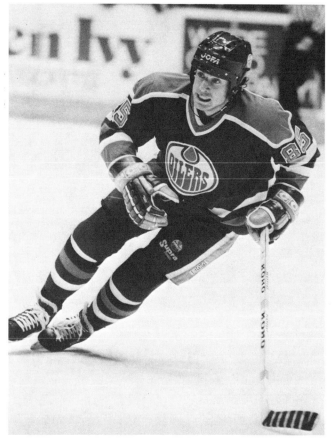

Petr Klima's goal at 15:13 of the third overtime period in Game 1 of last year's finals against Boston ended the longest game (115:13) in Stanley Cup finals history.

EDMONTON OILERS

CLUB DIRECTORY

Owner/Governor
Peter Pocklington
Alternate Governor
Glen Sather
General Counsels
Bob Lloyd, Gary Frohlich
President/General Manager
Glen Sather
Coach
John Muckler
Co-Coach
Ted Green
Assistant Coach
Ron Low
Assistant General Manager
Bruce MacGregor
Director of Player Personnel/Chief Scout
Barry Fraser
Scouting Staff
Lorne Davis, Ace Bailey, Ed Chadwick, Matti Vaisanen, Harry Howell
Controller
Werner Baum
Executive Secretary
Lana Anderson

Director of Public Relations
Bill Tuele
Assistant Public Relations Director
Steve Knowles
Trainer
Barrie Stafford
Assistant Trainer
Lyle Kulchisky
Athletic Therapist
Ken Lowe
Team Physician
Dr. Gordon Cameron
Home Ice
Northlands Coliseum
Address
Edmonton, Alta. T5B 4M9
Seating Capacity
17,313 (Standing 190)
Club Colors
Blue, Orange and White
Phone
(403) 474-8561
FAX
(403) 471-2171

YEAR-BY-YEAR RESULTS

Season	W.	L.	T.	Pts.	Position	Season	W.	L.	T.	Pts.	Position
1972-73	38	37	3	79	Fifth—*	1982-83	47	21	12	106	First—c
1973-74	38	37	3	79	Third—a	1983-84	57	18	5	119	First—xx
1974-75	36	38	4	76	Fifth—*	1984-85	49	20	11	109	First—xx
1975-76	27	49	5	59	Fourth—a	1985-86	56	17	7	119	First—a
1976-77	34	43	4	72	Fourth—a	1986-87	50	24	6	106	First—xx
1977-78	38	39	3	79	Fifth—a	1987-88	44	25	11	99	Second—xx
1978-79	48	30	2	98	First—c	1988-89	38	34	8	84	Third—†
1979-80	28	39	13	69	Fourth—†	1989-90	38	28	14	90	Second—xx
1980-81	29	35	16	74	Fourth—a	**Totals**	**743**	**551**	**142**	**1628**	
1981-82	48	17	15	111	First—†						

Key to standings: *—Missed playoffs. †—Eliminated in first round of new playoff format (1974-75). a—Eliminated in quarterfinal round. b—Eliminated in semifinal round. c—Eliminated in final round. xx—Stanley Cup champion.

NOTE: Records for Edmonton Oilers, Hartford Whalers, Quebec Nordiques and Winnipeg Jets include World Hockey Association results prior to their entrance into NHL in 1979-80. Key to WHA standings: *—Missed playoffs. †—Preliminary round (established for 1975-76 season). a—Eliminated in quarterfinal round. b—Eliminated in semifinal round. c—Eliminated in final round. xx—Avco World Cup champion.

Wayne Gretzky

Jari Kurri

1990-91 SCHEDULE

Home games shaded.

* At Chicago Stadium.

OCTOBER

Sun	Mon	Tue	Wed	Thu	Fri	Sat
	1	2	3	4	5	6 WIN
7 TOR	8	9	10	11 LA	12	13
14 VAN	15	16 STL	17	18	19 BOS	20
21 CAL	22	23	24 WIN	25 CAL	26	27
28 WAS	29	30	31 WIN			

NOVEMBER

Sun	Mon	Tue	Wed	Thu	Fri	Sat
				1	2	3 NJ
4	5	6 STL	7	8 CHI	9	10 LA
11	12	13	14 VAN	15	16 BUF	17
18 NYI	19	20 CHI	21	22	23 BUF	24 TOR
25	26	27 PIT	28	29 BOS	30	

DECEMBER

Sun	Mon	Tue	Wed	Thu	Fri	Sat
						1 HAR
2 PHI	3	4	5 QUE	6	7 NYR	8
9 CAL	10	11	12 VAN	13	14	15 LA
16	17	18 LA	19	20 VAN	21	22 CAL
23 VAN	24	25	26	27 CAL	28 VAN	29
30 HAR	31					

JANUARY

Sun	Mon	Tue	Wed	Thu	Fri	Sat
		1	2 MON	3	4 DET	5
6	7	8 PIT	9 DET	10	11	12 NJ
13 PHI	14	15 NYR	16	17 NYI	18	19 ALL STAR GAME*
20	21	22 LA	23 VAN	24	25 NYR	26
27 WIN	28	29	30 VAN	31		

FEBRUARY

Sun	Mon	Tue	Wed	Thu	Fri	Sat
					1 CHI	2
3 BUF	4	5 BOS	6 HAR	7	8 WAS	9
10	11 PIT	12 STL	13	14 LA	15	16 TOR
17	18 NJ	19	20 MIN	21	22 DET	23
24 QUE	25	26	27 CAL	28		

MARCH

Sun	Mon	Tue	Wed	Thu	Fri	Sat
					1 MIN	2 MON
3	4	5 WIN	6 MIN	7	8 PHI	9
10 WAS	11	12	13 NYI	14	15 WIN	16
17 MON	18	19	20 QUE	21	22	23 WIN
24 LA	25	26 LA	27	28 CAL	29 CAL	30
31 WIN						

1989-90 RESULTS

Oct.	5—At Vancouver	W	4-1
	7—At Los Angeles	W	6-5
	11—Vancouver	L	2-5
	13—Boston	T	3-3 (OT)
	15—Los Angeles	L	4-5 (OT)
	18—Winnipeg	W	7-2
	20—Boston	L	0-3
	22—At Winnipeg	L	4-5
	24—At N.Y. Islanders	T	3-3 (OT)
	25—At N.Y. Rangers	T	3-3 (OT)
	28—At Quebec	W	6-3
	29—At Montreal	L	4-5
Nov.	1—New Jersey	T	6-6 (OT)
	3—Calgary	W	5-2
	4—Pittsburgh	L	1-3
	6—At Calgary	L	1-5
	9—At Boston	L	2-6
	11—At Washington	W	5-3
	12—At Buffalo	L	5-6
	15—Los Angeles	T	2-2 (OT)
	17—Buffalo	W	3-0
	19—Chicago	W	5-4 (OT)
	21—Vancouver	W	4-3
	24—At Philadelphia	L	1-5
	25—At N.Y. Islanders	W	7-2
	27—At Detroit	W	6-2
	30—At Los Angeles	W	7-6
Dec.	2—Minnesota	W	6-1
	3—Toronto	W	5-3
	8—Los Angeles	W	5-4 (OT)
	11—Calgary	T	3-3 (OT)
	13—Quebec	W	5-1
	16—At St. Louis	T	3-3 (OT)
	17—At Chicago	L	5-6
	19—At Minnesota	W	5-0
	21—Winnipeg	W	3-2
	23—Calgary	W	2-1
	27—Philadelphia	W	2-1
	29—Montreal	W	6-2
	31—At Winnipeg	L	2-3
Jan.	2—At St. Louis	W	6-4
	3—At Chicago	L	2-3
	6—Hartford	T	4-4 (OT)
	7—Calgary	L	1-3
	9—At Calgary	W	3-2 (OT)
	11—At Los Angeles	T	3-3 (OT)
	16—Detroit	L	4-6
	17—Winnipeg	W	6-3
	23—N.Y. Rangers	L	3-4
	25—Los Angeles	W	7-6
	27—Vancouver	W	6-2
	30—At Hartford	T	4-4 (OT)
	31—At Detroit	L	5-7
Feb.	2—At Pittsburgh	L	3-6
	4—At Washington	W	5-4 (OT)
	6—At New Jersey	T	2-2 (OT)
	7—At N.Y. Rangers	L	2-5
	11—Winnipeg	W	7-4
	14—Washington	L	3-4
	16—At Vancouver	T	2-2 (OT)
	18—Minnesota	W	3-2
	20—At Vancouver	W	4-2
	21—Buffalo	W	7-3
	23—Toronto	L	5-6
	25—At Calgary	L	4-10
	28—At Los Angeles	L	2-4
Mar.	3—Philadelphia	W	5-3
	4—Vancouver	W	6-3
	6—Pittsburgh	W	4-3 (OT)
	9—At Winnipeg	L	5-7
	10—At Toronto	L	2-3
	13—At Quebec	W	4-1
	14—At Montreal	T	3-3 (OT)
	17—New Jersey	L	1-4
	18—Hartford	L	1-3
	21—St. Louis	W	8-6
	24—N.Y. Islanders	T	5-5 (OT)
	27—At Vancouver	W	4-1
	30—At Calgary	L	2-6
Apr.	1—At Winnipeg	W	4-2

1990-91 ROSTER

No.	FORWARDS	Hgt./Wt.	Place of Birth	Age	NHL exp.	1989-90 club (league)	G.	A.	Pts.
9	Glenn Anderson	6-01/190	Vancouver, B.C.	30	10	Edmonton (NHL)	34	38	72
32	Dave Brown	6-05/205	Saskatoon, Sask.	27	8	Edmonton (NHL)	0	6	6
16	Kelly Buchberger	6-02/210	Largenburg, Sask.	23	4	Edmonton (NHL)	2	6	8
	Dan Currie	6-02/195	Burlington, Ont.	22	0	Cape Breton (AHL)	36	40	76
20	Martin Gelinas	5-11/195	Shawinigan, Que.	20	2	Edmonton (NHL)	17	8	25
12	Adam Graves	5-11/185	Toronto, Ont.	22	3	Detroit (NHL)	0	1	1
						Edmonton (NHL)	9	12	21
	Kim Issel	6-04/196	Regina, Sask.	23	1	Cape Breton (AHL)	36	32	68
	Tomas Kapusta	6-00/187	Zlin, Czechoslovakia	23	0	Zlin (Czech.)	9	5	14
						Cape Breton (AHL)	12	37	49
85	Petr Klima	6-00/190	Chaomutov, Czech.	25	5	Detroit (NHL)	5	5	10
						Edmonton (NHL)	25	28	53
7	Mark Lamb	5-09/180	Ponteix, Sask.	26	5	Edmonton (NHL)	12	16	28
	Ken Linseman	5-11/175	Kingston, Ont.	32	12	Boston (NHL)	6	16	22
						Philadelphia (NHL)	5	9	14
14	Craig MacTavish	6-01/195	London, Ont.	32	11	Edmonton (NHL)	21	22	43
11	Mark Messier	6-01/210	Edmonton, Alta.	29	11	Edmonton (NHL)	45	84	129
8	Joe Murphy	6-01/190	London, Ont.	22	4	Detroit (NHL)	3	1	4
						Edmonton (NHL)	7	18	25
29	Vladimir Ruzicka	6-03/212	Most, Czechoslovakia	27	1	Litvinov (Czech.)	21	23	44
						Edmonton (NHL)	11	6	17
	Anatoli Semenov	6-02/190	Moscow, USSR	28	0	Moscow Dynamo	13	20	33
15	Trevor Sim	6-02/192	Calgary, Alta.	20	1	Swift Current (WHL)	3	2	5
						Kamloops (WHL)	27	35	62
						Edmonton (NHL)	0	1	1
18	Craig Simpson	6-02/195	London, Ont.	23	5	Edmonton (NHL)	29	32	61
10	Esa Tikkanen	6-01/200	Helsinki, Finland	25	6	Edmonton (NHL)	30	33	63
34	Mike Ware	6-05/216	York, Ont.	23	2	Edmonton (NHL)	0	0	0
						Cape Breton (AHL)	6	13	19

	DEFENSEMEN								
	Mario Barbe	6-01/204	Cadillac, Que.	23	0	Cape Breton (AHL)	0	15	15
6	Jeff Beukeboom	6-04/215	Ajax, Ont.	25	5	Edmonton (NHL)	1	12	13
	Corey Foster	6-03/200	Ottawa, Ont.	20	1	Cape Breton (AHL)	7	17	24
21	Randy Gregg	6-04/215	Edmonton, Alta.	34	9	Edmonton (NHL)	4	20	24
22	Charlie Huddy	6-00/210	Oshawa, Ont.	31	10	Edmonton (NHL)	1	23	24
2	Chris Joseph	6-02/210	Burnaby, B.C.	20	3	Cape Breton (AHL)	10	20	30
						Edmonton (NHL)	0	2	2
	Marc Laforge	6-2/210	Sudbury, Ont.	22	1	Hartford (NHL)	0	0	0
						Binghamton (AHL)	2	6	8
						Cape Breton (AHL)	0	1	1
35	Francois Leroux	6-06/221	Ste.-Adele, Que.	20	2	Edmonton (NHL)	0	1	1
						Victoriaville (QMJHL)	4	33	37
4	Kevin Lowe	6-02/195	Lachute, Que.	31	11	Edmonton (NHL)	7	26	33
28	Craig Muni	6-03/200	Toronto, Ont.	28	7	Edmonton (NHL)	5	12	17
25	Geoff Smith	6-03/200	Edmonton, Alta.	21	1	Edmonton (NHL)	4	11	15
5	Steve Smith	6-04/215	Glasgow, Scotland	27	6	Edmonton (NHL)	7	34	41

	GOALTENDERS						Ga.	SO	Avg.
35	Randy Exelby	5-09/170	Toronto, Ont.	25	2	Edmonton (NHL)	1	0	5.00
						Phoenix (IHL)	41	0	4.56
31	Grant Fuhr	5-10/186	Spruce Grove, Alta.	28	9	Edmonton (NHL)	21	1	3.89
						Cape Breton (AHL)	2	0	3.00
	Mike Greenlay	6-03/200	Vitoria, Brazil	22	0	Cape Breton (AHL)	46	2	3.38
30	Bill Ranford	5-10/170	Brandon, Man.	23	5	Edmonton (NHL)	56	1	3.19
33	Eldon Reddick	5-08/170	Halifax, N.S.	25	4	Edmonton (NHL)	11	0	3.08
						Cape Breton (AHL)	15	0	3.95
						Phoenix (IHL)	3	0	2.27

1989-90 RECORDS

1989-90 regular-season records: 38-28-14 (.563, 90 points, 2nd in Smythe Division); 23-11-6 at home; 15-17-8 on road; 5-1-14 in overtime; 18-10-4 vs. Smythe (3-4-1 vs. Flames; 4-2-2 vs. Kings; 6-1-1 vs. Canucks; 5-3-0 vs. Jets); 8-6-1 vs. Norris; 6-5-4 vs. Adams; 6-7-5 vs. Patrick.

MISCELLANEOUS DATA

1989-90 team rankings: Shorthanded goals for, 22 (1st in NHL); shorthanded goals against, 6 (T2nd); power play, 20.6% (12th); penalty killing, 80.3% (T10th); penalty minutes/game, 25.6.

TEAM HAT TRICKS, CAREER, ACTIVE

Glenn Anderson (20)	Craig MacTavish (1)
Martin Gelinas (1)	Mark Messier (13)
Adam Graves (1)	Craig Simpson (3)
Petr Klima (3)	Esa Tikkanen (2)

MINOR LEAGUE AFFILIATIONS

Cape Breton (AHL), Kansas City (IHL) with Hartford

Charlie Huddy

1990 DRAFT SELECTIONS

Rnd.	Player	Hgt.	Wgt.	Overall	(Pos.)	1989-90 Club	(League)
1	Scott Allison	6:04	194	17	(C)	Prince Albert	(WHL)
2	Alexandre Legault	6:01	205	38	(RW)	Boston University	
3	Joe Crowley	6:02	195	59	(LW)	Lawrence Academy	(Mass.)
4	Joel Blain	6:00	194	67	(LW)	Hull	(QMJHL)
5	Greg Louder	6:01	185	101	(G)	Cushing Academy	(Ct.)
6	Keijo Sailynoja	6:02	187	122	(LW)	Jokerit, Finland	
7	Mike Power	6:02	190	143	(G)	Western Michigan University	
8	Roman Mejzlik	6:02	187	164	(LW)	Dukla Jihlava, Czech.	
9	Richard Zemlicka	6:01	189	185	(RW)	Sparta Praha, Czech.	
10	Petr Korinek	6:00	200	206	(C)	Skoda Plzen, Czech.	
11	Pick voided			227			
12	Sami Nuutinen	6:00	178	248	(D)	K-Espoo, Finland	

FIRST-ROUND ENTRY DRAFT SELECTIONS

Year Name	Overall	Last Amateur Team	(League)	Years in NHL
1979—Kevin Lowe	21	Quebec	(QMJHL)	11
1980—Paul Coffey	6	Kitchener	(OHL)	10
1981—Grant Fuhr	8	Victoria	(WHL)	9
1982—Jim Playfair	20	Portland	(WHL)	3
1983—Jeff Beukeboom	19	Sault Ste. Marie	(OHL)	4
1984—Selmar Odelein	21	Regina	(WHL)	3
1985—Scott Metcalfe	20	Kingston	(OHL)	3
1986—Kim Issel	21	Prince Albert	(WHL)	1
1987—Peter Soberlak	21	Swift Current	(WHL)	0
1988—Francois Leroux	19	St. Jean	(QMJHL)	2
1989—Jason Soules	15	Niagara Falls	(OHL)	0
1990—Scott Allison	17	Prince Albert	(WHL)	0

PRIORITY SELECTIONS BEFORE 1979 EXPANSION DRAFT

Dave Dryden   Bengt Gustafsson   Ed Mio

Kevin Lowe

COACHING HISTORY

Glen Sather, 1979-80 to 1988-89   John Muckler since 1989-90

FRANCHISE LEADERS

Current players in bold type
(1979-80 through 1989-90)

Games
1. 838—Kevin Lowe
2. 798—Mark Messier
3. 754—Glenn Anderson
   754—Jari Kurri
5. 696—Wayne Gretzky
6. 653—Dave Hunter
7. **641—Charlie Huddy**
8. 586—Lee Fogolin
9. 532—Paul Coffey
10. 454—Dave Semenko

Goals
1. 583—Wayne Gretzky
2. 474—Jari Kurri
3. **389—Glenn Anderson**
4. **380—Mark Messier**
5. 209—Paul Coffey
6. **125—Esa Tikkanen**
7. 119—Dave Hunter
8. **107—Craig Simpson**
9. **100—Craig MacTavish**
10. 95—Mike Krushelnyski

Assists
1. 1086—Wayne Gretzky
2. **590—Mark Messier**
3. 569—Jari Kurri
4. 460—Paul Coffey
5. **452—Glenn Anderson**
6. **275—Kevin Lowe**
7. **265—Charlie Huddy**
8. **181—Esa Tikkanen**
9. 171—Dave Hunter
10. 148—Randy Gregg

Points
1. 1669—Wayne Gretzky
2. 1043—Jari Kurri
3. **970—Mark Messier**
4. **841—Glenn Anderson**
5. 669—Paul Coffey
6. **343—Kevin Lowe**
7. **341—Charlie Huddy**
8. **306—Esa Tikkanen**
9. 290—Dave Hunter
10. 230—Dave Lumley

Penalty Minutes
1. 1298—Kevin McClelland
2. **1088—Mark Messier**
3. 976—Dave Semenko
4. **944—Kevin Lowe**
5. **887—Steve Smith**
6. 886—Lee Fogolin
7. 776—Dave Hunter
8. **712—Glenn Anderson**
9. 693—Paul Coffey
10. 667—Marty McSorley

Goaltenders

Games
1. 410—Grant Fuhr
2. 235—Andy Moog
3. **91—Bill Ranford**
4. 77—Eddie Mio
5. 67—Ron Low
6. 26—Jim Corsi
7. 15—Gary Edwards

Shutouts (entire roster)
1. 8—Grant Fuhr
2. 4—Andy Moog
3. **2—Bill Ranford**
4. 1—Eddie Mio

Goals Against Average (entire roster)
(2400 minutes minimum)
1. **3.27—Bill Ranford**
2. 3.61—Andy Moog
3. **3.71—Grant Fuhr**
4. 4.02—Eddie Mio
5. 4.03—Ron Low

Wins
1. 220—Grant Fuhr
2. 143—Andy Moog
3. **42—Bill Ranford**
4. 30—Ron Low
5. 25—Eddie Mio
6. 8—Jim Corsi

Ron Francis has scored at least 23 goals in each of his nine years with the Whalers.

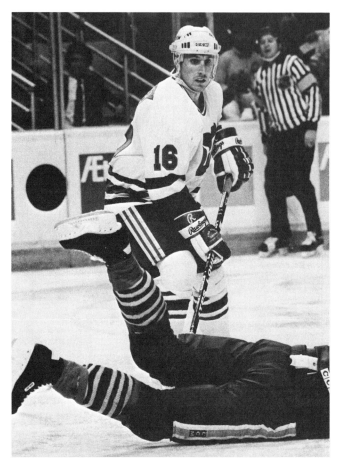

Pat Verbeek was the only NHL player last season to lead his team in both goals and penalty minutes.

Dave Babych has scored 71 of his 117 career goals while his team has enjoyed the man advantage.

Todd Krygier is the first University of Connecticut alumnus to play in the National Hockey League.

HARTFORD WHALERS

CLUB DIRECTORY

Managing General Partner and Governor
Richard H. Gordon
General Partner and Alternate Governor
Benjamin J. Sisti
President and Alternate Governor
Emile Francis
Vice-President and General Manager
Ed Johnston
Assistant General Manager
Robert Crocker
Special Assistant to the Managing General Partner
Gordie Howe
Coach
Rick Ley
Assistant Coaches
Jay Leach, Brent Peterson
Goaltending Coach
Jacques Caron
Director of Player Personnel and Scouting
Ken Schinkel
Scouts
Leo Boivin, Steve Brklacich, Claude Larose, Bruce Haralson, Fred Gore, Jiri Chra
Trainer
Frank (Bud) Goveira
Equipment Manager
Skip Cunningham
Strength and Conditioning Coach
Doug McKenney

Executive Vice-President for Administration and Finance
W. David Andrews
Vice-President, Marketing and Public Relations
William E. Barnes
Treasurer
Michael J. Amendola
Director of Public Relations
Phil Langan
Assistant Director of Public Relations
Mark Willand
Chief Statistician, Assistant Director of Public Relations and Archivist
Frank Polnaszek
Director of Advertising Sales
Rick Francis
Director of Ticket Operations and Sales
Jeff Morander
Home Ice
Hartford Civic Center
Address
242 Trumbull Street, 8th Floor, Hartford, CT 06103
Seating Capacity
15,635
Club Colors
Blue, Green and White
Phone
(203) 728-3366
FAX
(203) 522-7707

YEAR-BY-YEAR RESULTS

Season	W.	L.	T.	Pts.	Position
1972-73	46	30	2	94	First—xx
1973-74	43	31	4	90	First—a
1974-75	43	30	5	91	First—a
1975-76	33	40	7	73	Third—b
1976-77	35	40	6	76	Fourth—a
1977-78	44	31	5	93	Second—c
1978-79	37	34	9	83	Fourth—b
1979-80	27	34	19	73	Fourth—†
1980-81	21	41	18	60	Fourth—*
1981-82	21	41	18	60	Fifth—*

Season	W.	L.	T.	Pts.	Position
1982-83	19	54	7	45	Fifth—*
1983-84	28	42	10	66	Fifth—*
1984-85	30	41	9	69	Fifth—*
1985-86	40	36	4	84	Fourth—a
1986-87	43	30	7	93	First—†
1987-88	35	38	7	77	Fourth—†
1988-89	37	38	5	79	Fourth—†
1989-90	38	33	9	85	Fourth—†
Totals	620	664	151	1391	

Key to standings: *—Missed playoffs. †—Eliminated in first round of new playoff format (1974-75). a—Eliminated in quarterfinal round. b—Eliminated in semifinal round. c—Eliminated in final round. xx—Stanley Cup champion.

NOTE: Records for Edmonton Oilers, Hartford Whalers, Quebec Nordiques and Winnipeg Jets include World Hockey Association results prior to their entrance into NHL in 1979-80. Key to WHA standings: *—Missed playoffs. †—Preliminary round (established for 1975-76 season). a—Eliminated in quarterfinal round. b—Eliminated in semifinal round. c—Eliminated in final round. xx—Avco World Cup champion.

Mike Rogers

Blaine Stoughton

1990-91 SCHEDULE

▨ Home games shaded.

* At Chicago Stadium.

OCTOBER

Sun	Mon	Tue	Wed	Thu	Fri	Sat
	1	2	3	4 QUE	5	6 NYR
7	8 MON	9	10 BUF	11	12 DET	13 MON
14	15	16 QUE	17 TOR	18	19 LA	20
21	22	23	24 MIN	25	26	27 VAN
28 BUF	29	30	31 MON			

NOVEMBER

Sun	Mon	Tue	Wed	Thu	Fri	Sat
				1	2	3 STL
4	5	6 CHI	7	8	9 WIN	10 MIN
11	12	13	14 BOS	15 NJ	16	17 WAS
18	19	20	21 QUE	22	23 BOS	24 BOS
25	26	27	28 QUE	29 PIT	30	

DECEMBER

Sun	Mon	Tue	Wed	Thu	Fri	Sat
						1 EDM
2	3 MON	4	5 MON	6	7 BUF	8 PIT
9	10	11	12 BOS	13 BOS	14	15 WAS
16	17	18 BUF	19	20 NYI	21	22 PHI
23 MIN	24	25	26 QUE	27	28	29 CAL
30 EDM	31					

JANUARY

Sun	Mon	Tue	Wed	Thu	Fri	Sat
.	1	2 VAN	3	4	5 WIN	
6	7	8 LA	9	10 VAN	11	12 TOR
13 NYR	14	15	16 LA	17	18	19 ALL-STAR GAME*
20	21	22	23 CAL	24 BOS	25	26 PHI
27	28	29 NYI	30	31 STL		

FEBRUARY

Sun	Mon	Tue	Wed	Thu	Fri	Sat
					1	2 PHI
3 NYI	4	5	6 EDM	7	8	9 CAL
10 CHI	11	12	13 DET	14	15 NYR	16 MON
17	18	19	20 MON	21	22	23 BUF
24 BUF	25	26 WIN	27	28 CHI		

MARCH

Sun	Mon	Tue	Wed	Thu	Fri	Sat
					1	2 QUE
3 TOR	4	5 STL	6	7	8	9 PIT
10 QUE	11	12 WAS	13	14 DET	15	16 NJ
17 BUF	18	19 BOS	20	21	22	23 QUE
24	25 MON	26	27 NJ	28	29	30 BUF
31 BOS						

1989-90 RESULTS

Oct.	5—Montreal	L	1-4
	7—Minnesota	L	4-6
	8—At Quebec	W	9-6
	11—Washington	W	4-1
	13—At Buffalo	L	1-4
	14—New Jersey	L	2-3
	18—Buffalo	W	2-1
	19—At N.Y. Rangers	L	3-7
	21—Detroit	T	3-3 (OT)
	23—At Montreal	L	2-3
	25—Quebec	W	2-0
	26—At New Jersey	W	7-3
	28—At Boston	W	1-0
Nov.	1—St. Louis	L	3-5
	3—At Detroit	W	4-3
	4—Los Angeles	W	6-3
	8—Buffalo	L	3-6
	10—At Winnipeg	W	4-2
	12—At Chicago	L	2-4
	14—At Detroit	W	3-0
	15—Boston	L	2-5
	18—N.Y. Rangers	L	2-3
	22—Quebec	L	2-4
	25—Philadelphia	W	5-2
	26—At Buffalo	L	2-4
	28—Buffalo	L	2-4
	30—At St. Louis	W	5-3
Dec.	2—At Montreal	W	4-3
	6—N.Y. Islanders	L	3-4
	7—At Boston	W	4-3
	9—New Jersey	W	7-3
	13—Los Angeles	L	2-5
	14—At Philadelphia	W	3-2
	16—Washington	L	2-5
	19—At Pittsburgh	W	8-4
	20—Boston	W	4-3
	23—Minnesota	W	4-3
	26—At Quebec	T	3-3 (OT)
	30—At Chicago	L	3-7
Jan.	3—Winnipeg	L	2-4
	5—At Calgary	L	4-6
	6—At Edmonton	T	4-4 (OT)
	10—At Vancouver	W	3-1
	13—At Los Angeles	W	6-3
	15—At Boston	L	1-4
	17—Boston	T	5-5 (OT)
	19—Calgary	T	3-3 (OT)
	23—N.Y. Islanders	W	4-2
	25—At St. Louis	L	2-3
	27—Chicago	W	6-4
	30—Edmonton	T	4-4 (OT)
Feb.	1—At Philadelphia	L	1-2
	3—At Quebec	W	5-1
	4—At Montreal	L	0-2
	7—At Minnesota	W	5-3
	9—Vancouver	L	1-4
	10—Toronto	W	6-2
	14—At Toronto	T	6-6 (OT)
	17—At Montreal	L	3-7
	18—At Buffalo	W	6-4
	21—Quebec	W	3-2
	23—At Buffalo	L	3-7
	24—Winnipeg	L	1-3
	28—Montreal	W	3-1
Mar.	2—At Washington	W	4-3
	3—N.Y. Rangers	W	6-4
	6—At N.Y. Islanders	W	4-2
	8—Toronto	L	6-7
	10—Buffalo	L	0-5
	11—Boston	L	3-4
	13—At Vancouver	W	1-0
	17—At Calgary	L	4-5
	18—At Edmonton	W	3-1
	21—Quebec	W	4-1
	24—Montreal	W	7-4
	25—Pittsburgh	W	4-2
	27—At Pittsburgh	T	3-3 (OT)
	29—At Boston	L	2-3
	31—At Quebec	W	3-2
Apr.	1—Montreal	T	1-1 (OT)

1990-91 ROSTER

No.	FORWARDS	Hgt./Wt.	Place of Birth	Age	NHL exp.	1989-90 club (league)	G.	A.	Pts.
34	Mikael Andersson	5-11/185	Malmo, Sweden	24	1	Hartford (NHL)	13	24	37
	Blair Atcheynum	6-02/190	Estevan, Sask.	21	1	Binghamton (AHL)	20	21	41
23	James Black	5-11/185	Regina, Sask.	21	1	Binghamton (AHL)	37	35	72
						Hartford (NHL)	0	0	0
31	Bob Bodak	6-02/190	Thunder Bay, Ont.	29	2	Binghamton (AHL)	32	25	57
						Hartford (NHL)	0	0	0
20	Yvon Corriveau	6-01/195	Welland, Ont.	23	5	Washington (NHL)	9	6	15
						Hartford (NHL)	4	1	5
7	Randy Cunneyworth	6-00/180	Etobicoke, Ont.	29	7	Winnipeg (NHL)	5	6	11
						Hartford (NHL)	9	9	18
11	Kevin Dineen	5-11/190	Quebec City, Que.	27	7	Hartford (NHL)	25	41	66
12	Dean Evason	5-10/180	Flin Flon, Man.	26	8	Hartford (NHL)	18	25	43
26	Ray Ferraro	5-10/185	Trail, B.C.	26	6	Hartford (NHL)	25	29	54
10	Ron Francis	6-02/200	Sault Ste. Marie, Ont.	27	9	Hartford (NHL)	32	69	101
14	Chris Govedaris	6-00/200	Toronto, Ont.	20	1	Hartford (NHL)	0	1	1
						Binghamton (AHL)	3	3	6
	Robert Holik	6-01/195	Jihlava, Czech.	19	0	Dukla J'Lava (Czech.)	...	...	...
22	Ed Kastelic	6-04/215	Toronto, Ont.	26	5	Hartford (NHL)	6	2	8
17	Todd Krygier	5-11/180	Northville, Mich.	24	1	Hartford (NHL)	18	12	30
						Binghamton (AHL)	1	9	10
	Chris Lindbergh	6-01/190	Fort Francis, Ont.	23	0	Binghamton (AHL)	4	4	8
	Michel Picard	5-11/190	Beauport, Que.	20	0	Binghamton (AHL)	16	24	40
	Raymond Saumier	6-00/195	Hull, Que.	21	0	Binghamton (AHL)	9	11	20
15	Dave Tippett	5-10/180	Moosomin, Sask.	29	7	Hartford (NHL)	8	19	27
28	Mike Tomlak	6-03/205	Thunder Bay, Ont.	25	1	Hartford (NHL)	7	14	21
16	Pat Verbeek	5-09/190	Sarnia, Ont.	26	8	Hartford (NHL)	44	45	89
	Carey Wilson	6-02/205	Winnipeg, Man.	28	9	N.Y. Rangers (NHL)	9	17	26
38	Terry Yake	5-11/185	N. Westminster, B.C.	21	2	Binghamton (AHL)	13	42	55
						Hartford (NHL)	0	1	1
27	Scott Young	6-00/190	Clinton, Mass.	23	3	Hartford (NHL)	24	40	64
	DEFENSEMEN								
44	Dave Babych	6-02/215	Edmonton, Alta.	29	10	Hartford (NHL)	6	37	43
	Corey Beaulieu	6-01/210	Winnipeg, Man.	21	0	Binghamton (AHL)	0	2	2
6	Adam Burt	6-00/190	Detroit, Mich.	21	2	Hartford (NHL)	4	8	12
	Brian Chapman	6-00/195	Brockville, Ont.	22	0	Binghamton (AHL)	2	15	17
21	Sylvain Cote	5-11/185	Duberger, Que.	24	6	Hartford (NHL)	4	2	6
	Scott Humeniuk	6-00/190	Saskatoon, Sask.	21	0	Moose Jaw (WHL)	23	47	70
						Binghamton (AHL)	0	1	1
25	Grant Jennings	6-03/200	Hudson Bay, Sask.	25	2	Hartford (NHL)	3	6	9
29	Randy Ladouceur	6-02/220	Brockville, Ont.	30	8	Hartford (NHL)	3	12	15
31	Jim McKenzie	6-03/205	Gull Lake, Sask.	20	1	Binghamton (AHL)	4	12	16
						Hartford (NHL)	0	0	0
3	Joel Quenneville	6-01/200	Windsor, Ont.	32	12	Hartford (NHL)	1	4	5
5	Ulf Samuelsson	6-01/195	Fagersta, Sweden	26	6	Hartford (NHL)	2	11	13
32	Brad Shaw	6-00/190	Cambridge, Ont.	26	5	Hartford (NHL)	3	32	35

No.	GOALTENDERS	Hgt./Wt.	Place of Birth	Age	NHL exp.	1989-90 club (league)	Ga.	SO	Avg.
	Daryl Reaugh	5-08/175	Prince George, B.C.	25	2	Binghamton (AHL)	52	0	4.21
30	Peter Sidorkiewicz	5-09/180	D'br'n B'l'st'cka, Pol.	27	3	Hartford (NHL)	46	1	3.57
35	Kay Whitmore	5-11/175	Sudbury, Ont.	23	2	Hartford (NHL)	9	0	3.53
						Binghamton (AHL)	24	0	4.72

1989-90 RECORDS

1989-90 regular-season records: 38-33-9 (.531, 85 points, 4th in Adams Division); 17-18-5 at home; 21-15-4 on road; 0-0-9 in overtime; 14-15-3 vs. Adams (3-4-1 vs. Bruins; 2-6-0 vs. Sabres; 3-4-1 vs. Canadiens; 6-1-1 vs. Nordiques); 11-6-1 vs. Patrick; 7-6-2 vs. Norris; 6-6-3 vs. Smythe.

MISCELLANEOUS DATA

1989-90 team rankings: Shorthanded goals for, 12 (7th in NHL); shorthanded goals against, 10 (11th); power play, 20.1% (13th); penalty killing, 81.5% (4th); penalty minutes/game, 26.3.

TEAM HAT TRICKS, CAREER, ACTIVE

Randy Cunneyworth (2)	Ron Francis (8)
Kevin Dineen (5)	Mark Howe (1)
Dean Evason (1)	Pat Verbeek (5)
Ray Ferraro (5)	Carey Wilson (2)

MINOR LEAGUE AFFILIATIONS

Kansas City (IHL) with Edmonton, Springfield (AHL)

Brad Shaw

1990 DRAFT SELECTIONS

Rnd.	Player	Hgt.	Wgt.	Overall	(Pos.)	1989-90 Club	(League)
1	Mark Greig	5:11	188	15	(RW)	Lethbridge	(WHL)
2	Geoff Sanderson	6:00	185	36	(C)	Swift Current	(WHL)
3	Mike Lenarduzzi	6:00	165	57	(G)	Sault Ste. Marie	(OHL)
4	Chris Bright	6:00	187	78	(C)	Moose Jaw	(WHL)
6	Cory Keenan	6:01	182	120	(D)	Kitchener	(OHL)
7	Jergus Baca	6:02	211	141	(D)	Kosice, Czech.	
8	Martin D'Orsonnens	5:11	185	162	(D)	Clarkson University	
9	Corey Osmak	6:01	180	183	(C)	Nipiwan (Alta.) Tier II	
10	Espen Knutsen	5:11	172	204	(C)	Valerengen, Norway	
11	Tommie Eriksen	6:04	188	225	(D)	Prince Albert	(WHL)
12	Denis Chalifoux	5:08	165	246	(C)	Laval	(QMJHL)

FIRST-ROUND ENTRY DRAFT SELECTIONS

Year	Name	Overall	Last Amateur Team	(League)	Years in NHL
1979	Ray Allison	18	Brandon	(WHL)	7
1980	Fred Arthur	8	Cornwall	(QMJHL)	3
1981	Ron Francis	4	Sault Ste. Marie	(OHL)	9
1982	Paul Lawless	14	Windsor	(OHL)	7
1983	Sylvain Turgeon	2	Hull	(QMJHL)	7
	David A. Jensen	20	Lawrence Academy H.S.	(Mass.)	4
1984	Sylvain Cote	11	Quebec	(QMJHL)	6
1985	Dana Murzyn	5	Calgary	(WHL)	5
1986	Scott Young	11	Boston University		3
1987	Jody Hull	18	Peterborough	(OHL)	2
1988	Chris Govedaris	11	Toronto	(OHL)	1
1989	Robert Holik	10	Jihlava	(Czechoslovakia)	0
1990	Mark Greig	15	Lethbridge	(WHL)	0

PRIORITY SELECTIONS BEFORE 1979 EXPANSION DRAFT

Jordy Douglas	John Garrett	Mark Howe

Sylvain Cote

COACHING HISTORY

Don Blackburn, 1979-80
Don Blackburn and Larry Pleau, 1980-81
Larry Pleau, 1981-82
Larry Kish, Larry Pleau and John Cunniff, 1982-83

Jack Evans, 1983-84 to 1986-87
Jack Evans and Larry Pleau, 1987-88
Larry Pleau, 1988-89
Rick Ley since 1989-90

FRANCHISE LEADERS

Current players in bold type
(1979-80 through 1989-90)

Games

1. 647—Ron Francis
2. 483—Dave Tippett
3. 457—Joel Quenneville
4. 427—Ray Ferraro
5. 412—Kevin Dineen
6. 401—Ulf Samuelsson
7. 373—Paul MacDermid
8. 370—Sylvain Turgeon
9. 359—Dean Evason
10. 357—Blaine Stoughton

Goals

1. 243—Ron Francis
2. 219—Blaine Stoughton
3. 193—Kevin Dineen
4. 178—Sylvain Turgeon
5. 155—Ray Ferraro
6. 106—Ray Neufeld
7. 85—Mark Johnson
   85—Mike Rogers
9. 81—Dean Evason
10. 75—Dave Tippett

Assists

1. 502—Ron Francis
2. 200—Kevin Dineen
3. 190—Dave Babych
4. 189—Ray Ferraro
5. 158—Blaine Stoughton
6. 150—Sylvain Turgeon
7. 147—Mark Howe
8. 131—Ray Neufeld
9. 126—Mike Rogers
   126—Ulf Samuelsson

Points

1. 745—Ron Francis
2. 393—Kevin Dineen
2. 377—Blaine Stoughton
4. 344—Ray Ferraro
5. 328—Sylvain Turgeon
6. 234—Dave Babych
7. 226—Ray Neufeld
8. 210—Mike Rogers
9. 206—Dean Evason
10. 203—Mark Johnson

Penalty Minutes

1. 1,368—Torrie Robertson
2. 924—Ulf Samuelsson
3. 904—Kevin Dineen
4. 706—Paul MacDermid
5. 489—Ron Francis
6. 447—Dean Evason
7. 443—Chris Kotsopoulos
8. 417—Ray Ferraro
9. 408—Joel Quenneville
10. 400—Ray Neufeld

Goaltenders

Games

1. 252—Mike Liut
2. 219—Greg Millen
3. 122—John Garrett
4. 94—Steve Weeks
5. 91—Peter Sidorkiewicz
6. 69—Mike Veisor
7. 30—Al Smith

Shutouts

1. 13—Mike Liut
2. 5—Peter Sidorkiewicz
3. 4—Greg Millen
   4—Steve Weeks

Goals Against Average (entire roster)
(2400 minutes minimum)

1. 3.33—Peter Sidorkiewicz
2. 3.36—Mike Liut
3. 3.68—Steve Weeks
4. 4.25—Greg Millen
5. 4.28—John Garrett
6. 4.87—Mike Veisor

Wins

1. 115—Mike Liut
2. 62—Greg Millen
3. 42—Steve Weeks
4. 41—Peter Sidorkiewicz
5. 36—John Garrett

Luc Robitaille is the only NHL player to be named to the league's All-Star first team in each of the last three seasons.

Tony Granato scored a shorthanded goal at 8:37 of overtime in the Kings' 2-1 win over the Calgary Flames on April 8, 1990.

Fifteen of John Tonelli's 31 goals in 1989-90 were scored on the power play. Two years earlier, just one of Tonelli's 31 goals with the New York Islanders came with the man advantage.

Tomas Sandstrom (above), Dave Taylor and Tony Granato set an NHL record when each scored a hat trick in the Kings' 12-4 victory over Calgary on April 10, 1990.

LOS ANGELES KINGS

CLUB DIRECTORY

Governor/President
Bruce McNall
Alternate Governors
Roy A. Mlakar, Rogatien Vachon
Executive Vice-President
Roy A. Mlakar
Vice-Presidents
Steven H. Nesenblatt, Suzan A. Waks
Vice-President Administration/Finance
Robert Moor
General Manager
Rogatien Vachon
Assistant General Manager
Nick Beverley
Coach
Tom Webster
Assistant Coaches
Cap Raeder, Rick Wilson
Administrative Assistant to General Manager
John Wolf
Director of Amateur Scouting
Bob Owen
Scouting Staff
Alex Smart, Jim Anderson, Serge Blanchard, Jan

Lindgren, Mark Miller, Al Murray, Don Perry, Ted O'Connor
Executive Director, Communications
Scott J. Carmichael
Media Relations
Susan Carpenter
Trainers
Pete Demers, Mark O'Neill, Peter Millar
Home Ice
The Great Western Forum
Address
3900 West Manchester Blvd., P. O. Box 17013
Inglewood, Calif. 90308
Seating Capacity
16,005
Club Colors
Black, White and Silver
Phone
(213) 419-3160
FAX
(213) 673-8927

YEAR-BY-YEAR RESULTS

Season	W.	L.	T.	Pts.	Position	Season	W.	L.	T.	Pts.	Position
1967-68	31	33	10	72	Second—a	1979-80	30	36	14	74	Second—†
1968-69	24	42	10	58	Fourth—b	1980-81	43	24	13	99	Second—†
1969-70	14	52	10	38	Sixth—*	1981-82	24	41	15	63	Fourth—a
1970-71	25	40	13	63	Fifth—*	1982-83	27	41	12	66	Fifth—*
1971-72	20	49	9	49	Seventh—*	1983-84	23	44	13	59	Fifth—*
1972-73	31	36	11	73	Sixth—*	1984-85	34	32	14	82	Fourth—†
1973-74	33	33	12	78	Third—a	1985-86	23	49	8	54	Fifth—†
1974-75	42	17	21	105	Second—†	1986-87	31	41	8	70	Fourth—†
1975-76	38	33	9	85	Second—a	1987-88	30	42	8	68	Fourth—†
1976-77	34	31	15	83	Second—a	1988-89	42	31	7	91	Second—a
1977-78	31	34	15	77	Third—†	1989-90	34	39	7	75	Fourth—a
1978-79	34	34	12	80	Third—†	Totals	698	754	266	1662	

Key to standings: *—Missed playoffs. †—Eliminated in first round of new playoff format (1974-75). a—Eliminated in quarterfinal round. b—Eliminated in semifinal round. c—Eliminated in final round. xx—Stanley Cup champion.

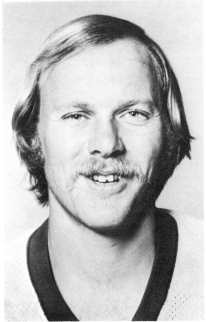

Butch Goring

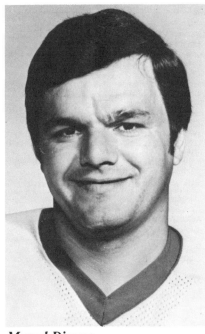

Marcel Dionne

1990-91 SCHEDULE

Home games shaded.
* At Chicago Stadium.

OCTOBER

Sun	Mon	Tue	Wed	Thu	Fri	Sat
	1	2	3	4 NYI	5	6 VAN
7	8	9 VAN	10	11 EDM	12	13 BOS
14 STL	15	16	17 MIN	18	19 HAR	20
21	22	23 CAL	24	25	26 WIN	27
28 WIN	29	30 NYI	31 NYR			

NOVEMBER

Sun	Mon	Tue	Wed	Thu	Fri	Sat
				1	2 WAS	3
4 CHI	5	6	7	8 DET	9	10 EDM
11	12	13	14 BUF	15	16	17 PIT
18	19	20 NJ	21	22 CAL	23	24 MON
25 QUE	26	27 DET	28	29 STL	30	

DECEMBER

Sun	Mon	Tue	Wed	Thu	Fri	Sat
						1 TOR
2	3	4	5 WIN	6	7	8 WIN
9	10	11 NYR	12	13 CAL	14	15 EDM
16	17	18 EDM	19	20 CAL	21	22 VAN
23	24	25	26	27 PHI	28	29 MON
30	31 MIN					

JANUARY

Sun	Mon	Tue	Wed	Thu	Fri	Sat
		1 NYR	2 NYI	3	4	5 TOR
6 CHI	7	8 HAR	9	10 BUF	11	12 VAN
13	14 NJ	15	16 HAR	17 BOS	18	19 ALL-STAR GAME*
20	21	22 EDM	23	24	25 VAN	26 VAN
27	28	29	30 NJ	31		

FEBRUARY

Sun	Mon	Tue	Wed	Thu	Fri	Sat
					1	2 VAN
3	4 DET	5 PHI	6	7	8 BUF	9 STL
10	11	12 CAL	13	14 EDM	15	16 BOS
17	18 WAS	19	20 QUE	21	22 WIN	23
24 WIN	25	26 PIT	27	28 WIN		

MARCH

Sun	Mon	Tue	Wed	Thu	Fri	Sat
					1	2 WIN
3	4	5 WAS	6	7 PIT	8	9 QUE
10 MON	11	12 PHI	13	14 CHI	15	16 CAL
17 VAN	18	19	20 TOR	21	22	23 CAL
24 EDM	25	26 EDM	27	28 MIN	29	30
31 CAL						

1989-90 RESULTS

Oct.	5—Toronto	W	4-2
	7—Edmonton	L	5-6
	8—Detroit	W	5-0
	11—N.Y. Islanders	L	4-7
	13—At Vancouver	W	6-5
	15—At Edmonton	W	5-4 (OT)
	17—Boston	L	2-3
	21—At St. Louis	W	6-4
	22—At Chicago	L	4-7
	25—Calgary	L	0-5
	27—At Winnipeg	W	3-1
	29—At Winnipeg	L	1-6
	31—At Pittsburgh	W	8-4
Nov.	2—At Boston	L	4-5 (OT)
	4—At Hartford	L	3-6
	5—At Buffalo	L	3-5
	8—Calgary	L	4-5
	11—Montreal	W	5-4
	14—At Calgary	W	8-6
	15—At Edmonton	T	2-2 (OT)
	18—Washington	W	5-3
	22—Chicago	W	6-3
	25—Vancouver	W	7-4
	26—At Vancouver	T	3-3 (OT)
	30—Edmonton	L	6-7
Dec.	2—N.Y. Rangers	W	6-0
	6—Vancouver	W	5-4 (OT)
	8—At Edmonton	L	4-5 (OT)
	10—At Quebec	W	8-4
	11—At Montreal	T	2-2 (OT)
	13—At Hartford	W	5-2
	15—At New Jersey	L	5-7
	16—At Philadelphia	L	2-5
	19—Winnipeg	W	9-5
	21—Quebec	W	6-1
	23—Vancouver	W	4-1
	27—Calgary	T	5-5 (OT)
	30—Philadelphia	L	3-6
Jan.	1—At Washington	W	7-4
	2—At N.Y. Islanders	L	3-5
	4—At New Jersey	L	2-4
	6—At Toronto	L	4-7
	9—St. Louis	L	3-4
	11—Edmonton	T	3-3 (OT)
	13—Hartford	L	3-6
	16—Buffalo	L	2-4
	18—Detroit	W	9-4
	23—At Vancouver	T	3-3 (OT)
	25—At Edmonton	L	6-7
	27—N.Y. Rangers	L	1-3
	30—New Jersey	W	5-2
Feb.	1—Chicago	L	4-7
	3—Calgary	W	4-3
	6—At Calgary	W	5-3
	8—Winnipeg	L	1-5
	10—At Pittsburgh	L	6-7
	12—At Toronto	L	3-5
	14—At Detroit	L	5-6
	15—At Minnesota	L	3-6
	17—Quebec	W	7-1
	19—Washington	W	3-2
	21—Minnesota	W	4-2
	24—Vancouver	L	4-6
	28—Edmonton	W	4-2
Mar.	2—At Winnipeg	L	3-9
	4—At Winnipeg	L	2-5
	5—At Calgary	L	0-5
	7—Montreal	L	2-5
	10—Pittsburgh	W	8-2
	12—At N.Y. Rangers	W	6-2
	14—At Buffalo	W	6-5 (OT)
	17—At Boston	W	5-4
	18—At Philadelphia	L	4-7
	20—At Minnesota	L	2-5
	22—N.Y. Islanders	W	3-1
	24—St. Louis	W	9-3
	27—Winnipeg	T	4-4 (OT)
	29—Winnipeg	L	0-1
	31—At Vancouver	L	3-6
Apr.	1—At Calgary	L	4-8

1990-91 ROSTER

No.	FORWARDS	Hgt./Wt.	Place of Birth	Age	NHL exp.	1989-90 club (league)	G.	A.	Pts.
	Micah Aivazoff	6-00/185	Powell River, B.C.	21	0	New Haven (AHL)	20	39	59
10	Mike Allison	6-00/202	Fort Francis, Ont.	29	10	New Haven (AHL)	2	2	4
						Los Angeles (NHL)	2	11	13
8	Scott Bjugstad	6-01/185	St. Paul, Minn.	29	7	New Haven (AHL)	45	21	66
						Los Angeles (NHL)	1	2	3
	Francois Breault	5-11/185	Acton Vale, Que.	23	0	New Haven (AHL)	17	21	38
23	Keith Crowder	6-00/190	Windsor, Ont.	31	10	Los Angeles (NHL)	4	13	17
6	Todd Elik	6-02/190	Brampton, Ont.	24	1	Los Angeles (NHL)	10	23	33
						New Haven (AHL)	20	23	43
14	Tony Granato	5-10/185	Downers Grove, Ill.	26	2	N.Y. Rangers (NHL)	7	18	25
						Los Angeles (NHL)	5	6	11
99	Wayne Gretzky	6-00/170	Brantford, Ont.	29	11	Los Angeles (NHL)	40	102	142
11	Steve Kasper	5-08/159	Montreal, Que.	29	10	Los Angeles (NHL)	17	28	45
15	Chris Kontos	6-01/200	Toronto, Ont.	26	7	New Haven (AHL)	10	20	30
						Los Angeles (NHL)	2	2	4
26	Mike Krushelnyski	6-02/200	Montreal, Que.	30	9	Los Angeles (NHL)	16	25	41
37	Bob Kudelski	6-01/200	Springfield, Mass.	26	3	Los Angeles (NHL)	23	13	36
51	Mikael Lindholm	6-01/194	Gavle, Sweden	25	1	Los Angeles (NHL)	2	2	4
						New Haven (AHL)	4	16	20
24	Mikko Makela	6-02/195	Tampere, Finland	25	5	N.Y. Islanders (NHL)	2	3	5
						Los Angeles (NHL)	7	14	21
29	Jay Miller	6-02/215	Wellesley, Mass.	30	5	Los Angeles (NHL)	10	2	12
20	Luc Robitaille	6-00/180	Montreal, Que.	24	4	Los Angeles (NHL)	52	49	101
7	Tomas Sandstrom	6-02/200	Fagersta, Sweden	26	6	N.Y. Rangers (NHL)	19	19	38
						Los Angeles (NHL)	13	20	33
18	Dave Taylor	6-00/200	Levack, Ont.	34	13	Los Angeles (NHL)	15	26	41
27	John Tonelli	6-01/190	Hamilton, Ont.	33	12	Los Angeles (NHL)	31	37	68
14	Gord Walker	6-00/178	Castlegar, B.C.	25	4	Los Angeles (NHL)	0	0	0
						New Haven (AHL)	14	7	21
	DEFENSEMEN								
2	Brian Benning	6-00/175	Edmonton, Alta.	24	5	St. Louis (NHL)	1	1	2
						Los Angeles (NHL)	5	18	23
4	Rob Blake	6-03/205	Simcoe, Ont.	20	1	Bowling Green Univ. (CCHA)	23	36	59
						Los Angeles (NHL)	0	0	0
28	Steve Duchesne	5-11/195	Sept-Illes, Que.	25	4	Los Angeles (NHL)	20	42	62
	Eric Germain	6-01/190	Quebec City, Que.	24	1	New Haven (AHL)	3	12	15
22	Bob Halkidis	5-11/195	Toronto, Ont.	24	5	Rochester (AHL)	1	13	14
						Los Angeles (NHL)	0	4	4
						New Haven (AHL)	3	17	20
3	Tom Laidlaw	6-02/215	Brampton, Ont.	32	10	Los Angeles (NHL)	1	8	9
33	Marty McSorley	6-01/190	Hamilton, Ont.	27	7	Los Angeles (NHL)	15	21	36
25	Petr Prajsler	6-03/200	Hr'd'c Kr'l've, Czech.	25	3	Los Angeles (NHL)	3	7	10
						New Haven (AHL)	1	7	8
19	Larry Robinson	6-03/210	Winchester, Ont.	39	18	Los Angeles (NHL)	7	32	39
5	Tim Watters	5-11/180	Kamloops, B.C.	31	9	Los Angeles (NHL)	1	10	11

	GOALTENDERS						Ga.	SO	Avg.
	Daniel Berthiaume	5-09/150	Longueuil, Que.	24	5	Winnipeg (NHL)	24	1	3.72
						Minnesota (NHL)	5	0	3.50
31	Mario Gosselin	5-08/160	Thetford Mines, Que.	27	7	Los Angeles (NHL)	26	0	3.87
32	Kelly Hrudey	5-10/183	Edmonton, Alta.	29	7	Los Angeles (NHL)	52	2	4.07
1	Ron Scott	5-08/155	Guelph, Ont.	30	5	Los Angeles (NHL)	12	0	3.67
						New Haven (AHL)	22	1	3.87
35	Robb Stauber	5-10/165	Duluth, Minn.	22	1	Los Angeles (NHL)	2	0	7.95
						New Haven (AHL)	14	0	3.03

1989-90 RECORDS

1989-90 regular-season records: 34-39-7 (.469, 75 points, 4th in Smythe Division); 21-16-3 at home; 13-23-4 on road; 3-2-7 in overtime; 11-15-6 vs. Smythe (3-4-1 vs. Flames; 2-4-2 vs. Oilers; 4-2-2 vs. Canucks; 2-5-1 vs. Jets); 7-8-0 vs. Norris; 7-7-1 vs. Adams; 9-9-0 vs. Patrick.

MISCELLANEOUS DATA

1989-90 team rankings: Shorthanded goals for, 11 (T8th in NHL); shorthanded goals against, 14 (16th); power play, 22.2% (8th); penalty killing, 76.0% (17th); penalty minutes/game, 23.1.

TEAM HAT TRICKS, CAREER, ACTIVE

Mike Allison (1)	Mike Krushelnyski (1)
Scott Bjugstad (3)	Larry Robinson (1)
Keith Crowder (2)	Luc Robitaille (7)
Steve Duchesne (1)	Tomas Sandstrom (4)
Tony Granato (3)	Dave Taylor (8)
Wayne Gretzky (46)	John Tonelli (5)
Steve Kasper (3)	

MINOR LEAGUE AFFILIATIONS

New Haven (AHL), Phoenix (IHL)

Kelly Hrudey

1990 DRAFT SELECTIONS

Rnd.	Player	Hgt.	Wgt.	Overall	(Pos.)	1989-90 Club (League)
1	Darryl Sydor	6:00	205	7	(D)	Kamloops (WHL)
2	Brandy Semchuk	6:01	187	28	(RW)	Canadian National Team
3	Bob Berg	6:01	190	49	(LW)	Belleville (OHL)
5	David Goverde	6:00	210	91	(G)	Sudbury (OHL)
6	Erik Andersson	6:02	187	112	(LW)	Danderyd, Sweden
7	Robert Lang	6:02	180	133	(C)	Litvinov, Czech.
8	Dean Hulett	6:06	205	154	(RW)	Lake Superior State Univ.
9	Denis LeBlanc	6:00	207	175	(C)	St. Hyacinthe (QMJHL)
10	Patrik Ross	6:01	186	196	(RW)	HV 71, Sweden
11	Kevin White	6:01	186	217	(C)	Windsor (OHL)
12	Troy Mohns	6:00	185	238	(D)	Colgate University

FIRST-ROUND ENTRY DRAFT SELECTIONS

Year	Name	Overall	Last Amateur Team (League)	Years in NHL
1969	No first round selection			
1970	No first round selection			
1971	No first round selection			
1972	No first round selection			
1973	No first round selection			
1974	No first round selection			
1975	Tim Young	16	Ottawa (OHL)	10
1976	No first round selection			
1977	No first round selection			
1978	No first round selection			
1979	Jay Wells	16	Kingston (OHL)	11
1980	Larry Murphy	4	Peterborough (OHL)	10
	Jim Fox	10	Ottawa (OHL)	10
1981	Doug Smith	2	Ottawa (OHL)	9
1982	No first round selection			
1983	No first round selection			
1984	Craig Redmond	6	Canadian Olympic Team	5
1985	Craig Duncanson	9	Sudbury (OHL)	5
	Dan Gratton	10	Oshawa (OHL)	1
1986	Jimmy Carson	2	Verdun (QMJHL)	4
1987	Wayne McBean	4	Medicine Hat (WHL)	3
1988	Martin Gelinas	7	Hull (QMJHL)	2
1989	No first round selection			
1990	Darryl Sydor	7	Kamloops (WHL)	0

Larry Murphy

COACHING HISTORY

Red Kelly, 1967-68 to 1968-69
Hal Laycoe and Johnny Wilson, 1969-70
Larry Regan, 1970-71
Larry Regan and Fred Glover, 1971-72
Bob Pulford, 1972-73 to 1976-77
Ron Stewart, 1977-78
Bob Berry, 1978-79 to 1980-81
Parker MacDonald and Don Perry, 1981-82

Don Perry, 1982-83
Don Perry, Rogie Vachon and Roger Neilson, 1983-84
Pat Quinn, 1984-85 to 1985-86
Pat Quinn and Mike Murphy 1986-87
Mike Murphy, Rogie Vachon & Robbie Ftorek, 1987-88
Robbie Ftorek, 1988-89
Tom Webster since 1989-90

FRANCHISE LEADERS

Current players in bold type
(1967-68 through 1989-90)

Games
1. 921—Marcel Dionne
2. **880—Dave Taylor**
3. 736—Butch Goring
4. 673—Mike Murphy
5. 604—Jay Wells
6. 602—Bernie Nicholls
7. 589—Mark Hardy
8. 578—Jim Fox
9. 539—Bob Berry
10. 502—Juha Widing

Goals
1. 550—Marcel Dionne
2. **388—Dave Taylor**
3. 327—Bernie Nicholls
4. 275—Butch Goring
5. 222—Charlie Simmer
6. **196—Luc Robitaille**
7. 194—Mike Murphy
8. 186—Jim Fox
9. 159—Bob Berry
10. 131—Juha Widing

Assists
1. 757—Marcel Dionne
2. **577—Dave Taylor**
3. 431—Bernie Nicholls
4. 384—Butch Goring
5. 292—Jim Fox
6. 262—Mike Murphy
7. 244—Mark Hardy
   244—Charlie Simmer
9. **216—Wayne Gretzky**
10. 211—Juha Widing

Points
1. 1307—Marcel Dionne
2. **965—Dave Taylor**
3. 758—Bernie Nicholls
4. 659—Butch Goring
5. 478—Jim Fox
6. 466—Charlie Simmer
7. 456—Mike Murphy
8. **394—Luc Robitaille**
9. 350—Bob Berry
10. 342—Juha Widing

Penalty Minutes
1. 1446—Jay Wells
2. **1301—Dave Taylor**
3. 827—Mark Hardy
4. 765—Bernie Nicholls
5. 727—Dave Williams

Goaltenders

Games
1. 389—Rogie Vachon
2. 240—Mario Lessard
3. 155—Gary Edwards
4. 119—Roland Melanson
5. 103—Gerry Desjardins
6. 102—Bob Janecyk
7. 86—Dennis DeJordy
8. 84—Darren Eliot
9. 83—Glenn Healy

Shutouts
1. 32—Rogie Vachon
2. 9—Mario Lessard
3. 7—Gerry Desjardins
   7—Gary Edwards

Goals Against Average
(2400 minutes minimum)
1. 2.86—Rogie Vachon
2. 3.34—Wayne Rutledge
3. 3.39—Gary Edwards
4. 3.52—Gerry DesJardins
5. 3.73—Dennis DeJordy
6. 3.74—Mario Lessard
7. **3.77—Kelly Hrudey**
8. 4.08—Doug Keans

Wins
1. 171—Rogie Vachon
2. 92—Mario Lessard
3. 54—Gary Edwards
4. 41—Bob Janecyk
5. 40—Roland Melanson
6. 37—Glenn Healy

Brian Bellows is one of only two players (Dino Ciccarelli is the other) to score 50 goals in a season for the Minnesota North Stars.

Mike Modano led all NHL rookies with 12 power-play goals last year.

Dave Gagner has scored 75 goals in the last two years after scoring only 19 goals in parts of four previous seasons.

Jon Casey's 61 games in 1989-90 was the most by a North Stars goaltender since Cesare Maniago played in 64 games during the 1968-69 season.

MINNESOTA NORTH STARS

CLUB DIRECTORY

Owner, President, CEO and Governor
Norman N. Green
Alternate Governors
Morris Belzberg, Bobby Clarke, Lou Nanne
Vice-President/General Manager
Bobby Clarke
Vice-President/Administration
Dick Arneson
Vice-President/Marketing and Public Relations
Lou Nanne
Vice-President/Finance
George Wettstaedt
Coach
Bob Gainey
Assistant Coaches
Doug Jarvis, Andy Murray
Goaltending Coach
Glenn Resch
Director of Player Personnel
Les Jackson
Team Services
Doug Armstrong
Chief Scout
Dennis Patterson
Scouts
Craig Button, Doug Overton, Wayne Simpson
Director of Merchandising
Peter Jocketty
Director of Ticket Sales
Bill Cox

Director of Public Relations and Advertising
Elaine Waddell
Director of Met Center
Jack Larson
Director of Operations
Eric Kruse
Advertising Sales Manager
Conrad Smith
Communications Manager
Joan Preston
Legal Counsel
Jim Erickson
Athletic Trainer
Dave Surprenant
Assistant Trainer
Dave Smith
Equipment Manager
Mark Baribeau
Home Ice
Metropolitan Sports Center
Address
7901 Cedar Avenue S., Bloomington, Minn. 55425
Seating Capacity
15,093 (15,593 standing room)
Club Colors
Green, White, Gold and Black
Phone
(612) 853-9333
FAX
(612) 853-9467

YEAR-BY-YEAR RESULTS

Season	W.	L.	T.	Pts.	Position	Season	W.	L.	T.	Pts.	Position
1967-68	27	32	15	69	Fourth—b	1979-80	36	28	16	88	Third—b
1968-69	18	43	15	51	Sixth—*	1980-81	35	28	17	87	Third—c
1969-70	19	35	22	60	Third—a	1981-82	37	23	20	94	First—†
1970-71	28	34	16	72	Fourth—b	1982-83	40	24	16	96	Second—a
1971-72	37	29	12	86	Second—a	1983-84	39	31	10	88	First—b
1972-73	37	30	11	85	Third—a	1984-85	25	43	12	62	Fourth—a
1973-74	23	38	17	63	Seventh—*	1985-86	38	33	9	85	Second—†
1974-75	23	50	7	53	Fourth—*	1986-87	30	40	10	70	Fifth—*
1975-76	20	53	7	47	Fourth—*	1987-88	19	48	13	51	Fifth—*
1976-77	23	39	18	64	Second—†	1988-89	27	37	16	70	Third—†
1977-78	18	53	9	45	Fifth—*	1989-90	36	40	4	76	Fourth—†
1978-79	28	40	12	68	Fourth—*	Totals	663	851	304	1630	

Key to standings: *—Missed playoffs. †—Eliminated in first round of new playoff format (1974-75). a—Eliminated in quarterfinal round. b—Eliminated in semifinal round. c—Eliminated in final round. xx—Stanley Cup champion.

Lou Nanne

Steve Payne

1990-91 SCHEDULE

▨ Home games shaded.

* At Chicago Stadium.

OCTOBER

Sun	Mon	Tue	Wed	Thu	Fri	Sat
	1	2	3	4 STL	5	6 NYI
7	8 NYR	9 NJ	10	11 BOS	12	13 CHI
14	15	16	17 LA	18	19	20 STL
21 CHI	22	23	24 HAR	25	26 DET	27 DET
28	29	30 TOR	31			

NOVEMBER

Sun	Mon	Tue	Wed	Thu	Fri	Sat
				1 PHI	2	3 QUE
4 MON	5	6	7	8 QUE	9	10 HAR
11	12	13 PIT	14	15 NYR	16	17 STL
18	19 NYR	20	21 DET	22	23 VAN	24 NJ
25	26	27 VAN	28	29	30 WIN	

DECEMBER

Sun	Mon	Tue	Wed	Thu	Fri	Sat
						1 PIT
2	3	4	5 TOR	6 TOR	7	8 PHI
9	10	11 CAL	12	13 STL	14	15 CHI
16 CHI	17	18	19	20 PIT	21	22 BOS
23 HAR	24	25	26 WIN	27	28	29 BOS
30	31 LA					

JANUARY

Sun	Mon	Tue	Wed	Thu	Fri	Sat
		1	2 DET	3 TOR	4	5 VAN
6	7	8 NYI	9	10	11	12 BUF
13 CHI	14	15 MON	16	17 WAS	18	19 ALL-STAR GAME*
20	21 WIN	22 STL	23	24	25 WAS	26 NJ
27	28 TOR	29	30 DET	31		

FEBRUARY

Sun	Mon	Tue	Wed	Thu	Fri	Sat
					1	2 QUE
3	4 MON	5	6	7 TOR	8	9 DET
10	11	12 NYI	13 BUF	14	15	16 DET
17	18	19	20 EDM	21	22	23 CHI
24	25	26 PHI	27	28		

MARCH

Sun	Mon	Tue	Wed	Thu	Fri	Sat
					1 EDM	2 CAL
3	4	5	6 EDM	7	8	9 DET
10 CAL	11	12 BUF	13	14 STL	15	16 TOR
17 TOR	18	19	20	21	22 WAS	23
24 CHI	25 STL	26	27	28 LA	29	30 CHI
31 STL						

1989-90 RESULTS

Oct.	5—N.Y. Islanders	W	6-5
	7—At Hartford	W	6-4
	8—At Buffalo	T	2-2 (OT)
	12—St. Louis	W	3-0
	14—Quebec	W	3-2
	17—At N.Y. Islanders	W	6-3
	18—At Detroit	L	3-4
	21—At Quebec	L	2-7
	25—Buffalo	W	4-2
	26—At St. Louis	L	1-4
	28—Philadelphia	W	6-5
	31—Toronto	L	4-6
Nov.	2—At Chicago	L	3-4 (OT)
	4—Chicago	W	3-0
	6—At Toronto	L	1-2
	9—Detroit	W	5-1
	11—Calgary	W	3-2 (OT)
	12—Toronto	W	6-3
	15—At New Jersey	W	2-1 (OT)
	16—At Philadelphia	L	3-6
	18—St. Louis	W	3-0
	21—At St. Louis	L	4-7
	22—Toronto	W	6-3
	24—New Jersey	W	7-6
	26—Chicago	W	5-3
	30—At Calgary	L	2-5
Dec.	2—At Edmonton	L	1-6
	3—At Vancouver	L	5-6
	6—Montreal	L	1-4
	8—At Detroit	L	1-2
	9—Detroit	L	1-3
	12—Vancouver	L	2-4
	14—Pittsburgh	T	4-4 (OT)
	16—At Toronto	W	4-3
	19—Edmonton	L	0-5
	21—At Boston	L	2-4
	23—At Hartford	L	3-4
	26—At Winnipeg	L	3-5
	28—At Chicago	T	1-1 (OT)
	30—At St. Louis	L	2-3
	31—St. Louis	W	2-1 (OT)
Jan.	4—N.Y. Rangers	W	8-2
	6—Detroit	W	4-3
	9—At Detroit	L	0-9
	11—N.Y. Islanders	L	4-8
	13—Detroit	W	6-4
	15—At Montreal	L	3-4
	17—At Chicago	L	1-3
	18—Quebec	W	7-4
	24—At Toronto	L	3-7
	26—At Vancouver	W	6-3
	27—At Calgary	L	1-3
	29—Winnipeg	W	4-2
	31—Washington	L	3-4 (OT)
Feb.	3—At Philadelphia	L	6-7 (OT)
	4—At N.Y. Rangers	L	3-4
	7—Hartford	L	3-5
	10—Chicago	W	6-4
	11—At Washington	L	3-5
	13—St. Louis	L	1-2 (OT)
	15—Los Angeles	W	6-3
	18—At Edmonton	L	2-3
	21—At Los Angeles	L	2-4
	24—Boston	L	2-3
	27—Winnipeg	W	8-3
Mar.	3—Montreal	W	3-2
	4—At Pittsburgh	L	6-8
	7—Chicago	W	5-4
	10—N.Y. Rangers	T	2-2 (OT)
	12—At Toronto	W	4-1
	13—New Jersey	L	1-3
	17—At Pittsburgh	W	6-2
	18—Washington	L	3-4
	20—Los Angeles	W	5-2
	22—At Detroit	W	5-1
	24—At Boston	W	7-6
	26—Toronto	W	5-4
	29—At Buffalo	L	2-4
	31—At St. Louis	W	6-3
Apr.	1—At Chicago	L	1-4

1990-91 ROSTER

No.	FORWARDS	Hgt./Wt.	Place of Birth	Age	NHL exp.	1989-90 club (league)	G.	A.	Pts.
43	Helmut Balderis	5-11/195	Riga, Latvia	38	1	Minnesota (NHL)	3	6	9
37	Don Barber	6-02/205	Victoria, B.C.	25	2	Minnesota (NHL)	15	19	34
						Kalamazoo (IHL)	4	4	8
23	Brian Bellows	5-11/195	St. Catharines, Ont.	26	8	Minnesota (NHL)	55	44	99
21	Perry Berezan	6-02/190	Edmonton, Alta.	25	6	Minnesota (NHL)	3	12	15
14	Aaron Broten	5-10/180	Roseau, Minn.	29	9	New Jersey (NHL)	10	8	18
						Minnesota (NHL)	9	9	18
7	Neal Broten	5-09/170	Roseau, Minn.	30	10	Minnesota (NHL)	23	62	85
27	Shane Churla	6-01/200	Fernie, B.C.	25	4	Minnesota (NHL)	2	3	5
22	Ulf Dahlen	6-02/195	Ostersund, Sweden	22	3	N.Y. Rangers (NHL)	18	18	36
						Minnesota (NHL)	2	4	6
16	Clark Donatelli	5-10/190	Providence, R.I.	24	1	Kalamazoo (IHL)	8	9	17
						Minnesota (NHL)	3	3	6
10	Gaetan Duchesne	5-11/200	Les Saulles Que.	28	9	Minnesota (NHL)	12	8	20
	Gary Emmons	5-09/170	Winnipeg, Man.	26	0	Kalamazoo (IHL)	41	59	100
	Kevin Evans	5-09/185	Peterborough, Ont.	25	0	Kalamazoo (IHL)	30	54	84
18	Curt Fraser	6-02/200	Cincinnati, O.	32	12	Minnesota (NHL)	1	0	1
15	Dave Gagner	5-10/180	Chatham, Ont.	25	6	Minnesota (NHL)	40	38	78
12	Stewart Gavin	6-00/190	Ottawa, Ont.	30	10	Minnesota (NHL)	12	13	25
20	Peter Lappin	5-11/180	St. Charles, Ill.	24	1	Kalamazoo (IHL)	45	35	80
						Minnesota (NHL)	0	0	0
17	Basil McRae	6-02/205	Beaverton, Ont.	29	9	Minnesota (NHL)	9	17	26
22	Mitch Messier	6-02/200	Regina, Sask.	25	3	Kalamazoo (IHL)	26	58	84
						Minnesota (NHL)	0	0	0
9	Mike Modano	6-03/190	Livonia, Mich.	20	2	Minnesota (NHL)	29	46	75
	Brian Propp	5-10/195	Lanigan, Sask.	31	11	Philadelphia (NHL)	13	15	28
3	J.F. Quintin	6-01/180	St. Jean, Que.	21	0	Boston (NHL)	3	9	12
						Kalamazoo (IHL)	20	18	38
48	Scott Robinson	6-02/180	100 Mile House, B.C.	26	1	Kalamazoo (IHL)	13	12	25
						Minnesota (NHL)	0	0	0
	Ilkka Sinisalo	6-01/190	Valeskoski, Finland	32	9	Philadelphia (NHL)	23	23	46
	Bobby Smith	6-04/214	North Sydney, N.S.	32	12	Montreal (NHL)	12	14	26
47	Mario Thyer	5-11/170	Montreal, Que.	24	1	Kalamazoo (IHL)	19	42	61
						Minnesota (NHL)	0	0	0
DEFENSEMEN									
26	Shawn Chambers	6-02/200	Sterling Hts., Mich.	23	3	Minnesota (NHL)	8	18	26
36	Link Gaetz	6-04/210	Vancouver, B.C.	22	2	Kalamazoo (IHL)	5	16	21
						Minnesota (NHL)	0	0	0
2	Curt Giles	5-08/175	The Pas, Man.	32	11	Minnesota (NHL)	1	12	13
	Dean Kolstad	6-06/210	Edmonton, Alta.	22	1	Kalamazoo (IHL)	10	40	50
	Pat MacLeod	5-11/190	Melfort, Sask.	21	0	Kalamazoo (IHL)	9	38	47
38	Jayson More	6-01/190	Souris, Man.	21	2	Kalamazoo (IHL)	9	25	34
						Minnesota (NHL)	0	0	0
8	Larry Murphy	6-02/210	Scarborough, Ont.	29	10	Minnesota (NHL)	10	58	68
6	Frantisek Musil	6-03/205	Pardubice, Czech.	25	4	Minnesota (NHL)	2	8	10
5	Ville Siren	6-01/185	Tempere, Finland	26	5	Minnesota (NHL)	1	13	14
24	Mark Tinordi	6-04/205	Red Deer, Alta.	24	3	Minnesota (NHL)	3	7	10
39	Neil Wilkinson	6-03/190	Selkirk, Man.	22	1	Minnesota (NHL)	0	5	5
						Kalamazoo (IHL)	6	7	13
41	Rob Zettler	6-03/190	Sept Iles, Que.	22	2	Minnesota (NHL)	0	8	8
						Kalamazoo (IHL)	6	10	16

No.	GOALTENDERS	Hgt./Wt.	Place of Birth	Age	NHL exp.	1989-90 club (league)	Ga.	SO	Avg.
30	Jon Casey	5-10/155	Grand Rapids, Minn.	28	5	Minnesota (NHL)	61	3	3.22
35	Jarmo Myllys	5-08/160	Sovanlinna, Finland	25	2	Kalamazoo (IHL)	49	1	3.51
						Minnesota (NHL)	4	0	6.15
1	Kari Takko	6-02/185	Kaupunki, Finland	27	5	Minnesota (NHL)	21	0	4.03
						Kalamazoo (IHL)	1	0	5.08

1989-90 RECORDS

1989-90 regular-season records: 36-40-4 (.475, 76 points, 4th in Norris Division); 26-12-2 at home; 10-28-2 on road; 3-4-4 in overtime; 17-14-1 vs. Norris (4-3-1 vs. Blackhawks; 4-4-0 vs. Red Wings; 4-4-0 vs. Blues; 5-3-0 vs. Maple Leafs); 6-9-0 vs. Smythe; 6-8-1 vs. Adams; 7-9-2 vs. Patrick.

MISCELLANEOUS DATA

1989-90 team rankings: Shorthanded goals for, 14 (T4th in NHL); shorthanded goals against, 16 (19th); power play, 21.0% (11th); penalty killing, 81.4% (5th); penalty minutes/game, 25.5.

TEAM HAT TRICKS, CAREER, ACTIVE

Don Barber (1)	Dave Gagner (2)
Brian Bellows (4)	Mike Modano (1)
Aaron Broten (1)	Brian Propp (4)
Neal Broten (6)	Ilkka Sinisalo (3)
Ulf Dahlen (1)	Bobby Smith (6)
Curt Fraser (1)	

MINOR LEAGUE AFFILIATIONS

Kalamazoo (IHL)

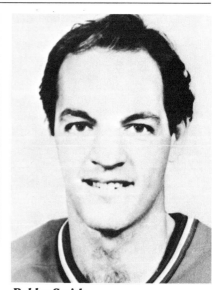

Bobby Smith

1990 DRAFT SELECTIONS

Rnd.	Player	Hgt.	Wgt.	Overall	(Pos.)	1989-90 Club	(League)
1—	Derian Hatcher	6:05	204	8	(D)	North Bay	(OHL)
3—	Laurie Billeck	6:03	207	50	(D)	Prince Albert	(WHL)
4—	Cal McGowan	6:01	182	70	(C)	Kamloops	(WHL)
4—	Frank Kovacs	6:02	205	71	(LW)	Regina	(WHL)
5—	Enrico Ciccone	6:04	196	92	(D)	Trois-Rivieres	(QMJHL)
6—	Roman Turek	6:03	189	113	(G)	Plzen, Czech.	
7—	Jeff Levy	5:11	160	134	(G)	Rochester Jr. A	(Minn.)
8—	Doug Barrault	6:02	203	155	(RW)	Lethbridge	(WHL)
9—	Joe Biondi	6:01	175	176	(C)	Univ. of Minnesota-Duluth	
10—	Troy Binnie	6:01	200	197	(RW)	Ottawa	(OHL)
11—	Ole Dahlstrom	6:00	187	218	(C)	Furuset, Norway	
12—	John McKersie	6:00	209	239	(G)	West High	(Minn.)

FIRST-ROUND ENTRY DRAFT SELECTIONS

Year	Name	Overall	Last Amateur Team	(League)	Years in NHL
1969—	Dick Redmond	5	St. Catharines	(OHL)	13
	Dennis O'Brien	14	St. Catharines	(OHL)	10
1970—	No first round selection				
1971—	No first round selection				
1972—	Jerry Byers	12	Kitchener	(OHL)	4
1973—	No first round selection				
1974—	Doug Hicks	6	Flin Flon	(WCHL)	9
1975—	Brian Maxwell	4	Medicine Hat	(WCHL)	8
1976—	Glen Sharpley	3	Hull	(QMJHL)	6
1977—	Brad Maxwell	7	New Westminster	(WCHL)	10
1978—	*Bobby Smith	1	Ottawa	(OHL)	12
1979—	Craig Hartsburg	6	Birmingham	(WHA)	10
	Tom McCarthy	10	Oshawa	(OHL)	9
1980—	Brad Palmer	16	Victoria	(WHL)	3
1981—	Ron Meighan	13	Niagara Falls	(OHL)	2
1982—	Brian Bellows	2	Kitchener	(OHL)	8
1983—	*Brian Lawton	1	Mt. St. Charles H.S.	(R.I.)	7
1984—	David Quinn	13	Kent H.S.	(Ct.)	0
1985—	No first round selection				
1986—	Warren Babe	12	Lethbridge	(WHL)	2
1987—	Dave Archibald	6	Portland	(WHL)	3
1988—	*Mike Modano	1	Prince Albert	(WHL)	1
1989—	Doug Zmolek	7	John Marshall H.S.	(Minn.)	0
1990—	Derian Hatcher	8	North Bay	(OHL)	0

*Designates first player chosen in draft.

Craig Hartsburg

COACHING HISTORY

Wren Blair, 1967-68
Wren Blair and John Muckler, 1968-69
Wren Blair and Charlie Burns, 1969-70
Jack Gordon, 1970-71 to 1972-73
Jack Gordon and Parker MacDonald, 1973-74
Jack Gordon and Charlie Burns, 1974-75
Ted Harris, 1975-76 to 1976-77
Ted Harris, Andre Beaulieu and Lou Nanne, 1977-78
Harry Howell and Glen Sonmor, 1978-79

Glen Sonmor, 1979-80 to 1980-81
Glen Sonmor and Murray Oliver, 1981-82 to 1982-83
Bill Mahoney, 1983-84
Bill Mahoney and Glen Sonmor, 1984-85
Lorne Henning, 1985-86
Lorne Henning and Glen Sonmor, 1986-87
Herb Brooks, 1987-88
Pierre Page, 1988-89 to 1989-90
Bob Gainey for 1990-91

FRANCHISE LEADERS

Current players in bold face
(1967-68 through 1989-90)

Games
1. 730—Fred Barrett
2. **690—Curt Giles**
3. 670—Bill Goldsworthy
4. **639—Neal Broten**
5. 635—Lou Nanne
6. 615—Tom Reid
7. 613—Steve Payne
8. 602—Dino Ciccarelli
9. **593—Brian Bellows**
10. 588—J.P. Parise

Goals
1. 332—Dino Ciccarelli
2. **277—Brian Bellows**
3. 267—Bill Goldsworthy
4. 228—Steve Payne
5. **216—Neal Broten**
6. 178—Tim Young
7. 176—Danny Grant
8. **156—Bobby Smith**
9. 154—J.P. Parise
10. 146—Tom McCarthy

Assists
1. **444—Neal Broten**
2. 319—Dino Ciccarelli
3. 316—Tim Young
4. 315—Craig Hartsburg
5. **295—Brian Bellows**
6. **294—Bobby Smith**
7. 242—J.P. Parise
8. 239—Bill Goldsworthy
9. 238—Steve Payne
10. 224—Gordie Roberts

Points
1. **660—Neal Broten**
2. 651—Dino Ciccarelli
3. **572—Brian Bellows**
4. 506—Bill Goldsworthy
5. 494—Tim Young
6. 466—Steve Payne
7. **450—Bobby Smith**
8. 413—Craig Hartsburg
9. 396—J.P. Parise
10. 353—Danny Grant

Penalty Minutes
1. 1137—Willi Plett
2. **1098—Basil McRae**
3. 1031—Brad Maxwell
4. 836—Dennis O'Brien
5. 832—Gordie Roberts
6. 818—Craig Hartsburg
7. 735—Bob Rouse

Goaltenders

Games
1. 420—Cesare Maniago
2. 328—Gilles Meloche
3. 316—Don Beaupre
4. 173—Pete LoPresti
5. **158—Jon Casey**
6. **108—Kari Takko**
7. 107—Gump Worsley

Shutouts
1. 26—Cesare Maniago
2. 9—Gilles Meloche
3. 5—Pete LoPresti
4. **4—Jon Casey**

Goals Against Average (entire roster)
(2400 minutes minimum)
1. 2.62—Gump Worsley
2. 3.17—Cesare Maniago
3. **3.33—Jon Casey**
4. 3.39—Gilles Gilbert
5. 3.44—Gary Edwards
6. 3.51—Gilles Meloche
7. 3.74—Don Beaupre
8. **3.83—Kari Takko**
9. 3.98—Fern Rivard
10. 4.06—Pete LoPresti

Wins
1. 143—Cesare Maniago
2. 141—Gilles Meloche
3. 126—Don Beaupre
4. **62—Jon Casey**
5. 43—Pete LoPresti

Stephane Richer is only the second player in Montreal history with at least two 50-goal seasons. Guy Lafleur had six 50-goal seasons in 14 seasons.

Just one of Mike McPhee's 124 goals in seven years with the Canadiens has come on the power play.

Shayne Corson (above, plus-33) and Stephane Richer (plus-35) finished in the top five in the NHL's plus-minus ratings last year. Two years earlier, Corson and Richer had the worst plus-minus ratings (minus-1 and plus-4, respectively) among Montreal regulars.

Denis Savard scored over 100 points five times in 10 seasons with the Chicago Blackhawks. Bobby Hull, with 107 points in 1968-69, is the only other Blackhawk to reach that level.

MONTREAL CANADIENS

CLUB DIRECTORY

Chairman of the Board, President and Governor
Ronald Corey
Vice-President Hockey and Managing Director
Serge Savard
Senior Vice-President, Corporate Affairs
Jean Beliveau
Vice-President, Forum Operations
Aldo Giampaolo
Vice-President, Finance and Administration
Fred Steer
Vice-President, Planning and Development
Louis-Joseph Regimbal
Assistant to Managing Director
Jacques Lemaire
Director of Recruitment and Assistant to Managing Director
Andre Boudrias
Coach
Pat Burns
Assistant Coaches
Jacques Laperriere, Charlie Thiffault
Goaltending Instructor
Francois Allaire
Director of Player Development and Scout
Claude Ruel
Chief Scout
Doug Robinson
Director of Special Events
Camil Desroches

Director of Advertising Sales
Floyd Curry
Director of Public Relations
Claude Mouton
Director of Press Relations
Michele Lapointe
Club Physician
Dr. D.G. Kinnear
Athletic Trainer
Gaetan Lefebvre
Equipment Manager
Eddy Palchak
Assistants to the Equipment Manager
Pierre Gervais, Sylvain Toupin
Home Ice
Montreal Forum
Address
2313 St. Catherine Street West, Montreal, Que.
H3H 1N2
Seating Capacity
16,197
Club Colors
Red, White and Blue
Phone
(514) 932-2582

YEAR-BY-YEAR RESULTS

Season	W.	L.	T.	Pts.	Position
1917-18	13	9	0	26	First and Third
1918-19	10	8	0	20	Second
1919-20	13	11	0	26	Second
1920-21	13	11	0	26	Third
1921-22	12	11	1	25	Third
1922-23	13	9	2	28	Second
1923-24	13	11	0	26	Second—xx
1924-25	17	11	2	36	Third
1925-26	11	24	1	23	Seventh
1926-27	28	14	2	58	Second—c
1927-28	26	11	7	59	First—b
1928-29	22	7	15	59	First—b
1929-30	21	14	9	51	Second—xx
1930-31	26	10	8	60	First—xx
1931-32	25	16	7	57	First—b
1932-33	18	25	5	41	Third—a
1933-34	22	20	6	50	Second—a
1934-35	19	23	6	44	Third—a
1935-36	11	26	11	33	Fourth—*
1936-37	24	18	6	54	First—b
1937-38	18	17	13	49	Third—a
1938-39	15	24	9	39	Sixth—a
1939-40	10	33	5	25	Seventh—*
1940-41	16	26	6	38	Sixth—a
1941-42	18	27	3	39	Sixth—a
1942-43	19	19	12	50	Fourth—b
1943-44	38	5	7	83	First—xx
1944-45	38	8	4	80	First—b
1945-46	28	17	5	61	First—xx
1946-47	34	16	10	78	First—c
1947-48	20	29	11	51	Fifth—*
1948-49	28	23	9	65	Third—b
1949-50	29	22	19	77	Second—b
1950-51	25	30	15	65	Third—c
1951-52	34	26	10	78	Second—c
1952-53	28	23	19	75	Second—xx
1953-54	35	24	11	81	Second—c

Season	W.	L.	T.	Pts.	Position
1954-55	41	18	11	93	Second—c
1955-56	45	15	10	100	First—xx
1956-57	35	23	12	82	Second—xx
1957-58	43	17	10	96	First—xx
1958-59	39	18	13	91	First—xx
1959-60	40	18	12	92	First—xx
1960-61	41	19	10	92	First—b
1961-62	42	14	14	98	First—b
1962-63	28	19	23	79	Third—b
1963-64	36	21	13	85	First—b
1964-65	36	23	11	83	Second—xx
1965-66	41	21	8	90	First—xx
1966-67	32	25	13	77	Second—c
1967-68	42	22	10	94	First—xx
1968-69	46	19	11	103	First—xx
1969-70	38	22	16	92	Fifth—*
1970-71	42	23	13	97	Third—xx
1971-72	46	16	16	108	Third—a
1972-73	52	10	16	120	First—xx
1973-74	45	24	9	99	Second—a
1974-75	47	14	19	113	First—b
1975-76	58	11	11	127	First—xx
1976-77	60	8	12	132	First—xx
1977-78	59	10	11	129	First—xx
1978-79	52	17	11	115	First—xx
1979-80	47	20	13	107	First—a
1980-81	45	22	13	103	First—†
1981-82	46	17	17	109	First—†
1982-83	42	24	14	98	Second—†
1983-84	35	40	5	75	Fourth—b
1984-85	41	27	12	94	First—a
1985-86	40	33	7	87	Second—xx
1986-87	41	29	10	92	Second—b
1987-88	45	22	13	103	First—a
1988-89	53	18	9	115	First—c
1989-90	41	28	11	93	Third—a
Totals	**2352**	**1385**	**695**	**5399**	

From 1917-18 through the 1925-26 season, National Hockey League champions played against the Pacific Coast Hockey League for the Stanley Cup. So, only Stanley Cup championships are designated in the following club records for that period.

Key to standings: *—Missed playoffs. †—Eliminated in first round of new playoff format (1974-75). a—Eliminated in quarterfinal round. b—Eliminated in semifinal round. c—Eliminated in final round. xx—Stanley Cup champion.

1990-91 SCHEDULE

▨ Home games shaded.

* At Chicago Stadium.

OCTOBER

Sun	Mon	Tue	Wed	Thu	Fri	Sat
	1	2	3	4 BUF	5	6 BUF
7	8 HAR	9	10	11	12 NYR	13 HAR
14	15 WAS	16	17 BUF	18 DET	19	20 PHI
21	22	23 PIT	24 NYI	25	26	27 STL
28 CHI	29	30	31 HAR			

NOVEMBER

Sun	Mon	Tue	Wed	Thu	Fri	Sat
				1	2	3 DET
4 MIN	5	6	7 BOS	8	9	10 NJ
11 QUE	12	13 NJ	14	15 PHI	16	17 BOS
18	19 QUE	20	21	22	23	24 LA
25 WIN	26	27	28 BUF	29	30 WAS	

DECEMBER

Sun	Mon	Tue	Wed	Thu	Fri	Sat
						1 CAL
2	3 HAR	4	5 HAR	6 BOS	7	8 BOS
9	10	11	12 TOR	13	14	15 WIN
16	17	18 QUE	19 QUE	20	21	22 NYR
23 PHI	24	25	26	27 VAN	28	29 LA
30	31 CAL					

JANUARY

Sun	Mon	Tue	Wed	Thu	Fri	Sat
		1	2 EDM	3	4	5 QUE
6 PIT	7	8	9 NYI	10	11	12 WAS
13 STL	14	15 MIN	16	17 STL	18	19 ALL-STAR GAME*
20	21	22	23 TOR	24	25	26 BUF
27 BOS	28	29	30 WIN	31 BOS		

FEBRUARY

Sun	Mon	Tue	Wed	Thu	Fri	Sat
					1	2 NYI
3	4 MIN	5	6 CHI	7 QUE	8	9 NYR
10	11	12	13 BOS	14	15 BUF	16 HAR
17	18	19	20 HAR	21	22	23 TOR
24	25	26	27 DET	28		

MARCH

Sun	Mon	Tue	Wed	Thu	Fri	Sat
					1 VAN	2 EDM
3	4 CAL	5	6 CHI	7	8	9 VAN
10 LA	11	12 PIT	13	14 BOS	15	16 BUF
17 EDM	18	19 BUF	20	21	22	23 NJ
24	25 HAR	26	27	28	29	30 QUE
31 QUE						

1989-90 RESULTS

Oct.	5—At Hartford	W	4-1
	7—Buffalo	W	5-1
	9—At Boston	L	0-2
	11—Boston	W	4-2
	13—At New Jersey	W	4-3 (OT)
	14—At Pittsburgh	L	1-2 (OT)
	16—Washington	L	3-4 (OT)
	18—Calgary	W	2-1
	20—At Buffalo	L	2-6
	21—New Jersey	L	4-5
	23—Hartford	W	3-2
	26—At Chicago	L	3-5
	28—Pittsburgh	W	5-1
	29—Edmonton	W	5-4
	31—At N.Y. Islanders	W	3-0
Nov.	2—Buffalo	L	3-4
	4—N.Y. Rangers	W	3-2
	6—St. Louis	T	3-3 (OT)
	8—At N.Y. Rangers	W	3-2
	9—At St. Louis	T	1-1 (OT)
	11—At Los Angeles	L	4-5
	15—Winnipeg	W	5-1
	16—At Boston	L	2-3
	18—Toronto	W	4-3 (OT)
	20—Calgary	W	3-2
	22—At Philadelphia	L	1-5
	25—Boston	W	5-3
	29—Quebec	W	5-2
	30—At Quebec	W	6-2
Dec.	2—Hartford	L	3-4
	6—At Minnesota	W	4-1
	8—At Winnipeg	T	6-6 (OT)
	9—At Toronto	L	4-7
	11—Los Angeles	T	2-2 (OT)
	13—Chicago	L	1-3
	16—Detroit	W	3-1
	17—At N.Y. Rangers	W	2-0
	22—At Buffalo	T	2-2 (OT)
	23—Philadelphia	L	3-5
	27—At Vancouver	L	1-2
	29—At Edmonton	L	2-6
	30—At Calgary	L	3-5
Jan.	6—Buffalo	W	6-3
	7—Vancouver	W	5-3
	9—At Quebec	L	2-5
	12—At New Jersey	W	5-2
	13—Philadelphia	T	2-2 (OT)
	15—Minnesota	W	4-3
	17—N.Y. Islanders	L	3-6
	24—Quebec	W	7-3
	26—At Washington	L	3-6
	27—At Toronto	W	5-3
	29—Boston	L	1-2
Feb.	1—At Boston	W	4-2
	3—Buffalo	W	1-0
	4—Hartford	W	2-0
	7—At Buffalo	L	1-3
	10—Quebec	W	7-2
	14—Vancouver	W	10-1
	16—At Buffalo	L	3-5
	17—Hartford	W	7-3
	19—At Detroit	T	5-5 (OT)
	22—At Quebec	W	6-5
	24—Pittsburgh	W	11-1
	25—St. Louis	W	6-5 (OT)
	28—At Hartford	L	1-3
Mar.	1—At Boston	L	3-5
	3—At Minnesota	L	2-3
	7—At Los Angeles	W	5-2
	10—Detroit	T	3-3 (OT)
	13—At N.Y. Islanders	W	4-2
	14—Edmonton	T	3-3 (OT)
	17—Chicago	W	3-2 (OT)
	18—Quebec	W	8-3
	21—At Winnipeg	L	2-3
	23—At Washington	W	4-2
	24—At Hartford	L	4-7
	29—At Quebec	W	5-2
	31—Boston	T	2-2 (OT)
Apr.	1—At Hartford	T	1-1 (OT)

1990-91 ROSTER

No.	FORWARDS	Hgt./Wt.	Place of Birth	Age	NHL exp.	1989-90 club (league)	G.	A.	Pts.
	Benoit Brunet	5-11/184	Montreal, Que.	22	1	Sherbrooke (AHL)	32	35	67
21	Guy Carbonneau	5-11/175	Sept Iles, Que.	30	9	Montreal (NHL)	19	36	55
43	Andrew Cassels	6-00/192	Bramalea, Ont.	21	1	Sherbrooke (AHL)	22	45	67
						Montreal (NHL)	2	0	2
31	Tom Chorske	6-01/204	Minneapolis, Minn.	24	1	Montreal (NHL)	3	1	4
						Sherbrooke (AHL)	22	24	46
27	Shayne Corson	6-00/201	Barrie, Ont.	24	5	Montreal (NHL)	31	44	75
6	Russ Courtnall	5-11/183	Victoria, B.C.	25	7	Montreal (NHL)	27	32	59
46	Ed Cristofoli	6-02/203	Trail, B.C.	23	1	Sherbrooke (AHL)	16	19	35
						Montreal (NHL)	0	1	1
	Martin Desjardins	5-11/165	Ste. Rose, Que.	23	1	Sherbrooke (AHL)	21	26	47
						Montreal (NHL)	0	2	2
36	Todd Ewen	6-02/220	Saskatoon, Sask.	24	4	St. Louis (NHL)	0	0	0
						Peoria (IHL)	0	0	0
						Montreal (NHL)	4	6	10
41	Brent Gilchrist	5-11/181	Moose Jaw, Sask.	23	2	Montreal (NHL)	9	15	24
12	Mike Keane	5-10/178	Winnipeg, Man.	23	2	Montreal (NHL)	9	15	24
47	Stephan Lebeau	5-10/172	Sherbrooke, Que.	22	2	Montreal (NHL)	15	20	35
8	Steve Martinson	6-01/206	Minnetonka, Minn.	31	3	Sherbrooke (AHL)	6	20	26
						Montreal (NHL)	0	0	0
35	Mike McPhee	6-01/203	Sydney, N.S.	30	7	Montreal (NHL)	23	18	41
14	Mark Pederson	6-02/196	Prelate, Sask.	22	1	Sherbrooke (AHL)	53	42	95
						Montreal (NHL)	0	2	2
44	Stephane Richer	6-02/212	Ripon, Que.	24	6	Montreal (NHL)	51	40	91
	Serge Roberge	6-01/195	Quebec City, Que.	25	0	Sherbrooke (AHL)	8	5	13
18	Denis Savard	5-09/157	Pointe Gatineau, Que.	29	10	Chicago (NHL)	27	53	80
39	Brian Skrudland	6-00/196	Peace River, Alta.	27	5	Montreal (NHL)	11	31	42
	Sylvain Turgeon	6-00/200	Noranda, Que.	25	7	New Jersey (NHL)	30	17	47
11	Ryan Walter	6-00/200	N. Westminster, B.C.	32	12	Montreal (NHL)	8	16	24
	DEFENSEMEN								
48	J.J. Daigneault	5-11/185	Montreal, Que.	24	5	Montreal (NHL)	2	10	12
						Sherbrooke (AHL)	8	19	27
28	Eric Desjardins	6-01/200	Rougn, Que.	21	2	Montreal (NHL)	3	13	16
	Gerald Diduck	6-02/207	Edmonton, Alta.	25	6	N.Y. Islanders (NHL)	3	17	20
34	Donald Dufresne	6-01/206	Quebec City, Que.	23	2	Montreal (NHL)	0	4	4
						Sherbrooke (AHL)	2	11	13
3	Sylvain Lefebvre	6-02/204	Richmond, Que.	22	1	Montreal (NHL)	3	10	13
38	Lyle Odelein	5-10/206	Quill Lake, Sask.	22	1	Sherbrooke (AHL)	7	24	31
						Montreal (NHL)	0	2	2
	Todd Richards	6-00/180	Robindale, Minn.	23	0	Sherbrooke (AHL)	6	18	24
	Mathieu Schneider	5-11/189	New York, N.Y.	21	1	Sherbrooke (AHL)	6	13	19
						Montreal (NHL)	7	14	21
25	Petr Svoboda	6-01/174	Most, Czechoslovakia	24	6	Montreal (NHL)	5	31	36

No.	GOALTENDERS	Hgt./Wt.	Place of Birth	Age	NHL exp.	1989-90 club (league)	Ga.	SO	Avg.
	J.-Claude Bergeron	6-02/192	Hauterive, Que.	21	0	Sherbrooke (AHL)	40	2	2.74
1	Brian Hayward	5-10/180	Weston, Ont.	30	8	Montreal (NHL)	29	1	3.37
53	Andre Racicot	5-11/165	Rouyn-Noranda, Que.	21	1	Sherbrooke (AHL)	33	1	2.99
						Montreal (NHL)	1	0	13.85
33	Patrick Roy	6-00/182	Quebec City, Que.	24	6	Montreal (NHL)	54	3	2.53

1989-90 RECORDS

1989-90 regular-season records: 41-28-11 (.581, 93 points, 3rd in Adams Division); 26-8-6 at home; 15-20-5 on road; 4-2-11 in overtime; 17-12-3 vs. Adams (3-4-1 vs. Bruins; 3-4-1 vs. Sabres; 4-3-1 vs. Whalers; 7-1-0 vs. Nordiques); 10-7-1 vs. Patrick; 7-4-4 vs. Norris; 7-5-3 vs. Smythe.

MISCELLANEOUS DATA

1989-90 team rankings: Shorthanded goals for, 4 (21st in NHL); shorthanded goals against, 7 (T4th); power play, 15.9% (21st); penalty killing, 80.7% (9th); penalty minutes/game, 19.9.

TEAM HAT TRICKS, CAREER, ACTIVE

Guy Carbonneau (1)	Stephane Richer (5)
Shayne Corson (2)	Denis Savard (11)
Russ Courtnall (2)	Sylvain Turgeon (4)
Mike McPhee (2)	Ryan Walter (1)

MINOR LEAGUE AFFILIATIONS

Fort Wayne (IHL) with Winnipeg, Fredericton (AHL)

Petr Svoboda

1990 DRAFT SELECTIONS

Rnd. Player	Hgt.	Wgt.	Overall	(Pos.)	1989-90 Club (League)
1—Turner Stevenson	6:03	200	12	(RW)	Seattle (WHL)
2—Ryan Kuwabara	6:00	205	39	(RW)	Ottawa (OHL)
3—Charles Poulin	6:00	172	58	(C)	St. Hyacinthe (QMJHL)
3—Robert Guillet	5:11	189	60	(RW)	Longueuil (QMJHL)
4—Gilbert Dionne	6:00	194	81	(LW)	Kitchener (OHL)
5—Paul DiPietro	5:09	181	102	(C)	Sudbury (OHL)
6—Craig Conroy	6:01	181	123	(C)	Northwood Prep (N.Y.)
7—Stephen Rohr	6:02	180	144	(RW)	Culver Military Academy (Ind.)
8—Brent Fleetwood	6:01	180	165	(LW)	Portland (WHL)
9—Derek Maguire	6:00	185	186	(D)	Delbarton H.S. (N.J.)
10—Mark Kettlehut	6:00	195	207	(D)	Duluth East H.S. (Minn.)
11—John Uniac	5:11	210	228	(D)	Kitchener (OHL)
12—Sergei Martinyuk	6:00	178	249	(LW)	Torpedo Jaroslav, USSR

FIRST-ROUND ENTRY DRAFT SELECTIONS

Year	Name	Overall	Last Amateur Team (League)	Years in NHL
1969	*Rejean Houle	1	Montreal (OHL)	11
	Marc Tardif	2	Montreal (OHL)	8
1970	Ray Martiniuk	5	Flin Flon (WCHL)	0
	Chuck Lefley	6	Canadian Nationals	9
1971	*Guy Lafleur	1	Quebec (QMJHL)	16
	Chuck Arnason	7	Flin Flon (WCHL)	6
	Murray Wilson	11	Ottawa (OHL)	7
1972	Steve Shutt	4	Toronto (OHL)	13
	Michel Larocque	6	Ottawa (OHL)	11
	Dave Gardner	8	Toronto (OHL)	7
	John Van Boxmeer	14	Guelph (SOJHL)	11
1973	Bob Gainey	8	Peterborough (OHL)	16
1974	Cam Connor	5	Flin Flon (WCHL)	5
	Doug Risebrough	7	Kitchener (OHL)	14
	Rick Chartraw	10	Kitchener (OHL)	10
	Mario Tremblay	12	Montreal (OHL)	12
	Gord McTavish	15	Sudbury (OHL)	2
1975	Robin Sadler	9	Edmonton (WCHL)	0
	Pierre Mondou	15	Montreal (QMJHL)	9
1976	Peter Lee	12	Ottawa (OHL)	6
	Rod Schutt	13	Sudbury (OHL)	8
	Bruce Baker	18	Ottawa (OHL)	0
1977	Mark Napier	10	Birmingham (WHA)	11
	Normand Dupont	18	Montreal (QMJHL)	5
1978	Danny Geoffrion	8	Cornwall (QMJHL)	3
	Dave Hunter	17	Sudbury (OHL)	10
1979	No first round selection			
1980	*Doug Wickenheiser	1	Regina (WHL)	10
1981	Mark Hunter	7	Brantford (OHL)	8
	Gilbert Delorme	18	Chicoutimi (QMJHL)	9
	Jan Ingman	19	Farjestads (Sweden)	0
1982	Alain Heroux	19	Chicoutimi (QMJHL)	0
1983	Alfie Turcotte	17	Portland (WHL)	6
1984	Petr Svoboda	5	Czechoslovakia	6
	Shayne Corson	8	Brantford (OHL)	5
1985	Jose Charbonneau	12	Drummondville (QMJHL)	2
	Tom Chorske	16	Minneapolis SW H.S. (Minn.)	1
1986	Mark Pederson	15	Medicine Hat (WHL)	1
1987	Andrew Cassels	17	Ottawa (OHL)	1
1988	Eric Charron	20	Trois-Rivieres (QMJHL)	0
1989	Lindsay Vallis	13	Seattle (WHL)	0
1990	Turner Stevenson	12	Seattle (WHL)	0

*Designates first player chosen in draft.

COACHING HISTORY

George Kennedy, 1917-18 to 1920-21
Leo Dandurand, 1921-22 to 1924-25
Cecil Hart, 1925-26 to 1931-32
Newsy Lalonde, 1932-33 to 1933-34
Newsy Lalonde and Leo Dandurand, 1934-35
Sylvio Mantha, 1935-36
Cecil Hart, 1936-37 to 1937-38
Cecil Hart and Jules Dugal, 1938-39
Pit Lepine, 1939-40
Dick Irvin 1940-41 to 1954-55
Toe Blake, 1955-56 to 1967-68

Claude Ruel, 1968-69 to 1969-70
Claude Ruel and Al MacNeil, 1970-71
Scotty Bowman, 1971-72 to 1978-79
Bernie Geoffrion and Claude Ruel, 1979-80
Claude Ruel, 1980-81
Bob Berry, 1981-82 to 1982-83
Bob Berry and Jacques Lemaire, 1983-84
Jacques Lemaire, 1984-85
Jean Perron, 1985-86 to 1987-88
Pat Burns since 1988-89

FRANCHISE LEADERS

Current players in bold type
(1917-18 through 1989-90)

Games

1. 1256—Henri Richard
2. 1202—Larry Robinson
3. 1160—Bob Gainey
4. 1125—Jean Beliveau
5. 1005—Claude Provost
6. 978—Maurice Richard
7. 968—Yvan Cournoyer
8. 961—Guy Lafleur
9. 917—Serge Savard
10. 890—Doug Harvey

Goals

1. 544—Maurice Richard
2. 518—Guy Lafleur
3. 507—Jean Beliveau
4. 428—Yvan Cournoyer
5. 408—Steve Shutt
6. 371—Bernie Geoffrion
7. 366—Jacques Lemaire
8. 358—Henri Richard
9. 270—Aurele Joliat
10. 258—Mario Tremblay

Assists

1. 728—Guy Lafleur
2. 712—Jean Beliveau
3. 688—Henri Richard
4. 686—Larry Robinson
5. 469—Jacques Lemaire
6. 435—Yvan Cournoyer
7. 421—Maurice Richard
8. 408—Elmer Lach
9. 406—Guy Lapointe
10. 388—Bernie Geoffrion

Points

1. 1246—Guy Lafleur
2. 1219—Jean Beliveau
3. 1046—Henri Richard
4. 965—Maurice Richard
5. 883—Larry Robinson
6. 863—Yvan Cournoyer
7. 835—Jacques Lemaire
8. 776—Steve Shutt
9. 759—Bernie Geoffrion
10. 623—Elmer Lach

Penalty Minutes

1. 2174—Chris Nilan
2. 1285—Maurice Richard
3. 1214—John Ferguson
4. 1043—Mario Tremblay
5. 1042—Doug Harvey
6. 1029—Jean Beliveau
7. 959—Doug Risebrough
8. 928—Henri Richard
9. 897—Tom Johnson
10. 884—Jean-Guy Talbot

Goaltenders

Games

1. 556—Jacques Plante
2. 397—Ken Dryden
3. 383—Bill Durnan
4. 328—Georges Vezina
5. 321—George Hainsworth
6. 276—Gerry McNeil
7. 249—Wilf Cude
8. 241—Patrick Roy
9. 236—Charlie Hodge
10. 231—Michel Larocque

Shutouts

1. 74—George Hainsworth
2. 58—Jacques Plante
3. 46—Ken Dryden
4. 34—Bill Durnan
5. 28—Gerry McNeil
6. 22—Wilf Cude
7. 21—Charlie Hodge
8. 17—Michel Larocque
9. 16—Lorne Worsley
10. 15—Georges Vezina

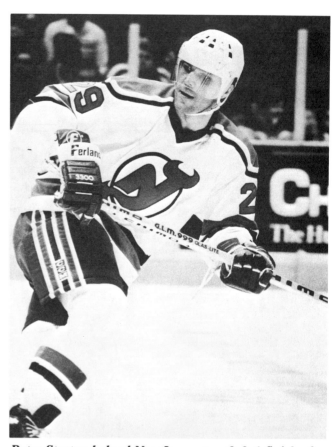

Kirk Muller tied a team record for most points in a period with two goals and two assists in the third period of a 5-3 win over Washington on February 9, 1990.

Peter Stastny helped New Jersey to a 9-3-1 finish after joining the team late last year.

John MacLean is the only Devils player to have two 40-goal seasons since the team moved from Colorado to New Jersey in 1982. MacLean scored 42 goals two seasons ago and 41 last year.

John Cunniff, who led the Devils to a 31-28-7 record after replacing Jim Schoenfeld last season, is the only coach in franchise history with a winning record.

NEW JERSEY DEVILS

CLUB DIRECTORY

Chairman
John J. McMullen
President and General Manager
Lou Lamoriello
Executive Vice-President
Max McNab
Coach
John Cunniff
Assistant Coach
Tim Burke, Doug Sulliman
Goaltending Coach
Warren Strelow
Goaltending Coach/Scout
Bob Bellemore
Director of Player Personnel
Marshall Johnston
Assistant Director of Player Personnel
David Conte
Scouts
Claude Carrier, Frank Jay, Ed Thomlinson, Milt Fisher, Glen Dirk, Dan Labraaten, Les Widdifield, Marcel Pronovost

Strength Coach
Dimitri Lopuchin
Director, Public and Media Relations
David Freed
Public Relations Assistants
Mike Levine, Nelson Rodriguez
Executive Offices
Byrne Meadowlands Arena
Home Ice
Byrne Meadowlands Arena
Address
Meadowlands Arena, P.O. Box 504, East Rutherford, N.J. 07073
Seating Capacity
19,040
Club Colors
Red, Green and White
Phone
(201) 935-6050
FAX
(201) 935-2127

YEAR-BY-YEAR RESULTS

Season	W.	L.	T.	Pts.	Position	Season	W.	L.	T.	Pts.	Position
1974-75	15	54	11	41	Fifth—*	1983-84	17	56	7	41	Fifth—*
1975-76	12	56	12	36	Fifth—*	1984-85	22	48	10	54	Fifth—*
1976-77	20	46	14	54	Fifth—*	1985-86	28	49	3	59	Fifth—*
1977-78	19	40	21	59	Second—†	1986-87	29	45	6	64	Sixth—*
1978-79	15	53	12	42	Fourth—*	1987-88	38	36	6	82	Fourth—b
1979-80	19	48	13	51	Sixth—*	1988-89	27	41	12	66	Fifth—*
1980-81	22	45	13	57	Fifth—*	1989-90	37	34	9	83	Second—†
1981-82	18	49	13	49	Fifth—*	**Totals**	355	749	176	886	
1982-83	17	49	14	48	Fifth—*						

Key to standings: *—Missed playoffs. †—Eliminated in first round of new playoff format (1974-75). a—Eliminated in quarterfinal round. b—Eliminated in semifinal round. c—Eliminated in final round. xx—Stanley Cup champion.

Barry Beck

Glenn Resch

1990-91 SCHEDULE

▦ Home games shaded.

* At Chicago Stadium.

OCTOBER

Sun	Mon	Tue	Wed	Thu	Fri	Sat
	1	2	3	4 DET	5	6 PHI
7 PIT	8	9 MIN	10	11 PHI	12	13 CAL
14	15	16	17 WAS	18	19 NYR	20 WAS
21	22	23 NYI	24	25 BUF	26	27 PIT
28	29	30 CAL	31			

NOVEMBER

Sun	Mon	Tue	Wed	Thu	Fri	Sat
				1 VAN	2	3 EDM
4	5	6	7 NYI	8	9 NYR	10 MON
11	12	13 MON	14	15 HAR	16	17 PHI
18 PHI	19	20 LA	21	22	23	24 MIN
25	26	27	28 PHI	29	30 NYI	

DECEMBER

Sun	Mon	Tue	Wed	Thu	Fri	Sat
						1 STL
2	3 WIN	4	5 VAN	6	7 WAS	8 WAS
9	10	11 NYI	12	13 PIT	14	15 BOS
16	17	18 BOS	19	20 PHI	21	22 QUE
23 TOR	24	25	26	27 NYI	28	29 BUF
30 NYR	31					

JANUARY

Sun	Mon	Tue	Wed	Thu	Fri	Sat
		1 WAS	2	3 CHI	4	5 PIT
6	7	8 STL	9	10	11	12 EDM
13	14 LA	15	16 CHI	17	18	19 ALL-STAR GAME*
20	21	22 PIT	23	24 QUE	25	26 MIN
27	28 DET	29	30 LA	31		

FEBRUARY

Sun	Mon	Tue	Wed	Thu	Fri	Sat
					1	2 STL
3	4	5 CAL	6	7	8	9 QUE
10 VAN	11	12	13 NYR	14 WIN	15	16 PHI
17	18 EDM	19	20	21	22 PIT	23
24 NYR	25 WAS	26	27 TOR	28		

MARCH

Sun	Mon	Tue	Wed	Thu	Fri	Sat
					1 DET	2
3 BOS	4	5 NYI	6 BUF	7	8	9
10 WIN	11	12	13 TOR	14	15 NYR	16 HAR
17	18	19 PIT	20	21 CHI	22	23 MON
24	25	26 NYR	27 HAR	28	29	30 WAS
31 NYI						

1989-90 RESULTS

Oct.	5—At Philadelphia	W	6-2
	7—Pittsburgh	T	4-4 (OT)
	10—Calgary	L	2-4
	13—Montreal	L	3-4 (OT)
	14—At Hartford	W	3-2
	18—Philadelphia	W	5-3
	20—Vancouver	L	2-3
	21—At Montreal	W	5-4
	23—At Toronto	W	5-4
	26—Hartford	L	3-7
	28—Chicago	W	3-2
	31—At Vancouver	L	3-4
Nov.	1—At Edmonton	T	6-6 (OT)
	4—At Calgary	L	3-7
	8—Quebec	W	6-3
	11—Philadelphia	L	5-7
	12—At Philadelphia	T	3-3 (OT)
	15—Minnesota	L	1-2 (OT)
	17—N.Y. Rangers	W	5-4 (OT)
	18—At Boston	L	4-6
	22—At Pittsburgh	W	6-3
	24—At Minnesota	L	6-7
	25—At Winnipeg	W	3-1
	28—N.Y. Islanders	W	3-2 (OT)
Dec.	1—At Buffalo	L	4-6
	2—Washington	L	3-5
	6—At N.Y. Rangers	L	3-5
	8—Pittsburgh	L	2-3
	9—At Hartford	L	3-7
	12—At N.Y. Islanders	W	7-2
	13—N.Y. Islanders	W	5-2
	15—Los Angeles	W	7-5
	17—Boston	W	3-1
	19—At N.Y. Islanders	L	4-5 (OT)
	22—At Philadelphia	W	5-4 (OT)
	23—St. Louis	W	3-2
	26—At N.Y. Rangers	T	4-4 (OT)
	27—Washington	L	1-3
	29—N.Y. Rangers	W	3-2
	31—At Detroit	L	4-6
Jan.	2—Buffalo	W	5-3
	4—Los Angeles	W	4-2
	8—Winnipeg	L	3-4
	10—Pittsburgh	W	6-3
	12—Montreal	L	2-5
	13—At Quebec	W	5-4
	16—At Washington	L	6-9
	23—At Pittsburgh	W	4-2
	24—Washington	W	3-2
	26—Toronto	L	1-5
	28—At N.Y. Islanders	T	4-4 (OT)
	30—At Los Angeles	L	2-5
Feb.	4—At Vancouver	L	2-4
	6—Edmonton	T	2-2 (OT)
	9—At Washington	W	5-3
	10—At St. Louis	L	0-7
	12—Detroit	T	1-1 (OT)
	16—N.Y. Rangers	L	1-2
	17—At Toronto	L	4-5
	19—At N.Y. Rangers	L	3-4 (OT)
	22—Winnipeg	L	2-4
	24—Chicago	W	3-2
	25—At N.Y. Islanders	T	3-3 (OT)
	28—At Pittsburgh	L	1-2
Mar.	2—Pittsburgh	W	6-5
	4—At Washington	L	3-4
	6—St. Louis	W	2-1
	8—N.Y. Islanders	W	4-2
	10—Quebec	W	9-3
	13—At Minnesota	W	3-1
	15—At Calgary	L	4-5
	17—At Edmonton	W	4-1
	20—Philadelphia	L	2-3
	22—At Chicago	L	3-6
	24—At Philadelphia	W	5-2
	25—At Buffalo	W	4-3
	27—Washington	W	4-1
	29—N.Y. Rangers	W	6-4
	31—Detroit	W	5-1
Apr.	1—At Boston	T	3-3 (OT)

1990-91 ROSTER

No.	FORWARDS	Hgt./Wt.	Place of Birth	Age	NHL exp.	1989-90 club (league)	G.	A.	Pts.
	Laurie Boschman	6-00/185	Major, Sask.	30	11	Winnipeg (NHL)	10	17	27
24	Doug Brown	5-10/180	Southborough, Mass.	26	4	New Jersey (NHL)	14	20	34
32	Pat Conacher	5-08/190	Edmonton, Alta.	31	7	Utica (AHL)	13	36	49
						New Jersey (NHL)	3	3	6
25	Troy Crowder	6-04/215	Sudbury, Ont.	22	1	Nashville (ECHL)	0	0	0
						New Jersey (NHL)	0	0	0
	Claude Lemieux	6-01/213	Buckingham, Que.	25	7	Montreal (NHL)	8	10	18
15	John MacLean	6-00/200	Oshawa, Ont.	25	7	New Jersey (NHL)	41	38	79
	Jeff Madill	5-11/195	Oshawa, Ont.	23	0	Utica (AHL)	43	26	69
8	David Maley	6-02/195	Beaver Dam, Wis.	27	5	New Jersey (NHL)	8	17	25
	Jason Miller	6-01/190	Edmonton, Alta.	19	0	Medicine Hat (WHL)	43	56	99
20	Jon Morris	6-00/175	Lowell, Mass.	24	2	Utica (AHL)	27	37	64
						New Jersey (NHL)	6	7	13
9	Kirk Muller	5-11/185	Kingston, Ont.	24	6	New Jersey (NHL)	30	56	86
22	Janne Ojanen	6-02/200	Tampere, Finland	22	2	New Jersey (NHL)	17	13	30
21	Walt Poddubny	6-01/210	Thunder Bay, Ont.	30	9	New Jersey (NHL)	4	10	14
						Utica (AHL)	1	2	3
11	Brendan Shanahan	6-03/210	Mimico, Ont.	21	3	New Jersey (NHL)	30	42	72
	Jarrod Skalde	6-00/170	Niagara Falls, Ont.	19	0	Oshawa (OHL)	40	52	92
29	Peter Stastny	6-01/200	Bratislava, Czech.	34	10	Quebec (NHL)	24	38	62
						New Jersey (NHL)	5	6	11
17	Patrik Sundstrom	6-01/200	Skelleftea, Czech.	28	8	New Jersey (NHL)	27	49	76
	Jim Thomson	6-02/205	Edmonton, Alta.	24	3	Utica (AHL)	20	23	43
						New Jersey (NHL)	0	0	0
	Claude Vilgrain	6-01/205	Port-au-Prince, Haiti	27	2	Utica (AHL)	37	52	89
						New Jersey (NHL)	1	2	3
	Paul Ysebaert	6-01/190	Sarnia, Ont.	24	2	Utica (AHL)	53	52	105
						New Jersey (NHL)	1	2	3
	DEFENSEMEN								
26	Tommy Albelin	6-01/190	Stockholm, Sweden	26	3	New Jersey (NHL)	6	23	29
3	Ken Daneyko	6-00/210	Windsor, Ont.	26	7	New Jersey (NHL)	6	15	21
23	Bruce Driver	6-00/185	Toronto, Ont.	28	7	New Jersey (NHL)	7	46	53
2	Viacheslav Fetisov	6-01/220	Moscow, USSR	32	1	New Jersey (NHL)	8	34	42
18	Jamie Huscroft	6-02/200	Creston, B.C.	23	2	Utica (AHL)	3	6	9
						New Jersey (NHL)	2	3	5
7	Alexei Kasatonov	6-01/215	Leningrad, USSR	30	0	Central Red Army (USSR)	6	7	13
						Utica (AHL)	0	2	2
						New Jersey (NHL)	6	15	21
	Chris Kiene	6-05/220	S. Windsor, Conn.	24	0	Utica (AHL)	5	17	22
	Dave Marcinyshyn	6-03/210	Edmonton, Alta.	23	0	Utica (AHL)	6	18	24
	Myles O'Connor	5-11/185	Calgary, Alta.	23	0	Utica (AHL)	14	33	47
	Jeff Sharples	6-01/195	Terrace, B.C.	23	3	Adirondack (AHL)	2	5	7
						Cape Breton (AHL)	4	13	17
						Utica (AHL)	2	5	7
4	Sergei Starikov	5-10/225	Chelyabinsk, USSR	31	1	New Jersey (NHL)	0	1	1
						Utica (AHL)	8	11	19
5	Eric Weinrich	6-01/210	Roanoke, Va.	23	2	Utica (AHL)	12	48	60
						New Jersey (NHL)	2	7	9

No.	GOALTENDERS	Hgt./Wt.	Place of Birth	Age	NHL exp.	1989-90 club (league)	Ga.	SO	Avg.
	Craig Billington	5-10/170	London, Ont.	24	3	Utica (AHL)	38	0	3.97
1	Sean Burke	6-04/210	Windsor, Ont.	23	3	New Jersey (NHL)	52	0	3.60
	Roland Melanson	5-10/185	Moncton, N.B.	30	9	Utica (AHL)	48	1	3.66
31	Chris Terreri	5-08/155	Providence, R.I.	25	3	New Jersey (NHL)	35	0	3.42

1989-90 RECORDS

1989-90 regular-season records: 37-34-9 (.519, 83 points, 2nd in Patrick Division); 22-15-3 at home; 15-19-6 on road; 3-4-9 in overtime; 18-12-5 vs. Patrick (4-1-2 vs. Islanders; 3-3-1 vs. Rangers; 4-2-1 vs. Flyers; 4-2-1 vs. Penguins; 3-4-0 vs. Capitals); 8-6-1 vs. Adams; 7-7-1 vs. Norris; 4-9-2 vs. Smythe.

MISCELLANEOUS DATA

1989-90 team rankings: Shorthanded goals for, 10 (T11th in NHL); shorthanded goals against, 12 (T12th); power play, 19.0% (15th); penalty killing, 80.3% (T10th); penalty minutes/game, 20.7.

TEAM HAT TRICKS, CAREER, ACTIVE

Perry Anderson (1)	Walt Poddubny (5)
Bob Brooke (1)	Brendan Shanahan (1)
Mark Johnson (5)	Peter Stastny (16)
Claude Lemieux (1)	Patrik Sundstrom (2)
John MacLean (4)	Peter Sundstrom (2)
Kirk Muller (3)	

MINOR LEAGUE AFFILIATIONS

Utica (AHL)

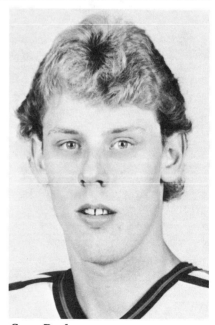

Sean Burke

1990 DRAFT SELECTIONS

Rnd.	Player	Hgt.	Wgt.	Overall	(Pos.)	1989-90 Club	(League)
1—	Martin Brodeur	6:00	189	20	(G)	St. Hyacinthe	(QMJHL)
2—	David Harlock	6:02	195	24	(D)	University of Michigan	
2—	Chris Gotziaman	6:02	200	29	(RW)	Roseau H.S.	(Minn.)
3—	Michael Dunham	6:02	162	53	(G)	Canterbury Prep	(Ct.)
3—	Brad Bombardir	6:02	187	56	(D)	Powell River Tier II	
4—	Mike Bodnarchuk	6:00	176	64	(RW)	Kingston	(OHL)
5—	Dean Malkoc	6:02	202	95	(D)	Kamloops	(WHL)
5—	Peter Kuchyna	6:02	180	104	(D)	Dukla Jihlava, Czech.	
6—	Lubomir Kolnik	5:11	178	116	(RW)	Dukla Trencin, Czech.	
7—	Chris McAlpine	5:10	173	137	(D)	Roseville H.S.	(Minn.)
9—	Jaroslav Modry	6:02	186	179	(D)	Budejovice, Czech.	
10—	Corey Schwab	5:11	179	200	(G)	Seattle	(WHL)
11—	Valeri Zelepukin	5:11	180	221	(RW)	Himik, USSR	
12—	Todd Reirden	6:04	175	242	(D)	Tabor H.S.	(Mass.)

FIRST-ROUND ENTRY DRAFT SELECTIONS

Year	Name	Overall	Last Amateur Team	(League)	Years in NHL
1974—	Wilf Paiement	2	St. Catharines	(OHL)	14
1975—	Barry Dean	2	Medicine Hat	(WCHL)	3
1976—	Paul Gardner	11	Oshawa	(OHL)	7
1977—	Barry Beck	2	New Westminster	(WCHL)	10
1978—	Mike Gillis	5	Kingston	(OHL)	6
1979—	*Rob Ramage	1	Birmingham	(WHA)	11
1980—	Paul Gagne	19	Windsor	(OHL)	8
1981—	Joe Cirella	5	Oshawa	(OHL)	8
1982—	Rocky Trottier	8	Billings	(WHL)	2
	Ken Daneyko	18	Seattle	(WHL)	7
1983—	John MacLean	6	Oshawa	(OHL)	7
1984—	Kirk Muller	2	Guelph	(OHL)	6
1985—	Craig Wolanin	3	Kitchener	(OHL)	5
1986—	Neil Brady	3	Medicine Hat	(WHL)	0
1987—	Brendan Shanahan	2	London	(OHL)	3
1988—	Corey Foster	12	Peterborough	(OHL)	1
1989—	Bill Guerin	5	Springfield (Mass.) Jr.		0
	Jason Miller	18	Medicine Hat	(WHL)	0
1990—	Martin Brodeur	20	St. Hyacinthe	(QMJHL)	0

*Designates first player chosen in draft.

Wilf Paiement

COACHING HISTORY

Bep Guidolin, 1974-75
Bep Guidolin, Sid Abel, and Eddie Bush, 1975-76
John Wilson, 1976-77
Pat Kelly, 1977-78
Pat Kelly and Bep Guidolin, 1978-79
Don Cherry, 1979-80
Billy MacMillan, 1980-81
Bert Marshall and Marshall Johnston, 1981-82

Billy MacMillan, 1982-83
Billy MacMillan and Tom McVie, 1983-84
Doug Carpenter, 1984-85 to 1986-87
Doug Carpenter and Jim Schoenfeld, 1987-88
Jim Schoenfeld, 1988-89
Jim Schoenfeld and John Cunniff, 1989-90
John Cunniff for 1990-91

FRANCHISE LEADERS

Current players in bold type
(1974-75 through 1989-90)

Games
1. 641—Aaron Broten
2. 503—Joe Cirella
3. **476—Kirk Muller**
4. 474—Mike Kitchen
5. **468—John MacLean**
6. 463—Pat Verbeek
7. 392—Wilf Paiement
8. 390—Gary Croteau
9. **369—Ken Daneyko**
10. 365—Paul Gagne

Goals
1. **172—John MacLean**
2. 170—Pat Verbeek
3. **166—Kirk Muller**
4. 162—Aaron Broten
5. 153—Wilf Paiement
6. 106—Paul Gagne
7. 92—Gary Croteau
8. **89—Mark Johnson**
9. 86—Doug Sulliman
10. 83—Paul Gardner

Assists
1. 307—Aaron Broten
2. **284—Kirk Muller**
3. **191—John MacLean**
4. 183—Wilf Paiement
5. **169—Bruce Driver**
6. 159—Joe Cirella
7. 151—Pat Verbeek
8. 148—Mel Bridgman
9. **140—Mark Johnson**
10. **126—Patrik Sundstrom**

Points
1. 469—Aaron Broten
2. **450—Kirk Muller**
3. **363—John MacLean**
4. 336—Wilf Paiement
5. 321—Pat Verbeek
6. **229—Mark Johnson**
7. 224—Mel Bridgman
8. **210—Bruce Driver**
9. 209—Joe Cirella
10. 205—Paul Gagne

Penalty Minutes
1. **1048—Ken Daneyko**
2. 943—Pat Verbeek
3. 938—Joe Cirella
4. **635—John MacLean**
5. 558—Wilf Paiement
6. **548—Perry Anderson**
7. 529—Rob Ramage
8. **496—Kirk Muller**
9. **474—David Maley**
10. 469—Craig Wolanin

Goaltenders

Games
1. 267—Chico Resch
2. 150—Michel Plasse
3. **127—Sean Burke**

Shutouts (entire roster)
1. **4—Sean Burke**
2. 1—Alain Chevrier
1—Doug Favell
1—Ron Low
1—Bill McKenzie
1—Bill Oleschuk
1—Chico Resch
1—Sam St. Laurent

Goals-Against Average
(2400 minutes minimum)
1. **3.67—Sean Burke**
2. 3.76—Hardy Astrom
3. 3.84—Doug Favell

Wins
1. 67—Chico Resch
2. **54—Sean Burke**
3. 53—Alain Chevrier

Pat LaFontaine's 11-game goal-scoring streak in 1989-90 was the longest in Islanders history.

Doug Crossman has been in the playoffs every year since his 1981-82 rookie season.

Mark Fitzpatrick's three shutouts last season were the most by an Islander goalie since Chico Resch had four in 1976-77.

Brent Sutter (above) has scored an overtime playoff goal in each of the last two years. Along with an overtime goal by Pat LaFontaine in 1988, they account for the Islanders' last three playoff victories.

NEW YORK ISLANDERS

CLUB DIRECTORY

Owner
John O. Pickett, Jr.
Chairman of the Board and General Manager
William A. Torrey
President
John H. Krumpe
General Counsel
William M. Skehan
Vice-President/Administration
Joseph H. Dreyer
Vice-President/Finance
Arthur J. McCarthy
Vice-President/Media Sales
Arthur Adler
Coach
Al Arbour
Assistant Coaches
Darcy Regier, Lorne Henning
Assistant General Manager/Director of Scouting
Gerry Ehman
Scouting Staff
Harry Boyd, Richard Green, Hal Laycoe, Mario Saraceno, Jack Vivian, Earl Ingarfield, Bert Marshall, Anders Kallur
Publicity Director
Greg Bouris

Assistant Publicity Director
Catherine Schutte
Controller
Ralph Sellitti
Director of Public Affairs
Jill Knee
Director of Sales
Jim Johnson
Director of Special Projects
Bob Nystrom
Athletic Trainer
Ed Tyburski
Assistant Trainers
John Doolan, Terry Murphy
Home Ice
Nassau Veterans Memorial Coliseum
Address
Uniondale, N. Y. 11553
Seating Capacity
16,297
Club Colors
Blue, White and Orange
Phone
(516) 794-4100
FAX
(516) 542-9348

YEAR-BY-YEAR RESULTS

Season	W.	L.	T.	Pts.	Position	Season	W.	L.	T.	Pts.	Position
1972-73	12	60	6	30	Eighth—*	1982-83	42	26	12	96	Second—xx
1973-74	19	41	18	56	Eighth—*	1983-84	50	26	4	104	First—c
1974-75	33	25	22	88	Third—b	1984-85	40	34	6	86	Third—a
1975-76	42	21	17	101	Second—b	1985-86	39	29	12	90	Third—†
1976-77	47	21	12	106	Second—b	1986-87	35	33	12	82	Third—a
1977-78	48	17	15	111	First—a	1987-88	39	31	10	88	First—†
1978-79	51	15	14	116	First—b	1988-89	28	47	5	61	Sixth—*
1979-80	39	28	13	91	Second—xx	1989-90	31	38	11	73	Fourth—†
1980-81	48	18	14	110	First—xx	**Totals**	697	526	213	1607	
1981-82	54	16	10	118	First—xx						

Key to standings: *—Missed playoffs. †—Eliminated in first round of new playoff format (1974-75). a—Eliminated in quarterfinal round. b—Eliminated in semifinal round. c—Eliminated in final round. xx—Stanley Cup champion.

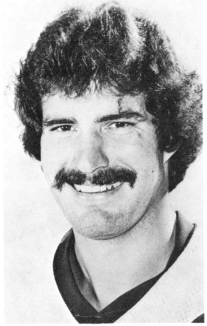

Clark Gillies

Billy Smith

1990-91 SCHEDULE

▦ Home games shaded.

* At Chicago Stadium.

OCTOBER

Sun	Mon	Tue	Wed	Thu	Fri	Sat
	1	2	3	4 LA	5	6 MIN
7 CHI	8	9	10	11	12	13 PIT
14	15	16 WIN	17	18	19 WAS	20 BUF
21	22	23 NJ	24 MON	25	26	27 PHI
28 PIT	29	30 LA	31			

NOVEMBER

Sun	Mon	Tue	Wed	Thu	Fri	Sat
				1	2 NYR	3 WAS
4	5	6 TOR	7 NJ	8	9	10 CAL
11	12	13	14	15 CAL	16 VAN	17
18 EDM	19	20	21	22 WIN	23	24 NYR
25 PHI	26	27 PHI	28	29	30 NJ	

DECEMBER

Sun	Mon	Tue	Wed	Thu	Fri	Sat
						1 WAS
2	3	4 VAN	5	6 CHI	7	8
9	10	11 NJ	12	13 PHI	14	15 QUE
16	17	18 TOR	19	20 HAR	21	22 PIT
23 PIT	24	25	26	27 NJ	28	29 CHI
30	31 QUE					

JANUARY

Sun	Mon	Tue	Wed	Thu	Fri	Sat
		1	2 BUF	3 LA	4	5 PHI
6	7	8 MIN	9 MON	10	11	12 DET
13 QUE	14	15 BOS	16	17 EDM	18	19 ALL-STAR GAME*
20	21	22 NYR	23	24	25 WIN	26
27 WAS	28	29 HAR	30	31 WAS		

FEBRUARY

Sun	Mon	Tue	Wed	Thu	Fri	Sat
					1	2 MON
3 HAR	4	5	6 NYR	7	8 DET	9 TOR
10	11	12 MIN	13	14 PIT	15	16 PIT
17	18 NYR	19	20	21 STL	22	23 PHI
24 PHI	25	26 BUF	27	28 BOS		

MARCH

Sun	Mon	Tue	Wed	Thu	Fri	Sat
					1	2 WAS
3	4	5 NJ	6	7 DET	8	9 NYR
10 PIT	11	12	13 EDM	14 CAL	15	16 VAN
17	18	19	20	21 WAS	22	23 STL
24 NYR	25	26	27	28 STL	29	30 BOS
31 NJ						

1989-90 RESULTS

Oct.	5—At Minnesota	L	5-6
	7—At Calgary	L	3-6
	9—At Vancouver	W	5-2
	11—At Los Angeles	W	7-4
	14—Philadelphia	T	3-3 (OT)
	17—Minnesota	L	3-6
	20—At Washington	W	5-3
	21—Vancouver	L	1-2
	24—Edmonton	T	3-3 (OT)
	27—At N.Y. Rangers	T	5-5 (OT)
	28—N.Y. Rangers	L	1-4
	31—Montreal	L	0-3
Nov.	2—At Pittsburgh	L	2-5
	4—Detroit	W	3-2
	5—At Philadelphia	L	2-3
	7—Washington	L	3-5
	9—Quebec	L	5-7
	11—Chicago	L	3-5
	12—At N.Y. Rangers	L	2-4
	14—Philadelphia	L	4-5
	16—Toronto	W	6-2
	18—At Pittsburgh	L	3-5
	21—Winnipeg	L	3-4
	22—At Washington	L	3-5
	25—Edmonton	L	2-7
	28—At New Jersey	L	2-3 (OT)
	30—At Chicago	W	2-0
Dec.	2—At Winnipeg	W	6-3
	5—Buffalo	W	3-0
	6—At Hartford	W	4-3
	9—N.Y. Rangers	T	0-0 (OT)
	12—New Jersey	L	2-7
	13—At New Jersey	L	2-5
	15—At Washington	W	5-3
	16—N.Y. Rangers	W	4-3
	19—New Jersey	W	5-4 (OT)
	23—Pittsburgh	W	8-6
	28—St. Louis	W	3-2
	30—At Quebec	L	3-6
	31—At Buffalo	W	4-2
Jan.	2—Los Angeles	W	5-3
	6—Quebec	W	5-2
	10—At Toronto	W	3-1
	11—At Minnesota	W	8-4
	13—Washington	W	4-2
	16—Vancouver	W	3-0
	17—At Montreal	W	6-3
	19—At Winnipeg	W	6-4
	23—At Hartford	L	2-4
	25—At Boston	L	2-5
	27—Pittsburgh	W	9-3
	28—New Jersey	T	4-4 (OT)
	30—St. Louis	L	1-2
Feb.	2—Washington	W	5-3
	4—At Buffalo	W	1-0
	6—At Pittsburgh	W	8-7 (OT)
	8—At Philadelphia	T	5-5 (OT)
	10—At Boston	W	4-3 (OT)
	13—Calgary	L	2-4
	17—Chicago	L	1-3
	18—At Philadelphia	L	2-3
	22—At Pittsburgh	L	3-4 (OT)
	24—Detroit	T	3-3 (OT)
	25—New Jersey	T	3-3 (OT)
	28—At Detroit	L	3-4
Mar.	2—At N.Y. Rangers	L	3-6
	3—At St. Louis	L	4-5
	6—Hartford	L	2-4
	8—At New Jersey	L	2-4
	10—Boston	T	3-3 (OT)
	13—Montreal	L	2-4
	15—At Philadelphia	L	4-5
	17—N.Y. Rangers	W	6-3
	18—Pittsburgh	T	2-2 (OT)
	20—At Washington	L	0-3
	22—At Los Angeles	L	1-3
	24—At Edmonton	T	5-5 (OT)
	27—Calgary	L	2-4
	28—At Toronto	W	6-3
	31—Philadelphia	W	6-2

1990-91 ROSTER

No.	FORWARDS	Hgt./Wt.	Place of Birth	Age	NHL exp.	1989-90 club (league)	G.	A.	Pts.
9	David Chyzowski	6-01/190	Edmonton, Alta.	19	1	Kamloops (WHL)	5	2	7
						Springfield (AHL)	0	0	0
						N.Y. Islanders (NHL)	8	6	14
17	Brad Dalgarno	6-03/216	Vancouver, B.C.	23	4	Did not play	...	...	...
34	Rob DiMaio	5-08/175	Calgary, Alta.	22	2	Springfield (AHL)	25	27	52
						N.Y. Islanders (NHL)	0	0	0
7	Tom Fitzgerald	6-01/190	Melrose, Mass.	22	2	Springfield (AHL)	30	23	53
						N.Y. Islanders (NHL)	2	5	7
26	Patrick Flatley	6-02/197	Toronto, Ont.	27	7	N.Y. Islanders (NHL)	17	32	49
	Travis Green	6-00/196	Creston, B.C.	19	0	Medicine Hat (WHL)	15	24	39
						Spokane (WHL)	45	44	89
10	Alan Kerr	5-11/190	Hazelton, B.C.	26	6	N.Y. Islanders (NHL)	15	21	36
27	Derek King	6-01/210	Hamilton, Ont.	23	4	N.Y. Islanders (NHL)	13	27	40
						Springfield (AHL)	11	12	23
16	Pat LaFontaine	5-10/177	St. Louis, Mo.	25	7	N.Y. Islanders (NHL)	54	51	105
32	Brad Lauer	6-00/195	Humbolt, Sask.	23	4	N.Y. Islanders (NHL)	6	18	24
						Springfield (AHL)	4	2	6
38	Derek Laxdal	6-01/175	St. Boniface, Man.	24	5	Newmarket (AHL)	7	8	15
						Springfield (AHL)	13	12	25
						N.Y. Islanders (NHL)	3	1	4
28	Don Maloney	6-01/190	Lindsay, Ont.	32	12	N.Y. Islanders (NHL)	16	27	43
39	Hubie McDonough	5-09/180	Manchester, N.H.	27	2	Los Angeles (NHL)	3	4	7
						N.Y. Islanders (NHL)	18	11	29
	Scott Scissons	6-01/201	Saskatoon, Sask.	18	0	Saskatoon (WHL)	40	47	87
21	Brent Sutter	5-11/175	Viking, Alta.	28	10	N.Y. Islanders (NHL)	33	35	68
25	David Volek	6-00/185	Prague, Czech.	24	2	N.Y. Islanders (NHL)	17	22	39
12	Mick Vukota	6-02/195	Saskatoon, Sask.	24	3	N.Y. Islanders (NHL)	4	8	12
11	Randy Wood	6-00/195	Manchester, Mass.	26	4	N.Y. Islanders (NHL)	24	24	48
	DEFENSEMEN								
24	Ken Baumgartner	6-01/200	Flin Flon, Man.	24	3	Los Angeles (NHL)	1	0	1
						N.Y. Islanders (NHL)	0	5	5
	Bill Berg	6-00/190	St. Catharines, Ont.	22	1	Springfield (AHL)	12	42	54
33	Mark Bergevin	6-00/185	Montreal, Que.	25	7	Springfield (AHL)	7	16	23
						N.Y. Islanders (NHL)	0	4	4
	Kevin Cheveldayoff	6-00/202	Saskatoon, Sask.	20	0	Brandon (WHL)	5	12	17
						Springfield (AHL)	0	0	0
2	Dean Chynoweth	6-02/190	Saskatoon, Sask.	21	2	Springfield (AHL)	0	7	7
						N.Y. Islanders (NHL)	0	2	2
3	Doug Crossman	6-02/190	Peterborough, Ont.	30	10	N.Y. Islanders (NHL)	15	44	59
37	Jeff Finley	6-02/185	Edmonton, Alta.	23	3	Springfield (AHL)	1	15	16
						N.Y. Islanders (NHL)	0	1	1
44	Jari Gronstrand	6-03/195	Tampere, Finland	27	4	Quebec (NHL)	0	1	1
						Springfield (AHL)	0	1	1
						N.Y. Islanders (NHL)	3	4	7
	Craig Ludwig	6-03/222	Rhinelander, Wis.	29	8	Montreal (NHL)	1	15	16
6	Wayne McBean	6-02/190	Calgary, Alta.	21	4	Springfield (AHL)	6	33	39
						N.Y. Islanders (NHL)	0	1	1
8	Jeff Norton	6-02/190	Cambridge, Mass.	24	3	N.Y. Islanders (NHL)	4	49	53
36	Gary Nylund	6-04/210	Surrey, B.C.	26	8	N.Y. Islanders (NHL)	4	21	25
47	Richard Pilon	6-00/202	Saskatoon, Sask.	22	2	N.Y. Islanders (NHL)	0	2	2

No.	GOALTENDERS	Hgt./Wt.	Place of Birth	Age	NHL exp.	1989-90 club (league)	Ga.	SO	Avg.
30	Mark Fitzpatrick	6-01/190	Toronto, Ont.	22	3	N.Y. Islanders (NHL)	47	3	3.39
	Jeff Hackett	6-01/176	London, Ont.	22	2	Springfield (AHL)	54	1	3.68
35	Glen Healy	5-10/185	Pickering, Ont.	28	4	N.Y. Islanders (NHL)	39	2	3.50

1989-90 RECORDS

1989-90 regular-season records: 31-38-11 (.456, 73 points, 4th in Patrick Division); 15-17-8 at home; 16-21-3 on road; 3-2-11 in overtime; 11-17-7 vs. Patrick (1-4-2 vs. Devils; 2-3-2 vs. Rangers; 1-4-2 vs. Flyers; 3-3-1 vs. Penguins; 4-3-0 vs. Capitals); 7-7-1 vs. Adams; 7-7-1 vs. Norris; 6-7-2 vs. Smythe.

MISCELLANEOUS DATA

1989-90 team rankings: Shorthanded goals for, 10 (T11th in NHL); shorthanded goals against, 8 (T7th); power play, 23.6% (T2nd); penalty killing, 76.5% (16th); penalty minutes/game, 22.2.

TEAM HAT TRICKS, CAREER, ACTIVE

Patrick Flatley (1)	Don Maloney (4)
Paul Gagne (1)	Brent Sutter (6)
Derek King (1)	Mick Vukota (1)
Pat LaFontaine (6)	Randy Wood (1)

MINOR LEAGUE AFFILIATIONS

Capital District (AHL)

Craig Ludwig

1990 DRAFT SELECTIONS

Rnd.	Player	Hgt.	Wgt.	Overall	(Pos.)	1989-90 Club	(League)
1	Scott Scissons	6:01	201	6	(C)	Saskatoon	(WHL)
2	Chris Taylor	5:11	186	27	(C)	London	(OHL)
3	Dan Plante	5:11	198	48	(RW)	Edina H.S.	(Minn.)
5	Chris Marinucci	6:00	175	90	(C)	Grand Rapids H.S.	(Minn.)
6	Joni Lehto	6:00	190	111	(D)	Ottawa	(OHL)
7	Michael Guilbert	6:02	195	132	(D)	Governor Dummer H.S.	(Mass.)
8	Sylvain Fleury	5:11	189	153	(LW)	Longueuil	(QMJHL)
9	John Joyce	6:03	185	174	(C)	Avon Old Farms H.S.	(Ct.)
10	Richard Enga	5:10	156	195	(C)	Culver Military Academy	(Ind.)
11	Martin Lacroix	5:11	155	216	(RW)	St. Lawrence University	
12	Andy Shier	5:11	165	237	(C)	Detroit Compuware	

FIRST-ROUND ENTRY DRAFT SELECTIONS

Year	Name	Overall	Last Amateur Team	(League)	Years in NHL
1972	*Billy Harris	1	Toronto	(OHL)	12
1973	*Denis Potvin	1	Ottawa	(OHL)	15
1974	Clark Gillies	4	Regina	(WCHL)	14
1975	Pat Price	11	Vancouver	(WHA)	13
1976	Alex McKendry	14	Sudbury	(OHL)	4
1977	Mike Bossy	15	Laval	(QMJHL)	10
1978	Steve Tambellini	15	Lethbridge	(WCHL)	10
1979	Duane Sutter	17	Lethbridge	(WHL)	11
1980	Brent Sutter	17	Red Deer	(AJHL)	10
1981	Paul Boutilier	21	Sherbrooke	(QMJHL)	8
1982	Pat Flatley	21	University of Wisconsin		7
1983	Pat LaFontaine	3	Verdun	(QMJHL)	7
	Gerald Diduck	16	Lethbridge	(WHL)	6
1984	Duncan MacPherson	20	Saskatoon	(WHL)	0
1985	Brad Dalgarno	6	Hamilton	(OHL)	3
	Derek King	13	Sault Ste. Marie	(OHL)	4
1986	Tom Fitzgerald	17	Austin Prep	(Mass.)	2
1987	Dean Chynoweth	13	Medicine Hat	(WHL)	2
1988	Kevin Cheveldayoff	16	Brandon	(WHL)	0
1989	Dave Chyzowski	2	Kamloops	(WHL)	1
1990	Scott Scissons	6	Saskatoon	(WHL)	0

*Designates first player chosen in draft.

Denis Potvin

COACHING HISTORY

Phil Goyette and Earl Ingarfield, 1972-73
Al Arbour, 1973-74 to 1985-86
Terry Simpson, 1986-87 to 1987-88

Terry Simpson and Al Arbour, 1988-89
Al Arbour since 1989-90

FRANCHISE LEADERS

Current players in bold type
(1972-73 through 1989-90)

Games
1. 1123—Bryan Trottier
2. 1080—Denis Potvin
3. 900—Bob Nystrom
4. 872—Clark Gillies
5. 814—Bob Bourne
6. 752—Mike Bossy
7. 675—Billy Smith
8. 623—Billy Harris
9. 622—Stefan Persson
10. **611—Brent Sutter**

Goals
1. 573—Mike Bossy
2. 500—Bryan Trottier
3. 310—Denis Potvin
4. 304—Clark Gillies
5. **262—Brent Sutter**
6. **246—Pat LaFontaine**
7. 238—Bob Bourne
8. 235—Bob Nystrom
9. 206—John Tonelli
10. 184—Billy Harris

Assists
1. 853—Bryan Trottier
2. 742—Denis Potvin
3. 553—Mike Bossy
4. 359—Clark Gillies
5. 338—John Tonelli
6. 317—Stefan Persson
7. 304—Bob Bourne
8. **285—Brent Sutter**
9. 278—Bob Nystrom
10. 259—Billy Harris

Points
1. 1353—Bryan Trottier
2. 1128—Mike Bossy
3. 1052—Denis Potvin
4. 663—Clark Gillies
5. **547—Brent Sutter**
6. 544—John Tonelli
7. 542—Bob Bourne
8. 513—Bob Nystrom
9. **481—Pat LaFontaine**
10. 443—Billy Harris

Penalty Minutes
1. 1466—Garry Howatt
2. 1354—Denis Potvin
3. 1248—Bob Nystrom
4. 891—Clark Gillies
   891—Duane Sutter
6. 798—Bryan Trottier
7. 783—Gerry Hart
8. **706—Brent Sutter**
9. **686—Alan Kerr**
10. 614—Gord Lane

Goaltenders
Games
1. 675—Billy Smith
2. 282—Chico Resch
3. 241—Kelly Hrudey
4. 136—Roland Melanson
5. 80—Gerry Desjardins
6. **58—Mark Fitzpatrick**
7. 39—Glenn Healy

Shutouts
1. 25—Chico Resch
2. 22—Billy Smith
3. 6—Kelly Hrudey

Goals Against Average (entire roster)
(2400 minutes minimum)
1. 2.56—Chico Resch
2. 3.14—Roland Melanson
3. 3.16—Billy Smith
4. 3.46—Kelly Hrudey
5. **3.49—Mark Fitzpatrick**
6. 4.00—Gerry Desjardins

Wins
1. 304—Billy Smith
2. 157—Chico Resch
3. 106—Kelly Hrudey
4. 77—Roland Melanson
5. **22—Mark Fitzpatrick**
6. 14—Gerry Desjardins
7. 12—Glenn Healy

Mike Gartner's hat trick against the Islanders on April 13, 1990, was the Rangers' first in the playoffs since Ron Duguay did it against Philadelphia on April 20, 1980.

John Vanbiesbrouck was the Rangers' goalie on December 9, 1989, when the Rangers and Islanders battled to a 0-0 tie. It was the Rangers' first scoreless tie in almost nine years.

John Ogrodnick scored 19 power-play goals last year to pace a Ranger attack that led the NHL with 103 power-play tallies.

Darren Turcotte's hat trick against Boston on February 26, 1990, helped the Rangers to a 6-1 victory and their first-ever season series sweep over the Bruins.

NEW YORK RANGERS

CLUB DIRECTORY

Chief Executive Officer and Governor
Richard H. Evans
President
John C. Diller
Vice-President and General Manager
Neil Smith
Vice-President, Business Affairs and Administration
David Peterson
Vice-President, Legal Affairs
Kevin Billet
Director of Communications
Barry Watkins
Director of Marketing
Kevin Kennedy
Alternate NHL Governors
John C. Diller, Neil Smith, Kenneth W. Munoz, Michael D. Walker, Thomas A. Conway
Assistant General Manager, Player Development
Larry Pleau
Director of Administration
Mark Piazza
Coach
Roger Neilson
Assistant Coaches
Wayne Cashman, Ron Smith, Colin Campbell
Scouting Staff
John Chapman, Tony Feltrin, Herb Hammond, Lou Jankowski, David McNab, Christer Rockstrom
Scouting Coordinator
Bill Short

Manager of Team Services
Matthew Loughran
Assistant to the Director, Communications
Kevin McDonald
Communications Assistant
Tina Pietroluongo
Statistician
Arthur Friedman
Team Physician and Orthopedic Surgeon
Barton Nisonson, M.D.
Medical Trainer
Dave Smith
Equipment Trainer
Joe Murphy
Assistant Trainers
Larry Nastasi, Tim Paris
Home Ice
Madison Square Garden
Address
4 Pennsylvania Plaza, New York, N. Y. 10001
Seating Capacity
17,520
Club Colors
Blue, Red and White
Phone
(212) 465-6000
FAX
(212) 465-6494

YEAR-BY-YEAR RESULTS

Season	W.	L.	T.	Pts.	Position	Season	W.	L.	T.	Pts.	Position
1926-27	25	13	6	56	First—a	1959-60	17	38	15	49	Sixth—*
1927-28	19	16	9	47	Second—xx	1960-61	22	38	10	54	Fifth—*
1928-29	21	13	10	52	Second—c	1961-62	26	32	12	64	Fourth—b
1929-30	17	17	10	44	Third—b	1962-63	22	36	12	56	Fifth—*
1930-31	19	16	9	47	Third—b	1963-64	22	38	10	54	Fifth—*
1931-32	23	17	8	54	First—c	1964-65	20	38	12	52	Fifth—*
1932-33	23	17	8	54	Third—xx	1965-66	18	41	11	47	Sixth—*
1933-34	21	19	8	50	Third—a	1966-67	30	28	12	72	Fourth—b
1934-35	22	20	6	50	Third—b	1967-68	39	23	12	90	Second—a
1935-36	19	17	12	50	Fourth—*	1968-69	41	26	9	91	Third—a
1936-37	19	20	9	47	Third—c	1969-70	38	22	16	92	Fourth—a
1937-38	27	15	6	60	Second—a	1970-71	49	18	11	109	Second—b
1938-39	26	16	6	58	Second—b	1971-72	48	17	13	109	Second—c
1939-40	27	11	10	64	Second—xx	1972-73	47	23	8	102	Third—b
1940-41	21	19	8	50	Fourth—a	1973-74	40	24	14	94	Third—b
1941-42	29	17	2	60	First—b	1974-75	37	29	14	88	Second—†
1942-43	11	31	8	30	Sixth—*	1975-76	29	42	9	67	Fourth—*
1943-44	6	39	5	17	Sixth—*	1976-77	29	37	14	72	Fourth—*
1944-45	11	29	10	32	Sixth—*	1977-78	30	37	13	73	Fourth—†
1945-46	13	28	9	35	Sixth—*	1978-79	40	29	11	91	Third—c
1946-47	22	32	6	50	Fifth—*	1979-80	38	32	10	86	Third—a
1947-48	21	26	13	55	Fourth—b	1980-81	30	36	14	74	Fourth—b
1948-49	18	31	11	47	Sixth—*	1981-82	39	27	14	92	Second—a
1949-50	28	31	11	67	Fourth—c	1982-83	35	35	10	80	Fourth—a
1950-51	20	29	21	61	Fifth—*	1983-84	42	29	9	93	Fourth—†
1951-52	23	34	13	59	Fifth—*	1984-85	26	44	10	62	Fourth—†
1952-53	17	37	16	50	Sixth—*	1985-86	36	38	6	78	Fourth—b
1953-54	29	31	10	68	Fifth—*	1986-87	34	38	8	76	Fourth—†
1954-55	17	35	18	52	Fifth—*	1987-88	36	34	10	82	Fourth—*
1955-56	32	28	10	74	Third—b	1988-89	37	35	8	82	Third—†
1956-57	26	30	14	66	Fourth—b	1989-90	36	31	13	85	First—a
1957-58	32	25	13	77	Second—b	Totals	1743	1786	677	4163	
1958-59	26	32	12	64	Fifth—*						

Key to standings: *—Missed playoffs. †—Eliminated in first round of new playoff format (1974-75). a—Eliminated in quarterfinal round. b—Eliminated in semifinal round. c—Eliminated in final round. xx—Stanley Cup champion.

—DID YOU KNOW—

That last year marked the first time since the 1941-42 season that the Rangers finished in first place in either the overall league standings or in their own division?

1990-91 SCHEDULE

☒ Home games shaded.

* At Chicago Stadium.

OCTOBER

Sun	Mon	Tue	Wed	Thu	Fri	Sat
	1	2	3	4 CHI	5	6 HAR
7	8 MIN	9	10 WAS	11	12 MON	13 WAS
14	15	16	17 WIN	18	19 NJ	20 PIT
21	22 TOR	23	24	25 PHI	26	27 QUE
28	29 QUE	30	31 LA			

NOVEMBER

Sun	Mon	Tue	Wed	Thu	Fri	Sat
				1	2 NYI	3 PIT
4	5 BOS	6	7 BUF	8	9 NJ	10
11 CAL	12	13 PHI	14	15 MIN	16 WIN	17
18	19 MIN	20	21 BUF	22	23	24 NYI
25	26 BUF	27	28 WAS	29	30 PHI	

DECEMBER

Sun	Mon	Tue	Wed	Thu	Fri	Sat
						1 BOS
2	3 PIT	4	5 CAL	6	7 EDM	8
9	10	11 LA	12	13	14 VAN	15
16	17 WAS	18	19 TOR	20	21	22 MON
23 BOS	24	25	26	27	28 WAS	29
30 NJ	31					

JANUARY

Sun	Mon	Tue	Wed	Thu	Fri	Sat
		1	2 LA	3 PIT	4	5 STL
6	7 PHI	8	9 STL	10	11 DET	12
13 HAR	14	15 EDM	16	17 CHI	18	19 ALL-STAR GAME*
20	21	22 NYI	23	24	25 EDM	26
27	28	29 CAL	30 VAN	31		

FEBRUARY

Sun	Mon	Tue	Wed	Thu	Fri	Sat
					1	2
3 WIN	4	5	6 NYI	7	8 VAN	9 MON
10	11	12	13 NJ	14	15 HAR	16
17	18 NYI	19	20	21 PHI	22 WAS	23
24 NJ	25	26	27 WAS	28 STL		

MARCH

Sun	Mon	Tue	Wed	Thu	Fri	Sat
					1	2 TOR
3	4 PHI	5	6	7 QUE	8	9 NYI
10 CHI	11	12	13 DET	14	15 NJ	16
17 PIT	18	19	20	21 PIT	22	23 PHI
24 NYI	25	26 NJ	27	28	29	30 DET
31 PIT						

1989-90 RESULTS

Oct.	6—At Winnipeg	W	4-1
	8—At Chicago	W	5-3
	11—Calgary	W	5-4
	13—At Washington	L	4-7
	15—Pittsburgh	W	4-2
	17—Chicago	T	3-3 (OT)
	19—Hartford	W	7-3
	21—At Philadelphia	W	3-1
	23—Vancouver	W	5-3
	25—Edmonton	T	3-3 (OT)
	27—N.Y. Islanders	T	5-5 (OT)
	28—At N.Y. Islanders	W	4-1
	30—Philadelphia	L	1-3
Nov.	2—Quebec	W	6-1
	4—At Montreal	L	2-3
	6—Detroit	W	6-1
	8—Montreal	L	2-3
	12—N.Y. Islanders	W	4-2
	14—At Pittsburgh	L	0-6
	17—At New Jersey	L	4-5 (OT)
	18—At Hartford	W	3-2
	20—Winnipeg	T	3-3 (OT)
	22—At Buffalo	L	1-4
	25—At Toronto	L	4-7
	26—Quebec	W	3-1
	29—At Winnipeg	L	4-5
Dec.	1—At Vancouver	W	4-3
	2—At Los Angeles	L	0-6
	6—New Jersey	W	5-3
	9—At N.Y. Islanders	T	0-0 (OT)
	10—Philadelphia	L	2-4
	13—St. Louis	L	1-3
	16—At N.Y. Islanders	L	3-4
	17—Montreal	L	0-2
	20—Buffalo	T	2-2 (OT)
	23—At Washington	L	2-3
	26—New Jersey	T	4-4 (OT)
	27—At Pittsburgh	L	4-7
	29—At New Jersey	L	2-3
	31—Pittsburgh	L	4-5
Jan.	3—Washington	W	2-1
	4—At Minnesota	L	2-8
	6—At St. Louis	L	3-4
	8—Pittsburgh	L	5-7
	10—Chicago	T	2-2 (OT)
	13—At Boston	W	3-2
	14—Philadelphia	W	4-3 (OT)
	18—At Pittsburgh	T	3-3 (OT)
	23—At Edmonton	W	4-3
	25—At Calgary	L	5-8
	27—At Los Angeles	W	3-1
	31—St. Louis	T	2-2 (OT)
Feb.	3—At Boston	W	2-1
	4—Minnesota	W	4-3
	7—Edmonton	W	5-2
	9—At Buffalo	L	2-3
	11—Calgary	L	2-5
	13—At Philadelphia	W	4-3
	14—Pittsburgh	L	3-4 (OT)
	16—At New Jersey	W	2-1
	19—New Jersey	W	4-3 (OT)
	21—At Detroit	T	4-4 (OT)
	23—At Washington	W	6-3
	26—Boston	W	6-1
	28—Washington	W	3-2
Mar.	2—N.Y. Islanders	W	6-3
	3—At Hartford	L	4-6
	5—Detroit	W	3-2
	8—At Philadelphia	W	7-5
	10—At Minnesota	T	2-2 (OT)
	12—Los Angeles	L	2-6
	14—At Toronto	W	8-2
	17—At N.Y. Islanders	L	3-6
	18—Vancouver	W	5-2
	21—Toronto	T	5-5 (OT)
	25—Philadelphia	W	7-5
	27—At Quebec	W	7-4
	29—At New Jersey	L	4-6
	31—At Washington	L	1-2
Apr.	1—Washington	L	2-3

1990-91 ROSTER

No.	FORWARDS	Hgt./Wt.	Place of Birth	Age	NHL exp.	1989-90 club (league)	G.	A.	Pts.
27	Rick Bennett	6-03/215	Springfield, Mass.	23	1	Providence (Hockey East)	12	24	36
						N.Y. Rangers (NHL)	1	0	1
37	Paul Broten	5-11/175	Roseau, Minn.	24	1	Flint (IHL)	17	9	26
						N.Y. Rangers (NHL)	5	3	8
	Tahir Domi	5-10/200	Windsor, Ont.	20	1	Newmarket (AHL)	14	11	25
						Toronto (NHL)	0	0	0
20	Jan Erixon	6-00/196	Skelleftea, Sweden	28	7	N.Y. Rangers (NHL)	4	9	13
22	Mike Gartner	6-00/190	Ottawa, Ont.	30	11	Minnesota (NHL)	34	36	70
						N.Y. Rangers (NHL)	11	5	16
	Jody Hull	6-01/200	Petrolia, Ont.	21	2	Binghamton (AHL)	7	10	17
						Hartford (NHL)	7	10	17
15	Mark Janssens	6-03/195	Surrey, B.C.	22	3	N.Y. Rangers (NHL)	5	8	13
12	Kris King	5-11/210	Bracebridge, Ont.	24	3	N.Y. Rangers (NHL)	6	7	13
11	Kelly Kisio	5-09/180	Peace River, Alta.	31	8	N.Y. Rangers (NHL)	22	44	66
	Daniel Lacroix	6-02/185	Montreal, Que.	21	0	Flint (IHL)	12	16	28
	James Latos	6-01/200	Wakaw, Sask.	24	1	Flint (IHL)	12	15	27
23	Corey Millen	5-07/165	Cloquet, Minn.	26	1	N.Y. Rangers (NHL)	0	0	0
						Flint (IHL)	4	5	9
32	Kevin Miller	5-10/180	Lansing, Mich.	25	2	Flint (IHL)	19	23	42
						N.Y. Rangers (NHL)	0	5	5
9	Bernie Nicholls	6-00/185	Haliburton, Ont.	29	9	Los Angeles (NHL)	27	48	75
						N.Y. Rangers (NHL)	12	25	37
25	John Ogrodnick	6-00/205	Ottawa, Ont.	21	11	N.Y. Rangers (NHL)	43	31	74
	Joe Paterson	6-02/207	Toronto, Ont.	30	10	Flint (IHL)	21	26	47
29	Rudy Poeschek	6-01/210	Kamloops, B.C.	24	3	N.Y. Rangers (NHL)	0	0	0
						Flint (IHL)	8	13	21
	Steve Rice	6-00/210	Waterloo, Ont.	19	0	Kitchener (OHL)	39	37	76
44	Lindy Ruff	6-02/200	Warburg, Alta.	30	11	N.Y. Rangers (NHL)	3	6	9
	Ray Sheppard	6-01/185	Pembroke, Ont.	24	3	Rochester (AHL)	3	5	8
						Buffalo (NHL)	4	2	6
8	Darren Turcotte	6-00/185	Boston, Mass.	22	2	N.Y. Rangers (NHL)	32	34	66
	DEFENSEMEN								
38	Jeff Bloemberg	6-02/200	Listowel, Ont.	22	2	Flint (IHL)	7	21	28
						N.Y. Rangers (NHL)	3	3	6
36	Todd Charlesworth	6-01/190	Calgary, Alta.	25	6	Cape Breton (AHL)	0	9	9
						Flint (IHL)	3	6	9
						N.Y. Rangers (NHL)	0	0	0
	Peter Fiorentino	6-01/200	Niagara Falls, Ont.	21	0	Flint (IHL)	2	7	9
14	Mark Hardy	5-11/195	Semaden, Switzerland	31	11	N.Y. Rangers (NHL)	0	15	15
6	Miroslav Horava	6-00/190	Kladno, Czech.	29	2	N.Y. Rangers (NHL)	4	10	14
2	Brian Leetch	5-11/185	Corpus Christi, Tex.	22	3	N.Y. Rangers (NHL)	11	45	56
24	Randy Moller	6-02/207	Red Deer, Alta.	27	8	N.Y. Rangers (NHL)	1	12	13
3	James Patrick	6-02/192	Winnipeg, Man.	27	7	N.Y. Rangers (NHL)	14	43	57
5	Normand Rochefort	6-01/200	Trois Rivieres, Que.	29	10	N.Y. Rangers (NHL)	3	1	4
21	David Shaw	6-02/204	St. Thomas, Ont.	26	8	N.Y. Rangers (NHL)	2	10	12
	Dennis Vial	6-01/190	Sault Ste. Marie, Ont.	21	0	Flint (IHL)	6	29	35

No.	GOALTENDERS	Hgt./Wt.	Place of Birth	Age	NHL exp.	1989-90 club (league)	Ga.	SO	Avg.
33	Bob Froese	5-11/178	St. Catharines, Ont.	32	8	N.Y. Rangers (NHL)	15	0	3.33
	Mark Laforest	5-10/175	Welland, Ont.	28	5	Newmarket (AHL)	10	0	4.05
						Toronto (NHL)	27	0	3.89
35	Mike Richter	5-10/185	Abington, Minn.	24	1	Flint (IHL)	13	0	3.76
						N.Y. Rangers (NHL)	23	0	3.00
	Sam St. Laurent	5-10/190	Arvida, Que.	31	4	Adirondack (AHL)	13	0	3.06
						Detroit (NHL)	14	0	3.76
34	John Vanbiesbrouck	5-08/179	Detroit, Mich.	27	8	N.Y. Rangers (NHL)	47	1	3.38

1989-90 RECORDS

1989-90 regular-season records: 36-31-13 (.531, 85 points, 1st in Patrick Division); 20-11-9 at home; 16-20-4 on road; 2-2-13 in overtime; 15-16-4 vs. Patrick (3-3-1 vs. Devils; 3-2-2 vs. Islanders; 5-2-0 vs. Flyers; 1-5-1 vs. Penguins; 3-4-0 vs. Capitals); 8-6-1 vs. Adams; 5-4-6 vs. Norris; 8-5-2 vs. Smythe.

MISCELLANEOUS DATA

1989-90 team rankings: Shorthanded goals for, 7 (T17th in NHL); shorthanded goals against, 8 (T7th); power play, 23.3% (T4th); penalty killing, 78.7% (14th); penalty minutes/game, 25.3.

TEAM HAT TRICKS, CAREER, ACTIVE

Paul Cyr (1)
Mike Gartner (14)
Jody Hull (1)
Brian Mullen (2)
Bernie Nicholls (14)

John Ogrodnick (6)
Lindy Ruff (2)
Ray Sheppard (2)
Darren Turcotte (2)

MINOR LEAGUE AFFILIATIONS

Binghamton (AHL)

Kelly Kisio

1990 DRAFT SELECTIONS

Rnd.	Player	Hgt.	Wgt.	Overall	(Pos.)	1989-90 Club	(League)
1	Michael Stewart	6:02	197	13	(D)	Michigan State University	
2	Doug Weight	5:11	185	34	(C)	Lake Superior State Univ.	
3	John Vary	6:01	207	55	(D)	North Bay (OHL)	
4	Jeff Nielsen	6:00	170	69	(RW)	Grand Rapids H.S. (Minn.)	
4	Rick Willis	6:00	185	76	(LW)	Pingree H.S. (Mass.)	
5	Sergei Zubov	6:00	187	85	(D)	CSKA, Russia	
5	Lubos Rob	5:11	183	99	(C)	Budejovice, Czech.	
6	Jason Weinrich	6:02	189	118	(D)	Springfield (Mass.) Olympics	
7	Bryan Lonsinger	6:03	193	139	(D)	Choate Academy (Ct.)	
8	Todd Hedlund	6:01	177	160	(RW)	Roseau H.S. (Minn.)	
9	Andrew Silverman	6:03	210	181	(D)	Beverly H.S. (Mass.)	
10	Jon Hillebrandt	5:10	160	202	(G)	Monona Grove H.S. (Wis.)	
11	Brett Lievers	6:00	170	223	(C)	Wayzata H.S. (Minn.)	
12	Sergei Nemchinov	.....	....	244	(C)	Krlja Sovetov, USSR	

FIRST-ROUND ENTRY DRAFT SELECTIONS

Year	Name	Overall	Last Amateur Team	(League)	Years in NHL
1969	Andre Dupont	8	Montreal (OHL)		13
	Pierre Jarry	12	Ottawa (OHL)		7
1970	Normand Gratton	11	Montreal (OHL)		5
1971	Steve Vickers	10	Toronto (OHL)		10
	Steve Durbano	13	Toronto (OHL)		6
1972	Albert Blanchard	10	Kitchener (OHL)		0
	Bobby MacMillan	15	St. Catharines (OHL)		11
1973	Rick Middleton	14	Oshawa (OHL)		14
1974	Dave Maloney	14	Kitchener (OHL)		11
1975	Wayne Dillon	12	Toronto (WHA)		4
1976	Don Murdoch	6	Medicine Hat (WCHL)		6
1977	Lucien DeBlois	8	Sorel (QMJHL)		13
	Ron Duguay	13	Sudbury (OHL)		12
1978	No first round selection				
1979	Doug Sulliman	13	Kitchener (OHL)		11
1980	Jim Malone	14	Toronto (OHL)		0
1981	James Patrick	9	Prince Albert (AJHL)		7
1982	Chris Kontos	15	Toronto (OHL)		7
1983	Dave Gagner	12	Brantford (OHL)		6
1984	Terry Carkner	14	Peterborough (OHL)		4
1985	Ulf Dahlen	7	Ostersund (Sweden)		3
1986	Brian Leetch	9	Avon Old Farms Prep (Ct.)		3
1987	Jayson More	10	New Westminster (WHL)		2
1988	No first round selection				
1989	Steven Rice	20	Kitchener (OHL)		0
1990	Michael Stewart	13	Michigan State University		0

James Patrick

COACHING HISTORY

Lester Patrick, 1926-27 to 1938-39
Frank Boucher, 1939-40 to 1947-48
Frank Boucher and Lynn Patrick, 1948-49
Lynn Patrick, 1949-50
Neil Colville, 1950-51
Neil Colville and Bill Cook, 1951-52
Bill Cook, 1952-538
Frank Boucher and Muzz Patrick, 1953-54
Muzz Patrick, 1954-55
Phil Watson, 1955-56 to 1958-59
Phil Watson and Alf Pike, 1959-60
Alf Pike, 1960-61
Doug Harvey, 1961-62
Muzz Patrick and Red Sullivan, 1962-63
Red Sullivan, 1963-64 to 1964-65
Red Sullivan and Emile Francis, 1965-66
Emile Francis, 1966-67 to 1967-68

Bernie Geoffrion and Emile Francis, 1968-69
Emile Francis, 1969-70 to 1972-73
Larry Popein and Emile Francis, 1973-74
Emile Francis, 1974-75
Ron Stewart and John Ferguson, 1975-76
John Ferguson, 1976-77
Jean-Guy Talbot, 1977-78
Fred Shero, 1978-79 to 1979-80
Fred Shero and Craig Patrick, 1980-81
Herb Brooks, 1981-82 to 1983-84
Herb Brooks and Craig Patrick, 1984-85
Ted Sator, 1985-86
Ted Sator, Tom Webster and Phil Esposito, 1986-87
Michel Bergeron, 1987-88
Michel Bergeron and Phil Esposito, 1988-89
Roger Neilson since 1989-90

FRANCHISE LEADERS

Current players in bold type
(1926-27 through 1989-90)

Games
1. 1160—Harry Howell
2. 1065—Rod Gilbert
3. 982—Ron Greschner
4. 945—Walt Tkaczuk
5. 862—Jean Ratelle
6. 838—Vic Hadfield
7. 810—Jim Neilson
8. 719—Andy Bathgate
9. 698—Steve Vickers
10. 666—Dean Prentice

Goals
1. 406—Rod Gilbert
2. 336—Jean Ratelle
3. 272—Andy Bathgate
4. 262—Vic Hadfield
5. 256—Camille Henry
6. 246—Steve Vickers
7. 228—Bill Cook
8. 227—Walt Tkaczuk
9. 195—Don Maloney
10. 187—Bryan Hextall

Assists
1. 615—Rod Gilbert
2. 481—Jean Ratelle
3. 457—Andy Bathgate
4. 451—Walt Tkaczuk
5. 431—Ron Greschner
6. 340—Steve Vickers
7. 310—Vic Hadfield
8. 307—Don Maloney
9. 283—Brad Park
10. 263—Harry Howell

Points
1. 1021—Rod Gilbert
2. 817—Jean Ratelle
3. 729—Andy Bathgate
4. 678—Walt Tkaczuk
5. 610—Ron Greschner
6. 586—Steve Vickers
7. 572—Vic Hadfield
8. 502—Don Maloney
9. 478—Camille Henry
10. 422—Dean Prentice

Penalty Minutes
1. 1226—Ron Greschner
2. 1147—Harry Howell
3. 1113—Dave Maloney
4. 1036—Vic Hadfield
5. 970—Nick Fotiu

Goaltenders

Games
1. 583—Gump Worsley
2. 539—Ed Giacomin
3. 377—Chuck Rayner
4. 324—Dave Kerr
5. **316—John Vanbiesbrouck**
6. 222—John Davidson
7. 184—Gilles Villemure

Shutouts
1. 49—Ed Giacomin
2. 40—Dave Kerr
3. 30—John Ross Roach
4. 24—Chuck Rayner
   24—Gump Worsley
6. 21—Lorne Chabot

Goals Against Average
(2400 minutes minimum)
1. 1.61—Lorne Chabot
2. 2.07—Dave Kerr
3. 2.16—John Ross Roach
4. 2.42—Andy Aitkenhead
5. 2.62—Johnny Bower
   2.62—Gilles Villemure
7. 2.73—Ed Giacomin

Wins
1. 266—Ed Giacomin
2. 204—Gump Worsley
3. 157—Dave Kerr
4. **138—John Vanbiesbrouck**
5. 123—Chuck Rayner
6. 96—Gilles Villemure
7. 93—John Davidson

Rick Tocchet has increased his point total in each of the last five seasons.

Ken Wregget's team-leading 22 victories in 1989-90 was the second-lowest total for a Flyers' goaltender in 17 years.

Ron Hextall, who played in only eight games last year, was a big reason for the Flyers' failure to make the playoffs for the first time since 1971-72.

Tim Kerr, who missed half the 1989-90 season because of a shoulder injury, is Philadelphia's career leader in power-play goals (138) and hat tricks (17).

56

PHILADELPHIA FLYERS

CLUB DIRECTORY

Chairman of the Executive Committee
Edward M. Snider
President
Jay T. Snider
Chairman of the Board Emeritus
Joseph C. Scott
Executive Vice-Presidents
Keith Allen, Ron Ryan
General Manager
Russ Farwell
Assistant General Manager
John Blackwell
Coach
Paul Holmgren
Assistant Coaches
Craig Hartsburg, Ken Hitchcock
Goaltending Instructor
Bernie Parent
Physical Conditioning and Rehabilitation Coach
Pat Croce
Director of Pro Scouting
Bill Barber
Scouts
Inge Hammarstrom, Jerry Melnyk, Glen Sonmor, Red Sullivan, Walt Atanas, Simon Nolet, Kevin Maxwell, Bill Dineen
Pro Scout and Player Development Coordinator
Kevin McCarthy
Vice-President, Communications
John Brogan

Director of Public Relations
Rodger Gottlieb
Assistant Director of Public Relations
Jill Vogel
Ticket Manager
Ceil Baker
Vice-President, Sales
Jack Betson
Director of Team Services
Joe Kadlec
Trainer
Dave Settlemyre
Assistant Trainer
Jim Evers
Vice-President, Finance
Bob Baer
Team Physician
Jeffrey Hartzell, M.D.
Home Ice
The Spectrum
Address
Pattison Place, Philadelphia, Pa. 19148
Seating Capacity
17,423
Club Colors
Orange, White and Black
Phone
(215) 465-4500
FAX
(215) 389-9403

YEAR-BY-YEAR RESULTS

Season	W.	L.	T.	Pts.	Position	Season	W.	L.	T.	Pts.	Position
1967-68	31	32	11	73	First—a	1979-80	48	12	20	116	First—c
1968-69	20	35	21	61	Third—a	1980-81	41	24	15	97	Second—a
1969-70	17	35	24	58	Fifth—*	1981-82	38	31	11	87	Third—†
1970-71	28	33	17	73	Third—a	1982-83	49	23	8	106	First—†
1971-72	26	38	14	66	Fifth—*	1983-84	44	26	10	98	Third—†
1972-73	37	30	11	85	Second—b	1984-85	53	20	7	113	First—c
1973-74	50	16	12	112	First—xx	1985-86	53	23	4	110	First—†
1974-75	51	18	11	113	First—xx	1986-87	46	26	8	100	First—c
1975-76	51	13	16	118	First—c	1987-88	38	33	9	85	Second—†
1976-77	48	16	16	112	First—b	1988-89	36	36	8	80	Fourth—b
1977-78	45	20	15	105	Second—b	1989-90	30	39	11	71	Sixth—*
1978-79	40	25	15	95	Second—a	**Totals**	920	604	294	2134	

Key to standings: *—Missed playoffs. †—Eliminated in first round of new playoff format (1974-75). a—Eliminated in quarterfinal round. b—Eliminated in semifinal round. c—Eliminated in final round. xx—Stanley Cup champion.

Bobby Clarke

Bernie Parent

1990-91 SCHEDULE

▦ Home games shaded.

* At Chicago Stadium.

OCTOBER

Sun	Mon	Tue	Wed	Thu	Fri	Sat
	1	2	3	4 BOS	5	6 NJ
7 DET	8	9	10	11 NJ	12	13 WIN
14	15	16 PIT	17	18 QUE	19	20 MON
21	22	23 WAS	24	25 NYR	26	27 NYI
28	29	30 PIT	31			

NOVEMBER

Sun	Mon	Tue	Wed	Thu	Fri	Sat
				1 MIN	2	3 CHI
4 TOR	5	6 WIN	7	8 CAL	9	10 QUE
11 VAN	12	13 NYR	14	15 MON	16	17 NJ
18 NJ	19	20	21 PIT	22	23 TOR	24
25 NYI	26	27 NYI	28 NJ	29	30 NYR	

DECEMBER

Sun	Mon	Tue	Wed	Thu	Fri	Sat
						1
2 EDM	3	4	5	6 BUF	7	8 MIN
9 CHI	10	11 WAS	12	13 NYI	14	15 DET
16 WIN	17	18 DET	19	20 NJ	21	22 HAR
23 MON	24	25	26	27 LA	28	29 STL
30	31 BUF					

JANUARY

Sun	Mon	Tue	Wed	Thu	Fri	Sat
		1	2	3	4 WAS	5 NYI
6	7 NYR	8	9	10	11	12 BOS
13 EDM	14	15 PIT	16	17 QUE	18	19 ALL-STAR GAME*
20	21	22 CAL	23	24 WAS	25	26 HAR
27	28	29	30	31 PIT		

FEBRUARY

Sun	Mon	Tue	Wed	Thu	Fri	Sat
					1	2 HAR
3	4	5 LA	6	7 VAN	8	9
10 WAS	11	12	13 TOR	14	15	16 NJ
17	18 CHI	19	20	21 NYR	22	23 NYI
24 NYI	25	26 MIN	27	28		

MARCH

Sun	Mon	Tue	Wed	Thu	Fri	Sat
					1	2 STL
3	4 NYR	5	6	7 CAL	8 EDM	9
10	11	12 LA	13 VAN	14	15	16 WAS
17 BOS	18	19	20	21 STL	22	23 NYR
24 BUF	25	26 PIT	27	28 WAS	29	30 PIT
31						

1989-90 RESULTS

Oct.	5—New Jersey	L	2-6
	6—At Washington	L	3-5
	8—At Winnipeg	L	3-5
	12—Quebec	W	4-2
	14—At N.Y. Islanders	T	3-3 (OT)
	15—Calgary	L	2-3
	18—At New Jersey	L	3-5
	21—N.Y. Rangers	L	1-3
	24—St. Louis	W	6-1
	28—At Minnesota	L	5-6
	30—At N.Y. Rangers	W	3-1
Nov.	1—At Detroit	T	5-5 (OT)
	4—At Toronto	W	7-4
	5—N.Y. Islanders	W	3-2
	9—Toronto	L	1-4
	11—At New Jersey	W	7-5
	12—New Jersey	T	3-3 (OT)
	14—At N.Y. Islanders	W	5-4
	16—Minnesota	W	6-3
	18—Winnipeg	L	0-1 (OT)
	22—Montreal	W	5-1
	24—Edmonton	W	5-1
	25—At Hartford	L	2-5
	28—At Pittsburgh	W	6-3
	30—Pittsburgh	W	4-1
Dec.	1—At Washington	W	3-2
	3—Boston	L	1-2
	5—Washington	L	3-4
	7—Buffalo	W	4-3 (OT)
	9—At Quebec	T	6-6 (OT)
	10—At N.Y. Rangers	W	4-2
	14—Hartford	L	2-3
	16—Los Angeles	W	5-2
	17—At Buffalo	L	3-4
	19—Washington	L	1-2
	22—New Jersey	L	4-5 (OT)
	23—At Montreal	W	5-3
	27—At Edmonton	L	1-2
	30—At Los Angeles	W	6-3
	31—At Vancouver	T	2-2 (OT)
Jan.	2—At Calgary	T	4-4 (OT)
	4—At St. Louis	L	4-5
	6—At Chicago	L	5-8
	11—Chicago	L	4-5
	13—At Montreal	T	2-2 (OT)
	14—At N.Y. Rangers	L	3-4 (OT)
	16—At Pittsburgh	L	3-4
	18—Vancouver	L	2-3 (OT)
	23—Buffalo	L	2-3
	25—Winnipeg	W	8-6
	27—At Boston	L	1-2
	28—At Washington	L	2-7
	30—At Pittsburgh	W	6-3
Feb.	1—Hartford	W	2-1
	3—Minnesota	W	7-6 (OT)
	8—N.Y. Islanders	T	5-5 (OT)
	11—Pittsburgh	L	1-4
	13—N.Y. Rangers	L	3-4
	15—Toronto	W	3-0
	16—At Detroit	L	6-9
	18—N.Y. Islanders	W	3-2
	20—At Pittsburgh	L	4-6
	22—At St.Louis	W	7-4
	25—At Chicago	L	1-4
	28—At Vancouver	T	7-7 (OT)
Mar.	1—At Calgary	W	4-2
	3—At Edmonton	L	3-5
	6—Boston	L	1-2
	8—N.Y. Rangers	L	5-7
	10—Washington	L	3-4
	15—N.Y. Islanders	W	5-4
	17—At Quebec	L	3-6
	18—Los Angeles	W	7-4
	20—At New Jersey	W	3-2
	22—Pittsburgh	W	5-3
	24—New Jersey	L	2-5
	25—At N.Y. Rangers	L	3-7
	29—Washington	T	2-2 (OT)
	31—At N.Y. Islanders	L	2-6
Apr.	1—Detroit	T	3-3 (OT)

1990-91 ROSTER

No.	FORWARDS	Hgt./Wt.	Place of Birth	Age	NHL exp.	1989-90 club (league)	G.	A.	Pts.
25	Keith Acton	5-08/170	Newmarket, Ont.	32	11	Philadelphia (NHL)	13	14	27
20	Len Barrie	6-00/195	Kimberly, B.C.	21	1	Kamloops (WHL)	85	100	185
						Philadelphia (NHL)	0	0	0
17	Craig Berube	6-02/195	Calihoo, Alta.	24	4	Philadelphia (NHL)	4	14	18
32	Murray Craven	6-03/190	Medicine Hat, Alta.	26	8	Philadelphia (NHL)	25	50	75
18	Brian Dobbin	5-11/195	Petrolia, Ont.	24	4	Hershey (AHL)	38	47	85
						Philadelphia (NHL)	1	1	2
9	Pelle Eklund	5-10/177	Stockholm, Sweden	27	5	Philadelphia (NHL)	23	39	62
7	Craig Fisher	6-01/170	Oshawa, Ont.	20	1	Miami of Ohio U. (CCHA)	37	29	66
						Philadelphia (NHL)	0	0	0
37	Mark Freer	5-11/175	Peterborough, Ont.	22	4	Hershey (AHL)	28	36	64
						Philadelphia (NHL)	0	0	0
34	Jeff Harding	6-04/207	Toronto, Ont.	21	2	Hershey (AHL)	0	2	2
						Philadelphia (NHL)	0	0	0
21	Tony Horacek	6-03/200	Vancouver, B.C.	23	1	Hershey (AHL)	0	5	5
						Philadelphia (NHL)	5	5	10
45	Chris Jensen	5-11/165	Fort St. John, B.C.	26	4	Hershey (AHL)	16	26	42
						Philadelphia (NHL)	0	0	0
12	Tim Kerr	6-03/215	Windsor, Ont.	30	10	Philadelphia (NHL)	24	24	48
36	Normand Lacombe	5-11/205	Pierrefond, Que.	25	6	Edmonton (NHL)	5	2	7
						Philadelphia (NHL)	0	2	2
19	Scott Mellanby	6-01/195	Montreal, Que.	24	5	Philadelphia (NHL)	6	17	23
42	Don Nachbaur	6-02/200	Kitimat, B.C.	31	8	Philadelphia (NHL)	0	1	1
						Hershey (AHL)	10	9	19
24	Derrick Smith	6-01/185	Scarborough, Ont.	25	6	Philadelphia (NHL)	3	6	9
15	Doug Sulliman	5-09/195	Glace Bay, N.S.	30	11	Philadelphia (NHL)	3	4	7
14	Ron Sutter	6-00/180	Viking, Alta.	26	8	Philadelphia (NHL)	22	26	48
22	Rick Tocchet	6-00/195	Scarborough, Ont.	26	6	Philadelphia (NHL)	37	59	96
	DEFENSEMEN								
8	Murray Baron	6-03/215	Prince George, B.C.	23	1	Hershey (AHL)	0	10	10
						Philadelphia (NHL)	2	2	4
29	Terry Carkner	6-03/200	Smith Falls, Ont.	24	3	Philadelphia (NHL)	4	18	22
6	Jeff Chychrun	6-04/190	Lasalle, Que.	24	4	Philadelphia (NHL)	2	7	9
26	Dave Fenyves	5-10/188	Dunnville, Ont.	30	8	Philadelphia (NHL)	0	0	0
						Hershey (AHL)	6	37	43
2	Mark Howe	5-11/180	Detroit, Mich.	35	13	Philadelphia (NHL)	7	21	28
5	Kerry Huffman	6-03/185	Peterborough, Ont.	22	4	Philadelphia (NHL)	1	12	13
11	Jiri Latal	6-00/190	Olomouc, Czech.	23	1	Hershey (AHL)	10	18	28
						Philadelphia (NHL)	6	13	19
3	Gord Murphy	6-01/180	Willowdale, Ont.	23	2	Philadelphia (NHL)	14	27	41
47	Shawn Sabol	6-03/215	Fargo, N.D.	24	1	Hershey (AHL)	6	16	22
						Philadelphia (NHL)	0	0	0
28	Kjell Samuelsson	6-06/227	Tingsryd, Sweden	33	5	Philadelphia (NHL)	5	17	22

No.	GOALTENDERS	Hgt./Wt.	Place of Birth	Age	NHL exp.	1989-90 club (league)	Ga.	SO	Avg.
27	Ron Hextall	6-03/170	Winnipeg, Man.	26	4	Philadelphia (NHL)	8	0	4.15
						Hershey (AHL)	1	0	3.67
30	Bruce Hoffort	5-10/185	N. Battleford, Sask.	24	1	Hershey (AHL)	40	1	3.65
						Philadelphia (NHL)	7	0	3.47
33	Pete Peeters	6-00/180	Edmonton, Alta.	33	12	Philadelphia (NHL)	24	1	3.79
35	Ken Wregget	6-01/180	Brandon, Man.	26	7	Philadelphia (NHL)	51	0	3.42

1989-90 RECORDS

1989-90 regular-season records: 30-39-11 (.444, 71 points, 6th in Patrick Division); 17-19-4 at home; 13-20-7 on road; 2-5-11 in overtime; 13-18-4 vs. Patrick (2-4-1 vs. Devils; 4-1-2 vs. Islanders; 2-5-0 vs. Rangers; 4-3-0 vs. Penguins; 1-5-1 vs. Capitals); 5-8-2 vs. Adams; 6-7-2 vs. Norris; 6-6-3 vs. Smythe.

MISCELLANEOUS DATA

1989-90 team rankings: Shorthanded goals for, 14 (T4th in NHL); shorthanded goals against, 13 (T14th); power play, 19.2% (14th); penalty killing, 81.0% (6th); penalty minutes/game, 25.8.

TEAM HAT TRICKS, CAREER, ACTIVE

Keith Acton (3)	Normand Lacombe (1)
Mike Bullard (7)	Ken Linseman (3)
Murray Craven (2)	Derrick Smith (1)
Tony Horacek (1)	Doug Sulliman (2)
Tim Kerr (17)	Rick Tocchet (7)

MINOR LEAGUE AFFILIATIONS

Hershey (AHL)

Ron Sutter

1990 DRAFT SELECTIONS

Rnd. Player	Hgt.	Wgt.	Overall	(Pos.)	1989-90 Club (League)
1—Mike Ricci	6:00	191	4	(C)	Peterborough (OHL)
2—Chris Simon	6:03	220	25	(LW)	Ottawa (OHL)
2—Mikael Renberg	6:02	183	40	(LW)	Pitea, Sweden
2—Terran Sandwith	6:04	210	42	(D)	Tri-City (WHL)
3—Kimbi Daniels	5:10	175	44	(C)	Swift Current (WHL)
3—Bill Armstrong	6:04	216	46	(D)	Oshawa (OHL)
3—Chris Therien	6:03	205	47	(D)	Northwood Prep (N.Y.)
3—Al Kinisky	6:04	220	52	(LW)	Seattle (WHL)
5—Dan Kordic	6:05	220	88	(D)	Medicine Hat (WHL)
6—Vjateslav Butsayev	6:02	200	109	(C)	CSKA, Russia
8—Patrik Englund	6:00	172	151	(LW)	AIK, Sweden
9—Toni Porkka	6:02	189	172	(D)	Lukko, Finland
10—Greg Hanson	6:03	215	193	(D)	Bloomington-Kennedy H.S. (Minn.)
11—Tommy Soderstrom	5:09	163	214	(G)	Djurgarden, Sweden
12—William Lund	5:09	165	235	(C)	Roseau H.S. (Minn.)

FIRST-ROUND ENTRY DRAFT SELECTIONS

Year Name	Overall	Last Amateur Team (League)	Years in NHL
1969—Bob Currier	6	Cornwall (QMJHL)	0
1970—No first round selection			
1971—Larry Wright	8	Regina (WCHL)	5
Pierre Plante	9	Drummondville (QMJHL)	9
1972—Bill Barber	7	Kitchener (OHL)	13
1973—No first round selection			
1974—No first round selection			
1975—*Mel Bridgeman	1	Victoria (WCHL)	14
1976—Mark Suzor	17	Kingston (OHL)	2
1977—Kevin McCarthy	17	Winnipeg (WCHL)	10
1978—Behn Wilson	6	Kingston (OHL)	9
Ken Linseman	7	Birmingham (WHA)	12
Dan Lucas	14	Sault Ste. Marie (OHL)	1
1979—Brian Propp	14	Brandon (WHL)	11
1980—Mike Stothers	21	Kingston (OHL)	4
1981—Steve Smith	16	Sault Ste. Marie (OHL)	0
1982—Ron Sutter	4	Lethbridge (WHL)	8
1983—No first round selection			
1984—No first round selection			
1985—Glen Seabrooke	21	Peterborough (OHL)	3
1986—Kerry Huffman	20	Guelph (OHL)	4
1987—Darren Rumble	20	Kitchener (OHL)	0
1988—Claude Boivin	14	Drummondville (QMJHL)	0
1989—No first round selection			
1990—Mike Ricci	4	Peterborough (OHL)	0

*Designates first player chosen in draft.

Bill Barber

COACHING HISTORY

Keith Allen, 1967-68 to 1968-69
Vic Stasiuk, 1969-70 to 1970-71
Fred Shero, 1971-72 to 1977-78
Bob McCammon and Pat Quinn, 1978-79
Pat Quinn, 1979-80 to 1980-81

Pat Quinn and Bob McCammon, 1981-82
Bob McCammon, 1982-83 to 1983-84
Mike Keenan, 1984-85 to 1987-88
Paul Holmgren since 1988-89

FRANCHISE LEADERS

Current players in bold type
(1967-68 through 1989-90)

Games
1. 1144—Bobby Clarke
2. 903—Bill Barber
3. 790—Brian Propp
4. 746—Joe Watson
5. 741—Bob Kelly
   741—Rick MacLeish
7. 725—Gary Dornhoefer
8. 617—Ed Van Impe
9. 613—Jim Watson
10. 606—Reggie Leach

Goals
1. 420—Bill Barber
2. 369—Brian Propp
3. 358—Bobby Clarke
4. **353—Tim Kerr**
5. 328—Rick MacLeish
6. 306—Reggie Leach
7. 202—Gary Dornhoefer
8. 199—Ilkka Sinisalo
9. **162—Rick Tocchet**
10. 161—Dave Poulin

Assists
1. 852—Bobby Clarke
2. 480—Brian Propp
3. 463—Bill Barber
4. 369—Rick MacLeish
5. 316—Gary Dornhoefer
6. **314—Mark Howe**
7. **273—Tim Kerr**
8. 233—Dave Poulin
9. **222—Murray Craven**
10. **214—Pelle Eklund**

Points
1. 1210—Bobby Clarke
2. 883—Bill Barber
3. 849—Brian Propp
4. 697—Rick MacLeish
5. **626—Tim Kerr**
6. 518—Gary Dornhoefer
7. 514—Reggie Leach
8. **445—Mark Howe**
9. 409—Ilkka Sinisalo
10. 394—Dave Poulin

Penalty Minutes
1. 1600—Paul Holmgren
2. 1505—Andre Dupont
3. 1453—Bobby Clarke
4. **1431—Rick Tocchet**
5. 1386—Dave Schultz
6. 1285—Bob Kelly
7. 1256—Gary Dornhoefer
8. 1110—Glen Cochrane
9. 1031—Dave Brown

Goaltenders
Games
1. 486—Bernie Parent
2. 215—Doug Favell
3. **200—Ron Hextall**
4. 165—Wayne Stephenson
5. 157—Pelle Lindbergh
6. **153—Pete Peeters**
7. 144—Bob Froese

Shutouts
1. 50—Bernie Parent
2. 16—Doug Favell
3. 12—Bob Froese
4. 10—Wayne Stephenson

Goals Against Average
(2400 minutes minimum)
1. 2.42—Bernie Parent
2. 2.74—Bob Froese
3. 2.77—Wayne Stephenson
4. 2.78—Doug Favell
5. 3.23—Rick St. Croix
6. **3.24—Pete Peeters**
7. **3.27—Ron Hextall**
8. 3.30—Pelle Lindbergh

Wins
1. 232—Bernie Parent
2. **101—Ron Hextall**
3. 93—Wayne Stephenson
4. 92—Bob Froese
5. 87—Pelle Lindbergh

Mario Lemieux's goals-per-game average of .808 is the highest in NHL history.

Paul Coffey has topped the 100-point plateau five times in 10 seasons. Bobby Orr (six times) and Denis Potvin (one) are the only other NHL defensemen to accomplish the feat.

Mark Recchi led Pittsburgh forwards with a plus-6 rating last season.

Joe Mullen has averaged 43 goals per season over the last seven years.

PITTSBURGH PENGUINS

CLUB DIRECTORY

Chairman of the Board
Edward J. DeBartolo, Sr.
President
Marie Denise DeBartolo York
Secretary and Treasurer
Anthony W. Liberati
Vice-President & General Counsel
Paul Martha
General Manager
Craig Patrick
Director of Player Development & Recruitment
Scotty Bowman
Coach
Bob Johnson
Assistant Coaches
Rick Kehoe, Rick Paterson, Barry Smith
Scouts
Greg Malone, Les Binkley, John Gill, Charlie Hodge, Doug McCauley, Ralph Cox, Pierre Maguire, Gilles Meloche
Vice-President, Communications & Sales
Bill Strong
Vice-President, Marketing
Tinsy Labrie
Director of Press Relations
Cindy Himes

Assistant Director of Press Relations
Harry Sanders
Trainer
Skip Thayer
Conditioning Coach
John Welday
Equipment Manager
Steve Latin
Director of Ticket Sales
Jeff Mercer
Team Physician
Dr. Charles Burke
Home Ice
Civic Arena
Address
Civic Arena, Gate No. 9, Pittsburgh, Pa. 15219
Seating Capacity
16,236
Club Colors
Black, Gold and White
Phone
(412) 642-1800
FAX
(412) 642-1925

YEAR-BY-YEAR RESULTS

Season	W.	L.	T.	Pts.	Position	Season	W.	L.	T.	Pts.	Position
1967-68	27	34	13	67	Fifth—*	1979-80	30	37	13	73	Third—†
1968-69	20	45	11	51	Fifth—*	1980-81	30	37	13	73	Third—†
1969-70	26	38	12	64	Second—b	1981-82	31	36	13	75	Fourth—†
1970-71	21	37	20	62	Sixth—*	1982-83	18	53	9	45	Sixth—*
1971-72	26	38	14	66	Fourth—a	1983-84	16	58	6	38	Sixth—*
1972-73	32	37	9	73	Fifth—*	1984-85	24	51	5	53	Fifth—*
1973-74	28	41	9	65	Fifth—*	1985-86	34	38	8	76	Fifth—*
1974-75	37	28	15	89	Third—a	1986-87	30	38	12	72	Fifth—*
1975-76	35	33	12	82	Third—†	1987-88	36	35	9	81	Sixth—*
1976-77	34	33	13	81	Third—†	1988-89	40	33	7	87	Second—a
1977-78	25	37	18	68	Fourth—*	1989-90	32	40	8	72	Fifth—*
1978-79	36	31	13	85	Second—a	**Totals**	668	888	262	1598	

Key to standings: *—Missed playoffs. †—Eliminated in first round of new playoff format (1974-75). a—Eliminated in quarterfinal round. b—Eliminated in semifinal round. c—Eliminated in final round. xx—Stanley Cup champion.

Dave Burrows

Rick Kehoe

1990-91 SCHEDULE

▦ Home games shaded.

* At Chicago Stadium.

OCTOBER

Sun	Mon	Tue	Wed	Thu	Fri	Sat
	1	2	3	4	5 WAS	6
7 NJ	8	9 STL	10	11 CHI	12	13 NYI
14	15	16 PHI	17	18	19 BUF	20 NYR
21	22	23 MON	24	25 QUE	26	27 NJ
28 NYI	29	30 PHI	31			

NOVEMBER

Sun	Mon	Tue	Wed	Thu	Fri	Sat
				1	2	3 NYR
4	5	6 CAL	7	8 STL	9	10 BOS
11	12	13 MIN	14 WIN	15	16	17 LA
18	19	20	21 PHI	22	23 WAS	24 WAS
25	26	27 EDM	28	29 HAR	30	

DECEMBER

Sun	Mon	Tue	Wed	Thu	Fri	Sat
						1 MIN
2	3 NYR	4	5 WAS	6	7 VAN	8 HAR
9	10	11 CHI	12	13 NJ	14 BUF	15
16 DET	17	18 WIN	19	20 MIN	21	22 NYI
23 NYI	24	25 WAS	26	27	28 DET	29 TOR
30	31 STL					

JANUARY

Sun	Mon	Tue	Wed	Thu	Fri	Sat
		1	2	3 NYR	4	5 NJ
6 MON	7	8 EDM	9	10 CAL	11	12
13	14	15 PHI	16	17 TOR	18	19 ALL-STAR GAME*
20	21	22 NJ	23	24	25	26 QUE
27	28	29 WAS	30	31 PHI		

FEBRUARY

Sun	Mon	Tue	Wed	Thu	Fri	Sat
					1	2 BOS
3 BOS	4	5	6	7	8 WIN	9
10	11 EDM	12	13	14 NYI	15	16 NYI
17	18	19 BUF	20	21 TOR	22 NJ	23
24 WAS	25	26 LA	27 VAN	28		

MARCH

Sun	Mon	Tue	Wed	Thu	Fri	Sat
					1 CAL	2
3	4	5 VAN	6	7 LA	8	9 HAR
10 NYI	11	12 MON	13	14	15	16 QUE
17 NYR	18	19 NJ	20	21 NYR	22	23 CHI
24	25	26 PHI	27 DET	28	29	30 PHI
31 NYR						

1989-90 RESULTS

Oct.	5—At Boston	L	4-5
	7—At New Jersey	T	4-4 (OT)
	10—Winnipeg	W	5-1
	14—Montreal	W	2-1 (OT)
	15—At N.Y. Rangers	L	2-4
	17—Toronto	W	7-5
	18—St. Louis	L	3-9
	21—Buffalo	L	2-4
	25—Toronto	L	6-8
	26—At Detroit	T	3-3 (OT)
	28—At Montreal	L	1-5
	31—Los Angeles	L	4-8
Nov.	2—N.Y. Islanders	W	5-2
	4—At Edmonton	W	3-1
	5—At Vancouver	L	3-5
	9—At Chicago	L	3-4
	11—At St. Louis	L	3-8
	14—N.Y. Rangers	W	6-0
	16—Quebec	W	8-2
	18—N.Y. Islanders	W	5-3
	22—New Jersey	L	3-6
	24—At Washington	W	7-4
	25—Washington	L	1-4
	28—Philadelphia	L	3-6
	30—At Philadelphia	L	1-4
Dec.	2—At Quebec	W	7-4
	6—Washington	W	5-3
	8—At New Jersey	W	3-2
	9—Chicago	L	4-6
	12—Boston	W	7-5
	14—At Minnesota	T	4-4 (OT)
	16—At Calgary	L	3-4
	19—Hartford	L	4-8
	21—Washington	W	5-2
	23—At N.Y. Islanders	L	6-8
	26—At Washington	L	3-6
	27—N.Y. Rangers	W	7-4
	31—At N.Y. Rangers	W	5-4
Jan.	2—Boston	L	2-5
	4—Vancouver	W	4-3
	6—Winnipeg	W	5-3
	8—At N.Y. Rangers	W	7-5
	10—At New Jersey	L	3-6
	12—At Washington	W	6-4
	16—Philadelphia	W	4-3
	18—N.Y. Rangers	T	3-3 (OT)
	23—New Jersey	L	2-4
	25—At Detroit	W	5-3
	27—At N.Y. Islanders	L	3-9
	28—At Buffalo	L	2-7
	30—Philadelphia	L	3-6
Feb.	2—Edmonton	W	6-3
	3—At Toronto	L	4-8
	6—N.Y. Islanders	L	7-8 (OT)
	8—Washington	W	7-5
	10—Los Angeles	W	7-6
	11—At Philadelphia	W	4-1
	14—At N.Y. Rangers	W	4-3 (OT)
	16—At Winnipeg	T	3-3 (OT)
	18—At Chicago	L	4-6
	20—Philadelphia	W	6-4
	22—N.Y. Islanders	W	4-3 (OT)
	24—At Montreal	L	1-11
	26—At Quebec	L	2-3
	28—New Jersey	W	2-1
Mar.	2—At New Jersey	L	5-6
	4—Minnesota	W	8-6
	6—At Edmonton	L	3-4 (OT)
	7—At Calgary	L	3-6
	10—At Los Angeles	L	2-8
	11—At Vancouver	L	3-5
	15—Detroit	W	6-1
	17—Minnesota	L	2-6
	18—At N.Y. Islanders	T	2-2 (OT)
	22—At Philadelphia	L	3-5
	24—Calgary	T	3-3 (OT)
	25—At Hartford	L	2-4
	27—Hartford	T	3-3 (OT)
	29—At St. Louis	L	4-5
	31—Buffalo	L	2-3 (OT)

1990-91 ROSTER

No.	FORWARDS	Hgt./Wt.	Place of Birth	Age	NHL exp.	1989-90 club (league)	G.	A.	Pts.
29	Phil Bourque	6-01/196	Chelmsford, Mass.	28	5	Pittsburgh (NHL)	22	17	39
44	Rob Brown	5-11/185	Kingston, Ont.	22	3	Pittsburgh (NHL)	33	47	80
14	Jock Callander	6-01/187	Regina, Sask	29	3	Muskegon (IHL)	29	49	78
						Pittsburgh (NHL)	4	7	11
16	Jay Caufield	6-04/237	Philadelphia, Pa.	30	4	Pittsburgh (NHL)	1	2	3
11	John Cullen	5-10/187	Puslinch, Ont.	26	2	Pittsburgh (NHL)	32	60	92
12	Bob Errey	5-10/183	Montreal, Que.	26	7	Pittsburgh (NHL)	20	19	39
	Daniel Gauthier	6-01/186	Charlemagne, Que.	20	0	Victoriaville (QMJHL)	45	69	114
19	Randy Gilhen	5-10/190	Zweibrucken, W. Ger.	27	3	Pittsburgh (NHL)	5	11	16
	Jaromir Jagr	6-02/198	Kladno, Czech.	18	0	Kladno (Czech.)	30	30	60
	Mark Kachowski	5-10/196	Edmonton, Alta.	25	3	Muskegon (IHL)	23	8	31
						Pittsburgh (NHL)	0	1	1
20	Jamie Leach	6-01/197	Winnipeg, Man.	21	1	Muskegon (IHL)	22	36	58
						Pittsburgh (NHL)	0	3	3
66	Mario Lemieux	6-04/210	Montreal, Que.	24	6	Pittsburgh (NHL)	45	78	123
24	Troy Loney	6-03/209	Bow Island, Alta.	27	7	Pittsburgh (NHL)	11	16	27
	Joe Mullen	5-09/180	New York, N.Y.	33	10	Calgary (NHL)	36	33	69
	Mike Needham	5-10/198	Calgary, Alta.	20	0	Kamloops (WHL)	59	66	125
10	Barry Pederson	5-11/185	Big River, Sask.	29	10	Vancouver (NHL)	2	7	9
						Pittsburgh (NHL)	4	18	22
8	Mark Recchi	5-10/189	Kamloops, Alta.	22	2	Muskegon (IHL)	7	4	11
						Pittsburgh (NHL)	30	37	67
15	Doug Smith	6-00/185	Ottawa, Ont.	27	9	Vancouver (NHL)	3	4	7
						Pittsburgh (NHL)	1	1	2
25	Kevin Stevens	6-03/217	Brockton, Mass.	25	3	Pittsburgh (NHL)	29	41	70
9	Tony Tanti	5-09/185	Toronto, Ont.	26	8	Vancouver (NHL)	14	18	32
						Pittsburgh (NHL)	14	18	32
	Bryan Trottier	5-10/205	Val Marie, Sask.	34	15	N.Y. Islanders (NHL)	13	11	24
18	Richard Zemlak	6-02/190	Wynard, Sask.	27	4	Muskegon (IHL)	17	39	56
						Pittsburgh (NHL)	1	5	6
	DEFENSEMEN								
7	Rod Buskas	6-01/205	Wetaskiwin, Alta.	29	8	Vancouver (NHL)	0	3	3
						Pittsburgh (NHL)	0	0	0
77	Paul Coffey	6-01/205	Weston, Ont.	29	10	Pittsburgh (NHL)	29	74	103
4	Chris Dahlquist	6-01/191	Fridley, Minn.	28	5	Muskegon (IHL)	1	1	2
						Pittsburgh (NHL)	4	10	14
27	Gilbert Delorme	6-01/199	Boucherville, Que.	27	9	Pittsburgh (NHL)	3	7	10
5	Gord Dineen	6-00/191	Quebec City, Que.	28	8	Pittsburgh (NHL)	1	8	9
23	Randy Hillier	6-01/188	Toronto, Ont.	30	9	Pittsburgh (NHL)	3	12	15
6	Jim Johnson	6-01/193	New Hope, Minn.	28	5	Pittsburgh (NHL)	3	13	16
3	Jim Kyte	6-05/220	Ottawa, Ont.	26	8	Pittsburgh (NHL)	3	1	4
	Paul Laus	6-01/200	Beamsville, Ont.	20	0	Niagara Falls (OHL)	13	35	48
	Paul Stanton	6-00/190	Boston, Mass.	23	0	Muskegon (IHL)	5	27	32
33	Zarley Zalapski	6-01/200	Edmonton, Alta.	22	3	Pittsburgh (NHL)	6	25	31
	GOALTENDERS						Ga.	SO	Avg.
35	Tom Barrasso	6-03/211	Boston, Mass.	25	7	Pittsburgh (NHL)	24	0	4.68
40	Frank Pietrangelo	5-09/182	Niagara Falls, Ont.	25	3	Muskegon (IHL)	12	0	3.30
						Pittsburgh (NHL)	21	0	4.33
	Bruce Racine	6-00/178	Cornwall, Ont.	24	0	Muskegon (IHL)	49	1	3.75
1	Wendell Young	5-09/181	Halifax, N.S.	27	5	Pittsburgh (NHL)	43	1	4.17

1989-90 RECORDS

1989-90 regular-season records: 32-40-8 (.450, 72 points, 5th in Patrick Division); 22-15-3 at home; 10-25-5 on road; 3-3-8 in overtime; 18-14-3 vs. Patrick (2-4-1 vs. Devils; 3-3-1 vs. Islanders; 5-1-1 vs. Rangers; 3-4-0 vs. Flyers; 5-2-0 vs. Capitals); 4-10-1 vs. Adams; 4-9-2 vs. Norris; 6-7-2 vs. Smythe.

MISCELLANEOUS DATA

1989-90 team rankings: Shorthanded goals for, 7 (T17th in NHL); shorthanded goals against, 21 (21st); power play, 21.3% (10th); penalty killing, 74.7% (20th); penalty minutes/game, 26.7.

TEAM HAT TRICKS, CAREER, ACTIVE

Rob Brown (7)	Barry Pederson (7)
Paul Coffey (5)	Kevin Stevens (1)
John Cullen (1)	Tony Tanti (11)
Mario Lemieux (25)	Bryan Trottier (16)
Joe Mullen (7)	

MINOR LEAGUE AFFILIATIONS

Muskegon (IHL)

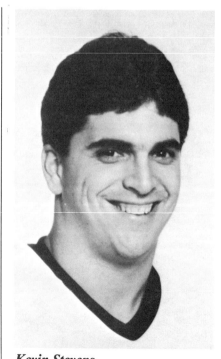

Kevin Stevens

1990 DRAFT SELECTIONS

Rnd.	Player	Hgt.	Wgt.	Overall	(Pos.)	1989-90 Club	(League)
1	Jaromir Jagr	6:02	198	5	(LW)	Poldi Kladno, Czech.	
3	Joe Dziedzic	6:03	200	61	(LW)	Edison H.S. (Minn.)	
4	Chris Tamer	6:02	185	68	(D)	University of Michigan	
5	Brian Farrell	5:11	182	89	(C)	Avon Old Farms H.S. (Ct.)	
6	Ian Moran	5:11	170	107	(D)	Belmont Hill H.S. (Mass.)	
6	Denis Casey	5:10	180	110	(G)	Colorado College	
7	Mika Valila	6:00	172	130	(C)	Tappara, Finland	
7	Ken Plaquin	6:02	190	131	(D)	Michigan Tech University	
7	Pat Neaton	6:00	180	145	(D)	University of Michigan	
8	Petteri Koskimaki	6:01	180	152	(C)	Boston University	
9	Ladislav Karabin	6:01	189	173	(LW)	Bratislava, Czech.	
10	Timothy Fingerhut	6:00	175	194	(LW)	Canterbury H.S. (Mass.)	
11	Michael Thompson	6:00	202	215	(RW)	Michigan State University	
12	Brian Bruininks	6:00	180	236	(D)	Colorado College	

FIRST-ROUND ENTRY DRAFT SELECTIONS

Year	Name	Overall	Last Amateur Team (League)	Years in NHL
1969	No first round selection			
1970	Greg Polis	7	Estevan (WCHL)	10
1971	No first round selection			
1972	No first round selection			
1973	Blaine Stoughton	7	Flin Flon (WCHL)	8
1974	Pierre Larouche	8	Sorel (QMJHL)	14
1975	Gord Laxton	13	New Westminster (WCHL)	4
1976	Blair Chapman	2	Saskatoon (WCHL)	7
1977	No first round selection			
1978	No first round selection			
1979	No first round selection			
1980	Mike Bullard	9	Brantford (OHL)	10
1981	No first round selection			
1982	Rich Sutter	10	Lethbridge (WHL)	8
1983	Bob Errey	15	Peterborough (OHL)	7
1984	*Mario Lemieux	1	Laval (QMJHL)	6
	Doug Bodger	9	Kamloops (WHL)	6
	Roger Belanger	16	Kingston (OHL)	1
1985	Craig Simpson	2	Michigan State University	5
1986	Zarley Zalapski	4	Team Canada	3
1987	Chris Joseph	5	Seattle (WHL)	3
1988	Darrin Shannon	4	Windsor (OHL)	2
1989	Jamie Heward	16	Regina (WHL)	0
1990	Jaromir Jagr	5	Poldi Kladno (Czech.)	0

*Designates first player chosen in draft.

Pierre Larouche

COACHING HISTORY

Red Sullivan, 1967-68 to 1968-69
Red Kelly, 1969-70 to 1971-72
Red Kelly and Ken Schinkel, 1972-73
Ken Schinkel and Marc Boileau, 1973-74
Marc Boileau, 1974-75
Marc Boileau and Ken Schinkel, 1975-76
Ken Schinkel, 1976-77
Johnny Wilson, 1977-78 to 1979-80

Eddie Johnston, 1980-81 to 1982-83
Lou Angotti, 1983-84
Bob Berry, 1984-85 to 1986-87
Pierre Creamer, 1987-88
Gene Ubriaco, 1988-89
Gene Ubriaco and Craig Patrick, 1989-90
Bob Johnson for 1990-91

FRANCHISE LEADERS

Current players in bold type
(1967-68 through 1989-90)

Games
1. 753—Jean Pronovost
2. 722—Rick Kehoe
3. 621—Ron Stackhouse
4. 619—Ron Schock
5. 573—Dave Burrows
6. 495—Syl Apps
   495—Greg Malone
8. 431—Rod Buskas
   431—Peter Lee
10. 427—**Mario Lemieux**

Goals
1. 345—**Mario Lemieux**
2. 316—Jean Pronovost
3. 312—Rick Kehoe
4. 186—Mike Bullard
5. 151—Syl Apps
6. 143—Greg Malone
7. 140—Lowell MacDonald
8. 124—Ron Schock
9. 123—Doug Shedden
10. 119—Pierre Larouche

Assists
1. 493—**Mario Lemieux**
2. 349—Syl Apps
3. 324—Rick Kehoe
4. 287—Jean Pronovost
5. 280—Ron Schock
6. 277—Ron Stackhouse
7. 257—Randy Carlyle
8. 221—Greg Malone
9. 209—**Paul Coffey**
10. 175—Mike Bullard

Points
1. 838—**Mario Lemieux**
2. 636—Rick Kehoe
3. 603—Jean Pronovost
4. 500—Syl Apps
5. 404—Ron Schock
6. 364—Greg Malone
7. 361—Mike Bullard
8. 343—Ron Stackhouse
9. 323—Randy Carlyle
10. 306—Lowell MacDonald

Penalty Minutes
1. 959—Rod Buskas
2. 871—Bryan Watson
3. 851—Paul Baxter
4. 832—Gary Rissling
5. 684—Russ Anderson
6. 671—**Troy Loney**
7. 635—**Jim Johnson**

Goaltenders

Games
1. 290—Denis Herron
2. 196—Les Binkley
3. 151—Michel Dion
4. 135—Greg Millen
5. 123—Roberto Romano
6. 115—Jim Rutherford
7. 104—Gilles Meloche
8. 100—Gary Inness

Shutouts
1. 11—Les Binkley
2. 6—Denis Herron
3. 5—Dunc Wilson

Goals Against Average
(2400 minutes minimum)
1. 3.07—Al Smith
2. 3.12—Les Binkley
3. 3.14—Jim Rutherford
4. 3.34—Gary Inness
5. 3.53—Dunc Wilson
6. 3.59—Michel Plasse
7. 3.65—Gilles Meloche
8. 3.78—Andy Brown
9. 3.83—Greg Millen
10. 3.87—Denis Herron

Wins
1. 88—Denis Herron
2. 58—Les Binkley
3. 57—Greg Millen
4. 45—Roberto Romano
5. 44—Jim Rutherford

Following the departures of Peter Stastny and Michel Goulet, Joe Sakic (above) finished as Quebec's leading scorer (with 102 points) last year.

Guy Lafleur needs just 36 assists to earn a spot in the NHL's all-time top 10 in three categories: goals, assists and points.

Quebec players posted the five poorest plus-minus ratings in the NHL last year, with Bryan Fogarty's minus-47 being the lowest figure of any player.

Tony McKegney, who is with the Nordiques for the second time in his career, has played for five different NHL teams in the last four years.

QUEBEC NORDIQUES

CLUB DIRECTORY

President and Governor
Marcel Aubut
Vice-President of Hockey Operations
Maurice Filion
General Manager
Pierre Page
Assistant to the General Manager
Gilles Leger
Coach
Dave Chambers
Associate Coach
Jacques Martin
Assistant Coach
Robbie Ftorek
Scout-Professional Hockey and Special Assignments
Andre Savard
Chief Scout
Pierre Gauthier
Assistant to the Chief Scout
Darwin Bennett
Scouts
Michel Georges, Bob Manclni, Frank Moberg, Don Paarup, Don Boyd, Mark Kelley
General Counsel
Jean Pelletier
Vice-President/Administration and Finance
Jean Laflamme

Vice-President/Marketing and Communications
Jean D. Legault
Supervisor of Press Relations
Jean Martineau
Coordinator—Public Relations
Nicole Bouchard
Supervisor of Public Relations
Marius Fortier
Team Doctor
Dr. Pierre Beauchemin
Trainers
Rene Lacasse, Rene Lavigueur, Jacques Lavergne
Home Ice
Quebec Colisee
Address
2205 Ave. du Colisee, Quebec, Que. G1L 4W7
Seating Capacity
15,399
Club Colors
Blue, White and Red
Phone
(418) 529-8441
FAX
(418) 529-1052

YEAR-BY-YEAR RESULTS

Season	W.	L.	T.	Pts.	Position	Season	W.	L.	T.	Pts.	Position
1972-73	33	40	5	71	Fifth—*	1982-83	34	34	12	80	Fourth—†
1973-74	38	36	4	80	Fifth—*	1983-84	42	28	10	94	Third—a
1974-75	46	32	0	92	First—c	1984-85	41	30	9	91	Second—b
1975-76	50	27	4	104	Second—a	1985-86	43	31	6	92	First—†
1976-77	47	31	3	97	First—xx	1986-87	31	39	10	72	Fourth—a
1977-78	40	37	3	83	Fourth—b	1987-88	32	43	5	69	Fifth—*
1978-79	41	34	5	87	Second—b	1988-89	27	46	7	61	Fifth—*
1979-80	25	44	11	61	Fifth—*	1989-90	12	61	7	31	Fifth—*
1980-81	30	32	18	78	Fourth—†	**Totals**	645	653	135	1425	
1981-82	33	31	16	82	Fourth—b						

Key to standings: *—Missed playoffs. †—Eliminated in first round of new playoff format (1974-75). a—Eliminated in quarterfinal round. b—Eliminated in semifinal round. c—Eliminated in final round. xx—Stanley Cup champion.

NOTE: Records for Edmonton Oilers, Hartford Whalers, Quebec Nordiques and Winnipeg Jets include World Hockey Association results prior to their entrance into NHL in 1979-80. Key to WHA standings: *—Missed playoffs. †—Preliminary round (established for 1975-76 season). a—Eliminated in quarterfinal round. b—Eliminated in semifinal round. c—Eliminated in final round. xx—Avco World Cup champion.

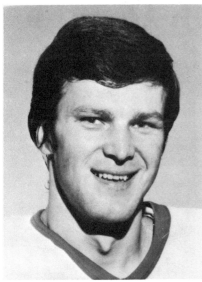

Peter Stastny

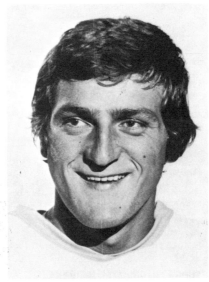

Anton Stastny

1990-91 SCHEDULE

▨ Home games shaded.

* At Chicago Stadium.

OCTOBER

Sun	Mon	Tue	Wed	Thu	Fri	Sat
	1	2	3	4 HAR	5	6 BOS
7 BOS	8	9	10 TOR	11	12 BUF	13 BUF
14	15	16 HAR	17	18 PHI	19	20 DET
21 VAN	22	23	24	25 PIT	26	27 NYR
28	29 NYR	30	31			

NOVEMBER

Sun	Mon	Tue	Wed	Thu	Fri	Sat
			1 CHI	2	3 MIN	
4	5	6 WAS	7	8 MIN	9	10 PHI
11 MON	12	13 STL	14	15 BOS	16	17 CHI
18	19 MON	20	21 HAR	22	23	24 WIN
25 LA	26	27	28 HAR	29	30	

DECEMBER

Sun	Mon	Tue	Wed	Thu	Fri	Sat
						1 BUF
2 CAL	3	4	5 EDM	6	7 CAL	8
9	10 VAN	11	12 DET	13	14	15 NYI
16	17	18 MON	19 MON	20	21	22 NJ
23 BUF	24	25	26 HAR	27	28	29 WAS
30	31 NYI					

JANUARY

Sun	Mon	Tue	Wed	Thu	Fri	Sat
		1	2	3 STL	4	5 MON
6	7	8 BOS	9	10 BOS	11	12 STL
13 NYI	14	15	16	17 PHI	18	19 ALL-STAR GAME*
20	21	22 TOR	23	24 NJ	25	26 PIT
27	28	29 WIN	30	31 BUF		

FEBRUARY

Sun	Mon	Tue	Wed	Thu	Fri	Sat
					1	2 MIN
3	4	5	6	7 MON	8	9 NJ
10 BOS	11	12 BUF	13	14 CHI	15	16
17 WIN	18 VAN	19	20 LA	21	22	23 CAL
24 EDM	25	26	27	28 BUF		

MARCH

Sun	Mon	Tue	Wed	Thu	Fri	Sat
					1	2 HAR
3	4	5 DET	6	7 NYR	8	9 LA
10 HAR	11	12 TOR	13	14 WAS	15	16 PIT
17	18	19 EDM	20	21 BOS	22	23 HAR
24	25	26 BOS	27	28 BUF	29	30 MON
31 MON						

1989-90 RESULTS

Oct.	5—At Buffalo	L	3-4
	7—Boston	W	4-1
	8—Hartford	L	6-9
	12—At Philadelphia	L	2-4
	14—At Minnesota	L	2-3
	17—Calgary	T	8-8 (OT)
	19—At Chicago	W	5-3
	21—Minnesota	W	7-2
	25—At Hartford	L	0-2
	26—At Boston	L	2-4
	28—Edmonton	L	3-6
	31—Chicago	L	3-5
Nov.	2—At NY. Rangers	L	1-6
	4—St. Louis	L	2-5
	5—Washington	L	0-3
	8—At New Jersey	L	3-6
	9—At N.Y. Islanders	W	7-5
	11—Vancouver	W	3-2
	14—Winnipeg	L	3-5
	16—At Pittsburgh	L	2-8
	18—Detroit	L	1-8
	21—Calgary	T	4-4 (OT)
	22—At Hartford	W	4-2
	25—Buffalo	L	2-3
	26—At N.Y. Rangers	L	1-3
	29—At Montreal	L	2-5
	30—Montreal	L	2-6
Dec.	2—Pittsburgh	L	4-7
	5—Boston	T	3-3 (OT)
	9—Philadelphia	T	6-6 (OT)
	10—Los Angeles	L	4-8
	13—At Edmonton	L	1-5
	14—At Calgary	L	2-8
	17—At Vancouver	T	2-2 (OT)
	21—At Los Angeles	L	1-6
	23—Buffalo	L	5-6
	26—Hartford	T	3-3 (OT)
	30—N.Y. Islanders	W	6-3
Jan.	3—At Toronto	L	4-5
	4—At Detroit	L	1-4
	6—At N.Y. Islanders	L	2-5
	9—Montreal	W	5-2
	11—At Boston	L	1-3
	13—New Jersey	L	4-5
	16—At Winnipeg	W	8-6
	18—At Minnesota	L	4-7
	23—Boston	L	2-9
	24—At Montreal	L	3-7
	27—Detroit	L	6-8
	30—Buffalo	L	2-5
	31—At Buffalo	L	3-6
Feb.	3—Hartford	L	1-5
	4—Boston	L	2-3
	6—At Washington	L	2-12
	8—At Boston	L	1-5
	10—At Montreal	L	2-7
	13—Vancouver	W	5-3
	15—At St. Louis	L	2-9
	17—At Los Angeles	L	1-7
	21—At Hartford	L	2-3
	22—Montreal	L	5-6
	24—St. Louis	L	1-6
	26—Pittsburgh	W	3-2
	28—At Toronto	L	4-5
Mar.	3—Buffalo	T	3-3 (OT)
	4—At Buffalo	L	3-5
	7—At Winnipeg	L	3-6
	9—At Washington	L	3-4
	10—At New Jersey	L	3-9
	13—Edmonton	L	1-4
	15—Chicago	L	3-6
	17—Philadelphia	W	6-3
	18—At Montreal	L	3-8
	21—At Hartford	L	1-4
	22—At Boston	L	3-7
	24—Toronto	L	3-4 (OT)
	27—N.Y. Rangers	L	4-7
	29—Montreal	L	2-5
	31—Hartford	L	2-3
Apr.	1—At Buffalo	L	2-5

1990-91 ROSTER

No.	FORWARDS	Hgt./Wt.	Place of Birth	Age	NHL exp.	1989-90 club (league)	G.	A.	Pts.
21	Jamie Baker	6-00/190	Ottawa, Ont.	24	1	Quebec (NHL)	0	0	0
						Halifax (AHL)	17	43	60
32	Lucien DeBlois	5-11/200	Joliette, Que.	33	13	Quebec (NHL)	9	8	17
33	Daniel Dore	6-03/202	Ferme-Neuve, Que.	20	1	Quebec (NHL)	2	3	5
						Chicoutimi (QMJHL)	6	23	29
9	Marc Fortier	6-00/192	Windsor, Que.	24	3	Quebec (NHL)	13	17	30
						Halifax (AHL)	5	6	11
23	Paul Gillis	5-11/198	Toronto, Ont.	26	8	Quebec (NHL)	8	14	22
18	Mike Hough	6-01/192	Montreal, Que.	27	4	Quebec (NHL)	13	13	26
28	Tony Hrkac	5-11/170	Thunder Bay, Ont.	24	4	St. Louis (NHL)	5	12	17
						Quebec (NHL)	4	8	12
						Halifax (AHL)	12	21	33
25	Jeff Jackson	6-01/195	Dresden, Ont.	25	6	Quebec (NHL)	8	12	20
11	Iiro Jarvi	6-01/198	Helsinki, Finland	25	2	Quebec (NHL)	7	13	20
						Halifax (AHL)	4	13	17
17	Kevin Kaminski	5-09/170	Churchbridge, Sask.	21	2	Quebec (NHL)	0	0	0
						Halifax (AHL)	3	4	7
15	Darin Kimble	6-02/205	Lucky Lake, Sask.	22	2	Quebec (NHL)	5	5	10
						Halifax (AHL)	6	6	12
10	Guy Lafleur	6-00/185	Thurso, Que.	39	16	Quebec (NHL)	12	22	34
	Claude Lapointe	5-09/173	Lachine, Que.	22	0	Halifax (AHL)	18	19	37
	David Latta	6-01/190	Thunder Bay, Ont.	23	3	Halifax (AHL)	11	5	16
20	Claude Loiselle	5-11/195	Ottawa, Ont.	27	9	Quebec (NHL)	11	14	25
14	Tony McKegney	6-01/200	Montreal, Que.	32	12	Detroit (NHL)	2	1	3
						Quebec (NHL)	16	11	27
12	Ken McRae	6-01/195	Winchester, Ont.	22	3	Quebec (NHL)	7	8	15
48	Max Middendorf	6-04/210	Syracuse, N.Y.	23	3	Quebec (NHL)	0	0	0
						Halifax (AHL)	20	17	37
22	Stephane Morin	6-00/175	Montreal, Que.	21	1	Quebec (NHL)	0	2	2
						Halifax (AHL)	28	32	60
	Owen Nolan	6-01/194	Belfast, Ireland	18	0	Cornwall (OHL)	51	60	111
19	Joe Sakic	5-11/185	Burnaby, B.C.	21	2	Quebec (NHL)	39	63	102
21	Everett Sanipass	6-02/204	Big Cove, N.B.	22	4	Chicago (NHL)	2	2	4
						Quebec (NHL)	3	3	6
						Indianapolis (IHL)	15	13	28
	Trevor Stienburg	6-01/200	Kingston, Ont.	24	4	Halifax (AHL)	3	3	6
27	Mark Vermette	6-01/203	Cochenour, Ont.	23	2	Quebec (NHL)	1	5	6
						Halifax (AHL)	20	17	37
	DEFENSEMEN								
2	Joe Cirella	6-03/210	Hamilton, Ont.	27	9	Quebec (NHL)	4	14	18
28	Mario Doyon	6-00/174	Quebec City, Que.	22	2	Indianapolis (IHL)	9	25	34
						Quebec (NHL)	2	3	5
29	Steven Finn	6-00/198	Laval, Que.	24	5	Quebec (NHL)	3	9	12
43	Bryan Fogarty	6-02/198	Brantford, Ont.	21	1	Quebec (NHL)	4	10	14
						Halifax (AHL)	5	14	19
6	Stephane Guerard	6-02/198	St. Elizabeth, Que.	22	2	Quebec (NHL)	0	0	0
						Halifax (AHL)	0	0	0
7	Curtis Leschyshyn	6-01/205	Thompson, Man.	21	2	Quebec (NHL)	2	6	8
44	Mario Marois	5-11/190	Quebec City, Que.	32	13	Quebec (NHL)	3	15	18
24	Michel Petit	6-01/205	Quebec City, Que.	26	8	Quebec (NHL)	12	24	36
5	Brent Severyn	6-02/210	Vegreville, Alta.	24	1	Halifax (AHL)	6	9	15
						Quebec (NHL)	0	2	2
4	Greg Smyth	6-03/212	Oakville, Ont.	24	4	Quebec (NHL)	0	0	0
						Halifax (AHL)	5	14	19
	Jim Sprott	6-01/200	Oakville, Ont.	21	0	Halifax (AHL)	2	1	3
	Randy Velischek	6-00/200	Montreal, Que.	28	8	New Jersey (NHL)	0	6	6

	GOALTENDERS						Ga.	SO	Avg.
	Stephane Fiset	6-00/175	Montreal, Que.	20	1	Victoriaville (QMJHL)	24	1	2.73
						Quebec (NHL)	6	0	5.96
	Scott Gordon	5-10/175	Brockton, Mass.	27	1	Quebec (NHL)	10	0	5.33
						Halifax (AHL)	48	0	3.33
1	Ron Tugnutt	5-11/155	Scarborough, Ont.	22	3	Quebec (NHL)	35	0	4.61
						Halifax (AHL)	6	0	3.77

1989-90 RECORDS

1989-90 regular-season records: 12-61-7 (.194, 31 points, 5th in Adams Division); 8-26-6 at home; 4-35-1 on road; 0-1-7 in overtime; 3-26-3 vs. Adams (1-6-1 vs. Bruins; 0-7-1 vs. Sabres; 1-6-1 vs. Whalers; 1-7-0 vs. Canadiens); 4-13-1 vs. Patrick; 2-13-0 vs. Norris; 3-9-3 vs. Smythe.

MISCELLANEOUS DATA

1989-90 team rankings: Shorthanded goals for, 8 (T15th in NHL); shorthanded goals against, 15 (T17th); power play, 18.9% (16th); penalty killing, 74.3% (21st); penalty minutes/game, 26.3.

TEAM HAT TRICKS, CAREER, ACTIVE

Lucien DeBlois (1)	Lane Lambert (2)
Paul Gillis (1)	Tony McKegney (8)
Guy Lafleur (17)	Joe Sakic (3)

MINOR LEAGUE AFFILIATIONS

Halifax (AHL)

Mats Sundin

1990 DRAFT SELECTIONS

Rnd.	Player	Hgt.	Wgt.	Overall	(Pos.)	1989-90 Club	(League)
1	Owen Nolan	6:01	194	1	(RW)	Cornwall (OHL)	
2	Ryan Hughes	6:01	180	22	(C)	Cornell University	
3	Bradley Zavisha	6:01	195	43	(LW)	Seattle (WHL)	
6	Jeff Parrott	6:01	195	106	(D)	Univ. of Minnesota-Duluth	
7	Dwayne Norris	5:10	175	127	(RW)	Michigan State University	
8	Andrei Kovalenko	5:09	161	148	(RW)	CSKA, Russia	
8	Alexander Karpovtsev	6:02	189	158	(D)	Moscow Dynamo	
9	Pat Mazzoli	5:10	170	169	(G)	Humboldt Tier II (Sask.)	
10	Scott Davis	6:00	188	190	(D)	University of Manitoba	
11	Mika Stromberg	5:11	178	211	(D)	Jokerit, Finland	
12	Wade Klippenstein	6:03	219	232	(LW)	Univ. of Alaska-Fairbanks	

FIRST-ROUND ENTRY DRAFT SELECTIONS

Year	Name	Overall	Last Amateur Team	(League)	Years in NHL
1979	Michel Goulet	20	Birmingham (WHA)		11
1980	No first round selection				
1981	Randy Moller	11	Lethbridge (WHL)		8
1982	David Shaw	13	Kitchener (OHL)		8
1983	No first round selection				
1984	Trevor Stienburg	15	Guelph (OHL)		4
1985	Dave Latta	15	Kitchener (OHL)		3
1986	Ken McRae	18	Sudbury (OHL)		3
1987	Bryan Fogarty	9	Kingston (OHL)		1
	Joe Sakic	15	Swift Current (WHL)		2
1988	Curtis Leschyshyn	3	Saskatoon (WHL)		2
	Daniel Dore	5	Drummondville (QMJHL)		1
1989	*Mats Sundin	1	Nacka (Sweden)		0
1990	*Owen Nolan	1	Cornwall (OHL)		0

*Designates first player chosen in draft.

PRIORITY SELECTIONS BEFORE 1979 EXPANSION DRAFT

Paul Baxter   Richard Brodeur   Garry Larivierre

Michel Goulet

COACHING HISTORY

Jacques Demers, 1979-80
Maurice Filion and Michel Bergeron, 1980-81
Michel Bergeron, 1981-82 to 1986-87
Andre Savard and Ron Lapointe, 1987-88

Ron Lapointe and Jean Perron, 1988-89
Michel Bergeron, 1989-90
Dave Chambers for 1990-91

FRANCHISE LEADERS

Current players in bold type
(1979-80 through 1989-90)

Games
1. 813—Michel Goulet
2. 737—Peter Stastny
3. 696—Alain Cote
4. 650—Anton Stastny
5. **527—Paul Gillis**
6. 523—Dale Hunter
7. 508—Randy Moller
8. 480—Normand Rochefort
9. 403—Mario Marois
10. 289—Robert Picard

Goals
1. 456—Michel Goulet
2. 380—Peter Stastny
3. 252—Anton Stastny
4. 140—Dale Hunter
5. 122—Real Cloutier
6. 116—Marc Tardif
7. 103—Alain Cote
8. 102—Wilf Paiement
9. 98—Marian Stastny
10. **84—Paul Gillis**

Assists
1. 668—Peter Stastny
2. 489—Michel Goulet
3. 384—Anton Stastny
4. 318—Dale Hunter
5. 190—Alain Cote
6. 162—Real Cloutier
    162—Mario Marois
8. 143—Marian Stastny
9. **138—Paul Gillis**
10. 128—Marc Tardif

Points
1. 1048—Peter Stastny
2. 945—Michel Goulet
3. 636—Anton Stastny
4. 450—Dale Hunter
5. 293—Alain Cote
6. 284—Real Cloutier
7. 244—Marc Tardif
8. 241—Marian Stastny
9. 223—Wilf Paiement
10. **222—Paul Gillis**

Penalty Minutes
1. 1545—Dale Hunter
2. **1260—Paul Gillis**
3. 1002—Randy Moller
4. 778—Mario Marois
5. **706—Steven Finn**
6. 687—Peter Stastny
7. 668—Gord Donnelly
8. 619—Wilf Paiement
9. 613—Michel Goulet
10. 535—Wally Weir

Goaltenders

Games
1. 225—Dan Bouchard
2. 192—Mario Gosselin
3. 140—Clint Malarchuk
4. **66—Ron Tugnutt**
5. 62—Michel Dion
6. 41—Michel Plasse
7. 40—Mario Brunetta
8. 35—Richard Sevigny

Shutouts
1. 6—Mario Gosselin
2. 5—Dan Bouchard
    5—Clint Malarchuk

Goals Against Average (entire roster)
(2400 minutes minimum)
1. 3.59—Dan Bouchard
2. 3.63—Clint Malarchuk
3. 3.67—Mario Gosselin
4. 4.02—Michel Dion
5. **4.15—Ron Tugnutt**

Wins
1. 107—Dan Bouchard
2. 79—Mario Gosselin
3. 62—Clint Malarchuk
4. **17—Ron Tugnutt**
5. 15—Michel Dion
6. 13—Richard Sevigny

Brett Hull accounted for 24 percent of St. Louis' goals last year and established a league record for goals by a right winger with 72.

Adam Oates, who set a team record with 79 assists last season, is only the fourth player in Blues history to score 100 points in a season.

Paul Cavallini has a plus-70 rating in regular-season play since joining St. Louis in December 1987.

Newcomer Jeff Brown scored 10 goals in 1989-90 with the Blues to become only the third St. Louis defenseman in the 1980s to score at least 10 goals in a season.

ST. LOUIS BLUES

CLUB DIRECTORY

Board of Directors
Michael F. Shanahan, Jerome V. LaBarbera, Bob Mohrmann, Philip McCarty, Jack J. Quinn
Advisor to Board
Lewis N. Wolff
Chairman of the Board
Michael F. Shanahan
Vice-Chairman
Jerome V. LaBarbera
President
Jack J. Quinn
Vice-President/General Manager
Ronald Caron
Vice-Present/Director of Sales
Bruce Affleck
Vice-President/Director of Player Personnel and Scouting
Ted Hampson
Vice-President/Director of Broadcast Sales
Matt Hyland
Vice-President/Director of Finance and Administration
Jerry Jasiek
Vice-President/Director of Marketing and Public Relations
Susie Mathieu
Secretary and General Counsel
Timothy R. Wolf
Assistant Director of Scouting
Jack Evans

Western Canada/U.S. Scout
Pat Ginnell
Coach
Brian Sutter
Assistant Coaches
Bob Berry, Wayne Thomas
Promotions/Community Relations
Tracy Lovasz
Assistant Director of Public Relations
Jeff Trammel
Assistant Director of Public Relations
Mike Caruso
Head Trainer
Mike Folga
Equipment Manager
Frank Burns
Home Ice
St. Louis Arena
Address
5700 Oakland Avenue, St. Louis, Missouri 63110-1397
Seating Capacity
17,188
Club Colors
Blue, Gold, Red and White
Phone
(314) 781-5300

YEAR-BY-YEAR RESULTS

Season	W.	L.	T.	Pts.	Position	Season	W.	L.	T.	Pts.	Position
1967-68	27	31	16	70	Third—c	1979-80	34	34	12	80	Second—†
1968-69	37	25	14	88	First—c	1980-81	45	18	17	107	First—a
1969-70	37	27	12	86	First—c	1981-82	32	40	8	72	Third—a
1970-71	34	25	19	87	Second—a	1982-83	25	40	15	65	Fourth—†
1971-72	28	39	11	67	Third—b	1983-84	32	41	7	71	Second—a
1972-73	32	34	12	76	Fourth—a	1984-85	37	31	12	86	First—†
1973-74	26	40	12	64	Sixth—*	1985-86	37	34	9	83	Third—b
1974-75	35	31	14	84	Second—†	1986-87	32	33	15	79	First—†
1975-76	29	37	14	72	Third—†	1987-88	34	38	8	76	Second—a
1976-77	32	39	9	73	First—a	1988-89	33	35	12	78	Second—a
1977-78	20	47	13	53	Fourth—*	1989-90	37	34	9	83	Second—a
1978-79	18	50	12	48	Third—*	Totals	733	803	282	1748	

Key to standings: *—Missed playoffs. †—Eliminated in first round of new playoff format (1974-75). a—Eliminated in quarterfinal round. b—Eliminated in semifinal round. c—Eliminated in final round. xx—Stanley Cup champion.

Red Berenson

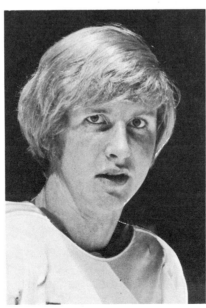

Garry Unger

1990-91 SCHEDULE

☐ Home games shaded.

* At Chicago Stadium.

OCTOBER

Sun	Mon	Tue	Wed	Thu	Fri	Sat
	1	2	3	4 MIN	5	6 CHI
7	8	9 PIT	10	11	12 VAN	13
14 LA	15	16 EDM	17	18 CAL	19	20 MIN
21	22	23	24 TOR	25 TOR	26	27 MON
28	29	30 DET	31			

NOVEMBER

Sun	Mon	Tue	Wed	Thu	Fri	Sat
				1 BOS	2	3 HAR
4	5	6 EDM	7	8 PIT	9	10 DET
11	12	13 QUE	14	15	16	17 MIN
18 WIN	19	20 WIN	21	22	23 DET	24 VAN
25	26	27 TOR	28	29 LA	30	

DECEMBER

Sun	Mon	Tue	Wed	Thu	Fri	Sat
						1 NJ
2 CHI	3	4	5	6	7 DET	8 DET
9	10	11 WIN	12	13 MIN	14	15 TOR
16 BUF	17	18	19	20 WAS	21	22 CHI
23	24	25	26 CHI	27 TOR	28	29 PHI
30	31 PIT					

JANUARY

Sun	Mon	Tue	Wed	Thu	Fri	Sat
		1	2	3 QUE	4	5 NYR
6	7	8 NJ	9 NYR	10	11	12 QUE
13 MON	14	15 WAS	16	17 MON	18	19 ALL-STAR GAME*
20	21	22 MIN	23	24	25 DET	26 DET
27	28	29 BUF	30	31 HAR		

FEBRUARY

Sun	Mon	Tue	Wed	Thu	Fri	Sat
					1	2 NJ
3	4 TOR	5	6 BUF	7	8	9 LA
10	11	12 EDM	13	14 VAN	15	16
17 CAL	18	19 TOR	20	21 NYI	22	23 BOS
24 CHI	25	26 CHI	27	28 NYR		

MARCH

Sun	Mon	Tue	Wed	Thu	Fri	Sat
					1	2 PHI
3	4	5 HAR	6	7 BOS	8	9 CAL
10 DET	11	12	13	14 MIN	15	16 CHI
17 CHI	18	19 WAS	20	21 PHI	22	23 NYI
24	25 MIN	26	27	28 NYI	29	30 TOR
31 MIN						

1989-90 RESULTS

Oct.	5—At Chicago	W	8-3
	7—Toronto	L	5-8
	12—At Minnesota	L	0-3
	14—Chicago	W	2-1
	18—At Pittsburgh	W	9-3
	19—Detroit	L	3-4
	21—Los Angeles	L	4-6
	24—At Philadelphia	L	1-6
	26—Minnesota	W	4-1
	28—Washington	W	1-0
	31—At Washington	T	1-1 (OT)
Nov.	1—At Hartford	W	5-3
	4—At Quebec	W	5-2
	6—At Montreal	T	3-3 (OT)
	9—Montreal	T	1-1 (OT)
	11—Pittsburgh	W	8-3
	15—At Toronto	L	2-5
	16—At Detroit	W	7-2
	18—At Minnesota	L	0-3
	21—Minnesota	W	7-4
	23—At Winnipeg	W	5-2
	25—Calgary	T	3-3 (OT)
	28—Boston	L	1-5
	30—Hartford	L	3-5
Dec.	2—At Boston	W	2-1
	3—At Buffalo	L	3-4
	5—At Detroit	T	2-2 (OT)
	7—Toronto	L	2-5
	9—Vancouver	W	6-4
	11—At Toronto	L	1-3
	13—At N.Y. Rangers	W	3-1
	16—Edmonton	T	3-3 (OT)
	18—At Toronto	L	3-6
	20—At Chicago	L	6-9
	23—At New Jersey	L	2-3
	26—Chicago	W	8-3
	28—At N.Y. Islanders	L	2-3
	30—Minnesota	W	3-2
	31—At Minnesota	L	1-2 (OT)
Jan.	2—Edmonton	L	4-6
	4—Philadelphia	W	5-4 (OT)
	6—N.Y. Rangers	W	4-3
	9—At Los Angeles	W	4-3
	12—At Vancouver	W	5-2
	14—At Winnipeg	L	5-6
	16—Calgary	L	2-5
	18—Toronto	L	1-4
	23—At Detroit	W	6-3
	25—Hartford	W	3-2
	27—Winnipeg	T	3-3 (OT)
	30—At N.Y. Islanders	W	2-1
	31—At N.Y. Rangers	T	2-2 (OT)
Feb.	3—Detroit	W	4-2
	6—Toronto	W	6-4
	7—At Toronto	L	1-7
	10—New Jersey	W	7-0
	11—Buffalo	W	4-2
	13—At Minnesota	W	2-1 (OT)
	15—Quebec	W	9-2
	17—Detroit	W	6-1
	20—Chicago	L	3-8
	22—Philadelphia	L	4-7
	24—At Quebec	W	6-1
	25—At Montreal	L	5-6 (OT)
	27—Buffalo	W	4-1
Mar.	1—At Chicago	W	6-4
	3—N.Y. Islanders	W	5-4
	6—At New Jersey	L	1-2
	8—At Detroit	L	2-3
	10—Chicago	T	2-2 (OT)
	11—At Chicago	W	6-4
	13—At Washington	W	4-1
	15—Vancouver	L	5-6 (OT)
	17—Detroit	L	3-4 (OT)
	19—At Calgary	L	2-5
	21—At Edmonton	L	6-8
	24—At Los Angeles	L	3-9
	27—Boston	L	0-3
	29—Pittsburgh	W	5-4
	31—Minnesota	L	3-6

1990-91 ROSTER

No.	FORWARDS	Hgt./Wt.	Place of Birth	Age	NHL exp.	1989-90 club (league)	G.	A.	Pts.
19	Rod Brind'Amour	6-01/202	Ottawa, Ont.	20	2	St. Louis (NHL)	26	35	61
17	Gino Cavallini	6-01/218	Toronto, Ont.	27	6	St. Louis (NHL)	15	15	30
39	Kelly Chase	5-11/192	Porcupine, Sask.	22	1	Peoria (IHL)	1	2	3
						St. Louis (NHL)	1	3	4
	Geoff Courtnall	6-01/190	Victoria, B.C.	28	7	Washington (NHL)	35	39	74
	Nelson Emerson	5-11/174	Hamilton, Ont.	23	0	Bowling Green U. (CCHA)	30	52	82
						Peoria (IHL)	1	1	2
16	Brett Hull	5-10/201	Belleville, Ont.	26	5	St. Louis (NHL)	72	41	113
10	Dave Lowry	6-01/191	Sudbury, Ont.	25	5	St. Louis (NHL)	19	6	25
15	Paul MacLean	6-02/218	Gronstenquin, France	32	10	St. Louis (NHL)	34	33	67
22	Rick Meagher	5-08/172	Belleville, Ont.	36	11	St. Louis (NHL)	8	17	25
27	Sergio Momesso	6-03/218	Montreal, Que.	25	6	St. Louis (NHL)	24	32	56
41	Michel Mongeau	5-09/188	Nun's Island, Que.	25	0	Peoria (IHL)	39	78	117
						St. Louis (NHL)	1	5	6
12	Adam Oates	5-11/189	Weston, Ont.	28	5	St. Louis (NHL)	23	79	102
28	Keith Osborne	6-01/188	Toronto, Ont.	21	1	Peoria (IHL)	23	24	47
						St. Louis (NHL)	0	2	2
25	Herb Raglan	6-00/200	Peterborough, Ont.	23	5	St. Louis (NHL)	0	1	1
7	Cliff Ronning	5-08/175	Vancouver, B.C.	25	4	Italy	74	60	134
23	Rich Sutter	5-11/165	Viking, Alta.	26	8	Vancouver (NHL)	9	9	18
						St. Louis (NHL)	2	0	2
40	Dave Thomlinson	6-01/196	Edmonton, Alta.	23	1	Peoria (IHL)	27	40	67
						St. Louis (NHL)	1	2	3
35	Steve Tuttle	6-01/193	Vancouver, B.C.	24	2	St. Louis (NHL)	12	10	22
33	Jim Vesey	6-01/202	Columbus, Mass.	24	2	Peoria (IHL)	47	44	91
						St. Louis (NHL)	0	1	1
18	Ron Wilson	5-09/180	Toronto, Ont.	34	10	Moncton	16	37	53
						St. Louis (NHL)	3	17	20
	DEFENSEMEN								
21	Jeff Brown	6-01/204	Ottawa, Ont.	24	5	Quebec (NHL)	6	10	16
						St. Louis (NHL)	10	28	38
14	Paul Cavallini	6-01/210	Toronto, Ont.	24	4	St. Louis (NHL)	8	39	47
	Rick Corriveau	5-11/205	Welland, Ont.	19	0	London (OHL)	22	55	77
37	Robert Dirk	6-04/210	Regina, Sask.	24	3	Peoria (IHL)	1	2	3
						St. Louis (NHL)	1	1	2
36	Glen Featherstone	6-04/216	Toronto, Ont.	22	2	Peoria (IHL)	1	4	5
						St. Louis (NHL)	0	12	12
38	Dominic Lavoie	6-02/199	Montreal, Que.	22	2	Peoria (IHL)	19	23	42
						St. Louis (NHL)	1	1	2
	Rob Robinson	6-01/214	St. Catharines, Ont.	23	0	Peoria (IHL)	2	11	13
34	Randy Skarda	6-01/205	St. Paul, Minn.	22	1	St. Louis (NHL)	0	5	5
						Peoria (IHL)	7	17	24
5	Harold Snepsts	6-03/210	Edmonton, Alta.	35	16	Vancouver (NHL)	1	3	4
						St. Louis (NHL)	0	1	1
	Scott Stevens	6-02/215	Kitchener, Ont.	26	8	Washington (NHL)	11	29	40
20	Tom Tilley	6-00/189	Trenton, Ont.	25	2	St. Louis (NHL)	0	5	5
						Peoria (IHL)	1	8	9
6	Tony Twist	6-00/212	Sherwood Park, Alta.	22	1	St. Louis (NHL)	0	0	0
						Peoria (IHL)	1	5	6

No.	GOALTENDERS	Hgt./Wt.	Place of Birth	Age	NHL exp.	1989-90 club (league)	Ga.	SO	Avg.
	Guy Hebert	5-11/180	Troy, N.Y.	23	0	Peoria (IHL)	30	1	4.36
1	Pat Jablonski	6-00/178	Toledo, O.	23	1	Peoria (IHL)	36	0	4.85
						St. Louis (NHL)	4	0	4.90
31	Curtis Joseph	5-10/182	Keswick, Ont.	23	1	Peoria (IHL)	23	0	3.87
						St. Louis (NHL)	15	0	3.38
30	Vincent Riendeau	5-10/181	St. Hyacinthe, Que.	24	3	St. Louis (NHL)	43	1	3.50

1989-90 RECORDS

1989-90 regular-season records: 37-34-9 (.519, 83 points, 2nd in Norris Division); 20-15-5 at home; 17-19-4 on road; 2-4-9 in overtime; 14-16-2 vs. Norris (5-2-1 vs. Blackhawks; 4-3-1 vs. Red Wings; 4-4-0 vs. North Stars; 1-7-0 vs. Maple Leafs); 4-8-3 vs. Smythe; 8-5-2 vs. Adams; 11-5-2 vs. Patrick.

MISCELLANEOUS DATA

1989-90 team rankings: Shorthanded goals for, 9 (T13th in NHL); shorthanded goals against, 12 (T12th); power play, 22.5% (7th); penalty killing, 80.9% (7th); penalty minutes/game, 22.6.

TEAM HAT TRICKS, CAREER, ACTIVE

Gino Cavallini (1)	Rick Meagher (2)
Geoff Courtnall (2)	Sergio Momesso (1)
Brett Hull (6)	Cliff Ronning (1)
Paul MacLean (8)	Rich Sutter (1)

MINOR LEAGUE AFFILIATIONS

Peoria (IHL)

Geoff Courtnall

70

1990 DRAFT SELECTIONS

Rnd.	Player	Hgt.	Wgt.	Overall	(Pos.)	1989-90 Club	(League)
2—	Craig Johnson	6:02	185	33	(LW)	Hill-Murray H.S.	(Minn.)
3—	Patrice Tardif	6:02	175	54	(C)	Champlain (Ont.) JC	
5—	Jason Ruff	6:02	192	96	(LW)	Lethbridge	(WHL)
6—	Kurtis Miller	5:11	180	117	(LW)	Rochester Jr. A	(Minn.)
7—	Wayne Conlan	5:10	170	138	(C)	Trinity-Pawling H.S.	(N.Y.)
9—	Parris Duffus	6:02	192	180	(G)	Melfort Tier II	(Sask.)
10—	Steve Widmeyer	6:02	200	201	(RW)	University of Maine	
11—	Joe Hawley	5:10	186	222	(RW)	Peterborough	(OHL)
12—	Joe Fleming	6:04	220	243	(D)	Xaverian Brothers H.S.	(Mass.)

FIRST-ROUND ENTRY DRAFT SELECTIONS

Year	Name	Overall	Last Amateur Team	(League)	Years in NHL
1969—	No first round selection				
1970—	No first round selection				
1971—	Gene Carr	4	Flin Flon	(WCHL)	8
1972—	Wayne Merrick	9	Ottawa	(OHL)	12
1973—	John Davidson	5	Calgary	(WCHL)	10
1974—	No first round selection				
1975—	No first round selection				
1976—	Bernie Federko	7	Saskatoon	(WCHL)	14
1977—	Scott Campbell	9	London	(OHL)	3
1978—	Wayne Babych	3	Portland	(WCHL)	9
1979—	Perry Turnbull	2	Portland	(WHL)	9
1980—	Rik Wilson	12	Kingston	(OHL)	6
1981—	Marty Ruff	20	Lethbridge	(WHL)	0
1982—	No first round selection				
1983—	No first round selection				
1984—	No first round selection				
1985—	No first round selection				
1986—	Jocelyn Lemieux	10	Laval	(QMJHL)	4
1987—	Keith Osborne	12	North Bay	(OHL)	1
1988—	Rod Brind'Amour	9	Notre Dame Academy	(Sask.)	1
1989—	Jason Marshall	9	Vernon (B.C.) Tier II		0
1990—	No first round selection				

Bernie Federko

COACHING HISTORY

Lynn Patrick and Scotty Bowman, 1967-68
Scotty Bowman, 1968-69 to 1969-70
Al Arbour and Scotty Bowman, 1970-71
Sid Abel, Bill McCreary and Al Arbour, 1971-72
Al Arbour and Jean-Guy Talbot, 1972-73
Jean-Guy Talbot and Lou Angotti, 1973-74
Lou Angotti, Lynn Patrick and Garry Young, 1974-75
Garry Young, Lynn Patrick and Leo Boivin, 1975-76
Emile Francis, 1976-77

Leo Boivin and Barclay Plager, 1977-78
Barclay Plager, 1978-79
Barclay Plager and Red Berenson, 1979-80
Red Berenson, 1980-81
Red Berenson and Emile Francis, 1981-82
Emile Francis and Barclay Plager, 1982-83
Jacques Demers, 1983-84 to 1985-86
Jacques Martin, 1986-87 to 1987-88
Brian Sutter since 1988-89

FRANCHISE LEADERS

Current players in bold type
(1967-68 through 1989-90)

Games
1. 927—Bernie Federko
2. 779—Brian Sutter
3. 662—Garry Unger
4. 615—Bob Plager
5. 614—Barclay Plager
6. 603—Larry Patey
7. 519—Red Berenson
8. 463—Gary Sabourin
9. 455—Jack Brownschidle
10. 441—Rob Ramage

Goals
1. 352—Bernie Federko
2. 303—Brian Sutter
3. 292—Garry Unger
4. 172—Red Berenson
5. 161—Jorgen Pettersson
6. 155—Wayne Babych
7. 151—Joe Mullen
8. 149—Doug Gilmour
9. 139—Perry Turnbull
10. 136—Gary Sabourin

Assists
1. 721—Bernie Federko
2. 334—Brian Sutter
3. 283—Garry Unger
4. 240—Red Berenson
5. 229—Rob Ramage
6. 205—Doug Gilmour
7. 201—Blake Dunlop
8. 190—Wayne Babych
9. 187—Barclay Plager
10. 184—Joe Mullen

Points
1. 1073—Bernie Federko
2. 636—Brian Sutter
3. 575—Garry Unger
4. 412—Red Berenson
5. 354—Doug Gilmour
6. 345—Wayne Babych
7. 335—Joe Mullen
8. 332—Jorgen Pettersson
9. 296—Rob Ramage
10. 287—Blake Dunlop

Penalty Minutes
1. 1786—Brian Sutter
2. 1115—Barclay Plager
3. 998—Rob Ramage
4. 866—Bob Gassoff
5. 829—Perry Turnbull

Goaltenders
Games
1. 347—Mike Liut
2. 209—Greg Millen
3. 154—Rick Wamsley
4. 140—Glenn Hall
5. 137—Ed Staniowski
6. 111—Ernie Wakely
7. 108—Eddie Johnston

Shutouts
1. 16—Glenn Hall
2. 10—Mike Liut
   10—Jacques Plante
4. 8—Greg Millen
   8—Ernie Wakely

Goals Against Average
(2400 minutes minimum)
1. 2.07—Jacques Plante
2. 2.43—Glenn Hall
3. 2.77—Ernie Wakely
4. 3.02—Jacques Caron
5. 3.12—Wayne Stephenson
6. 3.36—Eddie Johnston
7. 3.37—John Davidson
8. 3.41—Rick Wamsley
9. 3.43—Greg Millen
10. **3.51—Vincent Riendeau**

Wins
1. 151—Mike Liut
2. 85—Greg Millen
3. 75—Rick Wamsley
4. 58—Glenn Hall
5. 41—Eddie Johnston

Vincent Damphousse's 61 assists last year was the third-highest total in Toronto history.

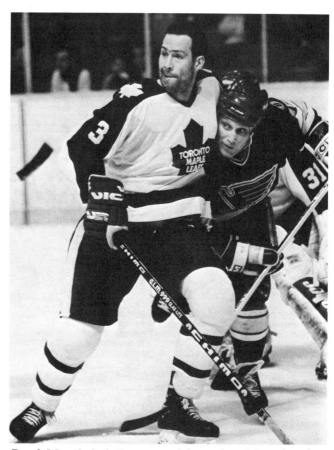

Brad Marsh led Toronto with a plus-14 rating last year.

Gary Leeman scored 51 goals last year to become only the second Toronto player to score 50 goals in one season. Former Leaf Rick Vaive did it three times.

Newcomers Tom Kurvers (above) and Lou Franceschetti combined to score 36 goals for Toronto last season. The Maple Leafs scored a league-leading 78 more goals in 1989-90 than they had the previous year.

TORONTO MAPLE LEAFS

CLUB DIRECTORY

President, Governor and C.E.O.
  Donald P. Giffin
General Manager
  Floyd Smith
Coach
  Doug Carpenter
Assistant Coaches
  Tom Watt, Mike Kitchen
Director of Scouting
  Pierre Dorion
Scouts
  Dick Duff, Jack Gardiner, Jim Bzdel, Bob Johnson,
  Doug Woods, George Armstrong, Dan Marr
Director of Business Operations & Communications
  Bob Stellick
Public Relations Coordinator
  Pat Park
Public Relations Assistant
  Mark Hillier

Box Office Manager
  I.M. 'Patty' Patoff
Athletic Therapist
  Chris Broadhurst
Trainers
  Dan Lemelin, Brian Papineau, Brent Smith
Home Ice
  Maple Leaf Gardens
Address
  60 Carlton Street, Toronto, Ont. M5B 1L1
Seating Capacity
  16,382 (including standees)
Club Colors
  Blue and White
Phone
  (416) 977-1641
FAX
  (416) 977-5364

YEAR-BY-YEAR RESULTS

Season	W.	L.	T.	Pts.	Position
1917-18	13	9	0	26	Second, First
1918-19	5	13	0	10	Third
1919-20	12	12	0	24	Third
1920-21	15	9	0	30	First
1921-22	13	10	1	27	Second—xx
1922-23	13	10	1	27	Third
1923-24	10	14	0	20	Third
1924-25	19	11	0	38	Second
1925-26	12	21	3	27	Sixth
1926-27	15	24	5	35	Fifth—*
1927-28	18	18	8	44	Fourth—*
1928-29	21	18	5	47	Third—b
1929-30	17	21	6	40	Fourth—*
1930-31	22	13	9	53	Second—a
1931-32	23	18	7	53	Second—xx
1932-33	24	18	6	54	First—c
1933-34	26	13	9	61	First—b
1934-35	30	14	4	64	First—c
1935-36	23	19	6	52	Second—c
1936-37	22	21	5	49	Third—a
1937-38	24	15	9	57	First—c
1938-39	19	20	9	47	Third—c
1939-40	25	17	6	56	Third—c
1940-41	28	14	6	62	Second—b
1941-42	27	18	3	57	Second—xx
1942-43	22	19	9	53	Third—b
1943-44	23	23	4	50	Third—b
1944-45	24	22	4	52	Third—xx
1945-46	19	24	7	45	Fifth—*
1946-47	31	19	10	72	Second—xx
1947-48	32	15	13	77	First—xx
1948-49	22	25	13	57	Fourth—xx
1949-50	31	27	12	74	Third—b
1950-51	41	16	13	95	Second—xx
1951-52	29	25	16	74	Third—b
1952-53	27	30	13	67	Fifth—*
1953-54	32	24	14	78	Third—b

Season	W.	L.	T.	Pts.	Position
1954-55	24	24	22	70	Third—b
1955-56	24	33	13	61	Fourth—b
1956-57	21	34	15	57	Fifth—*
1957-58	21	38	11	53	Sixth—*
1958-59	27	32	11	65	Fourth—c
1959-60	35	26	9	79	Second—c
1960-61	39	19	12	90	Second—b
1961-62	37	22	11	85	Second—xx
1962-63	35	23	12	82	First—xx
1963-64	33	25	12	78	Third—xx
1964-65	30	26	14	74	Fourth—b
1965-66	34	25	11	79	Third—b
1966-67	32	27	11	75	Third—xx
1967-68	33	31	10	76	Fifth—*
1968-69	35	26	15	85	Fourth—a
1969-70	29	34	13	71	Sixth—*
1970-71	37	33	8	82	Fourth—a
1971-72	33	31	14	80	Fourth—a
1972-73	27	41	10	64	Sixth—*
1973-74	35	27	16	86	Fourth—a
1974-75	31	33	16	78	Third—a
1975-76	34	31	15	83	Third—b
1976-77	33	32	15	81	Third—a
1977-78	41	29	10	92	Third—b
1978-79	34	33	13	81	Third—a
1979-80	35	40	5	75	Fourth—†
1980-81	28	37	15	71	Fifth—†
1981-82	20	44	16	56	Fifth—*
1982-83	28	40	12	68	Third—†
1983-84	26	45	9	61	Fifth—*
1984-85	20	52	8	48	Fifth—*
1985-86	25	48	7	57	Fourth—a
1986-87	32	42	6	70	Fourth—a
1987-88	21	49	10	52	Fourth—†
1988-89	28	46	6	62	Fifth—*
1989-90	38	38	4	80	Third—†
Totals	**1904**	**1875**	**653**	**4461**	

From 1917-18 through the 1925-26 season, National Hockey League champions played against the Pacific Coast Hockey League for the Stanley Cup. So, only Stanley Cup championships are designated in the following club records for that period.

Key to standings: *—Missed playoffs. †—Eliminated in first round of new playoff format (1974-75). a—Eliminated in quarterfinal round. b—Eliminated in semifinal round. c—Eliminated in final round. xx—Stanley Cup champion.

—DID YOU KNOW—

That the Maple Leafs' 38-38-4 record in 1989-90 was their first non-losing record since they finished 34-33-13 in 1978-79?

1990-91 SCHEDULE

Home games shaded.

* At Chicago Stadium.

OCTOBER

Sun	Mon	Tue	Wed	Thu	Fri	Sat
	1	2	3	4 WIN	5	6 CAL
7 EDM	8	9	10 QUE	11	12	13 DET
14	15	16	17 HAR	18 CHI	19	20 CHI
21	22 NYR	23	24 STL	25 STL	26	27 BUF
28	29	30 MIN	31			

NOVEMBER

Sun	Mon	Tue	Wed	Thu	Fri	Sat
				1 DET	2	3 CAL
4 PHI	5	6 NYI	7	8 VAN	9	10 CHI
11	12 WIN	13	14 WAS	15	16 DET	17 DET
18	19 BOS	20	21 WAS	22	23 PHI	24 EDM
25	26	27 STL	28	29 VAN	30	

DECEMBER

Sun	Mon	Tue	Wed	Thu	Fri	Sat
						1 LA
2	3	4	5 MIN	6 MIN	7	8 CHI
9	10	11	12 MON	13	14	15 STL
16	17	18 NYI	19 NYR	20	21	22 WAS
23 NJ	24	25	26	27 STL	28	29 PIT
30	31					

JANUARY

Sun	Mon	Tue	Wed	Thu	Fri	Sat
		1	2	3 MIN	4	5 LA
6	7	8 CAL	9	10 CHI	11	12 HAR
13	14 BUF	15	16	17 PIT	18	19 ALL-STAR GAME*
20	21	22 QUE	23 MON	24	25	26 CHI
27	28 MIN	29	30	31		

FEBRUARY

Sun	Mon	Tue	Wed	Thu	Fri	Sat
					1 DET	2 DET
3	4 STL	5	6 WIN	7 MIN	8	9 NYI
10	11	12	13 PHI	14	15	16 EDM
17 BUF	18	19 STL	20	21 PIT	22	23 MON
24	25	26	27 NJ	28		

MARCH

Sun	Mon	Tue	Wed	Thu	Fri	Sat
					1	2 NYR
3 HAR	4	5 BOS	6	7 VAN	8	9 BOS
10	11	12 QUE	13 NJ	14	15	16 MIN
17 MIN	18	19	20 LA	21	22 DET	23 DET
24	25	26 CHI	27	28 CHI	29	30 STL
31						

1989-90 RESULTS

Oct.	5—At Los Angeles	L	2-4
	7—At St. Louis	W	8-5
	11—Buffalo	L	1-7
	12—At Chicago	L	6-9
	14—Winnipeg	L	1-5
	17—At Pittsburgh	L	5-7
	18—Vancouver	W	4-3
	21—Washington	W	8-4
	23—New Jersey	L	4-5
	25—At Pittsburgh	W	8-6
	27—At Buffalo	L	5-6 (OT)
	28—Detroit	W	6-4
	31—At Minnesota	W	6-4
Nov.	3—At Washington	L	1-2
	4—Philadelphia	L	4-7
	6—Minnesota	W	2-1
	9—At Philadelphia	W	4-1
	11—Detroit	W	4-2
	12—At Minnesota	L	3-6
	15—St. Louis	W	5-2
	16—At N.Y. Islanders	L	2-6
	18—At Montreal	L	3-4 (OT)
	22—At Minnesota	L	3-6
	23—At Boston	L	0-6
	25—N.Y. Rangers	W	7-4
	29—At Vancouver	W	3-2 (OT)
Dec.	2—At Calgary	L	4-7
	3—At Edmonton	L	3-5
	6—At Chicago	L	4-6
	7—At St. Louis	W	5-2
	9—Montreal	W	7-4
	11—St. Louis	W	3-1
	13—At Detroit	W	4-2
	16—Minnesota	L	3-4
	18—St. Louis	W	6-3
	20—At Detroit	L	2-4
	22—At Chicago	W	5-3
	23—Chicago	L	5-7
	26—At Boston	L	4-6
	27—Detroit	T	7-7 (OT)
	30—Boston	W	7-6 (OT)
Jan.	3—Quebec	W	5-4
	6—Los Angeles	W	7-4
	8—Washington	W	8-6
	10—N.Y. Islanders	L	1-3
	13—Calgary	W	6-5
	15—Chicago	W	7-6
	18—At St. Louis	W	4-1
	24—Minnesota	W	7-3
	26—At New Jersey	W	5-1
	27—Montreal	L	3-5
	31—At Winnipeg	T	5-5 (OT)
Feb.	2—At Detroit	L	2-5
	3—Pittsburgh	W	8-4
	6—At St. Louis	L	4-6
	7—St. Louis	W	7-1
	10—At Hartford	L	2-6
	12—Los Angeles	W	5-3
	14—Hartford	T	6-6 (OT)
	15—At Philadelphia	L	0-3
	17—New Jersey	W	5-4
	22—At Calgary	L	2-12
	23—At Edmonton	W	6-5
	26—At Vancouver	L	2-5
	28—Quebec	W	5-4
Mar.	2—At Detroit	L	2-3 (OT)
	3—Detroit	L	4-5
	8—At Hartford	W	7-6
	10—Edmonton	W	3-2
	12—Minnesota	L	1-4
	14—N.Y. Rangers	L	2-8
	16—At Buffalo	W	4-3
	17—Winnipeg	L	4-5 (OT)
	19—Chicago	L	2-3
	21—At N.Y. Rangers	T	5-5 (OT)
	24—At Quebec	W	4-3 (OT)
	26—At Minnesota	L	3-6
	28—N.Y. Islanders	L	3-6
	29—At Chicago	L	2-4
	31—Chicago	W	6-4

1990-91 ROSTER

No.	FORWARDS	Hgt./Wt.	Place of Birth	Age	NHL exp.	1989-90 club (league)	G.	A.	Pts.
17	Wendel Clark	5-11/194	Kelvington, Sask.	23	5	Toronto (NHL)	18	8	26
10	Vincent Damphousse	6-01/190	Montreal, Que.	22	4	Toronto (NHL)	33	61	94
19	Tom Fergus	6-03/210	Chicago, Ill.	28	9	Toronto (NHL)	19	26	45
15	Lou Franceschetti	6-00/190	Toronto, Ont.	32	9	Toronto (NHL)	21	15	36
9	David Hannan	5-10/185	Sudbury, Ont.	28	9	Toronto (NHL)	6	9	15
	Greg Johnston	6-01/190	Barrie, Ont.	25	6	Boston (NHL)	1	1	2
						Maine (AHL)	16	26	42
27	John Kordic	6-01/190	Edmonton, Alta.	25	5	Toronto (NHL)	9	4	13
11	Gary Leeman	5-11/180	Toronto, Ont.	26	7	Toronto (NHL)	51	44	95
	Kevin Maguire	6-02/200	Toronto, Ont.	27	4	Buffalo (NHL)	6	9	15
						Philadelphia (NHL)	1	0	1
32	Daniel Marois	6-01/190	Montreal, Que.	21	2	Toronto (NHL)	39	37	76
44	John McIntyre	6-01/175	Ravenswood, Ont.	21	1	Toronto (NHL)	5	12	17
						Newmarket (AHL)	2	2	4
16	Ed Olczyk	6-01/200	Chicago, Ill.	24	6	Toronto (NHL)	32	56	88
12	Mark Osborne	6-02/205	Toronto, Ont.	29	9	Toronto (NHL)	23	50	73
	Rob Pearson	6-01/173	Oshawa, Ont.	19	0	Belleville (OHL)	48	40	88
22	Scott Pearson	6-01/203	Cornwall, Ont.	20	2	Toronto (NHL)	5	10	15
						Newmarket (AHL)	12	11	23
14	Dave Reid	6-00/205	Toronto, Ont.	26	7	Toronto (NHL)	9	19	28
20	Bobby Reynolds	5-11/175	Flint, Mich.	23	1	Newmarket (AHL)	22	28	50
						Toronto (NHL)	1	1	2
	Joe Sacco	6-01/180	Medford, Mass.	21	0	Boston U. (Hockey East)	28	24	52
26	Mike Stevens	5-11/195	Kitchener, Ont.	24	4	Newmarket (AHL)	16	28	44
						Toronto (NHL)	0	0	0
7	Gilles Thibaudeau	5-10/170	Montreal, Que.	27	4	N.Y. Islanders (NHL)	4	4	8
						Springfield (AHL)	5	8	13
						Newmarket (AHL)	7	13	20
						Toronto (NHL)	7	11	18
	Scott Thornton	6-02/200	London, Ont.	19	0	Belleville (OHL)	21	28	49
	DEFENSEMEN								
	Steve Bancroft	6-01/214	Toronto, Ont.	19	0	Belleville (OHL)	10	33	43
	Drake Berehowsky	6-01/211	Toronto, Ont.	18	0	Kingston (OHL)	3	11	14
28	Brian Curran	6-05/215	Toronto, Ont.	26	7	Toronto (NHL)	2	9	11
23	Todd Gill	6-01/185	Brockville, Ont.	24	6	Toronto (NHL)	1	14	15
33	Al Iafrate	6-03/215	Dearborn, Mich.	24	6	Toronto (NHL)	21	42	63
25	Tom Kurvers	6-02/195	Minneapolis, Minn.	28	6	New Jersey (NHL)	0	0	0
						Toronto (NHL)	15	37	52
3	Brad Marsh	6-03/220	London, Ont.	32	12	Toronto (NHL)	1	13	14
8	Rob Ramage	6-02/195	Byron, Ont.	31	11	Toronto (NHL)	8	41	49
2	Luke Richardson	6-04/210	Ottawa, Ont.	21	3	Toronto (NHL)	4	14	18
4	Darryl Shannon	6-02/190	Barrie, Ont.	22	2	Newmarket (AHL)	4	15	19
						Toronto (NHL)	0	1	1
	Darren Veitch	6-01/180	Saskatoon, Sask.	30	9	Newmarket (AHL)	13	54	67

	GOALTENDERS						Ga.	SO	Avg.
30	Allan Bester	5-07/150	Hamilton, Ont.	26	7	Toronto (NHL)	42	0	4.49
						Newmarket (AHL)	5	0	4.09
31	Peter Ing	6-02/165	Toronto, Ont.	21	1	Newmarket (AHL)	48	1	3.90
						Toronto (NHL)	3	0	5.93
35	Jeff Reese	5-09/170	Brantford, Ont.	24	3	Toronto (NHL)	21	0	4.41
						Newmarket (AHL)	7	0	4.04

1989-90 RECORDS

1989-90 regular-season records: 38-38-4 (.500, 80 points, 3rd in Norris Division); 24-14-2 at home; 14-24-2 on road; 3-4-4 in overtime; 16-15-1 vs. Norris (3-5-0 vs. Blackhawks; 3-4-1 vs. Red Wings; 3-5-0 vs. North Stars; 7-1-0 vs. Blues); 7-7-1 vs. Smythe; 7-7-1 vs. Adams; 8-9-1 vs. Patrick.

MISCELLANEOUS DATA

1989-90 team rankings: Shorthanded goals for, 16 (3rd in NHL); shorthanded goals against, 17 (20th); power play, 23.3% (T4th); penalty killing, 78.2% (15th); penalty minutes/game, 30.2.

TEAM HAT TRICKS, CAREER, ACTIVE

Wendel Clark (3)	Gary Leeman (4)
Vincent Damphousse (3)	Daniel Marois (3)
Dan Daoust (1)	Sean McKenna (1)
Tom Fergus (4)	Ed Olczyk (2)
Dave Hannan (1)	Mark Osborne (1)
Peter Ihnacak (1)	Doug Shedden (2)
Paul Lawless (1)	

MINOR LEAGUE AFFILIATIONS

Newmarket (AHL)

Ed Olczyk

1990 DRAFT SELECTIONS

Rnd.	Player	Hgt.	Wgt.	Overall	(Pos.)	1989-90 Club	(League)
1	Drake Berehowsky	6:01	211	10	(D)	Kingston (OHL)	
2	Felix Potvin	6:01	181	31	(G)	Chicoutimi (QMJHL)	
4	Darby Hendrickson	6:00	174	73	(C)	Richfield H.S. (Minn.)	
4	Greg Walters	6:01	195	80	(C)	Ottawa (OHL)	
6	Alexander Godynyuk	6:00	207	115	(D)	Sokol Kiev, USSR	
7	Eric Lacroix	6:01	200	136	(LW)	Governor Dummer H.S. (Mass.)	
8	Dan Stiver	6:00	185	157	(RW)	University of Michigan	
9	Robert Horyna	5:11	183	178	(G)	Dukla Jihlava, Czech.	
10	Rob Chebator	6:00	170	199	(D)	Arlington H.S. (Mass.)	
11	Scott Malone	6:00	180	220	(D)	Northfield-Mt. Hermon H.S. (Mass.)	
12	Nick Vachon	5:10	190	241	(C)	Governor Dummer H.S. (Mass.)	

FIRST-ROUND ENTRY DRAFT SELECTIONS

Year Name	Overall	Last Amateur Team (League)	Years in NHL
1969—Ernie Moser	9	Estevan (WCHL)	0
1970—Darryl Sittler	8	London (OHL)	15
1971—No first round selection			
1972—George Ferguson	11	Toronto (OHL)	12
1973—Lanny McDonald	4	Medicine Hat (WCHL)	16
Bob Neely	10	Peterborough (OHL)	5
Ian Turnbull	15	Ottawa (OHL)	10
1974—Jack Valiquette	13	Sault Ste. Marie (OHL)	7
1975—Don Ashby	6	Calgary (WCHL)	3
1976—No first round selection			
1977—John Anderson	11	Toronto (OHA)	12
Trevor Johansen	12	Toronto (OHA)	5
1978—No first round selection			
1979—Laurie Boschman	9	Brandon (WHL)	11
1980—No first round selection			
1981—Jim Benning	6	Portland (WHL)	9
1982—Gary Nylund	3	Portland (WHL)	8
1983—Russ Courtnall	7	Victoria (WHL)	7
1984—Al Iafrate	4	U.S. Olympics/Belleville (OHL)	6
1985—*Wendel Clark	1	Saskatoon (WHL)	5
1986—Vincent Damphousse	6	Laval (QMJHL)	4
1987—Luke Richardson	7	Peterborough (OHL)	3
1988—Scott Pearson	6	Kingston (OHL)	2
1989—Scott Thornton	3	Belleville (OHL)	0
Rob Pearson	12	Belleville (OHL)	0
Steve Bancroft	21	Belleville (OHL)	0
1990—Drake Berehowsky	10	Kingston (OHL)	0

*Designates first player chosen in draft.

Darryl Sittler

COACHING HISTORY

Alex Romeril and Conn Smythe, 1927-28 to 1929-30
Conn Smythe and Art Duncan, 1930-31
Art Duncan and Dick Irvin, 1931-32
Dick Irvin, 1932-33 to 1939-40
Hap Day, 1940-41 to 1949-50
Joe Primeau, 1950-51 to 1952-53
King Clancy, 1953-54 to 1955-56
Howie Meeker, 1956-57
Billy Reay, 1957-58
Billy Reay and Punch Imlach, 1958-59
Punch Imlach, 1959-60 to 1968-69

John McLellan, 1969-70 to 1972-73
Red Kelly, 1973-74 to 1976-77
Roger Neilson, 1977-78 to 1978-79
Floyd Smith, 1979-80
Punch Imlach and Joe Crozier, 1980-81
Mike Nykoluk, 1981-82 to 1983-84
Dan Maloney, 1984-85 to 1985-86
John Brophy, 1986-87 to 1987-88
John Brophy and George Armstrong, 1988-89
Doug Carpenter since 1989-90

FRANCHISE LEADERS

Current players in bold type
(1917-18 through 1989-90)

Games
1. 1187—George Armstrong
2. 1185—Tim Horton
3. 1099—Borje Salming
4. 1062—Dave Keon
5. 1034—Ron Ellis
6. 947—Bob Pulford
7. 844—Darryl Sittler
8. 838—Ron Stewart
9. 739—Bob Baun
10. 720—Frank Mahovlich

Goals
1. 389—Darryl Sittler
2. 365—Dave Keon
3. 332—Ron Ellis
4. 299—Rick Vaive
5. 296—George Armstrong
   296—Frank Mahovlich
7. 251—Bob Pulford
8. 231—Ted Kennedy
9. 219—Lanny McDonald
10. 201—Syl Apps

Assists
1. 620—Borje Salming
2. 527—Darryl Sittler
3. 493—Dave Keon
4. 417—George Armstrong
5. 349—Tim Horton
6. 329—Ted Kennedy
7. 312—Bob Pulford
8. 308—Ron Ellis
9. 305—Norm Ullman
10. 302—Ian Turnbull

Points
1. 916—Darryl Sittler
2. 858—Dave Keon
3. 768—Borje Salming
4. 713—George Armstrong
5. 640—Ron Ellis
6. 597—Frank Mahovlich
7. 563—Bob Pulford
8. 560—Ted Kennedy
9. 537—Rick Vaive
10. 471—Norm Ullman

Penalty Minutes
1. 1670—Dave Williams
2. 1389—Tim Horton
3. 1292—Borje Salming
4. 1264—Red Horner
5. 1155—Bob Baun
6. 954—Bob McGill

Goaltenders

Games
1. 629—Turk Broda
2. 472—Johnny Bower
3. 296—Mike Palmateer
4. 267—Harry Lumley
5. 214—Lorne Chabot
6. 210—Bruce Gamble
7. 200—Ken Wregget

Shutouts
1. 62—Turk Broda
2. 34—Harry Lumley
3. 33—Lorne Chabot
4. 32—Johnny Bower
5. 19—George Hainsworth

Goals Against Average
(2400 minutes minimum)
1. 2.00—John Ross Roach
2. 2.05—Al Rollins
3. 2.20—Lorne Chabot
4. 2.21—Harry Lumley
5. 2.26—George Hainsworth
6. 2.46—Jacques Plante
7. 2.51—Johnny Bower
8. 2.53—Turk Broda
9. 2.59—Bernie Parent
10. 2.71—Don Simmons

Wins
1. 302—Turk Broda
2. 220—Johnny Bower
3. 129—Mike Palmateer
4. 108—Lorne Chabot
5. 104—Harry Lumley

Kirk McLean's 21 victories last year were the most by a Canucks goaltender since Gary Smith won a team-record 32 games in 1974-75.

Trevor Linden is the only player in Vancouver history to score more than 100 career points before his 20th birthday.

Jyrki Lumme became the second Vancouver defenseman ever to score a regular-season overtime goal when he helped the Canucks to a 6-5 win at St. Louis on March 15, 1990.

Stan Smyl will be entering his team-record 13th season with Vancouver in 1990-91. He has been the Canucks' captain since 1982-83, the NHL's longest such streak.

VANCOUVER CANUCKS

CLUB DIRECTORY

Chairman of the Board
Frank A. Griffiths
Vice-Chairman and Governor
Arthur R. Griffiths
President and General Manager
Pat Quinn
Vice-President and Director of Hockey Operations
Brian Burke
Vice-President and Director of Marketing and Communications
Glen Ringdal
Vice-President of Finance and Administration
Carlos Mascarenhas
Senior Advisor
Jack Gordon
Director of Public and Media Relations
To be announced
Coach
Bob McCammon
Assistant Coaches
Jack McIlhargey, Ron Wilson
Strength Coach
Wayne Wilson
Director of Scouting
Mike Penny

Director of Pro Scouting
Murray Oliver
Scouts
Jack McCartan, Ken Slater, Ron Delorme, Ed McColgan, Paul McIntosh, Scott Carter, Ron Lapointe, Noel Price
Director of Special Events and Ticket Operations
Lynn Harrison
Trainers
Larry Ashley, Pat O'Neil, Ed Georgica
Home Ice
Pacific Coliseum
Address
100 North Renfrew St., Vancouver, B.C. V5K 3N7
Seating Capacity
16,123
Club Colors
White, Black, Red and Gold
Phone
(604) 254-5141
FAX
(604) 251-5123

YEAR-BY-YEAR RESULTS

Season	W.	L.	T.	Pts.	Position	Season	W.	L.	T.	Pts.	Position
1970-71	24	46	8	56	Sixth—*	1981-82	30	33	17	77	Second—c
1971-72	20	50	8	48	Seventh—*	1982-83	30	35	15	75	Third—†
1972-73	22	47	9	53	Seventh—*	1983-84	32	39	9	73	Third—†
1973-74	24	43	11	59	Seventh—*	1984-85	25	46	9	59	Fifth—*
1974-75	38	32	10	86	First—a	1985-86	23	44	13	59	Fourth—†
1975-76	33	32	15	81	Second—†	1986-87	29	43	8	66	Fifth—*
1976-77	25	42	13	63	Fourth—*	1987-88	25	46	9	59	Fifth—*
1977-78	20	43	17	57	Third—*	1988-89	33	39	8	74	Fourth—†
1978-79	25	42	13	63	Second—†	1989-90	25	41	14	64	Fifth—*
1979-80	27	37	16	70	Third—†	**Totals**	538	812	242	1318	
1980-81	28	32	20	76	Third—†						

Key to standings: *—Missed playoffs. †—Eliminated in first round of new playoff format (1974-75). a—Eliminated in quarterfinal round. b—Eliminated in semifinal round. c—Eliminated in final round. xx—Stanley Cup champion.

Richard Brodeur

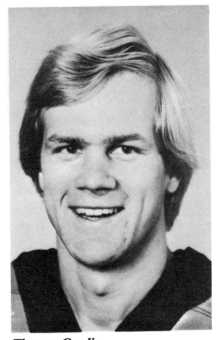

Thomas Gradin

1990-91 SCHEDULE

▨ Home games shaded.

* At Chicago Stadium.

OCTOBER

Sun	Mon	Tue	Wed	Thu	Fri	Sat
	1	2	3	4 CAL	5	6 LA
7	8	9 LA	10	11	12 STL	13
14 EDM	15	16	17 BOS	18	19 WIN	20
21 QUE	22	23 DET	24	25 BOS	26	27 HAR
28	29	30 WAS	31			

NOVEMBER

Sun	Mon	Tue	Wed	Thu	Fri	Sat
				1 NJ	2	3 WIN
4	5	6 DET	7	8 TOR	9 BUF	10
11 PHI	12	13	14 EDM	15	16 NYI	17
18	19 CAL	20	21 CHI	22	23 MIN	24 STL
25	26	27 MIN	28	29 TOR	30	

DECEMBER

Sun	Mon	Tue	Wed	Thu	Fri	Sat
						1
2 WIN	3	4 NYI	5 NJ	6	7 PIT	8
9	10 QUE	11	12 EDM	13	14 NYR	15
16 CAL	17	18 CAL	19	20 EDM	21	22 LA
23 EDM	24	25	26	27 MON	28 EDM	29
30	31 WIN					

JANUARY

Sun	Mon	Tue	Wed	Thu	Fri	Sat
		1	2 HAR	3 BOS	4	5 MIN
6	7	8 BUF	9	10 HAR	11	12 LA
13	14	15	16 WIN	17	18	19 ALL-STAR GAME*
20	21	22	23 EDM	24	25 LA	26 LA
27	28 CHI	29	30 EDM	31 NYR		

FEBRUARY

Sun	Mon	Tue	Wed	Thu	Fri	Sat
					1	2 LA
3	4	5 WAS	6	7 PHI	8 NYR	9
10 NJ	11	12	13	14 STL	15	16 WAS
17	18 QUE	19	20 WIN	21 CAL	22	23 DET
24	25 CAL	26	27 PIT	28		

MARCH

Sun	Mon	Tue	Wed	Thu	Fri	Sat
					1 MON	2
3 CHI	4	5 PIT	6	7 TOR	8	9 MON
10 BUF	11	12	13 PHI	14	15	16 NYI
17 LA	18	19	20 CAL	21	22 WIN	23
24	25	26 CAL	27	28 WIN	29	30
31						

1989-90 RESULTS

Oct.	5—Edmonton	L	1-4
	7—Detroit	W	5-3
	9—N.Y. Islanders	L	2-5
	11—At Edmonton	W	5-2
	13—Los Angeles	L	5-6
	15—Boston	W	7-6
	18—At Toronto	L	3-4
	20—At New Jersey	W	3-2
	21—At N.Y. Islanders	W	2-1
	23—At N.Y. Rangers	L	3-5
	27—At Calgary	T	5-5 (OT)
	28—Calgary	W	4-3
	31—New Jersey	W	4-3
Nov.	3—Winnipeg	L	2-3
	5—Pittsburgh	W	5-3
	8—At Winnipeg	L	2-3 (OT)
	10—At Buffalo	L	2-4
	11—At Quebec	L	2-3
	14—Washington	T	4-4 (OT)
	16—Chicago	W	4-3
	19—Buffalo	T	2-2 (OT)
	21—At Edmonton	L	3-4
	25—At Los Angeles	L	4-7
	26—Los Angeles	T	3-3 (OT)
	29—Toronto	L	2-3 (OT)
Dec.	1—N.Y. Rangers	L	3-4
	3—Minnesota	W	6-5
	6—At Los Angeles	L	4-5 (OT)
	9—At St. Louis	L	4-6
	10—At Chicago	L	1-7
	12—At Minnesota	W	4-2
	13—At Winnipeg	T	3-3 (OT)
	15—Winnipeg	T	3-3 (OT)
	17—Quebec	T	2-2 (OT)
	19—Calgary	L	1-2
	20—At Calgary	L	1-2 (OT)
	23—At Los Angeles	L	1-4
	27—Montreal	W	2-1
	31—Philadelphia	T	2-2 (OT)
Jan.	2—At Detroit	L	1-4
	4—At Pittsburgh	L	3-4
	5—At Washington	W	5-2
	7—At Montreal	L	3-5
	10—Hartford	L	1-3
	12—St. Louis	L	2-5
	13—Buffalo	L	3-5
	16—At N.Y. Islanders	L	0-3
	18—At Philadelphia	W	3-2 (OT)
	19—At Chicago	L	2-5
	23—Los Angeles	T	3-3 (OT)
	26—Minnesota	L	3-6
	27—At Edmonton	L	2-6
	30—Calgary	L	2-7
Feb.	1—At Calgary	L	3-4 (OT)
	2—At Winnipeg	L	1-8
	4—New Jersey	W	4-2
	6—Winnipeg	W	5-3
	9—At Hartford	W	4-1
	11—At Boston	W	4-2
	13—At Quebec	L	3-5
	14—At Montreal	L	1-10
	16—Edmonton	T	2-2 (OT)
	18—Boston	L	2-7
	20—Edmonton	L	2-4
	24—At Los Angeles	W	6-4
	26—Toronto	W	5-2
	28—Philadelphia	T	7-7 (OT)
Mar.	3—At Calgary	L	1-5
	4—At Edmonton	L	3-6
	9—Calgary	T	4-4 (OT)
	11—Pittsburgh	W	5-3
	13—Hartford	L	0-1
	15—At St. Louis	W	6-5 (OT)
	17—At Washington	W	3-1
	18—At N.Y. Rangers	L	2-5
	20—At Detroit	T	4-4 (OT)
	23—At Winnipeg	W	4-2
	25—Winnipeg	T	3-3 (OT)
	27—Edmonton	L	1-4
	31—Los Angeles	W	6-3

1990-91 ROSTER

No.	FORWARDS	Hgt./Wt.	Place of Birth	Age	NHL exp.	1989-90 club (league)	G.	A.	Pts.
8	Greg Adams	6-03/190	Nelson, B.C.	27	6	Vancouver (NHL)	30	20	50
	Shawn Antoski	6-04/235	Brantford, Ont.	20	0	North Bay (OHL)	25	31	56
14	Steve Bozek	5-11/180	Kelowna, B.C.	29	9	Vancouver (NHL)	14	9	23
10	Brian Bradley	5-10/180	Kitchener, Ont.	25	5	Vancouver (NHL)	19	29	48
	Cam Brown	6-01/205	Saskatoon, Sask.	21	0	Brandon (WHL)	34	41	75
28	Dave Capuano	6-02/190	Warwick, R.I.	22	1	Muskegon (IHL)	15	15	30
						Milwaukee (IHL)	0	4	4
						Pittsburgh (NHL)	0	0	0
						Vancouver (NHL)	3	5	8
38	Todd Hawkins	6-01/195	Kingston, Ont.	24	2	Vancouver (NHL)	0	0	0
						Milwaukee (IHL)	23	17	40
	Robert Kron	5-10/174	Brno, Czechoslovakia	23	0	Zetor Brno (Czech.)	...	...	...
17	Vladimir Krutov	5-09/200	Moscow, USSR	30	1	Vancouver (NHL)	11	23	34
18	Igor Larionov	5-09/165	Voskresensk, USSR	29	1	Vancouver (NHL)	17	27	44
16	Trevor Linden	6-04/205	Medicine Hat, Alta.	20	2	Vancouver (NHL)	21	30	51
	Dave Mackey	6-04/200	Richmond, B.C.	24	3	Minnesota (NHL)	2	0	2
33	Jay Mazur	6-02/205	Hamilton, Ont.	25	2	Milwaukee (IHL)	20	27	47
						Vancouver (NHL)	0	0	0
44	Rob Murphy	6-03/205	Hull, Que.	21	3	Vancouver (NHL)	1	1	2
						Milwaukee (IHL)	24	47	71
	Petr Nedved	6-03/178	Liberec, Czech.	18	0	Seattle (WHL)	65	80	145
7	Dan Quinn	5-10/175	Ottawa, Ont.	25	7	Pittsburgh (NHL)	9	20	29
						Vancouver (NHL)	16	18	34
19	Jim Sandlak	6-03/219	Kitchener, Ont.	23	4	Vancouver (NHL)	15	8	23
26	Petri Skriko	5-10/180	Laapeenranta, Finland	28	6	Vancouver (NHL)	15	33	48
12	Stan Smyl	5-08/195	Glendon, Alta.	32	12	Vancouver (NHL)	1	15	16
20	Ronnie Stern	6-00/195	Ste. Agathe, Que.	23	3	Vancouver (NHL)	2	3	5
						Milwaukee (IHL)	8	9	17
	Garry Valk	6-01/190	Edmonton, Alta.	22	0	North Dakota (WCHA)	22	17	39
	DEFENSEMEN								
36	Jim Agnew	6-01/190	Hartney, Man.	24	3	Milwaukee (IHL)	4	10	14
						Vancouver (NHL)	0	0	0
5	Garth Butcher	6-00/200	Regina, Sask.	27	9	Vancouver (NHL)	6	14	20
	Jack Capuano	6-02/210	Cranston, R.I.	24	0	Newmarket (AHL)	0	2	2
						Springfield (AHL)	0	4	4
						Milwaukee (IHL)	3	10	13
	Don Gibson	6-01/210	Deloraine, Man.	22	0	Michigan State U. (CCHA)	5	22	27
						Milwaukee (IHL)	0	0	0
2	Kevan Guy	6-03/202	Edmonton, Alta.	25	4	Vancouver (NHL)	2	5	7
						Milwaukee (IHL)	2	11	13
	Ian Kidd	5-11/195	Gresham, Ore.	26	2	Milwaukee (IHL)	11	36	47
3	Doug Lidster	6-01/200	Kamloops, B.C.	29	7	Vancouver (NHL)	8	28	36
21	Jyrki Lumme	6-01/207	Tampere, Finland	24	2	Montreal (NHL)	1	19	20
						Vancouver (NHL)	3	7	10
24	Larry Melnyk	6-00/195	Saskatoon, Sask.	30	10	Vancouver (NHL)	0	2	2
6	Robert Nordmark	6-01/200	Lulea, Sweden	28	3	Vancouver (NHL)	2	11	13
15	Adrien Plavsic	6-01/190	Montreal, Que.	20	1	Peoria (IHL)	7	14	21
						St. Louis (NHL)	0	1	1
						Vancouver (NHL)	3	2	5
						Milwaukee (IHL)	1	2	3
	Carl Valimont	6-01/200	Southington, Conn.	24	0	Milwaukee (IHL)	13	28	41

No.	GOALTENDERS	Hgt./Wt.	Place of Birth	Age	NHL exp.	1989-90 club (league)	Ga.	SO	Avg.
	Troy Gamble	5-11/195	New Glasgow, N.S.	23	2	Milwaukee (IHL)	56	2	4.21
1	Kirk McLean	6-00/185	Willowdale, Ont.	24	5	Vancouver (NHL)	63	0	3.47
31	Steve Weeks	5-11/170	Scarborough, Ont.	32	10	Vancouver (NHL)	21	0	4.15

1989-90 RECORDS

1989-90 regular-season records: 25-41-14 (.400, 64 points, 5th in Smythe Division); 13-16-11 at home; 12-25-3 on road; 2-5-14 in overtime; 6-18-8 vs. Smythe (1-5-2 vs. Flames; 1-6-1 vs. Oilers; 2-4-2 vs. Kings; 2-3-3 vs. Jets); 6-8-1 vs. Norris; 4-9-2 vs. Adams; 9-6-3 vs. Patrick.

MISCELLANEOUS DATA

1989-90 team rankings: Shorthanded goals for, 8 (T15th in NHL); shorthanded goals against, 8 (T7th); power play, 17.1% (18th); penalty killing, 74.9% (19th); penalty minutes/game, 20.6.

TEAM HAT TRICKS, CAREER, ACTIVE

Greg Adams (2) Dan Quinn (4)
Steve Bozek (2) Jim Sandlak (1)
Trevor Linden (2) Petri Skriko (5)
Andrew McBain (1) Stan Smyl (7)

MINOR LEAGUE AFFILIATIONS

Albany (IHL), Milwaukee (IHL)

Petri Skriko

78

1990 DRAFT SELECTIONS

Rnd.	Player	Hgt.	Wgt.	Overall	(Pos.)	1989-90 Club	(League)
1	Petr Nedved	6:02	178	2	(C)	Seattle (WHL)	
1	Shawn Antoski	6:04	234	18	(LW)	North Bay (OHL)	
2	Jiri Slegr	5:11	182	23	(D)	Litvinov, Czech.	
4	Darin Bader	6:00	202	65	(LW)	Saskatoon (WHL)	
5	Gino Odjick	6:02	220	86	(LW)	Laval (QMJHL)	
7	Daryl Filipek	6:01	185	128	(D)	Ferris State University	
8	Paul O'Hagan	6:02	204	149	(D)	Oshawa (OHL)	
9	Mark Cipriano	5:09	191	170	(RW)	Victoria (WHL)	
10	Troy Neumier	6:02	187	191	(D)	Prince Albert (WHL)	
11	Tyler Ertel	5:11	182	212	(C)	North Bay (OHL)	
12	Karri Kivi	6:00	172	233	(D)	Ilves Tampere, Finland	

FIRST-ROUND ENTRY DRAFT SELECTIONS

Year	Name	Overall	Last Amateur Team (League)	Years in NHL
1970	Dale Tallon	2	Toronto (OHL)	10
1971	Jocelyn Guevremont	3	Montreal (OHL)	9
1972	Don Lever	3	Niagara Falls (OHL)	15
1973	Dennis Ververgaert	3	London (OHL)	8
	Bob Dailey	9	Toronto (OHL)	9
1974	No first round selection			
1975	Rick Blight	10	Brandon (WCHL)	7
1976	No first round selection			
1977	Jere Gillis	4	Sherbrooke (QMJHL)	9
1978	Bill Derlago	4	Brandon (WCHL)	9
1979	Rick Vaive	5	Birmingham (WHA)	11
1980	Rick Lanz	7	Oshawa (OHL)	9
1981	Garth Butcher	10	Regina (WHL)	9
1982	Michel Petit	11	Sherbrooke (QMJHL)	8
1983	Cam Neely	9	Portland (WHL)	7
1984	J. J. Daigneault	10	Canadian Olympics/Longuevil (QMJHL)	5
1985	Jim Sandlak	4	London (OHL)	5
1986	Dan Woodley	7	Portland (WHL)	1
1987	No first round selection			
1988	Trevor Linden	2	Medicine Hat (WHL)	2
1989	Jason Herter	8	University of North Dakota	0
1990	Petr Nedved	2	Seattle (WHL)	0
	Shawn Antoski	18	North Bay (OHL)	0

Jim Sandlak

COACHING HISTORY

Hal Laycoe, 1970-71 to 1971-72
Vic Stasiuk, 1972-73
Bill McCreary and Phil Maloney, 1973-74
Phil Maloney, 1974-75 to 1975-76
Phil Maloney and Orland Kurtenbach, 1976-77
Orland Kurtenbach, 1977-78
Harry Neale, 1978-79 to 1980-81

Harry Neale and Roger Neilson, 1981-82
Roger Neilson, 1982-83
Roger Neilson and Harry Neale, 1983-84
Bill Laforge and Harry Neale, 1984-85
Tom Watt, 1985-86 to 1986-87
Bob McCammon since 1987-88

FRANCHISE LEADERS

Current players in bold type
(1970-71 through 1989-90)

Games
1. 851—Stan Smyl
2. 781—Harold Snepsts
3. 677—Dennis Kearns
4. 613—Thomas Gradin
5. 593—Don Lever

Goals
1. 260—Stan Smyl
2. 250—Tony Tanti
3. 197—Thomas Gradin
4. 186—Don Lever
5. **167—Petri Skriko**

Assists
1. 399—Stan Smyl
2. 353—Thomas Gradin
3. 290—Dennis Kearns
4. 267—Andre Boudrias
5. 221—Don Lever

Points
1. 659—Stan Smyl
2. 550—Thomas Gradin
3. 470—Tony Tanti
4. 407—Don Lever
5. 388—Andre Boudrias

Penalty Minutes
1. 1469—Stan Smyl
2. 1446—Harold Snepsts
3. **1411—Garth Butcher**
4. 1314—Tiger Williams
5. 651—Curt Fraser

Goaltenders

Games
1. 377—Richard Brodeur
2. 208—Gary Smith
3. 148—Dunc Wilson
4. **146—Kirk McLean**
5. 137—Glen Hanlon
6. 102—Frank Caprice
7. 96—Curt Ridley
8. 93—Cesare Maniago
9. 73—Gary Bromley
10. **65—Steve Weeks**

Shutouts (entire roster)
1. 11—Gary Smith
2. 6—Richard Brodeur
3. 5—Glen Hanlon
   5—Kirk McLean
5. 3—Gary Bromley
6. 2—Ken Lockett
   2—Cesare Maniago
   2—Dunc Wilson
9. 1—Frank Caprice
   1—Ed Dyck
   1—John Garrett
   1—Rick Heinz
   1—Curt Ridley

Goals Against Average
(2400 minutes minimum)
1. 3.33—Gary Smith
2. **3.39—Steve Weeks**
3. **3.42—Kirk McLean**
4. 3.56—Glen Hanlon
5. 3.63—Gary Bromley
6. 3.68—Cesare Maniago
7. 3.80—Curt Ridley
8. 3.87—Richard Brodeur
9. 3.93—Dunc Wilson
10. 4.11—John Garrett

Wins
1. 126—Richard Brodeur
2. 72—Gary Smith
3. **52—Kirk McLean**
4. 43—Glen Hanlon
5. 31—Frank Caprice
6. 27—Cesare Maniago
7. 25—Gary Bromley
   25—Curt Ridley
9. 24—Dunc Wilson
10. 22—John Garrett

Dino Ciccarelli has scored at least 40 goals the last five years.

Rod Langway has never finished with a negative plus-minus rating in his 12-year NHL playing career.

Mike Liut (above) and Don Beaupre combined for a 3.15 goals-against-average in last year's playoffs to help the Capitals advance to the Wales Conference championship series for the first time in team history.

John Druce scored 14 goals in 15 playoff games last year and led all NHL players with four game-winning playoff goals. He had scored just 16 goals in 93 regular-season games before the 1990 playoffs began.

WASHINGTON CAPITALS

CLUB DIRECTORY

Chairman and Governor
Abe Pollin
President and Alternate Governor
Richard M. Patrick
Vice-President and General Manager
David Poile
Legal Counselors and Alternate Governors
David M. Osnos, Peter F. O'Malley
Vice-President and Comptroller
Edmund Stelzer
Coach
Terry Murray
Assistant Coach
John Perpich
Strength and Conditioning Coach
Frank Costello
Director of Player Personnel and Recruitment
Jack Button
Coordinator of Scouting
Hugh Rogers
Chief U.S. Scout
Jack Barzee
Chief Eastern Scout
Jack Ferguson
Scouts
Gilles Cote, Fred Devereaux, Bruce Hamilton, Eje Johansson, Richard Rothermel, Bob Schmidt, Dan Sylvester, John Stanton, Darrell Young
Vice-President/Marketing
Lew Strudler

Director of Public Relations
Lou Corletto
Assistant Director of Marketing
Debi Angus
Director of Community Relations
Yvon Labre
Director of Promotions
Charles Copeland
Director of Season Subscriptions
Joanne Kowalski
Assistant Director of Public Relations
David Ferry
Administrative Assistant to the General Manager
Pat Young
Trainer
Stan Wong
Assistant Trainer/Head Equipment Manager
Doug Shearer
Home Ice
Capital Centre
Address
Landover, Md. 20785
Seating Capacity
18,130
Club Colors
Red, White and Blue
Phone
(301) 386-7000
FAX
(301) 386-7012

YEAR-BY-YEAR RESULTS

Season	W.	L.	T.	Pts.	Position
1974-75	8	67	5	21	Fifth—*
1975-76	11	59	10	32	Fifth—*
1976-77	24	42	14	62	Fourth—*
1977-78	17	49	14	48	Fifth—*
1978-79	24	41	15	63	Fourth—*
1979-80	27	40	13	67	Fifth—*
1980-81	26	36	18	70	Fifth—*
1981-82	26	41	13	65	Fifth—*
1982-83	39	25	16	94	Third—†
1983-84	48	27	5	101	Second—a
1984-85	46	25	9	101	Second—†
1985-86	50	23	7	107	Second—†
1986-87	38	32	10	86	Second—†
1987-88	38	33	9	85	Second—a
1988-89	41	29	10	92	First—†
1989-90	36	38	6	78	Third—b
Totals	499	607	174	1172	

Key to standings: *—Missed playoffs. †—Eliminated in first round of new playoff format (1974-75). a—Eliminated in quarterfinal round. b—Eliminated in semifinal round. c—Eliminated in final round. xx—Stanley Cup champion.

Bengt Gustafsson

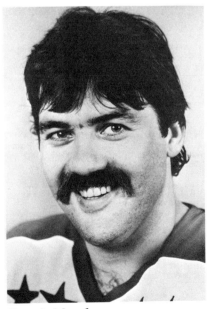

Dennis Maruk

1990-91 SCHEDULE

Home games shaded.

* At Chicago Stadium.

OCTOBER

Sun	Mon	Tue	Wed	Thu	Fri	Sat
	1	2	3	4	5 PIT	6 DET
7	8	9	10 NYR	11	12 WIN	13 NYR
14	15 MON	16	17 NJ	18	19 NYI	20 NJ
21	22	23 PHI	24	25 CHI	26	27 CAL
28 EDM	29	30 VAN	31			

NOVEMBER

Sun	Mon	Tue	Wed	Thu	Fri	Sat
				1	2 LA	3 NYI
4	5	6 QUE	7	8	9	10 BUF
11 BOS	12	13	14 TOR	15	16 CHI	17 HAR
18	19 DET	20	21 TOR	22	23 PIT	24 PIT
25	26	27	28 NYR	29	30 MON	

DECEMBER

Sun	Mon	Tue	Wed	Thu	Fri	Sat
						1 NYI
2	3	4	5 PIT	6	7 NJ	8 NJ
9	10	11 PHI	12	13	14	15 HAR
16	17 NYR	18	19 CHI	20 STL	21	22 TOR
23	24	25	26 PIT	27	28 NYR	29 QUE
30	31					

JANUARY

Sun	Mon	Tue	Wed	Thu	Fri	Sat
		1 NJ	2	3	4 PHI	5 BOS
6	7	8	9	10	11 CAL	12 MON
13	14	15 STL	16	17 MIN	18	19 ALL-STAR GAME*
20	21	22 DET	23	24 PHI	25 MIN	26
27 NYI	28	29 PIT	30	31 NYI		

FEBRUARY

Sun	Mon	Tue	Wed	Thu	Fri	Sat
					1	2 WIN
3	4	5 VAN	6	7	8 EDM	9
10 PHI	11	12	13	14	15 CAL	16 VAN
17	18 LA	19	20	21	22 NYR	23
24 PIT	25 NJ	26	27 NYR	28		

MARCH

Sun	Mon	Tue	Wed	Thu	Fri	Sat
					1	2 NYI
3	4	5 LA	6	7	8 WIN	9
10 EDM	11	12 HAR	13	14 QUE	15	16 PHI
17	18	19 STL	20	21 NYI	22 MIN	23
24 BOS	25	26 BUF	27	28 PHI	29	30 NJ
31 BUF						

1989-90 RESULTS

Oct.	6—Philadelphia	W	5-3
	7—Chicago	L	2-3
	11—At Hartford	L	1-4
	13—N.Y. Rangers	W	7-4
	14—Calgary	T	4-4 (OT)
	16—At Montreal	W	4-3 (OT)
	20—N.Y. Islanders	L	3-5
	21—At Toronto	L	4-8
	23—At Calgary	T	3-3 (OT)
	25—At Winnipeg	L	4-6
	28—At St. Louis	L	0-1
	29—At Chicago	L	0-1
	31—St. Louis	T	1-1 (OT)
Nov.	3—Toronto	W	2-1
	5—At Quebec	W	3-0
	7—At N.Y. Islanders	W	5-3
	10—Boston	L	3-5
	11—Edmonton	L	3-5
	14—At Vancouver	T	4-4 (OT)
	18—At Los Angeles	L	3-5
	22—N.Y. Islanders	W	5-3
	24—Pittsburgh	L	4-7
	25—At Pittsburgh	W	4-1
	29—At Detroit	W	5-3
Dec.	1—Philadelphia	L	2-3
	2—At New Jersey	W	5-3
	5—At Philadelphia	W	4-3
	6—At Pittsburgh	L	3-5
	9—At Boston	W	7-3
	10—At Buffalo	L	3-4
	15—N.Y. Islanders	L	3-5
	16—At Hartford	W	5-2
	19—At Philadelphia	W	2-1
	21—At Pittsburgh	L	2-5
	23—N.Y. Rangers	W	3-2
	26—Pittsburgh	W	6-3
	27—At New Jersey	W	3-1
	29—Detroit	W	2-1
Jan.	1—Los Angeles	L	4-7
	3—At N.Y. Rangers	L	1-2
	5—Vancouver	L	2-5
	6—At Boston	L	3-5
	8—At Toronto	L	6-8
	10—At Winnipeg	L	1-6
	12—Pittsburgh	L	4-6
	13—At N.Y. Islanders	L	2-4
	16—New Jersey	W	9-6
	19—At Buffalo	W	6-3
	23—Winnipeg	L	3-4
	24—At New Jersey	L	2-3
	26—Montreal	W	6-3
	28—Philadelphia	W	7-2
	31—At Minnesota	W	4-3 (OT)
Feb.	2—At N.Y. Islanders	L	3-5
	4—Edmonton	L	4-5 (OT)
	6—Quebec	W	12-2
	8—At Pittsburgh	L	5-7
	9—New Jersey	L	3-5
	11—Minnesota	W	5-3
	14—At Edmonton	W	4-3
	19—At Los Angeles	L	2-3
	23—N.Y. Rangers	L	3-6
	25—Detroit	W	9-4
	27—Chicago	W	4-0
	28—At N.Y. Rangers	L	2-3
Mar.	2—Hartford	L	3-4
	4—New Jersey	W	4-3
	6—Buffalo	T	1-1 (OT)
	9—Quebec	W	4-3
	10—At Philadelphia	W	4-3
	13—St. Louis	L	1-4
	17—Vancouver	L	1-3
	18—At Minnesota	W	4-3
	20—N.Y. Islanders	W	3-0
	23—Montreal	L	2-4
	25—Calgary	W	4-1
	27—At New Jersey	L	1-4
	29—At Philadelphia	T	2-2 (OT)
	31—N.Y. Rangers	W	2-1
Apr.	1—At N.Y. Rangers	W	3-2

1990-91 ROSTER

No.	FORWARDS	Hgt./Wt.	Place of Birth	Age	NHL exp.	1989-90 club (league)	G.	A.	Pts.
25	Robin Bawa	6-02/200	Chemainus, B.C.	24	1	Baltimore (AHL)	7	18	25
						Washington (NHL)	1	0	1
11	Tim Bergland	6-03/180	Crookston, Minn.	25	1	Baltimore (AHL)	12	19	31
						Washington (NHL)	2	5	7
22	Dino Ciccarelli	5-11/185	Sarnia, Ont.	30	10	Washington (NHL)	41	38	79
19	John Druce	6-01/190	Peterborough, Ont.	24	2	Baltimore (AHL)	15	16	31
						Washington (NHL)	8	3	11
32	Dale Hunter	5-09/189	Petrolia, Ont.	30	10	Washington (NHL)	23	39	62
27	Bob Joyce	6-01/180	St. Johns, N.B.	24	3	Boston (NHL)	1	2	3
						Washington (NHL)	5	8	13
9	Nick Kypreos	6-00/190	Toronto, Ont.	24	1	Washington (NHL)	5	4	9
						Baltimore (AHL)	6	5	11
39	Tyler Larter	5-10/180	Charlottetown, P.E.I.	22	1	Baltimore (AHL)	31	36	67
						Washington (NHL)	0	0	0
21	Steve Leach	5-11/180	Cambridge, Mass.	24	5	Washington (NHL)	18	14	32
26	Steve Maltais	6-01/190	Ottawa, Ont.	21	1	Baltimore (AHL)	29	37	66
						Washington (NHL)	0	0	0
16	Alan May	6-01/215	Barrhead, Alta.	25	3	Washington (NHL)	7	10	17
10	Kelly Miller	5-11/185	Lansing, Mich.	27	6	Washington (NHL)	18	22	40
23	Rob Murray	6-01/175	Toronto, Ont.	23	1	Baltimore (AHL)	5	4	9
						Washington (NHL)	2	7	9
20	Michal Pivonka	6-02/192	Kladno, Czech.	24	4	Washington (NHL)	25	39	64
	John Purves	6-02/185	Toronto, Ont.	22	0	Baltimore (AHL)	29	35	64
34	Mike Richard	5-09/175	Toronto, Ont.	24	2	Baltimore (AHL)	41	42	83
						Washington (NHL)	0	2	2
17	Mike Ridley	6-01/200	Winnipeg, Man.	27	5	Washington (NHL)	30	43	73
	Reggie Savage	5-10/177	Montreal, Que.	20	0	Victoriaville (QMJHL)	49	39	88
12	John Tucker	6-00/185	Windsor, Ont.	26	7	Buffalo (NHL)	1	2	3
						Washington (NHL)	9	19	28
39	Alfie Turcotte	5-10/175	Gary, Ind.	25	6	Baltimore (AHL)	26	40	66
						Washington (NHL)	0	2	2
	Peter Zezel	5-10/195	Toronto, Ont.	25	6	St. Louis (NHL)	25	47	72
	DEFENSEMEN								
28	Chris Felix	5-11/185	Bramalea, Ont.	26	2	Baltimore (AHL)	19	42	61
						Washington (NHL)	1	0	1
40	Mark Ferner	6-00/170	Regina, Sask.	25	3	Baltimore (AHL)	7	28	35
						Washington (NHL)	0	0	0
4	Kevin Hatcher	6-03/185	Detroit, Mich.	24	6	Washington (NHL)	13	41	54
2	Bill Houlder	6-02/192	Thunder Bay, Ont.	23	3	Baltimore (AHL)	3	7	10
						Washington (NHL)	1	11	12
6	Calle Johansson	5-11/198	Goteborg, Sweden	23	3	Washington (NHL)	8	31	39
	Mike Lalor	6-00/190	Fort Erie, Ont.	27	5	St. Louis (NHL)	0	16	16
5	Rod Langway	6-03/215	Maag, Taiwan	33	12	Washington (NHL)	0	8	8
	Rob Mendel	6-01/185	Los Angeles, Calif.	22	0	Univ. of Wisconsin (WCHA)	1	13	14
36	Kent Paynter	6-00/186	Summerside, P.E.I.	25	2	Baltimore (AHL)	7	20	27
						Washington (NHL)	1	2	3
8	Bob Rouse	6-01/210	Surrey, B.C.	26	7	Washington (NHL)	4	16	20

No.	GOALTENDERS	Hgt./Wt.	Place of Birth	Age	NHL exp.	1989-90 club (league)	Ga.	SO	Avg.
33	Don Beaupre	5-08/155	Kitchener, Ont.	29	10	Washington (NHL)	48	2	3.22
	Byron Dafoe	5-11/175	Duncan, B.C.	19	0	Portland (WHL)	40	...	5.11
	Jim Hrivnak	6-02/185	Montreal, Que.	22	1	Baltimore (AHL)	47	4	3.06
						Washington (NHL)	11	0	3.55
	Olaf Kolzig	6-03/207	J'h'nn'sb'rg, S. Afr.	20	1	Tri-City (WHL)	48	...	4.48
						Washington (NHL)	2	0	6.00
1	Mike Liut	6-02/195	Weston, Ont.	34	11	Hartford (NHL)	29	3	2.64
						Washington (NHL)	8	1	2.13

1989-90 RECORDS

1989-90 regular-season records: 36-38-6 (.488, 78 points, 3rd in Patrick Division); 19-18-3 at home; 17-20-3 on road; 2-1-6 in overtime; 18-16-1 vs. Patrick (4-3-0 vs. Devils; 3-4-0 vs. Islanders; 4-3-0 vs. Rangers; 5-1-1 vs. Flyers; 2-5-0 vs. Penguins); 8-6-1 vs. Adams; 8-6-1 vs. Norris; 2-10-3 vs. Smythe.

MISCELLANEOUS DATA

1989-90 team rankings: Shorthanded goals for, 9 (T13th in NHL); shorthanded goals against, 15 (T17th); power play, 17.0% (19th); penalty killing, 80.8% (8th); penalty minutes/game, 27.6.

TEAM HAT TRICKS, CAREER, ACTIVE

Dino Ciccarelli (16)
Dale Hunter (3)
Mike Ridley (3)
Doug Wickenheiser (2)
Peter Zezel (1)

MINOR LEAGUE AFFILIATIONS

Baltimore (AHL)

Peter Zezel

1990 DRAFT SELECTIONS

Rnd.	Player	Hgt.	Wgt.	Overall	(Pos.)	1989-90 Club	(League)
1	John Slaney	5:11	186	9	(D)	Cornwall	(OHL)
2	Rod Pasma	6:04	207	30	(D)	Cornwall	(OHL)
3	Chris Longo	5:10	180	51	(RW)	Peterborough	(OHL)
4	Randy Pearce	5:11	203	72	(LW)	Kitchener	(OHL)
5	Brian Sakic	5:10	179	93	(C)	Tri-City	(WHL)
5	Mark Ouimet	5:10	165	94	(C)	University of Michigan	
6	Andrei Kovalev	5:11	189	114	(RW)	Moscow Dynamo	
7	Roman Kontsek	5:11	183	135	(RW)	Dukla Trencin, Czech.	
8	Peter Bondra	5:11	180	156	(C)	Kosice, Czech.	
8	Steve Martell	5:10	185	159	(RW)	London	(OHL)
9	Ken Klee	6:01	200	177	(D)	Bowling Green State Univ.	
10	Michael Boback	5:11	180	198	(C)	Providence College	
11	Alan Brown	6:00	180	219	(D)	Colgate University	
12	Todd Hlushko	5:11	180	240	(LW)	London	(OHL)

FIRST-ROUND ENTRY DRAFT SELECTIONS

Year	Name	Overall	Last Amateur Team	(League)	Years in NHL
1974	*Greg Joly	1	Regina	(WCHL)	9
1975	Alex Forsyth	18	Kingston	(OHA)	1
1976	*Rick Green	1	London	(OHL)	13
	Greg Carroll	15	Medicine Hat	(WCHL)	2
1977	Robert Picard	3	Montreal	(QMJHL)	13
1978	Ryan Walter	2	Seattle	(WCHL)	12
	Tim Coulis	18	Hamilton	(OHL)	4
1979	Mike Gartner	4	Cincinnati	(WHA)	11
1980	Darren Veitch	5	Regina	(WHL)	9
1981	Bobby Carpenter	3	St. John's H.S.	(Mass.)	9
1982	Scott Stevens	5	Kitchener	(OHL)	8
1983	No first round selection				
1984	Kevin Hatcher	17	North Bay	(OHL)	6
1985	Yvon Corriveau	19	Toronto	(OHL)	5
1986	Jeff Greenlaw	19	Team Canada		1
1987	No first round selection				
1988	Reggie Savage	15	Victoriaville	(QMJHL)	0
1989	Olaf Kolzig	19	Tri-City	(WHL)	1
1990	John Slaney	9	Cornwall	(OHL)	0

*Designates first player chosen in draft.

Rick Green

COACHING HISTORY

Jim Anderson, Red Sullivan and Milt Schmidt, 1974-75
Milt Schmidt and Tom McVie, 1975-76
Tom McVie, 1976-77 to 1977-78
Dan Belisle, 1978-79
Dan Belisle and Gary Green, 1979-80

Gary Green, 1980-81
Gary Green, Roger Crozier and Bryan Murray, 1981-82
Bryan Murray, 1982-83 to 1988-89
Bryan Murray and Terry Murray, 1989-90
Terry Murray for 1990-91

FRANCHISE LEADERS

Current players in bold type
(1974-75 through 1989-90)

Games
1. 786—Mike Gartner
2. 629—Bengt Gustafsson
3. 606—Bobby Gould
4. 601—Scott Stevens
5. **585—Rod Langway**
6. 494—Dave Christian
7. 453—Larry Murphy
8. 451—Gaetan Duchesne
9. 428—Craig Laughlin
10. 422—Bobby Carpenter

Goals
1. 397—Mike Gartner
2. 196—Bengt Gustafsson
3. 193—Dave Christian
4. 182—Dennis Maruk
5. 177—Bobby Carpenter
6. 134—Bobby Gould
7. 129—Alan Haworth
8. 118—Guy Charron
9. **114—Mike Ridley**
   114—Ryan Walter

Assists
1. 392—Mike Gartner
2. 359—Bengt Gustafsson
3. 331—Scott Stevens
4. 249—Dennis Maruk
   249—Larry Murphy
6. 224—Dave Christian
7. 190—Bobby Carpenter
8. 173—Craig Laughlin
9. 164—Ryan Walter
10. **157—Rod Langway**

Points
1. 789—Mike Gartner
2. 555—Bengt Gustafsson
3. 431—Dennis Maruk
4. 429—Scott Stevens
5. 417—Dave Christian
6. 367—Bobby Carpenter
7. 334—Larry Murphy
8. 283—Craig Laughlin
9. 278—Ryan Walter
10. 276—Bobby Gould

Penalty Minutes
1. 1630—Scott Stevens
2. 770—Mike Gartner
3. 756—Yvon Labre
4. 694—Greg Adams
5. **692—Dale Hunter**
6. 614—Gord Lane
7. **605—Kevin Hatcher**
8. 562—Lou Franceschetti

Goaltenders
Games
1. 173—Al Jensen
2. 145—Ron Low
3. 143—Pat Riggin
4. 139—Pete Peeters
5. 120—Bernie Wolfe
6. 96—Clint Malarchuk
7. 77—Dave Parro

Goals Against Average
(2400 minutes minimum)
1. 3.02—Pat Riggin
2. 3.06—Pete Peeters
3. 3.16—Bob Mason
4. **3.17—Don Beaupre**
5. 3.26—Al Jensen
6. 3.31—Clint Malarchuk
7. 3.64—Gary Inness
8. 3.65—Wayne Stephenson
9. 3.94—Jim Bedard
10. 4.03—Mike Palmateer

Wins
1. 94—Al Jensen
2. 70—Pete Peeters
3. 67—Pat Riggin
4. 40—Clint Malarchuk
5. 35—Bob Mason
6. 30—Ron Low
7. **28—Don Beaupre**
8. 22—Wayne Stephenson
9. 21—Dave Parro

Thomas Steen had 47 points in 40 games before a back injury limited him to 15 games in the second half of the 1989-90 season.

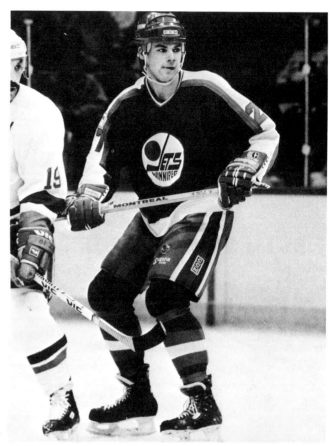

Defenseman Teppo Numminen had a solid sophomore season with Winnipeg, scoring 11 goals and 32 assists for 43 points in 79 games.

Peter Taglianetti led the Jets with a plus-20 rating last year after compiling a minus-23 mark in 1988-89.

Newcomer Phil Housley surpassed the 20-goal plateau for the fourth straight year in 1989-90 while adding a career-high 60 assists.

WINNIPEG JETS

CLUB DIRECTORY

President and Governor
Barry L. Shenkarow
Alternate Governors
Michael A. Smith, Bill Davis
Vice-President and General Manager
Michael A. Smith
Assistant General Manager—Director of Hockey Operations
Dennis McDonald
Director of Finance and Administration
Don Binda
Coach
Bob Murdoch
Assistant Coaches
Clare Drake, Terry Simpson
Director of Amateur Scouting
Bill Lesuk
Scouts
Mike Antonovich, Connie Broden, Sean Coedy, Larry Hornung, Tom Savage, Joe Yannetti
Executive Assistant to Vice-President and General Manager
Pat MacDonald
Director of Communications
Mike O'Hearn

Director of Community Relations
Lori Summers
Vice-President of Marketing
Madeline Hanson
Director of Team Services
Murray Harding
Athletic Therapists
Jim Ramsay, Phil Walker
Equipment Manager
Craig Heisinger
Home Ice
Winnipeg Arena
Address
15-1430 Maroons Road, Winnipeg, Man. R3G 0L5
Seating Capacity
15,393
Club Colors
Blue, Red and White
Phone
(204) 783-5387
FAX
(204) 788-4668

YEAR-BY-YEAR RESULTS

Season	W.	L.	T.	Pts.	Position	Season	W.	L.	T.	Pts.	Position
1972-73	43	31	4	90	First—c	1982-83	33	39	8	74	Fourth—†
1973-74	34	39	5	73	Fourth—a	1983-84	31	38	11	73	Third—†
1974-75	38	35	5	81	Third—*	1984-85	43	27	10	96	Second—a
1975-76	52	27	2	106	First—xx	1985-86	26	47	7	59	Third—†
1976-77	46	32	2	94	Second—c	1986-87	40	32	8	88	Third—a
1977-78	50	28	2	102	First—xx	1987-88	33	36	11	77	Third—†
1978-79	39	35	6	84	Third—xx	1988-89	26	42	12	64	Fifth—*
1979-80	20	49	11	51	Fifth—*	1989-90	37	32	11	85	Third—†
1980-81	9	57	14	32	Sixth—*	Totals	633	659	143	1409	
1981-82	33	33	14	80	Second—†						

Key to standings: *—Missed playoffs. †—Eliminated in first round of new playoff format (1974-75). a—Eliminated in quarterfinal round. b—Eliminated in semifinal round. c—Eliminated in final round. xx—Stanley Cup champion.

NOTE: Records for Edmonton Oilers, Hartford Whalers, Quebec Nordiques and Winnipeg Jets include World Hockey Association results prior to their entrance into NHL in 1979-80. Key to WHA standings: *—Missed playoffs. †—Preliminary round (established for 1975-76 season). a—Eliminated in quarterfinal round. b—Eliminated in semifinal round. c—Eliminated in final round. xx—Avco World Cup champion.

Randy Carlyle

Dale Hawerchuk

1990-91 SCHEDULE

Home games shaded.

* At Chicago Stadium.

OCTOBER

Sun	Mon	Tue	Wed	Thu	Fri	Sat
	1	2	3	4 TOR	5	6 EDM
7	8 CAL	9	10 BOS	11	12 WAS	13 PHI
14	15	16 NYI	17 NYR	18	19 VAN	20
21	22	23	24 EDM	25	26 LA	27
28 LA	29	30	31 EDM			

NOVEMBER

Sun	Mon	Tue	Wed	Thu	Fri	Sat
				1 CAL	2	3 VAN
4	5	6 PHI	7	8	9 HAR	10
11 CHI	12 TOR	13	14 PIT	15	16 NYR	17
18 STL	19	20 STL	21	22 NYI	23	24 QUE
25 MON	26	27	28 CAL	29	30 MIN	

DECEMBER

Sun	Mon	Tue	Wed	Thu	Fri	Sat
						1
2 VAN	3 NJ	4	5 LA	6	7	8 LA
9	10	11 STL	12	13 CHI	14	15 MON
16 PHI	17	18 PIT	19	20 DET	21	22 DET
23	24	25	26 MIN	27	28 BOS	29
30	31 VAN					

JANUARY

Sun	Mon	Tue	Wed	Thu	Fri	Sat
		1	2 CAL	3	4 BUF	5 HAR
6	7 BOS	8	9	10	11 CHI	12
13 CAL	14	15 CAL	16 VAN	17	18	19 ALL-STAR GAME*
20	21 MIN	22	23	24	25 NYI	26
27 EDM	28	29 QUE	30 MON	31		

FEBRUARY

Sun	Mon	Tue	Wed	Thu	Fri	Sat
					1	2 WAS
3 NYR	4	5	6 TOR	7	8 PIT	9
10 BUF	11	12 DET	13	14 NJ	15	16
17 QUE	18	19	20 VAN	21	22 LA	23
24 LA	25	26 HAR	27	28 LA		

MARCH

Sun	Mon	Tue	Wed	Thu	Fri	Sat
					1	2 LA
3	4	5 EDM	6	7	8 WAS	9
10 NJ	11	12 CAL	13 BUF	14	15 EDM	16
17	18 CAL	19	20	21	22 VAN	23 EDM
24	25	26	27	28 VAN	29	30
31 EDM						

1989-90 RESULTS

Oct.	6—N.Y. Rangers	L	1-4
	8—Philadelphia	W	5-3
	10—At Pittsburgh	L	1-5
	12—At Detroit	L	4-5
	14—At Toronto	W	5-1
	18—At Edmonton	L	2-7
	20—Chicago	L	2-4
	22—Edmonton	W	5-4
	25—Washington	W	6-4
	27—Los Angeles	L	1-3
	29—Los Angeles	W	6-1
Nov.	1—At Calgary	L	3-5
	3—At Vancouver	W	3-2
	5—At Chicago	L	3-4 (OT)
	8—Vancouver	W	3-2 (OT)
	10—Hartford	L	2-4
	12—Calgary	W	3-2
	14—At Quebec	W	5-3
	15—At Montreal	L	1-5
	18—At Philadelphia	W	1-0 (OT)
	20—At N.Y. Rangers	T	3-3 (OT)
	21—At N.Y. Islanders	W	4-3
	23—St. Louis	L	2-5
	25—New Jersey	L	1-3
	29—N.Y. Rangers	W	5-4
Dec.	1—Detroit	T	3-3 (OT)
	2—N.Y. Islanders	L	3-6
	6—At Calgary	W	4-3
	8—Montreal	T	6-6 (OT)
	10—Calgary	W	4-1
	13—Vancouver	T	3-3 (OT)
	15—At Vancouver	T	3-3 (OT)
	19—At Los Angeles	L	5-9
	21—At Edmonton	L	2-3
	26—Minnesota	W	5-3
	29—At Calgary	W	2-1 (OT)
	31—Edmonton	W	3-2
Jan.	3—At Hartford	W	4-2
	4—At Boston	L	2-4
	6—At Pittsburgh	L	3-5
	8—At New Jersey	W	4-3
	10—Washington	W	6-1
	12—Detroit	W	7-5
	14—St. Louis	W	6-5
	16—Quebec	L	6-8
	17—At Edmonton	L	3-6
	19—N.Y. Islanders	L	4-6
	23—At Washington	W	4-3
	25—At Philadelphia	L	6-8
	27—At St. Louis	T	3-3 (OT)
	29—At Minnesota	L	2-4
	31—Toronto	T	5-5 (OT)
Feb.	2—Vancouver	W	8-1
	4—Chicago	W	7-3
	6—At Vancouver	L	3-5
	8—At Los Angeles	W	5-1
	11—At Edmonton	L	4-7
	14—Boston	W	3-2
	16—Pittsburgh	T	3-3 (OT)
	18—Calgary	W	5-1
	20—Buffalo	L	3-4 (OT)
	22—At New Jersey	W	4-2
	24—At Hartford	W	3-1
	25—At Buffalo	L	1-3
	27—At Minnesota	L	3-8
Mar.	2—Los Angeles	W	9-3
	4—Los Angeles	W	5-2
	7—Quebec	W	6-3
	9—Edmonton	W	7-5
	11—Calgary	L	4-6
	12—At Calgary	L	4-5 (OT)
	15—At Boston	T	3-3 (OT)
	17—At Toronto	W	5-4 (OT)
	18—At Buffalo	L	3-4 (OT)
	21—Montreal	W	3-2
	23—Vancouver	L	2-4
	25—At Vancouver	T	3-3 (OT)
	27—At Los Angeles	T	4-4 (OT)
	29—At Los Angeles	W	1-0
Apr.	1—Edmonton	L	2-4

1990-91 ROSTER

No.	FORWARDS	Hgt./Wt.	Place of Birth	Age	NHL exp.	1989-90 club (league)	G.	A.	Pts.
	Scott Arniel	6-01/188	Kingston, Ont.	28	9	Buffalo (NHL)	18	14	32
7	Brent Ashton	6-01/210	Saskatoon, Sask.	30	11	Winnipeg (NHL)	22	34	56
	Stu Barnes	5-10/175	Edmonton, Alta.	19	0	Tri-City (WHL)	52	92	144
	Bob Brooke	5-11/195	Acton, Me.	29	7	Minnesota (NHL)	4	4	8
						New Jersey (NHL)	8	10	18
36	Danton Cole	5-11/189	Lansing, Mich.	23	1	Moncton (AHL)	31	42	73
						Winnipeg (NHL)	1	1	2
	Craig Duncanson	6-00/190	Sudbury, Ont.	23	5	Los Angeles (NHL)	3	2	5
						New Haven (AHL)	17	30	47
15	Pat Elynuik	6-00/185	Foam Lake, Sask.	22	3	Winnipeg (NHL)	32	42	74
39	Doug Evans	5-09/185	Peterborough, Ont.	27	5	St. Louis (NHL)	0	0	0
						Peoria (IHL)	19	28	47
						Winnipeg (NHL)	10	8	18
11	Paul Fenton	5-11/180	Springfield, Mass.	30	7	Winnipeg (NHL)	32	18	50
21	Mark Kumpel	6-00/190	Wakefield, Mass.	29	5	Winnipeg (NHL)	8	9	17
23	Paul MacDermid	6-01/205	Chesley, Ont.	27	9	Hartford (NHL)	6	12	18
						Winnipeg (NHL)	7	10	17
20	Dave McLlwain	6-00/190	Seaforth, Ont.	23	3	Winnipeg (NHL)	25	26	51
	Jeff Parker	6-03/194	St. Paul, Minn.	26	4	Buffalo (NHL)	4	5	9
28	Greg Paslawski	5-11/190	Kindersley, Sask.	29	7	Winnipeg (NHL)	18	30	48
	Pekka Peltola	6-02/196	Helsinki, Finland	25	0	HPK (Finland)	25	24	49
	Teemu Selanne	6-00/176	Helsinki, Finland	20	0	Finland	...	...	...
12	Doug Smail	5-09/175	Moose Jaw, Sask.	33	10	Winnipeg (NHL)	25	24	49
25	Thomas Steen	5-10/195	Tockmark, Sweden	30	9	Winnipeg (NHL)	18	48	66
17	Phil Sykes	6-00/175	Dawson Creek, B.C.	31	8	Winnipeg (NHL)	9	6	15
	DEFENSEMEN								
29	Brad Berry	6-02/190	Barshaw, Alta.	25	5	Winnipeg (NHL)	1	2	3
						Moncton (AHL)	1	9	10
8	Randy Carlyle	5-10/200	Sudbury, Ont.	34	14	Winnipeg (NHL)	3	15	18
44	Shawn Cronin	6-02/210	Flushing, Mich.	27	2	Winnipeg (NHL)	0	4	4
34	Gord Donnelly	6-01/202	Montreal, Que.	28	7	Winnipeg (NHL)	3	3	6
2	Dave Ellett	6-01/200	Cleveland, O.	26	6	Winnipeg (NHL)	17	29	46
5	Todd Flichel	6-03/195	Osgoode, Ont.	28	3	Moncton (AHL)	7	14	21
						Winnipeg (NHL)	0	1	1
	Phil Housley	5-10/179	St. Paul, Minn.	26	8	Buffalo (NHL)	21	60	81
22	Moe Mantha	6-02/210	Lakewood, O.	29	10	Winnipeg (NHL)	2	26	28
3	Bryan Marchment	6-01/198	Toronto, Ont.	21	2	Moncton (AHL)	4	19	23
						Winnipeg (NHL)	0	2	2
27	Teppo Numminen	6-01/190	Tampere, Finland	22	2	Winnipeg (NHL)	11	32	43
4	Fredrik Olausson	6-02/200	Vaxsjo, Sweden	24	4	Winnipeg (NHL)	9	46	55
	Daryl Stanley	6-02/200	Winnipeg, Man.	27	6	Vancouver (NHL)	1	1	2
32	Peter Taglianetti	6-02/200	Framingham, Mass.	27	6	Winnipeg (NHL)	3	6	9
						Moncton (AHL)	0	2	2

No.	GOALTENDERS	Hgt./Wt.	Place of Birth	Age	NHL exp.	1989-90 club (league)	Ga.	SO	Avg.
30	Stephane Beauregard	5-11/182	Cowansville, Que.	22	1	Fort Wayne (IHL)	33	1	3.54
						Winnipeg (NHL)	19	0	3.28
37	Tom Draper	5-11/180	Outremont, Que.	24	2	Moncton (AHL)	51	1	3.52
						Winnipeg (NHL)	6	0	4.35
35	Bob Essensa	6-00/160	Toronto, Ont.	25	2	Moncton (AHL)	6	0	2.51
						Winnipeg (NHL)	36	1	3.15
	Richard Tabaracci	5-10/186	Toronto, Ont.	21	1	Moncton (AHL)	27	2	4.06
						Fort Wayne (IHL)	22	0	4.12

1989-90 RECORDS

1989-90 regular-season records: 37-32-11 (.531, 85 points, 3rd in Smythe Division); 22-13-5 at home; 15-19-6 on road; 4-4-11 in overtime; 16-12-4 vs. Smythe (5-3-0 vs. Flames; 3-5-0 vs. Oilers; 5-2-1 vs. Kings; 3-2-3 vs. Canucks); 6-6-3 vs. Norris; 6-7-2 vs. Adams; 9-7-2 vs. Patrick.

MISCELLANEOUS DATA

1989-90 team rankings: Shorthanded goals for, 14 (T4th in NHL); shorthanded goals against, 7 (T4th); power play, 18.7% (17th); penalty killing, 82.9% (3rd); penalty minutes/game, 20.5.

TEAM HAT TRICKS, CAREER, ACTIVE

Scott Arniel (1)	Phil Housley (2)
Brent Ashton (6)	Greg Paslawski (2)
Laurie Boschman (2)	Doug Smail (2)
Iain Duncan (1)	Thomas Steen (3)

MINOR LEAGUE AFFILIATIONS

Fort Wayne (IHL), Moncton (AHL)

Brent Ashton

1990 DRAFT SELECTIONS

Rnd.	Player	Hgt.	Wgt.	Overall	(Pos.)	1989-90 Club (League)
1—Keith Tkachuk		6:02	212	19	(LW)	Malden Catholic H.S. (Mass.)
2—Mike Muller		6:02	205	35	(D)	Wayzata H.S. (Minn.)
4—Roman Meluzin		6:00	174	74	(RW)	Zetor Brno, Czech.
4—Scott Levins		6:03	200	75	(RW)	Tri-City (WHL)
4—Alexei Zhamnov		6:01	187	77	(C)	Moscow Dynamo
5—Craig Martin		6:02	219	98	(RW)	Hull (QMJHL)
6—Daniel Jardemyr		6:02	183	119	(D)	Uppsala, Sweden
7—John Lilley		5:09	170	140	(C)	Cushing Academy (Ct.)
8—Henrik Andersson		6:04	187	161	(D)	Vasteras, Sweden
9—Rauli Raitanen		6:02	183	182	(C)	Assat, Finland
10—Mika Alatalo		5:11	183	203	(LW)	Kookoo, Finland
11—Sergei Selyanin		6:02	198	224	(D)	Himik, USSR
12—Keith Morris		6:01	185	245	(C)	Univ. of Alaska-Anchorage

FIRST-ROUND ENTRY DRAFT SELECTIONS

Year	Name	Overall	Last Amateur Team (League)	Years in NHL
1979—Jimmy Mann		19	Sherbrooke (QMJHL)	8
1980—David Babych		2	Portland (WHL)	10
1981—*Dale Hawerchuk		1	Cornwall (QMJHL)	9
1982—Jim Kyte		12	Cornwall (OHL)	8
1983—Andrew McBain		8	North Bay (OHL)	7
Bobby Dollas		14	Laval (QMJHL)	5
1984—No first round selection				
1985—Ryan Stewart		18	Kamloops (WHL)	1
1986—Pat Elynuik		8	Prince Albert (WHL)	3
1987—Bryan Marchment		16	Belleville (OHL)	2
1988—Teemu Selanne		10	Jokerit (Finland)	0
1989—Stu Barnes		4	Tri-City (WHL)	0
1990—Keith Tkachuk		19	Malden Catholic H.S. (Mass.)	0

*Designates first player chosen in draft.

PRIORITY SELECTIONS BEFORE 1979 EXPANSION DRAFT

Scott Campbell	Morris Lukowich	Markus Mattsson

Dave Babych

COACHING HISTORY

Tom McVie, 1979-80
Tom McVie, Bill Sutherland and Mike Smith, 1980-81
Tom Watt, 1981-82 to 1982-83
Tom Watt and Barry Long, 1983-84
Barry Long, 1984-85

Barry Long and John Ferguson, 1985-86
Dan Maloney, 1986-87 to 1987-88
Dan Maloney and Rick Bowness, 1988-89
Bob Murdoch since 1989-90

FRANCHISE LEADERS

Current players in bold type
(1979-80 through 1989-90)

Games
1. 713—Dale Hawerchuk
2. **676—Doug Smail**
3. **667—Thomas Steen**
4. 536—Ron Wilson
5. 528—Paul MacLean

Goals
1. 379—Dale Hawerchuk
2. 248—Paul MacLean
3. **188—Doug Smail**
4. **186—Thomas Steen**
5. 168—Morris Lukowich

Assists
1. 550—Dale Hawerchuk
2. **388—Thomas Steen**
3. 270—Paul MacLean
4. 248—David Babych
5. 227—Laurie Boschman

Points
1. 929—Dale Hawerchuk
2. **574—Thomas Steen**
3. 518—Paul MacLean
4. **394—Doug Smail**
5. 379—Laurie Boschman

Penalty Minutes
1. **1338—Laurie Boschman**
2. 772—Jim Kyte
3. 760—Tim Watters
4. 726—Paul MacLean
5. **624—Randy Carlyle**

Goaltenders

Shutouts
1. 4—Daniel Berthiaume
2. 3—Markus Mattsson
3. 2—Ed Staniowski
  2—Dan Bouchard
  2—Doug Soetaert
  2—Bob Essensa

Wins
1. 63—Brian Hayward
2. 50—Daniel Berthiaume
3. 41—Eldon Reddick

NHL DEPARTMENTAL LEADERS

FORWARDS AND DEFENSEMEN

Goals
1. Brett Hull, St. Louis 72
2. Steve Yzerman, Detroit..................62
3. Cam Neely, Boston 55
   Brian Bellows, Minnesota 55
5. Pat LaFontaine, N.Y. Islanders 54

Assists
1. Wayne Gretzky, Los Angeles 102
2. Mark Messier, Edmonton..............84
3. Adam Oates, St. Louis 79
4. Mario Lemieux, Pittsburgh 78
5. Paul Coffey, Pittsburgh 74

Power-Play Goals
1. Brett Hull, St. Louis 27
2. Cam Neely, Boston 25
3. Mike Gartner, Minn.-N.Y. Rangers ...21
   Brian Bellows, Minnesota 21
5. Luc Robitaille, Los Angeles 20

Shorthanded Goals
1. Steve Yzerman, Detroit 7
   Dave McIlwain, Winnipeg 7
3. Mark Messier, Edmonton................6
   Craig MacTavish, Edmonton 6
5. Esa Tikkanen, Edmonton 4
   Wayne Gretzky, Los Angeles 4
   Mike Gartner, Minn.-N.Y. Rangers 4
   Dave Reid, Toronto..........................4

Game-Winning Goals
1. Cam Neely, Boston 12
   Brett Hull, St. Louis 12
3. John MacLean, New Jersey 11
4. Pierre Turgeon, Buffalo 10
5. Brian Bellows, Minnesota 9

Game-Tying Goals
1. Theo Fleury, Calgary 3
2. 14 Players tied with 2

First Goals
1. Cam Neely, Boston 12
   Mark Messier, Edmonton...............12
3. Dave Andreychuk, Buffalo 10
4. Dave Gagner, Minnesota 9

Shots
1. Brett Hull, St. Louis 385
2. Steve Yzerman, Detroit................332
3. Paul Coffey, Pittsburgh 324
4. John MacLean, New Jersey 322
5. Ray Bourque, Boston 310

Shooting Percentage (Min. 80 shots)
1. Luc Robitaille, Los Angeles 24.8
2. Pat Elynuik, Winnipeg 24.2
   Mike Ridley, Washington 24.2
4. Paul MacLean, St. Louis 24.1
5. Craig Janney, Boston 22.9

Plus/Minus Leaders
1. Paul Cavallini, St. Louis 38
2. Stephane Richer, Montreal 35
3. Jamie Macoun, Calgary.................34
4. Shayne Corson, Montreal 33
   Sergei Makarov, Calgary 33

Worst Plus/Minus Leaders
1. Bryan Fogarty, Quebec ....—47
2. Peter Stastny, Quebec-New Jersey ....—46
3. Mario Marois, Quebec ....—45
4. Curtis Leschyshyn, Quebec...........—41
5. Joe Sakic, Quebec ....—40

Penalty Minutes
1. Basil McRae, Minnesota 351
2. Alan May, Washington 339
3. Marty McSorley, Los Angeles 322
4. Troy Mallette, N.Y. Rangers 305
5. Wayne Van Dorp, Chicago 303

1989-90 FINAL NHL STANDINGS

CLARENCE CAMPBELL CONFERENCE

JAMES NORRIS DIVISION

	G.	W.	L.	T.	Pts.	G.F.	G.A.	Home	Away	Div. Rec.
Chicago Blackhawks	80	41	33	6	88	316	294	25-13-2	16-20-4	14-15-3
St. Louis Blues	80	37	34	9	83	295	279	20-15-5	17-19-4	14-16-2
Toronto Maple Leafs	80	38	38	4	80	337	358	24-14-2	14-24-2	16-15-1
Minnesota North Stars	80	36	40	4	76	284	291	26-12-2	10-28-2	17-14-1
Detroit Red Wings	80	28	38	14	70	288	323	20-14-6	8-24-8	14-15-3

CONN SMYTHE DIVISION

	G.	W.	L.	T.	Pts.	G.F.	G.A.	Home	Away	Div. Rec.
Calgary Flames	80	42	23	15	99	348	265	28-7-5	14-16-10	16-12-4
Edmonton Oilers	80	38	28	14	90	315	283	23-11-6	15-17-8	18-10-4
Winnipeg Jets	80	37	32	11	85	298	290	22-13-5	15-19-6	16-12-4
Los Angeles Kings	80	34	39	7	75	338	337	21-16-3	13-23-4	11-15-6
Vancouver Canucks	80	25	41	14	64	245	306	13-16-11	12-25-3	6-18-8

PRINCE OF WALES CONFERENCE

CHARLES F. ADAMS DIVISION

	G.	W.	L.	T.	Pts.	G.F.	G.A.	Home	Away	Div. Rec.
Boston Bruins	80	46	25	9	101	289	232	23-13-4	23-12-5	18-10-4
Buffalo Sabres	80	45	27	8	98	286	248	27-11-2	18-16-6	20-9-3
Montreal Canadiens	80	41	28	11	93	288	234	26-8-6	15-20-5	17-12-3
Hartford Whalers	80	38	33	9	85	275	268	17-18-5	21-15-4	14-15-3
Quebec Nordiques	80	12	61	7	31	240	407	8-26-6	4-35-1	3-26-3

LESTER PATRICK DIVISION

	G.	W.	L.	T.	Pts.	G.F.	G.A.	Home	Away	Div. Rec.
New York Rangers	80	36	31	13	85	279	267	20-11-9	16-20-4	15-16-4
New Jersey Devils	80	37	34	9	83	295	288	22-15-3	15-19-6	18-12-5
Washington Capitals	80	36	38	6	78	284	275	19-18-3	17-20-3	18-16-1
New York Islanders	80	31	38	11	73	281	288	15-17-8	16-21-3	11-17-7
Pittsburgh Penguins	80	32	40	8	72	318	359	22-15-3	10-25-5	18-14-3
Philadelphia Flyers	80	30	39	11	71	290	297	17-19-4	13-20-7	13-18-4

TOP 20 SCORERS FOR THE ART ROSS MEMORIAL TROPHY

*Indicates league-leading figure.

	Games	G.	A.	Pts.	Pen.	+/−	PPG	SHG	Shots	Shooting Pct.
1. Wayne Gretzky, Los Angeles	73	40	*102	*142	42	8	10	4	236	16.9
2. Mark Messier, Edmonton	79	45	84	129	79	19	13	6	211	21.3
3. Steve Yzerman, Detroit	79	62	65	127	79	− 6	16	*7	332	18.7
4. Mario Lemieux, Pittsburgh	59	45	78	123	78	− 18	14	3	226	19.9
5. Brett Hull, St. Louis	80	*72	41	113	24	− 1	*27	0	*385	18.7
6. Bernie Nicholls, Los Angeles	47	27	48	75	66	− 6	8	0	172	15.7
N.Y. Rangers	32	12	25	37	20	− 3	7	0	115	10.4
Totals	79	39	73	112	86	− 9	15	0	287	13.6
7. Pierre Turgeon, Buffalo	80	40	66	106	29	10	17	1	193	20.7
8. Pat LaFontaine, N.Y. Islanders	74	54	51	105	38	− 13	13	2	286	18.9
9. Paul Coffey, Pittsburgh	80	29	74	103	95	− 25	10	0	324	9.0
10. Joe Sakic, Quebec	80	39	63	102	27	− 40	8	1	234	16.7
Adam Oates, St. Louis	80	23	79	102	30	9	6	2	168	13.7
12. Luc Robitaille, Los Angeles	80	52	49	101	38	8	20	0	210	*24.8
Ron Francis, Hartford	80	32	69	101	73	13	15	1	170	18.8
14. Brian Bellows, Minnesota	80	55	44	99	72	− 3	21	1	300	18.3
15. Rick Tocchet, Philadelphia	75	37	59	96	196	4	15	1	269	13.8
16. Gary Leeman, Toronto	80	51	44	95	63	4	14	1	256	19.9
Joe Nieuwendyk, Calgary	79	45	50	95	40	32	18	0	226	19.9
18. Vincent Damphousse, Toronto	80	33	61	94	56	2	9	0	229	14.4
19. Jari Kurri, Edmonton	78	33	60	93	48	18	10	2	201	16.4
20. Cam Neely, Boston	76	55	37	92	117	10	25	0	271	20.3
John Cullen, Pittsburgh	72	32	60	92	138	− 13	9	0	197	16.2

TEAM-BY-TEAM INDIVIDUAL SCORING

*Indicates league-leading figure.

BOSTON BRUINS

	Games	G.	A.	Pts.	Pen.	+/−	PPG	SHG	Shots	Shooting Pct.
Cam Neely	76	55	37	92	117	10	25	0	271	20.3
Ray Bourque	76	19	65	84	50	31	8	0	310	6.1
Craig Janney	55	24	38	62	4	3	11	0	105	22.9

	Games	G.	A.	Pts.	Pen.	+/−	PPG	SHG	Shots	Shooting Pct.
Bobby Carpenter	80	25	31	56	97	− 3	5	0	220	11.4
Bob Sweeney	70	22	24	46	93	2	5	2	147	15.0
Dave Poulin, Philadelphia	28	9	8	17	12	5	0	0	46	19.6
Boston	32	6	19	25	12	11	0	1	42	14.3
Totals	60	15	27	42	24	16	0	1	88	17.0
Brian Propp, Philadelphia	40	13	15	28	31	3	5	0	108	12.0
Boston	14	3	9	12	10	2	0	1	45	6.7
Totals	54	16	24	40	41	5	5	1	153	10.5
Dave Christian, Washington	28	3	8	11	4	− 12	0	0	54	5.6
Boston	50	12	17	29	8	4	2	0	99	12.1
Totals	78	15	25	40	12	− 8	2	0	153	9.8
Andy Brickley	43	12	28	40	8	11	6	0	69	17.4
John Carter	76	17	22	39	26	17	2	1	142	12.0
Greg Hawgood	77	11	27	38	76	12	2	0	127	8.7
Glen Wesley	78	9	27	36	48	6	5	0	166	5.4
Garry Galley	71	8	27	35	75	2	1	0	142	5.6
Randy Burridge	63	17	15	32	47	9	7	0	118	14.4
Bob Gould	77	8	17	25	92	− 3	0	0	92	8.7
Jim Wiemer	61	5	14	19	63	11	0	0	90	5.6
Rob Cimetta	47	8	9	17	33	4	0	0	28	28.6
Brian Lawton, Hartford	13	2	1	3	6	− 2	1	0	17	11.8
Quebec	14	5	6	11	10	− 9	3	0	25	20.0
Boston	8	0	0	0	14	− 4	0	0	10	0.0
Totals	35	7	7	14	30	− 15	4	0	52	13.5
Peter Douris	36	5	6	11	15	8	1	0	63	7.9
Lyndon Byers	43	4	4	8	159	0	0	0	43	9.3
Don Sweeney	58	3	5	8	58	11	0	0	49	6.1
Mike Millar	15	1	4	5	0	− 2	0	0	18	5.6
Jarmo Kekalainen	11	2	2	4	8	2	0	0	7	28.6
Stephane Quintal	38	2	2	4	22	− 11	0	0	43	4.7
Nevin Markwart	8	1	2	3	15	− 2	1	0	6	16.7
Allen Pedersen	68	1	2	3	71	− 5	0	0	32	3.1
Andy Moog (Goalie)	46	0	3	3	18	0	0	0	0	0.0
Wes Walz	2	1	1	2	0	− 1	1	0	1	100.0
Greg Johnston	9	1	1	2	6	− 1	0	0	9	11.1
Michael Thelven	6	0	2	2	23	3	0	0	8	0.0
Gord Kluzak	8	0	2	2	11	4	0	0	8	0.0
Bob Beers	3	0	1	1	6	2	0	0	7	0.0
Bill O'Dwyer	6	0	1	1	2	− 2	0	0	7	0.0
Ray Neufeld	1	0	0	0	0	0	0	0	1	0.0
John Blum	2	0	0	0	0	− 1	0	0	0	0.0
Ron Hoover	2	0	0	0	0	− 2	0	0	2	0.0
Bruce Shoebottom	2	0	0	0	4	0	0	0	3	0.0
Graeme Townshend	4	0	0	0	7	− 1	0	0	3	0.0
Lou Crawford	7	0	0	0	20	1	0	0	6	0.0
Rejean Lemelin (Goalie)	43	0	0	0	32	0	0	0	0	0.0

BUFFALO SABRES

	Games	G.	A.	Pts.	Pen.	+/−	PPG	SHG	Shots	Shooting Pct.
Pierre Turgeon	80	40	66	106	29	10	17	1	193	20.7
Dave Andreychuk	73	40	42	82	42	6	18	0	206	19.4
Phil Housley	80	21	60	81	32	11	8	1	201	10.4
Christian Ruuttu	75	19	41	60	66	9	4	1	160	11.9
Rick Vaive	70	29	19	48	74	9	8	0	195	14.9
Doug Bodger	71	12	36	48	64	0	8	0	167	7.2
Alexander Mogilny	65	15	28	43	16	8	4	0	130	11.5
Mike Foligno	61	15	25	40	99	13	3	0	107	14.0
Scott Arniel	79	18	14	32	77	4	1	1	123	14.6
Dave Snuggerud	80	14	16	30	41	8	1	2	120	11.7
Mike Ramsey	73	4	21	25	47	21	1	0	91	4.4
Uwe Krupp	74	3	20	23	85	15	0	1	69	4.3
Mike Hartman	60	11	10	21	211	− 10	2	0	97	11.3
Jay Wells, Philadelphia	59	3	16	19	129	4	0	0	76	3.9
Buffalo	1	0	1	1	0	1	0	0	0	0.0
Totals	60	3	17	20	129	5	0	0	76	3.9
Benoit Hogue	45	11	7	18	79	0	1	0	73	15.1
Grant Ledyard	67	2	13	15	37	2	0	0	91	2.2
Ken Priestlay	35	7	7	14	14	− 1	1	0	66	10.6
Dean Kennedy	80	2	12	14	53	− 12	0	0	51	3.9
Jeff Parker	61	4	5	9	70	− 9	0	0	61	6.6
Darrin Shannon	17	2	7	9	4	6	0	0	20	10.0
Ray Sheppard	18	4	2	6	0	3	1	0	31	12.9
Shawn Anderson	16	1	3	4	8	2	0	0	16	6.3
Daren Puppa (Goalie)	56	0	4	4	4	0	0	0	0	0.0
Rob Ray	27	2	1	3	99	− 2	0	0	20	10.0
Mike Donnelly	12	1	2	3	8	− 4	0	0	20	5.0
Bob Corkum	8	2	0	2	4	2	0	0	6	33.3
Clint Malarchuk (Goalie)	29	0	2	2	14	0	0	0	0	0.0
Larry Playfair	4	0	1	1	2	− 2	0	0	0	0.0
Steve Ludzik	11	0	1	1	6	− 2	0	0	15	0.0
Francois Guay	1	0	0	0	0	0	0	0	0	0.0
Reed Larson	1	0	0	0	0	1	0	0	1	0.0
Brad Miller	1	0	0	0	0	1	0	0	0	0.0
Kevin Haller	2	0	0	0	0	0	0	0	1	0.0
Mitch Molloy	2	0	0	0	10	0	0	0	0	0.0
Darcy Loewen	4	0	0	0	4	− 3	0	0	1	0.0
Don McSween	4	0	0	0	6	− 3	0	0	4	0.0
Dale DeGray	6	0	0	0	6	− 4	0	0	5	0.0
Scott Metcalfe	7	0	0	0	5	0	0	0	5	0.0

Craig Janney

Bob Sweeney

Rick Vaive

Christian Ruuttu

Gary Suter

Gary Roberts

Dirk Graham

Jeremy Roenick

CALGARY FLAMES

	Games	G.	A.	Pts.	Pen.	+/−	PPG	SHG	Shots	Shooting Pct.
Joe Nieuwendyk	79	45	50	95	40	32	18	0	226	19.9
Doug Gilmour	78	24	67	91	54	20	12	1	152	15.8
Al MacInnis	79	28	62	90	82	20	14	1	304	9.2
Sergei Makarov	80	24	62	86	55	33	6	0	118	20.3
Gary Suter	76	16	60	76	97	4	5	0	211	7.6
Gary Roberts	78	39	33	72	222	31	5	0	175	22.3
Joe Mullen	78	36	33	69	24	6	8	3	236	15.3
Theo Fleury	80	31	35	66	157	22	9	3	200	15.5
Paul Ranheim	80	26	28	54	23	27	1	3	197	13.2
Brian MacLellan	65	20	18	38	26	− 3	10	0	127	15.7
Jamie Macoun	78	8	27	35	70	34	1	0	120	6.7
Joel Otto	75	13	20	33	116	4	7	0	96	13.5
Jiri Hrdina	64	12	18	30	31	10	0	0	96	12.5
Dana Murzyn	78	7	13	20	140	19	1	0	97	7.2
Brad McCrimmon	79	4	15	19	78	18	0	0	97	4.1
Ric Nattress	49	1	14	15	26	14	0	0	65	1.5
Colin Patterson	61	5	3	8	20	− 4	0	0	56	8.9
Jonas Bergqvist	22	2	5	7	10	10	0	0	30	6.7
Jim Korn, New Jersey	37	2	3	5	99	− 1	0	0	18	11.1
Calgary	9	0	2	2	26	1	0	0	3	0.0
Totals	46	2	5	7	125	0	0	0	21	9.5
Mark Hunter	10	2	3	5	39	0	2	0	15	13.3
Tim Hunter	67	2	3	5	279	− 9	0	0	69	2.9
Roger Johansson	35	0	5	5	48	9	0	0	23	0.0
Sergei Priakin	20	2	2	4	0	− 7	0	0	17	11.8
Mike Vernon (Goalie)	47	0	3	3	21	0	0	0	0	0.0
Jim Peplinski	6	1	0	1	4	− 1	0	0	12	8.3
Brian Glynn	1	0	0	0	0	− 1	0	0	0	0.0
Steve Guenette (Goalie)	2	0	0	0	2	0	0	0	0	0.0
Stu Grimson	3	0	0	0	17	− 1	0	0	0	0.0
Marc Bureau	5	0	0	0	4	− 1	0	0	3	0.0
Ken Sabourin	5	0	0	0	10	1	0	0	3	0.0
Rick Wamsley (Goalie)	36	0	0	0	4	0	0	0	0	0.0

CHICAGO BLACKHAWKS

	Games	G.	A.	Pts.	Pen.	+/−	PPG	SHG	Shots	Shooting Pct.
Steve Larmer	80	31	59	90	40	25	8	2	265	11.7
Denis Savard	60	27	53	80	56	8	10	2	181	14.9
Doug Wilson	70	23	50	73	40	13	13	1	242	9.5
Steve Thomas	76	40	30	70	91	− 3	13	0	235	17.0
Adam Creighton	80	34	36	70	224	4	12	0	156	21.8
Jeremy Roenick	78	26	40	66	54	2	6	0	173	15.0
Troy Murray	68	17	38	55	86	− 2	3	1	111	15.3
Dirk Graham	73	22	32	54	102	1	2	3	180	12.2
Michel Goulet, Quebec	57	16	29	45	42	− 33	8	0	144	11.1
Chicago	8	4	1	5	9	1	1	1	10	40.0
Totals	65	20	30	50	51	− 32	9	1	154	13.0
Greg Gilbert	70	12	25	37	54	27	0	0	108	11.1
Dave Manson	59	5	23	28	301	4	1	0	126	4.0
Jocelyn Lemieux, Montreal	34	4	2	6	61	− 1	0	0	34	11.8
Chicago	39	10	11	21	47	0	1	0	78	12.8
Totals	73	14	13	27	108	− 1	1	0	112	12.5
Keith Brown	67	5	20	25	87	26	2	0	111	4.5
Bob Murray	49	5	19	24	45	3	3	0	84	6.0
Al Secord	43	14	7	21	131	5	1	0	68	20.6
Mike Hudson	49	9	12	21	56	− 3	0	0	51	17.6
Trent Yawney	70	5	15	20	82	− 6	1	0	58	8.6
Duane Sutter	72	4	14	18	156	− 2	0	0	70	5.7
Steve Konroyd	75	3	14	17	34	6	1	0	93	3.2
Wayne Presley	49	6	7	13	69	− 19	1	0	75	8.0
Bob McGill	69	2	10	12	204	− 7	0	1	53	3.8
Wayne Van Dorp	61	7	4	11	303	− 3	0	0	38	18.4
Mike Eagles	23	1	2	3	34	− 4	0	0	23	4.3
Bruce Cassidy	2	1	1	2	0	− 1	1	0	3	33.3
Bob Bassen	6	1	1	2	8	1	0	0	7	14.3
Brian Noonan	8	0	2	2	6	0	0	0	13	0.0
Cam Russell	19	0	1	1	27	− 3	0	0	10	0.0
Greg Millen, St. Louis (Goalie)	21	0	0	0	0	0	0	0	0	0.0
Quebec (Goalie)	18	0	0	0	0	0	0	0	0	0.0
Chicago (Goalie)	10	0	1	1	0	0	0	0	0	0.0
Totals	49	0	1	1	0	0	0	0	0	0.0
Mike Peluso	2	0	0	0	15	0	0	0	0	0.0
Jimmy Waite (Goalie)	4	0	0	0	0	0	0	0	0	0.0
Jacques Cloutier (Goalie)	43	0	0	0	8	0	0	0	0	0.0

DETROIT RED WINGS

	Games	G.	A.	Pts.	Pen.	+/−	PPG	SHG	Shots	Shooting Pct.
Steve Yzerman	79	62	65	127	79	− 6	16	*7	332	18.7
Gerard Gallant	69	36	44	80	254	− 6	12	0	219	16.4
Bernie Federko	73	17	40	57	24	− 8	3	0	108	15.7
Shawn Burr	76	24	32	56	82	14	4	3	173	13.9

	Games	G.	A.	Pts.	Pen.	+/−	PPG	SHG	Shots	Shooting Pct.
John Chabot	69	9	40	49	24	5	0	2	91	9.9
Steve Chiasson	67	14	28	42	114	− 16	4	0	190	7.4
Jimmy Carson, Edmonton	4	1	2	3	0	− 2	1	0	11	9.1
Detroit	44	20	16	36	8	− 6	10	0	127	15.7
Totals	48	21	18	39	8	− 8	11	0	138	15.2
Joey Kocur	71	16	20	36	268	− 4	1	0	128	12.5
Dave Barr	62	10	25	35	45	5	2	3	96	10.4
Marc Habscheid	66	15	11	26	33	1	0	0	114	13.2
Rick Zombo	77	5	20	25	95	13	0	0	62	8.1
Daniel Shank	57	11	13	24	143	1	0	0	61	18.0
Lee Norwood	64	8	14	22	95	14	1	0	60	13.3
Borje Salming	49	2	17	19	52	20	2	0	52	3.8
Mike O'Connell	66	4	14	18	22	− 12	0	0	57	7.0
Greg C. Adams, Quebec	7	1	3	4	17	− 2	0	0	8	12.5
Detroit	28	3	7	10	16	0	0	0	19	15.8
Totals	35	4	10	14	33	− 2	0	0	27	14.8
Yves Racine	28	4	9	13	23	− 3	1	0	49	8.2
Kevin McClelland, Edmonton	10	1	1	2	13	− 1	0	0	7	14.3
Detroit	61	4	5	9	183	− 5	0	0	24	16.7
Totals	71	5	6	11	196	− 6	0	0	31	16.1
Doug Houda	73	2	9	11	127	− 5	0	0	59	3.4
Randy McKay	33	3	6	9	51	1	0	0	33	9.1
Sheldon Kennedy	20	2	7	9	10	0	0	0	23	8.7
Robert Picard, Quebec	24	0	5	5	28	− 5	0	0	25	0.0
Detroit	20	0	3	3	20	2	0	0	14	0.0
Totals	44	0	8	8	48	− 3	0	0	39	0.0
Torrie Robertson	42	1	5	6	112	− 3	0	0	20	5.0
Brent Fedyk	27	1	4	5	6	− 1	0	0	28	3.6
Bob Probert	4	3	0	3	21	0	0	0	12	25.0
Glen Hanlon (Goalie)	45	0	3	3	24	0	0	0	0	0.0
Jim Nill	15	0	2	2	18	− 3	0	0	10	0.0
Dean Morton	1	1	0	1	2	− 1	0	0	2	50.0
Chris McRae	7	1	0	1	45	0	0	0	1	100.0
Greg Stefan (Goalie)	7	0	1	1	4	0	0	0	0	0.0
Tim Cheveldae (Goalie)	28	0	1	1	2	0	0	0	0	0.0
John Mokosak	33	0	1	1	82	− 9	0	0	15	0.0
Murray Eaves	1	0	0	0	0	− 2	0	0	2	0.0
Peter Dineen	2	0	0	0	5	0	0	0	0	0.0
Chris Kotsopoulos	2	0	0	0	10	− 1	0	0	0	0.0
Glenn Merkosky	3	0	0	0	0	0	0	0	0	0.0
Sam St. Laurent (Goalie)	14	0	0	0	2	0	0	0	0	0.0

EDMONTON OILERS

	Games	G.	A.	Pts.	Pen.	+/−	PPG	SHG	Shots	Shooting Pct.
Mark Messier	79	45	84	129	79	19	13	6	211	21.3
Jari Kurri	78	33	60	93	48	18	10	2	201	16.4
Glenn Anderson	73	34	38	72	107	− 1	17	1	204	16.7
Petr Klima, Detroit	13	5	5	10	6	− 8	2	0	37	13.5
Edmonton	63	25	28	53	66	− 1	7	0	149	16.8
Totals	76	30	33	63	72	− 9	9	0	186	16.1
Esa Tikkanen	79	30	33	63	161	17	6	4	199	15.1
Craig Simpson	80	29	32	61	180	− 2	7	0	129	22.5
Craig MacTavish	80	21	22	43	89	13	1	6	109	19.3
Steve Smith	75	7	34	41	171	6	3	0	125	5.6
Kevin Lowe	78	7	26	33	140	18	2	1	74	9.5
Joe Murphy, Detroit	9	3	1	4	4	4	0	0	16	18.8
Edmonton	62	7	18	25	56	1	2	0	101	6.9
Totals	71	10	19	29	60	5	2	0	117	8.5
Mark Lamb	58	12	16	28	42	10	2	0	81	14.8
Martin Gelinas	46	17	8	25	30	0	5	0	71	23.9
Randy Gregg	48	4	20	24	42	24	0	0	41	9.8
Charlie Huddy	70	1	23	24	56	− 13	1	0	119	0.8
Adam Graves, Detroit	13	0	1	1	13	− 5	0	0	10	0.0
Edmonton	63	9	12	21	123	5	1	0	84	10.7
Totals	76	9	13	22	136	0	1	0	94	9.6
Vladimir Ruzicka	25	11	6	17	10	− 21	4	0	52	21.2
Craig Muni	71	5	12	17	81	22	0	2	42	11.9
Geoff Smith	74	4	11	15	52	13	1	0	66	6.1
Reijo Ruotsalainen, New Jersey	31	2	5	7	14	− 4	1	0	52	3.8
Edmonton	10	1	7	8	6	− 1	0	0	28	3.6
Totals	41	3	12	15	20	− 5	1	0	80	3.8
Jeff Beukeboom	46	1	12	13	86	5	0	0	36	2.8
Kelly Buchberger	55	2	6	8	168	− 8	0	0	35	5.7
Peter Eriksson	20	3	3	6	24	− 1	1	0	23	13.0
Dave Brown	60	0	6	6	145	− 3	0	0	32	0.0
Chris Joseph	4	0	2	2	2	− 2	0	0	5	0.0
Bill Ranford (Goalie)	56	0	2	2	18	0	0	0	0	0.0
Mike Greenlay (Goalie)	2	0	1	1	0	0	0	0	0	0.0
Francois Leroux	3	0	1	1	0	− 2	0	0	0	0.0
Trevor Sim	3	0	1	1	2	0	0	0	0	0.0
Bruce Bell	1	0	0	0	0	0	0	0	1	0.0
Randy Exelby (Goalie)	1	0	0	0	0	0	0	0	0	0.0
Tommy Lehmann	1	0	0	0	0	1	0	0	0	0.0
Norm Maciver	1	0	0	0	0	− 1	0	0	0	0.0
Mike Ware	3	0	0	0	4	− 1	0	0	1	0.0
Eldon Reddick (Goalie)	11	0	0	0	0	0	0	0	0	0.0
Grant Fuhr (Goalie)	21	0	0	0	2	0	0	0	0	0.0

Steve Chiasson

Shawn Burr

Esa Tikkanen

Glenn Anderson

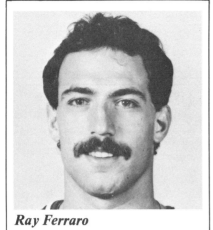

Ray Ferraro

Kevin Dineen

Wayne Gretzky

Steve Duchesne

HARTFORD WHALERS

	Games	G.	A.	Pts.	Pen.	+/–	PPG	SHG	Shots	Shooting Pct.
Ron Francis	80	32	69	101	73	13	15	1	170	18.8
Pat Verbeek	80	44	45	89	228	1	14	0	219	20.1
Kevin Dineen	67	25	41	66	164	7	8	2	214	11.7
Scott Young	80	24	40	64	47	– 24	10	2	239	10.0
Ray Ferraro	79	25	29	54	109	– 15	7	0	138	18.1
Dean Evason	78	18	25	43	138	7	2	2	150	12.0
Dave Babych	72	6	37	43	62	– 16	4	0	164	3.7
Mikael Andersson	50	13	24	37	6	0	1	2	86	15.1
Brad Shaw	64	3	32	35	30	2	3	0	65	4.6
Todd Krygier	58	18	12	30	52	4	5	1	103	17.5
Randy Cunneyworth, Winnipeg	28	5	6	11	34	– 7	2	0	51	9.8
Hartford	43	9	9	18	41	– 4	2	0	70	12.9
Totals	71	14	15	29	75	– 11	4	0	121	11.6
Dave Tippett	66	8	19	27	32	0	0	1	91	8.8
Mike Tomlak	70	7	14	21	48	5	1	1	64	10.9
Yvon Corriveau, Washington	50	9	6	15	50	– 1	1	0	76	11.8
Hartford	13	4	1	5	22	3	0	0	14	28.6
Totals	63	13	7	20	72	2	1	0	90	14.4
Jody Hull	38	7	10	17	21	– 6	2	0	46	15.2
Randy Ladouceur	71	3	12	15	126	– 6	0	0	45	6.7
Ulf Samuelsson	55	2	11	13	177	15	0	0	57	3.5
Adam Burt	63	4	8	12	105	3	1	0	83	4.8
Grant Jennings	64	3	6	9	171	– 4	0	0	45	6.7
Ed Kastelic	67	6	2	8	198	– 3	0	0	35	17.1
Sylvain Cote	28	4	2	6	14	2	1	0	50	8.0
Joel Quenneville	44	1	4	5	34	9	0	0	17	5.9
Tom Martin	21	1	2	3	37	0	0	0	13	7.7
Terry Yake	2	0	1	1	0	– 1	0	0	2	0.0
Jim Culhane	6	0	1	1	4	3	0	0	6	0.0
Kay Whitmore (Goalie)	9	0	1	1	4	0	0	0	0	0.0
Chris Govedaris	12	0	1	1	6	0	0	0	13	0.0
Peter Sidorkiewicz (Goalie)	46	0	1	1	4	0	0	0	0	0.0
James Black	1	0	0	0	0	0	0	0	0	0.0
Bob Bodak	1	0	0	0	7	0	0	0	1	0.0
Allan Tuer	2	0	0	0	6	– 1	0	0	0	0.0
Jim McKenzie	5	0	0	0	4	0	0	0	0	0.0
Steve Dykstra	9	0	0	0	2	2	0	0	10	0.0
Marc LaForge	9	0	0	0	43	– 1	0	0	0	0.0

LOS ANGELES KINGS

	Games	G.	A.	Pts.	Pen.	+/–	PPG	SHG	Shots	Shooting Pct.
Wayne Gretzky	73	40	*102	*142	42	8	10	4	236	16.9
Luc Robitaille	80	52	49	101	38	8	20	0	210	*24.8
Tomas Sandstrom, N.Y. Rangers	48	19	19	38	100	– 10	6	0	166	11.4
Los Angeles	28	13	20	33	28	– 1	1	1	83	15.7
Totals	76	32	39	71	128	– 11	7	1	249	12.9
John Tonelli	73	31	37	68	62	– 8	15	0	163	19.0
Steve Duchesne	79	20	42	62	36	– 3	6	0	224	8.9
Steve Kasper	77	17	28	45	27	4	1	1	72	23.6
Mike Krushelnyski	63	16	25	41	50	7	2	2	101	15.8
Dave Taylor	58	15	26	41	96	17	2	0	100	15.0
Larry Robinson	64	7	32	39	34	7	1	0	80	8.8
Bob Kudelski	62	23	13	36	49	– 7	2	2	135	17.0
Marty McSorley	75	15	21	36	322	2	2	1	127	11.8
Tony Granato, N.Y. Rangers	37	7	18	25	77	1	1	0	79	8.9
Los Angeles	19	5	6	11	45	– 2	1	0	41	12.2
Totals	56	12	24	36	122	– 1	2	0	120	10.0
Todd Elik	48	10	23	33	41	4	1	0	86	11.6
Mikko Makela, N.Y. Islanders	20	2	3	5	2	– 10	1	0	24	8.3
Los Angeles	45	7	14	21	16	– 4	0	0	58	12.1
Totals	65	9	17	26	18	– 14	1	0	82	11.0
Brian Benning, St. Louis	7	1	1	2	2	– 3	0	0	8	12.5
Los Angeles	48	5	18	23	104	1	3	0	114	4.4
Totals	55	6	19	25	106	– 2	3	0	122	4.9
Keith Crowder	55	4	13	17	93	2	0	0	48	8.3
Mike Allison	55	2	11	13	78	– 6	0	0	25	8.0
Jay Miller	68	10	2	12	224	– 6	0	0	44	22.7
Tim Watters	62	1	10	11	92	23	0	0	50	2.0
Petr Prajsler	34	3	7	10	47	– 9	1	0	49	6.1
Tom Laidlaw	57	1	8	9	42	4	0	0	27	3.7
Barry Beck	52	1	7	8	53	3	0	0	36	2.8
Craig Duncanson	10	3	2	5	9	1	0	0	12	25.0
Chris Kontos	6	2	2	4	4	3	0	0	9	22.2
Mikael Lindholm	18	2	2	4	2	2	0	0	10	20.0
Bob Halkidis	20	0	4	4	56	4	0	0	19	0.0
Scott Bjugstad	11	1	2	3	2	2	0	0	10	10.0
Jim Fox	11	1	1	2	0	– 1	0	0	7	14.3
Gord Walker	1	0	0	0	0	0	0	0	0	0.0
Robb Stauber (Goalie)	2	0	0	0	0	0	0	0	0	0.0
Rob Blake	4	0	0	0	4	0	0	0	3	0.0
Ron Scott (Goalie)	12	0	0	0	2	0	0	0	0	0.0
Mario Gosselin (Goalie)	26	0	0	0	0	0	0	0	0	0.0
Kelly Hrudey (Goalie)	52	0	0	0	18	0	0	0	1	0.0

MINNESOTA NORTH STARS

	Games	G.	A.	Pts.	Pen.	+/−	PPG	SHG	Shots	Shooting Pct.
Brian Bellows	80	55	44	99	72	− 3	21	1	300	18.3
Neal Broten	80	23	62	85	45	− 16	9	1	212	10.8
Dave Gagner	79	40	38	78	54	− 1	10	0	238	16.8
Mike Modano	80	29	46	75	63	− 7	12	0	172	16.9
Larry Murphy	77	10	58	68	44	− 13	4	0	173	5.8
Ulf Dahlen, N.Y. Rangers	63	18	18	36	30	− 4	13	0	111	16.2
Minnesota	13	2	4	6	0	1	0	0	24	8.3
Totals	76	20	22	42	30	− 3	13	0	135	14.8
Aaron Broten, New Jersey	42	10	8	18	36	− 15	1	2	83	12.0
Minnesota	35	9	9	18	22	− 8	0	0	65	13.8
Totals	77	19	17	36	58	− 23	1	2	148	12.8
Don Barber	44	15	19	34	32	4	4	0	100	15.0
Basil McRae	66	9	17	26	*351	− 5	2	0	95	9.5
Shawn Chambers	78	8	18	26	81	− 2	0	1	116	6.9
Stewart Gavin	80	12	13	25	76	9	0	3	146	8.2
Gaetan Duchesne	72	12	8	20	33	5	0	1	93	12.9
Perry Berezan	64	3	12	15	31	− 4	0	0	75	4.0
Ville Siren	53	1	13	14	60	1	0	0	53	1.9
Curt Giles	74	1	12	13	48	3	0	0	55	1.8
Mark Tinordi	66	3	7	10	240	0	1	0	50	6.0
Frantisek Musil	56	2	8	10	109	0	0	0	78	2.6
Helmut Balderis	26	3	6	9	2	0	2	0	30	10.0
Rob Zettler	31	0	8	8	45	− 7	0	0	21	0.0
Clark Donatelli	25	3	3	6	17	− 11	0	0	25	12.0
Shane Churla	53	2	3	5	292	− 4	0	0	40	5.0
Neil Wilkinson	36	0	5	5	100	− 1	0	0	36	0.0
Jon Casey (Goalie)	61	0	3	3	18	0	0	0	0	0.0
Dave Mackey	16	2	0	2	28	− 3	0	0	8	25.0
Curt Fraser	8	1	0	1	22	− 5	0	0	7	14.3
Kari Takko (Goalie)	21	0	1	1	2	0	0	0	0	0.0
Daniel Berthiaume, Winnipeg (G.)	24	0	1	1	6	0	0	0	0	0.0
Minnesota (Goalie)	5	0	0	0	2	0	0	0	0	0.0
Totals	29	0	1	1	8	0	0	0	0	0.0
Scott Robinson	1	0	0	0	2	0	0	0	0	0.0
Mitch Messier	2	0	0	0	0	− 2	0	0	1	0.0
Mike McHugh	3	0	0	0	0	− 1	0	0	2	0.0
Ken Leiter	4	0	0	0	0	− 2	0	0	5	0.0
Jarmo Myllys (Goalie)	4	0	0	0	0	0	0	0	0	0.0
Link Gaetz	5	0	0	0	33	− 5	0	0	4	0.0
Jayson More	5	0	0	0	16	1	0	0	4	0.0
Mario Thyer	5	0	0	0	0	− 3	0	0	4	0.0
Peter Lappin	6	0	0	0	2	− 5	0	0	8	0.0

Neal Broten

Larry Murphy

MONTREAL CANADIENS

	Games	G.	A.	Pts.	Pen.	+/−	PPG	SHG	Shots	Shooting Pct.
Stephane Richer	75	51	40	91	46	35	9	0	269	19.0
Shayne Corson	76	31	44	75	144	33	7	0	192	16.1
Russ Courtnall	80	27	32	59	27	14	3	0	294	9.2
Guy Carbonneau	68	19	36	55	37	21	1	1	125	15.2
Brian Skrudland	59	11	31	42	56	21	4	0	70	15.7
Mike McPhee	56	23	18	41	47	28	0	1	118	19.5
Mats Naslund	72	21	20	41	19	3	6	0	136	15.4
Petr Svoboda	60	5	31	36	98	20	2	0	90	5.6
Stephan Lebeau	57	15	20	35	11	13	5	0	79	19.0
Chris Chelios	53	9	22	31	136	20	1	2	123	7.3
Bobby Smith	53	12	14	26	35	− 4	4	0	102	11.8
Brent Gilchrist	57	9	15	24	28	3	1	0	80	11.3
Mike Keane	74	9	15	24	78	0	1	0	92	9.8
Ryan Walter	70	8	16	24	59	4	1	0	109	7.3
Mathieu Schneider	44	7	14	21	25	2	5	0	84	8.3
Claude Lemieux	39	8	10	18	106	− 8	3	0	104	7.7
Eric Desjardins	55	3	13	16	51	1	1	0	48	6.3
Craig Ludwig	73	1	15	16	108	24	0	0	49	2.0
Sylvain Lefebvre	68	3	10	13	61	18	0	0	89	3.4
J.J. Daigneault	36	2	10	12	14	11	0	0	40	5.0
Todd Ewen, St. Louis	3	0	0	0	11	− 2	0	0	3	0.0
Montreal	41	4	6	10	158	1	0	0	26	15.4
Totals	44	4	6	10	169	− 1	0	0	29	13.8
Patrick Roy (Goalie)	54	0	5	5	0	0	0	0	0	0.0
Tom Chorske	14	3	1	4	2	2	0	0	19	15.8
Donald Dufresne	18	0	4	4	23	1	0	0	6	0.0
Andrew Cassels	6	2	0	2	2	1	0	0	5	40.0
Martin Desjardins	8	0	2	2	2	− 4	0	0	7	0.0
Lyle Odelin	8	0	2	2	33	− 1	0	0	1	0.0
Mark Pederson	9	0	2	2	2	0	0	0	10	0.0
Ed Cristofoli	9	0	1	1	4	− 1	0	0	6	0.0
Andre Racicot (Goalie)	1	0	0	0	0	0	0	0	0	0.0
Steve Martinson	13	0	0	0	64	− 2	0	0	2	0.0
Brian Hayward (Goalie)	29	0	0	0	4	0	0	0	0	0.0

Guy Carbonneau

Patrick Roy

Patrik Sundstrom

Brendan Shanahan

Patrick Flatley

Jeff Norton

NEW JERSEY DEVILS

	Games	G.	A.	Pts.	Pen.	+/−	PPG	SHG	Shots	Shooting Pct.
Kirk Muller	80	30	56	86	74	− 1	9	0	200	15.0
John MacLean	80	41	38	79	80	17	10	3	322	12.7
Patrik Sundstrom	74	27	49	76	34	15	8	1	142	19.0
Peter Stastny, Quebec	62	24	38	62	24	− 45	10	0	131	18.3
New Jersey	12	5	6	11	16	− 1	2	0	25	20.0
Totals	74	29	44	73	40	− 46	12	0	156	18.6
Brendan Shanahan	73	30	42	72	137	15	8	0	196	15.3
Bruce Driver	75	7	46	53	63	6	1	0	185	3.8
Sylvain Turgeon	72	30	17	47	81	− 8	7	0	218	13.8
Mark Johnson	63	16	29	45	12	− 8	4	0	82	19.5
Viacheslav Fetisov	72	8	34	42	52	9	2	0	108	7.4
Doug Brown	69	14	20	34	16	7	1	3	135	10.4
Janne Ojanen	64	17	13	30	12	− 5	1	0	76	22.4
Tommy Albelin	68	6	23	29	63	− 1	4	0	125	4.8
Bob Brooke, Minnesota	38	4	4	8	33	− 5	0	3	65	6.2
New Jersey	35	8	10	18	30	3	0	0	44	18.2
Totals	73	12	14	26	63	− 2	0	3	109	11.0
David Maley	67	8	17	25	160	− 2	0	0	82	9.8
Alexei Kasatonov	39	6	15	21	16	15	1	0	60	10.0
Ken Daneyko	74	6	15	21	216	15	0	1	64	9.4
Walt Poddubny	33	4	10	14	28	− 4	1	0	50	8.0
Jon Morris	20	6	7	13	8	12	2	0	17	35.3
Eric Weinrich	19	2	7	9	11	1	1	0	16	12.5
Pat Conacher	19	3	3	6	4	2	0	0	18	16.7
Randy Velischek	62	0	6	6	72	4	0	0	34	0.0
Jamie Huscroft	42	2	3	5	149	− 2	0	0	19	10.5
Neil Brady	19	1	4	5	13	− 1	0	0	10	10.0
Paul Ysebaert	5	1	2	3	0	0	0	0	6	16.7
Claude Vilgrain	6	1	2	3	4	− 1	0	0	13	7.7
Peter Sundstrom	21	1	2	3	4	1	0	0	16	6.3
Sergei Starikov	16	0	1	1	8	− 8	0	0	6	0.0
Sean Burke (Goalie)	52	0	1	1	38	0	0	0	0	0.0
Jim Thomson	3	0	0	0	31	− 3	0	0	3	0.0
Troy Crowder	10	0	0	0	23	0	0	0	4	0.0
Chris Terreri (Goalie)	35	0	0	0	0	0	0	0	0	0.0

NEW YORK ISLANDERS

	Games	G.	A.	Pts.	Pen.	+/−	PPG	SHG	Shots	Shooting Pct.
Pat LaFontaine	74	54	51	105	38	− 13	13	2	286	18.9
Brent Sutter	67	33	35	68	65	9	17	3	198	16.7
Doug Crossman	80	15	44	59	54	3	8	0	159	9.4
Jeff Norton	60	4	49	53	65	− 9	4	0	104	3.8
Patrick Flatley	62	17	32	49	101	10	4	0	136	12.5
Randy Wood	74	24	24	48	39	− 10	6	1	185	13.0
Don Maloney	79	16	27	43	47	6	0	1	113	14.2
Derek King	46	13	27	40	20	2	5	0	91	14.3
Dave Volek	80	17	22	39	41	− 2	6	0	181	9.4
Hubie McDonough, Los Angeles	22	3	4	7	10	4	0	0	13	23.1
N.Y. Islanders	54	18	11	29	26	10	0	3	92	19.6
Totals	76	21	15	36	36	14	0	3	105	20.0
Alan Kerr	75	15	21	36	129	− 1	3	0	127	11.8
Gary Nylund	64	4	21	25	144	8	2	0	65	6.2
Bryan Trottier	59	13	11	24	29	− 11	4	0	84	15.5
Brad Lauer	63	6	18	24	19	5	0	0	86	7.0
Gerald Diduck	76	3	17	20	163	2	1	0	102	2.9
Dave Chyzowski	34	8	6	14	45	− 4	3	0	59	13.6
Mick Vukota	76	4	8	12	290	10	0	0	55	7.3
Joe Reekie	31	1	8	9	43	13	0	0	22	4.5
Jari Gronstrand, Quebec	7	0	1	1	2	− 1	0	0	3	0.0
N.Y. Islanders	41	3	4	7	27	0	0	0	23	13.0
Totals	48	3	5	8	29	− 1	0	0	26	11.5
Tom Fitzgerald	19	2	5	7	4	− 3	0	0	24	8.3
Ken Baumgartner, Los Angeles	12	1	0	1	28	− 10	0	0	7	14.3
N.Y. Islanders	53	0	5	5	194	6	0	0	41	0.0
Totals	65	1	5	6	222	− 4	0	0	48	2.1
Derek Laxdal	12	3	1	4	4	− 4	0	0	20	15.0
Marc Bergevin	18	0	4	4	30	− 8	0	0	12	0.0
Richard Pilon	14	0	2	2	31	2	0	0	5	0.0
Dean Chynoweth	20	0	2	2	39	0	0	0	8	0.0
Dale Henry	20	0	2	2	2	− 4	0	0	6	0.0
Mark Fitzpatrick (Goalie)	47	0	2	2	18	0	0	0	0	0.0
Shawn Evans	2	1	0	1	0	− 1	1	0	4	25.0
Paul Gagne	9	1	0	1	4	− 1	0	0	10	10.0
Wayne McBean	5	0	1	1	2	− 1	0	0	3	0.0
Jeff Finley	11	0	1	1	0	0	0	0	7	0.0
Glenn Healy (Goalie)	39	0	1	1	7	0	0	0	0	0.0
Dale Kushner	2	0	0	0	2	0	0	0	0	0.0
Rob DiMaio	7	0	0	0	2	0	0	0	2	0.0
Chris Pryor	10	0	0	0	24	− 7	0	0	2	0.0

NEW YORK RANGERS

	Games	G.	A.	Pts.	Pen.	+/−	PPG	SHG	Shots	Shooting Pct.
Bernie Nicholls, Los Angeles	47	27	48	75	66	− 6	8	0	172	15.7
N.Y. Rangers............................	32	12	25	37	20	− 3	7	0	115	10.4
Totals......................................	79	39	73	112	86	− 9	15	0	287	13.6
Mike Gartner, Minnesota..............	67	34	36	70	32	− 8	15	4	240	14.2
N.Y. Rangers............................	12	11	5	16	6	4	6	0	48	22.9
Totals......................................	79	45	41	86	38	− 4	21	4	288	15.6
John Ogrodnick...........................	80	43	31	74	44	11	19	0	215	20.0
Brian Mullen...............................	76	27	41	68	42	7	7	3	186	14.5
Darren Turcotte...........................	76	32	34	66	32	3	10	1	205	15.6
Kelly Kisio.................................	68	22	44	66	105	11	7	2	128	17.2
James Patrick.............................	73	14	43	57	50	4	9	0	136	10.3
Brian Leetch..............................	72	11	45	56	26	− 18	5	0	222	5.0
Troy Mallette.............................	79	13	16	29	305	− 8	4	0	107	12.1
Carey Wilson..............................	41	9	17	26	57	4	4	0	64	14.1
Mark Hardy.................................	54	0	15	15	94	4	0	0	55	0.0
Miloslav Horava..........................	45	4	10	14	26	10	1	0	50	8.0
Kris King...................................	68	6	7	13	286	2	0	0	49	12.2
Mark Janssens............................	80	5	8	13	161	− 26	0	0	61	8.2
Jan Erixon.................................	58	4	9	13	8	− 17	0	0	61	6.6
Randy Moller..............................	60	1	12	13	139	− 1	0	0	47	2.1
David Shaw................................	22	2	10	12	22	− 3	1	1	24	8.3
David Archibald, Minnesota..........	12	1	5	6	6	1	1	0	26	3.8
N.Y. Rangers............................	19	2	3	5	6	0	1	0	30	6.7
Totals......................................	31	3	8	11	12	1	2	0	56	5.4
Ron Greschner............................	55	1	9	10	53	− 7	0	0	26	3.8
Lindy Ruff.................................	56	3	6	9	80	− 10	0	0	59	5.1
Paul Broten................................	32	5	3	8	26	− 4	0	0	43	11.6
Jeff Bloemberg............................	28	3	3	6	25	− 8	2	0	20	15.0
Kevin Miller................................	16	0	5	5	2	− 1	0	0	9	0.0
Normand Rochefort.....................	31	3	1	4	24	2	0	0	30	10.0
Chris Nilan.................................	25	1	2	3	59	− 8	0	0	24	4.2
Mike Richter (Goalie)...................	23	0	3	3	0	0	0	0	0	0.0
John Vanbiesbrouck (Goalie)	47	0	2	2	24	0	0	0	0	0.0
Rick Bennett...............................	6	1	0	1	5	− 4	0	0	6	16.7
Cory Millen.................................	4	0	0	0	2	− 2	0	0	4	0.0
Todd Charlesworth	7	0	0	0	6	− 3	0	0	4	0.0
Bob Froese (Goalie).....................	15	0	0	0	0	0	0	0	0	0.0
Rudy Poeschek............................	15	0	0	0	55	− 1	0	0	1	0.0

PHILADELPHIA FLYERS

	Games	G.	A.	Pts.	Pen.	+/−	PPG	SHG	Shots	Shooting Pct.
Rick Tocchet...............................	75	37	59	96	196	4	15	1	269	13.8
Murray Craven	76	25	50	75	42	2	7	2	175	14.3
Mike Bullard..............................	70	27	37	64	67	0	6	0	181	14.9
Pelle Eklund...............................	70	23	39	62	16	7	5	3	126	18.3
Tim Kerr...................................	40	24	24	48	34	− 3	9	0	162	14.8
Ron Sutter.................................	75	22	26	48	104	2	0	2	157	14.0
Ilkka Sinisalo.............................	59	23	23	46	26	6	4	3	102	22.5
Gordon Murphy............................	75	14	27	41	95	− 7	4	0	160	8.8
Ken Linseman, Boston	32	6	16	22	66	12	1	0	47	12.8
Philadelphia.............................	29	5	9	14	30	− 7	1	0	32	15.6
Totals......................................	61	11	25	36	96	5	2	0	79	13.9
Mark Howe.................................	40	7	21	28	24	22	3	1	63	11.1
Keith Acton................................	69	13	14	27	80	− 2	0	2	94	13.8
Scott Mellanby............................	57	6	17	23	77	− 4	0	0	104	5.8
Kjell Samuelsson.........................	66	5	17	22	91	20	0	0	88	5.7
Terry Carkner.............................	63	4	18	22	169	− 8	1	0	60	6.7
Jiri Latal...................................	32	6	13	19	6	4	3	0	59	10.2
Craig Berube..............................	74	4	14	18	291	− 7	0	0	52	7.7
Kevin Maguire, Buffalo.................	61	6	9	15	115	− 3	0	0	62	9.7
Philadelphia.............................	5	1	0	1	6	− 1	0	0	7	14.3
Totals......................................	66	7	9	16	121	− 4	0	0	69	10.1
Kerry Huffman.............................	43	1	12	13	34	− 3	0	0	70	1.4
Tony Horacek..............................	48	5	5	10	117	6	0	0	31	16.1
Normand Lacombe, Edmonton......	15	5	2	7	21	4	0	0	15	33.3
Philadelphia.............................	18	0	2	2	7	0	0	0	21	0.0
Totals......................................	33	5	4	9	28	4	0	0	36	13.9
Derrick Smith.............................	55	3	6	9	32	− 15	0	0	72	4.2
Jeff Chychrun.............................	79	2	7	9	248	− 12	0	0	52	3.8
Doug Sulliman............................	28	3	4	7	0	4	0	0	28	10.7
Murray Baron.............................	16	2	2	4	12	− 1	0	0	18	11.1
Don Biggs..................................	11	2	0	2	8	− 4	1	0	14	14.3
Brian Dobbin..............................	9	1	1	2	11	1	1	0	11	9.1
Ken Wregget (Goalie)	51	0	2	2	12	0	0	0	0	0.0
Don Nachbaur............................	2	0	1	1	0	1	0	0	0	0.0
Pete Peeters (Goalie)	24	0	1	1	2	0	0	0	0	0.0
Len Barrie.................................	1	0	0	0	0	− 2	0	0	0	0.0
Chris Jensen..............................	1	0	0	0	2	− 1	0	0	0	0.0
Craig Fisher	2	0	0	0	0	0	0	0	5	0.0
Mark Freer	2	0	0	0	0	0	0	0	2	0.0
Shawn Sabol..............................	2	0	0	0	0	0	0	0	2	0.0
Bruce Hoffort (Goalie).................	7	0	0	0	2	0	0	0	0	0.0
Ron Hextall (Goalie)....................	8	0	0	0	14	0	0	0	0	0.0
Jeff Harding	9	0	0	0	18	− 1	0	0	11	0.0
Dave Fenyves.............................	12	0	0	0	4	− 6	0	0	10	0.0

Brian Leetch

Bernie Nicholls

Pelle Eklund

Murray Craven

Rob Brown

John Cullen

Michel Petit

Claude Loiselle

PITTSBURGH PENGUINS

	Games	G.	A.	Pts.	Pen.	+/−	PPG	SHG	Shots	Shooting Pct.
Mario Lemieux	59	45	78	123	78	− 18	14	3	226	19.9
Paul Coffey	80	29	74	103	95	− 25	10	0	324	9.0
John Cullen	72	32	60	92	138	− 13	9	0	197	16.2
Rob Brown	80	33	47	80	102	− 10	12	0	157	21.0
Kevin Stevens	76	29	41	70	171	− 13	12	0	179	16.2
Mark Recchi	74	30	37	67	44	6	6	2	143	21.0
Tony Tanti, Vancouver	41	14	18	32	50	1	5	0	103	13.6
Pittsburgh	37	14	18	32	22	− 11	7	0	89	15.7
Totals	78	28	36	64	72	− 10	12	0	192	14.6
Phil Bourque	76	22	17	39	108	− 7	2	1	110	20.0
Bob Errey	78	20	19	39	109	3	0	1	127	15.7
Zarley Zalapski	51	6	25	31	37	− 14	5	0	85	7.1
Barry Pederson, Vancouver	16	2	7	9	10	− 3	0	0	22	9.1
Pittsburgh	38	4	18	22	29	− 10	1	0	58	6.9
Totals	54	6	25	31	39	− 13	1	0	80	7.5
Troy Loney	67	11	16	27	168	− 9	0	0	78	14.1
Randy Gilhen	61	5	11	16	54	− 8	0	0	67	7.5
Jim Johnson	75	3	13	16	154	− 20	1	0	72	4.2
Randy Hillier	61	3	12	15	71	11	0	0	45	6.7
Chris Dahlquist	62	4	10	14	56	− 2	0	0	57	7.0
Jock Callander	30	4	7	11	49	0	0	0	22	18.2
Gilbert Delorme	54	3	7	10	44	3	0	0	37	8.1
Doug Smith, Vancouver	30	3	4	7	72	1	0	1	40	7.5
Pittsburgh	10	1	1	2	25	− 2	0	0	11	9.1
Totals	40	4	5	9	97	− 1	0	1	51	7.8
Gord Dineen	69	1	8	9	125	6	0	0	38	2.6
Richard Zemlak	19	1	5	6	43	− 6	1	0	11	9.1
Jim Kyte	56	3	1	4	125	− 10	0	0	23	13.0
Wendell Young (Goalie)	43	0	4	4	8	0	0	0	0	0.0
Jay Caufield	37	1	2	3	123	0	0	0	6	16.7
Jamie Leach	10	0	3	3	0	3	0	0	10	0.0
Rod Buskas, Vancouver	17	0	3	3	36	1	0	0	11	0.0
Pittsburgh	6	0	0	0	13	− 4	0	0	1	0.0
Totals	23	0	3	3	49	− 3	0	0	12	0.0
Alain Chevrier, Chicago (Goalie)	39	0	2	2	6	0	0	0	0	0.0
Pittsburgh (Goalie)	3	0	1	1	2	0	0	0	0	0.0
Totals	42	0	3	3	8	0	0	0	0	0.0
Mark Kachowski	14	0	1	1	40	1	0	0	4	0.0
Frank Pietrangelo (Goalie)	21	0	0	0	2	0	0	0	0	0.0
Tom Barrasso (Goalie)	24	0	0	0	8	0	0	0	0	0.0

QUEBEC NORDIQUES

	Games	G.	A.	Pts.	Pen.	+/−	PPG	SHG	Shots	Shooting Pct.
Joe Sakic	80	39	63	102	27	− 40	8	1	234	16.7
Michel Petit	63	12	24	36	215	− 38	5	0	137	8.8
Guy Lafleur	39	12	22	34	4	− 15	6	0	100	12.0
Tony McKegney, Detroit	14	2	1	3	8	2	0	0	18	11.1
Quebec	48	16	11	27	45	− 31	5	0	89	18.0
Totals	62	18	12	30	53	− 29	5	0	107	16.8
Marc Fortier	59	13	17	30	28	− 16	3	1	89	14.6
Tony Hrkac, St. Louis	28	5	12	17	8	1	1	0	41	12.2
Quebec	22	4	8	12	2	− 5	2	0	29	13.8
Totals	50	9	20	29	10	− 4	3	0	70	12.9
Mikc Hough	43	13	13	26	84	24	3	1	93	14.0
Claude Loiselle	72	11	14	25	104	− 27	0	3	128	8.6
Paul Gillis	71	8	14	22	234	− 24	0	1	68	11.8
Jeff Jackson	65	8	12	20	71	− 21	0	1	73	11.0
Iiro Jarvi	41	7	13	20	18	− 11	1	0	52	13.5
Joe Cirella	56	4	14	18	67	− 27	1	0	76	5.3
Mario Marois	67	3	15	18	104	− 45	2	0	108	2.8
Lucien DeBlois	70	9	8	17	45	− 29	1	0	83	10.8
Ken McRae	66	7	8	15	191	− 38	0	0	83	8.4
Bryan Fogarty	45	4	10	14	31	− 47	2	0	93	4.3
Steven Finn	64	3	9	12	208	− 33	1	0	74	4.1
Craig Wolanin, New Jersey	37	1	7	8	47	− 13	0	0	35	2.9
Quebec	13	0	3	3	10	2	0	0	25	0.0
Totals	50	1	10	11	57	− 11	0	0	60	1.7
Everett Sanipass, Chicago	12	2	2	4	17	0	0	0	16	12.5
Quebec	9	3	3	6	8	− 4	2	0	16	18.8
Totals	21	5	5	10	25	− 4	2	0	32	15.6
Darin Kimble	44	5	5	10	185	− 20	2	0	40	12.5
Curtis Leschyshyn	68	2	6	8	44	− 41	1	0	42	4.8
Mark Vermette	11	1	5	6	8	− 3	0	0	16	6.3
Mario Doyon	9	2	3	5	6	− 1	1	0	19	10.5
Daniel Dore	16	2	3	5	59	− 8	1	0	5	40.0
Stephane Morin	6	0	2	2	2	1	0	0	11	0.0
Jaroslav Sevcik	13	0	2	2	2	− 5	0	0	9	0.0
Brent Severyn	35	0	2	2	42	− 19	0	0	28	0.0
Dan Vincelette, Chicago	2	0	0	0	4	− 1	0	0	2	0.0
Quebec	11	0	1	1	25	− 6	0	0	15	0.0
Totals	13	0	1	1	29	− 7	0	0	17	0.0
Jamie Baker	1	0	0	0	0	− 1	0	0	0	0.0
Kevin Kaminski	1	0	0	0	0	− 1	0	0	0	0.0
Jean-Marc Richard	1	0	0	0	0	− 1	0	0	0	0.0
John Tanner (Goalie)	1	0	0	0	0	0	0	0	0	0.0

	Games	G.	A.	Pts.	Pen.	+/−	PPG	SHG	Shots	Shooting Pct.
Max Middendorf	3	0	0	0	0	− 9	0	0	5	0.0
Stephane Guerard	4	0	0	0	6	− 5	0	0	9	0.0
Mario Brunetta (Goalie)	6	0	0	0	0	0	0	0	0	0.0
Stephane Fiset (Goalie)	6	0	0	0	0	0	0	0	0	0.0
Jean-Marc Routhier	8	0	0	0	9	− 3	0	0	8	0.0
Scott Gordon (Goalie)	10	0	0	0	0	0	0	0	0	0.0
Sergei Mylnikov (Goalie)	10	0	0	0	0	0	0	0	0	0.0
Greg Smyth	13	0	0	0	57	− 8	0	0	4	0.0
Ron Tugnutt (Goalie)	35	0	0	0	2	0	0	0	0	0.0

ST. LOUIS BLUES

	Games	G.	A.	Pts.	Pen.	+/−	PPG	SHG	Shots	Shooting Pct.
Brett Hull	80	*72	41	113	24	− 1	*27	0	*385	18.7
Adam Oates	80	23	79	102	30	9	6	2	168	13.7
Peter Zezel	73	25	47	72	30	− 9	7	0	158	15.8
Paul MacLean	78	34	33	67	100	2	12	0	141	24.1
Rod Brind'Amour	79	26	35	61	46	23	10	0	160	16.3
Sergio Momesso	79	24	32	56	199	− 15	4	0	182	13.2
Jeff Brown, Quebec	29	6	10	16	18	− 14	2	0	104	5.8
St. Louis	48	10	28	38	37	− 12	6	1	180	5.6
Totals	77	16	38	54	55	− 26	8	1	284	5.6
Paul Cavallini	80	8	39	47	106	* 38	2	1	135	5.9
Gino Cavallini	80	15	15	30	77	− 8	1	0	134	11.2
Dave Lowry	78	19	6	25	75	1	0	2	98	19.4
Rick Meagher	76	8	17	25	47	4	0	2	99	8.1
Steve Tuttle	71	12	10	22	4	− 6	1	1	92	13.0
Rich Sutter, Vancouver	62	9	9	18	133	− 1	0	1	100	9.0
St. Louis	12	2	0	2	22	− 2	0	0	22	9.1
Totals	74	11	9	20	155	− 3	0	1	122	9.0
Ron Wilson	33	3	17	20	23	5	1	0	40	7.5
Gordie Roberts	75	3	14	17	140	− 12	0	0	56	5.4
Mike Lalor	78	0	16	16	81	− 6	0	0	79	0.0
Glen Featherstone	58	0	12	12	145	− 1	0	0	34	0.0
Michel Mongeau	7	1	5	6	2	4	0	0	2	50.0
Harold Snepsts, Vancouver	39	1	3	4	26	3	1	0	13	7.7
St. Louis	7	0	1	1	10	− 4	0	0	2	0.0
Totals	46	1	4	5	36	− 1	1	0	15	6.7
Randy Skarda	25	0	5	5	11	2	0	0	8	0.0
Tom Tilley	34	0	5	5	6	10	0	0	19	0.0
Kelly Chase	43	1	3	4	244	− 1	0	0	9	11.1
Dave Thomlinson	19	1	2	3	12	− 4	0	0	17	5.9
Dominic Lavoie	13	1	1	2	16	− 5	1	0	20	5.0
Robert Dirk	37	1	1	2	128	9	0	0	14	7.1
Keith Osborne	5	0	2	2	8	− 2	0	0	4	0.0
Jim Vesey	6	0	1	1	0	− 3	0	0	3	0.0
Herb Raglan	11	0	1	1	21	− 5	0	0	13	0.0
Curtis Joseph (Goalie)	15	0	1	1	0	0	0	0	0	0.0
Dave Richter	2	0	0	0	0	− 2	0	0	3	0.0
Pat Jablonski (Goalie)	4	0	0	0	0	0	0	0	0	0.0
Tony Twist	28	0	0	0	124	− 2	0	0	2	0.0
Vincent Riendeau (Goalie)	43	0	0	0	6	0	0	0	0	0.0

TORONTO MAPLE LEAFS

	Games	G.	A.	Pts.	Pen.	+/−	PPG	SHG	Shots	Shooting Pct.
Gary Leeman	80	51	44	95	63	4	14	1	256	19.9
Vincent Damphousse	80	33	61	94	56	2	9	0	229	14.4
Ed Olczyk	79	32	56	88	78	0	6	0	208	15.4
Dan Marois	68	39	37	76	82	1	14	0	183	21.3
Mark Osborne	78	23	50	73	91	2	3	1	137	16.8
Al Iafrate	75	21	42	63	135	− 4	6	1	153	13.7
Tom Kurvers, New Jersey	1	0	0	0	0	− 1	0	0	0	0.0
Toronto	70	15	37	52	29	− 8	9	1	156	9.6
Totals	71	15	37	52	29	− 9	9	1	156	9.6
Rob Ramage	80	8	41	49	202	− 1	3	0	196	4.1
Tom Fergus	54	19	26	45	62	− 18	4	0	120	15.8
Lou Franceschetti	80	21	15	36	127	− 12	0	2	76	27.6
Dave Reid	70	9	19	28	9	− 8	0	4	97	9.3
Wendel Clark	38	18	8	26	116	2	7	0	85	21.2
Gilles Thibaudeau, N.Y. Islanders	20	4	4	8	17	2	0	0	23	17.4
Toronto	21	7	11	18	13	6	3	0	44	15.9
Totals	41	11	15	26	30	8	3	0	67	16.4
Dan Daoust	65	7	11	18	89	1	0	4	53	13.2
Luke Richardson	67	4	14	18	122	− 1	0	0	80	5.0
John McIntyre	59	5	12	17	117	− 12	0	1	44	11.4
Dave Hannan	39	6	9	15	55	− 12	0	1	39	15.4
Scott Pearson	41	5	10	15	90	− 7	0	0	66	7.6
Todd Gill	48	1	14	15	92	− 8	0	0	44	2.3
Brad Marsh	79	1	13	14	95	14	0	0	50	2.0
John Kordic	55	9	4	13	252	− 8	3	0	48	18.8
Brian Curran	72	2	9	11	301	− 2	0	0	21	9.5
Bobby Reynolds	7	1	1	2	0	− 3	0	0	13	7.7
Peter Ihnacak	5	0	2	2	0	3	0	0	5	0.0
Allan Bester (Goalie)	42	0	2	2	4	0	0	0	0	0.0
Paul Lawless	6	0	1	1	0	− 4	0	0	6	0.0
Darryl Shannon	10	0	1	1	12	− 10	0	0	16	0.0
Jeff Reese (Goalie)	21	0	1	1	10	0	0	0	0	0.0

Rick Meagher

Paul MacLean

Al Iafrate

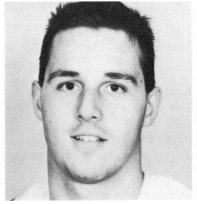

Dan Marois

Greg Adams

Dan Quinn

Michal Pivonka

Kevin Hatcher

	Games	G.	A.	Pts.	Pen.	+/−	PPG	SHG	Shots	Shooting Pct.
Mark Laforest (Goalie)	27	0	1	1	23	0	0	0	0	0.0
Jack Capuano	1	0	0	0	0	− 1	0	0	1	0.0
Mike Stevens	1	0	0	0	0	0	0	0	2	0.0
Tie Domi	2	0	0	0	42	0	0	0	0	0.0
Peter Ing (Goalie)	3	0	0	0	0	0	0	0	0	0.0
Rocky Dundas	5	0	0	0	14	− 1	0	0	1	0.0
Sean McKenna	5	0	0	0	20	− 3	0	0	6	0.0

VANCOUVER CANUCKS

	Games	G.	A.	Pts.	Pen.	+/−	PPG	SHG	Shots	Shooting Pct.
Dan Quinn, Pittsburgh	41	9	20	29	22	− 15	5	0	86	10.5
Vancouver	37	16	18	34	27	− 2	6	0	95	16.8
Totals	78	25	38	63	49	− 17	11	0	181	13.8
Paul Reinhart	67	17	40	57	30	− 2	9	1	139	12.2
Trevor Linden	73	21	30	51	43	− 17	6	2	171	12.3
Greg Adams	65	30	20	50	18	− 8	13	0	181	16.6
Brian Bradley	67	19	29	48	65	5	2	0	121	15.7
Petri Skriko	77	15	33	48	36	− 21	3	1	172	8.7
Igor Larionov	74	17	27	44	20	− 5	8	0	118	14.4
Doug Lidster	80	8	28	36	36	− 16	1	0	143	5.6
Vladimir Krutov	61	11	23	34	20	− 5	2	0	81	13.6
Jyrki Lumme, Montreal	54	1	19	20	41	17	0	0	79	1.3
Vancouver	11	3	7	10	8	0	0	0	30	10.0
Totals	65	4	26	30	49	17	0	0	109	3.7
Jim Sandlak	70	15	8	23	104	− 15	1	0	135	11.1
Steve Bozek	58	14	9	23	32	− 3	0	1	105	13.3
Andrew McBain, Pittsburgh	41	5	9	14	51	− 8	1	0	56	8.9
Vancouver	26	4	5	9	22	− 3	3	0	50	8.0
Totals	67	9	14	23	73	− 11	4	0	106	8.5
Garth Butcher	80	6	14	20	205	− 10	1	0	87	6.9
Stan Smyl	47	1	15	16	71	− 14	0	0	58	1.7
Robert Nordmark	44	2	11	13	34	− 16	1	0	86	2.3
Jim Benning	45	3	9	12	26	4	0	1	49	6.1
Dave Capuano, Pittsburgh	6	0	0	0	2	0	0	0	1	0.0
Vancouver	27	3	5	8	10	− 7	0	0	25	12.0
Totals	33	3	5	8	12	− 7	0	0	26	11.5
Kevan Guy	30	2	5	7	32	− 12	0	0	44	4.5
Adrien Plavsic, St. Louis	4	0	1	1	2	3	0	0	1	0.0
Vancouver	11	3	2	5	8	− 2	2	0	13	23.1
Totals	15	3	3	6	10	1	2	0	14	21.4
Ronnie Stern	34	2	3	5	208	− 17	0	0	27	7.4
Craig Coxe	25	1	4	5	66	− 4	0	0	11	9.1
Kirk McLean (Goalie)	63	0	3	3	6	0	0	0	0	0.0
Rob Murphy	12	1	1	2	0	− 13	0	0	6	16.7
Daryl Stanley	23	1	1	2	27	− 2	0	0	7	14.3
Larry Melnyk	67	0	2	2	91	− 27	0	0	45	0.0
Tim Lenardon	8	1	0	1	4	− 2	0	0	9	11.1
Todd Hawkins	4	0	0	0	6	− 1	0	0	3	0.0
Jay Mazur	5	0	0	0	4	− 2	0	0	4	0.0
Jim Agnew	7	0	0	0	36	− 1	0	0	3	0.0
Steve Weeks (Goalie)	21	0	0	0	0	0	0	0	0	0.0

WASHINGTON CAPITALS

	Games	G.	A.	Pts.	Pen.	+/−	PPG	SHG	Shots	Shooting Pct.
Dino Ciccarelli	80	41	38	79	122	− 5	10	0	267	15.4
Geoff Courtnall	80	35	39	74	104	27	9	0	307	11.4
Mike Ridley	74	30	43	73	27	0	8	3	124	24.2
Michal Pivonka	77	25	39	64	54	− 7	10	3	149	16.8
Dale Hunter	80	23	39	62	233	17	9	1	123	18.7
Kevin Hatcher	80	13	41	54	102	4	4	0	240	5.4
Kelly Miller	80	18	22	40	49	− 2	3	2	107	16.8
Scott Stevens	56	11	29	40	154	1	7	0	143	7.7
Calle Johansson	70	8	31	39	25	7	4	0	103	7.8
Stephen Leach	70	18	14	32	104	10	0	0	122	14.8
John Tucker, Buffalo	8	1	2	3	2	− 3	1	0	8	12.5
Washington	38	9	19	28	10	11	1	0	61	14.8
Totals	46	10	21	31	12	8	2	0	69	14.5
Bob Rouse	70	4	16	20	123	− 2	0	0	72	5.6
Alan May	77	7	10	17	339	− 1	1	0	67	10.4
Bob Joyce, Boston	23	1	2	3	22	− 8	0	0	32	3.1
Washington	24	5	8	13	4	2	1	0	30	16.7
Totals	47	6	10	16	26	− 6	1	0	62	9.7
Bill Houlder	41	1	11	12	28	8	0	0	49	2.0
John Druce	45	8	3	11	52	− 3	1	0	66	12.1
Nick Kypreos	31	5	4	9	82	2	0	0	27	18.5
Rob Murray	41	2	7	9	58	− 10	0	0	29	6.9
Doug Wickenheiser	27	1	8	9	20	1	0	0	44	2.3
Rod Langway	58	0	8	8	39	7	0	0	46	0.0
Tim Bergland	32	2	5	7	31	2	0	0	20	10.0
Neil Sheehy	59	1	5	6	291	8	0	0	32	3.1
Scot Kleinendorst	15	1	3	4	16	4	0	0	13	7.7
Kent Paynter	13	1	2	3	18	− 7	0	0	15	6.7
Mike Richard	3	0	2	2	2	0	0	0	5	0.0
Alfie Turcotte	4	0	2	2	0	0	0	0	4	0.0
Robin Bawa	5	1	0	1	6	− 3	0	0	1	100.0
Chris Felix	6	1	0	1	2	− 6	1	0	3	33.3

	Games	G.	A.	Pts.	Pen.	+/−	PPG	SHG	Shots	Shooting Pct.
Brian Tutt....................	7	1	0	1	2	− 4	0	0	5	20.0
Jim Hrivnak (Goalie).................	11	0	1	1	0	0	0	0	0	0.0
Don Beaupre (Goalie)...............	48	0	1	1	24	0	0	0	0	0.0
Tyler Larter....................	1	0	0	0	0	− 1	0	0	2	0.0
Alain Cote....................	2	0	0	0	7	− 2	0	0	2	0.0
Mark Ferner....................	2	0	0	0	0	− 1	0	0	2	0.0
Olaf Kolzig (Goalie)................	2	0	0	0	0	0	0	0	0	0.0
Jim Mathieson....................	2	0	0	0	4	0	0	0	0	0.0
Dennis Smith....................	4	0	0	0	0	0	0	0	0	0.0
Steve Maltais....................	8	0	0	0	2	− 2	0	0	11	0.0
Bob Mason (Goalie)................	16	0	0	0	4	0	0	0	0	0.0
Mike Liut, Hartford (Goalie)........	29	0	0	0	0	0	0	0	0	0.0
Washington (Goalie)	8	0	0	0	0	0	0	0	0	0.0
Totals....................	37	0	0	0	0	0	0	0	0	0.0

WINNIPEG JETS

	Games	G.	A.	Pts.	Pen.	+/−	PPG	SHG	Shots	Shooting Pct.
Dale Hawerchuk....................	79	26	55	81	70	− 11	8	0	211	12.3
Pat Elynuik....................	80	32	42	74	83	2	14	0	132	24.2
Thomas Steen....................	53	18	48	66	35	2	5	0	129	14.0
Brent Ashton....................	79	22	34	56	37	4	3	0	167	13.2
Fredrik Olausson....................	77	9	46	55	32	− 1	3	0	147	6.1
Dave McLlwain....................	80	25	26	51	60	− 1	1	*7	180	13.9
Paul Fenton....................	80	32	18	50	40	2	4	1	152	21.1
Doug Smail....................	79	25	24	49	63	15	1	1	165	15.2
Greg Paslawski....................	71	18	30	48	14	− 4	7	0	122	14.8
Dave Ellett....................	77	17	29	46	96	− 15	8	0	205	8.3
Teppo Numminen....................	79	11	32	43	20	− 4	1	0	105	10.5
Paul MacDermid, Hartford..........	29	6	12	18	69	1	3	0	37	16.2
Winnipeg....................	44	7	10	17	100	4	1	0	48	14.6
Totals....................	73	13	22	35	169	5	4	0	85	15.3
Moe Mantha....................	73	2	26	28	28	8	0	1	114	1.8
Laurie Boschman....................	66	10	17	27	103	− 11	3	1	87	11.5
Doug Evans, St. Louis..........	3	0	0	0	0	0	0	0	1	0.0
Winnipeg....................	27	10	8	18	33	7	2	1	36	27.8
Totals....................	30	10	8	18	33	7	2	1	37	27.0
Randy Carlyle....................	53	3	15	18	50	8	2	0	92	3.3
Mark Kumpel....................	56	8	9	17	21	− 5	0	1	74	10.8
Phil Sykes....................	48	9	6	15	26	− 8	0	1	50	18.0
Peter Taglianetti....................	49	3	6	9	136	20	0	0	57	5.3
Gord Donnelly....................	55	3	3	6	222	3	0	0	43	7.0
Shawn Cronin....................	61	0	4	4	243	− 16	0	0	30	0.0
Brent Hughes....................	11	1	2	3	33	− 4	0	0	7	14.3
Brad Berry....................	12	1	2	3	6	− 2	0	0	7	14.3
Danton Cole....................	2	1	1	2	0	− 1	0	0	2	50.0
Bryan Marchment....................	7	0	2	2	28	0	0	0	5	0.0
Brian McReynolds....................	9	0	2	2	4	− 4	0	0	11	0.0
Bob Essensa (Goalie)....................	36	0	2	2	0	0	0	0	0	0.0
Todd Flichel....................	3	0	1	1	2	0	0	0	1	0.0
Brad Jones....................	2	0	0	0	0	− 2	0	0	0	0.0
Tom Draper (Goalie)....................	6	0	0	0	0	0	0	0	0	0.0
Stephane Beauregard (Goalie).....	19	0	0	0	4	0	0	0	0	0.0

Dave Ellett

Pat Elynuik

COMPLETE GOALTENDING RECORDS

	Games	Mins.	Goals	SO.	Avg.	W.	L.	T.	Sv. Pct.
Rejean Lemelin....................	43	2310	108(2)	2	2.81	22	15	2	89.2
Andy Moog....................	46	2536	122	3	2.89	24	10	7	89.3
BOSTON TOTALS....................	80	4856	232	5	2.87	46	25	9	89.2
Patrick Roy....................	54	3173	134(2)	3	2.53	*31	16	5	*91.2
Brian Hayward....................	29	1674	94(1)	2	3.37	10	12	6	87.8
Andre Racicot....................	1	13	3	0	13.85	0	0	0	50.0
MONTREAL TOTALS....................	80	4870	234	4	2.88	41	28	11	89.8
Daren Puppa....................	56	3241	156(2)	1	2.89	*31	16	6	90.3
Clint Malarchuk....................	29	1596	89(1)	0	3.35	14	11	2	90.3
BUFFALO TOTALS....................	80	4850	248	1	3.07	45	27	8	90.2
Mike Vernon....................	47	2795	146(2)	0	3.13	23	14	9	87.0
Rick Wamsley....................	36	1969	107(2)	2	3.26	18	8	6	87.5
Steve Guenette....................	2	119	8	0	4.03	1	1	0	84.0
CALGARY TOTALS....................	80	4895	265	2	3.25	42	23	15	86.9
Mike Richter....................	23	1320	66	0	3.00	12	5	5	90.4
Bob Froese....................	15	812	45(1)	0	3.33	5	7	1	87.3
John Vanbiesbrouck....................	47	2734	154(1)	1	3.38	19	19	7	88.7
NEW YORK RANGERS TOTALS.	80	4878	267	1	3.28	36	31	13	88.9
Mike Liut (a)....................	29	1683	74(3)	3	2.64	15	12	1	90.1
Kay Whitmore....................	9	442	26	0	3.53	4	2	1	85.8
Peter Sidorkiewicz....................	46	2703	161(4)	1	3.57	19	19	7	86.6
HARTFORD TOTALS....................	80	4843	268	4	3.32	38	33	9	87.4
Mike Liut (a)....................	8	478	17(3)	1	2.13	4	4	0	92.2
Don Beaupre....................	48	2793	150(2)	2	3.22	23	18	5	89.0
Bob Mason....................	16	822	48(4)	0	3.50	4	9	1	87.7
Jim Hrivnak....................	11	609	36(2)	0	3.55	5	5	0	87.7
Olaf Kolzig....................	2	120	12	0	6.00	0	2	0	81.0
WASHINGTON TOTALS....................	80	4837	275	3	3.41	36	38	6	88.2

Daren Puppa

GOALTENDING LEADERS

Games Played
1. Kirk MacLean, Vancouver 63
2. Jon Casey, Minnesota 61
3. Daren Puppa, Buffalo 56
   Bill Ranford, Edmonton 56
5. Patrick Roy, Montreal 54

Minutes Played
1. Kirk MacLean, Vancouver 3739
2. Jon Casey, Minnesota 3407
3. Daren Puppa, Buffalo 3241
4. Patrick Roy, Montreal 3173
5. Bill Ranford, Edmonton 3107

Goals Allowed Leaders
1. Kirk MacLean, Vancouver 216
2. Kelly Hrudey, Los Angeles 194
3. Greg Millen, St. Louis-Quebec-Chicago.....188
4. Jon Casey, Minnesota 183
5. Sean Burke, New Jersey 175

Shutouts
1. Mike Liut, Hartford-Washington 4
2. Andy Moog, Boston 3
   Mark Fitzpatrick, N.Y. Islanders 3
   Patrick Roy, Montreal 3
   Jon Casey, Minnesota 3

Lowest Goals-Against Average
1. Mike Liut, Hartford-Washington 2.527
2. Patrick Roy, Montreal 2.534
3. Rejean Lemelin, Boston 2.805
4. Andy Moog, Boston 2.886
5. Daren Puppa, Buffalo 2.888

Highest Goals-Against Average
1. Ron Tugnutt, Quebec...........................4.61
2. Allan Bester, Toronto 4.49
3. Alain Chevrier, Chicago-Pittsburgh 4.25
4. Wendell Young, Pittsburgh 4.17
5. Kelly Hrudey, Los Angeles 4.07

Games Won Leaders
1. Patrick Roy, Montreal 31
   Daren Puppa, Buffalo 31
   Jon Casey, Minnesota 31
4. Andy Moog, Boston 24
   Bill Ranford, Edmonton 24

Games Lost Leaders
1. Kirk MacLean, Vancouver 30
2. Greg Millen, St. Louis-Quebec-Chicago.....25
3. Ron Tugnutt, Quebec 24
   Ken Wregget, Philadelphia 24
5. Sean Burke, New Jersey 22
   Jon Casey, Minnesota 22

Save Leaders
1. Kirk MacLean, Vancouver 1804
2. Jon Casey, Minnesota 1757
3. Daren Puppa, Buffalo 1610
4. Ken Wregget, Philadelphia 1560
5. Kelly Hrudey, Los Angeles 1532

Save Percentage Leaders
1. Patrick Roy, Montreal...........................91.2%
2. Mike Liut, Hartford-Washington 90.5%
3. Daren Puppa, Buffalo 90.3%
   Clint Malarchuk, Buffalo 90.3%
5. Mark Fitzpatrick, N.Y. Islanders............89.8%

Lowest Save Percentage Leaders
1. Alain Chevrier, Chicago-Pittsburgh 85.2%
2. Ron Tugnutt, Quebec...........................85.9%
3. Mario Gosselin, Los Angeles 86.5%
4. Peter Sidorkiewicz, Hartford................86.6%
5. Glen Hanlon, Detroit...........................86.7%

Best Winning Percentage Leaders
	W.	L.	T.	Pct.
1. Andy Moog, Boston	24	10	7	.671
2. Rick Wamsley, Calgary	18	8	6	.656
3. Patrick Roy, Montreal	31	16	5	.644
4. Daren Puppa, Buffalo	31	16	6	.642
5. Bob Essensa, Winnipeg	18	9	5	.641

Worst Winning Percentage Leaders
	W.	L.	T.	Pct.
1. Ron Tugnutt, Quebec............	5	24	3	.203
2. Mark Laforest, Toronto..........	9	14	0	.391
3. Mario Gosselin, Los Angeles....	7	11	1	.395
4. Glenn Healy, N.Y. Islanders ...	12	19	6	.405
5. Kirk MacLean, Vancouver	21	30	10	.426

	Games	Mins.	Goals	SO.	Avg.	W.	L.	T.	Sv. Pct.
Greg Millen (b).............	21	1245	61(2)	1	2.94	11	7	3	89.0
Curtis Joseph..............	15	852	48	0	3.38	9	5	1	89.0
Vincent Riendeau........	43	2551	149(2)	1	3.50	17	19	5	88.3
Pat Jablonski.............	4	208	17	0	4.90	0	3	0	82.7
ST. LOUIS TOTALS	80	4861	279	2	3.44	37	34	9	88.2
Eldon Reddick............	11	604	31(2)	0	3.08	5	4	2	89.0
Bill Ranford	56	3107	165(5)	1	3.19	24	16	9	88.7
Grant Fuhr	21	1081	70	0	3.89	9	7	3	86.8
Randy Exelby...........	1	60	5(1)	0	5.00	0	1	0	83.3
Mike Greenlay	2	20	4	0	12.00	0	0	0	76.5
EDMONTON TOTALS.......	80	4882	283	2	3.48	38	28	14	87.8
Chris Terreri.............	35	1931	110(3)	0	3.42	15	12	3	89.0
Sean Burke	52	2914	175	0	3.60	22	22	6	88.0
NEW JERSEY TOTALS.......	80	4864	288	0	3.55	37	34	9	88.3
Mark Fitzpatrick	47	2653	150(4)	3	3.39	19	19	5	89.8
Glenn Healy	39	2197	128(6)	2	3.50	12	19	6	89.4
N.Y. ISLANDERS TOTALS ...	80	4872	288	5	3.55	31	38	11	89.3
Bob Essensa.............	36	2035	107(5)	1	3.15	18	9	5	89.2
Stephane Beauregard......	19	1079	59(4)	0	3.28	7	8	3	89.6
Daniel Berthiaume (c)	24	1387	86(2)	1	3.72	10	11	3	87.1
Tom Draper	6	359	26(1)	0	4.35	2	4	0	83.0
WINNIPEG TOTALS	80	4873	290	2	3.57	37	32	11	87.8
Jon Casey................	61	3407	183(5)	3	3.22	*31	22	4	89.6
Daniel Berthiaume (c)	5	240	14	0	3.50	1	3	0	86.5
Kari Takko	21	1012	68(4)	0	4.03	4	12	0	85.9
Jarmo Myllys.............	4	156	16(1)	0	6.15	0	3	0	80.7
MINNESOTA TOTALS.......	80	4833	291	3	3.61	36	40	4	88.0
Jacques Cloutier	43	2178	112(2)	2	3.09	18	15	2	88.0
Greg Millen (b)	10	575	32(1)	0	3.34	5	4	1	88.0
Alain Chevrier (d)	39	1894	132(1)	0	4.18	16	14	3	85.3
Jimmy Waite	4	183	14	0	4.59	2	0	0	84.8
CHICAGO TOTALS	80	4835	294	2	3.65	41	33	6	86.6
Ken Wregget	51	2961	169(3)	0	3.42	22	24	3	89.2
Bruce Hoffort............	7	329	19	0	3.47	3	0	2	88.1
Pete Peeters	24	1140	72(5)	1	3.79	1	13	5	88.1
Ron Hextall	8	419	29	0	4.15	4	2	1	86.8
PHILADELPHIA TOTALS	80	4870	297	1	3.66	30	39	11	88.3
Kirk McLean.............	*63	*3739	*216(7)	0	3.47	21	*30	*10	88.0
Steve Weeks	21	1142	79(4)	0	4.15	4	11	4	87.3
VANCOUVER TOTALS.......	80	4892	306	0	3.75	25	41	14	87.4
Sam St. Laurent	14	607	38(2)	0	3.76	2	6	1	88.3
Tim Cheveldae	28	1600	101(1)	0	3.79	10	9	8	88.2
Greg Stefan	7	359	24	0	4.01	1	5	0	83.7
Glen Hanlon	45	2290	154(3)	1	4.03	15	18	5	86.7
DETROIT TOTALS	80	4880	323	1	3.97	28	38	14	87.0
Ron Scott	12	654	40(2)	0	3.67	5	6	0	87.5
Mario Gosselin	26	1226	79(4)	0	3.87	7	11	1	86.5
Kelly Hrudey	52	2860	194(7)	2	4.07	22	21	6	87.3
Robb Stauber	2	83	11	0	7.95	0	1	0	74.4
LOS ANGELES TOTALS ...	80	4846	337	2	4.17	34	39	7	86.4
Wendell Young............	43	2318	161(4)	1	4.17	16	20	3	87.3
Frank Pietrangelo	21	1066	77	0	4.33	8	6	2	86.7
Tom Barrasso	24	1294	101(2)	0	4.68	7	12	3	86.5
Alain Chevrier (d)	3	166	14	0	5.06	1	2	0	84.3
PITTSBURGH TOTALS	80	4856	359	1	4.44	32	40	8	86.6
Mark Laforest	27	1343	87(2)	0	3.89	9	14	0	88.6
Jeff Reese...............	21	1101	81	0	4.41	9	6	3	87.1
Allan Bester	42	2206	165(4)	0	4.49	20	16	0	87.3
Peter Ing	3	182	18(1)	0	5.93	0	2	1	83.2
TORONTO TOTALS.......	80	4842	358	0	4.44	38	38	4	87.2
John Tanner	1	60	3	0	3.00	0	1	0	90.0
Mario Brunetta	6	191	13	0	4.08	1	2	0	86.9
Ron Tugnutt	35	1978	152(4)	0	4.61	5	24	3	85.9
Sergei Mylnikov	10	568	47(1)	0	4.96	1	7	2	85.8
Greg Millen (b)	18	1080	95(3)	0	5.28	3	14	1	85.3
Scott Gordon	10	597	53(1)	0	5.33	2	8	0	85.6
Stephane Fiset	6	342	34(1)	0	5.96	0	5	1	82.9
QUEBEC TOTALS	80	4836	407	0	5.05	12	61	7	85.2

( )—Empty Net Goals. Do not count against a Goaltender's average.
(a)—Liut played for Hartford and Washington.
(b)—Millen played for St. Louis, Chicago and Quebec.
(c)—Berthiaume played for Winnipeg and Minnesota.
(d)—Chevrier played for Chicago and Pittsburgh.

NOTE: Liut led all goaltenders in shutouts with 4 (3 with Hartford and 1 with Washington) and goals against average with 2.527 (2.64 with Hartford and 2.13 with Washington). Roy was second in goals against average with 2.534.

MISCELLANEOUS STATISTICS

TEAM-BY-TEAM PENALTY KILLING RANKING

	Times Short-handed	Goals Against	Success Pct.	Short-handed Goals For	Short-handed Goals Against
1. Buffalo	351	58	83.5	7	7
2. Boston	316	53	83.2	5	3
3. Winnipeg	333	57	82.9	14	7
4. Hartford	401	74	81.5	12	10
5. Minnesota	397	74	81.4	14	16
6. Philadelphia	406	77	81.0	14	13
7. St. Louis	351	67	80.9	9	12
8. Washington	370	71	80.8	9	15
9. Montreal	295	57	80.7	4	7
10. New Jersey	340	67	80.3	10	12
Edmonton	417	82	80.3	22	6
12. Chicago	379	75	80.2	11	9
13. Calgary	366	76	79.2	11	6
14. N.Y. Rangers	362	77	78.7	7	8
15. Toronto	408	89	78.2	16	17
16. N.Y. Islanders	371	87	76.5	10	8
17. Los Angeles	366	88	76.0	11	14
18. Detroit	372	92	75.3	18	13
19. Vancouver	342	86	74.9	8	8
20. Pittsburgh	372	94	74.7	7	21
21. Quebec	382	98	74.3	8	15
League Average	....	....	79.2	11	11

PENALTY SHOT INFORMATION

Date	Shooter	Goaltender	Scored	Final Score
10-7-89	Doug Gilmour, CGY	Mark Fitzpatrick, NYI	No	CGY 6-NYI 3
10-10-89	Doug Smail, WPG	Tom Barrasso, PIT	No	PIT 5-WPG 1
10-19-89	Kevin Dineen, HFD	Mike Richter, NYR	No	NYR 7-HFD 3
10-28-89	Claude Loiselle, QUE	Bill Ranford, EDM	No	EDM 6-QUE 3
11-3-89	Jimmy Carson, DET	Mike Liut, HFD	No	HFD 4-DET 3
11-24-89	Mario Lemieux, PIT	Bob Mason, WSH	Yes	PIT 7-WSH 4
11-26-89	Lindy Ruff, NYR	Mario Brunetta, Que	Yes	NYR 3-QUE 1
12-6-89	Dale Hunter, WSH	Wendell Young, PIT	No	PIT 5-WSH 3
12-9-89	Joe Sakic, QUE	Ken Wregget, PHI	Yes	PHI 6-QUE 6
12-10-89	Greg Adams, VAN	Jacques Cloutier, CHI	No	CHI 7-VAN 1
1-14-90	Pelle Eklund, PHI	Mike Richter, NYR	No	NYR 4-PHI 3
2-10-90	Tomas Sandstrom, LA	Wendell Young, PIT	Yes	PIT 7-LA 6
2-19-90	Russ Courtnall, MTL	Tim Cheveldae, DET	Yes	MTL 5-DET 5
2-26-90	Kelly Kisio, NYR	Reggie Lemelin, BOS	No	NYR 6-BOS 1
3-10-90	Tom Kurvers, TOR	Bill Ranford, EDM	No	TOR 3-EDM 2
3-25-90	Keith Acton, PHI	J. Vanbiesbrouck, NYR	Yes	NYR 7-PHI 3

OVERTIME RESULTS

	Games	W.	L.	T.	Pts.	Win. Pct.
1. Edmonton	20	5	1	14	24	.600
2. Montreal	17	4	2	11	19	.559
3. Washington	9	2	1	6	10	.556
4. Los Angeles	12	3	2	7	13	.542
5. Boston	14	3	2	9	15	.536
6. Buffalo	15	4	3	8	16	.533
7. N.Y. Islanders	16	3	2	11	17	.531
8. Detroit	17	2	1	14	18	.529
9. Calgary	21	3	3	15	21	.500
Winnipeg	19	4	4	11	19	.500
N.Y. Rangers	17	2	2	13	17	.500
Pittsburgh	14	3	3	8	14	.500
Chicago	10	2	2	6	10	.500
Hartford	9	0	0	9	9	.500
15. New Jersey	16	3	4	9	15	.469
16. Minnesota	11	3	4	4	10	.455
Toronto	11	3	4	4	10	.455
18. Quebec	8	0	1	7	7	.438
19. St. Louis	15	2	4	9	13	.433
20. Vancouver	21	2	5	14	18	.429
21. Philadelphia	18	2	5	11	15	.417

Players with more than one overtime goal

Scorer Team	Date	Time	Final Score
Theo Fleury, Calgary	2- 1-90	4:51	CGY 4-VAN 3
	3-12-90	1:40	CGY 5-WPG 4
Kirk Muller, New Jersey	11-17-89	3:37	NJ 5-NYR 4
	12-22-89	1:18	NJ 5-PHI 4
Don Maloney, N.Y. Islanders	12-19-89	3:18	NYI 5-NJ 4
	2- 6-90	4:28	NYI 8-PIT 7
Bob Sweeney, Boston	11- 2-89	1:43	BOS 5-LA 4
	11-21-89	2:09	BOS 2-DET 1

TEAM-BY-TEAM POWER PLAY RANKING

	Advantages	Goals Scored	Success Pct.
1. Calgary	357	99	27.7
2. Boston	352	83	23.6
N.Y. Islanders	330	78	23.6
4. Toronto	348	81	23.3
N.Y. Rangers	442	103	23.3
6. Chicago	349	80	22.9
7. St. Louis	351	79	22.5
8. Los Angeles	343	76	22.2
9. Buffalo	358	79	22.1
10. Pittsburgh	403	86	21.3
11. Minnesota	386	81	21.0
12. Edmonton	407	84	20.6
13. Hartford	398	80	20.1
14. Philadelphia	338	65	19.2
15. New Jersey	337	64	19.0
16. Quebec	371	70	18.9
17. Winnipeg	347	65	18.7
18. Vancouver	374	64	17.1
19. Washington	412	70	17.0
20. Detroit	354	58	16.4
21. Montreal	340	54	15.9
League Average	...	...	20.8

PENALTY MINUTES PER TEAM

	Minutes	Game Avg.
1. Buffalo	1449	18.1
2. Boston	1458	18.2
3. Montreal	1590	19.9
4. Winnipeg	1639	20.5
5. Vancouver	1644	20.6
6. New Jersey	1659	20.7
7. Calgary	1751	21.9
8. N.Y. Islanders	1777	22.2
9. St. Louis	1809	22.6
10. Los Angeles	1844	23.1
11. N.Y. Rangers	2021	25.3
12. Minnesota	2041	25.5
13. Edmonton	2046	25.6
14. Philadelphia	2067	25.8
15. Hartford	2102	26.3
Quebec	2104	26.3
17. Pittsburgh	2132	26.7
18. Detroit	2140	26.8
19. Washington	2204	27.6
20. Toronto	2419	30.2
21. Chicago	2426	30.3
League Average	......	24.0

ROOKIE SCORING LEADERS

	G.	A.	Pts.
Sergei Makarov, Calgary	24	62	86
Mike Modano, Minnesota	29	46	75
Mark Recchi, Pittsburgh	30	37	67
Darren Turcotte, N.Y. Rangers	32	34	66
Jeremy Roenick, Chicago	26	40	66

CONSECUTIVE WINS

Games Team	Period Covered
9—N.Y. Islanders	Dec. 31 to Jan. 19
7—Boston	Nov. 9 to Nov. 23
6—Edmonton	Nov. 25 to Dec. 8

1990 STANLEY CUP PLAYOFFS

PRELIMINARY ROUNDS

(Division Semifinals)

(Best-of-seven Series)

ADAMS DIVISION
Series "A"

	W.	L.	Pts.	GF.	GA.
Boston Bruins	4	3	8	23	21
Hartford Whalers	3	4	6	21	23

(Boston won Adams Division semifinal, 4-3)

Thur.	April 5—Hartford 4, at Boston 3	
Sat.	April 7—Hartford 1, at Boston 3	
Mon.	April 9—Boston 3, at Hartford 5	
Wed.	April 11—Boston 6, at Hartford 5	
Fri.	April 13—Hartford 2, at Boston 3	
Sun.	April 15—Boston 2, at Hartford 3 (a)	
Tues.	April 17—Hartford 1, at Boston 3	

(a)—Kevin Dineen scored at 12:30 (OT) for Hartford.

Series "B"

	W.	L.	Pts.	GF.	GA.
Montreal Canadiens	4	2	8	17	13
Buffalo Sabres	2	4	4	13	17

(Montreal won Adams Division semifinal, 4-2)

Thur.	April 5—Montreal 1, at Buffalo 4
Sat.	April 7—Montreal 3, at Buffalo 0
Mon.	April 9—Buffalo 1, at Montreal 2 (b)
Wed.	April 11—Buffalo 4, at Montreal 2
Fri.	April 13—Montreal 4, at Buffalo 2
Sun.	April 15—Buffalo 2, at Montreal 5

(b)—Brian Skrudland scored at 12:35 (OT) for Mont.

PATRICK DIVISION
Series "C"

	W.	L.	Pts.	GF.	GA.
New York Rangers	4	1	8	22	13
New York Islanders	1	4	2	13	22

(N.Y. Rangers won Patrick Division semifinal, 4-1)

Thur.	April 5—N.Y. Islanders 1, at N.Y. Rangers 2
Sat.	April 7—N.Y. Islanders 2, at N.Y. Rangers 5
Mon.	April 9—N.Y. Rang. 3, at N.Y. Isl'nd'rs 4 (c)
Wed.	April 11—N.Y. Rangers 6, at N.Y. Islanders 1
Fri.	April 13—N.Y. Islanders 5, at N.Y. Rangers 6

(c)—Brent Sutter scored at 20:59 (OT) for N.Y. Isl.

Series "D"

	W.	L.	Pts.	GF.	GA.
Washington Capitals	4	2	8	21	18
New Jersey Devils	2	4	4	18	21

(Washington won Patrick Division semifinal, 4-2)

Thur.	April 5—Washington 5, at New Jersey 4 (d)
Sat.	April 7—Washington 5, at New Jersey 6
Mon.	April 9—New Jersey 2, at Washington 1
Wed.	April 11—New Jersey 1, at Washington 3
Fri.	April 13—Washington 4, at New Jersey 3
Sun.	April 15—New Jersey 2, at Washington 3

(d)—Dino Ciccarelli scored at 5:34 (OT) for Wash.

NORRIS DIVISION
Series "E"

	W.	L.	Pts.	GF.	GA.
Chicago Blackhawks	4	3	8	21	18
Minnesota North Stars	3	4	6	18	21

(Chicago won Norris Division semifinal, 4-3)

Wed.	April 4—Minnesota 2, at Chicago 1
Fri.	April 6—Minnesota 3, at Chicago 5
Sun.	April 8—Chicago 2, at Minnesota 1
Tues.	April 10—Chicago 0, at Minnesota 4
Thur.	April 12—Minnesota 1, at Chicago 5
Sat.	April 14—Chicago 3, at Minnesota 5
Mon.	April 16—Minnesota 2, at Chicago 5

Series "F"

	W.	L.	Pts.	GF.	GA.
St. Louis Blues	4	1	8	20	16
Toronto Maple Leafs	1	4	2	16	20

(St. Louis won Norris Division semifinal, 4-1)

Wed.	April 4—Toronto 2, at St. Louis 4
Fri.	April 6—Toronto 2, at St. Louis 4
Sun.	April 8—St. Louis 6, at Toronto 5 (e)
Tues.	April 10—St. Louis 2, at Toronto 4

Top 10 Playoff Scoring Leaders

	Games	G.	A.	Pts.	Pen.
1. Craig Simpson, Edmonton	22	*16	15	*31	8
Mark Messier, Edmonton	22	9	*22	*31	20
3. Cam Neely, Boston	21	12	16	28	51
4. Jari Kurri, Edmonton	22	10	15	25	18
5. Esa Tikkanen, Edmonton	22	13	11	24	26
6. Glenn Anderson, Edmonton	22	10	12	22	20
Steve Larmer, Chicago	20	7	15	22	8
Denis Savard, Chicago	20	7	15	22	41
Craig Janney, Boston	18	3	19	22	2
10. Brett Hull, St. Louis	12	13	8	21	17

*Indicates a league-leading figure.

Thur.	April 12—Toronto 3, at St. Louis 4

(e)—Sergio Momesso scored at 6:04 (OT) for St. L.

SMYTHE DIVISION
Series "G"

	W.	L.	Pts.	GF.	GA.
Los Angeles Kings	4	2	8	29	24
Calgary Flames	2	4	4	24	29

(Los Angeles won Smythe Division semifinal, 4-2)

Wed.	April 4—Los Angeles 5, at Calgary 3
Fri.	April 6—Los Angeles 5, at Calgary 8
Sun.	April 8—Calgary 1, at Los Angeles 2 (f)
Tues.	April 10—Calgary 4, at Los Angeles 12
Thur.	April 12—Los Angeles 1, at Calgary 5
Sat.	April 14—Calgary 3, at Los Angeles 4 (g)

(f)—Tony Granato scored at 8:37 (OT) for L.A.
(g)—Mike Krushelnyski scored at 23:14 (OT) for L.A.

Series "H"

	W.	L.	Pts.	GF.	GA.
Edmonton Oilers	4	3	8	24	22
Winnipeg Jets	3	4	6	22	24

(Edmonton won Smythe Division semifinal, 4-3)

Wed.	April 4—Winnipeg 7, at Edmonton 5
Fri.	April 6—Winnipeg 2, at Edmonton 3 (h)
Sun.	April 8—Edmonton 1, at Winnipeg 2
Tues.	April 10—Edmonton 3, at Winnipeg 4 (i)
Thur.	April 12—Winnipeg 3, at Edmonton 4
Sat.	April 14—Edmonton 4, at Winnipeg 3
Mon.	April 16—Winnipeg 1, at Edmonton 4

(h)—Mark Lamb scored at 4:21 (OT) for Edmonton.
(i)—Dave Ellett scored at 21:08 (OT) for Winnipeg.

QUARTERFINAL ROUNDS

(Division Finals)

(Best-of-seven Series)

ADAMS DIVISION
Series "I"

	W.	L.	Pts.	GF.	GA.
Boston Bruins	4	1	8	16	12
Montreal Canadiens	1	4	2	12	16

(Boston won Division final, 4-1)

Thur.	April 19—Montreal 0, at Boston 1
Sat.	April 21—Montreal 1, at Boston 5 (j)
Mon.	April 23—Boston 6, at Montreal 3
Wed.	April 25—Boston 1, at Montreal 4
Fri.	April 27—Montreal 1, at Boston 3

(j)—Garry Galley scored at 3:42 of overtime for Boston.

PATRICK DIVISION
Series "J"

	W.	L.	Pts.	GF.	GA.
Washington Capitals	4	1	8	22	15
New York Rangers	1	4	2	15	22

(Washington won Division final, 4-1)

Thur.	April 19—Washington 3, at N.Y. Rangers 7
Sat.	April 21—Washington 6, at N.Y. Rangers 3
Mon.	April 23—N.Y. Rangers 1, at Washington 7
Wed.	April 25—N.Y. Rangers 3, at Washington 4 (k)
Fri.	April 27—Washington 2, at N.Y. Rangers 1 (l)

(k)—Rod Langway scored at 0:34 (OT) for Wash.
(l)—John Druce scored at 6:48 (OT) for Washington.

NORRIS DIVISION
Series "K"

	W.	L.	Pts.	GF.	GA.
Chicago Blackhawks	4	3	8	28	22
St. Louis Blues	3	4	6	22	28

(Chicago won Division final, 4-3)

Wed.	April 18—St. Louis 4, at Chicago 3
Fri.	April 20—St. Louis 3, at Chicago 5
Sun.	April 22—Chicago 4, at St. Louis 5
Tues.	April 24—Chicago 3, at St. Louis 2
Thur.	April 26—St. Louis 3, at Chicago 3
Sat.	April 28—Chicago 2, at St. Louis 4
Mon.	April 30—St. Louis 2, at Chicago 8

SMYTHE DIVISION
Series "L"

	W.	L.	Pts.	GF.	GA.
Edmonton Oilers	4	0	8	24	10
Los Angeles Kings	0	4	0	10	24

(Edmonton won Division final, 4-0)

Wed.	April 18—Los Angeles 0, at Edmonton 7
Fri.	April 20—Los Angeles 1, at Edmonton 6
Sun.	April 22—Edmonton 5, at Los Angeles 4
Tues.	April 24—Edmonton 6, at Los Angeles 5 (m)

(m)—Joe Murphy scored at 4:42 (OT) for Edmonton.

SEMIFINAL ROUNDS

(Conference Championships)

(Best-of-seven Series)

PRINCE OF WALES CONFERENCE
Series "M"

	W.	L.	Pts.	GF.	GA.
Boston Bruins	4	0	8	15	6
Washington Capitals	0	4	0	6	15

(Boston won Conference title, 4-0)

Thur.	May 3—Washington 3, at Boston 5
Sat.	May 5—Washington 0, at Boston 3
Mon.	May 7—Boston 4, at Washington 1
Wed.	May 9—Boston 3, at Washington 2

CLARENCE CAMPBELL CONFERENCE
Series "N"

	W.	L.	Pts.	GF.	GA.
Edmonton Oilers	4	2	8	25	20
Chicago Blackhawks	2	4	4	20	25

(Edmonton won Conference title, 4-2)

Wed.	May 2—Chicago 2, at Edmonton 5
Fri.	May 4—Chicago 4, at Edmonton 3
Sun.	May 6—Edmonton 1, at Chicago 5
Tues.	May 8—Edmonton 4, at Chicago 2
Thur.	May 10—Chicago 3, at Edmonton 4
Sat.	May 12—Edmonton 8, at Chicago 4

FINALS FOR THE STANLEY CUP

GAME 1—TUESDAY, MAY 15
at Boston (Edmonton won, 3-2)

Edmonton..............................1 1 0 0 0 1–3
Boston..................................0 0 2 0 0 0–2

FIRST PERIOD—1. Edmonton—Graves 4 (Murphy, Simpson), 9:46. Penalties—Anderson, Edmonton (cross-checking), 3:05; Neely, Boston (interference), 4:41; Messier, Edmonton (tripping), 12:24; Carter, Boston (roughing), 15:53.

SECOND PERIOD—2. Edmonton—Anderson 7 (Messier, Ruotsalainen), 13:00. Penalties—Tikkanen, Edmonton (holding), 9:44; Huddy, Edmonton (hooking), 14:38.

THIRD PERIOD—3. Boston—Bourque 3 (Hawgood, Neely), 3:43. 4. Boston—Bourque 4 (Hawgood, Neely), 18:31. Penalties—None.

FIRST OVERTIME—None. Penalties—None.

SECOND OVERTIME—None. Penalties—None.

THIRD OVERTIME—5. Edmonton—Klima 5 (Kurri, MacTavish), 15:13. Penalties—S. Smith, Edmonton (roughing), 2:41; Neely, Boston (roughing), 2:41; Tikkanen, Edmonton (slashing), 13:48; Moog, Boston, served by Gould (slashing), 13:48.

Shots on goal—Edmonton 6-4-6-7-5-3–31. Boston 10-6-15-6-7-8–52. Power-play Opportunities—Edmonton 0 of 2; Boston 0 of 4. Goalies—Edmonton, Ranford, 13-5 (52 shots-50 saves). Boston, Moog, 12-4 (31-28). A—14,448.

GAME 2—FRIDAY, MAY 18
at Boston (Edmonton won, 7-2)

Edmonton.............................2 4 1–7
Boston..................................1 1 0–2

FIRST PERIOD—1. Edmonton—Graves 5 (Gregg, Murphy), 8:38. 2. Edmonton—Kurri 8 (Tikkanen), 10:53 (pp). 3. Boston—Bourque 5 (Neely), 19:07. Penalties—Messier, Edmonton (roughing), 0:49; Anderson, Edmonton (tripping), 4:45; Carter, Boston, major-game misconduct (high-sticking), 6:20; S. Smith, Edmonton (hooking), 6:45; Buchberger, Edmonton (unsportsmanlike conduct), 12:55; D. Sweeney, Boston (elbowing), 12:55; Lamb, Edmonton (tripping), 14:56.

SECOND PERIOD—4. Boston—Hawgood 1 (Bourque, Burridge), 2:56 (pp). 5. Edmonton—Kurri 9 (Tikkanen), 4:21. 6. Edmonton—Simpson 13 (Kurri), 15:28. 7. Edmonton—Tikkanen 11 (Kurri), 17:10. 8. Boston—Murphy 5 (S. Smith), 19:12. Penalties—Tikkanen, Edmonton (holding), 1:14; Neely, Boston (roughing) 2:27; S. Smith, Edmonton (roughing), 2:27; Tikkanen, Edmonton (roughing), 11:00; Hawgood, Boston (rough-

ing), 11:00; Ranford, Edmonton, served by Simpson (delay of game), 11:14.

THIRD PERIOD—9. Edmonton—Kurri 10 (Ruotsalainen, Lamb), 7:27 (pp). Penalties—B. Sweeney, Boston (holding), 5:30; Murphy, Edmonton, double minor (unsportsmanlike conduct, roughing), 12:50; Johnston, Boston, double minor (roughing), 12:50.

Shots on goal—Edmonton 2-9-11—22. Boston 10-12-5—27. Missed penalty shots—Klima, Edmonton, 19:00 second. Power-play Opportunities—Edmonton 2 of 3; Boston 1 of 5. Goalies—Edmonton, Ranford, 14-5 (27 shots-25 saves). Boston, Moog, 12-5 (4-1), Lemelin (4:21 second, 18-14). A—14,448.

GAME 3—SUNDAY, MAY 20
at Edmonton (Boston won 2-1)

Boston..................................2 0 0–2
Edmonton.............................0 0 1–1

FIRST PERIOD—1. Boston—Byce 2 (Neely), 0:10. 2. Boston—Johnston 1 (Burridge, B. Sweeney), 15:04. Penalties—D. Sweeney, Boston (holding), 3:16; Gelinas, Edmonton (hooking), 6:32; MacTavish, Edmonton (tripping), 12:18; Kurri, Edmonton (interference), 17:17.

SECOND PERIOD—None. Penalties—Simpson, Edmonton (interference), 12:28; Pedersen, Boston (holding), 15:37.

THIRD PERIOD—3. Edmonton—Tikkanen 12 (Kurri, S. Smith), 5:54 (pp). Penalties—D. Sweeney, Boston (holding), 1:30; Galley, Boston (holding), 5:32; Bourque, Boston (holding), 6:01; S. Smith, Edmonton (interference), 6:33.

Shots on goal—Boston 13-7-2—22. Edmonton 11-4-14—29. Power-play Opportunities—Boston 0 of 5; Edmonton 1 of 5. Goalies—Boston, Moog, 13-5 (29 shots-28 saves). Edmonton, Ranford, 14-6 (22-20). A—17,503.

GAME 4—TUESDAY, MAY 22
at Edmonton (Edmonton won, 5-1)

Boston..................................0 0 1–1
Edmonton.............................2 2 1–5

FIRST PERIOD—1. Edmonton—Anderson 8 (Simpson, Lamb), 2:13 (pp). 2. Edmonton—Anderson 9 (Messier, Simpson), 16:27. Penalties—Carpenter, Boston (interference), 0:24; Neely, Boston (roughing), 3:16; Muni, Edmonton (roughing), 3:16; Messier, Edmonton (boarding), 13:33; Ruotsalainen, Edmonton (unsportsmanlike conduct), 16:11; Carter, Boston (unsportsmanlike conduct), 16:11; Hawgood, Boston (slashing), 18:52.

SECOND PERIOD—3. Edmonton—Simpson 14 (Messier, Anderson), 1:00. 4. Edmonton—Tikkanen 13 (Kurri, MacTavish), 19:15. Penalties—Wesley, Boston (hooking), 6:20; Simpson, Edmonton (tripping), 12:39; Anderson, Edmonton (tripping), 19:50.

THIRD PERIOD—5. Boston—Carter 6 (unassisted) 15:02. 6. Edmonton—Simpson 15 (Anderson, Messier), 18:26. Penalties—Simpson, Edmonton (elbowing), 5:04; Burridge, Boston (slashing), 12:14; Neely, Boston (high-sticking), 15:14; S. Smith, Edmonton, major (fighting), 17:06; B. Sweeney, Boston, major (fighting), 17:06.

Shots on goal—Boston 7-11-7—25. Edmonton 12-10-11—33. Power-play Opportunities—Boston 0 of 4; Edmonton 1 of 5. Goalies—Boston, Moog, 13-6 (33 shots-28 saves), Edmonton, Ranford, 15-6 (25-24). A—17,503.

GAME 5—THURSDAY, MAY 24
at Boston (Edmonton won, 4-1)

Edmonton.............................0 2 2–4
Boston..................................0 0 1–1

FIRST PERIOD—None. Penalties—Bourque, Boston (cross-checking), 2:56; Tikkanen, Edmonton (holding), 4:32; Galley, Boston (holding), 4:45.

SECOND PERIOD—1. Edmonton—Anderson 10 (unassisted) 1:17. 2. Edmonton—Simpson 16 (Anderson), 9:31. Penalties—None.

THIRD PERIOD—3. Edmonton—S. Smith 5 (Messier, Simpson), 6:09. 4. Edmonton—Murphy 6 (Lamb, Gelinas), 14:53. 5. Boston—Byers 1 (D. Sweeney, Bourque), 16:30. Penalties—Huddy, Edmonton (hooking), 7:09; Bourque, Boston (holding), 11:46.

Shots on goal—Edmonton 10-5-7—22. Boston 10-10-10—30. Power-play Opportunities—Edmonton 0 of 3; Boston 0 of 1. Goalies—Edmonton, Ranford, 16-6 (30 shots-29 saves). Boston, Moog, 13-7 (22-18). A—14,448.

(Best-of-seven Series)					
Series "O"					
	W.	L.	Pts.	GF.	GA.
Edmonton Oilers...............	4	1	8	20	8
Boston Bruins	1	4	2	8	20

(Edmonton Oilers won Stanley Cup Championship, 4-1)

Tues.	May 15—Edmonton 3, at Boston 2 (3 OT)	
Fri.	May 18—Edmonton 7, at Boston 2	
Sun.	May 20—Boston 2, at Edmonton 1	
Tues.	May 22—Boston 1, at Edmonton 5	
Thur.	May 24—Edmonton 4, at Boston 1	

TEAM-BY-TEAM PLAYOFF SCORING

BOSTON BRUINS

(Lost Stanley Cup finals to Edmonton, 4-1)

	Games	G.	A.	Pts.	Pen.
Cam Neely	21	12	16	28	51
Craig Janney	18	3	19	22	2
Ray Bourque	17	5	12	17	16
Randy Burridge	21	4	11	15	14
Dave Poulin	18	8	5	13	8
Brian Propp	20	4	9	13	2
Bobby Carpenter	21	4	6	10	39
John Carter	21	6	3	9	45
Glen Wesley	21	2	6	8	36
Garry Galley	21	3	3	6	34
Don Sweeney	21	1	5	6	18
Dave Christian	21	4	1	5	4
Greg Hawgood	15	1	3	4	12
John Byce	8	2	0	2	2
Bob Beers	14	1	1	2	18
Bob Sweeney	20	0	2	2	30
Greg Johnston	5	1	0	1	4
Lyndon Byers	17	1	0	1	12
Peter Douris	8	0	1	1	5
Jim Wiemer	8	0	1	1	4

	Games	G.	A.	Pts.	Pen.
Lou Crawford	1	0	0	0	0
Bill O'Dwyer	1	0	0	0	2
Andy Brickley	2	0	0	0	0
Rejean Lemelin (Goalie)	3	0	0	0	0
Bob Gould	17	0	0	0	4
Andy Moog (Goalie)	20	0	0	0	6
Allen Pedersen	21	0	0	0	41

BUFFALO SABRES

(Lost Adams Division semifinals to Montreal, 4-2)

	Games	G.	A.	Pts.	Pen.
Dave Andreychuk	6	2	5	7	2
Rick Vaive	6	4	2	6	6
Pierre Turgeon	6	2	4	6	2
Doug Bodger	6	1	5	6	6
Phil Housley	6	1	4	5	4
Dean Kennedy	6	1	1	2	12
Scott Arniel	5	1	0	1	4
Bob Corkum	5	1	0	1	4
Alexander Mogilny	4	0	1	1	2
Mike Foligno	6	0	1	1	12
Mike Ramsey	6	0	1	1	8
Darrin Shannon	6	0	1	1	4

	Games	G.	A.	Pts.	Pen.
Don Audette	2	0	0	0	0
Benoit Hogue	3	0	0	0	10
Ken Priestlay	5	0	0	0	8
Mike Hartman	6	0	0	0	18
Uwe Krupp	6	0	0	0	4
Daren Puppa (Goalie)	6	0	0	0	0
Christian Ruuttu	6	0	0	0	4
Dave Snuggerud	6	0	0	0	2
Jay Wells	6	0	0	0	12

CALGARY FLAMES

(Lost Smythe Division semifinals to Los Angeles, 4-2)

	Games	G.	A.	Pts.	Pen.
Joe Nieuwendyk	6	4	6	10	4
Gary Roberts	6	2	5	7	41
Sergei Makarov	6	0	6	6	0
Theo Fleury	6	2	3	5	10
Al MacInnis	6	2	3	5	8
Doug Gilmour	6	3	1	4	8
Dana Murzyn	6	2	2	4	2
Joel Otto	6	2	2	4	2
Paul Ranheim	6	1	3	4	2
Joe Mullen	6	3	0	3	0

	Games	G.	A.	Pts.	Pen.
Jamie Macoun	6	0	3	3	10
Ric Nattress	6	2	0	2	8
Brian MacLellan	6	0	2	2	8
Brad McCrimmon	6	0	2	2	8
Jim Korn	4	1	0	1	12
Jiri Hrdina	6	0	1	1	2
Gary Suter	6	0	1	1	14
Rick Wamsley (Goalie)	1	0	0	0	0
Sergei Priakin	2	0	0	0	0
Tim Hunter	6	0	0	0	4
Mike Vernon (Goalie)	6	0	0	0	0

CHICAGO BLACKHAWKS

(Lost Clarence Campbell Conf. title to Edmonton, 4-2)

	Games	G.	A.	Pts.	Pen.
Steve Larmer	20	7	15	22	8
Denis Savard	20	7	15	22	41
Jeremy Roenick	20	11	7	18	8
Wayne Presley	19	9	6	15	29
Doug Wilson	20	3	12	15	18
Steve Thomas	20	7	6	13	33
Greg Gilbert	19	5	8	13	34
Adam Creighton	20	3	6	9	59
Jocelyn Lemieux	18	1	8	9	28
Troy Murray	20	4	4	8	22
Trent Yawney	20	3	5	8	27
Michel Goulet	14	2	4	6	6
Bob Murray	16	2	4	6	8
Dave Manson	20	2	4	6	46
Dirk Graham	5	1	5	6	2
Steve Konroyd	20	1	3	4	19
Keith Brown	18	0	4	4	43
Duane Sutter	20	1	1	2	48
Ed Belfour (Goalie)	9	0	1	1	6
Bob Bassen	1	0	0	0	2
Cam Russell	1	0	0	0	0
Jacques Cloutier (Goalie)	4	0	0	0	0
Mike Hudson	4	0	0	0	2
Bob McGill	5	0	0	0	2
Wayne Van Dorp	8	0	0	0	23
Al Secord	12	0	0	0	8
Greg Millen (Goalie)	14	0	0	0	4

EDMONTON OILERS

(Winners of 1990 Stanley Cup Playoffs)

	Games	G.	A.	Pts.	Pen.
Craig Simpson	22	*16	15	*31	8
Mark Messier	22	9	*22	*31	20
Jari Kurri	22	10	15	25	18
Esa Tikkanen	22	13	11	24	26
Glenn Anderson	22	10	12	22	20
Mark Lamb	22	6	11	17	2
Steve Smith	22	5	10	15	37
Joe Murphy	22	6	8	14	16
Reijo Ruotsalainen	22	2	11	13	12
Adam Graves	22	5	6	11	17
Randy Gregg	20	2	6	8	16
Craig MacTavish	22	2	6	8	29
Charlie Huddy	22	0	6	6	10
Petr Klima	21	5	0	5	8
Martin Gelinas	20	2	3	5	6
Kelly Buchberger	19	0	5	5	13
Craig Muni	22	0	3	3	16
Kevin Lowe	20	0	2	2	10
Bill Ranford (Goalie)	22	0	2	2	4
Eldon Reddick (Goalie)	1	0	0	0	0
Jeff Beukeboom	2	0	0	0	0
Anatoli Semenov	2	0	0	0	0
Dave Brown	3	0	0	0	0
Geoff Smith	3	0	0	0	0

HARTFORD WHALERS

(Lost Adams Division semifinals to Boston, 4-3)

	Games	G.	A.	Pts.	Pen.
Brad Shaw	7	2	5	7	0
Ron Francis	7	3	3	6	8
Kevin Dineen	6	3	2	5	18
Dean Evason	7	2	2	4	22
Pat Verbeek	7	2	2	4	26
Dave Tippett	7	1	3	4	2
Todd Krygier	7	2	1	3	4
Dave Babych	7	1	2	3	0
Mikael Andersson	5	0	3	3	2
Ray Ferraro	7	0	3	3	2
Scott Young	7	2	0	2	2

	Games	G.	A.	Pts.	Pen.
Yvon Corriveau	4	1	0	1	0
Randy Ladouceur	7	1	0	1	10
Ulf Samuelsson	7	1	0	1	18
Jody Hull	5	0	1	1	2
Mike Tomlak	7	0	1	1	2
Adam Burt	2	0	0	0	0
Chris Govedaris	2	0	0	0	2
Ed Kastelic	2	0	0	0	0
Randy Cunneyworth	4	0	0	0	2
Sylvain Cote	5	0	0	0	2
Grant Jennings	7	0	0	0	17
Peter Sidorkiewicz (G.)	7	0	0	0	0

LOS ANGELES KINGS

(Lost Smythe Division Finals to Edmonton, 4-0)

	Games	G.	A.	Pts.	Pen.
Todd Elik	10	3	9	12	10
Steve Duchesne	10	2	9	11	6
Luc Robitaille	10	5	5	10	12
Wayne Gretzky	7	3	7	10	0
Tony Granato	10	5	4	9	12
Tomas Sandstrom	10	5	4	9	19
Dave Taylor	6	4	4	8	6
Larry Robinson	10	2	3	5	10
Rob Blake	8	1	3	4	4
Mike Krushelnyski	10	1	3	4	12
Marty McSorley	10	1	3	4	18
Bob Kudelski	8	1	2	3	2
John Tonelli	10	1	2	3	6
Steve Kasper	10	1	1	2	2
Jay Miller	10	1	1	2	10
Brian Benning	7	0	2	2	6
Mike Allison	4	1	0	1	2
Chris Kontos	5	1	0	1	0
Keith Crowder	7	1	0	1	9
Bob Halkidis	8	0	1	1	8
Kelly Hrudey (Goalie)	9	0	1	1	0
Mikko Makela	1	0	0	0	0
Ron Scott (Goalie)	1	0	0	0	0
Scott Bjugstad	2	0	0	0	2
Mario Gosselin (Goalie)	3	0	0	0	0
Petr Prajsler	3	0	0	0	0
Tim Watters	4	0	0	0	6

MINNESOTA NORTH STARS

(Lost Norris Division semifinals to Chicago, 4-3)

	Games	G.	A.	Pts.	Pen.
Brian Bellows	7	4	3	7	10
Don Barber	7	3	3	6	8
Dave Gagner	7	2	3	5	16
Ulf Dahlen	7	1	4	5	2
Aaron Broten	7	0	5	5	8
Neal Broten	7	2	2	4	18
Shawn Chambers	7	2	1	3	10
Larry Murphy	7	1	2	3	31
Mike Modano	7	1	1	2	12
Stewart Gavin	7	0	2	2	12
Neil Wilkinson	7	0	2	2	11
Perry Berezan	5	1	0	1	0
Basil McRae	7	1	0	1	24
Curt Giles	7	0	1	1	6
Mark Tinordi	7	0	1	1	16
Kari Takko (Goalie)	1	0	0	0	0
Mario Thyer	1	0	0	0	2
Ville Siren	3	0	0	0	2
Frantisek Musil	4	0	0	0	14
Jon Casey (Goalie)	7	0	0	0	8
Shane Churla	7	0	0	0	44
Gaetan Duchesne	7	0	0	0	6

MONTREAL CANADIENS

(Lost Adams Division finals to Boston, 4-1)

	Games	G.	A.	Pts.	Pen.
Stephane Richer	9	7	3	10	2
Shayne Corson	11	2	8	10	20
Brian Skrudland	11	3	5	8	30
Russ Courtnall	11	5	1	6	10
Guy Carbonneau	11	2	3	5	6
Bobby Smith	11	1	4	5	6
Petr Svoboda	10	0	5	5	2
Mathieu Schneider	9	1	3	4	31
Claude Lemieux	11	1	3	4	38
Stephane Lebeau	2	3	0	3	0
Brent Gilchrist	8	2	0	2	2
Mats Naslund	3	1	1	2	0

	Games	G.	A.	Pts.	Pen.
Mike McPhee	9	1	1	2	16
Ryan Walter	11	0	2	2	0
Chris Chelios	5	0	1	1	8
Donald Dufresne	10	0	1	1	18
Mike Keane	11	0	1	1	8
Craig Ludwig	11	0	1	1	16
Patrick Roy (Goalie)	11	0	1	1	0
Brian Hayward (Goalie)	1	0	0	0	0
Mark Pederson	2	0	0	0	0
Eric Desjardins	6	0	0	0	10
Sylvain Lefebvre	6	0	0	0	0
J.J. Daigneault	9	0	0	0	2
Todd Ewen	10	0	0	0	4

NEW JERSEY DEVILS

(Lost Patrick Division semifinals to Washington, 4-2)

	Games	G.	A.	Pts.	Pen.
Brendan Shanahan	6	3	3	6	20
Bruce Driver	6	1	5	6	6
John MacLean	6	4	1	5	12
Peter Stastny	6	3	2	5	4
Jon Morris	6	1	3	4	23
Kirk Muller	6	1	3	4	11
Patrik Sundstrom	6	1	3	4	2
Eric Weinrich	6	1	3	4	17
Alexei Kasatonov	6	0	3	3	14
Ken Daneyko	6	2	0	2	21
Viacheslav Fetisov	6	0	2	2	10
Pat Conacher	5	1	0	1	10
Doug Brown	6	0	1	1	2
Sylvain Turgeon	1	0	0	0	0
Sean Burke (Goalie)	2	0	0	0	2
Troy Crowder	2	0	0	0	10
Mark Johnson	2	0	0	0	0
Chris Terreri (Goalie)	4	0	0	0	0
Claude Vilgrain	4	0	0	0	0
Bob Brooke	5	0	0	0	14
Jamie Huscroft	5	0	0	0	16
David Maley	6	0	0	0	25
Randy Velischek	6	0	0	0	4

NEW YORK ISLANDERS

(Lost Patrick Division semifinals to N.Y. Rangers, 4-1)

	Games	G.	A.	Pts.	Pen.
Brent Sutter	5	2	3	5	2
Dave Volek	5	1	4	5	0
Jeff Norton	4	1	3	4	17
Patrick Flatley	5	3	0	3	2
Wayne McBean	2	1	1	2	0
Randy Wood	5	1	1	2	4
Derek Laxdal	1	0	2	2	2
Brad Lauer	4	0	2	2	10
Jeff Finley	5	0	2	2	2
Gary Nylund	5	0	2	2	17
Rob DiMaio	1	1	0	1	0
Tom Fitzgerald	4	1	0	1	4
Bryan Trottier	4	1	0	1	4
Hubie McDonough	5	1	0	1	4
Rod Dallman	1	0	1	1	6
Pat LaFontaine	2	0	1	1	0
Glenn Healy (Goalie)	4	0	1	1	0
Doug Crossman	5	0	1	1	6
Marc Bergevin	1	0	0	0	2
Mick Vukota	1	0	0	0	17
Jari Gronstrand	3	0	0	0	4
Ken Baumgartner	4	0	0	0	27
Mark Fitzpatrick (Goalie)	4	0	0	0	19
Alan Kerr	4	0	0	0	10
Derek King	4	0	0	0	4
Gerald Diduck	5	0	0	0	12
Don Maloney	5	0	0	0	2

NEW YORK RANGERS

(Lost Patrick Division finals to Washington, 4-1)

	Games	G.	A.	Pts.	Pen.
Bernie Nicholls	10	7	5	12	16
James Patrick	10	3	8	11	0
Kelly Kisio	10	2	8	10	8
John Ogrodnick	10	6	3	9	0
Mike Gartner	10	5	3	8	12
Randy Moller	10	1	6	7	32
Darren Turcotte	10	1	6	7	4
Troy Mallette	10	2	2	4	81
Brian Mullen	10	2	2	4	8
Mark Janssens	9	2	1	3	10

	Games	G.	A.	Pts.	Pen.
Normand Rochefort	10	2	1	3	26
Carey Wilson	10	2	1	3	0
Jeff Bloemberg	7	0	3	3	5
Lindy Ruff	8	0	3	3	12
Paul Broten	6	1	1	2	2
Jan Erixon	10	1	0	1	2
Miloslav Horava	2	0	1	1	0
Mark Hardy	3	0	1	1	2
Chris Nilan	4	0	1	1	19
Kris King	10	0	1	1	30
Kevin Miller	1	0	0	0	0
Mike Richter (Goalie)	6	0	0	0	0
John Vanbiesbrouck (G.)	6	0	0	0	4
Ron Greschner	10	0	0	0	16

ST. LOUIS BLUES

(Lost Norris Division finals to Chicago, 4-3)

	Games	G.	A.	Pts.	Pen.
Brett Hull	12	13	8	21	17
Adam Oates	12	2	12	14	4
Rod Brind'Amour	12	5	8	13	6
Jeff Brown	12	2	10	12	4
Ron Wilson	12	3	5	8	18
Peter Zezel	12	1	7	8	4
Paul MacLean	12	4	3	7	20
Sergio Momesso	12	3	2	5	63
Paul Cavallini	12	2	3	5	20
Gino Cavallini	12	1	3	4	2
Dave Lowry	12	2	1	3	39
Rich Sutter	12	2	1	3	39
Harold Snepsts	11	0	3	3	38
Gordie Roberts	10	0	2	2	26
Glen Featherstone	12	0	2	2	47
Mike Lalor	12	0	2	2	31
Rick Meagher	8	1	0	1	2
Kelly Chase	9	1	0	1	46
Michel Mongeau	2	0	1	1	0
Steve Tuttle	5	0	1	1	2
Robert Dirk	3	0	0	0	0
Curtis Joseph (Goalie)	6	0	0	0	2
Vincent Riendeau (Goalie)	8	0	0	0	0

TORONTO MAPLE LEAFS

(Lost Norris Division semifinals to St. Louis, 4-1)

	Games	G.	A.	Pts.	Pen.
Gary Leeman	5	3	3	6	16
Mark Osborne	5	2	3	5	12
Dan Marois	5	2	2	4	12
Tom Fergus	5	2	1	3	4
Ed Olczyk	5	1	2	3	14
Rob Ramage	5	1	2	3	20
Todd Gill	5	0	3	3	16
Tom Kurvers	5	0	3	3	4
Scott Pearson	2	2	0	2	10
Wendel Clark	5	1	1	2	19
Vincent Damphousse	5	0	2	2	2
Dave Hannan	3	1	0	1	4
Brad Marsh	5	1	0	1	2
Brian Curran	5	0	1	1	19
Dan Daoust	5	0	1	1	20
Lou Franceschetti	5	0	1	1	26
John Kordic	5	0	1	1	33
John McIntyre	2	0	0	0	2
Jeff Reese (Goalie)	2	0	0	0	0
Dave Reid	3	0	0	0	0
Allan Bester (Goalie)	4	0	0	0	0
Luke Richardson	5	0	0	0	22

WASHINGTON CAPITALS

(Lost Prince Of Wales Conference finals to Boston, 4-0)

	Games	G.	A.	Pts.	Pen.
John Druce	15	14	3	17	23
Geoff Courtnall	15	4	9	13	32
Dale Hunter	15	4	8	12	61
Dino Ciccarelli	8	8	3	11	6
Scott Stevens	15	2	7	9	25
Kelly Miller	15	3	5	8	23
John Tucker	12	1	7	8	0
Kevin Hatcher	11	0	8	8	32
Mike Ridley	14	3	4	7	8
Calle Johansson	15	1	6	7	4

	Games	G.	A.	Pts.	Pen.
Bob Rouse	15	2	3	5	47
Rod Langway	15	1	4	5	12
Stephen Leach	14	2	2	4	8
Bob Joyce	14	2	1	3	9
Tim Bergland	15	1	1	2	10
Michal Pivonka	11	0	2	2	6
Nick Kypreos	7	1	0	1	15
Neil Sheehy	13	0	1	1	*92
Steve Maltais	1	0	0	0	0
Scot Kleinendorst	3	0	0	0	0
Kent Paynter	3	0	0	0	10
Don Beaupre (Goalie)	8	0	0	0	2
Mike Liut (Goalie)	9	0	0	0	0
Rob Murray	9	0	0	0	18
Alan May	15	0	0	0	37

WINNIPEG JETS

(Lost Smythe Division semifinals to Edmonton, 4-3)

	Games	G.	A.	Pts.	Pen.
Dale Hawerchuk	7	3	5	8	2
Thomas Steen	7	2	5	7	16
Pat Elynuik	7	2	4	6	2
Moe Mantha	7	1	5	6	2
Brent Ashton	7	3	1	4	2
Doug Evans	7	2	2	4	10
Greg Paslawski	7	1	3	4	0
Teppo Numminen	7	1	2	3	10
Dave Ellett	7	2	0	2	6
Paul Fenton	7	2	0	2	23
Mark Kumpel	7	2	0	2	2
Paul MacDermid	7	0	2	2	8
Fredrik Olausson	7	0	2	2	2
Doug Smail	5	1	0	1	0
Gord Donnelly	6	0	1	1	8
Dave McLlwain	7	0	1	1	2
Brad Berry	1	0	0	0	0
Laurie Boschman	2	0	0	0	2
Stephane Beauregard (G.)	4	0	0	0	0
Bob Essensa (Goalie)	4	0	0	0	0
Phil Sykes	4	0	0	0	0
Shawn Cronin	5	0	0	0	7
Peter Taglianetti	5	0	0	0	6

COMPLETE STANLEY CUP GOALTENDING

	Games	Mins.	Goals	SO.	Avg.
Eldon Reddick	1	2	0	0	0.00
Bill Ranford	*22	*1401	*59(1)	1	2.53
EDMONTON TOTALS	22	1405	60	1	2.56
Patrick Roy	11	641	26(1)	1	2.43
Brian Hayward	1	33	2	0	3.64
MONTREAL TOTALS	11	676	29	1	2.57
Andy Moog	20	1195	44(2)	*2	*2.21
Rejean Lemelin	3	135	13	0	5.78
BOSTON TOTALS	21	1331	59	2	2.66
Daren Puppa	6	370	15(2)	0	2.43
BUFFALO TOTALS	6	373	17	0	2.73
Kari Takko	1	4	0	0	0.00
Jon Casey	7	415	21	1	3.04
MINNESOTA TOTALS	7	420	21	1	3.00
Don Beaupre	8	401	18(1)	0	2.69
Mike Liut	9	507	28(1)	0	3.31
WASHINGTON TOTALS	15	913	48	0	3.15
Peter Sidorkiewicz	7	429	23	0	3.22
HARTFORD TOTALS	7	433	23	0	3.19
Stephane Beauregard	4	238	12	0	3.03
Bob Essensa	4	206	12	0	3.50
WINNIPEG TOTALS	7	445	24	0	3.24
Ed Belfour	9	409	17	0	2.49
Jacques Cloutier	4	175	8	0	2.74
Greg Millen	14	613	40	0	3.92
CHICAGO TOTALS	20	1200	65	0	3.25
John Vanbiesbrouck	6	298	15	0	3.02
Mike Richter	6	330	19(1)	0	3.45
NEW YORK RANGERS TOTALS	10	628	35	0	3.34
Chris Terreri	4	238	13	0	3.28
Sean Burke	2	125	8	0	3.84
NEW JERSEY TOTALS	6	366	21	0	3.44
Curtis Joseph	6	327	18(1)	0	3.30

	Games	Mins.	Goals	SO.	Avg.
Vincent Riendeau	8	397	24(1)	0	3.63
ST. LOUIS TOTALS	12	726	44	0	3.64
Jeff Reese	2	108	6	0	3.33
Allan Bester	4	196	14	0	4.29
TORONTO TOTALS	5	306	20	0	3.92
Glenn Healy	4	166	9	0	3.25
Mark Fitzpatrick	4	152	13	0	5.13
NEW YORK ISLANDERS TOTALS	5	321	22	0	4.11
Mike Vernon	6	342	19(1)	0	3.33
Rick Wamsley	1	49	9	0	11.02
CALGARY TOTALS	6	392	29	0	4.44
Mario Gosselin	3	62	3(1)	0	2.90
Kelly Hrudey	9	539	39(1)	0	4.34
Ron Scott	1	32	4	0	7.50
LOS ANGELES TOTALS	10	637	48	0	4.52

( )—Empty Net Goals. Do not count against a Goaltender's average.

INDIVIDUAL STANLEY CUP LEADERS

Goals	Craig Simpson, Edmonton—16
Assists	Mark Messier, Edmonton—22
Points	Craig Simpson, Edmonton—31
	Mark Messier, Edmonton—31
Penalty Minutes	Neil Sheehy, Washington—92
Goaltender's average (420 minutes)	Andy Moog, Boston—2.21
Shutouts	Andy Moog, Boston—2

STANLEY CUP PENALTY SHOT INFORMATION

Date	Shooter	Goaltender	Scored	Final Score
4-4-90	Al MacInnis, Calg.	Kelly Hrudey, L.A.	Yes	L.A. 5-Calg. 3
4-5-90	Randy Wood, N.Y.I.	Mike Richter, N.Y.R.	No	N.Y.R. 2-N.Y.I. 1
5-3-90	Kelly Miller, Wash.	Andy Moog, Bos.	No	Bos. 5-Wash. 3
5-18-90	Petr Klima, Edm.	Rejean Lemelin, Bos.	No	Edm. 7-Bos. 2

Gordie Howe

NHL STANLEY CUP WINNERS

Season	Club	Coach	Season	Club	Coach	Season	Club	Coach
1917-18	Toronto Arenas	Dick Carroll	1943-44	Montreal Canadiens	Dick Irvin	1968-69	Montreal Canadiens	Claude Ruel
1919-20	Ottawa Senators	Pete Green	1944-45	Toronto Maple Leafs	Hap Day	1969-70	Boston Bruins	Harry Sinden
1920-21	Ottawa Senators	Pete Green	1945-46	Montreal Canadiens	Dick Irvin	1970-71	Montreal Canadiens	Al MacNeil
1921-22	Toronto St. Pats	Eddie Powers	1946-47	Toronto Maple Leafs	Hap Day	1971-72	Boston Bruins	Tom Johnson
1922-23	Ottawa Senators	Pete Green	1947-48	Toronto Maple Leafs	Hap Day	1972-73	Montreal Canadiens	Scotty Bowman
1923-24	Montreal Canadiens	Leo Dandurand	1948-49	Toronto Maple Leafs	Hap Day	1973-74	Philadelphia Flyers	Fred Shero
1924-25	Victoria Cougars	Lester Patrick	1949-50	Detroit Red Wings	Tommy Ivan	1974-75	Philadelphia Flyers	Fred Shero
1925-26	Montreal Maroons	Eddie Gerard	1950-51	Toronto Maple Leafs	Joe Primeau	1975-76	Montreal Canadiens	Scotty Bowman
1926-27	Ottawa Senators	Dave Gill	1951-52	Detroit Red Wings	Tommy Ivan	1976-77	Montreal Canadiens	Scotty Bowman
1927-28	New York Rangers	Lester Patrick	1952-53	Montreal Canadiens	Dick Irvin	1977-78	Montreal Canadiens	Scotty Bowman
1928-29	Boston Bruins	Cy Denneny	1953-54	Detroit Red Wings	Tommy Ivan	1978-79	Montreal Canadiens	Scotty Bowman
1929-30	Montreal Canadiens	Cecil Hart	1954-55	Detroit Red Wings	Jimmy Skinner	1979-80	New York Islanders	Al Arbour
1930-31	Montreal Canadiens	Cecil Hart	1955-56	Montreal Canadiens	Toe Blake	1980-81	New York Islanders	Al Arbour
1931-32	Toronto Maple Leafs	Dick Irvin	1956-57	Montreal Canadiens	Toe Blake	1981-82	New York Islanders	Al Arbour
1932-33	New York Rangers	Lester Patrick	1957-58	Montreal Canadiens	Toe Blake	1982-83	New York Islanders	Al Arbour
1933-34	Chicago Black Hawks	Tommy Gorman	1958-59	Montreal Canadiens	Toe Blake	1983-84	Edmonton Oilers	Glen Sather
1934-35	Montreal Maroons	Tommy Gorman	1959-60	Montreal Canadiens	Toe Blake	1984-85	Edmonton Oilers	Glen Sather
1935-36	Detroit Red Wings	Jack Adams	1960-61	Chicago Black Hawks	Rudy Pilous	1985-86	Montreal Canadiens	Jean Perron
1936-37	Detroit Red Wings	Jack Adams	1961-62	Toronto Maple Leafs	Punch Imlach	1986-87	Edmonton Oilers	Glen Sather
1937-38	Chicago Black Hawks	Bill Stewart	1962-63	Toronto Maple Leafs	Punch Imlach	1987-88	Edmonton Oilers	Glen Sather
1938-39	Boston Bruins	Art Ross	1963-64	Toronto Maple Leafs	Punch Imlach	1988-89	Calgary Flames	Terry Crisp
1939-40	New York Rangers	Frank Boucher	1964-65	Montreal Canadiens	Toe Blake	1989-90	Edmonton Oilers	John Muckler
1940-41	Boston Bruins	Cooney Weiland	1965-66	Montreal Canadiens	Toe Blake			
1941-42	Toronto Maple Leafs	Hap Day	1966-67	Toronto Maple Leafs	Punch Imlach			
1942-43	Detroit Red Wings	Jack Adams	1967-68	Montreal Canadiens	Toe Blake			

NOTE: 1918-19 series between Montreal and Seattle cancelled after five games because of influenza epidemic.

INDIVIDUAL RECORDS

SINGLE SEASON RECORDS

1—GOALS

NHL—Wayne Gretzky, Edmonton Oilers—92 (1981-82 season).
WHA—Bobby Hull, Winnipeg Jets—77 (1974-75 season).
CHL—Alain Caron, St. Louis Braves—77 (1963-64 season).
AHL—Stephan Lebeau, Sherbrooke Canadiens—70 (1988-89 season).
IHL—Dan Lecours, Milwaukee Admirals—75 (1982-83 season).

2—ASSISTS

NHL—Wayne Gretzky, Edmonton Oilers—163 (1985-86 season).
WHA—Andre Lacroix, San Diego Mariners—106 (1974-75 season).
CHL—Richie Hansen, Salt Lake Golden Eagles—81 (1981-82 season).
AHL—George "Red" Sullivan, Hershey Bears—89 (1953-54 season).
IHL—John Cullen, Flint Spirits—109 (1987-88 season).

3—POINTS

NHL—Wayne Gretzky, Edmonton Oilers—215 (1985-86 season).
WHA—Marc Tardif, Quebec Nordiques—154 (1977-78 season).
CHL—Alain Caron, St. Louis Braves—125 (1963-64 season).
AHL—Stephan Lebeau, Sherbrooke Canadiens—134 (1988-89 season).
IHL—John Cullen, Flint Spirits—157 (1987-88 season).

4—PENALTY MINUTES

NHL—Dave Schultz, Philadelphia Flyers—472 (1974-75 season).
WHA—Curt Brackenbury, Minnesota Fighting Saints and Quebec Nordiques—365 (1975-76 season).
CHL—Randy Holt, Dallas Black Hawks—411 (1974-75 season).
AHL—Robert Ray, Rochester Americans—446 (1988-89 season).
IHL—Kevin Evans, Kalamazoo—648 (1986-87 season).

5—SHUTOUTS

NHL—George Hainsworth, Montreal Canadiens—22 (1928-29 season).

MODERN ERA

NHL—Tony Esposito, Chicago Black Hawks—15 (1969-70 season).
WHA—Gerry Cheevers, Cleveland Crusaders—5 (1972-73 season).
Joe Daley, Winnipeg Jets—5 (1975-76 season).
CHL—Marcel Pelletier, St. Paul Rangers—9 (1963-64 season).
AHL—Gordie Bell, Buffalo Bisons—9 (1942-43 season).
IHL—Charlie Hodge, Cincinnati Mohawks—10 (1953-54 season).

6—GOALS AGAINST AVERAGE

NHL—George Hainsworth, Montreal Canadiens—0.98 (1928-29 season).
WHA—Don McLeod, Houston Aeros—2.57 (1973-74 season).
CHL—Russ Gillow, Oklahoma City Blazers—2.16 (1967-68 season).
AHL—Frank Brimsek, Providence Reds—1.79 (1937-38 season).
IHL—Glenn Ramsay, Cincinnati Mohawks—1.88 (1956-57 season).

CAREER (Regular Season Only)

(No WHA Records Listed for Most Seasons Played.)

1—MOST SEASONS

NHL—Gordie Howe, Detroit Red Wings and Hartford Whalers—26 (1946-47 through 1970-71 and 1979-80).

CHL—Richie Hansen, Fort Worth Texans, Salt Lake Golden Eagles, Wichita Wind—9 (1975-76 through 1983-84 seasons).
AHL—Fred Glover, Indianapolis Caps, St. Louis Flyers, Cleveland Barons—20. Willie Marshall, Pittsburgh Hornets, Rochester Americans, Hershey Bears, Providence Reds, Baltimore Clippers—20.
IHL—Glenn Ramsay, Cincinnati Mohawks, Fort Wayne Komets, Troy Bruins, Toledo Blades, St. Paul Saints, Omaha Knights, Des Moines Oak Leafs, Toledo Hornets, Port Huron Flags—18 (1956-57 through 1973-74).

2—GAMES PLAYED

NHL—Gordie Howe, Detroit Red Wings and Hartford Whalers—1,767 (26 seasons).
WHA—Andre Lacroix, Philadelphia Blazers, New York Golden Blades, Jersey Knights, San Diego Mariners, Houston Aeros and New England Whalers—551 (7 seasons).
CHL—Richie Hansen, Fort Worth Texans, Salt Lake Golden Eagles, Wichita Wind—575 (9 seasons).
AHL—Willie Marshall, Pittsburgh Hornets, Rochester Americans, Hershey Bears, Providence Reds, Baltimore Clippers—1,205 (20 seasons).
IHL—Glenn Ramsay, Cincinnati Mohawks, Fort Wayne Komets, Troy Bruins, Toledo Blades, St. Paul Saints, Omaha Knights, Des Moines Oak Leafs, Toledo Hornets, Port Huron Flags—1,053 (18 seasons).

3—GOALS SCORED

NHL—Gordie Howe, Detroit Red Wings, Hartford Whalers—801 (26 seasons).
WHA—Marc Tardif, Quebec Nordiques—316 (6 seasons).
CHL—Richie Hansen, Fort Worth Texans, Salt Lake Golden Eagles, Wichita Wind—204 (9 seasons).
AHL—Willie Marshall, Pittsburgh Hornets, Rochester Americans, Hershey Bears, Providence Reds, Baltimore Clippers—523 (20 seasons).
IHL—Joe Kastelic, Fort Wayne Komets, Troy Bruins, Louisville Rebels, Muskegon Zephyrs, Muskegon Mohawks—526 (15 seasons).

4—ASSISTS

NHL—Wayne Gretzky, Edmonton Oilers, Los Angeles Kings—1,302 (11 seasons).
WHA—Andre Lacroix, Philadelphia Blazers, Jersey Knights, San Diego Mariners, Houston Aeros, New England Whalers—547 (7 seasons).
CHL—Richie Hansen, Fort Worth Texans, Salt Lake Golden Eagles, Wichita Wind—374 (9 seasons).
AHL—Willie Marshall, Pittsburgh Hornets, Hershey Bears, Rochester Americans, Providence Reds, Baltimore Clippers—852 (20 seasons).
IHL—Len Thornson, Huntington Hornets, Indianapolis Chiefs, Fort Wayne Komets—826 (13 seasons).

5—TOTAL POINTS

NHL—Wayne Gretzky, Edmonton Oilers, Los Angeles Kings—1979 (11 seasons).
WHA—Andre Lacroix, Philadelphia Blazers, Jersey Knights, San Diego Mariners, Houston Aeros, New England Whalers—798 (7 seasons).
CHL—Richie Hansen, Fort Worth Texans, Salt Lake Golden Eagles, Wichita Wind—578 (9 seasons).
AHL—Willie Marshall, Pittsburgh Hornets, Hershey Bears, Rochester Americans, Providence Reds, Baltimore Clippers—1,375 (20 seasons).
IHL—Len Thornson, Huntington Hornets, Indianapolis Chiefs, Fort Wayne Komets—1,252 (13 seasons).

Bobby Orr

6—PENALTY MINUTES

NHL—Dave (Tiger) Williams, Toronto Maple Leafs, Vancouver Canucks, Detroit Red Wings, Los Angeles Kings, Hartford Whalers—3,966 (13 seasons).
WHA—Paul Baxter, Cleveland Crusaders, Quebec Nordiques—962 (5 seasons).
CHL—Brad Gassoff, Tulsa Oilers, Dallas Black Hawks—899 (5 seasons).
AHL—Fred Glover, Indianapolis Caps, St. Louis Flyers, Cleveland Barons—2,402 (20 seasons).
IHL—Gord Malinoski, Dayton Gems, Saginaw Gears—2,175 (9 seasons).

7—SHUTOUTS

NHL—Terry Sawchuk, Detroit Red Wings, Boston Bruins, Los Angeles Kings, New York Rangers, Toronto Maple Leafs—103 (20 seasons).
WHA—Ernie Wakely, Winnipeg Jets, San Diego Mariners, Houston Aeros—16 (6 seasons).
CHL—Michel Dumas, Dallas Black Hawks—12 (4 seasons).
Mike Veisor, Dallas Black Hawks—12 (5 seasons).
AHL—Johnny Bower, Cleveland Barons, Providence Reds—45 (11 seasons).
IHL—Glenn Ramsay, Cincinnati Mohawks, Fort Wayne Komets, Troy Bruins, Toledo Blades, St. Paul Saints, Omaha Knights, Des Moines Oak Leafs, Toledo Hornets, Port Huron Flags—45 (18 seasons).

SINGLE GAME RECORDS

1—GOALS

NHL—Joe Malone, Quebec Bulldogs (January 31, 1920 vs. Toronto St. Pats)—7.

MODERN ERA

NHL—Syd Howe, Detroit Red Wings (Feb. 3, 1944 vs. N.Y. Rangers)—6.
Gordon Berenson, St. Louis Blues (Nov. 7, 1968 vs. Philadelphia)—6.
Darryl Sittler, Toronto Maple Leafs (Feb. 7, 1976 vs. Boston Bruins)—6.
WHA—Ron Ward, New York Raiders (January 4, 1973 vs. Ottawa)—5.
Ron Climie, Edmonton Oilers (vs. N.Y. Golden Blades, November 6, 1973)—5.
Andre Hinse, Houston Aeros (Jan. 16, 1975 vs. Edmonton)—5.
Vaclav Nedomansky, Toronto Toros (Nov. 13, 1975 vs. Denver Spurs)—5.
Wayne Connelly, Minnesota Fighting Saints (Nov. 27, 1975 vs. Cincinnati Stingers)—5.
Ron Ward, Cleveland Crusaders (Nov. 30, 1975 vs. Toronto Toros)—5.
Real Cloutier, Quebec Nordiques (Oct. 26, 1976 vs. Phoenix Roadrunners)—5.
CHL—Jim Mayer, Dallas Black Hawks (February 23, 1979)—6.
AHL—Bob Heron, Pittsburgh Hornets (1941-42)—6.
Harry Pidhirny, Springfield Indians (1953-54)—6.
Camille Henry, Providence Reds (1955-56)—6.
IHL—Pierre Brillant, Indianapolis Chiefs (Feb. 18, 1959)—6.
Bryan McLay, Muskegon Zephyrs (Mar. 8, 1961)—6.
Elliott Chorley, St. Paul Saints (Jan. 17, 1962)—6.
Joe Kastelic, Muskegon Zephyrs (Mar. 1, 1962)—6.
Tom St. James, Flint Generals (Mar. 15, 1985)—6.

2—ASSISTS

NHL—Billy Taylor, Detroit Red Wings (Mar. 16, 1947 vs. Chicago)—7.
Wayne Gretzky, Edmonton Oilers (Feb. 15, 1980 vs. Washington)—7.
WHA—Jim Harrison, Alberta Oilers (January 30, 1973 vs. New York)—7.
Jim Harrison, Cleveland Crusaders (Nov. 30, 1975 vs. Toronto Toros)—7.
CHL—Art Stratton, St. Louis Braves (1966-67)—6.
Ron Ward, Tulsa Oilers (1967-68)—6.
Bill Hogaboam, Omaha Knights, January 15, 1972—6.
Jim Wiley, Tulsa Oilers, (1974-75)—6.
AHL—Art Stratton, Buffalo Bisons (Mar. 17, 1963 vs. Pittsburgh)—9.
IHL—Jean-Paul Denis, St. Paul Saints (Jan. 17, 1962)—9.

3—POINTS

NHL—Darryl Sittler, Toronto Maple Leafs (Feb. 7, 1976 vs. Boston Bruins)—10.
WHA—Jim Harrison, Alberta Oilers (January 30, 1973 vs. New York)—10.
CHL—Steve Vickers, Omaha Knights (Jan. 15, 1972 vs. Kansas City)—8.
AHL—Art Stratton, Buffalo Bisons (Mar. 17, 1963 vs. Pittsburgh)—9.
IHL—Elliott Chorley, St. Paul Saints (Jan. 17, 1962)—11.
Jean-Paul Denis, St. Paul Saints (Jan. 17, 1962)—11.

4—PENALTY MINUTES

NHL—Randy Holt, Los Angeles Kings (March 11, 1979 vs. Philadelphia)—67.
WHA—Dave Hanson, Birmingham Bulls (Feb. 5, 1978 vs. Indianapolis)—46.
CHL—Gary Rissling, Birmingham Bulls (Dec. 5, 1980 vs. Salt Lake)—49.
AHL—Wally Weir, Rochester Americans (Jan. 16, 1981 vs. New Brunswick)—54.
IHL—Willie Trognitz, Dayton Gems (Oct. 29, 1977)—63.

DEFENSEMEN'S RECORDS

SINGLE SEASON

1—GOALS

NHL—Paul Coffey, Edmonton Oilers (1985-86 season)—48.
WHA—Kevin Morrison, Jersey Knights (1973-74 season)—24.
CHL—Dan Poulin, Nashville South Stars (1981-82 season)—29.
AHL—Greg Tebbutt, Baltimore Skipjacks (1982-83 season)—28.
IHL—Roly McLenahan, Cincinnati Mohawks (1955-56 season)—34.

2—ASSISTS

NHL—Bobby Orr, Boston Bruins (1970-71 season)—102.
WHA—J. C. Tremblay, Quebec Nordiques (1975-76 season)—77.
CHL—Barclay Plager, Omaha Knights (1963-64 season)—61.
AHL—Craig Levie, Nova Scotia Voyageurs (1980-81 season)—62.
Shawn Evans, Nova Scotia Oilers (1987-88 season)—62.
IHL—Gerry Glaude, Muskegon Zephyrs (1962-63 season)—86.

3—POINTS

NHL—Bobby Orr, Boston Bruins (1970-71 season)—139.
WHA—J. C. Tremblay, Quebec Nordiques (1972-73 and 1975-76 seasons)—89.
CHL—Dan Poulin, Nashville South Stars (1981-82 season)—85.
AHL—Greg Tebbutt, Baltimore Skipjacks (1982-83 season)—84.
IHL—Gerry Glaude, Muskegon Zephyrs (1962-63 season)—101.

STANLEY CUP PLAYOFF RECORDS

Team

Most Stanley Cup Championships: Montreal Canadiens (23).
Most Final Series Appearances: Montreal Canadiens (31).
Most Years in Playoffs: Montreal Canadiens (65).
Most Consecutive Stanley Cup Championships: Montreal Canadiens (5).
Most Consecutive Playoff Appearances: Boston Bruins (23).
Most Goals, One Team, One Game: Edmonton (13) vs. Los Angeles, April 9, 1987.
Most Goals, One Team, One Period: Montreal Canadiens (7) vs. Toronto, March 30, 1944—3rd period.
Most Consecutive Playoff Game Victories: Edmonton Oilers (12).

Individual

Most Years in Playoffs: Gordie Howe (Detroit 19, Hartford 1)—20.
Most Consecutive Years in Playoffs: Brad Park (N.Y. Rangers, Boston, Detroit)—17.
Most Playoff Games: Larry Robinson (Montreal, Los Angeles)—213.
Most Points in Playoffs: Wayne Gretzky (Edmonton, Los Angeles)—284.
Most Goals in Playoffs: Jari Kurri (Edmonton)—92.
Most Assists in Playoffs: Wayne Gretzky (Edmonton, Los Angeles)—195.
Most Shutouts in Playoffs: Jacques Plante (Montreal, St. Louis)—14.
Most Games Played by Goaltender: Billy Smith (N.Y. Islanders)—131.
Most Points One Year: Wayne Gretzky (Edmonton)—47 in 1984-85.
Most Goals One Year:
Reggie Leach (Philadelphia)—19 in 1975-76.
Jari Kurri (Edmonton)—19 in 1984-85.

Most Assists One Year: Wayne Gretzky (Edmonton)—31 in 1987-88.
Most Points By Defenseman One Year: Paul Coffey (Edmonton)—37 in 1984-85.
Most Goals By Defenseman One Year: Paul Coffey (Edmonton)—12 in 1984-85.
Most Assists By Defenseman One Year: Paul Coffey (Edmonton)—25 in 1984-85.
Most Penalty Minutes One Year: Chris Nilan (Montreal)—141 in 1985-86.
Most Shutouts One Year:
Clint Benedict (Montreal Maroons)—4 in 1927-28.
Dave Kerr (N.Y. Rangers)—4 in 1936-37.
Frank McCool (Toronto)—4 in 1944-45.
Terry Sawchuk (Detroit)—4 in 1951-52.
Bernie Parent (Philadelphia)—4 in 1974-75.
Ken Dryden (Montreal)—4 in 1976-77.
Most Consecutive Shutouts: Frank McCool (Toronto)—3 in 1944-45.
Most Points One Game:
Patrik Sundstrom (New Jersey)—8 vs. Washington, April 22, 1988.
Mario Lemieux (Pittsburgh)—8 vs. Philadelphia, April 25, 1989.
Most Goals One Game:
Maurice Richard (Montreal)—5 vs. Toronto, March 23, 1944.
Darryl Sittler (Toronto)—5 vs. Philadelphia, April 22, 1976.
Reggie Leach (Philadelphia)—5 vs. Boston, May 6, 1976.
Mario Lemieux (Pittsburgh)—5 vs. Philadelphia, April 25, 1989.
Most Assists One Game:
Mikko Leinonen (N.Y. Rangers)—6 vs. Philadelphia, April 8, 1982.
Wayne Gretzky (Edmonton)—6 vs. Los Angeles, April 9, 1987.
Most Penalty Minutes in Playoffs: Dave (Tiger) Williams (Toronto, Vancouver, Los Angeles)—455.

Stan Mikita (left) and Phil Esposito

INDIVIDUAL 1989-90 NHL TROPHY WINNERS

ART ROSS TROPHY (Scoring leader) ....Wayne Gretzky, Los Angeles
HART MEMORIAL TROPHY (Most Valuable) ....Mark Messier, Edmonton
JAMES NORRIS MEMORIAL TROPHY (Top Defenseman) ....Ray Bourque, Boston
VEZINA TROPHY (Top Goaltender) ....Patrick Roy, Montreal
BILL JENNINGS TROPHY (Goaltending Trophy) ....Rejean Lemelin, Boston
                                                       Andy Moog, Boston
CALDER MEMORIAL TROPHY (Top Rookie) ....Sergei Makarov, Calgary

LADY BYNG TROPHY (Most Gentlemanly) ....Brett Hull, St. Louis
CONN SMYTHE TROPHY (Playoff MVP) ....Bill Ranford, Edmonton
BILL MASTERTON MEMORIAL TROPHY
  (Perseverance, Sportsmanship and Dedication) ....Gord Kluzak, Boston
FRANK J. SELKE TROPHY (Best Defensive Forward) ....Rick Meagher, St. Louis
JACK ADAMS AWARD (Coach of the Year) ....Bob Murdoch, Winnipeg
KING CLANCY TROPHY (Humanitarian Contributions) ....Kevin Lowe, Edmonton

INDIVIDUAL AWARDS

ART ROSS TROPHY

Leading Scorer—Regular Season

(Originally Leading Scorer Trophy. Present trophy presented to NHL by Art Ross, former manager-coach of Boston Bruins, in 1947. In event of tie, player with most goals receives the award.)

Season	Player Club	Pts.
1917-18	Joe Malone, Montreal	44
1918-19	Newsy Lalonde, Montreal	32
1919-20	Joe Malone, Quebec Bulldogs	45
1920-21	Newsy Lalonde, Montreal	41
1921-22	Punch Broadbelt, Ottawa	46
1922-23	Babe Dye, Toronto	37
1923-24	Cy Denneny, Ottawa	23
1924-25	Babe Dye, Toronto	44
1925-26	Nels Stewart, Montreal Maroons	42
1926-27	Bill Cook, New York Rangers	37
1927-28	Howie Morenz, Montreal	51
1928-29	Ace Bailey, Toronto	32
1929-30	Cooney Weiland, Boston	73
1930-31	Howie Morenz, Montreal	51
1931-32	Harvey Jackson, Toronto	53
1932-33	Bill Cook, New York Rangers	50
1933-34	Charlie Conacher, Toronto	52
1934-35	Charlie Conacher, Toronto	57
1935-36	Dave Schriner, New York Americans	45
1936-37	Dave Schriner, New York Americans	46
1937-38	Gordie Drillon, Toronto	52
1938-39	Toe Blake, Montreal	47
1939-40	Milt Schmidt, Boston	52
1940-41	Bill Cowley, Boston	62
1941-42	Bryan Hextall, New York Rangers	56
1942-43	Doug Bentley, Chicago	73
1943-44	Herbie Cain, Boston	82
1944-45	Elmer Lach, Montreal	80
1945-46	Max Bentley, Chicago	61
1946-47	Max Bentley, Chicago	72
1947-48	Elmer Lach, Montreal	61
1948-49	Roy Conacher, Chicago	68
1949-50	Ted Lindsay, Detroit	78
1950-51	Gordie Howe, Detroit	86
1951-52	Gordie Howe, Detroit	86
1952-53	Gordie Howe, Detroit	95
1953-54	Gordie Howe, Detroit	81
1954-55	Bernie Geoffrion, Montreal	75
1955-56	Jean Beliveau, Montreal	88
1956-57	Gordie Howe, Detroit	89
1957-58	Dickie Moore, Montreal	84
1958-59	Dickie Moore, Montreal	96
1959-60	Bobby Hull, Chicago	81
1960-61	Bernie Geoffrion, Montreal	95
1961-62	Bobby Hull, Chicago	84
1962-63	Gordie Howe, Detroit	86
1963-64	Stan Mikita, Chicago	89
1964-65	Stan Mikita, Chicago	87
1965-66	Bobby Hull, Chicago	97
1966-67	Stan Mikita, Chicago	97
1967-68	Stan Mikita, Chicago	87
1968-69	Phil Esposito, Boston	126
1969-70	Bobby Orr, Boston	120
1970-71	Phil Esposito, Boston	152
1971-72	Phil Esposito, Boston	133
1972-73	Phil Esposito, Boston	130
1973-74	Phil Esposito, Boston	145
1974-75	Bobby Orr, Boston	135
1975-76	Guy Lafleur, Montreal	125
1976-77	Guy Lafleur, Montreal	136
1977-78	Guy Lafleur, Montreal	132
1978-79	Bryan Trottier, New York Islanders	134
1979-80	Marcel Dionne, Los Angeles	137
1980-81	Wayne Gretzky, Edmonton	164
1981-82	Wayne Gretzky, Edmonton	212
1982-83	Wayne Gretzky, Edmonton	196
1983-84	Wayne Gretzky, Edmonton	205
1984-85	Wayne Gretzky, Edmonton	208

Season	Player Club	Pts.
1985-86	Wayne Gretzky, Edmonton	215
1986-87	Wayne Gretzky, Edmonton	183
1987-88	Mario Lemieux, Pittsburgh	168
1988-89	Mario Lemieux, Pittsburgh	199
1989-90	Wayne Gretzky, Los Angeles	142

HART MEMORIAL TROPHY

Most Valuable Player

Season	Player Club
1923-24	Frank Nighbor, Ottawa
1924-25	Billy Burch, Hamilton
1925-26	Nels Stewart, Montreal Maroons
1926-27	Herb Gardiner, Montreal
1927-28	Howie Morenz, Montreal
1928-29	Roy Worters, N.Y. Americans
1929-30	Nels Stewart, Montreal Maroons
1930-31	Howie Morenz, Montreal
1931-32	Howie Morenz, Montreal
1932-33	Eddie Shore, Boston
1933-34	Aurel Joliat, Montreal
1934-35	Eddie Shore, Boston
1935-36	Eddie Shore, Boston
1936-37	Babe Siebert, Montreal
1937-38	Eddie Shore, Boston
1938-39	Toe Blake, Montreal
1939-40	Ebbie Goodfellow, Detroit
1940-41	Bill Cowley, Boston
1941-42	Tom Anderson, N.Y. Americans
1942-43	Bill Cowley, Boston
1943-44	Babe Pratt, Toronto
1944-45	Elmer Lach, Montreal
1945-46	Max Bentley, Chicago
1946-47	Maurice Richard, Montreal
1947-48	Buddy O'Connor, N.Y. Rangers
1948-49	Sid Abel, Detroit
1949-50	Chuck Rayner, N.Y. Rangers
1950-51	Milt Schmidt, Boston
1951-52	Gordie Howe, Detroit
1952-53	Gordie Howe, Detroit
1953-54	Al Rollins, Chicago
1954-55	Ted Kennedy, Toronto
1955-56	Jean Beliveau, Montreal
1956-57	Gordie Howe, Detroit
1957-58	Gordie Howe, Detroit
1958-59	Andy Bathgate, N.Y. Rangers
1959-60	Gordie Howe, Detroit
1960-61	Bernie Geoffrion, Montreal
1961-62	Jacques Plante, Montreal
1962-63	Gordie Howe, Detroit
1963-64	Jean Beliveau, Montreal
1964-65	Bobby Hull, Chicago
1965-66	Bobby Hull, Chicago
1966-67	Stan Mikita, Chicago
1967-68	Stan Mikita, Chicago
1968-69	Phil Esposito, Boston
1969-70	Bobby Orr, Boston
1970-71	Bobby Orr, Boston
1971-72	Bobby Orr, Boston
1972-73	Bobby Clarke, Philadelphia
1973-74	Phil Esposito, Boston
1974-75	Bobby Clarke, Philadelphia
1975-76	Bobby Clarke, Philadelphia
1976-77	Guy Lafleur, Montreal
1977-78	Guy Lafleur, Montreal
1978-79	Bryan Trottier, N.Y. Islanders
1979-80	Wayne Gretzky, Edmonton
1980-81	Wayne Gretzky, Edmonton
1981-82	Wayne Gretzky, Edmonton
1982-83	Wayne Gretzky, Edmonton
1983-84	Wayne Gretzky, Edmonton
1984-85	Wayne Gretzky, Edmonton
1985-86	Wayne Gretzky, Edmonton
1986-87	Wayne Gretzky, Edmonton
1987-88	Mario Lemieux, Pittsburgh

Season	Player Club
1988-89	Wayne Gretzky, Los Angeles
1989-90	Mark Messier, Edmonton

JAMES NORRIS MEMORIAL TROPHY

Outstanding Defenseman

Season	Player Club
1953-54	Red Kelly, Detroit
1954-55	Doug Harvey, Montreal
1955-56	Doug Harvey, Montreal
1956-57	Doug Harvey, Montreal
1957-58	Doug Harvey, Montreal
1958-59	Tom Johnson, Montreal
1959-60	Doug Harvey, Montreal
1960-61	Doug Harvey, Montreal
1961-62	Doug Harvey, N.Y. Rangers
1962-63	Pierre Pilote, Chicago
1963-64	Pierre Pilote, Chicago
1964-65	Pierre Pilote, Chicago
1965-66	Jacques Laperriere, Montreal
1966-67	Harry Howell, N.Y. Rangers
1967-68	Bobby Orr, Boston
1968-69	Bobby Orr, Boston
1969-70	Bobby Orr, Boston
1970-71	Bobby Orr, Boston
1971-72	Bobby Orr, Boston
1972-73	Bobby Orr, Boston
1973-74	Bobby Orr, Boston
1974-75	Bobby Orr, Boston
1975-76	Denis Potvin, N.Y. Islanders
1976-77	Larry Robinson, Montreal
1977-78	Denis Potvin, N.Y. Islanders
1978-79	Denis Potvin, N.Y. Islanders
1979-80	Larry Robinson, Montreal
1980-81	Randy Carlyle, Pittsburgh
1981-82	Doug Wilson, Chicago
1982-83	Rod Langway, Washington
1983-84	Rod Langway, Washington
1984-85	Paul Coffey, Edmonton
1985-86	Paul Coffey, Edmonton
1986-87	Ray Bourque, Boston
1987-88	Ray Bourque, Boston
1988-89	Chris Chelios, Montreal
1989-90	Ray Bourque, Boston

VEZINA TROPHY

(Awarded to goalkeeper(s) having played a minimum 25 games for the team with fewest goals scored against. Beginning with 1981-82 season, awarded to outstanding goaltender.)

Season	Player Club	GAA
1926-27	George Hainsworth, Montreal	1.52
1927-28	George Hainsworth, Montreal	1.09
1928-29	George Hainsworth, Montreal	0.98
1929-30	Tiny Thompson, Boston	2.23
1930-31	Roy Worters, N.Y. Amercians	1.68
1931-32	Charlie Gardiner, Chicago	2.10
1932-33	Tiny Thompson, Boston	1.83
1933-34	Charlie Gardiner, Chicago	1.73
1934-35	Lorne Chabot, Chicago	1.83
1935-36	Tiny Thompson, Boston	1.71
1936-37	Normie Smith, Detroit	2.13
1937-38	Tiny Thompson, Boston	1.85
1938-39	Frank Brimsek, Boston	1.60
1939-40	Dave Kerr, N.Y. Rangers	1.60
1940-41	Turk Broda, Toronto	2.60
1941-42	Frank Brimsek, Boston	2.38
1942-43	Johnny Mowers, Detroit	2.48
1943-44	Bill Durnan, Montreal	2.18
1944-45	Bill Durnan, Montreal	2.42
1945-46	Bill Durnan, Montreal	2.60
1946-47	Bill Durnan, Montreal	2.30

Bobby Hull (Inset Bobby (left) and Brett Hull)

Season	Player	Club	GAA
1947-48—	Turk Broda, Toronto		2.38
1948-49—	Bill Durnan, Montreal		2.10
1949-50—	Bill Durnan, Montreal		2.20
1950-51—	Al Rollins, Toronto		1.75
1951-52—	Terry Sawchuk, Detroit		1.98
1952-53—	Terry Sawchuk, Detroit		1.94
1953-54—	Harry Lumley, Toronto		1.85
1954-55—	Terry Sawchuk, Detroit		1.94
1955-56—	Jacques Plante, Montreal		1.86
1956-57—	Jacques Plante, Montreal		2.02
1957-58—	Jacques Plante, Montreal		2.09
1958-59—	Jacques Plante, Montreal		2.15
1959-60—	Jacques Plante, Montreal		2.54
1960-61—	Johnny Bower, Toronto		2.50
1961-62—	Jacques Plante, Montreal		2.37
1962-63—	Glenn Hall, Chicago		2.51
1963-64—	Charlie Hodge, Montreal		2.26
1964-65—	Terry Sawchuk, Toronto		2.56
	Johnny Bower, Toronto		2.38
1965-66—	Lorne Worsley, Montreal		2.36
	Charlie Hodge, Montreal		2.58
1966-67—	Glenn Hall, Chicago		2.38
	Denis DeJordy, Chicago		2.46
1967-68—	Lorne Worsley, Montreal		1.98
	Rogatien Vachon, Montreal		2.48
1968-69—	Glenn Hall, St. Louis		2.17
	Jacques Plante, St. Louis		1.96
1969-70—	Tony Esposito, Chicago		2.17
1970-71—	Ed Giacomin, N.Y. Rangers		2.15
	Gilles Villemure, N.Y. Rangers		2.29
1971-72—	Tony Esposito, Chicago		1.76
	Gary Smith, Chicago		2.41
1972-73—	Ken Dryden, Montreal		2.26
1973-74—	Bernie Parent, Philadelphia		1.89
	Tony Esposito, Chicago (tie)		2.04
1974-75—	Bernie Parent, Philadelphia		2.03
1975-76—	Ken Dryden, Montreal		2.03
1976-77—	Ken Dryden, Montreal		2.14
	Michel Larocque, Montreal		2.09
1977-78—	Ken Dryden, Montreal		2.05
	Michel Larocque, Montreal		2.67
1978-79—	Ken Dryden, Montreal		2.30
	Michel Larocque, Montreal		2.84
1979-80—	Bob Sauve, Buffalo		2.36
	Don Edwards, Buffalo		2.57
1980-81—	Richard Sevigny, Montreal		2.40
	Michel Larocque, Montreal		3.03
	Denis Herron, Montreal		3.50
1981-82—	Billy Smith, N.Y. Islanders		2.97
1982-83—	Pete Peeters, Boston		2.36
1983-84—	Tom Barrasso, Buffalo		2.84
1984-85—	Pelle Lindbergh, Philadelphia		3.02
1985-86—	John Vanbiesbrouck, N.Y. Rangers		3.32
1986-87—	Ron Hextall, Philadelphia		3.00
1987-88—	Grant Fuhr, Edmonton		3.43
1988-89—	Patrick Roy, Montreal		2.47
1989-90—	Patrick Roy, Montreal		2.53

BILL JENNINGS TROPHY

(Awarded to goalkeeper(s) having played a minimum of 25 games for the team with fewest goals scored against, beginning with 1981-82 season.)

Season	Player	Club	GAA
1981-82—	Denis Herron, Montreal		2.64
	Rick Wamsley, Montreal		2.75
1982-83—	Roland Melanson, N.Y. Islanders		2.66
	Billy Smith, N.Y. Islanders		2.87
1983-84—	Pat Riggin, Washington		2.66
	Al Jensen, Washington		2.91
1984-85—	Tom Barrasso, Buffalo		2.66
	Bob Sauve, Buffalo		3.22
1985-86—	Bob Froese, Philadelphia		2.55
	Darren Jensen, Philadelphia		3.68
1986-87—	Brian Hayward, Montreal		2.81
	Patrick Roy, Montreal		2.93
1987-88—	Brian Hayward, Montreal		2.86
	Patrick Roy, Montreal		2.90
1988-89—	Patrick Roy, Montreal		2.47
	Brian Hayward, Montreal		2.90
1989-90—	Rejean Lemelin, Boston		2.81
	Andy Moog, Boston		2.89

CALDER MEMORIAL TROPHY

Rookie of the Year

(Award was originally Leading Rookie Award. Named Calder Trophy in 1936-37 and became Calder Memorial Trophy when NHL President Frank Calder passed away —1942-43 season.)

Season	Player	Club
1932-33—	Carl Voss, Detroit	
1933-34—	Russ Blinco, Montreal Maroons	
1934-35—	Dave Schriner, N.Y. Americans	
1935-36—	Mike Karakas, Chicago	
1936-37—	Syl Apps, Toronto	
1937-38—	Cully Dahlstrom, Chicago	
1938-39—	Frank Brimsek, Boston	
1939-40—	Kilby Macdonald, N.Y. Rangers	
1940-41—	John Quilty, Montreal	
1941-42—	Grant Warwick, N.Y. Rangers	
1942-43—	Gaye Stewart, Toronto	
1943-44—	Gus Bodnar, Toronto	
1944-45—	Frank McCool, Toronto	
1945-46—	Edgar Laprade, N.Y. Rangers	
1946-47—	Howie Meeker, Toronto	
1947-48—	Jim McFadden, Detroit	
1948-49—	Pentti Lund, N.Y. Rangers	
1949-50—	Jack Gelineau, Boston	
1950-51—	Terry Sawchuk, Detroit	
1951-52—	Bernie Geoffrion, Montreal	
1952-53—	Lorne Worsley, N.Y. Rangers	
1953-54—	Camille Henry, N.Y. Rangers	
1954-55—	Ed Litzenberger, Chicago	
1955-56—	Glenn Hall, Detroit	
1956-57—	Larry Regan, Boston	
1957-58—	Frank Mahovlich, Toronto	
1958-59—	Ralph Backstrom, Montreal	
1959-60—	Bill Hay, Chicago	
1960-61—	Dave Keon, Toronto	
1961-62—	Bobby Rousseau, Montreal	
1962-63—	Kent Douglas, Toronto	
1963-64—	Jacques Laperriere, Montreal	
1964-65—	Roger Crozier, Detroit	
1965-66—	Brit Selby, Toronto	
1966-67—	Bobby Orr, Boston	
1967-68—	Derek Sanderson, Boston	
1968-69—	Danny Grant, Minnesota	
1969-70—	Tony Esposito, Chicago	
1970-71—	Gilbert Perreault, Buffalo	
1971-72—	Ken Dryden, Montreal	
1972-73—	Steve Vickers, N.Y. Rangers	
1973-74—	Denis Potvin, N.Y. Islanders	
1974-75—	Eric Vail, Atlanta	
1975-76—	Bryan Trottier, N.Y. Islanders	
1976-77—	Willi Plett, Atlanta	
1977-78—	Mike Bossy, N.Y. Islanders	
1978-79—	Bobby Smith, Minnesota	
1979-80—	Ray Bourque, Boston	
1980-81—	Peter Stastny, Quebec	
1981-82—	Dale Hawerchuk, Winnipeg	
1982-83—	Steve Larmer, Chicago	
1983-84—	Tom Barrasso, Buffalo	
1984-85—	Mario Lemieux, Pittsburgh	
1985-86—	Gary Suter, Calgary	
1986-87—	Luc Robitaille, Los Angeles	
1987-88—	Joe Nieuwendyk, Calgary	
1988-89—	Brian Leetch, N.Y. Rangers	
1989-90—	Sergei Makarov, Calgary	

LADY BYNG MEMORIAL TROPHY

Most Gentlemanly Player

(Originally Lady Byng Trophy. After winning award seven times, Frank Boucher received permanent possession and a new trophy was donated to NHL in 1936. After Lady Byng's death in 1949, NHL changed name to Lady Byng Memorial Trophy.)

Season	Player	Club
1924-25—	Frank Nighbor, Ottawa	
1925-26—	Frank Nighbor, Ottawa	
1926-27—	Billy Burch, N.Y. Americans	
1927-28—	Frank Boucher, N.Y. Rangers	
1928-29—	Frank Boucher, N.Y. Rangers	
1929-30—	Frank Boucher, N.Y. Rangers	
1930-31—	Frank Boucher, N.Y. Rangers	
1931-32—	Joe Primeau, Toronto	
1932-33—	Frank Boucher, N.Y. Rangers	
1933-34—	Frank Boucher, N.Y. Rangers	
1934-35—	Frank Boucher, N.Y. Rangers	
1935-36—	Doc Romnes, Chicago	
1936-37—	Marty Barry, Detroit	
1937-38—	Gordie Drillon, Toronto	
1938-39—	Clint Smith, N.Y. Rangers	
1939-40—	Bobby Bauer, Boston	
1940-41—	Bobby Bauer, Boston	
1941-42—	Syl Apps, Toronto	
1942-43—	Max Bentley, Chicago	
1943-44—	Clint Smith, Chicago	
1944-45—	Bill Mosienko, Chicago	
1945-46—	Toe Blake, Montreal	

Season	Player	Club
1946-47—	Bobby Bauer, Boston	
1947-48—	Buddy O'Connor, N.Y. Rangers	
1948-49—	Bill Quackenbush, Detroit	
1949-50—	Edgar Laprade, N.Y. Rangers	
1950-51—	Red Kelly, Detroit	
1951-52—	Sid Smith, Toronto	
1952-53—	Red Kelly, Detroit	
1953-54—	Red Kelly, Detroit	
1954-55—	Sid Smith, Toronto	
1955-56—	Earl Reibel, Detroit	
1956-57—	Andy Hebenton, N.Y. Rangers	
1957-58—	Camille Henry, N.Y. Rangers	
1958-59—	Alex Delvecchio, Detroit	
1959-60—	Don McKenney, Boston	
1960-61—	Red Kelly, Toronto	
1961-62—	Dave Keon, Toronto	
1962-63—	Dave Keon, Toronto	
1963-64—	Ken Wharram, Chicago	
1964-65—	Bobby Hull, Chicago	
1965-66—	Alex Delvecchio, Detroit	
1966-67—	Stan Mikita, Chicago	
1967-68—	Stan Mikita, Chicago	
1968-69—	Alex Delvecchio, Detroit	
1969-70—	Phil Goyette, St. Louis	
1970-71—	John Bucyk, Boston	
1971-72—	Jean Ratelle, N.Y. Rangers	
1972-73—	Gilbert Perreault, Buffalo	
1973-74—	John Bucyk, Boston	
1974-75—	Marcel Dionne, Detroit	
1975-76—	Jean Ratelle, N.Y. R.-Boston	
1976-77—	Marcel Dionne, Los Angeles	
1977-78—	Butch Goring, Los Angeles	
1978-79—	Bob MacMillan, Atlanta	
1979-80—	Wayne Gretzky, Edmonton	
1980-81—	Butch Goring, N.Y. Islanders	
1981-82—	Rick Middleton, Boston	
1982-83—	Mike Bossy, N.Y. Islanders	
1983-84—	Mike Bossy, N.Y. Islanders	
1984-85—	Jari Kurri, Edmonton	
1985-86—	Mike Bossy, N.Y. Islanders	
1986-87—	Joe Mullen, Calgary	
1987-88—	Mats Naslund, Montreal	
1988-89—	Joe Mullen, Calgary	
1989-90—	Brett Hull, St. Louis	

CONN SMYTHE TROPHY

Most Valuable Player in Playoffs

Season	Player	Club
1964-65—	Jean Beliveau, Montreal	
1965-66—	Roger Crozier, Detroit	
1966-67—	Dave Keon, Toronto	
1967-68—	Glenn Hall, St. Louis	
1968-69—	Serge Savard, Montreal	
1969-70—	Bobby Orr, Boston	
1970-71—	Ken Dryden, Montreal	
1971-72—	Bobby Orr, Boston	
1972-73—	Yvan Cournoyer, Montreal	
1973-74—	Bernie Parent, Philadelphia	
1974-75—	Bernie Parent, Philadelphia	
1975-76—	Reggie Leach, Philadelphia	
1976-77—	Guy Lafleur, Montreal	
1977-78—	Larry Robinson, Montreal	
1978-79—	Bob Gainey, Montreal	
1979-80—	Bryan Trottier, N.Y. Islanders	
1980-81—	Butch Goring, N.Y. Islanders	
1981-82—	Mike Bossy, N.Y. Islanders	
1982-83—	Billy Smith, N.Y. Islanders	
1983-84—	Mark Messier, Edmonton	
1984-85—	Wayne Gretzky, Edmonton	
1985-86—	Patrick Roy, Montreal	
1986-87—	Ron Hextall, Philadelphia	
1987-88—	Wayne Gretzky, Edmonton	
1988-89—	Al MacInnis, Calgary	
1989-90—	Bill Ranford, Edmonton	

BILL MASTERTON MEMORIAL TROPHY

(Presented by Professional Hockey Writers' Association to player who best exemplifies the qualities of perseverance, sportsmanship and dedication to hockey.)

Season	Player	Club
1967-68—	Claude Provost, Montreal	
1968-69—	Ted Hampson, Oakland	
1969-70—	Pit Martin, Chicago	
1970-71—	Jean Ratelle, N.Y. Rangers	
1971-72—	Bobby Clarke, Philadelphia	
1972-73—	Lowell MacDonald, Pittsburgh	
1973-74—	Henri Richard, Montreal	

Season	Player	Club
1974-75—	Don Luce, Buffalo	
1975-76—	Rod Gilbert, N.Y. Rangers	
1976-77—	Ed Westfall, N.Y. Islanders	
1977-78—	Butch Goring, Los Angeles	
1978-79—	Serge Savard, Montreal	
1979-80—	Al MacAdam, Minnesota	
1980-81—	Blake Dunlop, St. Louis	
1981-82—	Glenn Resch, Colorado	
1982-83—	Lanny McDonald, Calgary	
1983-84—	Brad Park, Detroit	
1984-85—	Anders Hedberg, N.Y. Rangers	
1985-86—	Charlie Simmer, Boston	
1986-87—	Doug Jarvis, Hartford	
1987-88—	Bob Bourne, Los Angeles	
1988-89—	Tim Kerr, Philadelphia	
1989-90—	Gord Kluzak, Boston	

FRANK J. SELKE TROPHY

Best Defensive Forward

Season	Player	Club
1977-78—	Bob Gainey, Montreal	

Season	Player	Club
1978-79—	Bob Gainey, Montreal	
1979-80—	Bob Gainey, Montreal	
1980-81—	Bob Gainey, Montreal	
1981-82—	Steve Kasper, Boston	
1982-83—	Bobby Clarke, Philadelphia	
1983-84—	Doug Jarvis, Washington	
1984-85—	Craig Ramsay, Buffalo	
1985-86—	Troy Murray, Chicago	
1986-87—	Dave Poulin, Philadelphia	
1987-88—	Guy Carbonneau, Montreal	
1988-89—	Guy Carbonneau, Montreal	
1989-90—	Rick Meagher, St. Louis	

JACK ADAMS AWARD

Coach of the Year

Season	Coach	Club
1973-74—	Fred Shero, Philadelphia	
1974-75—	Bob Pulford, Los Angeles	
1975-76—	Don Cherry, Boston	
1976-77—	Scotty Bowman, Montreal	
1977-78—	Bobby Kromm, Detroit	

Season	Coach	Club
1978-79—	Al Arbour, N.Y. Islanders	
1979-80—	Pat Quinn, Philadelphia	
1980-81—	Red Berenson, St. Louis	
1981-82—	Tom Watt, Winnipeg	
1982-83—	Orval Tessier, Chicago	
1983-84—	Bryan Murray, Washington	
1984-85—	Mike Keenan, Philadelphia	
1985-86—	Glen Sather, Edmonton	
1986-87—	Jacques Demers, Detroit	
1987-88—	Jacques Demers, Detroit	
1988-89—	Pat Burns, Montreal	
1989-90—	Bob Murdoch, Winnipeg	

KING CLANCY TROPHY

Humanitarian Contributions

Season	Player	Club
1987-88—	Lanny McDonald, Calgary	
1988-89—	Bryan Trottier, N.Y. Islanders	
1989-90—	Kevin Lowe, Edmonton	

NHL ENTRY DRAFT—JUNE 16, 1990

FIRST ROUND

NHL Club	Player	(Pos.)	1989-90 Club (League)
1—Quebec	Owen Nolan	(RW)	Cornwall (OHL)
2—Vancouver	Petr Nedved	(C)	Seattle (WHL)
3—Detroit	Keith Primeau	(C)	Niagara Falls (OHL)
4—Philadelphia	Mike Ricci	(C)	Peterborough (OHL)
5—Pittsburgh	Jaromir Jagr	(LW)	Poldi Kladno, Czech.
6—New York Islanders	Scott Scissons	(C)	Saskatoon (WHL)
7—Los Angeles	Darryl Sydor	(D)	Kamloops (WHL)
8—Minnesota	Derian Hatcher	(D)	North Bay (OHL)
9—Washington	John Slaney	(D)	Cornwall (OHL)
10—Toronto	Drake Berehowsky	(D)	Kingston (OHL)
11—Calgary (From N.J.)	Trevor Kidd	(G)	Brandon (WHL)
12—Montreal (From St.L.)	Turner Stevenson	(RW)	Seattle (WHL)
13—New York Rangers	Michael Stewart	(D)	Michigan State University
14—Buffalo (From Wpg.)	Brad May	(LW)	Niagara Falls (OHL)
15—Hartford	Mark Greig	(RW)	Lethbridge (WHL)
16—Chicago	Karl Dykhuis	(D)	Hull (QMJHL)
17—Edmonton	Scott Allison	(C)	Prince Albert (WHL)
18—Van. (From Mtl.)	Shawn Antoski	(LW)	North Bay (OHL)
19—Winnipeg (From Buf.)	Keith Tkachuk	(LW)	Malden Cath. H.S. (Mass.)
20—N.J. (From Cgy.)	Martin Brodeur	(G)	St. Hyacinthe (QMJHL)
21—Boston	Bryan Smolinski	(C)	Michigan State University

SECOND ROUND

NHL Club	Player	(Pos.)	1989-90 Club (League)
22—Quebec	Ryan Hughes	(C)	Cornell University
23—Vancouver	Jiri Slegr	(D)	Litvinov, Czech.
24—N.J. (From Cgy.-Det.)	David Harlock	(D)	University of Michigan
25—Philadelphia	Chris Simon	(LW)	Ottawa (OHL)
26—Calgary (From Pit.)	Nicolas Perreault	(D)	Hawkesbury Tier II
27—New York Islanders	Chris Taylor	(C)	London (OHL)
28—Los Angeles	Brandy Semchuk	(RW)	Canadian National Team
29—N.J. (From Cgy.-Min.)	Chris Gotziaman	(RW)	Roseau H.S. (Minn.)
30—Washington	Rod Pasma	(D)	Cornwall (OHL)
31—Toronto	Felix Potvin	(G)	Chicoutimi (QMJHL)
32—Calgary (From N.J.)	Vesa Viitakoski	(LW)	Saipa, Finland
33—St. Louis	Craig Johnson	(LW)	Hill-Murray H.S. (Minn.)
34—New York Rangers	Doug Weight	(C)	Lake Superior State Univ.
35—Winnipeg	Mike Muller	(D)	Wayzata H.S. (Minn.)
36—Hartford	Geoff Sanderson	(C)	Swift Current (WHL)
37—Chicago	Ivan Droppa	(D)	L. Mikulas, Czech.
38—Edmonton	Alexandre Legault	(RW)	Boston University
39—Montreal	Ryan Kuwabara	(RW)	Ottawa (OHL)
40—Phila. (From Buf.)	Mikael Renberg	(LW)	Pitea, Sweden
41—Calgary	Etienne Belzile	(D)	Cornell University
42—Phila. (From Bos.)	Terran Sandwith	(D)	Tri-City (WHL)

THIRD ROUND

NHL Club	Player	(Pos.)	1989-90 Club (League)
43—Quebec	Bradley Zavisha	(LW)	Seattle (WHL)
44—Phila. (From Vanc.)	Kimbi Daniels	(C)	Swift Current (WHL)
45—Detroit	Viacheslav Kozlov	(C)	Chimik, USSR
46—Philadelphia	Bill Armstrong	(D)	Oshawa (OHL)
47—Phila. (From Pit.)	Chris Therien	(D)	Northwood Prep (N.Y.)
48—New York Islanders	Dan Plante	(RW)	Edina H.S. (Minn.)
49—Los Angeles	Bob Berg	(LW)	Belleville (OHL)
50—Minnesota	Laurie Billeck	(D)	Prince Albert (WHL)
51—Washington	Chris Longo	(RW)	Peterborough (OHL)
52—Phila. (From Tor.)	Al Kinisky	(LW)	Seattle (WHL)
53—New Jersey	Michael Dunham	(G)	Canterbury Prep (Ct.)
54—St. Louis	Patrice Tardif	(C)	Champlain (Ont.) JC
55—New York Rangers	John Vary	(D)	North Bay (OHL)
56—N.J. (From Wpg.)	Brad Bombardir	(D)	Powell River Tier II
57—Hartford	Mike Lenarduzzi	(G)	Sault Ste. Marie (OHL)
58—Montreal (From Chi.)	Charles Poulin	(C)	St. Hyacinthe (QMJHL)
59—Edmonton	Joe Crowley	(LW)	Lawrence Acad. (Mass.)
60—Montreal	Robert Guillet	(RW)	Longueuil (QMJHL)
61—Pitts. (From Buf.)	Joe Dziedzic	(LW)	Edison H.S. (Minn.)
62—Calgary	Glen Mears	(D)	Rochester (Minn.) Jr. A.
63—Boston	Cameron Stewart	(C)	Elmira (Ont.) Jr. B.

FOURTH ROUND

NHL Club	Player	(Pos.)	1989-90 Club (League)
64—N.J. (From Que.)	Mike Bodnarchuk	(RW)	Kingston (OHL)
65—Vancouver	Darin Bader	(LW)	Saskatoon (WHL)
66—Detroit	Stewart Malgunas	(D)	Seattle (WHL)
67—Edm. (From Phila.)	Joel Blain	(LW)	Hull (QMJHL)
68—Pittsburgh	Chris Tamer	(D)	University of Michigan
69—N.Y.R. (From N.Y.I.)	Jeff Nielsen	(RW)	Grand Rapids H.S. (Minn.)
70—Minn. (From L.A.)	Cal McGowan	(C)	Kamloops (WHL)
71—Minnesota	Frank Kovacs	(LW)	Regina (WHL)
72—Washington	Randy Pearce	(LW)	Kitchener (OHL)
73—Toronto	Darby Hendrickson	(C)	Richfield H.S. (Minn.)
74—Winnipeg (From N.J.)	Roman Meluzin	(RW)	Zetor Brno, Czech.
75—Win. (From St.L.)	Scott Levins	(RW)	Tri-City (WHL)
76—New York Rangers	Rick Willis	(LW)	Pingree H.S. (Mass.)
77—Winnipeg	Alexei Zhamnov	(C)	Moscow Dynamo
78—Hartford	Chris Bright	(C)	Moose Jaw (WHL)
79—Chicago	Chris Tucker	(C)	Jefferson H.S. (Minn.)
80—Toronto (From Edm.)	Greg Walters	(C)	Ottawa (OHL)
81—Montreal	Gilbert Dionne	(LW)	Kitchener (OHL)
82—Buffalo	Brian McCarthy	(C)	Pingree H.S. (Mass.)
83—Calgary	Paul Kruse	(LW)	Kamloops (WHL)
84—Boston	Jerome Buckley	(RW)	Northwood Prep (N.Y.)

FIFTH ROUND

NHL Club	Player	(Pos.)	1989-90 Club (League)
85—N.Y.R. (From Que.)	Sergei Zubov	(D)	CSKA, Russia
86—Vancouver	Gino Odjick	(LW)	Laval (QMJHL)
87—Detroit	Tony Burns	(D)	Duluth-Denf. H.S. (Minn.)
00—Philadelphia	Dan Kordic	(D)	Medicine Ilat (WIIL)
89—Pittsburgh	Brian Farrell	(C)	Avon Old Farms H.S. (Ct.)
90—New York Islanders	Chris Marinucci	(C)	Grand Rapids H.S. (Minn.)
91—Los Angeles	David Goverde	(G)	Sudbury (OHL)
92—Minnesota	Enrico Ciccone	(D)	Trois-Rivieres (QMJHL)
93—Washington	Brian Sakic	(C)	Tri-City (WHL)
94—Wash. (From Tor.)	Mark Ouimet	(C)	University of Michigan
95—New Jersey	Dean Malkoc	(D)	Kamloops (WHL)

114

NHL Club	Player	(Pos.)	1989-90 Club (League)
96—St. Louis	Jason Ruff	(LW)	Lethbridge (WHL)
97—Buffalo (From N.Y. R.)	Richard Smehlik	(D)	Vitkovice, Czech.
98—Winnipeg	Craig Martin	(RW)	Hull (QMJHL)
99—N.Y. R. (From Hfd.)	Lubos Rob	(C)	Budejovice, Czech.
100—Buffalo (From Chi.)	Todd Bojcun	(G)	Peterborough (OHL)
101—Edm. (From Wpg.)	Greg Louder	(G)	Cushing Academy (Ct.)
102—Montreal	Paul Dipietro	(C)	Sudbury (OHL)
103—Buffalo	Brad Pascall	(D)	University of North Dakota
104—N.J. (From Cgy.)	Peter Kuchyna	(D)	Dukla Jihlava, Czech.
105—Boston	Mike Bales	(G)	Ohio State University

SIXTH ROUND

NHL Club	Player	(Pos.)	1989-90 Club (League)
106—Quebec	Jeff Parrott	(D)	Univ. of Minnesota-Duluth
107—Pitts. (From Van.)	Ian Moran	(D)	Belmont Hill H.S. (Mass.)
108—Detroit	Claude Barthe	(D)	Victoriaville (QMJHL)
109—Philadelphia	Vjateslav Butsayev	(C)	CSKA, Russia
110—Pittsburgh	Denis Casey	(G)	Colorado College
111—New York Islanders	Joni Lehto	(D)	Ottawa (OHL)
112—Los Angeles	Erik Andersson	(LW)	Danderyd, Sweden
113—Minnesota	Roman Turek	(G)	Plzen, Czech.
114—Washington	Andrei Kovalev	(RW)	Moscow Dynamo
115—Toronto	Alexander Godynyuk	(D)	Sokol Kiev, USSR
116—New Jersey	Lubomir Kolnik	(RW)	Dukla Trencin, Czech.
117—St. Louis	Kurtis Miller	(LW)	Rochester Jr. A (Minn.)
118—New York Rangers	Jason Weinrich	(D)	Springfield (Mass.) Olym.
119—Winnipeg	Daniel Jardemyr	(D)	Uppsala, Sweden
120—Hartford	Cory Keenan	(D)	Kitchener (OHL)
121—Chicago	Brett Stickney	(C)	St. Paul's H.S. (N.H.)
122—Edmonton	Keijo Sailynoja	(LW)	Jokerit, Finland
123—Montreal	Craig Conroy	(C)	Northwood Prep (N.Y.)
124—Chicago (From Buf.)	Derek Edgerly	(C)	Stoneham H.S. (Mass.)
125—Calgary	Chris Tschupp	(C)	Trinity Pawling H.S. (N.Y.)
126—Boston	Mark Woolf	(RW)	Spokane (WHL)

SEVENTH ROUND

NHL Club	Player	(Pos.)	1989-90 Club (League)
127—Quebec	Dwayne Norris	(RW)	Michigan State University
128—Vancouver	Daryl Filipek	(D)	Ferris State University
129—Detroit	Jason York	(D)	Kitchener (OHL)
130—Pitts. (From Phi.)	Mika Valila	(C)	Tappara, Finland
131—Pittsburgh	Ken Plaquin	(D)	Michigan Tech University
132—New York Islanders	Michael Guilbert	(D)	Gov. Dummer H.S. (Mass.)
133—Los Angeles	Robert Lang	(C)	Litvinov, Czech.
134—Minnesota	Jeff Levy	(G)	Rochester Jr. A (Minn.)
135—Washington	Roman Kontsek	(RW)	Dukla Trencin, Czech.
136—Toronto	Eric Lacroix	(LW)	Gov. Dummer H.S. (Mass.)
137—New Jersey	Chris McAlpine	(D)	Roseville H.S. (Minn.)
138—St. Louis	Wayne Conlan	(C)	Trinity Pawling H.S. (N.Y.)
139—New York Rangers	Bryan Lonsinger	(D)	Choate Academy (Ct.)
140—Winnipeg	John Lilley	(C)	Cushing Academy (Ct.)
141—Hartford	Jergus Baca	(D)	Kosice, Czech.
142—Buffalo (From Chi.)	Viktor Gordijuk	(RW)	Krylja Sovetov, USSR
143—Edmonton	Mike Power	(G)	Western Michigan Univ.
144—Montreal	Stephen Rohr	(RW)	Culver Mil. Academy (Ind.)
145—Pittsburgh (From Buf.)	Pat Neaton	(D)	University of Michigan
146—Calgary	Dimitri Frolov	(D)	Moscow Dynamo
147—Boston	Jim Mackey	(D)	Hotchkiss H.S. (Ct.)

EIGHTH ROUND

NHL Club	Player	(Pos.)	1989-90 Club (League)
148—Quebec	Andrei Kovalenko	(RW)	CSKA, Russia
149—Vancouver	Paul O'Hagan	(D)	Oshawa (OHL)
150—Detroit	Wes McCauley	(D)	Michigan State University
151—Philadelphia	Patrik Englund	(LW)	AIK, Sweden
152—Pittsburgh	Petteri Koskimaki	(C)	Boston University
153—New York Islanders	Sylvain Fleury	(LW)	Longueuil (QMJHL)
154—Los Angeles	Dean Hulett	(RW)	Lake Superior State Univ.
155—Minnesota	Doug Barrault	(RW)	Lethbridge (WHL)
156—Washington	Peter Bondra	(C)	Kosice, Czech.
157—Toronto	Dan Stiver	(RW)	University of Michigan
158—Quebec (From N.J.)	Al'x'nd'r Karpovtsev	(D)	Moscow Dynamo
159—Wash. (From St.L.)	Steve Martell	(RW)	London (OHL)
160—New York Rangers	Todd Hedlund	(RW)	Roseau H.S. (Minn.)
161—Winnipeg	Henrik Andersson	(D)	Vasteras, Sweden
162—Hartford	Martin D'Orsonnens	(D)	Clarkson University
163—Chicago	Hugo Belanger	(LW)	Clarkson University
164—Edmonton	Roman Mejzlik	(LW)	Dukla Jihlava, Czech.
165—Montreal	Brent Fleetwood	(LW)	Portland (WHL)
166—Buffalo	Milan Nedoma	(D)	Zetor Brno, Czech.
167—Calgary	Shawn Murray	(G)	Hill-Murray H.S. (Minn.)
168—Boston	John Gruden	(D)	Waterloo (Ia.) Jr. A

NINTH ROUND

NHL Club	Player	(Pos.)	1989-90 Club (League)
169—Quebec	Pat Mazzoli	(G)	Humboldt Tier II (Sask.)
170—Vancouver	Mark Cipriano	(RW)	Victoria (WHL)
171—Detroit	Anthony Gruba	(RW)	Hill Murray H.S. (Minn.)
172—Philadelphia	Toni Porkka	(D)	Lukko, Finland
173—Pittsburgh	Ladislav Karabin	(LW)	Bratislava, Czech.
174—New York Islanders	John Joyce	(C)	Avon Old Farms H.S. (Ct.)
175—Los Angeles	Denis Leblanc	(C)	St. Hyacinthe (QMJHL)
176—Minnesota	Joe Biondi	(C)	Univ. of Minnesota-Duluth
177—Washington	Ken Klee	(D)	Bowling Green State Univ.
178—Toronto	Robert Horyna	(G)	Dukla Jihlava, Czech.
179—New Jersey	Jaroslav Modry	(D)	Budejovice, Czech.
180—St. Louis	Parris Duffus	(G)	Melfort Tier II (Sask.)
181—New York Rangers	Andrew Silverman	(D)	Beverly H.S. (Mass.)
182—Winnipeg	Rauli Raitanen	(C)	Assat, Finland
183—Hartford	Corey Osmak	(C)	Nipiwan (Alta.) Tier II
184—Chicago	Owen Lessard	(LW)	Owen Sound (OHL)
185—Edmonton	Richard Zemlicka	(RW)	Sparta Praha, Czech.
186—Montreal	Derek Maguire	(D)	Delbarton H.S. (N.J.)
187—Buffalo	Jason Winch	(LW)	Niagara Falls (OHL)
188—Calgary	Mike Murray	(RW)	Cushing Academy (Ct.)
189—Boston	Darren Wetherill	(D)	Minot T-II (N.D.)

TENTH ROUND

NHL Club	Player	(Pos.)	1989-90 Club (League)
190—Quebec	Scott Davis	(D)	University of Manitoba
191—Vancouver	Troy Neumier	(D)	Prince Albert (WHL)
192—Detroit	Travis Tucker	(D)	Avon Old Farms H.S. (Ct.)
193—Philadelphia	Greg Hanson	(D)	Bloom.-Kennedy H.S. (MN)
194—Pittsburgh	Timothy Fingerhut	(LW)	Canterbury H.S. (Mass.)
195—New York Islanders	Richard Enga	(C)	Culver Mil. Academy (Ind.)
196—Los Angeles	Patrik Ross	(RW)	HV 71, Sweden
197—Minnesota	Troy Binnie	(RW)	Ottawa (OHL)
198—Washington	Michael Boback	(C)	Providence College
199—Toronto	Rob Chebator	(D)	Arlington H.S. (Mass.)
200—New Jersey	Corey Schwab	(G)	Seattle (WHL)
201—St. Louis	Steve Widmeyer	(RW)	University of Maine
202—New York Rangers	Jon Hillebrandt	(G)	Monona Grove H.S. (Wis.)
203—Winnipeg	Mika Alatalo	(LW)	Kookoo, Finland
204—Hartford	Espen Knutsen	(C)	Valerengen, Norway
205—Chicago	Erik Peterson	(C)	Brockton H.S. (Mass.)
206—Edmonton	Petr Korinek	(C)	Skoda Plzen, Czech.
207—Montreal	Mark Kettelhut	(D)	Duluth East H.S. (Minn.)
208—Buffalo	Sylvain Naud	(RW)	Laval (QMJHL)
209—Calgary	Rob Sumner	(D)	Victoria (WHL)
210—Boston	Dean Capuano	(D)	Mount St. Charles (R.I.)

ELEVENTH ROUND

NHL Club	Player	(Pos.)	1989-90 Club (League)
211—Quebec	Mika Stromberg	(D)	Jokerit, Finland
212—Vancouver	Tyler Ertel	(C)	North Bay (OHL)
213—Detroit	Brett Larson	(D)	Duluth-Denf. H.S. (Minn.)
214—Philadelphia	Tommy Soderstrom	(G)	Djurgarden, Sweden
215—Pittsburgh	Michael Thompson	(RW)	Michigan State University
216—New York Islanders	Martin Lacroix	(RW)	St. Lawrence University
217—Los Angeles	Kevin White	(C)	Windsor (OHL)
218—Minnesota	Ole Dahlstrom	(C)	Furuset, Norway
219—Washington	Alan Brown	(D)	Colgate University
220—Toronto	Scott Malone	(D)	N'field-Mt. Her. H.S. (MA)
221—New Jersey	Valeri Zelepukin	(RW)	Himik, USSR
222—St. Louis	Joe Hawley	(RW)	Peterborough (OHL)
223—New York Rangers	Brett Lievers	(C)	Wayzata H.S. (Minn.)
224—Winnipeg	Sergei Selyanin	(D)	Himik, USSR
225—Hartford	Tommie Eriksen	(D)	Prince Albert (WHL)
226—Chicago	Steve Dubinsky	(C)	Clarkson University
227—Edmonton	Pick Voided	....	....
228—Montreal	John Uniac	(D)	Kitchener (OHL)
229—Buffalo	Kenneth Martin	(LW)	Belmont Hill H.S. (Mass.)
230—Calgary	Pick Voided	....	....
231—Boston	Andy Bezeau	(LW)	Niagara Falls (OHL)

TWELFTH ROUND

NHL Club	Player	(Pos.)	1989-90 Club (League)
232—Quebec	Wade Klippenstein	(LW)	Univ. of Alaska-Fairbanks
233—Vancouver	Karri Kivi	(D)	Ilves, Finland
234—Detroit	John Hendry	(LW)	Lake Superior State Univ.
235—Philadelphia	William Lund	(C)	Roseau H.S. (Minn.)
236—Pittsburgh	Brian Bruininks	(D)	Colorado College
237—New York Islanders	Andy Shier	(C)	Detroit Compuware
238—Los Angeles	Troy Mohns	(D)	Colgate University

NHL Club	Player	(Pos.)	1989-90 Club (League)
239—Minnesota	John McKersie	(G)	West High (Minn.)
240—Washington	Todd Hlushko	(LW)	London (OHL)
241—Toronto	Nick Vachon	(C)	Gov. Dummer H.S. (Mass.)
242—New Jersey	Todd Reirden	(D)	Tabor H.S. (Mass.)
243—St. Louis	Joe Fleming	(D)	Xaverian Bros. H.S. (MA)
244—New York Rangers	Sergei Nemchinov	(C)	Krlja Sovetov, USSR
245—Winnipeg	Keith Morris	(C)	Univ. of Alaska-Anchorage

NHL Club	Player	(Pos.)	1989-90 Club (League)
246—Hartford	Denis Chalifoux	(C)	Laval (QMJHL)
247—Chicago	Dino Grossi	(RW)	Northeastern University
248—Edmonton	Sami Nuutinen	(D)	K-Espoo, Finland
249—Montreal	Sergei Martinyuk	(LW)	Torpedo Jaroslav, USSR
250—Buffalo	Brad Rubachuk	(C)	Lethbridge (WHL)
251—Calgary	Leo Gudas	(D)	Sparta Praha, Czech.
252—Boston	Ted Miskolczi	(RW)	Belleville (OHL)

1989-90 NHL ATTENDANCE

Team	Home Ice	Capacity	1988-89 Attendance	1989-90 Attendance	Team	Home Ice	Capacity	1988-89 Attendance	1989-90 Attendance
Boston	Boston Garden	14,488	563,730	572,544	N.Y. Islanders	Nassau Coliseum	16,297	557,004	524,685
Buffalo	Memorial Auditorium	16,433	603,484	634,692	N.Y. Rangers	Madison Square Garden	16,651	696,480	653,640
Calgary	Saddledome	20,002	778,324	794,444	Philadelphia	Spectrum	17,423	696,202	696,268
Chicago	Chicago Stadium	17,317	656,326	719,382	Pittsburgh	Civic Arena	16,025	629,345	640,700
Detroit	Joe Louis Arena	19,275	788,102	781,679	Quebec	Quebec Colisee	15,399	581,795	603,193
Edmonton	Northlands Coliseum	17,503	673,802	680,334	St. Louis	St. Louis Arena	17,188	605,537	632,525
Hartford	Civic Center	15,580	552,823	535,115	Toronto	Maple Leaf Gardens	16,382	644,000	648,000
Los Angeles	Great Western Forum	16,005	595,000	613,201	Vancouver	Pacific Coliseum	16,160	550,880	616,715
Minnesota	Met Center	15,093	391,787	454,147	Washington	Capital Centre	18,130	680,506	690,023
Montreal	Forum	16,197	737,485	750,945	Winnipeg	Winnipeg Arena	15,405	512,635	524,016
New Jersey	Meadowlands Arena	19,040	608,670	599,227	Totals			13,103,917	13,365,475

Jeremy Roenick

The Sporting News
1989-90 NHL All-Star Team

First Team Player, Club and Votes	Position	Second Team Player, Club and Votes
Mark Messier, Edmonton (174)	Center	Pat LaFontaine, N.Y. Islanders (56)
Brett Hull, St. Louis (183)	Right Wing	Cam Neely, Boston (106)
Luc Robitaille, Los Angeles (145)	Left Wing	Brian Bellows, Minnesota (88)
Ray Bourque, Boston (269)	Defense	Doug Wilson, Chicago (76)
Al MacInnis, Calgary (127)	Defense	Paul Coffey, Pittsburgh (74)
Patrick Roy, Montreal (155)	Goalie	Daren Puppa, Buffalo (101)

THE SPORTING NEWS Player of the Year Voting: Messier, 119; Bourque, 84; Hull, 74.

THE SPORTING NEWS Rookie of the Year Voting: Jeremy Roenick, Chicago, 90; Mike Modano, Minnesota, 60; Mark Recchi, Pittsburgh, 41.

THE SPORTING NEWS Coach of the Year Voting: Mike Milbury, Boston, 7; Bob Murdock, Winnipeg, 4; Rick Dudley, Buffalo and Roger Neilson, N.Y. Rangers, 3.

THE SPORTING NEWS Executive of the Year Voting: Harry Sinden, Boston, 16; Glen Sather, Edmonton and Ron Caron, St. Louis, 5; Neil Smith, N.Y. Rangers, 3.

Note: THE SPORTING NEWS All-Star Team is selected by the NHL Players.

Mike Milbury

AMERICAN HOCKEY LEAGUE

Address
425 Union Street, West Springfield, MA 01089
Phone—(413) 781-2030
FAX—(413) 733-4767
Chairman of the Board
Robert W. Clarke
President and Treasurer
Jack A. Butterfield
Vice-President and General Counsel
Macgregor Kilpatrick
Vice-President, Secretary
Gordon C. Anziano
Director of Marketing and Communications
Robert Ohrablo
Statistician
Hellen Schoeder

Board Of Governors
Adirondack—Nick Polano
Baltimore—Thomas Ebright
Binghamton—Thomas Mitchell
Cape Breton—Bruce MacGregor
Capital District—Michael Cantanucci
Fredericton—Andre Boudrias
Halifax—Gilles Leger
Hershey—Frank Mathers
Maine—Edward Anderson
Moncton—Gary O'Neill
New Haven—Roy Mlakar
Newmarket—Floyd Smith
Rochester—George Bergantz
Springfield—Peter R. Cooney
Utica—Lou Lamoriello
Honorary Governor—George Sage

ADIRONDACK RED WINGS

President—Michael Ilitch
Governor—Nick Polano
Vice-President/Alternate Governor—James Devellano
General Counsel—Denise Ilitch Lites
Executive Vice President—Jim Lites
Director of Operations—Jack Kelley
General Manager/Coach—Barry Melrose
Dir. of Marketing and Promotions—Don Ostrom
Director of Media Relations—Bill Miller
Dir. of P.R./Broadcaster—Bob Crawford
Trainer—David Casey
Home Ice—Glens Falls Civic Center
Address—1 Civic Center Plaza,
Glens Falls, N.Y. 12801
Seating Capacity—4,804
NHL Affiliation—Detroit Red Wings
Phone—(518) 798-0366
FAX—(518) 798-0816

BALTIMORE SKIPJACKS

President and Governor—Thomas Ebright
Vice-President—John M. Haas
Secretary/Treasurer—Gary Fisher
Alt. Gov./Gen. Man./Coach—Rob Laird
Asst. GM/V.P. Communications—Jim Riggs
Assistant Coach—Barry Trotz
Director of Marketing/Sales—Alan Rakvin
Director of Operations—Stacey M. Riggs
Dir. Community Relations—Margaret Robinson
Director of Merchandising—Cliff Gault
Director of Special Events—Sherrie Petti
Athletic Trainer—Dan Redmond
Equipment Manager—Rich Oberlin
Home Ice—Baltimore Arena
Address—Suite 412,
201 W. Baltimore Street
Baltimore, Md. 21201
Seating Capacity—11,025
NHL Affiliation—Washington Capitals
Phone—(301) 727-0703
FAX—(301) 547-8445

BINGHAMTON RANGERS

President—James R. McCoy
Vice President—Robert W. Carr, Jr.
Gov./Mang. Part./Sec./Treas.—Thomas Mitchell
General Manager/Alt. Governor—Neil Smith

Coach—John Paddock
Dir. Marketing/Communications—Tracy Zega
Director of Broadcasting—Marc Shelanski
Director of Promotions—Chris Martell
Director of Group Sales—Patrick Snyder
Home Ice—Broome County
Veterans Memorial Arena
Address—One Stuart Street
Binghamton, N.Y. 13901
Seating Capacity—4,794
NHL Affiliation—New York Rangers
Phone—(607) 723-8937
FAX—(607) 724-6892

CAPE BRETON OILERS

President—Glen Sather
Governor/Vice President—Bruce MacGregor
General Manager—Dave Andrews
Coach—Don MacAdam
Office Manager—Cheryl Clarke
Director of Player Personnel—Barry Fraser
Trainer—Conrad Lackten
Equipment Manager—Ben Haighway
Home Ice—Centre 200
Address—481 George Street
Sydney, Nova Scotia B1T 6R7
Seating Capacity—4,700
NHL Affiliation—Edmonton Oilers
Phone—(902) 562-0780
FAX—(902) 562-1806

CAPITAL DISTRICT ISLANDERS

Governor/President—Michael J. Cantanucci
Vice-Pres./General Manager—Kevin P. Earl
Secretary/Alt. Governor—Anthony Ianniello
Coach—Butch Goring
Controller—Elizabeth Johnson
Director of Ticket Sales—Thomas J. Sheehan
Director of Marketing—Joseph P. Romano
Marketing Representative—Robert M. Conway
Marketing Representative—Christopher Leach
Home Ice—RPI Houston Field House
Address—Peoples Ave.
Troy, N.Y. 12180
Seating Capacity—5,203
NHL Affiliation—New York Islanders
Phone—(518) 276-8375
FAX—(518) 276-8669

FREDERICTON CANADIENS

President/Alt. Governor—Peter Adams
Governor—Andre Boudrias
General Manager/Coach—Paulin Bordeleau
Director of Operations—Wayne Gamble
Director of Sales—Russ Newton
Director of Concessions—Terry Blizzard
Controller—Jayne Wallace
Equipment Manager—Bobby Belanger
Athletic Therapist—Jacques Parent
Home Ice—Aitken University Centre
Address—P.O. Box HABS
Fredericton, N.B. E3B 4Y2
Seating Capacity—3,570
NHL Affiliation—Montreal Canadiens
Phone—(506) 459-4227
FAX—(506) 457-4250

HALIFAX CITADELS

Governor—Gilles Leger
V.P./Mark., Media, Comm.—Michael E. Doyle
General Manager/Coach—Clement Jodoin
Assistant Coach—Dean Hopkins
Director of Sales—Francis McKenzie
Marketing/Promotions—Neil Woodisiss
Home Ice—Halifax Metro-Centre
Address—5284 Duke Street
Halifax, N.S. B3J 3L2
Seating Capacity—9,629
NHL Affiliation—Quebec Nordiques
Phone—(902) 421-1600
FAX—(902) 425-5260

HERSHEY BEARS

Chairman/Chief Exec. Officer—J. Bruce McKinney
Governor/President—Frank Mathers
General Manager—Jay Feaster
Asst. G.M./Dir. Hockey Oper.—Doug Yingst
Coach—Mike Eaves
Head Trainer—Dan Stuck
Assistant Trainer—Harry Bricker
Home Ice—Hersheypark Arena
Address—P.O. Box 866
Hershey, Pa. 17033
Seating Capacity—7,256
NHL Affiliation—Philadelphia Flyers
Phone—(717) 534-3380
FAX—(717) 534-3383

MAINE MARINERS

Governor and President—Edward Anderson
Alternate Governor—Harry Sinden
Coach/Alternate Governor—Rick Bowness
Business Manager—Jeff Fear
Marketing/Sales—Doug Foerster
Media/Public Relations—Joe Beninati
Head Trainer—Jerry Foster
Equipment Manager—Roger Beaudoin
Home Ice—Cumberland County
Civic Center
Address—P.O. Box 1219
Portland, Me. 04104
Seating Capacity—6,726
NHL Affiliation—Boston Bruins
Phone—(207) 775-3411
FAX—(207) 775-0219

MONCTON HAWKS

Chairman—George T. Urquhart
Governor—Gary O'Neill
Coach/General Manager—Dave Farrish
Dir. Promotions/Pub. Rel.—Tom Nicholls
Home Ice—Moncton Coliseum
Address—P.O. Box 2940, Station A
Moncton, N.B. E1C 8T8
Seating Capacity—6,802
NHL Affiliation—Winnipeg Jets
Phone—(506) 857-4000
FAX—(506) 859-8919

NEW HAVEN NIGHTHAWKS

Governor and President—Roy Mlakar
Director of Operations—Pat Hickey
Dir. Hockey Oper./Coach—Marcel Comeau
Director of Press Relations—Jan MacDonald
Trainer—Scott Green
Equipment Manager—Sal Lombardi
Office Manager—Henry Bradbury
Home Ice—Veterans Memorial Coliseum
Address—P.O. Box 1444
New Haven, Conn. 06506
Seating Capacity—5,933
NHL Affiliation—Los Angeles Kings
Phone—(203) 787-0101
FAX—(203) 787-9461

NEWMARKET SAINTS

President—Donald P. Giffin
Governor/General Manager—Floyd Smith
Alternate Governor—Bob Stellick
Coach—Frank Anzalone
Director of Administration—Chris Reed
Executive Assistant—Alan Millar
Trainer—Ken Garrett
Home Ice—Newmarket Recreation Complex
Address—100 Eagle Street, West
P.O. Box 116
Newmarket, Ont., L3Y 4W3
Seating Capacity—3,387
NHL Affiliation—Toronto Maple Leafs
Phone—(416) 895-7078
FAX—(416) 853-4230

ROCHESTER AMERICANS

Chairman of the Board—Lawrence Lovejoy
Governor—George Bergantz
General Manager—Randy Scott
Coach—Don Lever
Assistant Coach—Terry Martin
P.R. Dir./Broadcast—Don Stevens
Director of Media Relations—Jeff Holbrook
Executive Assistant—Michele Butz
Director of Sales—Tony Gentile
Account Executive—Chris Palin
Director of Marketing—Joe Baumann
Athletic Trainer—Kent Weisbeck
Home Ice—Rochester War Memorial
Address—100 Exchange Street
　　　　Rochester, N.Y. 14614
Seating Capacity—6,973
NHL Affiliation—Buffalo Sabres
Phone—(716) 454-5335
FAX—(716) 454-3954

SPRINGFIELD INDIANS

President and Governor—Peter R. Cooney
Alternate Governor—Eddie Johnston
Accountant—Dennis J. Fusco
General Manager—Bruce Landon
Coach—Jimmy Roberts
Business Manager—Martha Dailey
Broadcaster/Publicity Dir.—John H. Forslund
Equipment Manager—Ralph Calvanese
Home Ice—Springfield Civic Center
Address—P.O. Box 4896
　　　　Springfield, Mass. 01101
Seating Capacity—7,602
NHL Affiliation—Hartford Whalers
Phone—(413) 736-4546
FAX—(413) 788-6786

UTICA DEVILS

Chairman—John J. McMullen
President and Governor—Lou Lamoriello
Exec. Dir./Alt. Gov.—Brian Petrovek
General Manager/Coach—Tom McVie
Associate Coach—Bob Hoffmeyer
Director of Marketing—Paul D'Aiuto
Asst. Dir. Marketing—Virginia Roher
Dir. Public/Media Rel.—William Dowsland
Athletic Trainer—Robert Bill
Equipment Manager—Scott Moon
Home Ice—Utica Memorial Auditorium
Address—400 Oriskany St., West
　　　　Utica, N.Y. 13502
Seating Capacity—3,971
NHL Affiliation—New Jersey Devils
Phone—(315) 724-2126
FAX—(315) 724-2136

1989-90 FINAL AHL STANDINGS

NORTH DIVISION

	G.	W.	L.	T.	Pts.	GF.	GA.
Sherbrooke Canadiens	80	45	23	12	102	301	247
Cape Breton Oilers	80	39	34	7	85	317	306
Springfield Indians	80	38	38	4	80	317	310
Halifax Citadels	80	37	37	6	80	317	300
Maine Mariners	80	31	38	11	73	294	317
Moncton Hawks	80	33	42	5	71	265	303
New Haven Nighthawks	80	32	41	7	71	283	316

SOUTH DIVISION

	G.	W.	L.	T.	Pts.	GF.	GA.
Rochester Americans	80	43	28	9	95	337	286
Adirondack Red Wings	80	42	27	11	95	330	304
Baltimore Skipjacks	80	43	30	7	93	302	265
Utica Devils	80	44	32	4	92	354	315
Newmarket Saints	80	31	33	16	78	305	318
Hershey Bears	80	32	38	10	74	298	296
Binghamton Whalers	80	11	60	9	31	229	366

TOP 20 SCORERS FOR THE JOHN B. SOLLENBERGER TROPHY

	Games	G.	A.	Pts.	Pen.
1. Paul Ysebaert, Utica	74	53	52	*105	61
2. Ross Fitzpatrick, Hershey	74	45	*58	103	26
3. Mike Donnelly, Rochester	68	43	55	98	71
4. Mark Pederson, Sherbrooke	72	53	42	95	60
5. Don Biggs, Hershey	66	39	53	92	125
6. Murray Eaves, Adirondack	78	40	49	89	35
Claude Vilgrain, Utica	73	37	52	89	32
8. John LeBlanc, Cape Breton	77	*54	34	88	50
Don Audette, Rochester	70	42	46	88	78
Dale Krentz, Adirondack	74	38	50	88	36
11. Fabian Joseph, Cape Breton	77	33	53	86	46
12. Brian Dobbin, Hershey	68	38	47	85	58

	Games	G.	A.	Pts.	Pen.
13. Jody Gage, Rochester	75	45	38	83	42
Mike Richard, Baltimore	53	41	42	83	14
15. Dan Currie, Cape Breton	77	36	40	76	28
16. Ladislav Tresl, Halifax	66	35	39	74	64
Paul Gagne, Newmarket	28	13	14	27	11
Springfield	36	18	29	47	6
Totals	64	31	43	74	17
18. Mike Millar, Maine	60	40	33	73	77
Danton Cole, Moncton	80	31	42	73	18
Petr Ihnacak, Newmarket	72	26	47	73	40

TEAM-BY-TEAM BREAKDOWN OF AHL SCORING

ADIRONDACK RED WINGS

	Games	G.	A.	Pts.	Pen.
Murray Eaves	78	40	49	89	35
Dale Krentz	74	38	50	88	36
Glenn Merkosky	75	33	31	64	29
Al Conroy	77	23	33	56	147
Kory Kocur	79	18	37	55	36
Dennis Holland	78	19	34	53	53
Randy McKay	36	16	23	39	99
Bob Wilkie	58	5	33	38	64
Yves Racine	46	8	27	35	31
Derek Mayer	62	4	26	30	56
Brent Fedyk	33	14	15	29	24
Mike Gober	44	14	12	26	85
Sheldon Kennedy	26	11	15	26	35
Chris Luongo	53	9	14	23	37
Chris McRae	46	9	10	19	290
Jim Nill	20	10	8	18	24
Bill McDougall	11	10	7	17	4
Daniel Shank	14	8	8	16	36
Torrie Robertson	27	3	13	16	47
Dean Morton	75	1	15	16	183
Tom Bissett	16	11	4	15	4
Dave Barr	9	1	14	15	17

	Games	G.	A.	Pts.	Pen.
Gord Kruppke	59	2	12	14	103
Rob Schena	43	5	8	13	36
Peter Dineen	27	3	6	9	28
John Mokosak	29	2	6	8	80
Shawn Burr	3	4	2	6	2
Craig Endean	7	3	3	6	4
Chris Kotsopoulos	24	2	4	6	4
Marc Potvin	5	2	1	3	9
Tim Cheveldae (Goalie)	31	0	3	3	2
Mark Reimer (Goalie)	36	0	1	1	8
Greg Stefan (Goalie)	3	0	0	0	0
Mark Holick	7	0	0	0	5
Sam St. Laurent (Goalie)	13	0	0	0	6

BALTIMORE SKIPJACKS

	Games	G.	A.	Pts.	Pen.
Mike Richard	53	41	42	83	14
Tyler Larter	79	31	36	67	124
Steve Maltais	67	29	37	66	54
Alfie Turcotte	65	26	40	66	42
John Purves	75	29	35	64	12
Chris Felix	73	19	42	61	115
Tim Taylor	74	22	21	43	63

	Games	G.	A.	Pts.	Pen.
Mark Ferner	74	7	28	35	76
Dennis Smith	74	8	25	33	103
John Druce	26	15	16	31	38
Tim Bergland	47	12	19	31	55
Steve Seftel	74	10	19	29	52
Doug Wickenheiser	35	9	19	28	22
Kent Paynter	60	7	20	27	110
Robin Bawa	61	7	18	25	189
Alain Cote	57	5	19	24	161
Brian Tutt	67	2	13	15	80
Steve Hollett	43	4	10	14	18
Nick Kypreos	14	6	5	11	6
Bill Houlder	26	3	7	10	12
Rob Murray	23	5	4	9	63
Jeff Greenlaw	10	3	2	5	26
Jim Hrivnak (Goalie)	47	0	4	4	2
Bobby Babcock	67	0	4	4	249
Scot Kleinendorst	2	2	0	2	6
Bob Mason (Goalie)	13	0	1	1	2
Dave Richter	13	0	1	1	13
Shawn Simpson (Goalie)	15	0	1	1	2
Scott Birnie	1	0	0	0	0
Jordan Fois	1	0	0	0	0
Dennis McEwen	1	0	0	0	0
David Buckley	4	0	0	0	0
Alain Raymond (Goalie)	11	0	0	0	0

BINGHAMTON WHALERS

	Games	G.	A.	Pts.	Pen.
James Black	80	37	35	72	34
Dallas Gaume	76	26	39	65	43
Bob Bodak	79	32	25	57	59
Terry Yake	77	13	42	55	37
Chris Cichocki, Utica	11	3	1	4	10
Binghamton	60	21	26	47	12
Totals	71	24	27	51	22
Blair Atcheynum	78	20	21	41	45
Michel Picard	67	16	24	40	98
Raymond Saumier	56	9	11	20	171
Jody Hull	21	7	10	17	6
Jim Culhane	73	6	11	17	69
Brian Chapman	68	2	15	17	180
Jim McKenzie	56	4	12	16	149
Jim Ennis	69	3	12	15	61
Tom Martin	24	4	10	14	113
Al Tuer	58	3	7	10	176
Todd Krygier	12	1	9	10	16
Jeff Sirkka, Maine	56	0	9	9	110
Binghamton	16	0	1	1	38
Totals	72	0	10	10	148
Chris Lindberg	32	4	4	8	36
Pat Bingham	24	3	4	7	63
Chris Govedaris	14	3	3	6	4
Vern Smith	17	3	2	5	14
Mike Berger	10	0	4	4	10
Mike Moller	12	1	2	3	6
Mike Haviland	4	2	0	2	0
John Anderson	3	1	1	2	0
Corey Beaulieu	56	0	2	2	191
Scott Humeniuk	4	0	1	1	11
Daryl Reaugh (Goalie)	52	0	1	1	4
Sean Clement	1	0	0	0	0
Jim Burke	2	0	0	0	5
Bill Whitfield	3	0	0	0	0
Jamie Russel	4	0	0	0	0
Mike Short	4	0	0	0	0
Ross McKay (Goalie)	18	0	0	0	0
Kay Whitmore (Goalie)	24	0	0	0	16

CAPE BRETON OILERS

	Games	G.	A.	Pts.	Pen.
John LeBlanc	77	*54	34	88	50
Fabian Joseph	77	33	53	86	46
Dan Currie	77	36	40	76	28
Shaun Van Allen	61	25	44	69	83
Kim Issel	62	36	32	68	46
Norm Maciver, Binghamton	2	0	0	0	0
Cape Breton	68	13	37	50	55
Totals	70	13	37	50	55
Tomas Kapusta	55	12	37	49	56
Tim Tisdale	66	15	21	36	24
Wade Campbell	77	4	31	35	84
Bruce Bell	52	8	26	34	64
Brian Wilks	53	13	20	33	85
Chris Joseph	61	10	20	30	69
Corey Foster	54	7	17	24	32
Peter Soberlak	60	15	8	23	22
Mike Ware	54	6	13	19	191
David Haas	53	6	12	18	230
Tommy Lehmann	19	6	11	17	7
Peter Eriksson	21	5	12	17	36
Mario Barbe	64	0	15	15	138
Stan Drulia	31	5	7	12	2
Marc LaForge, Binghamton	25	2	6	8	111
Cape Breton	3	0	1	1	24
Totals	28	2	7	9	135
Todd Charlesworth	32	0	9	9	13
Ivan Matulik	32	2	6	8	44
Denis LaRocque	26	2	4	6	39
Eldon Reddick (Goalie)	15	0	3	3	4
Alexandr Tyzhnych (G.)	24	0	3	3	2
Mike Greenlay (Goalie)	46	0	2	2	14
Grant Fuhr (Goalie)	2	0	0	0	0

HALIFAX CITADELS

	Games	G.	A.	Pts.	Pen.
Ladislav Tresl	66	35	39	74	64
Miroslav Ihnacak	57	33	37	70	43
Stephane Morin	65	28	32	60	60
Jamie Baker	74	17	43	60	47
Dean Hopkins	54	23	32	55	167
Claude Julian	77	6	37	43	65
Marc Vermette	47	20	17	37	44
Max Middendorf	48	20	17	37	60

	Games	G.	A.	Pts.	Pen.
Claude Lapointe	63	18	19	37	51
Jaroslav Sevcik	50	17	17	34	36
Tony Hrkac	20	12	21	33	4
Ken Quinney	44	9	16	25	63
Jean Richard	40	1	24	25	38
Gerald Bzdel	59	2	20	22	84
Dave Pichette	58	3	18	21	65
Greg Adams	10	6	13	19	18
Bryan Fogarty	22	5	14	19	6
Greg Smyth	49	5	14	19	235
Dave Espe	48	2	16	18	26
Iiro Jarvi	26	4	13	17	4
Dave Latta	34	11	5	16	45
Brent Severyn	43	6	9	15	105
Darin Kimble	18	6	6	12	37
Jean Routhier	17	4	8	12	29
Marc Fortier	15	5	6	11	6
Bruce Major	32	5	6	11	23
Scott Shaunessey	27	3	5	8	105
Kevin Kaminski	19	3	4	7	128
Trevor Stienburg	11	3	3	6	36
Marc West	10	0	5	5	0
Craig Kitteringham	8	0	4	4	6
Jim Sprott	22	2	1	3	103
Mario Doyon	5	1	2	3	0
Joe Ferras	6	1	2	3	2
Joel Baillargeon	21	0	3	3	39
Brian Martin	2	1	0	1	0
Ron Tugnutt (Goalie)	6	0	1	1	0
Francois Gravel, Sher. (G.)	12	0	1	1	4
Halifax (Goalie)	2	0	0	0	0
Totals	14	0	1	1	4
Scott Gordon (Goalie)	48	0	1	1	8
Stephan Guerard	1	0	0	0	5
Alan Perry (Goalie)	2	0	0	0	4
Stephan Carrier	3	0	0	0	0
Mario Brunetta (Goalie)	24	0	0	0	16

HERSHEY BEARS

	Games	G.	A.	Pts.	Pen.
Ross Fitzpatrick	74	45	*58	103	26
Don Biggs	66	39	53	92	125
Brian Dobbin	68	38	47	85	58
Mark Freer	65	28	36	64	31
Ray Allison	70	25	30	55	66
Dave Fenyves	66	6	37	43	57
Chris Jensen	43	16	26	42	101
Tim Tookey	42	18	22	40	28
Scott Sandelin	70	4	27	31	38
Rocky Trottier	49	15	13	28	18
Jiri Latal	22	10	18	28	10
Gord Paddock	65	4	19	23	60
Shawn Sabol	46	6	16	22	49
Don Nachbaur	30	10	9	19	72
Bill Armstrong	58	10	6	16	99
Darren Rumble	57	2	13	15	31
Mark Bassen	57	5	9	14	128
John Stevens	79	3	10	13	193
Kent Hawley	24	6	4	10	28
Murray Baron	50	0	10	10	101
Mike Stothers	56	1	6	7	170
Steve Scheifele	35	2	3	5	6
Tony Horacek	12	0	5	5	25
Reid Simpson	28	2	2	4	175
Bruce Rendall	9	2	1	3	4
Steve Fletcher	28	1	1	2	132
Jeff Harding	6	0	2	2	2
Bruce Hoffort (Goalie)	40	0	1	1	6
Marc D'Amour (Goalie)	43	0	1	1	16
John Blessman	1	0	0	0	0
Ron Hextall (Goalie)	1	0	0	0	2

MAINE MARINERS

	Games	G.	A.	Pts.	Pen.
Mike Millar	60	40	33	73	77
Billy O'Dwyer	71	26	45	71	56
Scott Harlow	80	31	32	63	68
Ray Neufeld	76	27	29	56	117
Ron Hoover	75	28	26	54	57
Bob Beers	74	7	36	43	63
Greg Johnston	52	16	26	42	45
Paul Beraldo	51	14	27	41	31
Peter Douris	38	17	20	37	14
Grame Townshend	64	15	13	28	162
Lou Crawford	62	11	15	26	241
Steve Dykstra, Binghamton	53	5	17	22	55
Maine	16	0	4	4	20
Totals	69	5	21	26	75

	Games	G.	A.	Pts.	Pen.
John Blum	77	1	20	21	134
Stephan Quintal	37	4	16	20	27
Gord Cruickshank	24	9	8	17	16
Greg Poss	50	8	8	16	54
Jarmo Kekalainen	18	5	11	16	6
Rob MacInnis	34	3	12	15	48
Bruce Shoebottom	66	3	11	14	228
Dave Buda	39	7	4	11	14
Mark Ziliotto	34	6	5	11	66
Mitch Lamoureaux	10	4	7	11	10
Don Sweeney	11	0	8	8	8
Jim Wiemer	6	3	4	7	27
Mark Montanari	17	0	7	7	90
Steve Tsujiura	8	2	4	6	10
Rob Cimetta	9	3	2	5	13
John Carter	2	2	2	4	2
Paul Boutilier	12	0	4	4	21
Norm Foster (Goalie)	64	0	4	4	6
Todd Lalonde	5	2	0	2	6
David Jensen	4	0	2	2	0
Rick Boyd, Binghamton	3	0	0	0	7
Maine	11	0	2	2	29
Totals	14	0	2	2	36
Scott Drevitch	13	0	1	1	10
Vince Guidotti	2	0	0	0	0
Brian Lawton	5	0	0	0	14
Ryan Kummu	8	0	0	0	11
Frank Caprice (Goalie)	10	0	0	0	0
Mike Jeffrey (Goalie)	13	0	0	0	0

MONCTON HAWKS

	Games	G.	A.	Pts.	Pen.
Danton Cole	80	31	42	73	18
Guy Larose	79	44	26	70	232
Brent Hughes	65	31	29	60	277
Brian McReynolds	72	18	41	59	87
Ron Wilson	47	16	37	53	64
Iain Duncan	49	16	25	41	81
Scott Schneider	61	17	23	40	57
Stu Kulak	56	14	23	37	72
Larry Bernard	66	14	17	31	93
Chris Norton	62	9	20	29	49
Bryan Marchment	56	4	19	23	217
Todd Flichel	65	7	14	21	74
Tony Joseph	61	9	9	18	74
Phil Sykes, New Haven	25	3	12	15	32
Moncton	5	0	1	1	20
Totals	30	3	13	16	52
Matt Hervey	47	3	13	16	168
Brian Hunt	43	4	11	15	19
Dallas Eakins	75	2	11	13	189
Grant Richison	50	2	10	12	28
Guy Gosselin	70	2	10	12	37
Neil Headmore	40	6	5	11	118
Brian Erickson	13	4	7	11	4
Brad Berry	38	1	9	10	58
Simon Gagne	28	4	5	9	27
Tim Hanley, Springfield	9	2	0	2	2
Moncton	16	1	4	5	2
Totals	25	3	4	7	4
Tom Draper (Goalie)	51	0	3	3	4
Peter Taglianetti	3	0	2	2	2
Luciano Borsato	1	1	0	1	0
Jacques Mailhot, C.B.	6	0	1	1	12
Moncton	6	0	0	0	20
Totals	12	0	1	1	32
F. Ronal Aubrey	1	0	0	0	0
David Farrish	1	0	0	0	2
Frank Furlan (Goalie)	2	0	0	0	0
William Hyatt	2	0	0	0	0
Bob Essensa (Goalie)	6	0	0	0	0
Rick Tabaracci (Goalie)	27	0	0	0	38

NEW HAVEN NIGHTHAWKS

	Games	G.	A.	Pts.	Pen.
Scott Bjugstad	47	45	21	66	40
Mikal Aivazoff	77	20	39	59	71
Craig Duncanson	51	17	30	47	152
Todd Elik	32	20	23	43	42
Len Hachborn	32	13	27	40	15
Francois Breault	37	17	21	38	33
Taylor Hall	51	14	23	37	10
Murray Brumwell	62	7	29	36	24
Bob Halkidis, Rochester	18	1	13	14	70
New Haven	30	3	17	20	67
Totals	48	4	30	34	137
Ross Wilson	61	19	14	33	39

	Games	G.	A.	Pts.	Pen.
Brad Jones, Moncton	15	5	6	11	47
New Haven	36	8	11	19	71
Totals	51	13	17	30	118
Chris Kontos	42	10	20	30	25
Tim Bothwell	75	3	26	29	56
Darryl Williams	51	9	13	22	124
Gordie Walker	24	14	7	21	8
Paul Kelly	38	5	15	20	43
Mikael Lindholm	28	4	16	20	24
Scott Young	58	7	11	18	62
Sylvain Couturier	50	9	8	17	47
Eric Germain	59	3	12	15	112
Darwin Bozek	36	6	7	13	20
Paul Brydges	37	6	7	13	38
Petr Prajsler	6	1	7	8	2
Graham Stanley	22	2	5	7	66
John Miner	7	1	6	7	2
Bob Logan	11	2	4	6	4
Chris Panek	21	1	5	6	7
Mike Allison	5	2	2	4	14
Nick Fotiu	31	0	3	3	40
Paul Holden	2	1	1	2	2
John VanKessel	6	1	1	2	9
Eric Ricard	28	1	1	2	55
Kevin MacDonald	27	0	1	1	111
Rene Chapdelaine	41	0	1	1	35
Ned Desmond	1	0	0	0	0
Sean Fitzgerald	1	0	0	0	0
Tom Karalis	2	0	0	0	0
Al Leggett	4	0	0	0	0
Robb Stauber (Goalie)	14	0	0	0	8
Ron Scott (Goalie)	22	0	0	0	4
Darryl Gilmour (Goalie)	23	0	0	0	4
Carl Repp (Goalie)	24	0	0	0	8

NEWMARKET SAINTS

	Games	G.	A.	Pts.	Pen.
Petr Ihnacak	72	26	47	73	40
Darren Veitch	78	13	54	67	30
Mike Stevens, Springfield	28	12	10	22	75
Newmarket	46	16	28	44	86
Totals	74	28	38	66	161
Tim Armstrong	63	25	37	62	24
Kent Hulst	80	26	34	60	29
Doug Shedden	47	26	33	59	12
Ken Hammond	75	9	45	54	106
Bobby Reynolds	66	22	28	50	55
Wes Jarvis	36	13	22	35	18
Sean McKenna	73	17	17	34	30
Rocky Dundas	62	18	15	33	158
Gilles Thibaudeau, Spring.	6	5	8	13	0
Newmarket	10	7	13	20	4
Totals	16	12	21	33	4
Alan Hepple	72	6	20	26	96
Tie Domi	57	14	11	25	285
Scott Pearson	18	21	11	23	64
Darryl Shannon	47	4	15	19	58
Derek Langille	64	5	12	17	75
Bill Root	47	8	7	15	20
Tim Bean	39	5	10	15	27
Steve Chartrand	20	4	4	8	0
Greg Hotham	24	0	8	8	31
Brian Hoard	40	2	4	6	146
Brian Blad	58	2	4	6	216
John McIntyre	6	2	2	4	12
Mike Moes	8	2	1	3	2
Peter Ing (Goalie)	48	0	2	2	4
Paul Lawless	3	1	0	1	0
Trevor Jobe	1	0	1	1	2
Mark Laforest (Goalie)	10	0	1	1	10
Brian Bellefeuille	3	0	0	0	0
Christi Lalonde	3	0	0	0	0
Allan Bester (Goalie)	5	0	0	0	0
Jeff Reese (Goalie)	7	0	0	0	4
Tim Bernhardt (Goalie)	14	0	0	0	0

ROCHESTER AMERICANS

	Games	G.	A.	Pts.	Pen.
Mike Donnelly	68	43	55	98	71
Don Audette	70	42	46	88	78
Jody Gage	75	45	38	83	42
Francois Guay	69	28	35	63	39
Don McSween	70	16	43	59	43
Ken Priestlay	40	19	39	58	46
Scott McCrory	51	14	41	55	46
Steve Ludzik	54	25	29	54	71
Jim Jackson	77	16	37	53	14
Darrin Shannon	50	20	23	43	25

	Games	G.	A.	Pts.	Pen.
Dale DeGray, New Haven	16	2	10	12	38
Rochester	50	6	25	31	118
Totals	66	8	35	43	156
Scott Metcalfe	43	12	17	29	93
Bob Corkum	43	8	11	19	45
Ken Sutton	57	5	14	19	83
Darcy Loewen	50	7	11	18	193
Dave Beseggio	41	3	15	18	41
Steve Smith	42	3	15	18	107
Shawn Anderson	39	2	16	18	41
Rob Ray	43	2	13	15	335
Richie Dunn	41	7	7	14	34
Joel Savage	43	6	7	13	39
Brad Miller	60	2	10	12	273
Jim Hofford	52	1	9	10	233
Ray Sheppard	5	3	5	8	2
Darcy Wakaluk (Goalie)	56	0	7	7	38
Mitch Molloy	15	1	1	2	43
David Littman (Goalie)	14	0	2	2	0
Kevin Kerr	8	0	1	1	22
Brian Ford (Goalie)	19	0	1	1	0

SHERBROOKE CANADIENS

	Games	G.	A.	Pts.	Pen.
Mark Pederson	72	53	42	95	60
Benoit Brunet	72	32	35	67	82
Andrew Cassels	55	22	45	67	25
Dan Woodley	65	18	40	58	144
Jim Nesich	62	21	31	52	79
Martin Desjardins	65	21	26	47	72
Tom Chorske	59	22	24	46	54
Mario Roberge	73	13	27	40	247
Ed Cristofoli	57	16	19	35	31
Norman Desjardins	58	13	19	32	91
Lyle Odelein	68	7	24	31	265
J.J. Daigneault	28	8	19	27	18
Steve Martinson	37	6	20	26	111
Luc Gauthier	79	3	23	26	139
Todd Richards	71	6	18	24	73
Stephane Richer	60	10	12	22	85
Mathieu Schneider	28	6	13	19	20
Roy Mitchell	77	5	12	17	98
Marc Saumier	28	3	11	14	83
Serge Roberge	66	8	5	13	*343
Donald Dufresne	38	2	11	13	104
John Ferguson Jr.	17	4	3	7	8
Guy Darveau	38	2	2	4	120
Paul Willett	2	0	1	1	2
Andre Racicot (Goalie)	33	0	1	1	2
Frederic Chabot (Goalie)	2	0	0	0	0
Jean Claude Bergeron (G.)	40	0	0	0	0

SPRINGFIELD INDIANS

	Games	G.	A.	Pts.	Pen.
Paul Gagne, Newmarket	28	13	14	27	11
Springfield	36	18	29	47	6
Totals	64	31	43	74	17
Mike Walsh	69	34	20	54	43
Greg Parks	49	22	32	54	30
Bill Berg	74	12	42	54	74
Tom Fitzgerald	53	30	23	53	32
Rob DiMaio	54	25	27	52	69
Guy Rouleau	52	18	26	44	14
Mike Kelfer	57	24	18	42	10
Sean LeBrun	63	9	33	42	20
Shawn Evans	63	6	35	41	102
Derek Laxdal, Newmarket	23	7	8	15	52
Springfield	28	13	12	25	42
Totals	51	20	20	40	94
Wayne McBean	68	6	33	39	48
Dale Henry	43	17	14	31	68
Rod Dallman	43	10	20	30	129
Dale Kushner	45	14	11	25	163
Derek King	21	11	12	23	33
Marc Bergevin	47	7	16	23	66
Dave Pasin, New Haven	7	7	4	11	14
Springfield	11	2	3	5	2
Totals	18	9	7	16	16
Jeff Finley	57	1	15	16	41
Chris Pryor	60	3	7	10	105
Shawn Byram	31	4	4	8	30
Richie Kromm	9	3	4	7	4
Dean Ewen	34	0	7	7	194
Dean Chynoweth	40	0	7	7	98
Brad Lauer	7	4	2	6	0
Jack Capuano, Newmarket	8	0	2	2	8
Springfield	14	0	4	4	8
Totals	22	0	6	6	15

	Games	G.	A.	Pts.	Pen.
Hank Lammens	43	0	6	6	27
Brad McCaughey	7	3	2	5	0
Joe Reekie	15	1	4	5	24
Jeff Rohlicek	12	1	2	3	4
Jari Gronstrand, Halifax	2	0	0	0	0
Springfield	1	0	1	1	0
Totals	3	0	1	1	0
Kerry Clark	21	0	1	1	73
Jeff Hackett (Goalie)	54	0	1	1	16
Andre Brassard	1	0	0	0	2
Jim Hughes	1	0	0	0	0
Len Soccio	1	0	0	0	0
Kevin Cheveldayoff	4	0	0	0	0
David Chyzowski	4	0	0	0	7
Paul Cohen (Goalie)	9	0	0	0	0
George Maneluk (Goalie)	27	0	0	0	4

UTICA DEVILS

	Games	G.	A.	Pts.	Pen.
Paul Ysebaert	74	53	52	*105	61
Claude Vilgrain	73	37	52	89	32
Jeff Madill	74	43	26	69	233
Jon Morris	49	27	37	64	6
Eric Weinrich	57	12	48	60	38
Paul Guay	75	25	30	55	103
Kevin Todd	71	18	36	54	72
Pat Conacher	57	13	36	49	53
Myles O'Connor	76	14	33	47	124
Jim Thomson, Binghamton	8	1	2	3	30
Utica	60	20	23	43	124
Totals	68	21	25	46	154
Peter Sundstrom	31	11	28	39	6
Jean Lanthier	50	13	19	32	32
Jeff Sharples, Adirondack	9	2	5	7	6
Cape Breton	38	4	13	17	28
Utica	13	2	5	7	19
Totals	60	8	23	31	53
Perry Anderson	71	13	17	30	128
Steve Rooney	57	9	16	25	134
Dave Marcinyshyn	74	6	18	24	164
Neil Brady	38	10	13	23	21
Chris Kiene	67	5	17	22	60
Sergei Starikov	43	8	11	19	14
Bob Woods	58	2	12	14	30
Jamie Huscroft	22	3	6	9	122
Bill Huard	27	1	7	8	67
Jason Simon	16	3	4	7	28
Craig Wolanin	6	2	4	6	2
Craig Billington (Goalie)	38	0	5	5	6
Roland Melanson (Goalie)	48	0	4	4	18
Walt Poddubny	2	1	2	3	0
Alexei Kasatonov	3	0	2	2	7
Allan Stewart	1	0	0	0	0
Marc Laniel	20	0	0	0	25

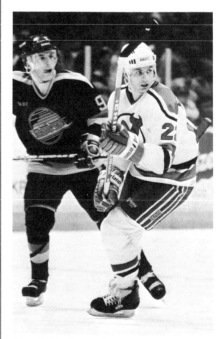

Paul Ysebaert

COMPLETE AHL GOALTENDING

	Games	Mins.	Goals	SO.	Avg.
Tim Cheveldae	31	1848	116(2)	0	3.77
Sam St. Laurent	13	785	40(1)	0	3.06
Mark Reimer	36	2092	131(7)	0	3.76
Greg Stefan	3	128	7	0	3.28
Adirondack Totals	80	4853	304	0	3.76
Jim Hrivnak	47	2722	139(3)	*4	3.06
Bob Mason	13	770	44	0	3.43
Shawn Simpson	15	733	45	0	3.68
Alain Raymond	11	612	34	0	3.33
Baltimore Totals	80	4837	265	4	3.29
Ross McKay	18	713	58(2)	0	4.88
Daryl Reaugh	52	2735	192(4)	0	4.21
Kay Whitmore	24	1386	109(1)	0	4.72
Binghamton Totals	80	4834	366	0	4.54
Mike Greenlay	46	2595	146(4)	2	3.38
Alexandr Tyzhnych	24	1309	94(2)	0	4.31
Grant Fuhr	2	120	6	0	3.00
Eldon Reddick	15	821	54	0	3.95
Cape Breton Totals	80	4845	306	2	3.79
Mario Brunetta	24	1444	99(4)	0	4.11
Scott Gordon	48	2851	158(3)	0	3.33
Alan Perry	2	38	3	0	4.74
Francois Gravel (a)	2	125	10	0	4.80
Ron Tugnutt	6	366	23	0	3.77
Halifax Totals	80	4824	300	0	3.73
Marc D'Amour	43	2505	148(1)	2	3.54
Bruce Hoffort	40	2284	139(5)	1	3.65
Ron Hextall	1	49	3	0	3.67
Hershey Totals	80	4838	296	3	3.67
Frank Caprice	10	550	46(1)	0	5.02
Norm Foster	*64	*3664	*217(7)	3	3.55
Mike Jeffrey	13	633	46	0	4.36
Maine Totals	80	4847	317	3	3.92
Bob Essensa	6	358	15	0	2.51
Rick Tabaracci	27	1580	107(2)	2	4.06
Frank Furlan	2	29	7	0	14.48
Tom Draper	51	2844	167(5)	1	3.52
Moncton Totals	80	4811	303	3	3.78
Carl Repp	24	1393	98(3)	0	4.22

	Games	Mins.	Goals	SO.	Avg.
Ron Scott	22	1224	79(4)	1	3.87
Robb Stauber	14	851	43	0	3.03
Darryl Gilmour	23	1356	85(4)	0	3.76
New Haven Totals	80	4824	316	1	3.93
Tim Bernhardt	14	755	51	0	4.05
Mark Laforest	10	604	33	1	3.28
Jeff Reese	7	431	29	0	4.04
Peter Ing	48	2829	184(2)	1	3.90
Allan Bester	5	264	18(1)	0	4.09
Newmarket Totals	80	4883	318	2	3.91
Brian Ford	19	1076	69(2)	0	3.85
Darcy Wakaluk	56	3095	173(4)	2	3.35
David Littman	14	681	37(1)	0	3.26
Rochester Totals	80	4852	286	2	3.54
Jean Claude Bergeron	40	2254	103	2	*2.74
Francois Gravel (a)	12	545	38	0	4.18
Andre Racicot	33	1948	97(1)	1	2.99
Frederic Chabot	2	119	8	0	4.03
Sherbrooke Totals	80	4866	247	3	3.05
Jeff Hackett	54	3045	187(3)	1	3.68
George Maneluk	27	1382	94	1	4.08
Paul Cohen	9	400	25(1)	0	3.75
Springfield Totals	80	4827	310	2	3.85
Craig Billington	38	2087	138(4)	0	3.97
Roland Melanson	48	2737	167(6)	1	3.66
Utica Totals	80	4824	315	1	3.92

( )—Empty Net Goals. Do not count against a Goaltender's average.
(a)—Gravel played for Halifax and Sherbrooke.

INDIVIDUAL 1989-90 LEADERS

Goals .... John LeBlanc, Cape Breton— 54
Assists .... Ross Fitzpatrick, Hershey— 58
Points .... Paul Ysebaert, Utica— 105
Penalty Minutes .... Serge Roberge, Sherbrooke— 343
Goaltending Average (25 Games) .... Jean Claude Bergeron, Sherbrooke—2.74
Shutouts .... Jim Hrivnak, Baltimore— 4

1990 CALDER CUP PLAYOFFS

(All series best-of-seven)

QUARTERFINALS

Series "A"

	W.	L.	Pts.	GF.	GA.
Sherbrooke	4	2	8	31	23
Halifax	2	4	4	23	31

(Sherbrooke wins series, 4 games to 2)

Series "B"

	W.	L.	Pts.	GF.	GA.
Springfield	4	2	8	31	24
Cape Breton	2	4	4	24	31

(Springfield wins series, 4 games to 2)

Series "C"

	W.	L.	Pts.	GF.	GA.
Rochester	4	1	8	20	15
Utica	1	4	2	15	20

(Rochester wins series, 4 games to 1)

Series "D"

	W.	L.	Pts.	GF.	GA.
Baltimore	4	2	8	29	17
Adirondack	2	4	4	17	29

(Baltimore wins series, 4 games to 2)

SEMIFINALS

Series "E"

	W.	L.	Pts.	GF.	GA.
Springfield	4	2	8	25	25
Sherbrooke	2	4	4	25	25

(Springfield wins series, 4 games to 2)

Series "F"

	W.	L.	Pts.	GF.	GA.
Rochester	4	2	8	24	19
Baltimore	2	4	4	19	24

(Rochester wins series, 4 games to 2)

FINALS FOR THE CALDER CUP

Series "G"

	W.	L.	Pts.	GF.	GA.
Springfield	4	2	8	22	22
Rochester	2	4	4	22	22

(Springfield wins series, and Calder Cup, 4 games to 2)

TOP 10 PLAYOFF SCORERS

	Games	G.	A.	Pts.
1. Greg Parks, Springfield	18	9	*13	*22
2. Mike Donnelly, Rochester	16	*12	7	19
3. Mark Pederson, Sherbrooke	11	10	8	18
Guy Rouleau, Springfield	18	9	9	18
5. Don Audette, Rochester	15	9	8	17
Shawn Evans, Springfield	18	6	11	17
Bill Berg, Springfield	15	5	12	17
Mike Richard, Baltimore	11	4	*13	17
Martin Desjardins, Sherbrooke	12	4	*13	17
10. Paul Gagne, Springfield	13	10	6	16
Alfie Turcotte, Baltimore	12	7	9	16
Steve Maltais, Baltimore	12	6	10	16

TEAM-BY-TEAM PLAYOFF SCORING

ADIRONDACK RED WINGS

(Lost quarterfinals to Baltimore, 4 games to 2)

	Games	G.	A.	Pts.	Pen.
Derek Mayer	5	0	6	6	4
Murray Eaves	6	2	3	5	2
Dale Krentz	6	2	3	5	11

	Games	G.	A.	Pts.	Pen.
Bob Wilkie	6	1	4	5	2
John Mokosak	6	1	3	4	13
Randy McKay	6	3	0	3	35
Brent Fedyk	6	2	1	3	4
Glenn Merkosky	6	2	1	3	6
Kory Kocur	6	1	2	3	2
Bill McDougall	2	1	1	2	2

	Games	G.	A.	Pts.	Pen.
Dennis Holland	6	1	1	2	10
Torrie Robertson	6	1	1	2	33
Marc Potvin	4	0	1	1	23
Peter Dineen	6	0	1	1	10
Mike Sillinger	1	0	0	0	0
Mark Reimer (Goalie)	2	0	0	0	0
Chris Luongo	3	0	0	0	0

	Games	G.	A.	Pts.	Pen.
Chris Kotsopoulos	4	0	0	0	2
Sam St. Laurent (Goalie)	4	0	0	0	0
Al Conroy	5	0	0	0	20
Dean Morton	6	0	0	0	30

BALTIMORE SKIPJACKS

(Lost semifinals to Rochester, 4 games to 2)

	Games	G.	A.	Pts.	Pen.
Mike Richard	11	4	*13	17	6
Alfie Turcotte	12	7	9	16	14
Steve Maltais	12	6	10	16	6
John Purves	9	5	7	12	4
Kent Paynter	11	5	6	11	34
Tyler Larter	12	5	6	11	57
Chris Felix	12	0	11	11	18
Steve Seftel	12	4	3	7	10
Doug Wickenheiser	12	2	5	7	22
Nick Kypreos	7	4	1	5	17
Tim Taylor	9	2	2	4	13
Robin Bawa	11	1	2	3	49
Mark Ferner	11	1	2	3	21
Dennis Smith	12	0	3	3	65
Bill Houlder	7	0	2	2	2
Jeff Greenlaw	7	1	0	1	13
Brian Tutt	9	1	0	1	14
Alain Cote	3	0	0	0	9
Victor Gervais	3	0	0	0	0
Jim Mathieson	3	0	0	0	4
Jim Hrivnak (Goalie)	6	0	0	0	2
Bob Mason (Goalie)	6	0	0	0	0
Bobby Babcock	7	0	0	0	23

CAPE BRETON OILERS

(Lost quarterfinals to Springfield, 4 games to 2)

	Games	G.	A.	Pts.	Pen.
Tomas Kapusta	6	2	7	9	4
Dan Currie	6	4	4	8	0
Bruce Bell	6	3	4	7	2
Norm Maciver	6	0	7	7	10
Wade Campbell	6	2	3	5	6
John LeBlanc	6	4	0	4	4
David Haas	4	2	2	4	15
Peter Eriksson	5	2	2	4	2
Tommy Lehmann	6	2	2	4	2
Kim Issel	6	1	3	4	10
Chris Joseph	6	2	1	3	4
Fabian Joseph	6	0	3	3	4
Mike Ware	6	0	3	3	29
Shaun Van Allen	4	0	2	2	8
Denis LaRocque	6	0	1	1	12
Corey Foster	1	0	0	0	0
Alexandr Tyzhnych (G.)	2	0	0	0	0
Marc LaForge	3	0	0	0	27
Tim Tisdale	3	0	0	0	0
Mario Barbe	4	0	0	0	4
Mike Greenlay (Goalie)	5	0	0	0	0

HALIFAX CITADELS

(Lost quarterfinals to Sherbrooke, 4 games to 2)

	Games	G.	A.	Pts.	Pen.
Tony Hrkac	6	5	9	14	4

	Games	G.	A.	Pts.	Pen.
Stephane Morin	6	3	4	7	6
Bryan Fogarty	6	4	2	6	0
Marc Vermette	6	1	5	6	6
Ladislav Tresl	6	3	2	5	6
Miroslav Ihnacak	5	1	4	5	6
Dean Hopkins	6	1	4	5	8
Mario Doyon	6	1	3	4	2
Brent Severyn	6	1	2	3	49
Darin Kimble	6	1	1	2	61
Claude Lapointe	6	1	1	2	34
Greg Smyth	6	1	0	1	52
Jaroslav Sevcik	3	0	1	1	0
Claude Julian	4	0	1	1	2
Gerald Bzdel	6	0	1	1	24
Mario Brunetta (Goalie)	1	0	0	0	0
Dave Espe	1	0	0	0	4
Kevin Kaminski	2	0	0	0	5
Ken Quinney	2	0	0	0	2
Dan Vincelette	2	0	0	0	4
Jamie Baker	6	0	0	0	7
Scott Gordon (Goalie)	6	0	0	0	2

ROCHESTER AMERICANS

(Lost finals to Springfield, 4 games to 2)

	Games	G.	A.	Pts.	Pen.
Mike Donnelly	16	*12	7	19	9
Don Audette	15	9	8	17	29
Ray Sheppard	17	8	7	15	9
Don McSween	17	3	10	13	12
Francois Guay	16	4	8	12	12
Steve Ludzik	16	5	6	11	57
Dale DeGray	17	5	6	11	59
Jody Gage	17	4	6	10	12
Scott McCrory	13	3	6	9	2
Bob Corkum	12	2	5	7	16
Ken Sutton	11	1	6	7	15
Jim Jackson	9	1	5	6	4
Darrin Shannon	9	4	1	5	2
Steve Smith	17	0	5	5	27
Rob Ray	17	1	3	4	*115
Richie Dunn	7	0	4	4	4
Jim Hofford	17	1	1	2	56
Darcy Loewen	5	1	0	1	6
Brad Miller	8	1	0	1	52
Shawn Anderson	9	1	0	1	8
Scott Metcalfe	2	0	1	1	0
Joel Savage	5	0	1	1	4
David Littman (Goalie)	1	0	0	0	0
Darcy Wakaluk (Goalie)	17	0	0	0	14

SHERBROOKE CANADIENS

(Lost semifinals to Springfield, 4 games to 2)

	Games	G.	A.	Pts.	Pen.
Mark Pederson	11	10	8	18	19
Martin Desjardins	12	4	*13	17	28
Benoit Brunet	12	8	7	15	20
Jim Nesich	12	2	*13	15	18
Stephane Richer	12	4	9	13	16
Andrew Cassels	12	2	11	13	6
Lyle Odelein	12	6	5	11	79
Tom Chorske	12	4	4	8	8
Mario Roberge	12	5	2	7	53
Norman Desjardins	12	4	3	7	15
Dan Woodley	10	1	6	7	58

	Games	G.	A.	Pts.	Pen.
Ed Cristofoli	12	2	4	6	14
Luc Gauthier	12	0	4	4	35
Todd Richards	5	1	2	3	6
Serge Roberge	12	2	0	2	44
Roy Mitchell	12	0	2	2	31
Herbert Hohenber	4	1	0	1	6
John Ferguson Jr.	1	0	0	0	0
Martin St. Amour	1	0	0	0	0
Eric Charron	2	0	0	0	0
Guy Darveau	2	0	0	0	2
Andre Racicot (Goalie)	5	0	0	0	0
Jean Claude Bergeron (G)	9	0	0	0	15

SPRINGFIELD INDIANS

(Winners of 1990 Calder Cup Playoffs)

	Games	G.	A.	Pts.	Pen.
Greg Parks	18	9	*13	*22	22
Guy Rouleau	18	9	9	18	20
Shawn Evans	18	6	11	17	35
Bill Berg	15	5	12	17	22
Paul Gagne	13	10	6	16	2
Wayne McBean	17	4	11	15	31
Derek Laxdal	13	8	6	14	47
Marc Bergevin	17	2	11	13	16
Rob DiMaio	16	4	7	11	45
Tom Fitzgerald	14	2	9	11	13
Rod Dallman	15	5	5	10	59
Dale Henry	18	3	5	8	33
Richie Kromm	16	1	5	6	4
Jeff Rohlicek	7	3	2	5	6
Dale Kushner	7	2	3	5	61
Jeff Finley	13	1	4	5	23
Mike Walsh	8	2	2	4	10
Chris Pryor	18	1	3	4	12
Dean Chynoweth	17	0	4	4	36
Dave Pasin	3	1	2	3	0
Jeff Hackett (Goalie)	17	0	1	1	0
George Maneluk (Goalie)	4	0	0	0	2
Hank Lammens	7	0	0	0	14

UTICA DEVILS

(Lost quarterfinals to Rochester, 4 games to 1)

	Games	G.	A.	Pts.	Pen.
Kevin Todd	5	2	4	6	2
Paul Ysebaert	5	2	4	6	0
Peter Sundstrom	5	4	1	5	0
Paul Guay	5	2	2	4	13
Jeff Madill	4	1	2	3	33
Myles O'Connor	5	1	2	3	26
Jeff Shaples	5	1	2	3	15
Sergei Starikov	4	0	3	3	0
Jean Lanthier	4	1	1	2	2
Dave Marcinyshyn	5	0	2	2	21
Jim Thomson	4	0	1	1	19
Neil Brady	5	0	1	1	10
Dill Huard	5	0	1	1	33
Steve Rooney	5	0	1	1	19
Chris Kiene	1	0	0	0	2
Allan Stewart	1	0	0	0	11
Jason Simon	2	0	0	0	12
Perry Anderson	5	0	0	0	24
Roland Melanson (Goalie)	5	0	0	0	2
Bob Woods	5	0	0	0	6

COMPLETE CALDER CUP GOALTENDING

	Games	Mins.	Goals	SO.	Avg.
Darcy Wakaluk, Rochester	*17	*1001	50(2)	0	*3.00
George Maneluk, Springfield	4	174	9(1)	0	3.10
Jim Hrivnak, Baltimore	6	360	19(2)	*1	3.17
Bob Mason, Baltimore	6	373	20	0	3.22
Jean Claude Bergeron, Sherbrooke	9	497	28	0	3.38
Jeff Hackett, Springfield	*17	934	*60(1)	0	3.85
Roland Melanson, Utica	5	298	20	0	4.03
Alexandr Tyzhnych, Cape Breton	2	67	5	0	4.48
Mark Reimer, Adirondack	2	127	10	0	4.72
Andre Racicot, Sherbrooke	5	227	18(2)	0	4.76
Sam St. Laurent, Adirondack	4	238	19	0	4.79
Scott Gordon, Halifax	6	340	28(1)	0	4.94
Mike Greenlay, Cape Breton	5	306	26	0	5.10
Mario Brunetta, Halifax	1	20	2	0	6.00
David Littman, Rochester	1	33	4	0	7.27

( )—Empty Net Goals. Do not count against a Goaltender's average.

INDIVIDUAL AHL PLAYOFF LEADERS

Goals	Mike Donnelly, Rochester— 12
Assists	Martin Desjardins, Sherbrooke— 13
	Jim Nesich, Sherbrooke— 13
	Greg Parks, Springfield— 13
	Mike Richard, Baltimore— 13
Points	Greg Parks, Springfield— 22
Penalty Minutes	Rob Ray, Rochester— 115
Goaltender's Average	Darcy Wakaluk, Rochester—3.00
Shutouts	Jim Hrivnak, Baltimore— 1

AHL 1989-90 ALL-STARS

First Team	Position	Second Team
Jean Claude Bergeron, Sherbrooke	Goalie	Jim Hrivnak, Baltimore
Eric Weinrich, Utica	Defense	Darren Veitch, Newmarket
Don McSween, Rochester	Defense	Dennis Smith, Baltimore
Paul Ysebaert, Utica	Center	Mike Richard, Baltimore
Don Audette, Rochester	Right Wing	Brian Dobbin, Hershey
Mark Pederson, Sherbrooke	Left Wing	Ross Fitzpatrick, Hershey

AHL 1989-90 TROPHY WINNERS

John B. Sollenberger Trophy (Leading Scorer) ....Paul Ysebaert, Utica
Les Cunningham Plaque (Most Valuable Player)............................Paul Ysebaert, Utica
Harry (Hap) Holmes Memorial Trophy (Top Team Goaltending)
Jean Claude Bergeron, Sherbrooke
Andre Racicot, Sherbrooke
Dudley (Red) Garrett Memorial Trophy (Top Rookie).................Don Audette, Rochester
Eddie Shore Plaque (Outstanding Defenseman)...............................Eric Weinrich, Utica
Fred Hunt Memorial Award (Sportsmanship, Determination, Dedication) .. Murray Eaves, Adirondack
Louis A.R. Pieri Memorial Award (Top AHL Coach)...............Jimmy Roberts, Springfield
Baz Bastien Trophy (Coaches pick as top AHL Goalie)........Jean Claude Bergeron, Sher.
Jack Butterfield Trophy (Calder Cup Playoffs MVP)...................Jeff Hackett, Springfield
Teddy Oke Trophy (North Division winner)....................................Sherbrooke Canadiens
John Chick Trophy (South Division winner) ....Rochester Americans

AHL ALL-TIME TROPHY WINNERS

JOHN B. SOLLENBERGER TROPHY

Leading Scorer

(Originally called Wally Kilrea Trophy, later changed to Carl Liscombe Trophy and during summer of 1955 given current name.)

Season	Player	Club	Points
1936-37	Jack Markle, Syracuse		60
1937-38	Jack Markle, Syracuse		54
1938-39	Don Deacon, Pittsburgh		65
1939-40	Norm Locking, Syracuse		63
1940-41	Les Cunningham, Cleveland		64
1941-42	Pete Kelly, Springfield		78
1942-43	Wally Kilrea, Hershey		99
1943-44	Tommy Burlington, Cleveland		82
1944-45	Bob Gracie, Pittsburgh		95
	Bob Walton, Pittsburgh		95
1945-46	Les Douglas, Indianapolis		90
1946-47	Phil Hergesheimer, Philadelphia		92
1947-48	Carl Liscombe, Providence		118
1948-49	Sid Smith, Pittsburgh		112
1949-50	Les Douglas, Cleveland		100
1950-51	Ab DeMarco, Buffalo		113
1951-52	Ray Powell, Providence		97
1952-53	Eddie Olson, Cleveland		86
1953-54	George Sullivan, Hershey		119
1954-55	Eddie Olson, Cleveland		88
1955-56	Zellio Toppazzini, Providence		113
1956-57	Fred Glover, Cleveland		99
1957-58	Willie Marshall, Hershey		104
1958-59	Bill Hicke, Rochester		97
1959-60	Fred Glover, Cleveland		107
1960-61	Bill Sweeney, Springfield		108
1961-62	Bill Sweeney, Springfield		101
1962-63	Bill Sweeney, Springfield		103
1963-64	Gerry Ehman, Rochester		85
1964-65	Art Stratton, Buffalo		109
1965-66	Dick Gamble, Rochester		98
1966-67	Gordon Labossiere, Quebec		95
1967-68	Simon Nolet, Quebec		96
1968-69	Jeannot Gilbert, Hershey		100
1969-70	Jude Drouin, Montreal		106
1970-71	Fred Speck, Baltimore		92
1971-72	Don Blackburn, Providence		99
1972-73	Yvon Lambert, Nova Scotia		104
1973-74	Steve West, New Haven		110
1974-75	Doug Gibson, Rochester		116
1975-76	Jean-Guy Gratton, Hershey		93
1976-77	Andre Peloffy, Springfield		99
1977-78	Gord Brooks, Philadelphia		98
	Rick Adduono, Rochester		98
1978-79	Bernie Johnston, Maine		95
1979-80	Norm Dube, Nova Scotia		101
1980-81	Mark Lofthouse, Hershey		103
1981-82	Mike Kasczyki, New Brunswick		118
1982-83	Ross Yates, Binghamton		125
1983-84	Claude Larose, Sherbrooke		120
1984-85	Paul Gardner, Binghamton		130
1985-86	Paul Gardner, Rochester		112
1986-87	Tim Tookey, Hershey		124
1987-88	Bruce Boudreau, Springfield		116
1988-89	Stephan Lebeau, Sherbrooke		134
1989-90	Paul Ysebaert, Utica		105

Stephan Lebeau

LES CUNNINGHAM PLAQUE

Most Valuable Player

Season	Player	Club
1947-48	Carl Liscombe, Providence	
1948-49	Carl Liscombe, Providence	
1949-50	Les Douglas, Cleveland	
1950-51	Ab DeMarco, Buffalo	
1951-52	Ray Powell, Providence	
1952-53	Eddie Olson, Cleveland	
1953-54	George "Red" Sullivan, Hershey	
1954-55	Ross Lowe, Springfield	
1955-56	Johnny Bower, Providence	
1956-57	Johnny Bower, Providence	
1957-58	Johnny Bower, Cleveland	
1958-59	Bill Hicke, Rochester	
	Rudy Migay, Rochester (tie)	
1959-60	Fred Glover, Cleveland	
1960-61	Phil Maloney, Buffalo	
1961-62	Fred Glover, Cleveland	
1962-63	Denis DeJordy, Buffalo	
1963-64	Fred Glover, Cleveland	
1964-65	Art Stratton, Buffalo	
1965-66	Dick Gamble, Rochester	
1966-67	Mike Nykoluk, Hershey	
1967-68	Dave Creighton, Providence	
1968-69	Gilles Villemure, Buffalo	
1969-70	Gilles Villemure, Buffalo	
1970-71	Fred Speck, Baltimore	
1971-72	Garry Peters, Boston	
1972-73	Billy Inglis, Cincinnati	
1973-74	Art Stratton, Rochester	
1974-75	Doug Gibson, Rochester	
1975-76	Ron Andruff, Nova Scotia	
1976-77	Doug Gibson, Rochester	
1977-78	Blake Dunlop, Maine	
1978-79	Rocky Saganiuk, New Brunswick	
1979-80	Norm Dube, Nova Scotia	
1980-81	Pelle Lindbergh, Maine	
1981-82	Mike Kasczyki, New Brunswick	
1982-83	Ross Yates, Binghamton	
1983-84	Mal Davis, Rochester	
	Garry Lariviere, St. Catharines (tie)	
1984-85	Paul Gardner, Binghamton	
1985-86	Paul Gardner, Rochester	
1986-87	Tim Tookey, Hershey	
1987-88	Jody Gage, Rochester	
1988-89	Stephan Lebeau, Sherbrooke	
1989-90	Paul Ysebaert, Utica	

HARRY (HAP) HOLMES MEMORIAL TROPHY

(Awarded to outstanding goaltender. Beginning with 1983-84, awarded to top team goaltending with each goaltender having played a minimum 25 games for the team with fewest goals scored against.)

Season	Player	Club	GAA
1936-37	Bert Gardiner, Philadelphia		2.29
1937-38	Frank Brimsek, Providence		1.79
1938-39	Alfie Moore, Hershey		1.98
1939-40	Moe Roberts, Cleveland		2.32

Season	Player	Club	GAA
1940-41	Chuck Rayner, Springfield		2.42
1941-42	Bill Beveridge, Cleveland		2.35
1942-43	Gordie Bell, Buffalo		2.40
1943-44	Nick Damore, Hershey		2.46
1944-45	Yves Nadon, Buffalo		2.90
1945-46	Connie Dion, St. Louis-Buffalo		2.95
1946-47	Baz Bastien, Pittsburgh		2.60
1947-48	Baz Bastien, Pittsburgh		2.50
1948-49	Baz Bastien, Pittsburgh		2.57
1949-50	Gil Mayer, Pittsburgh		2.84
1950-51	Gil Mayer, Pittsburgh		2.45
1951-52	Johnny Bower, Cleveland		2.43
1952-53	Gil Mayer, Pittsburgh		2.35
1953-54	Jacques Plante, Buffalo		2.69
1954-55	Gil Mayer, Pittsburgh		2.80
1955-56	Gil Mayer, Pittsburgh		2.70
1956-57	Johnny Bower, Providence		2.42
1957-58	Johnny Bower, Cleveland		2.19
1958-59	Bob Perreault, Hershey		2.68
1959-60	Ed Chadwick, Rochester		2.75
1960-61	Marcel Paille, Springfield		2.81
1961-62	Marcel Paille, Springfield		2.56
1962-63	Denis DeJordy, Buffalo		2.79
1963-64	Roger Crozier, Pittsburgh		2.34
1964-65	Gerry Cheevers, Rochester		2.68
1965-66	Les Binkley, Cleveland		2.93
1966-67	Andre Gill, Hershey		2.90
1967-68	Bob Perreault, Rochester		2.88
1968-69	Gilles Villemure, Buffalo		2.41
1969-70	Gilles Villemure, Buffalo		2.52
1970-71	Gary Kurt, Cleveland		2.67
1971-72	Dan Bouchard, Boston		2.51
	Ross Brooks, Boston		2.38
1972-73	Michel Larocque, Nova Scotia		2.50
1973-74	Jim Shaw, Nova Scotia		2.68
	Dave Elenbaas, Nova Scotia		2.96
1974-75	Ed Walsh, Nova Scotia		2.77
	Dave Elenbaas, Nova Scotia		3.15
1975-76	Dave Elenbaas, Nova Scotia		2.42
	Ed Walsh, Nova Scotia		3.06
1976-77	Ed Walsh, Nova Scotia		2.86
	Dave Elenbaas, Nova Scotia		2.61
1977-78	Bob Holland, Nova Scotia		3.17
	Maurice Barrette, Nova Scotia		2.74
1978-79	Pete Peeters, Maine		2.90
	Robbie Moore, Maine		3.38
1979-80	Rick St. Croix, Maine		2.90
	Robbie Moore, Maine		3.48
1980-81	Pelle Lindbergh, Maine		3.26
	Robbie Moore, Maine		3.86
1981-82	Bob Janecyk, New Brunswick		2.85
	Warren Skorodenski, New Brunswick		2.55
1982-83	Brian Ford, Fredericton		3.49
	Clint Malarchuk, Fredericton		3.11
1983-84	Brian Ford, Fredericton		2.94
1984-85	Jon Casey, Baltimore		2.63
1985-86	Sam St. Laurent, Maine		3.38
	Karl Friesen, Maine		3.48
1986-87	Vincent Riendeau, Sherbrooke		2.89
1987-88	Vincent Riendeau, Sherbrooke		2.67
	Jocelyn Perreault, Sherbrooke		3.71
1988 89	Randy Exolby, Shorbrooke		2.98
	Francois Gravel, Sherbrooke		3.51
1989-90	Jean Claude Bergeron, Sherbrooke		2.74
	Andre Racicot, Sherbrooke		2.99

DUDLEY (RED) GARRETT MEMORIAL TROPHY

Top Rookie

Season	Player	Club
1947-48	Bob Solinger, Cleveland	
1948-49	Terry Sawchuk, Indianapolis	
1949-50	Paul Meger, Buffalo	
1950-51	Wally Hergesheimer, Cleveland	
1951-52	Earl "Dutch" Reibel, Indianapolis	
1952-53	Guyle Fielder, St. Louis	
1953-54	Don Marshall, Buffalo	
1954-55	Jimmy Anderson, Springfield	
1955-56	Bruce Cline, Providence	
1956-57	Boris "Bo" Elik, Cleveland	
1957-58	Bill Sweeney, Providence	
1958-59	Bill Hicke, Rochester	
1959-60	Stan Baluik, Providence	
1960-61	Ronald "Chico" Maki, Buffalo	
1961-62	Les Binkley, Cleveland	
1962-63	Doug Robinson, Buffalo	
1963-64	Roger Crozier, Pittsburgh	
1964-65	Ray Cullen, Buffalo	
1965-66	Mike Walton, Rochester	
1966-67	Bob Rivard, Quebec	

Ron Hextall

Season	Player	Club
1967-68	Gerry Desjardins, Cleveland	
1968-69	Ron Ward, Rochester	
1969-70	Jude Drouin, Montreal	
1970-71	Fred Speck, Baltimore	
1971-72	Terry Caffery, Cleveland	
1972-73	Ron Anderson, Boston	
1973-74	Rick Middleton, Providence	
1974-75	Jerry Holland, Providence	
1975-76	Greg Holst, Providence	
	Pierre Mondou, Nova Scotia (tie)	
1976-77	Rod Schutt, Nova Scotia	
1977-78	Norm Dupont, Nova Scotia	
1978-79	Mike Meeker, Binghamton	
1979-80	Darryl Sutter, New Brunswick	
1980-81	Pelle Lindbergh, Maine	
1981-82	Bob Sullivan, Binghamton	
1982-83	Mitch Lamoureux, Baltimore	
1983-84	Claude Verret, Rochester	
1984-85	Steve Thomas, St. Catharines	
1985-86	Ron Hextall, Hershey	
1986-87	Brett Hull, Moncton	
1987-88	Mike Richard, Binghamton	
1988-89	Stephan Lebeau, Sherbrooke	
1989-90	Donald Audette, Rochester	

EDDIE SHORE PLAQUE

Outstanding Defenseman

Season	Player	Club
1958-59	Steve Kraftcheck, Rochester	
1959-60	Larry Hillman, Providence	
1960-61	Bob McCord, Springfield	
1961-62	Kent Douglas, Springfield	
1962-63	Marc Reaume, Hershey	
1963-64	Ted Harris, Cleveland	
1964-65	Al Arbour, Rochester	
1965-66	Jim Morrison, Quebec	
1966-67	Bob McCord, Pittsburgh	
1967-68	Bill Needham, Cleveland	
1968-69	Bob Blackburn, Buffalo	
1969-70	Noel Price, Springfield	
1970-71	Marshall Johnston, Cleveland	
1971-72	Noel Price, Nova Scotia	
1972-73	Ray McKay, Cincinnati	
1973-74	Gordon Smith, Springfield	
1974-75	Joe Zanussi, Providence	
1975-76	Noel Price, Nova Scotia	
1976-77	Brian Engblom, Nova Scotia	
1977-78	Terry Murray, Maine	
1978-79	Terry Murray, Maine	
1979-80	Rick Vasko, Adirondack	
1980-81	Craig Levie, Nova Scotia	

Season	Player	Club
1981-82	Dave Farrish, New Brunswick	
1982-83	Greg Tebbutt, Baltimore	
1983-84	Garry Lariviere, St. Catharines	
1984-85	Richie Dunn, Binghamton	
1985-86	Jim Wiemer, New Haven	
1986-87	Brad Shaw, Binghamton	
1987-88	Dave Fenyves, Hershey	
1988-89	Dave Fenyves, Hershey	
1989-90	Eric Weinrich, Utica	

FRED HUNT MEMORIAL AWARD

Sportsmanship, Determination and Dedication

Season	Player	Club
1977-78	Blake Dunlop, Maine	
1978-79	Bernie Johnston, Maine	
1979-80	Norm Dube, Nova Scotia	
1980-81	Tony Cassolato, Hershey	
1981-82	Mike Kasczyki, New Brunswick	
1982-83	Ross Yates, Binghamton	
1983-84	Claude Larose, Sherbrooke	
1984-85	Paul Gardner, Binghamton	
1985-86	Steve Tsujiura, Maine	
1986-87	Glenn Merkosky, Adirondack	
1987-88	Bruce Boudreau, Springfield	
1988-89	Murray Eaves, Adirondack	
1989-90	Murray Eaves, Adirondack	

LOUIS A. R. PIERI MEMORIAL AWARD

Top AHL Coach

Season	Coach	Club
1967-68	Vic Stasiuk, Quebec	
1968-69	Frank Mathers, Hershey	
1969-70	Fred Shero, Buffalo	
1970-71	Terry Reardon, Baltimore	
1971-72	Al MacNeil, Nova Scotia	
1972-73	Floyd Smith, Cincinnati	
1973-74	Don Cherry, Rochester	
1974-75	John Muckler, Providence	
1975-76	Chuck Hamilton, Hershey	
1976-77	Al MacNeil, Nova Scotia	
1977-78	Bob McCammon, Maine	
1978-79	Parker MacDonald, New Haven	
1979-80	Doug Gibson, Hershey	
1980-81	Bob McCammon, Maine	
1981-82	Orval Tessier, New Brunswick	
1982-83	Jacques Demers, Fredericton	
1983-84	Gene Ubriaco, Baltimore	
1984-85	Bill Dineen, Adirondack	

Season	Coach	Club
1985-86—	Bill Dineen, Adirondack	
1986-87—	Larry Pleau, Binghamton	
1987-88—	John Paddock, Hershey	
	Mike Milbury, Maine (tie)	
1988-89—	Tom McVie, Utica	
1989-90—	Jimmy Roberts, Springfield	

BAZ BASTIEN TROPHY

Coaches pick as top AHL Goalie

Season	Player	Club
1983-84—	Brian Ford, Fredericton	
1984-85—	Jon Casey, Baltimore	
1985-86—	Sam St. Laurent, Maine	
1986-87—	Mark Laforest, Adirondack	
1987-88—	Wendell Young, Hershey	
1988-89—	Randy Exelby, Sherbrooke	
1989-90—	Jean Claude Bergeron, Sherbrooke	

JACK BUTTERFIELD TROPHY

Calder Cup Playoffs MVP

Season	Player	Club
1983-84—	Bud Stefanski, Maine	
1984-85—	Brian Skrudland, Sherbrooke	
1985-86—	Tim Tookey, Hershey	
1986-87—	Dave Fenyves, Rochester	
1987-88—	Wendell Young, Hershey	
1988-89—	Sam St. Laurent, Adirondack	
1989-90—	Jeff Hackett, Springfield	

Jeff Hackett

AHL ALL-TIME CHAMPIONSHIP TEAMS

(Since 1989-90 season, Teddy Oke Trophy awarded to North Division winner, while John Chick Trophy awarded to South Division winner.)

Year	REGULAR SEASON Div. Championship Team (Coach)	PLAYOFFS (Calder Cup) Championship Team (Coach)
1936-37	E—Philadelphia (Herb Gardiner) W—Syracuse (Eddie Powers)	Syracuse Stars (E. Powers)
1937-38	E—Providence (Bun Cook) W—Cleveland (Bill Cook)	Providence Reds (Bun Cook)
1938-39	E—Philadelphia (Herb Gardiner) W—Hershey (Herb Mitchell)	Cleveland Barons (Bill Cook)
1939-40	E—Providence (Bun Cook) W—Indianapolis (Herb Lewis)	Providence Reds (Bun Cook)
1940-41	E—Providence (Bun Cook) W—Cleveland (Bill Cook)	Cleveland Barons (Bill Cook)
1941-42	E—Springfield (Johnny Mitchell) W—Indianapolis (Herb Lewis)	Indianapolis Caps (Herb Lewis)
1942-43	—Hershey (Cooney Weiland)	Buffalo Bisons (Art Chapman)
1943-44	E—Hershey (Cooney Weiland) W—Cleveland (Bun Cook)	Buffalo Bisons (Art Chapman)
1944-45	E—Buffalo (Art Chapman) W—Cleveland (Bun Cook)	Cleveland Barons (Bun Cook)
1945-46	E—Buffalo (Frank Beisler) W—Indianapolis (Earl Seibert)	Buffalo Bisons (Frank Beisler)
1946-47	E—Hershey (Don Penniston) W—Cleveland (Bun Cook)	Hershey Bears (Don Penniston)
1947-48	E—Providence (Terry Reardon) W—Cleveland (Bun Cook)	Cleveland Barons (Bun Cook)
1948-49	E—Providence (Terry Reardon) W—St. Louis (Ebbie Goodfellow)	Providence Reds (Terry Reardon)
1949-50	E—Buffalo (Roy Goldsworthy) W—Cleveland (Bun Cook)	Indianapolis Caps (Ott Heller)
1950-51	E—Buffalo (Roy Goldsworthy) W—Cleveland (Bun Cook)	Cleveland Barons (Bun Cook)
1951-52	E—Hershey (John Crawford) W—Pittsburgh (King Clancy)	Pittsburgh Hornets (King Clancy)
1952-53	—Cleveland (Bun Cook)	Cleveland Barons (Bun Cook)
1953-54	—Buffalo (Frank Eddolls)	Cleveland Barons (Bun Cook)
1954-55	—Pittsburgh (Howie Meeker)	Pittsburgh Hornets (Howie Meeker)
1955-56	—Providence (John Crawford)	Providence Reds (John Crawford)
1956-57	—Providence (John Crawford)	Cleveland Barons (Jack Gordon)
1957-58	—Hershey (Frank Mathers)	Hershey Bears (Frank Mathers)
1958-59	—Buffalo (Bobby Kirk)	Hershey Bears (Frank Mathers)
1959-60	—Springfield (Pat Egan)	Springfield Indians (Pat Egan)
1960-61	—Springfield (Pat Egan)	Springfield Indians (Pat Egan)
1961-62	E—Springfield (Pat Egan) W—Cleveland (Jack Gordon)	Springfield Indians (Pat Egan)
1962-63	E—Providence (Fern Flaman) W—Buffalo (Billy Reay)	Buffalo Bisons (Billy Reay)
1963-64	E—Quebec (Floyd Curry) W—Pittsburgh (Vic Stasiuk)	Cleveland Barons (Fred Glover)
1964-65	E—Quebec (Bernie Geoffrion) W—Rochester (Joe Crozier)	Rochester Americans (Joe Crozier)
1965-66	E—Quebec (Bernie Geoffrion) W—Rochester (Joe Crozier)	Rochester Americans (Joe Crozier)
1966-67	E—Hershey (Frank Mathers) W—Pittsburgh (Baz Bastien)	Pittsburgh Hornets (Baz Bastien)
1967-68	E—Hershey (Frank Mathers) W—Rochester (Joe Crozier)	Rochester Americans (Joe Crozier)
1968-69	E—Hershey (Frank Mathers) W—Buffalo (Fred Shero)	Hershey Bears (Frank Mathers)
1969-70	E—Montreal (Al MacNeil) W—Buffalo (Fred Shero)	Buffalo Bisons (Fred Shero)
1970-71	E—Providence (Larry Wilson) W—Baltimore (Terry Reardon)	Springfield Kings (John Wilson)
1971-72	E—Boston (Armond Guidolin) W—Baltimore (Terry Reardon)	Nova Scotia Voy'g'rs (Al MacNeil)
1972-73	E—Nova Scotia (Al MacNeil) W—Cincinnati (Floyd Smith)	Cincinnati Swords (Floyd Smith)
1973-74	N—Rochester (Don Cherry) S—Baltimore (Terry Reardon)	Hershey Bears (Chuck Hamilton)
1974-75	N—Providence (John Muckler) S—Virginia (Doug Barkley)	Springfield Indians (Ron Stewart)
1975-76	N—Nova Scotia (Al MacNeil) S—Hershey (Chuck Hamilton)	Nova Scotia Voy'g'rs (Al MacNeil)
1976-77	—Nova Scotia (Al MacNeil)	Nova Scotia Voy'g'rs (Al MacNeil)
1977-78	N—Maine (Bob McCammon) S—Rochester (Duane Rupp)	Maine Mariners (Bob McCammon)
1978-79	N—Maine (Bob McCammon) S—New Haven (Parker MacDonald)	Maine Mariners (Bob McCammon)
1979-80	N—New Brunswick (Crozier-Angotti) S—New Haven (Parker MacDonald)	Hershey Bears (Doug Gibson)
1980-81	N—Maine (Bob McCammon) S—Hershey (Bryan Murray)	Adirondack (Webster-LeBlanc)
1981-82	N—New Brunswick (Orval Tessier) S—Binghamton (Larry Kish)	New Brunswick (Orval Tessier)
1982-83	N—Fredericton (Jacques Demers) S—Rochester (Mike Keenan)	Rochester (Mike Keenan)
1983-84	N—Fredericton (Earl Jessiman) S—Baltimore (Gene Ubriaco)	Maine (John Paddock)
1984-85	N—Maine (McVie-Paddock) S—Binghamton (Larry Pleau)	Sherbrooke (Pierre Creamer)
1985-86	N—Adirondack (Bill Dineen) S—Hershey (John Paddock)	Adirondack (Bill Dineen)
1986-87	N—Sherbrooke (Pierre Creamer) S—Rochester (John Van Boxmeer)*	Rochester (John Van Boxmeer)
1987-88	N—Maine (Mike Milbury) S—Hershey (John Paddock)	Hershey (John Paddock)
1988-89	N—Sherbrooke (Jean Hamel) S—Adirondack (Bill Dineen)	Adirondack (Bill Dineen)
1989-90	N—Sherbrooke (Jean Hamel) S—Rochester (John Van Boxmeer)	Springfield (Jimmy Roberts)

*Rochester awarded division championship based on season-series record.

INTERNATIONAL HOCKEY LEAGUE

(Organized, December 21, 1945)

Commissioner
N. Thomas Berry Jr.
Chairman of the Board of Governors
I. John Snider
Vice-Chairman of the Board of Governors
N. R. (Bud) Poile
Legal Counsel
Robert P. Ufer
Director of Information
Michael A. Meyers
Address
3850 Priority Way
South Drive
Suite 104
Indianapolis, Ind. 46240
Phone—(317) 573-3888
FAX—(317) 573-3880
Board of Governors
Albany—David Welker
Fort Wayne—Steven Franke
Indianapolis—Ray Compton
Kalamazoo—Ted Parfet
Kansas City—Russ Parker
Milwaukee—Joseph E. Tierney Jr.
Muskegon—Larry Gordon
Peoria—Bruce Saurs
Phoenix—Lyle Abraham
Salt Lake—Tim Howells
San Diego—Vince Ciruzzi

ALBANY CHOPPERS

Governor—David Welker
General Manager—James Salfi
Coach—Dave Allison
Public Relations Director—Sam Karp
Marketing Director—John Wall
Home Ice—Knickerbocker Arena (15,008)
Address—51 South Pearl Street
Albany, N.Y. 12207
Affiliation—To be announced
Phone—(518) 487-2244
FAX—(518) 487-2248

FORT WAYNE KOMETS

Governor—Steven Franke
General Manager—David Franke
Coach—Al Sims
Public Relations Director—Tammy Franke
Marketing Director—Michael Franke
Home Ice—Allen County Memorial Coliseum (8,022)
Address—4000 Parnell
Fort Wayne, Ind. 46805
Affiliation—Montreal Canadiens and Winnipeg Jets
Phone—(219) 483-0011
FAX—(219) 483-3899

INDIANAPOLIS ICE

Governor and General Manager—Ray Compton

Coach—Dave McDowall
Director of Marketing—Dave Paitson
Director of Public Relations—Brad Beery
Home Ice—Indiana State Fairgrounds Col. (8,233)
Address—1202 East 38th Street
Indianapolis, Ind. 46205
Affiliation—Chicago Blackhawks
Phone—(317) 924-1234
FAX—(317) 924-1248

KALAMAZOO WINGS

Governor—Ted Parfet
General Manager—Bill Inglis
Coach—John Marks
Director of P.R./Marketing—Steve Doherty
Director of Broadcasting—Mike Miller
Home Ice—Wings Stadium (5,113)
Address—3620 Van Rick Drive,
Kalamazoo, Mich. 49002
Affiliation—Minnesota North Stars
Phone—(616) 349-9772
FAX—(616) 345-6584

KANSAS CITY BLADES

Governor—Russ Parker
General Manager—Tom Rieger
Coach—Doug Soetaert
Director of P.R./Marketing—Jim Loria
Home Ice—Kemper Arena (16,000)
Address—1800 Genessee
Kansas City, Mo. 64102
Affiliation—Edmonton Oilers and Hartford Whalers
Phone—(816) 842-5233
FAX—(816) 842-5610

MILWAUKEE ADMIRALS

Governor—Joseph E. Tierney Jr.
General Manager—Phil Wittliff
Coach—Mike Murphy
Public Relations Director—Stacey Johnson
Director of Marketing—Mike Wojciechowski
Home Ice—Bradley Center (17,809)
Address—1001 North Fourth Street
Milwaukee, Wis. 53203
Affiliation—Vancouver Canucks
Phone—(414) 227-0550
FAX—(414) 227-0568

MUSKEGON LUMBERJACKS

Governor and General Manager—Larry Gordon
Coach—Blair MacDonald
Director of Public Relations—Bob Heethuis
Director of Marketing—Mike Forbes
Home Ice—L.C. Walker Sports Arena (5,043)
Address—470 W. Western Avenue
Muskegon, Mich. 49440
Affiliation—Pittsburgh Penguins

Phone—(616) 726-5058
FAX—(616) 728-0428

PEORIA RIVERMEN

Governor—Bruce Saurs
General Manager—Denis Cyr
Coach—Bob Plager
Director of Public Relations—Brad Johnson
Director of Marketing—Mike Bonczyk
Home Ice—Peoria Civic Center (9,074)
Address—201 S. W. Jefferson
Peoria, Ill. 61602
Affiliation—St. Louis Blues
Phone—(309) 673-8900
FAX—(309) 676-2488

PHOENIX ROADRUNNERS

Governor—Lyle Abraham
General Manager—Adam Keller
Coach—Ralph Backstrom
Director of Public Relations—Dave Tunell
Director of Marketing—Ian MacPhee
Home Ice—Veterans Memorial Coliseum (13,737)
Address—1826 West McDowell Road
Phoenix, Ariz. 85005
Affiliation—Los Angeles Kings
Phone—(602) 340-0001
FAX—(602) 340-0041

SALT LAKE GOLDEN EAGLES

Governor—Tim Howells
General Manager—Mike Runge
Coach—Bob Francis
Director of Marketing—Dale Borg
Director of Public Relations—Mark Kelly
Home Ice—Salt Palace (10,466)
Address—5 Triad Center, Suite 525
Salt Lake City, Utah 84180
Affiliation—Calgary Flames
Phone—(801) 521-6120
FAX—(801) 521-9961

SAN DIEGO GULLS

Governor—Vince Ciruzzi
General Manager—Don Waddell
Coach—Mike O'Connell
Public Relations Director—Chris Ello
Marketing Director—Paul Mendez
Home Ice—San Diego Sports Arena (13,200)
Address—3780 Hancock Street
Suite "G"
San Diego, Calif. 92110
Affiliation—To be announced
Phone—(619) 688-1800
FAX—(619) 688-1808

1989-90 FINAL IHL STANDINGS

EAST DIVISION

	G.	W.	L.	OTL.	Pts.	GF.	GA.
Muskegon Lumberjacks	82	55	21	6	116	389	304
Kalamazoo Wings	82	53	23	6	112	389	311
Flint Spirits	82	40	36	6	86	326	358
Fort Wayne Komets	82	37	34	11	85	316	345

WEST DIVISION

	G.	W.	L.	OTL.	Pts.	GF.	GA.
Indianapolis Ice	82	53	21	8	114	315	237
Salt Lake Golden Eagles	82	37	36	9	83	326	311
Milwaukee Admirals	82	36	39	7	79	316	370
Peoria Rivermen	82	31	38	13	75	317	378
Phoenix Roadrunners	82	27	44	11	65	314	394

NOTE: OTL column includes overtime losses and shootout losses (teams receive a point for either).

TOP 20 SCORERS FOR THE LEO P. LAMOUREUX MEMORIAL TROPHY

	Games	G.	A.	Pts.	Pen.
1. Michel Mongeau, Peoria	73	39	*78	*117	53
2. Bruce Boudreau, Phoenix	82	41	68	109	89
3. Dave Michayluk, Muskegon	79	*51	51	102	80
4. Bob Lakso, Fort Wayne	82	42	58	100	6
Gary Emmons, Kalamazoo	81	41	59	100	38
6. Tim Sweeney, Salt Lake	81	46	51	97	32
7. Scott Gruhl, Muskegon	80	41	51	92	206
8. Jim Vesey, Peoria	60	47	44	91	75
Marc Bureau, Salt Lake	67	43	48	91	173
10. Ken Hodge, Kalamazoo	68	33	53	86	19

	Games	G.	A.	Pts.	Pen.
11. Perry Ganchar, Muskegon	79	40	45	85	111
12. Kevin Evans, Kalamazoo	76	30	54	84	346
Mitch Messier, Kalamazoo	65	26	58	84	56
14. Simon Wheeldon, Flint	76	34	49	83	61
15. Jim McGeough, Phoenix	77	35	46	81	90
16. Peter Lappin, Kalamazoo	74	45	35	80	42
17. Rob Zamuner, Flint	77	44	35	79	32
Larry Floyd, Phoenix	76	39	40	79	50
19. Dan Frawley, Muskegon	82	31	47	78	165
Jock Callander, Muskegon	46	29	49	78	118

TEAM-BY-TEAM BREAKDOWN OF IHL SCORING

FLINT SPIRITS

	Games	G.	A.	Pts.	Pen.
Simon Wheeldon	76	34	49	83	61
Rob Zamuner	77	44	35	79	32
Lee Giffin	73	30	44	74	68
Darren Lowe	67	31	35	66	44
Dave Archibald	41	14	38	52	16
Joe Paterson	69	21	26	47	198
Mike Golden	68	13	33	46	30
Kevin Miller	48	19	23	42	41
Mike Hurlbut	74	3	34	37	38
Dennis Vial	79	6	29	35	351
Soren True	54	15	17	32	49
Daniel LaCroix	61	12	16	28	128
Jeff Bloemberg	44	7	21	28	24
Jim Latos	71	12	15	27	244
Paul Broten	28	17	9	26	55
Peter Laviolette	62	6	18	24	82
Rudy Poeschek	38	8	13	21	109
Barry Chyzowski	30	3	8	11	6
Corey Millen	11	4	5	9	2
Todd Charlesworth	26	3	6	9	12
Peter Fiorentino	64	2	7	9	302
Normand Rochefort	7	3	2	5	4
Rick Knickle (Goalie)	55	0	5	5	6
Steve Richmond	10	1	3	4	19
Denis Larocque	31	1	2	3	66
Mike Richter (Goalie)	13	0	1	1	0
Craig Barnett (Goalie)	3	0	0	0	0
Stephane Brochu	5	0	0	0	2
Scott Brower, Phoe. (G.)	1	0	0	0	0
Flint (Goalie)	20	0	0	0	2
Totals	21	0	0	0	2
Jerry Tarrant, Salt Lake	8	0	0	0	12
Flint	23	0	0	0	27
Totals	31	0	0	0	39
Shootout Goals	...	6	...	6	...

FORT WAYNE KOMETS

	Games	G.	A.	Pts.	Pen.
Bob Kakso	82	42	58	100	6
Ron Handy	82	36	39	75	52
Colin Chin	74	21	38	59	79
Joe Stefan	67	22	33	55	72
Byron Lomow	79	29	24	53	230
Lonnie Loach, Indianapolis	3	0	1	1	0
Fort Wayne	54	15	33	48	40
Totals	57	15	34	49	40
Cam Plante	61	7	42	49	45
Keith Miller	51	26	19	45	10
Brad Aitken, Muskegon	46	10	23	33	172
Phoenix	8	2	1	3	18
Fort Wayne	13	5	2	7	57
Totals	67	17	26	43	247
Stephane Brochu	63	9	19	28	98
Kevin Kerr, Phoenix	6	0	0	0	25
Fort Wayne	43	11	16	27	219
Totals	49	11	16	27	244
Ron Shudra	67	11	16	27	48
Bob Fowler	59	8	14	22	75
Mike deCarle, Phoenix	24	5	4	9	44
Fort Wayne	12	4	5	9	7
Totals	36	9	9	18	51
Mark Vichorek, Phoenix	29	2	8	10	57
Fort Wayne	31	2	4	6	30
Totals	60	4	12	16	87
Brian Hannon	43	5	10	15	8
Carey Lucyk	79	2	12	14	119
Craig Endean	20	2	11	13	8

	Games	G.	A.	Pts.	Pen.
Bret Walter, Flint	6	1	1	2	4
Fort Wayne	24	5	5	10	47
Totals	30	6	6	12	51
Scott Shaunessy	45	3	9	12	267
Jean Marc Lanthier	7	4	7	11	4
Jason Hannigan	12	5	2	7	20
Serge Roy	19	1	4	5	13
Steve Bisson	23	1	4	5	14
Phil Berger	3	2	2	4	2
Rick Tabaracci (Goalie)	22	0	2	2	66
Bruce Rendall	2	1	0	1	0
Steve Hamilton	10	0	1	1	76
Ray LeBlanc, Ind. (G.)	23	0	0	0	6
Fort Wayne (Goalie)	15	0	1	1	4
Totals	38	0	1	1	10
Frank Furlin (Goalie)	1	0	0	0	0
Chris Wright (Goalie)	1	0	0	0	0
Tony Camazzola	2	0	0	0	15
Mike Chigasola	2	0	0	0	4
Brad Drury	2	0	0	0	9
Derek Ray	2	0	0	0	2
Doug Lawrence	3	0	0	0	0
Mike Bishop	12	0	0	0	0
Frederick Chabot (Goalie)	23	0	0	0	26
S. Beauregard (Goalie)	33	0	0	0	16
Shootout Goals	...	7	...	7	...

INDIANAPOLIS ICE

	Games	G.	A.	Pts.	Pen.
Brian Noonan	56	40	36	76	85
Mike Rucinski	80	28	41	69	27
Jim Johannson	82	22	41	63	74
Sean Williams	78	27	31	58	25
Bruce Cassidy	75	11	46	57	56
Jari Torkki	66	25	29	54	50
Bob Bassen	73	22	32	54	179
Mike McNeill	74	17	24	41	10
Warren Rychel	77	23	16	39	374
Mario Doyon	66	9	25	34	50
Jim Playfair	67	7	24	31	137
Dan Vincelette	49	16	13	29	262
Everett Sanipass	33	15	13	28	121
Ryan McGill	77	11	17	28	215
Mike Eagles	24	11	13	24	47
Craig Channell, Fort W.	37	6	11	17	86
Indianapolis	16	0	1	1	17
Totals	53	6	12	18	103
Cam Russell	46	3	15	18	114
Mike Peluso	75	7	10	17	279
Mike Stapleton	16	5	10	15	6
Guy Phillips	33	4	4	8	24
David Bassegio	10	1	7	8	2
Dale Marquette	32	3	3	6	13
Marty Nanne	50	3	3	6	36
Gary Moscaluk	31	0	4	4	30
Jimmy Waite (Goalie)	54	0	2	2	21
Jeff Cooper (Goalie)	1	0	0	0	0
Alex Roberts	4	0	0	0	2
Darren Pang (Goalie)	7	0	0	0	2
Mark Kurzawski	10	0	0	0	8
Shootout Goals	...	5	...	5	...

KALAMAZOO WINGS

	Games	G.	A.	Pts.	Pen.
Gary Emmons	81	41	59	100	38
Ken Hodge	68	33	53	86	19
Kevin Evans	76	30	54	84	346
Mitch Messier	65	26	58	84	56

	Games	G.	A.	Pts.	Pen.
Peter Lappin	74	45	35	80	42
Mario Thyer	68	19	42	61	12
Ed Courtenay	56	25	28	53	16
Dean Kolstad	77	10	40	50	172
Darcy Norton	66	22	25	47	55
Pat MacLeod	82	9	38	47	27
Jayson More, Flint	9	1	5	6	41
Kalamazoo	64	9	25	34	216
Totals	73	10	30	40	257
Jean-Francois Quintin	68	20	18	38	38
Mike McHugh	73	14	17	31	96
Paul Jerrard	60	9	18	27	134
Scott Robinson	48	13	12	25	97
Dusan Pasek	20	10	14	24	6
Larry DePalma	36	7	14	21	218
Link Gaetz	61	5	16	21	318
Clark Donatelli	27	8	9	17	47
Rob Zettler	41	6	10	16	64
Neil Wilkinson	20	6	7	13	62
Bret Barnett	35	5	5	10	38
Don Barber	10	4	4	8	38
Jarmo Myllys (Goalie)	49	0	8	8	39
Kevin Schamehorn	9	1	2	3	0
Ken Leiter	4	1	1	2	0
Larry Dyck (Goalie)	36	0	2	2	4
Steve Gotaas	1	1	0	1	0
Jordon Fois	2	0	1	1	0
Wade Flaherty (Goalie)	1	0	0	0	0
Kari Takko (Goalie)	1	0	0	0	0
Scott McCrady	3	0	0	0	11
Shootout Goals	...	9	...	9	...

MILWAUKEE ADMIRALS

	Games	G.	A.	Pts.	Pen.
David Bruce	68	40	35	75	148
Rob Murphy	64	24	47	71	87
Tim Lenardon	66	32	36	68	134
Jose Charbonneau	65	23	38	61	137
Peter Bakovic	56	19	30	49	230
Jeff Rohlicek	53	22	26	48	37
Jay Mazur	70	20	27	47	63
Ian Kidd	65	11	36	47	86
Carl Valimont	78	13	28	41	48
Todd Hawkins	61	23	17	40	273
Peter DeBoer	67	21	19	40	16
Dave Capuano, Muskegon	27	15	15	30	22
Milwaukee	2	0	4	4	0
Totals	29	15	19	34	22
Curtis Hunt	69	8	25	33	237
Ernie Vargas	63	15	15	30	79
Adrien Plavsic, Peoria	51	7	14	21	87
Milwaukee	3	1	2	3	14
Totals	54	8	16	24	101
Shaun Clouston	54	6	16	22	61
Keith Street	55	5	13	18	25
Ron Stern	26	8	9	17	165
Steve Veilleux	76	4	12	16	195
Terry Menard	22	6	9	15	14
Jim Agnew	51	4	10	14	238
Jack Capuano	17	3	10	13	60
Kevan Guy	29	2	11	13	33
Shannon Travis	39	2	9	11	13
Jim Revenberg	56	1	6	7	314
Craig Coxe	5	0	5	5	4
Dave Capuano	2	0	4	4	0
Troy Gamble (Goalie)	56	0	4	4	38
Grant Paranica	5	0	2	2	2
Don Gibson	1	0	0	0	4
Steve McKichan (Goalie)	1	0	0	0	0
Rob Sangster	1	0	0	0	4
Gus Morschauser (Goalie)	3	0	0	0	0

	Games	G.	A.	Pts.	Pen.
Dean Cook (Goalie)	15	0	0	0	0
Steve Herniman	15	0	0	0	102
Frank Caprice (Goalie)	20	0	0	0	0
Shootout Goals	...	3	...	3	...

MUSKEGON LUMBERJACKS

	Games	G.	A.	Pts.	Pen.
Dave Michayluk	79	*51	51	102	80
Scott Gruhl	80	41	51	92	206
Perry Ganchar	79	40	45	85	111
Dan Frawley	82	31	47	78	165
Jock Callander	46	29	49	78	118
Jeff Daniels	80	30	47	77	39
Jamie Leach	72	22	36	58	39
Richard Zemlak	61	17	39	56	263
Jim Paek	81	9	41	50	115
Duane Joyce, Kalamazoo	2	0	0	0	2
Fort Wayne	61	10	26	36	51
Muskegon	13	3	10	13	8
Totals	76	13	36	49	61
Mike Mersch	82	10	38	48	161
Glenn Mulvenna, Fort W.	6	2	5	7	2
Muskegon	52	14	21	35	17
Totals	58	16	26	42	19
Mitch Wilson	63	13	24	37	283
Paul Stanton	77	5	27	32	61
Mark Kachowski	62	23	8	31	129
Randy Taylor	63	2	22	24	29
Dave Goertz	51	3	18	21	64
Brian Wilks	15	6	11	17	10
Mark Recchi	4	7	4	11	2
Darren Stolk	65	3	3	6	59
Chris Dahlquist	6	1	1	2	8
Jeff Waver	4	0	2	2	2
Bruce Racine (Goalie)	49	0	2	2	0
Sandy Smith	3	1	0	1	0
Doug Hobson	9	0	1	1	4
Frank Pietrangelo (Goalie)	12	0	0	0	0
Chris Clifford (Goalie)	23	0	0	0	12
Shootout Goals	...	3	...	3	...

PEORIA RIVERMEN

	Games	G.	A.	Pts.	Pen.
Michel Mongeau	73	39	*78	*117	53
Jim Vesey	60	47	44	91	75
Dave Thomlinson	59	27	40	67	87
Kevin Miehm	76	23	38	61	20
Keith Osborne	56	23	24	47	58
Doug Evans	42	19	28	47	128
Dominic Lavoie	58	19	23	42	32
Terry MacLean	67	9	32	41	15
Scott Paluch	79	10	28	38	59
Richard Pion	69	10	21	31	58
Darin Smith	76	16	13	29	147
Toby Ducolon	62	11	14	25	22

	Games	G.	A.	Pts.	Pen.
Randy Skarda	38	7	17	24	40
Dave O'Brien	57	9	14	23	21
Mike Wolak	50	7	16	23	31
Marc Saumier	17	5	10	15	143
Brad McCaughey	23	8	6	14	2
Tom Karalis, Phoenix	21	1	3	4	35
Peoria	48	2	8	10	182
Totals	69	3	11	14	217
Rob Robinson	60	2	11	13	72
John Ferguson	18	1	8	9	14
Tom Tilley	22	1	8	9	13
Tony Twist	36	1	5	6	200
Yves Heroux	14	3	2	5	4
Glen Featherstone	15	1	4	5	43
Rik Wilson	15	1	4	5	34
Kelly Chase	10	1	2	3	76
Robert Dirk	24	1	2	3	79
Nelson Emerson	3	1	1	2	0
Darwin McPherson	18	1	0	1	94
Pat Jablonski (Goalie)	36	0	1	1	2
Todd Ewen	2	0	0	0	12
Curtis Joseph (Goalie)	23	0	0	0	0
Guy Hebert (Goalie)	30	0	0	0	0
Shootout Goals	...	4	...	4	...

PHOENIX ROADRUNNERS

	Games	G.	A.	Pts.	Pen.
Bruce Boudreau	82	41	68	109	89
Jim McGeough	77	35	46	81	90
Larry Floyd	76	39	40	79	50
Nick Beaulieu	71	26	46	72	93
Steve Johnson, Milwaukee	5	0	2	2	0
Phoenix	65	21	49	70	31
Totals	70	21	51	72	31
Jeff Lamb	78	20	33	53	152
Rob Nichols	69	25	25	50	265
Jason LaFreniere, Flint	41	9	25	34	13
Phoenix	14	4	9	13	0
Totals	55	13	34	47	13
Carl Mokosak, Fort W.	55	12	21	33	315
Phoenix	15	6	6	12	48
Totals	70	18	27	45	363
Grant Tkachuk	72	17	23	40	66
Brent Sapergia	43	19	13	32	159
Vern Smith	48	4	19	23	37
Ken Spangler	58	3	16	19	156
Marc Laniel	26	3	15	18	10
Mike Berger	51	5	12	17	75
Chris Luongo	23	5	9	14	41
Dave Korol	62	1	12	13	45
Keith Gretzky	23	6	6	12	2
Kerry Clark	38	4	8	12	262
Dave Richter, Peoria	12	1	4	5	28
Phoenix	20	0	5	5	49
Totals	32	1	9	10	77
Stan Drulia	16	6	3	9	2
Ivan Matulik	29	3	5	8	46
Richard Novak	16	2	5	7	2

	Games	G.	A.	Pts.	Pen.
Kevin MacDonald	30	1	5	6	201
Bryant Perrier	56	1	5	6	110
Randy Exelby (Goalie)	41	0	4	4	24
Paul Kelly	8	3	0	3	11
John Blue, Kal. (Goalie)	4	0	1	1	0
Phoenix (Goalie)	19	0	1	1	10
Totals	23	0	2	2	10
Don Martin	8	1	0	1	10
Trent Kaese	2	0	1	1	2
Shawn Dineen	15	0	1	1	27
David Littman (Goalie)	18	0	1	1	11
Darrin Beals (Goalie)	1	0	0	0	0
Mike Glover	1	0	0	0	4
Andrew MacVicar	1	0	0	0	0
Rob Schena	2	0	0	0	0
Eldon Reddick (Goalie)	3	0	0	0	0
Shawn Whitham	3	0	0	0	2
Mike Velucci	4	0	0	0	5
Bob Kennedy	7	0	0	0	12
Carl Repp (Goalie)	12	0	0	0	6
Jacques Mailhot	15	0	0	0	70
Shootout Goals	...	3	...	3	...

SALT LAKE GOLDEN EAGLES

	Games	G.	A.	Pts.	Pen.
Tim Sweeney	81	46	51	97	32
Marc Bureau	67	43	48	91	173
Rich Chernomaz	65	39	35	74	170
Darryl Olsen	72	16	50	66	90
Randy Bucyk	67	22	41	63	16
Brian Glynn	80	17	44	61	164
Stephane Matteau	81	23	35	58	130
Martin Simard	59	22	23	45	151
Rick Barkovich	71	20	23	43	55
Chris Biotti	60	9	19	28	73
Brian Deasley	71	16	11	27	46
Kevin Grant	78	7	17	24	117
Ken Sabourin	76	5	19	24	336
Rick Lessard	66	3	18	21	169
Rick Hayward	58	5	13	18	*419
Stu Grimson	62	8	8	16	319
Jonas Bergqvist	13	6	10	16	4
Mark Holmes	52	3	12	15	27
Randy Smith, Kalamazoo	8	1	2	3	12
Salt Lake	30	5	6	11	10
Totals	38	6	8	14	22
Jeff Wenaas	38	4	4	8	29
Jim Leavins	11	0	6	6	2
Kurt Kleinendorst	5	1	1	2	2
Doug Pickell	21	0	2	2	40
Serge Priakin	3	1	0	1	0
Darrin Banks, Fort Wayne	1	0	1	1	0
Salt Lake	4	0	0	0	11
Totals	5	0	1	1	11
Wayne Cowley (Goalie)	36	0	1	1	12
Warren Sharples (Goalie)	3	0	0	0	0
Steve Guenette (Goalie)	47	0	0	0	53
Shootout Goals	...	5	...	5	...

COMPLETE IHL GOALTENDING

	Games	Mins.	Goals	SO.	Avg.
Craig Barnett	3	102	8(2)	0	4.71
Mike Richter	13	782	49	0	3.76
Scott Brower (a)	21	1078	79(1)	0	4.40
Rick Knickle	55	2998	210(7)	1	4.20
Shootout losses	...	...	2	...	...
Flint Totals	82	4960	358	1	4.33
Frank Furlin	1	40	6	0	9.00
Craig Wright	1	53	5	0	5.66
Ray LeBlanc (b)	15	680	44(2)	0	3.88
Rick Tabaracci	22	1064	73(1)	0	4.12
Frederick Chabot	23	1208	87(4)	1	4.32
Stephane Beauregard	33	1949	115(1)	1	3.54
Shootout losses	...	...	7	...	...
Fort Wayne Totals	82	4994	345	2	4.15
Jeff Cooper	1	40	4	0	6.00
Darren Pang	7	401	17	1	2.54
Ray LeBlanc (b)	23	1334	71	2	3.19
Jimmy Waite	54	*3207	135(4)	*5	*2.53
Shootout losses	...	...	6	...	...
Indianapolis Totals	82	4982	237	8	2.85
Wade Flaherty	1	13	0	0	0.00
Kari Takko	1	59	5	0	5.08
John Blue (c)	4	232	18(1)	0	4.65
Larry Dyck	36	1959	116(2)	0	3.55
Jarmo Myllys	49	2715	159(7)	1	3.51

	Games	Mins.	Goals	SO.	Avg.
Shootout losses	...	...	3	...	...
Kalamazoo Totals	82	4978	311	1	3.75
Steve McKichan	1	40	2	0	3.00
Gus Morschauser	3	119	12	0	6.05
Dean Cook	15	669	55(1)	0	4.93
Frank Caprice	20	1098	79	0	4.32
Troy Gamble	*56	3033	*213(5)	2	4.21
Shootout losses	...	...	3	...	...
Milwaukee Totals	82	4959	370	2	4.48
Frank Pietrangelo	12	691	38(1)	0	3.30
Chris Clifford	23	1352	77	0	3.42
Bruce Racine	49	2911	182(2)	1	3.75
Shootout losses	...	...	4	...	...
Muskegon Totals	82	4954	304	1	3.68
Curtis Joseph	23	1241	80	0	3.87
Guy Hebert	30	1706	124(1)	1	4.36
Pat Jablonski	36	2043	165	0	4.85
Shootout losses	...	...	8	...	...
Peoria Totals	82	4990	378	1	4.54
Scott Brower (a)	1	20	1	0	3.00
Darren Beals	1	65	6	0	5.54
Eldon Reddick	3	185	7	0	2.27
Carl Repp	12	527	51	0	5.81
John Blue (c)	19	986	93(2)	0	5.66
David Littman	18	1047	64	0	3.67

	Games	Mins.	Goals	SO.	Avg.
Randy Exelby	41	2146	163(2)	0	4.56
Shootout losses	...	...	5	...	...
Phoenix Totals	82	4976	394	0	4.75
Warren Sharples	3	178	13	0	4.38
Wayne Cowley	36	2009	124(4)	1	3.70
Steve Guenette	47	2779	160(4)	0	3.45
Shootout losses	...	...	6	...	...
Salt Lake Totals	82	4966	311	1	3.76

( )—Empty Net Goals. Do not count against a Goaltender's average.
(a)—Brower played for Flint and Phoenix.
(b)—LeBlanc played for Fort Wayne and Indianapolis.
(c)—Blue played for Kalamazoo and Phoenix.

INDIVIDUAL 1989-90 LEADERS

Goals	Dave Michayluk, Muskegon— 51
Assists	Michel Mongeau, Peoria— 78
Points	Michel Mongeau, Peoria— 117
Penalty Minutes	Rick Hayward Salt Lake— 419
Goaltending Average (2,000 Minutes)	Jimmy Waite, Indianapolis—2.53
Shutouts	Jimmy Waite, Indianapolis— 5

1990 TURNER CUP PLAYOFFS

(All series best-of-seven)

QUARTERFINALS

Series "A"

	W.	L.	Pts.	GF.	GA.
Muskegon	4	1	8	32	22
Fort Wayne	1	4	2	22	32

(Muskegon wins series, 4 games to 1)

Series "B"

	W.	L.	Pts.	GF.	GA.
Kalamazoo	4	0	8	26	9
Flint	0	4	0	9	26

(Kalamazoo wins series, 4 games to 0)

Series "C"

	W.	L.	Pts.	GF.	GA.
Indianapolis	4	1	8	24	11
Peoria	1	4	2	11	24

(Indianapolis wins series, 4 games to 1)

Series "D"

	W.	L.	Pts.	GF.	GA.
Salt Lake	4	2	8	30	23
Milwaukee	2	4	4	23	30

(Salt Lake wins series, 4 games to 2)

SEMIFINALS

Series "E"

	W.	L.	Pts.	GF.	GA.
Muskegon	4	2	8	26	19
Kalamazoo	2	4	4	19	26

(Muskegon wins series, 4 games to 2)

Series "F"

	W.	L.	Pts.	GF.	GA.
Indianapolis	4	1	8	18	11
Salt Lake	1	4	2	11	18

(Indianapolis wins series, 4 games to 1)

FINALS FOR THE TURNER CUP

Series "G"

	W.	L.	Pts.	GF.	GA.
Indianapolis	4	0	8	17	9
Muskegon	0	4	0	9	17

(Indianapolis wins series, and N.R. (Bud) Poile Cup,
4 games to 0)

TOP 10 PLAYOFF SCORERS

	Games	G.	A.	Pts.
1. Dave Michayluk, Muskegon	15	8	*14	*22
2. Dan Frawley, Muskegon	15	9	12	21
3. Mike Eagles, Indianapolis	13	*10	10	20
Jock Callander, Muskegon	15	6	*14	20
5. Mike Stapleton, Indianapolis	14	9	10	19
6. Ken Hodge, Kalamazoo	10	5	13	18
7. Brian Wilks, Muskegon	15	7	10	17
8. Brian Noonan, Indianapolis	14	6	9	15
9. Scott Gruhl, Muskegon	15	8	6	14
10. Jamie Leach, Muskegon	14	9	4	13
Sean Williams, Indianapolis	14	8	5	13
Martin Simard, Salt Lake	11	5	8	13

TEAM-BY-TEAM PLAYOFF SCORING

FLINT SPIRITS

(Lost quarterfinals to Kalamazoo, 4 games to 0)

	Games	G.	A.	Pts.	Pen.
Dave Archibald	4	3	2	5	0
Darren Lowe	4	1	4	5	2
Lee Giffin	4	1	2	3	0
Simon Wheeldon	4	1	2	3	2
Daniel Lacroix	4	2	0	2	24
Rob Zamuner	4	1	0	1	6
Mike Hurlbut	3	0	1	1	2
Joe Paterson	4	0	1	1	2
Steve Richmond	4	0	1	1	16
Soren True	4	0	1	1	2
Barry Chyzowski	1	0	0	0	0
Rick Knickle (Goalie)	2	0	0	0	4
Scott Brower (Goalie)	3	0	0	0	0
Todd Charlesworth	4	0	0	0	4
Mike Golden	4	0	0	0	2
James Latos	4	0	0	0	4
Peter Laviolette	4	0	0	0	4
Rudy Poeschek	4	0	0	0	16
Dennis Vial	4	0	0	0	10

FORT WAYNE KOMETS

(Lost quarterfinals to Muskegon, 4 games to 1)

	Games	G.	A.	Pts.	Pen.
Mike deCarle	5	2	6	8	15
Cam Plante	5	1	6	7	2
Lonnie Loach	5	4	2	6	15
Bob Lakso	5	3	3	6	0
Joe Stefan	5	4	1	5	0
Byron Lomow	5	3	2	5	25
Ron Handy	5	3	1	4	0
Brad Aitken	5	1	3	4	12

	Games	G.	A.	Pts.	Pen.
Colin Chin	2	0	2	2	2
Stephane Brochu	5	0	2	2	6
Bob Fowler	5	0	2	2	19
Carey Lucyk	5	0	2	2	6
Mike Butters	5	0	1	1	11
Kevin Kerr	5	0	1	1	33
Scott Shaunessy	5	0	1	1	31
Mark Vichorek	5	0	1	1	19
Bret Walter	1	0	0	0	2
Ron Shudra	2	0	0	0	0
Ray LeBlanc (Goalie)	3	0	0	0	0
Rick Tabaracci (Goalie)	3	0	0	0	2

INDIANAPOLIS ICE

(Winners of 1990 Turner Cup Playoffs)

	Games	G.	A.	Pts.	Pen.
Mike Eagles	13	*10	10	20	34
Mike Stapleton	13	9	10	19	38
Brian Noonan	14	6	9	15	20
Sean Williams	14	8	5	13	12
Bob Bassen	12	3	8	11	33
Mike Rucinski	13	3	8	11	8
Bruce Cassidy	14	1	10	11	20
Mike McNeill	14	6	4	10	21
Jari Torkki	11	5	2	7	8
David Bassegio	10	2	4	6	6
Jim Playfair	14	1	5	6	24
Jim Johannson	14	1	4	5	6
Ryan McGill	14	2	2	4	29
Warren Rychel	14	1	3	4	64
Craig Channell	14	1	2	2	16
Darren Pang (Goalie)	5	0	1	1	12
Cam Russell	9	0	1	1	24
Mike Peluso	14	0	1	1	58
Guy Phillips	2	0	0	0	0
Jimmy Waite (Goalie)	10	0	0	0	2

KALAMAZOO WINGS

(Lost semifinals to Muskegon, 4 games to 2)

	Games	G.	A.	Pts.	Pen.
Ken Hodge	10	5	13	18	2
J.F. Quintin	10	8	4	12	14
Kevin Evans	10	4	8	12	86
Scott Robinson	10	4	7	11	21
Darcy Norton	6	3	6	9	6
Gary Emmons	8	2	7	9	2
Mario Thyer	10	2	6	8	4
Peter Lappin	8	5	2	7	4
Mitch Messier	8	4	3	7	25
Dean Kolstad	10	3	4	7	14
Pat MacLeod	10	1	6	7	2
Mike McHugh	10	0	6	6	16
Link Gaetz	9	2	2	4	59
Jayson More	10	0	3	3	13
Larry DePalma	4	1	1	2	32
Paul Jerrard	7	1	1	2	11
Clark Donatelli	4	0	2	2	12
Steve Gotaas	2	0	0	0	2
Ed Courtenay	3	0	0	0	0
Scott McCrady	4	0	0	0	19
Jarmo Myllys (Goalie)	5	0	0	0	0
Larry Dyck (Goalie)	7	0	0	0	2
Rob Zettler	7	0	0	0	6

MILWAUKEE ADMIRALS

(Lost quarterfinals to Salt Lake, 4 games to 2)

	Games	G.	A.	Pts.	Pen.
David Bruce	6	5	3	8	0
Rob Murphy	6	2	6	8	12
Ian Kidd	6	2	5	7	0
Dave Capuano	6	1	5	6	0
Todd Hawkins	5	4	1	5	19

	Games	G.	A.	Pts.	Pen.
Peter Bakovic	6	4	1	5	52
Adrien Plavsic	6	1	3	4	6
Jay Mazur	6	3	0	3	6
Ernie Vargas	5	0	3	3	0
Peter DeBoer	6	0	3	3	4
Tim Lenardon	6	1	1	2	4
Curtis Hunt	3	0	1	1	4
Carl Valimont	3	0	1	1	6
Jose Charbonneau	5	0	1	1	8
Don Gibson	5	0	1	1	41
Jack Capuano	6	0	1	1	12
Shawn Clouston	2	0	0	0	2
Terry Menard	2	0	0	0	4
Steve Veilleux	2	0	0	0	2
Frank Caprice (Goalie)	3	0	0	0	4
Jim Revenberg	4	0	0	0	45
Troy Gamble (Goalie)	5	0	0	0	0

MUSKEGON LUMBERJACKS

(Lost Finals to Indianapolis, 4 games to 0)

	Games	G.	A.	Pts.	Pen.
Dave Michayluk	15	8	*14	*22	10
Dan Frawley	15	9	12	21	51
Jock Callander	15	6	*14	20	54
Brian Wilks	15	7	10	17	41
Scott Gruhl	15	8	6	14	26
Jamie Leach	15	9	4	13	14
Jim Paek	15	1	10	11	41
Duane Joyce	12	3	7	10	13
Perry Ganchar	14	3	5	8	27
Richard Zemlak	14	3	4	7	*105
Glenn Mulvenna	11	2	5	7	0

	Games	G.	A.	Pts.	Pen.
Mark Kachowski	12	2	4	6	41
Paul Stanton	15	2	4	6	21
Mike Mersch	15	1	4	5	41
Mitch Wilson	15	1	4	5	97
Randy Taylor	15	0	4	4	8
Jeff Daniels	6	1	1	2	7
Darren Stolk	6	1	0	1	2
Bruce Racine (Goalie)	9	0	1	1	0
Chris Clifford (Goalie)	6	0	0	0	2

PEORIA RIVERMEN

(Lost quarterfinals to Indianapolis, 4 games to 1)

	Games	G.	A.	Pts.	Pen.
Michel Mongeau	5	3	4	7	6
Yves Heroux	5	2	2	4	0
Dominic Lavoie	5	2	2	4	16
Jim Vesey	5	1	3	4	21
Keith Osborne	5	1	1	2	4
David Thomlinson	5	1	1	2	15
Tom Karalis	5	0	2	2	48
Darin Smith	5	1	0	1	2
Scott Paluch	5	0	1	1	8
Rob Robinson	5	0	1	1	10
Tony Twist	5	0	1	1	38
David O'Brien	1	0	0	0	0
Guy Hebert (Goalie)	2	0	0	0	0
Marc Saumier	2	0	0	0	9
Toby Ducolon	3	0	0	0	12
John Ferguson	3	0	0	0	2
Kevin Miehm	3	0	0	0	4
Pat Jablonski (Goalie)	4	0	0	0	0
Terry MacLean	4	0	0	0	0

	Games	G.	A.	Pts.	Pen.
Randy Skarda	4	0	0	0	0
Richard Pion	5	0	0	0	0

SALT LAKE GOLDEN EAGLES

(Lost semifinals to Indianapolis, 4 games to 1)

	Games	G.	A.	Pts.	Pen.
Martin Simard	11	5	8	13	12
Rich Chernomaz	11	6	6	12	32
Marc Bureau	11	4	8	12	45
Stephane Matteau	10	6	3	9	38
Tim Sweeney	11	5	4	9	4
Darryl Olsen	11	3	6	9	2
Randy Bucyk	11	2	6	8	10
Jim Leavins	11	0	8	8	2
Brian Glynn	11	0	7	7	12
Mark Holmes	9	2	3	5	2
Brian Deasley	11	4	0	4	8
Rick Hayward	7	1	2	3	71
Rick Lessard	10	1	2	3	64
Rick Barkovich	7	1	1	2	4
Kevin Grant	11	0	2	2	22
Ken Sabourin	11	0	2	2	40
Chris Biotti	3	1	0	1	2
Steve Guenette (Goalie)	10	0	1	1	2
Darren Banks	1	0	0	0	10
Corey Lyons	1	0	0	0	0
Jeff Wenaas	1	0	0	0	0
Wayne Cowley (Goalie)	3	0	0	0	2
Randy Smith	3	0	0	0	0
Stu Grimson	4	0	0	0	8

COMPLETE TURNER CUP GOALTENDING

	Games	Mins.	Goals	SO.	Avg.
Jimmy Waite, Indianapolis	*10	*602	19	*1	*1.89
Jarmo Myllys, Kalamazoo	5	258	11	0	2.56
Darren Pang, Indianapolis	4	253	12	0	2.85
Wayne Cowley, Salt Lake	3	118	6	0	3.05
Bruce Racine, Muskegon	9	566	32(1)	0	3.39
Larry Dyck, Kalamazoo	7	356	22(2)	0	3.39
Steve Guenette, Salt Lake	*10	545	*35	*1	3.85
Guy Hebert, Peoria	2	76	5	0	3.95
Chris Clifford, Muskegon	6	360	24(1)	0	4.00
Frank Caprice, Milwaukee	3	142	10(1)	0	4.23
Ray LeBlanc, Fort Wayne	3	139	11(1)	0	4.75
Pat Jablonski, Peoria	4	223	19	0	5.11
Troy Gamble, Milwaukee	5	216	19(1)	0	5.28
Scott Brower, Flint	3	139	13	0	5.61
Rick Tabaracci, Fort Wayne	3	159	19(1)	0	7.17
Rick Knickle, Flint	2	101	13	0	7.72

( )—Empty Net Goals. Do not count against a Goaltender's average.

IHL 1989-90 ALL-STARS

First Team	Position	Second Team
Jimmy Waite, Indianapolis	Goalie	Jarmo Myllys, Kalamazoo
Brian Glynn, Salt Lake	Defense	Dean Kolstad, Kalamazoo
Bruce Cassidy, Indianapolis	Defense	Jim Agnew, Milwaukee
Michel Mongeau, Peoria	Center	Marc Bureau, Salt Lake
Bob Bassen, Indianapolis	Right Wing	Peter Lappin, Kalamazoo
David Bruce, Milwaukee		Brian Noonan, Indianapolis
Dave Michayluk, Muskegon	Left Wing	Tim Sweeney, Salt Lake

INDIVIDUAL IHL PLAYOFF LEADERS

Goals	Mike Eagles, Indianapolis—	10
Assists	Jock Callander, Muskegon—	14
	Dave Michayluk, Muskegon—	14
Points	Dave Michayluk, Muskegon—	22
Penalty Minutes	Richard Zemlak, Muskegon—	105
Goaltending Average	Jimmy Waite, Indianapolis—	1.89
Shutouts	Steve Guenette, Salt Lake—	1
	Jimmy Waite, Indianapolis—	1

IHL 1989-90 TROPHY WINNERS

James Gatschene Memorial Trophy (Most Valuable Player) ....Michel Mongeau, Peoria
Leo P. Lamoureux Memorial Trophy (Leading Scorer) ....Michel Mongeau, Peoria
James Norris Memorial Trophy (Outstanding Goaltender) ....Jimmy Waite, Indianapolis
Governors Trophy (Outstanding Defenseman) ....Brian Glynn, Salt Lake
Garry F. Longman Memorial Trophy (Outstanding Rookie) ....Rob Murphy, Milwaukee
Ken McKenzie Trophy (Outstanding American-Born Rookie) ......Tim Sweeney, Salt Lake
Commissioner's Trophy (Coach of the Year) ....Darryl Sutter, Indianapolis
N.R. (Bud) Poile Trophy (Playoff MVP) ....Mike McNeil, Indianapolis
Fred A. Huber Trophy (Regular Season Champion) ....Muskegon Lumberjacks
Joseph Turner Memorial Cup Winner (Playoff Champion)......................Indianapolis Ice

IHL ALL-TIME TROPHY WINNERS

JAMES GATSCHENE MEMORIAL TROPHY

Most Valuable Player

Season	Player	Club
1946-47	Herb Jones, Detroit Auto Club	
1947-48	Lyle Dowell, Det. Bright's Goodyears	
1948-49	Bob McFadden, Det. Jerry Lynch	
1949-50	Dick Kowcinak, Sarnia	
1950-51	John McGrath, Toledo	
1951-52	Ernie Dick, Chatham	
1952-53	Donnie Marshall, Cincinnati	
1953-54	No award given	
1954-55	Phil Goyette, Cincinnati	
1955-56	George Hayes, Grand Rapids	
1956-57	Pierre Brillant, Indianapolis	
1957-58	Pierre Brillant, Indianapolis	
1958-59	Len Thornson, Fort Wayne	
1959-60	Billy Reichart, Minneapolis	
1960-61	Len Thornson, Fort Wayne	
1961-62	Len Thornson, Fort Wayne	
1962-63	Len Thornson, Fort Wayne	
	Eddie Lang, Fort Wayne (tie)	
1963-64	Len Thornson, Fort Wayne	
1964-65	Chick Chalmers, Toledo	
1965-66	Gary Schall, Muskegon	
1966-67	Len Thornson, Fort Wayne	
1967-68	Len Thornson, Fort Wayne	
	Don Westbrooke, Dayton (tie)	
1968-69	Don Westbrooke, Dayton	
1969-70	Cliff Pennington, Des Moines	
1970-71	Lyle Carter, Muskegon	
1971-72	Len Fontaine, Port Huron	
1972-73	Gary Ford, Muskegon	
1973-74	Pete Mara, Des Moines	
1974-75	Gary Ford, Muskegon	
1975-76	Len Fontaine, Port Huron	
1976-77	Tom Mellor, Toledo	
1977-78	Dan Bonar, Fort Wayne	
1978-79	Terry McDougall, Fort Wayne	
1979-80	Al Dumba, Fort Wayne	

Season	Player	Club
1980-81	Marcel Comeau, Saginaw
1981-82	Brent Jarrett, Kalamazoo
1982-83	Claude Noel, Toledo
1983-84	Darren Jensen, Fort Wayne
1984-85	Scott Gruhl, Muskegon
1985-86	Darrell May, Peoria
1986-87	Jeff Pyle, Saginaw
	Jock Callander, Muskegon (tie)
1987-88	John Cullen, Flint
1988-89	Dave Michayluk, Muskegon
1989-90	Michel Mongeau, Peoria

LEO P. LAMOUREUX MEMORIAL TROPHY

Leading Scorer

(Originally called George H. Wilkinson Trophy from 1946-47 through 1959-60.)

Season	Player	Club
1946-47	Harry Marchand, Windsor
1947-48	Dick Kowcinak, Det. Auto Club
1948-49	Leo Richard, Toledo
1949-50	Dick Kowcinak, Sarnia
1950-51	Herve Parent, Grand Rapids
1951-52	George Parker, Grand Rapids
1952-53	Alex Irving, Milwaukee
1953-54	Don Hall, Johnstown
1954-55	Phil Goyette, Cincinnati
1955-56	Max Mekilok, Cincinnati
1956-57	Pierre Brillant, Indianapolis
1957-58	Warren Hynes, Cincinnati
1958-59	George Ranieri, Louisville
1959-60	Chick Chalmers, Louisville
1960-61	Ken Yackel, Minneapolis
1961-62	Len Thornson, Fort Wayne
1962-63	Moe Bartoli, Minneapolis
1963-64	Len Thornson, Fort Wayne
1964-65	Lloyd Maxfield, Port Huron
1965-66	Bob Rivard, Fort Wayne
1966-67	Len Thornson, Fort Wayne
1967-68	Gary Ford, Muskegon
1968-69	Don Westbrooke, Dayton
1969-70	Don Westbrooke, Dayton
1970-71	Darrel Knibbs, Muskegon
1971-72	Gary Ford, Muskegon
1972-73	Gary Ford, Muskegon
1973-74	Pete Mara, Des Moines
1974-75	Rick Bragnalo, Dayton
1975-76	Len Fontaine, Port Huron
1976-77	Jim Koleff, Flint
1977-78	Jim Johnston, Flint
1978-79	Terry McDougall, Fort Wayne
1979-80	Al Dumba, Fort Wayne
1980-81	Marcel Comeau, Saginaw
1981-82	Brent Jarrett, Kalamazoo
1982-83	Dale Yakiwchuk, Milwaukee
1983-84	Wally Schreiber, Fort Wayne
1984-85	Scott MacLeod, Salt Lake
1985-86	Scott MacLeod, Salt Lake
1986-87	Jock Callander, Muskegon
	Jeff Pyle, Saginaw (tie)
1987-88	John Cullen, Flint
1988-89	Dave Michayluk, Muskegon
1989-90	Michel Mongeau, Peoria

JAMES NORRIS MEMORIAL TROPHY

Outstanding Goaltender

Season	Player	Club
1955-56	Bill Tibbs, Troy
1956-57	Glenn Ramsey, Cincinnati
1957-58	Glenn Ramsey, Cincinnati
1958-59	Don Rigazio, Louisville
1959-60	Rene Zanier, Fort Wayne
1960-61	Ray Mikulan, Minneapolis
1961-62	Glenn Ramsey, Omaha
1962-63	Glenn Ramsey, Omaha
1963-64	Glenn Ramsey, Toledo
1964-65	Chuck Adamson, Fort Wayne
1965-66	Bob Sneddon, Port Huron
1966-67	Glenn Ramsey, Toledo
1967-68	Tim Tabor, Muskegon
	Bob Perani, Muskegon
1968-69	Pat Rupp, Dayton
	John Adams, Dayton
1969-70	Gaye Cooley, Des Moines
	Bob Perreault, Des Moines
1970-71	Lyle Carter, Muskegon

Michel Mongeau

Season	Player	Club
1971-72	Glenn Resch, Muskegon
1972-73	Robbie Irons, Fort Wayne
	Don Atchison, Fort Wayne
1973-74	Bill Hughes, Muskegon
1974-75	Bob Volpe, Flint
	Merlin Jenner, Flint
1975-76	Don Cutts, Muskegon
1976-77	Terry Richardson, Kalamazoo
1977-78	Lorne Molleken, Saginaw
	Pierre Chagnon, Saginaw
1978-79	Gord Laxton, Grand Rapids
1979-80	Larry Lozinski, Kalamazoo
1980-81	Claude Legris, Kalamazoo
	Georges Gagnon, Kalamazoo
1981-82	Lorne Molleken, Toledo
	Dave Tardich, Toledo
1982-83	Lorne Molleken, Toledo
1983-84	Darren Jensen, Fort Wayne
1984-85	Rick Heinz, Peoria
1985-86	Rick St. Croix, Fort Wayne
	Pokey Reddick, Fort Wayne
1986-87	Alain Raymond, Fort Wayne
	Michel Dufour, Fort Wayne
1987-88	Steve Guenette, Muskegon
1988-89	Rick Knickle, Fort Wayne
1989-90	Jimmy Waite, Indianapolis

GOVERNORS TROPHY

Outstanding Defenseman

Season	Player	Club
1964-65	Lionel Repka, Fort Wayne
1965-66	Bob Lemieux, Muskegon
1966-67	Larry Mavety, Port Huron
1967-68	Carl Brewer, Muskegon
1968-69	Al Breaule, Dayton
	Moe Benoit, Dayton (tie)
1969-70	John Gravel, Toledo
1970-71	Bob LaPage, Des Moines
1971-72	Rick Pagnutti, Fort Wayne
1972-73	Bob McCammon, Port Huron
1973-74	Dave Simpson, Dayton
1974-75	Murry Flegel, Muskegon
1975-76	Murry Flegel, Muskegon
1976-77	Tom Mellor, Toledo
1977-78	Michel LaChance, Milwaukee

Season	Player	Club
1978-79	Guido Tenesi, Grand Rapids
1979-80	John Gibson, Saginaw
1980-81	Larry Goodenough, Saginaw
1981-82	Don Waddell, Saginaw
1982-83	Jim Burton, Fort Wayne
	Kevin Willison, Milwaukee (tie)
1983-84	Kevin Willison, Milwaukee
1984-85	Lee Norwood, Peoria
1985-86	Jim Burton, Fort Wayne
1986-87	Jim Burton, Fort Wayne
1987-88	Phil Bourque, Muskegon
1988-89	Randy Boyd, Milwaukee
1989-90	Brian Glynn, Salt Lake

GARRY F. LONGMAN MEMORIAL TROPHY

Outstanding Rookie

Season	Player	Club
1961-62	Dave Richardson, Fort Wayne
1962-63	John Gravel, Omaha
1963-64	Don Westbrooke, Toledo
1964-65	Bob Thomas, Toledo
1965-66	Frank Golembrowsky, Port Huron
1966-67	Kerry Bond, Columbus
1967-68	Gary Ford, Muskegon
1968-69	Doug Volmar, Columbus
1969-70	Wayne Zuk, Toledo
1970-71	Corky Agar, Flint
	Herb Howdle, Dayton (tie)
1971-72	Glenn Resch, Muskegon
1972-73	Danny Gloor, Des Moines
1973-74	Frank DeMarco, Des Moines
1974-75	Rick Bragnalo, Dayton
1975-76	Sid Veysey, Fort Wayne
1976-77	Ron Zanussi, Fort Wayne
	Garth MacGuigan, Muskegon (tie)
1977-78	Dan Bonar, Fort Wayne
1978-79	Wes Jarvis, Port Huron
1979-80	Doug Robb, Milwaukee
1980-81	Scott Vanderburgh, Kalamazoo
1981-82	Scott Howson, Toledo
1982-83	Tony Fiore, Flint
1983-84	Darren Jensen, Fort Wayne
1984-85	Gilles Thibaudeau, Flint
1985-86	Guy Benoit, Muskegon
1986-87	Michel Mongeau, Saginaw

Season	Player	Club
1987-88	—Ed Belfour, Saginaw	
	John Cullen, Flint (tie)	
1988-89	—Paul Ranheim, Salt Lake	
1989-90	—Rob Murphy, Milwaukee	

KEN McKENZIE TROPHY

Outstanding American-Born Rookie

Season	Player	Club
1977-78	—Mike Eruzione, Toledo	
1978-79	—Jon Fontas, Saginaw	
1979-80	—Bob Janecyk, Fort Wayne	
1980-81	—Mike Labianca, Toledo	
	Steve Janaszak, Fort Wayne (tie)	
1981-82	—Steve Salvucci, Saginaw	
1982-83	—Paul Fenton, Peoria	
1983-84	—Mike Krensing, Muskegon	
1984-85	—Bill Schafhauser, Kalamazoo	
1985-86	—Brian Noonan, Saginaw	
1986-87	—Ray LeBlanc, Flint	
1987-88	—Dan Woodley, Flint	
1988-89	—Paul Ranheim, Salt Lake	
1989-90	—Tim Sweeney, Salt Lake	

COMMISSIONER'S TROPHY

Coach of the Year

Season	Coach	Club
1984-85	—Rick Ley, Muskegon	
	Pat Kelly, Peoria (tie)	
1985-86	—Rob Laird, Fort Wayne	
1986-87	—Wayne Thomas, Salt Lake	
1987-88	—Rick Dudley, Flint	
1988-89	—B. J. MacDonald, Muskegon	
	Phil Russell, Muskegon (tie)	
1989-90	—Darryl Sutter, Indianapolis	

N. R. (BUD) POILE TROPHY

Playoff MVP
(Originally called Turner Cup Playoff MVP
from 1984-85 through 1988-89.)

Season	Player	Club
1984-85	—Denis Cyr, Peoria	
1985-86	—Jock Callander, Muskegon	
1986-87	—Rick Heinz, Salt Lake	
1987-88	—Peter Lappin, Salt Lake	
1988-89	—Dave Michayluk, Muskegon	
1989-90	—Mike McNeill, Indianapolis	

Ed Belfour

IHL ALL-TIME CHAMPIONSHIP TEAMS
(Regular season championship award originally called J.P. McGuire Trophy from 1946-47 through 1953-54.)

FRED A. HUBER TROPHY

Season	Regular Season Championship Team (Coach)	Playoff Championship Team (Coach)
1945-46	No Trophy Awarded	Detroit Auto Club (Jack Ward)
1946-47	Windsor Staffords (Jack Ward)	Windsor Spitfires (Ebbie Goodfellow)
1947-48	Windsor Spitfires (Dent-Goodfellow)	Toledo Mercurys (Andy Mulligan)
1948-49	Toledo Mercurys (Andy Mulligan)	Windsor (Jimmy Skinner)
1949-50	Sarnia Sailors (Dick Kowcinak)	Chatham Maroons (Bob Stoddart)
1950-51	Grand Rapids Rockets (Lou Trudell)	Toledo Mercurys (Alex Wood)
1951-52	Grand Rapids Rockets (Lou Trudell)	Toledo Mercurys (Alex Wood)
1952-53	Cinc. Mohawks (Buddy O'Conner)	Cinc. Mohawks (Buddy O'Conner)
1953-54	Cinc. Mohawks (Roly McLenahan)	Cinc. Mohawks (Roly McLenahan)
1954-55	Cinc. Mohawks (Roly McLenahan)	Cinc. Mohawks (Roly McLenahan)
1955-56	Cinc. Mohawks (Roly McLenahan)	Cinc. Mohawks (Roly McLenahan)
1956-57	Cinc. Mohawks (Roly McLenahan)	Cinc. Mohawks (Roly McLenahan)
1957-58	Cincinnati Mohawks (Bill Gould)	Indiana. Chiefs (Leo Lamoureux)
1958-59	Louisville Rebels (Leo Gasparini)	Louisville Rebels (Leo Gasparini)
1959-60	Fort Wayne Komets (Ken Ullyot)	St. Paul Saints (Fred Shero)
1960-61	Minneapolis Millers (Ken Yackel)	St. Paul Saints (Fred Shero)
1961-62	Muskegon Zephyrs (Moose Lallo)	Muskegon Zephyrs (Moose Lallo)
1962-63	Fort Wayne Komets (Ken Ullyot)	Fort Wayne Komets (Ken Ullyot)
1963-64	Toledo Blades (Moe Benoit)	Toledo Blades (Moe Benoit)
1964-65	Port Huron Flags (Lloyd Maxfield)	Fort Wayne Komets (Eddie Long)
1965-66	Muskegon Mohawks (Moose Lallo)	Port Huron Flags (Lloyd Maxfield)
1966-67	Dayton Gems (Warren Back)	Toledo Blades (Terry Slater)
1967-68	Muskegon Mohawks (Moose Lallo)	Muskegon Mohawks (Moose Lallo)

JOSEPH TURNER MEMORIAL CUP WINNERS

Season	Regular Season Championship Team (Coach)	Playoff Championship Team (Coach)
1968-69	Dayton Gems (Larry Wilson)	Dayton Gems (Larry Wilson)
1969-70	Muskegon Mohawks (Moose Lallo)	Dayton Gems (Larry Wilson)
1970-71	Muskegon Mohawks (Moose Lallo)	Port Huron Flags (Ted Garvin)
1971-72	Muskegon Mohawks (Moose Lallo)	Port Huron Flags (Ted Garvin)
1972-73	Fort Wayne Komets (Marc Boileau)	Fort Wayne Komets (Marc Boileau)
1973-74	Des Moines Capitals (Dan Belisle)	Des Moines Capitals (Dan Belisle)
1974-75	Muskegon Mohawks (Moose Lallo)	Toledo Goaldiggers (Ted Garvin)
1975-76	Dayton Gems (Ivan Prediger)	Dayton Gems (Ivan Prediger)
1976-77	Saginaw Gears (Don Perry)	Saginaw Gears (Don Perry)
1977-78	Fort Wayne Komets (Gregg Pilling)	Toledo Goaldiggers (Ted Garvin)
1978-79	Grand Rapids Owls (Moe Bartoli)	Kalamazoo Wings (Bill Purcell)
1979-80	Kalamazoo Wings (Doug McKay)	Kalamazoo Wings (Doug McKay)
1980-81	Kalamazoo Wings (Doug McKay)	Saginaw Gears (Don Perry)
1981-82	Toledo Goaldiggers (Bill Inglis)	Toledo Goaldiggers (Bill Inglis)
1982-83	Toledo Goaldiggers (Bill Inglis)	Toledo Goaldiggers (Bill Inglis)
1983-84	Fort Wayne Komets (Ron Ullyot)	Flint Generals (Dennis Desrosiers)
1984-85	Peoria Rivermen (Pat Kelly)	Peoria Rivermen (Pat Kelly)
1985-86	Fort Wayne Komets (Rob Laird)	Muskegon Lumberjacks (Rick Ley)
1986-87	Fort Wayne Komets (Rob Laird)	S.L. Golden Eagles (Wayne Thomas)
1987-88	Musk. Lumberjacks (Rick Ley)	S.L. Golden Eagles (Paul Baxter)
1988-89	Musk. Lumberjacks (B.J. MacDonald)	Musk. Lumberjacks (B.J. MacDonald)
1989-90	Musk. Lumberjacks (B.J. MacDonald)	Indianapolis Ice (Darryl Sutter)

EAST COAST HOCKEY LEAGUE

Commissioner—Patrick Kelly
Director of Information—Chuck Harrison
Address
  P.O. Box 310
  Vinton, Va. 24179
  Phone—(703) 345-8626
  FAX—(703) 981-1723

ERIE PANTHERS

Team Owners—Henry Brabham IV, Jim Clark, Jim Wallin,
  Keith Lustig M.D., Duane Wallin
Coach and General Manager—Ron Hansis
Director of Marketing—Mike Van Natten
Address—Erie Civic Center
  809 French Street
  Erie, Pa. 16501-1260
Mailing Address—P.O. Box 6116
  Erie, Pa. 16512-6116
Phone—(814) 455-3936
FAX—(814) 456-8287

GREENSBORO MONARCHS

Team Owner—Cherokee Properties Inc. (Bill Coffey)
Coach and General Manager—Jeff Brubaker
Operations Manager—Brenda Coffey
Promotions—Judy Faucett
Director of Marketing—Bryan Gray
Address—Greensboro Coliseum
  1921 W. Lee Street
  Greensboro, N.C. 27403
Phone—(919) 852-6170
FAX—(919) 852-6259

HAMPTON ROADS ADMIRALS

Team Owner—Blake Cullen
Coach—John Brophy
General Manager—Pat Nugent

Public Relations—Julie Maner
Address—Scope Plaza
  P.O. Box 299
  Norfolk, Va. 23501
Phone—(804) 640-1212
FAX—(804) 640-8447

JOHNSTOWN CHIEFS

Team Owners—Henry Brabham IV, John Daley
General Manager—John Daley
Coach—Steve Carlson
Address—War Memorial Arena
  326 Napoleon Street
  Johnstown, Pa. 15901
Phone—(814) 539-1799
FAX—(814) 536-1316

KNOXVILLE CHEROKEES

Team Owners—Rob Stooksbury, President
  Kim Simmons Thomas, Vice-President
  Bob Thomas, Secretary/Treasurer
General Manager/Coach—Don Jackson
Operations Manager—Noelle Bean
Address—Civic Coliseum
  500 East Church Street
  Knoxville, Tenn. 37915
Phone—(615) 546-6707
FAX—(615) 546-5521

NASHVILLE KNIGHTS

Team Owner—Bob Polk
Owner and General Manager—Ron Fuller
Coach—Archie Henderson
Address—Municipal Auditorium
  417 4th Ave. North
  Nashville, Tenn. 37201

Phone—(615) 255-7825
FAX—(615) 255-0024

RICHMOND RENEGADES

Owner and General Manager—Allan B. Harvie, Jr.
Coach—Chris McSorley
Marketing—Matt Hodges
Address—Richmond Coliseum
  601 East Leigh Street
  Richmond, Va. 23219
Phone—(804) 643-7825

VIRGINIA LANCERS

Team Owner/General Manager—Richard Gerry
Coach/Assistant G.M.—David B. Allison
Director of Marketing—Jerry Hogan
Address—Lancerlot Sports Complex
  1111 Vinyard Road
  Vinton, Va. 24179
Phone—(703) 345-3557
FAX—(703) 344-2983

WINSTON-SALEM THUNDERBIRDS

President, Governor, Chairman of the Board—Steve Corns
General Manager and Coach—Jay Fraser
Office Manager—Connie Zavistoski
Secretary/Treasurer—W. Emmett Gladstone III
Address—Winston-Salem Coliseum
  2825 University Parkway
  Winston-Salem, N.C. 27105
Mailing Address—P.O. Box 4507
  Winston-Salem, N.C. 27115-4507
Phone—(919) 748-0919
FAX—(919) 724-3740

1989-90 FINAL ECHL STANDINGS

	G.	W.	L.	Pts.	GF.	GA.
Winston-Salem Thunderbirds	60	38	16(6)	82	312	257
Erie Panthers	60	38	16(6)	82	357	251
Virginia Lancers	60	36	18(6)	78	261	218
Greensboro Monarchs	60	29	27(4)	62	263	283
Hampton-Roads Admirals	60	29	29(2)	60	252	267
Nashville Knights	60	26	30(4)	56	248	289
Johnstown Chiefs	60	23	31(6)	52	233	291
Knoxville Cherokees	60	21	33(6)	48	230	300

( )—Indicates number of games lost in overtime and are worth one point.

TOP 10 ECHL SCORERS

	Games	G.	A.	Pts.
1. Bill McDougall, Erie	57	*80	68	*148
2. Len Soccio, Winston-Salem	60	51	62	113
3. Joe Ferras, Winston-Salem	49	45	63	108
4. Trent Kaese, Winston-Salem	57	56	51	107
5. Martin Bergeron, Erie	59	30	58	88
6. Glen Engevik, Nashville	53	45	39	84
Brian Martin, Hampton-Roads	58	40	44	84
Murray Hood, Hampton-Roads	56	15	*69	84
9. Phil Berger, Greensboro	46	38	44	82
10. Chris Robertson, Greensboro	59	32	43	75

TEAM-BY-TEAM BREAKDOWN OF ECHL SCORING

ERIE PANTHERS

	Games	G.	A.	Pts.	Pen.
Bill McDougall	57	*80	68	*148	226
Martin Bergeron	59	30	58	88	109
Daryl Harpe	60	28	44	72	123
Grant Ottenbreit	57	25	44	69	280
Doug Stromback	53	23	43	66	16
Rob McDougall	46	28	33	61	221
Rob Gador	60	21	33	54	67
Mike Vellucci, W.-Salem	10	2	7	9	21
Erie	22	7	20	27	57
Totals	32	9	27	36	78
Peter Buckridge	20	17	19	36	12
Ryan Kummu	45	5	30	35	71
Eric Legros	24	22	11	33	6
Craig Kitteringham	33	5	24	29	113
Steve Weinke	55	7	19	26	136
Barry Chyzowski	16	9	15	24	19
Doug Marsden	19	12	9	21	30

	Games	G.	A.	Pts.	Pen.
Guy Rouleau	13	9	10	19	9
Jerry Tarrant	10	1	16	17	36
Antti Autere	46	1	12	13	34
Simon Gagne	13	4	8	12	39
Chris Walsh	12	3	5	8	0
Craig Barnett (Goalie)	38	0	5	5	22
John Haley (Goalie)	2	0	2	2	0
Steve Moore	2	0	2	2	11
Mike Rosati (Goalie)	18	0	2	2	8
Dave Fentress	4	0	1	1	0
Scott Brower (Goalie)	5	0	0	0	0

GREENSBORO MONARCHS

	Games	G.	A.	Pts.	Pen.
Phil Berger	46	38	44	82	119
Chris Robertson	59	32	43	75	51
Boyd Sutton	60	32	26	58	25
Doug Lawrence	53	16	42	58	94

	Games	G.	A.	Pts.	Pen.
Daniel Bock	58	11	36	47	87
John Sullivan	37	15	27	42	125
Jamie Nicholls	28	15	11	26	12
Scott White	30	9	13	22	67
Steve McKinley	56	5	17	22	166
Scott Allen, Erie	16	5	3	8	10
Winston-Salem	10	1	4	5	26
Greensboro	19	2	6	8	16
Totals	45	8	13	21	52
Mike Butters	45	8	12	20	183
Chad Thompson	30	5	15	20	25
Mike McCormick	29	16	3	19	13
Chris Laganas	35	10	8	18	95
John Blessman, W.-Salem	17	1	6	7	108
Greensboro	19	0	7	7	81
Totals	36	1	13	14	189
Stephane Carrier	45	5	8	13	133
Pete Corbett	18	5	5	10	96
Bruce Major	12	4	3	7	6
Steve Hamilton	17	3	3	6	158
Doug Brown	16	1	4	5	47

	Games	G.	A.	Pts.	Pen.
Nick Vitucci, W-S (Goalie)	6	...	...	...	...
Greensboro (Goalie)	28	...	...	...	...
Totals	34	0	4	4	12
K. Kabot	2	1	1	2	2
Doug Brown	5	0	1	1	23
Dar. McClusky, John (G.)	7	0	0	0	8
Hampton-Roads (G.)	9	0	1	1	10
Greensboro (Goalie)	2	0	0	0	0
Totals	18	0	1	1	18
Elias Delaney (Goalie)	1	0	0	0	0
Jocelyn Perreault (Goalie)	8	0	0	0	14
Wade Flaherty (Goalie)	30	0	0	0	2

HAMPTON-ROADS ADMIRALS

	Games	G.	A.	Pts.	Pen.
Murray Hood	56	15	*69	84	37
Brian Martin, Greensboro	8	4	5	9	37
Hampton-Roads	50	36	39	75	71
Totals	58	40	44	84	108
Trevor Jobe	51	48	23	71	143
Don Gagne	59	33	20	53	150
Wayne Stripp	52	19	32	51	78
Dennis McEwen	58	25	22	47	114
Jody Praznik	55	7	35	42	40
Marc Vachon, Johnstown	58	18	21	39	38
Hampton-Roads	1	0	0	0	0
Totals	59	18	21	39	38
David Buckley	56	6	33	39	63
Steve Greenberg	55	11	23	34	50
Chris Lukey	53	14	17	31	87
Tom Bissett	5	7	7	14	2
Mike Flanagan	57	2	11	13	181
Al Murphy, Greensboro	3	0	0	0	0
Hampton-Roads	31	3	12	15	105
Totals	34	3	10	13	105
Kent Hanley	13	5	6	11	12
Frank Malone	18	5	5	10	31
Scott Taylor, Virginia	13	1	3	4	73
Hampton-Roads	16	1	5	6	92
Totals	29	2	8	10	165
Pat Cavanaugh	29	3	5	8	151
Jeff Turcotte	12	2	5	7	2
Jordan Fois	7	0	6	6	38
Rob Schenna	5	3	2	5	0
Alain Raymond (Goalie)	36	0	5	5	18
Bobby McGrath	16	3	1	4	4
Jamie Kompon	20	1	2	3	32
Darin Bannister	5	0	2	2	22
Jacques Mailhot	5	0	2	2	62
Chris Weseen	10	0	2	2	55
Randy Hansch (Goalie)	4	0	1	1	2
J. R. Reich (Goalie)	2	0	0	0	0
Ken Weiss, Virginia (G.)	2	0	0	0	0
Hampton-Roads (G.)	2	0	0	0	0
Totals	4	0	0	0	0
Frank Furlan (Goalie)	6	0	0	0	4
Trevor Kruger (Goalie)	7	0	0	0	2

JOHNSTOWN CHIEFS

	Games	G.	A.	Pts.	Pen.
John Messuri	55	25	47	72	45
Mike Rossetti	60	35	32	67	67
Darren Schwartz	50	26	27	53	270
Doug Weiss	40	19	23	42	32
E.J. Sauer, Winston-Salem	6	0	5	5	12
Johnstown	1	0	0	0	0
Greensboro	33	12	23	35	45
Totals	40	12	28	40	57
Bob Bennett, Knoxville	6	1	2	3	18
Johnstown	9	2	2	4	20
Winston-Salem	25	8	14	22	130
Virginia	6	1	4	5	16
Totals	46	12	22	34	184
Rich Stromback, Erie	25	7	18	25	130
Johnstown	20	6	2	8	44
Totals	45	13	20	33	174
Dean Hall	38	11	22	33	27
Darren Servatius	53	7	24	31	192
Danny Williams	50	11	18	29	251
Vince Guidotti	46	5	17	22	61
Mitch Malloy	18	10	10	20	102
Bob Goulet	52	6	14	20	57
Tim Hanley	16	6	12	18	28
Rick Boyd	45	5	12	17	284
Mark Bogoslowski	47	4	13	17	138
Rocky Johnson, Knoxville	40	5	7	12	36
Johnstown	1	0	0	0	0
Erie	4	2	0	2	4
Totals	45	7	7	14	40

	Games	G.	A.	Pts.	Pen.
Greg Parks	8	5	9	14	7
J.F. Nault	14	8	5	13	24
Mark Ziliotto	20	5	7	12	40
Shawn Byram	8	5	5	10	35
Gord Cruikshank	5	3	4	7	2
Rick McCarthy	6	2	3	5	10
Lee Odelein	24	1	4	5	60
Sean Finn	6	0	5	5	16
Jamie Kelly	10	2	2	4	0
Rick Burtchill (Goalie)	33	0	3	3	16
Ryan Schiff	5	0	2	2	2
Todd Lalonde	1	1	0	1	2
Dave Mellen	6	0	1	1	8
Bill Birks	8	0	1	1	12
Mike Jeffrey (Goalie)	16	0	1	1	12
Doug Smith	3	0	0	0	29
Will Putnam	4	0	0	0	0
Mark Benard (Goalie)	7	0	0	0	4
Tim Flanigan (Goalie)	8	0	0	0	2

KNOXVILLE CHEROKEES

	Games	G.	A.	Pts.	Pen.
Rob Hrytsak, Johnstown	10	1	7	8	33
Knoxville	38	17	37	54	51
Totals	48	18	44	62	84
Darren Banks	52	25	22	47	258
Brad Courteau	59	18	29	47	80
Gabby McDuff, Virginia	3	2	1	3	4
Knoxville	30	21	21	42	47
Totals	33	23	22	45	51
Greg Batters	46	13	29	42	210
Tom Sasso	43	17	23	40	10
Doug Davis	50	15	21	36	19
Quinton Brickley	24	14	18	32	0
Mike Murray	21	11	17	28	4
Jeff Lindsay	47	6	22	28	131
Perry Florio	53	8	16	24	114
Mike Paller	34	10	12	22	21
Patrick Noiseux	38	9	12	21	31
Barry Burkholder	23	10	9	19	17
Scott Callow	26	7	11	18	29
Sean Mangan	43	2	15	17	79
John O'Donnell	25	2	11	13	37
Mike Bishop	22	3	9	12	28
Scott Somerville	23	2	7	9	54
Max Daviault	22	0	8	8	47
Steve Ryding	27	0	6	6	58
Alex Daviault	12	2	3	5	120
Troy Pohle	10	2	2	4	56
Don Herczog	4	0	4	4	23
Marc Straub	5	2	1	3	2
Bryant Perrier	8	1	2	3	10
Arron Scott	6	1	1	2	0
Darren Srochenski	5	0	1	1	13
Mike Schwalb	11	0	1	1	0
Dean Anderson (Goalie)	17	0	1	1	10
Mike Kelly	1	0	0	0	0
Andre Lapensee (Goalie)	2	0	0	0	0
Larry Dyck (Goalie)	3	0	0	0	0
Andy Stewart	3	0	0	0	0
Ross McKay (Goalie)	8	0	0	0	2
Tony Mongillo (Goalie)	13	0	0	0	17
Steve Averill, Virginia (G.)	14	0	0	0	0
Knoxville (Goalie)	1	0	0	0	0
Totals	15	0	0	0	7
John Blue (Goalie)	19	...	...	...	...

NASHVILLE KNIGHTS

	Games	G.	A.	Pts.	Pen.
Glen Engevik	53	45	39	84	74
Rob Levasseur	60	35	30	65	115
Andre Brassard	56	20	41	61	131
Todd Jenkins	38	17	36	53	14
Bill Huard	34	24	27	51	212
Mike Marcinkiewicz, John.	9	2	3	5	42
Nashville	41	21	20	41	79
Totals	50	23	23	46	121
Mike Bukta	56	9	32	41	86
Jeff Salzbrun	44	17	22	39	155
Scott Rettew	27	10	28	38	121
Pat Bingam	39	7	30	37	175
Ed Krayer	55	7	25	32	23
Chris Cambio	52	13	16	29	21
Bob Kennedy	38	5	17	22	28
Scott Rettew	10	4	13	17	30
Dan O'Brien	33	4	9	13	88
Garth Lamb	33	1	10	11	67

	Games	G.	A.	Pts.	Pen.
Brock Kelly, Johnstown	7	0	1	1	68
Nashville	43	2	6	8	257
Totals	50	2	7	9	*325
Ron Servatius	27	3	5	8	72
Jason Simon	13	4	3	7	81
Guy Phillips	3	3	4	7	2
Greg Simeone	15	0	4	4	53
Darwin Bozek	11	0	3	3	20
John Reid (Goalie)	36	0	3	3	66
Steve Dickson	5	0	1	1	39
Darryle Gilmour (Goalie)	15	0	1	1	0
Scott Johnson	1	0	0	0	0
Terry McCutheon	1	0	0	0	0
Troy Crowder	3	0	0	0	15
Dan Deliandias (Goalie)	5	0	0	0	0

VIRGINIA LANCERS

	Games	G.	A.	Pts.	Pen.
Mike Chighisola	49	30	26	56	137
Jeff Waver	55	28	20	48	73
Greg Neish	49	19	28	47	215
Graham Stanley	33	23	23	46	217
Dan Richards	60	23	23	46	14
Scott Drevitch	40	14	31	45	46
Luke Vitale	59	14	27	41	20
Chris Linberg	26	11	23	34	27
Terry Menard	24	14	18	32	28
Bill Whitfield	60	9	22	31	113
Michelle Couvrette	11	12	11	23	10
Marco Fuster	29	7	16	23	118
Al Legget	59	3	17	20	79
Doug Hobson	46	2	16	18	135
Bill Gutenberg	31	8	7	15	13
Denis Paul	11	3	7	10	4
Darren Miciak, Knoxville	14	2	1	3	117
Virginia	2	2	0	2	15
Hampton-Roads	16	1	2	3	74
Totals	32	5	3	8	206
Randy Taylor	7	0	8	8	4
Jim Alcott	17	4	3	7	57
Shannon Travis	7	1	6	7	16
Steve Herniman	31	2	4	6	238
Shawn Clouston	5	3	2	5	14
Marty Rouse	4	3	1	4	2
Geoff Benic	5	2	2	4	6
Barry Niechar	5	2	2	4	27
Michael Black	9	1	3	4	2
Stephane Boudreau	10	1	3	4	8
Kurt Lackton	8	0	4	4	7
Wayne Muir	1	1	2	3	0
Ron Jones	3	1	2	3	4
Steve Chelios	5	1	2	3	4
Scott Sanders	6	1	1	2	0
Steve McKichan (Goalie)	27	0	1	1	48
Dana Demole	2	0	0	0	0
Chris Clifford (Goalie)	9	0	0	0	2
Dean Cook (Goalie)	11	0	0	0	2

WINSTON-SALEM THUNDERBIRDS

	Games	G.	A.	Pts.	Pen.
Len Soccio	60	51	62	113	87
Joe Ferras	49	45	63	108	56
Trent Kaese	57	56	51	107	110
John Devereaux	58	22	48	70	110
Troy Vohlhoffer	46	26	40	66	157
Dave Doucette, Erie	37	6	31	37	17
Winston-Salem	21	3	23	26	22
Totals	58	9	54	63	39
John Torchetti	47	23	21	44	82
Guy Jacob	28	13	17	30	49
Bob Wensley	53	7	19	26	65
Dan Shea	15	7	18	25	8
Marc West	18	6	17	23	13
Richard Novak	26	10	12	22	17
Randy Irving	45	0	22	22	85
Jeff Greene	54	4	11	15	159
Dave Wensley	16	9	5	14	4
Jamie Russell	29	5	9	14	41
Steve Shaunessey	51	2	12	14	247
Andy Black	13	4	3	7	2
Ron Rolston	7	1	5	6	2
Shane Doyle	7	1	4	5	44
Chris Delaney	6	1	3	4	0
Kenton Rein (Goalie)	24	0	3	3	18
Joe West	1	1	1	2	0
Ron Aubrey, Nashville	6	1	0	1	7
Winston-Salem	5	0	0	0	74
Totals	11	1	0	1	81

	Games	G.	A.	Pts.	Pen.
George Maneluk (Goalie) ..	3	0	1	1	7
Paul Cohen (Goalie)	18	0	1	1	10

	Games	G.	A.	Pts.	Pen.
Dan Olsen (Goalie)	1	0	0	0	2
Chris Pusey (Goalie)	3	0	0	0	4

	Games	G.	A.	Pts.	Pen.
Mike Schwalb, Nash. (G.) .	6	....	....	....	....
Winston-Salem (Goalie)	2	....	....	....	....
Totals............................	8	....	....	....	....

INDIVIDUAL ECHL GOALTENDING

	Games	Mins.	Goals	Avg.
Chris Clifford, Virginia	10	547	16	*1.76
Ross McKay, Knoxville	8	426	20	2.82
Steve Averill, Virginia	14	695	42	3.63
Knoxville	1	60	2	2.00
Totals..	15	755	44	3.50
Alain Raymond, Hampton-Roads.....................	31	2048	123	3.60
Frank Furlan, Hampton-Roads	7	380	24	3.79
Paul Cohen, Winston-Salem	18	1058	68	3.86
Mike Jeffery, Johnstown	14	755	49	3.89
Kenton Rein, Winston-Salem	24	1353	88	3.90
Larry Dyck, Knoxville	3	184	12	3.91
Craig Barnett, Erie	*38	*2244	147	3.93
Steve McKichan, Virginia	28	1445	97	4.03
Dan Deliandis, Nashville	5	264	18	4.09
Mike Rosati, Erie	18	1056	73	4.15
Dean Cook, Virginia	11	546	38	4.18
Chris Pusey, Winston-Salem	3	180	13	4.33
Dean Anderson, Knoxville	17	997	73	4.39
Wade Flaherty, Greensboro	27	1308	96	4.40
John Reid, Nashville	36	2004	*149	4.46
Richard Burtchill, Johnstown	32	1704	130	4.58
Nick Vitucci, Winston-Salem	6	360	28	4.67
Greensboro	28	1496	114	4.57
Totals..	34	1856	142	4.59
George Maneluk, Winston-Salem	3	140	11	4.71
Darryle Gilmour, Nashville	10	529	43	4.88
Jocelyn Perreault, Greensboro	6	294	24	4.90
Scott Brower, Erie	5	243	20	4.94
Randy Hansch, Hampton-Roads	4	240	20	5.00
Elias Delaney, Greensboro	1	60	5	5.00
John Blue, Knoxville	19	1000	85	5.10

	Games	Mins.	Goals	Avg.
Tim Flanagan Johnstown...............................	7	280	24	5.14
Mike Schwalb, Nashville	6	305	28	5.51
Winston-Salem	2	120	9	4.50
Totals..	8	425	37	5.22
John Haley, Erie	3	87	8	5.52
Tony Mongillo, Knoxville	11	444	41	5.54
Darren McClusky, Johnstown	7	379	34	5.38
Hampton-Roads	9	525	43	4.91
Greensboro	2	88	15	10.23
Totals..	18	992	92	5.56
Ken Weiss, Virginia	2	75	12	9.60
Hampton-Roads	2	120	8	4.00
Totals..	4	195	20	6.15
Trevor Kruger, Hampton-Roads	7	287	30	6.28
Mark Benard, Johnstown	9	385	47	7.32
Andre Lapensee, Knoxville	2	55	7	7.64
J. R. Reich, Hampton-Roads	2	10	2	12.00
Dan Olson, Winston-Salem	1	7	3	25.7

INDIVIDUAL 1989-90 LEADERS

Goals ....Bill McDougall, Erie— 80
Assists ....Murray Hood, Hampton-Roads— 69
Points ....Bill McDougall, Erie— 148
Penalty Minutes...............................Brock Kelly, Johnstown-Nashville— 325
Goaltending Average ....Chris Clifford, Virginia—1.76
Note: No regular-season shutouts recorded.

1990 ECHL PLAYOFFS

QUARTERFINALS

Series "A"
(Best-of-seven)

	W.	L.	Pts.	GF.	GA.
Winston-Salem................	4	1	8	26	15
Nashville	1	4	2	15	26

(Winston-Salem wins series, 4 games to 1)

Series "B"
(Best-of-five)

	W.	L.	Pts.	GF.	GA.
Erie	3	2	6	24	22
Hampton-Roads...............	2	3	4	22	24

(Erie wins series, 3 games to 2)

Series "C"
(Best-of-five)

	W.	L.	Pts.	GF.	GA.
Greensboro......................	3	1	6	14	11
Virginia	1	3	2	11	14

(Greensboro wins series, 3 games to 1)

SEMIFINALS

Series "D"
(Best-of-three)

	W.	L.	Pts.	GF.	GA.
Greensboro......................	2	0	4	7	5
Erie	0	2	0	5	7

(Greensboro wins series, 2 games to 0)

FINALS FOR THE RILEY CUP

Series "E"
(Best-of-seven)

	W.	L.	Pts.	GF.	GA.
Greensboro......................	4	1	8	21	14
Winston-Salem................	1	4	2	14	21

(Greensboro wins series and playoffs, 4 games to 1)

TOP 10 PLAYOFF SCORERS

	Games	G.	A.	Pts.
1. Len Soccio, Winston-Salem	10	5	12	*17
2. Joe Ferras, Winston-Salem	10	3	*13	16
3. Phil Berger, Greensboro............	10	*11	3	14
Troy Vohlhoffer, W.-S..............	9	8	6	14
Scott White, Greensboro............	11	4	10	14
6. Joe West, Winston-Salem	10	7	6	13
Chris Robertson, Greensboro	11	5	8	13
8. Mike McCormick, Greensboro	11	7	4	11
Dan Shea, Winston-Salem........	10	5	6	11
Boyd Sutton, Greensboro........	10	2	9	11

TEAM-BY-TEAM PLAYOFF SCORING

ERIE PANTHERS

(Lost semifinals to Greensboro, 2 games to 0)

	Games	G.	A.	Pts.	Pen.
Bill McDougall	7	5	5	10	20
Doug Stromback	7	4	5	9	0
Ryan Kummu	7	0	8	8	10
Martin Bergeron	7	3	4	7	20
Peter Buckridge	7	2	4	6	6
Barry Chyzowski	5	4	1	5	0
Daryl Harpe	7	2	3	5	22
Mike Vellucci	7	1	4	5	6
Doug Marsden	7	3	1	4	6
Steve Weinke	7	0	4	4	21
Rob McDougall	6	2	0	2	43

	Games	G.	A.	Pts.	Pen.
Rob Gador	7	1	1	2	14
Grant Ottenbreit................	7	1	1	2	46
Craig Barnett (Goalie)	7	0	2	2	2
Rich Stromback	1	1	0	1	0
Anti Autere	6	0	1	1	6
Craig Kitteringham	1	0	0	0	7
Jerry Tarrant....................	1	0	0	0	0

GREENSBORO MONARCHS

(Winners of ECHL Playoffs)

	Games	G.	A.	Pts.	Pen.
Phil Berger	10	*11	3	14	32

	Games	G.	A.	Pts.	Pen.
Scott White	11	4	10	14	24
Chris Robertson	11	5	8	13	7
Mike McCormick	11	7	4	11	19
Boyd Sutton	10	2	9	11	26
John Blessman	11	3	6	9	50
Doug Lawrence	11	2	7	9	67
Chad Thompson	11	0	9	9	6
Chris Laganas	10	4	2	6	30
John Sullivan	11	3	2	5	38
Mike Butters	11	1	4	5	*82
Bruce Major	10	2	2	4	12
Doug Brown	11	3	0	3	41
Daniel Bock	5	0	1	1	6
Wade Flaherty (Goalie)	9	0	1	1	2
Nick Vitucci (Goalie)	3	0	0	0	19
Steve McKinley	9	0	0	0	26

HAMPTON-ROADS ADMIRALS

(Lost quarterfinals to Erie, 3 games to 2)

	Games	G.	A.	Pts.	Pen.
Trevor Jobe	5	5	5	10	30
Dennis McEwen	5	5	1	6	30
Don Gagne	5	2	4	6	18
Kent Hawley	5	2	3	5	17
Brian Martin	5	1	4	5	6
Steve Greenberg	5	3	1	4	4
Chris Lukey	5	1	3	4	27
Wayne Stripp	5	1	3	4	9
Rob Krauss	5	0	4	4	23
Jody Praznik	5	0	4	4	0
Mark Vachon	4	1	1	2	13
Daren Banister	4	0	2	2	9
Alain Raymond (Goalie)	5	0	2	2	2
Pat Cavanaugh	1	1	0	1	11
David Buckley	5	0	1	1	11
Jamie Kompon	5	0	0	0	25

NASHVILLE KNIGHTS

(Lost quarterfinals to Winston-Salem, 4 games to 1)

	Games	G.	A.	Pts.	Pen.
Glen Engevik	5	3	2	5	27
Chris Cambio	5	2	3	5	0
Jeff Salzbrun	5	1	4	5	11

	Games	G.	A.	Pts.	Pen.
Mike Marcinkiewicz	4	2	2	4	4
Rob Levasseur	5	2	2	4	20
Jason Simon	5	1	3	4	17
Dan O'Brien	5	2	1	3	10
Scott Rettew	5	1	2	3	6
Ed Krayer	4	0	2	2	2
Darwin Bozek	5	0	2	2	0
Brock Kelly	5	0	2	2	32
Bob Kennedy	5	0	2	2	2
Andre Brassard	5	1	0	1	12
John Reid (Goalie)	3	0	1	1	0
Mike Bukta	5	0	1	1	8
Dan Deliandis (Goalie)	2	0	0	0	0

VIRGINIA LANCERS

(Lost quarterfinals to Greensboro, 3 games to 1)

	Games	G.	A.	Pts.	Pen.
Scott Drevitch	4	3	3	6	10
Jeff Waver	4	1	4	5	4
Dan Richards	4	3	0	3	4
Al Legget	4	1	2	3	4
Chris Lindberg	4	0	3	3	2
Luke Vitale	4	0	3	3	2
Graham Stanley	4	1	1	2	12
Marty Rouse	2	1	0	1	0
Bill Whitfield	2	1	0	1	0
Doug Hobson	4	0	1	1	10
Dean Cook (Goalie)	1	0	0	0	0
Rick Kelly	1	0	0	0	0

	Games	G.	A.	Pts.	Pen.
Wayne Muir	1	0	0	0	0
Marco Fuster	2	0	0	0	19
Steve Herniman	3	0	0	0	29
Ron Jones	3	0	0	0	6
Steve McKichan (Goalie)	3	0	0	0	25
Greg Neish	4	0	0	0	40
Shannon Travis	4	0	0	0	2

WINSTON-SALEM THUNDERBIRDS

(Lost finals to Greensboro, 4 games to 1)

	Games	G.	A.	Pts.	Pen.
Len Soccio	10	5	*12	*17	12
Joe Ferras	10	3	*13	16	30
Troy Vohlhoffer	9	8	6	14	23
Joe West	10	7	6	13	34
Dan Shea	10	5	6	11	17
Marc West	9	3	6	9	12
Dave Doucettte	10	0	8	8	4
Trent Kaese	8	5	1	6	18
Bob Wensley	10	2	2	4	20
John Devereaux	8	1	2	3	11
Randy Irving	9	0	2	2	31
Jeff Greene	10	0	2	2	39
John Torchetti	4	1	0	1	2
Jamie Russell	10	0	1	1	11
Steve Shaunessey	10	0	1	1	68
Paul Cohen (Goalie)	1	0	0	0	2
Kenton Rein (Goalie)	9	0	0	0	14

COMPLETE ECHL PLAYOFF GOALTENDING

	Games	Mins.	Goals	SO.	Avg.
Dean Cook, Virginia	1	60	2	0	2.00
Wade Flaherty, Greensboro	*9	567	21	0	*2.22
Nick Vitucci, Greensboro	3	153	7	0	2.75
Kenton Rein, Winston-Salem	*9	*570	28	0	2.95
Steve McKichan, Virginia	3	209	11	0	3.16
John Reid, Nashville	3	179	12	0	4.02
Craig Barnett, Erie	7	421	*29	0	4.13
Alain Raymond, Hampton-Roads	5	302	24	0	4.77
Dan Deliandis, Nashville	2	120	10	0	5.00
Paul Cohen, Winston-Salem	1	60	6	0	6.00

INDIVIDUAL ECHL PLAYOFF LEADERS

Goals .... Phil Berger, Greensboro— 11
Assists .... Joe Ferras, Winston-Salem— 13
Points .... Len Soccio, Winston-Salem— 17
Penalty Minutes .... Mike Butters, Greensboro— 82
Goaltending Average .... Wade Flaherty, Greensboro—2.22
Shutouts .... None

ECHL 1989-90 ALL-STARS

First Team	Position	Second Team
Alain Raymond, Hampton-Roads	Goalie	Craig Barnett, Erie
Dave Doucette, Winston-Salem	Defense	Jeff Lindsay, Knoxville
Bill Whitfield, Virginia	Defense	Scott Drevitch, Virginia
Andre Brassard, Nashville	Defense	
Bill McDougall, Erie	Forward	Joe Ferras, Winston-Salem
Trent Kaese, Winston-Salem	Forward	Glen Engevik, Nashville
Len Soccio, Winston-Salem	Forward	Trevor Jobe, Hampton-Roads
	Forward	Brian Martin, Hampton-Roads

ECHL 1989-90 TROPHY WINNERS

Most Valuable Player .... Bill McDougall, Erie
Top Scorer .... Bill McDougall, Erie
Top Defenseman .... Bill Whitfield, Virginia
Rookie of the Year .... Bill McDougall, Erie
Top Goaltender .... Alain Raymond, Hampton-Roads
Playoff MVP .... Wade Flaherty, Greensboro
Coach of the Year .... Dave Allison, Virginia

MOST VALUABLE PLAYER

Season	Player	Club
1981-82—	Dave MacQueen, Salem
1982-83—	Rory Cava, Carolina
1983-84—	Paul O'Neill, Virginia
1984-85—	Barry Tabobondung, Erie
1985-86—	Joe Curran, Carolina
1986-87—	Peter DeArmas, Virginia
1987-88—	John Torchetti, Carolina
1988-89—	Daryl Harpe, Erie
1989-90—	Bill McDougall, Erie

TOP SCORER

Season	Player	Club
1981-82—	Dave MacQueen, Salem
1982-83—	Dave Watson, Carolina
1983-84—	Rob Clavette, Pinebridge-Erie
1984-85—	Paul Mancini, Erie
1985-86—	Dave Herbst, Erie
1986-87—	Doug McCarthy, Carolina
1987-88—	John Torchetti, Carolina
1988-89—	Daryl Harpe, Erie
1989-90—	Bill McDougall, Erie

TOP GOALTENDER

Season	Player	Club
1981-82—	Gilles Moffet, Salem
1982-83—	Yves Dechene, Carolina
1983-84—	Darrell May, Erie
1984-85—	Dan Olson, Carolina
1985-86—	Ray LeBlanc, Carolina
1986-87—	Dana Demole, Virginia
1987-88—	Tim Flanigan, Virginia
1988-89—	Scott Gordon, Johnstown
1989-90—	Alain Raymond, Hampton-Roads

PLAYOFF MVP

Season	Player	Club
1984-85—	Brian Carroll, Carolina
1985-86—	Bob Dore, Carolina
1986-87—	Peter DeArmas, Virginia
	Dana Demole, Virginia (tie)
1987-88—	Tim Flanigan, Virginia
1988-89—	Nick Vitucci, Carolina
1989-90—	Wade Flaherty, Greensboro

ECHL CHAMPIONSHIP TEAMS

Regular Season Champion

Championship Team (Coach)
1981-82—Salem Raiders (Pat Kelly)
1982-83—Carolina Thunderbirds (Rick Dudley)
1983-84—Carolina Thunderbirds (Rick Dudley)
1984-85—Carolina Thunderbirds (Rick Dudley)
1985-86—Carolina Thunderbirds (Rick Dudley)
1986-87—Virginia Lancers (John Tortorella)
1987-88—Virginia Lancers (John Tortorella)
1988-89—Erie Panthers (Ron Hansis)
1989-90—Winston-Salem (McSorley, Fraser)

Bob Payne Trophy Playoff Champion

Championship Team (Coach)
Mohawk Valley Stars (Bill Horton)
Carolina Thunderbirds (Rick Dudley)
Erie Golden Blades (Bill Horton)
Carolina Thunderbirds (Rick Dudley)
Carolina Thunderbirds (Rick Dudley)
Virginia Lancers (John Tortorella)
Virginia Lancers (John Tortorella)
Carolina T'birds (Brendon Watson)
Erie Panthers (Ron Hansis)

ONTARIO HOCKEY LEAGUE

Commissioner
David E. Branch

Chairman of the Board
Dr. Robert Vaughan

Address
305 Milner Avenue
Suite 208
Scarborough, Ontario M1B 3V4
Phone—(416) 299-8700

Director of Administration
Herb Morell

Director of Information
Ted Baker

Director of Officiating
Ken Bodendistel

Director of Supervisors
Murray Darroch

Director of Central Scouting
Sheldon Ferguson

1989-90 FINAL OHL STANDINGS

MATT LEYDEN DIVISION

	G.	W.	L.	T.	Pts.	GF.	GA.
Oshawa Generals	66	42	20	4	88	334	244
Kingston Frontenacs	66	42	21	3	87	300	232
Peterborough Petes	66	37	23	6	80	294	236
Ottawa 67's	66	38	26	2	78	320	265
Belleville Bulls	66	36	26	4	76	301	247
Cornwall Royals	66	24	38	4	52	309	361
Dukes of Hamilton	66	11	49	6	28	211	371

HAP EMMS DIVISION

	G.	W.	L.	T.	Pts.	GF.	GA.
London Knights	66	41	19	6	88	313	246
Kitchener Rangers	66	38	21	7	83	358	259
Sudbury Wolves	66	36	23	7	79	295	267
Owen Sound Platers	66	28	31	7	63	265	305
North Bay Centennials	66	23	35	8	54	292	314
Niagara Falls Thunder	66	23	39	4	50	278	355
Sault Ste. Marie Greyhounds	66	18	42	6	42	229	289
Windsor Spitfires	66	17	41	8	42	233	341

NOTE: Sault Ste. Marie awarded seventh place in Emms Division based on 6-3-1, won-lost record over Windsor during regular season.

TOP 10 SCORERS FOR THE EDDIE POWERS MEMORIAL TROPHY

	Games	G.	A.	Pts.	Pen.
1. Keith Primeau, Niagara Falls	65	*57	70	*127	97
2. Paul DiPietro, Sudbury	66	56	63	119	57
3. Mike Ricci, Peterborough	60	52	64	116	39
4. Owen Nolan, Cornwall	58	51	60	111	240
5. Darcy Cahill, Cornwall	36	24	52	76	51
Sudbury	22	14	19	33	22
Totals	58	38	71	109	73

	Games	G.	A.	Pts.	Pen.
6. Brett Seguin, Ottawa	63	28	*80	108	30
7. Gilbert Dionne, Kitchener	64	48	57	105	85
Chris Taylor, London	66	45	60	105	60
Iain Fraser, Oshawa	56	40	65	105	75
10. Joey St. Aubin, Kitchener	66	36	68	104	102

TEAM-BY-TEAM BREAKDOWN OF OHL SCORING

BELLEVILLE BULLS

	Games	G.	A.	Pts.	Pen.
Bob Berg	66	48	49	97	124
John Porco	66	34	61	95	46
Rob Pearson	58	48	40	88	174
Richard Fatrola	66	17	46	63	72
Ted Miskolczi, Windsor	40	22	14	36	57
Belleville	28	12	13	25	32
Totals	68	34	27	61	89
Ken Rowbotham	66	29	31	60	46
Gord Pell, Cornwall	34	16	22	38	45
Belleville	21	8	9	17	25
Totals	55	24	31	55	70
Scott Thornton	47	21	28	49	91
Brent Gretzky	66	15	32	47	30
Steve Bancroft	53	10	33	43	135
Greg Bignell	58	6	35	41	141
Scott Boston	58	2	26	28	99
Darren McCarty	63	12	15	27	142
Jake Grimes	66	9	12	21	11
Sean O'Reilly	56	1	19	20	118
Craig Fraser	60	7	11	18	110
Derek Morin	56	5	11	16	118
Len DeVuono	30	4	8	12	52
Scott Feasby	26	1	4	5	39
Jason Skellett	39	0	5	5	49
Shawn Way	44	0	4	4	42
Jeff Fife (Goalie)	58	0	3	3	24
Norm Batherson	3	0	2	2	2
Brian Blaind	8	0	2	2	4
Bryan Helmer	6	0	1	1	0
Stu Tufts	6	0	1	1	0
Mike Kiley	1	0	0	0	0
Mark Rupnow	2	0	0	0	0
Jeff Smith	2	0	0	0	0
Rob Stopar (Goalie)	4	0	0	0	0
Greg Dreveny (Goalie)	14	0	0	0	6

CORNWALL ROYALS

	Games	G.	A.	Pts.	Pen.
Owen Nolan	58	51	60	111	240
John Slaney	64	38	59	97	60
Mike Jackson, Hamilton	15	8	13	21	41
Cornwall	26	15	29	44	59
Totals	41	23	42	65	100
Paul Cain	47	28	36	64	23
Jason Cirone	32	21	43	64	56
Darren Bell, Sudbury	43	8	16	24	50
Cornwall	25	6	13	19	29
Totals	68	14	29	43	79
Rob Knesaurek, Sudbury	25	5	12	17	38
Cornwall	32	11	14	25	52
Totals	57	16	26	42	90
Ron Jolie	62	10	28	38	90
Jeff Reid	62	13	20	33	30
Tom Nemeth	41	12	15	27	14
Guy Leveque	62	10	15	25	30
Chris Clancy	63	10	13	23	53
Craig Brocklehurst	52	9	14	23	19
Mark DeSantis	59	3	17	20	79
Rod Pasma	64	3	16	19	142
Todd Mondor	45	7	10	17	36
Jerry Ribble, London	25	1	4	5	18
Cornwall	37	5	5	10	41
Totals	62	6	9	15	59
Shawn Caplice	65	3	10	13	33
Jean Schneider	57	7	4	11	76
Marcus Middleton, Sby	25	1	1	2	28
Cornwall	25	2	3	5	48
Totals	50	3	4	7	76
Denis Leger	6	2	1	3	5
Darryl Paquette (Goalie)	44	0	4	4	16
Vern Ray	24	2	1	3	47
Jeff Murray	7	1	2	3	7

	Games	G.	A.	Pts.	Pen.
Kevin Meisner	6	0	3	3	10
Brent Brownlee (Goalie)	30	0	2	2	4
Troy Gleason	5	0	1	1	2
Jean-Paul Latreille	26	0	1	1	4
Todd Blackman, Kitchener	1	0	0	0	0
Cornwall	33	0	1	1	46
Totals	34	0	1	1	46
Jeff Nicholson	1	0	0	0	0
Justin Gray	2	0	0	0	0

DUKES OF HAMILTON

	Games	G.	A.	Pts.	Pen.
Joey Simon, Kingston	15	6	11	17	8
Hamilton	46	20	37	57	14
Totals	61	26	48	74	22
Shawn McCosh, Nia. Falls	9	6	10	16	24
Hamilton	39	24	28	52	65
Totals	48	30	38	68	89
Mike Reier	61	21	35	56	48
Steve Woods	62	24	30	54	33
Brad Gratton, Windsor	12	5	9	14	11
London	15	6	10	16	6
Hamilton	25	8	13	21	21
Totals	52	19	32	51	38
Chris Govedaris	23	11	21	32	53
Derek Booth, Sudbury	13	1	3	4	31
Hamilton	52	9	19	28	132
Totals	65	10	22	32	163
Clayton Martin	64	14	12	26	41
Rob Leask	43	6	18	24	50
Todd Gleason	64	5	12	17	79
Dale Chokan	37	7	7	14	71
Yvan Charrois, Ottawa	12	4	1	5	12
Hamilton	22	1	8	9	42
Totals	34	5	9	14	54
Bill Whistle	38	6	7	13	38

	Games	G.	A.	Pts.	Pen.
Jason Soules, Nia. Falls.....	9	2	8	10	20
Hamilton	18	0	2	2	42
Totals	27	2	10	12	62
Chris Code	35	5	6	11	31
Dave Ritchie	56	2	8	10	128
John Valo	31	3	6	9	38
Alek Stojanov	37	4	4	8	91
Kevin Mahony	27	2	6	8	177
Shawn Costello	38	5	2	7	19
Gary Taylor, Belleville	2	0	0	0	0
Hamilton	45	1	5	6	89
Totals	47	1	5	6	89
Jeff Smith	55	3	2	5	51
John Anger	11	1	3	4	2
Jason Braendle	5	1	1	2	7
Sloan Torti	9	0	2	2	6
Ralph DiPietro	3	0	1	1	0
Rob Ricketts	3	0	1	1	2
Rob Asselstine	5	0	1	1	0
Glen Craft	11	0	1	1	2
John Couch	21	0	1	1	21
Gus Morschauser, Kit. (G.)	6	0	0	0	6
Hamilton (Goalie)	38	0	1	1	26
Totals	44	0	1	1	32
Brad Costello	1	0	0	0	0
Steve Hanham (Goalie)	1	0	0	0	0
Jeff Bird (Goalie)	2	0	0	0	0
Dave Smeriglio (Goalie)	2	0	0	0	0
Mike LeBlanc	3	0	0	0	0
Luc Gagnon	6	0	0	0	7
Jamie Page	6	0	0	0	2
Dino Fellicetti	10	0	0	0	6
Andy Pearce	15	0	0	0	2
Dan Ryder, Sudbury (G.)	6	0	0	0	2
Hamilton (Goalie)	22	0	0	0	12
Totals	28	0	0	0	14

KINGSTON FRONTENACS

	Games	G.	A.	Pts.	Pen.
Mike Bodnarchuk	66	40	59	99	31
Wayne Doucet	66	32	47	79	127
Justin Morrison	65	27	40	67	201
Mark Major	62	29	32	61	168
Bob McKillop	66	28	33	61	42
Tony Iob	62	23	35	58	142
John Nelson, Hamilton	1	1	0	1	0
Kingston	45	20	36	56	125
Totals	46	21	36	57	125
Mike Cavanagh	66	11	38	49	55
Peter Liptrott, Windsor	40	10	28	38	89
Kingston	27	2	7	9	43
Totals	67	12	35	47	132
Jamie Allan	64	14	26	40	188
Tony Cimellaro	62	8	31	39	26
Matt Giesebrecht	64	17	21	38	52
Dave Stewart	52	5	24	29	94
Brock Woods	65	6	22	28	112
Brock Shyiak	57	3	21	24	55
Geoff Schneider	62	4	15	19	62
Gord Harris	51	7	7	14	50
Nathan LaFayette	53	6	8	14	14
Drake Berehowsky	9	3	11	14	28
Joel Washkurak	48	5	5	10	114
Sean Gauthier (Goalie)	32	0	3	3	6
Jeff Wilson (Goalie)	45	0	2	2	18
Derek MacNair	1	0	0	0	0
Greg Norman	1	0	0	0	0

KITCHENER RANGERS

	Games	G.	A.	Pts.	Pen.
Gilbert Dionne	64	48	57	105	85
Joey St. Aubin	66	36	68	104	102
Jason Firth	63	36	64	100	25
Shayne Stevenson	56	28	62	90	115
Steven Rice	58	39	37	76	102
Jason York, Windsor	39	9	30	39	38
Kitchener	25	11	25	36	17
Totals	64	20	55	75	55
Randy Pearce	62	31	34	65	139
Mark Montanari	33	15	36	51	71
Cory Keenan	66	13	35	48	88
Rival Fullum	61	20	25	45	64
John Uniac	57	9	35	44	38
Chris LiPuma	63	11	26	37	125
Richard Borgo	32	13	22	35	43
Rick Allain	55	5	16	21	156
Jack Williams	60	11	7	18	12
Steve Smith	47	6	9	15	35
Brad Barton	63	1	14	15	119

	Games	G.	A.	Pts.	Pen.
Gib Tucker	52	5	9	14	9
Tom Gemmell	18	8	5	13	6
Jamie Israel	52	3	1	4	33
John Copley	43	0	2	2	50
Mike Torchia (Goalie)	40	0	1	1	22
Mike Edwards (Goalie)	1	0	0	0	0
Ian Morgan	2	0	0	0	0
Neil Morgan	2	0	0	0	0
John Finnie (Goalie)	3	0	0	0	0
Gord Geisler	3	0	0	0	0
Vince Oldford	6	0	0	0	21
Mike Allen	11	0	0	0	0
Dave Schill, Hamilton (G.)	10	0	0	0	6
Kitchener (Goalie)	22	0	0	0	8
Totals	32	0	0	0	14

LONDON KNIGHTS

	Games	G.	A.	Pts.	Pen.
Chris Taylor	66	45	60	105	60
Rick Corriveau	63	22	55	77	63
Trevor Dam	56	20	54	74	91
Todd Hlushko, O. Sound	25	9	17	26	31
London	40	27	17	44	39
Totals	65	36	34	70	70
Dennis Purdie	63	23	39	62	143
Steve Boyd	64	15	39	54	85
Scott McKay	59	20	29	49	37
Steve Martell	63	19	24	43	91
Paul Holden	61	11	31	42	78
Louie DeBrusk	61	21	19	40	198
Doug Synishin	62	10	29	39	57
Dan LeBlanc	65	11	20	31	44
Dave Anderson, Niagara F.	21	6	10	16	29
London	30	5	9	14	26
Totals	51	11	19	30	55
Mark Guy	62	5	18	23	107
Aaron Nagy	61	9	13	22	12
Dave Noseworthy, O.S.	21	6	5	11	20
London	34	5	5	10	32
Totals	55	11	10	21	52
Chris Crombie	64	10	11	21	91
John Battice, Hamilton	4	0	1	1	14
London	25	4	16	20	35
Totals	29	4	17	21	49
Greg Ryan	65	4	10	14	73
Karl Taylor, Windsor	37	4	2	6	40
London	25	4	2	6	18
Totals	62	8	4	12	58
John Tanner, Peter. (G.)	18	0	1	1	37
London (Goalie)	19	0	5	5	24
Totals	37	0	6	6	61
Jeff Hogden	4	0	2	2	0
Barry Potomski	9	0	2	2	18
Pat Tenpenny (Goalie)	16	0	1	1	12
Brian Basque (Goalie)	1	0	0	0	0
Aurelio Cence	1	0	0	0	0
Dave Thompson	1	0	0	0	0
Mike Edwards (Goalie)	2	0	0	0	0
Steve Kavanagh	5	0	0	0	0
Peter Ing (Goalie)	8	0	0	0	0
Sean Basilio (Goalie)	28	0	0	0	6

NIAGARA FALLS THUNDER

	Games	G.	A.	Pts.	Pen.
Keith Primeau	65	*57	70	*127	97
Jason Winch, Hamilton	18	6	16	22	17
Niagara Falls	46	25	46	71	6
Totals	64	31	62	93	23
Brad May	61	33	58	91	223
John Johnson, Windsor	26	6	14	20	24
Niagara Falls	39	18	18	36	10
Totals	65	24	32	56	34
Greg Suchan, Hamilton	18	7	10	17	14
Niagara Falls	43	11	27	38	38
Totals	61	18	37	55	52
Paul Laus	60	13	35	48	231
Don McConnell, S.S.M.	16	2	6	8	6
Niagara Falls	48	13	19	32	18
Totals	64	15	25	40	24
Andy Bezeau	60	20	19	39	206
Greg Allen	60	13	23	36	79
Mark Lawrence	54	15	18	33	126
Paul Wolanski	63	8	20	28	57
Jeff Walker	60	7	17	24	75
Don Pancoe	61	2	16	18	114
Mike St. John, Peter.	28	5	5	10	9
Niagara Falls	28	3	4	7	2
Totals	56	8	9	17	11
Ken Ruddick	54	5	12	17	85

	Games	G.	A.	Pts.	Pen.
Todd Coopman, Oshawa	16	2	2	4	4
Niagara Falls	32	0	12	12	21
Totals	48	2	14	16	25
Geoff Rawson	62	3	5	8	63
Brian Mueggler, Kingston	8	0	0	0	6
Niagara Falls	48	2	5	7	10
Totals	56	2	5	7	16
David Benn	51	3	2	5	108
Trevor Renkers	1	1	0	1	4
Drew Rees	9	1	0	1	7
Dan Krisko	12	1	0	1	0
Rick Girhiny	1	0	1	1	0
Adrian VanDerSloot	6	0	1	1	20
Todd Simon	9	0	1	1	2
Roch Belley (Goalie)	23	0	1	1	10
Devon Colquhoun	24	0	1	1	24
Steve Udvari, S.S.M. (G.)	15	0	1	1	4
Niagara Falls (Goalie)	46	0	1	1	22
Totals	61	0	1	1	26
Joe Buote (Goalie)	2	0	0	0	0
Todd Reynolds (Goalie)	2	0	0	0	4
Tom Chapman	4	0	0	0	0
Ryan Hughes	8	0	0	0	2

NORTH BAY CENTENNIALS

	Games	G.	A.	Pts.	Pen.
John Spoltore	66	34	48	82	45
Derek Switzer	64	31	46	77	28
Tyler Ertel	63	31	43	74	108
Shawn Antoski	59	25	31	56	201
Jason Corrigan	66	24	29	53	53
Derian Hatcher	64	14	38	52	81
John Vary	59	7	39	46	79
Jamie Caruso	61	17	28	45	104
Trevor Halverson	54	22	20	42	162
Robert Deschamps	51	14	23	37	66
Jeff Gardiner	60	12	19	31	11
Gary Miller	50	5	26	31	69
Shayne Antoski	48	14	15	29	92
John Van Kessel	40	7	21	28	127
Colin Austin	52	12	15	27	91
Tom Purcell	60	4	17	21	107
Joel Morin	55	11	8	19	54
Tim Favot	64	4	9	13	43
Robert Frayn	43	1	10	11	40
Jason Beaton	53	1	4	5	126
Trevor Smith, Sudbury	18	1	1	2	19
North Bay	1	0	0	0	0
Totals	19	1	1	2	19
Chris Ottmann	12	0	2	2	7
Andy Hardy	25	0	2	2	8
Mike Short	1	0	0	0	2
Rob Krmpotic	2	0	0	0	0
Mike Matuszek (Goalie)	14	0	0	0	4
Rob Fournier, Niag. F. (G.)	1	0	0	0	0
North Bay (Goalie)	24	0	0	0	10
Totals	25	0	0	0	10
Ron Bertrand (Goalie)	35	0	0	0	20

OSHAWA GENERALS

	Games	G.	A.	Pts.	Pen.
Iain Fraser	56	40	65	105	75
Brent Grieve	62	46	47	93	125
Jarrod Skalde	62	40	52	92	66
Mike Craig	43	36	40	76	85
Dale Craigwell	64	22	41	63	39
Craig Donaldson	64	11	44	55	43
Joe Busillo	59	19	29	48	148
Cory Banika	63	17	22	39	201
Jean-Paul Davis	60	7	30	37	42
Eric Lindros	25	17	19	36	61
Matt Hoffman	61	16	17	33	68
Scott Luik	34	15	15	30	20
Clair Cornish	60	6	21	27	33
David Craievich	59	6	18	24	127
Paul O'Hagan	66	1	23	24	162
Trevor McIvor	49	5	13	18	25
Bill Armstrong, Hamilton	18	0	2	2	38
Niagara Falls	4	0	1	1	13
Oshawa	41	2	8	10	115
Totals	63	2	11	13	166
Scott Hollis	50	4	6	10	33
Brian Grieve	54	1	7	8	40
Wade Simpson	48	0	8	8	26
Mark Deazeley	27	3	1	4	56
Rick Cormier, Niagara Falls	1	0	0	0	0
Oshawa	5	3	0	3	0
Totals	6	3	0	3	0

	Games	G.	A.	Pts.	Pen.
Jan Benda	1	0	1	1	0
Fred Brathwaite (G.)	20	0	1	1	4
Kevin Butt (Goalie)	49	0	1	1	34
Derek Pifer	1	0	0	0	0
Chris Vanclief	3	0	0	0	0

OTTAWA 67's

	Games	G.	A.	Pts.	Pen.
Brett Seguin	63	28	80	108	30
Greg Walters	63	36	54	90	57
Chris Snell	63	18	62	80	36
Chris Simon	57	36	38	74	146
Troy Binnie	66	34	40	74	41
Joni Lehto	60	17	55	72	58
Ryan Kuwabara	66	30	38	68	62
Steve Kluczkowski	62	32	32	64	36
Jerrett DeFazio	54	22	30	52	18
Rob Sangster, Kitchener	24	6	18	24	151
Ottawa	21	2	8	10	100
Totals	45	8	26	34	251
Peter Ambroziak	60	13	19	32	37
Jeff Ricciardi	61	4	28	32	206
Greg Clancy	61	10	21	31	26
Jim Dean, Sault Ste. Marie	15	6	10	16	24
Ottawa	8	3	6	9	0
Totals	23	9	16	25	24
John East	62	5	19	24	103
Joey McTamney	56	11	11	22	26
Dan Poirier, Belleville	22	4	4	8	41
Ottawa	36	4	5	9	62
Totals	58	8	9	17	103
Gairin Smith	53	6	6	12	43
Scott McPherson	31	2	5	7	11
Wade Gibson	44	2	2	4	45
Andrew Brodie	24	0	2	2	54
Peter McGlynn (Goalie)	47	0	2	2	20
Chris Larkin	4	0	1	1	6
Bob McCleary	2	0	0	0	0
Luc Proulx (Goalie)	2	0	0	0	0
Kim Wahlsten	2	0	0	0	7
Craig Wilson	20	0	0	0	19
George Dourian (Goalie)	30	0	0	0	4

OWEN SOUND PLATERS

	Games	G.	A.	Pts.	Pen.
Jamey Hicks, Peterborough	2	0	3	3	4
Owen Sound	57	36	54	90	65
Totals	59	36	57	93	69
Jeff Christian, London	18	14	7	21	64
Owen Sound	37	19	26	45	145
Totals	55	33	33	66	209
Mike Speer	61	18	39	57	176
Owen Lessard	45	22	33	55	77
Grayden Reid	52	18	36	54	86
Sean Whyte	54	23	30	53	90
Ray Edwards	56	23	29	52	201
Jeff Perry	54	16	35	51	125
Keith Whitmore	64	11	34	45	105
Kirk Maltby	61	12	15	27	90
Steve Parson	58	13	12	25	51
Cory Pageau, North Bay	4	2	0	2	6
Owen Sound	54	8	13	21	138
Totals	58	10	13	23	144
Bryan Drury	65	5	18	23	74
Mark Strohack	66	4	17	21	63
Chris Driscoll	47	11	9	20	26
Jeff Ballantyne, Ottawa	15	1	4	5	51
Owen Sound	43	4	10	14	85
Totals	58	5	14	19	136
Jeff Grant	57	4	6	10	51
Maurice O'Brien	32	0	6	6	13
Mike Murray	32	1	4	5	40
Trent Cull	57	0	5	5	53
Jeff Cantlon, Belleville	2	0	0	0	11
Owen Sound	17	2	0	2	35
Totals	19	2	0	2	46
Todd Hunter (Goalie)	23	0	1	1	4
Mike Parson (Goalie)	49	0	1	1	10
Mark Henderson	1	0	0	0	0
Yanik Leduc	1	0	0	0	0
Marc Orr (Goalie)	1	0	0	0	0
Kevin Sutter	1	0	0	0	0
Scott Ballantyne (Goalie)	2	0	0	0	0
Dave Bonnar	3	0	0	0	0
Des Brown	3	0	0	0	0
Wade Laferriere	3	0	0	0	2
Jason Castellan	6	0	0	0	2

PETERBOROUGH PETES

	Games	G.	A.	Pts.	Pen.
Mike Ricci	60	52	64	116	39
Chris Longo	66	33	42	75	48
Troy Stephens	65	30	35	65	22
Dale McTavish	66	26	35	61	34
Dave Lorentz	57	22	32	54	55
Mark Myles	59	21	27	48	120
Joe Hawley	66	8	39	47	59
Geoff Ingram	66	13	29	42	103
Jamie Pegg	54	6	35	41	49
Mike Dagenais	44	14	26	40	74
Mike Tomlinson	66	21	15	36	60
Jason Dawe	50	15	18	33	19
Dan Brown	65	5	23	28	82
Scott Campbell	61	3	24	27	63
Paul Mitton	65	6	11	17	156
Bryan Gendron	46	4	9	13	96
Don O'Neill	51	5	6	11	110
Jassen Cullimore	59	2	6	8	61
Doug Searle	43	3	4	7	12
Brent Pope	31	0	7	7	14
Todd Bojcun (Goalie)	41	0	2	2	14
Tom Hopkins	16	0	1	1	32
Willie McGarvey	2	0	0	0	2
Andrew Verner (Goalie)	13	0	0	0	4

SAULT STE. MARIE GREYHOUNDS

	Games	G.	A.	Pts.	Pen.
Colin Miller, Niagara Falls	14	3	5	8	6
Sault Ste. Marie	44	25	46	71	33
Totals	58	28	51	79	39
Wayne Muir	62	40	21	61	210
Adam Foote	61	12	43	55	199
Denny Lambert	61	23	29	52	*276
Bob Jones	56	15	37	52	77
Brad Tiley	66	9	32	41	47
Jason Denomme, Oshawa	28	5	6	11	27
Sault Ste. Marie	28	13	10	23	34
Totals	56	18	16	34	61
Jim Ritchie	62	13	21	34	134
Bob Boughner	49	7	23	30	122
David Carrie, Niagara Falls	9	3	3	6	4
Sault Ste. Marie	34	10	13	23	14
Totals	43	13	16	29	18
Mike DeCoff, Oshawa	21	10	7	17	46
Sault Ste. Marie	13	6	5	11	10
Totals	34	16	12	28	56
Fred Goltz, Oshawa	3	0	1	1	0
Sault Ste. Marie	48	6	20	26	34
Totals	51	6	21	27	34
Kevin King	53	4	14	18	2
Dale Turnbull	21	8	5	13	16
Wade Whitten	60	6	6	12	46
Doug Minor	66	6	4	10	129
Shawn Simpson	22	5	3	8	8
Jeff Szeryk	40	5	2	7	42
Dave Matsos	53	2	5	7	31
David Doucette	42	2	3	5	15
Dan Ferguson	58	1	4	5	139
David Babcock	58	1	2	3	49
Derek Jefferson	5	0	2	2	0
Ron Solomon	13	0	2	2	0
Paul Silva	2	1	0	1	0
Rick Kowalsky	43	1	0	1	23
Chris Kraemer	2	0	1	1	7
Ian Northpeigan	2	0	0	0	0
Craig Wright	5	0	0	0	2
Steve Greenberg	6	0	0	0	2
Lyle Peel, Nia. Falls (G.)	5	0	0	0	0
Sault Ste. Marie (G.)	1	0	0	0	0
Totals	6	0	0	0	0
Rick Pracey (Goalie)	10	0	0	0	4
Graeme Harvey (Goalie)	29	0	0	0	12
Mike Lenarduzzi, Osh. (G.)	12	0	0	0	0
Sault Ste. Marie (G.)	20	0	0	0	0
Totals	32	0	0	0	0

SUDBURY WOLVES

	Games	G.	A.	Pts.	Pen.
Paul DiPietro	66	56	63	119	57
Darcy Cahill, Cornwall	36	24	52	76	51
Sudbury	22	14	19	33	22
Totals	58	38	71	109	73
Jason Young	62	26	47	73	64
Terry Chitaroni	65	21	47	68	173

	Games	G.	A.	Pts.	Pen.
Adam Bennett	65	18	43	61	116
Wade Bartley	60	23	36	59	53
Jim Sonmez	54	20	29	49	51
Glen Murray	62	8	28	36	17
Scott Mahoney	54	13	22	35	151
Jamie Matthews	60	16	17	33	25
Alastair Still	63	18	12	30	70
Andy MacVicar	41	12	16	28	47
Bill Kovacs, Hamilton	13	4	4	8	30
Sudbury	47	4	14	18	63
Totals	60	8	18	26	93
Sean O'Donnell	64	7	19	26	84
Alain Laforge, Nia. Falls	2	0	0	0	2
Sudbury	53	10	12	22	133
Totals	55	10	12	22	135
Kevin Falesy, Kitchener	37	3	8	11	53
Sudbury	21	2	2	4	28
Totals	58	5	10	15	81
Barry Young, Hamilton	13	2	0	2	24
Sudbury	47	1	11	12	62
Totals	60	3	11	14	86
Derek Etches	36	7	6	13	32
Leonard MacDonald	62	2	9	11	70
Neil Ethier	38	0	3	3	21
Derek Thompson	8	1	0	1	13
David Goverde (Goalie)	52	0	1	1	32
Tony MacAulay	2	0	0	0	5
Shane Sargant	8	0	0	0	9
Jon Boeve (Goalie)	17	0	0	0	4

WINDSOR SPITFIRES

	Games	G.	A.	Pts.	Pen.
Kevin White	66	22	49	71	63
Ron Jones	51	25	24	49	140
Ryan Merritt	66	22	23	45	87
Kevin MacKay, Belleville	27	8	9	17	13
Windsor	25	13	14	27	14
Totals	52	21	23	44	27
Jon Stos, London	11	2	8	10	8
Windsor	50	11	21	32	50
Totals	61	13	29	42	58
Mike Polano, Niagara Falls	27	3	15	18	56
Windsor	37	10	7	17	78
Totals	64	13	22	35	134
Bob Leeming	48	9	18	27	22
Sean Burns	65	8	18	26	197
Jason Stos	62	3	23	26	71
Jason Zohil	63	12	11	23	198
David Myles	52	11	8	19	75
Jason Snow, Kingston	37	4	5	9	30
Windsor	23	1	8	9	6
Totals	60	5	13	18	36
Brian Forestell	66	8	7	15	19
Steve Gibson	35	6	8	14	24
John Hartley	56	3	11	14	83
Trent Gleason	48	2	11	13	66
Trevor Walsh	42	6	5	11	121
Jamie Vargo, Kingston	5	0	1	1	5
Windsor	47	2	5	7	37
Totals	52	2	6	8	42
Chris Fraser, Ottawa	29	0	4	4	36
Windsor	19	0	4	4	26
Totals	48	0	8	8	62
Chris Lukey	7	2	2	4	4
Darren Dougan	25	1	3	4	4
Sean O'Hagan (Goalie)	43	0	4	4	14
Glen Craig	36	0	3	3	47
Kevin McDougall (Goalie)	32	0	2	2	12
Chad Badawey	2	0	0	0	4

COMPLETE OHL GOALTENDING

	Games	Mins.	Goals	SO.	Avg.
Jeff Fife	*58	*3206	188(5)	2	3.52
Greg Dreveny	14	632	44	0	4.18
Rob Stopar	4	146	10	0	4.11
Belleville Totals	66	3984	247	2	3.72
Darryl Paquette	44	2420	*213(5)	0	5.28
Brent Brownlee	30	1576	142(1)	0	5.41
Cornwall Totals	66	3996	361	0	5.42
David Schill (a)	10	585	45	1	4.62
Gus Morschauser (b)	38	2110	184(1)	0	5.23
Dan Ryder (c)	22	1121	115	0	6.16
Dave Smeriglio	2	125	15	0	7.20
Steve Hanham	1	29	5	0	10.34
Jeff Bird	2	25	6	0	14.40
Hamilton Totals	66	3995	371	1	5.57
Jeff Wilson	45	2383	129(1)	*3	3.25
Sean Gauthier	32	1602	101(1)	0	3.78
Kingston Totals	66	3985	232	3	3.49
Mike Torchia	40	2280	136(2)	1	3.58
Gus Morschauser (b)	6	345	22	0	3.83
David Schill (a)	22	1185	79(1)	1	4.00
John Finnie	3	129	10	0	4.65
Mike Edwards (d)	1	60	9	0	9.00
Kitchener Totals	66	3999	259	2	3.89
John Tanner (e)	19	1097	53(1)	1	2.90
Peter Ing	8	480	27	0	3.38
Brian Basque	1	53	3	0	3.40
Sean Basillo	28	1495	91(3)	1	3.65
Pat Tenpenny	16	811	61(1)	0	4.51
Mike Edwards (d)	2	72	6	0	5.00
London Totals	66	4008	246	2	3.68
Joe Buote	2	120	9	0	4.50
Steve Udvari (f)	46	2524	194	0	4.61
Roch Belley	23	1029	114	0	6.65
Lyle Peel (g)	5	171	19	0	6.67
Rob Fournier (h)	1	60	7	0	7.00
Todd Reynolds	2	94	12	0	7.66
Niagara Falls Totals	66	3998	355	0	5.33
Rob Fournier (h)	24	1342	92(2)	0	4.11
Ron Bertrand	35	1929	153(1)	1	4.76
Mike Matuszek	14	734	66	0	5.40
North Bay Totals	66	4005	314	1	4.70
Fred Brathwaite	20	901	45(1)	1	3.00
Kevin Butt	49	2640	164(1)	2	3.73
Mike Lenarduzzi (i)	12	444	32(1)	0	4.32
Oshawa Totals	66	3985	244	3	3.67
Peter McGlynn	47	2514	159(2)	0	3.79
George Dourian	30	1391	96(1)	0	4.14
Luc Proulx	2	84	7	0	5.00
Ottawa Totals	66	3989	265	0	3.99
Marc Orr	1	38	6	0	9.47
Todd Hunter	23	1149	84(3)	1	4.39
Mike Parson	49	2735	200(4)	1	4.39
Scott Ballantyne	2	80	8	0	6.00
Owen Sound Totals	66	4002	305	2	4.57
Todd Bojcun	41	2345	125(2)	1	*3.20
Andrew Verner	13	624	38	0	3.65
John Tanner (e)	18	1037	70(1)	0	4.05
Peterborough Totals	66	4006	236	1	3.53
Mike Lenarduzzi (i)	20	1117	66(2)	0	3.55
Steve Udvari (f)	15	788	53(1)	0	4.04
Graeme Harvey	29	1607	119	0	4.44
Rick Pracey	10	462	42	0	5.45
Lyle Peel (g)	1	26	6	0	13.85
Sault Ste. Marie Totals	66	4000	289	0	4.33
David Goverde	52	2941	182(2)	0	3.71
Dan Ryder (c)	6	218	15	0	4.13
Jon Boeve	17	850	64(4)	0	4.52
Sudbury Totals	66	4009	267	0	4.00
Sean O'Hagen	43	2416	193(4)	0	4.79
Kevin McDougall	32	1598	141(3)	0	5.29
Windsor Totals	66	4014	341	0	5.10

( )—Empty Net Goals. Do not count against a Goaltender's average.
(a)—Schill played for Hamilton and Kitchener.
(b)—Morschauser played for Hamilton and Kitchener.
(c)—Ryder played for Hamilton and Sudbury.
(d)—Edwards played for Kitchener and London.
(e)—Tanner played for London and Peterborough.
(f)—Udvari played for Niagara Falls and Sault Ste. Marie.
(g)—Peel played for Niagara Falls and Sault Ste. Marie.
(h)—Fournier played for Niagara Falls and North Bay.
(i)—Lenarduzzi played for Oshawa and Sault Ste. Marie.

INDIVIDUAL 1989-90 LEADERS

Goals	Keith Primeau, Niagara Falls— 57
Assists	Brett Seguin, Ottawa— 80
Points	Keith Primeau, Niagara Falls— 127
Penalty Minutes	Denny Lambert, Sault Ste. Marie— 276
Goaltender's Average	Todd Bojcun, Peterborough—3.20
Shutouts	Jeff Wilson, Kingston— 3

1990 J. ROSS ROBERTSON CUP PLAYOFFS

(All series best-of-seven)

QUARTERFINALS

LEYDEN DIVISION

Series "A"

	W.	L.	Pts.	GF.	GA.
Oshawa	4	2	8	39	27
Cornwall	2	4	4	27	39

(Oshawa wins series, 4 games to 2)

Series "B"

	W.	L.	Pts.	GF.	GA.
Belleville	4	3	8	27	25
Kingston	3	4	6	25	27

(Belleville wins series, 4 games to 3)

Series "C"

	W.	L.	Pts.	GF.	GA.
Peterborough	4	0	8	15	7
Ottawa	0	4	0	7	15

(Peterborough wins series, 4 games to 0)

EMMS DIVISION

Series "A"

	W.	L.	Pts.	GF.	GA.
Niagara Falls	4	2	8	26	22
London	2	4	4	22	26

(Niagara Falls wins series 4 games to 2)

Series "B"

	W.	L.	Pts.	GF.	GA.
Kitchener	4	1	8	35	19
North Bay	1	4	2	19	35

(Kitchener wins series, 4 games to 1)

Series "C"

	W.	L.	Pts.	GF.	GA.
Owen Sound	4	3	8	28	25
Sudbury	3	4	6	25	28

(Owen Sound wins series, 4 games to 3)

SEMIFINALS

Series "D"

	W.	L.	Pts.	GF.	GA.
Peterborough	4	0	8	20	6
Belleville	0	4	0	6	20

(Peterborough wins series, 4 games to 0)

Series "D"

	W.	L.	Pts.	GF.	GA.
Niagara Falls	4	1	8	28	18
Owen Sound	1	4	2	18	28

(Niagara Falls wins series, 4 games to 1)

FINALS

Series "E"

	W.	L.	Pts.	GF.	GA.
Oshawa	4	0	8	18	7
Peterborough	0	4	0	7	18

(Oshawa wins series, 4 games to 0)

Series "E"

	W.	L.	Pts.	GF.	GA.
Kitchener	4	1	8	30	17
Niagara Falls	1	4	2	17	30

(Kitchener wins series, 4 games to 1)

OHL FINAL SERIES FOR THE J. ROSS ROBERTSON CUP

Series "F"

	W.	L.	Pts.	GF.	GA.
Oshawa	4	3	8	26	19
Kitchener	3	4	6	19	26

(Oshawa wins series, & Robertson Cup, 4 games to 3)

TOP 10 PLAYOFF SCORERS

	Games	G.	A.	Pts.
1. Shayne Stevenson, Kitchener	17	16	21	*37
2. Eric Lindros, Oshawa	17	*18	18	36
3. Keith Primeau, Niagara Falls	16	16	17	33
4. Iain Fraser, Oshawa	17	10	*22	32
5. Mike Craig, Oshawa	17	10	16	26
6. Mark Montanari, Kitchener	16	9	16	25
7. Gilbert Dionne, Kitchener	17	13	10	23
Joey St. Aubin, Kitchener	17	9	14	23
Randy Pearce, Kitchener	17	8	15	23
10. Jason Firth, Kitchener	17	10	12	22
Brad May, Niagara Falls	16	9	13	22
Paul Laus, Niagara Falls	16	6	16	22
Jason York, Kitchener	17	3	19	22

TEAM-BY-TEAM PLAYOFF SCORING

BELLEVILLE BULLS

(Lost div. semifinals to Peterborough, 4 games to 0)

	Games	G.	A.	Pts.	Pen.
Steve Bancroft	11	3	9	12	38
Scott Thornton	11	2	10	12	15
Ken Rowbotham	11	8	3	11	10
Rob Pearson	11	5	5	10	26
Richard Fatrola	11	5	3	8	27
Ted Miskolczi	11	4	4	8	26
Greg Bignell	11	0	6	6	31
John Porco	11	1	4	5	18
Jake Grimes	11	0	5	5	14
Bob Berg	8	2	2	4	14
Darren McCarty	11	1	1	2	21
Derek Morin	11	0	2	2	10
Craig Fraser	10	1	0	1	11
Scott Boston	11	1	0	1	13
Gord Pell	6	0	1	1	0
Scott Feasby	11	0	1	1	17
Greg Dreveny (Goalie)	1	0	0	0	0
Jeff Fife (Goalie)	3	0	0	0	2
Shawn Way	4	0	0	0	0
Jason Skellett	5	0	0	0	4
Rob Stopar (Goalie)	7	0	0	0	6
Brent Gretzky	11	0	0	0	2
Sean O'Reilly	11	0	0	0	17

CORNWALL ROYALS

(Lost division quarterfinals to Oshawa, 4 games to 2)

	Games	G.	A.	Pts.	Pen.
Owen Nolan	6	7	5	12	26
Jason Cirone	6	4	6	10	14
John Slaney	6	0	8	8	11
Darren Bell	6	4	2	6	18
Paul Cain	6	4	2	6	2
Mike Jackson	6	2	4	6	33
Todd Mondor	6	1	5	6	4
Jeff Reid	6	2	1	3	6
Craig Brockelhurst	6	1	1	2	0
Rob Knesaurek	6	1	1	2	10
Mark DeSantis	6	0	2	2	13
Tom Nemeth	6	0	2	2	0
Rod Pasma	6	0	2	2	15
Jerry Ribble	6	0	2	2	6
Shawn Caplice	5	1	0	1	4
Chris Clancy	6	0	1	1	0
Marcus Middleton	2	0	0	0	5
Brent Brownlee (Goalie)	3	0	0	0	0
Ron Jolie	3	0	0	0	4
Guy Leveque	3	0	0	0	0
J.A. Schneider	4	0	0	0	6
Darryl Paquette (Goalie)	6	0	0	0	2

KINGSTON FRONTENACS

(Lost division quarterfinals to Belleville, 4 games to 3)

	Games	G.	A.	Pts.	Pen.
Justin Morrison	7	4	4	8	36
Wayne Doucet	7	2	5	7	18
Mark Major	6	3	3	6	12
Mike Bodnarchuk	7	2	4	6	4
John Nelson	4	4	1	5	25
Bob McKillop	7	3	2	5	2
Tony Cimellaro	7	1	4	5	2
Peter Liptrott	7	2	2	4	21
Jamie Allan	7	0	4	4	19
Matt Giesebrecht	7	0	4	4	4
Mike Cavanagh	7	0	3	3	12
Brock Shyiak	7	0	3	3	2
Tony Iob	7	2	0	2	21
Geoff Schneider	7	0	2	2	0
Gord Harris	6	1	0	1	2
Brock Woods	7	1	0	1	9
Nathan LaFayette	7	0	1	1	0
Sean Gauthier (Goalie)	2	0	0	0	0
Joel Washkurak	5	0	0	0	0
Jeff Wilson (Goalie)	6	0	0	0	11
Dave Stewart	7	0	0	0	8

KITCHENER RANGERS

(Lost league finals to Oshawa, 4 games to 3)

	Games	G.	A.	Pts.	Pen.
Shayne Stevenson	17	16	21	*37	31
Mark Montanari	16	9	16	25	54
Gilbert Dionne	17	13	10	23	22
Joey St. Aubin	17	9	14	23	31
Randy Pearce	17	8	15	23	42
Jason Firth	17	10	12	22	8
Jason York	17	3	19	22	10
Cory Keenan	17	2	11	13	14
Steven Rice	16	4	8	12	24
Richard Borgo	17	5	5	10	10
Rival Fullum	17	3	2	5	12
Chris LiPuma	17	1	4	5	16
Rick Allain	17	0	4	4	46
John Uniac	14	1	1	2	2
Mike Allen	1	0	0	0	0
John Copley	3	0	0	0	0
Gord Geisler	5	0	0	0	0
Gib Tucker	7	0	0	0	0
Steve Smith	11	0	0	0	0
Jamie Israel	12	0	0	0	0
Brad Barton	17	0	0	0	4
Mike Torchia (Goalie)	17	0	0	0	6
Jack Williams	17	0	0	0	0

LONDON KNIGHTS

(Lost division quarterfinals to Niag. Falls, 4 games to 2)

	Games	G.	A.	Pts.	Pen.
Rick Corriveau	6	4	3	7	12
Trevor Dam	6	2	5	7	15
Todd Hlushko	6	2	4	6	10
Steve Boyd	6	1	5	6	8
Chris Taylor	6	3	2	5	16
Louie Debrusk	6	2	2	4	24
Doug Synishin	6	1	3	4	4
Mark Guy	6	0	4	4	12
John Battice	6	1	2	3	8
Dan LeBlanc	6	1	2	3	13
Scott McKay	5	1	1	2	12
Paul Holden	6	1	1	2	7
Steve Martell	6	1	1	2	10
Dave Noseworthy	6	1	1	2	0
Karl Taylor	6	1	1	2	4
Dennis Purdie	3	0	2	2	10
Sean Basilio (Goalie)	1	0	0	0	0
Aaron Nagy	2	0	0	0	0
Dave Anderson	4	0	0	0	2
Greg Ryan	4	0	0	0	2
Chris Crombie	6	0	0	0	16
John Tanner (Goalie)	6	0	0	0	16

NIAGARA FALLS THUNDER

(Lost division finals to Kitchener, 4 games to 1)

	Games	G.	A.	Pts.	Pen.
Keith Primeau	16	16	17	33	49
Brad May	16	9	13	22	64
Paul Laus	16	6	16	22	71
Jason Winch	16	9	12	21	4
Andy Bezeau	16	6	9	15	73
Paul Wolanski	16	4	7	11	14
Greg Suchan	14	3	8	11	41
John Johnson	15	4	3	7	10
Mark Lawrence	16	2	5	7	42
Don McConnell	16	3	3	6	6
Don Pancoe	16	1	5	6	34
Jeff Walker	16	1	4	5	26
Todd Simon	11	3	1	4	2
Geoff Rawson	16	2	2	4	8
Greg Allen	16	1	3	4	17
Ken Ruddick	10	0	4	4	19
Mike St. John	13	1	0	1	0
Roch Belley (Goalie)	4	0	1	1	2
Dan Krisko	1	0	0	0	0
Todd Coopman	5	0	0	0	0
David Benn	10	0	0	0	4
Brian Mueggler	14	0	0	0	0
Steve Udvari (Goalie)	16	0	0	0	2

NORTH BAY CENTENNIALS

(Lost division quarterfinals to Kitchener, 4 games to 1)

	Games	G.	A.	Pts.	Pen.
John Spoltore	5	3	5	8	0
Derian Hatcher	5	2	3	5	8
Jason Corrigan	5	1	3	4	7
Derek Switzer	5	1	3	4	0
Trevor Halverson	2	2	1	3	2
Tyler Ertel	5	2	1	3	14
Shawn Antoski	5	1	2	3	17
Jamie Caruso	5	1	2	3	4
Joel Morin	5	1	2	3	6
Chris Ottman	5	1	2	3	7
John Van Kessel	5	0	3	3	16
Colin Austin	5	2	0	2	4
Tim Favot	5	1	1	2	0
John Vary	5	0	2	2	8
Jeff Gardiner	4	1	0	1	0
Shayne Antoski	5	0	1	1	23
Gary Miller	5	0	1	1	6
Tom Purcell	5	0	1	1	0
Ron Bertrand (Goalie)	2	0	0	0	2
Mike Matuszek (Goalie)	3	0	0	0	0
Jason Beaton	4	0	0	0	0

OSHAWA GENERALS

(Winners of 1990 J. Ross Robertson Cup Playoffs)

	Games	G.	A.	Pts.	Pen.
Eric Lindros	17	*18	18	36	*76
Iain Fraser	17	10	*22	32	8
Mike Craig	17	10	16	26	46
Brent Grieve	17	10	10	20	26
Jarrod Skalde	17	10	7	17	6
Dale Craigwell	17	7	7	14	11
Cory Banika	17	4	7	11	51
Craig Donaldson	17	1	10	11	17
Scott Luik	17	4	5	9	20
Joe Busillo	17	4	4	8	38
Paul O'Hagan	16	2	5	7	42
Bill Armstrong	17	0	7	7	39
Dave Craievich	17	0	6	6	28
Jean-Paul Davis	16	1	4	5	8
Brian Grieve	15	0	4	4	2
Scott Hollis	9	1	0	1	2
Matt Hoffman	17	1	0	1	10
Clair Cornish	6	0	0	0	0
Wade Simpson	6	0	0	0	4
Fred Brathwaite (Goalie)	10	0	0	0	0
Kevin Butt (Goalie)	14	0	0	0	6
Trevor McIvor	17	0	0	0	0

OTTAWA 67's

(Lost div. quarterfinals to Peterborough, 4 games to 0)

	Games	G.	A.	Pts.	Pen.
Chris Snell	3	2	4	6	4
Chris Simon	3	2	1	3	4
Greg Walters	4	1	2	3	12
Troy Binnie	4	1	1	2	2
Greg Clancy	4	1	1	2	0
Jeff Ricciardi	4	0	2	2	13
Jerrett DeFazio	4	0	1	1	2
Gairin Smith	4	0	1	1	0
Jeff Blondin	1	0	0	0	0
Bob McCleary	1	0	0	0	0
Rob Sangster	1	0	0	0	7
George Dourian	3	0	0	0	0
Steve Kluczkowski	3	0	0	0	0
Peter McGlynn (Goalie)	3	0	0	0	2
Peter Ambroziak	4	0	0	0	2
Andrew Brodie	4	0	0	0	0
John East	4	0	0	0	4
Wade Gibson	4	0	0	0	2
Ryan Kuwabara	4	0	0	0	0
Joey McTamney	4	0	0	0	4
Dan Poirier (Goalie)	4	0	0	0	4
Craig Wilson	4	0	0	0	2

OWEN SOUND PLATERS

(Lost division semifinals to Niagara Falls, 4 games to 1)

	Games	G.	A.	Pts.	Pen.
Jamey Hicks	12	8	12	20	20
Jeff Perry	12	8	5	13	26
Jeff Christian	10	6	7	13	43
Ray Edwards	12	4	8	12	38
Mike Speer	12	3	7	10	21
Grayden Reid	12	4	5	9	20
Owen Lessard	12	5	2	7	26
Kirk Maltby	12	1	6	7	15
Keith Whitmore	12	0	7	7	22
Cory Pageau	12	4	1	5	43
Mark Strohack	11	0	3	3	2
Jeff Ballantyne	12	1	1	2	14
Trent Cull	12	0	2	2	11
Chris Driscoll	4	1	0	1	2
Steve Parson	12	1	0	1	14
Sean Whyte	3	0	1	1	10
Bryan Drury	12	0	1	1	27
Todd Hunter (Goalie)	1	0	0	0	0
Mike Murray	1	0	0	0	0
Jeff Grant	9	0	0	0	4
Jeff Cantlon	12	0	0	0	9
Mike Parson (Goalie)	12	0	0	0	6

PETERBOROUGH PETES

(Lost division finals to Oshawa, 4 games to 0)

	Games	G.	A.	Pts.	Pen.
Mike Ricci	12	5	7	12	26
Jason Dawe	12	4	7	11	4
Jamie Pegg	12	4	6	10	10
Troy Stephens	12	2	8	10	11
Mark Myles	12	5	4	9	6
Geoff Ingram	2	3	6	9	14
Mike Tomlinson	8	2	4	6	2
Dale McTavish	12	1	5	6	2
Mike Dagenais	12	4	1	5	18
Dave Lorentz	12	3	2	5	8
Chris Longo	11	2	3	5	14
Joe Hawley	12	2	3	5	26
Scott Campbell	11	2	2	4	10
Bryan Gendron	10	2	1	3	9
Paul Mitton	12	2	1	3	15
Brent Pope	7	0	2	2	4
Dan Brown	11	0	2	2	10
Jassen Cullimore	11	0	2	2	8
Willie McGarvey	4	0	1	1	4
Todd Bojcun (Goalie)	10	0	1	1	4
Tom Hopkins	1	0	0	0	0
Doug Searle	1	0	0	0	0
Andrew Verner (Goalie)	2	0	0	0	0
Don O'Neill	8	0	0	0	30

SUDBURY WOLVES

(Lost div. quarterfinals to Owen Sound, 4 games to 3)

	Games	G.	A.	Pts.	Pen.
Darcy Cahill	7	1	13	14	14
Paul DiPietro	7	3	6	9	7
Andy MacVicar	7	2	5	7	10
Terry Chitaroni	7	4	1	5	15
Jason Young	7	3	2	5	8
Alain Laforge	7	2	3	5	16
Wade Bartley	7	1	4	5	10
Scott Mahoney	7	3	1	4	12
Derek Thompson	7	2	1	3	12
Adam Bennett	7	1	2	3	23
Sean O'Donnell	7	1	2	3	8
Bill Kovacs	7	1	1	2	15
Jamie Matthews	7	1	0	1	4
Derek Etches	4	0	1	1	4
Kevin Falesy	7	0	1	1	8
Jon Boeve (Goalie)	1	0	0	0	0
Jim Sonmez	3	0	0	0	0
Dave Goverde (Goalie)	7	0	0	0	2
Leonard McDonald	7	0	0	0	8
Glen Murray	7	0	0	0	4
Barry Young	7	0	0	0	12

COMPLETE ROBERTSON CUP GOALTENDING

	Games	Mins.	Goals	SO.	Avg.
Jeff Fife	3	244	11(2)	0	2.70
Rob Stopar	7	420	23(1)	1	3.29
Greg Dreveny	1	60	8	0	8.00
Belleville Totals	11	724	45	1	3.73
Brent Brownlee	3	72	4	0	3.33
Darryl Paquette	6	288	34(1)	0	7.08
Cornwall Totals	6	360	39	0	6.50
Jeff Wilson	6	408	21	0	3.09
Sean Gauthier	2	76	6	0	4.74
Kingston Totals	7	484	27	0	3.35
Mike Torchia	*17	*1023	60(2)	0	3.52
Kitchener Totals	17	1023	62	0	3.64
Sean Basilio	1	27	1	0	2.22
John Tanner	6	341	24(1)	0	4.22
London Totals	6	368	26	0	4.24
Steve Udvari	16	873	*62(1)	0	4.26
Roch Belley	4	98	7	0	4.29
Niagara Falls Totals	16	971	70	0	4.33
Mike Matuszek	3	180	19	0	6.33
Ron Bertrand	2	120	16	0	8.00
North Bay Totals	5	300	35	0	7.00
Fred Brathwaite	10	451	22(1)	0	2.93
Kevin Butt	14	569	30(1)	0	3.16
Oshawa Totals	17	1020	54	0	3.18
Peter McGlynn	3	189	8	0	2.54
George Dourian	3	141	7	0	2.98
Ottawa Totals	4	330	15	0	2.73
Mike Parson	12	722	51(1)	0	4.24
Todd Hunter	1	5	1	0	12.00
Owen Sound Totals	12	727	53	0	4.37
Todd Bojcun	10	689	25	*2	*2.18
Andrew Verner	2	121	6	0	2.98
Peterborough Totals	12	810	31	2	2.30
Dave Goverde	7	394	25	0	3.81
John Boeve	1	34	3	0	5.29
Sudbury Totals	7	428	28	0	3.93

( )—Empty Net Goals. Do not count against a goaltender's average.

INDIVIDUAL OHL PLAYOFF LEADERS

Goals .... Eric Lindros, Oshawa— 18
Assists .... Iain Fraser, Oshawa— 22
Points .... Shayne Stevenson, Kitchener— 37
Penalty Minutes .... Eric Lindros, Oshawa— 76
Goaltender's average .... Todd Bojcun, Peterborough—2.18
Shutouts .... Todd Bojcun, Peterborough— 2

OHL 1989-90 ALL-STARS

First Team	Position	Second Team
Jeff Fife, Belleville	Goal	Todd Bojcun, Peterborough
John Slaney, Cornwall	Defense	Paul Holden, London
Chris Snell, Ottawa	Defense	Joni Lehto, Ottawa
Mike Ricci, Peterborough	Center	Keith Primeau, Niagara Falls
Owen Nolan, Cornwall	Right Wing	Mike Bodnarchuk, Kingston
Bob Berg, Belleville	Left Wing	Brad May, Niagara Falls

OHL 1989-90 TROPHY WINNERS

Red Tilson Trophy (Outstanding Player) .... Mike Ricci, Peterborough
Eddie Powers Memorial Trophy (Scoring Champion) .... Keith Primeau, Niagara Falls
Dave Pinkney Trophy (Top Team Goaltending) .... Jeff Wilson, Kingston
.... Sean Gauthier, Kingston
Max Kaminsky Trophy (Outstanding Defenseman) .... John Slaney, Cornwall
William Hanley Trophy (Most Gentlemanly) .... Mike Ricci, Peterborough
Emms Family Award (Rookie of the Year) .... Chris Longo, Peterborough
Matt Leyden Trophy (Coach of the Year) .... Larry Mavety, Kingston
Jim Mahon Memorial Trophy (Top scoring Right Wing) .... Owen Nolan, Cornwall
F.W. Dinty Moore Trophy (Lowest average by a rookie goalie) ...... Sean Basilio, London
Leo Lalonde Memorial Trophy (Overage Player of the Year) .... Iain Fraser, Oshawa
Hamilton Spectator Trophy (Regular Season Champion) .... Oshawa Generals
J. Ross Robertson Cup (Playoff Champion) .... Oshawa Generals

HISTORICAL OHL TROPHY WINNERS

RED TILSON TROPHY

Outstanding Player

Season	Player	Club
1944-45—	Doug McMurdy, St. Catharines	
1945-46—	Tod Sloan, St. Michael's	
1946-47—	Ed Sanford, St. Michael's	
1947-48—	George Armstrong, Stratford	
1948-49—	Gil Mayer, Barrie	
1949-50—	George Armstrong, Marlboros	
1950-51—	Glenn Hall, Windsor	
1951-52—	Bill Harrington, Kitchener	
1952-53—	Bob Attersley, Oshawa	
1953-54—	Brian Cullen, St. Catharines	
1954-55—	Hank Ciesla, St. Catharines	
1955-56—	Ron Howell, Guelph	
1956-57—	Frank Mahovlich, St. Michael's	
1957-58—	Murray Oliver, Hamilton	
1958-59—	Stan Mikita, St. Catharines	
1959-60—	Wayne Connelly, Peterborough	
1960-61—	Rod Gilbert, Guelph	
1961-62—	Pit Martin, Hamilton	
1962-63—	Wayne Maxner, Niagara Falls	
1963-64—	Yvan Cournoyer, Montreal	
1964-65—	Andre Lacroix, Peterborough	
1965-66—	Andre Lacroix, Peterborough	
1966-67—	Mickey Redmond, Peterborough	
1967-68—	Walt Tkaczuk, Kitchener	
1968-69—	Rejean Houle, Montreal	
1969-70—	Gilbert Perreault, Montreal	
1970-71—	Dave Gardner, Marlboros	
1971-72—	Don Lever, Niagara Falls	
1972-73—	Rick Middleton, Oshawa	
1973-74—	Jack Valiquette, Sault Ste. Marie	
1974-75—	Dennis Maruk, London	
1975-76—	Peter Lee, Ottawa	
1976-77—	Dale McCourt, St. Catharines	
1977-78—	Bobby Smith, Ottawa	
1978-79—	Mike Foligno, Sudbury	
1979-80—	Jim Fox, Ottawa	
1980-81—	Ernie Godden, Windsor	
1981-82—	Dave Simpson, London	
1982-83—	Doug Gilmour, Cornwall	
1983-84—	John Tucker, Kitchener	
1984-85—	Wayne Groulx, Sault Ste. Marie	
1985-86—	Ray Sheppard, Cornwall	
1986-87—	Scott McCrory, Oshawa	
1987-88—	Andrew Cassels, Ottawa	
1988-89—	Bryan Fogarty, Niagara Falls	
1989-90—	Mike Ricci, Peterborough	

EDDIE POWERS MEMORIAL TROPHY

Scoring Champion

Season	Player	Club
1933-34—	J. Groboski, Oshawa	
1934-35—	J. Good, Toronto Lions	
1935-36—	John O'Flaherty, West Toronto	
1936-37—	Billy Taylor, Oshawa	
1937-38—	Hank Goldup, Tor. Marlboros	
1938-39—	Billy Taylor, Oshawa	
1939-40—	Jud McAtee, Oshawa	
1940-41—	Gaye Stewart, Tor. Marlboros	
1941-42—	Bob Wiest, Brantford	
1942-43—	Norman "Red" Tilson, Oshawa	
1943-44—	Ken Smith, Oshawa	
1944-45—	Leo Gravelle, St. Michael's	
1945-46—	Tod Sloan, St. Michael's	
1946-47—	Fleming Mackell, St. Michael's	
1947-48—	George Armstrong, Stratford	
1948-49—	Bert Giesebrecht, Windsor	
1949-50—	Earl Reibel, Windsor	
1950-51—	Lou Jankowski, Oshawa	
1951-52—	Ken Laufman, Guelph	
1952-53—	Jim McBurney, Galt	
1953-54—	Brian Cullen, St. Catharines	
1954-55—	Hank Ciesla, St. Catharines	
1955-56—	Stan Baliuk, Kitchener	
1956-57—	Bill Sweeney, Guelph	
1957-58—	John McKenzie, St. Catharines	
1958-59—	Stan Mikita, St. Catharines	
1959-60—	Chico Maki, St. Catharines	
1960-61—	Rod Gilbert, Guelph	
1961-62—	Andre Boudrias, Montreal	
1962-63—	Wayne Maxner, Niagara Falls	
1963-64—	Andre Boudrias, Montreal	
1964-65—	Ken Hodge, St. Catharines	
1965-66—	Andre Lacroix, Peterborough	

Season	Player	Club
1966-67—	Derek Sanderson, Niagara Falls	
1967-68—	Tom Webster, Niagara Falls	
1968-69—	Rejean Houle, Montreal	
1969-70—	Marcel Dionne, St. Catharines	
1970-71—	Marcel Dionne, St. Catharines	
1971-72—	Bill Harris, Toronto	
1972-73—	Blake Dunlop, Ottawa	
1973-74—	Jack Valiquette, Sault Ste. Marie	
	Rick Adduono, St. Catharines (tie)	
1974-75—	Bruce Boudreau, Toronto	
1975-76—	Mike Kaszycki, Sault Ste. Marie	
1976-77—	Dwight Foster, Kitchener	
1977-78—	Bobby Smith, Ottawa	
1978-79—	Mike Foligno, Sudbury	
1979-80—	Jim Fox, Ottawa	
1980-81—	John Goodwin, Sault Ste. Marie	
1981-82—	Dave Simpson, London	
1982-83—	Doug Gilmour, Cornwall	
1983-84—	Tim Salmon, Kingston	
1984-85—	Dave MacLean, Belleville	
1985-86—	Ray Sheppard, Cornwall	
1986-87—	Scott McCrory, Oshawa	
1987-88—	Andrew Cassels, Ottawa	
1988-89—	Bryan Fogarty, Niagara Falls	
1989-90—	Keith Primeau, Niagara Falls	

DAVE PINKNEY TROPHY

Top Team Goaltending

Season	Player	Club
1948-49—	Gil Mayer, Barrie	
1949-50—	Don Lockhart, Marlboros	
1950-51—	Don Lockhart, Marlboros	
	Lorne Howes, Barrie	
1951-52—	Don Head, Marlboros	
1952-53—	John Henderson, Marlboros	
1953-54—	Dennis Riggin, Hamilton	
1954-55—	John Albani, Marlboros	
1955-56—	Jim Crockett, Marlboros	
1956-57—	Len Broderick, Marlboros	
1957-58—	Len Broderick, Marlboros	
1958-59—	Jacques Caron, Peterborough	
1959-60—	Gerry Cheevers, St. Michael's	
1960-61—	Bud Blom, Hamilton	
1961-62—	George Holmes, Montreal	
1962-63—	Chuck Goddard, Peterborough	
1963-64—	Bernie Parent, Niagara Falls	
1964-65—	Bernie Parent, Niagara Falls	
1965-66—	Ted Quimet, Montreal	
1966-67—	Peter MacDuffe, St. Catharines	
1967-68—	Bruce Mullet, Montreal	
1968-69—	Wayne Wood, Montreal	
1969-70—	John Garrett, Peterborough	
1970-71—	John Garrett, Peterborough	
1971-72—	Michel Larocque, Ottawa	
1972-73—	Mike Palmateer, Toronto	
1973-74—	Don Edwards, Kitchener	
1974-75—	Greg Millen, Peterborough	
1975-76—	Jim Bedard, Sudbury	
1976-77—	Pat Riggin, London	
1977-78—	Al Jensen, Hamilton	
1978-79—	Nick Ricci, Niagara Falls	
1979-80—	Rick LaFerriere, Peterborough	
1980-81—	Jim Ralph, Ottawa	
1981-82—	Marc D'Amour, Sault Ste. Marie	
1982-83—	Peter Sidorkiewicz, Oshawa	
	Jeff Hogg, Oshawa	
1983-84—	Darren Pang, Ottawa	
	Greg Coram, Ottawa	
1984-85—	Scott Mosey, Sault Ste. Marie	
	Marty Abrams, Sault Ste. Marie	
1985-86—	Kay Whitmore, Peterborough	
	Ron Tugnutt, Peterborough	
1986-87—	Sean Evoy, Oshawa	
	Jeff Hackett, Oshawa	
1987-88—	Todd Bojcun, Peterborough	
	John Tanner, Peterborough	
1988-89—	Todd Bojcun, Peterborough	
	John Tanner, Peterborough	
1989-90—	Jeff Wilson, Kingston	
	Sean Gauthier, Kingston	

MAX KAMINSKY TROPHY

Outstanding Defenseman

Season	Player	Club
1969-70—	Ron Plumb, Peterborough	
1970-71—	Jocelyn Guevremont, Montreal	

Season	Player	Club
1971-72—	Denis Potvin, Ottawa	
1972-73—	Denis Potvin, Ottawa	
1973-74—	Jim Turkiewicz, Peterborough	
1974-75—	Mike O'Connell, Kingston	
1975-76—	Rick Green, London	
1976-77—	Craig Hartsburg, S. Ste. Marie	
1977-78—	Brad Marsh, London	
	Rob Ramage, London (tie)	
1978-79—	Greg Theberge, Peterborough	
1979-80—	Larry Murphy, Peterborough	
1980-81—	Steve Smith, Sault Ste. Marie	
1981-82—	Ron Meighan, Niagara Falls	
1982-83—	Allan MacInnis, Kitchener	
1983-84—	Brad Shaw, Ottawa	
1984-85—	Bob Halkidis, London	
1985-86—	Terry Carkner, Peterborough	
	Jeff Brown, Sudbury (tie)	
1986-87—	Kerry Huffman, Guelph	
1987-88—	Darryl Shannon, Windsor	
1988-89—	Bryan Fogarty, Niagara Falls	
1989-90—	John Slaney, Cornwall	

WILLIAM HANLEY TROPHY

Most Gentlemanly

Season	Player	Club
1960-61—	Bruce Draper, St. Michael's	
1961-62—	Lowell MacDonald, Hamilton	
1962-63—	Paul Henderson, Hamilton	
1963-64—	Fred Stanfield, St. Catharines	
1964-65—	Jimmy Peters, Hamilton	
1965-66—	Andre Lacroix, Peterborough	
1966-67—	Mickey Redmond, Peterborough	
1967-68—	Tom Webster, Niagara Falls	
1968-69—	Rejean Houle, Montreal	
1969-74—	No award presented	
1974-75—	Doug Jarvis, Peterborough	
1975-76—	Dale McCourt, Hamilton	
1976-77—	Dale McCourt, St. Catharines	
1977-78—	Wayne Gretzky, S.S. Marie	
1978-79—	Sean Simpson, Ottawa	
1979-80—	Sean Simpson, Ottawa	
1980-81—	John Goodwin, Sault Ste. Marie	
1981-82—	Dave Simpson, London	
1982-83—	Kirk Muller, Guelph	
1983-84—	Kevin Conway, Kingston	
1984-85—	Scott Tottle, Peterborough	
1985-86—	Jason Lafreniere, Belleville	
1986-87—	Scott McCrory, Oshawa	
	Keith Gretzky, Hamilton (tie)	
1987-88—	Andrew Cassels, Ottawa	
1988-89—	Kevin Miehm, Oshawa	
1989-90—	Mike Ricci, Peterborough	

EMMS FAMILY AWARD

Rookie of the Year

Season	Player	Club
1972-73—	Dennis Maruk, London	
1973-74—	Jack Valiquette, Sault Ste. Marie	
1974-75—	Danny Shearer, Hamilton	
1975-76—	John Travella, Sault Ste. Marie	
1976-77—	Yvan Joly, Ottawa	
1977-78—	Wayne Gretzky, S. S. Marie	
1978-79—	John Goodwin, Sault Ste. Marie	
1979-80—	Bruce Dowie, Toronto	
1980-81—	Tony Tanti, Oshawa	
1981-82—	Pat Verbeek, Sudbury	
1982-83—	Bruce Cassidy, Ottawa	
1983-84—	Shawn Burr, Kitchener	
1984-85—	Derek King, Sault Ste. Marie	
1985-86—	Lonnie Loach, Guelph	
1986-87—	Andrew Cassels, Ottawa	
1987-88—	Rick Corriveau, London	
1988-89—	Owen Nolan, Cornwall	
1989-90—	Chris Longo, Peterborough	

MATT LEYDEN TROPHY

Coach of the Year

Season	Coach	Club
1971-72—	Gus Bodnar, Oshawa	
1972-73—	George Armstrong, Toronto	
1973-74—	Jack Bownass, Kingston	
1974-75—	Bert Templeton, Hamilton	
1975-76—	Jerry Toppazzini, Sudbury	
1976-77—	Bill Long, London	
1977-78—	Bill White, Oshawa	
1978-79—	Gary Green, Peterborough	
1979-80—	Dave Chambers, Toronto	
1980-81—	Brian Kilrea, Ottawa	
1981-82—	Brian Kilrea, Ottawa	
1982-83—	Terry Crisp, Sault Ste. Marie	
1983-84—	Tom Barrett, Kitchener	
1984-85—	Terry Crisp, Sault Ste. Marie	
1985-86—	Jacques Martin, Guelph	
1986-87—	Paul Theriault, Oshawa	
1987-88—	Dick Todd, Peterborough	
1988-89—	Joe McDonnell, Kitchener	
1989-90—	Larry Mavety, Kingston	

JIM MAHON MEMORIAL TROPHY

Top Scoring Right Wing

Season	Player	Club
1971-72—	Bill Harris, Toronto	
1972-73—	Dennis Ververgaert, London	
1973-74—	Dave Gorman, St. Catharines	
1974-75—	Mark Napier, Toronto	
1975-76—	Peter Lee, Ottawa	
1976-77—	John Anderson, Toronto	
1977-78—	Dino Ciccarelli, London	
1978-79—	Mike Foligno, Sudbury	
1979-80—	Jim Fox, Ottawa	
1980-81—	Tony Tanti, Oshawa	
1981-82—	Tony Tanti, Oshawa	
1982-83—	Ian MacInnis, Cornwall	
1983-84—	Wayne Presley, Kitchener	
1984-85—	Dave MacLean, Belleville	
1985-86—	Ray Sheppard, Cornwall	
1986-87—	Ron Goodall, Kitchener	
1987-88—	Sean Williams, Oshawa	
1988-89—	Stan Drulia, Niagara Falls	
1989-90—	Owen Nolan, Cornwall	

F.W. DINTY MOORE TROPHY

Lowest Average by a Rookie Goalie

Season	Player	Club
1975-76—	Mark Locken, Hamilton	
1976-77—	Barry Heard, London	
1977-78—	Ken Ellacott, Peterborough	
1978-79—	Nick Ricci, Niagara Falls	
1979-80—	Mike Vezina, Ottawa	
1980-81—	John Vanbiesbrouck, Sault Ste. Marie	
1981-82—	Shawn Kilroy, Peterborough	
1982-83—	Dan Burrows, Belleville	
1983-84—	Jerry Iuliano, Sault Ste. Marie	
1984-85—	Ron Tugnutt, Peterborough	
1985-86—	Paul Henriques, Belleville	
1986-87—	Jeff Hackett, Oshawa	
1987-88—	Todd Bojcun, Peterborough	
1988-89—	Jeff Wilson, Kingston	
1989-90—	Sean Basilio, London	

LEO LALONDE MEMORIAL TROPHY

Overage Player of the Year

Season	Player	Club
1983-84—	Don McLaren, Ottawa	
1984-85—	Dunc MacIntyre, Belleville	
1985-86—	Steve Guenette, Guelph	
1986-87—	Mike Richard, Toronto	
1987-88—	Len Soccio, North Bay	
1988-89—	Stan Drulia, Niagara Falls	
1989-90—	Iain Fraser, Oshawa	

Wayne Gretzky

Rod Gilbert

HAMILTON SPECTATOR TROPHY

(Regular Season Champion)

Season	Club	Season	Club
1957-58—	St. Catharines Tee Pees	1974-75—	Toronto Marlboros
1958-59—	St. Catharines Tee Pees	1975-76—	Sudbury Wolves
1959-60—	Toronto Marlboros	1976-77—	St. Catharines Fincups
1960-61—	Guelph Royals	1977-78—	Ottawa 67's
1961-62—	Montreal Jr. Canadiens	1978-79—	Peterborough Petes
1962-63—	Niagara Falls Flyers	1979-80—	Peterborough Petes
1963-64—	Toronto Marlboros	1980-81—	Sault Ste. Marie Greyhounds
1964-65—	Niagara Falls Flyers	1981-82—	Ottawa 67's
1965-66—	Peterborough Petes	1982-83—	Sault Ste. Marie Greyhounds
1966-67—	Kitchener Rangers	1983-84—	Kitchener Rangers
1967-68—	Kitchener Rangers	1984-85—	Sault Ste. Marie Greyhounds
1968-69—	Montreal Jr. Canadiens	1985-86—	Peterborough Petes
1969-70—	Montreal Jr. Canadiens	1986-87—	Oshawa Generals
1970-71—	Peterborough Petes	1987-88—	Windsor Compuware Spitfires
1971-72—	Toronto Marlboros	1988-89—	Kitchener Rangers
1972-73—	Toronto Marlboros	1989-90—	Oshawa Generals
1973-74—	Kitchener Rangers		

THE J. ROSS ROBERTSON CUP

(Playoff Champion)

Season	Club	Season	Club
1933-34—	St. Michael's College	1962-63—	Niagara Falls Flyers
1934-35—	Kitchener	1963-64—	Toronto Marlboros
1935-36—	West Toronto Redmen	1964-65—	Niagara Falls Flyers
1936-37—	St. Michael's College	1965-66—	Oshawa Generals
1937-38—	Oshawa Generals	1966-67—	Toronto Marlboros
1938-39—	Oshawa Generals	1967-68—	Niagara Falls Flyers
1939-40—	Oshawa Generals	1968-69—	Montreal Jr. Canadiens
1940-41—	Oshawa Generals	1969-70—	Montreal Jr. Canadiens
1941-42—	Oshawa Generals	1970-71—	St. Catharines Black Hawks
1942-43—	Oshawa Generals	1971-72—	Peterborough Petes
1943-44—	Oshawa Generals	1972-73—	Toronto Marlboros
1944-45—	St. Michael's College	1973-74—	St. Catharines Black Hawks
1945-46—	St. Michael's College	1974-75—	Toronto Marlboros
1946-47—	St. Michael's College	1975-76—	Hamilton Steelhawks
1947-48—	Barrie Flyers	1976-77—	Ottawa 67's
1948-49—	Barrie Flyers	1977-78—	Peterborough Petes
1949-50—	Guelph Biltmores	1978-79—	Peterborough Petes
1950-51—	Barrie Flyers	1979-80—	Peterborough Petes
1951-52—	Guelph Biltmores	1980-81—	Kitchener Rangers
1952-53—	Barrie Flyers	1981-82—	Kitchener Rangers
1953-54—	St. Catharines Tee Pees	1982-83—	Oshawa Generals
1954-55—	Toronto Marlboros	1983 84	Ottawa 67's
1955-56—	Toronto Marlboros	1984-85—	Sault Ste. Marie Greyhounds
1956-57—	Guelph Biltmores	1985-86—	Guelph Platers
1957-58—	Toronto Marlboros	1986-87—	Oshawa Generals
1958-59—	Peterborough TPTs	1987-88—	Windsor Compuware Spitfires
1959-60—	St. Catharines Tee Pees	1988-89—	Peterborough Petes
1960-61—	St. Michael's College	1989-90—	Oshawa Generals
1961-62—	Hamilton Red Wings		

QUEBEC MAJOR JUNIOR HOCKEY LEAGUE

President and Executive Director	Vice-President	Statistician	Address
Gilles Courteau	To be announced	Douglas Horman	110, rue de la Barre, bureau 210, Longueuil, Quebec J4K 1A3 Phone—(514) 442-3590

FINAL 1989-90 QMJHL STANDINGS

	G.	W.	L.	T.	Pts.	GF.	GA.
Victoriaville Tigres	70	42	23	5	89	314	223
Trois-Rivieres Draveurs	70	44	26	0	88	345	278
Longueuil College-Francais	70	39	29	2	80	292	255
Shawinigan Cataractes	70	38	30	2	78	328	275
Laval Titans	70	37	30	3	77	332	274
Hull Olympiques	70	36	29	5	77	306	282
St. Hyacinthe Lasers	70	35	29	6	76	299	301
Chicoutimi Sagueneens	70	34	33	3	71	280	297
St. Jean Lynx	70	30	36	4	64	297	311
Granby Bisons	70	20	49	1	41	227	340
Drummondville Voltigeurs	70	14	55	1	29	232	416

TOP 10 SCORERS FOR THE JEAN BELIVEAU TROPHY

	Games	G.	A.	Pts.	Pen.
1. Patrick Lebeau, Victoriaville	72	68	*106	*174	109
2. Steve Cadieux, Shawinigan	67	*73	90	163	101
3. Steve Larouche, Trois-Rivieres	60	55	90	145	40
4. Martin St. Amour, Trois-Rivieres	60	57	79	136	162
5. Jan Alston, St. Jean	65	61	74	135	137
6. Paul Willett, Longueuil	68	57	75	132	68
7. Andrew McKim, Hull	70	66	64	130	44
8. Sylvain Fleury, Longueuil	70	50	74	124	26
9. Pierre Sevigny, St. Hyacinthe	67	47	72	119	205
10. Stephane Groleau, Shawinigan	70	47	68	115	128

TEAM-BY-TEAM BREAKDOWN OF QMJHL SCORING

CHICOUTIMI SAGUENEENS

	Games	G.	A.	Pts.	Pen.
Francois Belanger	70	41	52	93	91
Daniel Maurice	62	43	49	92	228
Denis Chasse	67	33	56	89	190
Eric Brule	70	12	60	72	157
Dany Duclos	51	21	34	55	214
Eric Dandenault	67	14	38	52	238
Patrice Martineau	67	21	27	48	68
Hughes Mongeon	66	24	18	42	16
Paul Brousseau	57	17	24	41	32
Daniel Dore	24	6	23	29	112
Martin Gagne	53	7	21	28	105
Pierre Paul Landry	67	1	26	27	148
Patrick Bisaillon	58	13	12	25	79
Eric Rochette	55	3	15	18	119
Sebastien Lavalliere	47	5	8	13	190
Martin Beaupre	63	0	12	12	105
Maxime Gagne	64	4	7	11	60
Jean Imbeau	50	3	4	7	30
Guy Lefebvre	57	1	5	6	166
Jasmin Ouellet	29	2	1	3	49
Rino Cormier	16	1	1	2	2
Richard Boivin	4	0	0	0	2
Patrick Chouinard (G.)	22	...	...	...	4
Felix Potvin (Goalie)	62	...	...	...	8

DRUMMONDVILLE VOLTIGEURS

	Games	G.	A.	Pts.	Pen.
Steve Chartrand	44	50	41	91	34
Roger Larche	61	23	51	74	139
Eric Meloche	62	21	34	55	170
Yanick Dupre	53	15	19	34	69
Christian Ratthe	68	8	24	32	157
Daniel Thibeault	61	9	21	30	47
Daniel Landry	62	16	12	28	46
Eric Plante	43	13	15	28	22
Dave Paquet	41	9	12	21	134
Michel Bergeron	68	8	13	21	111
Guy Lehoux	66	4	17	21	178
Alain Cote	67	4	15	19	34
Claude Jutras Jr	60	8	8	16	141
Joseph Napolitano	60	3	6	9	81
Stephane Desjardins	62	0	8	8	52
Marc Savard	61	1	5	6	50
Brad MacIsaac	52	0	6	6	18

	Games	G.	A.	Pts.	Pen.
Luc Doucet	42	1	3	4	28
Frederic Marion	9	1	2	3	4
Sylvain Brochu	14	1	2	3	6
Eric Cardinal	48	0	2	2	18
Rene Camire	57	0	2	2	4
Joel Chapdelaine	11	0	1	1	2
Steve Lupien (Goalie)	1	...	...	...	0
Rene Levesque (Goalie)	18	...	...	...	4
Jocelyn Provost (Goalie)	45	...	...	...	14

GRANBY BISONS

	Games	G.	A.	Pts.	Pen.
Jesse Belanger	67	53	54	107	53
Marc Rodgers	61	24	31	55	155
Benoit Therrien	69	13	31	44	79
Martin Balleux	69	15	23	38	10
Carl Leblanc	65	12	26	38	84
Carl Menard	70	11	24	35	22
Eric Cool	70	7	28	35	50
Claude Charles Sauriol	49	8	25	33	117
Jean Franco Gregoire	50	16	16	32	42
Simon Ouimette	48	9	18	27	111
Steve Searles	58	10	12	22	129
Christian Tardif	70	8	14	22	22
Mario Therrien	31	8	12	20	12
Sebastien Tremblay	28	10	6	16	132
Remi Belliveau	55	2	12	14	262
Sylvain Gourde	34	2	9	11	46
Patrick Tessier	57	4	6	10	63
Eric Prillo	51	1	5	6	51
Serge Bilodeau	53	0	6	6	36
Patrice Labrosse	37	0	3	3	36
Stephane Ricard	6	0	0	0	2
Patrick Taylor (Goalie)	16	...	...	...	2
Rock Chatel (Goalie)	30	...	...	...	8
Boris Rousson (Goalie)	39	...	...	...	6

HULL OLYMPIQUES

	Games	G.	A.	Pts.	Pen.
Andrew McKim	70	66	64	130	44
Bruno Villeneuve	61	34	50	84	36
Joel Blain	65	31	47	78	137
Herbert Hohenberger	65	16	50	66	125
Todd Sparks	69	26	37	63	107
Joe Suk	60	23	37	60	30

	Games	G.	A.	Pts.	Pen.
Karl Dykhuis	69	10	45	55	119
Guy Dupuis	70	8	41	49	96
Craig Martin	66	14	31	45	299
Patrick Lemay	68	17	25	42	164
Trevor Boland	55	15	26	41	77
Eric Lavigne	69	7	11	18	203
Frederic Boivin	67	7	7	14	170
Craig Williard	67	7	6	13	88
Steven Dion	54	7	5	12	82
Daniel Montmarquette	51	4	6	10	49
Dan Paolucci	55	4	6	10	85
John Osborne	39	3	3	6	12
Robert Melanson	69	3	3	6	249
Sylvain Ducharme	52	0	3	3	21
Sylvain Marcotte (Goalie)	31	...	...	...	19
Johnny Lorenzo (Goalie)	47	...	...	...	14

LAVAL TITANS

	Games	G.	A.	Pts.	Pen.
Denis Chalifoux	70	41	68	109	32
Martin Lapointe	65	42	54	96	77
Sylvain Naud	69	55	40	95	90
Carl Boudreau	68	31	63	94	57
Patrice Brisebois	56	18	70	88	108
Normand Demers	70	27	54	81	60
Claude Boivin	59	24	51	75	309
Michel Gingras	64	26	44	70	257
Patrick Caron	46	20	28	48	89
Eric Dubois	66	9	36	45	153
Gino Odjick	51	12	26	38	280
Jim Bermingham	68	11	23	34	118
Carl Mantha	52	4	29	33	33
Regis Tremblay	28	8	16	22	32
Sandy McCarthy	65	10	11	21	269
Serge Anglehart	48	2	19	21	131
Francois Pelletier	37	9	6	15	12
Eric Bissonnette	55	2	13	15	112
Greg MacEachern	53	0	13	13	14
Daniel Arsenault	69	2	7	9	55
Jason Brousseau	42	4	4	8	52
Allen Kerr	49	0	3	3	84
Stephane St. Pierre	4	1	0	1	2
Martin Duval	7	0	1	1	0
Robert Saaduldin	1	0	0	0	0
Jacques Leblanc	3	0	0	0	0
Martin Roy	4	0	0	0	0
Julian Cameron (Goalie)	27	...	...	...	6

	Games	G.	A.	Pts.	Pen.
Ghislain Lefebvre (Goalie)	27	...	...	...	4
Eric Raymond (Goalie)	37	...	...	...	47

LONGUEUIL COLLEGE-FRANCAIS

	Games	G.	A.	Pts.	Pen.
Paul Willett	68	57	75	132	68
Sylvain Fleury	70	50	74	124	26
Robert Guillet	69	32	40	72	132
David St. Pierre	63	33	24	57	24
Mario Nobili	67	11	34	45	64
Denis Cloutier	70	5	35	40	127
Dave Chouinard	63	13	23	36	18
Richard Ayotte	61	13	22	35	67
Nichol Cloutier	70	6	29	35	53
Martin Tanguay†	61	12	17	29	43
Yan Arsenault	61	7	22	29	60
Martin Tanguay‡	61	11	16	27	35
Donald Brashear	64	12	14	26	169
Stephane Perron	54	4	20	24	119
Dominic Rheaume	60	9	11	20	12
Christian Breton	52	6	10	16	157
Stephane Paradis	45	4	10	14	26
Dave Kallis	60	3	8	11	8
Martin Lajeunesse	61	2	9	11	61
Etienne Lavoie	50	2	5	7	187
Martin Wener	1	0	0	0	0
Steeve Milliard	3	0	0	0	0
J. Francois Gagnon (G.)	39	...	...	...	6
Francis Ouellette (Goalie)	45	...	...	...	12

†Wore uniform #66.
‡Wore uniform #27.

SHAWINIGAN CATARACTES

	Games	G.	A.	Pts.	Pen.
Steve Cadieux	67	*73	90	163	101
Stephane Groleau	70	47	68	115	128
Eric Nadeau	68	30	78	108	193
Yvan Bergeron	68	52	51	103	166
Stephane Charbonneau	62	37	58	95	154
Francois Groleau	66	11	54	65	80
Richard Hamelin	68	28	33	61	102
David Chernis	47	16	15	31	207
Patrick Hebert	65	6	15	21	86
Steve Dontigny	58	10	9	19	94
Pierre Cote	70	1	18	19	165
Francois Bourdeau	68	0	17	17	55
Dave Morissette	66	2	9	11	269
Hughes Bouchard	70	3	7	10	90
Mathieu Roy	56	4	4	8	21
Stephane Bourget	55	2	5	7	58
Shawn Simpson	18	3	3	6	26
Alain Cote	63	1	5	6	22
Eric Duchesne	67	0	4	4	148
Sandy Scalzo	4	0	0	0	0
Eric Trempe (Goalie)	1	...	...	...	0
Dominic Roussel (Goalie)	37	...	...	...	59
Andre Boulianne (Goalie)	40	...	...	...	10

ST. HYACINTHE LASERS

	Games	G.	A.	Pts.	Pen.
Pierre Sevigny	67	47	72	119	205
Charles Poulin	65	39	45	84	132
Denis Leblanc	69	44	33	77	74
Eric Bellerose	69	20	57	77	63
Marc Picard	61	16	43	59	38
Patrick Poulin	60	25	26	51	55
Eric Charron	68	13	38	51	152
Andy Ross	55	12	28	40	51
Pierre Allard	60	14	23	37	76
Yannik Lemay	56	5	31	36	101
Serge Renaud	53	20	11	31	147
Mil Sukovic	42	6	22	28	48
Christian Lariviere	69	5	19	24	129
Alain Vogin	45	8	15	23	38
Martin Fortin	60	6	15	21	94
Francois Paquette	54	0	14	14	39
Ronald Kay	55	5	7	12	77
Martin Cote	24	3	9	12	8
Lino Salvo	9	2	6	8	10
Patrick Chartrand	21	1	6	7	12
Joe Argento	39	1	2	3	77
Sylvain Gauthier	25	0	2	2	65
Carlo Colombi	16	0	0	0	2
Serge Labelle	59	0	0	0	277
Eric Charron (Goalie)	1	...	...	...	0
Yanick Degrace (Goalie)	34	...	...	...	4
Martin Brodeur (Goalie)	42	...	...	...	10

ST. JEAN LYNX

	Games	G.	A.	Pts.	Pen.
Jan Alston	65	61	74	135	137
Kenneth MacDermid	67	28	48	76	139
Marco Morin	69	20	34	54	36
Martin Lavallee	65	17	36	53	141
Martin Lefebvre	37	15	31	46	71
Stephane Ouellet	64	16	26	42	55
Yvan Corbin	70	14	17	31	24
Francois Chaput	65	10	20	30	236
Travor Duhaime	66	12	17	29	132
Martin Venne	44	5	17	22	33
Eric Marcoux	62	7	12	19	209
Stacy Dallaire	64	2	14	16	54
Serge Simard Jr.	67	3	10	13	62
Steve Armstrong	57	4	8	12	108
Pascal Vincent	70	4	7	11	45
Sylvain Bourgeois	17	0	11	11	14
Jason Underhill	69	4	4	8	22
Martin Thomas	24	3	4	7	32
Marco Lemay	31	1	4	5	53
Stephane Boudrias	36	1	2	3	100
Carl Henri Exantus	17	1	1	2	13
Jean Francois Poirier	2	0	1	1	0
Jean Franco Cardinal	8	0	0	0	2
Luc Masse	19	0	0	0	2
Yves Racine	20	0	0	0	0
Marc Delorme (Goalie)	30	...	...	...	8
Patrick Labrecque (G.)	48	...	...	...	26

TROIS-RIVIERES DRAVEURS

	Games	G.	A.	Pts.	Pen.
Steve Larouche	60	55	90	145	40
Martin St. Amour	60	57	79	136	162
Yanic Perreault	63	51	63	114	75
Chris Bartolone	60	14	66	80	112
Marco Pietroniro	58	25	47	72	47
Sebastien Parent	68	28	36	64	187
Christian Bertrand	40	26	36	62	190
Todd Gillingham	62	22	36	58	*349
Dominic Maltais	67	17	29	46	50
Pascal Dufault	46	6	23	29	75
Enrico Ciccone	40	4	24	28	227
Gilles Bouchard	68	12	15	27	46
Eric St. Amant	56	12	14	26	159
Paolo Racicot	53	3	16	19	41
Nicolas Lefebvre	54	6	11	17	43
Claude Poirier	68	5	11	16	58
Jacques Parent	56	5	5	10	92
Francis Couturier	60	3	5	8	55
Pierre Fillion	59	3	4	7	39
Martin Lacombe	48	0	7	7	119
Patrice Rene	40	1	4	5	61
Stephane Giard (Goalie)	1	...	...	...	0
Jean Francois Labbe (G.)	28	...	...	...	12
Alain Morissette (Goalie)	49	...	...	...	6

VICTORIAVILLE TIGRES

	Games	G.	A.	Pts.	Pen.
Patrick Lebeau	72	68	*106	*174	109
Daniel Gauthier	62	45	69	114	32
Reginald Savage	63	51	43	94	79
Claude Barthe	68	20	55	75	148
Jean Blouin	56	30	40	70	92
Alain Tardif	55	27	42	69	67
Christian Campeau	70	25	39	64	96
Steven Paiement	68	26	31	57	35
Dany Nolet	57	18	38	56	56
Yves Sarault	70	12	28	40	140
Marc Labelle	56	18	21	39	192
Martin Charrois	63	7	30	37	142
Francois Leroux	54	4	33	37	160
Patrick Cloutier	69	10	26	36	216
Karlo Pavich	40	11	15	26	90
Patrice Filiatrault	68	6	13	19	104
Claude Savoie	61	6	6	12	24
Serge Thibaudeau	62	5	7	12	24
Mathieu Lamothe	40	4	5	9	19
Jason Downey	44	0	9	9	49
Patrick Cote	38	1	2	3	16
Denis Beauchamps	44	0	3	3	20
Enrico Scardocchio	11	1	1	2	2
Richard Cartier Jr.	8	1	0	1	0
Marco Bussieres	7	0	0	0	2
Martin Houle (Goalie)	1	...	...	...	2
David Scott (Goalie)	4	...	...	...	2
Stephane Fiset (Goalie)	24	...	...	...	6
Pierre Gagnon (Goalie)	47	...	...	...	6

COMPLETE QMJHL GOALTENDING

	Games	Mins.	Goals	SO.	Avg.
Stephane Fiset, Victoriaville	24	1383	63	1	2.73
Pierre Gagnon, Victoriaville	47	2684	135	1	*3.02
Jean Francois Gagnon, Longueuil	39	1973	115	0	3.50
Francis Ouellette, Longueuil	45	2289	135	1	3.54
Eric Raymond, Laval	37	2068	123	1	3.57
Andre Boulianne, Shawinigan	40	2188	134	*2	3.67
Alain Morissette, Trois-Rivieres	49	2674	166	1	3.72
Johnny Lorenzo, Hull	47	2600	164	1	3.78
Ghislain Lefebvre, Laval	27	1580	101	*2	3.84
Felix Potvin, Chicoutimi	*62	*3478	231	*2	3.99
Martin Brodeur, St. Hyacinthe	42	2333	156	0	4.01
Dominic Roussel, Shawinigan	37	1985	133	0	4.02
Marc Delorme, St. Jean	30	1645	111	1	4.05
Yanick Degrace, St. Hyacinthe	34	1906	131	0	4.12
Sylvain Marcotte, Hull	31	1628	114	0	4.20
Jean Francois Labbe, Trois-Rivieres	28	1499	106	1	4.24
Julian Cameron, Laval	27	1252	90	0	4.31
Patrick Labrecque, St. Jean	48	2630	196	1	4.47
Boris Rousson, Granby	39	2076	158	0	4.57
Patrick Chouinard, Chicoutimi	22	766	60	0	4.70
Rock Chatel, Granby	30	1498	123	0	4.93
Patrick Taylor, Granby	16	753	63	0	5.02
David Scott, Victoriaville	4	167	14	0	5.03
Jocelyn Provost, Drummondville	45	2464	*242	0	5.89
Steve Lupien, Drummondville	1	60	6	0	6.00
Rene Levesque, Drummondville	18	912	97	0	6.38
Eric Trempe, Shawinigan	1	60	7	0	7.00
Stephane Giard, Trois-Rivieres	1	28	5	0	10.71
Martin Houle, Victoriaville	1	20	4	0	12.00
Eric Charron, St. Hyacinthe	1	30	6	0	12.00

INDIVIDUAL 1989-90 LEADERS

Goals	Steve Cadieux, Shawinigan— 73
Assists	Patrick Lebeau, Victoriaville— 106
Points	Patrick Lebeau, Victoriaville— 174
Penalty Minutes	Todd Gillingham, Trois-Rivieres— 349
Goaltending Average	Pierre Gagnon, Victoriaville—3.02
Shutouts	Andre Boulianne, Shawinigan— 2
	Ghislain Lefebvre, Laval— 2
	Felix Potvin, Chicoutimi— 2

1990 QMJHL PRESIDENT CUP PLAYOFFS

QUARTERFINALS

(Best-of-seven series)

Series "A"

	W.	L.	Pts.	GF.	GA.
Laval	4	2	8	36	23
Shawinigan	2	4	4	23	36

(Laval wins series, 4 games to 2)

Series "B"

	W.	L.	Pts.	GF.	GA.
Hull	4	3	8	24	21
Longueuil	3	4	6	21	24

(Hull wins series, 4 games to 3)

Series "C"

	W.	L.	Pts.	GF.	GA.
St. Hyacinthe	4	3	8	36	28
Trois-Rivieres	3	4	6	28	36

(St. Hyacinthe wins series, 4 games to 3)

Series "D"

	W.	L.	Pts.	GF.	GA.
Victoriaville	4	3	8	29	25
Chicoutimi	3	4	6	25	29

(Victoriaville wins series, 4 games to 3)

SEMIFINALS

(Best-of-seven series)

Series "E"

	W.	L.	Pts.	GF.	GA.
Laval	4	0	8	17	10
Hull	0	4	0	10	17

(Laval wins series, 4 games to 0)

Series "F"

	W.	L.	Pts.	GF.	GA.
Victoriaville	4	1	8	24	15
St. Hyacinthe	1	4	2	15	24

(Victoriaville wins series, 4 games to 1)

FINALS

(Best-of-seven series)

Series "G"

	W.	L.	Pts.	GF.	GA.
Laval	4	0	8	23	9
Victoriaville	0	4	0	9	23

(Laval wins series, and President Cup, 4 games to 0)

TOP 10 PLAYOFF SCORERS

	Games	G.	A.	Pts.
1. Denis Chalifoux, Laval	14	*14	14	*28
2. Daniel Gauthier, Victoriaville	16	8	*19	27
3. Martin Lapointe, Laval	14	8	17	25
4. Reginald Savage, Victoriaville	16	13	10	23
5. Patrick Lebeau, Victoriaville	16	7	15	22
6. Claude Boivin, Laval	13	7	13	20
7. Andrew McKim, Hull	11	8	10	18
8. Pierre Sevigny, St. Hyacinthe	12	8	8	16
Patrice Brisebois, Laval	13	7	9	16
Martin St. Amour, Trois-Rivieres	7	7	9	16

TEAM-BY-TEAM PLAYOFF SCORING

CHICOUTIMI SAGUEENEENS

(Lost quarterfinals to Victoriaville, 4 games to 3)

	Games	G.	A.	Pts.	Pen.
Daniel Maurice	7	4	8	12	30
Denis Chasse	7	7	4	11	60
Martin Beaupre	7	1	7	8	9
Dany Duclos	7	5	2	7	27
Francois Belanger	7	2	3	5	21
Eric Brule	7	0	5	5	8
Hughes Mongeon	7	3	1	4	4
Patrick Bisaillon	7	2	2	4	20
Patrice Martineau	7	1	2	3	6
Daniel Dore	6	0	3	3	27
Paul Brousseau	7	0	3	3	0
Pierre Paul Landry	7	0	3	3	16
Eric Dandenault	5	0	2	2	55
Maxime Gagne	7	0	1	1	10
Eric Rochette	7	0	1	1	20
Martin Gagne	4	0	0	0	4
Jasmin Ouellet	6	0	0	0	0
Jean Imbeau	7	0	0	0	0
Sebastien Lavalliere	7	0	0	0	25
Felix Potvin (Goalie)	7	...	...	...	0

HULL OLYMPIQUES

(Lost semifinals to Laval, 4 games to 0)

	Games	G.	A.	Pts.	Pen.
Andrew McKim	11	8	10	18	8
Joel Blain	11	6	6	12	16
Herbert Hohenberger	11	3	7	10	10
Bruno Villeneuve	11	3	7	10	4
Joe Suk	11	5	4	9	4
Karl Dykhuis	11	2	5	7	2
Todd Sparks	11	1	5	6	36
Guy Dupuis	11	1	3	4	8
Craig Martin	11	2	1	3	65
Steven Dion	11	1	2	3	12
Craig Williard	11	1	2	3	23
Trevor Boland	11	0	3	3	12
Patrick Lemay	11	1	0	1	65
Frederic Boivin	11	0	1	1	82
Sylvain Ducharme	11	0	0	0	0
Eric Lavigne	11	0	0	0	32
Robert Melanson	11	0	0	0	70
Dan Paolucci	11	0	0	0	2
Sylvain Marcotte (Goalie)	2	...	...	...	0
Johnny Lorenzo (Goalie)	10	...	...	...	17

LAVAL TITANS

(Winners of 1990 President Cup Playoffs)

	Games	G.	A.	Pts.	Pen.
Denis Chalifoux	14	*14	14	*28	14
Martin Lapointe	14	8	17	25	64
Claude Boivin	13	7	13	20	59
Patrice Brisebois	13	7	9	18	26
Sylvain Naud	13	6	8	14	17
Michel Gingras	13	4	10	14	45
Normand Demers	14	3	11	14	0
Carl Boudreau	14	5	7	12	8
Gino Odjick	13	6	5	11	*110
Eric Dubois	13	3	8	11	29
Jim Bermingham	14	1	8	9	19
Serge Anglehart	10	1	6	7	59
Regis Tremblay	11	3	3	6	10
Sandy McCarthy	14	3	3	6	60
Patrick Caron	14	3	2	5	34
Eric Bissonnette	14	1	4	5	35
Daniel Arsenault	14	1	3	4	41
Carl Mantha	9	0	3	3	6
Jason Brousseau	4	0	1	1	4
Greg MacEachern	10	0	1	1	0
Francois Pelletier	1	0	0	0	0
Richard Valois	3	0	0	0	0
Julian Cameron (Goalie)	4	...	...	...	0
Eric Raymond (Goalie)	10	...	...	...	2

LONGUEUIL COLLEGE-FRANCAIS

(Lost quarterfinals to Hull, 4 games to 3)

	Games	G.	A.	Pts.	Pen.
Sylvain Fleury	7	5	5	10	0
Paul Willett	7	3	7	10	12
Nichol Cloutier	7	2	6	8	21
Mario Nobili	7	2	3	5	17
Martin Tanguay†	7	1	4	5	9
Yan Arsenault	7	2	2	4	16
David St. Pierre	7	2	2	4	8
Robert Guillet	7	2	1	3	15
Dominic Rheaume	7	1	1	2	0
Dave Chouinard	2	1	0	1	0
Christian Breton	7	0	1	1	22
Denis Cloutier	7	0	1	1	14
Martin Lejeunesse	7	0	1	1	4
Martin Tanguay‡	7	0	1	1	2
Dave Kallis	5	0	0	0	0
Donald Brashear	7	0	0	0	11
Etienne Lavoie	7	0	0	0	31
Stephane Paradis	7	0	0	0	2
Stephane Perron	7	0	0	0	4
J. Francois Gagnon (G.)	2	...	...	...	0
Francis Ouellette (Goalie)	6	...	...	...	2

†Wore uniform #27.
‡Wore uniform #66.

SHAWINIGAN CATARACTES

(Lost quarterfinals to Laval, 4 games to 2)

	Games	G.	A.	Pts.	Pen.
Steve Cadieux	6	4	7	11	26
Eric Nadeau	6	4	7	11	14

	Games	G.	A.	Pts.	Pen.
Yvan Bergeron	6	7	3	10	29
Stephane Charbonneau	6	4	2	6	11
Stephane Groleau	6	1	4	5	35
Patrick Hebert	6	0	3	3	9
Richard Hamelin	5	1	1	2	36
Mathieu Roy	6	1	1	2	2
Francois Bourdeau	6	1	0	1	7
Alain Cote	5	0	1	1	19
Hughes Bouchard	6	0	1	1	14
Francois Groleau	6	0	1	1	12
Ugo Bellante	1	0	0	0	0
Steve Dontigny	3	0	0	0	0
Dave Morissette	4	0	0	0	18
David Chernis	5	0	0	0	47
Stephane Bourget	6	0	0	0	14
Pierre Cote	6	0	0	0	13
Eric Duchesne	6	0	0	0	34
Sandy Scalzo	6	0	0	0	5
Dominic Roussel (Goalie)	2	...	...	...	0
Andre Boulianne (Goalie)	4	...	...	...	0

ST. HYACINTHE LASERS

(Lost semifinals to Victoriaville, 4 games to 1)

	Games	G.	A.	Pts.	Pen.
Pierre Sevigny	12	8	8	16	42
Denis Leblanc	11	7	7	14	14
Charles Poulin	11	5	8	13	47
Eric Bellerose	12	4	8	12	21
Alain Vogin	11	4	7	11	4
Patrick Poulin	12	1	9	10	5
Serge Renaud	11	6	3	9	18
Marc Picard	12	2	6	8	17
Eric Charron	11	3	4	7	57
Martin Fortin	12	3	3	6	10
Christian Lariviere	12	1	5	6	41
Mil Sukovic	10	1	4	5	25
Yannik Lemay	12	1	4	5	38
Pierre Allard	11	3	0	3	22
Joe Argento	7	1	2	3	32
Andy Ross	3	1	1	2	2
Martin Cote	11	0	2	2	14
Patrick Chartrand	5	0	1	1	2
Sylvain Gauthier	7	0	1	1	16
Francois Paquette	6	0	0	0	0
Serge Labelle	8	0	0	0	50
Ronald Kay	9	0	0	0	12
Yanick Degrace (Goalie)	4	...	...	...	0
Martin Brodeur (Goalie)	12	...	...	...	14

TROIS-RIVIERES DRAVEURS

(Lost quarterfinals to St. Hyacinthe, 4 games to 3)

	Games	G.	A.	Pts.	Pen.
Martin St. Amour	7	7	9	16	19
Yanic Perreault	7	6	5	11	19
Marco Pietroniro	7	3	6	9	14

	Games	G.	A.	Pts.	Pen.
Christian Bertrand	7	1	8	9	34
Steve Larouche	7	3	5	8	8
Chris Bartolone	7	2	5	7	38
Todd Gillingham	6	3	1	4	72
Eric St. Amant	5	1	2	3	19
Paolo Racicot	5	0	3	3	4
Sebastien Parent	6	1	1	2	30
Pierre Fillion	5	0	2	2	16
Gilles Bouchard	7	0	2	2	2
Nicolas Lefebvre	7	1	0	1	28
Claude Poirier	6	0	1	1	4
Pascal Dufault	7	0	1	1	17
Dave Whitton	1	0	0	0	0
Jacques Parent	2	0	0	0	0
Enrico Ciccone	3	0	0	0	15
Patrice Rene	4	0	0	0	6
Francis Couturier	5	0	0	0	0

	Games	G.	A.	Pts.	Pen.
Martin Lacombe	5	0	0	0	26
Dominic Maltais	7	0	0	0	18
Jean Francois Labbe (G.)	3	...	...	...	2
Alain Morissette (Goalie)	5	...	...	...	0

VICTORIAVILLE TIGRES

(Lost finals to Laval, 4 games to 0)

	Games	G.	A.	Pts.	Pen.
Daniel Gauthier	16	8	*19	27	16
Reginald Savage	16	13	10	23	40
Patrick Lebeau	16	7	15	22	12
Alain Tardif	16	8	7	15	19
Dany Nolet	16	7	5	12	6
Marc Labelle	16	4	8	12	42

	Games	G.	A.	Pts.	Pen.
Patrick Cloutier	16	3	6	9	60
Claude Barthe	16	0	9	9	44
Patrice Filliatrault	11	3	5	8	44
Steven Paiement	15	3	5	8	0
Karlo Pavich	16	2	5	7	47
Christian Campeau	16	1	3	4	28
Jason Downey	16	1	3	4	25
Martin Charrois	15	1	2	3	48
Yves Sarault	16	0	3	3	26
Mathieu Lamothe	15	1	1	2	8
Jean Blouin	1	0	0	0	2
Denis Beauchamps	2	0	0	0	0
Patrick Cote	9	0	0	0	0
Serge Thibaudeau	12	0	0	0	2
Claude Savoie	16	0	0	0	2
Pierre Gagnon (Goalie)	4	...	...	...	0
Stephane Fiset (Goalie)	14	...	...	...	10

COMPLETE 1990 PRESIDENT CUP GOALTENDING

	Games	Mins.	Goals	SO.	Avg.
Eric Raymond, Laval	10	609	23	*1	*2.27
Jean Francois Gagnon, Longueuil	2	146	6	0	2.47
Johnny Lorenzo, Hull	10	624	29	0	2.79
Francis Ouellette, Longueuil	6	322	18	0	3.35
Jean Francois Labbe, Trois-Rivieres	3	132	8	0	3.64
Stephane Fiset, Victoriaville	*14	*790	*49	0	3.72
Felix Potvin, Chicoutimi	7	438	29	0	3.97
Martin Brodeur, St. Hyacinthe	12	678	46	0	4.07
Yanick Degrace, St. Hyacinthe	4	41	3	0	4.39
Pierre Gagnon, Victoriaville	4	189	14	0	4.44
Julian Cameron, Laval	4	238	19	0	4.79
Sylvain Marcotte, Hull	2	86	7	0	4.88
Alain Morissette, Trois-Rivieres	5	297	28	0	5.66
Andre Boulianne, Shawinigan	4	239	23	0	5.77
Dominic Roussel, Shawinigan	2	120	12	0	6.00

INDIVIDUAL PRESIDENT CUP PLAYOFF LEADERS

Goals	Denis Chalifoux, Laval—	14
Assists	Daniel Gauthier, Victoriaville—	19
Points	Denis Chalifoux, Laval—	28
Penalty Minutes	Gino Odjick, Laval—	110
Goaltender's Average	Eric Raymond, Laval—2.27	
Shutouts	Eric Raymond, Laval—	1

1989-90 QMJHL ALL-STAR TEAMS

First Team	Position	Second Team
Pierre Gagnon, Victoriaville	Goalie	Felix Potvin, Chicoutimi
Karl Dykhuis, Hull	Defense	Francois Groleau, Shawinigan
Claude Barthe, Victoriaville	Defense	Patrice Brisebois, Laval
Andrew McKim, Hull	Center	Steve Larouche, Trois-Rivieres
Martin Lapointe, Laval	Right Wing	Sylvain Naud, Laval
Patrick Lebeau, Victoriaville	Left Wing	Pierre Sevigny, St. Hyacinthe

1989-90 QMJHL TROPHY WINNERS

Frank Selke Trophy (Most Gentlemanly Player) .... Andrew McKim, Hull
Michel Bergeron Trophy (Top Rookie Forward) .... Martin Lapointe, Laval
Raymond Lagace Trophy (Top Rookie D'fens'm'n/G'lt'nd'r) ...... Francois Groleau, Shaw.
Jean Beliveau Trophy (Leading Point Scorer) .... Patrick Lebeau, Victoriaville
Michel Briere Trophy (Regular Season MVP) .... Andrew McKim, Hull
Marcel Robert Trophy (Top Scholastic/Athletic Performer) .... Yanic Perreault, Tr.-Riv.
Mike Bossy Trophy (Top Pro Prospect) .... Karl Dykhuis, Hull
Emile "Butch" Bouchard Trophy (Top Defenseman) .... Claude Barthe, Victoriaville
Jacques Plante Trophy (Best Goalie) .... Pierre Gagnon, Victoriaville
Guy Lafleur Trophy (Playoff MVP) .... Denis Chalifoux, Laval
Robert LeBel Trophy (Best Team Defensive Average) .... Victoriaville Tigres
John Rougeau Trophy (Regular Season Champion) .... Victoriaville Tigres
President Cup (Playoff Champion) .... Laval Titans

HISTORICAL QMJHL TROPHY WINNERS

FRANK SELKE TROPHY

(Most Gentlemanly Player)

Season	Player	Club
1970-71—	Norm Dube, Sherbrooke	
1971-72—	Gerry Teeple, Cornwall	
1972-73—	Claude Larose, Drummondville	
1973-74—	Gary MacGregor, Cornwall	
1974-75—	Jean-Luc Phaneuf, Montreal	
1975-76—	Norm Dupont, Montreal	
1976-77—	Mike Bossy, Laval	
1977-78—	Kevin Reeves, Montreal	
1978-79—	Ray Bourque, Verdun	
	Jean-Francois Sauve, Trois-Rivieres	
1979-80—	Jean-Francois Sauve, Trois-Rivieres	
1980-81—	Claude Verret, Trois-Rivieres	
1981-82—	Claude Verret, Trois-Rivieres	
1982-83—	Pat LaFontaine, Verdun	
1983-84—	Jerome Carrier, Verdun	
1984-85—	Patrick Emond, Chicoutimi	
1985-86—	Jimmy Carson, Verdun	
1986-87—	Luc Beausoleil, Laval	
1987-88—	Stephan Lebeau, Shawinigan	
1988-89—	Steve Cadieux, Shawinigan	
1989-90—	Andrew McKim, Hull	

MICHEL BERGERON TROPHY

(Top Rookie Forward)
(Prior to 1980-81 season, award was given to QMJHL Rookie-of-the-Year.)

Season	Player	Club
1969-70—	Serge Martel, Verdun	
1970-71—	Bob Murphy, Cornwall	
1971-72—	Bob Murray, Cornwall	
1972-73—	Pierre Larouche, Sorel	
1973-74—	Mike Bossy, Laval	
1974-75—	Dennis Pomerleau, Hull	
1975-76—	Jean-Marc Bonamie, Shawinigan	
1976-77—	Rick Vaive, Sherbrooke	
1977-78—	Norm Rochefort, Trois-Rivieres	
	Denis Savard, Montreal	
1978-79—	Alan Grenier, Laval	
1979-80—	Dale Hawerchuk, Cornwall	
1980-81—	Claude Verret, Trois-Rivieres	
1981-82—	Sylvain Turgeon, Hull	
1982-83—	Pat LaFontaine, Verdun	
1983-84—	Stephane Richer, Granby	
1984-85—	Jimmy Carson, Verdun	
1985-86—	Pierre Turgeon, Granby	
1986-87—	Rob Murphy, Laval	
1987-88—	Martin Gelinas, Hull	
1988-89—	Yanic Perreault, Trois-Rivieres	
1989-90—	Martin Lapointe, Laval	

RAYMOND LAGACE TROPHY

(Top Rookie Defenseman or Goaltender)

Season	Player	Club
1980-81—	Billy Campbell, Montreal	
1981-82—	Michel Petit, Sherbrooke	
1982-83—	Bobby Dollas, Laval	
1983-84—	James Gasseau, Drummondville	
1984-85—	Robert Desjardins, Shawinigan	
1985-86—	Stephane Guerard, Shawinigan	
1986-87—	Jimmy Waite, Chicoutimi	
1987-88—	Stephane Beauregard, St. Jean	
1988-89—	Karl Dykhuis, Hull	
1989-90—	Francois Groleau, Shawinigan	

JEAN BELIVEAU TROPHY

(Leading Point Scorer)

Season	Player	Club
1969-70—	Luc Simard, Trois-Rivieres	
1970-71—	Guy Lafleur, Quebec	
1971-72—	Jacques Richard, Quebec	
1972-73—	Andre Savard, Quebec	
1973-74—	Pierre Larouche, Sorel	
1974-75—	Norm Dupont, Montreal	
1975-76—	Richard Dalpe, Trois-Rivieres	
	Sylvain Locas, Chicoutimi	

Season	Player	Club
1976-77—	Jean Savard, Quebec	
1977-78—	Ron Carter, Sherbrooke	
1978-79—	Jean-Francois Sauve, Trois-Rivieres	
1979-80—	Jean-Francois Sauve, Trois-Rivieres	
1980-81—	Dale Hawerchuk, Cornwall	
1981-82—	Claude Verret, Trois-Rivieres	
1982-83—	Pat LaFontaine, Verdun	
1983-84—	Mario Lemieux, Laval	
1984-85—	Guy Rouleau, Longueuil	
1985-86—	Guy Rouleau, Hull	
1986-87—	Marc Fortier, Chicoutimi	
1987-88—	Patrice Lefebvre, Shawinigan	
1988-89—	Stephane Morin, Chicoutimi	
1989-90—	Patrick Lebeau, Victoriaville	

MICHEL BRIERE TROPHY

(Regular Season Most Valuable Player)

Season	Player	Club
1972-73—	Andre Savard, Quebec	
1973-74—	Gary MacGregor, Cornwall	
1974-75—	Mario Viens, Cornwall	
1975-76—	Peter Marsh, Sherbrooke	
1976-77—	Lucien DeBlois, Sorel	
1977-78—	Kevin Reeves, Montreal	
1978-79—	Pierre Lacroix, Trois-Rivieres	
1979-80—	Denis Savard, Montreal	
1980-81—	Dale Hawerchuk, Cornwall	
1981-82—	John Chabot, Sherbrooke	
1982-83—	Pat LaFontaine, Verdun	
1983-84—	Mario Lemieux, Laval	
1984-85—	Daniel Berthiaume, Chicoutimi	
1985-86—	Guy Rouleau, Hull	
1986-87—	Robert Desjardins, Longueuil	
1987-88—	Marc Saumier, Hull	
1988-89—	Stephane Morin, Chicoutimi	
1989-90—	Andrew McKim, Hull	

MARCEL ROBERT TROPHY

(Top Scholastic/Athletic Performer)

Season	Player	Club
1981-82—	Jacques Sylvestre, Granby	
1982-83—	Claude Gosselin, Quebec	
1983-84—	Gilbert Paiement, Chicoutimi	
1984-85—	Claude Gosselin, Longueuil	
1985-86—	Bernard Morin, Laval	
1986-87—	Patrice Tremblay, Chicoutimi	
1987-88—	Stephane Beauregard, St. Jean	
1988-89—	Daniel Lacroix, Granby	
1989-90—	Yanic Perreault, Trois-Rivieres	

MIKE BOSSY TROPHY

(Top Pro Prospect)
(Originally called Association of Journalism of
Hockey Trophy from 1980-81 through 1982-83.)

Season	Player	Club
1980-81—	Dale Hawerchuk, Cornwall	
1981-82—	Michel Petit, Sherbrooke	
1982-83—	Pat LaFontaine, Verdun	
	Sylvain Turgeon, Hull (tie)	
1983-84—	Mario Lemieux, Laval	
1984-85—	Jose Charbonneau, Drummondville	
1985-86—	Jimmy Carson, Verdun	
1986-87—	Pierre Turgeon, Granby	
1987-88—	Daniel Dore, Drummondville	
1988-89—	Patrice Brisebois, Laval	
1989-90—	Karl Dykhuis, Hull	

EMILE "BUTCH" BOUCHARD TROPHY

(Top Defenseman)

Season	Player	Club
1975-76—	Jean Gagnon, Quebec	
1976-77—	Robert Picard, Montreal	
1977-78—	Mark Hardy, Montreal	
1978-79—	Ray Bourque, Verdun	
1979-80—	Gaston Therrien, Quebec	
1980-81—	Fred Boimistruck, Cornwall	
1981-82—	Paul Andre Boutilier, Sherbrooke	
1982-83—	J.J. Daigneault, Longueuil	
1983-84—	Billy Campbell, Verdun	
1984-85—	Yves Beaudoin, Shawinigan	
1985-86—	Sylvain Cote, Hull	
1986-87—	Jean Marc Richard, Chicoutimi	
1987-88—	Eric Desjardins, Granby	

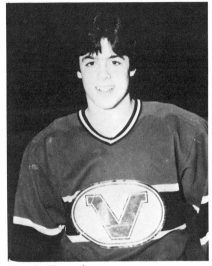

Pat LaFontaine

Mike Bossy

Season	Player	Club
1988-89—	Yves Racine, Victoriaville	
1989-90—	Claude Barthe, Victoriaville	

JACQUES PLANTE TROPHY

(Best Goalie)

Season	Player	Club
1969-70—	Michael Deguise, Sorel	
1970-71—	Reynald Fortier, Quebec	
1971-72—	Richard Brodeur, Cornwall	
1972-73—	Pierre Perusse, Quebec	
1973-74—	Claude Legris, Sorel	
1974-75—	Nick Sanza, Sherbrooke	
1975-76—	Tim Bernhardt, Cornwall	
1976-77—	Tim Bernhardt, Cornwall	
1977-78—	Tim Bernhardt, Cornwall	
1978-79—	Jacques Cloutier, Trois-Rivieres	
1979-80—	Corrado Micalef, Sherbrooke	
1980-81—	Michel Dufour, Sorel	
1981-82—	Jeff Barratt, Montreal	
1982-83—	Tony Haladuick, Laval	
1983-84—	Tony Haladuick, Laval	
1984-85—	Daniel Berthiaume, Chicoutimi	
1985-86—	Robert Desjardins, Hull	
1986-87—	Robert Desjardins, Longueuil	
1987-88—	Stephane Beauregard, St. Jean	
1988-89—	Stephane Fiset, Victoriaville	
1989-90—	Pierre Gagnon, Victoriaville	

GUY LAFLEUR TROPHY

(Most Valuable Player During Playoffs)

Season	Player	Club
1977-78—	Richard David, Trois-Rivieres	
1978-79—	Jean-Francois Sauve, Trois-Rivieres	
1979-80—	Dale Hawerchuk, Cornwall	
1980-81—	Alain Lemieux, Trois-Rivieres	
1981-82—	Michel Morissette, Sherbrooke	
1982-83—	Pat LaFontaine, Verdun	
1983-84—	Mario Lemieux, Laval	
1984-85—	Claude Lemieux, Verdun	
1985-86—	Sylvain Cote, Hull	
	Luc Robitaille, Hull (tie)	
1986-87—	Marc Saumier, Longueuil	
1987-88—	Marc Saumier, Hull	
1988-89—	Donald Audette, Laval	
1989-90—	Denis Chalifoux, Laval	

ROBERT LeBEL TROPHY

(Best Team Defensive Average)

Season	Club
1977-78—	Trois-Rivieres Draveurs
1978-79—	Trois-Rivieres Draveurs
1979-80—	Sherbrooke Beavers
1980-81—	Sorel Black Hawks
1981-82—	Montreal Juniors
1982-83—	Shawinigan Cataracts
1983-84—	Shawinigan Cataracts

Season	Club
1984-85—	Shawinigan Cataracts
1985-86—	Hull Olympiques
1986-87—	Longueuil Chevaliers
1987-88—	St. Jean Castors
1988-89—	Hull Olympiques
1989-90—	Victoriaville Tigres

JOHN ROUGEAU TROPHY

(Regular Season Champions)
(Originally called Governors Trophy from 1969-70
through 1982-83.)

Season	Club
1969-70—	Quebec Remparts
1970-71—	Quebec Remparts
1971-72—	Cornwall Royals
1972-73—	Quebec Remparts
1973-74—	Sorel Black Hawks
1974-75—	Sherbrooke Beavers
1975-76—	Sherbrooke Beavers
1976-77—	Quebec Remparts
1977-78—	Trois-Rivieres Draveurs
1978-79—	Trois-Rivieres Draveurs
1979-80—	Sherbrooke Beavers
1980-81—	Cornwall Royals
1981-82—	Sherbrooke Beavers
1982-83—	Laval Voisins
1983-84—	Laval Voisins
1984-85—	Shawinigan Cataracts
1985-86—	Hull Olympiques
1986-87—	Granby Bisons
1987-88—	Hull Olympiques
1988-89—	Trois-Rivieres Draveurs
1989-90—	Victoriaville Tigres

PRESIDENT CUP

(Playoff Champions)

Season	Club
1969-70—	Quebec Remparts
1970-71—	Quebec Remparts
1971-72—	Cornwall Royals
1972-73—	Quebec Remparts
1973-74—	Quebec Remparts
1974-75—	Sherbrooke Beavers
1975-76—	Quebec Remparts
1976-77—	Sherbrooke Beavers
1977-78—	Trois-Rivieres Draveurs
1978-79—	Trois-Rivieres Draveurs
1979-80—	Cornwall Royals
1980-81—	Cornwall Royals
1981-82—	Sherbrooke Beavers
1982-83—	Verdun Juniors
1983-84—	Laval Voisins
1984-85—	Verdun Junior Canadiens
1985-86—	Hull Olympiques
1986-87—	Longueuil Chevaliers
1987-88—	Hull Olympiques
1988-89—	Laval Titans
1989-90—	Laval Titans

WESTERN HOCKEY LEAGUE

(Canadian Major Junior Hockey League in 1966-67, renamed the Western Canadian Hockey League from 1967-68 to 1976-77. Has been named the Western Hockey League since 1977-78 season).

President
Ed Chynoweth
Vice-President
Richard Doerksen

Executive Assistant
Norman Dueck
Statistician
Randy Klassen

Address
616-5920 Macleod Trail S., Calgary, Alberta T2H 0K2
Phone
(403) 253-8113

FINAL 1989-90 WHL STANDINGS

EAST DIVISION

	G.	W.	L.	T.	Pts.	GF.	GA.
Lethbridge Hurricanes	72	51	17	4	106	465	270
Prince Albert Raiders	72	38	33	1	77	301	293
Regina Pats	72	34	31	7	75	332	329
Saskatoon Blades	72	33	34	5	71	325	354
Medicine Hat Tigers	72	32	38	2	66	298	331
Swift Current Broncos	72	29	39	4	62	323	351
Brandon Wheat Kings	72	28	38	6	62	276	325
Moose Jaw Warriors	72	28	41	3	59	287	330

WEST DIVISION

	G.	W.	L.	T.	Pts.	GF.	GA.
Kamloops Blazers	72	56	16	0	112	484	278
Seattle Thunderbirds	72	52	17	3	107	444	295
Tri-City Americans	72	39	28	5	83	433	354
Spokane Chiefs	72	30	37	5	65	334	344
Portland Winter Hawks	72	24	45	3	51	322	426
Victoria Cougars	72	5	65	2	12	221	565

NOTE: Swift Current defeated Brandon in a tie-breaker game and advanced to the playoffs.

TOP 20 SCORERS FOR THE BOB BROWNRIDGE MEMORIAL TROPHY

	Games	G.	A.	Pts.	Pen.
1. Len Barrie, Kamloops	70	*85	*100	*185	108
2. Glen Goodall, Seattle	67	76	87	163	83
3. Victor Gervais, Seattle	69	64	96	160	180
4. Brian Sakic, Swift Current	8	6	7	13	4
Tri-City	58	47	92	139	8
Totals	66	53	99	152	12
5. Phil Huber, Kamloops	72	63	89	152	176
6. Petr Nedved, Seattle	71	65	80	145	80
7. Stu Barnes, Tri-City	63	52	92	144	165
8. Corey Lyons, Lethbridge	72	63	79	142	26
9. Wes Walz, Lethbridge	56	54	86	140	69
10. Bryan Bosch, Lethbridge	72	48	90	138	34
11. Mark Greig, Lethbridge	65	55	80	135	149
12. Mike Sillinger, Regina	70	57	72	129	41

	Games	G.	A.	Pts.	Pen.
Peter Kasowski, Swift Current	28	19	34	53	28
Seattle	42	31	45	76	16
Totals	70	50	79	129	44
14. Travis Green, Spokane	50	45	44	89	80
Medicine Hat	25	15	24	39	19
Totals	75	60	68	128	99
15. Mike Needham, Kamloops	60	59	66	125	75
16. Pat Falloon, Spokane	71	60	64	124	48
17. Kelly Ens, Lethbridge	72	62	58	120	139
18. Jason Ruff, Lethbridge	72	55	64	119	114
Kevin Knopp, Swift Current	44	22	52	74	47
Medicine Hat	30	10	35	45	23
Totals	74	32	87	119	70
20. Brian Shantz, Kamloops	71	39	75	114	70

TEAM-BY-TEAM BREAKDOWN OF WHL SCORING

BRANDON WHEAT KINGS

	Games	G.	A.	Pts.	Pen.
Cam Brown	68	34	41	75	182
Brian Purdy	72	27	45	72	26
Jeff Odgers	64	37	28	65	209
Greg Hutchings	65	37	19	56	64
Troy Frederick	70	27	29	56	133
Bart Cote, Medicine Hat	14	2	6	8	23
Brandon	55	8	32	40	58
Totals	69	10	38	48	81
Gary Audette	62	19	23	42	39
Hardy Sauter	70	6	26	32	63
Pryce Wood	58	10	18	28	30
Merv Priest	59	11	15	26	21
Glen Gulutzan	36	6	19	25	24
Kevin Robertson, Tri-City	6	0	1	1	4
Brandon	54	8	11	19	28
Totals	60	8	12	20	32
Kevin Schmalz	64	8	12	20	83
Kevin Cheveldayoff	33	5	12	17	56
Chris Constant	32	9	5	14	32
Glen Webster	57	3	11	14	183
Dwayne Newman	72	0	14	14	99
Calvin Flint	62	2	9	11	18
Dwayne Gylywoychuk	58	2	8	10	37
Mike Vandenberghe	68	3	6	9	112
Jeff Hoad	11	4	1	5	4
Rob Puchniak	56	2	3	5	81
Trevor Kidd (Goalie)	63	0	2	2	14
Kelly Thiessen (Goalie)	18	0	1	1	7
Graham Garden	1	0	0	0	9
Chad Berezniuk	2	0	0	0	4
Mike Langen (Goalie)	2	0	0	0	0

KAMLOOPS BLAZERS

	Games	G.	A.	Pts.	Pen.
Len Barrie	70	*85	*100	*185	108
Phil Huber	72	63	89	152	176
Mike Needham	60	59	66	125	75
Brian Shantz	71	39	75	114	70
Daryl Sydor	67	29	66	95	129
Clayton Young, Victoria	25	23	14	37	45
Kamloops	38	22	25	47	88
Totals	63	45	39	84	133
Cal McGowan	71	33	44	77	78
Zac Boyer	71	24	47	71	63
Scott Niedermayer	64	14	55	69	64
Trevor Sim, Swift Current	6	3	2	5	21
Kamloops	43	27	35	62	53
Totals	49	30	37	67	74
Murray Duval, Tri-City	7	4	4	8	10
Swift Current	7	3	5	8	31
Kamloops	56	14	36	50	94
Totals	70	21	45	66	135
Paul Kruse	67	22	23	45	291
Joey Mittelsteadt	67	11	26	37	205
Dean Malkoc	48	3	18	21	209
Craig Bonner	64	1	17	18	77
Steve Yule	44	4	11	15	99
Todd Esselmont	50	7	5	12	37
Jarrett Bousquet	39	1	8	9	31
Jeff Watchorn	39	4	4	8	15
David Chyzowski	4	5	2	7	17
Lance Johnson	39	1	6	7	20
Shea Esselmont	22	1	2	3	2

	Games	G.	A.	Pts.	Pen.
David Linford, Swift Cur.	1	0	0	0	4
Kamloops	2	1	1	2	13
Totals	3	1	1	2	17
Dale Masson (Goalie)	22	0	1	1	2
Todd Harris	39	0	1	1	42
Corey Hirsch (Goalie)	63	0	1	1	10

LETHBRIDGE HURRICANES

	Games	G.	A.	Pts.	Pen.
Corey Lyons	72	63	79	142	26
Wes Walz	56	54	86	140	69
Bryan Bosch	72	48	90	138	34
Mark Greig	65	55	80	135	149
Kelly Ens	72	62	58	120	139
Jason Ruff	72	55	64	119	114
Brad Rubachuk	67	37	36	73	179
Peter Berthelsen	72	13	38	51	71
Neil Hawryluk	69	5	44	49	26
Kevin St. Jacques	63	24	19	43	49
Doug Barrault	54	14	16	30	36
Shane Peacock	65	7	23	30	60
Colin Gregor, Spokane	6	1	6	7	10
Lethbridge	48	3	9	12	104
Totals	54	4	15	19	114
Darcy Werenka	63	1	18	19	16
Ron Gunville, Prince Albert	4	1	1	2	11
Lethbridge	53	3	13	16	145
Totals	57	4	14	18	156
Rob Hale	65	8	9	17	213
Duane Maruschak	61	4	11	15	24
Pat Pylypuik	64	0	15	15	245

	Games	G.	A.	Pts.	Pen.
Brad Zimmer	50	4	8	12	34
Gary Reilly	44	3	9	12	9
David Holzer	24	0	4	4	15
Jamie Pushor	10	0	2	2	2
Dusty Imoo (Goalie)	48	0	1	1	0
Darcy Austin (Goalie)	1	0	0	0	0
Jeff Denham	1	0	0	0	0
Brian Dicken	1	0	0	0	0
Jamie McLennan (Goalie)	34	0	0	0	4

MEDICINE HAT TIGERS

	Games	G.	A.	Pts.	Pen.
Travis Green, Spokane	50	45	44	89	80
Medicine Hat	25	15	24	39	19
Totals	75	60	68	128	99
Kevin Knopp, Swift Current	44	22	52	74	47
Medicine Hat	30	10	35	45	23
Totals	74	32	87	119	70
Jason Miller	66	43	56	99	40
Kevin Riehl	72	38	47	85	71
Murray Garbutt	72	38	27	65	221
Brent Thompson	68	10	35	45	167
Jason Krywulak	70	18	26	44	51
Norm Batherson	63	11	28	39	52
Dave Shute, Victoria	14	4	5	9	25
Medicine Hat	48	13	15	28	56
Totals	62	17	20	37	81
Clayton Norris	72	13	18	31	176
Clayton Gainer	58	13	13	26	205
Jason Prosofsky	71	12	13	25	153
Jeff Knight, Swift Current	45	7	5	12	74
Medicine Hat	30	1	5	6	29
Totals	75	8	10	18	103
Dan Kordic	59	4	12	16	182
David Cooper	61	4	11	15	65
Dana Rieder	63	7	2	9	21
Jon Duval	67	0	9	9	113
Tyler Romanchuk	51	1	6	7	58
Kent Dochuk	8	2	3	5	10
Tomaz Vnuk	20	2	3	5	2
Chris Osgood (Goalie)	57	0	3	3	30
Patrick Backlund (Goalie)	14	0	1	1	0
Cam Moon, Sask. (Goalie)	13	0	1	1	0
Medicine Hat (Goalie)	10	0	0	0	2
Totals	23	0	1	1	2
Alec Sheflo (Goalie)	1	0	0	0	0
Mike Reimer	42	0	0	0	60

MOOSE JAW WARRIORS

	Games	G.	A.	Pts.	Pen.
Rob Harvey	71	40	62	102	24
Jerome Bechard	69	46	47	93	195
Rob Reimer	70	31	46	77	42
Chris Bright	72	36	38	74	107
Scott Humeniuk	71	23	47	70	141
Scott Barnstable	72	25	33	58	117
Kevin Masters	70	13	28	41	65
Derek Kletzel	66	15	17	32	54
Marty Loftsgard	65	4	22	26	54
Scott Reid	63	13	9	22	75
Scott Longstaff, Prince A.	1	0	0	0	0
Moose Jaw	58	6	16	22	20
Totals	59	6	16	22	20
Bob Loucks	64	8	13	21	121
Jason White, Brandon	21	3	4	7	28
Moose Jaw	43	2	8	10	114
Totals	64	5	12	17	142
Paul Dyck	72	5	10	15	86
Brad Boehm, Prince Albert	3	0	2	2	7
Moose Jaw	55	5	7	12	36
Totals	58	5	9	14	43
Darcy Jerome	41	4	7	11	17
Scott Thomas	61	2	9	11	42
Wade Smith, Swift Current	7	1	3	4	23
Tri-City	15	0	2	2	50
Moose Jaw	26	2	2	4	79
Totals	48	3	7	10	152
Jason Widmer	58	1	8	9	33
Jeff Rosner	21	3	1	4	182
Evan Anderson	12	1	1	2	6
Scott Ironside (Goalie)	30	0	2	2	8
Jeff Cowie	1	0	0	0	2
Jason Morris	1	0	0	0	0
Chris Bannerholt	3	0	0	0	0
Jay Dobrescu	4	0	0	0	2
Blaine Fomradas	6	0	0	0	15
Travis Kelln	7	0	0	0	0
Russ West	7	0	0	0	7
Jeff Petruic	9	0	0	0	0

	Games	G.	A.	Pts.	Pen.
Graham Waghorn	10	0	0	0	10
Kevin Messer	15	0	0	0	2
Jason Fitzsimmons (G.)	28	0	0	0	10
Jeff Calvert (Goalie)	32	0	0	0	4

PORTLAND WINTER HAWKS

	Games	G.	A.	Pts.	Pen.
Scott Mydan	71	36	61	97	70
Brent Fleetwood	72	41	43	84	114
Judson Innes	62	29	40	69	39
Dean Dorchak	72	32	35	67	97
Greg Leahy	50	20	43	63	131
Rob Krauss, Tri-City	33	5	19	24	107
Portland	31	4	24	28	95
Totals	64	9	43	52	202
Brad Harrison, Prince Alb.	5	3	1	4	8
Portland	42	24	21	45	108
Totals	47	27	22	49	116
Jamie Black	71	16	28	44	48
Jeff Sebastian, Regina	2	0	0	0	5
Portland	71	8	32	40	173
Totals	73	8	32	40	178
Steve Young, Moose Jaw	1	1	0	1	11
Prince Albert	10	1	1	2	39
Portland	42	15	17	32	169
Totals	53	17	18	35	219
Bryan Gourlie	70	18	15	33	69
Cam Danyluk	72	16	16	32	235
Mike Ruark	69	8	22	30	228
Rick Fry	64	9	19	28	100
Kim Deck	64	3	16	19	40
Brandon Smith	59	2	17	19	16
Ryan Slemko	30	6	8	14	44
Jamie Linden	67	5	7	12	124
Wayne Anchikoski	12	8	3	11	22
Kevin Jorgenson	26	2	5	7	125
Kelly Harris, Spokane	10	0	1	1	31
Portland	15	1	1	2	35
Totals	25	1	2	3	66
Byron Dafoe (Goalie)	40	0	3	3	10
Vince Cocciolo	29	0	2	2	80
Boyd Nolan	3	0	1	1	0
Dean Intwert (Goalie)	35	0	1	1	8
Terry Julian	1	0	0	0	0
Corey Andersen	3	0	0	0	6

PRINCE ALBERT RAIDERS

	Games	G.	A.	Pts.	Pen.
Jeff Nelson	72	28	69	97	79
Jackson Penney, Victoria	3	0	1	1	4
Prince Albert	55	53	32	85	51
Totals	58	53	33	86	55
Tracey Egeland	61	39	26	65	160
Todd Nelson	69	13	42	55	88
Scott Allison	66	22	16	38	73
David Neilson	67	16	19	35	189
Laurie Billeck	67	7	28	35	135
Mark Stowe	68	11	23	34	58
Troy Neumeier	72	8	26	34	73
Tom Fuller	56	13	20	33	18
Reid Simpson	29	15	17	32	121
Lee Leslie	62	14	16	30	13
Curt Regnier	57	8	19	27	8
Jeff Tomlinson	34	11	15	26	29
Terry Black, Portland	7	1	4	5	19
Prince Albert	33	4	15	19	31
Totals	40	5	19	24	50
Dean McAmmond	53	11	11	22	49
Brian Pellerin	53	6	15	21	175
Pat Odnokon	33	7	12	19	12
Tommie Eriksen	56	2	17	19	89
Dwayne Brook, Med. Hat	4	0	0	0	4
Saskatoon	5	0	0	0	10
Prince Albert	35	4	6	10	44
Totals	44	4	6	10	58
Dennis Sproxton (Goalie)	57	0	6	6	10
Troy Hjertaas	36	2	3	5	62
Darren Perkins	43	0	5	5	60
Chad Seibel, Lethbridge	4	1	0	1	2
Prince Albert	36	0	3	3	62
Totals	40	1	3	4	64
Donovan Hextall	7	1	2	3	4
Darren Van Impe	1	0	1	1	0
Steve Tillmanns	26	0	1	1	59
Scott Lindsay	5	0	0	0	0
Travis Laycock (Goalie)	9	0	0	0	6
Kevin Hennings	10	0	0	0	12

REGINA PATS

	Games	G.	A.	Pts.	Pen.
Mike Sillinger	70	57	72	129	41
Troy Mick	66	60	53	113	67
Scott Daniels	53	28	31	59	171
Frank Kovacs	71	26	32	58	165
Jamie Heward	72	14	44	58	42
Terry Hollinger	70	14	43	57	40
Kevin Haller	58	16	37	53	93
Jamie Splett	71	24	19	43	46
Cory Paterson	65	21	18	39	37
Greg Pankewicz	63	14	24	38	136
Gary Pearce	69	11	23	34	81
Martin Smith, Brandon	16	4	13	17	10
Victoria	1	1	0	1	0
Regina	21	3	7	10	16
Totals	38	8	20	28	26
Mike Kirby	65	11	16	27	23
Jim Mathieson	67	1	26	27	158
Kelly Markwart	35	7	14	21	47
Kelly Chotowetz, Tri-City	2	0	0	0	9
Swift Current	10	1	0	1	46
Regina	52	7	9	16	83
Totals	64	8	9	17	138
Cam McLellan	39	4	12	16	121
Cory Dosdall	25	5	6	11	86
Colin Ruck, Tri-City	28	1	3	4	46
Regina	29	1	3	4	33
Totals	57	2	6	8	79
Hal Christiansen	52	0	7	7	30
Wade Fennig	51	3	3	6	18
Brad McGinnis	3	2	3	5	0
Heath Weenk	43	0	4	4	14
Mikko Outinen	9	1	1	2	12
Gerry St. Cyr, Tri-City	3	1	0	1	6
Regina	3	0	0	0	17
Totals	6	1	0	1	23
Robin Poole, Brandon	2	1	0	1	0
Regina	1	0	1	1	0
Totals	3	1	0	1	5
Jamie Hayden	3	0	1	1	2
Ryan Reid	1	0	0	0	0
Jeff Shantz	1	0	0	0	0
Brad Scott	2	0	0	0	0
Craig Lumbard (Goalie)	4	0	0	0	0
Tim Olson, Saskatoon	3	0	0	0	2
Regina	1	0	0	0	0
Totals	4	0	0	0	2
Mike Risdale (Goalie)	30	0	0	0	4
Jason Glickman (Goalie)	52	0	0	0	13

SASKATOON BLADES

	Games	G.	A.	Pts.	Pen.
Jason Christie	69	42	65	107	70
Dean Holoien	70	43	49	92	121
Scott Scissons	61	40	47	87	81
David Struch	68	40	37	77	67
Jason Smart	66	27	48	75	187
Shawn Snesar	65	13	46	59	115
Darin Bauer	54	26	31	57	107
Derek Tibbatts	65	20	22	42	16
Todd Kinniburgh, Pr. Alb.	5	0	2	2	4
Portland	29	12	9	21	36
Medicine Hat	2	0	1	1	0
Saskatoon	24	2	8	10	2
Totals	60	14	20	34	42
Richard Matvichuk	56	8	24	32	126
Collin Bauer	29	4	25	29	49
Drew Sawtell	41	10	14	24	133
Shawn Yakimishyn	69	11	9	20	195
Jeff Buchanan	66	7	12	19	96
Rob Lelacheur	52	1	18	19	116
Grant Chorney, Victoria	12	2	3	5	43
Saskatoon	51	3	10	13	262
Totals	63	5	13	18	305
Trent Coghill	51	6	8	14	46
Dean Rambo	48	5	8	13	32
Shane Langager	58	9	2	11	12
Trevor Sherban	66	2	8	10	62
Shane Bogden, Regina	6	1	5	6	15
Saskatoon	5	0	0	0	7
Totals	11	1	5	6	22
Mark Wotton	51	2	3	5	31
Trevor Robins (Goalie)	51	0	5	5	16
Trent Hamm	32	2	2	4	12
Tim Cox	7	1	1	2	6
Mark Raiter	14	1	1	2	51
Damon Kustra (Goalie)	24	0	2	2	2
Dean Kuntz (Goalie)	2	0	0	0	0

SEATTLE THUNDERBIRDS

	Games	G.	A.	Pts.	Pen.
Glen Goodall	67	76	87	163	83
Victor Gervais	69	64	96	160	180
Petr Nedved	71	65	80	145	80
Peter Kasowski, Swift Cur..	28	19	34	53	28
Seattle	42	31	45	76	16
Totals	70	50	79	129	44
Lindsay Vallis	65	34	43	77	68
Stuart Malgunas	63	15	48	63	116
Turner Stevenson	62	29	32	61	276
Brad Zavisha	69	22	38	60	124
Vince Boe, Medicine Hat..	42	4	21	25	54
Seattle	28	4	22	26	58
Totals	70	8	43	51	112
Kevin Malgunas	67	22	26	48	209
Brent Bilodeau	68	14	29	43	170
Al Kinisky	72	9	29	38	103
Darren McAusland	62	14	18	32	28
Kevin Barrett, Swift Cur..	21	1	7	8	41
Seattle	44	7	9	16	109
Totals	65	8	16	24	150
Craig Chapman	70	8	15	23	64
Darcy Simon	63	5	13	18	285
Tom Sprague	68	1	10	11	93
Cregg Nicol	28	2	8	10	102
Scott Albert, Swift Current.	15	2	0	2	2
Seattle	37	1	7	8	5
Totals	52	3	7	10	7
Cam Brauer, Regina	4	0	0	0	20
Seattle	64	1	9	10	229
Totals	68	1	9	10	249
Mike Zakowich	10	1	6	7	2
Danny Lorenz (Goalie)	56	0	4	4	23
Brad Smith	4	0	1	1	4
Corey Schwab (Goalie)	27	0	1	1	10
Nick Majkovic	1	0	0	0	5
Trevor Mathias, M'se Jaw.	2	0	0	0	9
Seattle	1	0	0	0	4
Totals	3	0	0	0	13
Trevor Pennock	33	0	0	0	27

SPOKANE CHIEFS

	Games	G.	A.	Pts.	Pen.
Pat Falloon	71	60	64	124	48
Ray Whitney	71	57	56	113	50
Mark Woolf, Medicine Hat..	47	35	33	68	45
Spokane	21	17	19	36	28
Totals	68	52	52	104	73
Steve Junker	69	20	36	56	76
Barry Dreger, Brandon	6	1	2	3	26
Spokane	58	10	35	45	222
Totals	64	11	37	48	248
Brent Thurston, Victoria	36	5	12	17	148
Spokane	26	10	12	22	89
Totals	62	15	24	39	237
Dennis Saharchuk	45	17	21	38	20
Bobby House	64	18	16	34	74
Rob Dumas	57	8	23	31	134
John Klemm	66	3	28	31	100
Mike Chrun	72	11	17	28	40
Chris Rowland	69	13	14	27	128
Chris Lafreniere, Med. Hat.	40	2	9	11	60
Spokane	21	3	11	14	48
Totals	61	5	20	25	108
Calvin Thudium, Portland..	22	2	7	9	53
Spokane	34	6	9	15	49
Totals	56	8	16	24	102
Bram Vanderkracht	64	7	14	21	55
Frank Evans	52	2	17	19	141
Mike Jickling	64	4	14	18	90
Kerry Toporowski	65	1	13	14	*384
Shayne Sieker	18	7	5	12	20
Shane Maitland	47	3	9	12	92
Trevor Tovell	30	1	9	10	29
Curt Brennan, Lethbridge..	1	0	0	0	0
Spokane	6	2	0	2	0
Totals	7	2	0	2	0
Barcley Pearce	16	0	2	2	16
Mike Hawes	4	1	0	1	6
John Colvin (Goalie)	4	0	1	1	14
Shawn Dietrich (Goalie)	37	0	1	1	6
Jeff Ferguson (Goalie)	37	0	1	1	27
Chad Larsen	3	0	0	0	7
Brad Toporowski	3	0	0	0	2
Todd Patz	4	0	0	0	6
Greg Senio	7	0	0	0	18
Paul Checknita	13	0	0	0	12
Derek Harper	24	0	0	0	15

SWIFT CURRENT BRONCOS

	Games	G.	A.	Pts.	Pen.
Kimbi Daniels	69	43	51	94	84
Geoff Sanderson	70	32	62	94	56
Dan Lambert	50	17	51	68	119
Blake Knox	72	30	32	62	139
Mark McFarlane	61	31	30	61	275
Andy Schneider, Seattle..	28	10	12	22	55
Swift Current	42	16	21	37	43
Totals	70	26	33	59	98
Todd Holt	63	26	22	48	29
Jason Smith, Tri-City	5	0	1	1	0
Swift Current	61	9	35	44	26
Totals	66	9	36	45	26
Tyler Wright	67	14	18	32	119
Evan Marble	72	4	21	25	101
Lloyd Pelletier, Med. Hat..	26	0	3	3	19
Swift Current	27	13	8	21	7
Totals	53	13	11	24	26
Ed Bertuzzi, Kamloops..	20	3	7	10	87
Swift Current	19	7	5	12	48
Totals	39	10	12	22	135
Joel Dyck, Kamloops	13	0	7	7	14
Swift Current	45	5	7	12	38
Totals	58	5	14	19	52
Trent McCleary	70	3	15	18	43
Ed Patterson, Seattle	18	9	2	11	19
Swift Current	15	1	3	4	0
Totals	33	10	5	15	19
Kent Rogers	16	2	4	6	0
Stu Scantlebury	49	0	5	5	24
Kurt Seher	55	2	3	5	28
Scott Beed	61	1	3	4	21
Stan Reddick (Goalie)	61	0	2	2	11
Jay Macauley	2	0	1	1	9
Darren Naylor	2	0	1	1	2
Mike Mathers	5	1	0	1	0
Wade Sambrook	10	0	1	1	2
Dave Gerse, Regina	26	0	1	1	82
Swift Current	2	0	0	0	0
Totals	28	0	1	1	82
Curtis Friesen	2	0	0	0	0
Geoff Gerlitz	2	0	0	0	0
Chris Larkin	4	0	0	0	2
Matt Harasymuk (Goalie)..	8	0	0	0	2
Drew Schoneck	14	0	0	0	5
David Bell, Spo. (Goalie)..	12	0	0	0	6
Swift Current (Goalie)..	14	0	0	0	2
Totals	26	0	0	0	8
Randy Kerr	34	0	0	0	9

TRI-CITY AMERICANS

	Games	G.	A.	Pts.	Pen.
Brian Sakic, Swift Current.	8	6	7	13	4
Tri-City	58	47	92	139	8
Totals	66	53	99	152	12
Stu Barnes	63	52	92	144	165
Kyle Reeves, Swfit Current	2	1	1	2	2
Tri-City	67	67	36	103	94
Totals	69	68	37	105	96
Bill Lindsay	72	40	45	85	84
Steve Jaques	64	20	64	84	185
Steve McNutt	69	28	48	76	56
Greg Spenrath	67	36	32	68	256
Scott Levins	71	25	37	62	132
Terry Degner	70	21	39	60	27
Devin Derksen	69	15	43	58	137
Kalvin Knibbs	68	28	29	57	33
Steve Rennie	59	9	40	49	10
Dan Sherstenka	70	10	17	27	64
Scott Farrell, Lethbridge	4	1	1	2	22
Spokane	10	3	5	8	34
Tri-City	35	3	10	13	84
Totals	49	7	16	23	140
Terry Virtue, Victoria	24	1	9	10	85
Tri-City	34	1	10	11	82
Totals	58	2	19	21	167
Terran Sandwith	70	4	14	18	92
Jason Bowen	61	8	5	13	129
Don Blishen, Port. (G.)	1	0	0	0	0
Tri-City (Goalie)	34	0	11	11	8
Totals	35	0	11	11	8
David Podlubny	26	2	5	7	79
Brad Loring	55	3	2	5	126
Olaf Kolzig (Goalie)	48	0	5	5	36
Trevor Renkers	13	0	4	4	29
Adrian Van Der Sloot	9	2	1	3	35
Kevin Courchesne (Goalie)	1	0	0	0	0
Steve Passmore (Goalie)...	4	0	0	0	0

	Games	G.	A.	Pts.	Pen.
Jim Dean	6	0	0	0	7
Jeff Fancy	12	0	0	0	6

VICTORIA COUGARS

	Games	G.	A.	Pts.	Pen.
Terry Klapstein	64	25	39	64	35
Mike Seaton	67	25	39	64	43
Trevor Buchanan, Kam..	29	6	11	17	143
Victoria	43	21	20	41	193
Totals	72	27	31	58	336
Mark Cipriano	66	15	27	42	264
Dean Dyer	36	12	30	42	38
Ryan Harrison, Kamloops..	24	4	4	8	27
Victoria	43	13	16	29	43
Totals	67	17	20	37	70
Shayne Green	43	16	14	30	26
Milan Dragicevic, Spo..	27	4	5	9	98
Victoria	32	7	12	19	122
Totals	59	11	17	28	220
Blair Scott	69	4	18	22	101
Rob Sumner	58	2	19	21	206
Terry Bendera, Pr. Alb..	6	1	3	4	20
Victoria	57	5	9	14	70
Totals	63	6	12	18	90
Dino Caputo	59	10	6	16	40
Jarret Zukiwsky	67	7	8	15	100
Larry Woo	64	5	8	13	111
Pat Hodgins	11	4	5	9	0
Dwayne Keller	22	2	7	9	59
Jason Hicks, Portland	19	4	1	5	2
Victoria	4	1	0	1	2
Totals	23	5	1	6	4
Tommi Virkkunen, Kam. ...	3	1	2	3	0
Victoria	15	1	2	3	4
Totals	18	2	4	6	4
Craig Allan	22	2	4	6	8
Curtis Nykyforuk, Regina..	13	0	1	1	49
Victoria	27	2	3	5	68
Totals	40	2	4	6	117
Jason Peters, Moose Jaw..	29	1	2	3	20
Victoria	34	1	1	2	24
Totals	63	2	3	5	44
Chris Catellier	47	0	4	4	102
Andrew Wolf	4	1	2	3	7
John Badduke	49	1	2	3	138
John Bentham	35	0	3	3	30
Jason Knox	13	0	2	2	18
Jason Diesewich	17	0	2	2	4
Corey Jones, Port. (G.)	6	0	0	0	0
Victoria (Goalie)	31	0	2	2	13
Totals	37	0	2	2	13
Jaret Burgoyne (Goalie)	44	0	2	2	8
Len Jorgenson	7	1	0	1	4
Kirk Roworth	8	1	0	1	18
Jeff Greenwood	51	1	0	1	22
Rob Kreiger	2	0	1	1	12
Barry Rysz (Goalie)	19	0	1	1	4
Brad Hack	1	0	0	0	0
Jeff Kerr	1	0	0	0	2
Patrick Mullin, Brandon	1	0	0	0	0
Victoria	1	0	0	0	0
Totals	2	0	0	0	0
Brad Bagu	3	0	0	0	0
Doug Strang	3	0	0	0	0

COMPLETE WHL GOALTENDING

	Games	Mins.	Goals	SO.	Avg.
Mike Langen	2	17	0	0	0.00
Trevor Kidd	*63	*3676	254(1)	2	4.15
Kelly Thiessen	18	722	69(1)	0	5.73
Brandon Totals	72	4415	325	2	4.42
Dale Masson	22	745	46(1)	1	3.70
Corey Hirsch	*63	3608	230(1)	*3	3.82
Kamloops Totals	72	4353	278	4	3.83
Darcy Austin	1	20	0	0	0.00
Dusty Imoo	48	2667	159(1)	*3	*3.58
Jamie McLennan	34	1690	110	1	3.91
Lethbridge Totals	72	4377	270	4	3.70
Patrick Backlund	14	749	49	0	3.93
Chris Osgood	57	3094	228(4)	0	4.42
Cam Moon (a)	10	480	41(1)	0	5.13
Alec Sheflo	1	63	8	0	7.62
Medicine Hat Totals	72	4386	331	0	4.53
Jason Fitzsimmons	28	1392	90(2)	0	3.88
Scott Ironside	30	1558	117(2)	0	4.51
Jeff Calvert	32	1425	119	1	5.01
Moose Jaw Totals	72	4375	330	1	4.53
Don Blishen (b)	1	60	4	0	4.00
Byron Dafoe	40	2265	193(2)	0	5.11
Dean Intwert	35	1684	180(4)	0	6.41
Eric Badzgon (c)	2	120	15	0	7.50
Corey Jones (d)	6	223	28	0	7.53
Portland Totals	72	4352	426	0	5.87
Dennis Sproxton	57	3133	200(4)	0	3.83
Eric Badzgon (c)	16	805	56	0	4.17
Travis Laycock	9	405	33	0	4.89
Prince Albert Totals	72	4343	293	0	4.05
Jason Glickman	52	2836	195	0	4.13
Mike Risdale	30	1409	108(2)	0	4.60
Craig Lumbard	4	133	17	0	7.67
Willy MacDonald	1	40	7	0	10.50
Regina Totals	72	4418	329	0	4.47
Cam Moon (a)	13	573	42(2)	0	4.40
Trevor Robins	51	2616	203(2)	1	4.66
Damon Kustra	24	1073	91(1)	0	5.09
Dean Kuntz	2	120	13	0	6.50
Saskatoon Totals	72	4382	354	1	4.85

	Games	Mins.	Goals	SO.	Avg.
Corey Schwab	27	1150	69(1)	0	3.60
Danny Lorenz	56	3226	221(4)	0	4.11
Seattle Totals	72	4376	295	0	4.04
David Bell (e)	12	569	38(1)	0	4.01
Jeff Ferguson	37	2059	152(3)	0	4.43
Shawn Dietrich	37	1667	129(2)	1	4.64
John Colvin	4	111	19	0	10.27
Spokane Totals	72	4406	344	1	4.68
Stan Reddick	61	3423	250(5)	0	4.38
David Bell (e)	14	600	51(2)	0	5.10
Matt Harasymuk	8	357	43	0	7.23
Swift Current Totals	72	4380	351	0	4.81
Olaf Kolzig	48	2504	187(4)	1	4.48
Steve Passmore	4	215	17	0	4.74
Don Blishen (b)	34	1633	142	0	5.22
Kevin Courchesne	1	25	4	0	9.60
Tri-City Totals	72	4377	354	1	4.85
Barry Rysz	19	848	102(2)	0	7.22
Jaret Borgoyne	44	1975	*256(4)	0	7.78
Corey Jones (d)	31	1510	198(3)	0	7.87
Victoria Totals	72	4333	565	0	7.82

( )—Empty Net Goals. Do not count against a Goaltender's average.
(a)—Moon played for Medicine Hat and Saskatoon.
(b)—Blishen played for Portland and Tri-City.
(c)—Badzgon played for Portland and Prince Albert.
(d)—Jones played for Portland and Victoria.
(e)—Bell played for Spokane and Swift Current.

INDIVIDUAL 1989-90 LEADERS

Goals	Len Barrie, Kamloops— 85
Assists	Len Barrie, Kamloops— 100
Points	Len Barrie, Kamloops— 185
Penalty Minutes	Kerry Toporowski, Spokane— 384
Goaltender's Average	Dusty Imoo, Lethbridge—3.58
Shutouts	Corey Hirsch, Kamloops— 3
	Dusty Imoo, Lethbridge— 3

1990 WHL PLAYOFFS

EAST DIVISION QUARTERFINALS

(Best-of-five series)

Series "A"

	W.	L.	Pts.	GF.	GA.
Regina	3	1	6	17	16
Swift Current	1	3	2	16	17

(Regina wins series, 3 games to 1)

Series "B"

	W.	L.	Pts.	GF.	GA.
Saskatoon	3	0	6	18	9
Medicine Hat	0	3	0	9	18

(Saskatoon wins series, 3 games to 0)

WEST DIVISION SEMIFINALS

(Best-of-nine series)

Series "C"

	W.	L.	Pts.	GF.	GA.
Kamloops	5	1	10	34	20
Spokane	1	5	2	20	34

. (Kamloops wins series, 5 games to 1)

Series "D"

	W.	L.	Pts.	GF.	GA.
Seattle	5	2	10	35	17
Tri-City	2	5	4	17	35

(Seattle wins series, 5 games to 2)

EAST DIVISION SEMIFINALS

(Best-of-seven series)

Series "E"

	W.	L.	Pts.	GF.	GA.
Lethbridge	4	3	8	45	30
Saskatoon	3	4	6	30	45

(Lethbridge wins series, 4 games to 3)

Series "F"

	W.	L.	Pts.	GF.	GA.
Prince Albert	4	3	8	31	29
Regina	3	4	6	29	31

(Prince Albert wins series, 4 games to 3)

WEST DIVISION FINALS

(Best-of-nine series)

Series "G"

	W.	L.	Pts.	GF.	GA.
Kamloops	5	1	10	26	21
Seattle	1	5	2	21	26

(Kamloops wins series, 5 games to 1)

EAST DIVISION FINALS

(Best-of-seven series)

Series "H"

	W.	L.	Pts.	GF.	GA.
Lethbridge	4	3	8	32	28
Prince Albert	3	4	6	28	32

(Lethbridge wins series, 4 games to 3)

FINALS

(Best-of-seven series)

Series "I"

	W.	L.	Pts.	GF.	GA.
Kamloops	4	1	8	26	19
Lethbridge	1	4	2	19	26

(Kamloops wins WHL Playoffs, 4 games to 1)

TOP 10 WHL PLAYOFF SCORERS

	Games	G.	A.	Pts.
1. Len Barrie, Kamloops	17	*14	23	*37
Wes Walz, Lethbridge	19	13	*24	*37
3. Mark Greig, Lethbridge	18	11	21	32
4. Kelly Ens, Lethbridge	19	*14	14	28
5. Bryan Bosch, Lethbridge	19	13	13	26
Corey Lyons, Lethbridge	19	11	15	26
7. Mike Needham, Kamloops	17	11	13	24
8. Phil Huber, Kamloops	17	12	11	23
9. Mike Sillinger, Regina	11	12	10	22
Peter Kasowski, Seattle	13	8	14	22

TEAM-BY-TEAM PLAYOFF SCORING

KAMLOOPS BLAZERS

(Winners of 1990 WHL Playoffs)

	Games	G.	A.	Pts.	Pen.
Len Barrie	17	*14	23	*37	24
Mike Needham	17	11	13	24	10
Phil Huber	17	12	11	23	44
David Chyzowski	17	11	6	17	46
Clayton Young	17	6	11	17	29
Trevor Sim	17	3	13	16	28
Scott Niedermayer	17	2	14	16	35
Murray Duval	17	8	7	15	29
Daryl Sydor	17	2	9	11	28
Brian Shantz	14	4	6	10	14
Cal McGowan	17	4	5	9	42
Zac Boyer	17	4	4	8	8
Paul Kruse	17	3	5	8	79

	Games	G.	A.	Pts.	Pen.
Steve Yule	17	1	4	5	10
Craig Bonner	17	1	2	3	0
Dean Malkoc	17	0	3	3	56
Joey Mittelsteadt	17	0	3	3	21
Todd Esselmont	16	0	1	1	0
Corey Hirsch (Goalie)	17	0	1	1	10
Shea Esselmont	1	0	0	0	0
Lance Johnson	1	0	0	0	0
Paul Strand	1	0	0	0	0
Jeff Watchorn	1	0	0	0	0

LETHBRIDGE HURRICANES

(Lost WHL Finals to Kamloops, 4 games to 1)

	Games	G.	A.	Pts.	Pen.
Wes Walz	19	13	*24	*37	33
Mark Greig	18	11	21	32	35
Kelly Ens	19	*14	14	28	36
Bryan Bosch	19	13	13	26	10
Corey Lyons	19	11	15	26	4
Jason Ruff	19	9	10	19	18
Peter Berthelsen	19	5	12	17	20
Doug Barrault	19	7	3	10	0
Brad Rubachuk	16	3	7	10	51
Shane Peacock	19	2	8	10	42
Kevin St. Jacques	18	3	6	9	13
Neil Hawryluk	19	3	6	9	12
Ron Gunville	19	0	5	5	31
Pat Pylypuik	19	1	2	3	58
Rob Hale	19	1	1	2	23
Colin Gregor	8	0	2	2	6
Darcy Werenka	19	0	2	2	4
Gary Reilly	1	0	1	1	0
Dusty Imoo (Goalie)	9	0	0	0	2
Jamie McLennan (Goalie)	13	0	0	0	0
Brad Zimmer	15	0	0	0	4
Duane Maruschak	19	0	0	0	2

MEDICINE HAT TIGERS

(Lost East Div. quarterfinals to Sask., 3 games to 0)

	Games	G.	A.	Pts.	Pen.
Jason Miller	3	3	2	5	0
Kevin Knopp	3	1	3	4	2
Clayton Gainer	3	1	2	3	11
Jason Krywulak	3	2	0	2	4
Kevin Riehl	3	1	1	2	2
David Cooper	3	0	2	2	2
Chris Osgood (Goalie)	3	0	2	2	2
Murray Garbutt	3	1	0	1	21
Norm Batherson	3	0	1	1	5
Brent Thompson	3	0	1	1	14
Cam Moon (Goalie)	1	0	0	0	0
Jon Duval	3	0	0	0	6
Travis Green	3	0	0	0	2
Jeff Knight	3	0	0	0	4
Dan Kordic	3	0	0	0	9
Clayton Norris	3	0	0	0	15
Jason Prosofsky	3	0	0	0	8
Mike Reimer	3	0	0	0	5
Dana Rieder	3	0	0	0	5
Tyler Romanchuk	3	0	0	0	2

PRINCE ALBERT RAIDERS

(Lost East Division finals to Lethbridge, 4 games to 3)

	Games	G.	A.	Pts.	Pen.
Tracy Egeland	13	7	10	17	26
Jackson Penney	12	11	4	15	28
Todd Nelson	14	3	12	15	12
Jeff Nelson	14	2	11	13	10
Reid Simpson	14	4	7	11	34
Tom Fuller	14	4	5	9	4
David Neilson	14	4	4	8	31
Troy Neumeier	14	3	5	8	12
Mark Stowe	14	3	5	8	22
Troy Hjertaas	14	0	6	6	23
Tommie Eriksen	9	4	1	5	13
Laurie Billeck	14	2	3	5	24
Lee Leslie	14	2	3	5	4
Dean McAmmond	14	2	3	5	18
Scott Allison	11	1	4	5	8
Curt Regnier	14	3	1	4	8
Pat Odnokon	5	2	2	4	0
Brian Pellerin	10	1	3	4	26
Chad Seibel	14	0	4	4	11
Dwayne Brook	5	1	0	1	0
Travis Laycock (Goalie)	10	0	1	1	0

	Games	G.	A.	Pts.	Pen.
Steve Tillmanns	2	0	0	0	2
Darren Perkins	3	0	0	0	5
Dennis Sproxton (Goalie)	7	0	0	0	0

REGINA PATS

(Lost East Div. semifinals to Pr. Albert, 4 games to 3)

	Games	G.	A.	Pts.	Pen.
Mike Sillinger	11	12	10	22	2
Troy Mick	11	7	10	17	17
Kevin Haller	11	2	9	11	16
Frank Kovacs	11	4	4	8	10
Scott Daniels	11	3	5	8	21
Mike Kirby	11	3	5	8	6
Jamie Splett	11	4	3	7	6
Jim Mathieson	11	0	7	7	16
Cory Paterson	11	1	5	6	11
Jamie Heward	11	2	2	4	10
Greg Pankewicz	10	1	3	4	19
Terry Hollinger	11	1	3	4	10
Cam McLellan	11	2	1	3	35
Cory Dosdall	11	1	2	3	20
Kelly Chotowetz	11	1	1	2	28
Kelly Markwart	3	1	0	1	0
Colin Ruck	11	1	0	1	4
Jason Glickman (Goalie)	10	0	1	1	2
Garry Pearce	1	0	0	0	0
Robin Poole	1	0	0	0	0
Hal Christiansen	2	0	0	0	0
Mike Risdale (Goalie)	3	0	0	0	0
Heath Weenk	6	0	0	0	0
Wade Fennig	10	0	0	0	2

SASKATOON BLADES

(Lost East Div. semifinals to Lethbridge, 4 games to 3)

	Games	G.	A.	Pts.	Pen.
Jason Christie	10	10	8	18	15
Dean Holoien	10	6	11	17	11
David Struch	10	8	5	13	6
Scott Scissons	10	3	8	11	6
Darin Bader	10	6	4	10	30
Richard Matvichuk	10	2	8	10	16
Todd Kinninburgh	10	4	5	9	4
Collin Bauer	10	1	8	9	14
Jason Smart	10	1	5	6	19
Shawn Snesar	10	1	5	6	19
Derek Tibbatts	9	0	5	5	2
Shawn Yakimishyn	10	1	2	3	15
Drew Sawtell	9	2	0	2	34
Mark Wotton	7	1	1	2	15
Trevor Sherban	8	0	2	2	8
Jeff Buchanan	9	0	2	2	2
Trevor Robins (Goalie)	10	0	2	2	0
Trent Coghill	6	1	0	1	4
Grant Chorney	10	1	0	1	45
Damon Kustra (Goalie)	1	0	0	0	0
Cam Moon (Goalie)	1	0	0	0	0
Shane Langager	6	0	0	0	0
Rob Lelacheur	6	0	0	0	7

SEATTLE THUNDERBIRDS

(Lost West Division finals to Kamloops, 5 games to 1)

	Games	G.	A.	Pts.	Pen.
Peter Kasowski	13	8	14	22	10
Victor Gervais	13	8	9	17	30
Glen Goodall	10	7	7	14	2
Petr Nedved	11	4	9	13	2
Vince Boe	13	5	7	12	20
Lindsay Vallis	13	6	5	11	14
Stewart Malgunas	13	2	9	11	32
Brent Bilodeau	13	3	5	8	31
Kevin Malgunas	13	4	3	7	55
Brad Zavisha	13	1	6	7	16
Turner Stevenson	13	3	2	5	35
Al Kinisky	13	2	3	5	13
Kevin Barrett	13	1	2	3	20
Darren McAusland	13	1	2	3	4
Darcy Simon	13	1	2	3	79
Craig Chapman	13	0	2	2	8
Scott Albert	5	0	1	1	0
Danny Lorenz (Goalie)	13	0	1	1	0
Corey Schwab (Goalie)	3	0	0	0	0
Dody Wood	5	0	0	0	2
Cam Brauer	10	0	0	0	27
Tom Sprague	11	0	0	0	2

SPOKANE CHIEFS

(Lost West Div. semifinals to Kamloops, 5 games to 1)

	Games	G.	A.	Pts.	Pen.
Pat Falloon	6	5	8	13	4
Ray Whitney	6	3	4	7	6
Barry Dreger	6	1	3	4	24
Steve Junker	6	0	4	4	2
Mark Woolf	6	2	1	3	9
Mike Jickling	6	1	2	3	6
Brent Thurston	6	2	0	2	22
Bram Vanderkracht	3	1	1	2	0
Shane Maitland	4	1	1	2	10
Rob Dumas	6	1	1	2	17
Jon Klemm	6	1	1	2	5
Trevor Tovell	6	0	2	2	5
Frank Evans	6	1	0	1	6
Chris Lafreniere	6	1	0	1	6
Shayne Sieker	6	0	1	1	16
Chris Rowland	1	0	0	0	0
Bobby House	5	0	0	0	6
Calvin Thudium	5	0	0	0	9
Mike Chrun	6	0	0	0	6
Jeff Ferguson (Goalie)	6	0	0	0	7
Kerry Toporowski	6	0	0	0	37

SWIFT CURRENT BRONCOS

(Lost East Div. quarterfinals to Regina, 3 games to 1)

	Games	G.	A.	Pts.	Pen.
Lloyd Pelletier	4	3	3	6	4
Mark McFarlane	4	3	2	5	17
Dan Lambert	4	2	3	5	12
Geoff Sanderson	4	1	4	5	8
Kimbi Daniels	4	1	3	4	10
Blake Knox	4	1	3	4	14
Andy Schneider	4	2	1	3	2
Jason Smith	4	1	1	2	2
Joel Dyck	4	0	2	2	4
Evan Marble	4	0	2	2	4
Todd Holt	4	1	0	1	2
Trent McCleary	4	1	0	1	0
Scott Beed	4	0	0	0	0
Eddie Patterson	4	0	0	0	2
Stan Reddick (Goalie)	4	0	0	0	0
Kent Rogers	4	0	0	0	0
Stu Scantlebury	4	0	0	0	0
Kurt Seher	4	0	0	0	2
Tyler Wright	4	0	0	0	12

TRI-CITY AMERICANS

(Lost West Division semifinals to Seattle, 5 games to 2)

	Games	G.	A.	Pts.	Pen.
Stu Barnes	7	1	5	6	26
Steve Rennie	7	0	6	6	10
Kalvin Knibbs	7	5	0	5	6
Scott Levins	6	2	3	5	18
Bill Lindsay	7	3	0	3	17
Kyle Reeves	7	2	1	3	8
Steve Jaques	6	1	2	3	55
Terry Degner	7	1	2	3	6
Jason Bowen	7	0	3	3	4
Devin Derksen	7	0	2	2	13
Steve McNutt	7	0	2	2	9
Terran Sandwith	7	0	2	2	14
Brad Loring	6	1	0	1	13
Greg Spenrath	7	1	0	1	35
Scott Farrell	7	0	1	1	12
Dan Sherstenka	7	0	1	1	12
Jeff Fancy	2	0	0	0	0
Don Blishen (Goalie)	5	0	0	0	2
Olaf Kolzig (Goalie)	6	0	0	0	0
Terry Virtue	6	0	0	0	30

COMPLETE WHL PLAYOFF GOALTENDING

	Games	Mins.	Goals	SO.	Avg.
Corey Hirsch	*17	*1043	*60	0	3.45
Kamloops Totals	17	1043	60	0	3.45
Jamie McLennan	13	677	44	0	3.90
Dusty Imoo	9	496	39(1)	0	4.72
Lethbridge Totals	19	1173	84	0	4.30
Chris Osgood	3	173	17	0	5.90
Cam Moon	1	7	1	0	8.57
Medicine Hat Totals	3	180	18	0	6.00
Travis Laycock	10	562	36(1)	0	3.84
Denis Sproxton	7	317	23(1)	0	4.35
Prince Albert Totals	14	879	61	0	4.16
Jason Glickman	10	589	36(1)	0	3.67
Mike Risdale	3	100	10	0	6.00
Regina Totals	11	689	47	0	4.09
Damon Kustra	1	4	0	0	0.00
Cam Moon	1	21	1	0	2.86
Trevor Robins	10	587	53	0	5.42
Saskatoon Totals	10	612	54	0	5.29
Corey Schwab	3	49	2(1)	0	2.45
Danny Lorenz	13	751	40	0	*3.20
Seattle Totals	13	800	43	0	3.23
Jeff Ferguson	6	360	34	0	5.67
Spokane Totals	6	360	34	0	5.67
Stan Reddick	4	249	17	0	4.10
Swift Current Totals	4	249	17	0	4.10
Don Blishen	5	102	8	*1	4.71
Olaf Kolzig	6	318	27	0	5.09
Tri-City Totals	7	420	35	1	5.00

( )—Empty Net Goals. Do not count against a Goaltender's average.

INDIVIDUAL WHL PLAYOFF LEADERS

Goals	Len Barrie, Kamloops—	14
	Kelly Ens, Lethbridge—	14
Assists	Wes Walz, Kamloops—	24
Points	Len Barrie, Kamloops—	37
	Wes Walz, Kamloops—	37
Penalty Minutes	Paul Kruse, Kamloops—	79
	Darcy Simon, Seattle—	79
Goaltender's Average (60 minutes)	Danny Lorenz, Seattle—	3.20
Shutouts	Don Blishen, Tri-City—	1

1989-90 WHL ALL-STAR TEAMS

East Division	Position	West Division
Trevor Kidd, Brandon	Goal	Danny Lorenz, Seattle
Kevin Haller, Regina	Defense	Daryl Sydor, Kamloops
Dan Lambert, Swift Current	Defense	Stewart Malgunas, Seattle
Wes Walz, Lethbridge	Center	Len Barrie, Kamloops
Troy Mick, Regina	Left Wing	Phil Huber, Kamloops
Mark Greig, Lethbridge	Right Wing	Mike Needham, Kamloops

1990 WHL TROPHY WINNERS

Four Broncos Memorial Trophy (Most Valuable Player)	Glen Goodall, Seattle
Bob Clarke Trophy (Top Scorer)	Len Barrie, Kamloops
Jim Piggott Memorial Trophy (Rookie of the Year)	Petr Nedved, Seattle
Brad Hornung Trophy (Most Sportsmanlike Player)	Bryan Bosch, Lethbridge
Bill Hunter Trophy (Top Defenseman)	Kevin Haller, Regina
Del Wilson Trophy (Top Goaltender)	Trevor Kidd, Brandon
Player of the Year	Wes Walz, Lethbridge
Dunc McCallum Memorial Trophy (Coach of the Year)	Ken Hitchcock, Kamloops
Scott Munro Memorial Trophy (Regular Season Champion)	Kamloops Blazers
Msgr. Athol Murray Memorial Trophy (Playoff Champion)	Kamloops Blazers

HISTORICAL WHL TROPHY WINNERS

FOUR BRONCOS MEMORIAL TROPHY

Most Valuable Player selected by coaches

Season	Player	Club
1966-67	Gerry Pinder, Saskatoon	
1967-68	Jim Harrison, Estevan	
1968-69	Bobby Clarke, Flin Flon	
1969-70	Reggie Leach, Flin Flon	
1970-71	Ed Dyck, Calgary	
1971-72	John Davidson, Calgary	
1972-73	Dennis Sobchuk, Regina	
1973-74	Ron Chipperfield, Brandon	
1974-75	Bryan Trottier, Lethbridge	
1975-76	Bernie Federko, Saskatoon	
1976-77	Barry Beck, New Westminster	
1977-78	Ryan Walter, Seattle	
1978-79	Perry Turnbull, Portland	
1979-80	Doug Wickenheiser, Regina	
1980-81	Steve Tsujiura, Medicine Hat	
1981-82	Mike Vernon, Calgary	
1982-83	Mike Vernon, Calgary	
1983-84	Ray Ferraro, Brandon	
1984-85	Cliff Ronning, New Westminster	
1985-86	Emanuel Viveiros, Prince Albert (East Division)	
	Rob Brown, Kamloops (West Division)	
1986-87	Joe Sakic, Swift Current (East Division)	
	Rob Brown, Kamloops (West Division)	
1987-88	Joe Sakic, Swift Current	
1988-89	Stu Barnes, Tri-City	
1989-90	Glen Goodall, Seattle	

BOB CLARKE TROPHY

(Originally called Bob Brownridge Memorial Trophy)
Top Scorer

Season	Player	Club	Pts.
1966-67	Gerry Pinder, Saskatoon		140
1967-68	Bobby Clarke, Flin Flon		168
1968-69	Bobby Clarke, Flin Flon		137
1969-70	Reggie Leach, Flin Flon		111
1970-71	Chuck Arnason, Flin Flon		163
1971-72	Tom Lysiak, Medicine Hat		143
1972-73	Tom Lysiak, Medicine Hat		154
1973-74	Ron Chipperfield, Brandon		162
1974-75	Mel Bridgman, Victoria		157
1975-76	Bernie Federko, Saskatoon		187
1976-77	Bill Derlago, Brandon		178
1977-78	Brian Propp, Brandon		182
1978-79	Brian Propp, Brandon		194
1979-80	Doug Wickenheiser, Regina		170
1980-81	Brian Varga, Regina		187
1981-82	Jack Callander, Regina		190
1982-83	Dale Derkatch, Regina		179
1983-84	Ray Ferraro, Brandon		192
1984-85	Cliff Ronning, New Westminster		197
1985-86	Rob Brown, Kamloops		173
1986-87	Rob Brown, Kamloops		212
1987-88	Joe Sakic, Swift Current		160
	Theo Fleury, Moose Jaw		160
1988-89	Dennis Holland, Portland		167
1989-90	Len Barrie, Kamloops		185

JIM PIGGOTT MEMORIAL TROPHY

(Originally called Stewart "Butch" Paul Memorial Trophy)
Rookie of the Year

Season	Player	Club
1966-67	Ron Garwasiuk, Regina	
1967-68	Ron Fairbrother, Saskatoon	
1968-69	Ron Williams, Edmonton	
1969-70	Gene Carr, Flin Flon	
1970-71	Stan Weir, Medicine Hat	
1971-72	Dennis Sobchuk, Regina	
1972-73	Rick Blight, Brandon	
1973-74	Cam Connor, Flin Flon	
1974-75	Don Murdoch, Medicine Hat	
1975-76	Steve Tambellini, Lethbridge	
1976-77	Brian Propp, Brandon	
1977-78	John Ogrodnick, New Westminster	
	Keith Brown, Portland (tie)	
1978-79	Kelly Kisio, Calgary	
1979-80	Grant Fuhr, Victoria	
1980-81	Dave Michaluk, Regina	

Season	Player	Club
1981-82	Dale Derkatch, Regina	
1982-83	Dan Hodgson, Prince Albert	
1983-84	Cliff Ronning, New Westminster	
1984-85	Mark Mackay, Moose Jaw	
1985-86	Neil Brady, Medicine Hat (East Division)	
	Ron Shudra, Kamloops (West Division)	
	Dave Waldie, Portland (West Division)	
1986-87	Joe Sakic, Swift Current (East Division)	
	Dennis Holland, Portland (West Division)	
1987-88	Stu Barnes, New Westminster	
1988-89	Wes Walz, Lethbridge	
1989-90	Petr Nedved, Seattle	

BRAD HORNUNG TROPHY

(Originally called Frank Boucher Memorial Trophy for Most Gentlemanly Player)
Most Sportsmanlike Player

Season	Player	Club
1966-67	Morris Stefaniw, Estevan	
1967-68	Bernie Blanchette, Saskatoon	
1968-69	Bob Liddington, Calgary	
1969-70	Randy Rota, Calgary	
1970-71	Lorne Henning, Estevan	
1971-72	Ron Chipperfield, Brandon	
1972-73	Ron Chipperfield, Brandon	
1973-74	Mike Rogers, Calgary	
1974-75	Danny Arndt, Saskatoon	
1975-76	Blair Chapman, Saskatoon	
1976-77	Steve Tambellini, Lethbridge	
1977-78	Steve Tambellini, Lethbridge	
1978-79	Errol Rausse, Seattle	
1979-80	Steve Tsujiura, Medicine Hat	
1980-81	Steve Tsujiura, Medicine Hat	
1981-82	Mike Moller, Lethbridge	
1982-83	Darren Boyko, Winnipeg	
1983-84	Mark Lamb, Medicine Hat	
1984-85	Cliff Ronning, New Westminster	
1985-86	Randy Smith, Medicine Hat (East Division)	
	Ken Morrison, Kamloops (West Division)	
1986-87	Len Nielsen, Regina (East Division)	
	Dave Archibald, Portland (West Division)	

Season	Player	Club
1987-88	Craig Endean, Regina	
1988-89	Blair Atcheynum, Moose Jaw	
1989-90	Bryan Bosch, Lethbridge	

BILL HUNTER TROPHY

Top Defenseman

Season	Player	Club
1966-67	Barry Gibbs, Estevan	
1967-68	Gerry Hart, Flin Flon	
1968-69	Dale Hoganson, Estevan	
1969-70	Jim Hargreaves, Winnipeg	
1970-71	Ron Jones, Edmonton	
1971-72	Jim Watson, Calgary	
1972-73	George Pesut, Saskatoon	
1973-74	Pat Price, Saskatoon	
1974-75	Rick LaPointe, Victoria	
1975-76	Kevin McCarthy, Winnipeg	
1976-77	Barry Beck, New Westminster	
1977-78	Brad McCrimmon, Brandon	
1978-79	Keith Brown, Portland	
1979-80	David Babych, Portland	
1980-81	Jim Benning, Portland	
1981-82	Gary Nylund, Portland	
1982-83	Gary Leeman, Regina	
1983-84	Bob Rouse, Lethbridge	
1984-85	Wendel Clark, Saskatoon	
1985-86	Emanuel Viveiros, Prince Albert (East Division)	
	Glen Wesley, Portland (West Division)	
1986-87	Wayne McBean, Medicine Hat (East Division)	
	Glen Wesley, Portland (West Division)	
1987-88	Greg Hawgood, Kamloops	
1988-89	Dan Lambert, Swift Current	
1989-90	Kevin Haller, Regina	

DEL WILSON TROPHY

Top Goaltender

Season	Player	Club
1966-67	Ken Brown, Moose Jaw	
1967-68	Chris Worthy, Flin Flon	
1968-69	Ray Martyniuk, Flin Flon	
1969-70	Ray Martyniuk, Flin Flon	
1970-71	Ed Dyck, Calgary	
1971-72	John Davidson, Calgary	
1972-73	Ed Humphreys, Saskatoon	
1973-74	Garth Malarchuk, Calgary	
1974-75	Bill Oleschuk, Saskatoon	
1975-76	Carey Walker, New Westminster	
1976-77	Glen Hanlon, Brandon	
1977-78	Bart Hunter, Portland	
1978-79	Rick Knickle, Brandon	
1979-80	Kevin Eastman, Victoria	
1980-81	Grant Fuhr, Victoria	
1981-82	Mike Vernon, Calgary	
1982-83	Mike Vernon, Calgary	
1983-84	Ken Wregget, Lethbridge	
1984-85	Troy Gamble, Medicine Hat	

Season	Player	Club
1985-86	Mark Fitzpatrick, Medicine Hat	
1986-87	Kenton Rein, Prince Albert (East Division)	
	Dean Cook, Kamloops (West Division)	
1987-88	Troy Gamble, Spokane	
1988-89	Danny Lorenz, Seattle	
1989-90	Trevor Kidd, Brandon	

PLAYER OF THE YEAR

Selected by fans and media

Season	Player	Club
1974-75	Ed Staniowski, Regina	
1975-76	Bernie Federko, Saskatoon	
1976-77	Kevin McCarthy, Winnipeg	
1977-78	Ryan Walter, Seattle	
1978-79	Brian Propp, Brandon	
1979-80	Doug Wickenheiser, Regina	
1980-81	Barry Pederson, Victoria	
1981-82	Mike Vernon, Calgary	
1982-83	Dean Evason, Kamloops	
1983-84	Ray Ferraro, Brandon	
1984-85	Dan Hodgson, Prince Albert	
1985-86	Emanuel Viveiros, Prince Albert	
1986-87	Rob Brown, Kamloops	
1987-88	Joe Sakic, Swift Current	
1988-89	Dennis Holland, Portland	
1989-90	Wes Walz, Lethbridge	

DUNC McCALLUM MEMORIAL TROPHY

Coach of the Year

Season	Coach	Club
1968-69	Scotty Munro, Calgary	
1969-70	Pat Ginnell, Flin Flon	
1970-71	Pat Ginnell, Flin Flon	
1971-72	Earl Ingarfield, Regina	
1972-73	Pat Ginnell, Flin Flon	
1973-74	Stan Dunn, Swift Current	
1974-75	Pat Ginnell, Victoria	
1975-76	Ernie McLean, New Westminster	
1976-77	Dunc McCallum, Brandon	
1977-78	Jack Shupe, Victoria	
	Dave King, Billings (tie)	
1978-79	Dunc McCallum, Brandon	
1979-80	Doug Sauter, Calgary	
1980-81	Ken Hodge, Portland	
1981-82	Jack Sangster, Seattle	
1982-83	Darryl Lubiniecki, Saskatoon	
1983-84	Terry Simpson, Prince Albert	
1984-85	Doug Sauter, Medicine Hat	
1985-86	Terry Simpson, Prince Albert	
1986-87	Ken Hitchcock, Kam. (W. Division)	
	Graham James, S. Curr. (E. Div.)	
1987-88	Marcel Comeau, Saskatoon	
1988-89	Ron Kennedy, Medicine Hat	
1989-90	Ken Hitchcock, Kamloops	

SCOTT MUNRO MEMORIAL TROPHY

Regular Season Champions

Season	Team
1966-67	Edmonton Oil Kings
1967-68	Flin Flon Bombers
1968-69	Flin Flon Bombers
1969-70	Flin Flon Bombers
1970-71	Edmonton Oil Kings
1971-72	Calgary Centennials
1972-73	Saskatoon Blades
1973-74	Regina Pats
1974-75	Victoria Cougars
1975-76	New Westminster Bruins
1976-77	New Westminster Bruins
1977-78	Brandon Wheat Kings
1978-79	Brandon Wheat Kings
1979-80	Portland Winter Hawks
1980-81	Victoria Cougars
1981-82	Lethbridge Broncos
1982-83	Saskatoon Blades
1983-84	Kamloops Junior Oilers
1984-85	Prince Albert Raiders
1985-86	Medicine Hat Tigers
1986-87	Kamloops Blazers
1987-88	Saskatoon Blades
1988-89	Swift Current Broncos
1989-90	Kamloops Blazers

MSGR. ATHOL MURRAY MEMORIAL TROPHY

Playoff Champions

Season	Team
1966-67	Moose Jaw Canucks
1967-68	Estevan Bruins
1968-69	Flin Flon Bombers
1969-70	Flin Flon Bombers
1970-71	Edmonton Oil Kings
1971-72	Edmonton Oil Kings
1972-73	Medicine Hat Tigers
1973-74	Regina Pats
1974-75	New Westminster Bruins
1975-76	New Westminster Bruins
1976-77	New Westminster Bruins
1977-78	New Westminster Bruins
1978-79	Brandon Wheat Kings
1979-80	Regina Pats
1980-81	Victoria Cougars
1981-82	Portland Winter Hawks
1982-83	Lethbridge Broncos
1983-84	Kamloops Junior Oilers
1984-85	Prince Albert Raiders
1985-86	Kamloops Blazers
1986-87	Medicine Hat Tigers
1987-88	Medicine Hat Tigers
1988-89	Swift Current Broncos
1989-90	Kamloops Blazers

MEMORIAL CUP WINNERS

Season	Team
1918-19	University of Toronto Schools
1919-20	Toronto Canoe Club
1920-21	Winnipeg Falcons
1921-22	Fort William War Veterans
1922-23	Univ. of Manitoba-Winnipeg
1923-24	Owen Sound Greys
1924-25	Regina Pats
1925-26	Calgary Canadians
1926-27	Owen Sound Greys
1927-28	Regina Monarchs
1928-29	Toronto Marlboros
1929-30	Regina Pats
1930-31	Winnipeg Elmwoods
1931-32	Sudbury Wolves
1932-33	Newmarket
1933-34	Toronto St. Michael's
1934-35	Winnipeg Monarchs
1935-36	West Toronto Redmen
1936-37	Winnipeg Monarchs
1937-38	St. Boniface Seals
1938-39	Oshawa Generals
1939-40	Oshawa Generals
1940-41	Winnipeg Rangers
1941-42	Portage la Prairie

Season	Team
1942-43	Winnipeg Rangers
1943-44	Oshawa Generals
1944-45	Toronto St. Michael's
1945-46	Winnipeg Monarchs
1946-47	Toronto St. Michael's
1947-48	Port Arthur West End Bruins
1948-49	Montreal Royals
1949-50	Montreal Jr. Canadiens
1950-51	Barrie Flyers
1951-52	Guelph Biltmores
1952-53	Barrie Flyers
1953-54	St. Catharines Tee Pees
1954-55	Toronto Marlboros
1955-56	Toronto Marlboros
1956-57	Flin Flon Bombers
1957-58	Ottawa-Hull Jr. Canadiens
1958-59	Winnipeg Braves
1959-60	St. Catharines Tee Pees
1960-61	Toronto St. Michael's Majors
1961-62	Hamilton Red Wings
1962-63	Edmonton Oil Kings
1963-64	Toronto Marlboros
1964-65	Niagara Falls Flyers
1965-66	Edmonton Oil Kings

Season	Team
1966-67	Toronto Marlboros
1967-68	Niagara Falls Flyers
1968-69	Montreal Jr. Canadiens
1969-70	Montreal Jr. Canadiens
1970-71	Quebec Remparts
1971-72	Cornwall Royals
1972-73	Toronto Marlboros
1973-74	Regina Pats
1974-75	Toronto Marlboros
1975-76	Hamilton Fincups
1976-77	New Westminster Bruins
1977-78	New Westminster Bruins
1978-79	Peterborough Petes
1979-80	Cornwall Royals
1980-81	Cornwall Royals
1981-82	Kitchener Rangers
1982-83	Portland Winter Hawks
1983-84	Ottawa 67's
1984-85	Prince Albert Raiders
1985-86	Guelph Platers
1986-87	Medicine Hat Tigers
1987-88	Medicine Hat Tigers
1988-89	Swift Current Broncos
1989-90	Oshawa Generals

NATIONAL COLLEGIATE ATHLETIC ASSOCIATION

Year	Champion	Coach	Runner-Up
1948	Michigan	Vic Heyliger	Dartmouth
1949	Boston College	John Kelley	Dartmouth
1950	Colorado College	Cheddy Thompson	Boston University
1951	Michigan	Vic Heyliger	Brown
1952	Michigan	Vic Heyliger	Colorado College
1953	Michigan	Vic Heyliger	Minnesota
1954	Rensselaer Poly. Inst.	Ned Harkness	Minnesota
1955	Michigan	Vic Heyliger	Colorado College
1956	Michigan	Vic Heyliger	Michigan Tech
1957	Colorado College	Thomas Bedecki	Michigan
1958	Denver	Murray Armstrong	North Dakota
1959	North Dakota	Bob May	Michigan State
1960	Denver	Murray Armstrong	Michigan Tech
1961	Denver	Murray Armstrong	St. Lawrence
1962	Michigan Tech	John MacInnes	Clarkson
1963	North Dakota	Barry Thorndycraft	Denver
1964	Michigan	Al Renfrew	Denver
1965	Michigan Tech	John MacInnes	Boston College
1966	Michigan State	Amo Bessone	Clarkson
1967	Cornell	Ned Harkness	Boston University
1968	Denver	Murray Armstrong	North Dakota
1969	Denver	Murray Armstrong	Cornell
1970	Cornell	Ned Harkness	Clarkson
1971	Boston University	Jack Kelley	Minnesota
1972	Boston University	Jack Kelley	Cornell
1973	Wisconsin	Bob Johnson	Denver
1974	Minnesota	Herb Brooks	Michigan Tech
1975	Michigan Tech	John MacInnes	Minnesota
1976	Minnesota	Herb Brooks	Michigan Tech
1977	Wisconsin	Bob Johnson	Michigan
1978	Boston University	Jack Parker	Boston College
1979	Minnesota	Herb Brooks	North Dakota
1980	North Dakota	Gino Gasparini	Northern Michigan
1981	Wisconsin	Bob Johnson	Minnesota
1982	North Dakota	Gino Gasparini	Wisconsin
1983	Wisconsin	Jeff Sauer	Harvard
1984	Bowling Green State	Jerry York	Minnesota-Duluth
1985	Rensselaer Poly. Inst.	Mike Addesa	Providence College
1986	Michigan State	Ron Mason	Harvard
1987	North Dakota	Gino Gasparini	Michigan State
1988	Lake Superior State	Frank Anzalone	St. Lawrence
1989	Harvard	Bill Cleary	Minnesota
1990	Wisconsin	Jeff Sauer	Colgate

CENTRAL COLLEGIATE HOCKEY ASSOCIATION

	W.	L.	T.	GF.	GA.	Pct.
Michigan State (35-7-3)	26	3	3	190	93	.859
Lake Superior State (33-10-3)	24	6	2	169	91	.781
Bowling Green State (25-17-2)	20	10	2	153	142	.656
Michigan (24-12-6)	16	11	5	148	125	.578
*Western Michigan (14-24-2)	12	18	2	145	162	.406
Ohio State (11-24-5)	11	17	4	138	164	.406
Miami (O.) (12-24-4)	8	21	3	138	175	.297
Ferris State (11-23-6)	6	20	6	106	162	.281
Illinois-Chicago (10-27-1)	7	24	1	104	177	.234

*Western Michigan has tiebreaker over Ohio State based on 3-1 head-to-head record.

Overall record in parentheses.

1989-90 CCHA ALL-STARS

First Team	Position	Second Team
Jason Muzzatti, Michigan State	Goalie	Darrin Madeley, Lake Superior St.
Kord Cernich, Lake Superior State	Defenseman	Dan Keczmer, Lake Superior State
Rob Blake, Bowling Green State	Defenseman	Don Gibson, Michigan State
Craig Fisher, Miami (O.)	Forward	Pat Murray, Michigan State
Nelson Emerson, Bowling Green	Forward	Darryl Noren, Illinois-Chicago
Kip Miller, Michigan State	Forward	Jim Dowd, Lake Superior State

CCHA Player of the Year: Kip Miller, Michigan State
CCHA Rookie of the Year: David Roberts, Michigan
CCHA Coach of the Year: Ron Mason, Michigan State
CCHA Leading Scorer: Kip Miller, Michigan State
CCHA Playoff Most Valuable Player: Peter White, Michigan State

CCHA PLAYOFFS

QUARTERFINALS

(Best-of-three series)

Michigan State 6, Ferris State 4
Michigan State 13, Ferris State 1
(Michigan State wins series, 2-0)

Lake Superior State 5, Miami (O.) 3
Lake Superior State 7, Miami (O.) 4
(Lake Superior State wins series, 2-0)

Bowling Green State 7, Ohio State 1
Bowling Green State 6, Ohio State 5
(Bowling Green State wins series, 2-0)

Michigan 5, Western Michigan 3
Michigan 8, Western Michigan 2
(Michigan wins series, 2-0)

SEMIFINALS

Lake Superior St. 4, Bowling Green St. 2
Michigan State 4, Michigan 3 (OT)

CONSOLATION GAME

Michigan 5, Bowling Green State 4

CHAMPIONSHIP GAME

Michigan State 4, Lake Superior State 3

EASTERN COLLEGIATE ATHLETIC CONFERENCE

	W.	L.	T.	GF.	GA.	Pct.
Colgate (31-6-1)	18	3	1	101	62	.841
RPI (20-14-0)	14	8	0	131	107	.636
*Cornell (16-10-3)	12	7	3	86	69	.614
Clarkson (21-11-3)	12	7	3	91	77	.614
St. Lawrence (13-15-4)	12	8	2	87	74	.591
Harvard (13-14-1)	12	9	1	110	77	.568
Princeton (12-14-1)	11	10	1	95	91	.523
Brown (10-16-3)	8	11	3	78	94	.432
Vermont (9-20-2)	7	13	2	71	96	.364
Yale (8-20-1)	6	15	1	75	105	.295
Dartmouth (4-18-4)	4	14	4	58	98	.273
Army (10-16-4)	4	15	3	58	91	.250

*Cornell has tiebreaker over Clarkson based on better record versus others in the Top 8. They were even head-to-head and versus others in the Top 4.

Overall record in parentheses.

1989-90 ECAC ALL-STARS

First Team	Position	Second Team
Dave Gagnon, Colgate	Goalie	Chris Harvey, Brown
Mike Brewer, Brown	Defenseman	Mike McKee, Princeton
Dan Ratushny, Cornell	Defenseman	Dave Tretowicz, Clarkson
Joel Gardner, Colgate	Forward	Greg Polaski, Princeton
Mike Vukonich, Harvard	Forward	Andre Faust, Princeton
C.J. Young, Harvard	Forward	Joe Day, St. Lawrence

ECAC Player of the Year: Dave Gagnon, Colgate
ECAC Rookie of the Year: Kent Manderville, Cornell
ECAC Coach of the Year: Terry Slater, Colgate
ECAC Leading Scorer: Joe Juneau, RPI
ECAC Playoff Most Valuable Player: Craig Woodcroft, Colgate

ECAC PLAYOFFS

PRELIMINARY ROUND

Brown 7, Vermont 5

Yale 5, Princeton 1

QUARTERFINALS

(Best-of-three series)

Colgate 10, Yale 3
Colgate 5, Yale 4
(Colgate wins series, 2-0)

RPI 5, Brown 3
RPI 6, Brown 4
(RPI wins series, 2-0)

Cornell 6, Harvard 2
Cornell 4, Harvard 2
(Cornell wins series, 2-0)

Clarkson 4, St. Lawrence 1
Clarkson 5, St. Lawrence 2
(Clarkson wins series, 2-0)

SEMIFINALS

RPI 3, Cornell 2
Colgate 5, Clarkson 3

CHAMPIONSHIP GAME

Colgate 5, RPI 4
(No consolation game)

HOCKEY EAST

	W.	L.	T.	GF.	GA.	Pct.
Boston College (28-13-1)	15	6	0	101	69	.714
Maine (33-11-2)	14	6	1	88	57	.690
Boston University (25-17-2)	12	7	2	88	63	.619
Providence (22-10-3)	11	7	3	90	69	.595
New Hampshire (17-17-5)	8	9	4	86	86	.476
Northeastern (16-19-2)	9	10	2	96	100	.476
Lowell (13-20-2)	5	14	2	65	106	.286
Merrimack (10-24-1)	3	18	0	64	128	.143

Overall record in parentheses.

1989-90 HOCKEY EAST ALL-STARS

First Team	Position	Second Team
Scott King, Maine	Goalie	Scott Cashman, Boston University
Rob Cowie, Northeastern	Defenseman	Keith Carney, Maine
Greg Brown, Boston College	Defenseman	Jeff Serowik, Providence
Mike Boback, Providence	Forward	Harry Mews, Northeastern
David Emma, Boston College	Forward	Shawn McEachern, Boston Univ.
Steve Heinze, Boston College	Forward	Rick Bennett, Providence

Hockey East Player of the Year: Greg Brown, Boston College
Hockey East Rookie of the Year: Scott Cashman, Boston University
Hockey East Coach of the Year: Shawn Walsh, Maine

HOCKEY EAST PLAYOFFS

QUARTERFINALS

(Best-of-three series)

Boston College 3, Merrimack 1
Merrimack 6, Boston College 3
Boston College 8, Merrimack 5
 (Boston College wins series, 2-1)

Maine 7, Lowell 3
Maine 16, Lowell 0
 (Maine wins series, 2-0)

Northeastern 4, Boston University 3
Boston University 5, Northeastern 2
Boston University 5, Northeastern 3
 (Boston University wins series, 2-1)

Providence 5, New Hampshire 1
New Hampshire 2, Providence 0
New Hampshire 7, Providence 4
 (New Hampshire wins series, 2-1)

SEMIFINALS

Boston Col. 6, New Hampshire 5 (OT)
Maine 3, Boston University 1

CHAMPIONSHIP GAME

Boston College 4, Maine 3
 (No consolation game)

WESTERN COLLEGIATE HOCKEY ASSOCIATION

	W.	L.	T.	GF.	GA.	Pct.
Wisconsin (36-9-1)	19	8	1	147	111	.696
Minnesota (28-16-2)	17	9	2	147	124	.643
North Dakota (28-13-4)	15	10	3	149	114	.589
Northern Michigan (22-19-1)	15	12	1	130	129	.554
Denver (18-24-0)	13	15	0	130	139	.464
Minnesota-Duluth (20-19-1)	13	15	0	114	112	.464
Colorado College (18-20-2)	10	17	1	97	129	.375
Michigan Tech (10-30-0)	6	22	0	112	168	.214

Overall record in parentheses.

1989-90 WCHA ALL-STARS

First Team	Position	Second Team
Chad Erickson, Minnesota-Duluth	Goalie	Duane Derksen, Wisconsin
Russ Parent, North Dakota	Defenseman	Jason Herter, North Dakota
Kip Noble, Michigan Tech	Defenseman	Sean Hill, Wisconsin
Peter Hankinson, Minnesota	Forward	Eric Murano, Denver
Gary Shuchuk, Wisconsin	Forward	Lee Davidson, North Dakota
Dave Shields, Denver	Forward	John Byce, Wisconsin

WCHA Most Valuable Player: Gary Shuchuk, Wisconsin
WCHA Freshman of the Year: Scott Beattie, Northern Michigan
WCHA Coach of the Year: Doug Woog, Minnesota

WCHA PLAYOFFS

QUARTERFINALS

(Best-of-three series)

North Dakota 11, Minnesota-Duluth 3
North Dakota 2, Minnesota-Duluth 1
 (North Dakota wins series, 2-0)

Minnesota 9, Colorado College 3
Minnesota 9, Colorado College 2
 (Minnesota wins series, 2-0)

Northern Michigan 3, Denver 0
Northern Michigan 9, Denver 4
 (Northern Michigan wins series, 2-0)

Wisconsin 5, Michigan Tech 2
Wisconsin 4, Michigan Tech 3 (OT)
 (Wisconsin wins series, 2-0)

SEMIFINALS

Minnesota 5, North Dakota 4
Wisconsin 4, Northern Michigan 3 (OT)

CONSOLATION GAME

N. Dakota 6, Northern Michigan 5 (OT)

CHAMPIONSHIP GAME

Wisconsin 7, Minnesota 1

1990 NCAA TOURNAMENT

FIRST ROUND SERIES

(Best-of-three series)

Minnesota 6, Clarkson 1
Minnesota 5, Clarkson 1
 (Minnesota wins series, 2-0)

Maine 8, Bowling Green State 4
Maine 5, Bowling Green State 2
 (Maine wins series, 2-0)

Lake Superior 6, Alaska-Anchorage 2
Lake Superior 10, Alaska-Anchorage 3
 (Lake Superior State wins series, 2-0)

North Dakota 8, Boston University 5
Boston University 5, North Dakota 3
Boston University 5, North Dakota 0
 (Boston University wins series, 2-1)

QUARTERFINAL SERIES

(Best-of-three series)

Boston College 4, Minnesota 2
Minnesota 2, Boston College 1
Boston College 6, Minnesota 1
 (Boston College win series, 2-1)

Wisconsin 7, Maine 3
Wisconsin 4, Maine 3 (OT)
 (Wisconsin wins series, 2-0)

Colgate 3, Lake Superior State 2
Colgate 2, Lake Superior State 1
 (Colgate wins series, 2-0)

Michigan State 6, Boston University 3
Boston University 5, Michigan State 3
Boston University 5, Michigan State 3
 (Boston University wins series, 2-1)

SEMIFINAL SERIES

Played at Joe Louis Arena, Detroit, MI

Wisconsin 2, Boston College 1
Colgate 2, Boston University 1

CHAMPIONSHIP GAME

Wisconsin 7, Colgate 3
 (No consolation game)

1990 NCAA ALL-TOURNAMENT TEAM

Position	Player	College
Goalie	Duane Derksen	Wisconsin
Defenseman	Rob Andringa	Wisconsin
Defenseman	Mark Osiecki	Wisconsin
Forward	Joel Gardner	Colgate
Forward	John Byce	Wisconsin
Forward	Chris Tancill	Wisconsin

NCAA Tournament Most Outstanding Player: Chris Tancill, Wisconsin
NCAA Tournament Most Outstanding Goalie: Duane Derksen, Wisconsin

1989-90 COLLEGE HOCKEY ALL-AMERICA TEAMS

WEST

First Team	Position	Second Team
Chad Erickson, Minnesota-Duluth	Goalie	Jason Muzzatti, Michigan State
Rob Blake, Bowling Green State	Defenseman	Kord Cernich, Lake Superior State
Russ Parent, North Dakota	Defenseman	Kip Noble, Michigan Tech
Nelson Emerson, Bowling Green	Forward	Jim Dowd, Lake Superior State
Kip Miller, Michigan State	Forward	Dave Shields, Denver
Gary Shuchuk, Wisconsin	Forward	Lee Davidson, North Dakota

EAST

First Team	Position	Second Team
Dave Gagnon, Colgate	Goalie	Chris Harvey, Brown
Rob Cowie, Northeastern	Defenseman	Dan Ratushny, Cornell
Greg Brown, Boston College	Defenseman	Keith Carney, Maine
Joe Juneau, RPI	Forward	Joel Gardner, Colgate
David Emma, Boston College	Forward	C.J. Young, Harvard
Steve Heinze, Boston College	Forward	Jean-Yves Roy, Maine

ALL-TIME NCAA TOURNAMENT RECORDS AND FINISHES

	Tournament						Finished	
	Visits	W.	L.	GF	GA	Pct.	1st	2nd
Michigan	13	21	6	173	91	.778	7	2
Colgate	1	3	1	10	11	.750	0	1
‡Wisconsin	11	23	8	136	88	.742	5	1
North Dakota	13	22	11	132	102	.667	5	3
Denver	11	17	9	121	73	.654	5	2
*Northeastern	2	3	2	25	24	.600	0	0

	Tournament						Finished	
	Visits	W.	L.	GF	GA	Pct.	1st	2nd
Michigan Tech	10	13	9	118	85	.591	3	4
Minnesota	15	20	15	199	165	.571	3	6
†Michigan State	12	20	15	153	132	.571	2	6
#Rensselaer Polytechnic Institute	6	8	6	52	50	.567	2	0
#Lake Superior State	4	7	6	57	44	.538	1	0
Boston University	16	20	19	165	176	.513	3	2
Cornell	8	8	8	54	52	.500	2	2
Merrimack	1	2	2	14	16	.500	0	0
Yale	1	1	1	7	5	.500	0	0
Providence	5	8	9	55	54	.471	0	1
Maine	4	7	8	62	67	.467	0	0
Dartmouth	5	4	5	38	37	.444	0	2
Minnesota-Duluth	3	4	5	33	34	.444	0	1
*Bowling Green State	9	8	12	66	88	.400	1	0
Clarkson	9	7	11	50	78	.389	0	3
Colorado College	9	6	10	76	84	.375	2	2
†Harvard	14	13	22	132	159	.371	1	2
Brown	3	2	4	28	38	.333	0	1
Boston College	18	13	27	141	105	.325	1	2
Northern Michigan	3	2	5	21	30	.286	0	1
St. Lawrence	11	5	20	74	118	.200	0	0
New Hampshire	4	2	8	35	56	.200	0	0
‡Lowell	1	0	1	5	11	.000	0	0
Alaska-Anchorage	1	0	2	5	16	.000	0	0
St. Cloud State	1	0	2	5	10	.000	0	0
Vermont	1	0	2	2	10	.000	0	0
Western Michigan	1	0	2	4	11	.000	0	0

(Denver also participated in 1973 tournament but its record was voided by the NCAA in 1977 upon discovery of violations by the University. The team had finished second in '73.)

*Bowling Green State and Northeastern played to a 2-2 tie in 1981-82.
†Harvard and Michigan State played to a 3-3 tie in 1982-83.
#Lake Superior State and RPI played to a 3-3 tie in 1984-85.
‡Wisconsin and Lowell played to a 4-4 tie in 1987-88.
HOBEY BAKER MEMORIAL TROPHY (Top College hockey player in U.S.): Kip Miller, Michigan State.

AIR FORCE ACADEMY

Overall: 16-13-1

	Pos.	Class	Games	G.	A.	Pts.	Pen.
Matt Watson	D	Sr.	30	18	20	38	22
Mark Majewski	F	So.	30	20	15	35	62
Bob Ingraham	D	Fr.	27	13	17	30	26
Dan Greene	D	Jr.	29	8	22	30	20
Cal Ingraham	D	Fr	26	17	11	28	21
Mike Veneri	D	Jr.	26	6	19	25	29
Jason Mantaro	F	So.	30	9	12	21	38
Terry Courtney	F	Fr.	29	14	6	20	85
Eric Rice	F	Fr.	27	8	12	20	12
Kurt Rohloff	F	Sr.	30	3	11	14	44
Rob Haataja	F	Jr.	26	3	9	12	20
Mike Parent	D	Jr.	30	1	8	9	36
Kent Landreth	F	Jr.	22	1	3	4	24
Brett Gallagher	F	So.	24	1	3	4	8
Mark Skibinski	F	Jr.	23	0	4	4	28
Deron Christy	F	Fr.	25	0	4	4	6
Eric Nelson	D	Jr.	30	2	1	3	6
Tony Roe	D	So.	26	1	2	3	24
John Lyons	F	So.	23	1	0	1	8
Steve Banks	F	Jr.	4	0	1	1	0
Steven Masiello	D	Fr.	5	0	1	1	4
Mark Liebich	G	So.	19	0	1	1	0
Darec Liebel	G	Fr.	1	0	0	0	0
Matthew Snyder	F	So.	3	0	0	0	2
Mike Blank	G	Jr.	14	0	0	0	10

GOALTENDING

	G.	W.	L.	T.	Min.	Goals	Avg.
Darec Liebel	1	0	0	0	40	2	3.00
Mike Blank	14	7	5	0	715	41	3.44
Mark Liebich	19	9	8	1	1049	77	4.40

U.S. MILITARY ACADEMY (ARMY)

Overall: 10-16-4; ECAC: 4-15-3

	Pos.	Class	Games	G.	A.	Pts.	Pen.
Rich Sheridan	F	Sr.	28	10	19	29	62
Al Brenner	F	Jr.	29	10	16	26	10
Kevin Darby	F	So.	29	9	11	20	8
Scott Schulze	D	Sr.	30	8	12	20	42
Rick Randazzo	F	Fr.	27	10	9	19	16
Todd Tamburino	D	Jr.	30	6	10	16	68
Chris Kindgren	F	Jr.	28	6	9	15	26
Chris Mead	D	So.	30	2	11	13	20
Mike Gengler	F	Sr.	30	6	5	11	28
Phil Esposito	F	Fr.	23	6	4	10	48
Todd Traczyk	F	Sr.	26	5	5	10	31

	Pos.	Class	Games	G.	A.	Pts.	Pen.
Paul Haggerty	F	Jr.	29	5	5	10	16
Scott Tardif	F	So.	27	3	4	7	20
Chad Sundem	F	Fr.	26	2	4	6	4
Brad Hamacher	D	Jr.	28	1	5	6	30
Scott Williams	D	Jr.	29	1	5	6	26
Ross Erzar	F	So.	26	3	0	3	6
Neil Minihane	D	Sr.	29	0	3	3	67
Kevin Backus	D	Fr.	7	0	2	2	2
John Alissi	F	Fr.	16	0	2	2	2
Brooks Chretien	G	Jr.	23	0	1	1	4
Nick Meyer	F	Fr.	2	0	0	0	2
Brandon Hayes	G	So.	4	0	0	0	0
Dean Wegner	F	Fr.	5	0	0	0	2
Mike Kelsey	F	So.	6	0	0	0	2
Corey Averill	G	Sr.	8	0	0	0	2

GOALTENDING

	G.	W.	L.	T.	Min.	Goals	Avg.
Brooks Chretien	23	9	12	2	1306	72	3.31
Corey Averill	8	1	4	2	406	30	4.43
Brandon Hayes	4	0	0	0	104	9	5.19

BOSTON COLLEGE

Overall 28-13-1; Hockey East 15-6-0

	Pos.	Class	Games	G.	A.	Pts.	Pen.
David Emma	F	Jr.	42	38	34	72	46
Steve Heinze	F	So.	40	27	36	63	41
Marty McInnis	F	So.	41	24	29	53	43
Greg Brown	D	Jr.	42	5	35	40	42
Ted Crowley	D	Fr.	39	7	24	31	34
Jeff O'Neill	F	Jr.	42	12	17	29	30
David Franzosa	F	So.	42	8	20	28	20
Joe Cleary	D	So.	42	5	21	26	56
Bill Guerin	F	Fr.	39	14	11	25	64
Bill Nolan	F	Sr.	42	13	11	24	32
Marc Beran	F	Fr.	38	11	7	18	16
Matt Glennon	F	Jr.	31	7	11	18	16
Mark Dennehy	D	Jr.	30	2	14	16	8
Sean Farley	F	Jr.	31	5	7	12	24
Jason Rathbone	F	So.	37	4	7	11	20
Dave Pergola	F	Jr.	39	6	4	10	22
Steve Scheifele	F	Sr.	12	7	0	7	2
Pat Schafhauser	D	Fr.	39	1	6	7	30
Ron Pascucci	D	Fr.	37	0	6	6	12
John Reilly	F	Jr.	9	1	2	3	0
Scott Zygulski	D	Fr.	14	0	1	1	6
Chris Marshall	F	So.	17	0	1	1	40
Sandy Galuppo	G	Jr.	22	0	1	1	0
Dan Drew	G	Fr.	1	0	0	0	0
Mike Silva	G	So.	5	0	0	0	0
Mike Delay	D	So.	7	0	0	0	0
Scott Lagrand	G	Fr.	24	0	0	0	0

GOALTENDING

	G.	W.	L.	T.	Min.	Goals	Avg.
Scott Lagrand	24	17	4	0	1268	57	2.70
Sandy Galuppo	22	11	9	1	1235	73	3.55
Mike Silva	5	0	0	0	14	1	4.29
Dan Drew	1	0	0	0	3	1	20.00

BOSTON UNIVERSITY

Overall: 25-17-2; Hockey East: 12-7-2

	Pos.	Class	Games	G.	A.	Pts.	Pen.
Tony Amonte	F	Fr.	41	25	33	58	52
Shawn McEachern	F	So.	43	25	31	56	78
Joe Sacco	F	So.	44	28	24	52	70
Edward Ronan	F	Jr.	44	17	23	40	50
David Tomlinson	F	Jr.	43	15	22	37	53
Mike Sullivan	F	Fr.	38	11	20	31	26
Alexandre Legault	D	Fr.	43	9	21	30	54
Phillip Von Stefenelli	D	Jr.	44	8	20	28	40
Petteri Koskimaki	F	Fr.	44	12	12	24	15
Peter Ahola	D	Fr.	43	3	20	23	65
Robert Regan	F	Sr.	44	12	5	17	32
Mark Bavis	F	Fr.	44	2	11	13	28
Mike Bavis	F	Fr.	44	6	5	11	50
Stephen Foster	D	Fr.	28	0	8	8	26
Darin MacDonald	F	Jr.	38	4	3	7	29
Kevin O'Sullivan	D	Fr.	43	0	6	6	42
Mark Brownschidle	D	So.	38	1	4	5	12
David Sacco	F	So.	3	0	4	4	2
Mark Krys	D	Jr.	30	0	4	4	34
Dave Dahlberg	F	Fr.	18	1	1	2	6
Chris McCann	F	Jr.	23	1	0	1	12
Scott Cashman	G	Fr.	39	0	1	1	10
Tom Dion	D	Jr.	3	0	0	0	4
Ronald Trentini	F	Sr.	6	0	0	0	0
John Bradley	G	Jr.	7	0	0	0	0

GOALTENDING

	G.	W.	L.	T.	Min.	Goals	Avg.
John Bradley	7	2	3	1	377	20	3.18
Scott Cashman	39	23	14	1	2277	122	3.21

BOWLING GREEN STATE UNIVERSITY

Overall: 25-17-2; CCHA: 20-10-2

	Pos.	Class	Games	G.	A.	Pts.	Pen.
Nelson Emerson	F	Sr.	44	30	52	82	42
Rob Blake	D	Jr.	42	23	36	59	140
Brett Harkins	F	Fr.	41	11	43	54	45
Matt Ruchty	F	Jr.	42	28	21	49	135
Peter Holmes	F	So.	44	18	31	49	34
Marc Potvin	F	Sr.	40	19	17	36	72
Martin Jiranek	F	So.	41	13	21	34	38
Dan Bylsma	F	So.	44	13	17	30	32
Kevin Dahl	D	Sr.	43	8	22	30	74
Joe Quinn	F	Sr.	42	11	18	29	43
Jim Solly	F	So.	44	9	11	20	14
Otis Plageman	D	So.	44	6	14	20	52
Braden Shavchook	F	Jr.	44	8	6	14	4
Llew Ncwana	D	So.	37	4	8	12	22
Pierrick Maia	F	Jr.	39	4	5	9	16
Rick Mullins	F	Fr.	39	5	3	8	10
Ken Klee	D	Fr.	41	0	5	5	56
Paul Basic	D	Fr.	39	1	3	4	14
Derek Hopko	D	So.	14	0	1	1	6
Paul Connell	G	Sr.	18	0	1	1	2
Angelo Libertucci	G	Fr.	29	0	1	1	4
A.J. Plaskey	D	Fr.	2	0	0	0	0
John Burke	G	Jr.	3	0	0	0	0
Ty Eigner	F	So.	15	0	0	0	6

GOALTENDING

	G.	W.	L.	T.	Min.	Goals	Avg.
John Burke	3	1	1	0	124	6	2.90
Angelo Libertucci	28	16	10	1	1591	107	4.04
Paul Connell	18	8	6	1	943	79	5.03

BROWN UNIVERSITY

Overall: 10-16-3; ECAC: 8-11-3

	Pos.	Class	Games	G.	A.	Pts.	Pen.
Mike Brewer	F	So.	29	7	24	31	64
Bob Kenneally	F	Sr.	28	11	18	29	56
Steve King	F	Jr.	27	19	8	27	53
Mike Ross	F	Fr.	29	13	13	26	38
Derek Chauvette	F	Fr.	29	7	18	25	26
Scott Hanley	F	Fr.	29	12	7	19	32
Joey Beck	F	Fr.	27	4	15	19	18
James O'Brien	D	Fr.	29	3	12	15	78
Joe Verderber	F	So.	29	6	7	13	18
Sascha Pogor	F	Fr.	27	8	4	12	52
Darrin MacKay	F	So.	21	6	3	9	24
Brad Kraick	D	Jr.	29	1	8	9	37
Chris Schremp	F	Fr.	19	3	5	8	10
Jim Bickerton	D	Fr.	24	2	5	7	35
Rick Olczyk	D	So.	25	0	6	6	22
Paul Ohman	D	Jr.	23	1	4	5	14
Eric Bommer	F	Jr.	29	1	3	4	18
Bob Roche	F	Fr.	17	0	4	4	22
Chris Harvey	G	Sr.	27	0	2	2	6
Sean Murdoch	F	Fr.	17	1	0	1	10
Paul Stravato	D	Sr.	9	0	1	1	2
Dan Quinn	G	Sr.	3	0	0	0	0
Tim Chase	F	Fr.	8	0	0	0	0
Craig Pho	D	So.	8	0	0	0	4

GOALTENDING

	G.	W.	L.	T.	Min.	Goals	Avg.
Chris Harvey	28	10	15	3	1646	107	3.90
Dan Quinn	3	0	1	0	98	11	6.73

CLARKSON UNIVERSITY

Overall: 21-11-3; ECAC: 12-7-3

	Pos.	Class	Games	G.	A.	Pts.	Pen.
Mike Casselman	F	Jr.	34	22	21	43	69
Dave Trombley	F	Jr.	34	15	27	42	44
Mark Tretowicz	F	Sr.	35	15	24	39	34
Hugo Belanger	F	Fr.	35	14	25	39	12
Mark Green	F	Jr.	32	18	17	35	42
Scott Thomas	F	Fr.	34	19	13	32	95
Dave Tretowicz	D	Jr.	35	2	27	29	12
Mike Kozak	F	Jr.	32	6	14	20	38
Ed Sabo	D	So.	25	4	15	19	35
Janne Kekalainen	F	Fr.	8	9	9	18	4

	Pos.	Class	Games	G.	A.	Pts.	Pen.
Steve Dubinsky	F	Fr.	35	7	10	17	24
Steve Brennan	F	Sr.	33	7	6	13	48
Martin d'Orsonnens	D	Fr.	35	5	8	13	81
Jeff Torrey	F	So.	26	4	8	12	24
Ron Reagan	F	Sr.	34	3	3	6	10
David Green	F	Fr.	11	1	3	4	2
Paul Donovan	F	Sr.	29	0	4	4	84
Mikko Tavi	D	Fr.	30	2	1	3	14
Kent Anderson	D	So.	34	1	2	3	54
Todd Tyo	F	Sr.	3	1	1	2	4
Guy Sanderson	D	Fr.	21	1	1	2	76
John Bolton	D	Sr.	24	0	2	2	48
Bracken Gardner	F	Fr.	4	0	1	1	0
Rich Denicourt	F	So.	6	0	1	1	12
John Fletcher	G	Sr.	34	0	1	1	16
Phil Comtois	G	Fr.	4	0	0	0	0
Chris Rogles	G	Fr.	7	0	0	0	0

GOALTENDING

	G.	W.	L.	T.	Min.	Goals	Avg.
Chris Rogles	7	1	0	0	141	7	2.98
John Fletcher	34	20	11	3	1900	99	3.13
Phil Comtois	4	0	0	0	71	7	5.92

COLGATE UNIVERSITY

Overall: 31-6-1; ECAC: 18-3-1

	Pos.	Class	Games	G.	A.	Pts.	Pen.
Joel Gardner	F	Sr.	38	26	36	62	62
Marc Dupere	F	Sr.	38	23	29	52	22
Steve Spott	F	Sr.	37	20	29	49	91
Craig Woodcroft	F	Jr.	37	20	26	46	108
Shawn Lillie	F	Sr.	38	17	22	39	32
Jamie Cooke	F	So.	38	16	20	36	24
Dale Band	F	So.	37	12	24	36	24
Jason Greyerbiehl	F	So.	38	12	20	32	20
Grant Slater	F	Sr.	38	8	11	19	34
Steve Poapst	D	Jr.	38	4	15	19	54
Bob Haddock	D	Fr.	36	3	14	17	54
Troy Mohns	D	Fr.	38	2	13	15	42
Jeff Weber	F	Sr.	38	5	6	11	66
Karl Clauss	D	Sr.	38	2	8	10	34
Andrew Dickson	F	Fr.	38	1	9	10	6
Kelly Mills	F	Fr.	28	5	4	9	54
Dave Gagnon	G	Jr.	33	0	6	6	2
Alan Brown	F	Fr.	37	2	3	5	24
Gregg Wolf	D	Jr.	38	1	0	1	58
Jim White	F	Jr.	1	0	0	0	0
Greg Menges	G	Jr.	3	0	0	0	0
Ken Baker	G	So.	4	0	0	0	0
Scott Gordon	D	Jr.	13	0	0	0	8

GOALTENDING

	G.	W.	L.	T.	Min.	Goals	Avg.
Dave Gagnon	33	28	4	1	1986	93	2.81
Greg Menges	3	1	1	0	115	8	4.17
Ken Baker	4	2	1	0	184	15	4.89

COLORADO COLLEGE

Overall: 18-20-2; WCHA: 10-17-1

	Pos.	Class	Games	G.	A.	Pts.	Pen.
Chris Anderson	F	Sr.	40	20	26	46	22
Ed Zawatsky	F	Jr.	40	17	27	44	24
Doug Kirton	F	Sr.	37	19	21	40	47
John Mooney	F	Fr.	40	10	30	40	52
Steve Strunk	F	So.	40	13	18	31	40
Cal Brown	D	Sr.	39	4	21	25	74
Brent Mowery	F	Sr.	39	7	13	20	30
Grant Block	F	So.	35	13	6	19	24
Trevor Pochpnski	D	Jr.	40	5	13	18	54
Sean Foley	F	So.	26	9	8	17	98
Patrick Rafferty	F	Fr.	37	6	11	17	32
Alan Schuler	D	So.	32	1	13	14	16
Joe Schwartz	F	So.	38	8	3	11	36
Brian Bruininks	D	So.	31	3	7	10	8
Rik Duryea	D	So.	35	5	3	8	34
Rob Granato	F	Fr.	29	4	4	8	6
Marty Olson	F	Fr.	35	3	3	6	26
Brian Bethard	D	Fr.	38	1	5	6	40
Jon Manthey	F	Jr.	10	1	3	4	0
Mark Peterson	D	Fr.	30	0	4	4	12
Chris Hynnes	D	Fr.	17	0	3	3	10
Darren Leishman	D	Fr.	5	1	1	2	16
Jim Wilharm	D	Sr.	18	1	1	2	12
Denis Casey	F	Fr.	20	0	2	2	4
Derek Lamppa	F	Fr.	3	0	0	0	0
Jon Gustafson	G	Jr.	7	0	0	0	0
Paul Badalich	G	Fr.	22	0	0	0	0

GOALTENDING

	G.	W.	L.	T.	Min.	Goals	Avg.
Jon Gustafson	7	3	1	0	264	20	4.54
Paul Badalich	22	8	10	1	1084	75	4.15
Denis Casey	19	7	9	1	1060	77	4.36

CORNELL UNIVERSITY

Overall: 16-10-3; ECAC: 12-7-3

	Pos.	Class	Games	G.	A.	Pts.	Pen.
Joe Dragon	F	So.	29	15	24	39	26
Ross Lemon	F	Sr.	29	23	9	32	32
Doug Derraugh	F	Jr.	29	16	13	29	18
Casey Jones	F	Sr.	27	6	21	27	22
Kent Manderville	F	Fr.	26	11	15	26	28
Trent Andison	F	Jr.	25	8	16	24	12
Ryan Hughes	F	Fr.	28	7	16	23	35
Dan Ratushny	D	So.	26	5	14	19	54
Alex Nikolic	F	So.	28	6	9	15	45
Dave Burke	D	So.	29	0	12	12	28
Tim Vanini	D	Jr.	29	1	9	10	18
Phil Nobel	F	So.	29	4	5	9	20
Paul Dukovac	D	So.	29	1	8	9	34
Etieme Belzile	D	Fr.	28	1	4	5	18
Stephane Gauvin	F	So.	29	2	2	4	34
Jim Goerz	F	Sr.	14	1	3	4	8
Jason Vogel	F	Fr.	20	2	1	3	16
Karl Williams	F	So.	15	0	3	3	6
Bruce Frauley	D	Jr.	21	0	3	3	6
Marc Deschamps	D	So.	13	0	2	2	10
Corrie D'Alessio	G	Jr.	16	0	1	1	0
Jim McPhee	D	So.	2	0	0	0	0
Devin Mintz	F	So.	2	0	0	0	0
Jason Fairman	F	Jr.	7	0	0	0	2
Russ Hammond	F	Fr.	8	0	0	0	0
Jim Crozier	G	Jr.	16	0	0	0	0

GOALTENDING

	G.	W.	L.	T.	Min.	Goals	Avg.
Jim Crozier	16	10	3	1	866	38	2.63
Corrie D'Alessio	16	6	7	2	887	50	3.38

DARTMOUTH COLLEGE

Overall: 4-18-4; ECAC: 4-14-4

	Pos.	Class	Games	G.	A.	Pts.	Pen.
Jamie Hanlon	F	Sr.	25	12	18	30	44
Greg Chapman	F	Fr.	26	9	8	17	6
Dave Williams	D	Sr.	26	3	12	15	32
Sean Tomalty	F	Jr.	24	7	6	13	63
Mike Daly	F	Jr.	22	5	7	12	14
Roger Chiasson	F	Sr.	18	5	6	11	18
Tom Nieman	F	So.	26	6	3	9	16
Peter Clark	F	Fr.	26	1	7	8	8
Joe Gualtieri	D	Sr.	26	1	7	8	36
Shane Feeney	F	So.	24	4	3	7	8
Jeff Miller	D	Sr.	26	3	4	7	18
Nate Dudley	D	So.	26	2	5	7	16
Pat Wildman	D	Jr.	26	3	2	5	2
Paul Kinnaly	F	Jr.	23	1	4	5	14
Chris Clancy	F	Fr.	26	3	1	4	22
Nick Brown	F	So.	7	0	3	3	4
Will Geist	D	So.	15	1	1	2	12
Bill Fitzpatrick	F	Jr.	18	1	1	2	8
Shawn Burt	F	Fr.	11	0	2	2	12
Kevin Kiley	F	So.	17	0	2	2	12
Mike Fehm	D	Jr.	10	1	0	1	4
Kyle Flik	F	Jr.	14	1	0	1	2
Peter Lardner	F	Jr.	5	0	1	1	0
Cam McKennitt	F	Jr.	5	0	1	1	0
Chris Driscoll	F	Jr.	1	0	0	0	0
Butch Coughlin	D	Sr.	2	0	0	0	4
Vern Guetens	G	Fr.	7	0	0	0	4
Steve Laurin	G	Sr.	22	0	0	0	4

GOALTENDING

	G.	W.	L.	T.	Min.	Goals	Avg.
Steve Laurin	22	4	14	4	1386	100	4.32
Vern Guetens	7	0	4	0	276	22	4.78

UNIVERSITY OF DENVER

Overall: 18-24-0; WCHA: 13-15-0

	Pos.	Class	Games	G.	A.	Pts.	Pen.
Dave Shields	C	Sr.	42	31	43	74	24
Eric Murano	F	Sr.	42	33	35	68	52
Rick Berens	F	Jr.	38	27	25	52	48
Ken MacArthur	D	Jr.	38	12	29	41	96

	Pos.	Class	Games	G.	A.	Pts.	Pen.
Jay Moore	C	Jr.	38	15	22	37	66
Marc Rousseau	D	Sr.	42	6	26	32	62
Darren Biggs	F	So.	35	12	11	23	33
Corey Carlson	F	Fr.	39	8	15	23	74
Lance Momotani	F	So.	30	6	15	21	0
Mike Markovich	D	So.	42	4	17	21	34
Rod Summers	D	Sr.	42	3	18	21	42
Bruce Robinson	F	Jr.	42	5	6	11	24
Ryan O'Leary	F	Fr.	39	4	6	10	30
Brett Petersen	D	So.	34	3	6	9	23
Dan Brooks	D	Sr.	32	4	4	8	30
Don McLennan	D	Sr.	42	0	6	6	41
Brad Podiak	F	Fr.	40	4	1	5	33
Greg Stocklan	F	Jr.	31	3	2	5	32
Grant Ostir	F	Fr.	36	3	1	4	4
Bryan Schoen	G	Fr.	18	0	4	4	10
Rolf Beutel	F	So.	13	0	2	2	5
Lucien Carignan	G	Jr.	25	0	1	1	6
Brian Knieriem	F	Jr.	5	0	0	0	2

GOALTENDING

	G.	W.	L.	T.	Min.	Goals	Avg.
Bryan Schoen	18	8	9	0	1040	81	4.67
Lucien Carignan	25	10	15	0	1482	118	4.78

FERRIS STATE UNIVERSITY

Overall: 11-23-6; CCHA: 6-20-6

	Pos.	Class	Games	G.	A.	Pts.	Pen.
John dePourcq	F	Jr.	40	23	36	59	12
Rod Taylor	F	Jr.	38	28	16	44	81
Mike Jorgensen	F	Jr.	37	15	21	36	55
Daniel Chaput	D	Fr.	36	7	23	30	16
Bob Nardella	D	Jr.	38	10	14	24	46
Daryl Filipek	D	Fr.	38	4	20	24	44
Bill Thomas	F	Sr.	40	7	15	22	48
Chuck Wiegand	F	So.	34	10	11	21	50
Norm Krumpschmid	F	So.	36	6	14	20	22
Kelly Sorensen	F	So.	37	7	12	19	48
Clark Davies	D	Sr.	36	4	9	13	38
Jeff Jestadt	F	Fr.	35	7	2	9	52
Justin LaFayette	F	Jr.	34	4	5	9	38
John Bergeron	D	Sr.	39	2	7	9	76
Kevin Moore	F	Fr.	22	1	7	8	2
Don Rolfe	D	Jr.	31	0	6	6	48
Tim Corkery	D	Sr.	32	0	6	6	64
Tom O'Rourke	F	So.	22	3	2	5	42
Derek Frenette	F	So.	29	1	4	5	48
Mike Colman	D	So.	23	0	4	4	62
Mike LaLonde	F	Sr.	13	3	0	3	6
Matt Evo	F	Jr.	15	2	0	2	22
Aaron Asp	F	Fr.	10	1	1	2	2
Page Klostreich	F	Fr.	4	0	0	2	2
Marc Felicio	G	Jr.	17	0	0	0	2
Mike Williams	G	Sr.	31	0	0	0	4

GOALTENDING

	G.	W.	L.	T.	Min.	Goals	Avg.
Marc Felicio	17	2	7	3	738	59	4.80
Mike Williams	31	9	16	3	1697	138	4.88

HARVARD UNIVERSITY

Overall: 13-14-1; ECAC: 12-9-1

	Pos.	Class	Games	G.	A.	Pts.	Pen.
Mike Vukonich	F	Jr.	27	22	29	51	18
C.J. Young	F	Sr.	28	21	28	49	32
John Murphy	F	Sr.	28	9	27	36	18
Peter Ciavaglia	F	Jr.	28	17	18	35	22
John Weisbrod	F	Jr.	27	11	21	32	62
Ted Drury	F	Fr.	17	9	13	22	10
Tod Hartje	D	Sr.	28	6	10	16	29
Tim Burke	F	So.	28	6	7	13	24
Jim Coady	F	So.	28	3	10	13	6
Ted Donato	F	Jr.	16	5	6	11	34
Steven Flomenhoft	F	Fr.	28	5	5	10	44
Brian Popiel	D	Sr.	28	3	6	9	28
Scott Barringer	F	Jr.	25	0	9	9	30
Kevin Sneddon	D	So.	26	0	8	8	18
Kevan Melrose	D	Sr.	16	1	6	7	124
Matt Mallgrave	F	Fr.	26	3	3	6	33
Brian McCormack	D	So.	27	2	3	5	36
Scott McCormack	D	Sr.	24	1	4	5	36
Craig Miskovich	F	So.	14	1	1	2	12
Chuckie Hughes	G	So.	11	0	2	2	6
Greg Hess	D	So.	1	0	1	1	0
Aron Allen	F	Jr.	3	0	1	1	14
Rich DeFreitas	D	So.	28	0	1	1	18
Michael Francis	G	Jr.	3	0	0	0	0
Allain Roy	G	So.	15	0	0	0	0

GOALTENDING

	G.	W.	L.	T.	Min.	Goals	Avg.
Allain Roy	15	7	8	0	867	54	3.74
Michael Francis	3	1	1	0	143	9	3.78
Chuckie Hughes	11	5	5	1	669	43	3.86

UNIVERSITY OF ILLINOIS-CHICAGO

Overall: 10-27-1; CCHA: 7-24-1

	Pos.	Class	Games	G.	A.	Pts.	Pen.
Darryl Noren	F	Jr.	38	29	37	66	84
Rick Judson	F	So.	38	19	22	41	18
Dominic Dunlap	F	Jr.	38	20	18	38	40
Kevin Alexander	F	Sr.	31	12	19	31	24
Darin Banister	D	Sr.	37	5	22	27	72
Randy Zulinick	F	So.	29	10	13	23	34
Kurt Kabat	F	Sr.	27	7	13	20	31
Bob Melton	F	Jr.	31	5	15	20	24
Jim Maher	D	So.	38	4	12	16	64
Todd Finner	F	Fr.	36	3	11	14	33
Brad Smilev	F	So.	38	4	6	10	10
Ken Christison	F	Fr.	38	4	4	8	22
Trevor Wallace	D	Jr.	29	0	8	8	16
Chris Wolanin	D	Jr.	34	1	6	7	116
Mike Real	F	Fr.	38	4	2	6	28
Eric Schneider	D	So.	37	2	3	5	48
Jim Marchi	D	Jr.	22	0	4	4	45
Corv Hextall	F	Fr.	32	1	1	2	4
Erik Magsamen	F	So.	34	1	1	2	41
Rich Zeller	F	Fr.	2	0	0	0	0
Peter Wurm	F	Fr.	4	0	0	0	0
Gary Mangino	G	Jr.	12	0	0	0	0
Dan Marquardt	D	So.	22	0	0	0	10
Dave DePinto	G	Sr.	32	0	0	0	6

GOALTENDING

	G.	W.	L.	T.	Min.	Goals	Avg.
Gary Mangino	12	1	6	0	473	40	5.07
Dave DePinto	32	9	21	1	1812	158	5.23

LAKE SUPERIOR STATE UNIVERSITY

Overall: 33-10-3; CCHA: 24-6-2

	Pos.	Class	Games	G.	A.	Pts.	Pen.
Jim Dowd	F	Jr.	46	25	67	92	30
Jeff Jablonski	F	Sr.	46	38	33	71	82
Doug Weight	F	Fr.	46	21	48	69	44
Jeff Napierala	F	Jr.	44	33	26	59	32
Pete Stauber	F	Sr.	46	25	31	56	90
Karl Johnston	D	Jr.	43	12	28	40	32
Dan Keczmer	D	Sr.	43	13	23	36	48
Kord Cernich	D	Sr.	46	11	25	36	59
Sandy Moger	F	So.	46	17	15	32	76
Mark Astley	D	So.	43	7	25	32	74
Tim Breslin	F	Jr.	46	8	17	25	20
Tim Harris	F	Jr.	39	6	17	23	71
David DiVita	D	Jr.	46	4	12	16	58
Michael Smith	D	Fr.	41	4	10	14	6
John Hendry	F	Fr.	41	4	7	11	30
Paul Constantin	F	So.	29	6	2	8	10
Vincent Faucher	F	So.	16	5	3	8	12
Doug Laprade	F	Jr.	42	4	3	7	51
Dean Hulett	F	Fr.	13	1	4	5	18
Mike Bachusz	D	So.	31	0	4	4	8
Ken Blum	F	Fr.	19	2	1	3	14
Dean Dyer	F	Jr.	9	0	2	2	8
Darrin Madeley	G	Fr.	30	0	1	1	8
Brian Lukowski	G	Fr.	4	0	0	0	0
Brandon Reed	G	So.	19	0	0	0	0

GOALTENDING

	G.	W.	L.	T.	Min.	Goals	Avg.
Darrin Madeley	30	21	7	1	1683	68	2.42
Brandon Reed	19	11	3	2	975	61	3.75
Brian Lukowski	4	1	0	0	114	8	4.21

UNIVERSITY OF LOWELL

Overall: 13-20-2; Hockey East: 5-14-2

	Pos.	Class	Games	G.	A.	Pts.	Pen.
Craig Charron	F	Sr.	35	17	29	46	10
Scott MacPherson	F	Sr.	32	21	18	39	12
Brendan Flynn	F	Sr.	33	10	13	23	14
Dan O'Connell	F	Fr.	32	8	15	23	58
Dave Gatti	F	So.	34	6	13	19	14
Greg Carter	F	So.	34	10	8	18	22
Randy LeBrasseur	F	Sr.	33	10	6	16	30
Gerry Daley	F	Fr.	31	9	6	15	30

	Pos.	Class	Games	G.	A.	Pts.	Pen.
Dave Stevens	F	Fr.	33	2	12	14	36
Tim Smallwood	D	Fr.	33	5	7	12	28
Steve Ablitt	D/F	Jr.	21	2	10	12	75
Scott Wenham	D	Fr.	33	2	10	12	28
Jeff Flaherty	F	Sr.	18	5	5	10	58
Matt Robbins	F	Fr.	14	2	8	10	4
Don Parsons	D	So.	26	2	8	10	22
Dave Pensa	F	Fr.	28	2	5	7	36
Peter Sentner	F/D	Jr.	25	1	6	7	6
Glenn Seabury	F	Fr.	16	3	1	4	20
Mike Erickson	D	Jr.	32	1	3	4	42
Steve Roe	F	Fr.	5	2	0	2	8
Craig Seabury	F	Fr.	19	1	1	2	22
Garrett Burke	D	Fr.	4	0	2	2	4
Keith Carney	D	Fr.	8	0	2	2	0
Brian Seabury	F	Fr.	7	0	1	1	20
Matt Hayes	D	So.	14	0	1	1	1
Peter Harris	G	Sr.	1	0	0	0	0
Michael Tinkham	F	Fr.	1	0	0	0	0
Tyler Lovering	D/F	Fr.	6	0	0	0	4
Garry Scott	G	Fr.	8	0	0	0	2
Scott Meehan	D	Fr.	24	0	0	0	16
Mark Richards	G	Fr.	32	0	0	0	10

GOALTENDING

	G.	W.	L.	T.	Min.	Goals	Avg.
Mark Richards	32	11	18	2	1773	149	5.04
Peter Harris	1	0	0	0	31	3	5.81
Garry Scott	8	2	2	0	312	34	6.54

UNIVERSITY OF MAINE

Overall: 33-11-2; Hockey East: 14-6-1

	Pos.	Class	Games	G.	A.	Pts.	Pen.
Jean-Yves Roy	F	Fr.	46	39	26	65	52
Jim Montgomery	F	Fr.	45	26	34	60	35
Scott Pellerin	F	So.	42	22	34	56	68
Martin Robitaille	F	So.	46	24	28	52	24
Keith Carney	D	So.	41	3	41	44	43
Randy Olson	F	Fr.	37	17	25	42	21
Mike Barkley	F	So.	43	11	19	30	20
Claudio Scremin	D	Sr.	45	4	26	30	14
Jim Burke	D	Sr.	45	6	23	29	60
Guy Perron	F	Sr.	21	13	13	26	10
Brian Downey	F	Fr.	32	11	15	26	10
Brian Bellefeuille	F	Sr.	42	13	10	23	86
Brian Straub	D	So.	43	7	14	21	18
Justin Tomberlin	F	Fr.	35	10	7	17	6
Steve Tepper	F	So.	41	10	6	16	68
Kent Salfi	F	Fr.	37	6	10	16	21
Christian Lalonde	F	Sr.	41	2	13	15	44
Martin Mercier	F	Fr.	17	3	8	11	8
Dan Murphy	D	Fr.	42	1	9	10	26
Steve Widmeyer	F	So.	26	5	1	6	30
John Massara	F	Sr.	15	2	4	6	8
Eric Fenton	F	Fr.	7	2	2	4	2
Campbell Blair	D	So.	8	0	4	4	10
Tony Link	D	So.	15	0	3	3	6
Dave LaCouture	F	Fr.	9	0	2	2	6
Matt DelGuidice	G	Jr.	23	0	2	2	10
Claudio Kaiser	F	Fr.	5	1	0	1	2
Scott King	G	Sr.	29	0	1	1	2

GOALTENDING

	G.	W.	L.	T.	Min.	Goals	Avg.
Scott King	29	17	7	2	1526	67	2.63
Matt DelGuidice	23	16	4	0	1257	68	3.25

MERRIMACK COLLEGE

Overall: 10-24-1; Hockey East: 3-18-0

	Pos.	Class	Games	G.	A.	Pts.	Pen.
Andy Heinze	F	Sr.	35	20	27	47	14
Agostino Casale	F	So.	32	17	24	41	21
Howie Rosenblatt	F	Jr.	29	10	14	24	36
Claude Maillet	D	So.	32	8	15	23	55
Bryan Miller	D	Fr.	34	2	19	21	8
Jeff Massey	F	So.	28	7	13	20	16
Frank Schofield	F	Sr.	27	8	11	19	29
Ed Locke	F	So.	35	9	9	18	24
Brian Hayward	F	Sr.	34	7	11	18	10
Matt Crowley	F	Fr.	35	11	5	16	8
Ben Lebeau	F	Jr.	32	9	6	15	46
Teal Fowler	F	Fr.	25	5	7	12	42
David Moore	D	Jr.	28	2	6	8	14
Brendan Locke	F	Sr.	31	1	7	8	8
Doug Greschuk	D	Jr.	31	1	4	5	26
Dan Gravelle	F	Fr.	10	2	1	3	13
Sean Dooley	F	Jr.	22	1	2	3	31
Tim Doyle	D	Jr.	27	1	2	3	6

	Pos.	Class	Games	G.	A.	Pts.	Pen.
Matt Hentges	D	So.	33	1	2	3	40
John Barron	F	Fr.	16	1	1	2	16
Jamie Sullivan	D	Jr.	22	0	2	2	10
Jason Lawton	F	Fr.	2	0	0	0	0
Rusty Jordan	D	Jr.	8	0	0	0	4
Mike Doneghey	G	Fr.	9	0	0	0	0
Guy Ragault	F	Fr.	9	0	0	0	2
Steve Cardosi	F	Jr.	12	0	0	0	0
Yannick Gosselin	G	Fr.	13	0	0	0	2
Steve D'Amore	G	So.	19	0	0	0	2

GOALTENDING

	G.	W.	L.	T.	Min.	Goals	Avg.
Yannick Gosselin	13	3	7	0	638	60	5.64
Steve D'Amore	19	4	12	1	1042	88	5.07
Mike Doneghey	9	3	5	0	424	36	5.09

MIAMI (O.) UNIVERSITY

Overall: 12-24-4; CCHA: 8-21-3

	Pos.	Class	Games	G.	A.	Pts.	Pen.
Craig Fisher	F	So.	39	37	29	66	38
Todd Harkins	F	Jr.	40	27	17	44	78
Bob Wallwork	F	Jr.	40	12	30	42	60
Jim Bodden	F	Jr.	38	14	23	37	10
Rob Vanderydt	F	Jr.	30	10	14	24	14
Joey Saban	F	Fr.	36	12	9	21	12
Brendan Curley	F	Fr.	18	7	13	20	6
Dan Beaudette	F	Sr.	40	8	11	19	30
Tom Neziol	F	Sr.	31	11	4	15	14
Ken House	F	So.	37	10	5	15	32
Joe Tonello	D	Sr.	38	2	13	15	8
Scott Mazi	F	Jr.	33	2	11	13	42
Jaan Luik	D	Jr.	35	1	11	12	64
Chris Bergeron	F	Fr.	36	5	6	11	18
Scott Luik	F	Jr.	16	4	7	11	32
Rhys Hollyman	D	So.	37	2	8	10	54
Robert Fischer	D	So.	34	4	4	8	54
Steve Wilson	D	So.	40	2	3	5	46
Steve McGrinder	D	Sr.	20	0	5	5	18
Greg Island	D	Sr.	34	0	5	5	62
Tom Holdeman	F	Fr.	28	3	1	4	8
Mark Michaud	G	So.	33	0	2	2	8
Vito Mazzoli	G	Fr.	4	0	1	1	0
Robin McClain	D	Jr.	3	0	0	0	0
Terry Ouimet	F	Fr.	7	0	0	0	2
Craig Cowan	F	Jr.	9	0	0	0	0
Lee Cannon	G	So.	15	0	0	0	0

GOALTENDING

	G.	W.	L.	T.	Min.	Goals	Avg.
Vito Mazzoli	4	1	1	0	191	13	4.08
Mark Michaud	33	11	18	3	1754	149	5.10
Lee Cannon	16	0	5	1	471	42	5.35

UNIVERSITY OF MICHIGAN

Overall: 24-12-6; CCHA: 16-11-5

	Pos.	Class	Games	G.	A.	Pts.	Pen.
David Roberts	F	Fr.	42	21	32	53	46
Mike Moes	F	Sr.	42	19	29	48	10
Mark Ouimet	F	Fr.	38	15	32	47	14
Ted Kramer	F	So.	42	21	24	45	111
Don Stone	F	Jr.	42	20	24	44	12
Denny Felsner	F	So.	33	27	16	43	24
Alex Roberts	D	Sr.	41	14	21	35	105
Rob Brown	F	Sr.	42	12	18	30	20
Patrick Neaton	D	Fr.	42	3	23	26	36
Todd Copeland	D	Sr.	34	6	16	22	62
Dan Stiver	F	Fr.	40	9	10	19	6
Brad Turner	F	Sr.	32	8	9	17	34
Jim Ballantine	F	Jr.	41	6	11	17	8
David Harlock	D	Fr.	42	2	13	15	44
Ryan Pardoski	F	Sr.	33	4	5	9	16
Chris Tamer	D	Fr.	42	2	7	9	147
Mark Sorensen	D	Jr.	40	3	5	8	42
Mike Helber	F	So.	20	3	2	5	8
Doug Evans	D/F	So.	31	2	3	5	24
Tim Keough	G	So.	11	0	5	5	0
Vaclav Nedomansky	F	So.	9	2	0	2	6
Kent Brothers	F	Jr.	10	0	1	1	10
Tim Helber	F	Sr.	11	0	1	1	2
Warren Sharples	G	Sr.	39	0	1	1	2
Randy Kwong	D/F	Sr.	6	0	0	0	4

GOALTENDING

	G.	W.	L.	T.	Min.	Goals	Avg.
Warren Sharples	39	20	10	6	2165	117	3.24
Tim Keough	11	4	2	0	390	31	4.77

MICHIGAN STATE UNIVERSITY

Overall: 35-7-3; CCHA: 26-3-3

	Pos.	Class	Games	G.	A.	Pts.	Pen.
Kip Miller	F	Sr.	45	48	53	101	60
Pat Murray	F	Jr.	45	24	60	84	36
Peter White	F	So.	45	22	40	62	6
Shawn Heaphy	F	Jr.	45	28	31	59	54
Steve Beadle	D	Sr.	45	21	36	57	50
Jason Woolley	D	So.	45	10	38	48	26
Dwayne Norris	F	So.	36	19	26	45	30
Kerry Russell	F	Jr.	45	15	12	27	62
Bryan Smolinski	F	Fr.	39	10	17	27	45
Don Gibson	D	Sr.	44	5	22	27	167
Rob Woodward	F	Fr.	44	17	9	26	8
Walt Bartels	F	Jr.	45	7	15	22	16
Jim Cummins	F	So.	41	8	7	15	94
Joby Messier	D	So.	42	1	11	12	58
Wes McCauley	D	Fr.	42	2	7	9	15
Jason Muzzatti	G	Jr.	33	0	9	9	31
Michael Thompson	F	Fr.	19	4	4	8	4
Michael Stewart	D	Fr.	45	2	6	8	45
Craig Shepherd	F	Sr.	28	4	2	6	40
Jeff Pitawanakwat	F	Fr.	40	2	4	6	17
Doug Collins	D	So.	10	0	3	3	8
Mark Hirth	F	So.	5	1	1	2	4
Bill Shalawylo	F	Fr.	12	1	1	2	8
Mike Gilmore	G	So.	12	0	1	1	0
David McAuliffe	D	Sr.	1	0	0	0	0
Jamie Stewart	G	Jr.	4	0	0	0	0

GOALTENDING

	G.	W.	L.	T.	Min.	Goals	Avg.
Mike Gilmore	12	9	1	0	638	29	2.73
Jason Muzzatti	33	24	6	3	1976	99	3.01
Jamie Stewart	4	2	0	0	111	7	3.80

MICHIGAN TECHNOLOGICAL UNIVERSITY

Overall: 10-30-0; WCHA: 6-22-0

	Pos.	Class	Games	G.	A.	Pts.	Pen.
Kip Noble	D	Sr.	40	17	33	50	46
Jamie Steer	F	So.	40	21	21	42	26
John Young	F	Fr.	38	13	24	37	34
Jay Luknowsky	F	Jr.	40	15	19	34	30
Shawn Harrison	F	Sr.	36	13	19	32	46
Kelly Hurd	F	Jr.	37	12	13	25	50
Davis Payne	F	So.	30	11	10	21	81
Greg Parnell	F	So.	38	10	11	21	12
Darcy Martini	D	So.	36	3	16	19	150
Jim Carroll	F	Sr.	34	7	11	18	40
Rob Tustian	D	Jr.	37	6	9	15	74
Ken Plaquin	D	Fr.	33	2	13	15	20
Rod Ewacha	F	Fr.	34	3	6	9	7
Jeff St. Cyr	D	Sr.	36	2	7	9	81
Don Osborne	D	Fr.	28	4	2	6	18
Jim Bonner	D	Fr.	36	3	3	6	32
Dwight Degiacomo	F	Fr.	24	3	2	5	12
Reid McDonald	F	So.	31	3	2	5	6
Randy Lewis	F	Fr.	34	1	3	4	53
Rob Pallante	D	So.	12	1	2	3	6
Geoff Sarjeant	G	So.	19	0	3	3	4
Peter Grant	F/D	So.	14	0	1	1	10
Jay Boxer	F	So.	1	0	0	0	4
Mike Hauswirth	F	Fr.	4	0	0	0	0
Tim Hartnett	F	So.	14	0	0	0	2
Damian Rhodes	G	Jr.	25	0	0	0	16

GOALTENDING

	G.	W.	L.	T.	Min.	Goals	Avg.
Damian Rhodes	25	6	17	0	1358	119	5.26
Geoff Sarjeant	19	4	13	0	1043	94	5.41

UNIVERSITY OF MINNESOTA

Overall: 28-16-2; WCHA: 17-9-2

	Pos.	Class	Games	G.	A.	Pts.	Pen.
Peter Hankinson	F	Sr.	46	25	41	66	34
Scott Bloom	F	Sr.	43	24	28	52	22
Ken Gernander	F	Jr.	44	32	17	49	24
Larry Olimb	D	So.	46	6	36	42	44
Grant Bischoff	F	Jr.	45	21	19	40	18
Tom Pederson	D	So.	43	8	30	38	58
Trent Klatt	F	Fr.	38	22	14	36	16
Jason Miller	F	Jr.	41	10	26	36	16
Luke Johnson	D	Jr.	44	4	31	35	26
Ben Hankinson	F	Jr.	45	19	12	31	116
Jon Anderson	F	Sr.	42	15	14	29	41
Travis Richards	D	Fr.	45	4	24	28	38

	Pos.	Class	Games	G.	A.	Pts.	Pen.
Cory Laylin	F	So.	39	13	14	27	31
Dean Williamson	F	Sr.	46	10	11	21	24
Brett Strot	F	Sr.	42	8	8	16	23
Doug Zmolek	D	Fr.	40	1	10	11	52
John Brill	F	Fr.	34	2	8	10	22
Sean Fabian	D	So.	40	0	10	10	74
Lance Pitlick	D	Sr.	14	3	2	5	26
Eric Means	D	Fr.	22	0	4	4	12
Jake Enebak	F	Jr.	20	0	3	3	26
Tom Newman	G	Fr.	35	0	2	2	2
Lance Werness	F	Jr.	2	0	1	1	2
Nike Gerebi	F	So.	4	0	0	0	0
Jeff Stolp	G	So.	10	0	0	0	4
Scott Nelson	G	Jr.	11	0	0	0	0

GOALTENDING

	G.	W.	L.	T.	Min.	Goals	Avg.
Scott Nelson	11	4	2	0	364	19	3.13
Tom Newman	35	19	13	2	1982	127	3.84
Jeff Stolp	10	5	1	0	417	33	4.75

UNIVERSITY OF MINNESOTA-DULUTH

Overall: 20-19-1; WCHA: 13-15-0

	Pos.	Class	Games	G.	A.	Pts.	Pen.
Shjon Podein	F	Sr.	35	21	18	39	36
Darren Nauss	F	Jr.	37	21	17	38	24
Shawn Howard	F	Jr.	40	19	19	38	58
Greg Andrusak	D	Jr.	35	5	29	34	74
Sandy Smith	F	Sr.	39	15	16	31	53
Dennis Vaske	D	Sr.	37	5	24	29	72
Joey Biondi	F	Fr.	39	11	17	28	8
Scott Keller	F	Jr.	40	12	15	27	24
Doug Torrel	F	So.	39	11	11	22	48
Derek Plante	F	Fr.	28	10	11	21	12
Dale Jago	D	Sr.	33	9	11	20	24
Kevin Kaiser	F	So.	39	9	11	20	24
Kris Miller	D	Jr.	39	2	11	13	59
Jason Bortolussi	F	Fr.	39	7	5	12	26
Darrin Amundson	F	Jr.	23	5	6	11	12
Brad Penner	F/D	Fr.	32	3	5	8	10
Brett Hauer	D	Fr.	37	2	6	8	44
Jeff Parrott	D	Fr.	35	1	6	7	64
Wayne Sager	F	So.	13	1	5	6	0
Stu Plante	F	Sr.	20	0	2	2	10
Chad Erickson	G	So.	39	0	2	2	12
Scott Engen	F	Fr.	17	1	0	1	6
Jon Rohloff	D	So.	5	0	1	1	6
Steve Cronkhite	D	So.	1	0	0	0	2
Corey Chwialkowski	G	Fr.	5	0	0	0	0
Kevin Starren	D	So.	13	0	0	0	8

GOALTENDING

	G.	W.	L.	T.	Min.	Goals	Avg.
Chad Erickson	39	19	19	1	2301	141	3.68
Corey Chwialkowski	5	1	0	0	105	9	5.14

UNIVERSITY OF NEW HAMPSHIRE

Overall: 17-17-5; Hockey East: 8-9-4

	Pos.	Class	Games	G.	A.	Pts.	Pen.
Savo Mitrovic	F	So.	37	30	21	51	40
Donenic Amodeo	F	So.	39	19	26	45	12
Joe Flanagan	F	So.	34	12	24	36	6
Jeff Lazaro	D	Sr.	39	16	19	35	34
Greg Klym	F	Fr.	38	8	25	33	8
Riel Bellegrade	F	Jr.	39	12	20	32	28
David Aiken	F	Sr.	39	12	19	31	37
Chris Winnes	F	Jr.	24	10	13	23	12
Scott Morrow	F	So.	29	10	11	21	35
David MacIntyre	D	Jr.	37	5	15	20	20
Mark McGinn	F	So.	35	6	11	17	28
Chris Grassie	D	Sr.	39	3	12	15	52
Mark Johnson	F	Sr.	37	4	9	13	8
Kevin Thompson	F	Fr.	36	6	3	9	26
Jesse Cooper	D	Fr.	32	3	6	9	12
Steve Morrow	D	So.	35	2	7	9	40
Kevin Dean	F/D	Jr.	39	2	6	8	42
Bruce MacDonald	F	Jr.	35	2	3	5	16
Jim McGrath	D	Fr.	31	0	4	4	22
Adain Hayes	F	So.	4	2	0	2	2
Matt Trenovich	D	Jr.	11	1	1	2	0
Frank Messina	D/F	Jr.	11	1	0	1	10
Brett Abel	G	Fr.	2	0	0	0	0
Bill LaCouture	F	Jr.	2	0	0	0	0
Greg Blow	F	Fr.	7	0	0	0	4
Pat Morrison	G	Jr.	18	0	0	0	2
Pat Szturm	G	Sr.	21	0	0	0	0

GOALTENDING

	G.	W.	L.	T.	Min.	Goals	Avg.
Pat Szturm	21	....	....	....	1286	72	3.36
Pat Morrison	18	....	....	....	1003	72	4.31
Brett Abel	2	....	....	....	100	9	5.40

UNIVERSITY OF NORTH DAKOTA

Overall: 28-13-4; WCHA: 15-10-3

	Pos.	Class	Games	G.	A.	Pts.	Pen.
Lee Davidson	F	Sr.	45	26	49	75	66
Dixon Ward	F	So.	45	35	34	69	44
Russ Parent	D	Sr.	45	9	50	59	86
Greg Johnson	F	Fr.	44	17	38	55	11
Neil Eisenhut	F	Jr.	45	22	32	54	46
Russ Romaniuk	F	So.	45	36	15	51	54
Jason Herter	D	So.	38	11	39	50	40
Garry Valk	F	Jr.	43	22	17	39	92
Brent Bobyck	F	Jr.	44	16	21	37	47
Dane Jackson	F	So.	44	15	11	26	56
Jeff McLean	F	So.	45	10	16	26	42
David Marvin	D	Jr.	45	3	23	26	70
Dave Hakstol	D	So.	44	4	16	20	76
Justin Duberman	F	So.	42	10	9	19	50
Ross Johnson	F	Jr.	43	6	9	15	22
Brad Pascall	D	So.	45	1	9	10	98
Darryn Fossand	D	Jr.	33	1	6	7	8
Shane McFarlane	F	Jr.	23	3	2	5	10
John Hanson	F	So.	12	4	0	4	12
Chris Dickson	G	Jr.	23	0	3	3	2
Matt Morelli	F	Jr.	5	1	0	1	0
Mike McCormick	F	Jr.	2	0	1	1	4
Kevin McKinnon	F	Fr.	3	0	1	1	4
Jon Larson	D	Fr.	18	0	1	1	10
Tony Couture	G	Jr.	24	0	1	1	26
Steve Peters	G	Jr.	2	0	0	0	0
Jace Reed	D	Fr.	10	0	0	0	0

GOALTENDING

	G.	W.	L.	T.	Min.	Goals	Avg.
Tony Couture	24	16	6	1	1401	81	3.47
Chris Dickson	23	12	7	2	1227	84	4.11
Steve Peters	2	0	0	1	97	8	4.95

NORTHEASTERN UNIVERSITY

Overall: 16-19-2; Hockey East: 9-10-2

	Pos.	Class	Games	G.	A.	Pts.	Pen.
Harry Mews	F	Sr.	36	20	39	59	82
Brian Sullivan	F	Jr.	34	24	21	45	72
Rob Cowie	D	Jr.	34	14	31	45	54
Matt Saunders	F	So.	35	19	21	40	51
Jay Schiavo	F	So.	37	19	18	37	12
Andy May	F	Sr.	35	13	15	28	35
Tom Bivona	F	Sr.	36	8	17	25	8
Will Averill	D	Jr.	35	6	13	19	41
Mike Roberts	D	Sr.	36	7	11	18	16
Keith Cyr	F	Sr.	24	6	12	18	41
Sabastien Laplante	F	Fr.	32	10	6	16	19
Peter Schure	F	Jr.	27	6	10	16	64
Paul Sacco	D	Sr.	37	3	13	16	30
Dino Grossi	F	Fr.	31	6	9	15	43
Bob Kellogg	D	Fr.	36	3	12	15	30
Robbie Grant	F	Jr.	22	3	7	10	16
Rob Kenny	F	So.	32	2	7	9	20
Chris Foy	D	Fr.	37	0	5	5	48
Sean Curtin	F	Jr.	20	2	2	4	8
Paul Flanagan	D	So.	30	1	1	2	32
Tom Cole	G	So.	25	0	1	1	2
Bill Hartnett	F	Fr.	2	0	0	0	2
Tom Mutch	F	Jr.	2	0	0	0	2
Craig Stinehour	D	So.	3	0	0	0	0
John Schultz	F	So.	8	0	0	0	13
Scott Hopkins	G	Fr.	16	0	0	0	0

GOALTENDING

	G.	W.	L.	T.	Min.	Goals	Avg.
Tom Cole	25	10	12	2	1412	106	4.51
Scott Hopkins	16	6	7	0	819	72	5.28

NORTHERN MICHIGAN UNIVERSITY

Overall: 22-19-1; WCHA: 15-12-1

	Pos.	Class	Games	G.	A.	Pts.	Pen.
Scott Beattie	F	Fr.	36	30	29	59	24
Jim Hiller	F	Fr.	39	23	33	56	52
Eric LeMarque	F	Sr.	40	17	32	49	45
Dean Antos	F	Jr.	42	19	22	41	50
Dallas Drake	F	So.	36	13	24	37	42

	Pos.	Class	Games	G.	A.	Pts.	Pen.
Darryl Plandowski	F	Jr.	42	13	22	35	52
Kevin Scott	F	Jr.	34	20	14	34	46
Pete Podrasky	D	Sr.	35	6	22	28	36
Mark Beaufait	F	So.	34	10	14	24	12
Doug Garrow	F	Sr.	35	8	12	20	83
Phil Brown	F	Sr.	42	4	14	18	24
Ed Ward	F	Jr.	39	5	11	16	77
Dave Porter	F	Sr.	37	5	9	14	38
Lou Melone	D	So.	41	2	12	14	46
Geoff Simpson	D	Fr.	39	4	9	13	40
Phil Soukoroff	D	So.	23	1	8	9	39
Brad Werenka	D	Sr.	8	2	5	7	8
Dave Shyiak	F	Jr.	29	2	5	7	44
Dan Ruoho	D	Fr.	18	2	4	6	26
Phil Neururer	D	So.	27	1	5	6	28
Jeff Gawlicki	F	Sr.	36	3	2	5	67
David Huettl	D	Fr.	27	0	4	4	24
Bill Pye	G	Jr.	36	0	3	3	4
Mark Olson	F	So.	12	1	0	1	4
Willie Mitchell	G	So.	3	0	0	0	0
Rob Kruhlak	G	Fr.	9	0	0	0	0

GOALTENDING

	G.	W.	L.	T.	Min.	Goals	Avg.
Rob Kruhlak	9	1	4	0	357	22	3.70
Bill Pye	36	20	14	1	2035	149	4.39
Willie Mitchell	3	1	1	0	150	18	7.20

OHIO STATE UNIVERSITY

Overall: 11-24-5; CCHA: 11-17-4

	Pos.	Class	Games	G.	A.	Pts.	Pen.
Derek Higdon	F	Sr.	40	29	28	57	68
Don Oliver	F	Jr.	40	19	26	45	27
Glenn Painter	D	Fr.	40	12	28	40	32
Eddie Choi	F	Fr.	39	13	24	37	18
Scott Rex	F/D	Sr.	40	7	30	37	82
David Smith	F	So.	35	19	16	35	76
Paul Rutherford	F	Jr.	40	15	16	31	40
Stacey Hartnell	F	Jr.	40	12	10	22	32
Phil Cadman	F	Fr.	38	11	7	18	4
Rob Schriner	F	So.	40	6	9	15	50
Brian Baldrica	D	So.	40	0	15	15	38
Greg Beaucage	F/D	So.	37	5	7	12	71
Greg Burke	F	So.	40	5	5	10	50
Scott Walsh	F	So.	29	2	7	9	28
Tim Green	D	Fr.	21	0	5	5	20
Jeff Ladrow	F	Sr.	32	3	1	4	8
Sean Hartnell	D	Jr.	33	0	4	4	70
Eric Reisman	D	Jr.	39	1	2	3	91
Todd Fanning	G	Sr.	24	0	3	3	14
John Graham	D	Fr.	31	0	3	3	18
Paul Forfia	F	So.	14	1	0	1	0
Mike Bales	G	Fr.	21	0	1	1	2
Jim Slazyk	G	So.	1	0	0	0	0

GOALTENDING

	G.	W.	L.	T.	Min.	Goals	Avg.
Mike Bales	21	6	13	2	1117	95	5.10
Todd Fanning	24	5	11	3	1293	113	5.24
Jim Slazyk	1	0	0	0	15	3	11.78

PRINCETON UNIVERSITY

Overall: 12-14-1; ECAC: 11-10-1

	Pos.	Class	Games	G.	A.	Pts.	Pen.
Andre Faust	F	So.	27	15	29	44	28
Greg Polaski	F	Sr.	26	18	18	36	61
Mark Khozozian	F	Sr.	23	18	17	35	32
Sean Murphy	F	Jr.	27	10	17	27	24
Kevin Sullivan	F	Sr.	27	12	13	25	28
Mike McKee	D	So.	26	7	18	25	18
Bart Blaeser	F	Sr.	26	8	15	23	14
Jeff Kampersal	D	So.	27	3	7	10	26
Andy Cesarski	D	Jr.	27	1	9	10	22
Chris Tatum	F	Sr.	27	3	6	9	22
Danny Maze	F	Sr.	27	2	6	8	16
Sean Gorman	D	Jr.	27	2	4	6	8
Jim Sourges	D	Sr.	13	1	5	6	12
Nate Smith	D	Sr.	23	2	3	5	8
Terry Morris	F	Fr.	21	1	4	5	12
Tom Shimabukuro	F	Jr.	27	2	2	4	8
Brian Bigelow	F	Fr.	17	3	0	3	4
Chris Stewart	F	So.	7	2	1	3	0
Mike Cole	F	Jr.	24	1	0	1	10
Dan Gardner	F	Fr.	7	0	1	1	0
Sverre Sears	D	Fr.	18	0	1	1	14
Ron High	G	Jr.	20	0	1	1	0
Jack Craig	D	So.	1	0	0	0	0
Craig Fiander	G	Fr.	1	0	0	0	0

	Pos.	Class	Games	G.	A.	Pts.	Pen.
Scott Sinson	F	Fr.	3	0	0	0	0
Keith Merkler	F	Fr.	8	0	0	0	4
Mark Salsbury	G	Jr.	11	0	0	0	0

GOALTENDING

	G.	W.	L.	T.	Min.	Goals	Avg.
Mark Salsbury	11	5	3	0	480	24	3.00
Ron High	20	7	10	1	1140	88	4.63
Craig Fiander	1	0	1	0	12	2	10.00

PROVIDENCE COLLEGE

Overall: 22-10-3; Hockey East: 11-7-3

	Pos.	Class	Games	G.	A.	Pts.	Pen.
Mike Boback	F	So.	31	13	29	42	28
Rob Gaudreau	F	So.	32	20	18	38	12
Rick Bennett	F	Sr.	31	12	24	36	74
Lyle Wildgoose	F	Jr.	35	17	18	35	38
Andy Mattice	F	Sr.	31	13	19	32	10
Mario Aube	F	Jr.	32	13	16	29	10
Bob Cowan	F	Fr.	34	8	17	25	12
Jeff Serowik	D	Sr.	35	6	19	25	34
Larry Rooney	D	Jr.	33	7	12	19	24
Bob Creamer	F	So.	35	10	7	17	10
Shaun Kane	D	So.	31	9	8	17	46
Paul Saundercook	D	Sr.	35	2	13	15	58
Pat Becker	F	Sr.	27	4	7	11	12
Jeff Robison	D	So.	35	2	8	10	16
Pat Madigan	F	Jr.	24	4	4	8	14
Paul Flaherty	F	Jr.	14	3	4	7	4
Todd Whittemore	F	Sr.	16	4	2	6	30
Mark Devine	F	Fr.	13	0	6	6	8
Dave Guden	F	Sr.	27	4	0	4	28
Gary Socha	F	Fr.	25	2	2	4	8
Brian Jefferies	F	Fr.	13	1	1	2	0
Todd Huyber	D	Fr.	30	0	2	2	14
Mark Romaine	G	Sr.	19	0	1	1	0
Brad Mullahy	G	Fr.	5	0	0	0	0
Stephen Higgins	D	Sr.	11	0	0	0	8
Matt Merten	G	Sr.	16	0	0	0	6

GOALTENDING

	G.	W.	L.	T.	Min.	Goals	Avg.
Matt Merten	16	8	4	2	908	38	2.51
Mark Romaine	19	12	5	1	1023	52	3.05
Brad Mullahy	5	2	1	0	207	13	3.77

RENSSELAER POLYTECHNIC INSTITUTE (R.P.I.)

Overall: 20-14-0; ECAC: 14-8-0

	Pos.	Class	Games	G.	A.	Pts.	Pen.
Joey Juneau	F	Jr.	34	18	52	70	31
Bruce Coles	F	Jr.	34	28	24	52	142
Brian Ferreira	F	Sr.	34	10	35	45	36
Tony Hejna	F	Sr.	26	20	16	36	22
Bill Flanagan	F	Sr.	34	14	22	36	24
Gary Woolford	F	Jr.	27	13	18	31	46
Kevin Mazzella	F	Sr.	32	15	15	30	46
Francois Cadoret	F	Fr.	34	15	9	24	38
S. Robitaille	D	So.	30	3	21	24	16
Allen Kummu	D	Fr.	33	9	13	22	50
Derek DeCosty	F	Jr.	26	6	12	18	44
Mickey LeBlanc	F	Jr.	34	11	6	17	6
Tim Roberts	F	Jr.	26	2	10	12	31
Dan Vaillant	D	So.	33	3	8	11	36
Dave Casalena	F	Jr.	27	3	3	6	19
Denis Poissant	F	Sr.	16	2	4	6	4
Zachary Dargaty	D	So.	28	1	5	6	20
Todd Hilditch	D	So.	33	1	3	4	48
Ivan Moore	D	So.	33	1	3	4	24
Cam Matches	F	Fr.	19	0	3	3	8
Phil Kenner	F	Jr.	5	1	0	1	4
Steve Duncan	G	Sr.	16	0	1	1	2
Sean Kennedy	G	So.	18	0	1	1	6
Frank Balle	F	So.	1	0	0	0	0
Dennis Cesana	F	Jr.	3	0	0	0	0
Rick Borina	F	So.	10	0	0	0	8

GOALTENDING

	G.	W.	L.	T.	Min.	Goals	Avg.
Steve Duncan	17	7	9	0	926	73	4.73
Sean Kennedy	19	13	5	0	1108	75	4.06

ST. LAWRENCE UNIVERSITY

Overall: 13-15-4; ECAC: 12-8-2

	Pos.	Class	Games	G.	A.	Pts.	Pen.
Joe Day	F	Sr.	30	18	26	44	24
Andy Pritchard	F	Jr.	30	17	19	36	22

	Pos.	Class	Games	G.	A.	Pts.	Pen.
Doug Murray	F	Sr.	29	8	19	27	12
Dan Laperriere	D	So.	29	6	19	25	16
Chris Consorte	F	Sr.	29	8	16	24	53
Greg Carvel	F	Fr.	29	5	16	21	16
Martyn Ball	F	Sr.	29	8	11	19	34
Martin Lacroix	F	So.	30	11	7	18	14
Kevin Wright	F	Sr.	30	9	8	17	18
Shawn Rivers	D	So.	26	3	14	17	29
Rob White	D	Sr.	30	2	15	17	84
Jim Giacin	F	Fr.	26	4	2	6	30
Ted Beattie	D	Fr.	21	2	4	6	54
Ted Dent	F	So.	15	1	5	6	10
John Massoud	F	Fr.	19	2	1	3	18
Gerard Verbeek	F	Fr.	16	1	2	3	16
Chris Wells	F	So.	22	1	2	3	6
Bill MacCuaig	F	Jr.	18	0	3	3	6
Brad James	D	Sr.	28	2	0	2	52
Steve Torkos	D	Sr.	9	1	1	2	0
John Collins	F	So.	2	1	0	1	2
Mike Mudd	G	Sr.	14	0	1	1	0
Mike Terwilliger	D	Fr.	20	0	1	1	4
Brady Giroux	G	Fr.	2	0	0	0	0
Matt Dickson	F	Fr.	5	0	0	0	0
John Roderick	D	Fr.	15	0	0	0	18
Les Kuntar	G	Jr.	19	0	0	0	0

GOALTENDING

	G.	W.	L.	T.	Min.	Goals	Avg.
Mike Mudd	14	6	3	3	732	34	2.79
Les Kuntar	19	7	10	1	1076	76	4.24
Brady Giroux	2	0	0	0	19	3	9.09

UNIVERSITY OF VERMONT

Overall: 9-20-2; ECAC: 7-13-2

	Pos.	Class	Games	G.	A.	Pts.	Pen.
Jim Larkin	F	So.	28	20	15	35	14
Ricker Love	F	Jr.	24	9	18	27	32
Mike McLaughlin	F	So.	29	11	12	23	37
John LeClair	F	Jr.	10	10	6	16	38
Scott Jagod	F	Jr.	30	9	7	16	2
Aaron Miller	D	Fr.	31	1	15	16	24
Stephane Venne	D	Jr.	31	6	9	15	62
Travis Lehouiller	F	Fr.	30	6	8	14	29
Mike Doers	F	Fr.	30	2	11	13	26
Brendan Creagh	D	Fr.	30	4	7	11	12
David Browne	F	Jr.	25	2	9	11	34
Jeremy Benoit	D	So.	29	3	6	9	18
Jim Fernholz	F	Jr.	31	3	6	9	22
Dave Weber	D	Sr.	27	2	5	7	44
Toby Kearney	F	Fr.	25	2	3	5	24
Joel Muscatello	F	Fr.	25	2	2	4	18
Leif Selstad	F	So.	29	2	2	4	20
Chip Mason	F	Jr.	10	1	3	4	2
Rob Bateman	D	Sr.	31	0	4	4	62
Joe McCarthy	D/F	Fr.	31	2	1	3	21
Kevin Monty	F	Fr.	11	1	1	2	2
Matt Bertram	G	Fr.	11	0	1	1	4
Glenn Neary	G	Jr.	2	0	0	0	2
Ted Madden	D	So.	4	0	0	0	2
Mark Toof	F	So.	10	0	0	0	0
Mike Millham	G	Jr.	22	0	0	0	10

GOALTENDING

	G.	W.	L.	T.	Min.	Goals	Avg.
Glenn Neary	2	0	1	1	125	7	3.36
Mike Millham	22	5	15	1	1227	87	4.25
Matt Bertram	11	4	5	0	519	38	4.39

WESTERN MICHIGAN UNIVERSITY

Overall: 14-24-2; CCHA: 12-18-2

	Pos.	Class	Games	G.	A.	Pts.	Pen.
Shane Redshaw	F	Sr.	39	35	25	60	65
Jeff Green	F	Sr.	40	30	29	59	42
Paul Polillo	F	Sr.	40	19	35	54	34
Mike Eastwood	F	Jr.	40	25	27	52	36
Keith Jones	F	So.	40	19	18	37	82
Mike Posma	D	Sr.	39	8	28	36	28
Chris Clarke	D	Jr.	39	2	21	23	55
Rich Whitten	F	Sr.	40	11	10	21	26
Mike Ross	D	Jr.	39	1	19	20	48
Scott Garrow	F	So.	40	8	9	17	50
Tom Auge	F	Jr.	40	4	13	17	56
Doug Melnyk	D	Sr.	33	2	10	12	26
Gordie Frantti	F	Fr.	30	7	4	11	16

	Pos.	Class	Games	G.	A.	Pts.	Pen.
Andy Rymsha	D	Sr.	37	1	10	11	108
Andy Suhy	D	So.	34	3	5	8	52
Brad Dawson	F	So.	23	1	4	5	16
Jason Jennings	F	Fr.	28	3	1	4	50
J.P. LaRoche	F	Fr.	14	3	0	3	6
Byron Witkowski	F	Fr.	36	1	2	3	36
Brian Tulik	D	Jr.	6	0	2	2	12
Mike Power	G	Fr.	24	0	2	2	4
Joe Bonnett	F	So.	16	1	0	1	2
Rob Pallin	F	Sr.	18	0	1	1	6
Rob Laurie	G	So.	22	0	1	1	2
Dave Dimitri	D	So.	5	0	0	0	4

GOALTENDING

	G.	W.	L.	T.	Min.	Goals	Avg.
Mike Power	24	7	14	1	1304	105	4.83
Rob Laurie	22	7	10	1	1104	96	5.22

UNIVERSITY OF WISCONSIN

Overall: 36-9-1; WCHA: 19-8-1

	Pos.	Class	Games	G.	A.	Pts.	Pen.
Gary Shuchuk	F	Sr.	45	41	39	80	70
Chris Tancill	F	Sr.	45	39	32	71	44
John Byce	F	Sr.	46	27	44	71	20
Sean Hill	D	So.	42	14	39	53	78
Doug Macdonald	F	So.	44	16	35	51	52
Tom Sagissor	F	Sr.	43	19	28	47	122
Mark Osiecki	D	Sr.	46	5	38	43	78
Steve Rohlik	F	Sr.	46	17	23	40	52
Barry Richter	F/D	Fr.	42	13	23	36	26
Rob Andringa	D	Jr.	46	9	23	32	60
Dennis Snedden	F	Jr.	45	10	17	27	50
Don Granato	F	Jr.	45	12	11	23	40
John Parker	F	Jr.	35	11	9	20	22
Brett Kurtz	F	So.	42	8	12	20	28
Joe Decker	F	Jr.	36	4	10	14	14
Rob Mendel	D	Sr.	44	1	13	14	30
Rodger Sykes	D	Jr.	38	3	5	8	18
Tray Tuomie	F	Jr.	20	2	6	8	0
Jon Helgeson	F	Jr.	18	2	2	4	12
Chris Nelson	D	So.	37	1	3	4	38
Duane Derksen	G	So.	41	0	3	3	4
Jason Francisco	F	Fr.	7	0	1	1	0
Noel Rahn	F	Fr.	4	0	0	0	0
Jon Michelizzi	G	Fr.	9	0	0	0	0
Joe Harwell	D	Fr.	10	0	0	0	2

GOALTENDING

	G.	W.	L.	T.	Min.	Goals	Avg.
Duane Derksen	41	31	8	1	2345	133	3.40
Jon Michelizzi	9	5	1	0	427	30	4.22

YALE UNIVERSITY

Overall: 8-20-1; ECAC: 6-15-1

	Pos.	Class	Games	G.	A.	Pts.	Pen.
Jeff Blaeser	F	So.	29	17	14	31	16
Mark Kaufmann	F	Fr.	29	9	16	25	36
Bob Bowse	F	Jr.	29	16	8	24	10
Scott D'Orsi	F	Sr.	28	10	14	24	30
Craig Ferguson	F	So.	28	6	13	19	36
John Sather	F	So.	28	7	11	18	18
James Lavish	F	Fr.	27	6	11	17	40
Chris Gruber	F	Jr.	29	5	12	17	10
Scott Matusovich	D	So.	28	1	15	16	55
Mike Miller	F	Jr.	27	7	6	13	28
Greg Harrison	D	Sr.	29	5	5	10	32
Billy Matthews	D	Sr.	29	2	8	10	34
Yannick Chiasson	F	Fr.	22	2	7	9	16
Lance Marciano	D	Jr.	27	0	9	9	34
Julian Binavince	F	Sr.	15	3	4	7	14
Jack Duffy	D	Fr.	26	1	6	7	48
Peter Allen	D	Fr.	26	2	4	6	16
Mike O'Brien	F	So.	16	1	5	6	0
Bruce Wolanin	D	Jr.	28	1	5	6	26
Craig Forrest	F	Sr.	15	1	0	1	16
Dean Malish	D	Fr.	2	0	0	0	0
John Hockin	G	Fr.	4	0	0	0	0
Ray Letourneau	G	Jr.	28	0	0	0	0

GOALTENDING

	G.	W.	L.	T.	Min.	Goals	Avg.
Ray Letourneau	28	8	19	1	1631	126	4.64
John Hockin	4	0	1	0	111	15	8.11

NATIONAL HOCKEY LEAGUE SCHEDULE 1990-91

*Denotes afternoon game.

THURSDAY, OCTOBER 4
Philadelphia at Boston
Quebec at Hartford
Montreal at Buffalo
New York Islanders at Los Angeles
New York Rangers at Chicago
Detroit at New Jersey
Toronto at Winnipeg
St. Louis at Minnesota
Vancouver at Calgary

FRIDAY, OCTOBER 5
Pittsburgh at Washington

SATURDAY, OCTOBER 6
Quebec at Boston
New York Rangers at Hartford
Buffalo at Montreal
New York Islanders at Minnesota
Philadelphia at New Jersey
Detroit at Washington
Toronto at Calgary
Chicago at St. Louis
Winnipeg at Edmonton
Vancouver at Los Angeles

SUNDAY, OCTOBER 7
Boston at Quebec
New York Islanders at Chicago
New Jersey at Pittsburgh
Detroit at Philadelphia
Toronto at Edmonton

MONDAY, OCTOBER 8
Hartford at Montreal
Minnesota at New York Rangers
Calgary at Winnipeg

TUESDAY, OCTOBER 9
Minnesota at New Jersey
Pittsburgh at St. Louis
Los Angeles at Vancouver

WEDNESDAY, OCTOBER 10
Boston at Winnipeg
Buffalo at Hartford
Quebec at Toronto
Washington at New York Rangers
Calgary at Detroit

THURSDAY, OCTOBER 11
Boston at Minnesota
New Jersey at Philadelphia
Pittsburgh at Chicago
Edmonton at Los Angeles

FRIDAY, OCTOBER 12
Hartford at Detroit
Quebec at Buffalo
Montreal at New York Rangers
Winnipeg at Washington
St. Louis at Vancouver

SATURDAY, OCTOBER 13
Boston at Los Angeles
Montreal at Hartford
Buffalo at Quebec
Pittsburgh at New York Islanders
New York Rangers at Washington
Calgary at New Jersey
Winnipeg at Philadelphia
Detroit at Toronto
Chicago at Minnesota

SUNDAY, OCTOBER 14
*Calgary at Chicago
St. Louis at Los Angeles
*Edmonton at Vancouver

MONDAY, OCTOBER 15
Washington at Montreal

TUESDAY, OCTOBER 16
Hartford at Quebec
Winnipeg at New York Islanders
Philadelphia at Pittsburgh
Chicago at Detroit
St. Louis at Edmonton

WEDNESDAY, OCTOBER 17
Boston at Vancouver
Hartford at Toronto
Montreal at Buffalo

Winnipeg at New York Rangers
Washington at New Jersey
Minnesota at Los Angeles

THURSDAY, OCTOBER 18
Montreal at Detroit
Quebec at Philadelphia
Toronto at Chicago
St. Louis at Calgary

FRIDAY, OCTOBER 19
Boston at Edmonton
Hartford at Los Angeles
Pittsburgh at Buffalo
New York Islanders at Washington
New York Rangers at New Jersey
Vancouver at Winnipeg

SATURDAY, OCTOBER 20
Boston at Calgary
Buffalo at New York Islanders
Philadelphia at Montreal
*Detroit at Quebec
New York Rangers at Pittsburgh
New Jersey at Washington
Chicago at Toronto
Minnesota at St. Louis

SUNDAY, OCTOBER 21
*Vancouver at Quebec
Minnesota at Chicago
Calgary at Edmonton

MONDAY, OCTOBER 22
Toronto at New York Rangers

TUESDAY, OCTOBER 23
Montreal at Pittsburgh
New Jersey at New York Islanders
Washington at Philadelphia
Vancouver at Detroit
Calgary at Los Angeles

WEDNESDAY, OCTOBER 24
Hartford at Minnesota
New York Islanders at Montreal
St. Louis at Toronto
Edmonton at Winnipeg

THURSDAY, OCTOBER 25
Vancouver at Boston
Buffalo at New Jersey
Quebec at Pittsburgh
Philadelphia at New York Rangers
Washington at Chicago
Toronto at St. Louis
Edmonton at Calgary

FRIDAY, OCTOBER 26
Minnesota at Detroit
Los Angeles at Winnipeg

SATURDAY, OCTOBER 27
Chicago at Boston
Vancouver at Hartford
Buffalo at Toronto
Montreal at St. Louis
New York Rangers at Quebec
Philadelphia at New York Islanders
Pittsburgh at New Jersey
Washington at Calgary
Detroit at Minnesota

SUNDAY, OCTOBER 28
Hartford at Buffalo
Montreal at Chicago
New York Islanders at Pittsburgh
Washington at Edmonton
Los Angeles at Winnipeg

MONDAY, OCTOBER 29
Quebec at New York Rangers

TUESDAY, OCTOBER 30
Los Angeles at New York Islanders
New Jersey at Calgary
Pittsburgh at Philadelphia
Washington at Vancouver
Minnesota at Toronto
St. Louis at Detroit

WEDNESDAY, OCTOBER 31
Boston at Buffalo
Montreal at Hartford
Los Angeles at New York Rangers
Winnipeg at Edmonton

THURSDAY, NOVEMBER 1
St. Louis at Boston
Quebec at Chicago
New Jersey at Vancouver
Minnesota at Philadelphia
Toronto at Detroit
Winnipeg at Calgary

FRIDAY, NOVEMBER 2
N. York Islanders at N. York Rangers
Los Angeles at Washington

SATURDAY, NOVEMBER 3
Buffalo at Boston
St. Louis at Hartford
Detroit at Montreal
Minnesota at Quebec
Washington at New York Islanders
New York Rangers at Pittsburgh
New Jersey at Edmonton
*Chicago at Philadelphia
Calgary at Toronto
Winnipeg at Vancouver

SUNDAY, NOVEMBER 4
Calgary at Buffalo
Minnesota at Montreal
Philadelphia at Toronto
Los Angeles at Chicago

MONDAY, NOVEMBER 5
Boston at New York Rangers

TUESDAY, NOVEMBER 6
Chicago at Hartford
Washington at Quebec
Toronto at New York Islanders
Philadelphia at Winnipeg
Calgary at Pittsburgh
Detroit at Vancouver
Edmonton at St. Louis

WEDNESDAY, NOVEMBER 7
Boston at Montreal
Buffalo at New York Rangers
New York Islanders at New Jersey

THURSDAY, NOVEMBER 8
Quebec at Minnesota
Calgary at Philadelphia
St. Louis at Pittsburgh
Vancouver at Toronto
Detroit at Los Angeles
Edmonton at Chicago

FRIDAY, NOVEMBER 9
Hartford at Winnipeg
Vancouver at Buffalo
New York Rangers at New Jersey

SATURDAY, NOVEMBER 10
Pittsburgh at Boston
Hartford at Minnesota
Buffalo at Washington
New Jersey at Montreal
Philadelphia at Quebec
Calgary at New York Islanders
Chicago at Toronto
Detroit at St. Louis
Edmonton at Los Angeles

SUNDAY, NOVEMBER 11
Boston at Washington
Quebec at Montreal
Calgary at New York Rangers
Vancouver at Philadelphia
Winnipeg at Chicago

MONDAY, NOVEMBER 12
Winnipeg at Toronto

TUESDAY, NOVEMBER 13
Montreal at New Jersey
Quebec at St. Louis
New York Rangers at Philadelphia
Pittsburgh at Minnesota

WEDNESDAY, NOVEMBER 14
Boston at Hartford
Buffalo at Los Angeles
Pittsburgh at Winnipeg
Washington at Toronto
Chicago at Detroit
Vancouver at Edmonton

THURSDAY, NOVEMBER 15
Quebec at Boston
Hartford at New Jersey
Montreal at Philadelphia
New York Islanders at Calgary
New York Rangers at Minnesota

FRIDAY, NOVEMBER 16
Buffalo at Edmonton
New York Islanders at Vancouver
New York Rangers at Winnipeg
Chicago at Washington
Toronto at Detroit

SATURDAY, NOVEMBER 17
Montreal at Boston
Washington at Hartford
Buffalo at Calgary
Chicago at Quebec
*Philadelphia at New Jersey
Pittsburgh at Los Angeles
Detroit at Toronto
St. Louis at Minnesota

SUNDAY, NOVEMBER 18
New York Islanders at Edmonton
New Jersey at Philadelphia
St. Louis at Winnipeg

MONDAY, NOVEMBER 19
Boston at Toronto
Montreal at Quebec
Minnesota at New York Rangers
Washington at Detroit
Calgary at Vancouver

TUESDAY, NOVEMBER 20
New Jersey at Los Angeles
Chicago at Edmonton
Winnipeg at St. Louis

WEDNESDAY, NOVEMBER 21
Quebec at Hartford
New York Rangers at Buffalo
Philadelphia at Pittsburgh
Toronto at Washington
Minnesota at Detroit
Chicago at Vancouver

THURSDAY, NOVEMBER 22
Winnipeg at New York Islanders
Los Angeles at Calgary

FRIDAY, NOVEMBER 23
*Hartford at Boston
Edmonton at Buffalo
*Toronto at Philadelphia
Pittsburgh at Washington
St. Louis at Detroit
Vancouver at Minnesota

SATURDAY, NOVEMBER 24
Boston at Hartford
Los Angeles at Montreal
Winnipeg at Quebec
*N. York Rangers at N. York Islanders
New Jersey at Minnesota
Washington at Pittsburgh
Edmonton at Toronto
Chicago at Calgary
Vancouver at St. Louis

SUNDAY, NOVEMBER 25
Winnipeg at Montreal
Los Angeles at Quebec
New York Islanders at Philadelphia

MONDAY, NOVEMBER 26
Buffalo at New York Rangers

TUESDAY, NOVEMBER 27
Philadelphia at New York Islanders
Edmonton at Pittsburgh
Toronto at St. Louis
Los Angeles at Detroit
Minnesota at Vancouver

WEDNESDAY, NOVEMBER 28
Quebec at Hartford
Buffalo at Montreal
Washington at New York Rangers
Philadelphia at New Jersey
Calgary at Winnipeg

THURSDAY, NOVEMBER 29
Edmonton at Boston

Hartford at Pittsburgh
Toronto at Vancouver
Detroit at Chicago
Los Angeles at St. Louis

FRIDAY, NOVEMBER 30
Montreal at Washington
New York Islanders at New Jersey
New York Rangers at Philadelphia
Minnesota at Winnipeg

SATURDAY, DECEMBER 1
New York Rangers at Boston
Edmonton at Hartford
Buffalo at Quebec
Calgary at Montreal
Washington at New York Islanders
New Jersey at St. Louis
Pittsburgh at Minnesota
Toronto at Los Angeles
*Chicago at Detroit

SUNDAY, DECEMBER 2
Detroit at Buffalo
Calgary at Quebec
Edmonton at Philadelphia
St. Louis at Chicago
Vancouver at Winnipeg

MONDAY, DECEMBER 3
Hartford at Montreal
Pittsburgh at New York Rangers
New Jersey at Winnipeg

TUESDAY, DECEMBER 4
Boston at Detroit
Vancouver at New York Islanders

WEDNESDAY, DECEMBER 5
Montreal at Hartford
Quebec at Edmonton
New York Rangers at Calgary
Vancouver at New Jersey
Washington at Pittsburgh
Minnesota at Toronto
Winnipeg at Los Angeles

THURSDAY, DECEMBER 6
Montreal at Boston
Buffalo at Philadelphia
New York Islanders at Chicago
Toronto at Minnesota

FRIDAY, DECEMBER 7
Hartford at Buffalo
Quebec at Calgary
New York Rangers at Edmonton
New Jersey at Washington
Vancouver at Pittsburgh
St. Louis at Detroit

SATURDAY, DECEMBER 8
Boston at Montreal
Pittsburgh at Hartford
Washington at New Jersey
Philadelphia at Minnesota
Chicago at Toronto
Detroit at St. Louis
Winnipeg at Los Angeles

SUNDAY, DECEMBER 9
Boston at Buffalo
Philadelphia at Chicago
Calgary at Edmonton

MONDAY, DECEMBER 10
Quebec at Vancouver

TUESDAY, DECEMBER 11
Buffalo at Detroit
New Jersey at New York Islanders
New York Rangers at Los Angeles
Philadelphia at Washington
Chicago at Pittsburgh
Winnipeg at St. Louis
Calgary at Minnesota

WEDNESDAY, DECEMBER 12
Boston at Hartford
Montreal at Toronto
Vancouver at Edmonton

THURSDAY, DECEMBER 13
Hartford at Boston
Quebec at Detroit
New York Islanders at Philadelphia
New Jersey at Pittsburgh
Winnipeg at Chicago
Minnesota at St. Louis
Calgary at Los Angeles

FRIDAY, DECEMBER 14
Pittsburgh at Buffalo
New York Rangers at Vancouver

SATURDAY, DECEMBER 15
New Jersey at Boston
Hartford at Washington
Montreal at Winnipeg
New York Islanders at Quebec
*Detroit at Philadelphia
St. Louis at Toronto
*Chicago at Minnesota
Edmonton at Los Angeles

SUNDAY, DECEMBER 16
St. Louis at Buffalo
Philadelphia at Winnipeg
Detroit at Pittsburgh
*Minnesota at Chicago
*Calgary at Vancouver

MONDAY, DECEMBER 17
Washington at New York Rangers

TUESDAY, DECEMBER 18
Boston at New Jersey
Buffalo at Hartford
Montreal at Quebec
Toronto at New York Islanders
Philadelphia at Detroit
Winnipeg at Pittsburgh
Vancouver at Calgary
Los Angeles at Edmonton

WEDNESDAY, DECEMBER 19
Quebec at Montreal
Toronto at New York Rangers
Washington at Chicago

THURSDAY, DECEMBER 20
Buffalo at Boston
Hartford at New York Islanders
New Jersey at Philadelphia
Minnesota at Pittsburgh
Washington at St. Louis
Winnipeg at Detroit
Los Angeles at Calgary
Edmonton at Vancouver

SATURDAY, DECEMBER 22
Minnesota at Boston
Philadelphia at Hartford
New York Rangers at Montreal
New Jersey at Quebec
Pittsburgh at New York Islanders
*Toronto at Washington
Detroit at Winnipeg
Chicago at St. Louis
Edmonton at Calgary
Los Angeles at Vancouver

SUNDAY, DECEMBER 23
Boston at New York Rangers
Minnesota at Hartford
Quebec at Buffalo
Montreal at Philadelphia
New York Islanders at Pittsburgh
Toronto at New Jersey
Detroit at Chicago
Vancouver at Edmonton

WEDNESDAY, DECEMBER 26
Boston at Buffalo
Hartford at Quebec
Pittsburgh at Washington
St. Louis at Chicago
Winnipeg at Minnesota

THURSDAY, DECEMBER 27
Montreal at Vancouver
New York Islanders at New Jersey
Philadelphia at Los Angeles
St. Louis at Toronto
Calgary at Edmonton

FRIDAY, DECEMBER 28
Boston at Winnipeg
Chicago at Buffalo
New York Rangers at Washington
Detroit at Pittsburgh
Edmonton at Vancouver

SATURDAY, DECEMBER 29
Boston at Minnesota
Hartford at Calgary
Buffalo at New Jersey
Montreal at Los Angeles
Washington at Quebec
Chicago at New York Islanders

Philadelphia at St. Louis
Pittsburgh at Toronto

SUNDAY, DECEMBER 30
Hartford at Edmonton
New Jersey at New York Rangers

MONDAY, DECEMBER 31
Philadelphia at Buffalo
Montreal at Calgary
*Quebec at New York Islanders
*St. Louis at Pittsburgh
Chicago at Detroit
Los Angeles at Minnesota
Vancouver at Winnipeg

TUESDAY, JANUARY 1
*New Jersey at Washington

WEDNESDAY, JANUARY 2
Vancouver at Hartford
New York Islanders at Buffalo
Montreal at Edmonton
Los Angeles at New York Rangers
Minnesota at Detroit
Calgary at Winnipeg

THURSDAY, JANUARY 3
Vancouver at Boston
Quebec at St. Louis
Los Angeles at New York Islanders
New York Rangers at Pittsburgh
New Jersey at Chicago
Toronto at Minnesota

FRIDAY, JANUARY 4
Winnipeg at Buffalo
Philadelphia at Washington
Detroit at Edmonton

SATURDAY, JANUARY 5
Washington at Boston
Winnipeg at Hartford
Quebec at Montreal
Philadelphia at New York Islanders
New York Rangers at St. Louis
*New Jersey at Pittsburgh
Los Angeles at Toronto
Detroit at Calgary
Vancouver at Minnesota

SUNDAY, JANUARY 6
Pittsburgh at Montreal
Los Angeles at Chicago

MONDAY, JANUARY 7
Winnipeg at Boston
Philadelphia at New York Rangers

TUESDAY, JANUARY 8
Boston at Quebec
Hartford at Los Angeles
Buffalo at Vancouver
Minnesota at New York Islanders
St. Louis at New Jersey
Edmonton at Pittsburgh
Calgary at Toronto

WEDNESDAY, JANUARY 9
New York Islanders at Montreal
St. Louis at New York Rangers
Edmonton at Detroit

THURSDAY, JANUARY 10
Quebec at Boston
Hartford at Vancouver
Buffalo at Los Angeles
Calgary at Pittsburgh
Toronto at Chicago

FRIDAY, JANUARY 11
New York Rangers at Detroit
Calgary at Washington
Chicago at Winnipeg

SATURDAY, JANUARY 12
Philadelphia at Boston
Hartford at Toronto
Buffalo at Minnesota
Washington at Montreal
St. Louis at Quebec
Detroit at New York Islanders
*Edmonton at New Jersey
Vancouver at Los Angeles

SUNDAY, JANUARY 13
Hartford at New York Rangers
St. Louis at Montreal
New York Islanders at Quebec
Edmonton at Philadelphia
Minnesota at Chicago

Calgary at Winnipeg

MONDAY, JANUARY 14
Detroit at Boston
Buffalo at Toronto
Los Angeles at New Jersey

TUESDAY, JANUARY 15
Boston at New York Islanders
Montreal at Minnesota
Edmonton at New York Rangers
Pittsburgh at Philadelphia
Washington at St. Louis
Winnipeg at Calgary

WEDNESDAY, JANUARY 16
Los Angeles at Hartford
Detroit at Buffalo
Chicago at New Jersey
Winnipeg at Vancouver

THURSDAY, JANUARY 17
Los Angeles at Boston
Montreal at St. Louis
Quebec at Philadelphia
Edmonton at New York Islanders
Chicago at New York Rangers
Pittsburgh at Toronto
Washington at Minnesota

SATURDAY, JANUARY 19
All-Star Game at Chicago

MONDAY, JANUARY 21
Minnesota at Winnipeg

TUESDAY, JANUARY 22
Boston at Buffalo
Toronto at Quebec
N. York Rangers at N. York Islanders
New Jersey at Pittsburgh
Calgary at Philadelphia
Washington at Detroit
St. Louis at Minnesota
Los Angeles at Edmonton

WEDNESDAY, JANUARY 23
Calgary at Hartford
Toronto at Montreal
Edmonton at Vancouver

THURSDAY, JANUARY 24
Hartford at Boston
Buffalo at Chicago
Quebec at New Jersey
Washington at Philadelphia

FRIDAY, JANUARY 25
New York Islanders at Winnipeg
New York Rangers at Edmonton
Minnesota at Washington
St. Louis at Detroit
Los Angeles at Vancouver

SATURDAY, JANUARY 26
*Calgary at Boston
Philadelphia at Hartford
*Buffalo at Montreal
Pittsburgh at Quebec
Minnesota at New Jersey
Toronto at Chicago
Detroit at St. Louis
Vancouver at Los Angeles

SUNDAY, JANUARY 27
*Boston at Montreal
*Calgary at Buffalo
*New York Islanders at Washington
*Edmonton at Winnipeg

MONDAY, JANUARY 28
New Jersey at Detroit
Minnesota at Toronto
Chicago at Vancouver

TUESDAY, JANUARY 29
New York Islanders at Hartford
Buffalo at St. Louis
Winnipeg at Quebec
Washington at Pittsburgh

WEDNESDAY, JANUARY 30
Winnipeg at Montreal
New York Rangers at Calgary
New Jersey at Los Angeles
Detroit at Minnesota
Vancouver at Edmonton

THURSDAY, JANUARY 31
Montreal at Boston
Hartford at St. Louis

168

Quebec at Buffalo
Washington at New York Islanders
New York Rangers at Vancouver
Pittsburgh at Philadelphia

FRIDAY, FEBRUARY 1
Toronto at Detroit
Chicago at Edmonton

SATURDAY, FEBRUARY 2
*Boston at Pittsburgh
*Hartford at Philadelphia
Montreal at New York Islanders
Minnesota at Quebec
New Jersey at St. Louis
Winnipeg at Washington
Detroit at Toronto
Chicago at Calgary
Vancouver at Los Angeles

SUNDAY, FEBRUARY 3
Pittsburgh at Boston
Hartford at New York Islanders
Edmonton at Buffalo
Winnipeg at New York Rangers

MONDAY, FEBRUARY 4
Minnesota at Montreal
St. Louis at Toronto
Los Angeles at Detroit

TUESDAY, FEBRUARY 5
Edmonton at Boston
Calgary at New Jersey
Los Angeles at Philadelphia
Vancouver at Washington

WEDNESDAY, FEBRUARY 6
Edmonton at Hartford
St. Louis at Buffalo
Chicago at Montreal
N. York Islanders at N. York Rangers
Toronto at Winnipeg

THURSDAY, FEBRUARY 7
Calgary at Boston
Montreal at Quebec
Vancouver at Philadelphia
Toronto at Minnesota

FRIDAY, FEBRUARY 8
Los Angeles at Buffalo
New York Islanders at Detroit
Vancouver at New York Rangers
Pittsburgh at Winnipeg
Edmonton at Washington

SATURDAY, FEBRUARY 9
*Chicago at Boston
Calgary at Hartford
New York Rangers at Montreal
*New Jersey at Quebec
New York Islanders at Toronto
Detroit at Minnesota
Los Angeles at St. Louis

SUNDAY, FEBRUARY 10
*Boston at Quebec
Chicago at Hartford
*Buffalo at Winnipeg
*Vancouver at New Jersey
*Philadelphia at Washington

MONDAY, FEBRUARY 11
Pittsburgh at Edmonton

TUESDAY, FEBRUARY 12
Buffalo at Quebec
Minnesota at New York Islanders
Winnipeg at Detroit
St. Louis at Edmonton
Calgary at Los Angeles

WEDNESDAY, FEBRUARY 13
Boston at Montreal
Detroit at Hartford
Minnesota at Buffalo
New Jersey at New York Rangers
Philadelphia at Toronto

THURSDAY, FEBRUARY 14
Quebec at Chicago
New York Islanders at Pittsburgh
Winnipeg at New Jersey
St. Louis at Vancouver
Los Angeles at Edmonton

FRIDAY, FEBRUARY 15
Hartford at New York Rangers
Montreal at Buffalo
Washington at Calgary

SATURDAY, FEBRUARY 16
Boston at Los Angeles
Hartford at Montreal
Pittsburgh at New York Islanders
*Philadelphia at New Jersey
Washington at Vancouver
Edmonton at Toronto
*Minnesota at Detroit

SUNDAY, FEBRUARY 17
Toronto at Buffalo
*Quebec at Winnipeg
*Detroit at Chicago
St. Louis at Calgary

MONDAY, FEBRUARY 18
Quebec at Vancouver
*N. York Islanders at N. York Rangers
Edmonton at New Jersey
*Chicago at Philadelphia
*Washington at Los Angeles

TUESDAY, FEBRUARY 19
Buffalo at Pittsburgh
Toronto at St. Louis
Detroit at Calgary

WEDNESDAY, FEBRUARY 20
Montreal at Hartford
Quebec at Los Angeles
Edmonton at Minnesota
Vancouver at Winnipeg

THURSDAY, FEBRUARY 21
Boston at Chicago
New York Islanders at St. Louis
New York Rangers at Philadelphia
Toronto at Pittsburgh
Vancouver at Calgary

FRIDAY, FEBRUARY 22
New York Rangers at Washington
Pittsburgh at New Jersey
Detroit at Edmonton
Los Angeles at Winnipeg

SATURDAY, FEBRUARY 23
Boston at St. Louis
Buffalo at Hartford
Toronto at Montreal
Quebec at Calgary
Philadelphia at New York Islanders
Detroit at Vancouver
Chicago at Minnesota

SUNDAY, FEBRUARY 24
Hartford at Buffalo
Quebec at Edmonton
New York Islanders at Philadelphia
*New Jersey at New York Rangers
*Pittsburgh at Washington
St. Louis at Chicago
*Los Angeles at Winnipeg

MONDAY, FEBRUARY 25
Washington at New Jersey
Calgary at Vancouver

TUESDAY, FEBRUARY 26
Hartford at Winnipeg
Buffalo at New York Islanders
Philadelphia at Minnesota
Pittsburgh at Los Angeles
Chicago at St. Louis

WEDNESDAY, FEBRUARY 27
Montreal at Detroit
Washington at New York Rangers
New Jersey at Toronto
Pittsburgh at Vancouver
Edmonton at Calgary

THURSDAY, FEBRUARY 28
New York Islanders at Boston
Hartford at Chicago
Buffalo at Quebec
New York Rangers at St. Louis
Winnipeg at Los Angeles

FRIDAY, MARCH 1
Montreal at Vancouver
New Jersey at Detroit
Pittsburgh at Calgary
Minnesota at Edmonton

SATURDAY, MARCH 2
*Buffalo at Boston
Hartford at Quebec
Montreal at Edmonton
New York Islanders at Washington

New York Rangers at Toronto
St. Louis at Philadelphia
Minnesota at Calgary
Winnipeg at Los Angeles

SUNDAY, MARCH 3
Boston at New Jersey
Toronto at Hartford
Vancouver at Chicago

MONDAY, MARCH 4
Montreal at Calgary
Philadelphia at New York Rangers

TUESDAY, MARCH 5
Boston at Toronto
St. Louis at Hartford
Quebec at Detroit
New Jersey at New York Islanders
Vancouver at Pittsburgh
Los Angeles at Washington
Edmonton at Winnipeg

WEDNESDAY MARCH 6
New Jersey at Buffalo
Montreal at Chicago
Edmonton at Minnesota

THURSDAY, MARCH 7
St. Louis at Boston
New York Rangers at Quebec
New York Islanders at Detroit
Philadelphia at Calgary
Los Angeles at Pittsburgh
Vancouver at Toronto

FRIDAY, MARCH 8
Chicago at Buffalo
Philadelphia at Edmonton
Washington at Winnipeg

SATURDAY, MARCH 9
*Toronto at Boston
Pittsburgh at Hartford
Vancouver at Montreal
Los Angeles at Quebec
N. York Rangers at N. York Islanders
*Detroit at Minnesota
Calgary at St. Louis

SUNDAY, MARCH 10
Quebec at Hartford
Vancouver at Buffalo
Los Angeles at Montreal
Pittsburgh at New York Islanders
New York Rangers at Chicago
*New Jersey at Winnipeg
Washington at Edmonton
Detroit at St. Louis
Calgary at Minnesota

TUESDAY, MARCH 12
Hartford at Washington
Buffalo at Minnesota
Montreal at Pittsburgh
Toronto at Quebec
Philadelphia at Los Angeles
Winnipeg at Calgary

WEDNESDAY, MARCH 13
Buffalo at Winnipeg
New York Islanders at Edmonton
Detroit at New York Rangers
Toronto at New Jersey
Philadelphia at Vancouver

THURSDAY, MARCH 14
Montreal at Boston
Detroit at Hartford
Quebec at Washington
New York Islanders at Calgary
Chicago at Los Angeles
Minnesota at St. Louis

FRIDAY, MARCH 15
New York Rangers at New Jersey
Edmonton at Winnipeg

SATURDAY, MARCH 16
*Detroit at Boston
New Jersey at Hartford
Buffalo at Montreal
*Quebec at Pittsburgh
New York Islanders at Vancouver
Philadelphia at Washington
Minnesota at Toronto
Chicago at St. Louis
Los Angeles at Calgary

SUNDAY, MARCH 17

Boston at Philadelphia
Hartford at Buffalo
Edmonton at Montreal
*Pittsburgh at New York Rangers
Toronto at Minnesota
St. Louis at Chicago
Los Angeles at Vancouver

MONDAY, MARCH 18
Winnipeg at Calgary

TUESDAY, MARCH 19
Boston at Hartford
Edmonton at Quebec
Pittsburgh at New Jersey
St. Louis at Washington

WEDNESDAY, MARCH 20
Montreal at Buffalo
Toronto at Los Angeles
Calgary at Vancouver

THURSDAY, MARCH 21
Quebec at Boston
Washington at New York Islanders
New York Rangers at Pittsburgh
New Jersey at Chicago
St. Louis at Philadelphia

FRIDAY, MARCH 22
Minnesota at Washington
Toronto at Detroit
Winnipeg at Vancouver

SATURDAY, MARCH 23
*Buffalo at Boston
Hartford at Quebec
New Jersey at Montreal
St. Louis at New York Islanders
*New York Rangers at Philadelphia
*Chicago at Pittsburgh
Detroit at Toronto
Winnipeg at Edmonton
*Calgary at Los Angeles

SUNDAY, MARCH 24
*Boston at Washington
*Philadelphia at Buffalo
N. York Islanders at N. York Rangers
*Minnesota at Chicago
Los Angeles at Edmonton

MONDAY, MARCH 25
Hartford at Montreal
St. Louis at Minnesota

TUESDAY, MARCH 26
Boston at Quebec
Buffalo at Washington
New Jersey at New York Rangers
Pittsburgh at Philadelphia
Chicago at Toronto
Vancouver at Calgary
Edmonton at Los Angeles

WEDNESDAY, MARCH 27
Hartford at New Jersey
Pittsburgh at Detroit

THURSDAY, MARCH 28
Quebec at Buffalo
New York Islanders at St. Louis
Washington at Philadelphia
Toronto at Chicago
Minnesota at Los Angeles
Winnipeg at Vancouver
Edmonton at Calgary

FRIDAY, MARCH 29
Calgary at Edmonton

SATURDAY, MARCH 30
Boston at New York Islanders
Buffalo at Hartford
Quebec at Montreal
*New York Rangers at Detroit
New Jersey at Washington
*Philadelphia at Pittsburgh
Toronto at St. Louis
Chicago at Minnesota

SUNDAY, MARCH 31
Hartford at Boston
Washington at Buffalo
Montreal at Quebec
New York Islanders at New Jersey
Pittsburgh at New York Rangers
Detroit at Chicago
Minnesota at St. Louis
Winnipeg at Edmonton
*Los Angeles at Calgary

Wayne Gretzky needs only 21 points to become the first player in NHL history to reach the 2,000 point plateau.

HOCKEY REGISTER
EXPLANATION OF ABBREVIATIONS

A—Assists.
AHL—American Hockey League.
AJHL—Alberta Junior Hockey League.
ASHL—Alberta Senior Hockey League.
Avg.—Goals against per game average.
BCHL—British Columbia Hockey League.
CAHL—Central Alberta Hockey League.
CCHA—Central Collegiate Hockey Association.
Cent. OHL—Central Ontario Hockey Association.
CHL—California Hockey League or Central Hockey League.
CMJHL—Canadian Major Junior Hockey League.
CPHL—Central Pro Hockey League.
EHL—Eastern Hockey League.
EPHL—Eastern Pro Hockey League.
G—Goals scored.
Games—Games played.
Goals—Goals against.
IHL—International Hockey League.
Mins.—Minutes played.
MJHL—Manitoba Junior Hockey League or Midwest Junior Hockey League.
NAHL—North American Hockey League.
NEHL—Northeastern Hockey League.
NHL—National Hockey League.
NOHA—Northern Ontario Hockey Association.
NSHL—North Shore (New Brunswick) Hockey League.
NYMJHA—New York Metropolitan Junior Hockey Association.
OHA—Ontario Hockey Association.
OMJHL—Ontario Major Junior Hockey League.
OPHL—Ontario Provincial Hockey League.
Pen.—Minutes in penalties.
PHL—Prairie Hockey League.
Pts.—Points.
QJHL—Quebec Junior Hockey League.
QMJHL—Quebec Major Junior Hockey League.
SHL—Southern Hockey League.
SJHL—Saskatchewan Junior Hockey League.
SO.—Shutouts.
SOJHL—Southern Ontario Junior Hockey League.
TBJHL—Thunder Bay Junior Hockey League.
USHL—United States Hockey League.
WCHA—Western Collegiate Hockey Association.
WCHL—Western Canada Hockey League (Juniors).
WCJHL—Western Canada Junior League.
WHA—World Hockey Association.
WHL—Western Hockey League.
WHL—Western Hockey League (Junior "A" League since 1978-79).
WIHL—Western International Hockey League.
WOJHL—Western Ontario Junior Hockey League.
*—Indicates either led or was tied for league lead.
    Footnotes (a) indicates player was member of first all-star team.
    Footnotes (b) indicates player was member of second all-star team.
Scoring totals (goals plus assists) do not always balance in certain leagues due to un-balanced schedules and scoring system.
Junior "A" Ontario Hockey association also includes Metro League and OHA Major Junior.
Quebec Junior Hockey League also includes Montreal Metro League and OJHL Major.

FORWARDS AND DEFENSEMEN

(a)—First team all-star selection. (b)—Second team. *Indicates led league or tied for leadership.

KEITH EDWARD ACTON

Center . . . 5'10" . . . 167 lbs. . . . Born, Newmarket, Ont., April 15, 1958 . . . Shoots left . . . (April 20, 1984)—Injured left wrist in playoff game at St. Louis . . . (December 14, 1988)—Broke nose when struck by John Kordic's stick at Toronto . . . (May, 1989)—Played playoff series against Montreal with bruised ribs.

Year Team	League	Games	G.	A.	Pts.	Pen.
1974-75—Wexford Raiders	OPJHL	43	23	29	52	46
1975-76—Peterborough Petes	Jr."A"OHA	35	9	17	26	30
1976-77—Peterborough Petes	Jr."A"OHA	65	52	69	121	93
1977-78—Peterborough Petes (c)	Jr."A"OHA	68	42	86	128	52
1978-79—Nova Scotia Voyageurs	AHL	79	15	26	41	22
1979-80—Nova Scotia Voyageurs (b)	AHL	75	45	53	98	38
1979-80—Montreal Canadiens	NHL	2	0	1	1	0
1980-81—Montreal Canadiens	NHL	61	15	24	39	74
1981-82—Montreal Canadiens	NHL	78	36	52	88	88
1982-83—Montreal Canadiens	NHL	78	24	26	50	63
1983-84—Montreal Canadiens (d)	NHL	9	3	7	10	4
1983-84—Minnesota North Stars	NHL	62	17	38	55	60
1984-85—Minnesota North Stars	NHL	78	20	38	58	90
1985-86—Minnesota North Stars	NHL	79	26	32	58	100
1986-87—Minnesota North Stars	NHL	78	16	29	45	56
1987-88—Minnesota North Stars (e)	NHL	46	8	11	19	74
1987-88—Edmonton Oilers	NHL	26	3	6	9	21
1988-89—Edmonton Oilers (f)	NHL	46	11	15	26	47
1988-89—Philadelphia Flyers	NHL	25	3	10	13	64
1989-90—Philadelphia Flyers (g-h)	NHL	69	13	14	27	80
NHL TOTALS		747	195	303	498	821

(c)—Drafted from Peterborough Petes by Montreal Canadiens in sixth round of 1978 amateur draft.
(d)—October, 1983—Traded with Mark Napier and third round 1984 draft pick (Kenneth Hodge) by Montreal Canadiens to Minnesota North Stars for Bobby Smith.
(e)—January, 1988—Traded by Minnesota North Stars to Edmonton Oilers for Moe Mantha.
(f)—February 7, 1989—Traded with future considerations by Edmonton Oilers to Philadelphia Flyers for Dave Brown.
(g)—September 28, 1989—Traded with Pete Peeters by Philadelphia Flyers to Winnipeg Jets for future considerations.
(h)—October 3, 1989—Traded with Pete Peeters by Winnipeg Jets to Philadelphia Flyers for a draft pick. Also the Jets will not have to surrender future considerations in a previous deal for Shawn Cronin.

GREG G. ADAMS

Center . . . 6'2" . . . 185 lbs. . . . Born, Nelson, B.C., August 1, 1963 . . . Shoots left . . . (April, 1986)—Tore tendon in right wrist during World Championship game at Moscow while playing for Team Canada . . . (February, 1989)—Fractured ankle . . . (January 4, 1990)—Missed 12 games after fracturing a cheekbone at Pittsburgh when he was checked by Bob Errey.

Year Team	League	Games	G.	A.	Pts.	Pen.
1980-81—Kelowna Wings	BCJHL	47	40	50	90	16
1981-82—Kelowna Wings	BCJHL	45	31	42	73	24
1982-83—Northern Arizona Univ.	NCAA	29	14	21	35	46
1983-84—Northern Arizona Univ. (c)	NCAA	47	40	50	90	16
1984-85—Maine Mariners	AHL	41	15	20	35	12
1984-85—New Jersey Devils	NHL	36	12	9	21	14
1985-86—New Jersey Devils	NHL	78	35	43	78	30
1986-87—New Jersey Devils (d)	NHL	72	20	27	47	19
1987-88—Vancouver Canucks	NHL	80	36	40	76	30
1988-89—Vancouver Canucks	NHL	61	19	14	33	24
1989-90—Vancouver Canucks	NHL	65	30	20	50	18
NHL TOTALS		392	152	153	305	135

(c)—June, 1984—Signed by New Jersey Devils as a free agent.
(d)—September, 1987—Traded with Kirk McLean by New Jersey Devils to Vancouver Canucks for Patrik Sundstrom, fourth-round 1988 draft pick (Matt Ruchty) and the option to flip second-round picks in 1988 entry draft (New Jersey selected Jeff Christian and Vancouver selected Leif Rohlin).

GREGORY CHARLES ADAMS

Left Wing . . . 6'1" . . . 190 lbs. . . . Born, Duncan, B. C., May 31, 1960 . . . Shoots left . . . (September 26, 1986)—Suspended by NHL for first three games of season for an altercation in a pre-season game with Hartford . . . (February, 1987)—Hospitalized with a collapsed lung . . . (Summer, 1988)—Motorcycle accident. Needed a metal plate and six screws implanted into his left shoulder . . . (February, 1989)—Fractured ankle.

Year Team	League	Games	G.	A.	Pts.	Pen.
1977-78—Nanaimo	BCJHL	62	53	60	113	150
1978-79—Victoria Cougars	WHL	71	23	31	54	151
1979-80—Victoria Cougars (c)	WHL	71	62	48	110	212
1980-81—Philadelphia Flyers	NHL	6	3	0	3	8
1980-81—Maine Mariners	AHL	71	19	20	39	158
1981-82—Maine Mariners	AHL	45	16	21	37	241
1981-82—Philadelphia Flyers (d)	NHL	33	4	15	19	105
1982-83—Hartford Whalers	NHL	79	10	13	23	216
1983-84—Washington Capitals (e)	NHL	57	2	6	8	133
1984-85—Binghamton Whalers	AHL	28	9	16	25	58
1984-85—Washington Capitals	NHL	51	6	12	18	72
1985-86—Washington Capitals	NHL	78	18	38	56	152
1986-87—Washington Capitals	NHL	67	14	30	44	184
1987-88—Washington Capitals (f)	NHL	78	15	12	27	153
1988-89—Edmonton Oilers (g)	NHL	49	4	5	9	82
1988-89—Vancouver Canucks	NHL	12	4	2	6	35
1989-90—Halifax Citadels	AHL	10	6	13	19	18
1989-90—Quebec Nordiques (h-i)	NHL	7	1	3	4	17
1989-90—Detroit Red Wings (j)	NHL	28	3	7	10	16
NHL TOTALS		545	84	143	227	1173

(c)—August, 1980—Signed by Philadelphia Flyers as a free agent.
(d)—August, 1982—Traded by Philadelphia Flyers with Ken Linseman and Flyers' No. 1 draft choice (David A. Jensen) in 1983 to Hartford Whalers for Mark Howe. Hartford and Philadelphia also swapped third-round choices in 1983 draft (Philadelphia selected Derrick Smith and Hartford selected Leif Karlsson).
(e)—October, 1983—Traded by Hartford Whalers to Washington Capitals for Torrie Robertson.
(f)—July, 1988—Traded by Washington Capitals to Edmonton Oilers for Geoff Courtnall.
(g)—March 7, 1989—Traded with Doug Smith by Edmonton Oilers to Vancouver Canucks for Jean LeBlanc and a fifth-round 1989 draft pick (Peter White).
(h)—October 2, 1989—Selected by Quebec Nordiques in 1989 NHL waiver draft for $2,500.
(i)—December 3, 1989—Traded with Robert Picard by Quebec Nordiques to Detroit Red Wings for Tony McKegney.
(j)—March 3, 1990—Announced his retirement.

JIM AGNEW

Defense . . . 6'1" . . . 179 lbs. . . . Born, Deloraine, Man., March 21, 1966 . . . Shoots left . . . (March 18, 1990)—Tore knee ligaments in a collision with Kris King at N.Y. Rangers.

Year Team	League	Games	G.	A.	Pts.	Pen.
1982-83—Brandon Wheat Kings	WHL	14	1	1	2	9
1983-84—Brandon Wheat Kings (c)	WHL	71	6	17	23	107
1984-85—Brandon Wheat Kings	WHL	19	3	15	18	82
1984-85—Portland Winter Hawks	WHL	44	5	24	29	223
1985-86—Portland Winter Hawks (a)	WHL	70	6	30	36	386
1986-87—Vancouver Canucks	NHL	4	0	0	0	0
1986-87—Fredericton Express	AHL	67	0	5	5	261
1987-88—Vancouver Canucks	NHL	10	0	1	1	16
1987-88—Fredericton Express	AHL	63	2	8	10	188
1988-89—Milwaukee Admirals	IHL	47	2	10	12	181
1989-90—Milwaukee Admirals	IHL	51	4	10	14	238
1989-90—Vancouver Canucks	NHL	7	0	0	0	36
NHL TOTALS		21	0	1	1	52

(c)—June, 1984—Drafted as underage junior by Vancouver Canucks in NHL entry draft. Tenth Canucks pick, 157th overall, eighth round.

BRADLEY AITKEN

Left Wing and Center . . . 6'3" . . . 200 lbs. . . . Born, Scarborough, Ont., October 30, 1967 . . . Shoots left . . . (October, 1986)—Missed three weeks with a separated shoulder.

Year Team	League	Games	G.	A.	Pts.	Pen.
1984-85—Peterborough Petes	OHL	63	18	26	44	36
1985-86—Peterborough Petes (c)	OHL	48	9	28	37	77
1985-86—Sault Ste. Marie Greyhounds (d)	OHL	20	8	19	27	11
1986-87—Sault Ste. Marie Greyhounds	OHL	52	27	38	65	86
1987-88—Pittsburgh Penguins	NHL	5	1	1	2	0
1987-88—Muskegon Lumberjacks	IHL	74	32	31	63	128
1988-89—Muskegon Lumberjacks	IHL	74	35	30	65	139
1989-90—Muskegon Lumberjacks	IHL	46	10	23	33	172
1989-90—Fort Wayne Komets	IHL	13	5	2	7	57
1989-90—Phoenix Roadrunners	IHL	8	2	1	3	18
NHL TOTALS		5	1	1	2	0

(c)—February, 1986—Traded with future considerations by Peterborough Petes to Sault Ste. Marie Greyhounds for Graeme Bonar.
(d)—June, 1986—Drafted as underage junior by Pittsburgh Penguins in 1986 NHL entry draft. Third Penguins pick, 46th overall, third round.

MICAH AIVAZOFF

Center . . . 6' . . . 185 lbs. . . . Born, Powell River, B.C., May 4, 1969 . . . Shoots left.

Year Team	League	Games	G.	A.	Pts.	Pen.
1985-86—Victoria Cougars	WHL	27	3	4	7	25
1986-87—Victoria Cougars	WHL	72	18	39	57	112
1987-88—Victoria Cougars (c)	WHL	69	26	57	83	79
1988-89—Victoria Cougars	WHL	70	35	65	100	136
1989-90—New Haven Nighthawks	AHL	77	20	39	59	71

(c)—June, 1988—Drafted by Los Angeles Kings in 1988 NHL entry draft. Sixth Kings pick, 109th overall, sixth round.

TOMMY ALBELIN

Defense . . . 6'1" . . . 185 lbs. . . . Born, Stockholm, Sweden, May 21, 1964 . . . Shoots left.

Year	Team	League	Games	G.	A.	Pts.	Pen.
1982-83—Djurgardens (c)		Sweden	17	2	5	7	4
1983-84—Djurgardens		Sweden	37	9	8	17	36
1984-85—Djurgardens		Sweden	....	....	....	....	....
1985-86—Djurgardens		Sweden	....	....	....	....	....
1986-87—Djurgardens		Sweden	33	7	5	12	49
1987-88—Quebec Nordiques		NHL	60	3	23	26	47
1988-89—Halifax Citadels		AHL	8	2	5	7	4
1988-89—Quebec Nordiques (d)		NHL	14	2	4	6	27
1988-89—New Jersey Devils		NHL	46	7	24	31	40
1989-90—New Jersey Devils		NHL	68	6	23	29	63
NHL TOTALS			188	18	74	92	177

   (c)—June, 1983—Drafted by Quebec Nordiques in NHL entry draft. Seventh Nordiques pick, 152nd overall, eighth round.

   (d)—December 12, 1988—Traded by Quebec Nordiques to New Jersey Devils for a fourth-round 1989 draft pick (Niclas Andersson).

MICHAEL EARNEST ALLISON

Center . . . 6' . . . 202 lbs. . . . Born, Fort Francis, Ont., March 28, 1961 . . . Shoots right . . . Brother of Dave Allison . . . (January 13, 1981)—Strained ligaments in right knee . . . (October 25, 1981)—Bruised kneecap . . . (January 20, 1982)—Sprained medial collatoral ligament in right knee vs. N.Y. Islanders, requiring surgery . . . (November 20, 1982) Strained ligaments in right knee . . . (October, 1983)—Sprained left knee . . . (October, 1984)—Missed games with knee injury . . . (January, 1985)—Arthroscopic surgery to knee . . . (October, 1987)—Back injury . . . (January, 1988)—Groin injury . . . (October, 1988)—Sprained wrist . . . (January, 1989)—Strained knee . . . (September, 1989)—Strained groin in Los Angeles Kings training camp . . . (January, 1990)—Sore back . . . (March, 1990)—Food poisoning . . . (April, 1990)—Charley horse.

Year	Team	League	Games	G.	A.	Pts.	Pen.
1977-78—New Westminster Bruins		WCHL	5	0	1	1	2
1977-78—Kenora Thistles		MJHL	47	30	36	66	70
1978-79—Sudbury Wolves		OMJHL	59	24	32	56	41
1979-80—Sudbury Wolves (c)		OMJHL	67	24	71	95	74
1980-81—New York Rangers		NHL	75	26	38	64	83
1981-82—Springfield Indians		AHL	2	0	0	0	0
1981-82—New York Rangers		NHL	48	7	15	22	74
1982-83—Tulsa Oilers		CHL	6	2	2	4	2
1982-83—New York Rangers		NHL	39	11	9	20	37
1983-84—New York Rangers		NHL	45	8	12	20	64
1984-85—New York Rangers		NHL	31	9	15	24	17
1985-86—New Haven Nighthawks		AHL	9	6	6	12	4
1985-86—New York Rangers (d)		NHL	28	2	13	15	22
1986-87—Toronto Maple Leafs		NHL	71	7	16	23	66
1987-88—Toronto Maple Leafs (e)		NHL	15	0	3	3	10
1987-88—Los Angeles Kings		NHL	37	16	12	28	57
1988-89—Los Angeles Kings		NHL	55	14	22	36	122
1989-90—New Haven Nighthawks		AHL	5	2	2	4	14
1989-90—Los Angeles Kings		NHL	55	2	11	13	78
NHL TOTALS			499	102	166	268	630

   (c)—June, 1980—Drafted as underage junior by New York Rangers in NHL entry draft. Second Rangers pick, 35th overall, second round.

   (d)—August, 1986—Traded by New York Rangers to Toronto Maple Leafs for Walt Poddubny.

   (e)—December, 1987—Traded by Toronto Maple Leafs to Los Angeles Kings for Sean McKenna.

SCOTT ALLISON

Center . . . 6'4" . . . 194 lbs. . . . Born, St. Boniface, Man., April 22, 1972 . . . Shoots left.

Year	Team	League	Games	G.	A.	Pts.	Pen.
1988-89—Prince Albert Raiders		WHL	51	6	9	15	37
1989-90—Prince Albert Raiders (c)		WHL	66	22	16	38	73

   (c)—June 16, 1990—Selected by Edmonton Oilers in 1989 NHL entry draft. First Oilers pick, 17th overall, first round.

ANTHONY AMONTE

Right Wing . . . 6' . . . 165 lbs. . . . Born, Weymouth, Mass., August 2, 1970 . . . Shoots left.

Year	Team	League	Games	G.	A.	Pts.	Pen.
1986-87—Thayer Academy		Mass. H.S.	....	25	32	57	....
1987-88—Thayer Academy (c)		Mass. H.S.	....	30	38	68	....
1988-89—Team USA Juniors		......	7	1	3	4	....
1989-90—Boston University (d)		H. East	41	25	33	58	52

   (c)—June, 1988—Drafted by New York Rangers in 1988 NHL entry draft. Third Rangers pick, 68th overall, fourth round.

   (d)—Named to Hockey East All-Rookie team.

DARRIN AMUNDSON

Center . . . 6'2" . . . 180 lbs. . . . Born, Duluth, Minn., November 13, 1968 . . . Shoots left . . . Son of Art Amundson, coach at Duluth East High School in 1986-87.

Year	Team	League	Games	G.	A.	Pts.	Pen.
1985-86—Duluth East High School		Minn. H.S.	22	10	26	36	....
1986-87—Duluth East High School (c)		Minn. H.S.	24	20	37	57	....
1987-88—Univ. of Minnesota/Duluth		WCHA	16	0	6	6	4
1988-89—Univ. of Minnesota/Duluth		WCHA	37	5	11	16	10
1989-90—Univ. of Minnesota/Duluth		WCHA	23	5	6	11	12

   (c)—June, 1987—Drafted by Winnipeg Jets in 1987 NHL entry draft. Fifth Jets pick, 100th overall, fifth round.

GLENN CHRIS ANDERSON

Right Wing . . . 6'1" . . . 190 lbs. . . . Born, Vancouver, B.C., October 2, 1960 . . . Shoots left . . . Played on Canadian Olympic Team in 1980 . . . (November, 1980)—Knee surgery to remove bone chips . . . (Spring, 1982)—Nose surgery to correct breathing problem caused during a December 1, 1981 altercation with Mark Hunter of Montreal . . . (December 13, 1985)—Given eight-game suspension by NHL for stick-swinging incident at Winnipeg . . . Also plays Left Wing . . . (November, 1988)—Pulled side muscle . . . (February 28, 1990)—Fined $500 for deliberately breaking the cheekbone of Tomas Sanstrom with a punch.

Year	Team	League	Games	G.	A.	Pts.	Pen.
1977-78—New Westminster Bruins		WHL	1	0	1	1	2
1978-79—Seattle Breakers		WHL	2	0	1	1	0
1978-79—Denver University (c)		WCHA	40	26	29	55	58
1979-80—Canadian Olympic Team		Int'l	49	21	21	42	46
1979-80—Seattle Breakers		WHL	7	5	5	10	4
1980-81—Edmonton Oilers		NHL	58	30	23	53	24
1981-82—Edmonton Oilers		NHL	80	38	67	105	71
1982-83—Edmonton Oilers		NHL	72	48	56	104	70
1983-84—Edmonton Oilers		NHL	80	54	45	99	65
1984-85—Edmonton Oilers		NHL	80	42	39	81	69
1985-86—Edmonton Oilers		NHL	72	54	48	102	90
1986-87—Edmonton Oilers		NHL	80	35	38	73	65
1987-88—Edmonton Oilers		NHL	80	38	50	88	58
1988-89—Edmonton Oilers		NHL	79	16	48	64	93
1989-90—Edmonton Oilers		NHL	73	34	38	72	107
NHL TOTALS			754	389	452	841	712

   (c)—August, 1979—Drafted by Edmonton Oilers in NHL entry draft. Third Oilers pick, 69th overall, fourth round.

PERRY LYNN ANDERSON

Left Wing . . . 6' . . . 210 lbs. . . . Born, Barrie, Ont., October 14, 1961 . . . Shoots left . . . (March, 1984)—Broke bone in foot . . . (January 13, 1986)—Strained abdominal muscle at Chicago and missed eight games . . . (January, 1988)—Concussion . . . (October, 1988)—Strained rotator cuff . . . (January, 1989)—Sprained right knee . . . (March, 1989)—Separated left shoulder.

Year	Team	League	Games	G.	A.	Pts.	Pen.
1978-79—Kingston Canadians		OMJHL	60	6	13	19	85
1979-80—Kingston Canadians (c)		OMJHL	63	17	16	33	52
1980-81—Kingston Canadians		OHL	38	9	13	22	118
1980-81—Brantford Alexanders		OHL	31	8	27	35	43
1981-82—Salt Lake Golden Eagles (b)		CHL	71	32	32	64	117
1981-82—St. Louis Blues		NHL	5	1	2	3	0
1982-83—Salt Lake Golden Eagles		CHL	57	23	19	42	140
1982-83—St. Louis Blues		NHL	18	5	2	7	14
1983-84—Montana Magic		CHL	8	7	3	10	34
1983-84—St. Louis Blues		NHL	50	7	5	12	195
1984-85—St. Louis Blues (d)		NHL	71	9	9	18	146
1985-86—New Jersey Devils		NHL	51	7	12	19	91
1986-87—New Jersey Devils		NHL	57	10	9	19	105
1987-88—New Jersey Devils		NHL	60	4	6	10	222
1988-89—New Jersey Devils		NHL	39	3	6	9	128
1989-90—Utica Devils		AHL	71	13	17	30	128
NHL TOTALS			351	46	51	97	901

   (c)—June, 1980—Drafted by St. Louis Blues as an underage junior in NHL entry draft. Fifth Blues pick, 117th overall, sixth round.

   (d)—August, 1985—Traded by St. Louis Blues to New Jersey Devils for Rick Meagher and 1986 12th round draft choice (Bill Butler).

SHAWN ANDERSON

Defense . . . 6'1" . . . 190 lbs. . . . Born, Montreal, Que., February 7, 1968 . . . Shoots left . . . Also plays Left Wing . . . (October, 1986)—Sprained knee . . . (March 3, 1987)—Separated shoulder at Philadelphia . . . (March 28, 1987)—Reseparated shoulder vs. Montreal . . . (October, 1987)—Injured ankle . . . (December, 1987)—Injured ankle . . . (February, 1988)—Bruised knee.

Year	Team	League	Games	G.	A.	Pts.	Pen.
1984-85—Lac St. Louis Midget		Que.AAA Mid.	42	23	42	65	100
1985-86—University of Maine		H. East	16	5	8	13	22
1985-86—Team Canada (c)		Int'l	33	2	6	8	16
1986-87—Rochester Americans		AHL	15	2	5	7	11
1986-87—Buffalo Sabres		NHL	41	2	11	13	23
1987-88—Buffalo Sabres		NHL	23	1	2	3	17
1987-88—Rochester Americans		AHL	22	5	16	21	19
1988-89—Rochester Americans		AHL	31	5	14	19	24
1988-89—Buffalo Sabres		NHL	33	2	10	12	18
1989-90—Rochester Americans		AHL	39	5	16	18	41
1989-90—Buffalo Sabres		NHL	16	1	3	4	8
NHL TOTALS			113	6	26	32	66

   (c)—June, 1986—Drafted as underage player by Buffalo Sabres in 1986 NHL entry draft. First Sabres pick, fifth overall, first round.

BO MIKAEL ANDERSSON
(Known by middle name)

Center . . . 5'9" . . . 183 lbs. . . . Born, Malmo, Sweden, May 10, 1966 . . . Shoots left . . . (March 3, 1987)—Missed three weeks with sprained ankle at Philadelphia . . . (March, 1988)—Twisted ankle . . . (December, 1988)—Sprained neck and shoulder . . . (December 13, 1989)—Bruised left knee in collison with Keith Crowder vs. Los Angeles . . . (February 9, 1990)—Reinjured knee vs. Vancouver . . . (March 8, 1990)—Pulled right hamstring vs. Toronto . . . (March 17, 1990)—Reinjured hamstring in games at Vancouver and Calgary . . . (April, 1990)—Reinjured hamstring in playoff series vs. Boston . . . (May 14, 1990)—Had surgery to left knee in Sweden.

Year—Team	League	Games	G.	A.	Pts.	Pen.
1983-84—Vastra Frolunda (c)	Sweden	12	0	2	2	6
1984-85—Vastra Frolunda	Sweden	32	16	11	27	....
1985-86—Rochester Americans	AHL	20	10	4	14	6
1985-86—Buffalo Sabres	NHL	33	1	9	10	4
1986-87—Rochester Americans	AHL	42	6	20	26	14
1986-87—Buffalo Sabres	NHL	16	0	3	3	0
1987-88—Rochester Americans	AHL	35	12	24	36	16
1987-88—Buffalo Sabres	NHL	37	3	20	23	10
1988-89—Buffalo Sabres	NHL	14	0	1	1	4
1988-89—Rochester Americans	AHL	56	18	33	51	12
1989-90—Hartford Whalers (d)	NHL	50	13	24	37	6
NHL TOTALS		150	17	57	74	24

(c)—June, 1984—Drafted by Buffalo Sabres in NHL entry draft. First Sabres pick, 18th overall, first round.

(d)—October 2, 1989—Selected by Hartford Whalers in 1989 NHL waiver draft.

DAVID ANDREYCHUK

Left Wing . . . 6'4'' . . . 198 lbs. . . . Born, Hamilton, Ont., September 29, 1963 . . . Shoots right . . . (March, 1983)—Sprained knee . . . Played with Team Canada in 1982-83 World Junior Championship . . . (March, 1985)—Fractured collarbone . . . (September, 1985)—Twisted knee in first day of Buffalo training camp . . . (September, 1986)—Injured right knee during training camp when he collided with Phil Housley during a team scrimmage . . . (November 27, 1988)—Strained medial collateral ligaments in left knee . . . (February 18, 1990)—Broke left thumb when he struck Scott Young vs. Hartford.

Year—Team	League	Games	G.	A.	Pts.	Pen.
1980-81—Oshawa Generals	OHL	67	22	22	44	80
1981-82—Oshawa Generals (c)	OHL	67	58	43	101	71
1982-83—Oshawa Generals	OHL	14	8	24	32	6
1982-83—Buffalo Sabres	NHL	43	14	23	37	16
1983-84—Buffalo Sabres	NHL	78	38	42	80	42
1984-85—Buffalo Sabres	NHL	64	31	30	61	54
1985-86—Buffalo Sabres	NHL	80	36	51	87	61
1986-87—Buffalo Sabres	NHL	77	25	48	73	46
1987-88—Buffalo Sabres	NHL	80	30	48	78	112
1988-89—Buffalo Sabres	NHL	56	28	24	52	40
1989-90—Buffalo Sabres	NHL	73	40	42	82	42
NHL TOTALS		551	242	308	550	413

(c)—June, 1982—Drafted as underage junior by Buffalo Sabres in NHL entry draft. Third Sabres pick, 16th overall, first round.

GREG ANDRUSAK

Defense . . . 6'1'' . . . 180 lbs. . . . Born, Cranbrook, B.C., November 14, 1969 . . . Shoots right.

Year—Team	League	Games	G.	A.	Pts.	Pen.
1986-87—Kelowna Jr. A	BCJHL	45	10	24	34	95
1987-88—Univ. of Minnesota/Duluth (c)	WCHA	37	4	5	9	42
1988-89—Univ. of Minnesota/Duluth	WCHA	35	4	8	12	74
1988-89—Canadian National Team	Int'l	2	0	0	0	0
1989-90—Univ. of Minnesota/Duluth	WCHA	35	5	29	34	74

(c)—June, 1988—Drafted by Pittsburgh Penguins in 1988 NHL entry draft. Fifth Penguins pick, 88th overall, fifth round.

SERGE ANGLEHART

Defense . . . 6'2'' . . . 190 lbs. . . . Born, Hull, Que., April 18, 1970 . . . Shoots right . . . (March 26, 1989)—Suspended one game for being the aggressor in a fight with Reggie Savage at Victoriaville.

Year—Team	League	Games	G.	A.	Pts.	Pen.
1986-87—Outaouais Midget	Que. AAA	41	4	27	31	102
1987-88—Drummondville Voltigeurs (c)	QMJHL	44	1	8	9	122
1988-89—Drummondville Voltigeurs	QMJHL	39	6	15	21	89
1989-90—Laval Titans (d)	QMJHL	48	2	19	21	131

(c)—June, 1988—Drafted as underage junior by Detroit Red Wings in 1988 NHL entry draft. Second Red Wings pick, 38th overall, second round.

(d)—February 15, 1990—Traded with Claude Boivin and a fifth-round draft pick by Drummondville Voltigeurs to Laval Titans for Luc Doucet, Brad MacIsaac and second and third round draft picks.

SHAWN ANTOSKI

Left Wing . . . 6'4'' . . . 234 lbs. . . . Born, Brantford, Ont., May 25, 1970 . . . Shoots left . . . Also plays Right Wing and Defense . . . (December, 1988)—Injured knee ligament . . . (March, 1989)—Separated shoulder.

Year—Team	League	Games	G.	A.	Pts.	Pen.
1985-86—Don Mills Bantam	Toronto	27	10	15	25	50
1986-87—Don Mills Midgets	Toronto	33	12	13	25	75
1987-88—North Bay Centennials	OHL	52	3	4	7	163
1988-89—North Bay Centennials	OHL	57	6	21	27	201
1989-90—North Bay Centennials (c)	OHL	59	25	31	56	201

(c)—June 16, 1989—Selected by Vancouver Canucks in 1989 NHL entry draft. Second Canucks pick, 18th overall, first round.

DAVID ARCHIBALD

Center . . . 6'1'' . . . 195 lbs. . . . Born, Chilliwack, B.C., April 14, 1969 . . . Shoots left . . . (January, 1984)—Shoulder surgery . . . (October, 1986)—Lacerated hand . . . (September, 1987)—Injured shoulder . . . (February, 1989)—Sore lower back.

Year—Team	League	Games	G.	A.	Pts.	Pen.
1984-85—Portland Winter Hawks	WHL	47	7	11	18	10
1985-86—Portland Winter Hawks	WHL	70	29	35	64	56
1986-87—Portland Winter Hawks (c)	WHL	65	50	57	107	40
1987-88—Minnesota North Stars	NHL	78	13	20	33	26

Year—Team	League	Games	G.	A.	Pts.	Pen.
1988-89—Minnesota North Stars	NHL	72	14	19	33	14
1989-90—Minnesota North Stars (d)	NHL	12	1	5	6	6
1989-90—New York Rangers	NHL	19	2	3	5	6
1989-90—Flint Spirits	IHL	41	14	38	52	16
NHL TOTALS		181	30	47	77	52

(c)—June, 1987—Drafted as underage junior by Minnesota North Stars in 1987 NHL entry draft. First North Stars pick, sixth overall, first round.

(d)—November 1, 1989—Traded by Minnesota North Stars to New York Rangers for Jayson More.

BILL ARMSTRONG

Center . . . 6'2'' . . . 195 lbs. . . . Born, London, Ont., June 25, 1966 . . . Shoots left.

Year—Team	League	Games	G.	A.	Pts.	Pen.
1986-87—Western Michigan Univ.	CCHA	43	13	20	33	86
1987-88—Western Michigan Univ.	CCHA	41	22	17	39	88
1988-89—Western Michigan Univ. (c)	CCHA	40	23	19	42	97
1989-90—Hershey Bears	AHL	58	10	6	16	99

(c)—May 16, 1989—Signed by Philadelphia Flyers as a free agent.

TIM ARMSTRONG

Center . . . 5'11'' . . . 170 lbs. . . . Born, Toronto, Ont., May 12, 1967 . . . Shoots right.

Year—Team	League	Games	G.	A.	Pts.	Pen.
1983-84—Markham Tier II Jr. A	OHA	42	24	41	65	41
1984-85—Toronto Marlboros (c)	OHL	63	17	45	62	28
1985-86—Toronto Marlboros	OHL	64	35	69	104	36
1986-87—Toronto Marlboros	OHL	66	29	55	84	61
1986-87—Newmarket Saints	AHL	5	3	0	3	2
1987-88—Newmarket Saints	AHL	78	19	40	59	26
1988-89—Newmarket Saints	AHL	37	16	24	40	38
1988-89—Toronto Maple Leafs	NHL	11	1	0	1	6
1989-90—Newmarket Saints	AHL	63	25	37	62	24
NHL TOTALS		11	1	0	1	6

(c)—June, 1985—Drafted as underage junior by Toronto Maple Leafs in 1985 NHL entry draft. Eleventh Maple Leafs pick, 211th overall, 11th round.

WILLIAM ARMSTRONG

Defense . . . 6'4'' . . . 216 lbs. . . . Born, Richmond Hill, Ont., May 18, 1970 . . . Shoots left.

Year—Team	League	Games	G.	A.	Pts.	Pen.
1986-87—Barrie Flyers	OHA	45	1	11	12	45
1987-88—Toronto Marlboros	OHL	64	1	10	11	99
1988-89—Toronto Marlboros	OHL	64	1	16	17	82
1989-90—Dukes of Hamilton	OHL	18	0	2	2	38
1989-90—Niagara Falls Thunder	OHL	4	0	1	1	17
1989-90—Oshawa Generals	OHL	41	2	8	10	115

(c)—June 16, 1990—Selected by Philadelphia Flyers in 1990 NHL entry draft. Fifth Flyers pick, 46th overall, third round.

SCOTT ARNIEL

Left Wing . . . 6'1'' . . . 170 lbs. . . . Born, Kingston, Ont., September 17, 1962 . . . Shoots left . . . Also plays Center . . . (March, 1988)—Bruised abdominal muscle . . . (April 9, 1990)—Concussion in third playoff game vs. Montreal when checked by Brian Skrudland.

Year—Team	League	Games	G.	A.	Pts.	Pen.
1979-80—Cornwall Royals	QMJHL	61	22	28	50	51
1980-81—Cornwall Royals (c)	QMJHL	68	52	71	123	102
1981-82—Cornwall Royals	OHL	24	18	26	44	43
1981-82—Winnipeg Jets	NHL	17	1	8	9	14
1982-83—Winnipeg Jets	NHL	75	13	5	18	46
1983-84—Winnipeg Jets	NHL	80	21	35	56	68
1984-85—Winnipeg Jets	NHL	79	22	22	44	81
1985-86—Winnipeg Jets (d)	NHL	80	18	25	43	40
1986-87—Buffalo Sabres	NHL	63	11	14	25	59
1987-88—Buffalo Sabres	NHL	73	17	23	40	61
1988-89—Buffalo Sabres	NHL	80	18	23	41	46
1989-90—Buffalo Sabres (e)	NHL	79	18	14	32	77
NHL TOTALS		626	139	169	308	492

(c)—June, 1981—Drafted as underage junior by Winnipeg Jets in NHL entry draft. Second Jets pick, 22nd overall, second round.

(d)—June, 1986—Traded by Winnipeg Jets to Buffalo Sabres for Gilles Hamel.

(e)—June 16, 1990—Traded with Phil Housley, Jeff Parker and a first round 1990 draft pick (Keith Tkachuk) by Buffalo Sabres to Winnipeg Jets for Dale Hawerchuk and a first round 1990 draft pick (Brad May).

BRENT KENNETH ASHTON

Left Wing . . . 6'1'' . . . 200 lbs. . . . Born, Saskatoon, Sask., May 18, 1960 . . . Shoots left . . . Missed part of 1979-80 season with knee ligament injury . . . (October, 1985)—Missed two weeks with injured hip in training camp . . . Also plays Center . . . (September, 1986)—Tore left knee ligaments in pre-season altercation with Dave Semenko vs. Edmonton . . . (March 15, 1989)—Strained ligaments in right knee when checked by Michel Petit at N.Y. Rangers, missed three games and returned to play with a knee brace.

Year—Team	League	Games	G.	A.	Pts.	Pen.
1975-76—Saskatoon Blades	WCHL	11	3	4	7	11
1976-77—Saskatoon Blades	WCHL	54	26	25	51	84
1977-78—Saskatoon Blades	WCHL	46	38	28	66	47
1978-79—Saskatoon Blades (c)	WHL	62	64	55	119	80
1979-80—Vancouver Canucks	NHL	47	5	14	19	11
1980-81—Vancouver Canucks (d-e)	NHL	77	18	11	29	57

Year	Team	League	Games	G.	A.	Pts.	Pen.
1981-82—Colorado Rockies		NHL	80	24	36	60	26
1982-83—New Jersey Devils		NHL	76	14	19	33	47
1983-84—Minnesota North Stars (f)		NHL	68	7	10	17	54
1984-85—Minnesota North Stars (g)		NHL	29	4	7	11	15
1984-85—Quebec Nordiques		NHL	49	27	24	51	38
1985-86—Quebec Nordiques		NHL	77	26	32	58	64
1986-87—Quebec Nordiques (h)		NHL	46	25	19	44	17
1986-87—Detroit Red Wings		NHL	35	15	16	31	22
1987-88—Detroit Red Wings (i)		NHL	73	26	27	53	50
1988-89—Winnipeg Jets		NHL	75	31	37	68	36
1989-90—Winnipeg Jets		NHL	79	22	34	56	37
NHL TOTALS			811	244	286	530	474

(c)—August, 1979—Drafted by Vancouver Canucks as underage junior in NHL entry draft. Second Canucks pick, 26th overall, second round.

(d)—July, 1981—Traded with a fourth-round draft pick in 1982 by Vancouver to Winnipeg Jets as compensation for Canucks signing of Ivan Hlinka, a Czechoslovakian player drafted by Winnipeg in a special draft on May 28, 1981.

(e)—July, 1981—Traded with a third-round 1982 draft pick (Dave Kasper) by Winnipeg Jets to Colorado Rockies for Lucien DeBlois.

(f)—October, 1983—Traded by New Jersey Devils to Minnesota North Stars for Dave Lewis.

(g)—December, 1984—Traded with Brad Maxwell by Minnesota North Stars to Quebec Nordiques for Tony McKegney and Bo Berglund.

(h)—January, 1987—Traded with Gilbert Delorme and Mark Kumpel by Quebec Nordiques to Detroit Red Wings for John Ogrodnick, Doug Shedden and Basil McRae.

(i)—June, 1988—Traded by Detroit Red Wings to Winnipeg Jets for Paul MacLean.

MARK ASTLEY

Defense . . . 6' . . . 185 lbs. . . . Born, Calgary, Alta., March 30, 1969 . . . Shoots left . . . (March 14, 1990)—Hospitalized with strep pneumonia.

Year	Team	League	Games	G.	A.	Pts.	Pen.
1987-88—Calgary Canucks		AJHL	52	25	37	62	106
1988-89—Lake Superior State Univ. (c)		CCHA	42	3	12	15	26
1989-90—Lake Superior State Univ.		CCHA	43	7	25	32	74

(c)—June, 1989—Drafted by Buffalo Sabres in 1989 NHL entry draft. Ninth Sabres pick, 194th overall, 10th round.

BLAIR ATCHEYNUM

Right Wing . . . 6'2'' . . . 190 lbs. . . . Born, Estevan, Sask., April 20, 1969 . . . Shoots right.

Year	Team	League	Games	G.	A.	Pts.	Pen.
1984-85—North Battleford Midget		Sask.	26	26	26	52	150
1985-86—North Battleford Jrs.		SJHL	35	25	20	45	50
1986-87—Saskatoon Blades (c)		WHL	21	0	4	4	4
1986-87—Swift Current Broncos (d)		WHL	5	2	1	3	0
1986-87—Moose Jaw Warriors		WHL	12	3	0	3	2
1987-88—Moose Jaw Warriors		WHL	60	32	16	48	52
1988-89—Moose Jaw Warriors (a-e-f)		WHL	71	70	68	138	70
1989-90—Binghamton Whalers		AHL	78	20	21	41	45

(c)—February, 1987—Selected by Swift Current Broncos in special compensation draft to replace players injured and killed in a December 30, 1986 bus crash.

(d)—February, 1987—Traded by Swift Current Broncos to Moose Jaw Warriors for Tim Logan.

(e)—Won Brad Hornung Trophy (Most Sportsmanlike player).

(f)—June, 1989—Drafted by Hartford Whalers in 1989 NHL entry draft. Second Whalers pick, 52nd overall, third round.

DONALD AUDETTE

Right Wing . . . 5'8'' . . . 180 lbs. . . . Born, Laval, Que., September 23, 1969 . . . Shoots right . . . (February 11, 1990)—Broken left hand when slashed by Bruce Shoebottom vs. Maine and missed seven games.

Year	Team	League	Games	G.	A.	Pts.	Pen.
1986-87—St. Jean Castors		QMJHL	38	0	12	12	22
1987-88—Laval Titans		QMJHL	63	48	61	109	56
1988-89—Laval Titans (c)		QMJHL	70	76	85	161	123
1989-90—Rochester Americans (a-d)		AHL	70	42	46	88	78

(c)—June, 1989—Drafted by Buffalo Sabres in 1989 NHL entry draft. Eighth Sabres pick, 183rd overall, ninth round.

(d)—Won Dudley (Red) Garrett Award (Rookie of the Year).

WILLIAM AVERILL

Defense . . . 5'11'' . . . 175 lbs. . . . Born, Wayland, Mass., December 20, 1968 . . . Shoots right . . . Son of Bo Averill and brother of Jim and Bob Averill. All played for Northeastern University (Bo in the 1950's and Jim and Bob in the 1980's) . . . (November 28, 1989)—Suspended two games.

Year	Team	League	Games	G.	A.	Pts.	Pen.
1986-87—Belmont Hill (c)		Mass. H.S.	22	6	19	25	..
1987-88—Northeastern Univ.		H. East	36	2	23	25	36
1988-89—Northeastern Univ.		H. East	36	4	16	20	40
1989-90—Northeastern Univ.		H. East	35	6	13	19	41

(c)—June, 1987—Drafted by New York Islanders in 1987 NHL entry draft. Twelfth Islanders pick, 244th overall, 12th round.

BOB BABCOCK

Defense . . . 6'1'' . . . 190 lbs. . . . Born, Agincourt, Ont., August 3, 1968 . . . Shoots left . . . (December 10, 1989)—Suspended 10 games for fighting with Bryan Marchment before game vs. Moncton.

Year	Team	League	Games	G.	A.	Pts.	Pen.
1984-85—St. Michaels Midgets		OHA	40	8	30	38	140
1985-86—Sault Ste. Marie Greyhounds (c)		OHL	50	1	7	8	185
1986-87—Sault Ste. Marie Greyhounds		OHL	62	7	8	15	243

Year	Team	League	Games	G.	A.	Pts.	Pen.
1987-88—Sault Ste. Marie Greyhounds		OHL	8	0	2	2	30
1987-88—Cornwall Royals		OHL	42	0	16	16	120
1988-89—Cornwall Royals		OHL	42	0	9	9	163
1989-90—Baltimore Skipjacks		AHL	67	0	4	4	249

(c)—June, 1986—Drafted as underage junior by Washington Capitals in 1986 NHL entry draft. Eleventh Capitals pick, 208th overall, 10th round.

DAVID MICHAEL BABYCH

Defense . . . 6'2'' . . . 215 lbs. . . . Born, Edmonton, Alta., May 23, 1961 . . . Shoots left . . . Brother of Wayne Babych . . . First member of Winnipeg Jets to be voted to mid-season All-Star game (1983) starting team . . . (March, 1984)—Separated shoulder . . . (December, 1984)—Back spasms . . . (January, 1987)—Missed 12 games with a hip injury . . . (March 16, 1989)—Took 18 stitch cut across right hand when struck by skate of Uwe Krupp during altercation vs. Buffalo and missed six games . . . (March, 1990)—Bruised neck.

Year	Team	League	Games	G.	A.	Pts.	Pen.
1977-78—Portland Winter Hawks		WCHL	6	1	3	4	4
1977-78—Ft. Sask. Traders (a-c-d)		AJHL	56	31	69	100	37
1978-79—Portland Winter Hawks		WHL	67	20	59	79	63
1979-80—Portland Winter Hawks (a-e-f)		WHL	50	22	60	82	71
1980-81—Winnipeg Jets		NHL	69	6	38	44	90
1981-82—Winnipeg Jets		NHL	79	19	49	68	92
1982-83—Winnipeg Jets		NHL	79	13	61	74	56
1983-84—Winnipeg Jets		NHL	66	18	39	57	62
1984-85—Winnipeg Jets		NHL	78	13	49	62	78
1985-86—Winnipeg Jets (g)		NHL	19	4	12	16	14
1985-86—Hartford Whalers		NHL	62	10	43	53	36
1986-87—Hartford Whalers		NHL	66	8	33	41	44
1987-88—Hartford Whalers		NHL	71	14	36	50	54
1988-89—Hartford Whalers		NHL	70	6	41	47	54
1989-90—Hartford Whalers		NHL	72	6	37	43	62
NHL TOTALS			731	117	438	555	642

(c)—Named winner of AJHL Rookie of the Year Trophy.

(d)—Named winner of AJHL Top Defenseman Trophy.

(e)—Named winner of WHL Top Defenseman Trophy.

(f)—June, 1980—Drafted as underage junior by Winnipeg Jets in NHL entry draft. First Jets pick, second overall, first round.

(g)—November, 1985—Traded by Winnipeg Jets to Hartford Whalers for Ray Neufeld.

JERGUS BACA

Defense . . . 6'2'' . . . 210 lbs. . . . Born, Kosice, Czechoslovakia, April 1, 1965 . . . Shoots left.

Year	Team	League	Games	G.	A.	Pts.	Pen.
1989-90—Kosice (c)		Czech.	47	9	16	25	....

(c)—June 16, 1990—Selected by Hartford Whalers in 1990 NHL entry draft. Sixth Whalers pick, 141st overall, seventh round.

DARIN BADER

Left Wing . . . 6' . . . 200 lbs. . . . Born, Edmonton, Alta., April 2, 1971 . . . Shoots left . . . (August, 1989)—Injured knee and required surgery.

Year	Team	League	Games	G.	A.	Pts.	Pen.
1987-88—Saskatoon Blades		WHL	53	5	9	14	73
1988-89—Saskatoon Blades		WHL	66	19	14	33	214
1989-90—Saskatoon Blades (c)		WHL	54	26	31	57	107

(c)—June 16, 1990—Selected by Vancouver Canucks in 1990 NHL entry draft. Fourth Canucks pick, 65th overall, fourth round.

JAMIE BAKER

Center . . . 5'11'' . . . 180 lbs. . . . Born, Nepean, Que., August 31, 1966 . . . Shoots left . . . (December 30, 1988)—Broke left ankle vs. Western Michigan Univ. when his skates were knocked out from under him by Mike Posma and had surgery.

Year	Team	League	Games	G.	A.	Pts.	Pen.
1985-86—St. Lawrence Univ.		ECAC	31	9	16	25	52
1986-87—St. Lawrence Univ.		ECAC	32	8	24	32	59
1987-88—St. Lawrence Univ. (c)		ECAC	38	26	28	54	44
1988-89—St. Lawrence Univ.		ECAC	13	11	16	27	16
1989-90—Quebec Nordiques		NHL	1	0	0	0	0
1989-90—Halifax Citadels		AHL	74	17	43	60	47
NHL TOTALS			1	0	0	0	0

(c)—June, 1988—Selected by Quebec Nordiques in 1988 NHL supplemental draft.

PETER GEORGE BAKOVIC

Right Wing . . . 6'1'' . . . 190 lbs. . . . Born, Thunder Bay, Ont., January 31, 1965 . . . Shoots right . . . (November 12, 1988)—Given a two-game suspension for fighting at Indianapolis.

Year	Team	League	Games	G.	A.	Pts.	Pen.
1982-83—Thunder Bay Jr. B		OHA	40	30	29	59	159
1983-84—Kitchener Rangers		OHL	28	2	6	8	87
1983-84—Windsor Spitfires		OHL	35	10	25	35	74
1984-85—Windsor Spitfires		OHL	58	26	48	74	*259
1985-86—Moncton Golden Flames		AHL	80	18	36	54	349
1986-87—Moncton Golden Flames		AHL	77	17	34	51	280
1987-88—Vancouver Canucks (d)		NHL	10	2	0	2	48
1987-88—Salt Lake Golden Eagles		IHL	39	16	27	43	221
1988-89—Milwaukee Admirals		IHL	40	16	14	30	211
1989-90—Milwaukee Admirals		IHL	56	19	30	49	230
NHL TOTALS			10	2	0	2	48

(c)—October, 1985—Signed by Moncton Golden Flames as a free agent.

(d)—March, 1988—Traded with Brian Bradley and future considerations (Kevan Guy) by Calgary Flames to Vancouver Canucks for Craig Coxe.

HELMUT BALDERIS

Right Wing . . . 5'11" . . . 190 lbs. . . . Born, Riga, Latvia, June 30, 1952 . . . Shoots left . . . (December 27, 1989)—Strained groin in team practice and missed six games . . . (January 26, 1990)—Pulled groin at Vancouver and missed six games.

Year	Team	League	Games	G.	A.	Pts.	Pen.
1973-74—Dynamo Riga		Soviet	24	9	6	15	13
1974-75—Dynamo Riga		Soviet	36	34	14	48	20
1975-76—Dynamo Riga		Soviet	36	31	14	45	18
1976-77—Dynamo Riga		Soviet	35	40	23	63	57
1977-78—CSKA (Red Army) Moscow		Soviet	36	17	17	34	30
1978-79—CSKA (Red Army) Moscow		Soviet	41	24	24	48	53
1979-80—CSKA (Red Army) Moscow		Soviet	44	26	35	61	21
1980-81—Dynamo Riga		Soviet	44	26	24	50	28
1981-82—Dynamo Riga		Soviet	50	39	24	63	50
1982-83—Dynamo Riga		Soviet	40	32	31	63	39
1983-84—Dynamo Riga		Soviet	39	24	15	39	18
1984-85—Dynamo Riga		Soviet	39	31	20	51	52
1985-86—............			....	....	....	....	....
1986-87—............			....	....	....	....	....
1987-88—Coaching in Japan			....	....	....	....	....
1988-89—Coaching in Japan (c)			....	....	....	....	....
1989-90—Minnesota North Stars		NHL	26	3	6	9	2
NHL TOTALS			26	3	6	9	2

(c)—June, 1989—Drafted by Minnesota North Stars in 1989 NHL entry draft. Twelfth North Stars pick, 238th overall, 12th round.

STEVE BANCROFT

Defense . . . 6'1" . . . 215 lbs. . . . Born, Toronto, Ont., October 7, 1970 . . . Shoots left . . . (April, 1989)—Had surgery to left shoulder.

Year	Team	League	Games	G.	A.	Pts.	Pen.
1986-87—St. Catharines Jr. B	OHA	11	5	8	13	20
1987-88—Belleville Bulls	OHL	56	1	8	9	42
1988-89—Belleville Bulls (c)	OHL	66	7	30	37	99
1989-90—Belleville Bulls	OHL	53	10	33	43	135

(c)—June, 1989—Drafted by Toronto Maple Leafs in 1989 NHL entry draft. Third Maple Leafs pick, 21st overall, first round.

MARIO BARBE

Defense . . . 6'1" . . . 195 lbs. . . . Born, Abitibi, Que., March 17, 1967 . . . Shoots left.

Year	Team	League	Games	G.	A.	Pts.	Pen.
1983-84—Bourassa AAA	Que.Midget	42	7	13	20	63
1984-85—Chicoutimi Sagueneens (c)	QMJHL	64	2	13	15	211
1985-86—Granby Bisons	QMJHL	70	5	25	30	261
1986-87—Granby Bisons	QMJHL	65	7	25	32	356
1987-88—Granby Bisons	QMJHL	45	8	10	18	294
1988-89—Cape Breton Oilers	AHL	70	1	11	12	137
1989-90—Cape Breton Oilers	AHL	64	0	15	15	138

(c)—June, 1985—Drafted as underage junior by Edmonton Oilers in NHL entry draft. Ninth Oilers pick, 209th overall, 10th round.

DON BARBER

Left Wing . . . 6'1" . . . 205 lbs. . . . Born, Victoria, B.C., December 2, 1964 . . . Shoots left . . . (October, 1987)—Injured knee.

Year	Team	League	Games	G.	A.	Pts.	Pen.
1982-83—Kelowna Buckaroos (c)	BCJHL	35	26	31	57	54
1983-84—St. Albert Saints	AJHL	53	42	38	80	74
1984-85—Bowling Green Univ.	CCHA	39	15	12	27	44
1985-86—Bowling Green Univ. (d)	CCHA	35	21	22	43	64
1986-87—Bowling Green Univ.	CCHA	43	29	34	63	109
1987-88—Bowling Green Univ.	CCHA	38	18	47	65	60
1988-89—Minnesota North Stars	NHL	23	8	5	13	8
1988-89—Kalamazoo Wings	IHL	39	14	17	31	23
1989-90—Kalamazoo Wings	IHL	10	4	4	8	38
1989-90—Minnesota North Stars	NHL	44	15	19	34	32
NHL TOTALS		67	23	24	47	40

(c)—June, 1983—Drafted as underage junior by Edmonton Oilers in NHL entry draft. Fifth Oilers pick, 120th overall, sixth round.

(d)—December, 1985—Traded with Marc Habscheid and Emanuel Viveiros by Edmonton Oilers to Minnesota North Stars for Gord Sherven and Don Biggs.

MIKE BARKLEY

Right Wing . . . 6' . . . 185 lbs. . . . Born, Port Alberni, B.C., April 7, 1970 . . . Shoots right.

Year	Team	League	Games	G.	A.	Pts.	Pen.
1987-88—Vernon	BCJHL	47	50	42	92	92
1988-89—Univ. of Maine (c)	H. East	41	12	16	28	16
1989-90—Univ. of Maine	H. East	43	11	19	30	20

(c)—June, 1989—Drafted by Buffalo Sabres in 1989 NHL entry draft. Sixth Sabres pick, 119th overall, sixth round.

RICHARD BARKOVICH

Center . . . 5'10" . . . 185 lbs. . . . Born, Kirkland Lake, Ont., April 25, 1964 . . . Shoots right.

Year	Team	League	Games	G.	A.	Pts.	Pen.
1982-83—London Knights	OHL	65	14	14	28	40
1983-84—London Knights	OHL	67	25	29	54	83
1984-85—London Knights	OHL	63	41	40	81	56
1985-85—............	....	..	..	..	..	..
1986-87—Brantford (c)	OHA Senior	35	31	32	63	22
1987-88—Salt Lake Golden Eagles	IHL	79	34	25	59	65

Year	Team	League	Games	G.	A.	Pts.	Pen.
1988-89—Indianapolis Ice	IHL	78	32	35	67	81
1989-90—Salt Lake Golden Eagles	IHL	71	20	23	43	55

(c)—October 10, 1987—Signed by Calgary Flames as a free agent.

STU BARNES

Center . . . 5'10" . . . 175 lbs. . . . Born, Edmonton, Alta., December 25, 1970 . . . Shoots right.

Year	Team	League	Games	G.	A.	Pts.	Pen.
1986-87—St. Albert Saints	AJHL	57	43	32	75	80
1987-88—New Westminster Bruins (b-c)	WHL	71	37	64	101	88
1988-89—Tri-City Americans (a-d)	WHL	70	59	82	141	117
1989-90—Tri-City Americans	WHL	63	52	92	144	165

(c)—Won Jim Piggott Memorial Trophy (Top WHL Rookie).

(d)—June, 1989—Drafted by Winnipeg Jets in 1989 NHL entry draft. First Jets pick, fourth overall, first round.

MURRAY BARON

Defense . . . 6'3" . . . 210 lbs. . . . Born, Prince George, B.C., June 1, 1967 . . . Shoots left . . . (October 5, 1989)—Separated left shoulder vs. New Jersey . . . (April, 1990)—Surgery to have bone spur removed from foot.

Year	Team	League	Games	G.	A.	Pts.	Pen.
1984-85—Vernon Lakers	BCJHL	50	10	15	25	200
1985-86—Vernon Lakers (c)	BCJHL	46	12	32	44	....
1986-87—Univ. of North Dakota	WCHA	41	4	10	14	62
1987-88—Univ. of North Dakota	WCHA	41	1	10	11	95
1988-89—Univ. of North Dakota	WCHA	40	2	6	8	92
1988-89—Hershey Bears	AHL	9	0	3	3	8
1989-90—Hershey Bears	AHL	50	0	10	10	101
1989-90—Philadelphia Flyers	NHL	16	2	2	4	12
NHL TOTALS		16	2	2	4	12

(c)—June, 1986—Drafted as underage player by Philadelphia Flyers in 1986 NHL entry draft. Seventh Flyers pick, 167th overall, eighth round.

DAVID BARR

Center . . . 6'1" . . . 185 lbs. . . . Born, Edmonton, Alta., November 30, 1960 . . . Shoots right . . . Also plays Right Wing . . . (March 19, 1986)—Sprained knee vs. Hartford . . . (November, 1987)—Separated right shoulder . . . (December, 1987)—Broken right foot.

Year	Team	League	Games	G.	A.	Pts.	Pen.
1977-78—Pincher Creek	AJHL	60	16	32	48	53
1978-79—Edmonton Oil Kings	WHL	72	16	19	35	61
1979-80—Lethbridge Broncos	WHL	60	16	38	54	47
1980-81—Lethbridge Broncos	WHL	72	26	62	88	106
1981-82—Erie Blades	AHL	76	18	48	66	29
1981-82—Boston Bruins (c)	NHL	2	0	0	0	0
1982-83—Baltimore Skipjacks	AHL	72	27	51	78	67
1982-83—Boston Bruins	NHL	10	1	1	2	7
1983-84—New York Rangers (d)	NHL	6	0	0	0	2
1983-84—Tulsa Oilers	CHL	50	28	37	65	24
1983-84—St. Louis Blues (e)	NHL	1	0	0	0	0
1984-85—St. Louis Blues	NHL	75	16	18	34	32
1985-86—St. Louis Blues	NHL	75	13	38	51	70
1986-87—St. Louis Blues (f)	NHL	2	0	0	0	0
1986-87—Hartford Whalers (g)	NHL	30	2	4	6	19
1986-87—Detroit Red Wings	NHL	37	13	13	26	49
1987-88—Detroit Red Wings	NHL	51	14	26	40	58
1988-89—Detroit Red Wings	NHL	73	27	32	59	69
1989-90—Detroit Red Wings	NHL	62	10	25	35	45
1989-90—Adirondack Red Wings	AHL	9	1	14	15	17
NHL TOTALS		424	96	157	253	351

(c)—September, 1981—Signed by Boston Bruins as a free agent.

(d)—October, 1983—Traded by Boston Bruins to New York Rangers for Dave Silk.

(e)—March, 1984—Traded with third-round 1984 draft pick (Alan Perry) and cash by New York Rangers to St. Louis Blues for Larry Patey and NHL rights to Bob Brooke.

(f)—October, 1986—Traded by St. Louis Blues to Hartford Whalers for Tim Bothwell.

(g)—January, 1987—Traded by Hartford Whalers to Detroit Red Wings for Randy Ladouceur.

LEN BARRIE

Right Wing . . . 6' . . . 195 lbs. . . . Born, Kimberly, B.C., June 4, 1969 . . . Shoots right . . . (March, 1989)—Finger broken in WHL playoff game vs. Kamloops.

Year	Team	League	Games	G.	A.	Pts.	Pen.
1984-85—Kelowna	B.C. Mdgt.	20	51	55	106	24
1985-86—Calgary Spurs	AJHL	23	7	14	21	86
1985-86—Calgary Wranglers	WHL	32	3	0	3	18
1986-87—Victoria Cougars	WHL	68	20	19	39	173
1987-88—Victoria Cougars (c)	WHL	70	37	49	86	192
1988-89—Victoria Cougars	WHL	67	39	48	87	157
1989-90—Philadelphia Flyers	NHL	1	0	0	0	0
1989-90—Kamloops Blazers (d-e)	WHL	70	*85	*100	*185	108
NHL TOTALS		1	0	0	0	0

(c)—June, 1988—Drafted by Edmonton Oilers in 1988 NHL entry draft. Seventh Oilers pick, 124th overall, sixth round.

(d)—August, 1989—Traded by Victoria Cougars to Kamloops Blazers for Mark Cipriano.

(e)—February 8, 1990—Signed by Philadelphia Flyers as a free agent.

ROBIN BARTELL

Defense . . . 6' . . . 195 lbs. . . . Born, Drake, Sask., May 16, 1961 . . . Shoots left.

Year	Team	League	Games	G.	A.	Pts.	Pen.
1980-81—Prince Albert Raiders	SAJHL	86	22	63	85	....

Year	Team	League	Games	G.	A.	Pts.	Pen.
1981-82—Prince Albert Raiders		SAJHL	83	17	73	90	....
1982-83—Univ. of Saskatchewan		CAHA	24	4	14	18	....
1983-84—Canadian Olympic Team		Olympics	....	...	...	...	....
1984-85—Switzerland		Switzerland	....	...	...	...	....
1984-85—Moncton Golden Flames (c)		AHL	41	4	11	15	66
1985-86—Moncton Golden Flames		AHL	74	4	21	25	100
1985-86—Calgary Flames (d)		NHL	1	0	0	0	0
1986-87—Fredericton Express		AHL	10	0	2	2	15
1986-87—Vancouver Canucks		NHL	40	0	1	1	14
1987-88—Fredericton Express		AHL	37	1	10	11	54
1988-89—Milwaukee Admirals (e)		IHL	26	1	5	6	59
1988-89—Moncton Hawks		AHL	23	0	4	4	19
1989-90—Canadian National Team		Int'l.	23	1	1	2	10
NHL TOTALS			41	0	1	1	14

(c)—December, 1984—Signed by Moncton Golden Flames as a free agent.
(d)—July, 1986—Signed by Vancouver Canucks as a free agent.
(e)—February 8, 1989—Traded by Vancouver Canucks to Winnipeg Jets for Jamie Husgen.

CLAUDE BARTHE

Defense . . . 6'2'' . . . 195 lbs. . . . Born, St. Joseph de Sorel, Que., June 15, 1970 . . . Shoots right.

Year	Team	League	Games	G.	A.	Pts.	Pen.
1987-88—Verdun Jr. Canadiens		QMJHL	68	2	25	27	51
1988-89—Victoriaville Tigres		QMJHL	66	7	10	17	122
1989-90—Victoriaville Tigres (c-d)		QMJHL	68	20	55	75	148

(c)—Won Outstanding defenseman trophy.
(d)—June 16, 1990—Selected by Detroit Red Wings in 1990 NHL entry draft. Fifth Red Wings pick, 108th overall, sixth round.

WADE BARTLEY

Defense . . . 6'1'' . . . 190 lbs. . . . Born, Killarney, Manitoba, May 16, 1970 . . . Shoots right . . . (November, 1986)—Torn knee cartilage.

Year	Team	League	Games	G.	A.	Pts.	Pen.
1986-87—Dauphin Kings		MJHL	36	4	24	28	55
1987-88—Dauphin Kings (c)		MJHL	47	10	64	74	104
1988-89—Univ. of North Dakota		WCHA	32	1	1	2	8
1989-90—Sudbury Wolves		OHL	60	23	36	59	53

(c)—June, 1988—Drafted by Washington Capitals in 1988 NHL entry draft. Third Capitals pick, 41st overall, second round.

DAVID BASEGGIO

Defense . . . 6'1'' . . . 185 lbs. . . . Born, Niagara Falls, Ont., October 28, 1967 . . . Shoots left . . . Brother of Rob Basaggio (former teammate at Yale Univ.).

Year	Team	League	Games	G.	A.	Pts.	Pen.
1984-85—Niagara Falls Jr. B		OHA	39	16	45	61	88
1985-86—Yale University (c)		ECAC	30	7	17	24	54
1986-87—Yale University (b)		ECAC	29	8	17	25	52
1987-88—Yale University		ECAC	24	4	22	26	67
1988-89—Yale University		ECAC	28	10	23	33	41
1989-90—Indianapolis Ice		IHL	10	1	7	8	2
1989-90—Rochester Americans		AHL	41	3	15	18	41

(c)—June, 1986—Drafted by Buffalo Sabres in 1986 NHL entry draft. Fifth Sabres pick, 68th overall, fourth round.

BOB BASSEN

Center . . . 5'10'' . . . 180 lbs. . . . Born, Calgary, Alta., May 6, 1965 . . . Shoots left . . . Son of Hank Bassen (Goalie with Chicago, Detroit and Pittsburgh in NHL in mid '60s) . . . (October 12, 1985)—Injured knee at Los Angeles.

Year	Team	League	Games	G.	A.	Pts.	Pen.
1982-83—Medicine Hat Tigers		WHL	4	3	2	5	0
1983-84—Medicine Hat Tigers		WHL	72	29	29	58	93
1984-85—Medicine Hat Tigers (a-c)		WHL	65	32	50	82	143
1985-86—New York Islanders		NHL	11	2	1	3	6
1985-86—Springfield Indians		AHL	54	13	21	34	111
1986-87—New York Islanders		NHL	77	7	10	17	89
1987-88—New York Islanders		NHL	77	6	16	22	99
1988-89—New York Islanders (d)		NHL	19	1	4	5	21
1988-89—Chicago Black Hawks		NHL	49	4	12	16	62
1989-90—Indianapolis Ice		IHL	73	22	32	54	179
1989-90—Chicago Black Hawks		NHL	6	1	1	2	8
NHL TOTALS			239	21	44	65	285

(c)—June, 1985—Signed by New York Islanders as a free agent.
(d)—November 25, 1988—Traded with Steve Konroyd by New York Islanders to Chicago Black Hawks for Gary Nylund and Marc Bergevin.

JEFF BATTERS

Defense . . . 6'2'' . . . 215 lbs. . . . Born, Victoria, B.C., October 23, 1970 . . . Shoots right.

Year	Team	League	Games	G.	A.	Pts.	Pen.
1988-89—Univ. of Alaska/Anchorage (c)		Ind.	33	8	14	22	123
1989-90—Univ. of Alaska/Anchorage		Ind.	34	6	9	15	102

(c)—June, 1989—Drafted by St. Louis Blues in 1989 NHL entry draft. Seventh Blues pick, 135th overall, seventh round.

COLLIN BAUER

Defense . . . 6'1'' . . . 175 lbs. . . . Born, Edmonton, Alta., September 6, 1970 . . . Shoots left.

Year	Team	League	Games	G.	A.	Pts.	Pen.
1986-87—Saskatoon Blades		WHL	61	1	25	26	37

Year	Team	League	Games	G.	A.	Pts.	Pen.
1987-88—Saskatoon Blades (c)		WHL	70	9	53	62	66
1988-89—Saskatoon Blades		WHL	61	17	62	79	71
1989-90—Saskatoon Blades		WHL	29	4	25	29	49

(c)—June, 1988—Drafted by Edmonton Oilers in 1988 NHL entry draft. Fourth Oilers pick, 61st overall, third round.

KEN JAMES BAUMGARTNER

Defense . . . 6' . . . 200 lbs. . . . Born, Flin Flon, Manitoba, March 11, 1966 . . . Shoots left . . . (April 5, 1990)—Suspended one game for fighting in playoff game at N.Y. Rangers.

Year	Team	League	Games	G.	A.	Pts.	Pen.
1983-84—Prince Albert Raiders		WHL	57	1	6	7	203
1984-85—Prince Albert Raiders (c)		WHL	60	3	9	12	252
1985-86—Prince Albert Raiders (d)		WHL	70	4	23	27	277
1986-87—Chur		Switzerland	....	...	...	...	....
1986-87—New Haven Nighthawks		AHL	13	0	3	3	99
1987-88—Los Angeles Kings		NHL	30	2	3	5	189
1987-88—New Haven Nighthawks		AHL	48	1	5	6	181
1988-89—Los Angeles Kings		NHL	49	1	3	4	286
1988-89—New Haven Nighthawks		AHL	10	1	3	4	26
1989-90—Los Angeles Kings (e)		NHL	12	1	0	1	28
1989-90—New York Islanders		NHL	53	0	5	5	194
NHL TOTALS			144	4	11	15	697

(c)—June, 1985—Drafted as underage junior by Buffalo Sabres in 1985 NHL entry draft. Twelfth Sabres pick, 245th overall, 12th round.
(d)—January, 1986—Traded with Larry Playfair and Sean McKenna by Buffalo Sabres to Los Angeles Kings for Brian Engblom and Doug Smith.
(e)—November 29, 1989—Traded with Hubie McDonough by Los Angeles Kings to New York Islanders for Mikko Makela.

MARK BAVIS

Center . . . 6' . . . 175 lbs. . . . Born, Roslindale, Mass., March 13, 1970 . . . Shoots left . . . Twin brother of Mike Bavis (teammate at Boston University).

Year	Team	League	Games	G.	A.	Pts.	Pen.
1987-88—Catholic Memorial H.S.		Mass. H.S.	19	16	26	42	..
1988-89—Cushing Academy (c)		Mass. H.S.	29	27	31	58	18
1989-90—Boston University		H. East	44	6	5	11	50

(c)—June, 1989—Drafted by New York Rangers in 1989 NHL entry draft. Tenth Rangers pick, 181st overall, ninth round.

ROBIN BAWA

Right Wing . . . 6'2'' . . . 200 lbs. . . . Born, Chemainus, B.C., March 26, 1966 . . . Shoots right.

Year	Team	League	Games	G.	A.	Pts.	Pen.
1982-83—Kamloops Junior Oilers		WHL	66	10	24	34	17
1983-84—Kamloops Junior Oilers		WHL	64	16	28	44	40
1984-85—New Westminster Bruins		WHL	26	4	6	10	20
1984-85—Kamloops Blazers		WHL	26	2	13	15	25
1985-86—Kamloops Blazers		WHL	63	29	43	72	78
1986-87—Kamloops Blazers (a-c)		WHL	62	57	56	113	91
1987-88—Fort Wayne Komets		IHL	55	12	27	39	239
1988-89—Baltimore Skipjacks		AHL	75	23	24	47	205
1989-90—Baltimore Skipjacks		AHL	61	7	18	25	189
1989-90—Washington Capitals		NHL	5	1	0	1	6
NHL TOTALS			5	1	0	1	6

(c)—May 22, 1987—Signed by Washington Capitals as a free agent.

TIM BEAN

Left Wing . . . 6'1'' . . . 190 lbs. . . . Born, Sault Ste. Marie, Ont., March 9, 1967 . . . Shoots left.

Year	Team	League	Games	G.	A.	Pts.	Pen.
1982-83—North York Tier II		MTHL	45	9	11	20	57
1983-84—Belleville Bulls		OHL	63	12	13	25	131
1984-85—Belleville Bulls		OHL	31	10	11	21	60
1984-85—North Bay Centennials (c)		OHL	28	11	13	24	61
1985-86—North Bay Centennials		OHL	66	32	34	66	129
1986-87—North Bay Centennials		OHL	65	24	39	63	134
1987-88—Newmarket Saints		AHL	76	12	16	28	118
1988-89—Newmarket Saints		AHL	44	4	12	16	55
1988-89—Flint Spirits		IHL	3	1	3	4	4
1989-90—Newmarket Saints		AHL	39	5	10	15	27

(c)—June, 1985—Drafted by Toronto Maple Leafs in 1985 NHL entry draft as an underage junior. Seventh Maple Leafs pick, 127th overall, seventh round.

COREY BEAULIEU

Defense . . . 6'1'' . . . 210 lbs. . . . Born, Winnipeg, Man., September 9, 1969 . . . Shoots left.

Year	Team	League	Games	G.	A.	Pts.	Pen.
1984-85—Winnipeg Stars		Man. Mdgt.	48	2	19	21	168
1985-86—Moose Jaw Warriors		WHL	68	3	1	4	111
1986-87—Moose Jaw Warriors		WHL	63	2	7	9	188
1987-88—Seattle Thunderbirds (c)		WHL	67	2	9	11	225
1988-89—Seattle Thunderbirds (d)		WHL	32	0	3	3	134
1988-89—Moose Jaw Warriors		WHL	29	3	17	20	91
1989-90—Binghamton Whalers		AHL	56	0	2	2	191

(c)—June, 1988—Drafted by Hartford Whalers in 1988 NHL entry draft. Fifth Whalers pick, 116th overall, sixth round.
(d)—February 3, 1989—Traded by Seattle Thunderbirds to Moose Jaw Warriors for Brian Ilkuf and WHL rights to Petr Nedved.

NICHOLAS BEAULIEU

Left Wing . . . 6'1" . . . 200 lbs. . . . Born, Rimouski, Que., August 19, 1968 . . . Shoots left.

Year	Team	League	Games	G.	A.	Pts.	Pen.
1984-85—Richelieu Rivermen		Que. Midget	42	4	18	22	68
1985-86—Drummondville Voltigeurs (c)		QMJHL	70	11	20	21	93
1986-87—Drummondville Voltigeurs		QMJHL	69	19	34	53	198
1987-88—Laval Titans		QMJHL	64	39	56	95	240
1988-89—Cape Breton Oilers		AHL	60	10	13	23	85
1989-90—Phoenix Roadrunners		IHL	71	26	46	72	93

(c)—June, 1986—Drafted as underage junior by Edmonton Oilers in 1986 NHL entry draft. Eighth Oilers pick, 168th overall, eighth round.

JEROME BECHARD

Left Wing . . . 5'11" . . . 185 lbs. . . . Born, Regina, Sask., March 30, 1969 . . . Shoots left.

Year	Team	League	Games	G.	A.	Pts.	Pen.
1986-87—Moose Jaw Warriors		WHL	69	9	18	27	163
1987-88—Moose Jaw Warriors		WHL	72	16	21	37	280
1988-89—Moose Jaw Warriors (c)		WHL	70	29	52	81	242
1989-90—Moose Jaw Warriors		WHL	69	46	47	93	195

(c)—June, 1989—Drafted by Hartford Whalers in 1989 NHL entry draft. Fifth Whalers pick, 115th overall, sixth round.

ROBERT BEERS

Defense . . . 6'2" . . . 200 lbs. . . . Born, Cheektowaga, N.Y., May 20, 1967 . . . Shoots right . . . (May 9, 1990)—Broke right leg when checked by Tim Bergland vs. Washington.

Year	Team	League	Games	G.	A.	Pts.	Pen.
1985-86—Northern Arizona Univ. (c)		Ind.	28	11	39	50	96
1986-87—Univ. of Maine		H. East	38	0	13	13	46
1987-88—Univ. of Maine		H. East	41	3	11	14	72
1988-89—Univ. of Maine (b-d)		H. East	44	10	27	37	53
1989-90—Maine Mariners		AHL	74	7	36	43	63
1989-90—Boston Bruins		NHL	3	0	1	1	6
NHL TOTALS			3	0	1	1	6

(c)—June, 1985—Drafted by Boston Bruins in 1985 NHL entry draft. Tenth Bruins pick, 220th overall, 11th round.
(d)—Named Second team All-America (East).

BRUCE BELL

Defense . . . 5'11" . . . 195 lbs. . . . Born, Toronto, Ont., February 15, 1965 . . . Shoots left.

Year	Team	League	Games	G.	A.	Pts.	Pen.
1981-82—Sault Ste. Marie Greyhounds		OHL	67	11	18	29	63
1982-83—Sault Ste. Marie Greyhounds		OHL	5	0	2	2	2
1982-83—Windsor Spitfires (c)		OHL	61	10	35	45	39
1983-84—Brantford Alexanders		OHL	63	7	41	48	55
1984-85—Quebec Nordiques		NHL	75	6	31	37	44
1985-86—St. Louis Blues (d)		NHL	75	2	18	20	43
1986-87—St. Louis Blues (e)		NHL	45	3	13	16	18
1987-88—Colorado Rangers		IHL	65	11	34	45	107
1987-88—New York Rangers (f)		NHL	13	1	2	3	8
1988-89—Rapperswill		Switzerland	..	..	..	..	..
1988-89—Halifax Citadels (g)		AHL	12	1	2	3	29
1988-89—Adirondack Red Wings		AHL	9	1	4	5	4
1989-90—Edmonton Oilers		NHL	1	0	0	0	0
1989-90—Cape Breton Oilers		AHL	52	8	26	34	64
NHL TOTALS			209	12	64	76	113

(c)—June, 1983—Drafted by Quebec Nordiques in NHL entry draft. Second Nordiques pick, 52nd overall, third round.
(d)—October, 1985—Traded by Quebec Nordiques to St. Louis Blues for Gilbert Delorme.
(e)—June, 1987—Traded with fourth-round 1988 draft pick and future considerations by St. Louis Blues to New York Rangers for Tony McKegney and Rob Whistle.
(f)—August, 1988—Traded with Walt Poddubny, Jari Gronstrand and fourth-round draft choice in 1989 by New York Rangers to Quebec Nordiques for Normand Rochefort and Jason Lafreniere.
(g)—December 20, 1988—Claimed on waivers by Detroit Red Wings.

BRIAN BELLEFEUILLE

Left Wing . . . 6'2" . . . 185 lbs. . . . Born, Natick, Mass., March 21, 1967 . . . Shoots left.

Year	Team	League	Games	G.	A.	Pts.	Pen.
1984-85—Framingham North H.S.		Mass. H.S.	20	35	26	61	..
1985-86—Canterbury H.S. (c)		Mass. H.S.	31	57	58	115	..
1986-87—Univ. of Ill./Chicago		CCHA	2	0	0	0	2
1987-88—University of Maine		H. East	15	2	2	4	30
1988-89—University of Maine		H. East	36	5	10	15	32
1989-90—University of Maine		H. East	42	13	10	23	86
1989-90—Newmarket Saints		AHL	3	0	0	0	0

(c)—June, 1986—Drafted by Toronto Maple Leafs in 1986 NHL entry draft. Ninth Maple Leafs pick, 174th overall, ninth round.

BRIAN BELLOWS

Left Wing . . . 6' . . . 196 lbs. . . . Born, St. Catharines, Ont., September 1, 1964 . . . Shoots right . . . Also plays Center and Right Wing . . . (November, 1981)—Separated shoulder at Niagara Falls. Coached two games while recovering to become the youngest coach in OHL history (17) . . . (January, 1984)—Became youngest team captain in

Minnesota North Stars history . . . (October, 1984)—Tendinitis in elbow . . . (October, 1986)—Missed 13 games with an injured wrist . . . (February, 1989)—Missed last six weeks of the season due to strained abdominal muscles.

Year	Team	League	Games	G.	A.	Pts.	Pen.
1980-81—Kitchener Rangers		OHL	66	49	67	116	23
1981-82—Kitchener Rangers (a-c)		OHL	47	45	52	97	23
1982-83—Minnesota North Stars		NHL	78	35	30	65	27
1983-84—Minnesota North Stars		NHL	78	41	42	83	66
1984-85—Minnesota North Stars		NHL	78	26	36	62	72
1985-86—Minnesota North Stars		NHL	77	31	48	79	46
1986-87—Minnesota North Stars		NHL	65	26	27	53	54
1987-88—Minnesota North Stars		NHL	77	40	41	81	81
1988-89—Minnesota North Stars		NHL	60	23	27	50	55
1989-90—Minnesota North Stars (b)		NHL	80	55	44	99	72
NHL TOTALS			593	277	295	572	473

(c)—June, 1982—Drafted as underage junior by Minnesota North Stars in NHL entry draft. First North Stars pick, second overall, first round.

ETIENNE BELZILE

Defense . . . 6'1" . . . 180 lbs. . . . Born, Quebec City, Que., May 2, 1972 . . . Shoots left.

Year	Team	League	Games	G.	A.	Pts.	Pen.
1985-86—Jonquiere Orioles Pee Wees		Quebec	30	1	9	10	28
1986-87—Jonquiere Bantam '74		Quebec	27	2	8	10	18
1987-88—Jonquiere Bantam '74		Quebec	34	6	21	27	40
1988-89—Saguenay Cascades		Que. Midget	42	1	11	12	58
1989-90—Cornell University (c)		ECAC	28	1	4	5	18

(c)—June 16, 1989—Selected by Calgary Flames in 1990 NHL entry draft. Fourth Flames pick, 41st overall, second round.

ADAM BENNETT

Defense . . . 6'4" . . . 205 lbs. . . . Born, Georgetown, Ont., March 30, 1971 . . . Shoots right . . . (1987-88)—Separated both shoulders.

Year	Team	League	Games	G.	A.	Pts.	Pen.
1987-88—Georgetown Geminis		OHA	32	9	31	40	63
1988-89—Sudbury Wolves (c)		OHL	66	7	22	29	133
1989-90—Sudbury Wolves		OHL	65	18	43	61	116

(c)—June, 1989—Drafted by Chicago Black Hawks in 1989 NHL entry draft. First Black Hawks pick, sixth overall, first round.

ERIC (RICK) BENNETT

Left Wing . . . 6'3" . . . 200 lbs. . . . Born, Springfield, Mass., July 24, 1967 . . . Shoots left . . . (January 24, 1990)—Surgery to left knee.

Year	Team	League	Games	G.	A.	Pts.	Pen.
1985-86—Wilbraham Monson Acad. (c)		Mass. H.S.	20	30	39	69	25
1986-87—Providence College		H. East	32	15	12	27	34
1987-88—Providence College		H. East	33	9	16	25	70
1988-89—Providence College (d-e)		H. East	32	14	32	46	74
1989-90—Providence College (b)		H. East	31	12	24	36	74
1989-90—New York Rangers		NHL	6	1	0	1	5
NHL TOTALS			6	1	0	1	5

(c)—June, 1986—Drafted by Minnesota North Stars in 1986 NHL entry draft. Fourth North Stars pick, 54th overall, third round.
(d)—October 11, 1988—NHL rights traded with Brian Lawton and Igor Liba by Minnesota North Stars to New York Rangers for Mark Tinordi, Paul Jerrard, Mike Sullivan, Bret Barnett and the Los Angeles Kings third-round 1989 draft pick (Murray Garbutt).
(e)—Named Second team All-America (East).

BRIAN BENNING

Defense . . . 6' . . . 175 lbs. . . . Born, Edmonton, Alta., June 10, 1966 . . . Shoots left . . . Brother of Jim Benning . . . (December, 1983)—Cracked bone in his right wrist and missed 38 games . . . (December 28, 1984)—Broke right leg vs. Victoria . . . (March 6, 1990)—Missed three weeks following an appendectomy.

Year	Team	League	Games	G.	A.	Pts.	Pen.
1983-84—Portland Winter Hawks (c)		WHL	38	6	41	47	108
1984-85—Kamloops Blazers		WHL	17	3	18	21	26
1984-85—St. Louis Blues		NHL	4	0	2	2	0
1985-86—Team Canada		Int'l	60	6	13	19	43
1985-86—St. Louis Blues (d)		NHL	..	..	..	..	..
1986-87—St. Louis Blues		NHL	78	13	36	49	110
1987-88—St. Louis Blues		NHL	77	8	29	37	107
1988-89—St. Louis Blues		NHL	66	8	26	34	102
1989-90—St. Louis Blues (e)		NHL	7	1	1	2	2
1989-90—Los Angeles Kings		NHL	48	5	18	23	104
NHL TOTALS			280	35	112	147	425

(c)—June, 1984—Drafted as underage junior by St. Louis Blues in NHL entry draft. First Blues pick, 26th overall, second round.
(d)—No regular season record. Played six playoff games.
(e)—November 10, 1989—Traded by St. Louis Blues to Los Angeles Kings for a third-round 1991 draft pick.

JAMES BENNING

Defense . . . 6' . . . 183 lbs. . . . Born, Edmonton, Alta., April 29, 1963 . . . Shoots left . . . Brother of Brian Benning . . . (February 8, 1986)—Injured ligaments in right knee vs. St. Louis . . . (January, 1988)—Injured back.

Year	Team	League	Games	G.	A.	Pts.	Pen.
1978-79—Ft. Saskatchewan Traders		AJHL	45	14	57	71	10
1979-80—Portland Winter Hawks		WHL	71	11	60	71	42
1980-81—Portland Winter Hawks (a-c-d)		WHL	72	28	*111	139	61

Year	Team	League	Games	G.	A.	Pts.	Pen.
1981-82—Toronto Maple Leafs		NHL	74	7	24	31	46
1982-83—Toronto Maple Leafs		NHL	74	5	17	22	47
1983-84—Toronto Maple Leafs		NHL	79	12	39	51	66
1984-85—Toronto Maple Leafs		NHL	80	9	35	44	55
1985-86—Toronto Maple Leafs		NHL	52	4	21	25	71
1986-87—Newmarket Saints		AHL	10	1	5	6	0
1986-87—Toronto Maple Leafs (e)		NHL	5	0	0	0	4
1986-87—Vancouver Canucks		NHL	54	2	11	13	40
1987-88—Vancouver Canucks		NHL	77	7	26	33	58
1988-89—Vancouver Canucks		NHL	65	3	9	12	48
1989-90—Vancouver Canucks		NHL	45	3	9	12	26
NHL TOTALS			605	52	191	243	461

(c)—Winner of WHL Top Defenseman Trophy.

(d)—June, 1981—Drafted as underage junior by Toronto Maple Leafs in NHL entry draft. First Toronto pick, sixth overall, first round.

(e)—December, 1986—Traded with Dan Hodgson by Toronto Maple Leafs to Vancouver Canucks for Rick Lanz.

PAUL BERALDO

Right Wing . . . 6' . . . 180 lbs. . . . Born, Stoney Creek, Ont., October 5, 1967 . . . Shoots right.

Year	Team	League	Games	G.	A.	Pts.	Pen.
1984-85—Grimsby Jr.B.		OHA	25	9	4	13	24
1985-86—Sault Ste. Marie Greyhounds (c)		OHL	61	15	13	28	48
1986-87—Sault Ste. Marie Greyhounds		OHL	63	39	51	90	117
1987-88—Maine Mariners		AHL	62	22	15	37	112
1987-88—Boston Bruins		NHL	3	0	0	0	0
1988-89—Boston Bruins		NHL	7	0	0	0	4
1988-89—Maine Mariners		AHL	73	25	28	53	134
1989-90—Maine Mariners		AHL	51	14	27	41	31
1989-90—Canadian National Team		Int'l.	9	2	8	10	10
NHL TOTALS			10	0	0	0	4

(c)—June, 1986—Drafted as underage junior by Boston Bruins in 1986 NHL entry draft. Sixth Bruins pick, 139th overall, seventh round.

DRAKE BEREHOWSKY

Defense . . .6'1'' . . . 210 lbs. . . . Born, Toronto, Ont., January 3, 1972 . . . Shoots right . . . (October 13, 1989)—Smashed knees with Wade Bartley vs. Sudbury, had extensive reconstructive surgery and missed remainder of season.

Year	Team	League	Games	G.	A.	Pts.	Pen.
1987-88—Barrie Flyers		OHA	40	10	36	46	81
1988-89—Kingston Frontenacs		OHL	63	7	39	46	85
1989-90—Kingston Frontenacs (c)		OHL	9	3	11	14	28

(c)—June 16, 1990—Selected by Toronto Maple Leafs in 1990 NHL entry draft. First Maple Leafs pick, 10th overall, first round.

PERRY BEREZAN

Center . . . 6'2'' . . . 190 lbs. . . . Born, Edmonton, Alta., December 5, 1964 . . . Shoots right . . . (February, 1986)—Missed eight games with sinus problems . . . (March 19, 1986)—Broke ankle vs. Minnesota . . . (November, 1986)—Injured groin . . . (March, 1987)—Surgery for groin injury . . . (November, 1987)—Injured groin . . . (February, 1988)—Hand laceration . . . (October, 1989)—Concussion . . . (December 18, 1989)—Sprained ankle in team practice and missed eight games . . . (March, 1990)—Broken nose.

Year	Team	League	Games	G.	A.	Pts.	Pen.
1981-82—St. Albert Saints		AJHL	47	16	36	52	47
1982-83—St. Albert Saints (c)		AJHL	57	37	40	77	110
1983-84—Univ. of North Dakota		WCHA	44	28	24	52	29
1984-85—Univ. of North Dakota		WCHA	42	23	35	58	32
1984-85—Calgary Flames		NHL	9	3	2	5	4
1985-86—Calgary Flames		NHL	55	12	21	33	39
1986-87—Calgary Flames		NHL	24	5	3	8	24
1987-88—Calgary Flames		NHL	29	7	12	19	66
1988-89—Calgary Flames (d)		NHL	35	4	4	8	21
1988-89—Minnesota North Stars		NHL	16	1	4	5	4
1989-90—Minnesota North Stars		NHL	64	3	12	15	31
NHL TOTALS			232	35	58	93	189

(c)—June, 1983—Drafted as underage junior by Calgary Flames in NHL entry draft. Third Flames pick, 55th overall, third round.

(d)—March 4, 1989—Traded with Shane Churla by Calgary Flames to Minnesota North Stars for Brian MacLellan and a fourth-round 1989 draft pick (Robert Reichel).

BOB BERG

Left Wing . . . 6'2'' . . . 190 lbs. . . . Born, Beamsville, Ont., July 2, 1970 . . . Shoots left . . . Brother of Bill Berg.

Year	Team	League	Games	G.	A.	Pts.	Pen.
1986-87—Grimsby		OHA	36	13	16	29	115
1987-88—Belleville Bulls		OHL	61	15	27	42	59
1988-89—Belleville Bulls		OHL	66	33	51	84	88
1989-90—Belleville Bulls (a-c)		OHL	66	48	49	97	124

(c)—June 16, 1990—Selected by Los Angeles Kings in 1990 NHL entry draft. Third Kings pick, 49th overall, third round.

WILLIAM (BILL) BERG

Defense . . . 6' . . . 190 lbs. . . . Born, St. Catharines, Ont., October 21, 1967 . . . Shoots left . . . (March, 1985)—Broken ankle . . . (October, 1986)—Injured knee . . . (January, 1990)—Moved from Defense to Left Wing for the remainder of the season . . . (May, 1990)—Separated shoulder vs. Rochester . . . Brother of Bob Berg.

Year	Team	League	Games	G.	A.	Pts.	Pen.
1984-85—Grimsby Jr. B		OHA	42	10	22	32	153

Year	Team	League	Games	G.	A.	Pts.	Pen.
1985-86—Toronto Marlboros (c)		OHL	64	3	35	38	143
1986-87—Toronto Marlboros		OHL	57	3	15	18	138
1986-87—Springfield Indians		AHL	4	1	1	2	4
1987-88—Springfield Indians		AHL	76	6	26	32	148
1988-89—New York Islanders		NHL	7	1	2	3	10
1988-89—Springfield Indians		AHL	69	17	32	49	122
1989-90—Springfield Indians		AHL	74	12	42	54	74
NHL TOTALS			7	1	2	3	10

(c)—June, 1986—Drafted as underage junior by New York Islanders in 1986 NHL entry draft. Third Islanders pick, 59th overall, third round.

MIKE BERGER

Defense . . . 6'1'' . . . 197 lbs. . . . Born, Edmonton, Alta., June 2, 1967 . . . Shoots right . . . (November, 1983)—Separated shoulder . . . (January, 1985)—Hyperextended left knee . . . (October, 1985)—Shoulder injury . . . (September, 1987)—Injured in Minnesota training camp . . . (October 27, 1988)—Bruised foot . . . (January 27, 1989)—Tied IHL record for fastest opening goal when he scored five seconds into a game at Flint.

Year	Team	League	Games	G.	A.	Pts.	Pen.
1983-84—Lethbridge Broncos		WHL	41	2	9	11	60
1984-85—Lethbridge Broncos (c)		WHL	58	9	31	40	85
1985-86—Lethbridge Broncos		WHL	21	2	9	11	39
1985-86—Spokane Chiefs (b)		WHL	36	7	31	38	56
1986-87—Spokane Chiefs (b)		WHL	65	26	49	75	80
1986-87—Indianapolis Checkers		IHL	4	0	3	3	4
1987-88—Kalamazoo Wings		IHL	36	5	10	15	94
1987-88—Minnesota North Stars		NHL	29	3	1	4	65
1988-89—Kalamazoo Wings		IHL	67	9	16	25	96
1988-89—Minnesota North Stars		NHL	1	0	0	0	2
1989-90—Binghamton Whalers (d)		AHL	10	0	4	4	10
1989-90—Phoenix Roadrunners		IHL	51	5	12	17	75
NHL TOTALS			30	3	1	4	67

(c)—June, 1985—Drafted as underage junior by Minnesota North Stars in NHL entry draft. Second North Stars pick, 69th overall, fourth round.

(d)—October 7, 1989—Traded by Minnesota North Stars to Hartford Whalers for Kevin Sullivan.

PHILIP BERGER

Left Wing . . . 6' . . . 190 lbs. . . . Born, Dearborn, Mich., December 3, 1966 . . . Shoots left . . . Set WCHA record for hat tricks in one season (seven in 1987-88).

Year	Team	League	Games	G.	A.	Pts.	Pen.
1985-86—Northern Michigan Univ.		WCHA	21	5	2	7	20
1986-87—Northern Michigan Univ.		WCHA	24	11	10	21	6
1987-88—Northern Michigan Univ. (a-c-d)		WCHA	38	*40	32	72	22
1988-89—Northern Michigan Univ. (b)		WCHA	44	*30	33	*63	24
1989-90—Greensboro Monarchs (e)		ECHL	46	38	44	82	119
1989-90—Fort Wayne Komets		IHL	3	2	2	4	2

(c)—Named to Second Team All-America (West).

(d)—June, 1988—Selected by Quebec Nordiques in 1988 supplemental draft.

(e)—Led ECHL playoffs with 11 goals.

MARC BERGEVIN

Defense . . . 6' . . . 185 lbs. . . . Born, Montreal, Que., August 11, 1965 . . . Shoots left . . . (March 18, 1987)—Sprained neck at Toronto . . . (November 25, 1989)—Bruised ribs vs. Edmonton . . . (May, 1990)—Broke hand vs. Rochester.

Year	Team	League	Games	G.	A.	Pts.	Pen.
1982-83—Chicoutimi Sagueneens (c)		QMJHL	64	3	27	30	113
1983-84—Chicoutimi Sagueneens		QMJHL	70	10	35	45	125
1983-84—Springfield Indians		AHL	7	0	1	1	2
1984-85—Chicago Black Hawks		NHL	60	0	6	6	54
1985-86—Chicago Black Hawks		NHL	71	7	7	14	60
1986-87—Chicago Black Hawks		NHL	66	4	10	14	66
1987-88—Chicago Black Hawks		NHL	58	1	6	7	85
1987-88—Saginaw Hawks		IHL	10	2	7	9	20
1988-89—Chicago Black Hawks (d)		NHL	11	0	0	0	18
1988-89—New York Islanders		NHL	58	2	13	15	62
1989-90—New York Islanders		NHL	18	0	4	4	30
1989-90—Springfield Indians		AHL	47	7	16	23	66
NHL TOTALS			342	14	46	60	375

(c)—June, 1983—Drafted as underage junior by Chicago Black Hawks in NHL entry draft. Third Black Hawks pick, 59th overall, third round.

(d)—November 25, 1988—Traded with Gary Nylund by Chicago Black Hawks to New York Islanders for Steve Konroyd and Bob Bassen.

TIMOTHY BERGLUND

Center . . . 6'3'' . . . 180 lbs. . . . Born, Crookston, Minn., January 11, 1965 . . . Shoots right.

Year	Team	League	Games	G.	A.	Pts.	Pen.
1982-83—Lincoln High School (c)		Minn. H.S.	20	26	22	48	....
1983-84—Univ. of Minnesota		WCHA	24	4	11	15	4
1984-85—Univ. of Minnesota		WCHA	46	7	12	19	16
1985-86—Univ. of Minnesota		WCHA	48	11	16	27	26
1986-87—Univ. of Minnesota		WCHA	49	18	17	35	48
1987-88—Fort Wayne Komets		IHL	13	2	1	3	9
1987-88—Binghamton Whalers		AHL	63	21	26	47	31
1988-89—Baltimore Skipjacks		AHL	78	24	29	53	39
1989-90—Baltimore Skipjacks		AHL	47	12	19	31	55
1989-90—Washington Capitals		NHL	32	2	5	7	31
NHL TOTALS			32	2	5	7	31

(c)—June, 1983—Drafted by Washington Capitals as underage junior in NHL entry draft. First Capitals pick, 75th overall, fourth round.

JONAS BERGQVIST

Right Wing . . . 6' . . . 183 lbs. . . . Born, Hassleholm, Sweden, September 26, 1962 . . . Shoots left.

Year	Team	League	Games	G.	A.	Pts.	Pen.
1987-88—Leksland (c)	Sweden	37	19	12	31	....
1988-89—Leksland	Sweden	27	15	20	35	18
1989-90—Calgary Flames	NHL	21	1	5	6	8
1989-90—Salt Lake Golden Eagles (d)	IHL	13	6	10	16	4
NHL TOTALS		21	1	5	6	8

(c)—June, 1988—Drafted by Calgary Flames in 1988 NHL entry draft. Sixth Flames pick, 126th overall, sixth round.

(d)—April 28, 1990—Assigned to Mannheim of the German Hockey League.

LARRY BERNARD

Left Wing . . . 6'2" . . . 195 lbs. . . . Born, Prince George, B. C., April 16, 1967 . . . Shoots left . . . (January 26, 1990)—Suspended five AHL games for getting into a stick fight with Max Middendorf while both were in the penalty box vs. Halifax.

Year	Team	League	Games	G.	A.	Pts.	Pen.
1984-85—Seattle Thunderbirds (c)	WHL	63	18	26	44	66
1985-86—Seattle Thunderbirds	WHL	54	17	25	42	72
1986-87—Seattle Thunderbirds	WHL	70	40	46	86	159
1987-88—Colorado Rangers	IHL	64	14	13	27	68
1988-89—Denver Rangers (d)	IHL	21	4	5	9	44
1988-89—Kalamazoo Wings	IHL	45	9	16	25	47
1989-90—Moncton Hawks (e)	AHL	66	14	17	31	93

(c)—June, 1985—Drafted by New York Rangers in 1985 NHL entry draft. Eighth Rangers pick, 154th overall, eighth round.

(d)—December 10, 1988—Traded with a fifth-round 1989 draft pick (Rhys Hollyman) by New York Rangers to Minnesota North Stars for Mark Hardy.

(e)—October, 1989—Signed by Winnipeg Jets as a free agent.

BRAD BERRY

Defense . . . 6'2" . . . 190 lbs. . . . Born, Barshaw, Alta., April 1, 1965 . . . Shoots left . . . (November 9, 1987)—Broken nose.

Year	Team	League	Games	G.	A.	Pts.	Pen.
1982-83—St. Albert Junior Saints (c)	AJHL	55	9	33	42	97
1983-84—Univ. of North Dakota	WCHA	32	2	7	9	8
1984-85—Univ. of North Dakota	WCHA	40	4	26	30	26
1985-86—Univ. of North Dakota	WCHA	40	6	29	35	26
1985-86—Winnipeg Jets	NHL	13	1	0	1	10
1986-87—Winnipeg Jets	NHL	52	2	8	10	60
1987-88—Winnipeg Jets	NHL	48	0	6	6	75
1987-88—Moncton Golden Flames	AHL	10	1	3	4	14
1988-89—Moncton Hawks	AHL	38	3	16	19	39
1988-89—Winnipeg Jets	NHL	38	0	9	9	45
1989-90—Moncton Hawks	AHL	38	1	9	10	58
1989-90—Winnipeg Jets	NHL	12	1	2	3	6
NHL TOTALS		163	4	25	29	196

(c)—June, 1983—Drafted as underage junior by Winnipeg Jets in NHL entry draft. Third Jets pick, 29th overall, second round.

CRAIG BERUBE

Left Wing . . . 6'2" . . . 195 lbs. . . . Born, Calihoo, Alta., December 17, 1965 . . . Shoots left . . . (March, 1988)—Sprained left knee.

Year	Team	League	Games	G.	A.	Pts.	Pen.
1982-83—Kamloops Junior Oilers	WHL	4	0	0	0	0
1983-84—New Westminster Bruins	WHL	70	11	20	31	104
1984-85—New Westminster Bruins	WHL	70	25	44	69	191
1985-86—Kamloops Blazers	WHL	32	17	14	31	119
1985-86—Medicine Hat Tigers (c)	WHL	34	14	16	30	95
1986-87—Hershey Bears	AHL	63	7	17	24	325
1986-87—Philadelphia Flyers	NHL	7	0	0	0	57
1987-88—Hershey Bears	AHL	31	5	9	14	119
1987-88—Philadelphia Flyers	NHL	27	3	2	5	108
1988-89—Hershey Bears	AHL	7	0	2	2	19
1988-89—Philadelphia Flyers	NHL	53	1	1	2	199
1989-90—Philadelphia Flyers	NHL	74	4	14	18	291
NHL TOTALS		161	8	17	25	655

(c)—March, 1986—Signed as free agent by Philadelphia Flyers.

JEFF BEUKEBOOM

Defense . . . 6'4" . . . 210 lbs. . . . Born, Ajax, Ont., March 28, 1965 . . . Shoots right . . . Brother of John and Brian Beukeboom and nephew of Ed Kea (Atlanta/St. Louis, '73-'83) . . . First non-goalie to be drafted in first round not to have scored a goal in season prior to being drafted . . . (December, 1984)—Injured knee in World Junior Tournament vs. United States . . . (October 24, 1987)—Lacerated knuckle vs. Vancouver . . . (October 2, 1988)—Suspended 10 NHL games for leaving the bench in a pre-season game at Calgary . . . (January, 1989)—Sprained right knee.

Year	Team	League	Games	G.	A.	Pts.	Pen.
1981-82—Newmarket	OPJHL	49	5	30	35	218
1982-83—Sault Ste. Marie Greyhounds (c)	OHL	70	0	25	25	143
1983-84—Sault Ste. Marie Greyhounds	OHL	61	6	30	36	178
1984-85—Sault Ste. Marie Greyhounds (a)	OHL	37	4	20	24	85
1985-86—Nova Scotia Oilers	AHL	77	9	20	29	175
1985-86—Edmonton Oilers (d)	NHL	....	....	....	....	....
1986-87—Nova Scotia Voyageurs	AHL	14	1	7	8	35
1986-87—Edmonton Oilers	NHL	44	3	8	11	124
1987-88—Edmonton Oilers	NHL	73	5	20	25	201
1988-89—Cape Breton Oilers	AHL	8	0	4	4	36

Year	Team	League	Games	G.	A.	Pts.	Pen.
1988-89—Edmonton Oilers	NHL	36	0	5	5	94
1989-90—Edmonton Oilers	NHL	46	1	12	13	86
NHL TOTALS		199	9	45	54	505

(c)—June, 1983—Drafted as underage junior by Edmonton Oilers in NHL entry draft. First Oilers pick, 19th overall, first round.

(d)—No regular season record. Played one playoff game.

DON BIGGS

Center . . . 5'8" . . . 180 lbs. . . . Born, Mississauga, Ont., April 7, 1965 . . . Shoots right . . . (April, 1982)—Injured knee ligaments . . . (December 16, 1989)—Suspended five AHL games for biting Jim Culhane vs. Binghamton.

Year	Team	League	Games	G.	A.	Pts.	Pen.
1981-82—Mississauga Reds	MTHL	54	49	67	116	125
1982-83—Oshawa Generals (c)	OHL	70	22	53	75	145
1983-84—Oshawa Generals	OHL	58	31	60	91	149
1984-85—Oshawa Generals	OHL	60	48	69	117	105
1984-85—Springfield Indians	AHL	6	0	3	3	0
1984-85—Minnesota North Stars	NHL	1	0	0	0	0
1985-86—Springfield Indians (d)	AHL	28	15	16	31	46
1985-86—Nova Scotia Oilers	AHL	47	6	23	29	36
1986-87—Nova Scotia Oilers (e)	AHL	80	22	25	47	165
1987-88—Hershey Bears	AHL	77	38	41	79	151
1988-89—Hershey Bears	AHL	76	36	67	103	158
1989-90—Philadelphia Flyers	NHL	11	2	0	2	8
1989-90—Hershey Bears (f)	AHL	66	39	53	92	125
NHL TOTALS		12	2	0	2	8

(c)—June, 1983—Drafted as underage junior by Minnesota North Stars in NHL entry draft. Ninth North Stars pick, 156th overall, eighth round.

(d)—December, 1985—Traded with Gord Sherven by Minnesota North Stars to Edmonton Oilers for Marc Habscheid, Emanuel Viveiros and Don Barber.

(e)—July, 1987—Signed as free agent by Philadelphia Flyers.

(f)—May, 1990—Signed to play with Olten (Switzerland) for 1990-91.

LAURIE BILLECK

Defense . . . 6'3" . . . 205 lbs. . . . Born, Dolphin, Man., July 2, 1971 . . . Shoots right . . . (September, 1989)—Shoulder injury.

Year	Team	League	Games	G.	A.	Pts.	Pen.
1988-89—Prince Albert Raiders	WHL	60	2	4	6	65
1989-90—Prince Albert Raiders (c)	WHL	67	7	28	35	135

(c)—June 16, 1990—Selected by Minnesota North Stars in 1990 NHL entry draft. Second North Stars pick, 50th overall, third round.

CHRIS BIOTTI

Defense . . . 6'3" . . . 198 lbs. . . . Born, Waltham, Mass., April 22, 1967 . . . Shoots left . . . (August, 1985)—Injured knee during U.S. Sports festival and required major reconstructive surgery.

Year	Team	League	Games	G.	A.	Pts.	Pen.
1983-84—Belmont Hill H.S.	Mass. H.S.	23	10	20	30	....
1984-85—Belmont Hill H.S. (c)	Mass. H.S.	23	13	24	37	....
1985-86—Harvard University	ECAC	15	3	5	8	53
1986-87—Harvard University	ECAC	30	1	6	7	23
1987-88—Salt Lake Golden Eagles	IHL	72	5	19	24	73
1988-89—Salt Lake Golden Eagles	IHL	57	6	14	20	44
1989-90—Salt Lake Golden Eagles	IHL	60	9	19	28	73

(c)—June, 1985—Drafted by Calgary Flames in 1985 NHL entry draft. First Flames pick, 17th overall, first round.

GRANT BISCHOFF

Left Wing . . . 5'10" . . . 165 lbs. . . . Born, Anoka, Minn., October 26, 1968 . . . Shoots left . . . (March, 1986)—Broken thumb.

Year	Team	League	Games	G.	A.	Pts.	Pen.
1986-87—Grand Rapids H.S.	Minn. H.S.	23	26	31	57	....
1987-88—Univ. of Minnesota (c)	WCHA	40	14	22	36	14
1988-89—Univ. of Minnesota	WCHA	47	21	16	37	14
1989-90—Univ. of Minnesota	WCHA	45	21	19	40	18

(c)—June, 1988—Drafted by Minnesota North Stars in 1988 entry draft. Eighth North Stars pick, 211th overall, 11th round.

MICHAEL BISHOP

Defense . . . 6'2" . . . 187 lbs. . . . Born, Sarnia, Ont., June 15, 1966 . . . Shoots left . . . (December, 1986)—Knee surgery . . . (October, 1987)—Fractured wrist in ECAC pre-season game.

Year	Team	League	Games	G.	A.	Pts.	Pen.
1983-84—Mooretown Flags Jr. C	OHA	40	24	24	48	91
1984-85—Sarnia Bees Jr. B (c)	OHA	43	9	32	41	104
1985-86—Colgate University	ECAC	25	9	8	17	63
1986-87—Colgate University	ECAC	30	7	17	24	68
1987-88—Colgate University	ECAC	31	8	24	32	49
1988-89—Colgate University (b)	ECAC	31	8	13	21	92
1989-90—Fort Wayne Komets	IHL	12	0	0	0	6
1989-90—Knoxville Cherokees	ECHL	39	3	9	12	28

(c)—June, 1985—Drafted as underage junior by Montreal Canadiens in 1985 NHL entry draft. Fourteenth Canadiens pick, 226th overall, 11th round.

SCOTT BJUGSTAD

Left Wing . . . 6'1" . . . 185 lbs. . . . Born St. Paul, Minn., June 2, 1961 . . . Shoots left . . . 1979 graduate of Minnesota Irondale High School where he was All-Conference for three years and All-State as a senior . . . Named prep All-America in Soccer . . . Member of 1984 U.S. Olympic Team . . . Also plays Center. . . . (March 15,

1987)—Pulled abdominal muscle at Chicago . . . (October 31, 1987)—Separated shoulder vs. Washington . . . (December, 1987)—Strained knee ligaments . . . (February, 1988)—Knee surgery . . . (September, 1988)—Strained left knee ligaments during Minnesota North Stars training camp . . . (October, 1989)—Injured groin . . . (April, 1990)—Sprained knee.

Year	Team	League	Games	G.	A.	Pts.	Pen.
1979-80—University of Minnesota		WCHA	18	2	2	4	2
1980-81—University of Minnesota (c)		WCHA	35	12	13	25	34
1981-82—University of Minnesota		WCHA	36	29	14	43	24
1982-83—University of Minnesota		WCHA	44	43	48	91	30
1983-84—U.S. National Team		Int'l	54	31	20	51	28
1983-84—U.S. Olympic Team		Int'l	6	3	2	5	6
1983-84—Minnesota North Stars		NHL	5	0	0	0	2
1983-84—Salt Lake Golden Eagles		CHL	15	10	8	18	6
1984-85—Minnesota North Stars		NL	72	11	4	15	32
1984-85—Springfield Indians		AHL	5	2	3	5	2
1985-86—Minnesota North Stars		NHL	80	43	33	76	24
1986-87—Minnesota North Stars		NHL	39	4	9	13	43
1986-87—Springfield Indians		AHL	11	6	4	10	7
1987-88—Minnesota North Stars		NHL	33	10	12	22	15
1988-89—Geneva		Switzerland	....	...	....	....	....
1988-89—Pittsburgh Penguins (d-e)		NHL	24	3	0	3	4
1988-89—Kalamazoo Wings (f)		IHL	4	5	0	5	4
1989-90—New Haven Nighthawks		AHL	47	45	21	66	40
1989-90—Los Angeles Kings		NHL	11	1	2	3	2
NHL TOTALS			264	72	60	132	122

(c)—June, 1981—Drafted by Minnesota North Stars in NHL entry draft. Thirteenth North Stars pick, 181st overall, ninth round.

(d)—December 17, 1988—Traded with Gord Dineen by Minnesota North Stars to Pittsburgh Penguins for Ville Siren and Steve Gotaas.

(e)—March 10, 1989—Suspended by Pittsburgh Penguins for refusing to report to Muskegon Lumberjacks (IHL).

(f)—August, 1989—Signed by Los Angeles Kings as a free agent.

JAMES BLACK

Center . . . 5'11" . . . 185 lbs. . . . Born, Regina, Sask., August 15, 1969 . . . Shoots left.

Year	Team	League	Games	G.	A.	Pts.	Pen.
1987-88—Portland Winter Hawks		WHL	72	30	50	80	50
1988-89—Portland Winter Hawks (c)		WHL	71	45	51	96	57
1989-90—Hartford Whalers		NHL	1	0	0	0	0
1989-90—Binghamton Whalers		AHL	80	37	35	72	34
NHL TOTALS			1	0	0	0	0

(c)—June, 1989—Drafted by Hartford Whalers in 1989 NHL entry draft. Fourth Whalers pick, 94th overall, fifth round.

BRIAN BLAD

Defense . . . 6'2" . . . 195 lbs. . . . Born, Brockville, Ont., July 22, 1967 . . . Shoots left.

Year	Team	League	Games	G.	A.	Pts.	Pen.
1983-84—Windsor Spitfires		OHL	78	8	21	29	123
1984-85—Windsor Spitfires		OHL	56	1	7	8	126
1985-86—Windsor Spitfires		OHL	56	2	9	11	195
1986-87—Windsor Spitfires		OHL	15	1	1	2	30
1986-87—Belleville Bulls (c)		OHL	20	1	5	6	43
1987-88—Newmarket Saints		AHL	39	0	4	4	74
1987-88—Milwaukee Admirals		IHL	28	1	6	7	45
1988-89—Newmarket Saints		AHL	59	2	4	6	149
1989-90—Newmarket Saints		AHL	58	2	4	6	216

(c)—June, 1987—Drafted by Toronto Maple Leafs in 1987 NHL entry draft. Ninth Maple Leafs pick, 175th overall, ninth round.

JEFF BLAESER

Left Wing . . . 6'3" . . . 195 lbs. . . . Born, Parma, Ohio, November 5, 1970 . . . Shoots left.

Year	Team	League	Games	G.	A.	Pts.	Pen.
1986-87—St. John's Prep.		Mass. H.S.	..	15	22	37	..
1987-88—St. John's Prep. (c)		Mass. H.S.	..	14	20	34	..
1988-89—Princeton University		ECAC	26	11	19	30	26
1989-90—Yale University		ECAC	29	17	14	31	16

(c)—June, 1988—Drafted by Pittsburgh Penguins in 1988 NHL entry draft. Seventh Penguins pick, 130th overall, seventh round.

JOEL BLAIN

Left Wing . . . 6' . . . 195 lbs. . . . Born, Malartic, Que., October 12, 1971 . . . Shoots left.

Year	Team	League	Games	G.	A.	Pts.	Pen.
1986-87—Vald'or Canadiens		Que. Midget	29	19	30	49	....
1987-88—Hull Olympiques		QMJHL	51	2	7	9	25
1988-89—Hull Olympiques		QMJHL	64	14	16	30	105
1989-90—Hull Olympiques (c)		QMJHL	65	31	47	78	137

(c)—June 16, 1990—Selected by Edmonton Oilers in 1990 NHL entry draft. Fourth Oilers pick, 67th overall, fourth round.

MICHAEL WALTER BLAISDELL

Right Wing . . . 6'1" . . . 196 lbs. . . . Born, Moose Jaw, Sask., January 18, 1960 . . . Shoots right . . . (November 6, 1985)—Pulled groin vs. Washington and missed two games . . . (October 28, 1986)—Separated left shoulder at Hartford . . . (January, 1989)—Injured finger.

Year	Team	League	Games	G.	A.	Pts.	Pen.
1977-78—Regina Pats		WCHL	6	5	5	10	2
1977-78—Regina Blues		SJHL	60	70	46	116	43
1978-79—University of Wisconsin		WCHA	20	7	1	8	15
1979-80—Regina Pats (b-c)		WHL	63	71	38	109	62
1980-81—Adirondack Red Wings		AHL	41	10	4	14	8
1980-81—Detroit Red Wings		NHL	32	3	6	9	10
1981-82—Detroit Red Wings		NHL	80	23	32	55	48
1982-83—Detroit Red Wings (d)		NHL	80	18	23	41	22
1983-84—Tulsa Oilers		CHL	32	10	8	18	23
1983-84—New York Rangers		NHL	36	5	6	11	31
1984-85—New Haven Nighthawks		AHL	64	21	23	44	41
1984-85—New York Rangers		NHL	12	1	0	1	11
1985-86—Pittsburgh Penguins (e)		NHL	66	15	14	29	36
1986-87—Baltimore Skipjacks		AHL	43	12	12	24	47
1986-87—Pittsburgh Penguins		NHL	10	1	1	2	2
1987-88—Newmarket Saints		AHL	57	28	28	56	30
1987-88—Toronto Maple Leafs		NHL	18	3	2	5	2
1988-89—Toronto Maple Leafs		NHL	9	1	0	1	4
1988-89—Newmarket Saints		AHL	40	16	7	23	48
1989-90—Canadian National Team		Int'l.	50	12	18	30	40
NHL TOTALS			343	70	84	154	166

(c)—June, 1980—Drafted by Detroit Red Wings in NHL entry draft. First Red Wings pick, 11th overall, first round.

(d)—June, 1983—Traded with Mark Osborne and Willie Huber by Detroit Red Wings to New York Rangers for Ron Duguay, Eddie Johnstone and Eddie Mio.

(e)—October, 1985—Acquired by Pittsburgh Penguins in 1985 NHL waiver draft.

ROB BLAKE

Defense . . . 6'3" . . . 205 lbs. . . . Born, Simcoe, Ont., December 10, 1969 . . . Shoots right . . . (April, 1987)—Dislocated shoulder . . . (April, 1990)—Sprained knee in playoff game vs. Edmonton.

Year	Team	League	Games	G.	A.	Pts.	Pen.
1986-87—Stratford Junior B		OHA	31	11	20	31	115
1987-88—Bowling Green Univ. (c)		CCHA	36	5	8	13	72
1988-89—Bowling Green Univ. (b)		CCHA	46	11	21	32	140
1989-90—Bowling Green Univ. (a-d)		CCHA	42	23	36	59	140
1989-90—Los Angeles Kings		NHL	4	0	0	0	4
NHL TOTALS			4	0	0	0	4

(c)—June, 1988—Drafted by Los Angeles Kings in 1988 NHL entry draft. Fourth Kings pick, 70th overall, fourth round.

(d)—Named to All-America Team (West).

JEFF BLOEMBERG

Defense . . . 6'1" . . . 200 lbs. . . . Born, Listowel, Ont., January 31, 1968 . . . Shoots right.

Year	Team	League	Games	G.	A.	Pts.	Pen.
1984-85—Listowell Jr. B		OHA	31	7	14	21	73
1985-86—North Bay Centennials (c)		OHL	60	2	11	13	76
1986-87—North Bay Centennials		OHL	60	5	13	18	91
1987-88—North Bay Centennials		OHL	46	9	26	35	60
1987-88—Colorado Rangers		IHL	5	0	0	0	0
1988-89—New York Rangers		NHL	9	0	0	0	0
1988-89—Denver Rangers		AHL	64	7	22	29	55
1989-90—New York Rangers		NHL	28	3	3	6	25
1989-90—Flint Spirits		IHL	44	7	21	28	24
NHL TOTALS			37	3	3	6	25

(c)—June, 1986—Drafted as underage junior by New York Rangers in 1986 NHL entry draft. Fifth Rangers pick, 93rd overall, fifth round.

SCOTT BLOOM

Left Wing . . . 5'11" . . . 195 lbs. . . . Born, Edina, Minn., February 8, 1968 . . . Shoots left.

Year	Team	League	Games	G.	A.	Pts.	Pen.
1986-87—Univ. of Minnesota (c)		WCHA	44	6	11	17	28
1987-88—Univ. of Minnesota		WCHA	40	10	11	21	58
1988-89—Univ. of Minnesota		WCHA	19	2	5	7	22
1989-90—Univ. of Minnesota		WCHA	43	24	28	52	22

(c)—June, 1986—Drafted by Calgary Flames in 1986 NHL entry draft. Fourth Flames pick, 100th overall, fourth round.

JOHN BLUM

Defense . . . 6'3" . . . 205 lbs. . . . Born, Detroit, Mich., October 8, 1959 . . . Shoots right.

Year	Team	League	Games	G.	A.	Pts.	Pen.
1980-81—University of Michigan		WCHA	....	8	32	40	....
1981-82—Wichita Wind (c)		CHL	79	8	33	41	247
1982-83—Moncton Alpines		AHL	76	10	30	40	219
1982-83—Edmonton Oilers		NHL	5	0	3	3	24
1983-84—Moncton Alpines		AHL	57	3	22	25	202
1983-84—Edmonton Oilers (d)		NHL	4	0	1	1	2
1983-84—Boston Bruins		NHL	12	1	1	2	30
1984-85—Boston Bruins		NHL	75	3	13	16	263
1985-86—Boston Bruins		NHL	61	1	7	8	80
1985-86—Moncton Golden Flames		AHL	12	1	5	6	37
1986-87—Washington Capitals (e-f)		NHL	66	2	8	10	133
1987-88—Boston Bruins		NHL	19	0	1	1	70
1987-88—Maine Mariners (g)		AHL	43	5	18	23	136
1988-89—Adirondack Red Wings		AHL	56	1	19	20	168
1988-89—Detroit Red Wings (h)		NHL	6	0	0	0	8
1989-90—Maine Mariners		AHL	77	1	20	21	134
1989-90—Boston Bruins		NHL	2	0	0	0	0
NHL TOTALS			250	7	34	41	610

(c)—May, 1981—Signed by Edmonton Oilers as a free agent.
(d)—March, 1983—Traded by Edmonton Oilers to Boston Bruins for Larry Melnyk.
(e)—October, 1986—Selected by Washington Capitals in 1987 NHL waiver draft.
(f)—June, 1987—Traded by Washington Capitals to Boston Bruins for future considerations.
(g)—August, 1988—Signed by Detroit Red Wings as a free agent.
(h)—June, 1989—Signed by Boston Bruins as a free agent.

KENNETH BLUM

Center . . . 6'1" . . . 175 lbs. . . . Born, Hackensack, N.J., June 8, 1971 . . . Shoots left.

Year	Team	League	Games	G.	A.	Pts.	Pen.
1987-88—St. Joseph H.S.	N.J. H.S.	..	48	35	83	..
1988-89—St. Joseph H.S. (c)	N.J. H.S.	27	50	59	109	18
1989-90—Lake Superior State Univ.	CCHA	19	2	1	3	14

(c)—June, 1989—Drafted by New Jersey Devils in 1989 NHL entry draft. Tenth Devils pick, 175th overall, ninth round.

BRENT BOBYCK

Left Wing . . . 5'11" . . . 180 lbs. . . . Born, Regina, Sask., April 26, 1968 . . . Shoots left . . . (November 11, 1988)—Broken sternum vs. Wisconsin and missed a month.

Year	Team	League	Games	G.	A.	Pts.	Pen.
1985-86—Notre Dame Hounds (c)	Sask.	25	13	27	40	12
1986-87—Univ. of North Dakota	WCHA	46	8	11	19	16
1987-88—Univ. of North Dakota	WCHA	41	10	20	30	43
1988-89—Univ. of North Dakota	WCHA	28	11	8	19	16
1989-90—Univ. of North Dakota	WCHA	44	16	21	37	47

(c)—June, 1986—Drafted by Montreal Canadiens in 1986 NHL entry draft. Fourth Canadiens pick, 78th overall, fourth round.

BOB BODAK

Left Wing . . . 6'2" . . . 190 lbs. . . . Born, Thunder Bay, Ont., May 28, 1961 . . . Shoots left . . . (November, 1987)—Punctured sinus cavity.

Year	Team	League	Games	G.	A.	Pts.	Pen.
1983-84—Lakehead University	....	....	....	....	....	....
1984-85—Springfield Indians (c)	AHL	79	21	24	45	52
1985-86—Springfield Indians	AHL	4	0	0	0	4
1985-86—Moncton Golden Flames	AHL	58	27	15	42	114
1986-87—Moncton Golden Flames (d)	AHL	48	11	20	31	75
1987-88—Salt Lake Golden Eagles	IHL	44	12	10	22	117
1987-88—Calgary Flames	NHL	3	0	0	0	22
1988-89—Salt Lake Golden Eagles	IHL	4	0	0	0	2
1988-89—Binghamton Whalers	AHL	44	15	25	40	135
1989-90—Hartford Whalers	NHL	1	0	0	0	7
1989-90—Binghamton Whalers	AHL	79	32	25	57	59
NHL TOTALS		4	0	0	0	29

(c)—September, 1984—Signed by Springfield Indians as a free agent.
(d)—January, 1986—Signed by Calgary Flames as a free agent.

JAMIE BODDEN

Center . . . 5'10" . . . 180 lbs. . . . Born, Dundas, Ont., October 26, 1967 . . . Shoots right.

Year	Team	League	Games	G.	A.	Pts.	Pen.
1986-87—Chatham Jrs. (c)	SOHL	30	32	31	63	14
1987-88—Miami of Ohio Univ.	CCHA	38	10	14	24	30
1988-89—Miami of Ohio Univ.	CCHA	33	11	10	21	15
1989-90—Miami of Ohio Univ.	CCHA	38	14	23	37	10

(c)—June, 1987—Drafed by Pittsburgh Penguins in 1987 NHL entry draft. Seventh Penguins pick, 131st overall, seventh round.

DOUG BODGER

Defense . . . 6'2" . . . 200 lbs. . . . Born, Chemainus, B.C., June 18, 1966 . . . Shoots left . . . (April, 1985)—Surgery to remove bone chip near big toe of left foot . . . (December, 1987)—Sprained knee . . . (October, 1988)—Strained left knee . . . (October, 1989)—Missed eight games with sprained left knee.

Year	Team	League	Games	G.	A.	Pts.	Pen.
1982-83—Kamloops Junior Oilers (b)	WHL	72	26	66	92	98
1983-84—Kamloops Junior Oilers (a-c)	WHL	70	21	77	98	90
1984-85—Pittsburgh Penguins	NHL	65	5	26	31	67
1985-86—Pittsburgh Penguins	NHL	79	4	33	37	63
1986-87—Pittsburgh Penguins	NHL	76	11	38	49	52
1987-88—Pittsburgh Penguins	NHL	69	14	31	45	103
1988-89—Pittsburgh Penguins (d)	NHL	10	1	4	5	7
1988-89—Buffalo Sabres	NHL	61	7	40	47	52
1989-90—Buffalo Sabres	NHL	71	12	36	48	64
NHL TOTALS		431	54	208	262	408

(c)—June, 1984—Drafted as underage junior by Pittsburgh Penguins in NHL entry draft. Second Penguins pick, ninth overall, first round.
(d)—November 12, 1988—Traded with Darren Shannon by Pittsburgh Penguins to Buffalo Sabres for Tom Barrasso and a third-round 1990 draft pick.

MIKE BODNARCHUK

Right Wing . . . 6' . . . 176 lbs. . . . Born, Bramalea, Ont., March 26, 1970 . . . Shoots right.

Year	Team	League	Games	G.	A.	Pts.	Pen.
1986-87—Bramalea Blues	OHA	34	12	8	20	33
1987-88—Kingston Canadians	OHL	63	12	20	32	12
1988-89—Kingston Raiders	OHL	63	22	38	60	30
1989-90—Kingston Frontenacs (b-c)	OHL	66	40	59	99	31

(c)—June 16, 1990—Selected by New Jersey Devils in 1990 NHL entry draft. Sixth Devils pick, 64th overall, fourth round.

CLAUDE BOIVIN

Left Wing . . . 6'2" . . . 190 lbs. . . . Born, St. Foy, Que., March 1, 1970 . . . Shoots left.

Year	Team	League	Games	G.	A.	Pts.	Pen.
1986-87—Ste. Foy AAA	Que. Mdgt.	39	12	27	39	90
1987-88—Drummondville Voltigeurs (c)	QMJHL	63	23	26	49	233
1988-89—Drummondville Voltigeurs	QMJHL	63	20	36	56	218
1989-90—Laval Titans (d)	QMJHL	59	24	51	75	309

(c)—June, 1988—Drafted by Philadelphia Flyers in 1988 NHL entry draft. First Flyers pick, 14th overall, first round.
(d)—February 15, 1990—Traded with Serge Anglehart and a fifth-round draft pick by Drummondville Voltigeurs to Laval Titans for Luc Doucet, Brad MacIsaac and second and third round draft picks.

BRAD BOMBARDIR

Defense . . . 6'2" . . . 187 lbs. . . . Born, Powell River, B.C., May 5, 1972 . . . Shoots left.

Year	Team	League	Games	G.	A.	Pts.	Pen.
1989-90—Powell River Jrs. (c)	BCJHL	60	10	35	45	93

(c)—June 16, 1990—Selected by New Jersey Devils in 1990 NHL entry draft. Fifth Devils pick, 56th overall, third round.

RICHARD BORGO

Right Wing . . . 5'11" . . . 195 lbs. . . . Born, Thunder Bay, Ont., September 25, 1970 . . . Shoots right.

Year	Team	League	Games	G.	A.	Pts.	Pen.
1985-86—Thunder Bay Twins	USHL	41	11	19	30	37
1986-87—Kitchener Rangers	OHL	62	5	10	15	29
1987-88—Kitchener Rangers	OHL	64	24	22	46	81
1988-89—Kitchener Rangers (c)	OHL	66	23	23	46	75
1989-90—Kitchener Rangers	OHL	32	13	22	35	43

(c)—June, 1989—Drafted by Edmonton Oilers in 1989 NHL entry draft. Second Oilers pick, 36th overall, second round.

LUCIANO BORSATO

Center . . . 5'10" . . . 165 lbs. . . . Born, Richmond Hill, Ont., January 7, 1966 . . . Shoots right.

Year	Team	League	Games	G.	A.	Pts.	Pen.
1983-84—Bramalea Blues (c)	MTJHL	37	20	36	56	59
1984-85—Clarkson University	ECAC	33	15	17	32	37
1985-86—Clarkson University	ECAC	32	17	20	37	50
1986-87—Clarkson University	ECAC	31	16	*41	57	55
1987-88—Clarkson University (d)	ECAC	33	15	29	44	38
1987-88—Moncton Golden Flames	AHL	3	1	1	2	0
1988-89—Tappara	Finland	44	31	36	67	69
1988-89—Moncton Hawks	AHL	6	2	5	7	4
1989-90—Moncton Hawks	AHL	1	1	0	1	0

(c)—June, 1984—Drafted as underage junior by Winnipeg Jets in NHL entry draft. Seventh Jets pick, 135th overall, seventh round.
(d)—Named second-team All-America (East).

LAURIE JOSEPH BOSCHMAN

Center . . . 6' . . . 185 lbs. . . . Born, Major, Sask., June 4, 1960 . . . Shoots left . . . (December 7, 1980)—Finger tendon injury . . . (January, 1981)—Mononucleous . . . (December 7, 1983)—Dislocated shoulder at New Jersey . . . (April, 1988)—Surgery to reconstruct right shoulder . . . (October 16, 1988)—Ankle cut by a skate in Edmonton . . . (February 8, 1990)—Suspended eight games for high-sticking Tomas Sandstrom at Los Angeles.

Year	Team	League	Games	G.	A.	Pts.	Pen.
1976-77—Brandon	MJHL	47	17	40	57	139
1976-77—Brandon Wheat Kings	WCHL	3	0	1	1	0
1977-78—Brandon Wheat Kings	WCHL	72	42	57	99	227
1978-79—Brandon Wheat Kings (a-c)	WCHL	65	66	83	149	215
1979-80—Toronto Maple Leafs	NHL	80	16	32	48	78
1980-81—New Brunswick Hawks	AHL	4	4	1	5	47
1980-81—Toronto Maple Leafs	NHL	53	14	19	33	178
1981-82—Toronto Maple Leafs (d)	NHL	54	9	19	28	150
1981-82—Edmonton Oilers	NHL	11	2	3	5	37
1982-83—Edmonton Oilers (e)	NHL	62	8	12	20	183
1982-83—Winnipeg Jets	NHL	12	3	5	8	33
1983-84—Winnipeg Jets	NHL	61	28	46	74	234
1984-85—Winnipeg Jets	NHL	80	32	44	76	180
1985-86—Winnipeg Jets	NHL	77	27	42	69	241
1986-87—Winnipeg Jets	NHL	80	17	24	41	152
1987-88—Winnipeg Jets	NHL	80	25	23	48	227
1988-89—Winnipeg Jets	NHL	70	10	26	36	163
1989-90—Winnipeg Jets	NHL	66	10	17	27	103
NHL TOTALS		786	201	312	513	1959

(c)—August, 1979—Drafted by Toronto Maple Leafs in NHL entry draft. First Toronto pick, ninth overall, first round.
(d)—March, 1982—Traded by Toronto Maple Leafs to Edmonton Oilers for Walt Poddubny and Phil Drouillard.
(e)—March, 1983—Traded by Edmonton Oilers to Winnipeg Jets for Willy Lindstrom.

TIM BOTHWELL

Defense . . . 6'3" . . . 195 lbs. . . . Born, Vancouver, B.C., May 6, 1955 . . . Shoots left . . . Missed part of 1974-75 season with broken ankle . . . Missed part of 1978-79 season with fractured cheekbone that required surgery . . . (October, 1981)—Badly strained stomach muscles . . . (March 1, 1983)—Cut tendons in left hand vs. Los Angeles . . . (January, 1984)—Injured ligament in right knee during CHL game . . .

(October, 1985)—Missed seven games due to a parasitic infection caused by drinking tainted water . . . (January, 1989)—Pulled left groin.

Year	Team	League	Games	G.	A.	Pts.	Pen.
1973-74—Burlington Mohawks	.....	..	..	..	..	..	..
1974-75—Brown University JV	ECAC	9	6	9	15	14
1975-76—Brown University	ECAC	29	12	22	34	30
1976-77—Brown University (a)	ECAC	27	7	27	34	40
1977-78—Brown University (a-c)	ECAC	29	9	26	35	48
1978-79—New York Rangers	NHL	1	0	0	0	2
1978-79—New Haven Nighthawks	AHL	66	15	33	48	44
1979-80—New Haven Nighthawks	AHL	22	6	7	13	25
1979-80—New York Rangers	NHL	45	4	6	10	20
1980-81—New Haven Nighthawks	AHL	73	10	53	63	98
1980-81—New York Rangers	NHL	3	0	1	1	0
1981-82—Springfield Indians	AHL	10	0	4	4	7
1981-82—New York Rangers (d)	NHL	13	0	3	3	10
1982-83—St. Louis Blues	NHL	61	4	11	15	34
1983-84—Montana Magic	CHL	4	0	3	3	0
1983-84—St. Louis Blues	NHL	62	2	13	15	65
1984-85—St. Louis Blues	NHL	79	4	22	26	62
1985-86—Hartford Whalers (e)	NHL	62	2	8	10	53
1986-87—Hartford Whalers (f)	NHL	4	1	0	1	0
1986-87—St. Louis Blues	NHL	72	5	16	21	46
1987-88—St. Louis Blues	NHL	78	6	13	19	76
1988-89—Peoria Rivermen	IHL	14	0	7	7	14
1988-89—St. Louis Blues	NHL	22	0	0	0	14
1989-90—New Haven Nighthawks (g-h)	AHL	75	3	26	29	56
NHL TOTALS			502	28	93	121	382

(c)—Signed by New York Rangers, May, 1978.
(d)—October, 1982—Claimed by St. Louis Blues in NHL waiver draft.
(e)—October, 1985—Sold by St. Louis Blues to Hartford Whalers.
(f)—October, 1986—Traded by Hartford Whalers to St. Louis Blues for Dave Barr.
(g)—October, 1989—Named player/assistant coach of New Haven Nighthawks.
(h)—June 12, 1990—Named head coach of Medicine Hat Tigers.

BRUCE ALLAN BOUDREAU

Center . . . 5'10" . . . 170 lbs. . . . Born, Toronto, Ont., January 9, 1955 . . . Shoots left . . . Set OMJHL record with 165 pts. in '74-75 (Broken in '75-76 by Mike Kaszycki's 170 pts.) . . . Set OMJHL record with 68 goals in '74-75 (Broken in '77-78 by Bobby Smith's 69) . . . (1983-84)—Assistant coach at St. Catharines . . . (February, 1986)—Broke hand in AHL game . . . (December 11, 1988)—Broken left ankle when slashed by Kenton Rein vs. Rochester.

Year	Team	League	Games	G.	A.	Pts.	Pen.
1972-73—Toronto Marlboros	Jr."A"OHA	61	38	49	87	22
1973-74—Toronto Marlboros (b-c)	Jr."A"OHA	53	46	67	113	51
1974-75—Toronto Marlboros (d-e)	Jr."A"OHA	69	*68	97	*165	52
1975-76—Johnstown Jets	NAHL	34	25	35	60	14
1975-76—Minnesota Fighting Saints (f)	WHA	30	3	6	9	4
1976-77—Dallas Black Hawks	CHL	58	*37	34	71	40
1976-77—Toronto Maple Leafs	NHL	15	2	5	7	4
1977-78—Dallas Black Hawks	CHL	22	13	9	22	11
1977-78—Toronto Maple Leafs	NHL	40	11	18	29	12
1978-79—Toronto Maple Leafs	NHL	26	4	3	7	2
1978-79—New Brunswick Hawks	AHL	49	20	38	58	22
1979-80—Toronto Maple Leafs	NHL	2	0	0	0	2
1979-80—New Brunswick Hawks	AHL	75	36	54	90	47
1980-81—New Brunswick Hawks	AHL	40	17	41	58	22
1980-81—Toronto Maple Leafs	NHL	39	10	14	24	18
1981-82—Cincinnati Tigers (b)	AHL	65	42	61	103	42
1981-82—Toronto Maple Leafs	NHL	12	0	2	2	6
1982-83—St. Catharines Saints	AHL	80	50	72	122	65
1982-83—Toronto Maple Leafs (g)	NHL	..	..	..	..	..
1983-84—St. Catharines Saints	AHL	80	47	62	109	44
1984-85—Baltimore Skipjacks (h)	AHL	17	4	7	11	4
1985-86—Chicago Black Hawks (i)	NHL	7	1	0	1	2
1985-86—Nova Scotia Oilers	AHL	65	30	36	66	36
1986-87—Nova Scotia Oilers	AHL	78	35	47	82	40
1987-88—Springfield Indians	AHL	80	42	*74	*116	84
1988-89—Springfield Indians (j)	AHL	50	28	36	64	42
1988-89—Newmarket Saints (k)	AHL	20	7	16	23	12
1989-90—Phoenix Roadrunners	IHL	82	41	68	109	89
NHL TOTALS			141	28	42	70	46
WHA TOTALS			30	3	6	9	4

(c)—May, 1974—Selected by Minnesota Fighting Saints in World Hockey Association amateur player draft.
(d)—Won Eddie Powers Memorial Trophy (leading scorer).
(e)—Drafted from Toronto Marlboros by Toronto Maple Leafs in third round of 1975 amateur draft.
(f)—August, 1976—Signed by Toronto Maple Leafs.
(g)—No regular season record. Played four playoff games.
(h)—March, 1985—Signed by Baltimore Skipjacks as a free agent after completing season in West Germany.
(i)—August, 1985—Released by Detroit Red Wings and signed by Chicago Black Hawks as a free agent.
(j)—February 21, 1989—Traded by Springfield Indians to Newmarket Saints for future considerations.
(k)—June, 1989—Released by Newmarket Saints.

BOB BOUGHNER

Defense . . . 6' . . . 200 lbs. . . . Born, Windsor, Ont., March 8, 1971 . . . Shoots right.

Year	Team	League	Games	G.	A.	Pts.	Pen.
1987-88—St. Mary's Jr. B	OHA	36	4	18	22	177
1988-89—Sault Ste. Marie Greyhounds (c)	OHL	64	6	15	21	182
1989-90—Sault Ste. Marie Greyhounds	OHL	49	7	23	30	122

(c)—June, 1989—Drafted by Detroit Red Wings in 1989 NHL entry draft. Second Red Wings pick, 32nd overall, second round.

PHILLIPPE RICHARD BOURQUE

Left Wing . . . 6' . . . 180 lbs. . . . Born, Chelmsford, Mass., June 8, 1962 . . . Shoots left . . . Has also played Defense . . . (November, 1989)—Back spasms.

Year	Team	League	Games	G.	A.	Pts.	Pen.
1980-81—Kingston Canadians	OHL	47	4	4	8	46
1981-82—Kingston Canadians (c)	OHL	67	11	40	51	111
1982-83—Baltimore Skipjacks	AHL	65	1	15	16	93
1983-84—Baltimore Skipjacks	AHL	58	5	17	22	96
1983-84—Pittsburgh Penguins	NHL	5	0	1	1	12
1984-85—Baltimore Skipjacks	AHL	79	6	15	21	164
1985-86—Pittsburgh Penguins	NHL	4	0	0	0	2
1985-86—Baltimore Skipjacks	AHL	74	8	18	26	226
1986-87—Pittsburgh Penguins	NHL	22	2	3	5	32
1986-87—Baltimore Skipjacks	AHL	49	15	16	31	183
1987-88—Muskegon Lumberjacks (a-d)	IHL	52	16	36	52	66
1987-88—Pittsburgh Penguins	NHL	21	4	12	16	20
1988-89—Pittsburgh Penguins	NHL	80	17	26	43	97
1989-90—Pittsburgh Penguins	NHL	76	22	17	39	108
NHL TOTALS			208	45	59	104	271

(c)—July, 1982—Signed by Pittsburgh Penguins as a free agent.
(d)—Winner of Governors' Trophy (Top IHL defenseman).

RAYMOND JEAN BOURQUE

Defense . . . 5'11" . . . 197 lbs. . . . Born, Montreal, Que., December 28, 1960 . . . Shoots left . . . Set record for most points by a rookie defenseman 1979-80 (65 pts) (Broken by Larry Murphy of L.A. Kings in '80-81 with 76 pts). . . (November 11, 1980)—Broken jaw . . . Brother of Richard Bourque (203rd NHL '81 draft pick). (October, 1981)—Injured left shoulder . . . (April 21, 1982)—Broke left wrist vs. Quebec in playoffs. During the summer he refractured the wrist and his left forearm . . . (October, 1982)—Broke bone over left eye when hit by puck during preseason game vs. Montreal . . . (December 10, 1988)—Sprained left knee ligaments in a collision with Michel Petit vs. N.Y. Rangers . . . (April 7, 1990)—Bruised hip vs. Hartford when checked by Grant Jennings.

Year	Team	League	Games	G.	A.	Pts.	Pen.
1976-77—Sorel Black Hawks	QMJHL	69	12	36	48	61
1977-78—Verdun Black Hawks (a)	QMJHL	72	22	57	79	90
1978-79—Verdun Black Hawks (a-c)	QMJHL	63	22	71	93	44
1979-80—Boston Bruins (a-d-e)	NHL	80	17	48	65	73
1980-81—Boston Bruins (b)	NHL	67	27	29	56	96
1981-82—Boston Bruins (a)	NHL	65	17	49	66	51
1982-83—Boston Bruins (a)	NHL	65	22	51	73	20
1983-84—Boston Bruins (a)	NHL	78	31	65	96	57
1984-85—Boston Bruins (a)	NHL	73	20	66	86	53
1985-86—Boston Bruins (b)	NHL	74	19	57	76	68
1986-87—Boston Bruins (a-f)	NHL	78	23	72	95	36
1987-88—Boston Bruins (a-f)	NHL	78	17	64	81	72
1988-89—Boston Bruins (b)	NHL	60	18	43	61	52
1989-90—Boston Bruins (a-f)	NHL	76	19	65	84	50
NHL TOTALS			794	230	609	839	628

(c)—August, 1979—Drafted by Boston Bruins in 1979 entry draft. First Bruins pick, eighth overall, first round.
(d)—Selected NHL Rookie of the Year in poll of players by THE SPORTING NEWS.
(e)—Won Calder Memorial Trophy (Top NHL Rookie).
(f)—Won James Norris Memorial Trophy (Top NHL Defenseman).

PAUL ANDRE BOUTILIER

Defense . . . 5'11" . . . 188 lbs. . . . Born, Sydney, N.S., May 3, 1963 . . . Shoots left . . . (November, 1984)—Required 66 stitches to close cut when struck by a shot during a team practice.

Year	Team	League	Games	G.	A.	Pts.	Pen.
1980-81—Sherbrooke Beavers (c)	QMJHL	72	10	29	39	95
1981-82—Sherbrooke Beavers	QMJHL	57	20	60	80	62
1981-82—New York Islanders	NHL	1	0	0	0	0
1982-83—St. Jean Beavers (d)	QMJHL	22	5	14	19	30
1982-83—New York Islanders	NHL	29	4	5	9	24
1983-84—Indianapolis Checkers	CHL	50	6	17	23	56
1983-84—New York Islanders	NHL	28	0	11	11	36
1984-85—New York Islanders	NHL	78	12	23	35	90
1985-86—New York Islanders	NHL	77	4	30	34	100
1986-87—Boston Bruins (e)	NHL	52	5	9	14	84
1986-87—Minnesota North Stars (f)	NHL	10	2	4	6	8
1987-88—Moncton Golden Flames	AHL	41	9	29	38	40
1987-88—New Haven Nighthawks	AHL	9	0	3	3	10
1987-88—Colorado Rangers	IHL	9	2	6	8	4
1987-88—New York Rangers (g)	NHL	4	0	1	1	6
1987-88—Winnipeg Jets (h)	NHL	6	0	0	0	6
1988-89—Winnipeg Jets	NHL	3	0	0	0	4
1988-89—Moncton Hawks (a)	AHL	77	6	54	60	101
1989-90—..................	Switzerland	....	..	..	..	....
1989-90—Maine Mariners (i)	AHL	12	0	4	4	21
NHL TOTALS			288	27	83	110	358

(c)—June, 1981—Drafted as underage junior by New York Islanders in 1981 NHL entry draft. First Islanders pick, 21st overall, first round.
(d)—January, 1983—QHL rights traded by St. Jean Beavers to Shawinigan Cataracts for Yves Lapointe.
(e)—September, 1986—Sent to Boston Bruins by arbitration judge as compensation for New York Islanders signing of free agent Brian Curran.
(f)—March, 1987—Traded by Boston Bruins to Minnesota North Stars for a fourth-round 1987 draft pick (Darwin McPherson).
(g)—October, 1987—Traded with Jari Gronstrand by Minnesota North Stars to New York Rangers for Dave Gagner and Jay Caufield.
(h)—December, 1987—Traded by New York Rangers to Winnipeg Jets for a fifth-round 1989 draft pick (Aaron Miller) and future considerations.
(i)—March, 1990—Signed by Boston Bruins as a free agent.

STEVEN MICHAEL BOZEK

Left Wing . . . 5'11" . . . 170 lbs. . . . Born, Kelowna, B. C., November 26, 1960 . . . Shoots left . . . Set Los Angeles club record for most goals by a rookie in 1981-82 (since broken by Luc Robitaille) . . . (January 20, 1983)—Sprained left knee vs. Hartford . . . (October, 1984)—Torn ligament in baby finger of left hand in pre-season game . . . (March 12, 1986)—Injured knee vs. N.Y. Rangers . . . (October, 1987)—Strained knee ligaments . . . (March, 1988)—Hyperextended knee and strained back . . . (December, 1988)—Hyperextended knee.

Year	Team	League	Games	G.	A.	Pts.	Pen.
1978-79—Northern Michigan Univ.		CCHA	33	12	12	24	21
1979-80—Northern Michigan Univ. (a-c)		CCHA	41	42	47	89	32
1980-81—Northern Michigan Univ. (a-d)		CCHA	44	*35	*55	*90	46
1981-82—Los Angeles Kings		NHL	71	33	23	56	68
1982-83—Los Angeles Kings (e)		NHL	53	13	13	26	14
1983-84—Calgary Flames		NHL	46	10	10	20	16
1984-85—Calgary Flames		NHL	54	13	22	35	6
1985-86—Calgary Flames		NHL	64	21	22	43	24
1986-87—Calgary Flames		NHL	71	17	18	35	22
1987-88—Calgary Flames		NHL	26	3	7	10	12
1987-88—St. Louis Blues (f)		NHL	7	0	0	0	2
1988-89—Vancouver Canucks (g-h)		NHL	71	17	18	35	64
1989-90—Vancouver Canucks		NHL	58	14	9	23	32
NHL TOTALS			521	141	142	283	260

(c)—June, 1980—Drafted by Los Angeles Kings in 1980 NHL entry draft. Fifth Kings pick, 52nd overall, third round.

(d)—Selected to All-America (West) team.

(e)—June, 1983—Traded by Los Angeles Kings to Calgary Flames for Kevin LaVallee and Carl Mokosak.

(f)—March, 1988—Traded with Brett Hull by Calgary Flames to St. Louis Blues for Rob Ramage and Rick Wamsley.

(g)—September 5, 1988—Traded with Doug Gilmour, Mark Hunter and Michael Dark by St. Louis Blues to Calgary Flames for Mike Bullard, Craig Coxe and Tim Corkery.

(h)—September 6, 1988—Traded with Paul Reinhart by Calgary Flames to Vancouver Canucks for a third-round 1989 draft pick (Veli-Pekka Kautonen).

BRIAN BRADLEY

Center . . . 5'9" . . . 165 lbs. . . . Born, Kitchener, Ont., January 21, 1965 . . . Shoots right . . . (January, 1989)—Bruised knee . . . (February 1, 1990)—Cracked thumb knuckle at Calgary and missed seven games.

Year	Team	League	Games	G.	A.	Pts.	Pen.
1981-82—London Knights		OHL	62	34	44	78	34
1982-83—London Knights (c)		OHL	67	37	82	119	37
1983-84—London Knights		OHL	49	40	60	100	24
1984-85—London Knights		OHL	32	27	49	76	22
1985-86—Calgary Flames		NHL	5	0	1	1	0
1985-86—Moncton Golden Flames		AHL	59	23	42	65	40
1986-87—Moncton Golden Flames		AHL	20	12	16	28	8
1986-87—Calgary Flames		NHL	40	10	18	28	16
1987-88—Canadian Olympic Team		Int'l.	51	18	23	41	42
1987-88—Vancouver Canucks (d)		NHL	11	3	5	8	6
1988-89—Vancouver Canucks		NHL	71	18	27	45	42
1989-90—Vancouver Canucks		NHL	67	19	29	48	65
NHL TOTALS			194	50	80	130	129

(c)—June, 1983—Drafted by Calgary Flames as underage junior in 1983 NHL entry draft. Second Flames pick, 51st overall, third round.

(d)—March, 1988—Traded with Peter Bakovic and future considerations (Kevin Guy) by Calgary Flames to Vancouver Canucks for Craig Coxe.

NEIL BRADY

Center . . . 6'2" . . . 180 lbs. . . . Born, Montreal, Que., April 12, 1968 . . . Shoots left.

Year	Team	League	Games	G.	A.	Pts.	Pen.
1984-85—Calgary Northstars (b)		Alta. Midget	37	25	50	75	75
1985-86—Medicine Hat Tigers (c-d)		WHL	72	21	60	81	104
1986-87—Medicine Hat Tigers		WHL	57	19	64	83	126
1987-88—Medicine Hat Tigers		WHL	61	16	35	51	110
1988-89—Utica Devils		AHL	75	16	21	37	56
1989-90—New Jersey Devils		NHL	19	1	4	5	13
1989-90—Utica Devils		AHL	38	10	13	23	21
NHL TOTALS			19	1	4	5	13

(c)—WHL Rookie of the Year (East).

(d)—June, 1986—Drafted as underage junior by New Jersey Devils in 1986 NHL entry draft. First Devils pick, third overall, first round.

ANDRE BRASSARD

Defense . . . 6' . . . 190 lbs. . . . Born, Arvida, Que., April 18, 1968 . . . Shoots left.

Year	Team	League	Games	G.	A.	Pts.	Pen.
1985-86—Longueuil Chevaliers		QMJHL	61	3	15	18	70
1986-87—Longueuil Chevaliers		QMJHL	66	3	26	29	164
1987-88—Trois-Rivieres Draveurs (c)		QMJHL	56	5	31	36	141
1988-89—Trois-Rivieres Draveurs		QMJHL	60	10	40	50	102
1989-90—Springfield Indians		AHL	1	0	0	0	2
1989-90—Nashville Knights (a)		ECHL	56	20	41	61	131

(c)—June, 1988—Drafted by New York Islanders in 1988 NHL entry draft. Fifth Islanders pick, 79th overall, fourth round.

CAM BRAUER

Defense . . . 6'3" . . . 200 lbs. . . . Born, Calgary, Alta., January 4, 1970 . . . Shoots left.

Year	Team	League	Games	G.	A.	Pts.	Pen.
1986-87—Calgary Midget		Alta. Mgt.	34	4	7	11	112
1987-88—R.P.I. (c)		ECAC	18	0	1	1	4

Year	Team	League	Games	G.	A.	Pts.	Pen.
1988-89—Regina Pats		WHL	49	0	9	9	59
1989-90—Regina Pats (d)		WHL	4	0	0	0	20
1989-90—Seattle Thunderbirds (e)		WHL	64	1	9	10	229

(c)—June, 1988—Drafted by Edmonton Oilers in 1988 NHL entry draft. Fifth Oilers pick, 82nd overall, fourth round.

(d)—October 5, 1989—Traded by Regina Pats to Seattle Thunderbirds for Jason Glickman.

(e)—March 6, 1990—Traded by Edmonton Oilers to Hartford Whalers for Marc Laforge.

ANDY BRICKLEY

Left Wing . . . 5'11" . . . 185 lbs. . . . Born, Melrose, Mass., August 9, 1961 . . . Shoots left . . . (December, 1983)—Strained ankle . . . (December, 1985)—Tendinitis in shoulder . . . (September, 1987)—Injured foot . . . (December, 1988)—Strained groin . . . (September 24, 1989)—Sprained right ankle in training camp and missed first nine games of season . . . (January 27, 1990)—Torn right groin muscle vs. Philadelphia and missed eight games.

Year	Team	League	Games	G.	A.	Pts.	Pen.
1979-80—University of New Hampshire (c)		ECAC	27	15	17	32	8
1980-81—University of New Hampshire		ECAC	31	27	25	52	16
1981-82—University of New Hampshire (d)		ECAC	35	26	27	53	6
1982-83—Philadelphia Flyers		NHL	3	1	1	2	0
1982-83—Maine Mariners (b)		AHL	76	29	54	83	10
1983-84—Springfield Indians		AHL	7	1	5	6	2
1983-84—Pittsburgh Penguins (e)		NHL	50	18	20	38	9
1983-84—Baltimore Skipjacks		AHL	4	0	5	5	2
1984-85—Baltimore Skipjacks		AHL	31	13	14	27	8
1984-85—Pittsburgh Penguins		NHL	45	7	15	22	10
1985-86—Maine Mariners (f-g-h)		AHL	60	26	34	60	20
1986-87—New Jersey Devils		NHL	51	11	12	23	8
1987-88—Utica Devils		AHL	9	5	8	13	4
1987-88—New Jersey Devils		NHL	45	8	14	22	14
1988-89—Boston Bruins (i)		NHL	71	13	22	35	20
1989-90—Boston Bruins		NHL	43	12	28	40	8
NHL TOTALS			308	70	112	182	69

(c)—June, 1980—Drafted by Philadelphia Flyers in 1980 NHL entry draft. Tenth Flyers pick, 210th overall, 10th round.

(d)—Named to All-American Team (East).

(e)—October, 1983—Traded with Ron Flockhart, Mark Taylor and first-round 1984 draft pick (Roger Belanger) by Philadelphia Flyers to Pittsburgh Penguins for Rich Sutter and second (Greg Smyth) and third round (David McLay) 1984 draft picks.

(f)—August, 1985—Released by Pittsburgh Penguins.

(g)—September, 1985—Attended Hartford Whalers training camp as an unsigned free agent. Released at the conclusion of camp and signed with Maine Mariners as a free agent.

(h)—June, 1986—Signed by New Jersey Devils as a free agent.

(i)—October 3, 1988—Selected by Boston Bruins in 1988 waiver draft for $12,500.

CHRIS BRIGHT

Center . . . 6' . . . 185 lbs. . . . Born, Guelph, Ont., October 14, 1970 . . . Shoots left . . . Also plays Left Wing.

Year	Team	League	Games	G.	A.	Pts.	Pen.
1987-88—Calgary North Stars Midgets		Alta.	22	22	18	40	56
1987-88—Moose Jaw Warriors		WHL	20	2	2	4	10
1988-89—Moose Jaw Warriors		WHL	71	18	27	45	61
1989-90—Moose Jaw Warriors (c)		WHL	72	36	38	74	107

(c)—June 16, 1990—Selected by Hartford Whalers in 1990 NHL entry draft. Fourth Whalers pick, 78th overall, fourth round.

JOHN BRILL

Right Wing . . . 6'3" . . . 180 lbs. . . . Born, St. Paul, Minn., December 3, 1970 . . . Shoots left.

Year	Team	League	Games	G.	A.	Pts.	Pen.
1987-88—Grand Rapids H.S.		Minn. H.S.	28	15	13	28	..
1988-89—Grand Rapids H.S. (c)		Minn. H.S.	25	23	29	52	28
1989-90—Univ. of Minnesota		WCHA	34	2	8	10	22

(c)—June, 1989—Drafted by Pittsburgh Penguins in 1989 NHL entry draft. Third Penguins pick, 58th overall, third round.

ROD BRIND'AMOUR

Center . . . 6' . . . 185 lbs. . . . Born, Ottawa, Ont., August 9, 1970 . . . Shoots left . . . (November, 1985)—Broken wrist . . . Also plays Left Wing.

Year	Team	League	Games	G.	A.	Pts.	Pen.
1986-87—Notre Dame Midget		Sask. Mdgt.	33	38	50	88	66
1987-88—Notre Dame Jr. A (c)		SJHL	56	46	61	107	136
1988-89—Michigan State Univ. (d-e)		CCHA	42	27	32	59	63
1988-89—St. Louis Blues (f)		NHL	..	..	..	..	..
1989-90—St. Louis Blues		NHL	79	26	35	61	46
NHL TOTALS			79	26	35	61	46

(c)—June, 1988—Drafted by St. Louis Blues in 1988 NHL entry draft. First Blues pick, ninth overall, first round.

(d)—Named to CCHA All-Rookie Team.

(e)—Named CCHA Rookie-of-the-Year.

(f)—No regular season record. Played in five playoff games.

PATRICE BRISEBOIS

Defense . . . 6'1" . . . 175 lbs. . . . Born, Montreal, Que., January 27, 1971 . . . Shoots right . . . (August, 1988)—Broken left thumb . . . (March, 1988)—Torn ligaments in left knee . . . (February, 1988)—Operation on fractured right thumb.

Year Team	League	Games	G.	A.	Pts.	Pen.
1987-88—Laval Titans	QMJHL	48	10	34	44	95
1988-89—Laval Titans (c-d)	QMJHL	50	20	45	65	95
1989-90—Laval Titans (e)	QMJHL	56	18	70	88	108

(c)—June, 1989—Drafted by Montreal Canadiens in 1989 NHL entry draft. Second Canadiens pick, 30th overall, second round.
(d)—Won Mike Bossy Trophy (Top Pro Prospect).
(e)—May 26, 1990—Traded with Allen Kerr by Laval Titans to Drummondville Voltigeurs for second and third round 1990 draft picks.

STEPHANE BROCHU

Defense . . . 6'1" . . . 185 lbs. . . . Born, Sherbrooke, Que., August 15, 1967 . . . Shoots left . . . (December, 1983)—Separated shoulder.

Year Team	League	Games	G.	A.	Pts.	Pen.
1983-84—Magog Cantonniers	Que. Midget	38	7	24	31	36
1984-85—Quebec Remparts (c)	QMJHL	59	2	16	18	56
1985-86—St. Jean Castors	QMJHL	63	14	27	41	121
1986-87—Did not play		....	....	....	....	....
1987-88—Colorado Rangers	IHL	52	4	10	14	70
1988-89—Denver Rangers	IHL	67	5	14	19	109
1988-89—New York Rangers	NHL	1	0	0	0	0
1989-90—Flint Spirits	IHL	5	0	0	0	2
1989-90—Fort Wayne Komets	IHL	63	9	19	28	98
NHL TOTALS		1	0	0	0	0

(c)—June, 1985—Drafted by New York Rangers in 1985 NHL entry draft. Ninth Rangers pick, 175th overall, ninth round.

ROBERT W. BROOKE

Right Wing . . . 6'2" . . . 185 lbs. . . . Born, Melrose, Mass., December 18, 1960 . . . Shoots right . . . Holds Yale career records for goals (42), assists (113) and points (155) . . . Also plays Center and Defense . . . Played shortstop on Yale baseball team . Member of 1984 All-America Team . . . (October 11, 1984)—Separated shoulder in opening game of season vs. Hartford . . . (January, 1988)—Stiff neck. (September, 1988)—Separated left shoulder during Minnesota North Stars training camp . . . (March, 1990)—Bruised right foot.

Year Team	League	Games	G.	A.	Pts.	Pen.
1979-80—Yale University (c)	ECAC	24	7	22	29	38
1980-81—Yale University	ECAC	27	12	30	42	59
1981-82—Yale University	ECAC	25	12	30	42	60
1982-83—Yale University (a-d)	ECAC	27	11	31	42	50
1983-84—U.S. National Team	Int'l	54	7	18	25	75
1983-84—U.S. Olympic Team	Int'l	6	1	2	3	10
1983-84—New York Rangers (e)	NHL	9	1	2	3	4
1984-85—New York Rangers	NHL	72	7	9	16	79
1985-86—New York Rangers	NHL	79	24	20	44	111
1986-87—New York Rangers (f)	NHL	15	3	5	8	20
1986-87—Minnesota North Stars	NHL	65	10	18	28	78
1987-88—Minnesota North Stars	NHL	77	5	20	25	108
1988-89—Minnesota North Stars	NHL	57	7	9	16	57
1989-90—Minnesota North Stars (g)	NHL	38	4	4	8	33
1989-90—New Jersey Devils	NHL	35	8	10	18	30
NHL TOTALS		447	69	97	166	520

(c)—June, 1980—Drafted by St. Louis Blues in 1980 NHL entry draft. Third Blues pick, 75th overall, fourth round.
(d)—Named to All-America Team (East).
(e)—March, 1984—Traded with Larry Patey by St. Louis Blues to New York Rangers for Dave Barr, a third round (Alan Perry) 1984 draft pick and cash.
(f)—November, 1986—Traded with fourth-round 1988 draft pick by New York Rangers to Minnesota North Stars for Tony McKegney, Curt Giles and a second-round (Troy Mallette) 1988 draft pick.
(g)—January 5, 1990—Traded by Minnesota North Stars to New Jersey Devils for Aaron Broten.

DAN BROOKS

Defense . . . 6'3" . . . 210 lbs. . . . Born, St. Paul, Minn., April 26, 1967 . . . Shoots left . . . Son of Herb Brooks, former Coach of University of Minnesota, St. Cloud State and N.Y. Rangers.

Year Team	League	Games	G.	A.	Pts.	Pen.
1984-85—St. Thomas Academy (c)	Minn. H.S.	....	...	....	....	....
1985-86—St. Thomas Academy	Minn. H.S.	....	...	....	....	....
1986-87—Univ. of Denver	WCHA	7	0	0	0	4
1987-88—Univ. of Denver	WCHA	27	1	2	3	14
1988-89—Univ. of Denver	WCHA	41	0	6	6	36
1989-90—Univ. of Denver	WCHA	32	4	4	8	30

(c)—June, 1985—Drafted by St. Louis Blues in 1985 NHL entry draft. Fourth Blues pick, 100th overall, fifth round.

AARON BROTEN

Center . . . 5'10" . . . 168 lbs. . . . Born, Roseau, Minn., November 14, 1960 . . . Shoots left . . . Brother of Neal Broten and Paul Broten . . . Also plays Left Wing . . . (February 15, 1986)—Sprained ankle vs. N.Y. Islanders . . . (March 6, 1986)—Reinjured ankle vs. Detroit . . . (March 19, 1986)—Reinjured ankle vs. Pittsburgh . . . Holds New Jersey record for career assists . . . (March 17, 1990)—Slight concussion ended his playing streak at 318 games.

Year Team	League	Games	G.	A.	Pts.	Pen.
1979-80—University of Minnesota (c-d)	WCHA	41	25	47	72	8
1980-81—University of Minnesota (b-e)	WCHA	45	*47	*59	*106	24
1980-81—Colorado Rockies	NHL	2	0	0	0	0
1981-82—Fort Worth Texans	CHL	19	15	21	36	11
1981-82—Colorado Rockies	NHL	58	15	24	39	6
1982-83—Wichita Wind	CHL	4	0	4	4	0
1982-83—New Jersey Devils	NHL	73	16	39	55	28
1983-84—New Jersey Devils	NHL	80	13	23	36	36

Year Team	League	Games	G.	A.	Pts.	Pen.
1984-85—New Jersey Devils	NHL	80	22	35	57	38
1985-86—New Jersey Devils	NHL	66	19	25	44	26
1986-87—New Jersey Devils	NHL	80	26	53	79	36
1987-88—New Jersey Devils	NHL	80	26	57	83	80
1988-89—New Jersey Devils	NHL	80	16	43	59	81
1989-90—New Jersey Devils (f)	NHL	42	10	8	18	36
1989-90—Minnesota North Stars	NHL	35	9	9	18	22
NHL TOTALS		676	172	316	488	389

(c)—Named top WCHA Rookie.
(d)—June, 1980—Drafted by Colorado Rockies in 1980 NHL entry draft. Fifth Rockies pick, 106th overall, sixth round.
(e)—WCHA Scoring Leader.
(f)—January 5, 1990—Traded by New Jersey Devils to Minnesota North Stars for Bob Brooke.

NEAL LaMOY BROTEN

Center . . . 5'9" . . . 160 lbs. . . . Born, Roseau, Minn., November 29, 1959 . . . Shoots left . . . Brother of Aaron Broten and Paul Broten . . . Scored game winning goal to give University of Minnesota 1979 NCAA Championship over North Dakota . . . Member of 1980 U.S. Olympic Gold Medal Team . . . (December 26, 1981)—Ankle fracture . . . Set NHL record for most assists by American-born player (76), 1985-86 . . . (1985-86)—Became first American-born player to score 100 points in one season in NHL . . . (October 30, 1986)—Dislocated shoulder . . . (March, 1987)—Torn shoulder ligaments . . . (November, 1987)—Separated shoulder . . . (February, 1988)—Reconstructive shoulder surgery . . . (February 14, 1989)—Sterno-clavicular sprain when checked by Doug Wilson vs. Chicago.

Year Team	League	Games	G.	A.	Pts.	Pen.
1978-79—University of Minnesota (c-d)	WCHA	40	21	50	71	18
1979-80—U. S. Olympic Team	Int'l	62	27	31	58	22
1980-81—Univ. of Minnesota (a-e-f-g)	WCHA	36	17	54	71	56
1980-81—Minnesota North Stars	NHL	3	2	0	2	12
1981-82—Minnesota North Stars	NHL	73	38	60	98	42
1982-83—Minnesota North Stars	NHL	79	32	45	77	43
1983-84—Minnesota North Stars	NHL	76	28	61	89	43
1984-85—Minnesota North Stars	NHL	80	19	37	56	39
1985-86—Minnesota North Stars	NHL	80	29	76	105	47
1986-87—Minnesota North Stars	NHL	46	18	35	53	35
1987-88—Minnesota North Stars	NHL	54	9	30	39	32
1988-89—Minnesota North Stars	NHL	68	18	38	56	57
1989-90—Minnesota North Stars	NHL	80	23	62	85	45
NHL TOTALS		639	216	444	660	395

(c)—Named top WCHA Rookie player.
(d)—August, 1979—Drafted by Minnesota North Stars in 1979 NHL entry draft. Third North Stars pick, 42nd overall, second round.
(e)—Named to All-America Team (West).
(f)—Named to All-NCAA Tournament team.
(g)—First winner of Hobey Baker Memorial Trophy (Top U. S. College Hockey Player).

PAUL BROTEN

Center . . . 5'11" . . . 155 lbs. . . . Born, Roseau, Minn., October 27, 1965 . . . Shoots right . . . Brother of Aaron and Neal Broten . . . Also plays Right Wing.

Year Team	League	Games	G.	A.	Pts.	Pen.
1983-84—Roseau H.S. (c)	Minn. H.S.	26	26	29	55	4
1984-85—Univ. of Minnesota	WCHA	44	8	8	16	26
1985-86—Univ. of Minnesota	WCHA	38	6	16	22	24
1986-87—Univ. of Minnesota	WCHA	48	17	22	39	52
1987-88—Univ. of Minnesota	WCHA	62	19	26	45	54
1988-89—Denver Rangers	IHL	77	28	31	59	133
1989-90—Flint Spirits	IHL	28	17	9	26	55
1989-90—New York Rangers	NHL	32	5	3	8	26
NHL TOTALS		32	5	3	8	26

(c)—June, 1984—Drafted by New York Rangers in 1984 NHL entry draft. Third Rangers pick, 77th overall, fourth round.

DAVID BROWN

Right Wing . . . 6'5" . . . 205 lbs. . . . Born, Saskatoon, Sask., October 12, 1962 . . . Shoots right . . . (March, 1985)—Bruised shoulder . . . (March, 1987)—Suspended five games for stick swinging incident . . . (October 16, 1987)—Suspended 15 games by NHL for crosschecking Tomas Sandstrom vs. N.Y. Rangers . . . (January, 1988)—Bruised left hand and wrist vs. Pittsburgh . . . (March 3, 1989)—Took a five-stitch cut near his eye when struck by stick of Paul Fenton at Winnipeg . . . (March, 1989)—Sprained hand.

Year Team	League	Games	G.	A.	Pts.	Pen.
1980-81—Spokane Flyers	WHL	9	2	2	4	21
1981-82—Saskatoon Blades (c)	WHL	62	11	33	44	344
1982-83—Maine Mariners (d)	AHL	71	8	6	14	*418
1982-83—Philadelphia Flyers	NHL	2	0	0	0	5
1983-84—Philadelphia Flyers	NHL	19	1	5	6	98
1983-84—Springfield Indians	AHL	59	17	14	31	150
1984-85—Philadelphia Flyers	NHL	57	3	6	9	165
1985-86—Philadelphia Flyers	NHL	76	10	7	17	277
1986-87—Philadelphia Flyers	NHL	62	7	3	10	274
1987-88—Philadelphia Flyers	NHL	47	12	5	17	114
1988-89—Philadelphia Flyers (e)	NHL	50	0	3	3	100
1988-89—Edmonton Oilers	NHL	22	0	2	2	56
1989-90—Edmonton Oilers	NHL	60	0	6	6	145
NHL TOTALS		395	33	37	70	1234

(c)—June, 1982—Drafted by Philadelphia Flyers in 1982 NHL entry draft. Seventh Flyers pick, 140th overall, seventh round.
(d)—Led AHL Playoffs with 107 penalty minutes.
(e)—February 7, 1989—Traded by Philadelphia Flyers to Edmonton Oilers for Keith Acton and future considerations.

DOUG BROWN

Right Wing . . . 5'11" . . . 190 lbs. . . . Born, Southborough, Mass., June 12, 1964 . . . Shoots right . . . Brother of Greg Brown . . . (Summer, 1988)—Married to the granddaughter of New York Giants (NFL) owner Wellington Mara . . . (October, 1988)—Broken nose when struck by a puck at Quebec . . . (November 25, 1989)—Injured back at Winnipeg.

Year	Team	League	Games	G.	A.	Pts.	Pen.
1982-83—Boston College		ECAC	22	9	8	17	0
1983-84—Boston College		ECAC	38	11	10	21	6
1984-85—Boston College		H. East	45	37	31	68	10
1985-86—Boston College (c)		H. East	38	16	40	56	16
1986-87—Maine Mariners		AHL	73	24	34	58	15
1986-87—New Jersey Devils		NHL	4	0	1	1	0
1987-88—New Jersey Devils		NHL	70	14	11	25	20
1987-88—Utica Devils		AHL	2	0	2	2	2
1988-89—New Jersey Devils		NHL	63	15	10	25	15
1988-89—Utica Devils		AHL	4	1	4	5	0
1989-90—New Jersey Devils		NHL	69	14	20	34	16
NHL TOTALS			202	43	41	84	51

(c)—August, 1986—Signed by New Jersey Devils as a free agent.

GREGORY BROWN

Defense . . . 6' . . . 185 lbs. . . . Born, Hartford, Conn., March 7, 1963 . . . Shoots right . . . Brother of Doug Brown.

Year	Team	League	Games	G.	A.	Pts.	Pen.
1984-85—St. Marks H.S.		Mass. H.S.	24	16	24	40	12
1985-86—St. Marks H.S. (c)		Mass. H.S.	19	22	28	50	30
1986-87—Boston College		H. East	37	10	27	37	22
1987-88—U.S. Olympic Team		Int'l.	6	0	4	4	2
1988-89—Boston College (a-d-e)		H. East	40	9	34	43	24
1989-90—Boston College (a-d-e)		H. East	42	5	35	40	42

(c)—June, 1986—Drafted by Buffalo Sabres in 1986 NHL entry draft. Second Sabres pick, 26th overall, second round.
(d)—Named First team All-America (East).
(e)—Named Hockey East Player of the Year.

JEFF BROWN

Defense . . . 6'1" . . . 185 lbs. . . . Born, Ottawa, Ont., April 30, 1966 . . . Shoots right.

Year	Team	League	Games	G.	A.	Pts.	Pen.
1981-82—Hawkesbury Tier II		Ont. Jr.	49	12	47	59	72
1982-83—Sudbury Wolves		OHL	65	9	37	46	39
1983-84—Sudbury Wolves (c)		OHL	68	17	60	77	39
1984-85—Sudbury Wolves		OHL	56	16	48	64	26
1985-86—Sudbury Wolves (a-d)		OHL	45	22	28	50	24
1985-86—Quebec Nordiques		NHL	8	3	2	5	6
1985-86—Fredericton Express (e)		AHL	....	...	....	....	....
1986-87—Fredericton Express		AHL	26	2	14	16	16
1986-87—Quebec Nordiques		NHL	44	7	22	29	16
1987-88—Quebec Nordiques		NHL	78	16	37	53	64
1988-89—Quebec Nordiques		NHL	78	21	47	68	62
1989-90—Quebec Nordiques (f)		NHL	29	6	10	16	18
1989-90—St. Louis Blues		NHL	48	10	28	38	37
NHL TOTALS			285	63	146	209	203

(c)—June, 1984—Drafted as underage junior by Quebec Nordiques in 1984 NHL entry draft. Second Nordiques pick, 36th overall, second round.
(d)—Shared Max Kaminsky Trophy (Top OHL Trophy) with Terry Carkner.
(e)—No regular season record. Played one playoff game.
(f)—December 13, 1989—Traded by Quebec Nordiques to St. Louis Blues for Greg Millen and Tony Hrkac.

KEITH JEFFREY BROWN

Defense . . . 6'1" . . . 192 lbs. . . . Born, Corner Brook, Nfld., May 6, 1960 . . . Shoots right . . . (December 23, 1981)—Torn ligaments in right knee . . . (January 26, 1983)—Separated right shoulder vs. Vancouver . . . (January, 1985)—Strained leg . . . (October, 1985)—Broken finger in three places in weight training accident and missed 10 games . . . (October, 1987)—Torn ligaments and damaged cartilage in left knee . . . (January, 1990)—Bruised shoulder . . . (February 25, 1990)—Bruised ribs vs. Philadelphia and missed 10 games . . . (April, 1990)—Bruised elbow.

Year	Team	League	Games	G.	A.	Pts.	Pen.
1976-77—Ft. Saskatchewan Traders		AJHL	59	14	61	75	14
1976-77—Portland Winter Hawks		WCHL	2	0	0	0	0
1977-78—Portland Winter Hawks (b-c)		WCHL	72	11	53	64	51
1978-79—Portland Winter Hawks (a-d-e)		WHL	70	11	85	96	75
1979-80—Chicago Black Hawks		NHL	76	2	18	20	27
1980-81—Chicago Black Hawks		NHL	80	9	34	43	80
1981-82—Chicago Black Hawks		NHL	33	4	20	24	26
1982-83—Chicago Black Hawks		NHL	50	4	27	31	20
1983-84—Chicago Black Hawks		NHL	74	10	25	35	94
1984-85—Chicago Black Hawks		NHL	56	1	22	23	55
1985-86—Chicago Black Hawks		NHL	70	11	29	40	87
1986-87—Chicago Black Hawks		NHL	73	4	23	27	86
1987-88—Chicago Black Hawks		NHL	24	3	6	9	45
1988-89—Chicago Black Hawks		NHL	74	2	16	18	84
1989-90—Chicago Black Hawks		NHL	67	5	20	25	87
NHL TOTALS			677	55	240	295	691

(c)—Shared WCHL Top Rookie with John Ogrodnick.
(d)—Named outstanding WHL defenseman.
(e)—August, 1979—Drafted as underage junior by Chicago Black Hawks in 1979 NHL entry draft. First Black Hawks pick, seventh overall, first round.

ROBERT BROWN

Center . . . 6' . . . 180 lbs. . . . Born, Kingston, Ont., October 4, 1968 . . . Shoots left . . . Holds WHL records for career assists (343) and points (522) . . . Set single season WHL record with 212 points in 1986-87 . . . (October, 1987)—Scored goals on his first three NHL shots . . . (February 12, 1989)—Separated right shoulder when checked by Joe Nieuwendyk vs. Calgary and missed 12 games . . . Son of Bob Brown, General Manager of Kamloops Blazers.

Year	Team	League	Games	G.	A.	Pts.	Pen.
1983-84—Kamloops Jr. Oilers		WHL	50	16	42	58	80
1984-85—Kamloops Blazers		WHL	60	29	50	79	95
1985-86—Kamloops Blazers (a-c-d)		WHL	69	58	*115	*173	171
1986-87—Kamloops Blazers (a-c-e)		WHL	63	*76	*136	*212	101
1987-88—Pittsburgh Penguins		NHL	51	24	20	44	56
1988-89—Pittsburgh Penguins		NHL	68	49	66	115	118
1989-90—Pittsburgh Penguins		NHL	80	33	47	80	102
NHL TOTALS			199	106	133	239	276

(c)—Named WHL Most Valuable Player (West).
(d)—June, 1986—Drafted by Pittsburgh Penguins as underage junior in 1986 NHL entry draft. Fourth Penguins pick, 67th overall, fourth round.
(e)—Named WHL Player-of-the-Year.

MARK BROWNSCHIDLE

Defense . . . 6'2" . . . 185 lbs. . . . Born, East Amherst, N.Y., October 26, 1970 . . . Shoots right . . . Brother of Jack Brownschidle, who played for St. Louis Blues and Hartford Whalers, and Jeff Brownschidle, who played briefly for the Whalers.

Year	Team	League	Games	G.	A.	Pts.	Pen.
1987-88—Amherst Jr.		Buffalo	..	2	12	14	..
1988-89—Boston University (c)		H. East	35	0	7	7	12
1989-90—Boston University		H. East	38	1	4	5	12

(c)—June, 1989—Drafted by Winnipeg Jets in 1989 NHL entry draft. Fifth Jets pick, 64th overall, fourth round.

DAVID BRUCE

Right Wing . . . 5'11" . . . 170 lbs. . . . Born, Thunder Bay, Ont., October 7, 1964 . . . Shoots right . . . Also plays Center . . . (November, 1987)—Mononucleosis . . . (March, 1988)—Bruised foot . . . (March, 1989)—Torn cartilage near thumb on left hand and required surgery.

Year	Team	League	Games	G.	A.	Pts.	Pen.
1981-82—Thunder Bay Kings		Tier II	35	27	31	58	74
1982-83—Kitchener Rangers (c)		OHL	67	36	35	71	199
1983-84—Kitchener Rangers		OHL	62	52	40	92	203
1984-85—Fredericton Express		AHL	56	14	11	25	104
1985-86—Fredericton Express		AHL	66	25	16	41	151
1985-86—Vancouver Canucks		NHL	12	0	1	1	14
1986-87—Fredericton Express		AHL	17	7	6	13	73
1986-87—Vancouver Canucks		NHL	50	9	7	16	109
1987-88—Fredericton Express		AHL	30	27	18	45	115
1987-88—Vancouver Canucks		NHL	28	7	3	10	57
1988-89—Vancouver Canucks		NHL	53	7	7	14	65
1989-90—Salt Lake Golden Eagles (d)		IHL	67	22	41	63	16
NHL TOTALS			143	23	18	41	245

(c)—June, 1983—Drafted as underage junior by Vancouver Canucks in 1983 NHL entry draft. Second Canucks pick, 30th overall, second round.
(d)—July, 1990—Signed by St. Louis Blues as a free agent.

JAMES MURRAY BRUMWELL
(Known by middle name)

Defense . . . 6'1" . . . 190 lbs. . . . Born, Calgary, Alta., March 31, 1960 . . . Shoots left . . . (February, 1979)—Mononucleosis . . . (January, 1982)—Back injury.

Year	Team	League	Games	G.	A.	Pts.	Pen.
1977-78—Calgary Canucks		AJHL	59	4	40	44	79
1977-78—Calgary Wranglers		WCHL	1	0	0	0	2
1977-78—Saskatoon Blades		WCHL	1	0	2	2	0
1978-79—Billings Bighorns		WHL	61	11	32	43	62
1979-80—Billings Bighorns		WHL	67	18	54	72	50
1980-81—Minnesota North Stars (c)		NHL	1	0	0	0	0
1980-81—Oklahoma City Stars		CHL	79	12	43	55	79
1981-82—Nashville South Stars		CHL	55	4	21	25	66
1981-82—Minnesota North Stars (d)		NHL	21	0	3	3	18
1982-83—Wichita Wind		CHL	11	4	1	5	4
1982-83—New Jersey Devils		NHL	59	5	14	19	34
1983-84—Maine Mariners		AHL	34	4	25	29	16
1983-84—New Jersey Devils		NHL	42	7	13	20	14
1984-85—Maine Mariners		AHL	64	8	31	39	52
1985-86—New Jersey Devils		NHL	1	0	0	0	0
1985-86—Maine Mariners		AHL	66	9	28	37	35
1986-87—Maine Mariners		AHL	69	10	38	48	30
1986-87—New Jersey Devils		NHL	1	0	0	2	0
1987-88—Utica Devils		AHL	77	13	53	66	44
1987-88—New Jersey Devils		NHL	3	0	1	1	2
1988-89—Utica Devils (e)		AHL	73	5	29	34	29
1989-90—New Haven Nighthawks		AHL	62	7	29	36	24
NHL TOTALS			128	12	31	43	70

(c)—September, 1980—Signed by Minnesota North Stars as a free agent.
(d)—Claimed by New Jersey Devils in 1982 NHL waiver draft.
(e)—July 13, 1989—Announced his retirement.

BENOIT BRUNET

Left Wing . . . 5'11" . . . 180 lbs. . . . Born, Montreal, Que., August 24, 1968 . . . Shoots left . . . (September, 1987)—Injured ankle.

Year	Team	League	Games	G.	A.	Pts.	Pen.
1985-86—Hull Olympiques (c)		QMJHL	71	33	37	70	81
1986-87—Hull Olympiques (b)		QMJHL	60	43	67	110	105
1987-88—Hull Olympiques		QMJHL	62	54	89	143	131
1988-89—Montreal Canadiens		NHL	2	0	1	1	0
1988-89—Sherbrooke Canadiens (a)		AHL	73	41	76	117	95
1989-90—Sherbrooke Canadiens		AHL	72	32	35	67	82
NHL TOTALS			2	0	1	1	0

(c)—June, 1986—Drafted as underage junior by Montreal Canadiens in 1986 NHL entry draft. Second Canadiens pick, 27th overall, second round.

TREVOR BUCHANAN

Left Wing . . . 6' . . . 176 lbs. . . . Born, Thompson, Man., June 7, 1969 . . . Shoots left.

Year	Team	League	Games	G.	A.	Pts.	Pen.
1988-89—Kamloops Blazers (c)		WHL	63	13	21	34	217
1989-90—Kamloops Blazers		WHL	29	6	11	17	143
1989-90—Victoria Cougars		WHL	43	21	20	41	193

(c)—June, 1989—Drafted by Hartford Whalers in 1989 NHL entry draft. Ninth Whalers pick, 199th overall, tenth round.

KELLY BUCHBERGER

Left Wing . . . 6'2" . . . 190 lbs. . . . Born, Langenburg, Sask., December 12, 1966 . . . Shoots left . . . (March 30, 1988)—Suspended six games by AHL for leaving the bench in a fight . . . (March, 1989)—Fractured right ankle . . . (March 13, 1990)—Dislocated left shoulder in fight with Dan Vincelette at Quebec . . . (May 4, 1990)—Reinjured shoulder when Steve Konroyd fell on him vs. Chicago.

Year	Team	League	Games	G.	A.	Pts.	Pen.
1983-84—Melville Millionaires		SAJHL	60	14	11	25	139
1984-85—Moose Jaw Warriors (c)		WHL	51	12	17	29	114
1985-86—Moose Jaw Warriors		WHL	72	14	22	36	206
1986-87—Nova Scotia Oilers		AHL	70	12	20	32	257
1986-87—Edmonton Oilers (d)		NHL	....	...	...	...	....
1987-88—Edmonton Oilers		NHL	19	1	0	1	81
1987-88—Nova Scotia Oilers		AHL	49	21	23	44	206
1988-89—Edmonton Oilers		NHL	66	5	9	14	234
1989-90—Edmonton Oilers		NHL	55	2	6	8	168
NHL TOTALS			140	8	15	23	483

(c)—June, 1985—Drafted as underage junior by Edmonton Oilers in 1985 NHL entry draft. Eighth Oilers pick, 188th overall, ninth round.

(d)—No regular season record. Played three playoff games.

DAVID BUCKLEY

Defense . . . 6'4" . . . 195 lbs. . . . Born, Newton, Mass., January 27, 1966 . . . Shoots left.

Year	Team	League	Games	G.	A.	Pts.	Pen.
1983-84—Trinity Pawling Prep (c)		N.Y. H.S.	20	10	17	27	..
1984-85—		....	..	..	..	..	....
1985-86—Boston College		H. East	22	0	2	2	4
1986-87—Boston College		H. East	34	3	5	8	9
1987-88—Boston College		H. East	33	1	8	9	40
1988-89—Boston College		H. East	40	3	7	10	48
1989-90—Hampton Road Gulls		ECHL	56	6	33	39	63
1989-90—Baltimore Skipjacks		AHL	4	0	0	0	0

(c)—June, 1984—Drafted by Toronto Maple Leafs in 1984 NHL entry draft. Ninth Maple Leafs pick, 192nd overall, 10th round.

JEROME BUCKLEY

Right Wing . . . 6'2" . . . 200 lbs. . . . Born, Needham, Mass., June 27, 1971 . . . Shoots right.

Year	Team	League	Games	G.	A.	Pts.	Pen.
1986-87—St. Sebastian's Prep.		Mass. H.S.	25	2	6	8	8
1987-88—St. Sebastian's Prep.		Mass. H.S.	25	5	10	15	14
1988-89—St. Sebastian's Prep.		Mass. H.S.	25	20	15	35	40
1989-90—Northwood Prep. (c)		Mass. H.S.	37	35	33	68	....

(c)—June 16, 1990—Selected by Boston Bruins in 1990 NHL entry draft. Third Bruins pick, 84th overall, fourth round.

RANDY BUCYK

Center . . . 6' . . . 190 lbs. . . . Born, Edmonton, Alta., November 9, 1962 . . . Shoots left . . . Nephew of Johnny Bucyk (Hall of Famer and former Boston Bruin) . . . (November, 1989)—Injured knee.

Year	Team	League	Games	G.	A.	Pts.	Pen.
1980-81—Northeastern Univ.		ECAC	26	9	7	16	18
1981-82—Northeastern Univ.		ECAC	33	19	17	36	10
1982-83—Northeastern Univ.		ECAC	28	16	20	36	16
1983-84—Northeastern Univ.		ECAC	29	16	13	29	11
1984-85—Sherbrooke Canadiens (c)		AHL	62	21	26	47	20
1985-86—Sherbrooke Canadiens		AHL	43	18	33	51	22
1985-86—Montreal Canadiens		NHL	17	4	2	6	8
1986-87—Sherbrooke Canadiens (d)		AHL	70	24	39	63	28
1987-88—Salt Lake Golden Eagles		IHL	75	37	45	82	68
1987-88—Calgary Flames		NHL	2	0	0	0	0
1988-89—Salt Lake Golden Eagles		IHL	79	28	59	87	24
1988-89—Canadian National Team		Int'l	4	0	0	0	2
1989-90—Salt Lake Golden Eagles		IHL	67	22	41	63	16
NHL TOTALS			19	4	2	6	8

(c)—September, 1984—Signed by Montreal Canadiens as a free agent.

(d)—August, 1987—Signed by Calgary Flames as a free agent.

DAVID BUDA

Center . . . 6'4" . . . 190 lbs. . . . Born, Mississauga, Ont., March 14, 1966 . . . Shoots left.

Year	Team	League	Games	G.	A.	Pts.	Pen.
1984-85—Streetsville Jr. B (c)		OHA	..	..	..	..	..
1985-86—Northeastern Univ.		H. East	39	4	4	8	39
1986-87—Northeastern Univ.		H. East	37	15	15	30	32
1987-88—Northeastern Univ.		H. East	37	21	16	37	66
1988-89—Northeastern Univ. (a)		H. East	35	23	23	46	45
1989-90—Maine Mariners		AHL	39	7	4	11	14

(c)—June, 1985—Drafted by Boston Bruins in 1985 NHL entry draft. Ninth Bruins pick, 199th overall, 10th round.

MICHAEL BRIAN BULLARD

Center . . . 5'10" . . . 183 lbs. . . . Born, Ottawa, Ont., March 10, 1961 . . . Shoots left . . . (February 21, 1982)—Scored winning goal with 4:29 to play to stop N.Y. Islanders 15-game win streak in 4-3 win at Pittsburgh . . . (October, 1982)—Missed first 20 games of the season with mononucleosis . . . Set Pittsburgh club record for goals in a rookie season (36), 1981-82 . . . (Record broken by Mario Lemieux in 1984-85) . . . (December, 1984)—Chip fracture of left shoulder and missed 11 games . . . (January 31, 1985)—Arrested in Mount Lebanon, Pennsylvania when his car struck two people . . . (March, 1990)—Injured hip flexor.

Year	Team	League	Games	G.	A.	Pts.	Pen.
1978-79—Brantford Alexanders		OMJHL	66	43	56	99	66
1979-80—Brantford Alexanders (b-c)		OMJHL	66	66	84	150	86
1980-81—Brantford Alexanders		OHL	42	47	60	107	55
1980-81—Pittsburgh Penguins		NHL	15	1	2	3	19
1981-82—Pittsburgh Penguins		NHL	75	36	27	63	91
1982-83—Pittsburgh Penguins		NHL	57	22	22	44	60
1983-84—Pittsburgh Penguins		NHL	76	51	41	92	57
1984-85—Pittsburgh Penguins		NHL	57	9	11	20	125
1985-86—Pittsburgh Penguins		NHL	77	41	42	83	69
1986-87—Pittsburgh Penguins		NHL	14	2	10	12	17
1986-87—Calgary Flames (d)		NHL	57	28	26	54	34
1987-88—Calgary Flames		NHL	79	48	55	103	68
1988-89—St. Louis Blues (e-f)		NHL	20	4	12	16	46
1988-89—Philadelphia Flyers		NHL	54	23	26	49	60
1989-90—Philadelphia Flyers (g)		NHL	70	27	37	64	67
NHL TOTALS			651	292	311	603	713

(c)—June, 1980—Drafted as underage junior by Pittsburgh Penguins in 1980 NHL entry draft. First Penguins pick, ninth overall, first round.

(d)—November, 1986—Traded by Pittsburgh Penguins to Calgary Flames for Dan Quinn.

(e)—September 5, 1988—Traded with Craig Coxe and Tim Corkery by Calgary Flames to St. Louis Blues for Doug Gilmour, Mark Hunter, Steve Bozek and Michael Dark.

(f)—November 29, 1988—Traded by St. Louis Blues to Philadelphia Flyers for Peter Zezel.

(g)—June, 1990—Signed to play with team in Lausonne, Switzerland in 1990-91 season.

MARC BUREAU

Right Wing . . . 6' . . . 195 lbs. . . . Born, Trois-Rivieres, Que., May 17, 1966 . . . Shoots right . . . (March 25, 1990)—Eye contusion at Phoenix and missed final two weeks of season.

Year	Team	League	Games	G.	A.	Pts.	Pen.
1983-84—Chicoutimi Sagueneens		QMJHL	56	6	16	22	14
1984-85—Granby Bisons		QMJHL	68	50	70	120	29
1985-86—Chicoutimi Sagueneens		QMJHL	63	36	62	98	69
1986-87—Longueuil Chevaliers (c)		QMJHL	66	54	58	112	68
1987-88—Salt Lake Golden Eagles		IHL	69	7	20	27	86
1988-89—Salt Lake Golden Eagles		IHL	76	28	36	64	119
1989-90—Salt Lake Golden Eagles		IHL	67	43	48	91	173
1989-90—Calgary Flames		NHL	5	0	0	0	4
NHL TOTALS			5	0	0	0	4

(c)—May 16, 1987—Signed by Calgary Flames as a free agent.

DAVID BURKE

Defense . . . 6'1" . . . 185 lbs. . . . Born, Detroit, Mich., October 15, 1970 . . . Shoots left.

Year	Team	League	Games	G.	A.	Pts.	Pen.
1984-85—Little Caesers Bantams		MNHL	78	24	56	80	44
1985-86—Little Caesers Midget		MNHL	71	6	39	45	72
1986-87—Detroit Compuware		NAJHL	56	7	13	20	105
1987-88—Detroit Compuware		NAJHL	61	4	34	38	94
1988-89—Cornell Univ. (c)		ECAC	30	0	3	3	24
1989-90—Cornell Univ.		ECAC	29	0	12	12	28

(c)—June, 1989—Drafted by Toronto Maple Leafs in 1989 NHL entry draft. Sixth Maple Leafs pick, 108th overall, sixth round.

TONY BURNS

Defense . . . 6' . . . 195 lbs. . . . Born, Duluth, Minn., September 18, 1971 . . . Shoots left . . . (September 2, 1988)—Injured right knee.

Year	Team	League	Games	G.	A.	Pts.	Pen.
1988-89—Duluth Denfield H.S.		Minn. H.S.	29	17	25	42	....
1989-90—Duluth Denfield H.S. (c)		Minn. H.S.	25	21	23	44	....

(c)—June 16, 1990—Selected by Detroit Red Wings in 1990 NHL entry draft. Fourth Red Wings pick, 87th overall, fifth round.

SHAWN BURR

Center . . . 6'1" . . . 180 lbs. . . . Born, Sarnia, Ont., July 1, 1966 . . . Shoots left . . . (May, 1988)—Separated left shoulder at Edmonton.

Year	Team	League	Games	G.	A.	Pts.	Pen.
1982-83—Sarnia Midgets		OPHL	52	50	85	135	125
1983-84—Kitchener Rangers (c-d)		OHL	68	41	44	85	50
1984-85—Kitchener Rangers		OHL	48	24	42	66	50
1984-85—Detroit Red Wings		NHL	9	0	0	0	2
1984-85—Adirondack Red Wings		AHL	4	0	0	0	2
1985-86—Kitchener Rangers (b)		OHL	59	60	67	127	83
1985-86—Adirondack Red Wings		AHL	3	2	2	4	2
1985-86—Detroit Red Wings		NHL	5	1	0	1	4
1986-87—Detroit Red Wings		NHL	80	22	25	47	107
1987-88—Detroit Red Wings		NHL	78	17	23	40	97
1988-89—Detroit Red Wings		NHL	79	19	27	46	78
1989-90—Adirondack Red Wings		AHL	3	4	2	6	2
1989-90—Detroit Red Wings		NHL	76	24	32	56	82
NHL TOTALS			327	83	107	190	370

(c)—June, 1984—Drafted as underage junior by Detroit Red Wings in 1984 NHL entry draft. First Red Wings pick, seventh overall, first round.

(d)—Won Emms Family Award (Top OHL Rookie).

RANDY BURRIDGE

Left Wing . . . 5'9'' . . . 170 lbs. . . . Born, Fort Erie, Ont., January 7, 1966 . . . Shoots left . . . (March 1, 1986)—Strained groin vs. New Jersey . . . (April, 1987)—Suspended during AHL playoffs . . . (February 6, 1990)—Sprained medial collateral ligament in left knee vs. Detroit and missed 18 games . . . Has also played Center.

Year	Team	League	Games	G.	A.	Pts.	Pen.
1982-83—Fort Erie Jr. B		OHA	42	32	56	88	32
1983-84—Peterborough Petes		OHL	55	6	7	13	44
1984-85—Peterborough Petes (c)		OHL	66	49	57	106	88
1985-86—Peterborough Petes		OHL	17	15	11	26	23
1985-86—Boston Bruins		NHL	52	17	25	42	28
1985-86—Moncton Golden Flames (d)		AHL	..	..	..	..	..
1986-87—Moncton Golden Flames		AHL	47	26	41	67	139
1986-87—Boston Bruins		NHL	23	1	4	5	16
1987-88—Boston Bruins		NHL	79	27	28	55	105
1988-89—Boston Bruins		NHL	80	31	30	61	39
1989-90—Boston Bruins		NHL	63	17	15	32	47
NHL TOTALS			297	93	102	195	235

(c)—June, 1985—Drafted by Boston Bruins in 1985 NHL entry draft. Seventh Bruins pick, 157th overall, eighth round.

(d)—No regular season record. Played three playoff games.

ADAM BURT

Defense . . . 6'2'' . . . 195 lbs. . . . Born, Detroit, Mich., January 15, 1969 . . . Shoots left . . . (December, 1985)—Broken jaw . . . (September 13, 1988)—Separated left shoulder in collision with Paul MacDermid during Whalers training camp . . . (December, 1989)—Bruised hip . . . (January 19, 1990)—Dislocated left shoulder in collision with Joel Otto vs. Calgary.

Year	Team	League	Games	G.	A.	Pts.	Pen.
1985-86—North Bay Centennials		OHL	49	0	11	11	81
1986-87—North Bay Centennials (c)		OHL	57	4	27	31	138
1987-88—North Bay Centennials (b)		OHL	66	17	54	71	176
1988-89—North Bay Centennials		OHL	23	4	11	15	45
1988-89—Team USA Nat. Jrs.		Int'l	7	1	6	7	....
1988-89—Binghamton Whalers		AHL	5	0	2	2	13
1988-89—Hartford Whalers		NHL	5	0	0	0	6
1989-90—Hartford Whalers		NHL	63	4	8	12	105
NHL TOTALS			68	4	8	12	111

(c)—June, 1987—Drafted as underage junior by Hartford Whalers in 1987 NHL entry draft. Second Whalers pick, 39th overall, second round.

ROD DALE BUSKAS

Defense . . . 6'2'' . . . 195 lbs. . . . Born, Wetaskiwin, Alta., January 7, 1961 . . . Shoots right . . . (February, 1985)—Shoulder injury . . . (November, 1986)—Injured shoulder . . . (December 13, 1989)—Broke ankle at Winnipeg, required surgery and missed 29 games.

Year	Team	League	Games	G.	A.	Pts.	Pen.
1978-79—Red Deer Rustlers		AJHL	37	13	22	35	63
1978-79—Billings Bighorns		WHL	1	0	0	0	0
1978-79—Medicine Hat Tigers		WHL	35	1	12	13	60
1979-80—Medicine Hat Tigers		WHL	72	7	40	47	284
1980-81—Medicine Hat Tigers (c)		WHL	72	14	46	60	164
1981-82—Erie Blades		AHL	69	1	18	19	78
1982-83—Muskegon Mohawks		IHL	1	0	0	0	9
1982-83—Baltimore Skipjacks		AHL	31	2	8	10	45
1982-83—Pittsburgh Penguins		NHL	41	2	2	4	102
1983-84—Baltimore Skipjacks		AHL	33	2	12	14	100
1983-84—Pittsburgh Penguins		NHL	47	2	4	6	60
1984-85—Pittsburgh Penguins		NHL	69	2	7	9	191
1985-86—Pittsburgh Penguins		NHL	72	2	7	9	159
1986-87—Pittsburgh Penguins		NHL	68	3	15	18	123
1987-88—Pittsburgh Penguins		NHL	76	4	8	12	206
1988-89—Pittsburgh Penguins		NHL	52	1	5	6	105
1989-90—Vancouver Canucks (d-e)		NHL	17	0	3	3	36
1989-90—Pittsburgh Penguins		NHL	6	0	0	0	13
NHL TOTALS			448	16	51	67	995

(c)—June, 1981—Drafted by Pittsburgh Penguins in 1981 NHL entry draft. Fifth Penguins pick, 112th overall, sixth round.

(d)—October 24, 1989—Traded by Pittsburgh Penguins to Vancouver Canucks for a sixth-round 1990 draft pick (Ian Moran).

(e)—January 8, 1990—Traded with Tony Tanti and Barry Pederson by Vancouver Canucks to Pittsburgh Penguins for Dan Quinn, Andrew McBain and Dave Capuano.

GARTH BUTCHER

Defense . . . 6' . . . 194 lbs. . . . Born, Regina, Sask., January 8, 1963 . . . Shoots right . . . (October, 1984)—Shoulder separation.

Year	Team	League	Games	G.	A.	Pts.	Pen.
1978-79—Regina Canadians		AMHL	22	4	22	26	72
1979-80—Regina Tier II		SJHL	51	15	31	46	236
1979-80—Regina Pats		WHL	13	0	4	4	20
1980-81—Regina Pats (a-c)		WHL	69	9	77	86	230
1981-82—Regina Pats (a)		WHL	65	24	68	92	318
1981-82—Vancouver Canucks		NHL	5	0	0	0	9
1982-83—Kamloops Junior Oilers		WHL	5	4	2	6	4
1982-83—Vancouver Canucks		NHL	55	1	13	14	104
1983-84—Fredericton Express		AHL	25	4	13	17	43
1983-84—Vancouver Canucks		NHL	28	2	0	2	34
1984-85—Vancouver Canucks		NHL	75	3	9	12	152
1985-86—Vancouver Canucks		NHL	70	4	7	11	188
1986-87—Vancouver Canucks		NHL	70	5	15	20	207
1987-88—Vancouver Canucks		NHL	80	6	17	23	285
1988-89—Vancouver Canucks		NHL	78	0	20	20	227
1989-90—Vancouver Canucks		NHL	80	6	14	20	205
NHL TOTALS			541	27	95	122	1411

(c)—June, 1981—Drafted as underage junior by Vancouver Canucks in 1981 NHL entry draft. First Canucks pick, 10th overall, first round.

JOHN BYCE

Center . . . 6' . . . 175 lbs. . . . Born, Madison, Wis., September 8, 1967 . . . Shoots right . . . (November 18, 1988)—Injured knee.

Year	Team	League	Games	G.	A.	Pts.	Pen.
1984-85—Madison Memorial (c)		Wisc. H.S.	24	39	47	86	32
1985-86—....................			....	....	....	....	....
1986-87—Univ. of Wisconsin		WCHA	40	1	4	5	12
1987-88—Univ. of Wisconsin		WCHA	41	22	12	34	18
1988-89—Univ. of Wisconsin (b)		WCHA	42	27	28	55	16
1989-90—Univ. of Wisconsin		WCHA	46	27	44	71	20
1989-90—Boston Bruins (d)		NHL	....	....	....	....	....

(c)—June, 1985—Drafted by Boston Bruins in 1985 NHL entry draft. Eleventh Bruins pick, 220th overall, 11th round.

(d)—No regular season record. Played eight playoff games.

LYNDON BYERS

Right Wing . . . 6'2'' . . . 195 lbs. . . . Born, Nipawin, Sask., February 29, 1964 . . . Shoots right . . . (April, 1981)—Broken right wrist . . . (September, 1987)—Torn ligaments in right knee in collision in training camp . . . (November, 1987)—Separated left shoulder . . . (March, 1988)—Bruised right hand . . . (April, 1988)—Bruised left thigh . . . (September, 1988)—Dislocated jaw in training camp . . . (December, 1988)—Separated right shoulder . . . (February, 1989)—Inflammation of left elbow . . . (March 22, 1989)—Separated right shoulder . . . (September 29, 1989)—Injured left knee and missed first seven games of season . . . (December 9, 1989)—Tore tendon in left thumb in fight with Alan May vs. Washington and missed 14 games . . . (February, 1990)—Broke left foot and missed 14 games.

Year	Team	League	Games	G.	A.	Pts.	Pen.
1980-81—Notre Dame Hounds (b)		SCMHL	37	35	42	77	106
1981-82—Regina Pats (c-d)		WHL	57	18	25	43	169
1982-83—Regina Pats		WHL	70	32	38	70	153
1983-84—Regina Pats		WHL	58	32	57	89	154
1983-84—Boston Bruins		NHL	10	2	4	6	32
1984-85—Hershey Bears		AHL	27	4	6	10	55
1984-85—Boston Bruins		NHL	33	3	8	11	41
1985-86—Boston Bruins		NHL	5	0	2	2	9
1985-86—Moncton Golden Flames		AHL	14	2	4	6	26
1985-86—Milwaukee Admirals		IHL	8	0	2	2	22
1986-87—Moncton Golden Flames		AHL	27	5	5	10	63
1986-87—Boston Bruins		NHL	18	2	3	5	53
1987-88—Maine Mariners		AHL	2	0	1	1	18
1987-88—Boston Bruins		NHL	53	10	14	24	236
1988-89—Maine Mariners		AHL	4	1	3	4	12
1988-89—Boston Bruins		NHL	49	0	4	4	218
1989-90—Boston Bruins		NHL	43	4	4	8	159
NHL TOTALS			211	21	39	60	748

(c)—September, 1981—Traded by Saskatoon Blades to Regina Pats for Todd Strueby.

(d)—June, 1982—Drafted as underage junior by Boston Bruins in NHL entry draft. Third Bruins pick, 39th overall, second round.

DANIEL BYLSMA

Left Wing . . . 6'2'' . . . 205 lbs. . . . Born, Grand Rapids, Mich., September 19, 1970 . . . Shoots left.

Year	Team	League	Games	G.	A.	Pts.	Pen.
1987-88—St. Mary's Jr. B		WJBHL	40	30	39	69	33
1988-89—Bowling Green Univ. (c)		CCHA	39	4	7	11	16
1989-90—Bowling Green Univ.		CCHA	44	13	17	30	32

(c)—June, 1989—Drafted by Winnipeg Jets in 1989 NHL entry draft. Sixth Jets pick, 69th overall, fourth round.

SHAWN BYRAM

Left Wing . . . 6'2'' . . . 190 lbs. . . . Born, Neepawa, Man., September 12, 1968 . . . Shoots left . . . Also plays Center.

Year	Team	League	Games	G.	A.	Pts.	Pen.
1984-85—Regina Canadians		Sask. Midget	25	12	21	33	38
1985-86—Regina Pats (c)		WHL	46	7	6	13	45
1986-87—Prince Albert Raiders		WHL	67	19	21	40	147

Year	Team	League	Games	G.	A.	Pts.	Pen.
1987-88—Prince Albert Raiders		WHL	61	23	28	51	178
1988-89—Springfield Indians		AHL	45	5	11	16	195
1988-89—Indianapolis Ice		IHL	1	0	0	0	2
1989-90—Springfield Indians		AHL	31	4	4	8	30
1989-90—Johnstown Chiefs		ECHL	8	5	5	10	35

(c)—June, 1986—Drafted as underage junior by New York Islanders in 1986 NHL entry draft. Fourth Islanders pick, 80th overall, fourth round.

GERALD BZDEL

Defense . . . 6' . . . 190 lbs. . . . Born, Wyryard, Sask., March 13, 1968 . . . Shoots right . . . (March, 1985)—Torn ligaments in left knee.

Year	Team	League	Games	G.	A.	Pts.	Pen.
1984-85—Regina Pats		WHL	20	0	4	4	6
1985-86—Regina Pats (c)		WHL	72	2	15	17	107
1986-87—Seattle Thunderbirds		WHL	48	4	12	16	137
1987-88—Moose Jaw Warriors		WHL	72	4	17	21	217
1988-89—Halifax Citadels		AHL	36	1	3	4	46
1989-90—Halifax Citadels		AHL	59	2	20	22	84

(c)—June, 1986—Drafted as underage junior by Quebec Nordiques in 1986 NHL entry draft. Fifth Nordiques pick, 102nd overall, fifth round.

STEVE CADIEUX

Center . . . 5'10" . . . 175 lbs. . . . Born, Ste. Therese, Que., June 17, 1969 . . . Shoots left.

Year	Team	League	Games	G.	A.	Pts.	Pen.
1986-87—St. Jean Castors		QMJHL	65	28	22	50	26
1987-88—St. Jean Castors		QMJHL	66	43	50	93	18
1988-89—St. Jean/Shawinigan (c-d-e)		QMJHL	70	*80	86	166	22
1989-90—Shawinigan Cataracts		QMJHL	67	*73	90	163	101

(c)—November 5, 1988—Traded with Pierre Cote by St. Jean Castors to Shawinigan Cataracts for Patrice Lebeau and rights to Eric Metivier.
(d)—Won Frank Selke Trophy (Most Gentlemanly Player).
(e)—June, 1989—Drafted by Montreal Canadiens in 1989 NHL entry draft. Twelfth Canadiens pick, 251st overall, 12th round.

DARCY CAHILL

Center . . . 5'11" . . . 190 lbs. . . . Born, Kingston, Ont., August 19, 1970 . . . Shoots right.

Year	Team	League	Games	G.	A.	Pts.	Pen.
1985-86—Kingston Jr. B.		OHA	31	21	28	49	12
1986-87—North Bay Centennials		OHL	52	7	19	26	7
1987-88—Kingston Canadians		OHL	66	27	41	68	19
1988-89—Cornwall Royals (c-d)		OHL	66	35	57	92	49
1989-90—Cornwall Royals (e)		OHL	36	24	52	76	51
1989-90—Sudbury Wolves		OHL	22	14	19	33	22

(c)—November, 1988—Traded by Kingston Raiders to Cornwall Royals for Brad Gratton.
(d)—June, 1989—Drafted by Vancouver Canucks in 1989 NHL entry draft. Tenth Canucks pick, 239th overall, 12th round.
(e)—January, 1990—Traded by Cornwall Royals to Sudbury Wolves for Darren Bell, Markus Middleton and a sixth-round 1990 draft pick.

PAUL CAIN

Center . . . 5'10" . . . 180 lbs. . . . Born, Toronto, Ont., April 6, 1969 . . . Shoots right . . . Suspended by Cornwall Royals after drunk-driving accident.

Year	Team	League	Games	G.	A.	Pts.	Pen.
1984-85—Toronto Red Wings		Ont. Mdgt.	40	36	38	74	26
1985-86—Cornwall Royals		OHL	62	11	12	23	21
1986-87—Cornwall Royals		OHL	60	13	27	40	8
1987-88—Cornwall Royals (c)		OHL	21	14	9	23	6
1988-89—Cornwall Royals		OHL	44	19	47	66	26
1989-90—Cornwall Royals		OHL	47	28	36	64	23

(c)—June, 1988—Drafted by New York Rangers in 1988 NHL entry draft. Ninth Rangers pick, 194th overall, 10th round.

JOHN (JOCK) CALLANDER

Center . . . 6'1" . . . 170 lbs. . . . Born, Regina, Sask., April 23, 1961 . . . Shoots right . . . Brother of Drew Callander.

Year	Team	League	Games	G.	A.	Pts.	Pen.
1978-79—Regina Pats		WHL	19	3	2	5	0
1978-79—Regina Blues		SJHL	42	44	42	86	24
1979-80—Regina Pats		WHL	39	9	11	20	25
1980-81—Regina Pats		WHL	72	67	86	153	37
1981-82—Regina Pats (c-d)		WHL	71	79	111	*190	59
1982-83—Salt Lake Golden Eagles		CHL	68	20	27	47	26
1983-84—Montana Magic		CHL	72	27	32	59	69
1983-84—Toledo Goaldiggers		IHL	2	0	0	0	0
1984-85—Muskegon Lumberjacks		IHL	82	39	68	107	86
1985-86—Muskegon Lumberjacks (e)		IHL	82	39	72	111	121
1986-87—Muskegon Lumberjacks (a-f-g)		IHL	82	54	82	*136	110
1987-88—Muskegon Lumberjacks		IHL	31	20	36	56	49
1987-88—Pittsburgh Penguins		NHL	41	11	16	27	45
1988-89—Muskegon Lumberjacks		IHL	48	25	39	64	40
1988-89—Pittsburgh Penguins		NHL	30	6	5	11	20
1989-90—Muskegon Lumberjacks		IHL	46	29	49	78	118
1989-90—Pittsburgh Penguins		NHL	30	4	7	11	49
NHL TOTALS			101	21	28	49	114

(c)—Won Bob Brownridge Memorial Trophy (WHL scoring leader).
(d)—Led WHL playoffs with 26 assists.
(e)—Won Turner Cup Playoff MVP.
(f)—Co-winner of Leo P. Lamoureaux Memorial Trophy (IHL leading scorer) with Jeff Pyle.
(g)—Co-winner of James Gatschene Memorial Trophy (IHL MVP) with Jeff Pyle.

WADE CAMPBELL

Defense . . . 6'4" . . . 220 lbs. . . . Born, Peace River, Alta., February 1, 1961 . . . Shoots right.

Year	Team	League	Games	G.	A.	Pts.	Pen.
1980-81—University of Alberta		CWJAA	24	3	15	18	46
1981-82—University of Alberta (c)		CWJAA	24	6	12	18	....
1982-83—Sherbrooke Jets		AHL	18	4	2	6	23
1982-83—Winnipeg Jets		NHL	42	1	2	3	50
1983-84—Winnipeg Jets		NHL	79	7	14	21	147
1984-85—Winnipeg Jets		NHL	40	1	6	7	21
1984-85—Sherbrooke Canadiens		AHL	28	2	6	8	70
1985-86—Sherbrooke Canadiens		AHL	9	0	2	2	26
1985-86—Winnipeg Jets (d)		NHL	24	0	1	1	27
1985-86—Moncton Golden Flames		AHL	17	2	2	4	21
1985-86—Boston Bruins		NHL	8	0	0	0	15
1986-87—Moncton Golden Flames		AHL	64	12	23	35	34
1986-87—Boston Bruins		NHL	14	0	3	3	24
1987-88—Boston Bruins		NHL	6	0	1	1	21
1987-88—Maine Mariners		AHL	69	11	29	40	118
1988-89—Played in France			....	....	....	....	....
1989-90—Cape Breton Oilers (e)		AHL	77	4	31	35	84
NHL TOTALS			213	9	27	36	305

(c)—September, 1982—Signed by Winnipeg Jets as a free agent.
(d)—January, 1986—Traded by Winnipeg Jets to Boston Bruins for Bill Derlago.
(e)—September 28, 1989—Signed with Edmonton Oilers as a free agent.

DAVID CAPUANO

Center . . . 6'2" . . . 190 lbs. . . . Born, Warwick, R.I., July 27, 1968 . . . Shoots left . . . Brother of Jack Capuano. . . . (August, 1986)—Broke hand at U.S. National Junior Team tryout camp at Lake Placid, N.Y.

Year	Team	League	Games	G.	A.	Pts.	Pen.
1984-85—Mt. St. Charles H.S.		R.I. H.S.	....	41	38	79	....
1985-86—Mt. St. Charles H.S. (c)		R.I. H.S.	22	39	48	87	20
1986-87—University of Maine		H. East	38	18	41	59	14
1987-88—University of Maine		H. East	42	34	51	85	51
1988-89—University of Maine (a-d)		H. East	41	37	30	67	38
1989-90—Muskegon Lumberjacks		IHL	27	15	15	30	22
1989-90—Pittsburgh Penguins (e)		NHL	6	0	0	0	2
1989-90—Vancouver Canucks		NHL	27	3	5	8	10
1989-90—Milwaukee Admirals		IHL	2	0	4	4	0
NHL TOTALS			33	3	5	8	12

(c)—June, 1986—Drafted by Pittsburgh Penguins in 1986 NHL entry draft. Second Penguins pick, 25th overall, second round.
(d)—Named First team All-America (East).
(e)—January 8, 1990—Traded with Dan Quinn and Andrew McBain by Pittsburgh Penguins to Vancouver Canucks for Tony Tanti, Barry Pederson and Rod Buskas.

JACK CAPUANO

Defense . . . 6'2" . . . 210 lbs. . . . Born, Cranston, R.I., July 7, 1966 . . . Shoots left . . . Brother of Dave Capuano.

Year	Team	League	Games	G.	A.	Pts.	Pen.
1983-84—Kent Prep. (c)		Conn.	....	10	8	18	....
1984-85—University of Maine		H. East	...	...	...	...	...
1985-86—University of Maine		H. East	39	9	13	22	59
1986-87—University of Maine (b)		H. East	42	10	34	44	20
1987-88—University of Maine (d)		H. East	43	13	37	50	87
1988-89—Newmarket Saints		AHL	74	5	16	21	52
1989-90—Toronto Maple Leafs (e)		NHL	1	0	0	0	0
1989-90—Newmarket Saints		AHL	8	0	2	2	7
1989-90—Springfield Indians (f)		AHL	14	0	4	4	8
1989-90—Milwaukee Admirals		IHL	17	3	10	13	60
NHL TOTALS			1	0	0	0	0

(c)—June, 1984—Drafted by Toronto Maple Leafs in 1984 NHL entry draft. Fourth Maple Leafs pick, 88th overall, fifth round.
(d)—Named First team All-America (East).
(e)—December 20, 1989—Traded with Paul Gagne and Derek Laxdal by Toronto Maple Leafs to New York Islanders for Gilles Thibaudeau and Mike Stevens.
(f)—March 6, 1990—Traded by New York Islanders to Vancouver Canucks for Jeff Rohlicek.

GUY CARBONNEAU

Center . . . 5'11" . . . 175 lbs. . . . Born, Sept Iles, Que., March 18, 1960 . . . Shoots right . . . (October 7, 1989)—Strained right knee ligaments when checked by Mike Foligno vs. Buffalo and missed nine games . . . (October 28, 1989)—Nose broken by Kevin Lowe vs. Edmonton.

Year	Team	League	Games	G.	A.	Pts.	Pen.
1976-77—Chicoutimi Sagueneens		QMJHL	59	9	20	29	8
1977-78—Chicoutimi Sagueneens		QMJHL	70	28	55	83	60
1978-79—Chicoutimi Sagueneens (c)		QMJHL	72	62	79	141	47
1979-80—Chicoutimi Sagueneens (b)		QMJHL	72	72	110	182	66
1979-80—Nova Scotia Voyageurs (d)		AHL	....	....	....	....	....
1980-81—Montreal Canadiens		NHL	2	0	1	1	0
1980-81—Nova Scotia Voyageurs		AHL	78	35	53	88	87
1981-82—Nova Scotia Voyageurs		AHL	77	27	67	94	124
1982-83—Montreal Canadiens		NHL	77	18	29	47	68
1983-84—Montreal Canadiens		NHL	78	24	30	54	75
1984-85—Montreal Canadiens		NHL	79	23	34	57	43
1985-86—Montreal Canadiens		NHL	80	20	36	56	57
1986-87—Montreal Canadiens		NHL	79	17	21	45	68
1987-88—Montreal Canadiens (e)		NHL	80	17	21	38	61
1988-89—Montreal Canadiens (e)		NHL	79	26	30	56	44
1989-90—Montreal Canadiens		NHL	68	19	36	55	37
NHL TOTALS			622	165	244	409	453

189

(c)—August, 1979—Drafted by Montreal Canadiens as underage junior in NHL entry draft. Fourth Canadiens pick, 44th overall, third round.
(d)—No regular season record. Played one playoff game.
(e)—Won Frank Selke Trophy (Top NHL defensive forward).

TERRY CARKNER

Defense . . . 6'3" . . . 200 lbs. . . . Born, Smith Falls, Ont., March 7, 1966 . . . Shoots left . . . (January 24, 1988)—Suspended 10 games by NHL for leaving the bench during an altercation in game vs. Montreal . . . (September 23, 1989)—Left knee surgery vs. N.Y. Islanders and missed 15 games . . . (March, 1990)—Bruised ankle.

Year	Team	League	Games	G.	A.	Pts.	Pen.
1982-83—Brockville Braves	COJHL	47	8	32	40	94
1983-84—Peterborough Petes (c)	OHL	66	4	21	25	91
1984-85—Peterborough Petes (b)	OHL	64	14	47	61	125
1985-86—Peterborough Petes (a-d)	OHL	54	12	32	44	106
1986-87—New Haven Nighthawks	AHL	12	2	6	8	56
1986-87—New York Rangers (e)	NHL	52	2	13	15	120
1987-88—Quebec Nordiques (f)	NHL	63	3	24	27	159
1988-89—Philadelphia Flyers	NHL	78	11	32	43	149
1989-90—Philadelphia Flyers	NHL	63	4	18	22	167
NHL TOTALS		256	20	87	107	595

(c)—June, 1984—Drafted as underage junior by New York Rangers in NHL entry draft. First Rangers pick, 14th overall, first round.
(d)—Shared Max Kaminsky Trophy (Top OHL Defenseman) with Jeff Brown.
(e)—September, 1987—Traded with Jeff Jackson by New York Rangers to Quebec Nordiques for John Ogrodnick and David Shaw.
(f)—July, 1988—Traded by Quebec Nordiques to Philadelphia Flyers for Greg Smyth and third-round draft choice in 1989 (John Tanner).

RANDY ROBERT CARLYLE

Defense . . . 5'10" . . . 198 lbs. . . . Born, Sudbury, Ont., April 19, 1956 . . . Shoots left . . . Missed part of 1978-79 season with broken ankle . . . (October, 1982)—Injured back . . . (January, 1983)—Injured knee . . . (March, 1984)—Knee injury . . . (November 12, 1985)—Missed eight games with thigh injury . . . (November, 1986)—Missed nine games with whiplash injury after being checked by Tiger Williams vs. Los Angeles . . . Does not wear a helmet . . . (January 18, 1989)—Strained neck muscles when he struck the end boards head first after a check by Craig Muni vs. Edmonton . . . (November 5, 1989)—Bruised left knee at Chicago and missed nine games . . . (December, 1989)—Missed 10 games due to death of his parents . . . (March 15, 1990)—Torn ligaments in right knee.

Year	Team	League	Games	G.	A.	Pts.	Pen.
1973-74—Sudbury Wolves	Jr."A" OHA	12	0	8	8	21
1974-75—Sudbury Wolves	Jr."A" OHA	67	17	47	64	118
1975-76—Sudbury Wolves (b-c)	Jr."A" OHA	60	15	64	79	126
1976-77—Dallas Black Hawks	CHL	26	2	7	9	63
1976-77—Toronto Maple Leafs	NHL	45	0	5	5	51
1977-78—Dallas Black Hawks	CHL	21	3	14	17	31
1977-78—Toronto Maple Leafs (d)	NHL	49	2	11	13	31
1978-79—Pittsburgh Penguins	NHL	70	13	34	47	78
1979-80—Pittsburgh Penguins	NHL	67	8	28	36	45
1980-81—Pittsburgh Penguins (a-e)	NHL	76	16	67	83	136
1981-82—Pittsburgh Penguins	NHL	73	11	64	75	131
1982-83—Pittsburgh Penguins	NHL	61	15	41	56	110
1983-84—Pittsburgh Penguins (f)	NHL	50	3	23	26	82
1983-84—Winnipeg Jets	NHL	5	0	3	3	2
1984-85—Winnipeg Jets	NHL	71	13	38	51	98
1985-86—Winnipeg Jets	NHL	68	16	33	49	93
1986-87—Winnipeg Jets	NHL	71	16	26	42	93
1987-88—Winnipeg Jets	NHL	78	15	44	59	210
1988-89—Winnipeg Jets	NHL	78	6	38	44	78
1989-90—Winnipeg Jets	NHL	53	3	15	18	50
NHL TOTALS		915	137	470	607	1288

(c)—Drafted from Sudbury Wolves by Toronto Maple Leafs in second round of 1976 amateur draft.
(d)—Traded to Pittsburgh Penguins by Toronto Maple Leafs with George Ferguson for Dave Burrows, June, 1978.
(e)—Won James Norris Memorial Trophy (Top NHL Defenseman).
(f)—March, 1984—Traded by Pittsburgh Penguins to Winnipeg Jets for first round 1984 draft pick (Doug Bodger) and player to be named after the 1983-84 season (Moe Mantha).

KEITH CARNEY

Defense . . . 6'1" . . . 175 lbs. . . . Born, Cumberland, R.I. February 7, 1971 . . . Shoots left.

Year	Team	League	Games	G.	A.	Pts.	Pen.
1987-88—Mt. St. Charles H.S.	R.I. H.S.	....	8	15	23	....
1988-89—Mt. St. Charles H.S. (c)	R.I. H.S.	....	12	25	37	....
1989-90—Univ. of Maine (b)	H. East	41	3	41	44	43

(c)—June, 1989—Drafted by Toronto Maple Leafs in 1989 NHL entry draft. Fifth Maple Leafs pick, 96th overall, fifth round.

ROBERT CARPENTER

Center . . . 6' . . . 190 lbs. . . . Born, Beverly, Mass., July 13, 1963 . . . Shoots left . . . First to play in NHL directly from U.S. high school hockey . . . Set NHL record for most goals by American-born player (53), 1984-85 (Record broken by Jimmy Carson in 1987-88) . . . (January, 1988)—Torn rotator cuff . . . (December 31, 1988)—Broke right thumb and wrist in exhibition game against Dynamo Riga . . . (April, 1989)—Tore ligaments of right wrist vs. Montreal.

Year	Team	League	Games	G.	A.	Pts.	Pen.
1979-80—St. Johns Prep. H.S. (a)	Mass. H.S.	....	28	37	65	....
1980-81—St. Johns Prep. H.S. (a-c)	Mass. H.S.	....	14	24	38	....

Year	Team	League	Games	G.	A.	Pts.	Pen.
1981-82—Washington Capitals	NHL	80	32	35	67	69
1982-83—Washington Capitals	NHL	80	32	37	69	64
1983-84—Washington Capitals	NHL	80	28	40	68	51
1984-85—Washington Capitals	NHL	80	53	42	95	87
1985-86—Washington Capitals	NHL	80	27	29	56	105
1986-87—Washington Capitals (d)	NHL	22	5	7	12	21
1986-87—New York Rangers (e)	NHL	28	2	8	10	20
1986-87—Los Angeles Kings	NHL	10	2	3	5	6
1987-88—Los Angeles Kings	NHL	71	19	33	52	84
1988-89—Los Angeles Kings	NHL	39	11	15	26	16
1988-89—Boston Bruins (f)	NHL	18	5	9	14	10
1989-90—Boston Bruins	NHL	80	25	31	56	97
NHL TOTALS		668	241	289	530	630

(c)—June, 1981—Drafted as underage junior by Washington Capitals in 1981 NHL entry draft. First Capitals pick, third overall, first round.
(d)—January, 1987—Traded with second-round 1989 draft pick by Washington Capitals to New York Rangers for Mike Ridley, Kelly Miller and Bobby Crawford.
(e)—March, 1987—Traded with Tom Laidlaw by New York Rangers to Los Angeles Kings for Marcel Dionne, Jeff Crossman and a third-round 1989 draft pick.
(f)—January 23, 1989—Traded by Los Angeles Kings to Boston Bruins for Steve Kasper and Jay Miller.

JAMES CARSON

Center . . . 6' . . . 185 lbs. . . . Born, Southfield, Mich., July 20, 1968 . . . Shoots right . . . (October, 1986)—Youngest Los Angeles King in club history . . . Set NHL record for most goals by American-born player (55), 1987-88 . . . Set NHL record for most points by American-born player (107), 1987-88 (Record broken by Joe Mullen in 1988-89) . . . (September 27, 1989)—Bruised right knee at Calgary . . . (February 3, 1990)—Injured right knee ligaments at St. Louis and missed 14 games . . . (March, 1990)—Tonsillitis and mononucleosis.

Year	Team	League	Games	G.	A.	Pts.	Pen.
1984-85—Verdun Juniors	QMJHL	68	44	72	116	16
1985-86—Verdun Juniors (b-c-d-e)	QMJHL	69	70	83	153	46
1986-87—Los Angeles Kings	NHL	80	37	42	79	22
1987-88—Los Angeles Kings (f)	NHL	80	55	52	107	45
1988-89—Edmonton Oilers	NHL	80	49	51	100	36
1989-90—Edmonton Oilers (g)	NHL	4	1	2	3	0
1989-90—Detroit Red Wings	NHL	44	20	16	36	8
NHL TOTALS		288	162	163	325	111

(c)—Won Frank Selke Trophy (Most Gentlemanly player).
(d)—Won Mike Bossy Trophy (Top Pro Prospect).
(e)—June, 1986—Drafted as underage junior by Los Angeles Kings in 1986 NHL entry draft. First Kings pick, second overall, first round.
(f)—August, 1988—Traded with Martin Gelinas and first-round draft choices in 1989 (traded to New Jersey), '91 and '93, plus $15 million by Los Angeles Kings to Edmonton Oilers for Wayne Gretzky, Marty McSorley and Mike Krushelnyski.
(g)—November 2, 1989—Traded with Kevin McClelland and a fifth-round 1991 draft pick by Edmonton Oilers to Detroit Red Wings for Joe Murphy, Adam Graves, Petr Klima and Jeff Sharples.

JOHN CARTER

Left Wing . . . 5'10" . . . 175 lbs. . . . Born, Winchester, Mass., May 3, 1963 . . . Shoots left . . . (February, 1986)—Sprained knee in ECAC game . . . (March, 1987)—Bruised knee . . . (February, 1988)—Bruised knee.

Year	Team	League	Games	G.	A.	Pts.	Pen.
1982-83—R.P.I.	ECAC	29	16	22	38	33
1983-84—R.P.I. (b)	ECAC	38	35	39	74	52
1984-85—R.P.I. (a-c)	ECAC	37	43	29	72	52
1985-86—R.P.I. (d)	ECAC	27	23	18	41	68
1985-86—Boston Bruins	NHL	3	0	0	0	0
1986-87—Moncton Golden Flames	AHL	58	25	30	55	60
1986-87—Boston Bruins	NHL	8	0	1	1	0
1987-88—Boston Bruins	NHL	4	0	1	1	2
1987-88—Maine Mariners	AHL	76	38	38	76	145
1988-89—Maine Mariners	AHL	24	13	6	19	12
1988-89—Boston Bruins	NHL	44	12	10	22	24
1989-90—Maine Mariners	AHL	2	2	2	4	2
1989-90—Boston Bruins	NHL	76	17	22	39	26
NHL TOTALS		135	29	34	63	52

(c)—Named Second team All-America (East).
(d)—March, 1986—Signed by Boston Bruins as a free agent.

ANDREW CASSELS

Center . . . 6' . . . 167 lbs. . . . Born, Mississauga, Ont., July 23, 1969 . . . Shoots left . . . (January, 1986)—Broken wrist . . . (September, 1988)—First degree sprain of left knee ligaments vs. Hartford . . . (November 22, 1989)—Separated right shoulder at Philadelphia and missed 10 games.

Year	Team	League	Games	G.	A.	Pts.	Pen.
1985-86—Bramalea Jr. B	OHA	33	18	25	43	26
1986-87—Ottawa 67's (c-d)	OHL	66	26	66	92	28
1987-88—Ottawa 67's (a-e-f)	OHL	61	48	*103	*151	39
1988-89—Ottawa 67's (a)	OHL	56	37	97	134	66
1989-90—Sherbrooke Canadiens	AHL	55	22	45	67	25
1989-90—Montreal Canadiens	NHL	6	2	0	2	2
NHL TOTALS		6	2	0	2	2

(c)—Won Emms Family Award (OHL Rookie of the Year).
(d)—June, 1987—Drafted as underage junior by Montreal Canadiens in 1987 NHL entry draft. First Canadiens pick, 17th overall, first round.
(e)—Won Eddie Powers Memorial Trophy (Top OHL scorer).
(f)—Won Red Tilson Trophy (Outstanding Player).

BRUCE CASSIDY

Defense . . . 5'11" . . . 175 lbs. . . . Born, Ottawa, Ont., May 20, 1965 . . . Shoots left . . . (Summer, 1984)—Injured knee and missed training camp.

Year	Team	League	Games	G.	A.	Pts.	Pen.
1981-82—Hawkesbury Hawks	COJHL	37	13	30	43	32
1982-83—Ottawa 67's (c-d)	OHL	70	25	86	111	33
1983-84—Ottawa 67's (b)	OHL	67	27	68	95	58
1983-84—Chicago Black Hawks	NHL	1	0	0	0	0
1984-85—Ottawa 67's	OHL	28	13	27	40	15
1985-86—Chicago Black Hawks	NHL	1	0	0	0	0
1985-86—Nova Scotia Oilers	AHL	4	0	0	0	0
1986-87—Saginaw Generals	IHL	10	2	13	15	6
1986-87—Nova Scotia Oilers	IHL	19	2	8	10	4
1986-87—Chicago Black Hawks	NHL	2	0	0	0	0
1987-88—Chicago Black Hawks	NHL	21	3	10	13	6
1987-88—Saginaw Hawks	IHL	60	9	37	46	59
1988-89—Chicago Black Hawks	NHL	9	0	2	2	4
1988-89—Saginaw Hawks (a)	IHL	72	16	64	80	80
1989-90—Indianapolis Ice	IHL	75	11	46	57	56
1989-90—Chicago Black Hawks	NHL	2	1	1	2	0
NHL TOTALS		36	4	13	17	10

(c)—Won Emms Family Award (OHL Rookie-of-the-Year).
(d)—June, 1983—Drafted as underage junior by Chicago Black Hawks in NHL entry draft. First Black Hawks pick, 18th overall, first round.

JAY CAUFIELD

Right Wing . . . 6'4" . . . 220 lbs. . . . Born, Lansdale, Penn., July 17, 1965 . . . Shoots right . . . Linebacker at University of North Dakota. He gave up his football career following a neck injury. . . . (October, 1986)—Injured knee . . . (October, 1988)—Injured ankle and suffered blood poisining . . . (December, 1988)—Pinched nerve in neck . . . (February 2, 1990)—Dislocated finger on right hand during fight with Kelly Buchberger vs. Edmonton and missed 18 games following surgery.

Year	Team	League	Games	G.	A.	Pts.	Pen.
1984-85—University of North Dakota	WCHA	1	0	0	0	0
1985-86—New Haven Nighthawks (c)	AHL	42	2	3	5	40
1985-86—Toledo Goaldiggers	IHL	30	5	3	8	54
1986-87—New Haven Nighthawks	AHL	13	0	0	0	43
1986-87—Flint Spirit	IHL	14	4	3	7	59
1986-87—New York Rangers	NHL	13	2	1	3	45
1987-88—Kalamazoo Wings	IHL	65	5	10	15	273
1987-88—Minnesota North Stars (d)	NHL	1	0	0	0	0
1988-89—Pittsburgh Penguins (e)	NHL	58	1	4	5	285
1989-90—Pittsburgh Penguins	NHL	37	1	2	3	123
NHL TOTALS		109	4	7	11	453

(c)—October, 1985—Signed by New York Rangers as a free agent.
(d)—October, 1987—Traded with Dave Gagner by New York Rangers to Minnesota North Stars for Jari Gronstrand and Paul Boutilier.
(e)—October 3, 1988—Selected by Pittsburgh Penguins in 1988 NHL waiver draft for $40,000.

GINO CAVALLINI

Left Wing . . . 6'2" . . . 215 lbs. . . . Born, Toronto, Ont., November 24, 1962 . . . Shoots left . . . (January, 1988)—Missed 16 games with broken right hand . . . (February, 1989)—Strained left knee.

Year	Team	League	Games	G.	A.	Pts.	Pen.
1981-82—Toronto St. Mikes	OJHL	37	27	56	83	..
1982-83—Bowling Green Univ.	CCHA	40	8	16	24	52
1983-84—Bowling Green Univ. (c)	CCHA	43	25	23	48	16
1984-85—Moncton Golden Flames	AHL	51	29	19	48	28
1984-85—Calgary Flames	NHL	27	6	10	16	14
1985-86—Moncton Golden Flames	AHL	4	3	2	5	7
1985-86—Calgary Flames (d)	NHL	27	7	7	14	26
1985-86—St. Louis Blues	NHL	30	6	5	11	36
1986-87—St. Louis Blues	NHL	80	18	26	44	54
1987-88—St. Louis Blues	NHL	64	15	17	32	62
1988-89—St. Louis Blues	NHL	74	20	23	43	79
1989-90—St. Louis Blues	NHL	80	15	15	30	77
NHL TOTALS		382	87	103	190	348

(c)—July, 1984—Signed by Calgary Flames as a free agent.
(d)—February, 1986—Traded with Eddy Beers and Charles Bourgeois by Calgary Flames to St. Louis Blues for Terry Johnson, Joe Mullen and Rik Wilson.

PAUL CAVALLINI

Defense . . . 6'2" . . . 202 lbs. . . . Born, Toronto, Ont., October 13, 1965 . . . Shoots left . . . (December 11, 1987)—Broke hand when slashed by Darren Veitch at Detroit . . . (December 11, 1988)—Injured neck in Chicago . . . (February 25, 1989)—Dislocated left shoulder when checked by Mark Messier at Edmonton.

Year	Team	League	Games	G.	A.	Pts.	Pen.
1983-84—Henry Carr H.S. (c)	MTHL	54	20	41	61	190
1984-85—Providence College	H. East	45	5	14	19	64
1985-86—Team Canada	Int'l.	52	1	11	12	95
1985-86—Binghamton Whalers	AHL	15	3	4	7	20
1986-87—Binghamton Whalers	AHL	66	12	24	36	188
1986-87—Washington Capitals	NHL	6	0	2	2	8
1987-88—Washington Capitals (d)	NHL	24	2	3	5	66
1987-88—St. Louis Blues	NHL	48	4	7	11	86
1988-89—St. Louis Blues	NHL	65	4	20	24	128
1989-90—St. Louis Blues	NHL	80	8	39	47	106
NHL TOTALS		223	18	71	89	394

(c)—June, 1984—Drafted as underage junior by Washington Capitals in NHL entry draft. Ninth Capitals pick, 205th overall, 10th round.

(d)—December, 1987—Traded by Washington Capitals to St. Louis Blues for a second-round 1988 draft pick (Wade Bartley).

ANDY CESARSKI

Defense . . . 6'4" . . . 200 lbs. . . . Born, Fort Monmouth, N.J., September 21, 1968 . . . Shoots left.

Year	Team	League	Games	G.	A.	Pts.	Pen.
1986-87—Culver Military Academy (c)	N.J. H.S.	....				
1987-88—Princeton Univ.	ECAC	28	2	3	5	34
1988-89—Princeton Univ.	ECAC	26	6	10	16	34
1989-90—Princeton Univ.	ECAC	27	1	9	10	22

(c)—June, 1987—Drafted by St. Louis Blues in 1987 NHL entry draft. Eleventh Blues pick, 207th overall, 10th round.

JOHN DAVID CHABOT

(Given Name: John Kahibaitche)

Center . . . 6'1" . . . 185 lbs. . . . Born Summerside, P.E.I., May 18, 1962 . . . Shoots left . . . (February, 1988)—Fractured mastoin in ear . . . (November 23, 1988)—Strained tendons in right knee and required surgery . . . (March 15, 1990)—Severed tendon in instep of right foot when cut by Rob Brown's skate blade at Pittsburgh and had surgery.

Year	Team	League	Games	G.	A.	Pts.	Pen.
1979-80—Hull Olympics (c)	QMJHL	68	26	57	83	28
1980-81—Hull Olympics	QMJHL	70	27	62	89	24
1980-81—Nova Scotia Voyageurs	AHL	1	0	0	0	0
1981-82—Sherbrooke Beavers (a-d-e)	QMJHL	62	34	*109	143	40
1982-83—Nova Scotia Voyageurs	AHL	76	16	73	89	19
1983-84—Montreal Canadiens	NHL	56	18	25	43	13
1984-85—Montreal Canadiens (f)	NHL	10	1	6	7	2
1984-85—Pittsburgh Penguins	NHL	67	8	45	53	12
1985-86—Pittsburgh Penguins	NHL	77	14	31	45	6
1986-87—Pittsburgh Penguins (g)	NHL	72	14	22	36	8
1987-88—Detroit Red Wings	NHL	78	13	44	57	10
1988-89—Detroit Red Wings	NHL	52	2	10	12	6
1988-89—Adirondack Red Wings	AHL	8	3	12	15	0
1989-90—Detroit Red Wings	NHL	69	9	40	49	24
NHL TOTALS		481	79	223	302	81

(c)—June, 1980—Drafted as underage junior by Montreal Canadiens in 1980 NHL entry draft. Third Canadiens pick, 40th overall, second round.
(d)—September 1981—Traded by Hull Olympics to Sherbrooke Beavers for Tim Cranston and Rousell MacKenzie.
(e)—Won Michel Briere Trophy (Regular Season QMJHL MVP).
(f)—November, 1984—Traded by Montreal Canadiens to Pittsburgh Penguins for Ron Flockhart.
(g)—July, 1987—Signed by Detroit Red Wings as a free agent.

SEAN CHAMBERS

Defense . . . 6'2" . . . 215 lbs. . . . Born, Royal Oaks, Mich., October 11, 1966 . . . Shoots left . . . (February, 1988)—Dislocated shoulder at Toronto . . . (September, 1988)—Separated right shoulder during training camp.

Year	Team	League	Games	G.	A.	Pts.	Pen.
1985-86—Univ. Alaska/Fairbanks	GWHC	25	15	21	36	34
1986-87—Univ. Alaska/Fairbanks (c)	GWHC	17	11	19	30	....
1986-87—Seattle Thunderbirds	WHL	28	8	25	33	58
1986-87—Fort Wayne Komets	IHL	12	2	6	8	0
1987-88—Minnesota North Stars	NHL	19	1	7	8	21
1987-88—Kalamazoo Wings	IHL	19	1	6	7	22
1988-89—Minnesota North Stars	NHL	72	5	19	24	80
1989-90—Minnesota North Stars	NHL	78	8	18	26	81
NHL TOTALS		169	14	44	58	182

(c)—June, 1987—Selected by Minnesota North Stars in 1987 NHL supplemental draft.

CRAIG CHANNELL

Defense . . . 5'11" . . . 195 lbs. . . . Born, Moncton, N.B., April 24, 1962 . . . Shoots left.

Year	Team	League	Games	G.	A.	Pts.	Pen.
1979-80—Seattle Breakers	WHL	70	3	21	24	191
1980-81—Seattle Breakers	WHL	71	9	66	75	181
1981-82—Seattle Breakers (c)	WHL	71	9	79	88	244
1982-83—Sherbrooke Jets	AHL	65	0	15	15	109
1983-84—Sherbrooke Jets	AHL	80	5	18	23	112
1984-85—Sherbrooke Canadiens	AHL	1	0	0	0	0
1984-85—Fort Wayne Komets	IHL	78	10	35	45	110
1985-86—Fort Wayne Komets	IHL	69	7	28	35	116
1986-87—Fort Wayne Komets	IHL	81	12	42	54	90
1987-88—Fort Wayne Komets	IHL	81	11	29	40	108
1988-89—Fort Wayne Komets (b)	IHL	79	5	25	30	168
1989-90—Fort Wayne Komets (d)	IHL	37	6	11	17	86
1989-90—Indianapolis Ice	IHL	16	0	1	1	17

(c)—September, 1982—Signed by Winnipeg Jets as a free agent.
(d)—March 8, 1990—Traded by Fort Wayne Komets to Indianapolis Ice for Ray Leblanc. Both players will return to their original clubs at end of season.

RENE CHAPDELAINE

Defense . . . 6'1" . . . 195 lbs. . . . Born, Weyburn, Sask., September 27, 1966 . . . Shoots right.

Year	Team	League	Games	G.	A.	Pts.	Pen.
1984-85—Weyburn	SJHL	61	3	17	20	0
1985-86—Lake Superior State (c)	CCHA	40	2	7	9	24
1986-87—Lake Superior State	CCHA	28	1	5	6	51
1987-88—Lake Superior State	CCHA	35	1	9	10	44

Year	Team	League	Games	G.	A.	Pts.	Pen.
1988-89—Lake Superior State		CCHA	46	4	9	13	52
1989-90—New Haven Nighthawks		AHL	41	0	1	1	35

(c)—June, 1986—Drafted by Los Angeles Kings in 1986 NHL entry draft. Seventh Kings pick, 149th overall, eighth round.

BRIAN CHAPMAN

Defense . . . 6' . . . 185 lbs. . . . Born, Brockville, Ont., February 10, 1968 . . . Shoots left. . . . (October 5, 1986)—Suspended 10 games by OHL . . . (March 11, 1989)—Suspended six AHL games for fighting.

Year	Team	League	Games	G.	A.	Pts.	Pen.
1984-85—Brockville Braves	Jr.A. OPHL	50	11	32	43	145
1985-86—Belleville Bulls (c)	OHL	66	6	31	37	168
1986-87—Belleville Bulls	OHL	54	4	32	36	142
1986-87—Binghamton Whalers (d)	AHL	....	...	...	...	....
1987-88—Belleville Bulls	OHL	63	11	57	68	180
1988-89—Binghamton Whalers	AHL	71	5	25	30	216
1989-90—Binghamton Whalers	AHL	68	2	15	17	180

(c)—June, 1986—Drafted as underage junior by Hartford Whalers in 1986 NHL entry draft. Third Whalers pick, 74th overall, fourth round.

(d)—No regular season record. Played one playoff game.

JOSE CHARBONNEAU

Right Wing . . . 6' . . . 195 lbs. . . . Born, Ferme-Neuve, Que., November 2, 1966 . . . Shoots right . . . (November, 1984)—Separated right shoulder . . . (December, 1984)—Reinjured shoulder . . . (January, 1985)—Aggravated shoulder.

Year	Team	League	Games	G.	A.	Pts.	Pen.
1983-84—Drummondville Voltigeurs	QMJHL	65	31	59	90	110
1984-85—Drummondville Voltigeurs (c)	QMJHL	46	34	40	74	91
1985-86—Drummondville Voltigeurs	QMJHL	57	44	45	89	158
1986-87—Sherbrooke Canadiens	AHL	72	14	27	41	94
1987-88—Sherbrooke Canadiens	AHL	55	30	35	65	108
1987-88—Montreal Canadiens	NHL	16	0	2	2	6
1988-89—Sherbrooke Canadiens	AHL	33	13	15	28	95
1988-89—Milwaukee Admirals	IHL	13	8	5	13	46
1988-89—Montreal Canadiens (d)	NHL	9	1	3	4	6
1988-89—Vancouver Canucks	NHL	13	0	1	1	6
1989-90—Milwaukee Admirals	IHL	65	23	38	61	137
NHL TOTALS		38	1	6	7	18

(c)—June, 1985—Drafted as underage junior by Montreal Canadiens in NHL entry draft. First Canadiens pick, 12th overall, first round.

(d)—January 24, 1989—Traded by Montreal Canadiens to Vancouver Canucks for Dan Woodley.

TODD CHARLESWORTH

Defense . . . 6'1'' . . . 185 lbs. . . . Born, Calgary, Alta., March 22, 1965 . . . Shoots left.

Year	Team	League	Games	G.	A.	Pts.	Pen.
1981-82—Gloucester Rangers	COJHL	50	13	24	37	67
1982-83—Oshawa Generals (c)	OHL	70	6	23	29	55
1983-84—Oshawa Generals	OHL	57	11	35	46	54
1983-84—Pittsburgh Penguins	NHL	10	0	0	0	8
1984-85—Pittsburgh Penguins	NHL	67	1	8	9	31
1985-86—Baltimore Skipjacks	AHL	19	1	3	4	10
1985-86—Muskegon Lumberjacks	IHL	51	9	27	36	78
1985-86—Pittsburgh Penguins	NHL	2	0	1	1	0
1986-87—Baltimore Skipjacks	AHL	75	5	21	26	64
1986-87—Pittsburgh Penguins	NHL	1	0	0	0	0
1987-88—Pittsburgh Penguins	NHL	6	2	0	2	2
1987-88—Muskegon Lumberjacks	IHL	64	9	31	40	49
1988-89—Muskegon Lumberjacks (b-d)	IHL	74	10	53	63	85
1989-90—Cape Breton Oilers	AHL	32	0	9	9	13
1989-90—Flint Spirits	IHL	26	3	6	9	12
1989-90—New York Rangers	NHL	7	0	0	0	6
NHL TOTALS		93	3	9	12	47

(c)—June, 1983—Drafted as underage junior by Pittsburgh Penguins in NHL entry draft. Second Penguins pick, 22nd overall, second round.

(d)—June, 1989—Signed by Edmonton Oilers as a free agent.

ERIC CHARRON

Defense . . . 6'3'' . . . 190 lbs. . . . Born, Verdun, Que., January 14, 1970 . . . Shoots left.

Year	Team	League	Games	G.	A.	Pts.	Pen.
1986-87—Lac St. Louis AAA	Que. Mdgt.	41	1	8	9	92
1987-88—Trois-Rivieres Draveurs (c)	QMJHL	67	3	13	16	135
1988-89—Sherbrooke Canandiens	AHL	1	0	0	0	0
1988-89—Verdun Junior Canadiens	QMJHL	67	4	31	35	177
1989-90—St. Hyacinthe Lasers	QMJHL	68	13	38	51	152

(c)—June, 1988—Drafted by Montreal Canadiens in 1988 NHL entry draft. First Canadiens pick, 20th overall, first round.

STEVE CHARTRAND

Left Wing . . . 5'9'' . . . 158 lbs. . . . Born, Verdun, Que., January 8, 1969 . . . Shoots left.

Year	Team	League	Games	G.	A.	Pts.	Pen.
1986-87—Drummondville Voltigeurs	QMJHL	70	45	55	100	28
1987-88—Drummondville Voltigeurs	QMJHL	68	50	62	112	36
1988-89—Drummondville Voltigeurs (c)	QMJHL	70	74	83	157	46
1989-90—Drummondville Voltigeurs	QMJHL	44	50	41	91	34
1989-90—Newmarket Saints	AHL	20	4	4	8	0

(c)—June, 1989—Drafted by Toronto Maple Leafs in 1989 NHL entry draft. Thirteenth Maple Leafs pick, 234th overall, 12th round.

KELLY CHASE

Right Wing . . . 5'11'' . . . 200 lbs. . . . Born, Porcupine Plain, Sask., October 25, 1967 . . . Shoots right . . . (January, 1990)—Bruised right foot . . . (March, 1990)—Back spasms.

Year	Team	League	Games	G.	A.	Pts.	Pen.
1985-86—Saskatoon Blades	WHL	57	7	18	25	172
1986-87—Saskatoon Blades	WHL	68	17	29	46	285
1987-88—Saskatoon Blades (c)	WHL	70	21	34	55	*343
1988-89—Peoria Rivermen	IHL	38	14	7	21	278
1989-90—Peoria Rivermen	IHL	10	1	2	3	76
1989-90—St. Louis Blues	NHL	43	1	3	4	244
NHL TOTALS		43	1	3	4	244

(c)—May 24, 1988—Signed by St. Louis Blues as a free agent.

CHRIS CHELIOS

Defense . . . 6'1'' . . . 187 lbs. . . . Born, Chicago, Ill., January 25, 1962 . . . Shoots right. . . . Member of 1984 U.S. Olympic Team . . . (January, 1985)—Sprained right ankle . . . (April, 1985)—Injured left knee . . . Older brother of Steve Chelios (OHL player) . . . (December 19, 1985)—Sprained knee at Quebec . . . (January 20, 1986)—Reinjured knee at Quebec . . . (October, 1986)—Back spasms . . . (December, 1987)—Broke little finger of left hand vs. N.Y. Rangers . . . (February 7, 1988)—Bruised tailbone . . . (February, 1990)—Strained left knee ligaments . . . (April 30, 1990)—Surgery to repair torn abdominal muscle.

Year	Team	League	Games	G.	A.	Pts.	Pen.
1979-80—Moose Jaw Canucks	SJHL	53	12	31	43	118
1980-81—Moose Jaw Canucks (c)	SJHL	54	23	64	87	175
1981-82—University of Wisconsin	WCHA	43	6	43	49	50
1982-83—University of Wisconsin (b)	WCHA	45	16	32	48	62
1983-84—U.S. National Team	Int'l.	60	14	35	49	58
1983-84—U.S. Olympic Team	Int'l.	6	0	4	4	8
1983-84—Montreal Canadiens	NHL	12	0	2	2	12
1984-85—Montreal Canadiens	NHL	74	9	55	64	87
1985-86—Montreal Canadiens	NHL	41	8	26	34	67
1986-87—Montreal Canadiens	NHL	71	11	33	44	124
1987-88—Montreal Canadiens	NHL	71	20	41	61	172
1988-89—Montreal Canadiens (a-d)	NHL	80	15	58	73	185
1989-90—Montreal Canadiens (e)	NHL	53	9	22	31	136
NHL TOTALS		402	72	237	309	783

(c)—June, 1981—Drafted as underage junior by Montreal Canadiens in 1981 NHL entry draft. Fifth Canadiens pick, 40th overall, second round.

(d)—Won James Norris Memorial Trophy (Top NHL Defenseman).

(e)—June 29, 1990—Traded with a second-round 1991 draft pick by Montreal Canadiens to Chicago Black Hawks for Denis Savard.

RICHARD CHERNOMAZ

Right Wing . . . 5'10'' . . . 175 lbs. . . . Born, Selkirk, Man., September 1, 1963 . . . Shoots right . . . Missed parts of 1981-82 season with recurring pain caused by separated shoulder . . . (January, 1983)—Injured knee ligaments . . . (November 27, 1984)—Sprained left knee vs. Minnesota and needed arthroscopic surgery . . . (November, 1989)—Surgery to remove ligament from right knee and missed 13 games.

Year	Team	League	Games	G.	A.	Pts.	Pen.
1979-80—Saskatoon	SJHL	51	33	37	70	75
1979-80—Saskatoon Blades	WHL	25	9	10	19	33
1980-81—Victoria Cougars (c)	WHL	72	49	64	113	92
1981-82—Victoria Cougars	WHL	49	36	62	98	69
1981-82—Colorado Rockies	NHL	7	0	0	0	0
1982-83—Victoria Cougars (a)	WHL	64	71	53	124	113
1983-84—Maine Mariners	AHL	69	17	29	46	39
1983-84—New Jersey Devils	NHL	7	2	1	3	2
1984-85—New Jersey Devils	NHL	3	0	2	2	2
1984-85—Maine Mariners	AHL	64	17	34	51	64
1985-86—Maine Mariners	AHL	78	21	28	49	82
1986-87—Maine Mariners	AHL	58	35	27	62	65
1986-87—New Jersey Devils (d)	NHL	25	6	4	10	8
1987-88—Calgary Flames	NHL	2	1	0	1	0
1987-88—Salt Lake Golden Eagles	IHL	73	48	47	95	122
1988-89—Calgary Flames	NHL	1	0	0	0	0
1988-89—Salt Lake Golden Eagles (b)	IHL	81	33	68	101	122
1989-90—Salt Lake Golden Eagles	IHL	65	39	35	74	170
NHL TOTALS		40	9	7	16	12

(c)—June, 1981—Drafted as underage junior by Colorado Rockies in 1981 NHL entry draft. Third Rockies pick, 26th overall, second round.

(d)—August, 1987—Signed as free agent by Calgary Flames.

KEVIN CHEVELDAYOFF

Defense . . . 6'1'' . . . 200 lbs. . . . Born, Saskatoon, Sask., February 4, 1970 . . . Shoots right . . . (January 6, 1989)—Damaged ligaments in WHL game and had major reconstructive surgery to left knee . . . (1989-90)—Missed most of the season while rehabilitating from knee surgery.

Year	Team	League	Games	G.	A.	Pts.	Pen.
1986-87—Brandon Wheat Kings	WHL	70	0	16	16	259
1987-88—Brandon Wheat Kings (c)	WHL	71	3	29	32	265
1988-89—Brandon Wheat Kings	WHL	40	4	12	16	135
1989-90—Brandon Wheat Kings	WHL	33	5	12	17	56
1989-90—Springfield Indians	AHL	4	0	0	0	0

(c)—June, 1988—Drafted by New York Islanders in 1988 NHL entry draft. First Islanders pick, 16th overall, first round.

STEVE CHIASSON

Defense . . . 6'1'' . . . 200 lbs. . . . Born, Barrie, Ont., April 14, 1967 . . . Shoots left . . . (October, 1985)—Hand injury . . . (February, 1988)—Separated right shoulder

... (May, 1988)—Injured foot ... (October, 1988)—Injured groin ... (January, 1989)—Bruised ribs ... (February, 1989)—Injured ankle.

Year	Team	League	Games	G.	A.	Pts.	Pen.
1982-83—Peterborough Midgets	OHA	40	25	35	60	120
1983-84—Guelph Platers	OHL	55	1	9	10	112
1984-85—Guelph Platers (c)	OHL	61	8	22	30	139
1985-86—Guelph Platers	OHL	54	12	29	41	126
1986-87—Detroit Red Wings	NHL	45	1	4	5	73
1987-88—Adirondack Red Wings	AHL	23	6	11	17	58
1987-88—Detroit Red Wings	NHL	29	2	9	11	57
1988-89—Detroit Red Wings	NHL	65	12	35	47	149
1989-90—Detroit Red Wings	NHL	67	14	28	42	114
NHL TOTALS		206	29	76	105	393

(c)—June, 1985—Drafted as underage junior by Detroit Red Wings in 1985 NHL entry draft. Third Red Wings pick, 50th overall, third round.

COLIN CHIN

Center ... 5'8" ... 165 lbs. ... Born, Fort Wayne, Ind., August 28, 1961 ... Shoots left ... Brother of Gordon Chin.

Year	Team	League	Games	G.	A.	Pts.	Pen.
1983-84—Univ. Illinois-Chicago	CCHA	35	11	25	36	14
1984-85—Univ. Illinois-Chicago (c)	CCHA	38	23	42	65	22
1985-86—Baltimore Skipjacks	AHL	78	17	28	45	38
1986-87—Fort Wayne Komets	IHL	75	33	42	75	35
1987-88—Fort Wayne Komets	IHL	75	31	35	66	60
1988-89—Fort Wayne Komets	IHL	76	21	35	56	71
1989-90—Fort Wayne Komets	IHL	74	21	38	59	79

(c)—October, 1985—Signed by Pittsburgh Penguins as a free agent.

THOMAS CHORSKE

Right Wing ... 6'1" ... 185 lbs. ... Born, Minneapolis, Minn., September 18, 1966 ... Shoots right ... (November 18, 1988)—Separated shoulder vs. Univ. Minn./Duluth and missed 11 games ... (October 26, 1989)—Hip pointer at Chicago.

Year	Team	League	Games	G.	A.	Pts.	Pen.
1984-85—Minn. Southwest H.S. (c)	Minn. H.S.	23	44	26	70	..
1985-86—University of Minnesota	WCHA	39	6	4	10	6
1986-87—University of Minnesota	WCHA	47	20	22	42	20
1987-88—U.S. Olympic Team	Int'l	..	9	16	25	..
1988-89—University of Minnesota (a)	WCHA	37	25	24	49	28
1989-90—Montreal Canadiens	NHL	14	3	1	4	2
1989-90—Sherbrooke Canadiens	AHL	59	22	24	46	54
NHL TOTALS		14	3	1	4	2

(c)—June, 1985—Drafted by Montreal Canadiens in 1985 NHL entry draft. Second Canadiens pick, 16th overall, first round.

DAVE CHRISTIAN

Center ... 5'11" ... 170 lbs. ... Born, Warroad, Minn., May 12, 1959 ... Shoots right ... Member of 1978 U.S. National Junior Team and 1980 U.S. Olympic Gold Medal Team ... Son of Bill Christian ('60 & '64 Olympic Teams), nephew of Roger Christian ('60 & '64 Olympic Teams) and nephew of Gordon Christian ('56 Olympic Team) ... His father (Bill) and uncle (Roger) own the Christian Brothers Hockey Stick Company ... Also plays Right Wing ... Brother of Edward Christian (Winnipeg '80 draft pick) ... (December, 1982)—Torn shoulder muscles and missed 25 games.

Year	Team	League	Games	G.	A.	Pts.	Pen.
1977-78—University of North Dakota	WCHA	38	8	16	24	14
1978-79—University of North Dakota (c)	WCHA	40	22	24	46	22
1979-80—U.S. Olympic Team	Int'l	*66	10	28	38	32
1979-80—Winnipeg Jets	NHL	15	8	10	18	2
1980-81—Winnipeg Jets	NHL	80	28	43	71	22
1981-82—Winnipeg Jets	NHL	80	25	51	76	28
1982-83—Winnipeg Jets (d)	NHL	55	18	26	44	23
1983-84—Washington Capitals	NHL	80	29	52	81	28
1984-85—Washington Capitals	NHL	80	26	43	69	14
1985-86—Washington Capitals	NHL	80	41	42	83	15
1986-87—Washington Capitals	NHL	76	23	27	50	8
1987-88—Washington Capitals	NHL	80	37	21	58	26
1988-89—Washington Capitals	NHL	80	34	31	65	12
1989-90—Washington Capitals (e)	NHL	28	3	8	11	4
1989-90—Boston Bruins	NHL	50	12	17	29	8
NHL TOTALS		784	284	371	655	190

(c)—August, 1979—Drafted by Winnipeg Jets in 1979 NHL entry draft. Second Jets pick, 40th overall, second round.

(d)—June, 1983—Traded by Winnipeg Jets to Washington Capitals for first round pick in 1983 draft (Bobby Dollas).

(e)—December 13, 1989—Traded by Washington Capitals to Boston Bruins for Bob Joyce.

JEFF CHRISTIAN

Left Wing ... 6'1" ... 185 lbs. ... Born, Burlington, Ont., July 30, 1970 ... Shoots left ... Son of Gord Christian (Member of Hamilton Tiger Cats-CFL, 1967-72) ... (March 28, 1990)—Suspended three games for high sticking vs. Sudbury.

Year	Team	League	Games	G.	A.	Pts.	Pen.
1986-87—Dundas Blues	OHA Jr. 'C'	29	20	34	54	42
1987-88—London Knights (c)	OHL	64	15	29	44	154
1988-89—London Knights	OHL	60	27	30	57	221
1989-90—London Knights (d)	OHL	18	14	7	21	64
1989-90—Owen Sound Platers	OHL	37	19	26	45	145

(c)—June, 1988—Drafted by New Jersey Devils in 1988 NHL entry draft. Second Devils pick, 23rd overall, second round.

(d)—November 27, 1989—Traded by London Knights to Owen Sound Platers for Todd Hlushko and David Noseworthy.

SHANE CHURLA

Right Wing ... 6'1" ... 200 lbs. ... Born, Fernie, B.C., June 24, 1965 ... Shoots right ... (October, 1985)—Pulled stomach muscles ... (October 5, 1986)—Suspended three games by AHL ... (April 2, 1989)—Broken wrist when checked by Bryan Merchment at Winnipeg ... (November, 1989)—Bruised right hand ... (December 28, 1989)—Suspended 10 games for fighting at Chicago ... (April, 1990)—Surgery to wrist.

Year	Team	League	Games	G.	A.	Pts.	Pen.
1983-84—Medicine Hat Tigers	WHL	48	3	7	10	115
1984-85—Medicine Hat Tigers (c)	WHL	70	14	20	34	*370
1985-86—Binghamton Whalers	AHL	52	4	10	14	306
1986-87—Binghamton Whalers	AHL	24	1	5	6	249
1986-87—Hartford Whalers	NHL	20	0	1	1	789
1987-88—Binghamton Whalers	AHL	25	5	8	13	168
1987-88—Hartford Whalers (d)	NHL	2	0	0	0	14
1987-88—Calgary Flames	NHL	29	1	5	6	132
1988-89—Calgary Flames (e)	NHL	5	0	0	0	25
1988-89—Minnesota North Stars	NHL	13	1	0	1	54
1988-89—Salt Lake Golden Eagles	IHL	32	3	13	16	278
1989-90—Minnesota North Stars	NHL	53	2	3	5	292
NHL TOTALS		122	4	9	13	595

(c)—June, 1985—Drafted by Hartford Whalers in 1985 NHL entry draft. Fourth Whalers pick, 110th overall, sixth round.

(d)—January, 1988—Traded with Dana Murzyn by Hartford Whalers to Calgary Flames for Neil Sheehy, Carey Wilson and Lane McDonald.

(e)—March 4, 1989—Traded with Perry Berezan by Calgary Flames to Minnesota North Stars for Brian MacLellan and a fourth-round 1989 draft pick (Robert Reichel).

JEFF CHYCHRUN

Defense ... 6'4" ... 190 lbs. ... Born, Lasalle, Que., May 3, 1966 ... Shoots right ... (November, 1989)—Viral infection.

Year	Team	League	Games	G.	A.	Pts.	Pen.
1983-84—Kingston Canadians (c)	OHL	83	1	13	14	137
1984-85—Kingston Canadians	OHL	58	4	10	14	206
1985-86—Kingston Canadians	OHL	61	4	21	25	127
1985-86—Kalamazoo Wings (d)	IHL	....	...	...	....	....
1985-86—Hershey Bears (e)	AHL	....	...	....	....	....
1986-87—Hershey Bears	AHL	74	1	17	18	239
1986-87—Philadelphia Flyers	NHL	1	0	0	0	4
1987-88—Philadelphia Flyers	NHL	3	0	0	0	4
1987-88—Hershey Bears	AHL	55	0	5	5	210
1988-89—Philadelphia Flyers	NHL	80	1	4	5	245
1989-90—Philadelphia Flyers	NHL	79	2	7	9	250
NHL TOTALS		163	3	11	14	503

(c)—June, 1984—Drafted as underage junior by Philadelphia Flyers in 1984 NHL entry draft. Second Flyers pick, 37th overall, second round.

(d)—No regular season record. Played three playoff games.

(e)—No regular season record. Played four playoff games.

DEAN CHYNOWETH

Defense ... 6'1" ... 185 lbs. ... Born, Saskatoon, Sask., October 30, 1968 ... Shoots right ... Son of Ed Chynoweth, President of the Western Hockey League ... (April, 1987)—Fractured rib and punctured lung during WHL playoff game ... (September, 1985) April, 1986 and October, 1986)—Broken nose ... (October 27, 1988)—Left eye injured by Rick Tocchet vs. Philadelphia and missed nearly two months ... (December, 1988)—Suffers from Osgood-Schlatter disease, an abnormal relationship between the muscles and growing bones. He had grown an inch in the last year and was out the remainder of the season ... (October 31, 1989)—Injured ankle vs. Montreal ... (November, 1989)—Sprained ligaments in right thumb.

Year	Team	League	Games	G.	A.	Pts.	Pen.
1984-85—Calgary Buffaloes	Atla. Midget	26	5	13	18	104
1985-86—Medicine Hat Tigers	WHL	69	3	12	15	208
1986-87—Medicine Hat Tigers (c)	WHL	67	3	18	21	285
1987-88—Medicine Hat Tigers	WHL	64	1	21	22	274
1988-89—New York Islanders	NHL	6	0	0	0	48
1989-90—New York Islanders	NHL	20	0	2	2	39
1989-90—Springfield Indians	AHL	40	0	7	7	98
NHL TOTALS		26	0	2	2	87

(c)—June, 1987—Drafted as underage junior by New York Islanders in 1987 NHL entry draft. First Islanders pick, 13th overall, first round.

DAVID CHYZOWSKI

Left Wing ... 6'1" ... 190 lbs. ... Born, Edmonton, Alta., July 11, 1971 ... Shoots left ... Brother of Ron and Barry Chyzowski.

Year	Team	League	Games	G.	A.	Pts.	Pen.
1987-88—Kamloops Blazers	WHL	66	16	17	33	117
1988-89—Kamloops Blazers (a-c)	WHL	68	56	48	104	139
1989-90—Kamloops Blazers	WHL	4	5	2	7	17
1989-90—Springfield Indians	AHL	4	0	0	0	7
1989-90—New York Islanders	NHL	34	8	6	14	45
NHL TOTALS		34	8	6	14	45

(c)—June, 1989—Drafted by New York Islanders in 1989 NHL entry draft. First Islanders pick, second overall, first round.

PETER CIAVAGLIA

Center ... 5'10" ... 160 lbs. ... Born, Albany, N.Y., July 15, 1969 ... Shoots left.

Year	Team	League	Games	G.	A.	Pts.	Pen.
1985-86—Nichols/Wheatfield Mid.	NY Midget	60	84	113	197	..
1986-87—Nichols/Wheatfield Jr. B (c)	NY Jr. B	..	53	84	137	...
1987-88—Harvard University	ECAC	30	10	23	33	16

Year	Team	League	Games	G.	A.	Pts.	Pen.
1988-89—Harvard University (b)		ECAC	34	15	48	63	36
1989-90—Harvard University		ECAC	28	17	18	35	22

(c)—June, 1987—Drafted by Calgary Flames in 1987 NHL entry draft. Eighth Flames pick, 145th overall, seventh round.

DINO CICCARELLI

Right Wing . . . 5'11'' . . . 185 lbs. . . . Born, Sarnia, Ont., February 8, 1960 . . . Shoots right . . . (Spring, 1978)—Fractured midshaft of right femur that required the insertion of 16 inch metal rod in leg . . . Set NHL Playoff record for most goals as a rookie (14) in 1981 . . . First Minnesota player to score 50 goals in a season . . . (November, 1984)—Shoulder injury . . . (December, 1984)—Broken right wrist . . . (October 5, 1987)—Suspended three games by NHL for making contact with linesman Mark Pare during pre-season game vs. Chicago . . . (January 6, 1988)—Given 10-game suspension by NHL for stick swinging incident involving Luke Richardson at Toronto . . . (September 10, 1988)—Suspended by Minnesota for failure to report to North Stars training camp . . . (March 8, 1989)—Concussion when checked by Craig Ludwig against Montreal . . . (April 23, 1990)—Sprained left knee vs. N.Y. Rangers.

Year	Team	League	Games	G.	A.	Pts.	Pen.
1976-77—London Knights		OMJHL	66	39	43	82	45
1977-78—London Knights (b)		OMJHL	68	72	70	142	49
1978-79—London Knights (c)		OMJHL	30	8	11	19	25
1979-80—London Knights		OMJHL	62	50	53	103	72
1979-80—Oklahoma City Stars		CHL	6	3	2	5	0
1980-81—Oklahoma City Stars		CHL	48	32	25	57	45
1980-81—Minnesota North Stars		NHL	32	18	12	30	29
1981-82—Minnesota North Stars		NHL	76	55	51	106	138
1982-83—Minnesota North Stars		NHL	77	37	38	75	94
1983-84—Minnesota North Stars		NHL	79	38	33	71	58
1984-85—Minnesota North Stars		NHL	51	15	17	32	41
1985-86—Minnesota North Stars		NHL	75	44	45	89	53
1986-87—Minnesota North Stars		NHL	80	52	51	103	92
1987-88—Minnesota North Stars		NHL	67	41	45	86	79
1988-89—Minnesota North Stars (d)		NHL	65	32	27	59	64
1988-89—Washington Capitals		NHL	11	12	3	15	12
1989-90—Washington Capitals		NHL	80	41	38	79	122
NHL TOTALS			693	385	360	745	782

(c)—September, 1979—Signed by Minnesota North Stars as free agent.
(d)—March 7, 1989—Traded with Bob Rouse by Minnesota North Stars to Washington Capitals for Mike Gartner and Larry Murphy.

ENRICO CICCONE

Defense . . . 6'4'' . . . 196 lbs. . . . Born, Montreal, Que., April 10, 1970 . . . Shoots left.

Year	Team	League	Games	G.	A.	Pts.	Pen.
1986-87—Lac St. Louis Lions Midgets		Quebec	38	10	20	30	172
1987-88—Shawinigan Cataracts		QMJHL	61	2	12	14	324
1988-89—Shaw./Trois-Riv. Draveurs		QMJHL	58	7	19	26	289
1989-90—Trois-Rivieres Draveurs (c)		QMJHL	40	4	24	28	227

(c)—June 16, 1990—Selected by Minnesota North Stars in 1990 NHL entry draft. Fifth North Stars pick, 92nd overall, fifth round.

CHRIS CICHOCKI

Right Wing . . . 5'10'' . . . 185 lbs. . . . Born, Detroit, Mich., September 17, 1963 . . . Shoots right . . . Member of 1983 U.S. Junior National Team . . . (January, 1989)—Missed 17 games with a separated shoulder.

Year	Team	League	Games	G.	A.	Pts.	Pen.
1982-83—Michigan Tech.		CCHA	36	12	10	22	10
1983-84—Michigan Tech.		CCHA	40	25	20	45	36
1984-85—Michigan Tech. (c)		WCHA	40	30	24	54	14
1985-06—Adirondack Red Wings		AHL	9	4	4	8	6
1985-86—Detroit Red Wings		NHL	59	10	11	21	21
1986-87—Adirondack Red Wings		AHL	55	31	34	65	27
1986-87—Detroit Red Wings (d)		NHL	2	0	0	0	2
1986-87—Maine Mariners		AHL	7	2	2	4	0
1987-88—New Jersey Devils		NHL	5	1	0	1	2
1987-88—Utica Devils		AHL	69	36	30	66	66
1988-89—New Jersey Devils		NHL	2	0	1	1	2
1988-89—Utica Devils		AHL	59	32	31	63	50
1989-90—Utica Devils (e)		AHL	11	3	1	4	10
1989-90—Binghamton Whalers		AHL	60	21	26	47	12
NHL TOTALS			68	11	12	23	27

(c)—June, 1985—Signed by Detroit Red Wings as a free agent.
(d)—March, 1987—Traded with third-round 1987 draft pick by Detroit Red Wings to New Jersey Devils for Mel Bridgman. (The Devils later traded the pick to Buffalo who drafted Andrew MacIver).
(e)—October 31, 1989—Traded by New Jersey Devils to Hartford Whalers for Jim Thomson.

ROBERT CIMETTA

Left Wing . . . 6' . . . 190 lbs. . . . Born, Toronto, Ont., February 15, 1970 . . . Shoots left . . . (October, 1986)—Fractured wrist.

Year	Team	League	Games	G.	A.	Pts.	Pen.
1986-87—Toronto Marlboros		OHL	66	21	35	56	65
1987-88—Toronto Marlboros (c)		OHL	64	34	42	76	90
1988-89—Toronto Marlboros (a)		OHL	50	55	47	102	89
1988-89—Boston Bruins		NHL	7	2	0	2	0
1989-90—Boston Bruins		NHL	47	8	9	17	33
1989-90—Maine Mariners		AHL	9	3	2	5	13
NHL TOTALS			54	10	9	19	33

(c)—June, 1988—Drafted by Boston Bruins in 1988 NHL entry draft. First Bruins pick, 18th overall, first round.

JOE CIRELLA

Defense . . . 6'2'' . . . 205 lbs. . . . Born, Hamilton, Ont., May 9, 1963 . . . Shoots right . . . Brother of Carmine Cirella . . . (December 17, 1984)—Hit by stick vs. Edmonton and needed 12 stitches . . . (November 26, 1985)—Injured left knee vs. Winnipeg . . . (January 18, 1990)—Broken right foot at Minnesota . . . (February 28, 1990)—Strained lower back at Toronto.

Year	Team	League	Games	G.	A.	Pts.	Pen.
1979-80—Hamilton Major Midgets		....	21	5	26	31	....
1980-81—Oshawa Generals (c)		OHL	56	5	31	36	220
1981-82—Oshawa Generals		OHL	3	0	1	1	10
1981-82—Colorado Rockies		NHL	65	7	12	19	52
1982-83—Oshawa Generals (a)		OHL	56	13	55	68	110
1982-83—New Jersey Devils		NHL	2	0	1	1	4
1983-84—New Jersey Devils		NHL	79	11	33	44	137
1984-85—New Jersey Devils		NHL	66	6	18	24	143
1985-86—New Jersey Devils		NHL	66	6	23	29	147
1986-87—New Jersey Devils		NHL	65	9	22	31	111
1987-88—New Jersey Devils		NHL	80	8	31	39	191
1988-89—New Jersey Devils (d)		NHL	80	3	19	22	155
1989-90—Quebec Nordiques		NHL	56	4	14	18	67
NHL TOTALS			559	54	173	227	1007

(c)—June, 1981—Drafted as underage junior by Colorado Rockies in 1981 NHL entry draft. First Rockies pick, fifth overall, first round.
(d)—June 17, 1989—Traded by New Jersey Devils to Quebec Nordiques for Walt Poddubny.

JASON CIRONE

Center . . . 5'9'' . . . 184 lbs. . . . Born, Toronto, Ont., February 21, 1971 . . . Shoots left.

Year	Team	League	Games	G.	A.	Pts.	Pen.
1986-87—Toronto Red Wings		OHA Bantam	36	53	64	117	125
1987-88—Cornwall Royals		OHL	53	12	11	23	41
1988-89—Cornwall Royals (c)		OHL	64	39	44	83	67
1989-90—Cornwall Royals		OHL	32	21	43	64	56

(c)—June, 1989—Drafted by Winnipeg Jets in 1989 NHL entry draft. Third Jets pick, 46th overall, third round.

KERRY CLARK

Right Wing . . . 6'1'' . . . 195 lbs. . . . Born, Kelvington, Sask., August 21, 1968 . . . Shoots right . . . (October 15, 1988)—Suspended six AHL games for fighting . . . Brother of Wendel Clark . . . (1986-87)—Broke ankle when slashed by goaltender Kenton Rein.

Year	Team	League	Games	G.	A.	Pts.	Pen.
1984-85—Regina Pats		WHL	36	1	1	2	66
1985-86—Regina Pats		WHL	23	4	4	8	58
1985-86—Saskatoon Blades (c)		WHL	39	5	8	13	104
1986-87—Saskatoon Blades		WHL	54	12	10	22	229
1987-88—Saskatoon Blades		WHL	67	15	11	26	241
1988-89—Springfield Indians		AHL	63	7	7	14	264
1988-89—Indianapolis Ice		IHL	3	0	1	1	12
1989-90—Phoenix Roadrunners		IHL	38	4	8	12	262
1989-90—Springfield Indians		AHL	21	0	1	1	73

(c)—June, 1986—Drafted as underage junior by New York Islanders in 1986 NHL entry draft. Twelfth Islanders pick, 206th overall, 10th round.

WENDEL CLARK

Left Wing . . . 5'11'' . . . 190 lbs. . . . Born, Kelvington, Sask., October 25, 1966 . . . Shoots left . . . (November, 1985)—Virus . . . (November 26, 1985)—Missed 14 games with broken right foot at St. Louis . . . Also plays Defense . . . (November, 1987)—Missed 23 games with back spasms . . . (October, 1987)—Tendinitis in right shoulder . . . (February, 1988)—Reinjured back . . . (March 1, 1989)—Returned to the Toronto lineup after missing more than a year with chronic back problems . . . Brother of Kerry Clark . . . (October, 1989)—Recurrence of back problems . . . (November 4, 1989)—Bruised muscle above left knee vs. Philadelphia and missed seven games . . . (January 26, 1990)—Torn ligament of right knee when checked by Viacheslav Fetisov vs. New Jersey and missed 29 games.

Year	Team	League	Games	G.	A.	Pts.	Pen.
1983-84—Saskatoon Blades		WHL	72	23	45	68	225
1984-85—Saskatoon Blades (a-c-d)		WHL	64	32	55	87	253
1985-86—Toronto Maple Leafs (e)		NHL	66	34	11	45	227
1986-87—Toronto Maple Leafs		NHL	80	37	23	60	271
1987-88—Toronto Maple Leafs		NHL	28	12	11	23	80
1988-89—Toronto Maple Leafs		NHL	15	7	4	11	66
1989-90—Toronto Maple Leafs		NHL	38	18	8	26	116
NHL TOTALS			227	108	57	165	760

(c)—Won WHL Top Defenseman Trophy.
(d)—June, 1985—Drafted as underage junior by Toronto Maple Leafs in 1985 NHL entry draft. First Maple Leafs pick, first overall, first round.
(e)—Named NHL Rookie of the Year in poll of players by THE SPORTING NEWS.

CHRISTOPHER CLARKE

Defense . . . 6' . . . 180 lbs. . . . Born, Arnprior, Ont., August 6, 1967 . . . Shoots left . . . (January, 1989)—Injured jaw.

Year	Team	League	Games	G.	A.	Pts.	Pen.
1986-87—Pembrooke (c)		BCJHL	..	..	..	..	..
1987-88—Western Michigan Univ.		CCHA	42	7	32	39	64
1988-89—Western Michigan Univ.		CCHA	38	3	21	24	51
1989-90—Western Michigan Univ.		CCHA	39	2	21	23	55

(c)—June, 1987—Drafted by Washington Capitals in 1987 NHL entry draft. Eighth Capitals pick, 204th overall, 10th round.

JOSEPH CLEARY

Defense . . . 6' . . . 190 lbs. . . . Born, Buffalo, N.Y., January 17, 1970 . . . Shoots right.

Year	Team	League	Games	G.	A.	Pts.	Pen.
1986-87	Cushing Academy	Mass. H.S.	..	15	30	45	..
1987-88	Stratford Cullitons (c)	OHA	41	20	37	57	160
1988-89	Boston College	H. East	38	5	7	12	36
1989-90	Boston College	H. East	42	5	21	26	56

(c)—June, 1988—Drafted by Chicago Black Hawks in 1988 NHL entry draft. Fourth Black Hawks pick, 92nd overall, fifth round.

SHAUN CLOUSTON

Right Wing . . . 6' . . . 205 lbs. . . . Born, Viking, Alta., February 21, 1968 . . . Shoots left.

Year	Team	League	Games	G.	A.	Pts.	Pen.
1985-86	Univ. of Alberta (c)	CWUAA	25	10	9	19	59
1986-87	Portland Winter Hawks	WHL	70	6	25	31	93
1987-88	Portland Winter Hawks	WHL	68	29	50	79	144
1988-89	Portland Winter Hawks	WHL	72	45	47	92	150
1989-90	Milwaukee Admirals	IHL	54	6	16	22	61
1989-90	Virginia Lancers	ECHL	5	3	2	5	14

(c)—June, 1986—Drafted by New York Rangers in 1986 NHL entry draft. Third Rangers pick, 53rd overall, third round.

PAUL DOUGLAS COFFEY

Defense . . . 6'1" . . . 185 lbs. . . . Born, Weston, Ont., June 1, 1961 . . . Shoots left . . . Became only third defenseman in NHL history to have a 100-point season (Potvin & Orr) with 126 points in 1983-84 . . . (May, 1985)—Set NHL record for most goals (12) assists (25) and points (37) in playoffs by a defenseman . . . (1985-86)—Set NHL record for most goals in one season by a defenseman, breaking Bobby Orr's mark of 46 goals in 1974-75 . . . (December, 1986)—Missed 10 games with recurring back spasms . . . (December, 1987)—Slightly torn knee cartilage in a collision with referee Don Koharski . . . (November 16, 1988)—Bruised right shoulder at Toronto when checked by Brad Marsh . . . (May, 1990)—Broke finger during World Hockey Championships in Switzerland.

Year	Team	League	Games	G.	A.	Pts.	Pen.
1977-78	Kingston Canadians	OHL	8	2	2	4	11
1977-78	North York Rangers	MTHL	50	14	33	47	64
1978-79	Sault Ste. Marie Greyhounds	OPJHL	68	17	72	89	99
1979-80	Sault Ste. Marie Grehhounds	OPJHL	23	10	21	31	63
1979-80	Kitchener Rangers (b-c)	OPJHL	52	19	52	71	130
1980-81	Edmonton Oilers	NHL	74	9	23	32	130
1981-82	Edmonton Oilers (b)	NHL	80	29	60	89	106
1982-83	Edmonton Oilers (b)	NHL	80	29	67	96	87
1983-84	Edmonton Oilers (b)	NHL	80	40	86	126	104
1984-85	Edmonton Oilers (a-d)	NHL	80	37	84	121	97
1985-86	Edmonton Oilers (a-d)	NHL	79	48	90	138	120
1986-87	Edmonton Oilers	NHL	59	17	50	67	49
1987-88	Pittsburgh Penguins (e)	NHL	46	15	52	67	93
1988-89	Pittsburgh Penguins (a)	NHL	75	30	83	113	193
1989-90	Pittsburgh Penguins (b)	NHL	80	29	74	103	95
	NHL TOTALS		733	283	669	952	1074

(c)—June, 1980—Drafted by Edmonton Oilers in NHL entry draft. First Oilers pick, sixth overall, first round.

(d)—Won James Norris Memorial Trophy (Top NHL Defenseman).

(e)—November, 1987—Traded with Dave Hunter and Wayne Van Dorp by Edmonton Oilers to Pittsburgh Penguins for Craig Simpson, Dave Hannan, Moe Mantha and Chris Joseph.

DANTON COLE

Center . . . 5'10" . . . 180 lbs. . . . Born, Pontiac, Mich., January 10, 1967 . . . Shoots right . . . Also plays Right Wing.

Year	Team	League	Games	G.	A.	Pts.	Pen.
1984-85	Aurora Tigers (c)	OHA	41	51	44	95	91
1985-86	Michigan State Univ.	CCHA	43	11	10	21	22
1986-87	Michigan State Univ.	CCHA	44	9	15	24	16
1987-88	Michigan State Univ.	CCHA	46	20	36	56	38
1988-89	Michigan State Univ.	CCHA	47	29	33	62	46
1989-90	Winnipeg Jets	NHL	2	1	1	2	0
1989-90	Moncton Hawks	AHL	80	31	42	73	18
	NHL TOTALS		2	1	1	2	0

(c)—June, 1985—Drafted by Winnipeg Jets in 1985 NHL entry draft. Sixth Jets pick, 123rd overall, sixth round.

PATRICK JOHN CONACHER

Center . . . 5'8" . . . 188 lbs. . . . Born, Edmonton, Alta., May 1, 1959 . . . Shoots left . . . (September 21, 1980)—Fractured left ankle in rookie scrimmage vs. Washington that required surgery . . . (November, 1982)—Injured shoulder . . . (December, 1984)—Severe groin injury . . . (February, 1988)—Sprained back . . . (December, 1988)—Bruised left shoulder . . . (April 7, 1989)—Had major reconstructive surgery to left shoulder . . . (October 13, 1989)—Lost two teeth and required 50 stitches to close cuts in his mouth when boarded by Steve Seftel vs. Baltimore . . . (April 9, 1990)—Sprained left knee vs. New Jersey.

Year	Team	League	Games	G.	A.	Pts.	Pen.
1977-78	Billings Bighorns	WCHL	72	31	44	75	105
1978-79	Billings Bighorns	WHL	39	25	37	62	50
1978-79	Saskatoon Blades (c)	WHL	33	15	32	47	37
1979-80	New York Rangers	NHL	17	0	5	5	4
1979-80	New Haven Nighthawks	AHL	53	11	14	25	43

Year	Team	League	Games	G.	A.	Pts.	Pen.
1980-81	Did not play		..	..	..	..	..
1981-82	Springfield Indians	AHL	77	23	22	45	38
1981-82	Springfield Indians	AHL	77	23	22	45	38
1982-83	Tulsa Oilers	CHL	63	29	28	57	44
1982-83	New York Rangers	NHL	5	0	1	1	4
1983-84	Moncton Alpines	AHL	28	7	16	23	30
1983-84	Edmonton Oilers	NHL	45	2	8	10	31
1984-85	Nova Scotia Oilers (d)	AHL	68	20	45	65	44
1985-86	New Jersey Devils	NHL	2	0	2	2	2
1985-86	Maine Mariners	AHL	69	15	30	45	83
1986-87	Maine Mariners	AHL	56	12	14	26	47
1987-88	Utica Devils	AHL	47	14	33	47	32
1987-88	New Jersey Devils	NHL	24	2	5	7	12
1988-89	New Jersey Devils	NHL	55	7	5	12	14
1989-90	Utica Devils	AHL	57	13	36	49	53
1989-90	New Jersey Devils	NHL	19	3	3	6	4
	NHL TOTALS		167	14	29	43	71

(c)—August, 1979—Drafted by New York Rangers in 1979 NHL entry draft. Third Rangers pick, 76th overall, fourth round.

(d)—August, 1985—Signed by New Jersey Devils as a free agent.

JAMIE COOK

Right Wing . . . 6'1" . . . 195 lbs. . . . Born, Bramalea, Ont., November 5, 1968 . . . Shoots right.

Year	Team	League	Games	G.	A.	Pts.	Pen.
1986-87	Bramalea Jr. B	OHL	37	21	28	49	46
1987-88	Bramalea Jr. B (c)	OHL	37	26	44	70	56
1988-89	Colgate University	ECAC	28	13	11	24	26
1989-90	Colgate University	ECAC	38	16	20	36	24

(c)—June, 1988—Drafted by Philadelphia Flyers in 1988 NHL entry draft. Eighth Flyers pick, 140th overall, seventh round.

TODD COPELAND

Defense . . . 6'2" . . . 200 lbs. . . . Born, Ridgewood, N.J., May 18, 1968 . . . Shoots left . . . (February, 1986)—Knee injury.

Year	Team	League	Games	G.	A.	Pts.	Pen.
1984-85	Belmont Hill H.S.	Mass. H.S.	23	8	25	33	18
1985-86	Belmont Hill H.S. (c)	Mass. H.S.	19	4	19	23	19
1986-87	University of Michigan	CCHA	34	2	10	12	57
1987-88	University of Michigan	CCHA	41	3	10	13	58
1988-89	University of Michigan	CCHA	39	5	14	19	102
1989-90	University of Michigan	CCHA	34	6	16	22	62

(c)—June, 1986—Drafted by New Jersey Devils in 1986 NHL entry draft. Second Devils pick, 24th overall, second round.

TIM CORKERY

Defense . . . 6'4" . . . 210 lbs. . . . Born, Ponoka, Alaska, February 17, 1967 . . . Shoots left.

Year	Team	League	Games	G.	A.	Pts.	Pen.
1986-87	Ferris State Univ. (c)	CCHA	40	3	7	10	120
1987-88	Ferris State Univ.	CCHA	40	0	6	6	108
1988-89	Ferris State Univ. (d)	CCHA	23	2	5	7	53
1989-90	Ferris State Univ.	CCHA	32	0	6	6	64

(c)—June, 1987—Drafted by Calgary Flames in 1987 NHL entry draft. Sixth Flames pick, 103rd overall, fifth round.

(d)—September 5, 1988—Traded with Mike Bullard and Craig Coxe by Calgary Flames to St. Louis Blues for Doug Gilmour, Mark Hunter, Steve Bozek and Michael Dark.

BOB CORKUM

Right Wing . . . 6'2" . . . 200 lbs. . . . Born, Salisbury, Mass., December 18, 1967 . . . Shoots right.

Year	Team	League	Games	G.	A.	Pts.	Pen.
1984-85	Triton Regional H.S.	Mass. H.S.	18	35	36	71	....
1985-86	University of Maine (c)	H. East	39	7	16	23	53
1986-87	University of Maine	H. East	35	18	11	29	24
1987-88	University of Maine	H. East	40	14	18	32	64
1988-89	University of Maine	H. East	45	17	31	48	64
1989-90	Rochester Americans	AHL	43	8	11	19	45
1989-90	Buffalo Sabres	NHL	8	2	0	2	4
	NHL TOTALS		8	2	0	2	4

(c)—June, 1986—Drafted by Buffalo Sabres in 1986 NHL entry draft. Third Sabres pick, 47th overall, third round.

RICK CORRIVEAU

Defense . . . 5'11" . . . 205 lbs. . . . Born, Welland, Ont., January 6, 1971 . . . Shoots left . . . (November 6, 1988)—Injured right knee ligaments when checked by Mark Montanari at Kitchener . . . Brother of Yvon Corriveau.

Year	Team	League	Games	G.	A.	Pts.	Pen.
1986-87	Welland Jr. B	OHA	29	9	17	26	90
1987-88	London Knights	OHL	63	19	47	66	51
1988-89	London Knights (c)	OHL	12	4	10	14	23
1989-90	London Knights	OHL	63	22	55	77	63

(c)—June, 1989—Drafted by St. Louis Blues in 1989 NHL entry draft. Second Blues pick, 31st overall, second round.

YVON CORRIVEAU

Left Wing . . . 6'1" . . . 195 lbs. . . . Born, Welland, Ont., February 8, 1967 . . . Shoots left . . . (March, 1985)—Shoulder injury . . . (November, 1988)—Charley horse . . . Brother of Rick Corriveau.

Year	Team	League	Games	G.	A.	Pts.	Pen.
1983-84—Welland Cougars Jr. B	OHA	36	16	21	37	51
1984-85—Toronto Marlboros (c)	OHL	59	23	28	51	65
1985-86—Toronto Marlboros	OHL	59	54	36	90	75
1985-86—Washington Capitals	NHL	2	0	0	0	0
1986-87—Toronto Marlboros	OHL	23	14	19	33	23
1986-87—Binghamton Whalers	AHL	7	0	0	0	2
1986-87—Washington Capitals	NHL	17	1	1	2	24
1987-88—Binghamton Whalers	AHL	35	15	14	29	64
1987-88—Washington Capitals	NHL	44	10	9	19	84
1988-89—Baltimore Skipjacks	AHL	33	16	23	39	65
1988-89—Washington Capitals	NHL	33	3	2	5	62
1989-90—Washington Capitals (d)	NHL	50	9	6	15	50
1989-90—Hartford Whalers	NHL	13	4	1	5	22
NHL TOTALS		159	27	19	46	242

(c)—June, 1985—Drafted as underage junior by Washington Capitals in NHL entry draft. First Capitals pick, 19th overall, first round.

(d)—March 5, 1990—Traded by Washington Capitals to Hartford Whalers for Mike Liut.

SHAYNE CORSON

Center and Left Wing . . . 6' . . . 175 lbs. . . . Born, Barrie, Ont., August 13, 1966 . . . Shoots left . . . (1986)—Named to World Junior Hockey Championship All-Star team . . . (January 24, 1987)—Broke jaw at St. Louis . . . (September, 1987)—Strained ligament in right knee during training camp . . . (March, 1988)—Injured groin . . . (April, 1988)—Knee injury . . . (April, 1989)—Knee injury . . . (October 29, 1989)—Bruised left shoulder vs. Edmonton . . . (December, 1989)—Broke little toe on right foot.

Year	Team	League	Games	G.	A.	Pts.	Pen.
1982-83—Barrie Flyers	COJHL	23	13	29	42	87
1983-84—Brantford Alexanders (c)	OHL	66	25	46	71	165
1984-85—Hamilton Steelhawks	OHL	54	27	63	90	154
1985-86—Hamilton Steelhawks	OHL	47	41	57	98	153
1985-86—Montreal Canadiens	NHL	3	0	0	0	2
1986-87—Montreal Canadiens	NHL	55	12	11	23	144
1987-88—Montreal Canadiens	NHL	71	12	27	39	152
1988-89—Montreal Canadiens	NHL	80	26	24	50	193
1989-90—Montreal Canadiens	NHL	76	31	44	75	144
NHL TOTALS		285	81	106	187	635

(c)—June, 1984—Drafted as underage junior by Montreal Canadiens in 1984 NHL entry draft. Second Canadiens pick, eighth overall, first round.

ALAIN GABRIEL COTE

Defense . . . 6' . . . 200 lbs. . . . Born, Montmagny, Que., April 14, 1967 . . . Shoots right.

Year	Team	League	Games	G.	A.	Pts.	Pen.
1983-84—Quebec Remparts	QMJHL	60	3	17	20	40
1984-85—Quebec Remparts (c)	QMJHL	68	9	25	34	173
1985-86—Granby Bisons	QMJHL	22	4	12	16	48
1985-86—Moncton Golden Flames	AHL	3	0	0	0	0
1985-86—Boston Bruins	NHL	32	0	6	6	14
1986-87—Granby Bisons	QMJHL	43	7	24	31	185
1986-87—Boston Bruins	NHL	3	0	0	0	0
1987-88—Boston Bruins	NHL	2	0	0	0	0
1987-88—Maine Mariners	AHL	69	9	34	43	108
1988-89—Maine Mariners	AHL	37	5	16	21	111
1988-89—Boston Bruins	NHL	31	2	3	5	51
1989-90—Washington Capitals (d)	NHL	2	0	0	0	7
1989-90—Baltimore Skipjacks	AHL	57	5	19	24	161
NHL TOTALS		70	2	9	11	72

(c)—June, 1985—Drafted as underage junior by Boston Bruins in NHL entry draft. First Bruins pick, 31st overall, second round.

(d)—September 27, 1989—Traded by Boston Bruins to Washington Capitals for Bobby Gould.

SYLVAIN COTE

Defense . . . 6' . . . 170 lbs. . . . Born, Quebec City, Que., January 19, 1966 . . . Shoots right . . . (1986)—Named to World Junior Championship All-Star team . . . (November, 1988)—Played three games at Right Wing . . . (October 28, 1989)—Broke toe on left foot when struck by a John Carter shot at Boston . . . (December, 1989)—Sprained left knee . . . (January 22, 1990)—Fractured right foot when struck by a Pat Verbeek shot during a practice.

Year	Team	League	Games	G.	A.	Pts.	Pen.
1982-83—Quebec Remparts	QMJHL	66	10	24	34	50
1983-84—Quebec Remparts (c)	QMJHL	66	15	50	65	89
1984-85—Hartford Whalers	NHL	67	3	9	12	17
1985-86—Hartford Whalers	NHL	2	0	0	0	0
1985-86—Hull Olympiques (a-d-e)	QMJHL	26	10	33	43	14
1986-87—Binghamton Whalers	AHL	12	2	4	6	0
1986-87—Hartford Whalers	NHL	67	2	8	10	20
1987-88—Hartford Whalers	NHL	67	7	21	28	30
1988-89—Hartford Whalers	NHL	78	8	9	17	49
1989-90—Hartford Whalers	NHL	28	4	2	6	14
NHL TOTALS		309	24	49	73	130

(c)—June, 1984—Drafted as underage junior by Hartford Whalers in 1984 NHL entry draft. First Whalers pick, 11th overall, first round.

(d)—Won Emile "Butch" Bouchard Trophy (Top Defenseman).

(e)—Shared Guy Lafleur Trophy (Playoff MVP) with Luc Robitaille.

GEOFF COURTNALL

Left Wing . . . 6' . . . 165 lbs. . . . Born, Victoria, B.C., August 18, 1962 . . . Shoots left . . . Brother of Russ Courtnall.

Year	Team	League	Games	G.	A.	Pts.	Pen.
1980-81—Victoria Cougars	WHL	11	3	5	8	6
1981-82—Victoria Cougars	WHL	72	35	57	92	100
1983-84—Victoria Cougars	WHL	71	41	73	114	186
1983-84—Hershey Bears (c)	AHL	74	14	12	26	51
1983-84—Boston Bruins	NHL	5	0	0	0	0
1984-85—Hershey Bears	AHL	9	8	4	12	4
1984-85—Boston Bruins	NHL	64	12	16	28	82
1985-86—Moncton Golden Flames	AHL	12	8	8	16	6
1985-86—Boston Bruins	NHL	64	21	17	38	61
1986-87—Boston Bruins	NHL	65	13	23	36	117
1987-88—Boston Bruins (d)	NHL	62	32	26	58	108
1987-88—Edmonton Oilers (e)	NHL	12	4	4	8	15
1988-89—Washington Capitals	NHL	79	42	38	80	112
1989-90—Washington Capitals (f)	NHL	80	35	39	74	104
NHL TOTALS		431	159	163	322	599

(c)—September, 1983—Signed by Boston Bruins as a free agent.

(d)—March, 1988—Traded with Bill Ranford by Boston Bruins to Edmonton Oilers for Andy Moog.

(e)—July, 1988—Traded by Edmonton Oilers to Washington Capitals for Greg Adams.

(f)—July 13, 1990—Traded by Washington Capitals to St. Louis Blues for Peter Zezel and Mike Lalor.

RUSS COURTNALL

Center . . . 5'10" . . . 175 lbs. . . . Born, Victoria, B.C., June 3, 1965 . . . Shoots right . . . Member of 1984 Canadian Olympic Team . . . (November, 1987)—Bruised knee . . . (February, 1988)—Virus . . . (March, 1988)—Back spasms at Vancouver . . . Brother of Geoff Courtnall.

Year	Team	League	Games	G.	A.	Pts.	Pen.
1982-83—Victoria Cougars (c)	WHL	60	36	61	97	33
1983-84—Victoria Cougars	WHL	32	29	37	66	63
1983-84—Canadian Olympic Team	Int'l	16	4	7	11	10
1983-84—Toronto Maple Leafs	NHL	14	3	9	12	6
1984-85—Toronto Maple Leafs	NHL	69	12	10	22	44
1985-86—Toronto Maple Leafs	NHL	73	22	38	60	52
1986-87—Toronto Maple Leafs	NHL	79	29	44	73	90
1987-88—Toronto Maple Leafs	NHL	65	23	26	49	47
1988-89—Toronto Maple Leafs (d)	NHL	9	1	1	2	4
1988-89—Montreal Canadiens	NHL	64	22	17	39	15
1989-90—Montreal Canadiens	NHL	80	27	32	59	27
NHL TOTALS		453	139	177	316	285

(c)—June, 1983—Drafted by Toronto Maple Leafs as underage junior in NHL entry draft. First Maple Leafs pick, seventh overall, first round.

(d)—November 7, 1988—Traded by Toronto Maple Leafs to Montreal Canadiens for John Kordic and a sixth-round 1989 draft pick (Michael Doers).

SYLVAIN COUTURIER

Center . . . 6'1" . . . 200 lbs. . . . Born, Greenfield Park, Que., April 23, 1968 . . . Shoots left . . . Also plays Left Wing . . . (October, 1989)—Broken jaw.

Year	Team	League	Games	G.	A.	Pts.	Pen.
1984-85—Richelieu Riverain Midget	Que.	42	41	70	111	62
1985-86—Laval Titans (c)	QMJHL	68	21	37	58	649
1986-87—Laval Titans	QMJHL	67	39	51	90	77
1987-88—Laval Titans	QMJHL	67	70	67	137	115
1988-89—Los Angeles Kings	NHL	16	1	3	4	2
1988-89—New Haven Nighthawks	AHL	44	18	20	38	33
1989-90—New Haven Nighthawks	AHL	50	9	8	17	47
NHL TOTALS		16	1	3	4	2

(c)—June, 1986—Drafted as underage junior by Los Angeles Kings in 1986 NHL entry draft. Third Kings pick, 65th overall, fourth round.

CRAIG COXE

Center . . . 6'4" . . . 185 lbs. . . . Born, Chula Vista, Calif., January 21, 1964 . . . Shoots left . . . (October, 1985)—Broke hand in pre-season game with Calgary and missed 13 games . . . (September, 1987)—Suspended for first three regular season games by NHL after leaving the penalty box in a pre-season game vs. Los Angeles.

Year	Team	League	Games	G.	A.	Pts.	Pen.
1980-81—Los Angeles Midgets	Calif.	..	..	..	..	..
1981-82—St. Albert Saints (c)	AJHL	51	17	48	65	212
1982-83—Belleville Bulls	OHL	64	14	27	41	102
1983-84—Belleville Bulls	OHL	45	17	28	45	90
1984-85—Vancouver Canucks (d)	NHL	9	0	0	0	49
1984-85—Fredericton Express	AHL	62	8	7	15	242
1985-86—Vancouver Canucks	NHL	57	3	5	8	176
1986-87—Fredericton Express	AHL	46	1	12	13	168
1986-87—Vancouver Canucks	NHL	15	1	0	1	31
1987-88—Vancouver Canucks (e)	NHL	64	5	12	17	186
1987-88—Calgary Flames	NHL	7	2	3	5	32
1988-89—St. Louis Blues (f)	NHL	41	0	7	7	127
1988-89—Peoria Rivermen	IHL	8	2	7	9	38
1989-90—Vancouver Canucks (g-h)	NHL	25	1	4	5	66
1989-90—Milwaukee Admirals	IHL	5	0	5	5	4
NHL TOTALS		218	12	31	43	667

(c)—June, 1982—Drafted as underage junior by Detroit Red Wings in 1982 NHL entry draft. Fourth Red Wings pick, 66th overall, fourth round.

(d)—October, 1984—WHL rights traded by Portland Winter Hawks to Saskatoon Blades for future considerations.

(e)—March, 1988—Traded by Vancouver Canucks to Calgary Flames for Brian Bradley, Peter Bakovic and future considerations (Kevan Guy).

(f)—September 6, 1988—Traded with Mike Bullard and Tim Corkey by Calgary Flames to St. Louis Blues for Doug Gilmour, Mark Hunter, Steve Bozek and Michael Dark.

(g)—September 28, 1989—Sold by St. Louis Blues to Chicago Black Hawks to complete future consideration of Rik Wilson trade made on September 27.

(h)—October 2, 1989—Claimed by Vancouver Canucks in 1989 NHL waiver draft for $15,000.

MIKE CRAIG

Right Wing . . . 6' . . . 180 lbs. . . . Born, London, Ont., June 6, 1971 . . . Shoots right . . . (January 28, 1990)—Cracked fibula in leg when slashed by Shayne Antoski vs. North Bay.

Year	Team	League	Games	G.	A.	Pts.	Pen.
1986-87—Woodstock Navy Vets Jr. C.		OHA	32	29	19	48	64
1987-88—Oshawa Generals		OHL	61	6	10	16	39
1988-89—Oshawa Generals (c)		OHL	63	36	36	72	34
1989-90—Oshawa Generals		OHL	43	36	40	76	85

(c)—June, 1989—Drafted by Minnesota North Stars in 1989 NHL entry draft. Second North Stars pick, 28th overall, second round.

MURRAY CRAVEN

Center . . . 6'2'' . . . 175 lbs. . . . Born, Medicine Hat, Alta., July 20, 1964 . . . Shoots left . . . Also plays Left Wing . . . (January 15, 1983)—Injured left knee cartilage vs. Toronto . . . (April 16, 1987)—Broke foot vs. N.Y. Rangers . . . (November, 1988)—Hyperextended right knee and lacerated eye . . . (January, 1989)—Bruised right foot . . . (February 24, 1989)—Fractured left wrist at Philadelphia . . . (April 5, 1989)—Fractured right wrist in opening playoff game of Washington . . . (February, 1990)—Back spasms . . . (March 24, 1990)—Injured rotator cuff at New Jersey.

Year	Team	League	Games	G.	A.	Pts.	Pen.
1980-81—Medicine Hat Tigers		WHL	69	5	10	15	18
1981-82—Medicine Hat Tigers (c)		WHL	72	35	46	81	49
1982-83—Medicine Hat Tigers		WHL	28	17	29	46	35
1982-83—Detroit Red Wings		NHL	31	4	7	11	6
1983-84—Medicine Hat Tigers		WHL	48	38	56	94	53
1983-84—Detroit Red Wings		NHL	15	0	4	4	6
1984-85—Philadelphia Flyers (d)		NHL	80	26	35	61	30
1985-86—Philadelphia Flyers		NHL	78	21	33	54	34
1986-87—Philadelphia Flyers		NHL	77	19	30	49	38
1987-88—Philadelphia Flyers		NHL	72	30	46	76	58
1988-89—Philadelphia Flyers		NHL	51	9	28	37	52
1989-90—Philadelphia Flyers		NHL	76	25	50	75	42
NHL TOTALS			480	134	233	367	266

(c)—June, 1982—Drafted as underage junior by Detroit Red Wings in 1982 NHL entry draft. First Red Wings pick, 17th overall, first round.

(d)—October, 1984—Traded with Joe Paterson by Detroit Red Wings to Philadelphia Flyers for Darryl Sittler.

LOUIS CRAWFORD

Left Wing . . . 5'11'' . . . 175 lbs. . . . Born, Belleville, Ont., November 5, 1962 . . . Shoots left.

Year	Team	League	Games	G.	A.	Pts.	Pen.
1979-80—Belleville Jr. B		OHA	10	7	11	18	60
1980-81—Kitchener Rangers		OHL	53	2	7	9	134
1981-82—Kitchener Rangers		OHL	64	11	17	28	243
1982-83—Rochester Americans (c)		AHL	64	5	11	16	142
1983-84—Rochester Americans		AHL	76	7	6	13	234
1984-85—Rochester Americans		AHL	65	12	29	41	173
1985-86—Nova Scotia Oilers (d)		AHL	78	8	11	19	214
1986-87—Nova Scotia Oilers		AHL	35	3	4	7	48
1987-88—Nova Scotia Oilers		AHL	65	15	15	30	170
1988-89—Adirondack Red Wings		AHL	74	23	23	46	179
1989-90—Boston Bruins (e)		NHL	7	0	0	0	20
1989-90—Maine Mariners		AHL	62	11	15	26	241
NHL TOTALS			7	0	0	0	20

(c)—August, 1984—Signed by Buffalo Sabres as a free agent.

(d)—October, 1985—Signed by Nova Scotia Oilers as a free agent.

(e)—July 6, 1989—Signed by Boston Bruins as a free agent.

ADAM CREIGHTON

Center . . . 6'5'' . . . 210 lbs. . . . Born, Burlington, Ont., June 2, 1965 . . . Shoots left . . . Son of Dave Creighton (NHL, '50s-'60s) . . . (May, 1984)—Named MVP of 1984 Memorial Cup . . . (January, 1988)—Knee surgery . . . (September, 1988)—Sprained knee in Buffalo Sabres training camp.

Year	Team	League	Games	G.	A.	Pts.	Pen.
1981-82—Ottawa 67's		OHL	60	14	27	42	73
1982-83—Ottawa 67's (c)		OHL	68	44	46	90	88
1983-84—Ottawa 67's		OHL	56	42	49	91	79
1983-84—Buffalo Sabres		NHL	7	2	2	4	4
1984-85—Ottawa 67's		OHL	10	4	14	18	23
1984-85—Rochester Americans		AHL	6	5	3	8	2
1984-85—Buffalo Sabres		NHL	30	2	8	10	33
1985-86—Rochester Americans		AHL	32	17	21	38	27
1985-86—Buffalo Sabres		NHL	20	1	1	2	2
1986-87—Buffalo Sabres		NHL	56	18	22	40	26
1987-88—Buffalo Sabres		NHL	36	10	17	27	87
1988-89—Buffalo Sabres (d)		NHL	24	7	10	17	44
1988-89—Chicago Black Hawks		NHL	43	15	14	29	92
1989-90—Chicago Black Hawks		NHL	80	34	36	70	224
NHL TOTALS			296	89	110	199	512

(c)—June, 1983—Drafted as underage junior by Buffalo Sabres in 1983 NHL entry draft. Third Sabres pick, 11th overall, first round.

(d)—December 2, 1988—Traded by Buffalo Sabres to Chicago Black Hawks for Rick Vaive.

EDMUND (SPAGS) CRISTOFOLI

Center . . . 6'2'' . . . 205 lbs. . . . Born, Trail, B.C., May 14, 1967 . . . Shoots left . . . Also plays Left Wing . . . Son of Ed Cristofoli (Member of 1961 World Champion Trail Smoke Eaters) . . . (November 22, 1989)—Injured shoulder at Philadelphia.

Year	Team	League	Games	G.	A.	Pts.	Pen.
1984-85—Penticton Knights (c)		BCJHL	48	36	34	70	58
1985-86—Univ. of Denver		WCHA	46	10	9	19	32
1986-87—Univ. of Denver		WCHA	40	14	15	29	52
1987-88—Univ. of Denver		WCHA	38	12	27	39	64
1988-89—Univ. of Denver		WCHA	43	20	19	39	50
1989-90—Sherbrooke Canadiens		AHL	57	16	19	35	31
1989-90—Montreal Canadiens		NHL	9	0	1	1	4
NHL TOTALS			9	0	1	1	4

(c)—June, 1985—Drafted by Montreal Canadiens in 1985 NHL entry draft. Ninth Canadiens pick, 142nd overall, seventh round.

SHAWN CRONIN

Defense . . . 6'2'' . . . 210 lbs. . . . Born, Flushing, Mich., August 20, 1963 . . . Shoots left . . . (February, 1990)—Bruised hand.

Year	Team	League	Games	G.	A.	Pts.	Pen.
1982-83—U. of Illinois-Chicago		CCHA	36	1	5	6	52
1983-84—U. of Illinois-Chicago		CCHA	32	0	4	4	41
1984-85—U. of Illinois-Chicago		CCHA	31	2	6	8	52
1985-86—U. of Illinois-Chicago (c)		CCHA	38	3	8	11	70
1986-87—Binghamton Whalers		AHL	12	0	1	1	60
1986-87—Salt Lake Golden Eagles		IHL	53	8	16	24	118
1987-88—Binghamton Whalers (d)		AHL	66	3	8	11	212
1988-89—Washington Capitals (e)		NHL	1	0	0	0	0
1988-89—Baltimore Skipjacks		AHL	75	3	9	12	267
1989-90—Winnipeg Jets (f)		NHL	61	0	4	4	243
NHL TOTALS			62	0	4	4	243

(c)—March, 1986—Signed by Hartford Whalers as a free agent.

(d)—June, 1988—Signed by Washington Capitals as a free agent.

(e)—June 13, 1989—Signed by Philadelphia Flyers as a free agent.

(f)—July 24, 1989—Traded by Philadelphia Flyers to Winnipeg Jets for future considerations. The future considerations were later canceled.

DOUG CROSSMAN

Defense . . . 6'2'' . . . 190 lbs. . . . Born, Peterborough, Ont., June 30, 1960 . . . Shoots left . . . (February, 1983)—Injured thumb.

Year	Team	League	Games	G.	A.	Pts.	Pen.
1976-77—London Knights		OMJHL	1	0	0	0	0
1977-78—Ottawa 67's		OMJHL	65	4	17	21	17
1978-79—Ottawa 67's (c)		OMJHL	67	12	51	63	63
1979-80—Ottawa 67's (a)		OMJHL	66	20	96	116	48
1980-81—Chicago Black Hawks		NHL	9	0	2	2	2
1980-81—New Brunswick Hawks		AHL	70	13	43	56	90
1981-82—Chicago Black Hawks		NHL	70	12	28	40	24
1982-83—Chicago Black Hawks (d)		NHL	80	13	40	53	46
1983-84—Philadelphia Flyers		NHL	78	7	28	35	63
1984-85—Philadelphia Flyers		NHL	80	4	33	37	65
1985-86—Philadelphia Flyers		NHL	80	6	37	43	55
1986-87—Philadelphia Flyers		NHL	78	9	31	40	29
1987-88—Philadelphia Flyers		NHL	76	9	29	38	43
1988-89—New Haven Nighthawks		AHL	3	0	0	0	0
1988-89—Los Angeles Kings (e)		NHL	74	10	15	25	53
1989-90—New York Islanders		NHL	80	15	44	59	54
NHL TOTALS			705	85	287	372	434

(c)—August, 1979—Drafted by Chicago Black Hawks as underage junior in 1979 NHL entry draft. Sixth Black Hawks pick, 112th overall, sixth round.

(d)—June, 1983—Traded by Chicago Black Hawks with second-round draft pick (Scott Mellanby) in 1984 to Philadelphia Flyers for Behn Wilson.

(e)—May 23, 1989—Traded by Los Angeles Kings to New York Islanders to complete a February 22, 1989 trade that saw Kelly Hrudey traded to the Kings for Mark Fitzpatrick, Wayne McBean and future considerations.

KEITH SCOTT CROWDER

Right Wing . . . 6' . . . 190 lbs. . . . Born, Windsor, Ont., January 6, 1959 . . . Shoots right . . . Also plays Center . . . Brother of former NHLer Bruce Crowder . . . (February, 1978)—Broken ankle . . . Set Bruins team record for most penalty minutes by a rookie (172) in 1980-81 . . . (December, 1983)—Sprained right knee and missed 16 games . . . (October 26, 1986)—Separated right shoulder at Calgary . . . (May, 1987)—Surgery to right shoulder . . . (February, 1988)—Strained abdominal muscle . . . (March, 1988)—Strained right shoulder . . . (November, 1988)—Right thigh Charley horse . . . (October, 1989)—Missed 10 games with a strained neck . . . (March 17, 1990)—Strained left knee at Boston.

Year	Team	League	Games	G.	A.	Pts.	Pen.
1976-77—Peterborough Petes		Jr. ''A''OHA	58	13	19	32	99
1977-78—Peterborough Petes		Jr. ''A''OHA	58	30	30	60	139
1978-79—Birmingham Bulls (d)		WHA	5	1	0	1	17
1978-79—Peterborough Petes (e)		OMJHL	43	25	41	66	76
1979-80—Binghamton Dusters		AHL	13	4	0	4	15
1979-80—Grand Rapids Owls		IHL	20	10	13	23	22
1980-81—Springfield Indians		AHL	26	12	18	30	34
1980-81—Boston Bruins		NHL	47	13	12	25	172
1981-82—Boston Bruins		NHL	71	23	21	44	101
1982-83—Boston Bruins		NHL	74	35	39	74	105
1983-84—Boston Bruins		NHL	63	24	28	52	128
1984-85—Boston Bruins		NHL	79	32	38	70	142
1985-86—Boston Bruins		NHL	78	38	46	84	177
1986-87—Boston Bruins		NHL	58	22	30	52	106
1987-88—Boston Bruins		NHL	68	17	26	43	173
1988-89—Boston Bruins (f)		NHL	69	15	18	33	147
1989-90—Los Angeles Kings		NHL	55	4	13	17	93
WHA TOTALS			5	1	0	1	17
NHL TOTALS			662	223	271	494	1344

(c)—July, 1978—Signed by Birmingham Bulls (WHA) as underage player.

(d)—November, 1978—Returned to Peterborough to play final year of junior eligibility.

(e)—August, 1979—Drafted by Boston Bruins in entry draft. Fourth Boston pick, 57th overall, third round.

(f)—June 16, 1989—Signed with the Los Angeles Kings as a free agent.

TROY CROWDER

Right Wing . . . 6'3'' . . . 200 lbs. . . . Born, Sudbury, Ont., May 3, 1968 . . . Shoots right . . . (September, 1989)—Left training camp and returned in March, 1990 . . . Son of Brian Crowder.

Year	Team	League	Games	G.	A.	Pts.	Pen.
1984-85	Walden Midgets	NOHA	28	20	21	41	63
1985-86	Hamilton Steelhawks (c)	OHL	55	4	4	8	178
1986-87	North Bay Centennials	OHL	35	6	11	17	90
1986-87	Belleville Bulls	OHL	21	5	5	10	52
1987-88	North Bay Centennials	OHL	9	1	2	3	44
1987-88	Belleville Bulls	OHL	46	12	27	39	103
1987-88	Utica Devils	AHL	3	0	0	0	36
1988-89	Utica Devils	AHL	62	6	4	10	152
1989-90	Nashville Knights	ECHL	3	0	0	0	15
1989-90	New Jersey Devils	NHL	10	0	0	0	23
	NHL TOTALS		10	0	0	0	23

(c)—June, 1986—Drafted as underage junior by New Jersey Devils in 1986 NHL entry draft. Sixth Devils pick, 108th overall, sixth round.

JOSEPH CROWLEY

Left Wing . . . 6'2'' . . . 192 lbs. . . . Born, Concord, Mass., February 29, 1972 . . . Shoots left . . . (January, 1990)—Mononucleosis . . . Brother of Ted Crowley.

Year	Team	League	Games	G.	A.	Pts.	Pen.
1987-88	Lawrence Academy	Mass. H.S.	24	21	23	44	34
1988-89	Lawrence Academy	Mass. H.S.	20	13	22	35	42
1989-90	Lawrence Academy (c)	Mass. H.S.	10	8	5	13	14

(c)—June 16, 1990—Selected by Edmonton Oilers in 1990 NHL entry draft. Third Oilers pick, 59th overall, third round.

JIM CULHANE

Defense . . . 6' . . . 190 lbs. . . . Born, Haileybury, Ont., August 8, 1960 . . . Shoots left.

Year	Team	League	Games	G.	A.	Pts.	Pen.
1983-84	Western Michigan Univ. (c)	CCHA	42	1	14	15	88
1984-85	Western Michigan Univ.	CCHA	37	2	8	10	84
1985-86	Western Michigan Univ.	CCHA	40	1	21	22	61
1986-87	Western Michigan Univ.	CCHA	41	9	13	22	*163
1987-88	Binghamton Whalers	AHL	76	5	17	22	169
1988-89	Binghamton Whalers	AHL	72	6	11	17	200
1989-90	Hartford Whalers	NHL	6	0	1	1	4
1989-90	Binghamton Whalers	AHL	73	6	11	17	69
	NHL TOTALS		6	0	1	1	4

(c)—June, 1984—Drafted by Hartford Whalers in 1984 NHL entry draft. Sixth Whalers pick, 214th overall, 11th round.

JOHN CULLEN

Center . . . 5'10'' . . . 185 lbs. . . . Born, Puslinch, Ont., August 2, 1964 . . . Shoots right . . . Holds Boston University record for career points . . . (1987-88)—Set IHL record for points by a rookie . . . Son of Barry Cullen (Former NHL player with Toronto and Detroit, 1959-1964) and brother of Terry Cullen (Univ. of Michigan, 1978) . . . (October, 1989)—Missed seven games with hepatitis.

Year	Team	League	Games	G.	A.	Pts.	Pen.
1983-84	Boston Univ. (c)	ECAC	40	23	33	56	28
1984-85	Boston Univ. (a)	H. East	41	27	32	59	46
1985-86	Boston Univ. (a-d-e)	H. East	43	25	49	74	54
1986-87	Boston Univ. (b)	H. East	36	23	29	52	35
1987-88	Flint Spirits (a-f-g-h)	IHL	81	48	*109	*157	113
1988-89	Pittsburgh Penguins (i)	NHL	79	12	37	49	112
1989-90	Pittsburgh Penguins	NHL	72	32	60	92	138
	NHL TOTALS		151	44	97	141	250

(c)—Named ECAC Rookie of the Year.

(d)—Named Second team All-America (East).

(e)—Selected by Buffalo Sabres in 1986 NHL supplemental draft.

(f)—Won James Gatschene Trophy (IHL MVP).

(g)—Won Leo Lamoureux Trophy (IHL scoring leader).

(h)—Shared Gary Longman Trophy with Ed Belfour (IHL Rookie of the Year).

(i)—July, 1988—Signed by Pittsburgh Penguins as a free agent.

JIM CUMMINS

Right Wing . . . 6'2'' . . . 200 lbs. . . . Born, Dearborn, Mich., May 17, 1970 . . . Shoots right.

Year	Team	League	Games	G.	A.	Pts.	Pen.
1987-88	Detroit Compuware Jr. A.	NAJHL	31	11	15	26	146
1988-89	Michigan State Univ. (c)	CCHA	36	3	9	12	100
1989-90	Michigan State Univ.	CCHA	41	8	7	15	94

(c)—June, 1989—Drafted by New York Rangers in 1989 NHL entry draft. Fifth Rangers pick, 67th overall, fourth round.

RANDY WILLIAM CUNNEYWORTH

Center and Left Wing . . . 6' . . . 180 lbs. . . . Born, Etobicoke, Ont., May 10, 1961 . . . Shoots left . . . (January, 1988)—Suspended by NHL for three games and five games . . . (January 24, 1989)—Fractured right foot when struck by a Paul Coffey shot in a team practice . . . (October, 1989)—Cracked bone in right foot.

Year	Team	League	Games	G.	A.	Pts.	Pen.
1979-80	Ottawa 67's (c)	OMJHL	63	16	25	41	145
1980-81	Ottawa 67's	OHL	67	54	74	128	240
1980-81	Rochester Americans	AHL	1	0	1	1	2
1980-81	Buffalo Sabres	NHL	1	0	0	0	2
1981-82	Rochester Americans	AHL	57	12	15	27	86
1981-82	Buffalo Sabres	NHL	20	2	4	6	47
1982-83	Rochester Americans	AHL	78	23	33	56	111
1983-84	Rochester Americans	AHL	54	18	17	35	85
1984-85	Rochester Americans	AHL	72	30	38	68	148
1985-86	Pittsburgh Penguins (d)	NHL	75	15	30	45	74
1986-87	Pittsburgh Penguins	NHL	79	26	27	53	142
1987-88	Pittsburgh Penguins	NHL	71	35	39	74	141
1988-89	Pittsburgh Penguins (e)	NHL	70	25	19	44	156
1989-90	Winnipeg Jets (f)	NHL	28	5	6	11	34
1989-90	Hartford Whalers	NHL	43	9	9	18	41
	NHL TOTALS		387	117	134	251	637

(c)—June, 1980—Drafted as underage junior by Buffalo Sabres in 1980 NHL entry draft. Ninth Sabres pick, 167th overall, eighth round.

(d)—October, 1985—After attending Pittsburgh's training camp as an unsigned free agent, his equalization rights were traded with Mike Moller by Buffalo Sabres to Pittsburgh Penguins for future considerations.

(e)—June 17, 1989—Traded with Richard Tabaracci and Dave McLlwain by Pittsburgh Penguins to Winnipeg Jets for Andrew McBain, Jim Kyte and Randy Gilhen.

(f)—December 13, 1989—Traded by Winnipeg Jets to Hartford Whalers for Paul Mac-Dermid.

BRIAN CURRAN

Defense . . . 6'4'' . . . 200 lbs. . . . Born, Toronto, Ont., November 5, 1963 . . . Shoots left . . . (November, 1981)—Appendectomy . . . (September, 1982)—Broken ankle . . . (November, 1984)—Charley Horse . . . (February 1, 1986)—Broken leg at Montreal . . . Set a N.Y. Islanders record for penalty minutes in a season (356) in 1986-87 . . . (January 12, 1988)—Fractured jaw vs. Pittsburgh . . . (November, 1988)—Pulled pelvic muscle . . . (December 1, 1988)—Bruised spine when his head struck the knee of Steve Duchesne at Los Angeles . . . (February 25, 1989)—Dislocated right wrist at Minnesota.

Year	Team	League	Games	G.	A.	Pts.	Pen.
1980-81	Portland Winter Hawks	WHL	51	2	16	18	132
1981-82	Portland Winter Hawks (c)	WHL	59	2	28	30	275
1982-83	Portland Winter Hawks	WHL	56	1	30	31	187
1983-84	Hershey Bears	AHL	23	0	2	2	94
1983-84	Boston Bruins	NHL	16	1	1	2	57
1984-85	Hershey Bears	AHL	4	0	0	0	19
1984-85	Boston Bruins	NHL	56	0	1	1	158
1985-86	Boston Bruins	NHL	43	2	5	7	192
1986-87	New York Islanders (d)	NHL	68	0	10	10	356
1987-88	Springfield Indians	AHL	8	1	0	1	43
1987-88	New York Islanders (e)	NHL	22	0	1	1	68
1987-88	Toronto Maple Leafs	NHL	7	0	1	1	19
1988-89	Toronto Maple Leafs	NHL	47	1	4	5	185
1989-90	Toronto Maple Leafs	NHL	72	2	9	11	301
	NHL TOTALS		331	6	32	38	1336

(c)—June, 1982—Drafted as underage junior by Boston Bruins in 1982 NHL entry draft. Second Bruins pick, 22nd overall, second round.

(d)—August, 1986—Signed by New York Islanders as a free agent with compensation due Boston. When the two clubs could not agree, an arbitration judge awarded the Bruins Paul Boutilier.

(e)—March, 1988—Traded by New York Islanders to Toronto Maple Leafs for a sixth-round 1988 draft pick (Pavel Gross).

DAN CURRIE

Left Wing . . . 6'1'' . . . 180 lbs. . . . Born, Burlington, Ont., March 15, 1968 . . . Shoots left.

Year	Team	League	Games	G.	A.	Pts.	Pen.
1984-85	Burlington Midgets	OHA	29	28	27	55	35
1985-86	Sault Ste. Marie Greyhounds (c)	OHL	66	21	22	43	37
1986-87	Sault Ste. Marie Greyhounds	OHL	66	31	52	83	53
1987-88	Sault Ste. Marie Greyhounds (a)	OHL	57	50	59	109	53
1987-88	Nova Scotia Oilers	AHL	3	4	2	6	0
1988-89	Cape Breton Oilers	AHL	77	29	36	65	29
1989-90	Cape Breton Oilers	AHL	77	36	40	76	28

(c)—June, 1986—Drafted as underage junior by Edmonton Oilers in 1986 NHL entry draft. Fourth Oilers pick, 84th overall, fourth round.

PAUL CYR

Left Wing . . . 5'10'' . . . 180 lbs. . . . Born, Port Alberni, B.C., October 31, 1963 . . . Shoots left . . . (December 16, 1982)—Injured thumb while playing for Team Canada at World Junior Championships . . . (March 6, 1984)—Broke knuckle in finger at Montreal . . . (December 13, 1985)—Pulled groin vs. Hartford . . . (August, 1986)—Broke ankle in charity softball game and missed training camp . . . (October, 1987)—Sprained knee . . . (October, 1988)—Sprained right knee and required surgery . . . (October, 1989)—Ongoing problems with right knee . . . Uncle of Jason Brown.

Year	Team	League	Games	G.	A.	Pts.	Pen.
1979-80	Nanaimo	BCJHL	60	28	52	80	202
1980-81	Victoria Cougars	WHL	64	36	22	58	85
1981-82	Victoria Cougars (b-c)	WHL	58	52	56	108	167
1982-83	Victoria Cougars	WHL	20	21	22	43	61
1982-83	Buffalo Sabres	NHL	36	15	12	27	59
1983-84	Buffalo Sabres	NHL	71	16	27	43	52
1984-85	Buffalo Sabres	NHL	71	22	24	46	63
1985-86	Buffalo Sabres	NHL	71	20	31	51	120
1986-87	Buffalo Sabres	NHL	73	11	16	27	122

Year	Team	League	Games	G.	A.	Pts.	Pen.
1987-88—Buffalo Sabres (d)		NHL	20	1	1	2	38
1987-88—New York Rangers		NHL	40	4	13	17	41
1988-89—New York Rangers		NHL	1	0	0	0	2
1989-90—Did not play			....	....	....	....	....
NHL TOTALS			383	89	124	213	497

(c)—June, 1982—Drafted as underage junior by Buffalo Sabres in 1982 NHL entry draft. Second Sabres pick, ninth overall, first round.

(d)—December, 1987—Traded with 10th-round 1988 draft pick (Eric Fenton) by Buffalo Sabres to New York Rangers for Mike Donnelly and a fifth-round 1988 draft pick (Alexander Mogilny).

MIKE DAGENAIS

Defense . . . 6'3'' . . . 200 lbs. . . . Born, Ottawa, Ont., July 22, 1969 . . . Shoots left . . . Son of Dennis Degenais, 1967 scoring leader of the Quebec Professional Lacrosse League.

Year	Team	League	Games	G.	A.	Pts.	Pen.
1984-85—Gloucester Major Midget		ODHA	40	12	22	34	78
1985-86—Peterborough Petes		OHL	45	1	3	4	40
1986-87—Peterborough Petes (c)		OHL	56	1	17	18	66
1987-88—Peterborough Petes		OHL	66	11	23	34	125
1988-89—Peterborough Petes		OHL	62	14	23	37	122
1989-90—Peterborough Petes		OHL	44	14	26	40	74

(c)—June, 1987—Drafted by Chicago Black Hawks in 1979 NHL entry draft. Fourth Black Hawks pick, 60th overall, third round.

ULF DAHLEN

Center . . . 6'2'' . . . 194 lbs. . . . Born, Ostersund, Sweden, January 12, 1967 . . . Shoots right . . . (November, 1987)—Bruised shin . . . (November, 1988)—Bruised left shoulder . . . (January, 1989)—Separated right shoulder.

Year	Team	League	Games	G.	A.	Pts.	Pen.
1983-84—Ostersund		Sweden	36	15	11	26	10
1984-85—Ostersund (c)		Sweden	36	33	26	59	20
1985-86—Bjorkloven		Sweden	22	4	3	7	8
1986-87—Bjorkloven		Sweden	37	15	14	29	25
1987-88—New York Rangers		NHL	70	29	23	52	26
1987-88—Colorado Rangers		IHL	2	2	2	4	0
1988-89—New York Rangers		NHL	56	24	19	43	50
1989-90—New York Rangers (d)		NHL	63	18	18	36	30
1989-90—Minnesota North Stars		NHL	13	2	4	6	0
NHL TOTALS			202	73	64	137	106

(c)—June, 1985—Drafted by New York Rangers in 1985 NHL entry draft. First Rangers pick, seventh overall, first round.

(d)—March 6, 1990—Traded with a fourth-round 1990 draft pick and future considerations by New York Rangers to Minnesota North Stars for Mike Gartner.

CHRIS DAHLQUIST

Defense . . . 6'1'' . . . 190 lbs. . . . Born, Fridley, Minn., December 14, 1962. . . . Shoots left.

Year	Team	League	Games	G.	A.	Pts.	Pen.
1981-82—Lake Superior State		CCHA	39	4	10	14	18
1982-83—Lake Superior State		CCHA	35	0	12	12	63
1983-84—Lake Superior State		CCHA	40	4	19	23	76
1984-85—Lake Superior State (c)		CCHA	44	4	15	19	112
1985-86—Baltimore Skipjacks		AHL	65	4	21	25	64
1985-86—Pittsburgh Penguins		NHL	5	1	2	3	2
1986-87—Baltimore Skipjacks		AHL	51	1	16	17	50
1986-87—Pittsburgh Penguins		NHL	19	0	1	1	20
1987-88—Pittsburgh Penguins		NHL	44	3	6	9	69
1988-89—Pittsburgh Penguins		NHL	43	1	5	6	42
1988-89—Muskegon Lumberjacks		IHL	10	3	6	9	14
1989-90—Muskegon Lumberjacks		IHL	6	1	1	2	8
1989-90—Pittsburgh Penguins		NHL	62	4	10	14	56
NHL TOTALS			173	9	24	33	189

(c)—May, 1985—Signed by Pittsburgh Penguins as a free agent.

JEAN-JACQUES DAIGNEAULT

Defense . . . 5'11'' . . . 180 lbs. . . . Born, Montreal, Que., October 12, 1965 . . . Shoots left . . . (March, 1984)—Knee surgery . . . (March 19, 1986)—Broke finger vs. Toronto . . . (April 12, 1987)—Sprained ankle vs. N.Y. Rangers.

Year	Team	League	Games	G.	A.	Pts.	Pen.
1981-82—Laval Voisins		QMJHL	64	4	25	29	41
1982-83—Longueuil Chevaliers (a)		QMJHL	70	26	58	84	58
1983-84—Canadian Olympic Team		Int'l	62	6	15	21	40
1983-84—Longueuil Chevaliers (c)		QMJHL	10	2	11	13	6
1984-85—Vancouver Canucks		NHL	67	4	23	27	69
1985-86—Vancouver Canucks (d)		NHL	64	5	23	28	45
1986-87—Philadelphia Flyers		NHL	77	6	16	22	56
1987-88—Philadelphia Flyers		NHL	28	2	2	4	12
1987-88—Hershey Bears		AHL	10	1	5	6	8
1988-89—Hershey Bears (e)		AHL	12	0	10	10	13
1988-89—Sherbrooke Canadiens		AHL	63	10	33	43	48
1989-90—Sherbrooke Canadiens		AHL	28	8	19	27	18
1989-90—Montreal Canadiens		NHL	36	2	10	12	14
NHL TOTALS			272	19	74	93	196

(c)—June, 1984—Drafted as underage junior by Vancouver Canucks in 1984 NHL entry draft. First Canucks pick, 10th overall, first round.

(d)—June, 1986—Traded by Vancouver Canucks with second-round draft choice (Kent Hawley) in 1986 and a fifth round choice in 1987 to Philadelphia Flyers for Rich Sutter, Dave Richter and third-round choice in 1986.

(e)—November, 1988—Traded by Philadelphia Flyers to Montreal Canadiens for Scott Sandelin.

BRAD DALGARNO

Right Wing . . . 6'3'' . . . 205 lbs. . . . Born, Vancouver, B.C., August 8, 1967 . . . Shoots right . . . (November, 1988)—Concussion . . . (February 21, 1989)—Fractured left eye orbital bone in fight with Joe Kocur vs. Detroit . . . Sat out 1989-90 season in retirement.

Year	Team	League	Games	G.	A.	Pts.	Pen.
1983-84—Markham Travelways		MTJHL	40	17	11	28	59
1984-85—Hamilton Steelhawks (c)		OHL	66	23	30	53	86
1985-86—Hamilton Steelhawks		OHL	54	22	43	65	79
1985-86—New York Islanders		NHL	2	1	0	1	0
1986-87—Hamilton Steelhawks		OHL	60	27	32	59	100
1986-87—New York Islanders (d)		NHL	....	....	....	....	....
1987-88—New York Islanders		NHL	38	2	8	10	58
1987-88—Springfield Indians		AHL	39	13	11	24	76
1988-89—New York Islanders		NHL	55	11	10	21	86
1989-90—Did not play			....	....	....	....	....
NHL TOTALS			95	14	18	32	144

(c)—June, 1985—Drafted as underage junior by New York Islanders in 1985 NHL draft. First Islanders pick, sixth overall, first round.

(d)—No regular season record. Played one playoff game.

ROD DALLMAN

Left Wing . . . 5'11'' . . . 185 lbs. . . . Born, Quesnel, B.C., January 26, 1967 . . . Shoots left . . . (October, 1984)—Broken left ankle . . . (October, 1986)—Injured shoulder . . . (November 22, 1989)—Suspended five AHL games for knocking down linesman Mark Faucette at Adirondack . . . (May, 1990)—Strained knee ligaments vs. Rochester.

Year	Team	League	Games	G.	A.	Pts.	Pen.
1983-84—P. Albert Midget Raiders		BC-Midget	21	14	6	20	69
1984-85—Prince Albert Raiders (c)		WHL	40	8	11	19	133
1985-86—Prince Albert Raiders		WHL	59	20	21	41	198
1986-87—Prince Albert Raiders		WHL	47	13	21	34	240
1987-88—New York Islanders		NHL	3	1	0	1	6
1987-88—Springfield Indians		AHL	59	9	17	26	355
1988-89—New York Islanders		NHL	1	0	0	0	15
1988-89—Springfield Indians		AHL	67	12	12	24	360
1989-90—Springfield Indians (d)		AHL	43	10	20	30	129
NHL TOTALS			4	1	0	1	21

(c)—June, 1985—Drafted as underage junior by New York Islanders in 1985 NHL entry draft. Eighth Islanders pick, 118th overall, eighth round.

(d)—August, 1990—Signed by Philadelphia Flyers as a free agent.

TREVOR DAM

Right Wing . . . 5'10'' . . . 205 lbs. . . . Born, Scarborough, Ont., April 20, 1970 . . . Shoots right.

Year	Team	League	Games	G.	A.	Pts.	Pen.
1985-86—Toronto Marlboro Midget		OHA	38	11	23	34	46
1986-87—London Knights		OHL	64	6	17	23	88
1987-88—London Knights (c)		OHL	66	25	38	63	169
1988-89—London Knights		OHL	66	33	59	92	111
1989-90—London Knights		OHL	56	20	54	74	91

(c)—June, 1988—Drafted by Chicago Black Hawks in 1988 NHL entry draft. Second Black Hawks pick, 50th overall, third round.

VINCENT DAMPHOUSSE

Left Wing . . . 6'1'' . . . 190 lbs. . . . Born, Montreal, Que., December 17, 1967 . . . Shoots left . . . Also plays Center . . . (1989-90)—Set a Toronto record for points by a left wing, breaking the old record set by Frank Mahovlich (84 in 1960-61).

Year	Team	League	Games	G.	A.	Pts.	Pen.
1983-84—Laval Voisins		QMJHL	66	29	36	65	25
1984-85—Laval Voisins		QMJHL	68	35	68	103	62
1985-86—Laval Titans (b-c)		QMJHL	69	45	110	155	70
1986-87—Toronto Maple Leafs		NHL	80	21	25	46	26
1987-88—Toronto Maple Leafs		NHL	75	12	36	48	40
1988-89—Toronto Maple Leafs		NHL	80	26	42	68	75
1989-90—Toronto Maple Leafs		NHL	80	33	61	94	56
NHL TOTALS			315	92	164	256	197

(c)—June, 1986—Drafted as underage junior by Toronto Maple Leafs in 1986 NHL entry draft. First Maple Leafs pick, sixth overall, first round.

KENNETH DANEYKO

Defense . . . 6'1'' . . . 195 lbs. . . . Born, Windsor, Ont., April 17, 1964 . . . Shoots left. . . . (November 2, 1983)—Broke right fibula at Hartford . . . (October, 1985)—Given one game suspension and fined $500 by the NHL for playing hockey in West Germany (Manheim) without NHL permission . . . (February 25, 1987)—Injured wrist during an altercation with Mitch Wilson at Pittsburgh . . . (February 24, 1988)—Nose cut and broken by a Ray Neufeld shot vs. Winnipeg.

Year	Team	League	Games	G.	A.	Pts.	Pen.
1980-81—Spokane Flyers		WHL	62	6	13	19	140
1981-82—Spokane Flyers		WHL	26	1	11	12	147
1981-82—Seattle Breakers (c-d)		WHL	38	1	22	23	151
1982-83—Seattle Breakers		WHL	69	17	43	60	150
1983-84—Kamloops Junior Oilers		WHL	19	6	28	34	52
1983-84—New Jersey Devils		NHL	11	1	4	5	17
1984-85—New Jersey Devils		NHL	1	0	0	0	10
1984-85—Maine Mariners		AHL	80	4	9	13	206
1985-86—Maine Mariners		AHL	21	3	2	5	75
1985-86—New Jersey Devils		NHL	44	0	10	10	100
1986-87—New Jersey Devils		NHL	79	2	12	14	183

Year	Team	League	Games	G.	A.	Pts.	Pen.
1987-88—New Jersey Devils		NHL	80	5	7	12	239
1988-89—New Jersey Devils		NHL	80	5	5	10	283
1989-90—New Jersey Devils		NHL	74	6	15	21	216
NHL TOTALS			369	19	53	72	1048

(c)—December, 1981—Drafted by Seattle Breakers in WHL Dispersal draft of players from Spokane Flyers.

(d)—June, 1982—Drafted as underage junior by New Jersey Devils in 1982 entry draft. Second Devils pick, 18th overall, first round.

JEFF DANIELS

Left Wing . . . 6' . . . 190 lbs. . . . Born, Oshawa, Ont., June 24, 1968 . . . Shoots left.

Year	Team	League	Games	G.	A.	Pts.	Pen.
1984-85—Oshawa Generals		OHL	59	7	11	18	16
1985-86—Oshawa Generals (c)		OHL	62	13	19	32	23
1986-87—Oshawa Generals		OHL	54	14	9	23	22
1987-88—Oshawa Generals		OHL	64	29	39	68	59
1988-89—Muskegon Lumberjacks		IHL	58	21	21	42	58
1989-90—Muskegon Lumberjacks		IHL	80	30	47	77	39

(c)—June, 1986—Drafted as underage junior by Pittsburgh Penguins in 1986 NHL entry draft. Sixth Penguins pick, 109th overall, sixth round.

KIMBI DANIELS

Center . . . 5'10" . . . 175 lbs. . . . Born, Brandon, Man., January 19, 1972 . . . Shoots right.

Year	Team	League	Games	G.	A.	Pts.	Pen.
1988-89—Swift Current Broncos		WHL	68	30	31	61	48
1989-90—Swift Current Broncos (c)		WHL	69	43	51	94	84

(c)—June 16, 1990—Selected by Philadelphia Flyers in 1990 NHL entry draft. Fifth Flyers pick, 44th overall, third round.

RORY SCOTT DANIELS
(Known by middle name.)

Left Wing . . . 6'3" . . . 200 lbs. . . . Born, Prince Albert, B.C., September 19, 1969 . . . Shoots left . . . (1982)—Broke leg . . . (1986)—Broken finger.

Year	Team	League	Games	G.	A.	Pts.	Pen.
1986-87—Kamloops Blazers (c)		WHL	43	6	4	10	66
1986-87—New Westminister Bruins		WHL	19	4	7	11	30
1987-88—New Westminister Bruins		WHL	37	6	11	17	157
1987-88—Regina Pats		WHL	19	2	3	5	83
1988-89—Regina Pats (d)		WHL	64	21	26	47	241
1989-90—Regina Pats		WHL	53	28	31	59	171

(c)—February, 1987—Traded with Mario Desjardins, Wayne MacDonald, Jason Bennings and future considerations by Kamloops Blazers to New Westminister Bruins for Glenn Mulvenna and Garth Premak.

(d)—June, 1989—Drafted by Hartford Whalers in 1989 NHL entry draft. Sixth Whalers pick, 136th overall, seventh round.

DAN ARMAND DAOUST

Center . . . 5'11" . . . 160 lbs. . . . Born, Kirkland Lake, Ont., February 29, 1960 . . . Shoots left . . . (November 2, 1986)—Missed 45 games when he broke left ankle during an altercation with Gerard Gallant vs. Detroit . . . (March, 1988)—Strained right ankle ligaments.

Year	Team	League	Games	G.	A.	Pts.	Pen.
1977-78—Cornwall Royals		QMJHL	68	24	44	68	74
1978-79—Cornwall Royals		QMJHL	72	42	55	97	85
1979-80—Cornwall Royals (c)		QMJHL	70	40	62	102	82
1980-81—Nova Scotia Voyageurs (a)		AHL	80	38	60	98	106
1981-82—Nova Scotia Voyageurs		AHL	61	25	40	65	75
1982-83—Montreal Canadiens (d)		NHL	4	0	1	1	4
1982-83—Toronto Maple Leafs		NHL	48	18	33	51	31
1983-84—Toronto Maple Leafs		NHL	78	18	56	74	88
1984-85—Toronto Maple Leafs		NHL	79	17	37	54	98
1985-86—Toronto Maple Leafs		NHL	80	7	13	20	88
1986-87—Newmarket Saints		AHL	1	0	0	0	4
1986-87—Toronto Maple Leafs		NHL	33	4	3	7	35
1987-88—Toronto Maple Leafs		NHL	67	9	8	17	57
1988-89—Toronto Maple Leafs		NHL	68	7	5	12	54
1989-90—Toronto Maple Leafs (e)		NHL	65	7	11	18	89
NHL TOTALS			522	87	167	254	544

(c)—September, 1980—Signed by Montreal Canadiens as a free agent.

(d)—December, 1982—Traded by Montreal Canadiens with Gaston Gingras to Toronto Maple Leafs for future draft considerations.

(e)—May 1, 1990—Signed to play for Ajoie, Switzerland.

GUY DARVEAU

Defense . . . 6' . . . 200 lbs. . . . Born, Montreal, Que., April 7, 1968 . . . Shoots left.

Year	Team	League	Games	G.	A.	Pts.	Pen.
1985-86—Longueuil Chevaliers		QMJHL	55	0	8	8	139
1986-87—Longueuil Chevaliers		QMJHL	67	9	24	33	175
1987-88—Victoriaville Tigers		QMJHL	57	19	16	35	274
1988-89—Verdun Junior Canadiens		QMJHL	25	1	9	10	38
1989-90—Sherbrooke Canadiens		AHL	38	2	2	4	120

(c)—June, 1988—Drafted by Calgary Flames in 1988 NHL entry draft. Tenth Flames pick, 210th overall, 10th round.

LEE DAVIDSON

Center . . . 5'10" . . . 160 lbs. . . . Born, Winnipeg, Man., June 30, 1968 . . . Shoots left . . . Son of Roy Davidson (Former Univ. of North Dakota player).

Year	Team	League	Games	G.	A.	Pts.	Pen.
1985-86—Penticton Knights (c)		BCJHL	46	34	72	106	37
1986-87—Univ. of North Dakota		WCHA	41	16	12	28	65

Year	Team	League	Games	G.	A.	Pts.	Pen.
1987-88—Univ. of North Dakota		WCHA	40	22	24	46	74
1988-89—Univ. of North Dakota		WCHA	41	16	37	53	60
1989-90—Univ. of North Dakota		WCHA	45	26	49	75	66

(c)—June, 1986—Drafted by Washington Capitals in 1986 NHL entry draft. Ninth Capitals pick, 166th overall, eighth round.

CLARK DAVIES

Defense . . . 6' . . . 185 lbs. . . . Born, Yorkton, Sask., June 20, 1967 . . . Shoots left.

Year	Team	League	Games	G.	A.	Pts.	Pen.
1986-87—Ferris State Univ.		CCHA	42	5	20	25	42
1987-88—Ferris State Univ. (c)		CCHA	40	4	15	19	65
1988-89—Ferris State Univ.		CCHA	32	3	10	13	59
1989-90—Ferris State Univ.		CCHA	36	4	9	13	38

(c)—June, 1988—Selected by Buffalo Sabres in 1988 NHL supplemental draft.

JOSEPH DAY

Left Wing . . . 5'11" . . . 185 lbs. . . . Born, Chicago, Ill., May 11, 1968 . . . Shoots left.

Year	Team	League	Games	G.	A.	Pts.	Pen.
1985-86—Chicago Minor Hawks		Ill.	30	23	18	41	69
1986-87—St. Lawrence Univ. (c)		ECAC	33	9	11	20	25
1987-88—St. Lawrence Univ.		ECAC	33	23	17	40	40
1988-89—St. Lawrence Univ.		ECAC	36	21	27	48	44
1989-90—St. Lawrence Univ. (b)		ECAC	30	18	26	44	24

(c)—June, 1987—Drafted by Hartford Whalers in 1987 NHL entry draft. Eighth Whalers pick, 186th overall, ninth round.

KEVIN DEAN

Defense . . . 6' . . . 195 lbs. . . . Born, Madison, Wis., April 1, 1969 . . . Shoots left.

Year	Team	League	Games	G.	A.	Pts.	Pen.
1985-86—Culver Academy		Ill. H.S.	35	28	44	72	48
1986-87—Culver Academy (c)		Ill. H.S.	25	19	25	44	30
1987-88—Univ. of New Hampshire		ECAC	27	1	6	7	34
1988-89—Univ. of New Hampshire		ECAC	34	1	12	13	28
1989-90—Univ. of New Hampshire		ECAC	39	2	6	8	42

(c)—June, 1987—Drafted by New Jersey Devils in 1987 NHL entry draft. Fourth Devils pick, 86th overall, fourth round.

BRYAN THOMAS DEASLEY

Left Wing . . . 6'3" . . . 200 lbs. . . . Born, Toronto, Ont., November 26, 1968 . . . Shoots left . . . (February, 1986)—Broken ribs . . . (January, 1987)—Fractured wrist . . . (July, 1987)—Off-season ankle injury.

Year	Team	League	Games	G.	A.	Pts.	Pen.
1985-86—St. Michael's Jr. B		OHA	30	17	20	37	88
1986-87—Univ. of Michigan (c)		CCHA	38	13	10	23	74
1987-88—Univ. of Michigan		CCHA	27	18	4	22	38
1988-89—Canadien National Team		Int'l.	54	19	19	38	32
1988-89—Salt Lake Golden Eagles (d)		IHL	....	....	....	....	....
1989-90—Salt Lake Golden Eagles		IHL	71	16	11	27	46

(c)—June, 1987—Drafted by Calgary Flames in 1987 NHL entry draft. First Flames pick, 19th overall, first round.

(d)—No regular season record. Played seven playoff games.

LUCIEN DeBLOIS

Right Wing . . . 5'11" . . . 200 lbs. . . . Born, Joliette, Que., June 21, 1957 . . . Shoots right . . . (November, 1980)—Groin pull . . . (November 6, 1984)—Pulled groin at Detroit . . . (January 2, 1985)—Pulled stomach muscles at Detroit . . . (October 16, 1985)—Sprained right knee vs. Buffalo and missed 16 games . . . (January, 1988)—Hyper-extended right knee . . . (March, 1988)—Bursitis in right knee . . . (November, 1988)—Torn bicep tendon in right shoulder.

Year	Team	League	Games	G.	A.	Pts.	Pen.
1973-74—Sorel Black Hawks		QMJHL	56	30	35	65	53
1974-75—Sorel Black Hawks		QMJHL	72	46	53	99	62
1975-76—Sorel Black Hawks (a)		QMJHL	70	56	55	111	112
1976-77—Sorel Black Hawks (a-c-d)		QMJHL	72	56	78	134	131
1977-78—New York Rangers		NHL	71	22	8	30	27
1978-79—New York Rangers		NHL	62	11	17	28	26
1978-79—New Haven Nighthawks		AHL	7	4	6	10	6
1979-80—New York Rangers (e)		NHL	6	3	1	4	7
1979-80—Colorado Rockies (f)		NHL	70	24	19	43	36
1980-81—Colorado Rockies		NHL	74	26	16	42	78
1981-82—Winnipeg Jets		NHL	65	25	27	52	87
1982-83—Winnipeg Jets		NHL	79	27	27	54	69
1983-84—Winnipeg Jets (g)		NHL	80	34	45	79	50
1984-85—Montreal Canadiens		NHL	51	12	11	23	20
1985-86—Montreal Canadiens		NHL	61	14	17	31	48
1986-87—New York Rangers (h)		NHL	40	3	8	11	27
1987-88—New York Rangers		NHL	74	9	21	30	103
1988-89—New York Rangers (i)		NHL	73	9	24	33	107
1989-90—Quebec Nordiques		NHL	70	9	8	17	45
NHL TOTALS			876	228	249	477	730

(c)—Won Most Valuable Player Award.

(d)—Drafted from Sorel Black Hawks by New York Rangers in first round of 1977 amateur draft.

(e)—November, 1979—Traded with Mike McEwen, Pat Hickey, Dean Turner and future considerations (Bobby Sheehan and Bobby Crawford) by New York Rangers to Colorado Rockies for Barry Beck.

(f)—July, 1981—Traded by Colorado Rockies to Winnipeg Jets for Brent Ashton and a third-round 1982 draft pick (Dave Kasper).

(g)—June, 1984—Traded by Winnipeg Jets to Montreal Canadiens for Perry Turnbull.

(h)—September, 1986—Signed by New York Rangers as a free agent.

(i)—June 27, 1989—Signed by Quebec Nordiques as a free agent.

LOUIE DeBRUSK

Left Wing . . . 6'1" . . . 205 lbs. . . . Born, Cambridge, Ont., March 19, 1971 . . . Shoots left.

Year	Team	League	Games	G.	A.	Pts.	Pen.
1987-88—Stratford Jr. B		OHA	43	13	14	27	205
1988-89—London Knights (c)		OHL	59	11	11	22	149
1989-90—London Knights		OHL	61	21	19	40	198

(c)—June, 1989—Drafted by New York Rangers in 1989 NHL entry draft. Fourth Rangers pick, 49th overall, third round.

RICHARD DeFREITAS

Defense . . . 6'2" . . . 195 lbs. . . . Born, Manchester, N.H., January 28, 1969 . . . Shoots left.

Year	Team	League	Games	G.	A.	Pts.	Pen.
1985-86—St. Marks		N.H. H.S.	19	14	18	32	15
1986-87—St. Marks (c)		N.H. H.S.	23	13	32	45	14
1987-88—St. Marks		N.H. H.S.	23	12	29	41	..
1988-89—Harvard Univ.		ECAC	5	0	2	2	6
1989-90—Harvard Univ.		ECAC	28	0	1	1	18

(c)—June, 1987—Drafted by Washington Capitals in 1987 NHL entry draft. Fifth Capitals pick, 120th overall, sixth round.

DALE DeGRAY

Defense . . . 5'10" . . . 190 lbs. . . . Born, Oshawa, Ont., September 3, 1963 . . . Shoots right . . . (January, 1988)—Missed 15 games with separated left shoulder . . . (October, 1988)—Sprained knee . . . (December, 1988)—Concussion.

Year	Team	League	Games	G.	A.	Pts.	Pen.
1979-80—Oshawa Legionaires		Metro Jr.B	42	14	14	28	34
1979-80—Oshawa Generals		OMJHL	1	0	0	0	2
1980-81—Oshawa Generals (c)		OHL	61	11	10	21	93
1981-82—Oshawa Generals		OHL	66	11	22	33	162
1982-83—Oshawa Generals		OHL	69	20	30	50	149
1983-84—Colorado Flames		CHL	67	16	14	30	67
1984-85—Moncton Golden Flames (b)		AHL	77	24	37	61	63
1985-86—Moncton Golden Flames		AHL	76	10	31	41	128
1985-86—Calgary Flames		NHL	1	0	0	0	0
1986-87—Moncton Golden Flames		AHL	45	10	22	32	57
1986-87—Calgary Flames		NHL	27	6	7	13	29
1987-88—Toronto Maple Leafs (d)		NHL	56	6	18	24	63
1987-88—Newmarket Saints		AHL	8	2	10	12	8
1988-89—Los Angeles Kings (e)		NHL	63	6	22	28	97
1989-90—New Haven Nighthawks (f)		AHL	16	2	10	12	38
1989-90—Rochester Americans		AHL	50	6	25	31	118
1989-90—Buffalo Sabres		NHL	6	0	0	0	6
NHL TOTALS			153	18	47	65	195

(c)—June, 1981—Drafted as underage junior by Calgary Flames in 1981 NHL entry draft. Seventh Flames pick, 162nd overall, eighth round.

(d)—September, 1987—Traded by Calgary Flames to Toronto Maple Leafs for future considerations.

(e)—October 3, 1988—Selected by Los Angeles Kings in 1988 NHL waiver draft for $12,500.

(f)—November 24, 1989—Traded by Los Angeles Kings to Buffalo Sabres for Bob Halkidis.

GILBERT DELORME

Defense . . . 5'11" . . . 205 lbs. . . . Born, Boucherville, Que., November 25, 1962 . . . Shoots right . . . (January 3, 1982)—Dislocated left shoulder at Buffalo . . . (November 19, 1985)—Injured throat vs. Edmonton and missed two games . . . (January 25, 1986)—Bruised knee vs. Buffalo and missed seven games . . . (February, 1988)—Injured ankle . . . (November, 1988)—Pulled thigh muscle . . . (December, 1988)—Strained knee . . . (February, 1989)—Injured shoulder . . . (January 28, 1990)—Separated shoulder at N.Y. Islanders and missed 11 games . . . (March, 1990)—Bruised ankle.

Year	Team	League	Games	G.	A.	Pts.	Pen.
1978-79—Chicoutimi Sagueneens		QMJHL	72	13	47	60	53
1979-80—Chicoutimi Sagueneens		QMJHL	71	25	86	111	68
1980-81—Chicoutimi Sagueneens (b-c)		QMJHL	70	27	79	106	77
1981-82—Montreal Canadiens		NHL	60	3	8	11	55
1982-83—Montreal Canadiens		NHL	78	12	21	33	89
1983-84—Montreal Canadiens (d)		NHL	27	2	7	9	8
1983-84—St. Louis Blues		NHL	44	0	5	5	41
1984-85—St. Louis Blues		NHL	74	2	12	14	53
1985-86—Quebec Nordiques (e)		NHL	65	2	18	20	55
1986-87—Quebec Nordiques (f)		NHL	19	2	0	2	14
1986-87—Detroit Red Wings		NHL	24	2	3	5	33
1987-88—Detroit Red Wings		NHL	55	2	8	10	81
1988-89—Detroit Red Wings (g)		NHL	42	1	3	4	51
1989-90—Pittsburgh Penguins		NHL	54	3	7	10	44
NHL TOTALS			542	31	92	123	524

(c)—June, 1981—Drafted as underage junior by Montreal Canadiens in 1981 NHL entry draft. Second Canadiens pick, 18th overall, first round.

(d)—December, 1983—Traded with Doug Wickenheiser and Greg Paslawski by Montreal Canadiens to St. Louis Blues for Perry Turnbull.

(e)—October, 1985—Traded by St. Louis Blues to Quebec Nordiques for Bruce Bell.

(f)—January, 1987—Traded with Brent Ashton and Mark Kumpel by Quebec Nordiques to Detroit Red Wings for John Ogrodnick, Doug Shedden and Basil McRae.

(g)—June 16, 1989—Signed by Pittsburgh Penguins as a free agent.

LARRY DePALMA

Left Wing . . . 6' . . . 180 lbs. . . . Born, Trenton, Mich., October 27, 1965 . . . Shoots left . . . (October, 1987)—Injured wrist . . . (February, 1989)—Sprained ankle ligaments that will require off-season surgery.

Year	Team	League	Games	G.	A.	Pts.	Pen.
1984-85—New Westminister Bruins		WHL	65	14	16	30	87
1985-86—Saskatoon Blades (b)		WHL	65	61	51	112	232
1985-86—Minnesota North Stars (c)		NHL	1	0	0	0	0
1986-87—Springfield Indians		AHL	9	2	2	4	82
1986-87—Minnesota North Stars		NHL	56	9	6	15	219
1987-88—Baltimore Skipjacks		AHL	16	8	10	18	121
1987-88—Kalamazoo Wings		IHL	22	6	11	17	215
1987-88—Minnesota North Stars		NHL	7	1	1	2	15
1988-89—Minnesota North Stars		NHL	43	5	7	12	102
1989-90—Kalamazoo Wings		IHL	36	7	14	21	218
NHL TOTALS			107	15	14	29	336

(c)—March, 1986—Signed by Minnesota North Stars as a free agent.

ERIC DESJARDINS

Defense . . . 6'1" . . . 185 lbs. . . . Born, Rouyn, Que., June 14, 1969 . . . Shoots right . . . (January, 1989)—Flu . . . (November 2, 1989)—Pulled groin vs. Buffalo and missed seven games.

Year	Team	League	Games	G.	A.	Pts.	Pen.
1985-86—Laval Laurentides Midget		Que. Midget	42	6	30	36	54
1986-87—Granby Bisons (b-c)		QMJHL	66	14	24	38	75
1987-88—Granby Bisons		QMJHL	62	18	49	67	138
1987-88—Sherbrooke Canadiens		AHL	3	0	0	0	6
1988-89—Montreal Canadiens		NHL	36	2	12	14	26
1989-90—Montreal Canadiens		NHL	55	3	13	16	51
NHL TOTALS			91	5	25	30	77

(c)—June, 1987—Drafted as an underage junior by Montreal Canadiens in 1987 NHL entry draft. Third Canadiens pick, 38th overall, second round.

MARTIN DESJARDINS

Center . . . 5'11" . . . 165 lbs. . . . Born, Ste. Rose, Que., January 28, 1967 . . . Shoots left.

Year	Team	League	Games	G.	A.	Pts.	Pen.
1984-85—Trois-Rivieres Draveurs (c)		QMJHL	66	29	34	63	76
1985-86—Trois-Rivieres Draveurs		QMJHL	71	49	69	118	103
1986-87—Longueuil Chevaliers		QMJHL	68	39	61	100	89
1987-88—Sherbrooke Canadiens		AHL	75	34	36	70	117
1988-89—Sherbrooke Canadiens		AHL	70	17	27	44	104
1989-90—Sherbrooke Canadiens		AHL	65	21	26	47	72
1989-90—Montreal Canadiens		NHL	8	0	2	2	2
NHL TOTALS			8	0	2	2	2

(c)—June, 1985—Drafted by Montreal Canadiens in 1985 NHL entry draft. Fifth Canadiens pick, 75th overall, fourth round.

GERALD DIDUCK

Defense . . . 6'2" . . . 195 lbs. . . . Born, Edmonton, Alta., April 6, 1965 . . . Shoots right . . . (November, 1987)—Fractured left foot . . . (November, 1988)—Fractured right hand . . . (January, 1989)—Knee injury.

Year	Team	League	Games	G.	A.	Pts.	Pen.
1981-82—Lethbridge Broncos		WHL	71	1	15	16	81
1982-83—Lethbridge Broncos (c)		WHL	67	8	16	24	151
1983-84—Lethbridge Broncos		WHL	65	10	24	34	133
1984-85—New York Islanders		NHL	65	2	8	10	80
1985-86—New York Islanders		NHL	10	1	2	3	2
1985-86—Springfield Indians		AHL	61	6	14	20	175
1986-87—Springfield Indians		AHL	45	6	8	14	120
1986-87—New York Islanders		NHL	30	2	3	5	67
1987-88—New York Islanders		NHL	68	7	12	19	113
1988-89—New York Islanders		NHL	65	11	21	32	155
1989-90—New York Islanders (d)		NHL	76	3	17	20	163
NHL TOTALS			314	26	63	89	580

(c)—June, 1983—Drafted as underage junior by New York Islanders in 1983 NHL entry draft. Second Islanders pick, 16th overall, first round.

(d)—September 4, 1990—Traded by New York Islanders to Montreal Canadiens for Craig Ludwig.

ROB DiMAIO

Center . . . 5'8" . . . 175 lbs. . . . Born, Calgary, Alta., February 19, 1968 . . . Shoots right . . . (January 28, 1988)—Suspended two games for leaving the bench to fight . . . (February, 1989)—Bruised left hand . . . (November, 1989)—Sprained clavicle.

Year	Team	League	Games	G.	A.	Pts.	Pen.
1984-85—Kamloops Blazers		WHL	55	9	18	27	29
1985-86—Kamloops Blazers (c)		WHL	6	1	0	1	0
1985-86—Medicine Hat Tigers		WHL	55	20	30	50	82
1986-87—Medicine Hat Tigers (d)		WHL	70	27	43	70	130
1987-88—Medicine Hat Tigers		WHL	54	47	43	90	120
1988-89—New York Islanders		NHL	16	1	0	1	30
1988-89—Springfield Indians		AHL	40	13	18	31	67
1989-90—New York Islanders		NHL	7	0	0	0	2
1989-90—Springfield Indians		AHL	54	25	27	52	69
NHL TOTALS			23	1	0	1	32

(c)—December, 1985—Traded with Dave MacKay and Calvin Knibbs by Kamloops Blazers to Medicine Hat Tigers for Doug Pickel and Sean Pass.

(d)—June, 1987—Drafted by New York Islanders in 1987 NHL entry draft. Sixth Islanders pick, 118th overall, sixth round.

GORDON DINEEN

Defense . . . 5'11" . . . 180 lbs. . . . Born, Toronto, Ont., September 21, 1962 . . . Shoots right . . . Brother of Shawn, Peter, Jerry and Kevin Dineen and son of Bill Dineen (Detroit and Chicago, mid-1950s) . . . (January 15, 1985)—Bruised ribs vs. Vancouver . . . (February, 1988)—Sprained left ankle.

Year	Team	League	Games	G.	A.	Pts.	Pen.
1979-80—St. Michaels Junior 'B'		....	42	15	35	50	103
1980-81—Sault Ste. Marie Greyhounds (c)		OHL	68	4	26	30	158
1981-82—Sault Ste. Marie Greyhounds		OHL	68	9	45	54	185
1982-83—Indianapolis Racers (a-d-e)		CHL	73	10	47	57	78
1982-83—New York Islanders		NHL	2	0	0	0	4
1983-84—Indianapolis Checkers		IHL	26	4	13	17	63
1983-84—New York Islanders		NHL	43	1	11	12	32
1984-85—Springfield Indians		AHL	25	1	8	9	46
1984-85—New York Islanders		NHL	48	1	12	13	89
1985-86—New York Islanders		NHL	57	1	8	9	81
1985-86—Springfield Indians		AHL	11	2	3	5	20
1986-87—New York Islanders		NHL	71	4	10	14	110
1987-88—New York Islanders (f)		NHL	57	4	12	16	62
1987-88—Minnesota North Stars		NHL	13	1	1	2	21
1988-89—Kalamazoo Wings		IHL	25	2	6	8	49
1988-89—Minnesota North Stars (g)		NHL	2	0	1	1	2
1988-89—Pittsburgh Penguins		NHL	38	1	2	3	42
1989-90—Pittsburgh Penguins		NHL	69	1	8	9	125
NHL TOTALS			400	14	65	79	568

(c)—June, 1981—Drafted as underage junior by New York Islanders in 1981 NHL entry draft. Second Islanders pick, 42nd overall, second round.

(d)—Won Bobby Orr Trophy (Most Valuable CHL Defenseman).

(e)—Won Bob Gassoff Award (Most Improved CHL Defenseman).

(f)—March, 1988—Traded with future considerations by New York Islanders to Minnesota North Stars for Chris Pryor.

(g)—December 17, 1988—Traded with Scott Bjugstad by Minnesota North Stars to Pittsburgh Penguins for Ville Siren and Steve Gotaas.

KEVIN DINEEN

Right Wing . . . 5'10" . . . 180 lbs. . . . Born, Quebec, Que., October 28, 1963 . . . Shoots right . . . Brother of Shawn, Peter, Jerry and Gordon Dineen and son of Bill Dineen (Detroit and Chicago, mid-1950s.) . . . Set University of Denver penalty-minute record (105) as a freshman . . . Member of 1984 Canadian Olympic Team . . . (October 24, 1985)—Sprained left shoulder at Philadelphia and missed nine games . . . (January 12, 1986)—Broke knuckle at Chicago and missed seven games . . . (February 14, 1986)—Sprained knee at Winnipeg . . . (September, 1988)—Shoulder tendinitis during Hartford Whalers training camp . . . Suffers from Chrone's Disease.

Year	Team	League	Games	G.	A.	Pts.	Pen.
1980-81—St. Michaels Jr. B		MTJHL	40	15	28	43	167
1981-82—University of Denver (c)		WCHA	38	12	22	34	105
1982-83—University of Denver		WCHA	36	16	13	29	108
1983-84—Canadian Olympic Team		Int'l.	..	..	..	..	..
1984-85—Binghamton Whalers		AHL	25	15	8	23	41
1984-85—Hartford Whalers		NHL	57	25	16	41	120
1985-86—Hartford Whalers		NHL	57	33	35	68	124
1986-87—Hartford Whalers		NHL	78	40	69	109	110
1987-88—Hartford Whalers		NHL	74	25	25	50	219
1988-89—Hartford Whalers		NHL	79	45	44	89	167
1989-90—Hartford Whalers		NHL	67	25	41	66	164
NHL TOTALS			412	193	230	423	904

(c)—June, 1982—Drafted as underage player by Hartford Whalers in 1982 NHL entry draft. Third Whalers pick, 56th overall, third round.

PETER DINEEN

Defense . . . 5'11" . . . 181 lbs. . . . Born, Kingston, Ont., November 19, 1960 . . . Shoots right . . . Brother of Shawn, Gordon, Jerry and Kevin Dineen and son of Bill Dineen (Detroit and Chicago, mid-1950s) . . . (October, 1980)—Broken ankle . . . (December 5, 1989)—Separated shoulder vs. St. Louis . . . (December 28, 1989)—Filled in for coach Barry Melrose for five games while Melrose was serving an AHL suspension . . . (January 23, 1990)—Surgery on injured shoulder.

Year	Team	League	Games	G.	A.	Pts.	Pen.
1977-78—Seattle Breakers		WCHL	2	0	0	0	0
1978-79—Kingston Canadians		OMJHL	60	7	14	21	70
1979-80—Kingston Canadians (c)		OMJHL	32	4	10	14	54
1980-81—Maine Mariners		AHL	41	6	7	13	100
1981-82—Maine Mariners		AHL	71	6	14	20	156
1982-83—Maine Mariners (d)		AHL	2	0	0	0	0
1982-83—Moncton Alpines		AHL	59	0	10	10	76
1983-84—Moncton Alpines		AHL	63	0	10	10	120
1983-84—Hershey Bears (e)		AHL	12	0	1	1	32
1984-85—Hershey Bears (f)		AHL	79	4	19	23	144
1985-86—Binghamton Whalers		AHL	11	0	1	1	35
1985-86—Moncton Golden Flames (g)		AHL	55	5	13	18	136
1986-87—Los Angeles Kings		NHL	11	0	2	2	8
1986-87—New Haven Nighthawks		AHL	59	2	17	19	140
1987-88—Adirondack Red Wings		AHL	76	8	26	34	137
1988-89—Adirondack Red Wings		AHL	32	2	12	14	61
1989-90—Detroit Red Wings		NHL	2	0	0	0	5
1989-90—Adirondack Red Wings		AHL	27	3	6	9	28
NHL TOTALS			13	0	2	2	13

(c)—June, 1980—Drafted by Philadelphia Flyers in 1980 NHL entry draft. Ninth Flyers pick, 189th overall, ninth round.

(d)—October, 1982—Traded by Philadelphia Flyers to Edmonton Oilers for Bob Hoffmeyer.

(e)—September, 1984—Signed by Boston Bruins as a free agent.

(f)—August, 1985—Signed as free agent by Hartford Whalers.

(g)—July, 1986—Signed by Los Angeles Kings as a free agent.

GILBERT DIONNE

Left Wing . . . 6' . . . 194 lbs. . . . Born, Drummondville, Que., September 19, 1970 . . . Shoots left . . . Nephew of Marcel Dionne.

Year	Team	League	Games	G.	A.	Pts.	Pen.
1987-88—Niagara Falls Canucks Jr. B		OHA	38	36	48	84	60
1988-89—Kitchener Rangers		OHL	66	11	33	44	13
1989-90—Kitchener Rangers (c)		OHL	64	48	57	105	85

(c)—June 16, 1990—Selected by Montreal Canadiens in 1990 NHL entry draft. Fifth Canadiens pick, 81st overall, fourth round.

PAUL DiPIETRO

Center . . . 5'9" . . . 181 lbs. . . . Born, Sault Ste. Marie, Ont., September 8, 1970 . . . Shoots right.

Year	Team	League	Games	G.	A.	Pts.	Pen.
1985-86—Sault Ste. Marie Bantams		OHA	33	33	30	63	85
1986-87—Sudbury Wolves		OHL	49	5	11	16	13
1987-88—Sudbury Wolves		OHL	63	25	42	67	27
1988-89—Sudbury Wolves		OHL	57	31	48	79	27
1989-90—Sudbury Wolves (c)		OHL	66	56	63	119	57

(c)—June 16, 1990—Selected by Montreal Canadiens in 1990 NHL entry draft. Sixth Canadiens pick, 102nd overall, fifth round.

ROBERT DIRK

Defense . . . 6'4" . . . 210 lbs. . . . Born, Regina, Sask., August 20, 1966 . . . Shoots left.

Year	Team	League	Games	G.	A.	Pts.	Pen.
1982-83—Regina Pats		WHL	1	0	0	0	0
1983-84—Regana Pats (c)		WHL	62	2	10	12	64
1984-85—Regina Pats		WHL	69	10	34	44	97
1985-86—Regina Pats (b)		WHL	72	19	60	79	140
1986-87—Peoria Rivermen		IHL	76	5	17	22	155
1987-88—St. Louis Blues		NHL	7	0	1	1	16
1987-88—Peoria Rivermen		IHL	54	4	21	25	126
1988-89—St. Louis Blues		NHL	9	0	1	1	11
1988-89—Peoria Rivermen		IHL	22	0	2	2	54
1989-90—Peoria Rivermen		IHL	24	1	2	3	79
1989-90—St. Louis Blues		NHL	37	1	1	2	128
NHL TOTALS			53	1	3	4	155

(c)—June, 1984—Drafted as underage junior by St. Louis Blues in 1984 NHL entry draft. Fourth Blues pick, 53rd overall, third round.

DAVID DiVITA

Defense . . . 6'2" . . . 205 lbs. . . . Born, Detroit, Mich., February 3, 1969 . . . Shoots right . . . (February 5, 1988)—Separated shoulder.

Year	Team	League	Games	G.	A.	Pts.	Pen.
1987-88—Lake Superior State Univ. (c)		CCHA	26	1	0	1	20
1988-89—Lake Superior State Univ.		CCHA	25	1	4	5	28
1989-90—Lake Superior State Univ.		CCHA	46	4	12	16	58

(c)—June, 1988—Drafted by Buffalo Sabres in 1988 NHL entry draft. Sixth Sabres pick, 106th overall, sixth round.

PER DJOOS

Defense . . . 5'11" . . . 170 lbs. . . . Born, Mora, Sweden, May 11, 1968 . . . Shoots left.

Year	Team	League	Games	G.	A.	Pts.	Pen.
1984-85—Mora		Sweden-II	20	2	3	5	2
1985-86—Mora (c)		Sweden	30	9	5	14	14
1986-87—Brynas		Sweden	23	1	2	3	16
1987-88—Brynas		Sweden	34	4	11	15	18
1988-89—Brynas		Sweden	40	1	17	18	44
1989-90—Brynas		Sweden	37	5	13	18	34

(c)—June, 1986—Selected by Detroit Red Wings in 1986 NHL entry draft. Seventh Red Wings pick, 127th overall, seventh round.

BRIAN DOBBIN

Right Wing . . . 5'11" . . . 195 lbs. . . . Born, Petrolia, Ont., August 18, 1966 . . . Shoots right . . . (September, 1986)—Damaged ligament in right knee during Philadelphia training camp and required surgery.

Year	Team	League	Games	G.	A.	Pts.	Pen.
1981-82—Mooretown Flags Jr. C		GLOHA	38	31	24	55	50
1982-83—Kingston Canadians		OHL	69	16	39	55	35
1983-84—London Knights (c)		OHL	70	30	40	70	70
1984-85—London Knights		OHL	53	42	57	99	63
1985-86—London Knights		OHL	59	38	55	93	113
1985-86—Hershey Bears		AHL	2	1	0	1	0
1986-87—Hershey Bears		AHL	52	26	35	61	66
1986-87—Philadelphia Flyers		NHL	12	2	1	3	14
1987-88—Hershey Bears		AHL	54	36	47	83	58
1987-88—Philadelphia Flyers		NHL	21	3	5	8	6
1988-89—Philadelphia Flyers		NHL	14	0	1	1	8
1988-89—Hershey Bears (a)		AHL	59	43	48	91	61
1989-90—Hershey Bears (b)		AHL	68	38	47	85	58
1989-90—Philadelphia Flyers		NHL	9	1	1	2	11
NHL TOTALS			56	6	8	14	39

(c)—June, 1984—Drafted as underage junior by Philadelphia Flyers in 1984 NHL entry draft. Sixth Flyers pick, 100th overall, fifth round.

MICHAEL DOERS

Right Wing . . . 6' . . . 175 lbs. . . . Born, Madison, Wis., June 17, 1971 . . . Shoots right.

Year	Team	League	Games	G.	A.	Pts.	Pen.
1987-88—Northwood Prep.		N.Y. H.S.	28	14	20	34	....
1988-89—Northwood Prep. (c)		N.Y. H.S.	28	19	24	43	....
1989-90—Univ. of Vermont		ECAC	30	2	11	13	26

(c)—June, 1989—Drafted by Toronto Maple Leafs in 1989 NHL entry draft. Seventh Maple Leafs pick, 125th overall, sixth round.

BOBBY DOLLAS

Defense . . . 6'2" . . . 220 lbs. . . . Born, Montreal, Que., January 31, 1965 . . . Shoots left.

Year	Team	League	Games	G.	A.	Pts.	Pen.
1981-82—Lac St. Louis AAA		Que. Midget	44	9	31	40	138
1982-83—Laval Voisins (b-c-d)		QMJHL	63	16	45	61	144
1983-84—Laval Voisins		QMJHL	54	12	33	45	80
1983-84—Winnipeg Jets		NHL	1	0	0	0	0
1984-85—Winnipeg Jets		NHL	9	0	0	0	0
1984-85—Sherbrooke Canadiens		AHL	8	1	3	4	4
1985-86—Sherbrooke Canadiens		AHL	25	4	7	11	29
1985-86—Winnipeg Jets		NHL	46	0	5	5	66
1986-87—Sherbrooke Canadiens		AHL	75	6	18	24	87
1987-88—Quebec Nordiques (e)		NHL	9	0	0	0	2
1987-88—Moncton Golden Flames		AHL	26	4	10	14	20
1987-88—Fredericton Express		AHL	33	4	8	12	27
1988-89—Halifax Citadels		AHL	57	5	19	24	65
1988-89—Quebec Nordiques		NHL	16	0	3	3	16
1989-90—Canadian National Team		Int'l.	68	8	29	37	60
NHL TOTALS			72	0	8	8	84

(c)—Won Raymond Lagace Trophy (Top rookie defenseman).

(d)—June, 1983—Drafted as underage junior by Winnipeg Jets in 1983 NHL entry draft. Second Jets pick, 14th overall, first round.

(e)—December, 1987—Traded by Winnipeg Jets to Quebec Nordiques for Stu Kulak.

TAHIR (Tie) DOMI

Right Wing . . . 5'10" . . . 200 lbs. . . . Born, Windsor, Ont., November 1, 1969 . . . (November 2, 1986)—Given an indefinite suspension by OHL for leaving the bench during an on-ice altercation.

Year	Team	League	Games	G.	A.	Pts.	Pen.
1985-86—Windsor Junior B		OHL	32	8	17	25	346
1986-87—Peterborough Petes		OHL	18	1	1	2	79
1987-88—Peterborough Petes (c)		OHL	60	22	21	43	292
1988-89—Peterborough Petes		OHL	43	14	16	30	175
1989-90—Newmarket Saints		AHL	57	14	11	25	285
1989-90—Toronto Maple Leafs (d)		NHL	2	0	0	0	42
NHL TOTALS			2	0	0	0	42

(c)—June, 1988—Drafted by Toronto Maple Leafs in 1988 NHL entry draft. Second Maple Leafs pick, 27th overall, second round.

(d)—June 28, 1990—Traded with Mark Laforest by Toronto Maple Leafs to New York Rangers for Greg Johnston.

CLARK DONATELLI

Left Wing . . . 5'10" . . . 190 lbs. . . . Born, Providence, R.I., November 22, 1965 . . . Shoots left.

Year	Team	League	Games	G.	A.	Pts.	Pen.
1983-84—Stratford Collitons Jr. B (c)		MWOHA	38	41	49	90	46
1984-85—Boston University		H. East	40	17	18	35	46
1985-86—Boston University		H. East	43	28	34	62	30
1986-87—Boston University (d)		H. East	37	15	23	38	46
1987-88—U.S. Olympic Team		Int'l.	53	12	28	40	..
1988-89—Did not play (e)		......	....	....	....	....	....
1989-90—Kalamazoo Wings		IHL	27	8	9	17	47
1989-90—Minnesota North Stars		NHL	25	3	3	6	17
NHL TOTALS			25	3	3	6	17

(c)—June, 1984—Drafted by New York Rangers in 1984 NHL entry draft. Fourth Rangers pick, 98th overall, fifth round.

(d)—October, 1986—Traded with Reijo Ruotsalainen, Ville Horava and Jim Wiemer by New York Rangers to Edmonton Oilers to complete an earlier deal that saw the Rangers acquire Don Jackson and Mike Golden.

(e)—June, 1989—Signed by Minnesota North Stars as a free agent.

TED DONATO

Center . . . 5'10" . . . 170 lbs. . . . Born, Dedham, Mass., April 28, 1968 . . . Shoots left . . . (November 18, 1989)—Broke collarbone.

Year	Team	League	Games	G.	A.	Pts.	Pen.
1986-87—Catholic Memorial H.S. (c)		Mass. H.S.	22	29	34	63	30
1987-88—Harvard Univ.		ECAC	28	12	14	26	24
1988-89—Harvard Univ.		ECAC	34	14	37	51	30
1989-90—Harvard Univ.		ECAC	16	5	6	11	34

(c)—June, 1987—Drafted by Boston Bruins in 1987 NHL entry draft. Fifth Bruins pick, 98th overall, fifth round.

GORDON DONNELLY

Defense . . . 6'2" . . . 202 lbs. . . . Born, Montreal, Que., April 5, 1962 . . . Shoots right . . . (October 29, 1987)—Suspended five games by NHL for kneeing . . . (February 26, 1988)—Suspended five games and fined $100 for engaging in a pre-game fight at Montreal . . . (March 27, 1988)—Suspended 10 games by NHL for hitting Jim Johnson with his stick vs. Pittsburgh. He missed the final four games of the

1987-88 season, and the first six in 1988-89 . . . (April 12, 1990)—Fined $500 by NHL for kicking Kelly Buchberger on the chin vs. Winnipeg.

Year	Team	League	Games	G.	A.	Pts.	Pen.
1978-79—Laval Nationals		QMJHL	71	1	14	15	79
1979-80—Laval Nationals		QMJHL	44	5	10	15	47
1979-80—Chicoutimi Sagueneens		QMJHL	24	1	5	6	64
1980-81—Sherbrooke Beavers (c)		QMJHL	67	15	23	38	252
1981-82—Sherbrooke Beavers (d)		QMJHL	60	8	41	49	250
1982-83—Salt Lake Golden Eagles (e)		CHL	67	3	12	15	222
1983-84—Fredericton Express		AHL	30	2	3	5	146
1983-84—Quebec Nordiques		NHL	38	0	5	5	60
1984-85—Fredericton Express		AHL	42	1	5	6	134
1984-85—Quebec Nordiques		NHL	22	0	0	0	33
1985-86—Fredericton Express		AHL	37	3	5	8	103
1985-86—Quebec Nordiques		NHL	36	2	2	4	85
1986-87—Quebec Nordiques		NHL	38	0	2	2	143
1987-88—Quebec Nordiques		NHL	63	4	3	7	301
1988-89—Quebec Nordiques (f)		NHL	16	4	0	4	46
1988-89—Winnipeg Jets		NHL	57	6	10	16	228
1989-90—Winnipeg Jets		NHL	55	3	3	6	222
NHL TOTALS			325	19	25	44	1118

(c)—June, 1981—Drafted by St. Louis Blues in 1981 NHL entry draft. Third Blues pick, 62nd overall, third round.

(d)—Led QMJHL Playoffs with 106 penalty minutes.

(e)—August, 1983—Sent by St. Louis Blues along with Claude Julien to Quebec Nordiques as compensation for St. Louis signing coach Jacques Demers.

(f)—December 6, 1988—Traded by Quebec Nordiques to Winnipeg Jets for Mario Marois.

MIKE DONNELLY

Left Wing . . . 5'11" . . . 185 lbs. . . . Born, Livonia, Mich., October 10, 1963 . . . Shoots left . . . Set a CCHA single-season record with 59 goals in 1985-86 . . . (November, 1987)—Dislocated and fractured right index finger.

Year	Team	League	Games	G.	A.	Pts.	Pen.
1982-83—Michigan State University		CCHA	24	7	13	20	8
1983-84—Michigan State University		CCHA	44	18	14	32	40
1984-85—Michigan State University		CCHA	44	26	21	47	48
1985-86—Michigan State Univeristy (c-d)		CCHA	44	*59	38	97	65
1985-86—New York Rangers		NHL	5	1	1	2	0
1986-87—New Haven Nighthawks		AHL	58	27	34	61	52
1987-88—Colorado Rangers		IHL	8	7	11	19	15
1987-88—New York Rangers (e)		NHL	17	2	2	4	8
1987-88—Buffalo Sabres		NHL	40	6	8	14	44
1988-89—Buffalo Sabres		NHL	22	4	6	10	10
1988-89—Rochester Americans		AHL	53	32	37	69	53
1989-90—Rochester Americans		AHL	68	43	55	98	71
1989-90—Buffalo Sabres		NHL	12	1	2	3	8
NHL TOTALS			96	14	19	33	70

(c)—Named First team All-America (West).

(d)—August, 1986—Signed by New York Rangers as a free agent

(e)—December, 1987—Traded with a fifth-round 1988 draft pick (Alexander Mogilny) by New York Rangers to Buffalo Sabres for Paul Cyr and a 10th-round 1988 draft pick (Eric Fenton).

SEAN DOOLEY

Defense . . . 6'3" . . . 215 lbs. . . . Born, Ipswich, Mass., March 22, 1969 . . . Shoots left.

Year	Team	League	Games	G.	A.	Pts.	Pen.
1985-86—Groton H.S.		Mass. H.S.	....	11	18	29	....
1986-87—Groton H.S. (c)		Mass. H.S.	....	9	17	26	....
1987-88—Merrimack College		ECAC	3	0	0	0	0
1988-89—Merrimack College		ECAC	19	2	8	10	10
1989-90—Merrimack College		H. East	22	1	2	3	31

(c)—June, 1987—Drafted by Buffalo Sabres in 1987 NHL entry draft. Eighth Sabres pick, 148th overall, eighth round.

DANIEL DORE

Right Wing . . . 6'3" . . . 200 lbs. . . . Born, St. Jerome, Que., April 9, 1970 . . . Shoots right . . . (April, 1989)—Surgery to finger injured in a fight with Claude Boivin during Canadian National junior team training camp . . . (May, 1989)—Nose surgery.

Year	Team	League	Games	G.	A.	Pts.	Pen.
1986-87—Drummondville Voltigeurs		QMJHL	68	23	41	64	229
1987-88—Drummondville Voltigeurs (c-d)		QMJHL	64	24	39	63	218
1988-89—Drummondville Voltigeurs		QMJHL	62	33	58	91	236
1989-90—Quebec Nordiques		NHL	16	2	3	5	6
1989-90—Chicoutimi Sagueneens (e)		QMJHL	24	6	23	29	112
NHL TOTALS			16	2	3	5	6

(c)—June, 1988—Drafted by Quebec Nordiques in 1988 NHL entry draft. Second Nordiques pick, fifth overall, first round.

(d)—Won Mike Bossy Trophy (Top Pro Prospect).

(e)—December 19, 1989—Traded with Denis Chasse and Pierre-Paul Landry by Drummondville Voltigeurs to Chicoutimi Sagueneens for Yanick Dupre, Guy Lehoux and Eric Meloche.

WAYNE DOUCET

Left Wing . . . 6'1" . . . 200 lbs. . . . Born, Etobicoke, Ont., June 19, 1970 . . . Shoots left . . . (October, 1986)—Separated shoulder.

Year	Team	League	Games	G.	A.	Pts.	Pen.
1985-86—Toronto Marlboro Midget		OHA	34	17	18	35	101
1986-87—Sudbury Wolves		OHL	64	20	28	48	85
1987-88—Sudbury Wolves		OHL	23	9	4	13	53
1987-88—Hamilton Steelhawks (c)		OHL	37	11	14	25	74

Year	Team	League	Games	G.	A.	Pts.	Pen.
1988-89—Kingston Canadians		OHL	59	26	43	69	89
1988-89—Springfield Indians		AHL	6	2	2	4	4
1989-90—Kingston Frontenacs		OHL	66	32	47	79	127

(c)—June, 1988—Drafted by New York Islanders in 1988 NHL entry draft. Second Islanders pick, 29th overall, second round.

PETER DOURIS

Center . . . 6' . . . 195 lbs. . . . Born, Toronto, Ont., February 19, 1966 . . . Shoots right.

Year	Team	League	Games	G.	A.	Pts.	Pen.
1983-84—Univ. of New Hampshire (c)		ECAC	38	19	15	34	14
1984-85—Univ. of New Hampshire		H. East	42	27	24	51	34
1985-86—Team Canada		Int'l.	33	16	7	23	18
1985-86—Winnipeg Jets		NHL	11	0	0	0	0
1986-87—Sherbrooke Canadiens		AHL	62	14	28	42	24
1986-87—Winnipeg Jets		NHL	6	0	0	0	0
1987-88—Moncton Golden Flames		AHL	73	42	37	79	53
1987-88—Winnipeg Jets		NHL	4	0	2	2	0
1988-89—Peoria Rivermen (d)		IHL	81	28	41	69	32
1989-90—Maine Mariners (e)		AHL	38	17	20	37	14
1989-90—Boston Bruins		NHL	36	5	6	11	15
NHL TOTALS			57	5	8	13	15

(c)—June, 1984—Drafted by Winnipeg Jets in 1984 NHL entry draft. First Jets pick, 30th overall, second round.

(d)—September 29, 1988—Traded by Winnipeg Jets to St. Louis Blues for Kent Carlson and a 12th-round 1989 draft pick (Sergei Kharin).

(e)—September, 1989—Signed by Boston Bruins as a free agent.

JIM DOWD

Right Wing . . . 6'1" . . . 185 lbs. . . . Born, Brick, N.J., December 25, 1968 . . . Shoots right.

Year	Team	League	Games	G.	A.	Pts.	Pen.
1985-86—Brick H.S.		N.J. H.S.	..	47	51	98	..
1986-87—Brick H.S. (c)		N.J. H.S.	24	22	33	55	..
1987-88—Lake Superior State Univ.		CCHA	45	18	27	45	16
1988-89—Lake Superior State Univ.		CCHA	46	24	35	59	40
1989-90—Lake Superior State Univ. (b)		CCHA	46	25	67	92	30

(c)—June, 1987—Drafted by New Jersey Devils in 1987 NHL entry draft. Seventh Devils pick, 149th overall, eighth round.

MARIO DOYON

Defense . . . 6' . . . 175 lbs. . . . Born, Quebec City, Que., August 27, 1968 . . . Shoots right.

Year	Team	League	Games	G.	A.	Pts.	Pen.
1985-86—Drummondville Voltigeurs (c)		QMJHL	71	5	14	19	129
1986-87—Drummondville Voltigeurs		QMJHL	65	18	47	65	150
1987-88—Drummondville Voltigeurs		QMJHL	68	23	54	77	233
1988-89—Saginaw Hawks		IHL	71	16	32	48	69
1988-89—Chicago Black Hawks		NHL	7	1	1	2	6
1989-90—Indianapolis Ice (d)		IHL	66	9	25	34	50
1989-90—Halifax Citadels		AHL	5	1	2	3	0
1989-90—Quebec Nordiques		NHL	9	2	3	5	6
NHL TOTALS			16	3	4	7	12

(c)—June, 1986—Drafted by Chicago Black Hawks in 1986 NHL entry draft. Fifth Black Hawks pick, 119th overall, sixth round.

(d)—March 5, 1990—Traded with Everett Sanipass and Dan Vincelette by Chicago Black Hawks to Quebec Nordiques for Michel Goulet, Greg Millen and a sixth round 1991 draft pick.

DALLAS DRAKE

Center . . . 6' . . . 165 lbs. . . . Born, Trail, B.C., February 4, 1969 . . . Shoots left.

Year	Team	League	Games	G.	A.	Pts.	Pen.
1984-85—Rossland Warriors		KIJHL	30	13	37	50	....
1985-86—Rossland Warriors		KIJHL	41	53	73	126	....
1986-87—Rossland Warriors		KIJHL	40	55	80	135	....
1987-88—Vernon Lakers		BCJHL	47	39	85	124	50
1988-89—Northern Michigan Univ. (c)		WCHA	45	18	24	42	26
1989-90—Northern Michigan Univ.		WCHA	36	13	24	37	42

(c)—June, 1989—Drafted by Detroit Red Wings in 1989 NHL entry draft. Sixth Red Wings pick, 116th overall, sixth round.

KRIS DRAPER

Center . . . 5'11" . . . 190 lbs. . . . Born, Toronto, Ont., May 24, 1971 . . . Shoots left.

Year	Team	League	Games	G.	A.	Pts.	Pen.
1987-88—Don Mills Midgets		OHA	40	35	32	67	46
1988-89—Canadian National Team (c)		Int'l.	60	11	15	26	16
1989-90—Canadian National Team		Int'l.	61	12	22	34	44

(c)—June, 1989—Drafted by Winnipeg Jets in 1989 NHL entry draft. Fourth Jets pick, 62nd overall, third round.

SCOTT DREVITCH

Defense . . . 5'10" . . . 175 lbs. . . . Born, Brookline, Mass., September 9, 1965 . . . Shoots right.

Year	Team	League	Games	G.	A.	Pts.	Pen.
1985-86—Univ. of Lowell		H. East	32	1	8	9	10
1986-87—Univ. of Lowell		H. East	35	3	25	28	24
1987-88—Univ. of Lowell (c)		H. East	37	5	21	26	28
1988-89—Maine Mariners		AHL	75	10	21	31	51
1989-90—Virginia Lancers (b)		ECHL	40	14	31	45	46
1989-90—Maine Mariners		AHL	13	0	1	1	10

(c)—October, 1988—Signed as free agent by Maine Mariners.

BRUCE DRIVER

Defense . . . 6' . . . 195 lbs. . . . Born, Toronto, Ont., April 29, 1962 . . . Shoots left . . . Member of 1984 Canadian Olympic Team . . . (February, 1985)—Surgery to left knee . . . (April 2, 1985)—Reinjured knee when struck by stick at St. Louis . . . (March 9, 1986)—Bruised shoulder at Buffalo . . . (February, 1987)—Stiff neck . . . (February, 1988)—Sprained ankle . . . (December 7, 1988)—Broke right leg in three places when checked by Lou Franceschetti vs. Washington and had surgery to implant a plate and 10 screws.

Year	Team	League	Games	G.	A.	Pts.	Pen.
1979-80—Royal York Royals		OPJHL	43	13	57	70	102
1980-81—University of Wisconsin (c)		WCHA	42	5	15	20	42
1981-82—University of Wisconsin (a-d)		WCHA	46	7	37	44	84
1982-83—University of Wisconsin (b)		WCHA	39	16	34	50	50
1983-84—Canadian Olympic Team		Int'l	61	11	17	28	44
1983-84—Maine Mariners		AHL	12	2	6	8	15
1983-84—New Jersey Devils		NHL	4	0	2	2	0
1984-85—New Jersey Devils		NHL	67	9	23	32	36
1985-86—Maine Mariners		AHL	15	4	7	11	16
1985-86—New Jersey Devils		NHL	40	3	15	18	32
1986-87—New Jersey Devils		NHL	74	6	28	34	36
1987-88—New Jersey Devils		NHL	74	15	40	55	68
1988-89—New Jersey Devils		NHL	27	1	15	16	24
1989-90—New Jersey Devils		NHL	75	7	46	53	63
NHL TOTALS			361	41	169	210	259

(c)—June, 1981—Drafted as underage junior by Colorado Rockies in 1981 NHL entry draft. Sixth Rockies pick, 108th overall, sixth round.

(d)—Named to All-America Team (West).

JOHN DRUCE

Right Wing . . . 6'1" . . . 190 lbs. . . . Born, Peterborough, Ont., February 23, 1966 . . . Shoots right . . . (October, 1983)—Broken collarbone . . . (December, 1984)—Partially torn ligaments in ankle . . . (October, 1985)—Torn thumb ligaments.

Year	Team	League	Games	G.	A.	Pts.	Pen.
1983-84—Peterborough Jr. B		OHA	40	15	18	33	69
1984-85—Peterborough Petes (c)		OHL	54	12	14	26	90
1985-86—Peterborough Petes		OHL	49	22	24	46	84
1986-87—Binghamton Whalers		AHL	77	13	9	22	131
1987-88—Binghamton Whalers		AHL	68	32	29	61	82
1988-89—Washington Capitals		NHL	48	8	7	15	62
1988-89—Baltimore Skipjacks		AHL	16	2	11	13	10
1989-90—Washington Capitals		NHL	45	8	3	11	52
1989-90—Baltimore Skipjacks		AHL	26	15	16	31	38
NHL TOTALS			93	16	10	26	114

(c)—June, 1985—Drafted by Washington Capitals in 1985 NHL entry draft. Second Capitals pick, 40th overall, second round.

STAN DRULIA

Right Wing . . . 5'10" . . . 180 lbs. . . . Born, Elmira, N.Y., January 5, 1968 . . . Shoots right.

Year	Team	League	Games	G.	A.	Pts.	Pen.
1984-85—Belleville Bulls		OHL	63	24	31	55	33
1985-86—Belleville Bulls (c)		OHL	66	43	37	80	73
1986-87—Hamilton Steelhawks		OHL	55	27	51	78	26
1987-88—Hamilton Steelhawks		OHL	65	52	69	121	44
1988-89—Niagara Falls Thunder (a)		OHL	47	52	93	145	59
1988-89—Maine Mariners		AHL	3	1	1	2	0
1989-90—Cape Breton Oilers (d)		AHL	31	5	7	12	2
1989-90—Phoenix Roadrunners		IHL	6	3	6	9	2

(c)—June, 1986—Drafted as underage junior by Pittsburgh Penguins in 1986 NHL entry draft. Eleventh Penguins pick, 214th overall, 11th round.

(d)—May, 1909—Signed by Edmonton Oilers as a free agent.

THEODORE DRURY

Center . . . 6' . . . 185 lbs. . . . Born, Boston, Mass., September 13, 1971 . . . Shoots left . . . (January, 1988)—Broken ankle.

Year	Team	League	Games	G.	A.	Pts.	Pen.
1987-88—Fairfield Prep.		Mass. H.S.	....	21	28	49	....
1988-89—Fairfield Prep. (c)		Mass. H.S.	....	35	31	66	....
1989-90—Harvard University		ECAC	17	9	13	22	10

(c)—June, 1989—Drafted by Calgary Flames in 1989 NHL entry draft. Second Flames pick, 42nd overall, second round.

ERIC DuBOIS

Defense . . . 6' . . . 193 lbs. . . . Born, Montreal, Que., May 7, 1970 . . . Shoots right.

Year	Team	League	Games	G.	A.	Pts.	Pen.
1986-87—Laval Titans		QMJHL	61	1	17	18	29
1987-88—Laval Titans		QMJHL	69	8	32	40	132
1988-89—Laval Titans (c)		QMJHL	68	15	44	59	126
1989-90—Laval Titans		QMJHL	66	9	36	45	153

(c)—June, 1989—Drafted by Quebec Nordiques in 1989 NHL entry draft. Sixth Nordiques pick, 76th overall, fourth round.

GAETAN DUCHESNE

Left Wing . . . 5'11" . . . 195 lbs. . . . Born, Quebec City, Que., July 11, 1962 . . . Shoots left . . . (December 30, 1981)—Bruised right ankle at Pittsburgh . . . (October 11, 1984)—Broke index finger of left hand on a shot at Philadelphia . . . (January 26, 1988)—Sprained left knee on goal post . . . (November, 1988)—Sprained left shoulder . . . (November 11, 1989)—Sprained right knee vs. Calgary and missed eight games.

Year	Team	League	Games	G.	A.	Pts.	Pen.
1979-80—Quebec Remparts		QMJHL	46	9	28	37	22
1980-81—Quebec Remparts (c)		QMJHL	72	27	45	72	63
1981-82—Washington Capitals		NHL	74	9	14	23	46
1982-83—Hershey Bears		AHL	1	1	0	1	0
1982-83—Washington Capitals		NHL	77	18	19	37	52
1983-84—Washington Capitals		NHL	79	17	19	36	29
1984-85—Washington Capitals		NHL	67	15	23	38	32
1985-86—Washington Capitals		NHL	80	11	28	39	39
1986-87—Washington Capitals (d)		NHL	74	17	35	52	53
1987-88—Quebec Nordiques		NHL	80	24	23	47	83
1988-89—Quebec Nordiques (e)		NHL	70	8	21	29	56
1989-90—Minnesota North Stars		NHL	72	12	8	20	33
NHL TOTALS			673	131	190	321	423

(c)—June, 1981—Drafted by Washington Capitals in 1981 NHL entry draft. Eighth Capitals pick, 152nd overall, eighth round.

(d)—June, 1987—Traded with Alan Haworth and a first-round 1987 draft pick (Joe Sakic) by Washington Capitals to Quebec Nordiques for Dale Hunter and Clint Malarchuk.

(e)—June 18, 1989—Traded by Quebec Nordiques to Minnesota North Stars for Kevin Kaminski.

STEVE DUCHESNE

Defense . . . 5'11" . . . 195 lbs. . . . Born, Sept-Illes, Que., June 30, 1965 . . . Shoots left . . . (January 26, 1988)—Strained left knee in collision with goal post at Quebec . . . (November, 1988)—Separated left shoulder.

Year	Team	League	Games	G.	A.	Pts.	Pen.
1983-84—Drummondville Voltigeurs		QMJHL	67	1	34	35	79
1984-85—Drummondville Voltigeurs (c)		QMJHL	65	22	54	76	94
1985-86—New Haven Nighthawks		AHL	75	14	35	49	76
1986-87—Los Angeles Kings		NHL	75	13	25	38	74
1987-88—Los Angeles Kings		NHL	71	16	39	55	109
1988-89—Los Angeles Kings		NHL	79	25	50	75	92
1989-90—Los Angeles Kings		NHL	79	20	42	62	36
NHL TOTALS			304	74	156	230	311

(c)—October, 1984—Signed by Los Angeles Kings as a free agent.

TOBY DUCOLON

Left Wing . . . 6' . . . 195 lbs. . . . Born, St. Albans, Vt., June 18, 1966 . . . Shoots right.

Year	Team	League	Games	G.	A.	Pts.	Pen.
1983-84—Bellows Free Academy (c)		Ver. H.S.	22	38	26	64	36
1984-85—University of Vermont		ECAC	24	7	4	11	14
1985-86—University of Vermont		ECAC	30	10	6	16	48
1986-87—University of Vermont		ECAC	32	9	11	20	42
1987-88—University of Vermont		ECAC	34	21	18	39	62
1988-89—Peoria Rivermen		IHL	73	17	33	50	58
1989-90—Peoria Rivermen		IHL	62	11	14	25	22

(c)—June, 1984—Drafted by St. Louis Blues in 1984 NHL entry draft. Third Blues pick, 50th overall, third round.

DONALD DUFRESNE

Defense . . . 6' . . . 187 lbs. . . . Born, Quebec City, Que., April 10, 1967 . . . Shoots left . . . (November, 1984)—Pneumonia . . . (January 8, 1988)—Dislocated shoulder in AHL game at Rochester . . . (February, 1989)—Sprained ankle . . . (October 5, 1989)—Separated shoulder at Hartford and missed 15 games . . . (December 9, 1989)—Reinjured shoulder at Toronto.

Year	Team	League	Games	G.	A.	Pts.	Pen.
1983-84—Trois-Rivieres Draveurs		QMJHL	67	7	12	19	97
1984-85—Trois-Rivieres Draveurs (c)		QMJHL	65	5	30	35	112
1985-86—Trois-Rivieres Draveurs (b)		QMJHL	63	8	32	40	160
1986-87—Longueuil Chevaliers (b)		QMJHL	67	5	29	34	97
1987-88—Sherbrooke Canadiens		AHL	47	1	8	9	107
1988-89—Montreal Canadiens		NHL	13	0	1	1	43
1988-89—Sherbrooke Canadiens		AHL	47	0	12	12	170
1989-90—Montreal Canadiens		NHL	18	0	4	4	23
1989-90—Sherbrooke Canadiens		AHL	38	2	11	13	104
NHL TOTALS			31	0	5	5	66

(c)—June, 1985—Drafted as underage junior by Montreal Canadiens in 1985 entry draft. Eighth Canadiens pick, 117th overall, sixth round.

IAIN DUNCAN

Left Wing . . . 6'1" . . . 180 lbs. . . . Born, Weston, Ont., October 6, 1964 . . . Shoots left . . . (February, 1988)—Injured groin . . . (October, 1988)—Bruised ribs . . . (December, 1988)—Fractured elbow . . . (January 26, 1989)—Damaged nerves in shoulder . . . (October 6, 1989)—Strained medial colateral ligament of right knee during Winnipeg training camp and missed 15 games . . . (December 28, 1989)—Fractured hand vs. Cape Breton.

Year	Team	League	Games	G.	A.	Pts.	Pen.
1983-84—Bowling Green Univ. (c)		CCHA	44	9	11	20	65
1984-85—Bowling Green Univ.		CCHA	37	9	21	30	105
1985-86—Bowling Green Univ.		CCHA	41	26	26	52	124
1986-87—Bowling Green Univ. (a)		CCHA	39	28	41	69	141
1986-87—Winnipeg Jets		NHL	6	1	2	3	0
1987-88—Winnipeg Jets		NHL	62	19	23	42	73
1987-88—Moncton Golden Flames		AHL	8	1	3	4	26
1988-89—Winnipeg Jets		NHL	57	14	30	44	74
1989-90—Moncton Hawks		AHL	49	16	25	41	81
NHL TOTALS			125	34	55	89	147

(c)—June, 1983—Drafted by Winnipeg Jets in 1983 NHL entry draft. Eighth Jets pick, 129th overall, seventh round.

CRAIG DUNCANSON

Left Wing . . . 6' . . . 190 lbs. . . . Born, Sudbury, Ont., March 17, 1967 . . . Shoots left . . . (September, 1984)—Torn knee ligaments . . . (November 23, 1986)—Deep leg bruise in OHL game at Hamilton.

Year	Team	League	Games	G.	A.	Pts.	Pen.
1982-83—St. Michaels Jr. B		OHA	32	14	19	33	68
1983-84—Sudbury Wolves		OHL	62	38	38	76	178
1984-85—Sudbury Wolves (c)		OHL	53	35	28	63	129
1985-86—Sudbury Wolves		OHL	21	12	17	29	55
1985-86—Cornwall Royals		OHL	40	31	50	81	135
1985-86—Los Angeles Kings		NHL	2	0	1	1	0
1985-86—New Haven Nighthawks (d)		AHL	..	..	..	..	..
1986-87—Cornwall Royals		OHL	52	22	45	67	88
1986-87—Los Angeles Kings		NHL	2	0	0	0	24
1987-88—New Haven Nighthawks		AHL	57	15	25	40	170
1987-88—Los Angeles Kings		NHL	9	0	0	0	12
1988-89—New Haven Nighhawks		AHL	69	25	39	64	200
1988-89—Los Angeles Kings		NHL	5	0	0	0	0
1989-90—Los Angeles Kings		NHL	10	3	2	5	9
1989-90—New Haven Nighthawks (e)		AHL	51	17	30	47	152
NHL TOTALS			28	3	3	6	45

(c)—June, 1985—Drafted as underage junior by Los Angeles Kings in 1985 NHL entry draft. First Kings pick, ninth overall, first round.

(d)—No regular season record. Played two playoff games.

(e)—September 6, 1990—Traded by Los Angeles Kings to Minnesota North Stars for Daniel Berthiaume.

ROCKY DUNDAS

Right Wing . . . 6' . . . 195 lbs. . . . Born, Edmonton, Alta., January 30, 1967 . . . Shoots right . . . Brother of R.J. Dundas . . . Son of Ron Dundas (former CFL player).

Year	Team	League	Games	G.	A.	Pts.	Pen.
1983-84—Kelowna Wings		WHL	72	15	24	39	57
1984-85—Kelowna Wings (c)		WHL	71	32	44	76	117
1985-86—Spokane Chiefs		WHL	71	31	70	101	160
1986-87—Medicine Hat Tigers		WHL	48	35	41	76	132
1987-88—Baltimore Skipjacks		AHL	9	0	1	1	46
1987-88—Sherbrooke Canadiens		AHL	38	9	6	15	104
1988-89—Sherbrooke Canadiens		AHL	63	12	29	41	212
1989-90—Toronto Maple Leafs (d)		NHL	5	0	0	0	14
1989-90—Newmarket Saints		AHL	62	18	15	33	158
NHL TOTALS			5	0	0	0	14

(c)—June, 1985—Drafted as underage junior by Montreal Canadiens in 1985 NHL entry draft. Fourth Canadiens pick, 47th overall, third round.

(d)—October 4, 1989—Signed by Toronto Maple Leafs as a free agent.

RICHARD DUNN

Defense . . . 6' . . . 192 lbs. . . . Born, Canton, Mass., May 12, 1957 . . . Shoots left . . . (December, 1981)—Shoulder injury.

Year	Team	League	Games	G.	A.	Pts.	Pen.
1975-76—Kingston Canadians		Jr. "A"OHA	61	7	18	25	62
1976-77—Windsor Spitfires (c)		Jr. "A"OHA	65	5	21	26	98
1977-78—Hershey Bears		AHL	54	7	22	29	17
1977-78—Buffalo Sabres		NHL	25	0	3	3	16
1978-79—Buffalo Sabres		NHL	24	0	3	3	14
1978-79—Hershey Bears		AHL	34	5	18	23	10
1979-80—Buffalo Sabres		NHL	80	7	31	38	61
1980-81—Buffalo Sabres		NHL	79	7	42	49	34
1981-82—Buffalo Sabres (d)		NHL	72	7	19	26	73
1982-83—Calgary Flames (e)		NHL	80	3	11	14	47
1983-84—Hartford Whalers		NHL	63	5	20	25	30
1984-85—Hartford Whalers		NHL	13	1	4	5	2
1984-85—Binghamton Whalers (a-f-g)		AHL	64	9	39	48	43
1985-86—Buffalo Sabres		NHL	29	4	5	9	25
1985-86—Rochester Americans		AHL	34	6	17	23	12
1986-87—Buffalo Sabres		NHL	2	0	1	1	2
1986-87—Rochester Americans (a)		AHL	64	6	26	32	47
1987-88—Rochester Americans		AHL	68	12	35	47	52
1987-88—Buffalo Sabres		NHL	12	0	2	2	8
1988-89—Rochester Americans		AHL	69	9	35	44	81
1988-89—Buffalo Sabres		NHL	4	0	1	1	2
1989-90—Rochester Americans		AHL	41	7	7	14	34
NHL TOTALS			483	36	140	176	312

(c)—September, 1977—Signed by Buffalo Sabres as free agent.

(d)—June, 1982—Traded by Buffalo Sabres with goaltender Don Edwards and a second-round choice in 1982 NHL entry draft to Calgary Flames for Calgary's first and second round draft choices in 1982 and their second round pick in 1983 plus the option to switch first-round picks in '83.

(e)—July, 1983—Traded by Calgary Flames with Joel Quenneville to Hartford Whalers for Mickey Volcan.

(f)—Won Eddie Shore Plaque (Top AHL defenseman).

(g)—August, 1985—Signed by Buffalo Sabres as a free agent.

GUY DUPUIS

Defense . . . 6'2" . . . 200 lbs. . . . Born, Moncton, N.B., May 10, 1970 . . . Shoots right.

Year	Team	League	Games	G.	A.	Pts.	Pen.
1986-87—Hull Olympiques		QMJHL	69	5	10	15	35
1987-88—Hull Olympiques (c)		QMJHL	69	14	34	48	72
1988-89—Hull Olympiques		QMJHL	70	15	56	71	89
1989-90—Hull Olympiques		QMJHL	70	8	41	49	96

(c)—June, 1988—Drafted by Detroit Red Wings in 1988 NHL entry draft. Third Red Wings pick, 47th overall, third round.

MURRAY DUVAL

Defense . . . 6' . . . 195 lbs. . . . Born, Thompson, Man., January 22, 1970 . . . Shoots left . . . (January, 1987)—Stretched left knee ligaments.

Year	Team	League	Games	G.	A.	Pts.	Pen.
1986-87—Spokane Chiefs		WHL	27	2	6	8	21
1987-88—Spokane Chiefs (c)		WHL	70	26	37	63	104
1988-89—Spokane Chiefs		WHL	4	0	3	3	22
1988-89—Tri-City Americans		WHL	67	14	25	39	122
1989-90—Tri-City Americans (d)		WHL	7	4	4	8	10
1989-90—Swift Current Broncos		WHL	7	3	5	8	31
1989-90—Kamloops Blazers		WHL	56	14	36	50	94

(c)—June, 1988—Drafted by New York Rangers in 1988 NHL entry draft. Second Rangers pick, 26th overall, second round.

(d)—October 18, 1989—Traded with Jason Smith by Tri-City Americans to Swift Current Broncos for Brian Sakic and Wade Smith.

KARL DYKHUIS

Defense . . . 6'2'' . . . 185 lbs. . . . Born, Sept-Iles, Que., July 8, 1972 . . . Shoots left.

Year	Team	League	Games	G.	A.	Pts.	Pen.
1988-89—Hull Olympiques		QMJHL	63	2	29	31	59
1989-90—Hull Olympiques (c)		QMJHL	69	10	45	55	119

(c)—June 16, 1990—Selected by Chicago Black Hawks in 1990 NHL entry draft. First Black Hawks pick, 16th overall, first round.

STEVE DYKSTRA

Defense . . . 6'2'' . . . 190 lbs. . . . Born, Edmonton, Alta., February 3, 1962 . . . Shoots left . . . (February 19, 1986)—Injured shoulder at Hartford . . . (August 27, 1986) —Hospitalized after an automobile accident . . . (January, 1987)—Back spasms . . . (December, 1987)—Knee injury.

Year	Team	League	Games	G.	A.	Pts.	Pen.
1981-82—Seattle Flyers		WHL	57	8	26	34	139
1982-83—Rochester Americans (c)		AHL	70	2	16	18	100
1983-84—Rochester Americans		AHL	64	3	19	22	141
1984-85—Rochester Americans		AHL	51	9	23	32	113
1984-85—Flint Generals		IHL	15	1	7	8	36
1985-86—Buffalo Sabres		NHL	65	4	21	25	108
1986-87—Rochester Americans		AHL	18	0	0	0	77
1986-87—Buffalo Sabres		NHL	37	0	1	1	179
1987-88—Rochester Americans		AHL	7	0	1	1	33
1987-88—Buffalo Sabres (d)		NHL	27	1	1	2	91
1987-88—Edmonton Oilers		NHL	15	2	3	5	39
1988-89—Pittsburgh Penguins (e)		NHL	65	1	6	7	126
1989-90—Hartford Whalers (f)		NHL	9	0	0	0	2
1989-90—Binghamton Whalers (g)		AHL	53	5	17	22	55
1989-90—Maine Mariners		AHL	16	0	4	4	20
NHL TOTALS			218	8	32	40	545

(c)—October, 1982—Signed by Buffalo Sabres as a free agent.

(d)—February, 1988—Traded by Buffalo Sabres to Edmonton Oilers for Scott Metcalfe.

(e)—October 3, 1988—Selected by Pittsburgh Penguins in 1988 NHL waiver draft for $2,500.

(f)—October 14, 1989—Signed by Hartford Whalers as a free agent.

(g)—March 3, 1990—Traded by Hartford Whalers to Boston Bruins for Jeff Sirkka.

JOSEPH DZIEDZIC

Left Wing . . . 6'3'' . . . 200 lbs. . . . Born, Minneapolis, Minn., December 18, 1971 . . . Shoots left . . . Will be attending University of Minnesota.

Year	Team	League	Games	G.	A.	Pts.	Pen.
1988-89—Minneapolis Edison H.S.		Minn. H.S.	25	47	27	74	..
1989-90—Minneapolis Ed. H.S. (c)		Minn. H.S.	17	29	19	48	..

(c)—June 16, 1990—Selected by Pittsburgh Penguins in 1990 NHL entry draft. Second Penguins pick, 61st overall, third round.

MICHAEL EAGLES

Center . . . 5'10'' . . . 180 lbs. . . . Born, Sussex, N.B., March 7, 1963 . . . Shoots left . . . (October, 1984)—Broken hand . . . (February 21, 1986)—Injured ribs at Minnesota . . . (February, 1989)—Broken left hand . . . (January 15, 1990)— Bruised kidney at Toronto and missed eight games.

Year	Team	League	Games	G.	A.	Pts.	Pen.
1979-80—Melville		SJHL	55	46	30	76	77
1980-81—Kitchener Rangers (c)		OHL	56	11	27	38	64
1981-82—Kitchener Rangers		OHL	62	26	40	66	148
1982-83—Kitchener Rangers		OHL	58	26	36	62	133
1982-83—Quebec Nordiques		NHL	2	0	0	0	2
1983-84—Fredericton Express		AHL	68	13	29	42	85
1984-85—Fredericton Express		AHL	36	4	20	24	80
1985-86—Quebec Nordiques		NHL	73	11	12	23	49
1986-87—Quebec Nordiques		NHL	73	13	19	32	55
1987-88—Quebec Nordiques (d)		NHL	76	10	10	20	74
1988-89—Chicago Black Hawks		NHL	47	5	11	16	44
1989-90—Indianapolis Ice (e)		IHL	24	11	13	24	47
1989-90—Chicago Black Hawks		NHL	23	1	2	3	34
NHL TOTALS			294	40	54	94	258

(c)—June, 1981—Drafted as underage junior by Quebec Nordiques in 1981 NHL entry draft. Fifth Nordiques pick, 110th overall, sixth round.

(d)—July, 1988—Traded by Quebec Nordiques to Chicago Black Hawks for Bob Mason.

(e)—Led IHL playoffs with 10 goals.

DALLAS EAKINS

Defense . . . 6'1'' . . . 180 lbs. . . . Born, Dade City, Fla., January 20, 1967 . . . Shoots left . . . (October, 1988)—Back injury.

Year	Team	League	Games	G.	A.	Pts.	Pen.
1983-84—Peterborough Midgets		OHA	29	7	20	27	67
1984-85—Peterborough Petes (c)		OHL	48	0	8	8	96
1985-86—Peterborough Petes		OHL	60	6	16	22	134
1986-87—Peterborough Petes		OHL	54	3	11	14	145
1987-88—Peterborough Petes		OHL	64	11	27	38	129
1988-89—Baltimore Skipjacks		AHL	62	0	10	10	139
1989-90—Moncton Hawks (d)		AHL	75	2	11	13	189

(c)—June, 1985—Drafted as underage junior by Washington Capitals in 1985 NHL entry draft. Eleventh Capitals pick, 208th overall, 10th round.

(d)—September, 1989—Signed by Winnipeg Jets as a free agent.

MICHAEL EASTWOOD

Center . . . 6'3'' . . . 200 lbs. . . . Born, Cornwall, Ont., July 1, 1967 . . . Shoots right . . . Also plays Right Wing.

Year	Team	League	Games	G.	A.	Pts.	Pen.
1986-87—Pembrooke Lumberkings (c)		OHA	....	.....	....	.....	....
1987-88—Western Michigan Univ.		CCHA	42	5	8	13	14
1988-89—Western Michigan Univ.		CCHA	40	10	13	23	87
1989-90—Western Michigan Univ.		CCHA	40	25	27	52	36

(c)—June, 1987—Drafted by Toronto Maple Leafs in 1987 NHL entry draft. Fifth Maple Leafs pick, 91st overall, fifth round.

MURRAY EAVES

Center . . . 5'10'' . . . 185 lbs. . . . Born, Calgary, Alta., May 10, 1960 . . . Shoots right . . . Brother of Mike Eaves . . . (September, 1984)—Sprained ankle in training camp.

Year	Team	League	Games	G.	A.	Pts.	Pen.
1977-78—Windsor Spitfires		OMJHL	3	0	0	0	0
1978-79—University of Michigan		WCHA	23	12	22	34	14
1979-80—University of Michigan (a-c)		WCHA	33	36	49	85	34
1980-81—Winnipeg Jets		NHL	12	1	2	3	5
1980-81—Tulsa Oilers		CHL	59	24	34	58	59
1981-82—Tulsa Oilers		CHL	68	30	49	79	33
1981-82—Winnipeg Jets		NHL	2	0	0	0	0
1982-83—Winnipeg Jets		NHL	26	2	7	9	2
1982-83—Sherbrooke Jets		AHL	40	25	34	59	16
1983-84—Winnipeg Jets		NHL	2	0	0	0	0
1983-84—Sherbrooke Jets (a)		AHL	78	47	68	115	40
1984-85—Winnipeg Jets		NHL	3	0	3	3	0
1984-85—Sherbrooke Jets		AHL	47	26	42	68	28
1985-86—Sherbrooke Canadiens		AHL	68	22	51	73	26
1985-86—Winnipeg Jets (d)		NHL	4	1	0	1	0
1986-87—Nova Scotia Oilers		AHL	76	26	38	64	46
1987-88—Detroit Red Wings (e)		NHL	7	0	1	1	2
1987-88—Adirondack Red Wings		AHL	65	39	54	93	65
1988-89—Adirondack Red Wings (b-f)		AHL	80	46	72	118	84
1989-90—Adirondack Red Wings (g)		AHL	78	40	49	89	35
1989-90—Detroit Red Wings (h)		NHL	1	0	0	0	0
NHL TOTALS			150	29	93	122	16

(c)—June, 1980—Drafted by Winnipeg Jets in 1980 NHL entry draft. Third Jets pick, 44th overall, third round.

(d)—July, 1986—Traded by Winnipeg Jets to Edmonton Oilers for future considerations.

(e)—July, 1987—Signed by Detroit Red Wings as a free agent.

(f)—Won Fred C. Hunt Trophy (AHL Sportsmanship Trophy).

(g)—June 26, 1990—Won Fred Hunt Award (Sportsmanship).

(h)—May, 1990—Signed to play with Varese, Italy in 1990-91.

DEREK EDGERLY

Center . . . 6'1'' . . . 190 lbs. . . . Born, Malden, Mass., March 3, 1971 . . . Shoots left . . . Plans to attend Northeastern University.

Year	Team	League	Games	G.	A.	Pts.	Pen.
1988-89—Stoneham H.S.		Mass. H.S.	18	30	12	42	10
1989-90—Stoneham H.S. (c)		Mass. H.S.	18	28	23	51	12

(c)—June 16, 1990—Selected by Chicago Black Hawks in 1990 NHL entry draft. Fifth Black Hawks pick, 124th overall, sixth round.

TRACEY EGELAND

Left Wing . . . 6'1'' . . . 180 lbs. . . . Born, Lethbridge, Alta., August 20, 1970 . . . Shoots right . . . (November, 1986)—Missed two weeks with injured elbow.

Year	Team	League	Games	G.	A.	Pts.	Pen.
1986-87—Swift Current Broncos		WHL	48	3	2	5	20
1987-88—Swift Current Broncos		WHL	63	10	22	32	34
1988-89—Medicine Hat Tigers (c)		WHL	42	11	12	23	64
1988-89—Prince Albert Raiders (d)		WHL	24	17	10	27	24
1989-90—Prince Albert Raiders		WHL	61	39	26	65	160

(c)—August, 1988—Traded by Swift Current Broncos to Medicine Hat Tigers for Travis Kellin.

(d)—June, 1989—Drafted by Chicago Black Hawks in 1989 NHL entry draft. Fifth Black Hawks pick, 132nd overall, seventh round.

PER-ERIK (Pelle) EKLUND

Center . . . 5'10'' . . . 170 lbs. . . . Born, Stockholm, Sweden, March 22, 1963 . . . Shoots left . . . (October, 1985)—Named Sweden's Athlete of the Year for 1984. He was the second leading scorer in the elite league . . . (March, 1988)—Bruised hip . . . (October, 1989)—Strained left knee . . . (November 24, 1989)—Bruised right knee vs. Edmonton.

Year	Team	League	Games	G.	A.	Pts.	Pen.
1983-84—Stockholm AIK (c)		Sweden	35	9	18	27	24
1984-85—Stockholm AIK		Sweden	35	16	33	49	10
1985-86—Philadelphia Flyers		NHL	70	15	51	66	12
1986-87—Philadelphia Flyers		NHL	72	14	41	55	2

Year	Team	League	Games	G.	A.	Pts.	Pen.
1987-88—Philadelphia Flyers		NHL	71	10	32	42	12
1988-89—Philadelphia Flyers		NHL	79	18	51	69	23
1989-90—Philadelphia Flyers		NHL	70	23	39	62	16
NHL TOTALS			362	80	214	294	65

(c)—June, 1983—Drafted by Philadelphia Flyers in 1983 NHL entry draft. Seventh Flyers pick, 161st overall, eighth round.

TODD ELIK

Center . . . 6'2'' . . . 190 lbs. . . . Born, Brampton, Ont., April 15, 1966 . . . Shoots left.

Year	Team	League	Games	G.	A.	Pts.	Pen.
1982-83—St. Michaels Midgets		OHA	35	25	26	51	55
1983-84—Kingston Canadians		OHL	64	5	16	21	17
1984-85—Kingston Canadians		OHL	34	14	11	25	6
1984-85—North Bay Centennials		OHL	23	4	6	10	2
1985-86—North Bay Centennials		OHL	40	12	34	46	20
1986-87—Univ. of Regina		CWUAA	27	26	34	60	137
1987-88—Denver Rangers (c)		IHL	81	44	56	100	83
1988-89—Denver Rangers (d)		IHL	28	20	15	35	22
1988-89—New Haven Nighthawks		AHL	43	11	25	36	31
1989-90—Los Angeles Kings		NHL	48	10	23	33	41
1989-90—New Haven Nighthawks		AHL	32	20	23	43	42
NHL TOTALS			48	10	23	33	41

(c)—February 26, 1988—Signed by New York Rangers as a free agent.

(d)—December 12, 1988—Traded with Igor Liba, Michael Boyce and future considerations by New York Rangers to Los Angeles Kings for Dean Kennedy and Denis Larocque.

DAVE ELLETT

Defense . . . 6'1'' . . . 200 lbs. . . . Born, Cleveland, O., March 30, 1964 . . . Shoots left . . . Son of Dave Ellett Sr. who played for Cleveland Barons in AHL . . . (March 6, 1988)—Missed 10 games with a bruised thigh . . . (November 16, 1988)—Sprained ankle vs. Chicago.

Year	Team	League	Games	G.	A.	Pts.	Pen.
1981-82—Ottawa Senators		CJOHL	50	9	35	44	..
1982-83—Bowling Green Univ. (c)		CCHA	40	4	13	17	34
1983-84—Bowling Green Univ.		CCHA	43	15	39	54	9
1984-85—Winnipeg Jets		NHL	80	11	27	38	85
1985-86—Winnipeg Jets		NHL	80	15	31	46	96
1986-87—Winnipeg Jets		NHL	78	13	31	44	53
1987-88—Winnipeg Jets		NHL	68	13	45	58	106
1988-89—Winnipeg Jets		NHL	75	22	34	56	62
1989-90—Winnipeg Jets		NHL	77	17	29	46	96
NHL TOTALS			458	91	197	288	498

(c)—June, 1982—Drafted as underage player by Winnipeg Jets in NHL entry draft. Third Jets pick, 75th overall, fourth round.

PAT ELYNUIK

Right Wing . . . 6' . . . 185 lbs. . . . Born, Foam Lake, Sask., October 30, 1967 . . . Shoots right . . . (March 7, 1989)—Separated left shoulder at Calgary.

Year	Team	League	Games	G.	A.	Pts.	Pen.
1983-84—Prince Albert Midget Raiders		SAHA	26	33	30	63	54
1984-85—Prince Albert Raiders		WHL	70	23	20	43	54
1985-86—Prince Albert Raiders (a-c)		WHL	68	53	53	106	62
1986-87—Prince Albert Raiders (a)		WHL	64	51	62	113	40
1987-88—Winnipeg Jets		NHL	13	1	3	4	12
1987-88—Moncton Golden Flames		AHL	30	11	18	29	35
1988-89—Winnipeg Jets		NHL	56	26	25	51	29
1988-89—Moncton Hawks		AHL	7	8	2	10	2
1989-90—Winnipeg Jets		NHL	80	32	42	74	83
NHL TOTALS			149	59	70	129	124

(c)—June 1986—Drafted as underage junior by Winnipeg Jets in 1986 NHL entry draft. First Jets pick, eighth overall, first round.

NELSON EMERSON

Center . . . 5'11'' . . . 165 lbs. . . . Born, Hamilton, Ont., August 17, 1967 . . . Shoots right . . . Holds Bowling Green University career scoring record.

Year	Team	League	Games	G.	A.	Pts.	Pen.
1984-85—Stratford Cullitans Jr.B (c)		OHA	40	23	38	61	70
1985-86—Stratford Cullitans Jr.B		OHA	39	54	58	112	91
1986-87—Bowling Green Univ. (d)		CCHA	45	26	35	61	28
1987-88—Bowling Green Univ. (e)		CCHA	45	34	49	83	54
1988-89—Bowling Green Univ. (b)		CCHA	44	22	46	68	46
1989-90—Bowling Green Univ. (a-f)		CCHA	44	30	52	82	42
1989-90—Peoria Rivermen		IHL	3	1	1	2	0

(c)—June, 1985—Drafted by St. Louis Blues in 1985 NHL entry draft. Second Blues pick, 44th overall, third round.

(d)—Named CCHA Rookie-of-the-Year.

(e)—Named Second team All-America (West).

(f)—Named First team All-America (West).

DAVID EMMA

Center . . . 5'9'' . . . 175 lbs. . . . Born, Cranston, R.I., January 14, 1969 . . . Shoots left.

Year	Team	League	Games	G.	A.	Pts.	Pen.
1987-88—Boston College		H. East	30	19	16	35	30
1988-89—Boston College (b-c)		H. East	36	20	31	51	36
1989-90—Boston College (a-d)		H. East	42	38	34	*72	46

(c)—Drafted by New Jersey Devils in 1989 NHL entry draft. Sixth Devils pick, 110th overall, sixth round.

(d)—Named First team All-America (East).

GARY EMMONS

Center . . . 5'9'' . . . 170 lbs. . . . Born, Winnipeg, Man., December 30, 1963 . . . Shoots right.

Year	Team	League	Games	G.	A.	Pts.	Pen.
1983-84—Northern Michigan Univ.		CCHA	40	28	21	49	42
1984-85—Northern Michigan Univ.		WCHA	40	25	28	53	22
1985-86—Northern Michigan Univ. (c)		WCHA	36	45	30	75	34
1986-87—Northern Michigan Univ. (b)		WCHA	35	32	34	66	59
1987-88—Milwaukee Admirals (d)		IHL	13	3	4	7	4
1987-88—Nova Scotia Oilers		AHL	59	18	27	45	22
1988-89—Canadian National Team		Int'l.	49	16	26	42	42
1989-90—Kalamazoo Wings (e)		IHL	81	41	59	100	38

(c)—June, 1986—Selected by New York Rangers in 1986 NHL supplemental draft.

(d)—July 27, 1987—Signed by Edmonton Oilers as a free agent.

(e)—July 11, 1989—Signed by Minnesota North Stars as a free agent.

CRAIG T. ENDEAN

Right Wing . . . 6' . . . 170 lbs. . . . Born, Kamloops, B.C., April 13, 1968 . . . Shoots left . . . Also plays Center and Left Wing . . . Holds WHL career records for games played (351) and career points (529) . . . (November, 1988)—Suspended by Winnipeg for refusing to report to Moncton.

Year	Team	League	Games	G.	A.	Pts.	Pen.
1983-84—Seattle Breakers		WHL	67	16	6	22	14
1984-85—Seattle Breakers		WHL	69	37	60	97	28
1985-86—Seattle Thunderbirds (c)		WHL	70	58	70	128	34
1986-87—Regina Pats (b)		WHL	76	*69	77	*146	34
1986-87—Winnipeg Jets		NHL	2	0	1	1	0
1987-88—Regina Pats (d)		WHL	69	50	86	136	50
1988-89—Moncton Hawks		AHL	18	3	9	12	16
1988-89—Fort Wayne Komets		IHL	34	10	18	28	0
1989-90—Fort Wayne Komets (e-f)		IHL	20	2	11	13	8
1989-90—Adirondack Red Wings (g)		AHL	7	3	3	6	4
NHL TOTALS			2	0	1	1	0

(c)—June, 1986—Drafted as underage junior by Winnipeg Jets in 1986 NHL entry draft. Fifth Jets pick, 92nd overall, fifth round.

(d)—Won Brad Hornung Trophy (Most Sportsmanlike player).

(e)—September, 1989—Assigned to Tappara, Finland by Winnipeg Jets.

(f)—December 11, 1989—Released by Winnipeg Jets.

(g)—March 17, 1990—Signed by Adirondack Red Wings as a free agent.

JIM ENNIS

Defense . . . 6' . . . 200 lbs. . . . Born, Edmonton, Alta., July 10, 1967 . . . Shoots left.

Year	Team	League	Games	G.	A.	Pts.	Pen.
1985-86—Boston University (c)		H. East	40	1	4	5	22
1986-87—Boston University		H. East	26	3	4	7	27
1987-88—Nova Scotia Oilers		AHL	59	8	12	20	102
1987-88—Edmonton Oilers		NHL	5	1	0	1	10
1988-89—Cape Breton Oilers		AHL	67	3	15	18	94
1989-90—Binghamton Whalers (d)		AHL	69	3	12	15	61
NHL TOTALS			5	1	0	1	10

(c)—June, 1986—Drafted by Edmonton Oilers in 1986 NHL entry draft. Sixth Oilers pick, 126th overall, sixth round.

(d)—October 9, 1989—Traded by Edmonton Oilers to Hartford Whalers for Norm Maciver.

KELLY ENS

Center . . . 6'2'' . . . 195 lbs. . . . Born, Saskatoon, Sask., June 15, 1969 . . . Shoots left . . . (November, 1987)—Torn knee ligaments.

Year	Team	League	Games	G.	A.	Pts.	Pen.
1986-87—Calgary Wranglers		WHL	58	11	12	23	76
1987-88—Lethbridge Hurricanes		WHL	52	27	27	54	89
1988-89—Lethbridge Hurricanes (c)		WHL	72	46	36	82	146
1989-90—Lethbridge Hurricanes		WHL	72	62	58	120	139

(c)—June, 1989—Drafted by New York Islanders in 1989 NHL entry draft. Thirteenth Islanders pick, 212th overall, 11th round.

MICHAEL ERICKSON

Defense . . . 5'11'' . . . 175 lbs. . . . Born, Worcester, Mass., March 11, 1969 . . . Shoots left.

Year	Team	League	Games	G.	A.	Pts.	Pen.
1986-87—St. John's Hill H.S. (c)		Mass. H.S.	20	8	21	29	20
1987-88—Univ. of Lowell		H. East	35	14	9	23	8
1988-89—Univ. of Lowell		H. East	33	4	2	6	50

(c)—June, 1987—Drafted by New York Islanders in 1987 NHL entry draft. Eleventh Islanders pick, 223rd overall, 11th round.

PETER ERIKSSON

Right Wing . . . 6' . . . 200 lbs. . . . Born, Nassjo, Sweden, September 19, 1960 . . . Shoots right . . . (October, 1989)—Injured right knee during Edmonton Oilers training camp . . . (November, 1989)—Back injury.

Year	Team	League	Games	G.	A.	Pts.	Pen.
1986-87—HV-71 (c)		Sweden	36	10	14	24	24
1987-88—HV-71		Sweden	37	14	9	23	22
1988-89—HV-71 (d)		Sweden	40	10	27	37	48
1989-90—Cape Breton Oilers		AHL	21	5	12	17	36
1989-90—Edmonton Oilers		NHL	20	3	3	6	24
NHL TOTALS			20	3	3	6	24

(c)—June, 1987—Drafted by Edmonton Oilers in 1987 NHL entry draft. Fourth Oilers pick, 64th overall, third round.

(d)—May 3, 1989—Signed multi-year contract with Edmonton.

JAN ERIXON

Right Wing . . . 6' . . . 190 lbs. . . . Born, Skelleftea, Sweden, July 8, 1962 . . . Shoots left . . . (February, 1985)—Bruised foot . . . (December 8, 1985)—Bruised leg vs. Philadelphia . . . (January 12, 1986)—Fractured tibia vs. St. Louis . . . (December, 1986)—Hip injury . . . (October, 1988)—Sprained right knee . . . (February, 1989)—Sprained back . . . (December 2, 1989)—Back spasms after a game at Los Angeles . . . (May 2, 1990)—Surgery to lower back to repair a herniated disc.

Year	Team	League	Games	G.	A.	Pts.	Pen.
1979-80—Skelleftea AIK		Sweden	32	9	3	12	22
1980-81—Skelleftea AIK (c)		Sweden	32	6	6	12	4
1981-82—Skelleftea AIK		Sweden	30	7	7	14	26
1982-83—Skelleftea AIK		Sweden	36	10	18	28	..
1983-84—New York Rangers		NHL	75	5	25	30	16
1984-85—New York Rangers		NHL	66	7	22	29	33
1985-86—New York Rangers		NHL	31	2	17	19	4
1986-87—New York Rangers		NHL	68	8	18	26	24
1987-88—New York Rangers		NHL	70	7	19	26	33
1988-89—New York Rangers		NHL	44	4	11	15	27
1989-90—New York Rangers		NHL	58	4	9	13	8
NHL TOTALS			412	37	121	158	145

(c)—June, 1981—Drafted by New York Rangers in 1981 NHL entry draft. Second Rangers pick, 30th overall, second round.

BOB ERREY

Left Wing . . . 5'10" . . . 185 lbs. . . . Born, Montreal, Que., September 21, 1964 . . . Shoots left . . . (March 18, 1987)—Sprained right knee at St. Louis . . . (October, 1987)—Broken right wrist.

Year	Team	League	Games	G.	A.	Pts.	Pen.
1981-82—Peterborough Petes		OHL	68	29	31	60	39
1982-83—Peterborough Petes (a-c)		OHL	67	53	47	100	74
1983-84—Pittsburgh Penguins		NHL	65	9	13	22	29
1984-85—Baltimore Skipjacks		AHL	59	17	24	41	14
1984-85—Pittsburgh Penguins		NHL	16	0	2	2	7
1985-86—Baltimore Skipjacks		AHL	18	8	7	15	28
1985-86—Pittsburgh Penguins		NHL	37	11	6	17	8
1986-87—Pittsburgh Penguins		NHL	72	16	18	34	46
1987-88—Pittsburgh Penguins		NHL	17	3	6	9	18
1988-89—Pittsburgh Penguins		NHL	76	26	32	58	124
1989-90—Pittsburgh Penguins		NHL	78	20	19	39	109
NHL TOTALS			361	85	96	181	341

(c)—June, 1983—Drafted as underage junior by Pittsburgh Penguins in 1983 NHL entry draft. First Penguins pick, 15th overall, first round.

LEONARD ESAU

Defense . . . 6'3" . . . 190 lbs. . . . Born, Meadow Lake, Sask., March 16, 1968 . . . Shoots right.

Year	Team	League	Games	G.	A.	Pts.	Pen.
1986-87—Humboldt Broncos		SJHL	57	4	26	30	278
1987-88—Humboldt Broncos (c)		SJHL	57	16	37	53	229
1988-89—St. Cloud State Univ.		NCAA-II	35	12	27	39	69
1989-90—St. Cloud State Univ.		NCAA-II	29	8	11	19	83

(c)—June, 1988—Drafted by Toronto Maple Leafs in 1988 NHL entry draft. Fifth Maple Leafs pick, 86th overall, fifth round.

DAVID ESPE

Defense . . . 6' . . . 185 lbs. . . . Born, St. Paul, Minn., November 3, 1966 . . . Shoots left.

Year	Team	League	Games	G.	A.	Pts.	Pen.
1984-85—White Bear Lake H.S. (c)		Minn. H.S.	21	11	16	27	30
1985-86—Univ. of Minnesota		WCHA	27	0	6	6	18
1986-87—Univ. of Minnesota		WCHA	45	4	8	12	28
1987-88—Univ. of Minnesota		WCHA	43	4	10	14	68
1988-89—Univ. of Minnesota		WCHA	47	0	11	11	61
1989-90—Halifax Citadels		AHL	48	2	16	18	26

(c)—June, 1985—Drafted by Quebec Nordiques in 1985 NHL entry draft. Fifth Nordiques pick, 78th overall, fourth round.

DOUG EVANS

Center . . . 5'9" . . . 178 lbs. . . . Born, Peterborough, Ont., June 2, 1963 . . . Shoots left . . . (September, 1987)—Separated left shoulder during St. Louis training camp.

Year	Team	League	Games	G.	A.	Pts.	Pen.
1980-81—Peterborough Petes		OHL	51	9	24	33	139
1981-82—Peterborough Petes		OHL	56	17	49	66	176
1982-83—Peterborough Petes		OHL	65	31	55	86	165
1983-84—Peterborough Petes		OHL	61	45	79	124	98
1984-85—Peoria Prancers (c)		IHL	81	36	61	97	189
1985-86—St. Louis Blues		NHL	13	1	0	1	2
1985-86—Peoria Rivermen (a)		IHL	69	46	51	97	179
1986-87—Peoria Rivermen		IHL	18	10	15	25	39
1986-87—St. Louis Blues		NHL	53	3	13	16	91
1987-88—Peoria Rivermen		IHL	11	4	16	20	64
1987-88—St. Louis Blues		NHL	41	5	7	12	49
1988-89—St. Louis Blues		NHL	53	7	12	19	81
1989-90—Peoria Rivermen		IHL	42	19	28	47	128
1989-90—St. Louis Blues (d)		NHL	3	0	0	0	0
1989-90—Winnipeg Jets		NHL	27	10	8	18	33
NHL TOTALS			190	26	40	66	256

(c)—June, 1985—Signed by St. Louis Blues as a free agent.
(d)—January 22, 1990—Traded by St. Louis Blues to Winnipeg Jets for Ron Wilson.

DOUGLAS EVANS

Defense . . . 6' . . . 200 lbs. . . . Born, San Jose, Calif., July 12, 1971 . . . Shoots right . . . (July, 1988)—Strained knee ligament . . . Also plays Right Wing.

Year	Team	League	Games	G.	A.	Pts.	Pen.
1987-88—Detroit Compuware		NAJHL	30	2	16	18	119
1988-89—Univ. of Michigan (c)		CCHA	38	0	8	8	41
1989-90—Univ. of Michigan		CCHA	31	2	3	5	24

(c)—June, 1989—Drafted by Winnipeg Jets in 1989 NHL entry draft. Ninth Jets pick, 131st overall, seventh round.

KEVIN EVANS

Defense . . . 5'11" . . . 195 lbs. . . . Born, Peterborough, Ont., July 10, 1965 . . . Shoots left . . . (1986-87)—Set a pro-hockey record for penalty minutes in a season . . . (December 28, 1988)—Fined $100 and suspended for three games for fighting vs. Milwaukee . . . (February 24, 1989)—Five tendons and an artery cut when a skate ran over his right ankle vs. Flint . . . (November 25, 1989)—Fined $300 and suspended one IHL game for fighting with Byron Lomow vs. Kalamazoo.

Year	Team	League	Games	G.	A.	Pts.	Pen.
1983-84—Peterborough Jr. B		OHA	39	17	34	51	210
1984-85—London Knights		OHL	52	3	7	10	148
1985-86—Victoria Cougars		WHL	66	16	39	55	*441
1985-86—Kalamazoo Wings		IHL	11	3	5	8	97
1986-87—Kalamazoo Wings		IHL	73	19	31	50	*648
1987-88—Kalamazoo Wings		IHL	54	9	28	37	404
1988-89—Kalamazoo Wings (c)		IHL	54	22	32	54	328
1989-90—Kalamazoo Wings		IHL	76	30	54	84	346

(c)—August 8, 1988—Signed by Minnesota North Stars as a free agent.

SHAWN EVANS

Defense . . . 6'3" . . . 195 lbs. . . . Born, Kingston, Ont., September 7, 1965 . . . Shoots left . . . Cousin of Dennis Kearns (Vancouver, 1970s).

Year	Team	League	Games	G.	A.	Pts.	Pen.
1981-82—Kitchener Rangers MW Jr. B		OHA	21	9	13	22	55
1982-83—Peterborough Petes (c)		OHL	58	7	41	48	116
1983-84—Peterborough Petes (b)		OHL	67	21	88	109	116
1984-85—Peterborough Petes		OHL	66	16	83	99	78
1985-86—Peoria Rivermen		IHL	55	8	26	34	36
1985-86—St. Louis Blues (d)		NHL	7	0	0	0	2
1986-87—Nova Scotia Oilers (e)		AHL	55	7	28	35	29
1987-88—Nova Scotia Oilers		AHL	79	8	62	70	109
1988-89—Springfield Indians (f)		AHL	68	9	50	59	125
1989-90—New York Islanders		NHL	2	1	0	1	0
1989-90—Springfield Indians (g)		AHL	63	6	35	41	102
NHL TOTALS			9	1	0	1	2

(c)—June, 1983—Drafted by New Jersey Devils as underage junior in 1983 NHL entry draft. Second Devils pick, 24th overall, second round.
(d)—September, 1985—Traded with a fifth round 1986 draft pick (Mike Wolak) by New Jersey Devils to St. Louis Blues for Mark Johnson.
(e)—October, 1986—Traded by St. Louis Blues to Edmonton Oilers for Todd Ewen.
(f)—June 20, 1988—Signed by New York Islanders as a free agent.
(g)—May, 1990—Signed to play with Olten, Switerland for 1990-91.

DEAN EVASON

Center . . . 5'10" . . . 175 lbs. . . . Born, Flin Flon, Man., August 22, 1964 . . . Shoots left . . . Brother of Dan Evason (1984-85 assistant coach of Brandon Wheat Kings) . . . (December 14, 1988)—Strained left ankle ligaments when checked by Trent Yawney at Chicago.

Year	Team	League	Games	G.	A.	Pts.	Pen.
1980-81—Spokane Flyers		WHL	3	1	1	2	0
1981-82—Kamloops Junior Oilers (c-d)		WHL	70	29	69	98	112
1982-83—Kamloops Junior Oilers		WHL	70	71	93	164	102
1983-84—Kamloops Junior Oilers (a-e)		WHL	57	49	88	137	89
1983-84—Washington Capitals		NHL	2	0	0	0	2
1984-85—Binghamton Whalers		AHL	65	27	49	76	38
1984-85—Washington Capitals (f)		NHL	15	3	4	7	2
1984-85—Hartford Whalers		NHL	2	0	0	0	0
1985-86—Binghamton Whalers		AHL	26	9	17	26	29
1985-86—Hartford Whalers		NHL	55	20	28	48	65
1986-87—Hartford Whalers		NHL	80	22	37	59	67
1987-88—Hartford Whalers		NHL	77	10	18	28	117
1988-89—Hartford Whalers		NHL	67	11	17	28	60
1989-90—Hartford Whalers		NHL	78	18	25	43	138
NHL TOTALS			376	84	129	213	451

(c)—December, 1981—Drafted by Kamloops Junior Oilers in WHL disperal draft of players of Spokane Flyers.
(d)—June, 1982—Drafted as underage junior by Washington Capitals in 1982 NHL entry draft. Third Capitals pick, 89th overall, fifth round.
(e)—Shared WHL playoff scoring with Taylor Hall, each had 21 goals.
(f)—March, 1985—Traded with Peter Sidorkiewicz by Washington Capitals to Hartford Whalers for David A. Jensen.

DEAN EWEN

Left Wing . . . 6'1" . . . 185 lbs. . . . Born, St. Albert, Alta., February 28, 1969 . . . Shoots left . . . Brother of Todd Ewen . . . (November 1, 1987)—Suspended 12 games by WHL for fighting.

Year	Team	League	Games	G.	A.	Pts.	Pen.
1984-85—St. Albert Saints		AJHL	30	2	4	6	25
1985-86—New Westminster Bruins		WHL	61	7	15	22	154
1986-87—Spokane Chiefs (c)		WHL	66	8	14	22	236
1987-88—Spokane Chiefs		WHL	49	12	12	24	302
1988-89—Spokane Chiefs		WHL	5	0	0	0	53

Year	Team	League	Games	G.	A.	Pts.	Pen.
1988-89—Seattle Thunderbirds		WHL	56	22	30	52	254
1988-89—Springfield Indians		AHL	6	0	0	0	26
1989-90—Springfield Indians		AHL	34	0	7	7	194

(c)—June, 1987—Drafted as underage junior by New York Islanders in 1987 NHL entry draft. Third Islanders pick, 55th overall, third round.

TODD EWEN

Right Wing . . . 6'2" . . . 185 lbs. . . . Born, Saskatoon, Sask., March 26, 1966 . . . Shoots right . . . Brother of Dean Ewen . . . (October, 1987)—Sprained ankle . . . (January, 1988)—Suspended one game by NHL for his third game misconduct of the season . . . (October, 1988)—Pulled groin . . . (December, 1988)—Torn right eye muscle . . . (February, 1989)—Pulled left hamstring and bruised shoulder . . . (April 18, 1989)—Suspended 10 games by NHL for coming off the bench to instigate a fight with Wayne Van Dorp in a playoff game vs. Chicago. He served three games in the playoffs and will miss the first seven games of 1989-90 . . . (October 28, 1989)—Broke right hand in collision with Dino Ciccarelli vs. Washington.

Year	Team	League	Games	G.	A.	Pts.	Pen.
1982-83—Vernon Lakers		BCJHL	42	20	23	53	195
1982-83—Kamloops Junior Oilers		WHL	3	0	0	0	2
1983-84—New Westminster Bruins (c)		WHL	68	11	13	24	176
1984-85—New Westminster Bruins		WHL	56	11	20	31	304
1985-86—New Westminster Bruins		WHL	60	28	24	52	289
1985-86—Maine Mariners (d)		AHL	....	....	....	....	....
1986-87—Peoria Rivermen		IHL	16	3	3	6	110
1986-87—St. Louis Blues (e)		NHL	23	2	0	2	84
1987-88—St. Louis Blues		NHL	64	4	2	6	227
1988-89—St. Louis Blues		NHL	34	4	5	9	171
1989-90—Peoria Rivermen		IHL	2	0	0	0	12
1989-90—St. Louis Blues (f)		NHL	3	0	0	0	11
1989-90—Montreal Canadiens		NHL	41	4	6	10	158
NHL TOTALS			165	14	13	27	651

(c)—June, 1984—Drafted as underage junior by Edmonton Oilers in 1984 NHL entry draft. Eighth Oilers pick, 168th overall, eighth round.

(d)—No regular season record. Played three playoff games.

(e)—October, 1986—Traded by Edmonton Oilers to St. Louis Blues for Shawn Evans.

(f)—December 12, 1989—Traded by St. Louis Blues to Montreal Canadiens for the return of a draft pick dealt to Montreal for Mike Lalor.

BRIAN FARRELL

Center . . . 5'11" . . . 182 lbs. . . . Born, Hartford, Conn., April 16, 1972 . . . Shoots left . . . (1989-90)—Hampered by knee, groin and shoulder injuries.

Year	Team	League	Games	G.	A.	Pts.	Pen.
1988-89—Avon Old Farms		Conn. H.S.	27	13	24	37	....
1989-90—Avon Old Farms (c)		Conn. H.S.	24	22	23	45	....

(c)—June 16, 1990—Selected by Pittsburgh Penguins in 1990 NHL entry draft. Fourth Penguins pick, 89th overall, fifth round.

SCOTT FARRELL

Defense . . . 5'11" . . . 190 lbs. . . . Born, Richmond, B.C., April 15, 1970 . . . Shoots left . . . (October 9, 1989)—Suspended three WHL games for fighting vs. Kamloops.

Year	Team	League	Games	G.	A.	Pts.	Pen.
1984-85—Richmond Bantams		BC Bantam	72	68	107	175	339
1985-86—New Westminster Bruins		WHL	4	1	0	1	9
1986-87—New Westminster Bruins		WHL	67	4	8	12	47
1987-88—Spokane Chiefs		WHL	62	1	16	17	198
1988-89—Spokane Chiefs (c)		WHL	67	10	32	42	221
1989-90—Spokane Chiefs (d-e)		WHL	10	3	5	8	34
1989-90—Lethbridge Hurricanes		WHL	4	1	1	2	22
1989-90—Tri-City Americans		WHL	35	3	10	13	84

(c)—June, 1989—Selected by Pittsburgh Penguins in 1989 NHL entry draft. Twelfth Penguins pick, 226th overall, 11th round.

(d)—October 30, 1989—Traded by Spokane Chiefs to Lethbridge Hurricanes for Colin Gregor.

(e)—November 16, 1989—Left Lethbridge Hurricanes and was traded to Tri-City Americans.

ANDRE FAUST

Center . . . 6'1" . . . 180 lbs. . . . Born, Joliette, Que., October 7, 1969 . . . Shoots left.

Year	Team	League	Games	G.	A.	Pts.	Pen.
1984-85—Anjou Midget		Que. Midg.	36	34	34	68	14
1985-86—Anjou Midget		Que. Midg.	39	39	41	80	26
1986-87—Upper Canada College		Que. H.S.	32	40	38	78	20
1987-88—Upper Canada College		Que. H.S.	45	66	59	125	30
1988-89—Princeton University (c-d)		ECAC	26	18	16	34	34
1989-90—Princeton University (b)		ECAC	27	15	29	44	28

(c)—Named ECAC Rookie of the Year.

(d)—June, 1989—Drafted by New Jersey Devils in 1989 NHL entry draft. Eighth Devils pick, 173rd overall, ninth round.

GLEN FEATHERSTONE

Defense . . . 6'4" . . . 209 lbs. . . . Born, Toronto, Ont., July 8, 1968 . . . Shoots left . . . Father (Roy Featherstone) played professional soccer in Ireland.

Year	Team	League	Games	G.	A.	Pts.	Pen.
1984-85—Toronto National Midget		MTHL	45	7	24	31	94
1985-86—Windsor Spitfires (c)		OHL	49	0	6	6	135
1986-87—Windsor Spitfires		OHL	47	6	11	17	154
1987-88—Windsor Spitfires		OHL	53	7	27	34	201
1988-89—Peoria Rivermen		IHL	37	5	19	24	97
1988-89—St. Louis Blues		NHL	18	0	2	2	22

Year	Team	League	Games	G.	A.	Pts.	Pen.
1989-90—Peoria Rivermen		IHL	15	1	4	5	43
1989-90—St. Louis Blues		NHL	58	0	12	12	145
NHL TOTALS			76	0	14	14	167

(c)—June, 1986—Drafted as underage junior by St. Louis Blues in 1986 NHL entry draft. Fourth Blues pick, 73rd overall, fourth round.

BERNARD ALLAN FEDERKO

Center . . . 6' . . . 185 lbs. . . . Born, Foam Lake, Sask., May 12, 1956 . . . Shoots left . . . Brother of Ken Federko (Salt Lake—CHL 1980-82) . . . Missed final games of 1978-79 season with broken right wrist . . . (December 29, 1981)—Tore rib cartilage vs. Hartford . . . (November 20, 1984)—Bruised left ankle at Vancouver . . . (January, 1985)—Bruised lung and ribs . . . Holds St. Louis Blues career records in games (927), goals (352), assists (721) and points (1,073) . . . (January 9, 1987)—Broken jaw when struck by teammate Mark Hunter's stick at Edmonton . . . (December, 1988)—Missed 10 games with a lacerated left ankle . . . (March, 1989)—Infected cut above left elbow.

Year	Team	League	Games	G.	A.	Pts.	Pen.
1973-74—Saskatoon Blades		WCHL	68	22	28	50	19
1974-75—Saskatoon Blades (c)		WCHL	66	39	68	107	30
1975-76—Saskatoon Blades (a-d-e-f)		WCHL	72	72	*115	*187	108
1976-77—Kansas City Blues (b-g)		CHL	42	30	39	69	41
1976-77—St. Louis Blues		NHL	31	14	9	23	15
1977-78—St. Louis Blues		NHL	72	17	24	41	27
1978-79—St. Louis Blues		NHL	74	31	64	95	14
1979-80—St. Louis Blues		NHL	79	38	56	94	24
1980-81—St. Louis Blues		NHL	78	31	73	104	47
1981-82—St. Louis Blues		NHL	74	30	62	92	70
1982-83—St. Louis Blues		NHL	75	24	60	84	24
1983-84—St. Louis Blues		NHL	79	41	66	107	43
1984-85—St. Louis Blues		NHL	76	30	73	103	27
1985-86—St. Louis Blues		NHL	80	34	68	102	34
1986-87—St. Louis Blues		NHL	64	20	52	72	32
1987-88—St. Louis Blues		NHL	79	20	69	89	52
1988-89—St. Louis Blues (h)		NHL	66	22	45	67	54
1989-90—Detroit Red Wings (i)		NHL	73	17	40	57	24
NHL TOTALS			1000	369	761	1130	487

(c)—Led in goals (15) during playoffs.

(d)—Named Most Valuable Player in WCHL.

(e)—Drafted from Saskatoon Blades by St. Louis Blues in first round of 1976 amateur draft.

(f)—Led in assists (27) and points (45) during playoffs.

(g)—CHL Rookie-of-the-Year.

(h)—June 15, 1989—Traded with Tony McKegney by St. Louis Blues to Detroit Red Wings for Adam Oates and Paul MacLean.

(i)—June, 1990—Announced his retirement.

SERGEI FEDOROV

Center . . . 6'1" . . . 187 lbs. . . . Born, Minsk, USSR, December 13, 1969 . . . Shoots left.

Year	Team	League	Games	G.	A.	Pts.	Pen.
1985-86—Minsk Dynamo		USSR	15	6	1	7	10
1986-87—Central Red Army		USSR	29	6	6	12	12
1987-88—Central Red Army		USSR	48	7	9	16	20
1988-89—Central Red Army (c)		USSR	44	9	8	17	35
1989-90—Central Red Army		USSR	48	19	10	29	20

(c)—June, 1989—Selected by Detroit Red Wings in 1989 NHL entry draft. Fourth Red Wings pick, 74th overall, fourth round.

BRENT FEDYK

Right Wing . . . 6' . . . 180 lbs. . . . Born, Yorkton, Sask., March 8, 1967 . . . Shoots right . . . (Septmeber, 1985)—Strained hip in Detroit training camp and missed three weeks of WHL season.

Year	Team	League	Games	G.	A.	Pts.	Pen.
1982-83—Regina Pats		WHL	1	0	0	0	0
1983-84—Regina Pats		WHL	63	15	28	43	30
1984-85—Regina Pats (c)		WHL	66	35	35	70	48
1985-86—Regina Pats (b)		WHL	50	43	34	77	47
1986-87—Regina Pats (d)		WHL	12	9	6	15	9
1986-87—Seattle Thunderbirds (e)		WHL	13	5	11	16	9
1986-87—Portland Winter Hawks		WHL	11	5	4	9	6
1987-88—Detroit Red Wings		NHL	2	0	1	1	2
1987-88—Adirondack Red Wings		AHL	34	9	11	20	22
1988-89—Detroit Red Wings		NHL	5	2	0	2	0
1988-89—Adirondack Red Wings		AHL	66	40	28	68	33
1989-90—Detroit Red Wings		NHL	27	1	4	5	6
1989-90—Adirondack Red Wings		AHL	33	14	15	29	24
NHL TOTALS			34	3	5	8	8

(c)—June, 1985—Drafted as underage junior by Detroit Red Wings in 1985 NHL entry draft. First Red Wings pick, eighth overall, first round.

(d)—November, 1986—Traded with Ken MacIntyre, Grant Kazuik, Gerald Bzdel and the WHL rights to Kevin Kowalchuk by Regina Pats to Seattle Thunderbirds for Craig Endean, Ray Savard, Grant Chorney, Chris Ginnell and WHL rights to Frank Kovacs.

(e)—February, 1987—Traded by Seattle Thunderbirds to Portland Winter Hawks for future considerations.

CHRIS FELIX

Defense . . . 5'11" . . . 185 lbs. . . . Born, Bramalea, Ont., May 27, 1964 . . . Shoots right.

Year	Team	League	Games	G.	A.	Pts.	Pen.
1982-83—Sault Ste. Marie Greyhounds		OHL	68	16	57	73	39
1983-84—Sault Ste. Marie Greyhounds		OHL	70	32	61	93	75
1984-85—Sault Ste. Marie Greyhounds		OHL	66	29	72	101	89

Year	Team	League	Games	G.	A.	Pts.	Pen.
1985-86	Canadian National Team	Int'l	73	7	33	40	33
1986-87	Canadian National Team (c)	Int'l	78	14	38	52	36
1987-88	Canadian Olympic Team	Int'l	68	7	27	34	68
1987-88	Fort Wayne Komets	IHL	19	5	17	22	24
1988-89	Baltimore Skipjacks	AHL	50	8	29	37	44
1988-89	Washington Capitals	NHL	21	0	8	8	8
1989-90	Baltimore Skipjacks	AHL	73	19	42	61	115
1989-90	Washington Capitals	NHL	6	1	0	1	2
	NHL TOTALS		27	1	8	9	10

(c)—March, 1987—Signed by Washington Capitals as a free agent.

DENNY FELSNER

Left Wing . . . 6' . . . 180 lbs. . . . Born, Warren, Mich., April 29, 1970 . . . Shoots left . . . (December 29, 1989)—Injured knee vs. Northern Michigan.

Year	Team	League	Games	G.	A.	Pts.	Pen.
1986-87	Detroit Falcons	NAJHL	37	22	33	55	18
1987-88	Detroit Junior Wings	NAJHL	39	35	43	78	46
1988-89	Univ. of Michigan (c-d)	CCHA	39	30	19	49	22
1989-90	Univ. of Michigan	CCHA	33	27	16	43	24

(c)—Named to CCHA All-Rookie team.
(d)—June, 1989—Drafted by St. Louis Blues in 1989 NHL entry draft. Third Blues pick, 55th overall, third round.

PAUL FENTON

Center . . . 5'11" . . . 180 lbs. . . . Born, Springfield, Mass., December 22, 1959 . . . Shoots left.

Year	Team	League	Games	G.	A.	Pts.	Pen.
1979-80	Boston University	ECAC	28	12	21	33	18
1980-81	Boston University	ECAC	7	4	4	8	0
1981-82	Boston University	ECAC	28	20	13	33	28
1982-83	Peoria Prancers (b-c)	IHL	82	60	51	111	53
1982-83	Colorado Flames	CHL	1	0	1	1	0
1983-84	Binghamton Whalers (d)	AHL	78	41	24	65	67
1984-85	Binghamton Whalers	AHL	45	26	21	47	18
1984-85	Hartford Whalers	NHL	33	7	5	12	10
1985-86	Hartford Whalers	NHL	1	0	0	0	0
1985-86	Binghamton Whalers (a-e)	AHL	75	53	35	88	87
1986-87	New York Rangers (f)	NHL	8	0	0	0	2
1986-87	New Haven Nighthawks (b)	AHL	70	37	38	75	45
1987-88	New Haven Nighthawks	AHL	5	11	5	16	9
1987-88	Los Angeles Kings (g)	NHL	71	20	23	43	46
1988-89	Los Angeles Kings (h)	NHL	21	2	3	5	6
1988-89	Winnipeg Jets	NHL	59	14	9	23	33
1989-90	Winnipeg Jets	NHL	80	32	18	50	40
	NHL TOTALS		273	75	58	133	137

(c)—Won Ken McKenzie Trophy (Top U.S. born IHL Rookie).
(d)—October, 1983—Signed by Hartford Whalers as a free agent.
(e)—July, 1986—Released by Hartford Whalers.
(f)—September, 1986—Signed by New York Rangers as a free agent.
(g)—October, 1987—Acquired by Los Angeles Kings on waivers from New York Rangers.
(h)—November 25, 1988—Traded by Los Angeles Kings to Winnipeg Jets for Gilles Hamel.

DAVE ALAN FENYVES

Defense . . . 5'10" . . . 188 lbs. . . . Born, Dunnville, Ont., April 29, 1960 . . . Shoots left . . . (October, 1977)—Separated shoulder.

Year	Team	League	Games	G.	A.	Pts.	Pen.
1977-78	Peterborough Petes	OMJHL	59	3	12	15	36
1978-79	Peterborough Petes	OMJHL	66	2	23	25	122
1979-80	Peterborough Petes (c)	OMJHL	66	9	36	45	92
1980-81	Rochester Americans	AHL	77	6	16	22	146
1981-82	Rochester Americans	AHL	73	3	14	17	68
1982-83	Rochester Americans	AHL	51	2	19	21	45
1982-83	Buffalo Sabres	NHL	24	0	8	8	14
1983-84	Buffalo Sabres	NHL	10	0	4	4	9
1983-84	Rochester Americans	AHL	70	3	16	19	55
1984-85	Rochester Americans	AHL	9	0	3	3	8
1984-85	Buffalo Sabres	NHL	60	1	8	9	27
1985-86	Buffalo Sabres	NHL	47	0	7	7	37
1986-87	Rochester Americans (b-d)	AHL	71	6	16	22	57
1986-87	Buffalo Sabres	NHL	7	1	0	1	0
1987-88	Philadelphia Flyers (e)	NHL	5	0	0	0	0
1987-88	Hershey Bears	AHL	75	11	40	51	47
1988-89	Philadelphia Flyers	NHL	1	0	1	1	0
1988-89	Hershey Bears (a-f)	AHL	79	15	51	66	41
1989-90	Philadelphia Flyers	NHL	12	0	0	0	4
1989-90	Hershey Bears	AHL	66	6	37	43	57
	NHL TOTALS		166	2	28	30	91

(c)—October, 1979—Signed by Buffalo Sabres as a free agent.
(d)—Won Jack Butterfield Trophy (AHL Playoff MVP).
(e)—October, 1987—Selected by Philadelphia Flyers during 1988 NHL waiver draft as compensation for Buffalo Sabres drafting of Ed Hospodar.
(f)—Won Eddie Shore Plaque (Top AHL Defenseman).

TOM JOSEPH FERGUS

Center . . . 6' . . . 176 lbs. . . . Born, Chicago, Ill., June 16, 1962 . . . Shoots left . . . (January 20, 1982)—Tore ligaments in left knee at Pittsburgh . . . (February, 1984)—Damaged knee ligaments . . . (March, 1987)—Missed 23 games with a viral infection . . . (November, 1987)—Pulled groin . . . (March, 1988)—Bruised ribs . . . (February 6, 1990)—Pulled groin and stomach muscle at St. Louis.

Year	Team	League	Games	G.	A.	Pts.	Pen.
1979-80	Peterborough Petes (c)	OMJHL	63	8	6	14	14
1980-81	Peterborough Petes	OMJHL	63	43	45	88	33
1981-82	Boston Bruins	NHL	61	15	24	39	12
1982-83	Boston Bruins	NHL	80	28	35	63	39
1983-84	Boston Bruins	NHL	69	25	36	61	12
1984-85	Boston Bruins	NHL	79	30	43	73	75
1985-86	Toronto Maple Leafs (d)	NHL	78	31	42	73	64
1986-87	Newmarket Saints	AHL	1	0	1	1	0
1986-87	Toronto Maple Leafs	NHL	57	21	28	49	57
1987-88	Toronto Maple Leafs	NHL	63	19	31	50	81
1988-89	Toronto Maple Leafs	NHL	80	22	45	67	48
1989-90	Toronto Maple Leafs	NHL	54	19	26	45	62
	NHL TOTALS		621	210	310	520	450

(c)—June, 1980—Drafted as underage junior by Boston Bruins in 1980 NHL entry draft. Second Bruins pick, 60th overall, third round.
(d)—September, 1985—Traded by Boston Bruins to Toronto Maple Leafs for Bill Derlago.

JOHN FERGUSON JR.

Left Wing . . . 6' . . . 175 lbs. . . . Born, Winnipeg, Man., July 7, 1967 . . . Shoots left . . . Son of John Ferguson (Former NHL player with Montreal and former G.M. of New York Rangers and Winnipeg Jets).

Year	Team	League	Games	G.	A.	Pts.	Pen.
1984-85	Winnipeg South Blues (c)	MJHL	..	..	..	..	..
1985-86	Providence College	H. East	18	1	2	3	2
1986-87	Providence College	H. East	23	0	0	0	6
1987-88	Providence College	H. East	34	0	5	5	31
1988-89	Providence College	H. East	40	14	15	29	66
1989-90	Sherbrooke Canadiens	AHL	17	4	3	7	8
1989-90	Peoria Rivermen	IHL	18	1	8	9	14

(c)—June, 1985—Drafted by Montreal Canadiens in 1985 NHL entry draft. Fifteenth Canadiens pick, 247th overall, 12th round.

MARK FERNER

Defense . . . 6' . . . 170 lbs. . . . Born, Regina, Sask., September 5, 1965 . . . Shoots left . . . (March, 1986)—Broken foot.

Year	Team	League	Games	G.	A.	Pts.	Pen.
1982-83	Kamloops Junior Oilers (c)	WHL	69	6	15	21	81
1983-84	Kamloops Junior Oilers	WHL	72	9	30	39	162
1984-85	Kamloops Blazers (a)	WHL	69	15	39	54	91
1985-86	Rochester Americans	AHL	63	3	14	17	87
1986-87	Buffalo Sabres	NHL	13	0	3	3	9
1986-87	Rochester Americans	AHL	54	0	12	12	157
1987-88	Rochester Americans	AHL	69	1	25	26	165
1988-89	Buffalo Sabres	NHL	2	0	0	0	2
1988-89	Rochester Americans	AHL	55	0	18	18	97
1989-90	Washington Capitals	NHL	2	0	0	0	0
1989-90	Baltimore Skipjacks	AHL	74	7	28	35	76
	NHL TOTALS		17	0	3	3	11

(c)—June, 1983—Drafted as underage junior by Buffalo Sabres in 1983 NHL entry draft. Twelfth Sabres pick, 194th overall, 10th round.

RAY FERRARO

Center . . . 5'10" . . . 180 lbs. . . . Born, Trail, B.C., August 23, 1964 . . . Shoots left . . . (1983-84) Set WHL record for most goals in a season (108), most power-play goals (43) and most three-goal games (15).

Year	Team	League	Games	G.	A.	Pts.	Pen.
1981-82	Penticton (c)	BCJHL	48	65	70	135	50
1982-83	Portland Winter Hawks	WHL	50	41	49	90	39
1983-84	Brandon Wheat Kings (a-d-e-f)	WHL	72	*108	84	*192	84
1984-85	Binghamton Whalers	AHL	37	20	13	33	29
1984-85	Hartford Whalers	NHL	44	11	17	28	40
1985-86	Hartford Whalers	NHL	76	30	47	77	57
1986-87	Hartford Whalers	NHL	80	27	32	59	42
1987-88	Hartford Whalers	NHL	68	21	29	50	81
1988-89	Hartford Whalers	NHL	80	41	35	76	86
1989-90	Hartford Whalers	NHL	79	25	29	54	109
	NHL TOTALS		427	155	189	344	415

(c)—June, 1982—Drafted as underage junior by Hartford Whalers in 1982 NHL entry draft. Fifth Whalers pick, 88th overall, fifth round.
(d)—Named WHL's Most Valuable Player.
(e)—Won Bob Brownridge Memorial Trophy (Top WHL Scorer).
(f)—WHL's Molson Player of the Year.

BRIAN P. FERREIRA

Right Wing . . . 6' . . . 180 lbs. . . . Born, Falmouth, Mass., February 1, 1968 . . . Shoots right . . . Also plays Center and Defense . . . (January, 1989)—Knee surgery.

Year	Team	League	Games	G.	A.	Pts.	Pen.
1984-85	Falmouth H.S.	Mass.	24	31	32	63	....
1985-86	Falmouth H.S. (c)	Mass.	22	37	43	80	12
1986-87	R.P.I.	ECAC	30	19	17	36	24
1987-88	R.P.I.	ECAC	32	18	19	37	48
1988-89	R.P.I.	ECAC	15	3	13	16	28
1989-90	R.P.I.	ECAC	34	10	35	45	36

(c)—June, 1986—Drafted by Boston Bruins in 1986 NHL entry draft. Seventh Bruins pick, 160th overall, eighth round.

VIACHESLAV FETISOV

Defense . . . 6'1" . . . 200 lbs. . . . Born, Moscow, U.S.S.R., May 20, 1958 . . . Shoots left . . . Two-time winner of the Soviet Player of the Year Award (1982, 1986) . . . Winner of the 1984 Gold Stick Award as Europe's top player . . . (November 22,

1989)—Torn cartilage in left knee when checked by John Cullen in Pittsburgh and missed six games.

Year	Team	League	Games	G.	A.	Pts.	Pen.
1976-77	Central Red Army	USSR	28	3	4	7	14
1977-78	Central Red Army (c)	USSR	35	9	18	27	46
1978-79	Central Red Army	USSR	29	10	19	29	40
1979-80	Central Red Army	USSR	37	10	14	24	46
1980-81	Central Red Army	USSR	48	13	16	29	44
1981-82	Central Red Army	USSR	46	15	26	41	20
1982-83	Central Red Army	USSR	43	6	17	23	46
1983-84	Central Red Army (d)	USSR	44	19	30	49	38
1984-85	Central Red Army	USSR	20	13	12	25	6
1985-86	Central Red Army	USSR	40	15	19	34	12
1986-87	Central Red Army	USSR	39	13	20	33	18
1987-88	Central Red Army	USSR	46	18	17	35	26
1988-89	Central Red Army	USSR	23	9	8	17	18
1989-90	New Jersey Devils	NHL	72	8	34	42	52
NHL TOTALS			72	8	34	42	52

(c)—June, 1978—Drafted by Montreal Canadiens in 1978 NHL amateur draft. Fourteenth Canadiens pick, 201st overall, 12th round.

(d)—June, 1983—Drafted by New Jersey Devils in 1983 NHL entry draft. Sixth Devils pick, 150th overall, eighth round.

JEFF FINLEY

Defense . . . 6'2" . . . 185 lbs. . . . Born, Edmonton, Alta., April 14, 1967 . . . Shoots left . . . (September, 1988)—Swollen left knee during N.Y. Islanders training camp.

Year	Team	League	Games	G.	A.	Pts.	Pen.
1983-84	Portland Winter Hawks	WHL	5	0	0	0	0
1983-84	Summarland Buckeroos	BCJHL	49	0	21	21	14
1984-85	Portland Winter Hawks (c)	WHL	69	6	44	50	57
1985-86	Portland Winter Hawks	WHL	70	11	59	70	83
1986-87	Portland Winter Hawks	WHL	72	13	53	66	113
1987-88	Springfield Indians	AHL	52	5	18	23	50
1987-88	New York Islanders	NHL	10	0	5	5	15
1988-89	New York Islanders	NHL	4	0	0	0	6
1988-89	Springfield Indians	AHL	65	3	16	19	55
1989-90	New York Islanders	NHL	11	0	1	1	0
1989-90	Springfield Indians	AHL	57	1	15	16	41
NHL TOTALS			25	0	6	6	21

(c)—June, 1985—Drafted as underage junior by New York Islanders in 1985 NHL entry draft. Fourth Islanders pick, 55th overall, third round.

STEVEN FINN

Defense . . . 6' . . . 190 lbs. . . . Born, Laval, Que., August 20, 1966 . . . Shoots left . . . (January 31, 1990)—Separated left shoulder at Buffalo.

Year	Team	League	Games	G.	A.	Pts.	Pen.
1982-83	Laval Voisins	QMJHL	69	7	30	37	108
1983-84	Laval Voisins (c)	QMJHL	68	7	39	46	159
1984-85	Laval Voisins	QMJHL	61	20	33	53	169
1984-85	Fredericton Express	AHL	4	0	0	0	14
1985-86	Laval Titans	QMJHL	29	4	15	19	111
1985-86	Quebec Nordiques	NHL	17	0	1	1	28
1986-87	Fredericton Express	AHL	38	7	19	26	73
1986-87	Quebec Nordiques	NHL	36	2	5	7	40
1987-88	Quebec Nordiques	NHL	75	3	7	10	198
1988-89	Quebec Nordiques	NHL	77	2	6	8	235
1989-90	Quebec Nordiques	NHL	64	3	9	12	208
NHL TOTALS			269	10	28	38	709

(c)—June, 1984—Drafted as underage junior by Quebec Nordiques in 1984 NHL entry draft. Third Nordiques pick, 57th overall, third round.

PETER FIORENTINO

Defense . . . 6'1" . . . 200 lbs. . . . Born, Niagara Falls, Ont., December 22, 1968 . . . Shoots right.

Year	Team	League	Games	G.	A.	Pts.	Pen.
1984-85	Niagara Falls Junior 'B'	OHA	38	7	10	17	149
1985-86	Sault Ste. Marie Greyhounds	OHL	58	1	6	7	87
1986-87	Sault Ste. Marie Greyhounds	OHL	64	1	12	13	187
1987-88	Sault Ste. Marie Greyhounds (c)	OHL	65	5	27	32	252
1988-89	Sault Ste. Marie Greyhounds	OHL	55	5	24	29	220
1988-89	Denver Rangers	IHL	10	0	0	0	39
1989-90	Flint Spirits	IHL	64	2	7	9	302

(c)—June, 1988—Drafted by New York Rangers in 1988 NHL entry draft. Eleventh Rangers pick, 215th overall, 11th round.

CRAIG FISHER

Center . . . 6'1" . . . 170 lbs. . . . Born, Oshawa, Ont., June 30, 1970 . . . Shoots left . . . (October, 1987)—Concussion . . . (December 10, 1988)—Had a Miami school record 17-game point streak stopped at Ohio State.

Year	Team	League	Games	G.	A.	Pts.	Pen.
1986-87	Oshawa Legionaires Jr. B	OHA	34	22	26	48	18
1987-88	Oshawa Legionaires Jr. B (c)	OHA	36	42	34	76	48
1988-89	Miami of Ohio Univ. (d)	CCHA	37	22	20	42	37
1989-90	Miami of Ohio Univ. (a)	CCHA	39	37	29	66	38
1989-90	Philadelphia Flyers	NHL	2	0	0	0	0
NHL TOTALS			2	0	0	0	0

(c)—June, 1988—Drafted by Philadelphia Flyers in 1988 NHL entry draft. Third Flyers pick, 56th overall, third round.

(d)—Named to CCHA All-Rookie team.

THOMAS FITZGERALD

Center . . . 6'1" . . . 190 lbs. . . . Born, Melrose, Mass., August 28, 1968 . . . Shoots right . . . Also plays Right Wing.

Year	Team	League	Games	G.	A.	Pts.	Pen.
1984-85	Austin Prep.	Mass. H.S.	18	20	21	41	....
1985-86	Austin Prep. (c)	Mass. H.S.	24	35	38	73	....
1986-87	Providence College	H. East	15	2	0	2	2
1987-88	Providence College	H. East	36	19	15	34	50
1988-89	Springfield Indians	AHL	61	24	18	42	43
1988-89	New York Islanders	NHL	23	3	5	8	10
1989-90	Springfield Indians	AHL	53	30	23	53	32
1989-90	New York Islanders	NHL	19	2	5	7	4
NHL TOTALS			42	5	10	15	14

(c)—June, 1986—Drafted by New York Islanders in 1986 NHL entry draft. First Islanders pick, 17th overall, first round.

ROSS FITZPATRICK

Center . . . 6' . . . 195 lbs. . . . Born, Penticton, B.C., October 7, 1960 . . . Shoots left . . . (December, 1982)—Broke hand vs. Hershey . . . (January 10, 1985)—Surgery for shoulder separated vs. Sherbrooke . . . (January, 1987)—Knee surgery . . . (February 25, 1990)—Chip fracture of ankle bone when struck by a Ken Hammond shot vs. Newmarket and missed six games.

Year	Team	League	Games	G.	A.	Pts.	Pen.
1978-79	Univ. of Western Michigan	CCHA	35	16	21	37	31
1979-80	Univ. of Western Michigan (c)	CCHA	34	26	33	59	22
1980-81	Univ. of Western Michigan (a)	CCHA	36	28	43	71	22
1981-82	Univ. of Western Michigan	CCHA	33	30	28	58	34
1982-83	Maine Mariners	AHL	66	29	28	57	32
1982-83	Philadelphia Flyers	NHL	1	0	0	0	0
1983-84	Springfield Indians	AHL	45	33	30	63	28
1983-84	Philadelphia Flyers	NHL	12	4	2	6	0
1984-85	Hershey Bears	AHL	35	26	15	41	8
1984-85	Philadelphia Flyers	NHL	5	1	0	1	0
1985-86	Philadelphia Flyers	NHL	2	0	0	0	0
1985-86	Hershey Bears (b)	AHL	77	50	47	97	28
1986-87	Hershey Bears	AHL	66	45	40	85	34
1987-88	Hershey Bears	AHL	35	14	17	31	12
1988-89	Vienna	Austria	..	..	..	..	..
1988-89	Hershey Bears	AHL	11	6	9	15	4
1989-90	Hershey Bears (b-d)	AHL	74	45	*58	103	26
NHL TOTALS			20	5	2	7	0

(c)—June, 1980—Selected by Philadelphia Flyers in 1980 NHL entry draft. Seventh Flyers pick, 147th overall, seventh round.

(d)—August, 1990—Signed by New York Rangers as a free agent.

PATRICK FLATLEY

Right Wing . . . 6'3" . . . 200 lbs. . . . Born, Toronto, Ont., October 3, 1963 . . . Shoots right . . . Member of 1984 Canadian Olympic hockey team . . . (April, 1985)—Broke bone in left hand during playoff series with Washington . . . (February 4, 1987)—Strained left knee ligaments at Vancouver . . . (November, 1987)—Separated right shoulder . . . (January, 1988)—Injured right knee . . . (February, 1988)—Reconstructive knee surgery . . . (December, 1988)—Injured right knee . . . (February, 1989)—Sore right ankle . . . (March, 1989)—Reinjured right knee . . . (October, 1989)—Bruised right ankle . . . (February 13, 1990)—Pulled groin muscle . . . (March 2, 1990)—Reinjured groin at N.Y. Rangers and missed six games.

Year	Team	League	Games	G.	A.	Pts.	Pen.
1980-81	Henry Carr H.S.	Ont. Tier II	42	30	61	91	122
1981-82	University of Wisconsin (c)	WCHA	33	17	20	37	65
1982-83	University of Wisconsin (a-d)	WCHA	43	25	44	69	76
1983-84	Canadian Olympic Team	Int'l	57	33	17	50	136
1983-84	New York Islanders	NHL	16	2	7	9	6
1984-85	New York Islanders	NHL	78	20	31	51	106
1985-86	New York Islanders	NHL	73	18	34	52	66
1986-87	New York Islanders	NHL	63	16	35	51	81
1987-88	New York Islanders	NHL	40	9	15	24	28
1988-89	New York Islanders	NHL	41	10	15	25	31
1988-89	Springfield Indians	AHL	2	1	1	2	2
1989-90	New York Islanders	NHL	62	17	32	49	101
NHL TOTALS			373	92	169	261	419

(c)—June, 1982—Drafted as underage player by New York Islanders in 1982 NHL entry draft. First Islanders pick, 21st overall, first round.

(d)—Named to All-America Team (West).

STEVEN FLETCHER

Defense . . . 6'2" . . . 180 lbs. . . . Born, Montreal, Que., March 31, 1962 . . . Shoots left.

Year	Team	League	Games	G.	A.	Pts.	Pen.
1979-80	Hull Olympiques (c)	QMJHL	61	2	14	16	183
1980-81	Hull Olympiques	QMJHL	66	4	13	17	231
1981-82	Hull Olympiques	QMJHL	60	4	20	24	230
1982-83	Fort Wayne Komets	IHL	34	1	9	10	115
1982-83	Sherbrooke Jets	AHL	36	0	1	1	119
1983-84	Sherbrooke Jets	AHL	77	3	7	10	208
1984-85	Sherbrooke Canadiens	AHL	50	2	4	6	192
1985-86	Sherbrooke Canadiens	AHL	64	2	12	14	293
1986-87	Sherbrooke Canadiens	AHL	70	15	11	26	261
1987-88	Sherbrooke Canadiens	AHL	76	8	21	29	138
1988-89	Hershey Bears	AHL	29	5	8	13	91
1988-89	Moncton Hawks	AHL	23	1	1	2	89

Year	Team	League	Games	G.	A.	Pts.	Pen.
1988-89—Winnipeg Jets (d)		NHL	3	0	0	0	5
1989-90—Hershey Bears		AHL	28	1	1	2	132
NHL TOTALS			3	0	0	0	5

(c)—June, 1980—Drafted as underage junior by Calgary Flames in 1980 NHL entry draft. Eleventh Flames pick, 202nd overall, 10th round.

(d)—July 15, 1988—Signed by Winnipeg Jets as a free agent.

THEOREN FLEURY

Center ... 5'6" ... 155 lbs. ... Born, Oxbow, Sask., June 29, 1968 ... Shoots right.

Year	Team	League	Games	G.	A.	Pts.	Pen.
1983-84—St. James Canadians		Wpg. Midget	22	33	31	64	88
1984-85—Moose Jaw Warriors		WHL	71	29	46	75	82
1985-86—Moose Jaw Warriors		WHL	72	43	65	108	124
1986-87—Moose Jaw Warriors (a-c)		WHL	66	61	68	129	110
1987-88—Moose Jaw Warriors (b)		WHL	65	68	92	*160	235
1987-88—Salt Lake Golden Eagles		IHL	2	3	4	7	7
1988-89—Salt Lake Golden Eagles		IHL	40	37	37	74	81
1988-89—Calgary Flames		NHL	36	14	20	34	46
1989-90—Calgary Flames		NHL	80	31	35	66	157
NHL TOTALS			116	45	55	100	203

(c)—June, 1987—Drafted by Calgary Flames in 1987 NHL entry draft. Ninth Flames pick, 166th overall, eighth round.

TODD FLICHEL

Defense ... 6'3" ... 195 lbs. ... Born, Osgoode, Ont., September 14, 1964 ... Shoots right.

Year	Team	League	Games	G.	A.	Pts.	Pen.
1983-84—Bowling Green Univ. (c)		CCHA	44	1	3	4	12
1984-85—Bowling Green Univ.		CCHA	42	5	7	12	62
1985-86—Bowling Green Univ.		CCHA	42	3	10	13	84
1986-87—Bowling Green Univ.		CCHA	42	4	15	19	75
1987-88—Winnipeg Jets		NHL	2	0	0	0	14
1987-88—Moncton Golden Flames		AHL	65	5	12	17	102
1988-89—Moncton Hawks		AHL	74	2	29	31	81
1988-89—Winnipeg Jets		NHL	1	0	0	0	0
1989-90—Winnipeg Jets		NHL	3	0	1	1	2
1989-90—Moncton Hawks		AHL	65	7	14	21	74
NHL TOTALS			6	0	1	1	16

(c)—June, 1983—Drafted by Winnipeg Jets in 1983 NHL entry draft. Tenth Jets pick, 169th overall, ninth round.

LARRY FLOYD

Center ... 5'8" ... 180 lbs. ... Born, Peterborough, Ont., May 1, 1961 ... Shoots left.

Year	Team	League	Games	G.	A.	Pts.	Pen.
1979-80—Peterborough Petes		OMJHL	66	21	37	58	54
1980-81—Peterborough Petes		OHL	44	26	37	63	43
1981-82—Peterborough Petes		OHL	39	32	37	69	26
1981-82—Rochester Americans		AHL	1	0	2	2	0
1982-83—New Jersey Devils (c)		NHL	5	1	0	1	2
1982-83—Wichita Wind (d)		CHL	75	40	43	83	16
1983-84—New Jersey Devils		NHL	7	1	3	4	7
1983-84—Maine Mariners		AHL	69	37	49	86	40
1984-85—Maine Mariners		AHL	72	30	51	81	24
1985-86—Maine Mariners		AHL	80	29	58	87	25
1986-87—Maine Mariners		AHL	77	30	44	74	50
1987-88—Played in Austria			..	..	..	..	..
1987-88—Utica Devils		AHL	28	21	21	42	14
1988-89—Cape Breton Oilers		AHL	70	16	33	49	40
1989-90—Phoenix Roadrunners		IHL	76	39	40	79	50
NHL TOTALS			12	2	3	5	9

(c)—September, 1982—Signed by New Jersey Devils as a free agent.

(d)—Won Ken McKenzie Trophy (Top CHL Rookie).

BRYAN FOGARTY

Defense ... 6'1" ... 190 lbs. ... Born, Montreal, Que., June 11, 1969 ... Shoots left ... (1988-89)—Set junior hockey records for goals, assists and points by a defenseman ... (September, 1989)—Appendectomy during Quebec training camp.

Year	Team	League	Games	G.	A.	Pts.	Pen.
1984-85—Aurora Tigers Jr. A		OHA	66	18	39	57	180
1985-86—Kingston Canadians		OHL	47	2	19	21	14
1986-87—Kingston Canadians (a-c)		OHL	56	20	50	70	46
1987-88—Kingston Canadians		OHL	48	11	36	47	50
1988-89—Niag. Falls Thunder (a-d-e-f-g-h)		OHL	60	47	*108	*155	88
1989-90—Quebec Nordiques		NHL	45	4	10	14	31
1989-90—Halifax Citadels		AHL	22	5	14	19	6
NHL TOTALS			45	4	10	14	31

(c)—June, 1987—Drafted as an underage junior by Quebec Nordiques in 1987 NHL entry draft. First Nordiques pick, ninth overall, first round.

(d)—August, 1988—Traded by Kingston Haiders to Niagara Falls Thunder for Garth Joy, Jason Simon, Kevin Lune and a fourth-round 1989 draft pick.

(e)—Won Red Tilson Trophy (Outstanding OHL Player).

(f)—Won Eddie Powers Memorial Trophy (Leading OHL Scorer).

(g)—Won Max Kaminsky Trophy (Outstanding OHL Defenseman).

(h)—Named outstanding Canadian Major Junior Defenseman of the Year and Outstanding Canadian Major Junior Player of the Year. He also led all junior players in Canada with a +91.

MIKE ANTHONY FOLIGNO

Right Wing ... 6'2" ... 190 lbs. ... Born, Sudbury, Ont., January 29, 1959 ... Shoots right ... (December 27, 1980)—Set Detroit record for most penalty minutes in one game (37 vs. Philadelphia) ... (October 31, 1982)—Injured tailbone vs. Montreal ... (February 12, 1983)—Injured shoulder at Calgary ... (December 7, 1986)—Bruised kidney when he struck a goal post at New Jersey ... (February, 1988)—Back spasms ... (January 14, 1989)—Pulled rib cartilage at Quebec ... (February 18, 1990)—Fractured left thumb when he struck Scott Young vs. Hartford.

Year	Team	League	Games	G.	A.	Pts.	Pen.
1975-76—Sudbury Wolves		OMJHL	57	22	14	36	45
1976-77—Sudbury Wolves		OMJHL	66	31	44	75	62
1977-78—Sudbury Wolves		OMJHL	67	47	39	86	112
1978-79—Sudbury Wolves (a-c-d-e-f)		OMJHL	68	65	85	*150	98
1979-80—Detroit Red Wings		NHL	80	36	35	71	109
1980-81—Detroit Red Wings		NHL	80	28	35	63	210
1981-82—Detroit Red Wings (g)		NHL	26	13	13	26	28
1981-82—Buffalo Sabres		NHL	56	20	31	51	149
1982-83—Buffalo Sabres		NHL	66	22	25	47	135
1983-84—Buffalo Sabres		NHL	70	32	31	63	151
1984-85—Buffalo Sabres		NHL	77	27	29	56	154
1985-86—Buffalo Sabres		NHL	79	41	39	80	168
1986-87—Buffalo Sabres		NHL	75	30	29	59	176
1987-88—Buffalo Sabres		NHL	74	29	28	57	220
1988-89—Buffalo Sabres		NHL	75	27	22	49	156
1989-90—Buffalo Sabres		NHL	61	15	25	40	99
NHL TOTALS			819	320	342	662	1755

(c)—Won Red Tilson Memorial Trophy (OMJHL-MVP).

(d)—Won Eddie Powers Memorial Trophy (OMJHL Leading Scorer).

(e)—Won Jim Mahon Memorial Trophy (OMJHL Top Scoring Right Wing).

(f)—August, 1979—Drafted by Detroit Red Wings in 1979 NHL entry draft. First Red Wings pick, third overall, first round.

(g)—December, 1981—Traded with Dale McCourt, Brent Peterson and future considerations by Detroit Red Wings to Buffalo Sabres for Bob Sauve, Jim Schoenfeld and Derek Smith.

ADAM FOOTE

Defense ... 6'1" ... 180 lbs. ... Born, Toronto, Ont., July 10, 1971 ... Shoots right.

Year	Team	League	Games	G.	A.	Pts.	Pen.
1987-88—Whitby Midgets		OMHA	65	25	43	68	108
1988-89—Sault Ste. Marie Greyhounds (c)		OHL	66	7	32	39	120
1989-90—Sault Ste. Marie Greyhounds		OHL	61	12	43	55	199

(c)—June, 1989—Drafted by Quebec Nordiques in 1989 NHL entry draft. Second Nordiques pick, 22nd overall, second round.

MARC FORTIER

Center ... 6' ... 190 lbs. ... Born, Sherbrooke, Que., February 26, 1966 ... Shoots right.

Year	Team	League	Games	G.	A.	Pts.	Pen.
1984-85—Chicoutimi Sagueneens		QMJHL	68	35	63	98	114
1985-86—Chicoutimi Sagueneens		QMJHL	71	47	86	133	49
1986-87—Chicoutimi Sagueneens (a-c)		QMJHL	65	66	*135	*201	39
1987-88—Quebec Nordiques		NHL	27	4	10	14	12
1987-88—Fredericton Express		AHL	50	26	36	62	48
1988-89—Quebec Nordiques		NHL	57	20	19	39	45
1988-89—Halifax Citadels		AHL	16	11	11	22	14
1989-90—Halifax Citadels		AHL	15	5	6	11	6
1989-90—Quebec Nordiques		NHL	59	13	17	30	28
NHL TOTALS			143	37	46	83	85

(c)—February, 1987—Signed by Quebec Nordiques as a free agent.

COREY FOSTER

Defense ... 6'3" ... 200 lbs. ... Born, Ottawa, Ont., October 27, 1969 ... Shoots left.

Year	Team	League	Games	G.	A.	Pts.	Pen.
1985-86—Ottawa West Minor Midget		OHA	37	15	35	50	30
1986-87—Peterborough Petes		OHL	30	3	4	7	4
1987-88—Peterborough Petes (c)		OHL	66	13	31	44	58
1988-89—Peterborough Petes		OHL	55	14	42	56	42
1988-89—New Jersey Devils (d)		NHL	2	0	0	0	0
1989-90—Cape Breton Oilers		AHL	54	7	17	24	32
NHL TOTALS			2	0	0	0	0

(c)—June, 1988—Drafted by New Jersey Devils in 1988 NHL entry draft. First Devils pick, 12th overall, first round.

(d)—June 17, 1989—Traded by New Jersey Devils to Edmonton Oilers for a first-round 1989 draft pick (Jason Miller).

JAMES CHARLES FOX

Right Wing ... 5'8" ... 183 lbs. ... Born, Coniston, Ont., May 18, 1960 ... Shoots right ... (November 6, 1985)—Injured disc at Los Angeles and missed 24 games ... (January 29, 1986)—Bruised hip vs. Minnesota ... (March 10, 1988)—Injured right knee at Boston ... (September, 1988)—Knee surgery and out for the year.

Year	Team	League	Games	G.	A.	Pts.	Pen.
1975-76—North Bay Trappers		OPJHL	44	30	45	75	16
1976-77—North Bay Trappers (c)		OPJHL	38	44	64	*108	4
1977-78—Ottawa 67's		OMJHL	59	44	83	127	12
1978-79—Ottawa 67's		OMJHL	53	37	66	103	4
1979-80—Ottawa 67's (d-e-f-g)		OMJHL	52	65	*101	*166	30
1980-81—Los Angeles Kings		NHL	71	18	25	43	8
1981-82—Los Angeles Kings		NHL	77	30	38	68	23
1982-83—Los Angeles Kings		NHL	77	28	40	68	8

Year	Team	League	Games	G.	A.	Pts.	Pen.
1983-84—Los Angeles Kings		NHL	80	30	42	72	26
1984-85—Los Angeles Kings		NHL	79	30	53	83	10
1985-86—Los Angeles Kings		NHL	39	14	17	31	2
1986-87—Los Angeles Kings		NHL	76	19	42	61	48
1987-88—Los Angeles Kings		NHL	68	16	35	51	18
1988-89—Los Angeles Kings		NHL	....	...	...	...	...
1989-90—Los Angeles Kings (h)		NHL	11	1	1	2	0
NHL TOTALS			578	186	293	479	143

(c)—Led OPJHL Playoffs in points (38) and assists (25) in 19 games, and was co-leader (with teammate Jim Omiciolli) in goals (13).

(d)—Won Eddie Powers Memorial Trophy (OMJHL Leading Scorer).

(e)—Won Albert (Red) Tilson Memorial Trophy (OMJHL MVP).

(f)—Won Jim Mahon Memorial Trophy (Top Scoring OMJHL Right Wing).

(g)—June, 1980—Drafted by Los Angeles Kings in 1980 NHL entry draft. Second Kings pick, 10th overall, first round.

(h)—November 25, 1989—Announced his retirement.

LOU FRANCESCHETTI

Left Wing . . . 6' . . . 190 lbs. . . . Born, Toronto, Ont., March 28, 1958 . . . Shoots left . . . (March, 1988)—Bruised right leg.

Year	Team	League	Games	G.	A.	Pts.	Pen.
1975-76—St. Catharines Black Hawks		OMJHL	1	0	0	0	0
1976-77—Niagara Falls Flyers		OMJHL	61	23	30	53	80
1977-78—Niagara Falls Flyers (c)		OMJHL	62	40	50	90	46
1978-79—Saginaw Gears		IHL	2	1	1	2	0
1978-79—Port Huron Flags		IHL	76	45	58	103	131
1979-80—Port Huron Flags		IHL	15	3	8	11	31
1979-80—Hershey Bears		AHL	65	27	29	56	58
1980-81—Hershey Bears		AHL	79	32	36	68	173
1981-82—Washington Capitals		NHL	30	2	10	12	23
1981-82—Hershey Bears		AHL	50	22	33	55	89
1982-83—Hershey Bears		AHL	80	31	44	75	176
1983-84—Washington Capitals		NHL	2	0	0	0	0
1983-84—Hershey Bears		AHL	73	26	34	60	130
1984-85—Binghamton Whalers		AHL	52	29	43	72	75
1984-85—Washington Capitals		NHL	22	4	7	11	45
1985-86—Washington Capitals		NHL	76	7	14	21	131
1986-87—Washington Capitals		NHL	75	12	9	21	127
1987-88—Washington Capitals		NHL	59	4	8	12	113
1987-88—Binghamton Whalers		AHL	6	2	4	6	4
1988-89—Washington Capitals		NHL	63	7	10	17	123
1988-89—Baltimore Skipjacks (d)		AHL	10	8	7	15	30
1989-90—Toronto Maple Leafs		NHL	80	21	15	36	127
NHL TOTALS			407	57	73	130	689

(c)—June, 1978—Drafted by Washington Capitals in the 1978 NHL amateur draft. Seventh Capitals pick, 71st overall, fifth round.

(d)—July, 1989—Traded to Toronto Maple Leafs for future considerations.

RONALD FRANCIS

Center . . . 6'1" . . . 170 lbs. . . . Born, Sault Ste. Marie, Ont., March 1, 1963 . . . Shoots left . . . Cousin of Mike Liut . . . (January 27, 1982)—Out of lineup for three weeks with eye injury . . . (November 30, 1983)—Strained ligaments in right knee vs. Vancouver . . . (January 18, 1986)—Broke left ankle at Quebec and missed 27 games . . . (January 28, 1989)—Broke left index finger when slashed by Steven Finn vs. Quebec and missed 11 games.

Year	Team	League	Games	G.	A.	Pts.	Pen.
1979-80—Sault Ste. Marie Legion		OMHL	45	57	92	149	....
1980-81—Sault Ste. Marie Greyhounds (c)		OHL	64	26	43	69	33
1981-82—Sault Ste. Marie Greyhounds		OHL	25	18	30	48	46
1981-82—Hartford Whalers		NHL	59	25	43	68	51
1982-83—Hartford Whalers		NHL	79	31	59	90	60
1983-84—Hartford Whalers		NHL	72	23	60	83	45
1984-85—Hartford Whalers		NHL	80	24	57	81	66
1985-86—Hartford Whalers		NHL	53	24	53	77	24
1986-87—Hartford Whalers		NHL	75	30	63	93	45
1987-88—Hartford Whalers		NHL	80	25	50	75	89
1988-89—Hartford Whalers		NHL	69	29	48	77	36
1989-90—Hartford Whalers		NHL	80	32	69	101	73
NHL TOTALS			647	243	502	745	489

(c)—June, 1981—Drafted as underage junior by Hartford Whalers in 1981 NHL entry draft. First Whalers pick, fourth overall, first round.

DAVID FRANZOSA

Left Wing . . . 5'11" . . . 175 lbs. . . . Born, Reading, Mass., November 20, 1970 . . . Shoots left.

Year	Team	League	Games	G.	A.	Pts.	Pen.
1988-89—Boston College (c)		H. East	23	2	5	7	4
1989-90—Boston College		H. East	42	8	20	28	20

(c)—June, 1989—Drafted by Boston Bruins in 1989 NHL entry draft. Eleventh Bruins pick, 227th overall, 11th round.

CURT FRASER

Left Wing . . . 6' . . . 190 lbs. . . . Born, Cincinnati, Ohio, January 12, 1958 . . . Shoots left . . . (November, 1983)—Torn knee ligaments . . . (January 13, 1985)—Multiple fractures to face when struck by goalie stick of Billy Smith vs. N.Y. Islanders . . . (December 14, 1985)—Sprained ankle at Montreal and missed 19 games . . . (October, 1987)—Bruised ribs . . . (November, 1987)—Bacterial infection complicated by diabetes . . . (October, 1988)—Stretched rib cartilage . . . (January, 1989)—Injured wrist . . . (January 15, 1989)—Major reconstructive surgery to left

shoulder . . . (1989-90)—Missed most of season undergoing rehabilitation on shoulder.

Year	Team	League	Games	G.	A.	Pts.	Pen.
1973-74—Kelowna Buckaroos		Jr."A"BCHL	52	32	32	64	85
1974-75—Victoria Cougars		WCHL	68	17	32	49	105
1975-76—Victoria Cougars		WCHL	71	43	64	107	167
1976-77—Victoria Cougars		WCHL	60	34	41	75	82
1977-78—Victoria Cougars (c)		WCHL	66	48	44	92	256
1978-79—Vancouver Canucks		NHL	78	16	19	35	116
1979-80—Vancouver Canucks		NHL	78	17	25	42	143
1980-81—Vancouver Canucks		NHL	77	25	24	49	118
1981-82—Vancouver Canucks		NHL	79	28	39	67	175
1982-83—Vancouver Canucks (d)		NHL	36	6	7	13	99
1982-83—Chicago Black Hawks		NHL	38	6	13	19	77
1983-84—Chicago Black Hawks		NHL	29	5	12	17	26
1984-85—Chicago Black Hawks		NHL	73	25	25	50	109
1985-86—Chicago Black Hawks		NHL	61	29	39	68	84
1986-87—Chicago Black Hawks		NHL	75	25	25	50	182
1987-88—Chicago Black Hawks		NHL	27	4	6	10	57
1987-88—Minnesota North Stars (e)		NHL	10	1	1	2	20
1988-89—Minnesota North Stars		NHL	35	5	5	10	76
1989-90—Minnesota North Stars		NHL	8	1	0	1	22
NHL TOTALS			704	193	240	433	1304

(c)—Drafted from Victoria Cougars by Vancouver Canucks in second round of 1978 amateur draft.

(d)—January, 1983—Traded by Vancouver Canucks to Chicago Black Hawks for Tony Tanti.

(e)—January, 1988—Traded by Chicago Black Hawks to Minnesota North Stars for Dirk Graham.

IAIN FRASER

Center . . . 5'10" . . . 175 lbs. . . . Born, Scarborough, Ont., August 10, 1969 . . . Shoots left.

Year	Team	League	Games	G.	A.	Pts.	Pen.
1986-87—Oshawa Jr. B.		OHA	31	18	22	40	119
1987-88—Oshawa Generals		OHL	16	4	4	8	22
1988-89—Oshawa Generals (c)		OHL	62	33	57	90	87
1989-90—Oshawa Generals (d-e)		OHL	56	40	65	105	75

(c)—June, 1989—Drafted by New York Islanders in 1989 NHL entry draft. Fourteenth Islanders pick, 233rd overall, 12th round.

(d)—Won Leo LaLonde Memorial Trophy (top overage player).

(e)—Named MVP of Memorial Cup Tournament.

WILLIAM DANNY FRAWLEY
(Known by middle name.)

Right Wing . . . 6' . . . 193 lbs. . . . Born, Sturgeon Falls, Ont., June 2, 1962 . . . Shoots right . . . (December, 1987)—Knee surgery.

Year	Team	League	Games	G.	A.	Pts.	Pen.
1979-80—Sudbury Wolves (c)		OHL	63	21	26	47	67
1980-81—Cornwall Royals		QMJHL	28	10	14	24	76
1981-82—Cornwall Royals		OHL	64	27	50	77	239
1982-83—Springfield Indians		AHL	80	30	27	57	107
1983-84—Chicago Black Hawks		NHL	3	0	0	0	0
1983-84—Springfield Indians		AHL	69	22	34	56	137
1984-85—Milwaukee Admirals		IHL	26	11	12	23	125
1984-85—Chicago Black Hawks		NHL	30	4	3	7	64
1985-86—Pittsburgh Penguins (d)		NHL	69	10	11	21	174
1986-87—Pittsburgh Penguins		NHL	78	14	14	28	218
1987-88—Pittsburgh Penguins		NHL	47	6	8	14	152
1988-89—Muskegon Lumberjacks		IHL	24	12	16	28	35
1988-89—Pittsburgh Penguins		NHL	46	3	4	7	66
1989-90—Muskegon Lumberjacks		IHL	82	31	47	78	165
NHL TOTALS			273	37	40	77	674

(c)—June, 1980—Drafted as underage junior by Chicago Black Hawks in 1980 NHL entry draft. Fifteenth Black Hawks pick, 204th overall, 10th round.

(d)—October, 1985—Acquired by Pittsburgh Penguins in 1985 NHL waiver draft.

MARK FREER

Center . . . 5'11" . . . 175 lbs. . . . Born, Peterborough, Ont., July 14, 1968 . . . Shoots left.

Year	Team	League	Games	G.	A.	Pts.	Pen.
1984-85—Peterborough Midget		OHA	49	53	68	121	63
1985-86—Peterborough Petes		OHL	65	16	28	44	24
1986-87—Peterborough Petes		OHL	65	39	43	82	44
1986-87—Philadelphia Flyers (c)		NHL	1	0	1	1	0
1987-88—Philadelphia Flyers		NHL	1	0	0	0	0
1987-88—Peterborough Petes		OHL	63	38	71	109	63
1988-89—Philadelphia Flyers		NHL	5	0	1	1	0
1988-89—Hershey Bears		AHL	75	30	49	79	77
1989-90—Philadelphia Flyers		NHL	2	0	0	0	0
1989-90—Hershey Bears		AHL	65	28	36	64	31
NHL TOTALS			9	0	2	2	0

(c)—September, 1986—Signed by Philadelphia Flyers as a free agent.

DEREK FRENETTE

Left Wing . . . 6'1" . . . 175 lbs. . . . Born, Montreal, Que., July 13, 1971 . . . Shoots left.

Year	Team	League	Games	G.	A.	Pts.	Pen.
1987-88—Lac St. Louis Midget		Que. Midg.	42	30	34	64	66
1988-89—Ferris State Univ. (c)		CCHA	27	3	4	7	17
1989-90—Ferris State Univ.		CCHA	29	1	4	5	48

(c)—June, 1989—Drafted by St. Louis Blues in 1989 NHL entry draft. Sixth Blues pick, 124th overall, sixth round.

LINK GAETZ

Defense . . . 6'2" . . . 205 lbs. . . . Born, Vancouver, B.C., October 2, 1968 . . . Shoots left . . . (April 12, 1988)—Suspended indefinitely by Spokane Chiefs . . . (January 23, 1989)—Suspended four IHL games for high sticking.

Year	Team	League	Games	G.	A.	Pts.	Pen.
1986-87—New Westminster Bruins		WHL	44	2	7	9	52
1987-88—Spokane Chiefs (c)		WHL	59	9	20	29	313
1988-89—Minnesota North Stars		NHL	12	0	2	2	53
1988-89—Kalamazoo Wings		IHL	37	3	4	7	192
1989-90—Kalamazoo Wings		IHL	61	5	16	21	318
1989-90—Minnesota North Stars		NHL	5	0	0	0	33
NHL TOTALS			17	0	2	2	86

(c)—June, 1988—Drafted by Minnesota North Stars in 1988 NHL entry draft. Second North Stars pick, 40th overall, second round.

JOSEPH (JODY) GAGE

Right Wing . . . 5'11" . . . 182 lbs. . . . Born, Toronto, Ont., November 29, 1959 . . . Shoots right . . . (September 27, 1988)—Strained ankle and knee ligaments in AHL pre-season game at Newmarket and missed two months.

Year	Team	League	Games	G.	A.	Pts.	Pen.
1976-77—St. Catharines Black Hawks		OMJHL	47	13	20	33	2
1977-78—Hamilton Fincups		OMJHL	32	15	18	33	19
1977-78—Kitchener Rangers		OMJHL	36	17	27	44	21
1978-79—Kitchener Rangers (c)		OMJHL	59	46	43	89	40
1979-80—Adirondack Red Wings		AHL	63	25	21	46	15
1979-80—Kalamazoo Wings		IHL	14	17	12	29	0
1980-81—Detroit Red Wings		NHL	16	2	2	4	22
1980-81—Adirondack Red Wings		AHL	59	17	31	48	44
1981-82—Adirondack Red Wings		AHL	47	21	20	41	21
1981-82—Detroit Red Wings		NHL	31	9	10	19	2
1982-83—Adirondack Red Wings		AHL	65	23	30	53	33
1983-84—Detroit Red Wings		NHL	3	0	0	0	0
1983-84—Adirondack Red Wings		AHL	73	40	32	72	32
1984-85—Adirondack Red Wings		AHL	78	27	33	60	55
1985-86—Buffalo Sabres (d)		NHL	7	3	2	5	0
1985-86—Rochester Americans (a)		AHL	73	42	57	99	56
1986-87—Rochester Americans		AHL	70	26	39	65	60
1987-88—Rochester Americans		AHL	76	60	44	104	46
1987-88—Buffalo Sabres		NHL	2	0	0	0	0
1988-89—Rochester Americans		AHL	65	31	38	69	50
1989-90—Rochester Americans		AHL	75	45	38	83	42
NHL TOTALS			59	14	14	28	24

(c)—August, 1979—Drafted by Detroit Red Wings in 1979 NHL Entry draft. Second Detroit pick, 46th overall, third round.

(d)—August, 1985—Signed by Buffalo Sabres as a free agent.

PAUL GAGNE

Left Wing . . . 5'10" . . . 178 lbs. . . . Born, Iroquois Falls, Ont., February 6, 1962 . . . Shoots left . . . (December 18, 1980)—Tore knee ligaments . . . (October, 1981)—Fractured cheekbone . . . (January 2, 1982)—Shoulder separation vs. Detroit . . . (February 15, 1986)—Injured back at N.Y. Islanders . . . (March 2, 1986)—Injured back vs. Winnipeg . . . (March 25, 1986)—Injured back vs. N.Y. Rangers . . . (September, 1986)—Reinjured back in training camp and returned home for back therapy, missing the entire 1986-87 and 1987-88 seasons . . . (May, 1990)—Separated shoulder vs. Rochester.

Year	Team	League	Games	G.	A.	Pts.	Pen.
1978-79—Windsor Spitfires		OMJHL	67	24	18	42	64
1979-80—Windsor Spitfires (b-c)		OMJHL	65	48	53	101	67
1980-81—Colorado Rockies		NHL	61	25	16	41	12
1981-82—Colorado Rockies		NHL	59	10	12	22	17
1982-83—Wichita Wind		CHL	16	1	9	10	9
1982-83—New Jersey Devils		NHL	53	14	15	29	13
1983-84—New Jersey Devils		NHL	66	14	18	32	33
1984-85—New Jersey Devils		NHL	79	24	19	43	28
1985-86—New Jersey Devils		NHL	47	19	19	38	14
1986-87—Did not play			....	...	...	....	....
1987-88—Did not play (d)			....	...	...	....	....
1988-89—Toronto Maple Leafs		NHL	16	3	2	5	6
1988-89—Newmarket Saints		AHL	56	33	41	74	29
1989-90—Newmarket Saints (e)		AHL	28	13	14	27	11
1989-90—New York Islanders		NHL	9	1	0	1	4
1989-90—Springfield Indians		AHL	36	18	29	47	6
NHL TOTALS			390	110	101	211	127

(c)—June, 1980—Drafted by Colorado Rockies in 1980 NHL entry draft as an underage junior. First Rockies pick, 19th overall, first round.

(d)—July, 1988—Signed by Toronto Maple Leafs as a free agent.

(e)—December 20, 1989—Traded with Derek Laxdal and Jack Capuano from Toronto Maple Leafs to New York Islanders for Gilles Thibaudeau and Mike Stevens.

DAVE GAGNER

Center . . . 5'10" . . . 185 lbs. . . . Born, Chatham, Ont., December 11, 1964 . . . Shoots left . . . Member of 1984 Canadian Olympic Team . . . (February 5, 1986)—Fractured ankle at St. Louis . . . (December, 1986)—Emergency appendectomy . . . (March 31, 1989)—Broken kneecap when struck by a Steve Chiasson slapshot at Detroit.

Year	Team	League	Games	G.	A.	Pts.	Pen.
1981-82—Brantford Alexanders		OHL	68	30	46	76	31
1982-83—Brantford Alexanders (b-c)		OHL	70	55	66	121	57
1983-84—Canadian Olympic Team		Int'l	50	19	18	37	26
1983-84—Brantford Alexanders		OHL	12	7	13	20	4
1984-85—New Haven Nighthawks		AHL	38	13	20	33	23

Year	Team	League	Games	G.	A.	Pts.	Pen.
1984-85—New York Rangers		NHL	38	6	6	12	16
1985-86—New York Rangers		NHL	32	4	6	10	19
1985-86—New Haven Nighthawks		AHL	16	10	11	21	11
1986-87—New York Rangers		NHL	10	1	4	5	12
1986-87—New Haven Nighthawks		AHL	56	22	41	63	50
1987-88—Kalamazoo Wings		IHL	14	16	10	26	26
1987-88—Minnesota North Stars (d)		NHL	51	8	11	19	55
1988-89—Minnesota North Stars		NHL	75	35	43	78	104
1988-89—Kalamazoo Wings		IHL	1	0	1	1	4
1989-90—Minnesota North Stars		NHL	79	40	38	78	54
NHL TOTALS			285	94	108	202	260

(c)—June, 1983—Drafted as underage junior by New York Rangers in 1983 NHL entry draft. First Rangers pick, 12th overall, first round.

(d)—October, 1987—Traded with Jay Caufield by New York Rangers to Minnesota North Stars for Jari Gronstrad and Paul Boutilier.

GERARD GALLANT

Left Wing . . . 5'11" . . . 164 lbs. . . . Born, Summerside, P.E.I., September 2, 1963 . . . Shoots left . . . Also plays Center . . . (December 11, 1985)—Broke jaw vs. Minnesota and missed 25 games . . . (April 8, 1989)—Fined $500 by NHL for swinging his stick at Dave Manson vs. Chicago . . . (October 7, 1989)—Suspended five games for slashing Garth Butcher vs. Vancouver . . . (January 13, 1990)—Suspended three games for hitting linesman Jerry Pateman vs. Minnesota.

Year	Team	League	Games	G.	A.	Pts.	Pen.
1979-80—Summerside		PEIHA	45	60	55	115	90
1980-81—Sherbrooke Beavers (c)		QMJHL	68	41	60	101	220
1981-82—Sherbrooke Beavers		QMJHL	58	34	58	92	260
1982-83—St. Jean Beavers		QMJHL	33	28	25	53	139
1982-83—Verdun Juniors		QMJHL	29	26	49	75	105
1983-84—Adirondack Red Wings		AHL	77	31	33	64	195
1984-85—Adirondack Red Wings		AHL	46	18	29	47	131
1984-85—Detroit Red Wings		NHL	32	6	12	18	66
1985-86—Detroit Red Wings		NHL	52	20	19	39	106
1986-87—Detroit Red Wings		NHL	80	38	34	72	216
1987-88—Detroit Red Wings		NHL	73	34	39	73	242
1988-89—Detroit Red Wings (b)		NHL	76	39	54	93	230
1989-90—Detroit Red Wings		NHL	69	36	44	80	254
NHL TOTALS			382	173	202	375	1114

(c)—June, 1981—Drafted as underage junior by Detroit Red Wings in 1981 NHL entry draft. Fourth Red Wings pick, 107th overall, sixth round.

GARRY GALLEY

Defense . . . 5'11" . . . 190 lbs. . . . Born, Ottawa, Ont., April 16, 1963 . . . Shoots left . . . (December 8, 1985)—Injured knee at Winnipeg . . . (September 30, 1989)—Missed first nine games of season with sprained left shoulder suffered during training camp.

Year	Team	League	Games	G.	A.	Pts.	Pen.
1981-82—Bowling Green Univ.		CCHA	42	3	36	39	48
1982-83—Bowling Green Univ. (a-c)		CCHA	40	17	29	46	40
1983-84—Bowling Green Univ.		CCHA	44	15	52	67	61
1984-85—Los Angeles Kings		NHL	78	8	30	38	82
1985-86—Los Angeles Kings		NHL	49	9	13	22	46
1985-86—New Haven Nighthawks		AHL	4	2	6	8	6
1986-87—Los Angeles Kings (d)		NHL	30	5	11	16	57
1986-87—Washington Capitals		NHL	18	1	10	11	10
1987-88—Washington Capitals (e)		NHL	58	7	23	30	44
1988-89—Boston Bruins		NHL	78	8	21	29	80
1989-90—Boston Bruins		NHL	71	8	27	35	75
NHL TOTALS			382	46	135	181	394

(c)—June, 1983—Drafted by Los Angeles Kings in 1983 NHL entry draft. Fourth Kings pick, 100th overall, fifth round

(d)—February, 1987—Traded by Los Angeles Kings to Washington Capitals for Al Jensen.

(e)—July, 1988—Signed by Boston Bruins as a free agent with Washington Capitals getting third round draft choice in 1989 as compensation.

PERRY GANCHAR

Right Wing . . . 5'9" . . . 175 lbs. . . . Born, Saskatoon, Sask., October 28, 1963 . . . Shoots right . . . (January, 1988)—Injured knee . . . (January 4, 1989)—Set IHL record with three goals in 33 seconds (old record was 52 seconds set on February 23, 1956 by Cincinnati's Roly McLenahan.)

Year	Team	League	Games	G.	A.	Pts.	Pen.
1977-78—Saskatoon Blades		WHL	4	2	0	2	2
1978-79—Saskatoon		SJHL	50	21	33	54	72
1978-79—Saskatoon Blades		WHL	14	5	3	8	15
1979-80—Saskatoon Blades		WHL	70	41	24	65	116
1980-81—Saskatoon Blades		WHL	68	36	20	56	195
1981-82—Saskatoon Blades (c)		WHL	53	38	52	90	82
1982-83—Saskatoon Blades		WHL	68	68	48	116	105
1982-83—Salt Lake Golden Eagles (d)		CHL	..	..	..	..	..
1983-84—Montana Magic		CHL	59	23	22	45	77
1983-84—St. Louis Blues		NHL	1	0	0	0	0
1984-85—Peoria Rivermen (b)		IHL	63	41	29	70	114
1984-85—St. Louis Blues (e)		NHL	7	0	2	2	0
1985-86—Sherbrooke Canadiens		AHL	75	25	29	54	42
1986-87—Sherbrooke Canadiens		AHL	68	22	29	51	64
1987-88—Sherbrooke Canadiens		AHL	28	12	18	30	61
1987-88—Montreal Canadiens (f)		NHL	1	1	0	1	0
1987-88—Pittsburgh Penguins		NHL	30	2	5	7	36

Year Team	League	Games	G.	A.	Pts.	Pen.
1988-89—Pittsburgh Penguins	NHL	3	0	0	0	0
1988-89—Muskegon Lumberjacks	IHL	70	39	34	73	114
1989-90—Muskegon Lumberjacks	IHL	70	40	45	85	111
NHL TOTALS		42	3	7	10	36

(c)—June, 1982—Drafted as underage junior by St. Louis Blues in 1982 NHL entry draft. Third Blues pick, 113th overall, sixth round.

(d)—No regular season record. Played one playoff game.

(e)—August, 1985—Traded by St. Louis Blues to Montreal Canadiens for Ron Flockhart.

(f)—December, 1987—Traded by Montreal Canadiens to Pittsburgh Penguins for future considerations.

MURRAY GARBUTT

Center . . . 6'1" . . . 205 lbs. . . . Born, Hanna, Alta., July 29, 1971 . . . Shoots left . . . Also plays Left Wing.

Year Team	League	Games	G.	A.	Pts.	Pen.
1987-88—Medicine Hat Tigers	WHL	9	2	1	3	5
1988-89—Medicine Hat Tigers (c)	WHL	64	14	24	38	145
1989-90—Medicine Hat Tigers	WHL	72	38	27	65	221

(c)—June, 1989—Drafted by Minnesota North Stars in 1989 NHL entry draft. Third North Stars pick, 60th overall, third round.

JOEL GARDNER

Center . . . 6' . . . 175 lbs. . . . Born, Petrolia, Ont., September 16, 1967 . . . Shoots left . . . (December, 1986)—Broken wrist.

Year Team	League	Games	G.	A.	Pts.	Pen.
1985-86—Sarnia (c)	OPJHL	42	23	51	74	72
1986-87—Colgate Univ.	ECAC	31	10	20	30	20
1987-88—Colgate Univ.	ECAC	31	14	32	46	24
1988-89—Colgate Univ.	ECAC	30	21	25	46	38
1989-90—Colgate Univ. (a)	ECAC	38	26	36	62	62

(c)—June, 1986—Drafted by Boston Bruins in 1986 NHL entry draft. Tenth Bruins pick, 244th overall, 11th round.

JOHAN GARPENLOV

Left Wing . . . 5'11" . . . 185 lbs. . . . Born Stockholm, Sweden, March 21, 1968 . . . Shoots left.

Year Team	League	Games	G.	A.	Pts.	Pen.
1986-87—Djurgardens (c)	Sweden	29	5	8	13	20
1987-88—Djurgardens	Sweden	30	7	10	17	12
1988-89—Djurgardens	Sweden	36	12	19	31	20
1989-90—Djurgardens	Sweden	39	20	13	33	36

(c)—June, 1984—Selected by Detroit Red Wings in 1986 NHL entry draft. Fifth Red Wings pick, 85th overall, fifth round.

MICHAEL ALFRED GARTNER

Right Wing . . . 6' . . . 180 lbs. . . . Born, Ottawa, Ont., October 29, 1959 . . . Shoots right . . . (February, 1983)—Eye injury . . . (March, 1986)—Arthroscopic surgery to repair torn cartilage in left knee . . . (November, 1988)—Sprained right knee . . . (April 14, 1989)—Surgery to repair left knee cartilage injured late in the season.

Year Team	League	Games	G.	A.	Pts.	Pen.
1975-76—St. Cath. Black Hawks	Jr."A"OHA	3	1	3	4	0
1976-77—Niagara Falls Flyers	Jr."A"OHA	62	33	42	75	125
1977-78—Niagara Falls Flyers (a-c)	Jr."A"OHA	64	41	49	90	56
1978-79—Cincinnati Stingers (d)	WHA	78	27	25	52	123
1979-80—Washington Capitals	NHL	77	36	32	68	66
1980-81—Washington Capitals	NHL	80	48	46	94	100
1981-82—Washington Capitals	NHL	80	35	45	80	121
1982-83—Washington Capitals	NHL	73	38	38	76	54
1983-84—Washington Capitals	NHL	80	40	45	85	90
1984-85—Washington Capitals	NHL	80	50	52	102	71
1985-86—Washington Capitals	NHL	74	35	40	75	63
1986-87—Washington Capitals	NHL	78	41	32	73	61
1987-88—Washington Capitals	NHL	80	48	33	81	73
1988-89—Washington Capitals (e)	NHL	56	26	29	55	71
1988-89—Minnesota North Stars	NHL	13	7	7	14	2
1989-90—Minnesota North Stars (f)	NHL	67	34	36	70	32
1989-90—New York Rangers	NHL	12	11	5	16	6
WHA TOTALS		78	27	25	52	123
NHL TOTALS		850	449	440	889	810

(c)—August, 1978—Signed by Cincinnati Stingers (WHA) as underage junior.

(d)—August, 1979—Drafted by Washington Capitals in 1979 entry draft. First Capitals pick, fourth overall, first round.

(e)—March 7, 1989—Traded with Larry Murphy by Washington Capitals to Minnesota North Stars for Dino Ciccarelli and Bob Rouse.

(f)—March 6, 1990—Traded by Minnesota North Stars to New York Rangers for Ulf Dahlen and a fourth-round 1990 draft pick and future considerations.

ROBERT GAUDREAU

Right Wing . . . 6' . . . 180 lbs. . . . Born, Providence, R.I., January 20, 1970 . . . Shoots right . . . (February, 1987)—Separated shoulder.

Year Team	League	Games	G.	A.	Pts.	Pen.
1986-87—Bishop Hendricken	R.I. Met. 'A'	33	41	39	80	..
1987-88—Bishop Hendricken (c)	R.I. Met. 'A'	..	52	60	112	..
1988-89—Providence College (d-e-f)	H. East	42	28	29	57	32
1989-90—Providence College	H. East	32	20	18	38	12

(c)—June, 1988—Drafted by Pittsburgh Penguins in 1988 NHL entry draft. Eighth Penguins pick, 127nd overall, ninth round.

(d)—November 1, 1988—Traded by Pittsburgh Penguins to Minnesota North Stars for Richard Zemlak.

(e)—Named to Hockey East All-Rookie team.

(f)—Named Hockey East co-Rookie of the Year, sharing the honor with Scott Pellerin of Maine.

DALLAS GAUME

Center . . . 5'10" . . . 180 lbs. . . . Born, Innisfal, Alta., August 27, 1963 . . . Shoots left . . . Broke Bill Masterton record for career points at University of Denver.

Year Team	League	Games	G.	A.	Pts.	Pen.
1982-83—University of Denver	WCHA	37	19	47	66	12
1983-84—University of Denver	WCHA	32	12	25	37	22
1984-85—University of Denver	WCHA	39	15	48	63	28
1985-86—University of Denver (a-c-d)	WCHA	47	32	*67	*99	18
1986-87—Binghamton Whalers	AHL	77	18	39	57	31
1987-88—Binghamton Whalers	AHL	63	24	49	73	39
1988-89—Hartford Whalers	NHL	4	1	1	2	0
1988-89—Binghamton Whalers	AHL	57	23	43	66	16
1989-90—Binghamton Whalers	AHL	76	26	39	65	43
NHL TOTALS		4	1	1	2	0

(c)—Named WCHA MVP.

(d)—July, 1986—Signed by Hartford Whalers as a free agent.

DANIEL GAUTHIER

Left Wing . . . 6'1" . . . 180 lbs. . . . Born, Charlemagne, Que., May 17, 1970 . . . Shoots left . . . (January 2, 1990)—Left Victoriaville and returned on January 16.

Year Team	League	Games	G.	A.	Pts.	Pen.
1986-87—Longueuil Chevaliers	QMJHL	64	23	22	45	23
1987-88—Victoriaville Tigres (c)	QMJHL	66	43	47	90	53
1988-89—Victoriaville Tigres	QMJHL	64	41	75	116	84
1989-90—Victoriaville Tigres	QMJHL	62	45	69	114	32

(c)—June, 1988—Drafted by Pittsburgh Penguins in 1988 NHL entry draft. Third Penguins pick, 62nd overall, third round.

LUC GAUTHIER

Defense . . . 5'9" . . . 195 lbs. . . . Born, Longueuil, Que., April 19, 1964 . . . Shoots left . . . (October, 1987)—Broken ankle vs. Hershey.

Year Team	League	Games	G.	A.	Pts.	Pen.
1982-83—Longueuil Chevaliers	QMJHL	67	3	18	21	132
1983-84—Longueuil Chevaliers	QMJHL	70	8	54	62	207
1984-85—Longueuil Chevaliers	QMJHL	60	13	47	60	111
1984-85—Flint Generals	IHL	21	1	0	1	20
1985-86—Saginaw Generals	IHL	66	9	29	38	165
1986-87—Sherbrooke Canadiens (c)	AHL	78	5	17	22	81
1987-88—Sherbrooke Canadiens	AHL	61	4	10	14	105
1988-89—Sherbrooke Canadiens	AHL	77	8	20	28	178
1989-90—Sherbrooke Canadiens	AHL	79	3	23	26	139

(c)—October 7, 1986—Signed by Montreal Canadiens as a free agent.

ROBERT STEWART GAVIN
(Known By middle name.)

Left Wing . . . 6' . . . 180 lbs. . . . Born, Ottawa, Ont., March 15, 1960 . . . Shoots left . . . (October, 1981)—Shoulder separation . . . (December, 1981)—Reinjured shoulder . . . (October, 1982)—Sprained ankle . . . (December 8, 1987)—Missed 22 games with strained ligaments in right ankle at Quebec . . . (December 13, 1988)—Broken cheekbone when struck by a shot at Detroit.

Year Team	League	Games	G.	A.	Pts.	Pen.
1976-77—Ottawa 67's	OMJHL	1	0	0	0	0
1977-78—Toronto Marlboros	OMJHL	67	16	24	40	19
1978-79—Toronto Marlboros	OMJHL	61	24	25	49	83
1979-80—Toronto Marlboros (c)	OMJHL	66	27	30	57	52
1980-81—Toronto Maple Leafs	NHL	14	1	2	3	13
1980-81—New Brunswick Hawks	AHL	46	7	12	19	42
1981-82—Toronto Maple Leafs	NHL	38	5	6	11	29
1982-83—St. Catharines Saints	OHL	6	2	4	6	17
1982-83—Toronto Maple Leafs	NHL	63	6	5	11	44
1983-84—Toronto Maple Leafs	NHL	80	10	22	32	90
1984-85—Toronto Maple Leafs	NHL	73	12	13	25	38
1985-06—Hartford Whalers (d)	NHL	76	26	29	55	51
1986-87—Hartford Whalers	NHL	79	20	22	42	28
1987-88—Hartford Whalers	NHL	56	11	10	21	59
1988-89—Minnesota North Stars (e)	NHL	73	8	18	26	34
1989-90—Minnesota North Stars	NHL	80	12	12	24	76
NHL TOTALS		632	111	140	251	462

(c)—June, 1980—Drafted by Toronto Maple Leafs in 1980 NHL entry draft. Fourth Maple Leafs pick, 74th overall, fourth round.

(d)—October, 1985—Traded by Toronto Maple Leafs to Hartford Whalers for Chris Kotsopoulos.

(e)—October 3, 1988—Selected by Minnesota North Stars in 1988 NHL waiver draft for $7,500.

MARTIN GELINAS

Left Wing . . . 5'11" . . . 195 lbs. . . . Born, Shawinigan, Que., June 5, 1970 . . . Shoots left . . . (November, 1983)—Broken left clavicle . . . (July, 1986)—Hairline fracture of clavicle . . . (March 9, 1990)—Suspended five games for crosschecking Dave Ellett vs. Winnipeg.

Year Team	League	Games	G.	A.	Pts.	Pen.
1986-87—Magog Midgets	Quebec	41	36	42	78	36
1987-88—Hull Olympiques (c-d)	QMJHL	65	63	68	131	74
1988-89—Edmonton Oilers	NHL	6	1	2	3	0
1988-89—Hull Olympiques	QMJHL	41	38	39	77	31
1989-90—Edmonton Oilers	NHL	46	17	8	25	30
NHL TOTALS		52	18	10	28	30

(c)—June, 1988—Drafted by Los Angeles Kings in 1988 NHL entry draft. First Kings pick, seventh overall, first round.

(d)—August, 1988—Traded with Jimmy Carson, first-round draft choices in 1989 (traded to New Jersey), '91 and '93, plus $15 million by Los Angeles Kings to Edmonton Oilers for Wayne Gretzky, Marty McSorley and Mike Krushelnyski.

ERIC GERMAIN

Defense . . . 6'1'' . . . 190 lbs. . . . Born, Quebec City, Que., June 26, 1966 . . . Shoots left . . . (March 13, 1990)—Suspended 10 AHL games for bumping into referee Dave Jackson at Baltimore.

Year	Team	League	Games	G.	A.	Pts.	Pen.
1983-84—St. Jean Beavers		QMJHL	57	2	15	17	60
1984-85—St. Jean Beavers		QMJHL	66	10	31	41	243
1985-86—St. Jean Castors (c)		QMJHL	66	5	38	43	183
1986-87—Flint Spirit		IHL	21	0	2	2	23
1986-87—Fredericton Express		AHL	44	2	8	10	28
1987-88—Los Angeles Kings		NHL	4	0	1	1	13
1987-88—New Haven Nighthawks		AHL	69	0	10	10	82
1988-89—New Haven Nighthawks		AHL	55	0	9	9	93
1989-90—New Haven Nighthawks		AHL	59	3	12	15	112
NHL TOTALS			4	0	1	1	13

(c)—June, 1986—Signed by Los Angeles Kings as a free agent.

KENNETH GERNANDER

Center . . . 5'10'' . . . 155 lbs. . . . Born, Grand Rapids, Minn., June 30, 1969 . . . Shoots left . . . Son of Bob Gernander (Head coach of Greenway-Coleraine High School hockey team).

Year	Team	League	Games	G.	A.	Pts.	Pen.
1985-86—Greenway H.S.		Minn. H.S.	23	14	23	37	....
1986-87—Greenway H.S. (c)		Minn. H.S.	26	35	34	69	....
1987-88—Univ. of Minnesota		WCHA	44	14	14	28	14
1988-89—Univ. of Minnesota		WCHA	44	9	11	20	2
1989-90—Univ. of Minnesota		WCHA	44	32	17	49	24

(c)—June, 1987—Drafted by Winnipeg Jets in 1987 NHL entry draft. Fourth Jets pick, 96th overall, fifth round.

VICTOR GERVAIS

Center . . . 5'9'' . . . 170 lbs. . . . Born, Prince George, B.C., March 13, 1969 . . . Shoots left.

Year	Team	League	Games	G.	A.	Pts.	Pen.
1985-86—Seattle Thunderbirds		WHL	1	0	0	0	0
1986-87—Seattle Thunderbirds		WHL	66	13	30	43	58
1987-88—Seattle Thunderbirds		WHL	69	30	46	76	134
1988-89—Seattle Thunderbirds (c)		WHL	72	54	65	119	158
1989-90—Seattle Thunderbirds		WHL	69	64	96	160	180

(c)—June, 1989—Drafted by Washington Capitals in 1989 NHL entry draft. Eighth Capitals pick, 187th overall, ninth round.

DONALD SCOTT GIBSON

Defense . . . 6'1'' . . . 210 lbs. . . . Born, Deloraine, Man., March 17, 1967 . . . Shoots right . . . (February, 1988)—Suspended three CCHA games for spearing and fighting . . . (December, 1988)—Injured knee . . . (December, 1989)—Injured knee.

Year	Team	League	Games	G.	A.	Pts.	Pen.
1985-86—Winkler Flyers (c)		MJHL	34	24	29	53	210
1986-87—Michigan State Univ.		CCHA	43	3	3	6	74
1987-88—Michigan State Univ.		CCHA	43	7	12	19	118
1988-89—Michigan State Univ.		CCHA	39	7	10	17	107
1989-90—Michigan State Univ.		CCHA	44	5	22	27	167
1989-90—Milwaukee Admirals		IHL	1	0	0	0	4

(c)—June, 1986—Drafted by Vancouver Canucks in 1986 NHL entry draft. Second Canucks pick, 49th overall, third round.

LEE GIFFIN

Right Wing . . . 5'11'' . . . 177 lbs. . . . Born, Chatham, Ont., April 1, 1967 . . . Shoots right . . . (September, 1987)—Scratched left eye cornea and cut eyelid during a training camp scrimmage . . . (December 1, 1988)—Fractured two ribs and bruised kidney in collision with Ed Belfour vs. Saginaw.

Year	Team	League	Games	G.	A.	Pts.	Pen.
1982-83—Newmarket Flyers		OHA	47	10	21	31	123
1983-84—Oshawa Generals		OHL	70	23	27	50	88
1984-85—Oshawa Generals (c)		OHL	62	36	42	78	78
1985-86—Oshawa Generals		OHL	54	29	37	66	28
1986-87—Oshawa Generals (a)		OHL	48	31	69	100	46
1986-87—Pittsburgh Penguins		NHL	8	1	1	2	0
1987-88—Pittsburgh Penguins		NHL	19	0	2	2	9
1987-88—Muskegon Lumberjacks		IHL	48	26	37	63	61
1988-89—Muskegon Lumberjacks		IHL	63	30	44	74	93
1989-90—Flint Spirits (d)		IHL	73	30	44	74	68
NHL TOTALS			27	1	3	4	9

(c)—June, 1985—Drafted as underage junior by Pittsburgh Penguins in 1985 NHL entry draft. Second Penguins pick, 23rd overall, second round.
(d)—September, 1989—Signed by New York Rangers as a free agent.

GREG SCOTT GILBERT

Left Wing . . . 6' . . . 190 lbs. . . . Born, Mississauga, Ont., January 22, 1962 . . . Shoots left . . . (December, 1979)—Sprained ankle . . . (September, 1984)—Stretched ligaments in left ankle while jogging prior to training camp . . . (February 27, 1985)—Injured ligaments when checked into open door at players bench by Jamie Macoun at Calgary. He required major reconstructive surgery when the knee did not respond to therapy following arthroscopic surgery . . . (October 11, 1986)—Broke jaw in fight with Tiger Williams at Los Angeles, lost 13 pounds and missed 10 games . . . (December 7, 1986)—Bruised thigh at Boston . . . (February, 1987)—Bruised hip . . . (March, 1987)—Separated right shoulder . . . (February 20, 1988)—Bruised right knee . . . (April, 1988)—Injured left foot . . . (February, 1989)—Back

spasms and injured left shoulder. . . . (March, 1989)—Broken foot . . . (March 8, 1990)—Strained abdominal muscle during a practice.

Year	Team	League	Games	G.	A.	Pts.	Pen.
1979-80—Toronto Marlboros (c)		OMJHL	68	10	11	21	35
1980-81—Toronto Marlboros		OHL	64	30	37	67	73
1981-82—Toronto Marlboros		OHL	65	41	67	108	119
1981-82—New York Islanders		NHL	1	1	0	1	0
1982-83—Indianapolis Checkers		CHL	24	11	16	27	23
1982-83—New York Islanders		NHL	45	8	11	19	30
1983-84—New York Islanders		NHL	79	31	35	66	59
1984-85—New York Islanders		NHL	58	13	25	38	36
1985-86—Springfield Indians		AHL	2	0	0	0	2
1985-86—New York Islanders		NHL	60	9	19	28	82
1986-87—New York Islanders		NHL	51	6	7	13	26
1987-88—New York Islanders		NHL	76	17	28	45	46
1988-89—New York Islanders (d)		NHL	55	8	13	21	45
1988-89—Chicago Black Hawks		NHL	4	0	0	0	0
1989-90—Chicago Black Hawks		NHL	70	12	25	37	54
NHL TOTALS			499	105	163	268	378

(c)—June, 1980—Drafted as underage junior by New York Islanders in 1980 NHL entry draft. Fifth Islanders pick, 80th overall, fourth round.
(d)—March 7, 1989—Traded by New York Islanders to Chicago Black Hawks for a fifth-round 1989 draft pick (Steve Young).

BRENT GILCHRIST

Center . . . 5'10'' . . . 175 lbs. . . . Born, Moose Jaw, Sask., April 3, 1967 . . . Shoots left . . . (January, 1985)—Strained medial collateral ligament at Portland . . . (January, 1987)—Injured knee.

Year	Team	League	Games	G.	A.	Pts.	Pen.
1983-84—Kelowna Wings		WHL	69	16	11	27	16
1984-85—Kelowna Wings (c)		WHL	51	35	38	73	58
1985-86—Spokane Chiefs		WHL	52	45	45	90	57
1986-87—Spokane Chiefs		WHL	46	45	55	100	71
1986-87—Sherbrooke Canadiens (d)		AHL	....	...	....	....	....
1987-88—Sherbrooke Canadiens		AHL	77	26	48	74	83
1988-89—Montreal Canadiens		NHL	49	8	16	24	16
1988-89—Sherbrooke Canadiens		AHL	7	6	5	11	7
1989-90—Montreal Canadiens		NHL	57	9	15	24	28
NHL TOTALS			106	17	31	48	44

(c)—June, 1985—Drafted as underage junior by Montreal Canadiens in 1985 NHL entry draft. Sixth Canadiens pick, 79th overall, sixth round.
(d)—No regular season record. Played 10 playoff games.

CURT GILES

Defense . . . 5'8'' . . . 180 lbs. . . . Born, The Pas, Manitoba, November 30, 1958 . . . Shoots left . . . Named to All-American College teams in 1978 and 1979 . . . (February, 1981)—Right knee strain . . . (January, 1984)—Knee injury . . . (March 24, 1986)—Left ring finger amputated due to a tumor that had grown into the bone. He returned for the playoffs . . . (April 14, 1987)—Fractured elbow vs. Philadelphia . . . (November 6, 1989)—Injured groin at Toronto . . . (March, 1990)—Strained lower back.

Year	Team	League	Games	G.	A.	Pts.	Pen.
1975-76—Univ. of Minnesota-Duluth		WCHA	34	5	17	22	76
1976-77—Univ. of Minnesota-Duluth		WCHA	37	12	37	49	64
1977-78—Univ. of Minn.-Duluth (a-c)		WCHA	34	11	36	47	62
1978-79—Univ. of Minnesota-Duluth (a)		WCHA	30	3	38	41	38
1979-80—Oklahoma City Stars		CHL	42	4	24	28	35
1979-80—Minnesota North Stars		NHL	37	2	7	9	31
1980-81—Minnesota North Stars		NHL	67	5	22	27	56
1981-82—Minnesota North Stars		NHL	74	3	12	15	87
1982-03—Minnesota North Stars		NHL	76	2	21	23	70
1983-84—Minnesota North Stars		NHL	70	6	22	28	59
1984-85—Minnesota North Stars		NHL	77	5	25	30	49
1985-86—Minnesota North Stars		NHL	69	6	21	27	30
1986-87—Minnesota North Stars (d)		NHL	11	0	3	3	4
1986-87—New York Rangers		NHL	61	2	17	19	50
1987-88—New York Rangers (e)		NHL	13	0	0	0	10
1987-88—Minnesota North Stars		NHL	59	1	12	13	66
1988-89—Minnesota North Stars		NHL	76	5	10	15	77
1989-90—Minnesota North Stars		NHL	74	1	12	13	48
NHL TOTALS			764	38	184	222	637

(c)—June, 1978—Drafted by Minnesota North Stars in NHL amateur draft. Fourth North Stars pick, 54th overall, fourth round.
(d)—November, 1986—Traded with Tony McKegney and a second round 1988 draft pick (Troy Mallette) by Minnesota North Stars to New York Rangers for Bob Brooke and a fourth-round draft pick.
(e)—November, 1987—Traded by New York Rangers to Minnesota North Stars for Byron Lomow and future considerations.

RANDY GILHEN

Left Wing . . . 5'11'' . . . 195 lbs. . . . Born, Zweibrucken, West Germany, June 13, 1963 . . . Shoots left . . . (November 16, 1988)—Separated shoulder at Edmonton . . . (November 2, 1989)—Sprained knee vs. N.Y. Islanders.

Year	Team	League	Games	G.	A.	Pts.	Pen.
1979-80—Saskatoon		SJHL	55	18	34	52	112
1979-80—Saskatoon Blades		WHL	9	2	2	4	20
1980-81—Saskatoon Blades		WHL	68	10	5	15	154
1981-82—Winnipeg Warriors (c)		WHL	61	41	37	78	87
1982-83—Winnipeg Warriors		WHL	71	57	44	101	84
1982-83—Hartford Whalers		NHL	2	0	1	1	0
1982-83—Binghamton Whalers (d)		AHL	..	..	..	..	..
1983-84—Binghamton Whalers		AHL	73	8	12	20	72

Year	Team	League	Games	G.	A.	Pts.	Pen.
1984-85—Salt Lake Golden Eagles	IHL	57	20	20	40	28
1984-85—Binghamton Whalers (e)	AHL	18	3	3	6	9
1985-86—Fort Wayne Komets	IHL	82	44	40	84	48
1986-87—Winnipeg Jets	NHL	2	0	0	0	0
1986-87—Sherbrooke Canadiens	AHL	75	36	29	65	44
1987-88—Winnipeg Jets	NHL	13	3	2	5	15
1987-88—Moncton Golden Flames	AHL	68	40	47	87	51
1988-89—Winnipeg Jets (f)	NHL	64	5	3	8	38
1989-90—Pittsburgh Penguins	NHL	61	5	11	16	54
NHL TOTALS			142	13	17	30	107

(c)—June, 1982—Drafted as underage junior by Hartford Whalers in 1982 NHL entry draft. Sixth Whalers pick, 109th overall, sixth round.

(d)—No regular season record. Played five playoff games.

(e)—August, 1985—Signed by Winnipeg Jets as a free agent.

(f)—June 17, 1989—Traded with Andrew McBain and Jim Kyte by Winnipeg Jets to Pittsburgh Penguins for Randy Cunneyworth, Richard Tabaracci and Dave McLlwain.

TODD GILL

Left Wing . . . 6'1" . . . 175 lbs. . . . Born, Brockville, Ont., November 9, 1965 . . . Shoots left . . . (October, 1987)—Cracked bone in right foot . . . Also plays Defense . . . (March, 1989)—Bruised shoulder.

Year	Team	League	Games	G.	A.	Pts.	Pen.
1982-83—Windsor Spitfires	OHL	70	12	24	36	108
1983-84—Windsor Spitfires (c)	OHL	68	9	48	57	184
1984-85—Toronto Maple Leafs	NHL	10	1	0	1	13
1984-85—Windsor Spitfires	OHL	53	17	40	57	148
1985-86—St. Catharines Saints	AHL	58	8	25	33	90
1985-86—Toronto Maple Leafs	NHL	15	1	2	3	28
1986-87—Newmarket Saints	AHL	11	1	8	9	33
1986-87—Toronto Maple Leafs	NHL	61	4	27	31	92
1987-88—Newmarket Saints	AHL	2	0	1	1	2
1987-88—Toronto Maple Leafs	NHL	65	8	17	25	131
1988-89—Toronto Maple Leafs	NHL	59	11	14	25	72
1989-90—Toronto Maple Leafs	NHL	48	1	14	15	92
NHL TOTALS			258	26	74	100	428

(c)—June, 1984—Drafted as underage junior by Toronto Maple Leafs in 1984 NHL entry draft. Second Maple Leafs pick, 25th overall, second round.

PAUL C. GILLIS

Center . . . 6' . . . 195 lbs. . . . Born, Toronto, Ont., December 31, 1963 . . . Shoots left . . . Brother of Mike Gillis . . . (November 2, 1986)—Three-game NHL suspension for scratching Dean Evason's face in a fight vs. Hartford . . . (Summer, 1989)—Developed Guillian-Bare Syndrome, a neurological disorder brought on by a virus and missed first eight games of season . . . (November, 1989)—Sprained knee.

Year	Team	League	Games	G.	A.	Pts.	Pen.
1980-81—Niagara Falls Flyers	OHL	59	14	19	33	165
1981-82—Niagara Falls Flyers (c)	OHL	66	27	62	89	247
1982-83—North Bay Centennials	OHL	61	34	52	86	151
1982-83—Quebec Nordiques	NHL	7	0	2	2	2
1983-84—Fredericton Express	AHL	18	7	8	15	47
1983-84—Quebec Nordiques	NHL	57	8	9	17	59
1984-85—Quebec Nordiques	NHL	77	14	28	42	168
1985-86—Quebec Nordiques	NHL	80	19	24	43	203
1986-87—Quebec Nordiques	NHL	76	13	26	39	267
1987-88—Quebec Nordiques	NHL	80	7	10	17	164
1988-89—Quebec Nordiques	NHL	79	15	25	40	163
1989-90—Quebec Nordiques	NHL	71	8	14	22	234
NHL TOTALS			527	84	138	222	1260

(c)—June, 1982—Drafted as underage junior by Quebec Nordiques in 1982 NHL entry draft. Second Nordiques pick, 34th overall, second round.

DOUGLAS GILMOUR

Center . . . 5'11" . . . 164 lbs. . . . Born, Kingston, Ont., June 25, 1963 . . . Shoots left . . . (October 7, 1985)—Sprained ankle in training camp and missed four regular season games . . . (January, 1988)—Concussion . . . (March, 1988)—Bruised shoulder . . . (March, 1989)—Missed six games and lost 10 pounds with an abscessed jaw . . . (August 12, 1989)—Broke bone in right foot while jogging.

Year	Team	League	Games	G.	A.	Pts.	Pen.
1980-81—Cornwall Royals	QMJHL	51	12	23	35	35
1981-82—Cornwall Royals (c)	OHL	67	46	73	119	42
1982-83—Cornwall Royals (a-d-e)	OHL	68	*70	*107	*177	62
1983-84—St. Louis Blues	NHL	80	25	28	53	57
1984-85—St. Louis Blues	NHL	78	21	36	57	49
1985-86—St. Louis Blues	NHL	74	25	28	53	41
1986-87—St. Louis Blues	NHL	80	42	63	105	58
1987-88—St. Louis Blues	NHL	72	36	50	86	59
1988-89—Calgary Flames (f)	NHL	72	26	59	85	44
1989-90—Calgary Flames	NHL	78	24	67	91	54
NHL TOTALS			534	199	331	530	362

(c)—June, 1982—Drafted as underage junior by St. Louis Blues in 1982 NHL entry draft. Fourth Blues pick, 134th overall, seventh round.

(d)—Won Red Tilson Trophy (Outstanding OHL Player).

(e)—Won Eddie Powers Memorial Trophy (OHL Scoring Champion).

(f)—September 5, 1988—Traded with Mark Hunter, Steve Bozek and Michael Dark by St. Louis Blues to Calgary Flames for Mike Bullard, Craig Coxe and Tim Corkery.

MATT GLENNON

Left Wing . . . 6' . . . 185 lbs. . . . Born, Quincy, Mass., September 20, 1968 . . . Shoots left . . . Brother of Mike Glennon (Who played at Univ. of New Hampshire in 1984-88).

Year	Team	League	Games	G.	A.	Pts.	Pen.
1985-86—Archbishop Williams H.S.	Mass. H.S.	18	18	22	40	6
1986-87—Archbishop Williams H.S. (c)	Mass. H.S.	18	22	36	58	20
1987-88—Boston College	H. East	16	3	3	6	16
1988-89—Boston College	H. East	16	1	6	7	4
1989-90—Boston College	H. East	31	7	11	18	16

(c)—June, 1987—Drafted by Boston Bruins in 1987 NHL entry draft. Seventh Bruins pick, 119th overall, sixth round.

BRIAN GLYNN

Defense . . . 6'4" . . . 224 lbs. . . . Born, Iserlohn, West Germany, November 23, 1967 . . . Shoots left.

Year	Team	League	Games	G.	A.	Pts.	Pen.
1984-85—Melville Millionaires	SAJHL	12	1	0	1	2
1985-86—Saskatoon Blades (c)	WHL	66	7	25	32	131
1986-87—Saskatoon Blades	WHL	44	2	26	28	163
1987-88—Calgary Flames	NHL	67	5	14	19	87
1988-89—Salt Lake Golden Eagles	IHL	31	3	10	13	105
1988-89—Calgary Flames	NHL	9	0	1	1	19
1989-90—Calgary Flames	NHL	1	0	0	0	0
1989-90—Salt Lake Golden Eagles (d)	IHL	80	17	44	61	164
NHL TOTALS			77	5	15	20	106

(c)—June, 1986—Drafted by Calgary Flames in 1986 NHL entry draft. Second Flames pick, 37th overall, second round.

(d)—Won Governors Trophy (Top IHL Defenseman).

MICHAEL GOBER

Left Wing . . . 6' . . . 190 lbs. . . . Born, St. Louis, Mo., April 10, 1967 . . . Shoots left . . . (January, 1986)—Injured shoulder . . . (May, 1987)—Broke pelvis in automobile accident.

Year	Team	League	Games	G.	A.	Pts.	Pen.
1984-85—Verdun Jr. Canadiens	QMJHL	46	9	20	29	125
1985-86—Trois-Rivieres Draveurs	QMJHL	57	27	23	50	151
1986-87—Laval Titans (c)	QMJHL	63	49	47	96	292
1987-88—Trois-Rivieres Draveurs	QMJHL	19	5	10	15	96
1988-89—Adirondack Red Wings	AHL	41	15	7	22	55
1989-90—Adirondack Red Wings	AHL	44	14	12	26	85

(c)—June, 1987—Drafted by Detroit Red Wings in 1987 NHL entry draft. Eighth Red Wings pick, 137th overall, seventh round.

DAVE GOERTZ

Defense . . . 5'11" . . . 205 lbs. . . . Born, Edmonton, Alta., March 28, 1965 . . . Shoots right.

Year	Team	League	Games	G.	A.	Pts.	Pen.
1981-82—Regina Pats	WHL	67	5	19	24	181
1982-83—Regina Pats (c)	WHL	69	4	22	26	132
1983-84—Prince Albert Raiders	WHL	60	13	47	60	111
1983-84—Baltimore Skipjacks	AHL	1	0	0	0	0
1984-85—Prince Albert Raiders	WHL	48	3	48	51	62
1984-85—Baltimore Skipjacks (d)	AHL	....	...	...	...	....
1985-86—Baltimore Skipjacks	AHL	74	1	15	16	76
1986-87—Muskegon Lumberjacks	IHL	44	3	17	20	44
1986-87—Baltimore Skipjacks	AHL	16	0	3	3	8
1987-88—Pittsburgh Penguins	NHL	2	0	0	0	2
1987-88—Muskegon Lumberjacks	IHL	73	8	36	44	87
1988-89—Muskegon Lumberjacks	IHL	74	1	32	33	102
1989-90—Muskegon Lumberjacks	IHL	51	3	18	21	64
NHL TOTALS			2	0	0	0	2

(c)—June, 1983—Drafted as underage junior by Pittsburgh Penguins in 1983 NHL entry draft. Tenth Penguins pick, 223rd overall, 12th round.

(d)—No regular season record. Played two playoff games.

MICHAEL GOLDEN

Center . . . 6'1" . . . 194 lbs. . . . Born, Boston, Mass., June 17, 1965 . . . Shoots right.

Year	Team	League	Games	G.	A.	Pts.	Pen.
1982-83—Reading H.S. (c)	Mass. H.S.	23	22	41	63	..
1983-84—Univ. of New Hampshire	ECAC	7	1	1	2	2
1984-85—Stratford Jr. B.	OHL	23	..	..	66	4
1985-86—University of Maine (d)	H. East	24	13	16	29	10
1986-87—University of Maine	H. East	36	19	23	42	37
1987-88—Univ. of Maine (b-e)	H. East	44	31	44	75	46
1988-89—Denver Rangers	IHL	36	12	10	22	21
1989-90—Flint Spirits	IHL	68	13	33	46	30

(c)—June, 1983—Drafted as underage junior by Edmonton Oilers in 1983 NHL entry draft. Second Oilers pick, 40th overall, second round.

(d)—October, 1986—Traded with Don Jackson by Edmonton Oilers to New York Rangers for Reijo Ruotsalainen, NHL rights to Ville Horava, Clark Donatelli and Jim Wiemer.

(e)—Named NCAA second team All-American (East).

GLEN GOODALL

Center . . . 5'8" . . . 168 lbs. . . . Born, Fort Nelson, B.C., January 22, 1970 . . . Shoots right . . . Set WHL records for points by a 16-year-old (112) and goals (63) . . . (1989-90)—Set WHL records for career games, goals and points.

Year	Team	League	Games	G.	A.	Pts.	Pen.
1983-84—Thompson Bantam	Manitoba	74	163	157	320	40
1984-85—Seattle Breakers	WHL	59	5	21	26	6
1985-86—Seattle Thunderbirds	WHL	65	13	28	41	53
1986-87—Seattle Thunderbirds (b)	WHL	68	63	49	112	64
1987-88—Seattle Thunderbirds (c)	WHL	70	53	64	117	88

Year	Team	League	Games	G.	A.	Pts.	Pen.
1988-89—Seattle Thunderbirds		WHL	70	52	62	114	58
1988-89—Flint Spirits		IHL	9	5	4	9	4
1989-90—Seattle Thunderbirds		WHL	67	76	87	163	83

(c)—June, 1988—Drafted by Detroit Red Wings in 1988 NHL entry draft. Ninth Red Wings pick, 206th overall, 10th round.

GUY GOSSELIN

Defense . . . 5'10'' . . . 185 lbs. . . . Born, Rochester, Minn., January 6, 1964 . . . Shoots left . . . Son of Gordon Gosselin, a member of 1952 Fort Francis, Ontario Allen Cup Champions . . . (November 25, 1988)—Broken ankle.

Year	Team	League	Games	G.	A.	Pts.	Pen.
1981-82—Rochester J. Marshall H.L. (c)		Minn.H.S.	22	14	15	29	48
1982-83—Univ. of Minn.-Duluth		WCHA	4	0	0	0	0
1983-84—Univ. of Minn.-Duluth		WCHA	37	3	3	6	26
1984-85—Univ. of Minn.-Duluth		WCHA	47	3	7	10	50
1985-86—Univ. of Minn.-Duluth		WCHA	39	2	16	18	53
1986-87—Univ. of Minn.-Duluth (b)		WCHA	33	7	8	15	66
1987-88—U.S. Olympic Team		Int'l	53	3	22	25	....
1987-88—Winnipeg Jets		NHL	5	0	0	0	6
1988-89—Moncton Hawks		AHL	58	2	8	10	56
1989-90—Moncton Hawks		AHL	70	2	10	12	37
NHL TOTALS			5	0	0	0	6

(c)—June, 1982—Drafted as underage player by Winnipeg Jets in 1982 NHL entry draft. Sixth Jets pick, 159th overall, eighth round.

STEVE GOTAAS

Center . . . 5'9'' . . . 170 lbs. . . . Born, Cumrose, Sask., May 10, 1967 . . . Shoots right . . . (May, 1984)—Shoulder surgery . . . (September, 1987)—Bursitis in hip during Pittsburgh training camp . . . (September, 1988)—Injured shoulder in Pittsburgh Penguins training camp . . . (March, 1989)—Injured knee cap and required off-season surgery . . . (October 12, 1989)—Major reconstructive knee surgery and unable to return until final week of season.

Year	Team	League	Games	G.	A.	Pts.	Pen.
1983-84—Prince Albert Raiders		WHL	65	10	22	32	47
1984-85—Prince Albert Raiders (c)		WHL	72	32	41	73	66
1985-86—Prince Albert Raiders		WHL	61	40	61	101	31
1986-87—Prince Albert Raiders		WHL	68	53	55	108	94
1987-88—Pittsburgh Penguins		NHL	36	5	6	11	45
1987-88—Muskegon Lumberjacks		IHL	34	16	22	38	4
1988-89—Muskegon Lumberjacks (d)		IHL	19	9	16	25	34
1988-89—Kalamazoo Wings		IHL	30	24	22	46	12
1988-89—Minnesota North Stars		NHL	12	1	3	4	6
1989-90—Kalamazoo Wings		IHL	1	1	0	1	0
NHL TOTALS			48	6	9	15	51

(c)—June, 1985—Drafted as underage junior by Pittsburgh Penguins in 1985 NHL entry draft. Fourth Penguins pick, 86th overall, fifth round.

(d)—December 17, 1988—Traded with Ville Siren by Pittsburgh Penguins to Minnesota North Stars for Scott Bjugstad and Gord Dineen.

CHRIS GOTZIAMAN

Right Wing . . . 6'2'' . . . 190 lbs. . . . Born, Roseau, Minn., November 29, 1971 . . . Shoots right . . . (February, 1988)—Surgery on knee cartilage . . . Plans to attend University of North Dakota.

Year	Team	League	Games	G.	A.	Pts.	Pen.
1988-89—Roseau H.S.		Minn. H.S.	25	13	18	31	..
1989-90—Roseau H.S. (c)		Minn. H.S.	28	34	31	65	..

(c)—June 16, 1990—Selected by New Jersey Devils in 1990 NHL entry draft. Third Devils pick, 29th overall, second round.

ROBERT GOULD

Right Wing . . . 5'11'' . . . 195 lbs. . . . Born, Petrolia, Ont., September 2, 1957 . . . Shoots right . . . (October, 1987)—Hairline fracture of right foot . . . (April, 1990)—Sprained left knee.

Year	Team	League	Games	G.	A.	Pts.	Pen.
1975-76—University of New Hampshire		ECAC	31	13	14	27	16
1976-77—University of New Hampshire (c)		ECAC	39	24	25	49	36
1977-78—University of New Hampshire		ECAC	30	23	34	57	40
1978-79—University of New Hampshire		ECAC	....	24	17	41	....
1978-79—Tulsa Oilers		CHL	5	2	0	2	4
1979-80—Atlanta Flames		NHL	1	0	0	0	0
1979-80—Birmingham Bulls		CHL	79	27	33	60	73
1980-81—Calgary Flames		NHL	3	0	0	0	0
1980-81—Birmingham Bulls		CHL	58	25	25	50	43
1980-81—Fort Worth Texans		CHL	18	8	6	14	6
1981-82—Oklahoma City Stars		CHL	1	0	1	1	0
1981-82—Calgary Flames (d)		NHL	16	3	0	3	4
1981-82—Washington Capitals		NHL	60	18	13	31	69
1982-83—Washington Capitals		NHL	80	22	18	40	43
1983-84—Washington Capitals		NHL	78	21	19	40	74
1984-85—Washington Capitals		NHL	78	14	19	33	69
1985-86—Washington Capitals		NHL	79	19	19	38	26
1986-87—Washington Capitals		NHL	78	23	27	50	74
1907-00—Washington Capitals		NHL	72	12	14	26	56
1988-89—Washington Capitals		NHL	75	5	13	18	65
1989-90—Boston Bruins (e)		NHL	77	8	17	25	92
NHL TOTALS			698	145	159	304	572

(c)—June, 1977—Drafted by Atlanta Flames in 1977 amateur draft. Sixth Flames pick, 118th overall, seventh round.

(d)—November, 1981—Traded with Randy Holt by Calgary Flames to Washington Capitals for Pat Ribble.

(e)—September 27, 1989—Traded by Washington Capitals to Boston Bruins for Alain Cote.

MICHEL GOULET

Left Wing . . . 6'1'' . . . 195 lbs. . . . Born, Peribonqua, Que., April 21, 1960 . . . Shoots left . . . Set Nordiques NHL record for most goals in a season in 1982-83 (57) . . . (1983-84)—Set NHL record for most points by left wing in a season (121) and tied record for assists by a left wing (65) set by John Bucyk of Boston in 1970-71 . . . (January 2, 1985)—Fractured thumb vs. Hartford . . . (September, 1985)—Left training camp to renegotiate contract, suspended by Quebec and did not return until after the regular season had started . . . (October 13, 1986)—Broke finger on right hand when slashed by Brad Maxwell at Vancouver . . . (October 6, 1988)—Strained ligaments in left knee when hooked by Ulf Samuelsson in opening game of the season . . . (May, 1989)—Surgery to finger . . . (October 28, 1989)—Sprained right ankle vs. Edmonton and missed nine games . . . (March 11, 1990)—Bruised ribs and stretched rib cartilage when checked by Glen Featherstone vs. St. Louis.

Year	Team	League	Games	G.	A.	Pts.	Pen.
1976-77—Quebec Remparts		QMJHL	37	17	18	35	9
1977-78—Quebec Remparts (b-c)		QMJHL	72	73	62	135	109
1978-79—Birmingham Bulls (d)		WHA	78	28	30	58	64
1979-80—Quebec Nordiques		NHL	77	22	32	54	48
1980-81—Quebec Nordiques		NHL	76	32	39	71	45
1981-82—Quebec Nordiques		NHL	80	42	42	84	48
1982-83—Quebec Nordiques (b)		NHL	80	57	48	105	51
1983-84—Quebec Nordiques (a)		NHL	75	56	65	121	76
1984-85—Quebec Nordiques		NHL	69	55	40	95	55
1985-86—Quebec Nordiques (a)		NHL	75	53	50	103	64
1986-87—Quebec Nordiques (a)		NHL	75	49	47	96	61
1987-88—Quebec Nordiques		NHL	80	48	58	106	56
1988-89—Quebec Nordiques		NHL	69	26	38	64	67
1989-90—Quebec Nordiques (e)		NHL	57	16	29	45	42
1989-90—Chicago Black Hawks		NHL	8	4	1	5	9
WHA TOTALS			78	28	30	58	64
NHL TOTALS			821	460	489	949	622

(c)—July, 1978—Signed by Birmingham Bulls (WHA) as underage player.

(d)—August, 1979—Drafted by Quebec Nordiques in 1979 NHL entry draft. First Nordiques pick, 20th overall, first round.

(e)—March 5, 1990—Traded with Greg Millen and a sixth-round 1991 draft pick by Quebec Nordiques to Chicago Black Hawks for Everett Sanipass, Dan Vincelette and Mario Doyon.

CHRIS GOVEDARIS

Left Wing . . . 6' . . . 200 lbs. . . . Born, Toronto, Ont., February 2, 1970 . . . Shoots left . . . Also plays Center . . . (October, 1986)—Suspended two games by OHL . . . (January 22, 1989)—Suspended 15 games by OHL for shattering his stick across the hip of Mike Dagenais vs. Peterborough.

Year	Team	League	Games	G.	A.	Pts.	Pen.
1985-86—Toronto Young Nationals		MTHL	38	35	50	85	....
1986-87—Toronto Marlboros		OHL	64	36	28	64	148
1987-88—Toronto Marlboros (c)		OHL	62	42	38	80	118
1988-89—Toronto Marlboros		OHL	49	41	38	79	117
1989-90—Hartford Whalers		NHL	12	0	1	1	6
1989-90—Binghamton Whalers		AHL	14	3	3	6	4
1989-90—Hamilton Dukes		OHL	23	11	21	32	53
NHL TOTALS			12	0	1	1	6

(c)—June, 1988—Drafted by Hartford Whalers in 1988 NHL entry draft. First Whalers pick, 11th overall, first round.

DIRK GRAHAM

Right Wing . . . 5'11'' . . . 190 lbs. . . . Born, Regina, Sask., July 29, 1959 . . . Shoots right . . . (November, 1987)—Missed seven games with a sprained wrist . . . (December 28, 1989)—Fined $500 for fighting before game between Minnesota and Chicago . . . (March 17, 1990)—Cracked left kneecap at Montreal and missed six weeks.

Year	Team	League	Games	G.	A.	Pts.	Pen.
1975-76—Regina Blues		SJHL	54	36	32	68	82
1975-76—Regina Pats		WCHL	2	0	0	0	0
1976-77—Regina Pats		WCHL	65	37	28	65	66
1977-78—Regina Pats		WCHL	72	49	61	110	87
1978-79—Regina Pats (b-c)		WHL	71	48	60	108	252
1979-80—Dallas Black Hawks		CHL	62	17	15	32	96
1980-81—Fort Wayne Komets		IHL	6	1	2	3	12
1980-81—Toledo Goaldiggers		IHL	61	40	45	85	88
1981-82—Toledo Goaldiggers		IHL	72	49	56	105	68
1982-83—Toledo Goaldiggers (a-d)		IHL	78	70	55	125	86
1983-84—Minnesota North Stars		NHL	6	1	1	2	0
1983-84—Salt Lake Golden Eagles (a)		CHL	57	37	57	94	72
1984-85—Springfield Indians		AHL	37	20	28	48	41
1984-85—Minnesota North Stars		NHL	36	12	11	23	23
1985-86—Minnesota North Stars		NHL	80	22	33	55	87
1986-87—Minnesota North Stars		NHL	76	25	29	54	142
1987-88—Minnesota North Stars (e)		NHL	28	7	5	12	39
1987-88—Chicago Black Hawks		NHL	42	17	19	36	32
1900-09—Chicago Black Hawks		NHL	80	33	45	78	89
1989-90—Chicago Black Hawks		NHL	73	22	32	54	102
NHL TOTALS			421	139	175	314	514

(c)—August, 1979—Drafted by Vancouver Canucks in 1979 NHL entry draft. Fifth Canucks pick, 89th overall, fifth round.

(d)—Co-leader, with teammate Rick Hendricks, during IHL playoffs with 20 points.

(e)—January, 1988—Traded by Minnesota North Stars to Chicago Black Hawks for Curt Fraser.

TONY GRANATO

Center . . . 5'10" . . . 185 lbs. . . . Born, Downers Grove, Ill., July 25, 1964 . . . Shoots right . . . (February, 1989)—Bruised foot . . . (January 25, 1990)—Pulled groin at Edmonton and missed 12 games . . . (March 20, 1990)—Injured knee at Edmonton.

Year	Team	League	Games	G.	A.	Pts.	Pen.
1981-82—Northwood Prep. (c)		Ill. H.S.	..	..	..	..	..
1982-83—Northwood Prep.		Ill. H.S.	..	..	..	..	..
1983-84—Univ. of Wisconsin		WCHA	35	14	17	31	48
1984-85—Univ. of Wisconsin		WCHA	42	33	34	67	94
1985-86—Univ. of Wisconsin		WCHA	32	25	24	49	36
1986-87—Univ. of Wisconsin (b-d)		WCHA	42	28	45	73	64
1987-88—U.S. National Team		Int'l	49	40	31	71	55
1987-88—U.S. Olympic Team		Olympics	6	1	7	8	4
1987-88—Denver Rangers		IHL	22	13	14	27	36
1988-89—New York Rangers		NHL	78	36	27	63	140
1989-90—New York Rangers (e)		NHL	37	7	18	25	77
1989-90—Los Angeles Kings		NHL	19	5	6	11	45
NHL TOTALS			134	48	51	99	262

(c)—June, 1982—Drafted by New York Rangers in 1982 NHL entry draft. Fifth Rangers pick, 120th overall, sixth round.

(d)—Named Second team All-America (West).

(e)—January 20, 1990—Traded with Tomas Sandstrom by New York Rangers to Los Angeles Kings for Bernie Nicholls.

KEVIN GRANT

Defense . . . 6'4" . . . 210 lbs. . . . Born, Toronto, Ont., January 9, 1969 . . . Shoots right . . . (February 1, 1987)—Injured knee ligaments at North Bay.

Year	Team	League	Games	G.	A.	Pts.	Pen.
1984-85—Halifax McDonalds		N.S. Midget	35	15	20	35	50
1985-86—Kitchener Rangers		OHL	63	2	15	17	204
1986-87—Kitchener Rangers (c)		OHL	52	5	18	23	125
1987-88—Kitchener Rangers		OHL	48	3	20	23	138
1988-89—Sudbury Wolves (d)		OHL	60	9	41	50	186
1988-89—Salt Lake Golden Eagles		IHL	3	0	1	1	5
1989-90—Salt Lake Golden Eagles		IHL	78	7	17	24	117

(c)—June, 1987—Drafted as underage junior by Calgary Flames in 1987 NHL entry draft. Third Flames pick, 40th overall, second round.

(d)—November, 1988—Traded with Sean Stansfield and fourth-round 1989 (Traded to Sault Ste. Marie Greyhounds) and 1990 draft picks by Kitchener Rangers to Sudbury Wolves for Pierre Gagnon, John Uniac and a seventh round 1989 draft pick (Jamie Isreal).

DANNY GRATTON

Center and Left Wing . . . 6'1" . . . 185 lbs. . . . Born, Brantford, Ont., December 7, 1966 . . . Shoots left . . . Son of Ken Gratton (minor league player, 1967-1976).

Year	Team	League	Games	G.	A.	Pts.	Pen.
1981-82—Guelph Platers		OJHL	40	14	26	40	70
1982-83—Oshawa Generals		OHL	64	15	28	43	55
1983-84—Oshawa Generals		OHL	65	40	34	74	55
1984-85—Oshawa Generals (c)		OHL	56	24	48	72	67
1985-86—Oshawa Generals		OHL	10	3	5	8	15
1985-86—Belleville Bulls (d)		OHL	20	12	14	26	11
1985-86—Ottawa 67's		OHL	25	18	18	36	19
1986-87—New Haven Nighthawks		AHL	49	6	10	16	45
1987-88—New Haven Nighthawks		AHL	57	18	28	46	77
1987-88—Los Angeles Kings		NHL	7	1	0	1	5
1988-89—Flint Spirits		IHL	20	5	9	14	8
1988-89—New Haven Nighthawks		AHL	29	5	13	18	41
1989-90—Canadian National Team (e)		Int'l.	68	29	37	66	40
NHL TOTALS			7	1	0	1	5

(c)—June, 1985—Drafted as underage junior by Los Angeles Kings in 1985 NHL entry draft. Second Kings pick, 10th overall, first round.

(d)—February, 1986—Traded by Belleville Bulls to Ottawa 67's for Frank Dimuzio.

(e)—August, 1990—Signed by Los Angeles Kings as a free agent.

ADAM GRAVES

Center . . . 6' . . . 185 lbs. . . . Born, Toronto, Ont., April 12, 1968 . . . Shoots left . . . Also plays Left Wing . . . (February, 1986)—Bruised shoulder.

Year	Team	League	Games	G.	A.	Pts.	Pen.
1984-85—King City Jr. B.		OHL	25	23	33	56	29
1985-86—Windsor Spitfires (c)		OHL	62	27	37	64	35
1986-87—Windsor Spitfires		OHL	66	45	55	100	70
1986-87—Adirondack Red Wings (d)		AHL	....	....	....	....	....
1987-88—Detroit Red Wings		NHL	9	0	1	1	8
1987-88—Windsor Spitfires		OHL	37	28	32	60	107
1988-89—Detroit Red Wings		NHL	56	7	5	12	60
1988-89—Adirondack Red Wings		AHL	14	10	11	21	28
1989-90—Detroit Red Wings (e)		NHL	13	0	1	1	13
1989-90—Edmonton Oilers		NHL	63	9	12	21	123
NHL TOTALS			141	16	19	35	204

(c)—June, 1986—Drafted as underage junior by Detroit Red Wings in 1986 NHL entry draft. Second Red Wings pick, 22nd overall, second round.

(d)—No regular season record. Played five playoff games.

(e)—November 2, 1989—Traded with Joe Murphy, Petr Klima and Jeff Sharples by Detroit Red Wings to Edmonton Oilers for Jimmy Carson, Kevin McClelland and a fifth-round 1991 draft pick.

STEVE GRAVES

Left Wing and Center . . . 6' . . . 180 lbs. . . . Born, Kingston, Ont., April 7, 1964 . . . Shoots left . . . (February, 1986)—Torn groin muscle.

Year	Team	League	Games	G.	A.	Pts.	Pen.
1980-81—Ottawa Senators		OPJHL	44	21	17	38	47
1981-82—Sault Ste. Marie Greyhounds (c)		OHL	66	12	15	27	49
1982-83—Sault Ste. Marie Greyhounds		OHL	60	21	20	41	48
1983-84—Sault Ste. Marie Greyhounds		OHL	67	41	48	81	47
1983-84—Edmonton Oilers		NHL	2	0	0	0	0
1984-85—Nova Scotia Oilers		AHL	80	17	15	32	20
1985-86—Nova Scotia Oilers		AHL	78	19	18	37	22
1986-87—Edmonton Oilers		NHL	12	2	0	2	0
1986-87—Nova Scotia Oilers		AHL	59	18	10	28	22
1987-88—Edmonton Oilers		NHL	21	3	4	7	10
1987-88—Nova Scotia Oilers		AHL	11	6	2	8	4
1988-89—Canadian National Team		Int'l.	3	5	1	6	2
1988-89—TPS (d)		Finland	43	16	12	28	48
1989-90—Canadian National Team		Int'l.	53	24	19	43	50
NHL TOTALS			35	5	4	9	10

(c)—June, 1982—Drafted as underage junior by Edmonton Oilers in 1982 NHL entry draft. Second Oilers pick, 41st overall, second round.

(d)—September, 1988—Signed by TPS (Finland) as a free agent.

MARK GREEN

Center . . . 6'3" . . . 205 lbs. . . . Born, Massensa, N.Y., December 12, 1967 . . . Shoots left . . . Also plays Left Wing.

Year	Team	League	Games	G.	A.	Pts.	Pen.
1985-86—New Hampton Prep. (c)		N.Y. H.S.	26	26	28	54	20
1986-87—New Hampton Prep.		N.Y. H.S.	....	....	....	....	....
1987-88—Clarkson University		ECAC	18	3	6	9	18
1988-89—Clarkson University		ECAC	30	16	11	27	42
1989-90—Clarkson University		ECAC	32	18	17	35	42

(c)—June, 1986—Drafted by Winnipeg Jets in 1986 NHL entry draft. Eighth Jets pick, 176th overall, ninth round.

RICHARD DOUGLAS (RICK) GREEN

Defense . . . 6'3" . . . 200 lbs. . . . Born, Belleville, Ont., February 20, 1956 . . . Shoots left . . . Missed part of 1976-77 season with broken right wrist . . . (November, 1980)—Broken hand . . . (December 14, 1981)—Separated shoulder at Montreal . . . (March, 1983)—Hip injury . . . (October, 1983)—Broken right wrist . . . (February 21, 1984)—Broke rib at Buffalo . . . (September, 1985)—Injured ankle during training camp and missed first eight games of season . . . (December 31, 1985)—Broken thumb . . . (February 24, 1986)—Reinjured thumb at Edmonton . . . (October, 1986)—Cut eyelid . . . (October, 1987)—Bruised right foot . . . (March, 1988)—Injured back . . . (November 24, 1988)—Concussion when elbowed by Gord Donnelly at Quebec . . . (March, 1989)—Back spasms.

Year	Team	League	Games	G.	A.	Pts.	Pen.
1972-73—London Knights		Jr."A"OHA	7	0	1	1	2
1973-74—London Knights		Jr."A"OHA	65	6	30	36	45
1974-75—London Knights		Jr."A"OHA	65	8	45	53	68
1975-76—London Knights (a-c-d)		Jr."A"OHA	61	13	47	60	69
1976-77—Washington Capitals		NHL	45	3	12	15	16
1977-78—Washington Capitals		NHL	60	5	14	19	67
1978-79—Washington Capitals		NHL	71	8	33	41	62
1979-80—Washington Capitals		NHL	71	4	20	24	52
1980-81—Washington Capitals		NHL	65	8	23	31	91
1981-82—Washington Capitals (e)		NHL	65	3	25	28	93
1982-83—Montreal Canadiens		NHL	66	2	24	26	58
1983-84—Montreal Canadiens		NHL	7	0	1	1	7
1984-85—Montreal Canadiens		NHL	77	1	18	19	30
1985-86—Montreal Canadiens		NHL	46	3	2	5	20
1986-87—Montreal Canadiens		NHL	72	1	9	10	10
1987-88—Montreal Canadiens		NHL	59	2	11	13	33
1988-89—Montreal Canadiens		NHL	72	1	14	15	25
1989-90—Marano (f)		Italy	19	5	12	17	6
NHL TOTALS			776	41	206	247	564

(c)—Won Max Kaminsky Memorial Trophy (Outstanding Defenseman).

(d)—Drafted from London Knights by Washington Capitals in first round of 1976 amateur draft.

(e)—September, 1982—Traded by Washington Capitals with Ryan Walter to Montreal Canadiens for Rod Langway, Brian Engblom, Doug Jarvis and Craig Laughlin.

(f)—June 15, 1990—NHL rights traded by Montreal Canadiens to Detroit Red Wings for a fifth-round 1991 draft pick.

TRAVIS GREEN

Center . . . 6' . . . 195 lbs. . . . Born, Creston, B.C., December 20, 1970 . . . Shoots right.

Year	Team	League	Games	G.	A.	Pts.	Pen.
1985-86—Castlegar Rebels		BCJHL	35	30	40	70	41
1986-87—Spokane Chiefs		WHL	64	8	17	25	27
1987-88—Spokane Chiefs		WHL	72	33	53	86	42
1988-89—Spokane Chiefs (c)		WHL	72	51	51	102	79
1989-90—Spokane Chiefs (d)		WHL	50	45	44	89	80
1989-90—Medicine Hat Tigers		WHL	25	15	24	39	19

(c)—June, 1989—Drafted by New York Islanders in 1989 NHL entry draft. Second Islanders pick, 23rd overall, second round.

(d)—January 26, 1990—Traded by Spokane Chiefs to Medicine Hat Tigers for Mark Woolf, Chris Lafreniere and Frank Esposito.

JEFF GREENLAW

Left Wing . . . 6'3" . . . 220 lbs. . . . Born, Toronto, Ont., February 28, 1968 . . . Shoots left . . . (April, 1987)—Fitted for body cast to allow healing of a stress fracture of a vertebrae . . . (September, 1989)—Deep right leg bruise and missed 65 games.

Year	Team	League	Games	G.	A.	Pts.	Pen.
1984-85	—St. Catharines Jr. B	OHA	33	21	29	50	141
1985-86	—Team Canada (c)	Int'l.	57	3	16	19	81
1986-87	—Washington Capitals	NHL	22	0	3	3	44
1986-87	—Binghamton Whalers	AHL	4	0	2	2	0
1987-88	—Binghamton Whalers	AHL	56	8	7	15	142
1988-89	—Baltimore Skipjacks	AHL	55	12	15	27	115
1989-90	—Baltimore Skipjacks	AHL	10	3	2	5	26
NHL TOTALS			22	0	3	3	44

(c)—June, 1986—Drafted by Washington Capitals in 1986 NHL entry draft. First Capitals pick, 19th overall, first round.

RANDY GREGG

Defense . . . 6'4" . . . 215 lbs. . . . Born, Edmonton, Alta., February 19, 1956 . . . Shoots left . . . Has a degree in medicine . . . Furthered medical studies while he played hockey in Japan . . . (December, 1984)—Bruised left shoulder . . . (January, 1985)—Sprained left knee . . . (October 28, 1985)—Separated ribs at Calgary and missed 16 games . . . Won Senator Joseph Sullivan Award as the top Canadian College player in 1979 . . . (March 17, 1987)—Dislocated left shoulder . . . (December, 1988)—Pulled leg muscle in team practice . . . (September, 1989)—Pulled leg muscle during camp and missed first 21 games of season . . . (May 10, 1990)—Charley horse in collision with Steve Thomas vs. Chicago.

Year	Team	League	Games	G.	A.	Pts.	Pen.
1975-76	—University of Alberta	CWUAA	20	3	14	17	27
1976-77	—University of Alberta	CWUAA	24	9	17	26	34
1977-78	—University of Alberta	CWUAA	24	7	23	30	37
1978-79	—University of Alberta	CWUAA	24	5	16	21	47
1979-80	—Canadian National Team	Int'l	56	7	17	24	36
1979-80	—Canadian Olympic Team	Int'l	6	1	1	2	2
1980-81	—Kokudo Bunnies (c)	Japan	35	12	18	30	30
1981-82	—Kokudo Bunnies	Japan	36	12	20	32	25
1981-82	—Edmonton Oilers (d)	NHL	....	...	....	....	....
1982-83	—Edmonton Oilers	NHL	80	6	22	28	54
1983-84	—Edmonton Oilers	NHL	80	13	27	40	56
1984-85	—Edmonton Oilers	NHL	57	3	20	23	32
1985-86	—Edmonton Oilers	NHL	64	2	26	28	47
1986-87	—Edmonton Oilers (e)	NHL	52	8	16	24	42
1987-88	—Canadian Olympic Team	Int'l	45	3	8	11	45
1987-88	—Edmonton Oilers	NHL	15	1	2	3	8
1988-89	—Edmonton Oilers	NHL	57	3	15	18	28
1989-90	—Edmonton Oilers	NHL	48	4	20	24	42
NHL TOTALS			453	40	148	188	309

(c)—March, 1981—Signed by Edmonton Oilers as a free agent.
(d)—No regular season record. Played four playoff games.
(e)—September, 1986—Announced he was retiring. He returned to the Oilers in November.

MARK GREIG

Right Wing . . . 5'11" . . . 188 lbs. . . . Born, High River, Alta., January 25, 1970 . . . Shoots right.

Year	Team	League	Games	G.	A.	Pts.	Pen.
1985-86	—Blackie Bisons	Alta. Midget	31	12	43	55	44
1986-87	—Calgary North Stars	Alta. Midget	18	9	28	37	30
1986-87	—Calgary Wranglers	WHL	5	0	0	0	0
1987-88	—Lethbridge Hurricanes	WHL	65	9	18	27	38
1988-89	—Lethbridge Hurricanes	WHL	71	36	72	108	113
1989-90	—Lethbridge Hurricanes (c)	WHL	65	55	80	135	149

(c)—June 16, 1990—Selected by Hartford Whalers in 1990 NHL entry draft. First Whalers pick, 15th overall, first round.

RONALD JOHN GRESCHNER

Defense . . . 6'2" . . . 205 lbs. . . . Born, Goodsoil, Sask., December 22, 1954 . . . Shoots left . . . Set WCHL record for points by defenseman in season in 1973-74 (broken by Kevin McCarthy in 1975-76) . . . Missed part of 1978-79 season with shoulder separation . . . (November 18, 1981)—Pinched nerve in back vs. Philadelphia . . . (September, 1982)—Injured back in training camp and out until February, 1983 . . . (March, 1983)—Reinjured back . . . (November, 1984)—Shoulder separation that cost him 31 games at various points of the season . . . (May, 1985)—Surgery to resection the distal clavical of left shoulder . . . (April 15, 1986)—Fractured right hand at Philadelphia . . . Also plays Center . . . (October, 1986)—Fractured left foot . . . (March, 1988)—Strained left shoulder . . . (November, 1988)—Bruised ribs . . . (February, 1989)—Bruised left instep, strained back muscles and surgery to his nose . . . (March 26, 1989)—Suspended for final three games of the season for spitting water at linseman Ron Asselstine . . . (January, 1990)—Left knee contusion . . . (March 3, 1990)—Broke little toe on right foot when struck by a shot at Hartford.

Year	Team	League	Games	G.	A.	Pts.	Pen.
1971-72	—New Westminster Bruins	WCHL	44	1	9	10	126
1972-73	—New Westminster Bruins	WCHL	68	22	47	69	169
1973-74	—New Westminster Bruins (c)	WCHL	67	33	70	103	170
1974-75	—Providence Reds	AHL	7	5	6	11	10
1974-75	—New York Rangers	NHL	70	8	37	45	94
1975-76	—New York Rangers	NHL	77	6	21	27	93
1976-77	—New York Rangers	NHL	80	11	36	47	89
1977-78	—New York Rangers	NHL	78	24	48	72	100
1978-79	—New York Rangers	NHL	60	17	36	53	66
1979-80	—New York Rangers	NHL	76	21	37	58	103
1980-81	—New York Rangers	NHL	74	27	41	68	112
1981-82	—New York Rangers	NHL	29	5	11	16	16
1982-83	—New York Rangers	NHL	10	3	5	8	0
1983-84	—New York Rangers	NHL	77	12	44	56	117
1984-85	—New York Rangers	NHL	48	16	29	45	42
1985-86	—New York Rangers	NHL	78	20	28	48	104
1986-87	—New York Rangers	NHL	61	6	34	40	62
1987-88	—New York Rangers	NHL	51	1	5	6	82
1988-89	—New York Rangers	NHL	58	1	10	11	94
1989-90	—New York Rangers (d)	NHL	55	1	9	10	53
NHL TOTALS			982	179	431	610	1227

(c)—Drafted from New Westminster Bruins by New York Rangers in second round of 1974 amateur draft.
(d)—July, 1990—Released by New York Rangers.

WAYNE GRETZKY

Center . . . 6' . . . 170 lbs. . . . Born, Brantford, Ont., January 26, 1961 . . . Shoots left . . . In 1979-80, his first NHL season, he became the youngest player in history to win an NHL trophy, to score 50 goals, to collect 100 points (Broken by Dale Hawerchuk) and the youngest to ever be named to the NHL All-Star team . . . Set new regular season NHL record for goals (92 in 1981-82), assists (135 in 1984-85) and points (212 in 1981-82) . . . Set new NHL records for goals (97 in 1981-82), assists (165 in 1984-85) and points (255 in 1984-85) regular season plus playoffs . . . Set new NHL playoff records for assists (31) in 1987-88 and points (47) in 1984-85 . . . Tied single game record in playoffs for most assists in a period (3), and a game (5), in first game of 1981 playoffs (April 8, 1981) in a 6-3 win at Montreal despite not taking a single shot on goal . . . In 1981-82, also set NHL records for fastest (50) goals from the start of the year (39 games), fastest 500 career points (234 games), largest margin over second-place finisher in scoring race (65 points) and most 3-or-more goals in a season (10-later tied in 1983-84) . . . (December 27, 1981)—Became first hockey player to be named THE SPORTING NEWS MAN-OF-THE-YEAR . . . (March 19, 1982)—Youngest player to reach 500 NHL career points (21 years, 1 month, 21 days) . . . (February 8, 1983)—Set All-Star game record with four goals . . . Set NHL playoff record for most points in one game with 7 (vs. Calgary, April 17, 1983, vs. Winnipeg, April 25, 1985 and vs. Los Angeles, April 9, 1987)—Broken by Patrik Sundstrom with 8 in 1987-88 and Mario Lemieux with 8 in 1988-89) . . . (October 5, 1983-January 27, 1984)—Set NHL record by collecting points in 51 consecutive games (61g, 92a), the first 51 games of the season . . . (January 28, 1984)—Bruised right shoulder vs. Los Angeles and ended consecutive games played streak at 362, an Oilers club record . . . (June, 1984)—Surgery on left ankle to remove benign growth caused by lacing his skates too tight . . . Set NHL record with 12 shorthanded goals in 1983-84 (Broken by Mario Lemieux with 13 in 1988-89) . . . (November 26, 1983-January 4, 1984)—Set NHL record for collecting assists in 17 straight games . . . (December 19, 1984)—Collected his 1000th NHL point in fewer games than any player in history, 424 games (Previous fastest was 720 games by Guy Lafleur). He is also the youngest player to ever reach the plateau at 23 yrs., 10 mos., 23 days. The previous youngest was Lafleur at 29 yrs., 3 mos., 18 days . . . Set playoff record for most assists in a single series (14 vs. Chicago), 1985 . . . First player to have 100 point seasons in first 11 years of NHL . . . Named 1985 Canadian Athlete of the Year . . . Set new regular season NHL records for assists (163) and points (215) in 1985-86 . . . Set new NHL playoff records for most career assists (195) and points (284) . . . Tied playoff record for most assists in single playoff game (6 on April 9, 1987) . . . (December 30, 1987)—Twisted right knee as he scored a goal at Philadelphia . . . (February 19, 1988)—Missed three games due to corneal abrasion to left eye vs. Pittsburgh . . . All-time NHL career assist leader . . . (October 15, 1989)—Broke Gordie Howe's all-time NHL career point record of 1,851 at Edmonton . . . Brother of Keith, Brent and Glen Gretzky . . . (March 17, 1990)—Injured groin at Boston . . . (March 22, 1990)—Strained lower back when hit by Alan Kerr and Ken Baumgartner at N.Y. Islanders and missed final five games of season and first two playoff games against Calgary with muscle spasms. It marked the first time in his career he had missed a playoff game . . . (1989-90)—Collected 40 goals for the 11th consecutive season, an NHL record.

Year	Team	League	Games	G.	A.	Pts.	Pen.
1976-77	—Peterborough Petes	OMJHL	3	0	3	3	0
1977-78	—S. Ste. M. G'hounds (b-c)	OMJHL	64	70	112	182	14
1978-79	—Indianapolis Racers (d)	WHA	8	3	3	6	0
1978-79	—Edmonton Oilers (b-e-f-g)	WHA	72	43	61	104	19
1979-80	—Edmonton Oilers (b-h-i)	NHL	79	51	*86	*137	21
1980-81	—Edmonton Oilers (a-h-j-l)	NHL	80	55	*109	*164	28
1981-82	—Edmonton Oilers (a-h-j-l-p)	NHL	80	*92	*120	*212	26
1982-83	—Edmonton Oilers (a-h-j-k-l-p)	NHL	80	*71	*125	*196	59
1983-84	—Edmonton Oilers (a-h-j-l-m-p)	NHL	74	*87	*118	*205	39
1984-85	—Edmonton Oilers (a-h-j-l-n-o-p)	NHL	80	*73	*135	*208	52
1985-86	—Edmonton Oilers (a-h-j-l)	NHL	80	52	*163	*215	46
1986-87	—Edmonton Oilers (a-h-j-q)	NHL	79	*62	*121	*183	28
1987-88	—Edmonton Oilers (b-o-r-s)	NHL	64	40	*109	149	24
1988-89	—Los Angeles Kings (b-h)	NHL	78	54	*114	168	26
1989-90	—Los Angeles Kings (b-j)	NHL	73	40	*102	*142	42
NHL TOTALS			847	677	1302	1979	391
WHA TOTALS			80	46	64	110	19

(c)—May, 1978—Signed to multi-year contract by Indianapolis Racers (WHA) as an underage junior.
(d)—November, 1978—Traded by Indianapolis to Edmonton with Peter Driscoll, Ed Mio for cash and future considerations.
(e)—Won WHA Rookie award.
(f)—Named WHA Rookie of the Year in poll of players by THE SPORTING NEWS.
(g)—Led in points (20) and tied for lead in goals (10) during playoffs.
(h)—Won Hart Memorial Trophy (Most Valuable Player).

(i)—Won Lady Byng Memorial Trophy (Most Gentlemanly Player).
(j)—Won Art Ross Memorial Trophy (NHL Leading Scorer).
(k)—Led Stanley Cup Playoffs with 26 assists and 38 points.
(l)—Selected NHL Player of Year by THE SPORTING NEWS in poll of players.
(m)—Led Stanley Cup Playoffs with 22 assists and 35 points.
(n)—Led Stanley Cup Playoffs with 30 assists and 47 points.
(o)—Won Conn Smythe Trophy (Stanley Cup Playoff MVP).
(p)—Won Lester Pearson Award (NHL Players MVP).
(q)—Led Stanley Cup Playoffs with 29 assists and 34 points.
(r)—Led Stanley Cup Playoffs with 31 assists and 43 points.
(s)—August, 1988—Traded with Marty McSorley and Mike Krushelnyski by Edmonton Oilers to Los Angeles Kings for Jimmy Carson, Martin Gelinas, first-round draft choices in 1989 (traded to New Jersey), '91 and '93, plus $15 million.

JASON GREYERBIEHL

Left Wing . . . 6' . . . 175 lbs. . . . Born, Bramalea, Ont., March 24, 1970 . . . Shoots left.

Year	Team	League	Games	G.	A.	Pts.	Pen.
1987-88—Bramalea Jr. B		OHA	37	33	27	60	10
1988-89—Colgate Univ. (c)		ECAC	31	6	9	15	14
1989-90—Colgate Univ.		ECAC	38	12	20	32	20

(c)—June, 1989—Drafted by Chicago Black Hawks in 1989 NHL entry draft. Seventh Black Hawks pick, 174th overall, ninth round.

BRENT GRIEVE

Left Wing . . . 6'1" . . . 200 lbs. . . . Born, Oshawa, Ont., May 9, 1969 . . . Shoots left.

Year	Team	League	Games	G.	A.	Pts.	Pen.
1985-86—Oshawa Minor Midget		OHA	51	38	48	86	200
1986-87—Oshawa Generals		OHL	60	9	19	28	102
1987-88—Oshawa Generals		OHL	56	19	20	39	122
1988-89—Oshawa Generals (c)		OHL	49	34	33	67	105
1989-90—Oshawa Generals		OHL	62	46	47	93	125

(c)—June, 1989—Drafted by New York Islanders in 1989 NHL entry draft. Fourth Islanders pick, 65th overall, fourth round.

STUART GRIMSON

Left Wing . . . 6'5" . . . 210 lbs. . . . Born, Vancouver, B.C., May 20, 1965 . . . Shoots left . . . (February, 1983)—Fractured forearm . . . (January 9, 1990)—Broke cheekbone vs. Edmonton.

Year	Team	League	Games	G.	A.	Pts.	Pen.
1982-83—Regina Pats (c)		WHL	48	0	1	1	144
1983-84—Regina Pats		WHL	63	8	8	16	131
1984-85—Regina Pats (d-e)		WHL	71	24	32	56	248
1985-86—Univ. of Manitoba		CWUAA	12	7	4	11	113
1986-87—Univ. of Manitoba		CWUAA	29	8	8	16	67
1987-88—Salt Lake Golden Eagles		IHL	38	9	5	14	268
1988-89—Calgary Flames		NHL	1	0	0	0	5
1988-89—Salt Lake Golden Eagles		IHL	72	9	18	27	*397
1989-90—Salt Lake Golden Eagles		IHL	62	8	8	16	319
1989-90—Calgary Flames		NHL	3	0	0	0	17
NHL TOTALS			4	0	0	0	22

(c)—June, 1983—Drafted by Detroit Red Wings in 1983 NHL entry draft. Eleventh Red Wings pick, 186th overall, 10th round.
(d)—May, 1985—Not signed by Detroit and returned to entry draft pool.
(e)—June, 1985—Drafted by Calgary Flames in 1985 NHL entry draft. Eighth Flames pick, 143rd overall, seventh round.

JARI GRONSTRAND

Defense . . . 6'3" . . . 197 lbs. . . . Born, Tampere, Finland, November 14, 1962 . . . Shoots left . . . (December 16, 1986)—Separated shoulder at N.Y. Islanders . . . (February, 1987)—Strained knee ligaments . . . (March 11, 1987)—Hospitalized after being struck in the eye with a stick vs. Toronto . . . (February, 1988)—Strained ligaments in right knee . . . (February 9, 1989)—Fractured left cheekbone when struck by a shot at Pittsburgh . . . (September, 1989)—Fractured right cheekbone during Quebec Nordiques training camp.

Year	Team	League	Games	G.	A.	Pts.	Pen.
1984-85—Tappara		Finland	33	9	6	15	..
1985-86—Tappara (c)		Finland	44	10	7	17	32
1986-87—Minnesota North Stars		NHL	47	1	6	7	27
1987-88—New York Rangers (d)		NHL	62	3	11	14	63
1987-88—Colorado Rangers (e)		IHL	3	1	3	4	0
1988-89—Quebec Nordiques		NHL	25	1	3	4	14
1988-89—Halifax Citadels		AHL	8	0	1	1	6
1989-90—Halifax Citadels		AHL	2	0	0	0	0
1989-90—Quebec Nordiques (f)		NHL	7	0	1	1	2
1989-90—New York Islanders		NHL	41	3	4	7	27
1989-90—Springfield Indians		AHL	1	0	1	1	0
NHL TOTALS			182	8	25	33	133

(c)—June, 1986—Drafted by Minnesota North Stars in 1986 NHL entry draft. Eighth North Stars pick, 96th overall, fifth round.
(d)—October, 1987—Traded with Paul Boutilier by Minnesota North Stars to New York Rangers for Dave Gagner and Jay Caufield.
(e)—August, 1988—Traded with Walt Poddubny, Bruce Bell and fourth-round draft choice in 1989 (Eric Dubois) by New York Rangers to Quebec Nordiques for Normand Rochefort and Jason Lafreniere.
(f)—November 21, 1989—Claimed by New York Islanders on waivers from Quebec Nordiques.

SCOTT KENNETH GRUHL

Left Wing . . . 5'11" . . . 185 lbs. . . . Born, Port Colborne, Ont., September 13, 1959 . . . Shoots left . . . Also plays Defense . . . (March, 1988)—Fractured left hand in IHL game.

Year	Team	League	Games	G.	A.	Pts.	Pen.
1976-77—Northeastern University		ECAC	17	6	4	10	....
1977-78—Northeastern University		ECAC	28	21	38	59	46
1978-79—Sudbury Wolves		OMJHL	68	35	49	84	78
1979-80—Binghamton Dusters		AHL	4	1	0	1	6
1979-80—Saginaw Gears (b-c)		IHL	75	53	40	93	100
1980-81—Houston Apollos		CHL	4	0	0	0	0
1980-81—Saginaw Gears (d)		IHL	77	56	34	90	87
1981-82—New Haven Nighthawks		AHL	73	28	41	69	107
1981-82—Los Angeles Kings		NHL	7	2	1	3	2
1982-83—New Haven Nighthawks		AHL	68	25	38	63	114
1982-83—Los Angeles Kings		NHL	7	0	2	2	4
1983-84—Muskegon Mohawks (a)		IHL	56	40	56	96	49
1984-85—Muskegon Lumberjacks (a-e-f)		IHL	82	62	64	126	102
1985-86—Muskegon Lumberjacks		IHL	82	59	50	109	178
1986-87—Muskegon Lumberjacks		IHL	67	34	39	73	157
1987-88—Pittsburgh Penguins		NHL	6	1	0	1	0
1987-88—Muskegon Lumberjacks		IHL	55	28	47	75	115
1988-89—Muskegon Lumberjacks		IHL	79	37	55	92	163
1989-90—Muskegon Lumberjacks		IHL	80	41	51	92	206
NHL TOTALS			20	3	3	6	6

(c)—September, 1980—Signed by Los Angeles Kings as free agent.
(d)—Led IHL playoff with 11 goals and 19 assists.
(e)—Won James Gatchene Memorial Trophy (IHL MVP).
(f)—Led IHL playoffs with 16 assists.

FRANCOIS GUAY

Center . . . 6' . . . 185 lbs. . . . Born, Gatineau, Que., June 8, 1968 . . . Shoots left.

Year	Team	League	Games	G.	A.	Pts.	Pen.
1984-85—Laval Voisins		QMJHL	66	13	18	31	21
1985-86—Laval Titans (c)		QMJHL	71	19	55	74	46
1986-87—Laval Titans		QMJHL	63	52	77	129	67
1987-88—Laval Titans		QMJHL	66	60	84	144	142
1988-89—Rochester Americans		AHL	45	6	20	26	34
1989-90—Buffalo Sabres		NHL	1	0	0	0	0
1989-90—Rochester Americans		AHL	69	28	35	63	39
NHL TOTALS			1	0	0	0	0

(c)—June, 1986—Drafted as underage junior by Buffalo Sabres in 1986 NHL entry draft. Ninth Sabres pick, 152nd overall, eighth round.

PAUL GUAY

Right Wing . . . 6' . . . 185 lbs. . . . Born, Providence, R.I., September 2, 1963 . . . Shoots right . . . Member of 1984 U.S. Olympic Team.

Year	Team	League	Games	G.	A.	Pts.	Pen.
1979-80—Mt. St. Charles H.S.		R.I.H.S.	23	18	19	37	....
1980-81—Mt. St. Charles H.S. (c)		R.I.H.S.	23	28	38	66	....
1981-82—Providence College		ECAC	33	23	17	40	38
1982-83—Providence College (b)		ECAC	42	34	31	65	83
1983-84—U.S. National Team		Int'l	62	20	18	38	44
1983-84—U.S. Olympic Team		Int'l	6	1	0	1	8
1983-84—Philadelphia Flyers (d)		NHL	14	2	6	8	14
1984-85—Hershey Bears		AHL	74	23	30	53	123
1984-85—Philadelphia Flyers		NHL	2	0	1	1	0
1985-86—Los Angeles Kings (e)		NHL	23	3	3	6	18
1985-86—New Haven Nighthawks		AHL	57	15	36	51	101
1986-87—Los Angeles Kings		NHL	35	2	5	7	16
1986-87—New Haven Nighthawks		AHL	6	1	3	4	11
1987-88—New Haven Nighthawks		AHL	42	21	26	47	53
1987-88—Los Angeles Kings		NHL	33	4	4	8	40
1988-89—New Haven Nighthawks		AHL	4	4	6	10	20
1988-89—Los Angeles Kings (f)		NHL	2	0	0	0	2
1988-89—Boston Bruins		NHL	5	0	2	2	0
1988-89—Maine Mariners		AHL	61	15	29	44	77
1989-90—Utica Devils (g)		AHL	75	25	30	55	103
NHL TOTALS			114	11	21	32	90

(c)—June, 1981—Drafted as underage player by Minnesota North Stars in 1981 NHL entry draft. Tenth North Stars pick, 118th overall, sixth round.
(d)—February, 1984—Traded with third round 1985 draft pick by Minnesota North Stars to Philadelphia Flyers for Paul Holmgren.
(e)—October, 1985—Traded by Philadelphia Flyers to Los Angeles Kings for Steve Seguin.
(f)—November 3, 1988—Traded by Los Angeles Kings to Boston Bruins for Dave Pasin.
(g)—August, 1990—Signed by New York Islanders as a free agent.

STEPHANE GUERARD

Defense . . . 6'2" . . . 185 lbs. . . . Born, St. Elisabeth, Que., April 12, 1968 . . . Shoots left . . . (November 5, 1987)—Surgery to right knee . . . (September 19, 1988)—Left Quebec Nordiques training camp . . . (December, 1988)—Broke ring finger of right hand . . . (October 12, 1989)—Sprained right knee at Philadelphia . . . (December 19, 1989)—Sprained knee and pulled left thigh muscle.

Year	Team	League	Games	G.	A.	Pts.	Pen.
1984-85—Laurentides Midget		Que.	36	6	12	18	140
1985-86—Shawinigan Cataracts (c-d)		QMJHL	59	4	16	20	167
1986-87—Shawinigan Cataracts		QMJHL	31	5	16	21	57
1987-88—Quebec Nordiques		NHL	30	0	0	0	34
1988-89—Halifax Citadels		AHL	37	1	9	10	140
1989-90—Quebec Nordiques		NHL	4	0	0	0	6
1989-90—Halifax Citadels		AHL	10	0	0	0	5
NHL TOTALS			34	0	0	0	40

(c)—Won Raymond Lagace Trophy (Top Rookie Defenseman or Goaltender).
(d)—June, 1986—Drafted as underage junior by Quebec Nordiques in 1986 NHL entry draft. Third Nordiques pick, 41st overall, second round.

BILL GUERIN

Right Wing . . . 6'3" . . . 185 lbs. . . . Born, Wilbraham, Mass., November 9, 1970 . . . Shoots right.

Year	Team	League	Games	G.	A.	Pts.	Pen.
1985-86—Springfield Olympics		NEJHL	48	26	19	45	71
1986-87—Springfield Olympics		NEJHL	32	34	20	54	40
1987-88—Springfield Olympics		NEJHL	38	31	44	75	146
1988-89—Springfield Olympics (c)		NEJHL	31	32	37	69	90
1989-90—Boston College		H. East	39	14	11	25	64

(c)—June, 1989—Drafted by New Jersey Devils in 1989 NHL entry draft. First Devils pick, fifth overall, first round.

ROBERT GUILLET

Right Wing . . . 5'11" . . . 189 lbs. . . . Born, Montreal, Que., February 22, 1972 . . . Shoots right.

Year	Team	League	Games	G.	A.	Pts.	Pen.
1988-89—Richelieu Midget		Quebec	36	41	23	64	64
1989-90—Longueuil College Francais (c)		QMJHL	69	32	40	72	132

(c)—June 16, 1990—Selected by Montreal Canadiens in 1990 NHL entry draft. Fourth Canadiens pick, 60th overall, third round.

KEVAN GUY

Defense . . . 6'2" . . . 190 lbs. . . . Born, Edmonton, Alta., July 16, 1965 . . . Shoots right . . . (February 18, 1990)—Cracked bone in right foot when struck by a Ray Bourque shot vs. Boston and missed 10 games.

Year	Team	League	Games	G.	A.	Pts.	Pen.
1982-83—Medicine Hat Tigers (c)		WHL	69	7	20	27	89
1983-84—Medicine Hat Tigers		WHL	72	15	42	57	117
1984-85—Medicine Hat Tigers		WHL	31	7	17	24	46
1985-86—Moncton Golden Flames		AHL	73	4	20	24	56
1986-87—Moncton Golden Flames		AHL	46	2	10	12	38
1986-87—Calgary Flames		NHL	24	0	4	4	19
1987-88—Calgary Flames		NHL	11	0	3	3	8
1987-88—Salt Lake Golden Eagles (d)		IHL	61	6	30	36	49
1988-89—Vancouver Canucks		NHL	45	2	2	4	34
1989-90—Milwaukee Admirals		IHL	29	2	11	13	33
1989-90—Vancouver Canucks		NHL	30	2	5	7	32
NHL TOTALS			110	4	14	18	93

(c)—June, 1983—Drafted as underage junior by Calgary Flames in 1983 NHL entry draft. Fifth Flames pick, 71st overall, fourth round
(d)—June, 1988—Traded by Calgary Flames to Vancouver Canucks to complete March, 1988 deal in which Calgary sent Brian Bradley and Peter Bakovic to Vancouver for Craig Coxe.

DAVID HAAS

Left Wing . . . 6'2" . . . 185 lbs. . . . Born, Toronto, Ont., July 23, 1968 . . . Shoots left.

Year	Team	League	Games	G.	A.	Pts.	Pen.
1984-85—Don Mills Flyers Midgets		MTHL	38	38	38	76	80
1985-86—London Knights (c)		OHL	62	4	13	17	91
1986-87—London Knights (d)		OHL	5	1	0	1	5
1986-87—Kitchener Rangers		OHL	4	0	1	1	4
1986-87—Belleville Bulls		OHL	55	10	13	23	86
1987-88—Belleville Bulls		OHL	5	1	1	2	9
1987-88—Windsor Spitfires (b)		OHL	58	59	46	105	237
1988-89—Cape Breton Oilers		AHL	61	9	9	18	325
1989-90—Cape Breton Oilers		AHL	53	6	12	18	230

(c)—June, 1986—Drafted as underage junior by Edmonton Oilers in 1986 NHL entry draft. Fifth Oilers pick, 105th overall, fifth round.
(d)—October, 1986—Traded with Kelly Cain and Ed Kister by London Knights to Kitchener Rangers for Peter Lisy, Ian Pound, Stebe Marcolini and Greg Hankkio.

MARC JOSEPH HABSCHEID

Center and Right Wing . . . 6'2" . . . 180 lbs. . . . Born, Swift Current, Sask., March 1, 1963 . . . Shoots right . . . (November, 1982)—Head injury . . . (October, 1985)—Suspended by Edmonton Oilers for refusing to report to Nova Scotia Oilers (AHL).

Year	Team	League	Games	G.	A.	Pts.	Pen.
1980-81—Saskatoon Blades (c)		WHL	72	34	63	97	50
1981-82—Saskatoon Blades (b)		WHL	55	64	87	151	74
1981-82—Edmonton Oilers		NHL	7	1	3	4	2
1981-82—Wichita Wind (d)		CHL	..	..	..	..	..
1982-83—Kamloops Junior Oilers		WHL	6	7	16	23	8
1982-83—Edmonton Oilers		NHL	32	3	10	13	14
1983-84—Edmonton Oilers		NHL	9	1	0	1	6
1983-84—Moncton Alpines		AHL	71	19	37	56	32
1984-85—Edmonton Oilers		NHL	26	5	3	8	4
1984-85—Nova Scotia Oilers		AHL	48	29	29	58	65
1985-86—Minnesota North Stars (e)		NHL	6	2	3	5	0
1985-86—Springfield Indians		AHL	41	18	32	50	21
1986-87—Minnesota North Stars (f)		NHL	15	2	0	2	2
1987-88—Canadian Olympic Team		Int'l	69	24	37	61	48
1987-88—Minnesota North Stars		NHL	16	4	11	15	6
1988-89—Minnesota North Stars (g)		NHL	76	23	31	54	40
1989-90—Detroit Red Wings		NHL	66	15	11	26	33
NHL TOTALS			253	56	72	128	107

(c)—June, 1981—Drafted as underage junior by Edmonton Oilers in 1981 NHL entry draft. Sixth Oilers pick, 113th overall, sixth round.
(d)—No regular season record. Played three playoff games.
(e)—December, 1985—Traded with Don Barber and Emanuel Viveiros by Edmonton Oilers to Minnesota North Stars for Gord Sherven and Don Biggs.

(f)—November, 1986—Assigned to Springfield Indians (AHL) but refused to report. He was then allowed to join the Canadian National team in Calgary.
(g)—June 9, 1989—Signed with Detroit Red Wings as a free agent.

BOB HALKIDIS

Defense . . . 5'11" . . . 195 lbs. . . . Born, Toronto, Ont., March 5, 1966 . . . Shoots left . . . (September, 1982)—Broke ankle during training camp. In first game back, in November, he reinjured ankle and missed another two weeks . . . (December 4, 1985)—Dislocated right shoulder at St. Louis and missed 15 games . . . (October 23, 1987)—Given six-game AHL suspension for fighting . . . (December, 1987)—Injured ankle . . . (December, 1988)—Injured shoulder . . . (May, 1990)—Surgery to shoulder injured during AHL playoffs.

Year	Team	League	Games	G.	A.	Pts.	Pen.
1981-82—Toronto Young Nationals		MTMHL	40	9	27	36	54
1982-83—London Knights		OHL	37	3	12	15	52
1983-84—London Knights (c)		OHL	51	9	22	31	123
1984-85—London Knights (a-d)		OHL	62	14	50	64	154
1984-85—Buffalo Sabres (e)		NHL	..	..	..	..	..
1985-86—Buffalo Sabres		NHL	37	1	9	10	115
1986-87—Buffalo Sabres		NHL	6	1	1	2	19
1986-87—Rochester Americans		AHL	59	1	8	9	144
1987-88—Rochester Americans		AHL	15	2	5	7	50
1987-88—Buffalo Sabres		NHL	30	0	3	3	115
1988-89—Buffalo Sabres		NHL	16	0	1	1	66
1988-89—Rochester Americans		AHL	16	0	6	6	64
1989-90—Rochester Americans (f)		AHL	18	1	13	14	70
1989-90—Los Angeles Kings		NHL	20	0	4	4	56
1989-90—New Haven Nighthawks		AHL	30	3	17	20	67
NHL TOTALS			109	2	18	20	371

(c)—June, 1984—Drafted as underage junior by Buffalo Sabres in 1984 NHL entry draft. Fourth Sabres pick, 81st overall, fourth round.
(d)—Won Max Kaminsky Trophy (Top OHL Defenseman).
(e)—No regular season record. Played four playoff games.
(f)—November 24, 1989—Traded by Buffalo Sabres to Los Angeles Kings for Dale DeGray.

TAYLOR HALL

Left Wing . . . 5'11' . . . 177 lbs. . . . Born, Regina, Sask., February 20, 1964 . . . Shoots left . . . (October, 1984)—Damaged knee ligaments . . . (February, 1989)—Broke foot in Italy.

Year	Team	League	Games	G.	A.	Pts.	Pen.
1980-81—Regina Canadians		Midget	26	51	28	79	35
1981-82—Regina Pats (c)		WHL	48	14	15	29	43
1982-83—Regina Pats		WHL	72	37	57	94	78
1983-84—Regina Pats (a-d)		WHL	69	63	79	142	42
1983-84—Vancouver Canucks		NHL	4	1	0	1	0
1984-85—Vancouver Canucks		NHL	7	1	4	5	19
1985-86—Fredericton Express		AHL	45	21	14	35	28
1985-86—Vancouver Canucks		NHL	19	5	5	10	6
1986-87—Fredericton Express		AHL	36	21	20	41	53
1986-87—Vancouver Canucks (e)		NHL	4	0	0	0	0
1987-88—Maine Mariners		AHL	71	33	41	74	58
1987-88—Boston Bruins		NHL	7	0	0	0	4
1988-89—Asiago		Italy	26	25	21	46	....
1988-89—Maine Mariners		AHL	8	0	1	1	7
1988-89—Newmarket Saints		AHL	9	5	5	10	14
1989-90—Asiago		Italy	26	25	21	46	..
1989-90—New Haven Nighthawks		AHL	51	14	23	37	10
NHL TOTALS			41	9	16	29	29

(c)—June, 1982—Drafted as underage junior by Vancouver Canucks in 1982 NHL entry draft. Fourth Canucks pick, 116th overall, sixth round.
(d)—Shared WHL playoff goal-scoring lead (21) with Dean Evason of Kamloops.
(e)—July, 1987—Signed by Boston Bruins as a free agent.

KEVIN HALLER

Defense . . . 6'2" . . . 180 lbs. . . . Born, Trochu, Alta., December 5, 1970 . . . Shoots left . . . (October, 1986)—Broken leg . . . (May, 1987)—Broken leg.

Year	Team	League	Games	G.	A.	Pts.	Pen.
1986-87—Three Hills Braves		Alta. Midget	12	10	11	21	8
1987-88—Olds Grizzlys		AJHL	54	13	31	44	58
1988-89—Regina Pats (c)		WHL	72	10	31	41	99
1989-90—Regina Pats		WHL	58	16	37	53	93
1989-90—Buffalo Sabres		NHL	2	0	0	0	0
NHL TOTALS			2	0	0	0	0

(c)—June, 1989—Drafted by Buffalo Sabres in 1989 NHL entry draft. First Sabres pick, 14th overall, first round.

KEN HAMMOND

Defense . . . 6'1" . . . 190 lbs. . . . Born, London, Ont., August 23, 1963 . . . Shoots left . . . (March 13, 1988)—Sprained knee vs. St. Louis . . . (March, 1989)—Back spasms.

Year	Team	League	Games	G.	A.	Pts.	Pen.
1981-82—R.P.I.		ECAC	29	2	3	5	54
1982-83—R.P.I. (c)		ECAC	28	4	13	17	54
1983-84—R.P.I.		ECAC	34	5	11	16	72
1984-85—R.P.I. (a-d)		ECAC	38	11	28	39	90
1984-85—Los Angeles Kings		NHL	3	1	0	1	0
1985-86—New Haven Nighthawks		AHL	67	4	12	16	96
1985-86—Los Angeles Kings		NHL	3	0	1	1	2
1986-87—New Haven Nighthawks		AHL	66	1	15	16	76
1986-87—Los Angeles Kings		NHL	10	0	2	2	11

Year	Team	League	Games	G.	A.	Pts.	Pen.
1987-88—New Haven Nighthawks		AHL	26	3	8	11	27
1987-88—Los Angeles Kings		NHL	46	7	9	16	69
1988-89—Edmonton Oilers (e)		NHL	5	0	1	1	8
1988-89—New York Rangers (f-g)		NHL	3	0	0	0	0
1988-89—Toronto Maple Leafs		NHL	14	0	2	2	12
1988-89—Denver Rangers		IHL	38	5	18	23	24
1989-90—Newmarket Saints		AHL	75	9	45	54	106
NHL TOTALS			84	8	15	23	102

(c)—June, 1983—Drafted by Los Angeles Kings in 1983 NHL entry draft. Eighth Kings pick, 147th overall, eighth round.

(d)—Named First team All-America (East).

(e)—October 3, 1988—Selected by Edmonton Oilers in 1988 NHL waiver draft for $30,000.

(f)—November 1, 1988—Claimed on waivers from Edmonton Oilers by New York Rangers when the Oilers attempted to assign him to Cape Breton.

(g)—February 19, 1989—Traded by New York Rangers to Toronto Maple Leafs for Chris McRae.

RON HANDY

Left Wing . . . 5'11" . . . 165 lbs. . . . Born, Toronto, Ont., January 15, 1963 . . . Shoots left . . . (January, 1984)—Broken nose in CHL game.

Year	Team	League	Games	G.	A.	Pts.	Pen.
1979-80—Toronto Marlboro Midgets		Midget	39	48	60	108	....
1980-81—Sault Ste. Marie Greyhounds (c)		OHL	66	43	43	86	45
1981-82—Sault Ste. Marie Greyhounds		OHL	20	15	10	25	20
1981-82—Kingston Canadians		OHL	44	35	38	73	23
1982-83—Kingston Canadians		OHL	67	52	96	148	64
1982-83—Indianapolis Checkers		CHL	9	2	7	9	0
1983-84—Indianapolis Checkers (b)		CHL	66	29	46	75	40
1984-85—New York Islanders		NHL	10	0	2	2	0
1984-85—Springfield Indians		AHL	69	29	35	64	38
1985-86—Springfield Indians		AHL	79	31	30	61	66
1986-87—Indianapolis Checkers (b-d)		IHL	82	*55	80	135	57
1987-88—Peoria Rivermen (a)		IHL	78	53	63	116	61
1987-88—St. Louis Blues		NHL	4	0	1	1	0
1988-89—Indianapolis Ice (e-f)		IHL	81	43	57	100	52
1989-90—Fort Wayne Komets (g)		IHL	82	36	39	75	52
NHL TOTALS			14	0	3	3	0

(c)—June, 1981—Drafted as underage junior by New York Islanders in 1981 NHL entry draft. Third Islanders pick, 57th overall, third round.

(d)—September, 1987—Signed by St. Louis Blues as a free agent.

(e)—February, 1989—Named player/coach of Indianapolis Ice when head coach Archie Henderson had to step down due to a ruptured colon.

(f)—May 5, 1989—Released by St. Louis Blues.

(g)—September, 1989—Signed multi-year contract with Fort Wayne Komets as a free agent.

BENJAMIN HANKINSON

Center . . . 6'2" . . . 180 lbs. . . . Born, Edina, Minn., January 5, 1969 . . . Shoots right . . . Also plays Right Wing . . . Son of John Hankinson, former NFL player with Philadelphia Eagles and Minnesota Vikings.

Year	Team	League	Games	G.	A.	Pts.	Pen.
1985-86—Edina H.S.		Minn. H.S.	....	9	21	30	....
1986-87—Edina H.S. (c)		Minn. H.S.	26	14	20	34	....
1987-88—University of Minnesota		WCHA	24	4	7	11	36
1988-89—University of Minnesota		WCHA	43	7	11	18	115
1989-90—University of Minnesota		WCHA	46	25	41	66	34

(c)—June, 1987—Drafted by New Jersey Devils in 1987 NHL entry draft. Fifth Devils pick, 107th overall, sixth round.

DAVE HANNAN

Center . . . 5'11" . . . 174 lbs. . . . Born, Sudbury, Ont., November 26, 1961 . . . Shoots left . . . Missed part of '80-81 season with a bruised shoulder . . . (January 9, 1987)—Injured knee at Washington and required surgery . . . (October, 1988)—Hip pointer . . . (March, 1989)—Sprained knee . . . (November 22, 1989)—Injured left knee ligaments at Minnesota . . . (December 18, 1989)—Left knee surgery and missed 23 games.

Year	Team	League	Games	G.	A.	Pts.	Pen.
1977-78—Windsor Spitfires		OMJHL	68	14	16	30	43
1978-79—Sault Ste. Marie Greyhounds		OMJHL	26	7	8	15	13
1979-80—Sault Ste. Marie Greyhounds		OMJHL	28	11	10	21	31
1979-80—Brantford Alexanders		OMJHL	25	5	10	15	26
1980-81—Brantford Alexanders (c)		OHL	56	46	35	81	155
1981-82—Erie Blades		AHL	76	33	37	70	129
1981-82—Pittsburgh Penguins		NHL	1	0	0	0	0
1982-83—Baltimore Skipjacks		AHL	5	2	2	4	13
1982-83—Pittsburgh Penguins		NHL	74	11	22	33	127
1983-84—Baltimore Skipjacks		AHL	47	18	24	42	98
1983-84—Pittsburgh Penguins		NHL	24	2	3	5	33
1984-85—Baltimore Skipjacks		AHL	49	20	25	45	91
1984-85—Pittsburgh Penguins		NHL	30	6	7	13	43
1985-86—Pittsburgh Penguins		NHL	75	17	18	35	91
1986-87—Pittsburgh Penguins		NHL	58	10	15	25	56
1987-88—Pittsburgh Penguins (d)		NHL	21	4	3	7	23
1987-88—Edmonton Oilers		NHL	51	9	11	20	43
1988-89—Pittsburgh Penguins (e)		NHL	72	10	20	30	157
1989-90—Toronto Maple Leafs (f)		NHL	39	6	9	15	55
NHL TOTALS			445	75	108	183	628

(c)—June, 1981—Drafted by Pittsburgh Penguins in 1981 NHL entry draft. Ninth Penguins pick, 196th overall, 10th round.

(d)—November, 1987—Traded with Craig Simpson, Chris Joseph and Moe Mantha by Pittsburgh Penguins to Edmonton Oilers for Paul Coffey, Dave Hunter and Wayne Van Dorp.

(e)—October 3, 1988—Selected by Pittsburgh Penguins in 1988 NHL waiver draft. Dave Hunter was taken by Edmonton Oilers as compensation.

(f)—October 2, 1989—Selected by Toronto Maple Leafs in 1989 NHL waiver draft for a waiver price of $7,500.

JEFFREY HARDING

Right Wing . . . 6'4" . . . 207 lbs. . . . Born, Toronto, Ont., April 6, 1969 . . . Shoots right . . . Also plays Center . . . (October, 1985)—Injured knee . . . (November, 1988)—Infected elbow . . . (December 8, 1988)—Suspended three NHL games for shoving linesman Pat Dapuzzo . . . (January, 1989)—Lacerated kneecap . . . (September, 1989)—Viral infection and missed first three weeks of season.

Year	Team	League	Games	G.	A.	Pts.	Pen.
1985-86—Henry Carr Crusaders		OHA	23	14	10	24	30
1986-87—St. Michael's Buzzers (c)		OHA	22	22	8	30	97
1987-88—Michigan State Univ.		CCHA	43	17	10	27	129
1988-89—Philadelphia Flyers		NHL	6	0	0	0	29
1988-89—Hershey Bears		AHL	34	13	5	18	64
1989-90—Hershey Bears		AHL	6	0	2	2	2
1989-90—Philadelphia Flyers		NHL	9	0	0	0	18
NHL TOTALS			15	0	0	0	47

(c)—June, 1987—Drafted as underage junior by Philadelphia Flyers in 1987 NHL entry draft. Second Flyers pick, 30th overall, second round.

MARK LEA HARDY

Defense . . . 5'11" . . . 190 lbs. . . . Born, Semaden, Switzerland, February 1, 1959 . . . Shoots left . . . Mother was a member of 1952 Olympic Figure Skating team from England . . . (October, 1985)—Missed 25 games due to surgery to sublexation tendon in left wrist injured in final pre-season game vs. Calgary . . . (January, 1988)—Viral infection . . . (October 19, 1988)—Injured wrist when struck by a shot at Calgary . . . (March, 1989)—Sprained wrist . . . (March 3, 1990)—Sprained right ankle at Hartford, missed final 13 games of season and first two playoff games . . . (April 9, 1990)—Reinjured ankle in third game of playoff series at N.Y. Islanders and out for remainder of playoffs.

Year	Team	League	Games	G.	A.	Pts.	Pen.
1975-76—Montreal Juniors		QMJHL	64	6	17	23	44
1976-77—Montreal Juniors		QMJHL	72	20	40	60	137
1977-78—Montreal Juniors (a-c)		QMJHL	72	25	57	82	150
1978-79—Montreal Juniors (d)		QMJHL	67	18	52	70	117
1979-80—Binghamton Dusters		AHL	56	3	13	16	32
1979-80—Los Angeles Kings		NHL	15	0	1	1	10
1980-81—Los Angeles Kings		NHL	77	5	20	25	77
1981-82—Los Angeles Kings		NHL	77	6	39	45	130
1982-83—Los Angeles Kings		NHL	74	5	34	39	101
1983-84—Los Angeles Kings		NHL	79	8	41	49	122
1984-85—Los Angeles Kings		NHL	78	14	39	53	97
1985-86—Los Angeles Kings		NHL	55	6	21	27	71
1986-87—Los Angeles Kings		NHL	73	3	27	30	120
1987-88—Los Angeles Kings (e)		NHL	61	6	22	28	99
1987-88—New York Rangers (f)		NHL	19	2	2	4	31
1988-89—Minnesota North Stars (g)		NHL	15	2	4	6	26
1988-89—New York Rangers		NHL	45	2	12	14	45
1989-90—New York Rangers		NHL	54	0	15	15	94
NHL TOTALS			722	59	277	336	1023

(c)—Named top defenseman in QMJHL.

(d)—August, 1979—Drafted by Los Angeles Kings in 1979 entry draft. Third Kings pick, 30th overall, second round.

(e)—February, 1988—Traded by Los Angeles Kings to New York Rangers for Ron Duguay.

(f)—June, 1988—Traded by New York Rangers to Minnesota North Stars for future draft considerations.

(g)—December 10, 1988—Traded by Minnesota North Stars to New York Rangers for Larry Bernard and a fifth-round 1989 draft pick (Rhys Hollyman).

BRETT HARKINS

Left Wing . . . 6'1" . . . 170 lbs. . . . Born, North Ridgefield, Ohio, July 2, 1970 . . . Shoots left . . . Also plays Center . . . Brother of Todd Harkins.

Year	Team	League	Games	G.	A.	Pts.	Pen.
1987-88—Brockville Braves		OHA	55	21	55	76	36
1988-89—Detroit Compuware (c)		NAJHL	38	23	46	69	94
1989-90—Bowling Green Univ. (d)		CCHA	41	11	43	54	45

(c)—June, 1989—Drafted by New York Islanders in 1989 NHL entry draft. Ninth Islanders pick, 133rd overall, seventh round.

(d)—Named to CCHA All-Rookie team.

TODD HARKINS

Right Wing . . . 6'3" . . . 210 lbs. . . . Born, Cleveland, Ohio, October 8, 1968 . . . Shoots right . . . Brother of Brett Harkins.

Year	Team	League	Games	G.	A.	Pts.	Pen.
1986-87—Aurora Eagles		OHA	40	19	29	48	102
1987-88—Miami Univ. of Ohio (c)		CCHA	34	9	7	16	133
1988-89—Miami Univ. of Ohio		CCHA	36	8	7	15	77
1989-90—Miami Univ. of Ohio		CCHA	40	27	17	44	78

(c)—June, 1988—Drafted by Calgary Flames in 1988 NHL entry draft. Second Flames pick, 42nd overall, second round.

DAVID HARLOCK

Defense . . . 6'2'' . . . 195 lbs. . . . Born, Toronto, Ont., March 16, 1971 . . . Shoots left . . . (October, 1988)—Injured knee.

Year	Team	League	Games	G.	A.	Pts.	Pen.
1986-87—Toronto Red Wings		MTHL	86	17	55	72	60
1987-88—Toronto Red Wings		MTHL	70	16	56	72	100
1988-89—St. Michael's Jr. B		OHA	25	4	15	19	34
1989-90—Univ. of Michigan (c)		CCHA	42	2	13	15	44

(c)—June 16, 1990—Selected by New Jersey Devils in 1990 NHL entry draft. Second Devils pick, 24th overall, second round.

SCOTT HARLOW

Left Wing . . . 6' . . . 190 lbs. . . . Born, East Bridgewater, Mass., October 11, 1963 . . . Shoots left.

Year	Team	League	Games	G.	A.	Pts.	Pen.
1982-83—Boston College (c)		ECAC	24	6	19	25	19
1984-85—Boston College		ECAC	39	27	20	47	17
1984-85—Boston College		H. East	44	34	38	72	45
1985-86—Bostgn College (d)		H. East	42	38	41	79	48
1986-87—Sherbrooke Canadiens		AHL	66	22	26	48	6
1987-88—St. Louis Blues (e)		NHL	1	0	1	1	0
1987-88—Sherbrooke Canadiens		AHL	18	6	12	18	8
1987-88—Baltimore Skipjacks		AHL	29	24	27	51	21
1987-88—Peoria Rivermen		IHL	39	30	25	55	46
1988-89—Peoria Rivermen (f)		IHL	45	16	26	42	22
1988-89—Maine Mariners		AHL	30	16	17	33	8
1989-90—Maine Mariners		AHL	80	31	32	63	68
NHL TOTALS			1	0	1	1	0

(c)—June, 1982—Drafted by Montreal Canadiens in 1982 entry draft. Sixth Canadiens pick, 61st overall, third round.
(d)—Selected First team All-America (East).
(e)—January, 1988—Traded by Montreal Canadiens to St. Louis Blues for future considerations.
(f)—February 3, 1989—Traded by St. Louis Blues to Boston Bruins for Phil DeGaetano.

TIM HARRIS

Right Wing . . . 6'1'' . . . 180 lbs. . . . Born, Toronto, Ont., October 16, 1967 . . . Shoots right.

Year	Team	League	Games	G.	A.	Pts.	Pen.
1985-86—Pickering Jr. B		OHA	34	13	25	38	91
1986-87—Pickering Jr. B (c)		OHA	36	20	36	56	142
1987-88—Lake Superior State Univ.		CCHA	43	8	10	18	79
1988-89—Lake Superior State Univ.		CCHA	29	1	5	6	78
1989-90—Lake Superior State Univ.		CCHA	39	6	17	23	71

(c)—June, 1987—Drafted by Calgary Flames in 1987 NHL entry draft. Fifth Flames pick, 70th overall, fourth round.

TODD HARTJE

Center . . . 6' . . . 175 lbs. . . . Born, Anoka, Minn., February 27, 1968 . . . Shoots left.

Year	Team	League	Games	G.	A.	Pts.	Pen.
1985-86—Anoka H.S.		Minn. H.S.	22	25	34	59	....
1986-87—Harvard Univ. (c)		ECAC	34	3	9	12	36
1987-88—Harvard Univ.		ECAC	32	5	17	22	40
1988-89—Harvard Univ.		ECAC	33	4	17	21	40
1989-90—Harvard Univ. (d)		ECAC	28	6	10	16	29

(c)—June, 1987—Drafted by Winnipeg Jets in 1987 NHL entry draft. Seventh Jets pick, 142nd overall, seventh round.
(d)—April 9, 1990—Assigned to Sokol Kiev (USSR) for 1990-91 season.

MIKE HARTMAN

Left Wing . . . 5'11'' . . . 190 lbs. . . . Born, West Bloomfield, Mich., February 7, 1967 . . . Shoots left . . . Also plays Right Wing . . . (January, 1989)—Sore back . . . (December 1, 1989)—Sprained right ankle vs. New Jersey and missed five games . . . (December 29, 1989)—Retwisted right ankle vs. Boston and missed five games . . . (March 10, 1990)—Injured ankle at Hartford.

Year	Team	League	Games	G.	A.	Pts.	Pen.
1984-85—Belleville Bulls		OHL	49	13	12	25	119
1985-86—Belleville Bulls		OHL	4	2	1	3	5
1985-86—North Bay Centennials (c)		OHL	53	19	16	35	205
1986-87—North Bay Centennials		OHL	32	15	24	39	144
1986-87—Buffalo Sabres		NHL	17	3	3	6	69
1987-88—Rochester Americans		AHL	57	13	14	27	283
1987-88—Buffalo Sabres		NHL	18	3	1	4	90
1988-89—Buffalo Sabres		NHL	70	8	9	17	316
1989-90—Buffalo Sabres		NHL	60	11	10	21	211
NHL TOTALS			165	25	23	48	686

(c)—June, 1986—Drafted by Buffalo Sabres in 1986 NHL entry draft. Eighth Sabres pick, 131st overall, seventh round.

DERIAN HATCHER

Defense . . . 6'5'' . . . 204 lbs. . . . Born, Sterling Heights, Mich., June 4, 1972 . . . Shoots left . . . Brother of Kevin and Mark Hatcher . . . (January, 1989)—Knee surgery.

Year	Team	League	Games	G.	A.	Pts.	Pen.
1988-89—Detroit G.P.D.		MNHL	51	19	35	54	100
1989-90—North Bay Centennials (c)		OHL	64	14	38	52	81

(c)—June 16, 1990—Selected by Minnesota North Stars in 1990 NHL entry draft. First North Stars pick, eighth overall, first round.

KEVIN HATCHER

Defense . . . 6'3'' . . . 185 lbs. . . . Born, Detroit, Mich., September 9, 1966 . . . Shoots right . . . (October, 1987)—Torn cartilage in left knee . . . (January, 1989)—Pulled groin . . . (February 5, 1989)—Fractured two metatarsal bones in left foot when struck by Mike Bullard shot vs. Philadelphia and missed 15 games . . . (April 27, 1990)—Sprained left knee vs. N.Y. Rangers . . . Brother of Derian and Mark Hatcher.

Year	Team	League	Games	G.	A.	Pts.	Pen.
1982-83—Detroit Compuware		Mich. Midget	75	30	45	75	120
1983-84—North Bay Centennials (c)		OHL	67	10	39	49	61
1984-85—North Bay Centennials (b)		OHL	58	26	37	63	75
1984-85—Washington Capitals		NHL	2	1	0	1	0
1985-86—Washington Capitals		NHL	79	9	10	19	119
1986-87—Washington Capitals		NHL	78	8	16	24	144
1987-88—Washington Capitals		NHL	71	14	27	41	137
1988-89—Washington Capitals		NHL	62	13	27	40	101
1989-90—Washington Capitals		NHL	80	13	41	54	102
NHL TOTALS			372	58	121	179	603

(c)—June, 1984—Drafted as underage junior by Washington Capitals in 1984 NHL entry draft. First Capitals pick, 17th overall, first round.

BRETT HAUER

Defense . . . 6'2'' . . . 180 lbs. . . . Born, Edina, Minn., July 11, 1971 . . . Shoots right . . . Cousin of Don Jackson (former NHL player with Minnesota and Edmonton).

Year	Team	League	Games	G.	A.	Pts.	Pen.
1987-88—Richfield H.S.		Minn. H.S.	24	3	3	6	..
1988-89—Richfield H.S. (c)		Minn. H.S.	24	8	15	23	..
1989-90—Univ. of Minn./Duluth		WCHA	37	2	6	8	44

(c)—June, 1989—Drafted by Vancouver Canucks in 1989 NHL entry draft. Third Canucks pick, 71st overall, fourth round.

DALE HAWERCHUK

Center . . . 5'11'' . . . 170 lbs. . . . Born, Toronto, Ont., April 4, 1963 . . . Shoots left . . . Youngest player to have 100-point season (18 years, 351 days) . . . (March 7, 1984)—Set NHL record with five assists in a period at Los Angeles . . . (April 13, 1985)—Broken rib in playoff game when checked by Jamie Macoun at Calgary . . . President and part owner of Cornwall Royals of Quebec Major Junior Hockey League . . . (February 1, 1989)—Fractured cheekbone in collision with Dirk Graham at Chicago.

Year	Team	League	Games	G.	A.	Pts.	Pen.
1979-80—Cornwall Royals (c-d)		OMJHL	72	37	66	103	21
1980-81—Cornwall Royals (a-e-f-g-h-i)		OHL	72	*81	*102	*183	69
1981-82—Winnipeg Jets (j-k)		NHL	80	45	58	103	47
1982-83—Winnipeg Jets		NHL	79	40	51	91	31
1983-84—Winnipeg Jets		NHL	80	37	65	102	73
1984-85—Winnipeg Jets (b)		NHL	80	53	77	130	74
1985-86—Winnipeg Jets		NHL	80	46	59	105	44
1986-87—Winnipeg Jets		NHL	80	47	53	100	54
1987-88—Winnipeg Jets		NHL	80	44	77	121	59
1988-89—Winnipeg Jets		NHL	75	41	55	96	28
1989-90—Winnipeg Jets (l)		NHL	79	26	55	81	60
NHL TOTALS			713	379	550	929	470

(c)—Winner of The Instructeurs Trophy (QMJHL Top Rookie).
(d)—Winner of Guy Lafleur Trophy (QMJHL Playoff MVP).
(e)—Winner of Jean Beliveau Trophy (QMJHL Leading Scorer).
(f)—Winner of Michel Briere Trophy (QMJHL MVP).
(g)—Winner of The Association of Journalists for Major Junior League Hockey Trophy (Best Pro Prospect). First year awarded.
(h)—Winner of CCM Trophy (Top Canadian Major Junior League Player).
(i)—Drafted as underage junior by Winnipeg Jets in 1981 NHL entry draft. First Jets pick, first overall, first round.
(j)—Named NHL Rookie of the Year by The Sporting News in poll of players.
(k)—Winner of Calder Memorial Trophy (NHL Rookie of the Year).
(l)—June 16, 1990—Traded with a first-round 1990 draft pick (Brad May) by Winnipeg Jets to Buffalo Sabres for Scott Arniel, Jeff Parker and a first-round 1990 draft pick (Keith Tkachuk).

GREG HAWGOOD

Defense . . . 5'8'' . . . 175 lbs. . . . Born, St. Albert, Alta., August 10, 1968 . . . Shoots left . . . Holds record for career points by a WHL defenseman.

Year	Team	League	Games	G.	A.	Pts.	Pen.
1983-84—Kamloops Junior Oilers		WHL	49	10	23	33	39
1984-85—Kamloops Blazers		WHL	66	25	40	65	72
1985-86—Kamloops Blazers (a-c)		WHL	71	34	85	119	86
1986-87—Kamloops Blazers (a)		WHL	61	30	93	123	139
1987-88—Boston Bruins		NHL	1	0	0	0	0
1987-88—Kamloops Blazers		WHL	63	48	85	133	142
1988-89—Boston Bruins		NHL	56	16	24	40	84
1988-89—Maine Mariners		AHL	21	2	9	11	41
1989-90—Boston Bruins (d)		NHL	77	11	27	38	76
NHL TOTALS			134	27	51	78	160

(c)—June, 1986—Drafted as underage junior by Boston Bruins in 1986 NHL entry draft. Ninth Bruins pick, 202nd overall, 10th round.
(d)—July, 1990—Announced that he would play in Italy for 1990-91 season.

TODD HAWKINS

Right Wing . . . 5'11'' . . . 190 lbs. . . . Born, Kingston, Ont., August 2, 1966 . . . Shoots right . . . (October 1, 1986)—Suspended two games by OHL . . . (September, 1988)—Bruised hand in Vancouver Canucks training camp.

Year	Team	League	Games	G.	A.	Pts.	Pen.
1984-85—Belleville Bulls		OHL	58	7	16	23	117
1985-86—Belleville Bulls (c)		OHL	60	14	13	27	172

Year	Team	League	Games	G.	A.	Pts.	Pen.
1986-87—Belleville Bulls (b)		OHL	60	47	40	87	187
1987-88—Flint Spirits		IHL	50	13	13	26	337
1987-88—Fredericton Express		AHL	2	0	0	0	11
1988-89—Vancouver Canucks		NHL	4	0	0	0	9
1988-89—Milwaukee Admirals		IHL	63	12	14	26	307
1989-90—Vancouver Canucks		NHL	4	0	0	0	6
1989-90—Milwaukee Admirals		IHL	61	23	17	40	273
NHL TOTALS			8	0	0	0	15

(c)—June, 1986—Drafted by Vancouver Canucks in 1986 NHL entry draft. Tenth Canucks pick, 217th overall, 11th round.

KENT HAWLEY

Center ... 6'3" ... 215 lbs. ... Born, Kingston, Ont., February 20, 1968 ... Shoots left.

Year	Team	League	Games	G.	A.	Pts.	Pen.
1984-85—Ottawa Senators		CJHL	54	19	37	56	119
1985-86—Ottawa 67's (c)		OHL	64	21	30	51	96
1986-87—Ottawa 67's		OHL	64	29	53	82	86
1987-88—Ottawa 67's		OHL	55	29	49	78	84
1988-89—Hershey Bears		AHL	54	9	17	26	47
1989-90—Hershey Bears		AHL	24	6	4	10	28

(c)—June, 1986—Drafted as underage junior by Philadelphia Flyers in 1986 NHL entry draft. Third Flyers pick, 28th overall, second round.

RICK HAYWARD

Defense ... 6' ... 180 lbs. ... Born, Toledo, O., February 25, 1966 ... Shoots left ... (October 12, 1988)—Suspended by IHL for six games for abusing an official.

Year	Team	League	Games	G.	A.	Pts.	Pen.
1984-85—Hull Olympiques		QMJHL	56	7	27	34	367
1985-86—Hull Olympiques (c)		QMJHL	59	3	40	43	354
1986-87—Sherbrooke Canadiens		AHL	43	2	3	5	153
1987-88—Sherbrooke Canadiens (d)		AHL	22	1	5	6	91
1987-88—Saginaw Hawks		IHL	24	3	4	7	129
1987-88—Salt Lake Golden Eagles		IHL	17	1	3	4	124
1988-89—Salt Lake Golden Eagles		IHL	72	4	20	24	313
1989-90—Salt Lake Golden Eagles		IHL	58	5	13	18	419

(c)—June, 1986—Drafted by Montreal Canadiens in 1986 NHL entry draft. Ninth Canadiens pick, 162nd overall, eighth round.

(d)—February, 1988—Traded by Montreal Canadiens to Calgary Flames for Martin Nicoletti.

STEPHEN HEINZE

Center ... 5'11" ... 180 lbs. ... Born, Lawrence, Mass., January 30, 1970 ... Shoots right.

Year	Team	League	Games	G.	A.	Pts.	Pen.
1986-87—Lawrence Academy		Mass. H.S.	23	26	24	50	....
1987-88—Lawrence Academy (c)		Mass. H.S.	23	30	25	55	....
1988-89—Boston College (d)		H. East	36	26	23	49	26
1989-90—Boston College (a-e)		H. East	40	27	36	63	41

(c)—June, 1988—Drafted by Boston Bruins in 1988 NHL entry draft. Second Bruins pick, 60th overall, second round.

(d)—Named to Hockey East All-Rookie Team.

(e)—Named to NCAA All-America Team (East).

ANTHONY J. HEJNA

Left Wing ... 6' ... 190 lbs. ... Born, Buffalo, N.Y., January 8, 1968 ... Shoots left ... (November 22, 1989)—Surgery to remove scar tissue from disc in back and missed two months.

Year	Team	League	Games	G.	A.	Pts.	Pen.
1984-85—Nichols H.S.		N.Y.	34	46	40	86	20
1985-86—Nichols H.S. (c)		N.Y.	33	51	27	78	26
1986-87—R.P.I.		ECAC	33	12	18	30	18
1987-88—R.P.I.		ECAC	32	17	19	36	48
1988-89—R.P.I.		ECAC	29	12	9	21	14
1989-90—R.P.I.		ECAC	26	20	16	36	22

(c)—June, 1986—Drafted by St. Louis Blues in 1986 NHL entry draft. Third Blues pick, 52nd overall, third round.

DARBY HENDRICKSON

Center ... 6' ... 174 lbs. ... Born, Richfield, Minn., August 28, 1972 ... Shoots left.

Year	Team	League	Games	G.	A.	Pts.	Pen.
1987-88—Richfield H.S.		Minn. H.S.	22	12	9	21	10
1988-89—Richfield H.S.		Minn. H.S.	22	22	20	42	12
1989-90—Richfield H.S. (c)		Minn. H.S.	24	23	27	50	49

(c)—June 16, 1990—Selected by Toronto Maple Leafs in 1990 NHL entry draft. Third Maple Leafs pick, 73rd overall, fourth round.

DALE HENRY

Left Wing ... 6' ... 205 lbs. ... Born, Prince Albert, Sask., September 24, 1964 ... Shoots left ... (December, 1986)—Missed 12 games with a bruised left thigh ... (March 3, 1987)—Sprained left knee ligaments vs. Boston ... (November 20, 1987)—Given a four-game suspension by AHL for fighting.

Year	Team	League	Games	G.	A.	Pts.	Pen.
1981-82—Saskatoon Blades		WHL	32	5	4	9	50
1982-83—Saskatoon Blades (c)		WHL	63	21	19	40	213
1983-84—Saskatoon Blades		WHL	71	41	36	77	162
1984-85—Springfield Indians		AHL	67	11	20	31	133
1984-85—New York Islanders		NHL	16	2	1	3	19
1985-86—Springfield Indians		AHL	64	14	26	40	162

Year	Team	League	Games	G.	A.	Pts.	Pen.
1985-86—New York Islanders		NHL	7	1	3	4	15
1986-87—Springfield Indians		AHL	23	9	14	23	49
1986-87—New York Islanders		NHL	19	3	3	6	46
1987-88—Springfield Indians		AHL	24	9	12	21	103
1987-88—New York Islanders		NHL	48	5	15	20	115
1988-89—Springfield Indians		AHL	50	13	21	34	83
1988-89—New York Islanders		NHL	22	2	2	4	66
1989-90—New York Islanders		NHL	20	0	2	2	2
1989-90—Springfield Indians		AHL	43	17	14	31	68
NHL TOTALS			132	13	26	39	263

(c)—June, 1983—Drafted as underage junior by New York Islanders in 1983 NHL entry draft. Tenth Islanders pick, 157th overall, eighth round.

MATHEW HENTGES

Defense ... 6'4" ... 200 lbs. ... Born, St. Paul, Minn., December 19, 1969 ... Shoots left.

Year	Team	League	Games	G.	A.	Pts.	Pen.
1986-87—Edina H.S.		Minn. H.S.	24	3	10	13	34
1987-88—Edina H.S. (c)		Minn. H.S.	27	3	18	21	..
1988-89—Merrimack College		ECAC	33	0	16	16	22
1989-90—Merrimack College		H. East	33	1	2	3	40

(c)—June, 1988—Drafted by Chicago Black Hawks in 1988 NHL entry draft. Eighth Black Hawks pick, 176th overall, ninth round.

ALAN HEPPLE

Defense ... 5'10" ... 200 lbs. ... Born, Blaudon-on-Tyne, England, August 16, 1963 ... Shoots right ... Also plays Center ... (October, 1980)—Eye injury.

Year	Team	League	Games	G.	A.	Pts.	Pen.
1980-81—Ottawa 67's		OHL	64	3	13	16	110
1981-82—Ottawa 67's (c)		OHL	66	6	22	28	160
1982-83—Ottawa 67's		OHL	64	10	26	36	168
1983-84—Maine Mariners		AHL	64	4	23	27	117
1983-84—New Jersey Devils		NHL	1	0	0	0	7
1984-85—Maine Mariners		AHL	80	7	17	24	125
1984-85—New Jersey Devils		NHL	1	0	0	0	0
1985-86—Maine Mariners		AHL	69	4	21	25	104
1985-86—New Jersey Devils		NHL	1	0	0	0	0
1986-87—Maine Mariners		AHL	74	6	19	25	137
1987-88—Utica Devils		AHL	78	3	16	19	213
1988-89—Newmarket Saints		AHL	72	5	24	29	122
1989-90—Newmarket Saints		AHL	72	6	20	26	96
NHL TOTALS			3	0	0	0	7

(c)—June, 1982—Drafted as underage junior by New Jersey Devils in 1982 NHL entry draft. Ninth Devils pick, 169th overall, ninth round.

JASON HERTER

Defense ... 6'1" ... 180 lbs. ... Born, Hafford, Sask., October 2, 1970 ... Shoots right ... (September, 1988)—Strained shoulder.

Year	Team	League	Games	G.	A.	Pts.	Pen.
1987-88—Notre Dame Hounds		SJHL	54	5	33	38	152
1988-89—Univ. of North Dakota (c)		WCHA	41	8	24	32	62
1989-90—Univ. of North Dakota		WCHA	38	11	39	50	40

(c)—June, 1989—Drafted by Vancouver Canucks in 1989 NHL entry draft. First Canucks pick, eighth overall, first round.

MATT HERVEY

Defense ... 5'11" ... 195 lbs. ... Born, Los Angeles, Calif., May 16, 1966 ... Shoots right ... (November, 1986)—Suspended by WHL for six games for stick-swinging incident with Troy Pohl vs. Portland.

Year	Team	League	Games	G.	A.	Pts.	Pen.
1983-84—Victoria Cougars		WHL	67	4	19	23	89
1984-85—Victoria Cougars		WHL	14	1	3	4	17
1984-85—Lethbridge Broncos		WHL	54	3	9	12	88
1985-86—Lethbridge Broncos		WHL	60	9	17	26	110
1986-87—Seattle Thunderbirds		WHL	9	4	5	9	59
1987-88—Moncton Hawks (c)		AHL	69	9	20	29	265
1988-89—Moncton Hawks		AHL	73	8	28	36	295
1988-89—Winnipeg Jets		NHL	2	0	0	0	4
1989-90—Moncton Hawks		AHL	47	3	13	16	168
NHL TOTALS			2	0	0	0	4

(c)—October, 1987—Signed by Winnipeg Jets as a free agent.

JAMIE HEWARD

Right Wing ... 6'2" ... 185 lbs. ... Born, Regina, Sask., March 30, 1971 ... Shoots right ... (November, 1988)—Broken jaw ... (September, 1989)—Mononucleosis ... Also plays Defense.

Year	Team	League	Games	G.	A.	Pts.	Pen.
1987-88—Regina Pats (c)		WHL	68	10	17	27	17
1988-89—Regina Pats (d)		WHL	52	31	28	59	29
1989-90—Regina Pats		WHL	72	14	44	58	42

(c)—October, 1987—Traded by Spokane Chiefs to Regina Pats for Pat Falloon and future considerations.

(d)—June, 1989—Drafted by Pittsburgh Penguins in 1989 NHL entry draft. First Penguins pick, 16th overall, first round.

RANDY GEORGE HILLIER

Defense ... 6'1" ... 170 lbs. ... Born, Toronto, Ont., March 30, 1960 ... Shoots right ... (April 19, 1982)—Injured knee in playoff series vs. Quebec ... (December, 1982)—Injured left knee ... (April 2, 1983)—Strained ligaments in right knee at

Montreal . . . (December, 1984)—Surgery to remove bone chips from left shoulder and missed 20 games . . . (March, 1985)—Broken finger . . . (November 30, 1985)—Tore knee ligaments vs. N.Y. Rangers . . . (November, 1986)—Injured shoulder . . . (March 12, 1987)—Bruised left hand vs. Quebec . . . (October, 1987)—Torn hip muscles . . . (November, 1987)—Bruised heel . . . (February, 1989)—Bruised ribs . . . (March, 1989)—Bruised knee . . . (April, 1989)—Broken toe . . . (January 10, 1990)—Broke thumb at New Jersey and missed 10 games.

Year	Team	League	Games	G.	A.	Pts.	Pen.
1977-78—Sudbury Wolves	OMJHL	60	1	14	15	67
1978-79—Sudbury Wolves	OMJHL	61	9	25	34	173
1979-80—Sudbury Wolves (c)	OMJHL	60	16	49	65	143
1980-81—Springfield Indians	AHL	64	3	17	20	105
1981-82—Erie Blades	AHL	35	6	13	19	52
1981-82—Boston Bruins	NHL	25	0	8	8	29
1982-83—Boston Bruins	NHL	70	0	10	10	99
1983-84—Boston Bruins	NHL	69	3	12	15	125
1984-85—Pittsburgh Penguins (d)	NHL	45	2	19	21	56
1985-86—Baltimore Skipjacks	AHL	8	0	5	5	14
1985-86—Pittsburgh Penguins	NHL	28	0	3	3	53
1986-87—Pittsburgh Penguins	NHL	55	4	8	12	97
1987-88—Pittsburgh Penguins	NHL	55	1	12	13	144
1988-89—Pittsburgh Penguins	NHL	68	1	23	24	141
1989-90—Pittsburgh Penguins	NHL	61	3	12	15	71
NHL TOTALS		476	14	107	121	815

(c)—June, 1980—Drafted by Boston Bruins in 1980 NHL entry draft. Fourth Bruins pick, 102nd overall, fifth round.

(d)—October, 1984—Traded by Boston Bruins to Pittsburgh Penguins for fourth round draft choice in 1985.

BRIAN HOARD

Defense . . . 6'4" . . . 195 lbs. . . . Oshawa, Ont., March 10, 1968 . . . Shoots right . . . (February 1, 1990)—Suspended eight AHL games for crosschecking Rob Ray vs. Rochester.

Year	Team	League	Games	G.	A.	Pts.	Pen.
1985-86—Hamilton Steelhawks (c)	OHL	34	2	2	4	69
1986-87—Hamilton Steelhawks	OHL	1	0	1	1	0
1986-87—Belleville Bulls	OHL	9	0	0	0	31
1986-87—Sault Ste. Marie Greyhounds	OHL	44	4	8	12	137
1987-88—Sault Ste. Marie Greyhounds	OHL	59	1	12	13	187
1988-89—Newmarket Saints	AHL	54	2	5	7	208
1989-90—Newmarket Saints	AHL	40	2	4	6	146

(c)—June, 1989—Drafted by Toronto Maple Leafs in 1986 NHL entry draft. Twelfth Maple Leafs pick, 237th overall, 10th round.

KENNETH HODGE JR.

Center . . . 6'2" . . . 190 lbs. . . . Born, Windsor, Ontario, April 13, 1966 . . . Shoots left . . . Son of former NHL star Ken Hodge, who played for Chicago, Boston and New York Rangers from 1965 through 1978 . . . (November, 1987)—Injured his shoulders twice in IHL pre-season games.

Year	Team	League	Games	G.	A.	Pts.	Pen.
1983-84—St. John's Prep. (c)	Mass. H.S.	22	25	38	63	..
1984-85—Boston College (d)	H. East	41	20	44	64	28
1985-86—Boston College	H. East	21	11	17	28	16
1986-87—Boston College	H. East	37	29	33	62	30
1987-88—Kalamazoo Wings	IHL	70	15	35	50	24
1988-89—Minnesota North Stars	NHL	5	1	1	2	0
1988-89—Kalamazoo Wings	IHL	72	26	45	71	34
1989-90—Kalamazoo Wings (e)	IHL	68	33	53	86	19
NHL TOTALS		5	1	1	2	0

(c)—June, 1984—Drafted by Minnesota North Stars in 1984 NHL entry draft. Second North Stars pick, 46th overall, third round.

(d)—Named top Hockey East Freshman.

(e)—August 21, 1990—Traded by Minnesota North Stars to Boston Bruins for future considerations.

JIM HOFFORD

Defense . . . 6' . . . 190 lbs. . . . Born, Sudbury, Ont., October 4, 1964 . . . Shoots right . . . (September, 1981)—Broken nose . . . (November, 1987)—Concussion . . . (January, 1988)—Broke jaw.

Year	Team	League	Games	G.	A.	Pts.	Pen.
1981-82—Windsor Spitfires	OHL	67	5	9	14	214
1982-83—Windsor Spitfires (c)	OHL	63	8	20	28	171
1983-84—Windsor Spitfires	OHL	1	0	0	0	2
1984-85—Rochester Americans	AHL	70	2	13	15	166
1985-86—Rochester Americans	AHL	40	2	7	9	148
1985-86—Buffalo Sabres	NHL	5	0	0	0	5
1986-87—Rochester Americans	AHL	54	1	8	9	204
1986-87—Buffalo Sabres	NHL	12	0	0	0	40
1987-88—Rochester Americans	AHL	69	3	15	18	322
1988-89—Los Angeles Kings (d-e)	NHL	1	0	0	0	2
1988-89—Rochester Americans	AHL	34	1	9	10	139
1989-90—Rochester Americans	AHL	52	1	9	10	233
NHL TOTALS		18	0	0	0	47

(c)—June, 1983—Drafted as underage junior by Buffalo Sabres in 1983 NHL entry draft. Eighth Sabres pick, 114th overall, sixth round.

(d)—October 3, 1988—Selected by Los Angeles Kings in 1988 NHL waiver draft for $30,000.

(e)—October 20, 1988—Reclaimed by Buffalo Sabres on waivers from Los Angeles Kings.

BENOIT HOGUE

Center . . . 5'11" . . . 170 lbs. . . . Born, Repentigny, Que., October 28, 1966 . . . Shoots left . . . (October, 1987)—Suspended six games for fighting by AHL (March, 1988)—Sore back . . . (October 11, 1989)—Broke left checkbone at Toronto and missed 20 games . . . (March 14, 1990)—Sprained left ankle vs. Los Angeles.

Year	Team	League	Games	G.	A.	Pts.	Pen.
1984-85—St. Jean Beavers	QMJHL	59	14	11	25	42
1984-85—St. Jean Beavers (c)	QMJHL	63	46	44	90	92
1985-86—St. Jean Beavers	QMJHL	65	54	54	108	115
1986-87—Rochester Americans	AHL	52	14	20	34	52
1987-88—Buffalo Sabres	NHL	3	1	1	2	0
1987-88—Rochester Americans	AHL	62	24	31	55	141
1988-89—Buffalo Sabres	NHL	69	14	30	44	120
1989-90—Buffalo Sabres	NHL	45	11	7	18	79
NHL TOTALS		117	26	38	64	199

(c)—June, 1985—Drafted as underage junior by Buffalo Sabres in 1985 NHL entry draft. Second Sabres pick, 35th overall, second round.

PAUL HOLDEN

Defense . . . 6'3" . . . 210 lbs. . . . Born, Kitchener, Ont., March 15, 1970 . . . Shoots left.

Year	Team	League	Games	G.	A.	Pts.	Pen.
1986-87—St. Thomas Jr. B	OHL	23	5	11	16	112
1987-88—London Knights (c)	OHL	65	8	12	20	87
1988-89—London Knights	OHL	54	11	21	32	90
1989-90—London Knights (b)	OHL	61	11	31	42	78
1989-90—New Haven Nighthawks	AHL	2	1	1	2	2

(c)—June, 1988—Drafted by Los Angeles Kings in 1988 NHL entry draft. Second Kings pick, 28th overall, second round.

ROBERT HOLIK

Center . . . 6'3" . . . 210 lbs. . . . Born, Jihlava, Czechoslovakia, January 1, 1971 . . . Shoots right.

Year	Team	League	Games	G.	A.	Pts.	Pen.
1987-88—Dukla Jihlava	Czech.	31	5	9	14	..
1988-89—Dukla Jihlava (c)	Czech.	24	7	10	17	..
1989-90—Dukla Jihlava	Czech.	31	12	18	30	..

(c)—June, 1989—Drafted by Hartford Whalers in 1989 NHL entry draft. First Whalers pick, 10th overall, first round.

DENNIS HOLLAND

Center . . . 5'10" . . . 167 lbs. . . . Born, Vernon, B.C., January 30, 1969 . . . Shoots left . . . Brother of Ken Holland, former AHL goaltender and currently Detroit Red Wings western scout.

Year	Team	League	Games	G.	A.	Pts.	Pen.
1985-86—Vernon Lakers	BCJHL	51	43	62	105	40
1985-86—Portland Winter Hawks	WHL	1	3	2	5	0
1986-87—Portland Winter Hawks (c)	WHL	72	36	77	113	96
1987-88—Portland Winter Hawks	WHL	67	58	86	144	115
1988-89—Portland Winter Hawks (a)	WHL	69	82	85	167	120
1989-90—Adirondack Red Wings	AHL	78	19	34	53	53

(c)—June, 1987—Drafted by Detroit Red Wings in 1987 NHL entry draft as an underage junior. Fourth Red Wings pick, 52nd overall, third round.

RHYS HOLLYMAN

Defense . . . 6'3" . . . 210 lbs. . . . Born, Toronto, Ont., January 30, 1970 . . . Shoots right.

Year	Team	League	Games	G.	A.	Pts.	Pen.
1987-88—Barrie Colts Jr. A	OHA	40	24	28	52	50
1988-89—Miami Univ. of Ohio (c)	CCHA	33	8	5	13	60
1989-90—Miami Univ. of Ohio	CCHA	37	2	8	10	54

(c)—June, 1989—Drafted by Minnesota North Stars in 1989 NHL entry draft. Seventh North Stars pick, 97th overall, fifth round.

DEAN HOLOIEN

Defense . . . 6' . . . 197 lbs. . . . Born, Melford, Sask., April 18, 1969 . . . Shoots right.

Year	Team	League	Games	G.	A.	Pts.	Pen.
1986-87—Saskatoon Blades	WHL	7	1	1	2	13
1987-88—Saskatoon Blades	WHL	72	7	34	41	68
1988-89—Saskatoon Blades (c)	WHL	59	22	30	52	78
1989-90—Saskatoon Blades	WHL	70	43	49	92	121

(c)—June, 1989—Drafted by Washington Capitals in 1989 NHL entry draft. Seventh Capitals pick, 166th overall, eighth round.

RON HOOVER

Defense . . . 5'10" . . . 165 lbs. . . . Born, North Bay, Ont., January 9, 1965 . . . Shoots left.

Year	Team	League	Games	G.	A.	Pts.	Pen.
1985-86—Western Michigan Univ. (c)	CCHA	43	10	23	33	36
1986-87—Western Michigan Univ.	CCHA	34	7	10	17	22
1987-88—Western Michigan Univ. (b)	CCHA	42	39	23	62	40
1988-89—Western Michigan Univ.	CCHA	42	32	27	59	66
1989-90—Boston Bruins (d)	NHL	2	0	0	0	0
1989-90—Maine Mariners	AHL	75	28	26	54	57
NHL TOTALS		2	0	0	0	0

(c)—June, 1986—Drafted by Hartford Whalers in 1986 NHL entry draft. Seventh Whalers' pick, 158th overall, eighth round.

(d)—September, 1989—Signed by Boston Bruins as a free agent.

DEAN ROBERT HOPKINS

Right Wing . . . 6'1" . . . 205 lbs. . . . Born, Cobourg, Ont., June 6, 1959 . . . Shoots right . . . Played Center prior to 1978-79 . . . (1979-80)—Missed 14 games with broken ankle . . . (December, 1981)—Dislocated elbow . . . Brother of Brent Hopkins . . . (March, 1986)—Broken jaw.

Year	Team	League	Games	G.	A.	Pts.	Pen.
1975-76	London Knights	OMJHL	53	4	14	18	50
1976-77	London Knights	OMJHL	63	19	26	45	67
1977-78	London Knights	OMJHL	67	19	34	53	70
1978-79	London Knights (c)	OMJHL	65	37	55	92	149
1979-80	Los Angeles Kings	NHL	60	8	6	14	39
1980-81	Los Angeles Kings	NHL	67	8	18	26	118
1981-82	Los Angeles Kings	NHL	41	2	13	15	102
1982-83	New Haven Nighthawks	AHL	20	9	8	17	58
1982-83	Los Angeles Kings	NHL	49	5	12	17	43
1983-84	New Haven Nighthawks	AHL	79	35	47	82	162
1984-85	New Haven Nighthawks (d)	AHL	20	7	10	17	38
1984-85	Nova Scotia Voyageurs	AHL	49	13	17	30	93
1985-86	Edmonton Oilers (e)	NHL	1	0	0	0	0
1985-86	Nova Scotia Voyageurs	AHL	60	23	32	55	131
1986-87	Nova Scotia Oilers	AHL	59	20	25	45	84
1987-88	Nova Scotia Oilers	AHL	44	20	22	42	122
1988-89	Halifax Citadels	AHL	53	18	31	49	116
1988-89	Quebec Nordiques (f)	NHL	5	0	2	2	4
1989-90	Halifax Citadels	AHL	54	23	32	55	167
	NHL TOTALS		223	23	51	74	306

(c)—August, 1979—Drafted by Los Angeles Kings in 1979 entry draft. Second Kings pick, 29th overall, second round.

(d)—November, 1984—Traded with Mark Morrison by New Haven Nighthawks to Nova Scotia Oilers for Rob Tudor and Gerry Minor.

(e)—September, 1985—Signed by Edmonton Oilers as a free agent.

(f)—July 30, 1988—Signed by Quebec Nordiques as a free agent.

TONY HORACEK

Left Wing . . . 6'3" . . . 200 lbs. . . . Born, Vancouver, B.C., February 3, 1967 . . . Shoots left . . . (November 1, 1987)—Suspended one WHL game for swinging his stick at fans . . . (November 27, 1987)—Suspended eight WHL games for fighting . . . (December, 1989)—Broken knuckle.

Year	Team	League	Games	G.	A.	Pts.	Pen.
1984-85	Kelowna Wings (c)	WHL	67	9	18	27	114
1985-86	Spokane Chiefs	WHL	64	19	28	47	129
1986-87	Spokane Chiefs	WHL	64	23	37	60	177
1986-87	Hershey Bears	AHL	1	0	0	0	0
1987-88	Hershey Bears	AHL	1	0	0	0	0
1987-88	Spokane Chiefs	WHL	24	17	23	40	63
1987-88	Kamloops Blazers	WHL	26	14	17	31	51
1988-89	Hershey Bears	AHL	10	0	0	0	38
1988-89	Indianapolis Ice	IHL	43	11	13	24	138
1989-90	Philadelphia Flyers	NHL	48	5	5	10	117
1989-90	Hershey Bears	AHL	12	0	5	5	25
	NHL TOTALS		48	5	5	10	117

(c)—June, 1985—Drafted as underage junior by Philadelphia Flyers in 1985 NHL entry draft. Eighth Flyers pick, 147th overall, seventh round.

MILOSLAV HORAVA

Defense . . . 6' . . . 200 lbs. . . . Born Kladno, Czechoslovakia, August 14, 1961 . . . Shoots left.

Year	Team	League	Games	G.	A.	Pts.	Pen.
1986-87	Boldi Kladno (c-d)	Czech.	38	17	26	43	....
1987-88	Boldi Kladno	Czech.	29	7	11	18	....
1988-89	Boldi Kladno	Czech.	35	10	16	26	....
1988-89	New York Rangers	NHL	6	0	1	1	0
1989-90	New York Rangers	NHL	45	4	10	14	26
	NHL TOTALS		51	4	11	15	26

(c)—June, 1981—Drafted by Edmonton Oilers in 1981 NHL entry draft. Eighth Oilers pick, 176th overall, seventh round.

(d)—October 23, 1986—Traded with Don Jackson, Mike Golden and future considerations by Edmonton Oilers to New York Rangers for Reijo Ruotsalainen, Ville Kentala, Clark Donatelli and Jim Wiemer.

GREG HOTHAM

Defense . . . 5'11" . . . 183 lbs. . . . Born, London, Ont., March 7, 1956 . . . Shoots right . . . (November, 1982)—Injured knee . . . (1982-83)—Missed parts of season with sprained knee, separated shoulder and injured back . . . (September, 1984)—Missed first 20 games of season with mononucleosis.

Year	Team	League	Games	G.	A.	Pts.	Pen.
1973-74	Aurora Tigers	OPJHL	44	10	22	32	120
1974-75	Aurora Tigers	OPJHL	27	14	10	24	46
1974-75	Kingston Canadians	Jr."A"OHA	31	1	14	15	49
1975-76	Kingston Canadians (c)	Jr."A"OHA	49	10	32	42	76
1976-77	Saginaw Gears	IHL	69	4	33	37	100
1977-78	Saginaw Gears (b)	IHL	80	13	59	72	56
1977-78	Dallas Black Hawks (d)	CHL	....	....	....	....	....
1978-79	New Brunswick Hawks	AHL	76	9	27	36	88
1979-80	Toronto Maple Leafs	NHL	46	3	10	13	10
1979-80	New Brunswick Hawks	AHL	21	1	6	7	10
1980-81	Toronto Maple Leafs	NHL	11	1	1	2	11
1980-81	New Brunswick Hawks	AHL	68	8	48	56	80
1981-82	Cincinnati Tigers	CHL	46	10	33	43	94
1981-82	Toronto Maple Leafs (e)	NHL	3	0	0	0	0
1981-82	Pittsburgh Penguins	NHL	25	4	6	10	16
1982-83	Pittsburgh Penguins	NHL	58	2	30	32	39

Year	Team	League	Games	G.	A.	Pts.	Pen.
1983-84	Pittsburgh Penguins	NHL	76	5	25	30	59
1984-85	Baltimore Skipjacks	AHL	44	4	27	31	43
1984-85	Pittsburgh Penguins	NHL	11	0	2	2	4
1985-86	Baltimore Skipjacks	AHL	78	2	26	28	94
1986-87	Newmarket Saints	AHL	51	4	9	13	60
1987-88	Newmarket Saints	AHL	78	12	27	39	102
1988-89	Newmarket Saints	AHL	73	9	42	51	62
1989-90	Newmarket Saints	AHL	24	0	8	8	31
	NHL TOTALS		230	15	74	89	139

(c)—Drafted from Kingston Canadians by Toronto Maple Leafs in fifth round of 1976 amateur draft.

(d)—No regular season record. Played five playoff games.

(e)—January, 1982—Traded by Toronto Maple Leafs to Pittsburgh Penguins for future draft considerations.

DOUG HOUDA

Defense . . . 6'2" . . . 195 lbs. . . . Born, Blairmore, Alta., June 3, 1966 . . . Shoots right . . . (September 23, 1988)—Fractured left cheekbone when kicked by a skate in pre-season game at Buffalo . . . (November 21, 1989)—Injured knee vs. Boston and required surgery.

Year	Team	League	Games	G.	A.	Pts.	Pen.
1981-82	Calgary Wranglers	WHL	3	0	0	0	0
1982-83	Calgary Wranglers	WHL	71	5	23	28	99
1983-84	Calgary Wranglers (c)	WHL	69	6	30	36	195
1984-85	Calgary Wranglers (b)	WHL	65	20	54	74	182
1984-85	Kalamazoo Wings (d)	IHL	....	....	....	....	....
1985-86	Calgary Wranglers	WHL	16	4	10	14	60
1985-86	Medicine Hat Tigers	WHL	35	9	23	32	80
1985-86	Detroit Red Wings	NHL	6	0	0	0	4
1986-87	Adirondack Red Wings	AHL	77	6	23	29	142
1987-88	Detroit Red Wings	NHL	11	1	1	2	10
1987-88	Adirondack Red Wings	AHL	71	10	32	42	169
1988-89	Adirondack Red Wings	AHL	7	0	3	3	8
1988-89	Detroit Red Wings	NHL	57	2	11	13	67
1989-90	Detroit Red Wings	NHL	73	2	9	11	127
	NHL TOTALS		147	5	21	26	208

(c)—June, 1984—Drafted as underage junior by Detroit Red Wings in 1984 NHL entry draft. Second Red Wings pick, 28th overall, second round.

(d)—No regular season record. Played seven playoff games.

MIKE L. HOUGH

Left Wing . . . 6'1" . . . 195 lbs. . . . Born, Montreal, Que., February 6, 1963 . . . Shoots left . . . (November 5, 1989)—Sprained left shoulder vs. Washington, developed tendinitis and missed 14 games . . . (January 23, 1990)—Broke right thumb vs. Boston and missed 12 games.

Year	Team	League	Games	G.	A.	Pts.	Pen.
1980-81	Dixie Beehives	OPJHL	24	15	20	35	84
1981-82	Kitchener Rangers (c)	OHL	58	14	34	48	172
1982-83	Kitchener Rangers	OHL	61	17	27	44	156
1983-84	Fredericton Express	AHL	69	11	16	27	142
1984-85	Fredericton Express	AHL	76	21	27	48	49
1985-86	Fredericton Express	AHL	74	21	33	54	68
1986-87	Quebec Nordiques	NHL	56	6	8	14	79
1986-87	Fredericton Express	AHL	10	1	3	4	20
1987-88	Quebec Nordiques	NHL	17	3	2	5	2
1987-88	Fredericton Express	AHL	46	16	25	41	133
1988-89	Halifax Citadels	AHL	22	11	10	21	87
1988-89	Quebec Nordiques	NHL	46	9	10	19	39
1989-90	Quebec Nordiques	NHL	43	13	13	26	84
	NHL TOTALS		162	31	33	64	204

(c)—June, 1982—Drafted as underage junior by Quebec Nordiques in 1982 NHL entry draft. Seventh Nordiques pick, 181st overall, ninth round.

WILLIAM HOULDER

Defense . . . 6'2" . . . 192 lbs. . . . Born, Thunder Bay, Ont., March 11, 1967 . . . Shoots left . . . (January, 1989)—Pulled groin in AHL game.

Year	Team	League	Games	G.	A.	Pts.	Pen.
1983-84	Thunder Bay Beavers	TBAHA	23	4	18	22	37
1984-85	North Bay Centennials (c)	OHL	66	4	20	24	37
1985-86	North Bay Centennials	OHL	59	5	30	35	97
1986-87	North Bay Centennials	OHL	62	17	51	68	68
1987-88	Washington Capitals	NHL	30	1	2	3	10
1987-88	Fort Wayne Komets	IHL	43	10	14	24	32
1988-89	Baltimore Skipjacks	AHL	65	10	36	46	50
1988-89	Washington Capitals	NHL	8	0	3	3	4
1989-90	Baltimore Skipjacks	AHL	26	3	7	10	12
1989-90	Washington Capitals	NHL	41	1	11	12	28
	NHL TOTALS		79	2	16	18	42

(c)—June, 1985—Drafted as underage junior by Washington Capitals in 1985 NHL entry draft. Fourth Capitals pick, 82nd overall, fourth round.

PHIL HOUSLEY

Defense . . . 5'11" . . . 170 lbs. . . . Born, St. Paul, Minn., March 9, 1964 . . . Shoots left . . . Member of Team U.S.A. at World Junior Championships, 1982 . . . Also plays Center . . . Member of Team U.S.A. at World Cup Tournament, 1982 . . . Set Buffalo record for most assists by a rookie (47) in 1982-83 . . . (January, 1984)—Bruised shoulder . . . (March 18, 1984)—Became youngest defenseman in NHL history to have 30-goal season (20 years, 9 days—Bobby Orr was 22 years, 2 days) . . . Set Buffalo record for points by a defenseman with 77 in 1983-84 . . . (October, 1984) —Given three-game NHL suspension . . . Also plays Center . . . (November, 1987)—

Injured back . . . (January 12, 1989)—Bruised back at Chicago . . . (March 18, 1989)—Hip pointer and bruised back at Minnesota . . . (April, 1989)—Pulled shoulder ligaments while playing for Team USA at World Cup Tournament.

Year	Team	League	Games	G.	A.	Pts.	Pen.
1980-81—St. Paul Volcans		USHL	6	7	7	14	6
1981-82—South St. Paul H.S. (c)		Minn. H.S.	22	31	34	65	18
1982-83—Buffalo Sabres		NHL	77	19	47	66	39
1983-84—Buffalo Sabres		NHL	75	31	46	77	33
1984-85—Buffalo Sabres		NHL	73	16	53	69	28
1985-86—Buffalo Sabres		NHL	79	15	47	62	54
1986-87—Buffalo Sabres		NHL	78	21	46	67	57
1987-88—Buffalo Sabres		NHL	74	29	37	66	96
1988-89—Buffalo Sabres		NHL	72	26	44	70	47
1989-90—Buffalo Sabres (d)		NHL	80	21	60	81	32
NHL TOTALS			608	178	380	558	386

(c)—June, 1982—Drafted as underage player by Buffalo Sabres in 1982 NHL entry draft. First Sabres pick, sixth overall, first round.

(d)—June 16, 1990—Traded with Scott Arniel, Jeff Parker and a first-round 1990 draft pick (Keith Tkachuk) by Buffalo Sabres to Winnipeg Jets for Dale Hawerchuk and a first-round 1990 draft pick (Brad May).

SHAWN HOWARD

Center . . . 6' . . . 180 lbs. . . . Born, Anchorage, Alaska, March 20, 1968 . . . Shoots left.

Year	Team	League	Games	G.	A.	Pts.	Pen.
1986-87—Penticton		BCJHL	51	25	34	59	64
1987-88—Univ. of Minnesota/Duluth (c)		WCHA	37	13	8	21	42
1988-89—Univ. of Minnesota/Duluth		WCHA	39	7	9	16	31
1989-90—Univ. of Minnesota/Duluth		WCHA	40	19	19	38	58

(c)—June, 1987—Drafted by New York Islanders in 1987 NHL entry draft. Ninth Islanders pick, 181st overall, eighth round.

MARK STEVEN HOWE

Defense . . . 5'11" . . . 180 lbs. . . . Born, Detroit, Mich., May 28, 1955 . . . Shoots left . . . Brother of Marty Howe and son of Hall-of-Famer Gordie Howe . . . Was member of 1972 USA Olympic team . . . Missed most of 1971-72 season following corrective knee surgery and part of 1976-77 season with shoulder separation . . . Missed part of 1977-78 season with rib injury . . . (October 9, 1980)—First defenseman in NHL to score two shorthanded goals in one period at St. Louis . . . (December 27, 1980)—Five-inch puncture wound to upper thigh . . . Set NHL record for most assists (56) and points (80) by an American born player in 1979-80 (Broken by Neal Broten in '81-82) . . . (February, 1984)—Injured shoulder . . . (January, 1985)—Bruised collarbone . . . Also plays Left Wing . . . (January, 1987)—Back spasms . . . (September, 1987)—Broken rib and cracked vertebra when struck by a Ray Bourque shot during a pre-season game vs. Boston . . . (March, 1988)—Strained back . . . (October, 1988)—Bruised right foot . . . (December, 1988)—Pulled groin muscle . . . (February, 1989)—Missed eight games with sprained left knee cruciate ligament . . . (February 27, 1989)—Resprained left knee at Calgary . . . (December 22, 1989)—Injured groin vs. New Jersey . . . (January 27, 1990)—Injured back vs. Boston.

Year	Team	League	Games	G.	A.	Pts.	Pen.
1970-71—Detroit Jr. Wings (a-c)		SOJHL	44	37	*70	*107	....
1971-72—Detroit Jr. Wings		SOJHL	9	5	9	14	....
1971-72—USA Olympic Team			....	....	....	....	....
1972-73—Toronto Marlboros (d-e-f)		Jr."A"OHA	60	38	66	104	27
1973-74—Houston Aeros (b-g-h)		WHA	76	38	41	79	20
1974-75—Houston Aeros (i)		WHA	74	36	40	76	30
1975-76—Houston Aeros		WHA	72	39	37	76	38
1976-77—Houston Aeros (b-j)		WHA	57	23	52	75	46
1977-78—New England Whalers		WHA	70	30	61	91	32
1978-79—New England Whalers (a-k)		WHA	77	42	65	107	32
1979-80—Hartford Whalers		NHL	74	24	56	80	20
1980-81—Hartford Whalers		NHL	63	19	46	65	54
1981-82—Hartford Whalers (l)		NHL	76	8	45	53	18
1982-83—Philadelphia Flyers (a)		NHL	76	20	47	67	18
1983-84—Philadelphia Flyers		NHL	71	19	34	53	44
1984-85—Philadelphia Flyers		NHL	73	18	39	57	31
1985-86—Philadelphia Flyers (a)		NHL	77	24	58	82	36
1986-87—Philadelphia Flyers (a)		NHL	69	15	43	58	37
1987-88—Philadelphia Flyers		NHL	75	19	43	62	62
1988-89—Philadelphia Flyers		NHL	52	9	29	38	45
1989-90—Philadelphia Flyers		NHL	40	7	21	28	24
WHA TOTALS			426	208	296	504	198
NHL TOTALS			746	182	461	643	389

(c)—Won Most Valuable Player and Outstanding Forward Awards.

(d)—August, 1972—Traded to Toronto Marlboros by London Knights for Larry Goodenough and Dennis Maruk.

(e)—Led in points (26) during playoffs.

(f)—June, 1972—Signed by Houston Aeros (WHA).

(g)—Won WHA Rookie Award.

(h)—Drafted from Toronto Marlboros by Boston Bruins in second round of 1974 amateur draft.

(i)—Tied for lead in goals (10) and led in points (22) during playoffs.

(j)—June, 1977—Signed by New England Whalers as free agent.

(k)—June, 1979—Selected by Boston Bruins in NHL reclaim draft, but remained Hartford Whalers property as a priority selection for the expansion draft.

(l)—August, 1982—Traded by Hartford Whalers to Philadelphia Flyers for Ken Linseman, Greg Adams and Philadelphia's first-round choice (David A. Jensen) in 1983 entry draft. Philadelphia and Hartford also agreed to exchange third-round choices in 1983.

JIRI HRDINA

Center . . . 6' . . . 195 lbs. . . . Born, Prague, Czechoslovakia, January 5, 1958 . . . Shoots right . . . (December 16, 1989)—Strained ligaments in right knee vs. Pittsburgh when sideswiped by Randy Hillier.

Year	Team	League	Games	G.	A.	Pts.	Pen.
1985-86—Sparta Prava (c)		Czech.	44	18	19	37	30
1986-87—Sparta Prava		Czech.	31	18	18	36	24
1987-88—Sparta Prava		Czech.	....	....	....	....	....
1987-88—Calgary Flames		NHL	9	2	5	7	2
1988-89—Calgary Flames		NHL	70	22	32	54	26
1989-90—Calgary Flames		NHL	64	12	18	30	31
NHL TOTALS			143	36	55	91	59

(c)—June, 1984—Drafted by Calgary Flames in 1984 NHL entry draft. Eighth Flames pick, 159th overall, eighth round.

ANTHONY HRKAC

Center . . . 5'11" . . . 165 lbs. . . . Born, Thunder Bay, Ont., July 7, 1966 . . . Shoots left . . . (January, 1985)—Suspended six games by coach for disciplinary reasons . . . (January, 1987)—Bruised left leg . . . (January 12, 1988)—Sprained shoulder when checked by Dave Andreychuk vs. Buffalo . . . (March, 1988)—Lacerated ankle . . . (November 28, 1989)—Bruised left shoulder vs. Boston.

Year	Team	League	Games	G.	A.	Pts.	Pen.
1983-84—Orillia Travelways (c)		OJHL	42	*52	54	*106	20
1984-85—Univ. of North Dakota		WCHA	36	18	36	54	16
1985-86—Team Canada		Int'l.	62	19	30	49	36
1986-87—U. of N. Dakota (a-d-e-f-g)		WCHA	48	46	*70	*116	48
1986-87—St. Louis Blues (h)		NHL	....	....	....	....	....
1987-88—St. Louis Blues		NHL	67	11	37	48	22
1988-89—St. Louis Blues		NHL	70	17	28	45	8
1989-90—St. Louis Blues (i)		NHL	28	5	12	17	8
1989-90—Quebec Nordiques		NHL	22	4	8	12	2
1989-90—Halifax Citadels		AHL	20	12	21	33	4
NHL TOTALS			187	37	85	122	40

(c)—June, 1984—Drafted as underage junior by St. Louis Blues in 1984 NHL entry draft. Second Blues pick, 32nd overall, second round.

(d)—Named to NCAA All-Tournament Team.

(e)—Named NCAA Tournament MVP.

(f)—Named WCHA Player of the Year.

(g)—Won 1987 Hobey Baker Award (Top U.S. College Player).

(h)—No regular season record. Played three playoff games.

(i)—December 13, 1989—Traded with Greg Millen by St. Louis Blues to Quebec Nordiques for Jeff Brown.

PHIL HUBER

Left Wing . . . 5'10" . . . 195 lbs. . . . Born, Calgary, Alta., January 10, 1969 . . . Shoots left.

Year	Team	League	Games	G.	A.	Pts.	Pen.
1987-88—Kamloops Blazers		WHL	63	19	30	49	54
1988-89—Kamloops Blazers (c)		WHL	72	54	68	122	103
1989-90—Kamloops Blazers		WHL	72	63	89	152	176

(c)—June, 1989—Drafted by New York Islanders in 1989 NHL entry draft. Tenth Islanders pick, 149th overall, eighth round.

CHARLES WILLIAM HUDDY

Defense . . . 6' . . . 200 lbs. . . . Born, Oshawa, Ont., June 2, 1959 . . . Shoots left . . . (November 10, 1980)—Injured shoulder vs. N.Y. Islanders . . . (February, 1986)—Missed three games with back spasms . . . (April, 1986)—Broken finger . . . (May 7, 1988)—Charley Horse in thigh after colliding with Tim Higgins in playoff game vs. Detroit and required surgery . . . (January 2, 1989)—Strained hamstring at Minnesota.

Year	Team	League	Games	G.	A.	Pts.	Pen.
1977-78—Oshawa Generals		OMJHL	59	17	18	35	81
1978-79—Oshawa Generals		OMJHL	64	20	38	58	108
1979-80—Houston Apollos (c)		CHL	79	14	34	48	46
1980-81—Edmonton Oilers		NHL	12	2	5	7	6
1980-81—Wichita Wind		CHL	47	8	36	44	71
1981-82—Wichita Wind		CHL	32	7	19	26	51
1981-82—Edmonton Oilers		NHL	41	4	11	15	46
1982-83—Edmonton Oilers		NHL	76	20	37	57	58
1983-84—Edmonton Oilers		NHL	75	8	34	42	43
1984-85—Edmonton Oilers		NHL	80	7	44	51	46
1985-86—Edmonton Oilers		NHL	76	6	35	41	55
1986-87—Edmonton Oilers		NHL	58	4	15	19	35
1987-88—Edmonton Oilers		NHL	77	13	28	41	71
1988-89—Edmonton Oilers		NHL	76	11	33	44	52
1989-90—Edmonton Oilers		NHL	70	1	23	24	56
NHL TOTALS			641	76	265	341	468

(c)—September, 1979—Signed by Edmonton Oilers as a free agent.

MICHAEL HUDSON

Left Wing . . . 6'1" . . . 185 lbs. . . . Born, Guelph, Ont., February 6, 1967 . . . Shoots left . . . Also plays Center . . . (December 21, 1989)—Lacerated right hand when run over by a linesman at St. Louis and missed 12 games.

Year	Team	League	Games	G.	A.	Pts.	Pen.
1984-85—Hamilton Steelhawks		OHL	50	10	12	22	13
1985-86—Hamilton Steelhawks (c)		OHL	7	3	2	5	4
1985-86—Sudbury Wolves (d)		OHL	59	35	42	77	20
1986-87—Sudbury Wolves		OHL	63	40	57	97	18
1987-88—Saginaw Hawks		IHL	75	18	30	48	44

Year	Team	League	Games	G.	A.	Pts.	Pen.
1988-89—Chicago Black Hawks		NHL	41	7	16	23	20
1988-89—Saginaw Hawks		IHL	30	15	17	32	10
1989-90—Chicago Black Hawks		NHL	49	9	12	21	56
NHL TOTALS			90	16	28	44	76

(c)—October, 1985—Traded with Keith Vanrooyen by Hamilton Steelhawks to Sudbury Wolves for Brad Belland.

(d)—June, 1986—Drafted as underage junior by Chicago Black Hawks in 1986 NHL entry draft. Sixth Black Hawks pick, 140th overall, seventh round.

KERRY HUFFMAN

Defense . . . 6'3" . . . 185 lbs. . . . Born, Peterborough, Ont., January 3, 1968 . . . Shoots left . . . Brother-in-law of Mike Posavad (St. Louis Blues) . . . (November, 1987)—Sprained ankle . . . (January, 1988)—Missed 22 games with calcium deposits in thigh . . . (March 15, 1990)—Bruised right knee vs. N.Y. Islanders.

Year	Team	League	Games	G.	A.	Pts.	Pen.
1984-85—Peterborough Jr. B		Metro Jr.B	24	2	5	7	53
1985-86—Guelph Platers (c)		OHL	56	3	24	27	35
1986-87—Guelph Platers (a-d)		OHL	44	4	31	35	20
1986-87—Hershey Bears		AHL	3	0	1	1	0
1986-87—Philadelphia Flyers		NHL	9	0	0	0	2
1987-88—Philadelphia Flyers		NHL	52	6	17	23	34
1988-89—Hershey Bears		AHL	29	2	13	15	16
1988-89—Philadelphia Flyers		NHL	29	0	11	11	31
1989-90—Philadelphia Flyers		NHL	43	1	12	13	34
NHL TOTALS			133	7	40	47	101

(c)—June, 1986—Drafted as underage junior by Philadelphia Flyers in 1986 NHL entry draft. First Flyers pick, 20th overall, first round.

(d)—Won Max Kaminsky Trophy (Top OHL Defenseman).

BRENT HUGHES

Left Wing . . . 5'11" . . . 180 lbs. . . . Born, New Westminster, B.C., April 5, 1966 . . . Shoots left.

Year	Team	League	Games	G.	A.	Pts.	Pen.
1983-84—New Westminster Bruins		WHL	67	21	18	39	133
1984-85—New Westminster Bruins		WHL	64	25	32	57	135
1985-86—New Westminster Bruins		WHL	71	28	52	80	180
1986-87—Victoria Cougars (a-c)		WHL	69	43	65	108	168
1987-88—Moncton Golden Flames (d)		AHL	77	13	19	32	206
1988-89—Winnipeg Jets		NHL	28	3	2	5	82
1988-89—Moncton Hawks		AHL	54	34	34	68	286
1989-90—Moncton Hawks		AHL	65	31	29	60	277
1989-90—Winnipeg Jets		NHL	11	1	2	3	33
NHL TOTALS			39	4	4	8	115

(c)—October, 1986—Traded by New Westminster Bruins to Victoria Cougars for future considerations.

(d)—July, 1987—Signed by Winnipeg Jets as a free agent.

RYAN HUGHES

Center . . . 6'1" . . . 180 lbs. . . . Born, Montreal, Que., January 17, 1972 . . . Shoots left.

Year	Team	League	Games	G.	A.	Pts.	Pen.
1986-87—West Island Bantam		Quebec	14	14	18	32	....
1987-88—Lac St. Louis Midget		Quebec	38	20	30	50	....
1988-89—Lac St. Louis Midget		Quebec	42	25	62	87	48
1989-90—Cornell University (c)		ECAC	28	7	16	23	35

(c)—June 16, 1990—Selected by Quebec Nordiques in 1990 NHL entry draft. Second Nordiques pick, 22nd overall, second round.

BRETT HULL

Right Wing . . . 5'11" . . . 190 lbs. . . . Born, Belleville, Ont., August 9, 1964 . . . Shoots right . . . Brother of Blake Hull, son of Hall-of-Fame left wing Bobby Hull and nephew of Dennis Hull . . . (February-March, 1987)—Set AHL record by scoring goals in 14 straight games . . . (February 6, 1990)—Scored his 50th goal of season vs. Toronto to become the first son of an NHL 50-goal scorer to score 50 goals . . . (February 15, 1990)—Scored his 55th goal of the season to set a club record.

Year	Team	League	Games	G.	A.	Pts.	Pen.
1983-84—Penticton (c)		BCJHL	56	105	83	188	20
1984-85—Univ. of Minn.-Duluth (d)		WCHA	48	32	28	60	24
1985-86—Univ. of Minn.-Duluth (a)		WCHA	42	*52	32	84	46
1985-86—Calgary Flames (e)		NHL	....	....	....	....	....
1986-87—Moncton Golden Flames (a-f)		AHL	67	50	42	92	16
1986-87—Calgary Flames		NHL	5	1	0	1	0
1987-88—Calgary Flames (g)		NHL	52	26	24	50	12
1987-88—St. Louis Blues		NHL	13	6	8	14	4
1988-89—St. Louis Blues		NHL	78	41	43	84	33
1989-90—St. Louis Blues (a-h)		NHL	80	*72	41	113	24
NHL TOTALS			228	146	116	262	73

(c)—June, 1984—Drafted by Calgary Flames in 1984 NHL entry draft. Sixth Flames pick, 117th overall, sixth round.

(d)—WCHA Freshman of the Year.

(e)—No regular season record. Played two playoff games.

(f)—Won Red Garrett Trophy (AHL Top Rookie).

(g)—March, 1988—Traded with Steve Bozek by Calgary Flames to St. Louis Blues for Rob Ramage and Rick Wamsley.

(h)—Won Lady Byng Memorial Trophy (Most Gentlemanly). The first time a father and son have won the same NHL trophy.

JODY HULL

Center and Right Wing . . . 6'1" . . . 200 lbs. . . . Born, Petrolia, Ont., February 2, 1969 . . . Shoots right . . . (September, 1986)—Strained ankle ligaments . . . (February, 1987)—Pulled groin . . . (March, 1989)—Pulled hamstring.

Year	Team	League	Games	G.	A.	Pts.	Pen.
1984-85—Cambridge Winterhawks		OHA	38	13	17	30	39
1985-86—Peterborough Petes		OHL	61	20	22	42	29
1986-87—Peterborough Petes (c)		OHL	49	18	34	52	22
1987-88—Peterborough Petes (b)		OHL	60	50	44	94	33
1988-89—Hartford Whalers		NHL	60	16	18	34	10
1989-90—Binghamton Whalers		AHL	21	7	10	17	6
1989-90—Hartford Whalers (d)		NHL	38	7	10	17	21
NHL TOTALS			98	23	28	51	31

(c)—June, 1987—Drafted as underage junior by Hartford Whalers in 1987 NHL entry draft. First Whalers pick, 18th overall, first round.

(d)—July 9, 1990—Traded by Hartford Whalers to New York Rangers for Carey Wilson and future considerations.

KENT HULST

Center . . . 6'1" . . . 180 lbs. . . . Born, St. Thomas, Ont., April 8, 1968 . . . Shoots left . . . (September, 1988)—Separated shoulder when he collided with Luke Richardson at Toronto Maple Leafs training camp.

Year	Team	League	Games	G.	A.	Pts.	Pen.
1984-85—St. Thomas Jr. B		OHA	47	21	25	46	29
1985-86—Belleville Bulls (c)		OHL	43	6	17	23	20
1985-86—Windsor Spitfires (d)		OHL	17	6	10	16	9
1986-87—Windsor Spitfires		OHL	37	18	20	38	49
1986-87—Belleville Bulls		OHL	27	13	10	23	17
1987-88—Belleville Bulls		OHL	66	42	43	85	48
1988-89—Belleville Bulls		OHL	45	21	41	62	43
1988-89—Flint Spirits		IHL	7	0	1	1	4
1989-90—Newmarket Saints		AHL	80	26	34	60	29

(c)—February, 1986—Traded with future considerations by Belleville Bulls to Windsor Compuware Spitfires for Keith Gretzky.

(d)—June, 1986—Drafted as underage junior by Toronto Maple Leafs in 1986 NHL entry draft. Fourth Maple Leafs pick, 69th overall, fourth round.

BRIAN HUNT

Center . . . 6' . . . 185 lbs. . . . Born, Toronto, Ont., February 12, 1969 . . . Shoots left.

Year	Team	League	Games	G.	A.	Pts.	Pen.
1985-86—Oshawa Jr. B		OHA	17	14	8	22	13
1986-87—Oshawa Generals		OHL	61	13	22	35	22
1987-88—Oshawa Generals (c)		OHL	65	39	56	95	21
1988-89—Oshawa Generals		OHL	63	30	56	86	36
1989-90—Moncton Hawks		AHL	43	4	11	15	19

(c)—June, 1988—Drafted by Winnipeg Jets in 1988 NHL entry draft. Fourth Jets pick, 73rd overall, fourth round.

JEFF CURTIS HUNT
(Known by middle name.)

Defense . . . 6'1" . . . 175 lbs. . . . Born, North Battleford, Sask., January 28, 1967 . . . Shoots left.

Year	Team	League	Games	G.	A.	Pts.	Pen.
1984-85—Prince Albert Raiders (c)		WHL	64	2	13	15	61
1985-86—Prince Albert Raiders		WHL	72	5	29	34	108
1986-87—Prince Albert Raiders (b)		WHL	47	6	31	37	101
1987-88—Flint Spirits		WHL	76	4	17	21	181
1987-88—Fredericton Express		AHL	1	0	0	0	2
1988-89—Milwaukee Admirals		IHL	65	3	17	20	226
1989-90—Milwaukee Admirals		IHL	69	8	25	33	237

(c)—June, 1985—Drafted as underage junior by Vancouver Canucks in 1985 NHL entry draft. Ninth Canucks pick, 172nd overall, ninth round.

DALE ROBERT HUNTER

Center . . . 5'9" . . . 189 lbs. . . . Born, Petrolia, Ont., July 31, 1960 . . . Shoots left . . . Brother of Dave and Mark Hunter . . . (March, 1984)—Given three-game suspension by NHL . . . (April 21, 1985)—Hand infection occurred during playoff game with Montreal . . . (November 25, 1986)—Broke lower fibula of left leg when skate got caught in a rut at Montreal after checking Petr Svoboda . . . (September, 1988)—Broken thumb when slashed by Dave Brown in pre-season game vs. Philadelphia.

Year	Team	League	Games	G.	A.	Pts.	Pen.
1977-78—Kitchener Rangers		Jr."A"OHA	68	22	42	64	115
1978-79—Sudbury Wolves (c)		Jr."A"OHA	59	42	68	110	188
1979-80—Sudbury Wolves		OMJHL	61	34	51	85	189
1980-81—Quebec Nordiques		NHL	80	19	44	63	226
1981-82—Quebec Nordiques		NHL	80	22	50	72	272
1982-83—Quebec Nordiques		NHL	80	17	46	63	206
1983-84—Quebec Nordiques		NHL	77	24	55	79	232
1984-85—Quebec Nordiques (d)		NHL	80	20	52	72	209
1985-86—Quebec Nordiques		NHL	80	28	43	71	265
1986-87—Quebec Nordiques (e)		NHL	46	10	29	39	135
1987-88—Washington Capitals		NHL	79	22	37	59	238
1988-89—Washington Capitals		NHL	80	20	37	57	219
1989-90—Washington Capitals		NHL	80	23	39	62	233
NHL TOTALS			762	205	432	637	2235

(c)—August, 1979—Drafted as underage junior by Quebec Nordiques in entry draft. Second Nordiques pick, 41st overall, second round.

(d)—Led Stanley Cup playoffs with 97 penalty minutes.

(e)—June, 1987—Traded with Clint Malarchuk by Quebec Nordiques to Washington Capitals for Alan Haworth, Gaeten Duchesne and a first-round 1987 draft pick (Joe Sakic).

MARK HUNTER

Right Wing . . . 6'1" . . . 200 lbs. . . . Born, Petrolia, Ont., November 12, 1962 . . . Shoots right . . . Brother of Dale and Dave Hunter . . . (November 13, 1982)—Pulled tendon in right knee at Los Angeles . . . (November 29, 1982)—17-stitch cut under right arm vs. Winnipeg . . . (December 26, 1982)—Tore medial ligaments in right knee in collision with brother Dale vs. Quebec. Surgery was required and missed 42 games . . . (October, 1983)—Injured right knee that required surgery . . . (February 21, 1984)—Injured knee at Quebec . . . (February, 1985)—Recurring knee injury . . . (March, 1987)—Strained shoulder . . . (November 3, 1987)—Bruised thigh when checked by Stu Kulak vs. Quebec . . . (March 22, 1988)—Strained left knee at Washington . . . (November, 1988)—Dislocated right shoulder in fight with Mike Hartman vs. Buffalo . . . (December 26, 1988)—Concussion when struck by Garth Butcher in fight at Vancouver . . . (March 13, 1989)—Suspended three NHL games for striking Michel Petit with his stick vs. N.Y. Rangers . . . (April 13, 1989)—Broke hand in collision with Joel Otto in sixth game of playoff series vs. Vancouver . . . (October 11, 1989)—Strained anterior cruciate ligament of right knee vs. N.Y. Rangers and missed 11 games . . . (November 18, 1989)—Reinjured knee vs. Chicago . . . (December, 1989)—Reinjured knee during team practice . . . (December 15, 1989)—Major surgery to right knee.

Year	Team	League	Games	G.	A.	Pts.	Pen.
1979-80—Brantford Alexanders		OMJHL	66	34	55	89	171
1980-81—Brantford Alexanders (c)		OHL	53	39	40	79	157
1981-82—Montreal Canadiens		NHL	71	18	11	29	143
1982-83—Montreal Canadiens		NHL	31	8	8	16	73
1983-84—Montreal Canadiens		NHL	22	6	4	10	42
1984-85—Montreal Canadiens (d)		NHL	72	21	12	33	123
1985-86—St. Louis Blues		NHL	78	44	30	74	171
1986-87—St. Louis Blues		NHL	74	36	33	69	169
1987-88—St. Louis Blues		NHL	66	32	31	63	136
1988-89—Calgary Flames (e)		NHL	66	22	8	30	194
1989-90—Calgary Flames		NHL	10	2	3	5	39
NHL TOTALS			490	189	140	329	1090

(c)—June, 1981—Drafted as underage junior by Montreal Canadiens in 1981 NHL entry draft. First Canadiens pick, seventh overall, first round.

(d)—June, 1985—Traded with NHL rights to Michael Dark and second-round (Herb Raglan), third (Nelson Emerson), fifth (Dan Brooks) and sixth (Rich Burchill) round 1985 draft picks by Montreal Canadiens to St. Louis Blues for first (Jose Charbonneau), second (Todd Richards), fourth (Martin Desjardins), fifth (Tom Sagissor) and sixth (Donald Dufresne) round 1985 draft picks.

(e)—September 5, 1988—Traded with Doug Gilmour, Steve Bozek and Michael Dark by St. Louis Blues to Calgary Flames for Mike Bullard, Craig Coxe and Tim Corkery.

TIM ROBERT HUNTER

Defense . . . 6'2" . . . 186 lbs. . . . Born, Calgary, Alta., September 10, 1960 . . . Shoots right . . . Also plays Right Wing . . . (October, 1987)—Bruised hand . . . (October 17, 1988)—Injured right eye by finger of Marty McSorley vs. Los Angeles . . . (November 1, 1989)—Fined $500 and suspended 10 games after leaving the bench to fight with Gord Donnelly vs. Winnipeg.

Year	Team	League	Games	G.	A.	Pts.	Pen.
1977-78—Kamloops		BCJHL	51	9	28	37	266
1977-78—Seattle Breakers		WCHL	3	1	2	3	4
1978-79—Seattle Breakers (c)		WHL	70	8	41	49	300
1979-80—Seattle Breakers		WHL	72	14	53	67	311
1980-81—Birmingham Bulls		CHL	58	3	5	8	*236
1980-81—Nova Scotia Voyageurs		AHL	17	0	0	0	62
1981-82—Oklahoma City Stars		CHL	55	4	12	16	222
1981-82—Calgary Flames		NHL	2	0	0	0	9
1982-83—Calgary Flames		NHL	16	1	0	1	54
1982-83—Colorado Flames		CHL	46	5	12	17	225
1983-84—Calgary Flames		NHL	43	4	4	8	130
1984-85—Calgary Flames		NHL	71	11	11	22	259
1985-86—Calgary Flames		NHL	66	8	7	15	291
1986-87—Calgary Flames		NHL	73	6	15	21	357
1987-88—Calgary Flames		NHL	68	8	5	13	337
1988-89—Calgary Flames		NHL	75	3	9	12	*375
1989-90—Calgary Flames		NHL	67	2	3	5	279
NHL TOTALS			481	43	54	97	2091

(c)—August, 1979—Drafted by Atlanta Flames in 1979 NHL entry draft. Fourth Flames pick, 54th overall, third round.

KELLY HURD

Right Wing . . . 5'11" . . . 185 lbs. . . . Born, Castlegar, B.C., May 13, 1968 . . . Shoots right.

Year	Team	League	Games	G.	A.	Pts.	Pen.
1986-87—Kelowna Packers		BCJHL	50	40	53	93	121
1987-88—Michigan Tech. Univ. (c)		WCHA	41	18	22	40	34
1988-89—Michigan Tech. Univ.		WCHA	42	18	14	32	36
1989-90—Michigan Tech. Univ.		WCHA	37	12	13	25	50

(c)—June, 1988—Drafted by Detroit Red Wings in 1988 NHL entry draft. Sixth Red Wings pick, 143rd overall, seventh round.

JAMES HUSCROFT

Defense . . . 6'2" . . . 200 lbs. . . . Born, Creston, B.C., January 9, 1967 . . . Shoots right . . . (October, 1986)—Missed eight weeks with a broken arm . . . (October, 1988)—Fractured right wrist . . . (December, 1988)—Injured groin . . . (January, 1989)—Missed 19 games with a broken foot.

Year	Team	League	Games	G.	A.	Pts.	Pen.
1983-84—Portland Winter Hawks		WHL	63	0	12	12	77
1984-85—Seattle Breakers (c)		WHL	69	3	13	16	273
1985-86—Seattle Thunderbirds		WHL	66	6	20	26	394
1986-87—Seattle Thunderbirds (d)		WHL	21	1	18	19	99

Year	Team	League	Games	G.	A.	Pts.	Pen.
1986-87—Medicine Hat Tigers		WHL	35	4	21	25	170
1987-88—Flint Spirits		IHL	3	1	0	1	2
1987-88—Utica Devils		AHL	71	5	7	12	316
1988-89—Utica Devils		AHL	41	2	10	12	215
1988-89—New Jersey Devils		NHL	15	0	2	2	51
1989-90—New Jersey Devils		NHL	42	2	3	5	144
1989-90—Utica Devils		AHL	22	3	6	9	122
NHL TOTALS			57	2	5	7	195

(c)—June, 1985—Drafted as underage junior by New Jersey Devils in 1985 NHL entry draft. Ninth Devils pick, 171st overall, ninth round.

(d)—February, 1987—Traded by Seattle Thunderbirds to Medicine Hat Tigers for Mike Schwengler.

AL IAFRATE

Defense . . . 6'3" . . . 190 lbs. . . . Born, Dearborn, Mich., March 21, 1966 . . . Shoots left . . . Member of 1984 U.S. Olympic Team . . . (February, 1985)—Bruised knee . . . (October 2, 1985)—Broken nose in fight and missed five games . . . (January 29, 1986)—Strained neck vs. Washington and missed six games . . . (January, 1988)—Stiff back . . . (October 22, 1988)—Broken back vs. Calgary . . . (December 9, 1988)—Four-stitch cut on hand at Detroit . . . (March 24, 1990)—Tore right knee ligament at Quebec when he became entangled with Mike Hough . . . (April 9, 1990)—Knee surgery.

Year	Team	League	Games	G.	A.	Pts.	Pen.
1983-84—U.S. National Team		Int'l	55	4	17	21	26
1983-84—U.S. Olympic Team		Int'l	6	0	0	0	2
1983-84—Belleville Bulls (c)		OHL	10	2	4	6	2
1984-85—Toronto Maple Leafs		NHL	68	5	16	21	51
1985-86—Toronto Maple Leafs		NHL	65	8	25	33	40
1986-87—Toronto Maple Leafs		NHL	80	9	21	30	55
1987-88—Toronto Maple Leafs		NHL	77	22	30	52	80
1988-89—Toronto Maple Leafs		NHL	65	13	20	33	72
1989-90—Toronto Maple Leafs		NHL	75	21	42	63	135
NHL TOTALS			430	78	154	232	433

(c)—June, 1984—Drafted as underage junior by Toronto Maple Leafs in 1984 NHL entry draft. First Maple Leafs pick, fourth overall, first round.

MIROSLAV IHNACAK

Left Wing . . . 6' . . . 185 lbs. . . . Born, Poprad, Czechoslovakia, February 19, 1962 . . . Shoots left . . . Brother of Peter Ihnacak.

Year	Team	League	Games	G.	A.	Pts.	Pen.
1985-86—St. Catharines Saints (c)		AHL	13	4	4	8	2
1985-86—Toronto Maple Leafs		NHL	21	2	4	6	27
1986-87—Newmarket Saints		AHL	32	11	17	28	6
1986-87—Toronto Maple Leafs		NHL	34	6	5	11	12
1987-88—Newmarket Saints		AHL	51	11	17	28	24
1988-89—Detroit Red Wings (d-e)		NHL	1	0	0	0	0
1988-89—Adirondack Red Wings		AHL	62	34	37	71	32
1989-90—Halifax Citadels (f)		AHL	57	33	37	70	43
NHL TOTALS			56	8	9	17	39

(c)—June, 1982—Drafted by Toronto Maple Leafs in 1982 NHL entry draft. Twelfth Maple Leafs pick, 171st overall, ninth round.

(d)—August, 1988—Contract bought out by Toronto Maple Leafs.

(e)—October, 1988—Signed by Detroit Red Wings as a free agent.

(f)—September, 1989—Released by Detroit Red Wings and signed as free agent by Halifax Citadels.

PETER IHNACAK

Center . . . 6' . . . 180 lbs. . . . Born, Prague, Czechoslovakia, May 5, 1957 . . . Shoots right . . . Set Toronto club rookie record with 66 points in 1982-83, and tied rookie record with 28 goals . . . Brother of Miroslav Ihnacak . . . (October 16, 1983)—Injured knee ligaments at New Jersey . . . (February 29, 1984)—Injured shoulder vs. N.Y. Rangers and missed remainder of season . . . (October, 1984)—Knee injury . . . (November 30, 1985)—Suffered concussion vs. Buffalo and missed nine games . . . (January, 1986)—Missed five games with a shoulder injury.

Year	Team	League	Games	G.	A.	Pts.	Pen.
1978-79—Dukla Jihlava		Czech.	44	22	12	34	....
1979-80—Sparta CKD Praha		Czech.	44	19	28	47	....
1980-81—Sparta CKD Praha		Czech.	44	23	22	45	....
1981-82—Sparta CKD Praha		Czech.	39	16	22	38	30
1982-83—Toronto Maple Leafs (c)		NHL	80	28	38	66	44
1983-84—Toronto Maple Leafs		NHL	47	10	13	23	24
1984-85—Toronto Maple Leafs		NHL	70	22	22	44	24
1985-86—Toronto Maple Leafs		NHL	63	18	27	45	16
1986-87—Toronto Maple Leafs		NHL	58	12	27	39	16
1986-87—Newmarket Saints		AHL	8	2	6	8	0
1987-88—Toronto Maple Leafs		NHL	68	10	20	30	41
1988-89—Newmarket Saints		AHL	38	14	16	30	8
1988-89—Toronto Maple Leafs		NHL	26	2	16	18	10
1989-90—Newmarket Saints		AHL	72	26	47	73	40
1989-90—Toronto Maple Leafs		NHL	5	0	2	2	0
NHL TOTALS			417	102	165	267	175

(c)—July, 1983—Signed by Toronto Maple Leafs as a free agent.

KIM ISSEL

Right Wing . . . 6'3" . . . 185 lbs. . . . Born, Regina, Sask., September 25, 1967 . . . Shoots left . . . Also plays Left Wing.

Year	Team	League	Games	G.	A.	Pts.	Pen.
1983-84—Prince Albert Raiders		WHL	31	9	9	18	24
1984-85—Prince Albert Raiders		WHL	44	8	15	23	43
1985-86—Prince Albert Raiders (b-c)		WHL	68	29	39	68	41

Year	Team	League	Games	G.	A.	Pts.	Pen.
1986-87—Prince Albert Raiders		WHL	70	31	44	75	55
1987-88—Nova Scotia Oilers		AHL	68	20	25	45	31
1988-89—Cape Breton Oilers		AHL	65	34	28	62	62
1988-89—Edmonton Oilers		NHL	4	0	0	0	0
1989-90—Cape Breton Oilers		AHL	62	36	32	68	46
NHL TOTALS			4	0	0	0	0

(c)—June, 1986—Drafted as underage junior by Edmonton Oilers in 1986 NHL entry draft. First Oilers pick, 21st overall, first round.

JEFF JABLONSKI

Left Wing . . . 6' . . . 175 lbs. . . . Born, Toledo, Ohio, June 20, 1967 . . . Shoots left . . . Brother of Pat Jablonski.

Year	Team	League	Games	G.	A.	Pts.	Pen.
1985-86—London Diamonds Jr. B (c)		OHA	42	28	32	60	47
1986-87—Lake Superior State Univ.		CCHA	40	17	10	27	42
1987-88—Lake Superior State Univ.		CCHA	45	13	12	25	54
1988-89—Lake Superior State Univ.		CCHA	45	11	12	23	50
1989-90—Lake Superior State Univ.		CCHA	46	38	33	71	82

(c)—June, 1986—Drafted by New York Islanders in 1986 NHL entry draft. Eleventh Islanders pick, 185th overall, ninth round.

DANE JACKSON

Right Wing . . . 6'1" . . . 190 lbs. . . . Born, Winnipeg, Man., May 17, 1970 . . . Shoots right.

Year	Team	League	Games	G.	A.	Pts.	Pen.
1987-88—Vernon Lakers (c)		BCJHL	50	28	32	60	99
1988-89—Univ. of North Dakota		WCHA	30	4	5	9	33
1989-90—Univ. of North Dakota		WCHA	44	15	11	26	56

(c)—June, 1988—Drafted by Vancouver Canucks in 1988 NHL entry draft. Third Canucks pick, 44th overall, third round.

JAMES KENNETH JACKSON

Center . . . 5'8" . . . 190 lbs. . . . Born, Oshawa, Ont., February 1, 1960 . . . Shoots right . . . Also plays Right Wing and Defense . . . (January, 1981)—Groin injury.

Year	Team	League	Games	G.	A.	Pts.	Pen.
1976-77—Oshawa Generals		OMJHL	65	13	40	53	26
1977-78—Oshawa Generals		OMJHL	68	33	47	80	60
1978-79—Niagara Falls Flyers		OMJHL	64	26	39	65	73
1979-80—Niagara Falls Flyers		OMJHL	66	29	57	86	55
1980-81—Richmond Rifles (b)		EHL	58	17	43	60	42
1981-82—Muskegon Mohawks (b)		IHL	82	24	51	75	72
1982-83—Colorado Flames		CHL	30	10	16	26	4
1982-83—Calgary Flames		NHL	48	8	12	20	7
1983-84—Calgary Flames		NHL	49	6	14	20	13
1983-84—Colorado Flames		CHL	25	5	27	32	4
1984-85—Moncton Golden Flames		AHL	24	2	5	7	6
1984-85—Calgary Flames		NHL	10	1	4	5	0
1985-86—Rochester Americans (c)		AHL	65	16	32	48	10
1986-87—Rochester Americans		AHL	71	19	38	57	48
1987-88—Buffalo Sabres		NHL	5	2	0	2	0
1987-88—Rochester Americans		AHL	74	23	48	71	23
1988-89—Rochester Americans		AHL	73	19	50	69	14
1989-90—Rochester Americans		AHL	77	16	37	53	14
NHL TOTALS			112	17	30	47	20

(c)—November, 1985—Signed by Rochester Americans as a free agent.

JEFF JACKSON

Left Wing . . . 6'1" . . . 193 lbs. . . . Born, Chatham, Ont., April 24, 1965 . . . Shoots left . . . Also plays Center . . . (January, 1982)—Stretched knee ligaments . . . (March, 1987)—Has a deteriorating hip condition . . . (January, 1988)—Sprained left knee . . . (March, 1988)—Sprained both knees . . . (January 26, 1989)—Sprained right knee at Minnesota . . . (February, 1989)—Sprained ligaments in left knee.

Year	Team	League	Games	G.	A.	Pts.	Pen.
1981-82—Newmarket Flyers		OJHL	45	30	39	69	105
1982-83—Brantford Alexanders (c)		OHL	64	18	25	43	63
1983-84—Brantford Alexanders		OHL	58	27	42	69	78
1984-85—Hamilton Steelhawks		OHL	20	13	14	27	51
1984-85—Toronto Maple Leafs		NHL	17	0	1	1	24
1985-86—St. Catharines Saints		AHL	74	17	28	45	122
1985-86—Toronto Maple Leafs		NHL	5	1	2	3	2
1986-87—Newmarket Saints		AHL	7	3	6	9	13
1986-87—Toronto Maple Leafs (d)		NHL	55	8	7	15	64
1986-87—New York Rangers		NHL	9	5	1	6	15
1987-88—Quebec Nordiques (e)		NHL	68	9	18	27	103
1988-89—Quebec Nordiques		NHL	33	4	6	10	28
1989-90—Quebec Nordiques		NHL	65	8	12	20	71
NHL TOTALS			252	35	47	82	307

(c)—June, 1983—Drafted as underage junior by Toronto Maple Leafs in 1983 NHL entry draft. Second Maple Leafs pick, 28th overall, second round.

(d)—March, 1987—Traded with a third-round 1989 draft pick by Toronto Maple Leafs to New York Rangers for Mark Osborne.

(e)—September, 1987—Traded with Terry Carkner by New York Rangers to Quebec Nordiques for David Shaw and John Ogrodnick.

JAROMIR JAGR

Left Wing . . . 6'3" . . . 198 lbs. . . . Born, Kladno, Czechoslovakia, February 15, 1972 . . . Shoots left.

Year	Team	League	Games	G.	A.	Pts.	Pen.
1988-89—Poldi Kladno		Czech.	39	8	10	18	....
1989-90—Poldi Kladno (c)		Czech.	51	30	30	60	....

(c)—June 16, 1990—Selected by Pittsburgh Penguins in 1990 NHL entry draft. First Penguins pick, fifth overall, first round.

CRAIG JANNEY

Center . . . 6'1" . . . 180 lbs. . . . Born, Hartford, Conn., September 26, 1967 . . . Shoots left . . . (December, 1985)—Broken collarbone . . . (December, 1986)—Mononucleosis . . . (December, 1988)—Missed seven games with a pulled right groin . . . October 26, 1989)—Torn right groin muscle vs. Quebec and missed 21 games . . . (April 5, 1990)—Strained left shoulder vs. Hartford.

Year	Team	League	Games	G.	A.	Pts.	Pen.
1984-85—Deerfield Academy		Conn.	17	33	35	68	6
1985-86—Boston College (c)		H. East	34	13	14	27	8
1986-87—Boston College (a-d)		H. East	37	28	*55	*83	6
1987-88—U.S. Olympic Team		Int'l	54	28	44	72	....
1987-88—Boston Bruins		NHL	15	7	9	16	0
1988-89—Boston Bruins		NHL	62	16	46	62	12
1989-90—Boston Bruins		NHL	55	24	38	62	4
NHL TOTALS			132	47	93	140	16

(c)—June, 1986—Drafted by Boston Bruins in 1986 NHL entry draft. First Bruins pick, 13th overall, first round.

(d)—Named First team All-America (East).

MARK JANSSENS

Center . . . 6'3" . . . 195 lbs. . . . Born, Surrey, B.C., May 19, 1968 . . . Shoots left . . . Also plays Left Wing . . . (December 10, 1988)—Fractured skull and had cerebral concussion in fight with Martin Simard at Salt Lake City when his helmet came off and his head struck the ice.

Year	Team	League	Games	G.	A.	Pts.	Pen.
1983-84—Surrey Midgets		B.C.	48	40	58	98	64
1984-85—Regina Pats		WHL	70	8	22	30	51
1985-86—Regina Pats (c)		WHL	71	25	38	63	146
1986-87—Regina Pats		WHL	68	24	38	62	209
1987-88—Colorado Rangers		IHL	6	2	2	4	24
1987-88—Regina Pats		WHL	71	39	51	90	202
1987-88—New York Rangers		NHL	1	0	0	0	0
1988-89—New York Rangers		NHL	5	0	0	0	0
1988-89—Denver Rangers		IHL	38	19	19	38	104
1989-90—New York Rangers		NHL	80	5	8	13	161
NHL TOTALS			86	5	8	13	161

(c)—June, 1986—Drafted as underage junior by New York Rangers in 1986 NHL entry draft. Fourth Rangers pick, 72nd overall, fourth round.

STEVE JAQUES

Defense . . . 5'11" . . . 180 lbs. . . . Born, Burnaby, B.C., February 21, 1969 . . . Shoots right . . . (March 26, 1989)—Injured knee ligaments vs. Portland.

Year	Team	League	Games	G.	A.	Pts.	Pen.
1987-88—New Westminster Bruins		WHL	69	15	31	46	336
1988-89—Tri-City Americans (a-c)		WHL	61	18	34	52	233
1989-90—Tri-City Americans		WHL	64	20	64	84	185

(c)—June, 1989—Drafted by Los Angeles Kings in 1989 NHL entry draft. Eleventh Kings pick, 228th overall, 11th round.

IIRVO JARVI

Right Wing . . . 6'2" . . . 200 lbs. . . . Born, Helsinki, Finland, March 23, 1965 . . . Shoots right.

Year	Team	League	Games	G.	A.	Pts.	Pen.
1985-86—Helsinki IFK (c)		Finland	29	7	6	13	19
1986-87—Helsinki IFK		Finland	43	23	30	53	82
1987-88—Helsinki IFK		Finland	44	21	20	41	68
1988-89—Quebec Nordiques		NHL	75	11	30	41	40
1989-90—Halifax Citadels		AHL	26	4	13	17	4
1989-90—Quebec Nordiques		NHL	41	7	13	20	18
NHL TOTALS			116	18	43	61	58

(c)—June, 1983—Drafted by Quebec Nordiques in 1983 NHL entry draft. Third Nordiques pick, 54th overall, third round.

GRANT JENNINGS

Defense . . . 6'3" . . . 190 lbs. . . . Born, Hudson Bay, Sask., May 5, 1965 . . . Shoots left . . . (1984-85)—Shoulder injury . . . (October, 1986)—Knee injury . . . (October 6, 1988)—Broke left hand vs. Quebec . . . (October, 1988)—Bruised right foot . . . (December, 1988)—Sprained left shoulder . . . (April 14, 1989)—Surgery to left shoulder . . . (February 7, 1990)—Sprained left knee vs. Toronto . . . (March 14, 1990)—Twisted knee when checked by Jim Sandlak at Vancouver.

Year	Team	League	Games	G.	A.	Pts.	Pen.
1983-84—Saskatoon Blades		WHL	64	5	13	18	102
1984-85—Saskatoon Blades (c)		WHL	47	10	14	24	134
1985-86—Binghamton Whalers		AHL	51	0	4	4	109
1986-87—Fort Wayne Komets		IHL	3	0	0	0	0
1986-87—Binghamton Whalers		AHL	47	1	5	6	125
1987-88—Binghamton Whalers (d)		AHL	56	2	12	14	195
1988-89—Hartford Whalers		NHL	55	3	10	13	159
1988-89—Binghamton Whalers		AHL	2	0	0	0	2
1989-90—Hartford Whalers		NHL	64	3	6	9	154
NHL TOTALS			119	6	16	22	313

(c)—June, 1985—Signed by Washington Capitals as a free agent.

(d)—July, 1988—Traded with Ed Kastelic by Washington Capitals to Hartford Whalers for Neil Sheehy and Mike Millar.

CHRIS JENSEN

Center . . . 5'11" . . . 165 lbs. . . . Born, Fort St. John, B.C., October 28, 1963 . . . Shoots right . . . (October, 1985)—Injured knee . . . (October, 1986)—Strained shoulder . . . (April, 1987)—Shoulder surgery . . . (February, 1989)—Missed five weeks following knee surgery . . . (October, 1989)—Injured hand.

Year	Team	League	Games	G.	A.	Pts.	Pen.
1980-81—Kelowna		BCJHL	53	51	45	96	120
1981-82—Kelowna (c)		BCJHL	48	46	46	92	212
1982-83—University of North Dakota		WCHA	13	3	3	6	28
1983-84—University of North Dakota		WCHA	44	24	25	49	100
1984-85—University of North Dakota		WCHA	40	25	27	52	80
1985-86—University of North Dakota		WCHA	34	25	40	65	53
1985-86—New York Rangers		NHL	9	1	3	4	0
1986-87—New York Rangers		NHL	37	6	7	13	21
1986-87—New Haven Nighthawks		AHL	14	4	9	13	41
1987-88—New York Rangers		NHL	7	0	1	1	2
1987-88—Colorado Rangers		IHL	43	10	23	33	68
1988-89—Hershey Bears (d)		AHL	45	27	31	58	66
1989-90—Philadelphia Flyers		NHL	1	0	0	0	2
1989-90—Hershey Bears		AHL	43	16	26	42	101
NHL TOTALS			54	7	11	18	25

(c)—June, 1982—Drafted as underage player by New York Rangers in 1982 NHL entry draft. Fourth Rangers pick, 78th overall, fourth round.

(d)—September 28, 1988—Traded by New York Rangers to Philadelphia Flyers for Michael Boyce.

PAUL JERRARD

Defense . . . 6'1" . . . 185 lbs. . . . Born, Winnipeg, Man., April 20, 1965 . . . Shoots right . . . (October, 1987)—Fractured cheekbone when struck by a shot during an IHL game.

Year	Team	League	Games	G.	A.	Pts.	Pen.
1982-83—Notre Dame H.S. (c)		Man. Juv.	60	34	37	71	150
1983-84—Lake Superior State College		CCHA	40	8	18	26	48
1984-85—Lake Superior State College		CCHA	43	9	25	34	61
1985-86—Lake Superior State College		CCHA	40	13	11	24	34
1986-87—Lake Superior State College		CCHA	34	10	17	27	54
1987-88—Colorado Rangers		IHL	77	20	28	48	182
1988-89—Denver Rangers (d)		IHL	2	1	1	2	21
1988-89—Kalamazoo Wings		IHL	68	15	25	40	195
1988-89—Minnesota North Stars		IHL	5	0	0	0	4
1989-90—Kalamazoo Wings		IHL	60	9	18	27	134
NHL TOTALS			5	0	0	0	4

(c)—June, 1983—Drafted by New York Rangers in 1983 NHL entry draft. Tenth Rangers pick, 173rd overall, ninth round.

(d)—October 11, 1988—Traded with Mark Tinordi, Mike Sullivan, Bret Barnett and Los Angeles Kings third-round 1989 draft pick (Murray Garbutt) by New York Rangers to Minnesota North Stars for Igor Liba, Brian Lawton and the NHL rights to Eric Bennett.

JIM JOHANNSON

Center . . . 6'1" . . . 195 lbs. . . . Born, Rochester, Minn., March 10, 1964 . . . Shoots right.

Year	Team	League	Games	G.	A.	Pts.	Pen.
1982-83—Univ. of Wisconsin		WCHA	43	12	9	21	16
1983-84—Univ. of Wisconsin		WCHA	35	17	21	38	52
1984-85—Univ. of Wisconsin		WCHA	40	16	24	40	54
1985-86—Univ. of Wisconsin		WCHA	30	18	13	31	44
1986-87—Landsberg		W. Germ.	57	46	56	102	90
1987-88—U.S. National Team		Int'l	47	16	14	30	64
1987-88—U.S. Olympic Team (c)		Olym.	4	0	1	1	4
1987-88—Salt Lake Golden Eagles		IHL	18	14	7	21	50
1988-89—Salt Lake Golden Eagles		IHL	82	35	40	75	87
1989-90—Indianapolis Ice		IHL	82	22	41	63	74

(c)—February, 1988—Signed by Calgary Flames as a free agent.

CARL (Calle) JOHANSSON

Defense . . . 5'11" . . . 198 lbs. . . . Born, Goteborg, Sweden, February 14, 1967 . . . Shoots left . . . (October 9, 1988)—Dislocated thumb at Philadelphia . . . (October 7, 1989)—Injured back vs. Chicago and missed 10 games.

Year	Team	League	Games	G.	A.	Pts.	Pen.
1983-84—Vastra Frolunda		Sweden	34	5	10	15	20
1984-85—Vastra Frolunda (c)		Sweden	36	14	15	29	20
1985-86—Bjorkloven		Sweden	17	1	1	2	14
1986-87—Bjorkloven		Sweden	30	2	13	15	18
1987-88—Buffalo Sabres		NHL	71	4	38	42	37
1988-89—Buffalo Sabres (d)		NHL	47	2	11	13	33
1988-89—Washington Capitals		NHL	12	1	7	8	4
1989-90—Washington Capitals		NHL	70	8	31	39	25
NHL TOTALS			200	15	87	102	99

(c)—June, 1985—Drafted by Buffalo Sabres in 1985 NHL entry draft. First Sabres pick, 14th overall, first round.

(d)—March 6, 1989—Traded with a second-round 1989 draft pick (Byron Dafoe) by Buffalo Sabres to Washington Capitals for Grant Ledyard, Clint Malarchuk and a sixth-round 1991 draft pick.

ROGER JOHANSSON

Defense . . . 6'4" . . . 190 lbs. . . . Born, Ljungby, Sweden, April 17, 1967 . . . Shoots left.

Year	Team	League	Games	G.	A.	Pts.	Pen.
1983-84—Troja Sr.		Sweden	8	2	1	3	8
1984-85—Troja Sr. (c)		Sweden	30	1	10	11	28
1985-86—Troja Sr		Sweden	32	5	16	21	42
1986-87—Farjestads		Sweden	31	6	11	17	22
1987-88—Farjestads		Sweden	24	3	11	14	20
1988-89—Farjestads		Sweden	40	5	15	20	36
1989-90—Calgary Flames		NHL	35	0	5	5	48
NHL TOTALS			35	0	5	5	48

(c)—June, 1985—Drafted by Calgary Flames in 1985 NHL entry draft. Fifth Flames pick, 80th overall, fourth round.

CRAIG JOHNSON

Center . . . 6'1" . . . 180 lbs. . . . Born, St. Paul, Minn., March 18, 1972 . . . Shoots left . . . (February, 1987)—Stress fracture of vertebrae . . . Plans to attend Univ. of Minnesota.

Year	Team	League	Games	G.	A.	Pts.	Pen.
1987-88—Hill Murray H.S.		Minn. H.S.	28	14	20	34	4
1988-89—Hill Murray H.S.		Minn. H.S.	24	22	30	52	10
1989-90—Hill Murray H.S. (c)		Minn. H.S.	23	15	36	51	....

(c)—June 16, 1990—Selected by St. Louis Blues in 1990 NHL entry draft. First Blues pick, 33rd overall, second round.

GREG JOHNSON

Center . . . 5'10" . . . 170 lbs. . . . Born, Thunder Bay, Ont., March 16, 1971 . . . Shoots left.

Year	Team	League	Games	G.	A.	Pts.	Pen.
1988-89—Thunder Bay Jrs. (a-c)		USHL	47	32	64	96	4
1989-90—University of North Dakota		WCHA	44	17	38	55	11

(c)—June, 1989—Drafted by Philadelphia Flyers in 1989 NHL entry draft. First Flyers pick, 33rd overall, second round.

JIM JOHNSON

Defense . . . 6' . . . 190 lbs. . . . Born, New Hope, Minn., August 9, 1962 . . . Shoots left . . . (January, 1988)—Torn cartilage in right knee.

Year	Team	League	Games	G.	A.	Pts.	Pen.
1981-82—Univ. of Minnesota-Duluth		WCHA	40	0	10	10	62
1982-83—Univ. of Minnesota-Duluth		WCHA	44	3	18	21	118
1983-84—Univ. of Minnesota-Duluth		WCHA	43	3	13	16	116
1984-85—Univ. of Minnesota-Duluth (c)		WCHA	47	7	29	36	49
1985-86—Pittsburgh Penguins		NHL	80	3	26	29	115
1986-87—Pittsburgh Penguins		NHL	80	5	25	30	116
1987-88—Pittsburgh Penguins		NHL	55	1	12	13	87
1988-89—Pittsburgh Penguins		NHL	76	2	14	16	163
1989-90—Pittsburgh Penguins		NHL	75	3	13	16	154
NHL TOTALS			366	14	90	104	635

(c)—June, 1985—Signed by Pittsburgh Penguins as a free agent.

MARK JOHNSON

Center . . . 5'9" . . . 160 lbs. . . . Born, Minneapolis, Minn., September 22, 1957 . . . Shoots left . . . Member of 1978 and 1979 U.S. National teams and 1980 U.S. Gold Medal Winning Hockey Team . . . Son of Bob Johnson (Former coach of Calgary Flames and currently Executive Director of U.S. Amateur Hockey Assoc.) . . . (September, 1980)—Took 20 stitches near right eye in preseason game . . . (November, 1980)—Wrist injury . . . (February, 1985)—Rib injury . . . (October, 1987)—Strained left knee . . . (November, 1987)—Knee surgery . . . (January, 1988)—Bruised right instep . . . (November, 1988)—Missed six weeks with a fractured jaw when a clearing pass by teammate goalie Bob Sauve went off his face . . . (December, 1988)—Strained left knee . . . (January, 1989)—Pulled hamstring in a team practice.

Year	Team	League	Games	G.	A.	Pts.	Pen.
1976-77—University of Wisconsin (c-d)		WCHA	43	36	44	80	16
1977-78—University of Wisconsin (a-e)		WCHA	42	*48	38	86	24
1978-79—Univ. of Wisconsin (a-e-f)		WCHA	40	*41	49	*90	34
1979-80—U.S. Olympic Team		Int'l	60	*38	*54	*92	31
1979-80—Pittsburgh Penguins		NHL	17	3	5	8	4
1980-81—Pittsburgh Penguins		NHL	73	10	23	33	50
1981-82—Pittsburgh Penguins (g)		NHL	46	10	11	21	30
1981-82—Minnesota North Stars (h)		NHL	10	2	2	4	10
1982-83—Hartford Whalers		NHL	73	31	38	69	28
1983-84—Hartford Whalers		NHL	79	35	52	87	27
1984-85—Hartford Whalers (i)		NHL	49	19	28	47	21
1984-85—St. Louis Blues		NHL	17	4	6	10	2
1985-86—New Jersey Devils (j)		NHL	80	21	41	62	16
1986-87—New Jersey Devils		NHL	68	25	26	51	22
1987-88—New Jersey Devils		NHL	54	14	19	33	14
1988-89—New Jersey Devils		NHL	40	13	25	38	24
1989-90—New Jersey Devils (k)		NHL	63	16	29	45	12
NHL TOTALS			669	203	305	508	260

(c)—June, 1977—Drafted by Pittsburgh Penguins in 1977 NHL amateur draft. Third Penguins pick, 66th overall, fourth round.

(d)—Named WCHA Outstanding Freshman.

(e)—Named to All-America Team (West).

(f)—Named WCHA MVP and NCAA Player of the Year.

(g)—March, 1982—Traded by Pittsburgh Penguins to Minnesota North Stars for second-round 1982 entry draft pick (Tim Hrynewich).

(h)—October, 1982—Traded by Minnesota North Stars with Kent-Erik Andersson to Hartford Whalers for 1984 fifth-round pick (Jiri Poner) in NHL entry draft and future considerations (Jordy Douglas).

(i)—February, 1985—Traded with Greg Millen by Hartford Whalers to St. Louis Blues for Mike Liut and future considerations (Jorgen Pettersson).

(j)—September, 1985—Traded by St. Louis Blues to New Jersey Devils for Shawn Evans and a fifth round 1986 draft pick (Mike Wolak).

(k)—August, 1990—Signed with team in Italy for 1990-91 season.

STEVE JOHNSON

Right Wing . . . 6'1" . . . 190 lbs. . . . Born, Grand Forks, N.D., March 3, 1966 . . . Shoots right . . . Brother of Chad Johnson.

Year	Team	League	Games	G.	A.	Pts.	Pen.
1984-85—Univ. of North Dakota		WCHA	41	18	16	34	10
1985-86—Univ. of North Dakota		WCHA	38	31	28	59	40
1986-87—Univ. of North Dakota (c)		WCHA	48	26	44	70	38

Year	Team	League	Games	G.	A.	Pts.	Pen.
1987-88—Univ. of North Dakota (d)		WCHA	42	34	51	85	28
1988-89—Milwaukee Admirals		IHL	64	18	34	52	37
1989-90—Milwaukee Admirals		IHL	5	0	2	2	0
1989-90—Phoenix Roadrunners		IHL	65	21	49	70	31

(c)—June, 1987—Selected by Vancouver Canucks in 1987 NHL supplemental draft.
(d)—Named First team All-America (West).

GREG JOHNSTON

Right Wing . . . 6'1" . . . 195 lbs. . . . Born, Barrie, Ont., January 14, 1965 . . . Shoots right . . . Also plays Center . . . (September, 1982)—Broken ankle . . . (November, 1988)—Strained abdominal muscle.

Year	Team	League	Games	G.	A.	Pts.	Pen.
1981-82—Barrie		OHA Midget	42	31	46	77	74
1982-83—Toronto Marlboros (c)		OHL	58	18	19	37	58
1983-84—Toronto Marlboros		OHL	57	38	35	73	67
1983-84—Boston Bruins		NHL	15	2	1	3	2
1984-85—Boston Bruins		NHL	6	0	0	0	0
1984-85—Hershey Bears		AHL	3	1	0	1	0
1984-85—Toronto Marlboros		OHL	42	22	28	50	55
1985-86—Moncton Golden Flames		AHL	60	19	26	45	56
1985-86—Boston Bruins		NHL	20	0	2	2	0
1986-87—Boston Bruins		NHL	76	12	15	27	79
1987-88—Maine Mariners		AHL	75	21	32	53	105
1987-88—Boston Bruins		NHL	57	11	10	21	32
1988-89—Maine Mariners		AHL	15	5	7	12	31
1989-90—Maine Mariners		AHL	52	16	26	42	45
1989-90—Boston Bruins (d)		NHL	9	1	1	2	6
NHL TOTALS			183	26	29	55	119

(c)—June, 1983—Drafted as underage junior by Boston Bruins in 1983 NHL entry draft. Second Bruins pick, 42nd overall, second round.
(d)—June 28, 1990—Traded with future considerations by Boston Bruins to New York Rangers for Chris Nilan. Johnston was then traded by the Rangers to Toronto Maple Leafs for Tie Domi and Mark Laforest.

BRAD JONES

Center . . . 6' . . . 175 lbs. . . . Born, Sterling Heights, Mich., June 26, 1965 . . . Shoots left . . . (November, 1984)—Injured knee vs. Lake Superior State . . . (February, 1987)—Set record for career assists at Michigan.

Year	Team	League	Games	G.	A.	Pts.	Pen.
1983-84—University of Michigan (c)		CCHA	37	8	26	34	32
1984-85—University of Michigan		CCHA	34	21	27	48	69
1985-86—University of Michigan (b)		CCHA	36	28	39	67	40
1986-87—University of Michigan (a-d)		CCHA	40	32	46	78	64
1986-87—Winnipeg Jets		NHL	4	1	0	1	0
1987-88—Winnipeg Jets		NHL	19	2	5	7	15
1987-88—U.S. Olympic Team		Int'l	50	27	23	50	59
1988-89—Winnipeg Jets		NHL	22	6	5	11	6
1988-89—Moncton Hawks		AHL	44	20	19	39	62
1989-90—Winnipeg Jets (e)		NHL	2	0	0	0	0
1989-90—Moncton Hawks		AHL	15	5	6	11	47
1989-90—New Haven Nighthawks		AHL	36	8	11	19	71
NHL TOTALS			47	9	10	19	21

(c)—June, 1984—Drafted by Winnipeg Jets in 1984 NHL entry draft. Eighth Jets pick, 156th overall, eighth round.
(d)—Named Second team All-America (West).
(e)—November, 1989—Traded by Winnipeg Jets to Los Angeles Kings for Phil Sykes.

CASEY JONES

Center . . . 5'11" . . . 170 lbs. . . . Born, North Bay, Ont., May 30, 1968 . . . Shoots left.

Year	Team	League	Games	G.	A.	Pts.	Pen.
1986-87—Cornell University (c)		ECAC	27	6	12	18	38
1987-88—Cornell University		ECAC	27	10	22	32	26
1988-89—Cornell University		ECAC	29	8	27	35	22
1989-90—Cornell University		ECAC	27	6	21	27	22

(c)—June, 1987—Drafted by Boston Bruins in 1987 NHL entry draft. Eleventh Bruins pick, 203rd overall, 10th round.

ANTHONY JOSEPH

Right Wing . . . 6'4" . . . 203 lbs. . . . Born, Cornwall, Ont., March 1, 1969 . . . Shoots right.

Year	Team	League	Games	G.	A.	Pts.	Pen.
1984-85—Cornwall Midget		OHA	37	33	30	63	48
1985-86—Oshawa Generals		OHL	41	3	1	4	28
1986-87—Oshawa Generals		OHL	44	2	5	7	93
1987-88—Oshawa Generals (c)		OHL	49	9	18	27	126
1988-89—Winnipeg Jets		NHL	2	1	0	1	0
1988-89—Oshawa Generals		OHL	52	20	16	36	106
1989-90—Tappara		Finland	5	0	0	0	2
1989-90—Moncton Hawks		AHL	61	9	9	18	74
NHL TOTALS			2	1	0	1	0

(c)—June, 1988—Drafted by Winnipeg Jets in 1988 NHL entry draft. Fifth Jets pick, 94th overall, fifth round.

CHRIS JOSEPH

Defense . . . 6'1" . . . 195 lbs. . . . Born, Burnaby, B.C., September 10, 1969 . . . Shoots right . . . (January, 1989)—Strained knee ligaments.

Year	Team	League	Games	G.	A.	Pts.	Pen.
1984-85—Burnaby Midget		B.C. Midget	52	18	48	66	52
1985-86—Seattle Breakers		WHL	72	4	8	12	50
1986-87—Seattle Thunderbirds (c)		WHL	67	13	45	58	155

Year	Team	League	Games	G.	A.	Pts.	Pen.
1987-88—Pittsburgh Penguins (d)		NHL	17	0	4	4	12
1987-88—Edmonton Oilers		NHL	7	0	4	4	6
1987-88—Nova Scotia Oilers		AHL	8	0	2	2	8
1987-88—Seattle Thunderbirds		WHL	23	5	14	19	49
1988-89—Cape Breton Oilers		AHL	5	1	1	2	18
1988-89—Edmonton Oilers		NHL	44	4	5	9	54
1989-90—Edmonton Oilers		NHL	4	0	2	2	2
1989-90—Cape Breton Oilers		AHL	61	10	20	30	69
NHL TOTALS			72	4	15	19	74

(c)—June, 1987—Drafted by Pittsburgh Penguins in 1988 NHL entry draft. First Penguins pick, fifth overall, first round.
(d)—November, 1987—Traded with Craig Simpson, Dave Hannan and Moe Mantha by Pittsburgh Penguins to Edmonton Oilers for Paul Coffey, Dave Hunter and Wayne Van Dorp.

FABIAN JOSEPH

Center . . . 5'8" . . . 165 lbs. . . . Born, Sydney, N.S., December 5, 1965 . . . Shoots left.

Year	Team	League	Games	G.	A.	Pts.	Pen.
1982-83—Victoria Cougars		WHL	69	42	48	90	50
1983-84—Victoria Cougars (c)		WHL	72	52	75	127	27
1984-85—Toronto Marlboros		OHL	60	32	43	75	16
1985-86—Canadian Olympic Team		Int'l	71	26	18	44	51
1986-87—Canadian Olympic Team		Int'l	74	15	30	45	26
1987-88—Nova Scotia Oilers		AHL	77	31	39	70	20
1988-89—Cape Breton Oilers		AHL	70	32	34	66	30
1989-90—Cape Breton Oilers		AHL	77	33	53	86	46

(c)—June, 1984—Drafted as underage junior by Toronto Maple Leafs in 1984 NHL entry draft. Fifth Maple Leafs pick, 109th overall, sixth round.

ROBERT JOYCE

Left Wing . . . 6'1" . . . 180 lbs. . . . Born, St. Johns, N.B., July 11, 1966 . . . Shoots left . . . (October, 1985)—Tied a WCHA record with five goals vs. Michigan Tech . . . (January 24, 1987)—Set WCHA record with six goals vs. Michigan Tech. He also had three assists to tie a WCHA record in a nine-point game . . . (September, 1988)—Sprained right knee in Boston Bruins training camp . . . (October 6, 1988)—Concussion and six-stitch cut to lip in a collision with Brad Marsh vs. Toronto . . . (March, 1989)—Pulled groin muscle . . . (November 23, 1989)—Dislocated shoulder . . . (January 3, 1990)—Sprained right knee in collision with Brian Leetch vs. N.Y. Rangers, had surgery and missed 17 games.

Year	Team	League	Games	G.	A.	Pts.	Pen.
1983-84—Wilcox Notre Dame H.S. (c)		Sask. HS	30	33	37	70	..
1984-85—Univ. of North Dakota		WCHA	41	18	16	34	10
1985-86—Univ. of North Dakota		WCHA	38	31	28	59	40
1986-87—Univ. of North Dakota (a-d)		WCHA	48	*52	37	89	42
1987-88—Canadian Olympic Team		Int'l	50	13	10	23	28
1987-88—Boston Bruins		NHL	15	7	5	12	10
1988-89—Boston Bruins		NHL	77	18	31	49	46
1989-90—Boston Bruins (e)		NHL	23	1	2	3	22
1989-90—Washington Capitals		NHL	24	5	8	13	4
NHL TOTALS			139	31	46	77	82

(c)—June, 1984—Drafted by Boston Bruins in 1984 NHL entry draft. Fourth Bruins pick, 82nd overall, fourth round.
(d)—Named First Team All-America (West).
(e)—December 13, 1989—Traded by Boston Bruins to Washington Capitals for Dave Christian.

RICK JUDSON

Left Wing . . . 5'11" . . . 180 lbs. . . . Born, Lambentville, Mich., August 13, 1969 . . . Shoots left.

Year	Team	League	Games	G.	A.	Pts.	Pen.
1987-88—Rochester Mustangs (a)		USHL	..	56	35	91	..
1988-89—Univ. of Illinois/Chicago (c)		CCHA	42	14	20	34	20
1989-90—Univ. of Illinois/Chicago		CCHA	38	19	22	41	18

(c)—June, 1989—Drafted by Detroit Red Wings in 1989 NHL entry draft. Eleventh Red Wings pick, 204th overall, 10th round.

CLAUDE JULIEN

Defense . . . 6' . . . 195 lbs. . . . Born, Orleans, Ont., November 11, 1958 . . . Shoots right . . . (February 1, 1986)—Broken nose at Quebec.

Year	Team	League	Games	G.	A.	Pts.	Pen.
1977-78—Newmarket Flyers		OPJHL	45	18	26	44	137
1977-78—Oshawa Generals		OMJHL	11	0	5	5	14
1978-79—..................			....	....	....	....	....
1979-80—Windsor Spitfires		OMJHL	68	14	37	51	148
1980-81—Windsor Spitfires		OHL	3	1	2	3	21
1980-81—Port Huron Flags		IHL	77	15	40	55	153
1981-82—Salt Lake Golden Eagles (c)		CHL	70	4	18	22	134
1982-83—Salt Lake Golden Eagles (b-d)		CHL	76	14	47	61	176
1983-84—Milwaukee Admirals		IHL	5	0	3	3	2
1983-84—Fredericton Express		AHL	57	7	22	29	58
1984-85—Fredericton Express		AHL	77	6	28	34	97
1984-85—Quebec Nordiques		NHL	1	0	0	0	0
1985-86—Quebec Nordiques		NHL	13	0	1	1	25
1985-86—Fredericton Express		AHL	49	3	18	21	74
1986-87—Fredericton Express (e)		AHL	17	1	6	7	22
1987-88—Fredericton Express		AHL	35	1	14	15	52
1987-88—Baltimore Skipjacks		AHL	30	1	14	20	22
1988-89—Halifax Citadels (b)		AHL	79	8	52	60	72
1989-90—Halifax Citadels		AHL	77	6	37	43	65
NHL TOTALS			14	0	1	1	25

(c)—September, 1981—Signed by St. Louis Blues as a free agent.
(d)—August, 1983—Sent by St. Louis Blues along with Gordon Donnelly to Quebec Nordiques as compensation for St. Louis signing coach Jacques Demers.
(e)—March, 1987—Signed by Fredericton Express after completing a season in Europe.

JOE JUNEAU

Center . . . 6' . . . 175 lbs. . . . Born, Pont-Rouge, Que., January 5, 1968 . . . Shoots right.

Year	Team	League	Games	G.	A.	Pts.	Pen.
1986-87—Levis-Lauzon Cegep AAA	Que. Midget	38	27	57	84	....
1987-88—R.P.I. (c)	ECAC	31	16	29	45	18
1988-89—R.P.I.	ECAC	30	12	23	35	40
1989-90—R.P.I. (a-d)	ECAC	34	18	*52	*70	31

(c)—June, 1988—Drafted by Boston Bruins in 1988 NHL entry draft. Third Bruins pick, 81st overall, fourth round.
(d)—Named to NCAA All-America Team (East).

MARK KACHOWSKI

Left Wing . . . 5'10" . . . 195 lbs. . . . Born, Edmonton, Alta., February 20, 1965 . . . Shoots left.

Year	Team	League	Games	G.	A.	Pts.	Pen.
1983-84—Kamloops Blazers	WHL	57	6	9	15	156
1984-85—Kamloops Blazers	WHL	68	22	15	37	185
1985-86—Kamloops Blazers	WHL	61	21	31	52	182
1986-87—Flint Spirits (c)	IHL	75	18	13	31	273
1987-88—Pittsburgh Penguins	NHL	38	5	3	8	126
1987-88—Muskegon Lumberjacks	IHL	25	3	6	9	72
1988-89—Pittsburgh Penguins	NHL	12	1	1	2	43
1988-89—Muskegon Lumberjacks	IHL	57	8	8	16	167
1989-90—Pittsburgh Penguins	NHL	14	0	1	1	40
1989-90—Muskegon Lumberjacks	IHL	62	23	8	31	129
NHL TOTALS		64	6	5	11	209

(c)—August, 1987—Signed by Pittsburgh Penguins as a free agent.

TRENT KAESE

Right Wing . . . 6' . . . 205 lbs. . . . Born, Nanaimo, B.C., September 4, 1967 . . . Shoots right.

Year	Team	League	Games	G.	A.	Pts.	Pen.
1983-84—Lethbridge Broncos	WHL	64	6	6	12	33
1984-85—Lethbridge Broncos (c)	WHL	67	20	18	38	107
1985-86—Lethbridge Broncos	WHL	67	24	41	65	67
1986-87—Flint Spirits	IHL	1	0	0	0	0
1986-87—Calgary Wranglers	WHL	70	31	24	55	121
1987-88—Rochester Americans	AHL	37	6	11	17	32
1987-88—Flint Spirits	IHL	43	11	26	37	58
1988-89—Buffalo Sabres	NHL	1	0	0	0	0
1988-89—Flint Spirits	IHL	9	2	3	5	61
1988-89—Rochester Americans	AHL	45	9	11	20	68
1989-90—Phoenix Roadrunners	IHL	2	0	1	1	2
1989-90—Winston-Salem Thunderbirds (a)	ACHL	57	56	51	107	110
NHL TOTALS		1	0	0	0	0

(c)—June, 1985—Drafted as underage junior by Buffalo Sabres in 1985 NHL entry draft. Eighth Sabres pick, 161st overall, eighth round.

KEVIN KAISER

Left Wing . . . 6' . . . 185 lbs. . . . Born, Winnipeg, Man., July 26, 1970 . . . Shoots left.

Year	Team	League	Games	G.	A.	Pts.	Pen.
1986-87—Winnipeg South Monarchs	Man. Midg.	40	43	44	87	100
1987-88—Winnipeg South Blues	MJHL	74	69	52	121	80
1988-89—Univ. Minnesota/Duluth (c)	WCHA	40	2	5	7	26
1989-90—Univ. Minnesota/Duluth	WCHA	39	9	11	20	24

(c)—June, 1989—Drafted by Quebec Nordiques in 1989 NHL entry draft. Seventh Nordiques pick, 85th overall, fifth round.

KEVIN KAMINSKI

Center . . . 5'9" . . . 168 lbs. . . . Born, Churchbridge, Sask., March 13, 1969 . . . Shoots left . . . (November 4, 1987)—Suspended 12 WHL games for cross checking . . . (September, 1989)—Separated shoulder in Quebec Nordiques training camp . . . (January 26, 1990)—Suspended two games for head-butting Simon Gagne vs. Moncton.

Year	Team	League	Games	G.	A.	Pts.	Pen.
1984-85—Saskatoon Blades	WHL	5	0	1	1	17
1985-86—Saskatoon Blades	WHL	4	1	1	2	35
1986-87—Saskatoon Blades (c)	WHL	67	26	44	70	235
1987-88—Saskatoon Blades	WHL	55	38	61	99	247
1988-89—Saskatoon Blades	WHL	52	25	43	68	199
1988-89—Minnesota North Stars (d)	NHL	1	0	0	0	0
1989-90—Quebec Nordiques	NHL	1	0	0	0	0
1989-90—Halifax Citadels	AHL	19	3	4	7	128
NHL TOTALS		2	0	0	0	0

(c)—June, 1987—Drafted by Minnesota North Stars in 1987 NHL entry draft as an underage junior. Third North Stars pick, 48th overall, third round.
(d)—June 18, 1989—Traded by Minnesota North Stars to Quebec Nordiques for Gaetan Duchesne.

SHAUN KANE

Defense . . . 6'2" . . . 180 lbs. . . . Born, Holyoke, Mass., February 24, 1970 . . . Shoots left.

Year	Team	League	Games	G.	A.	Pts.	Pen.
1986-87—Springfield Olympics	NEJHL	....	20	36	56	....
1987-88—Springfield Olympics (c)	NEJHL	....	23	40	63	....

Year	Team	League	Games	G.	A.	Pts.	Pen.
1988-89—Providence College (d)	H. East	37	2	9	11	54
1989-90—Providence College	H. East	31	9	8	17	46

(c)—June, 1988—Drafted by Minnesota North Stars in 1988 NHL entry draft. Third North Stars pick, 43rd overall, third round.
(d)—Named to Hockey East all-rookie team.

THOMAS KAPUSTA

Center . . . 6' . . . 187 lbs. . . . Born, Zlin, Czechoslovakia (formerly Gottwaldov, Czech.), February 23, 1967 . . . Shoots left.

Year	Team	League	Games	G.	A.	Pts.	Pen.
1984-85—Gottwaldov (c)	Czech.	36	5	7	12	14
1985-86—Gottwaldov	Czech.	..	..	..	..	..
1986-87—Gottwaldov	Czech.	..	..	..	..	..
1987-88—Dukla Trencin	Czech.	..	..	..	..	..
1988-89—Dukla Trencin	Czech.	44	8	25	33	..
1989-90—Zlin	Czech.	..	..	..	..	..
1989-90—Cape Breton Oilers	AHL	55	12	37	49	56

(c)—June, 1985—Selected by Edmonton Oilers in 1985 NHL entry draft. Fourth Oilers pick, 104th overall, fifth round.

ALEXEI KASATONOV

Defense . . . 6'1" . . . 210 lbs. . . . Born, Leningrad, Soviet Union, October 14, 1959 . . . Shoots left . . . (February, 1990)—Broken toe on right foot.

Year	Team	League	Games	G.	A.	Pts.	Pen.
1976-77—Leningrad SKA	USSR	7	0	0	0	0
1977-78—Leningrad SKA	USSR	35	4	7	11	15
1978-79—CSKA Moscow	USSR	40	5	14	19	30
1979-80—CSKA Moscow (a)	USSR	37	5	8	13	26
1980-81—CSKA Moscow (a)	USSR	47	10	12	22	38
1981-82—CSKA Moscow (a)	USSR	46	12	27	39	45
1982-83—CSKA Moscow (a-c)	USSR	44	12	19	31	37
1983-84—CSKA Moscow (a)	USSR	39	12	24	36	20
1984-85—CSKA Moscow (a)	USSR	40	18	18	36	26
1985-86—CSKA Moscow (a)	USSR	40	6	17	23	27
1986-87—CSKA Moscow (a)	USSR	40	13	17	30	16
1987-88—CSKA Moscow (a)	USSR	43	8	12	20	8
1988-89—CSKA Moscow	USSR	41	8	14	22	8
1989-90—New Jersey Devils	NHL	39	6	15	21	16
1989-90—Utica Devils	AHL	3	0	2	2	7
NHL TOTALS		39	6	15	21	16

(c)—June, 1983—Selected by New Jersey Devils in 1983 NHL entry draft. Ninth Devils pick, 225th overall, 12th round.

PETER KASOWSKI

Center . . . 5'11" . . . 180 lbs. . . . Born, Edmonton, Alta., March 19, 1969 . . . Shoots left . . . (March, 1989)—Mononucleosis.

Year	Team	League	Games	G.	A.	Pts.	Pen.
1987-88—Swift Current Broncos	WHL	70	33	31	64	27
1988-89—Swift Current Broncos (c)	WHL	72	58	73	131	46
1989-90—Swift Current Broncos	WHL	28	19	34	53	28
1989-90—Seattle Thunderbirds	WHL	42	31	45	76	16

(c)—June, 1989—Drafted by Hartford Whalers in 1989 NHL entry draft. Eleventh Whalers pick, 241st overall, 12th round.

STEPHEN NEIL KASPER

Center . . . 5'8" . . . 159 lbs. . . . Born, Montreal, Que., September 28, 1961 . . . Shoots left . . . Brother of David Kasper (New Jersey, '82 pick) . . . (October 17, 1981)—Hip pointer at Los Angeles . . . (November 9, 1982)—Surgery to remove torn shoulder cartilage . . . (December 7, 1982)—Surgery to left shoulder for a torn capsule . . . (April, 1983)—Concussion during playoff series vs. Buffalo . . . (November, 1983)—Separated left shoulder . . . (January 7, 1984)—Surgery to shoulder . . . (February, 1984)—Reinjured shoulder.

Year	Team	League	Games	G.	A.	Pts.	Pen.
1977-78—Verdun Black Hawks	QMJHL	63	26	45	71	16
1978-79—Verdun Black Hawks	QMJHL	67	37	67	104	53
1979-80—Sorel Black Hawks (c)	QMJHL	70	57	65	122	117
1980-81—Sorel Black Hawks	QMJHL	2	5	2	7	0
1980-81—Boston Bruins	NHL	76	21	35	56	94
1981-82—Boston Bruins (d)	NHL	73	20	31	51	72
1982-83—Boston Bruins	NHL	24	2	6	8	24
1983-84—Boston Bruins	NHL	27	3	11	14	19
1984-85—Boston Bruins	NHL	77	16	24	40	33
1985-86—Boston Bruins	NHL	80	17	23	40	73
1986-87—Boston Bruins	NHL	79	20	30	50	51
1987-88—Boston Bruins	NHL	79	26	44	70	35
1988-89—Boston Bruins (e)	NHL	49	10	16	26	49
1988-89—Los Angeles Kings	NHL	29	9	15	24	14
1989-90—Los Angeles Kings	NHL	77	17	28	45	27
NHL TOTALS		668	161	263	424	491

(c)—June, 1980—Drafted by Boston Bruins in 1980 NHL entry draft. Third Bruins pick, 81st overall, fourth round.
(d)—Winner of Frank Selke Trophy (Best Defensive Forward).
(e)—January 23, 1989—Traded with Jay Miller by Boston Bruins to Los Angeles Kings for Bobby Carpenter.

EDWARD KASTELIC

Right Wing . . . 6'3" . . . 203 lbs. . . . Born, Toronto, Ont., January 29, 1964 . . . Shoots right . . . Played Defense prior to 1981-82 season . . . (September 30, 1985)—Fractured left cheekbone in pre-season game at Hartford . . . (January 20, 1986)—Suspended by Washington Capitals . . . (December 30, 1988)—Suspended 20 games by AHL for biting linesman Frank Quigley during a fight at Springfield.

Year	Team	League	Games	G.	A.	Pts.	Pen.
1980-81—Mississauga Reps		Midget	51	4	10	14	....
1981-82—London Knights (c)		OHL	68	5	18	23	63
1982-83—London Knights		OHL	68	12	11	23	96
1983-84—London Knights		OHL	68	17	16	33	218
1984-85—Fort Wayne Komets		IHL	5	1	0	1	37
1984-85—Binghamton Whalers		AHL	4	0	0	0	7
1984-85—Moncton Golden Flames		AHL	62	5	11	16	187
1985-86—Washington Capitals		NHL	15	0	0	0	73
1985-86—Binghamton Whalers		AHL	23	7	9	16	76
1986-87—Binghamton Whalers		AHL	48	17	11	28	124
1986-87—Washington Capitals		NHL	23	1	1	2	83
1987-88—Binghamton Whalers		AHL	6	4	1	5	6
1987-88—Washington Capitals (d)		NHL	35	1	0	1	78
1988-89—Hartford Whalers		NHL	10	0	2	2	15
1988-89—Binghamton Whalers		AHL	35	9	6	15	124
1989-90—Hartford Whalers		NHL	67	6	2	8	198
NHL TOTALS			150	8	5	13	447

(c)—June, 1982—Selected by Washington Capitals in 1982 NHL entry draft as an underage junior. Fourth Capitals pick, 110th overall, sixth round.

(d)—July, 1988—Traded with Grant Jennings by Washington Capitals to Hartford Whalers for Neil Sheehy and Mike Millar.

MIKE KEANE

Right Wing . . . 5'11" . . . 170 lbs. . . . Born, Winnipeg, Man., May 29, 1967 . . . Shoots right . . . (December 21, 1988)—Separated right shoulder when checked by Grant Jennings vs. Hartford.

Year	Team	League	Games	G.	A.	Pts.	Pen.
1983-84—Winnipeg Warriors		WHL	1	0	0	0	0
1984-85—Moose Jaw Warriors		WHL	65	17	26	43	141
1985-86—Moose Jaw Warriors		WHL	67	34	49	83	162
1986-87—Moose Jaw Warriors (c)		WHL	53	25	45	70	107
1986-87—Sherbrooke Canadiens (d)		AHL	....	...	...	...	...
1987-88—Sherbrooke Canadiens		AHL	78	25	43	68	70
1988-89—Montreal Canadiens		NHL	69	16	19	35	69
1989-90—Montreal Canadiens		NHL	74	9	15	24	78
NHL TOTALS			143	25	34	59	147

(c)—March, 1987—Signed by Montreal Canadiens as a free agent.

(d)—No regular season record. Played nine playoff games.

FRANCIS TOBY KEARNEY

(Known by middle name.)

Left Wing . . . 6'2" . . . 185 lbs. . . . Born, Newburyport, Mass., September 2, 1970 . . . Shoots left.

Year	Team	League	Games	G.	A.	Pts.	Pen.
1987-88—Belmont Hill		Mass. H.S.	..	9	12	21	..
1988-89—Belmont Hill (c)		Mass. H.S.	..	15	17	32	..
1989-90—University of Vermont		ECAC	25	2	3	5	24

(c)—June, 1989—Drafted by Calgary Flames in 1989 NHL entry draft. Seventh Flames pick, 105th overall, fifth round.

DANIEL KECZMER

Defense . . . 6'1" . . . 180 lbs. . . . Born, Mt. Clemens, Mich., May 25, 1968 . . . Shoots left . . . (February 2, 1990)—Injured shoulder vs. Ferris State.

Year	Team	League	Games	G.	A.	Pts.	Pen.
1985-86—Little Caesars Midget (c)		Mich.	65	6	48	54	116
1986-87—Lake Superior State Univ.		CCHA	38	3	5	8	28
1987-88—Lake Superior State Univ.		CCHA	41	2	15	17	34
1988-89—Lake Superior State Univ.		CCHA	46	3	26	29	70
1989-90—Lake Superior State Univ. (b)		CCHA	43	13	23	36	48

(c)—June, 1986—Drafted by Minnesota North Stars in 1986 NHL entry draft. Eleventh North Stars pick, 201st overall, 10th round.

CORY KEENAN

Defense . . . 6'2" . . . 185 lbs. . . . Born, St. Louis, Mo., March 19, 1970 . . . Shoots left . . . Son of Larry Keenan (former NHL player with Toronto, St. Louis, Buffalo and Philadelphia, 1961 through 1972).

Year	Team	League	Games	G.	A.	Pts.	Pen.
1986-87—St. Mary's Lincolns		OHA	29	3	8	11	52
1987-88—Kitchener Rangers		OHL	66	2	18	20	32
1988-89—Kitchener Rangers		OHL	66	15	35	50	69
1989-90—Kitchener Rangers (c)		OHL	66	13	35	48	88

(c)—June 16, 1990—Selected by Hartford Whalers in 1990 NHL entry draft. Fifth Whalers pick, 120th overall, sixth round.

JARMO KEKALAINEN

Left Wing . . . 6' . . . 190 lbs. . . . Born, Kuopio, Finland, July 3, 1966 . . . Shoots right . . . Brother of Janne Kekalainen.

Year	Team	League	Games	G.	A.	Pts.	Pen.
1987-88—Clarkson University		ECAC	32	7	11	18	38
1988-89—Clarkson University (b-c)		ECAC	31	19	25	44	47
1989-90—Boston Bruins		NHL	11	2	2	4	8
1989-90—Maine Mariners		AHL	18	5	11	16	6
NHL TOTALS			11	2	2	4	8

(c)—May 3, 1989—Signed by Boston Bruins as a free agent.

MICHAEL KELFER

Center . . . 5'10" . . . 180 lbs. . . . Born, Peabody, Mass., January 2, 1967 . . . Shoots right.

Year	Team	League	Games	G.	A.	Pts.	Pen.
1984-85—St. John's Prep. (c)		Mass. H.S.	25	33	48	81	....
1985-86—Boston University		H. East	39	13	14	27	40
1986-87—Boston University		H. East	33	21	19	40	20
1987-88—Boston University		H. East	54	26	27	53	33
1988-89—Boston University (b-d)		H. East	33	23	29	52	22
1989-90—Springfield Indians		AHL	57	24	18	42	10

(c)—June, 1985—Drafted by Minnesota North Stars in 1985 NHL entry draft. Fifth North Stars pick, 132nd overall, seventh round.

(d)—May 17, 1989—Traded by Minnesota North Stars to New York Islanders to complete a March 7 deal that saw the North Stars acquire Reed Larson for a seventh-round 1989 draft pick (Brett Hawkins) and future considerations.

ROBERT EDWARD KELLOGG

Defense . . . 6'4" . . . 200 lbs. . . . Born, Springfield, Mass., February 16, 1971 . . . Shoots left.

Year	Team	League	Games	G.	A.	Pts.	Pen.
1987-88—Springfield Olympics		NEJHL	38	8	36	44	54
1988-89—Springfield Olympics (c)		NEJHL	..	13	34	47	..
1989-90—Northeastern Univ.		H. East	36	3	12	15	30

(c)—June, 1989—Drafted by Chicago Black Hawks in 1989 NHL entry draft. Third Black Hawks pick, 48th overall, third round.

PAUL KELLY

Defense . . . 6' . . . 190 lbs. . . . Born, Hamilton, Ont., April 17, 1967 . . . Shoots left.

Year	Team	League	Games	G.	A.	Pts.	Pen.
1983-84—Hamilton Midget		OHA	36	37	32	69	52
1984-85—Guelph Platers		OHL	64	15	27	42	50
1985-86—Guelph Platers (c)		OHL	59	26	32	58	95
1986-87—Guelph Platers		OHL	61	27	48	75	67
1987-88—New Haven Nighthawks		AHL	60	14	25	39	23
1988-89—New Haven Nighthawks		AHL	12	4	5	9	22
1988-89—Utica Devils (d)		AHL	34	6	8	14	25
1988-89—Flint Spirits		IHL	4	0	1	1	0
1989-90—New Haven Nighthawks		AHL	38	5	15	20	43
1989-90—Phoenix Roadrunners		IHL	8	3	0	3	11

(c)—June, 1986—Drafted by Los Angeles Kings in 1986 NHL entry draft. Ninth Kings pick, 191st overall, 10th round.

(d)—December 13, 1988—Loaned to Utica Devils by Los Angeles Kings.

EDWARD DEAN KENNEDY

(Known by middle name.)

Defense . . . 6'2" . . . 200 lbs. . . . Born, Redvers, Sask., January 18, 1963 . . . Shoots right . . . (February 18, 1983)—Given four-game suspension by NHL after off-ice altercation with Ken Linseman at Edmonton (February 3) . . . Missed part of 1981-82 season with a knee injury . . . (March, 1987)—Hip pointer . . . (November, 1987)—Broken finger . . . (March, 1988)—Injured groin . . . (November 10, 1988)—Spent two days in hospital with concussion suffered vs. Hartford.

Year	Team	League	Games	G.	A.	Pts.	Pen.
1979-80—Weyburn Red Wings		SJHL	57	12	20	32	64
1979-80—Brandon Wheat Kings		WHL	1	0	0	0	0
1980-81—Brandon Wheat Kings (c)		WHL	71	3	29	32	157
1981-82—Brandon Wheat Kings		WHL	49	5	38	43	103
1982-83—Brandon Wheat Kings		WHL	14	2	15	17	22
1982-83—Los Angeles Kings		NHL	55	0	12	12	97
1982-83—Saskatoon Blades (d)		WHL	....	...	...	...	...
1983-84—New Haven Nighthawks		AHL	26	1	7	8	23
1983-84—Los Angeles Kings		NHL	37	1	5	6	50
1984-85—New Haven Nighthawks		AHL	76	3	14	17	104
1985-86—Los Angeles Kings		NHL	78	2	10	12	132
1986-87—Los Angeles Kings		NHL	66	6	14	20	91
1987-88—Los Angeles Kings		NHL	58	1	11	12	158
1988-89—New York Rangers (e-f)		NHL	16	0	1	1	40
1988-89—Los Angeles Kings		NHL	51	3	10	13	63
1989-90—Buffalo Sabres (g)		NHL	80	2	12	14	53
NHL TOTALS			441	15	75	90	684

(c)—June, 1981—Drafted as underage junior by Los Angeles Kings in 1981 NHL entry draft. Second Kings pick, 39th overall, second round.

(d)—No regular season record. Played four playoff games.

(e)—December 12, 1988—Traded with Denis Larocque by Los Angeles Kings to New York Rangers for Igor Liba, Todd Elik, Michael Boyce and future considerations.

(f)—February 3, 1989—Traded by New York Rangers to Los Angeles Kings for a fifth-round 1990 draft pick.

(g)—October 4, 1989—Traded by Los Angeles Kings to Buffalo Sabres for a fourth-round 1990 draft pick.

SHELDON KENNEDY

Right Wing . . . 5'10" . . . 170 lbs. . . . Born, Brandon, Manitoba, June 15, 1969 . . . Shoots right . . . Brother of Troy Kennedy . . . (January 18, 1987)—Missed six weeks with a broken ankle . . . (December 5, 1989)—Separated shoulder vs. St. Louis . . . (March 2, 1990)—Injured thumb vs. Toronto . . . (March 21, 1990)—Took leave of absence to attend an alcohol treatment program.

Year	Team	League	Games	G.	A.	Pts.	Pen.
1986-87—Swift Current Broncos		WHL	49	23	41	64	64
1987-88—Swift Current Broncos (c)		WHL	59	53	64	117	45
1988-89—Swift Current Broncos		WHL	51	58	48	106	92
1989-90—Detroit Red Wings		NHL	20	2	7	9	10
1989-90—Adirondack Red Wings		AHL	26	11	15	26	35
NHL TOTALS			20	2	7	9	10

(c)—June, 1988—Drafted by Detroit Red Wings in 1988 NHL entry draft. Fifth Red Wings pick, 80th overall, fourth round.

ALAN KERR

Right Wing . . . 5'11" . . . 190 lbs. . . . Born, Hazelton, B.C., March 28, 1964 . . . Shoots right . . . (April, 1988)—Took 40 stitches above right eye when grazed by a Ken Daneyko skate in playoff game vs. New Jersey . . . Cousin of former NHLer Reg Kerr . . . (December, 1988)—Sprained left knee . . . (April, 1990)—Bruised left knee.

Year	Team	League	Games	G.	A.	Pts.	Pen.
1981-82—Seattle Breakers (c)		WHL	68	15	18	33	1079
1982-83—Seattle Breakers		WHL	71	38	53	91	183
1983-84—Seattle Breakers (a)		WHL	66	46	66	112	141
1984-85—Springfield Indians		AHL	62	32	27	59	140
1984-85—New York Islanders		NHL	19	3	1	4	24
1985-86—Springfield Indians		AHL	71	35	36	71	127
1985-86—New York Islanders		NHL	7	0	1	1	16
1986-87—New York Islanders		NHL	72	7	10	17	175
1987-88—New York Islanders		NHL	80	24	34	58	198
1988-89—New York Islanders		NHL	71	20	18	38	144
1989-90—New York Islanders		NHL	75	15	20	35	129
NHL TOTALS			324	69	84	153	686

(c)—June, 1982—Drafted by New York Islanders as underage junior in 1982 NHL entry draft. Fourth Islanders pick, 84th overall, fourth round.

KEVIN KERR

Right Wing . . . 5'10" . . . 175 lbs. . . . Born, North Bay, Ont., September 18, 1967 . . . Shoots right . . . (October 28, 1988)—Suspended two games for striking linesman John Galipeau with his stick during an altercation with Mike Ware vs. Cape Breton . . . (March 11, 1989)—Suspended for remainder of AHL season for biting Ed Kastelic at Binghamton.

Year	Team	League	Games	G.	A.	Pts.	Pen.
1984-85—Windsor Spitfires		OHL	57	5	16	21	189
1985-86—Windsor Spitfires (c)		OHL	59	21	51	72	*266
1986-87—Windsor Spitfires		OHL	63	27	41	68	*264
1987-88—Rochester Americans		AHL	72	18	11	29	352
1988-89—Rochester Americans		AHL	66	20	18	38	306
1989-90—Rochester Americans		AHL	8	0	1	1	22
1989-90—Fort Wayne Komets		IHL	43	11	16	27	219
1989-90—Phoenix Roadrunners		IHL	6	0	0	0	25

(c)—June, 1986—Drafted as underage junior by Buffalo Sabres in 1986 NHL entry draft. Fourth Sabres pick, 56th overall, third round.

TIM KERR

Right Wing and Center . . . 6'3" . . . 215 lbs. . . . Born, Windsor, Ont., January 5, 1960 . . . Shoots right . . . (November 1, 1980)—Injured shoulder . . . (October, 1981)—Injured knee cartilage . . . (September, 1982)—Hernia surgery . . . (November 10, 1982)—Stretched knee ligaments at Buffalo that required surgery . . . (March, 1983)—Cracked fibula of left leg . . . (March, 1985)—Strained knee ligaments . . . (April 13, 1985)—Set NHL playoff records for most goals (4) and power-play goals (3) in a single period in the 2nd period at N.Y. Rangers . . . (May 5, 1985)—Strained right knee in collision with teammate Todd Bergen vs. Quebec . . . (September, 1985)—Hospitalized with aseptic meningitis, a viral infection of the brain lining . . . (1985-86)—Set NHL record for most power-play goals in one season with 34, breaking mark of 28 held jointly by Phil Esposito (1971-72) and Mike Bossy (1980-81) . . . (November 29, 1986)—Missed three games with pulled hamstring at N.Y. Islanders . . . (June, 1987)—Had two off-season operations to repair injury to his left shoulder that caused him to miss last two rounds of playoffs . . . (October, 1987)—Two more shoulder surgeries . . . (November, 1987)—A fifth shoulder operation since June, 1987, to remove a screw that was causing an infection . . . (December, 1987)—Served as assistant coach behind the Flyer's bench . . . (March, 1988)—Returned to the Flyers' lineup after missing 315 days . . . (December 27, 1988)—Pulled muscle in left shoulder at Washington . . . (October 6, 1989)—Bruised left shoulder at Washington and missed four games . . . (November 12, 1989)—Torn rotator cuff in left shoulder and missed 33 games following surgery to remove bone chips and scar tissue . . . (March 18, 1990)—Separated left shoulder vs. Los Angeles . . . (March, 1990)—Had his eighth surgery to his left shoulder.

Year	Team	League	Games	G.	A.	Pts.	Pen.
1976-77—Windsor Spitfires		OMJHL	9	2	4	6	7
1977-78—Kingston Canadians		OMJHL	67	14	25	39	33
1978-79—Kingston Canadians		OMJHL	57	17	25	42	27
1979-80—Kingston Canadians (c)		OMJHL	63	40	33	73	39
1979-80—Maine Mariners		AHL	7	2	4	6	2
1980-81—Philadelphia Flyers		NHL	68	22	23	45	84
1981-82—Philadelphia Flyers		NHL	61	21	30	51	138
1982-83—Philadelphia Flyers		NHL	24	11	8	19	6
1983-84—Philadelphia Flyers		NHL	79	54	39	93	29
1984-85—Philadelphia Flyers		NHL	74	54	44	98	57
1985-86—Philadelphia Flyers		NHL	76	58	26	84	79
1986-87—Philadelphia Flyers (b)		NHL	75	58	37	95	57
1987-88—Philadelphia Flyers		NHL	8	3	2	5	12
1988-89—Philadelphia Flyers (d)		NHL	69	48	40	88	73
1989-90—Philadelphia Flyers		NHL	40	24	24	48	34
NHL TOTALS			574	353	273	626	569

(c)—January, 1980—Signed by Philadelphia Flyers as a free agent.
(d)—Won Bill Masterton Memorial Trophy (Perseverance, sportsmanship and dedication).

IAN KIDD

Defense . . . 6' . . . 197 lbs. . . . Born, Gresham, Ore., May 11, 1964 . . . Shoots right.

Year	Team	League	Games	G.	A.	Pts.	Pen.
1985-86—Univ. of North Dakota (c)		WCHA	37	6	16	22	65
1986-87—Univ. of North Dakota (d-e)		WCHA	47	13	47	60	58
1987-88—Fredericton Express		AHL	53	1	21	22	70

Year	Team	League	Games	G.	A.	Pts.	Pen.
1987-88—Vancouver Canucks		NHL	19	4	7	11	25
1988-89—Vancouver Canucks		NHL	1	0	0	0	0
1988-89—Milwaukee Admirals		IHL	76	13	40	53	124
1989-90—Milwaukee Admirals		IHL	65	11	36	47	86
NHL TOTALS			20	4	7	11	25

(c)—October, 1986—First overall selection in NHL supplemental draft by Detroit Red Wings. However, choice was later voided by NHL.
(d)—Selected First team All-America (West).
(e)—August, 1987—Signed by Vancouver Canucks as a free agent.

DARIN KIMBLE

Right Wing . . . 6'2" . . . 210 lbs. . . . Born, Lucky Lake, Sask., November 22, 1968 . . . Shoots right . . . (March 23, 1989)—Suspended eight games for slashing Ulf Samuelsson vs. Hartford, missed final four games of season and will miss first four games of 1989-90 . . . (September, 1989)—Sprained right wrist during Quebec Nordiques training camp . . . (November 5, 1989)—Bruised ribs vs. Washington.

Year	Team	League	Games	G.	A.	Pts.	Pen.
1984-85—Swift Current Jr. A		SAJHL	59	28	32	60	264
1984-85—Calgary Wranglers (c)		WHL	..	..	..	..	..
1985-86—Calgary Wranglers		WHL	37	14	8	22	93
1985-86—New Westminster Bruins		WHL	11	1	1	2	22
1985-86—Brandon Wheat Kings		WHL	15	1	6	7	39
1986-87—Prince Albert Raiders (d)		WHL	68	17	13	30	190
1987-88—Prince Albert Raiders (e)		WHL	67	35	36	71	307
1988-89—Halifax Citadels		AHL	39	8	6	14	188
1988-89—Quebec Nordiques		NHL	26	3	1	4	149
1989-90—Quebec Nordiques		NHL	44	5	5	10	185
1989-90—Halifax Citadels		AHL	18	6	6	12	37
NHL TOTALS			70	8	6	14	334

(c)—No regular season record. Played one playoff game.
(d)—September, 1986—Traded with Kerry Angus by Brandon Wheat Kings to Prince Albert Raiders for Graham Garden, Ryan Stewart and Kim Rasmussen.
(e)—June, 1988—Drafted by Quebec Nordiques in 1988 NHL entry draft. Fifth Nordiques pick, 66th overall, fourth round.

DEREK KING

Left Wing . . . 6'1" . . . 210 lbs. . . . Born, Hamilton, Ont., February 11, 1967 . . . Shoots left . . . (September, 1985)—Sprained right wrist in N.Y. Islanders training camp . . . (December 12, 1987)—Fractured left wrist at Pittsburgh . . . (November 23, 1988)—Separated shoulder in collision with Lou Franceschetti at Washington.

Year	Team	League	Games	G.	A.	Pts.	Pen.
1983-84—Hamilton Jr.A.		OHA	37	10	14	24	142
1984-85—Sault Ste. Marie Greyhounds (c-d)		OHL	63	35	38	73	106
1985-86—Sault Ste. Marie Greyhounds		OHL	25	12	17	29	33
1985-86—Oshawa Generals		OHL	19	8	13	21	15
1986-87—Oshawa Generals (a)		OHL	57	53	53	106	74
1986-87—New York Islanders		NHL	2	0	0	0	0
1987-88—New York Islanders		NHL	55	12	24	36	30
1987-88—Springfield Indians		AHL	10	7	6	13	6
1988-89—Springfield Indians		AHL	4	4	0	4	0
1988-89—New York Islanders		NHL	60	14	29	43	14
1989-90—Springfield Indians		AHL	21	11	12	23	33
1989-90—New York Islanders		NHL	46	13	27	40	20
NHL TOTALS			163	39	80	119	64

(c)—Won Emms Family Award (OHL Top Rookie).
(d)—June, 1985—Drafted as underage junior by New York Islanders in 1985 NHL entry draft. Second Islanders pick, 13th overall, first round.

KRIS KING

Center . . . 5'10" . . . 185 lbs. . . . Born, Bracebridge, Ont., February 18, 1966 . . . Shoots left.

Year	Team	League	Games	G.	A.	Pts.	Pen.
1982-83—Gravenhurst		SOJHL	32	72	53	125	115
1983-84—Peterborough Petes (c)		OHL	62	13	18	31	168
1984-85—Peterborough Petes		OHL	61	18	35	53	222
1985-86—Peterborough Petes		OHL	58	19	40	59	254
1986-87—Peterborough Petes		OHL	46	23	33	56	160
1986-87—Binghamton Whalers (d)		AHL	7	0	0	0	18
1987-88—Adirondack Red Wings		AHL	78	21	32	53	337
1987-88—Detroit Red Wings		NHL	3	1	0	1	2
1988-89—Detroit Red Wings		NHL	55	2	3	5	168
1989-90—New York Rangers (e)		NHL	68	6	7	13	286
NHL TOTALS			126	9	10	19	456

(c)—June, 1984—Drafted as underage junior by Washington Capitals in 1984 NHL entry draft. Fourth Capitals pick, 80th overall, fourth round.
(d)—June, 1987—Signed by Detroit Red Wings as a free agent.
(e)—September 7, 1989—Traded by Detroit Red Wings to New York Rangers for Chris McRae and a fifth-round 1990 draft pick.

AL KINISKY

Left Wing . . . 6'4" . . . 220 lbs. . . . Born, Coquitlan, B.C., May 31, 1972 . . . Shoots left.

Year	Team	League	Games	G.	A.	Pts.	Pen.
1989-90—Nipawin		SJHL	28	2	4	6	92
1989-90—Seattle Thunderbirds (c)		WHL	72	9	29	38	103

(c)—June 16, 1990—Selected by Philadelphia Flyers in 1990 NHL entry draft. Seventh Flyers pick, 52nd overall, third round.

DOUG KIRTON

Ring Wing . . . 6'2'' . . . 190 lbs. . . . Born, Pentanguishene, Ont., March 21, 1966 . . . Shoots right . . . (November, 1987)—Broken kneecap.

Year	Team	League	Games	G.	A.	Pts.	Pen.
1985-86—Orilla (c)		OHL	46	34	45	79	158
1986-87—Colorado College		WCHA	38	10	10	20	42
1987-88—Colorado College		WCHA	31	11	17	28	42
1988-89—Colorado College		WCHA	38	8	16	24	33
1989-90—Colorado College		WCHA	39	19	21	40	47

(c)—June, 1986—Drafted by New Jersey Devils in 1986 NHL entry draft. Twelfth Devils pick, 236th overall, 12th round.

KELLY KISIO

Center . . . 5'9'' . . . 170 lbs. . . . Born, Wetaskwin, Alta., September 18, 1959 . . . Shoots right . . . Also plays Right Wing . . . (February, 1985)—Given five-game suspension by NHL for stick-swinging incident . . . (October, 1986)—Dislocated left shoulder . . . (April, 1987)—Surgery on shoulder . . . (February, 1988)—Bruised and twisted left knee . . . (October, 1988)—Missed five games with a fractured left hand . . . (November, 1988)—Back spasms . . . (November 9, 1989)—Bruised left thigh and back spasms and missed 11 games.

Year	Team	League	Games	G.	A.	Pts.	Pen.
1976-77—Red Deer Rustlers		AJHL	60	53	48	101	101
1977-78—Red Deer Rustlers (a)		AJHL	58	74	68	142	66
1978-79—Calgary Wranglers		WHL	70	60	61	121	73
1979-80—Calgary Wranglers		WHL	71	65	73	138	64
1980-81—Adirondack Red Wings		AHL	41	10	14	24	43
1980-81—Kalamazoo Wings (c)		IHL	31	27	16	43	48
1981-82—Dallas Black Hawks (d)		CHL	78	*62	39	101	59
1982-83—Davos HC		Switzerland	....	49	38	87	....
1982-83—Detroit Red Wings (e)		NHL	15	4	3	7	0
1983-84—Detroit Red Wings		NHL	70	23	37	60	34
1984-85—Detroit Red Wings		NHL	75	20	41	61	56
1985-86—Detroit Red Wings (f)		NHL	76	21	48	69	85
1986-87—New York Rangers		NHL	70	24	40	64	73
1987-88—New York Rangers		NHL	77	23	55	78	88
1988-89—New York Rangers		NHL	70	26	36	62	91
1989-90—New York Rangers		NHL	68	22	44	66	105
NHL TOTALS			521	163	304	467	532

(c)—February, 1981—Traded by Toledo Goaldiggers to Kalamazoo Wings for Jean Chouinard.
(d)—Led CHL Adams Cup Playoffs with 12 goals and 29 points and was co-leader (with Bruce Affleck) with 17 assists.
(e)—February, 1983—Signed by Detroit as a free agent at the conclusion of season in Switzerland.
(f)—July, 1986—Traded with Lane Lambert, Jim Leavins and a fifth-round 1988 draft pick by Detroit Red Wings to New York Rangers for Glen Hanlon, third round 1987 (Dennis Holland) and 1988 draft picks and future considerations.

TRENT KLATT

Center . . . 6'1'' . . . 205 lbs. . . . Born, Robbinsdale, Minn., January 30, 1971 . . . Shoots right.

Year	Team	League	Games	G.	A.	Pts.	Pen.
1987-88—Ossea H.S.		Minn. H.S.	22	19	17	36	....
1988-89—Ossea H.S. (c)		Minn. H.S.	22	24	39	63	....
1989-90—University of Minnesota		WCHA	38	22	14	36	16

(c)—June, 1989—Drafted by Washington Capitals in 1989 NHL entry draft. Fifth Capitals pick, 82nd overall, fourth round.

SCOT KLEINENDORST

Defense . . . 6'3'' . . . 205 lbs. . . . Born, Grand Rapids, Minn., January 16, 1960 . . . Shoots left . . . (September, 1982)—Preseason surgery for off-season knee injury . . . Brother of Kurt Kleinendorst . . . (February, 1984)—Suffered groin injury and out for the season . . . (February, 1985)—Knee sprain . . . (October 30, 1985)—Broken right foot vs. Quebec and missed 18 games . . . (February 11, 1986)—Bruised ribs at St. Louis . . . (August, 1987)—Broken foot while training for Team USA in Canada Cup Tournament . . . (November, 1987)—Injured back . . . (February, 1988)—Separated shoulder . . . (September, 1988)—Sprained right knee during Hartford training camp and missed first 15 games of season . . . (December 6, 1988)—Depressed left cheekbone during fight with Mike Hartman vs. Buffalo . . . (January 28, 1989)—Bruised left hand in fight with Paul Gillis vs. Quebec . . . (March, 1989)—Back spasms . . . (October 7, 1989)—Torn left knee ligaments vs. Chicago and required surgery.

Year	Team	League	Games	G.	A.	Pts.	Pen.
1979-80—Providence College (b-c-d)		ECAC	30	1	12	13	38
1980-81—Providence College		ECAC	32	3	31	34	75
1981-82—Providence College (a)		ECAC	33	30	27	57	14
1981-82—Springfield Indians		AHL	5	0	4	4	11
1982-83—Tulsa Oilers		CHL	10	0	7	7	14
1982-83—New York Rangers		NHL	30	2	9	11	8
1983-84—Tulsa Oilers		CHL	24	4	9	13	10
1983-84—New York Rangers (e)		NHL	23	0	2	2	35
1984-85—Binghamton Whalers		AHL	30	3	7	10	42
1984-85—Hartford Whalers		NHL	35	1	8	9	69
1985-86—Hartford Whalers		NHL	41	2	7	9	62
1986-87—Hartford Whalers		NHL	66	3	9	12	130
1987-88—Hartford Whalers		NHL	44	3	6	9	86
1988-89—Binghamton Whalers		AHL	4	0	1	1	19
1988-89—Hartford Whalers (f)		NHL	24	0	1	1	36
1988-89—Washington Capitals		NHL	3	0	1	1	10
1989-90—Washington Capitals		NHL	15	1	3	4	16
1989-90—Baltimore Skipjacks		AHL	2	2	0	2	6
NHL TOTALS			281	12	46	58	452

(c)—Named to All-New England Collegiate All-Star Team (Second team).
(d)—June, 1980—Drafted by New York Rangers in 1980 NHL entry draft. Fourth Rangers pick, 98th overall, fifth round.
(e)—February, 1984—Traded by New York Rangers to Hartford Whalers for Blaine Stoughton.
(f)—March 6, 1989—Traded by Hartford Whalers to Washington Capitals for Jim Thomson.

PETR KLIMA

Left Wing . . . 6' . . . 190 lbs. . . . Born, Chaomutov, Czechoslovakia, December 23, 1964 . . . Shoots right . . . (May, 1988)—Broke right thumb at Edmonton when slashed by Charlie Huddy . . . (November 12, 1988)—Sprained right ankle in collision with Ron Hextall at Philadelphia . . . (December, 1988)—Groin pull . . . (February, 1989)—Injured back.

Year	Team	League	Games	G.	A.	Pts.	Pen.
1982-83—Czechoslovakian Nationals (c)		Czech.	44	19	17	36	74
1983-84—Dukla Jihlava		Czech.	41	20	16	36	46
1983-84—Czechoslovakian Nationals		Czech.	7	6	5	11	....
1984-85—Dukla Jihlava		Czech.	35	23	22	45	....
1985-86—Detroit Red Wings		NHL	74	32	24	56	16
1986-87—Detroit Red Wings		NHL	77	30	23	53	42
1987-88—Detroit Red Wings		NHL	78	37	25	62	46
1988-89—Adirondack Red Wings		AHL	5	5	1	6	4
1988-89—Detroit Red Wings		NHL	51	25	16	41	44
1989-90—Detroit Red Wings (d)		NHL	13	5	5	10	6
1989-90—Edmonton Oilers		NHL	63	25	28	53	66
NHL TOTALS			356	154	121	275	220

(c)—June, 1983—Drafted by Detroit Red Wings in NHL entry draft. Fifth Red Wings pick, 88th overall, fifth round.
(d)—November 2, 1989—Traded with Joe Murphy, Adam Graves and Jeff Sharples by Detroit Red Wings to Edmonton Oilers for Jimmy Carson, Kevin McClelland and a fifth-round 1991 draft pick.

GORD KLUZAK

Defense . . . 6'3'' . . . 214 lbs. . . . Born, Climax, Sask., March 4, 1964 . . . Shoots left . . . (February 9, 1982)—Injured knee vs. Medicine Hat that required surgery . . . (March 12, 1983)—Eye injured vs. Philadelphia . . . (October 7, 1984)—Tore ligaments in left knee when he collided with Dave Lewis vs. New Jersey, underwent major reconstructive surgery the following day and was lost for the season . . . (January 29, 1986)—Injured shoulder at Washington and missed nine games . . . (September, 1986)—Surgery to left knee and missed season . . . (May 29, 1987)—Had his fourth knee operation . . . (October, 1987)—Sprained left knee . . . (February, 1988)—Sprained right knee . . . (September 17, 1988)—Eighth operation on left knee and missed 71 games . . . (March 19, 1989)—Reinjured left knee vs. Hartford . . . (April 17, 1989)—Ninth operation to left knee . . . (August, 1989)—Tenth operation to left knee . . . (October 27, 1989)—Missed first 39 games of season with knee problem . . . (January, 1990)—Strained left knee.

Year	Team	League	Games	G.	A.	Pts.	Pen.
1980-81—Billings Bighorns		WHL	68	4	34	38	160
1981-82—Billings Bighorns (b-c)		WHL	38	9	24	33	110
1982-83—Boston Bruins		NHL	70	1	6	7	105
1983-84—Boston Bruins		NHL	80	10	27	37	135
1984-85—Boston Bruins		NHL	....	....	....	....	....
1985-86—Boston Bruins		NHL	70	8	31	39	155
1986-87—Boston Bruins		NHL	....	....	....	....	....
1987-88—Boston Bruins		NHL	66	6	31	37	135
1988-89—Boston Bruins		NHL	3	0	1	1	2
1989-90—Boston Bruins (d)		NHL	8	0	2	2	11
NHL TOTALS			297	25	98	123	543

(c)—June, 1982—Drafted as underage junior by Boston Bruins in 1982 NHL entry draft. First Bruins pick, first overall, first round.
(d)—Won Bill Masterton Memorial Trophy (Perseverance and dedication to hockey).

JOE KOCUR

Right Wing . . . 6' . . . 204 lbs. . . . Born, Calgary, Alta., December 21, 1964 . . . Shoots right . . . (December, 1981)—Stretched knee ligaments . . . (January, 1985)—Took 20 stitches to back of right hand in fight with Jim Playfair in game with Nova Scotia Oilers . . . (December 11, 1985)—Sprained thumb at Minnesota . . . (March 26, 1986)—Strained ligaments at Chicago . . . (October, 1987)—Sore right elbow . . . (November, 1987)—Strained sternum and collarbone . . . (December, 1987)—Injured shoulder . . . (May, 1988)—Separated shoulder . . . Cousin of Kory Kocur . . . (November, 1988)—Injured knee . . . (February, 1989)—Injured back . . . (February 16, 1990)—Struck by a Gerard Gallant shot vs. Detroit and bruised right foot . . . (March, 1990)—Strained right knee ligaments.

Year	Team	League	Games	G.	A.	Pts.	Pen.
1980-81—Yorkton Terriers		SJHL	48	6	9	15	307
1981-82—Yorkton Terriers		SJHL	47	20	21	41	199
1982-83—Saskatoon Blades (c)		WHL	62	23	17	40	289
1983-84—Saskatoon Blades		WHL	69	40	41	81	258
1984-85—Detroit Red Wings		NHL	17	1	0	1	64
1984-85—Adirondack Red Wings		AHL	47	12	7	19	171
1985-86—Adirondack Red Wings		AHL	9	6	2	8	34
1985-86—Detroit Red Wings		NHL	59	9	6	15	*377
1986-87—Detroit Red Wings		NHL	77	9	9	18	276
1987-88—Detroit Red Wings		NHL	64	7	7	14	263
1988-89—Detroit Red Wings		NHL	60	9	9	18	213
1989-90—Detroit Red Wings		NHL	71	16	20	36	268
NHL TOTALS			348	51	51	102	1461

(c)—June, 1983—Drafted as underage junior by Detroit Red Wings in 1983 NHL entry draft. Sixth Red Wings pick, 88th overall, fifth round.

KORY KOCUR

Right Wing . . . 5'11" . . . 188 lbs. . . . Born, Kelvington, Sask., March 6, 1969 . . . Shoots right . . . Cousin of Joe Kocur.

Year	Team	League	Games	G.	A.	Pts.	Pen.
1986-87—Saskatoon Blades		WHL	62	13	17	30	98
1987-88—Saskatoon Blades (c)		WHL	69	34	37	71	95
1988-89—Saskatoon Blades		WHL	66	45	57	102	111
1989-90—Adirondack Red Wings		AHL	79	18	37	55	36

(c)—June, 1988—Drafted by Detroit Red Wings in 1988 NHL entry draft. First Red Wings pick, 17th overall, first round.

DEAN KOLSTAD

Defense . . . 6'6" . . . 200 lbs. . . . Born, Edmonton, Alta., June 16, 1968 . . . Shoots left.

Year	Team	League	Games	G.	A.	Pts.	Pen.
1984-85—New Westminster Bruins		WHL	13	0	0	0	16
1985-86—New Westminster Bruins		WHL	16	0	5	5	19
1985-86—Prince Albert Raiders (c)		WHL	54	2	15	17	80
1986-87—Prince Albert Raiders (a)		WHL	72	17	37	54	112
1987-88—Prince Albert Raiders		WHL	72	14	37	51	121
1988-89—Minnesota North Stars		NHL	25	1	5	6	42
1988-89—Kalamazoo Wings		IHL	51	10	23	33	91
1989-90—Kalamazoo Wings (b)		IHL	77	10	40	50	172
NHL TOTALS			25	1	5	6	42

(c)—June, 1986—Drafted as underage junior by Minnesota North Stars in 1986 NHL entry draft. Third North Stars pick, 33rd overall, second round.

STEPHEN MARK KONROYD

Defense . . . 6'1" . . . 195 lbs. . . . Born, Scarborough, Ont., February 10, 1961 . . . Shoots left . . . (December, 1984)—Dislocated elbow . . . (February, 1986)—Pulled chest muscle vs. Toronto . . . (December, 1986)—Bruised collarbone . . . (January, 1988)—Suspended four NHL games for stick-swinging incident with Randy Cunneyworth vs. Pittsburgh . . . (January, 1990)—Charley horse.

Year	Team	League	Games	G.	A.	Pts.	Pen.
1978-79—Oshawa Generals		OMJHL	65	4	19	23	63
1979-80—Oshawa Generals (c-d)		OMJHL	62	11	23	34	133
1980-81—Calgary Flames		NHL	4	0	0	0	4
1980-81—Oshawa Generals (b)		OHL	59	19	49	68	232
1981-82—Oklahoma City Stars		CHL	14	2	3	5	15
1981-82—Calgary Flames		NHL	63	3	14	17	78
1982-83—Calgary Flames		NHL	79	4	13	17	73
1983-84—Calgary Flames		NHL	80	1	13	14	94
1984-85—Calgary Flames		NHL	64	3	23	26	73
1985-86—Calgary Flames (e)		NHL	59	7	20	27	64
1985-86—New York Islanders		NHL	14	0	5	5	16
1986-87—New York Islanders		NHL	72	5	16	21	70
1987-88—New York Islanders		NHL	62	2	15	17	99
1988-89—New York Islanders (f)		NHL	21	1	5	6	2
1988-89—Chicago Black Hawks		NHL	57	5	7	12	40
1989-90—Chicago Black Hawks		NHL	75	3	14	17	34
NHL TOTALS			650	34	145	179	647

(c)—June, 1980—Drafted as underage junior by Calgary Flames in 1980 NHL entry draft. Fourth Flames pick, 39th overall, second round.

(d)—Named winner of Bobby Smith Award (OHL player who best combines high standards of play with academic excellence).

(e)—March, 1986—Traded by Calgary Flames with Richard Kromm to New York Islanders for John Tonelli.

(f)—November 25, 1988—Traded with Bob Bassen by New York Islanders to Chicago Black Hawks for Gary Nylund and Marc Bergevin.

CHRIS KONTOS

Center . . . 6'1" . . . 200 lbs. . . . Born, Toronto, Ont., December 10, 1963 . . . Shoots left . . . Also plays Left Wing . . . (November, 1983)—Suspended by N.Y. Rangers when he refused to report to Tulsa Oilers and was reinstated in January, 1984.

Year	Team	League	Games	G.	A.	Pts.	Pen.
1979-80—North York Flames		OPJHL	42	39	55	94	37
1980-81—Sudbury Wolves		OHL	56	17	27	44	36
1981-82—Sudbury Wolves (c)		OHL	12	6	6	12	18
1981-82—Toronto Marlboros (d)		OHL	59	36	56	92	68
1982-83—Toronto Marlboros		OHL	28	21	33	54	23
1982-83—New York Rangers		NHL	44	8	7	15	33
1983-84—New York Rangers		NHL	6	0	1	1	8
1983-84—Tulsa Oilers		CHL	21	5	13	18	8
1984-85—New Haven Nighthawks		AHL	48	19	24	43	30
1984-85—New York Rangers		NHL	28	4	8	12	24
1985-86—New Haven Nighthawks		AHL	21	8	15	23	12
1986-87—New Haven Nighthawks (e)		AHL	36	14	17	31	29
1986-87—Pittsburgh Penguins		NHL	31	8	9	17	6
1987-88—Pittsburgh Penguins (f)		NHL	36	1	7	8	12
1987-88—Los Angeles Kings		NHL	6	2	10	12	2
1987-88—New Haven Nighthawks		AHL	16	8	16	24	4
1987-88—Muskegon Lumberjacks		IHL	10	3	6	9	8
1988-89—Kloten		Switzerland	..	..	..	..	..
1988-89—Los Angeles Kings		NHL	7	2	1	3	2
1989-90—New Haven Nighthawks		AHL	42	10	20	30	25
1989-90—Los Angeles Kings		NHL	6	2	2	4	4
NHL TOTALS			164	27	45	72	91

(c)—October, 1981—Traded by Sudbury Wolves to Toronto Marlboros for Keith Knight.

(d)—June, 1982—Drafted as underage junior by New York Rangers in 1982 NHL entry draft. First Rangers pick, 15th overall, first round.

(e)—January, 1987—Traded by New York Rangers to Pittsburgh Penguins for Ron Duguay.

(f)—February, 1988—Traded with a sixth-round 1988 draft pick (Micah Aivazoff) by Pittsburgh Penguins to Los Angeles Kings for Bryan Erickson.

DAN KORDIC

Defense . . . 6'5" . . . 220 lbs. . . . Born, Edmonton, Alta., April 18, 1971 . . . Shoots left . . . Brother of John Kordic.

Year	Team	League	Games	G.	A.	Pts.	Pen.
1986-87—Knights of Columbus		AAMMHL	42	1	16	17	88
1987-88—Medicine Hat Tigers		WHL	63	1	5	6	75
1988-89—Medicine Hat Tigers		WHL	70	1	13	14	190
1989-90—Medicine Hat Tigers (c)		WHL	59	4	12	16	182

(c)—June 16, 1990—Selected by Philadelphia Flyers in 1990 NHL entry draft. Eighth Flyers pick, 88th overall, fifth round.

JOHN KORDIC

Right Wing . . . 6'1" . . . 190 lbs. . . . Born, Edmonton, Alta., March 22, 1965 . . . Shoots right . . . Uncle played pro soccer in Yugoslavia . . . (February 26, 1988)—Suspended five NHL games and fined $100 for fighting prior to a game vs. Quebec . . . (December 14, 1988)—Suspended 10 games for crosschecking Keith Acton and breaking his nose . . . (November 23, 1989)—Suspended one game after his third game misconduct of the season . . . (January 24, 1990)—Suspended four games for attacking Mike Modano vs. Minnesota and fined $500 . . . Brother of Dan Kordic.

Year	Team	League	Games	G.	A.	Pts.	Pen.
1981-82—Edmonton K. of C. AA		Edm. Midget	48	23	41	64	178
1982-83—Portland Winter Hawks (c)		WHL	72	3	22	25	235
1983-84—Portland Winter Hawks		WHL	67	9	50	59	232
1984-85—Portland Winter Hawks		WHL	25	6	22	28	73
1984-85—Seattle Breakers (b)		WHL	46	17	36	53	154
1984-85—Sherbrooke Canadiens		AHL	4	0	0	0	4
1985-86—Sherbrooke Canadiens		AHL	68	3	14	17	238
1985-86—Montreal Canadiens		NHL	5	0	1	1	12
1986-87—Sherbrooke Canadiens		AHL	10	4	4	8	49
1986-87—Montreal Canadiens		NHL	44	5	3	8	151
1987-88—Montreal Canadiens		NHL	60	2	6	8	159
1988-89—Montreal Canadiens (d)		NHL	6	0	0	0	13
1988-89—Toronto Maple Leafs		NHL	46	1	2	3	185
1989-90—Toronto Maple Leafs		NHL	55	9	4	13	252
NHL TOTALS			216	17	16	33	772

(c)—June, 1983—Drafted as underage junior by Montreal Canadiens in 1983 NHL entry draft. Sixth Canadiens pick, 78th overall, fourth round.

(d)—November 7, 1988—Traded with a sixth-round 1989 draft pick (Michael Doers) by Montreal Canadiens to Toronto Maple Leafs for Russ Courtnall.

JAMES A. KORN

Left Wing and Defense . . . 6'5" . . . 220 lbs. . . . Born, Hopkins, Minn., July 28, 1957 . . . Shoots left . . . (January 13, 1981)—Injured ligaments in right knee . . . (February 8, 1984)—Injured ribs vs. Boston . . . (November 5, 1984)—Dislocated shoulder when he collided with goal post at Minnesota . . . (January, 1985)—Given three-game NHL suspension . . . (February 9, 1985)—Separated shoulder during fight with Chris Nilan at Montreal . . . Missed entire 1985-86 season with knee injury . . . (February 12, 1988)—Surgery to remove cartilage, calcium and tissue from rotator cuff in left shoulder . . . (January 21, 1989)—Fined $500 and suspended three games for scuffling with Boston Bruins head coach Terry O'Reilly after a game . . . (April 7, 1989)—Surgery to right knee cartilage.

Year	Team	League	Games	G.	A.	Pts.	Pen.
1976-77—Providence College (c)		ECAC	29	6	9	15	73
1977-78—Providence College		ECAC	33	7	14	21	47
1978-79—Providence College		ECAC	27	5	19	24	72
1979-80—Adirondack Red Wings		AHL	14	2	7	9	40
1979-80—Detroit Red Wings		NHL	63	5	13	18	108
1980-81—Adirondack Red Wings		AHL	9	3	7	10	53
1980-81—Detroit Red Wings		NHL	63	5	15	20	246
1981-82—Detroit Red Wings (d)		NHL	59	1	7	8	104
1981-82—Toronto Maple Leafs		NHL	11	1	3	4	44
1982-83—Toronto Maple Leafs		NHL	80	8	21	29	238
1983-84—Toronto Maple Leafs		NHL	65	12	14	26	257
1984-85—Toronto Maple Leafs		NHL	41	5	5	10	171
1985-86—Toronto Maple Leafs		NHL	..	..	..	..	..
1986-87—Buffalo Sabres (e-f)		NHL	51	4	10	14	158
1987-88—New Jersey Devils		NHL	52	8	13	21	140
1988-89—New Jersey Devils		NHL	65	15	16	31	212
1989-90—New Jersey Devils (g)		NHL	37	2	3	5	99
1989-90—Calgary Flames		NHL	9	0	2	2	26
NHL TOTALS			596	66	122	188	1803

(c)—June, 1977—Drafted by Detroit Red Wings in 1977 amateur draft. Fourth Detroit pick, 73rd overall, fifth round.

(d)—March, 1982—Traded by Detroit Red Wings to Toronto Maple Leafs for 1982 fourth-round pick (Craig Coxe) and a 1983 fifth-round pick (Joey Kocur) in the NHL entry draft.

(e)—October, 1986—Traded by Toronto Maple Leafs to Buffalo Sabres as part of a three-club trade that saw the Sabres send Brian Engblom to Calgary and the Flames send Terry Johnson to Toronto.

(f)—May, 1987—Traded by Buffalo Sabres to New Jersey Devils for Jan Ludvig.

(g)—March 6, 1990—Traded by New Jersey Devils to Calgary Flames for a fifth-round 1990 draft pick (Peter Kuchyna).

DAVID KOROL

Defense . . . 6' . . . 180 lbs. . . . Born, Winnipeg, Man., March 1, 1965 . . . Shoots left . . . (January, 1982)—Thumb surgery.

Year	Team	League	Games	G.	A.	Pts.	Pen.
1981-82—Winnipeg Warriors		WHL	64	4	22	26	55
1982-83—Winnipeg Warriors (c)		WHL	72	14	43	57	90
1983-84—Winnipeg Warriors		WHL	57	15	48	63	49
1983-84—Adirondack Red Wings		AHL	2	0	4	4	0

Year	Team	League	Games	G.	A.	Pts.	Pen.
1984-85—Regina Pats		WHL	48	4	30	34	61
1985-86—Adirondack Red Wings		AHL	74	3	9	12	56
1986-87—Adirondack Red Wings		AHL	48	1	4	5	67
1987-88—Adirondack Red Wings		AHL	53	2	17	19	61
1988-89—Adirondack Red Wings		AHL	73	3	24	27	57
1989-90—Phoenix Roadrunners		IHL	62	1	12	13	45

(c)—June, 1983—Drafted by Detroit Red Wings in 1983 NHL entry draft. Fourth Red Wings pick, 68th overall, fourth round.

CHRIS KOTSOPOULOS

Defense . . . 6'3" . . . 215 lbs. . . . Born, Toronto, Ont., November 27, 1958 . . . Shoots right . . . Brother of George Kotsopoulos . . . (October, 1980)—Broke right thumb during exhibition game . . . (January, 1981)—Infection in right arm . . . (January 24, 1981)—Hand infection developed after treatment for cut hand . . . (February, 1983)—Pulled stomach muscles . . . (January 24, 1984)—Strained ligaments in right knee at Montreal . . . (December 28, 1984)—Broke bone in left foot when hit by a Moe Mantha shot at Pittsburgh . . . (March 3, 1985)—Sprained left knee and ankle vs. Vancouver . . . (January 13, 1985)—Bruised shoulder vs. Detroit . . . (March 8, 1986)—Strained Achilles tendon vs. Chicago . . . (January, 1987)—Missed 38 games with a groin pull . . . (October, 1987)—Concussion . . . (November, 1987)—Badly stretched groin muscle . . . (October, 1988)—Bruised left ankle and strained shoulder . . . (March, 1989)—Bruised left ankle and missed eight games . . . (1989-90)—Chronic groin injury.

Year	Team	League	Games	G.	A.	Pts.	Pen.
1975-76—Windsor Spitfires		OMJHL	59	3	13	16	169
1978-79—Toledo Goaldiggers		IHL	64	6	22	28	153
1979-80—New Haven Nighthawks		AHL	75	7	27	34	149
1980-81—New York Rangers (c)		NHL	54	4	12	16	153
1981-82—Hartford Whalers		NHL	68	13	20	33	147
1982-83—Hartford Whalers		NHL	68	6	24	30	125
1983-84—Hartford Whalers		NHL	72	5	13	18	118
1984-85—Hartford Whalers		NHL	33	5	3	8	53
1985-86—Toronto Maple Leafs (d)		NHL	61	6	11	17	83
1986-87—Toronto Maple Leafs		NHL	43	2	10	12	75
1987-88—Toronto Maple Leafs		NHL	21	2	2	4	19
1988-89—Toronto Maple Leafs (e)		NHL	57	1	14	15	44
1989-90—Detroit Red Wings		NHL	2	0	0	0	10
1989-90—Adirondack Red Wings		AHL	24	2	4	6	4
NHL TOTALS			479	44	109	153	827

(c)—October, 1981—Traded with Doug Sulliman and Gerry McDonald by New York Rangers to Hartford Whalers for Mike Rogers and a 10th-round 1982 draft pick (Simo Saarinen).

(d)—October, 1985—Traded by Hartford Whalers to Toronto Maple Leafs for Stewart Gavin.

(e)—June, 1989—Signed by Detroit Red Wings as a free agent rather than accept a termination contract with Toronto.

FRANK KOVACS

Right Wing . . . 6'2" . . . 205 lbs. . . . Born, Regina, Sask., June 3, 1971 . . . Shoots left.

Year	Team	League	Games	G.	A.	Pts.	Pen.
1987-88—Regina Pats (c)		WHL	70	10	8	18	48
1988-89—Regina Pats		WHL	70	16	27	43	90
1989-90—Regina Pats (d)		WHL	71	26	32	58	165

(c)—November, 1986—WHL Rights traded with Craig Endean, Ray Savard, Grant Chorney by Seattle Thunderbirds to Regina Pats for Ken MacIntyre, Brent Fedyk, Grant Kazuik, Gerald Bzdel and WHL rights to Kevin Kowalchuk.

(d)—June 16, 1990—Selected by Minnesota North Stars in 1990 NHL entry draft. Fourth North Stars pick, 71st overall, fourth round.

TED KRAMER

Right Wing . . . 6' . . . 190 lbs. . . . Born, Findlay, Ohio, October 29, 1969 . . . Shoots right . . . (June, 1988)—Surgery to repair stretched knee ligaments.

Year	Team	League	Games	G.	A.	Pts.	Pen.
1984-85—Findley H.S.		Ohio H.S.	24	63	32	95	..
1985-86—Little Caesars Midget		Mich.	60	40	30	70	..
1986-87—Little Caesars Midget		Mich.	60	55	50	105	..
1987-88—St. Michaels Jr. B		OHA	35	36	25	61	54
1988-89—Univ. of Michigan (c)		CCHA	40	17	15	32	78
1989-90—Univ. of Michigan		CCHA	42	21	24	45	111

(c)—June, 1989—Drafted by Los Angeles Kings in 1989 NHL entry draft. Sixth Kings pick, 144th overall, seventh round.

ROB KRAUSS

Defense . . . 6'1" . . . 210 lbs. . . . Born, Grand Prairie, Alta., October 28, 1969 . . . Shoots left.

Year	Team	League	Games	G.	A.	Pts.	Pen.
1983-84—Red Deer Moose Bantams		WHL	27	12	33	45	77
1984-85—Lethbridge Broncos		WHL	20	0	0	0	9
1985-86—Olds Grizzlys		AJHL	19	1	10	11	100
1985-86—Lethbridge Broncos		WHL	12	0	2	2	15
1986-87—Calgary Wranglers		WHL	70	3	17	20	130
1987-88—Lethbridge Hurricanes (c)		WHL	69	6	21	27	245
1988-89—Tri-City Americans		WHL	66	4	23	27	257
1989-90—Tri-City Americans		WHL	33	5	19	24	107
1989-90—Portland Winter Hawks		WHL	31	4	24	28	95

(c)—June, 1988—Drafted by Washington Capitals in 1988 NHL entry draft. Fifth Capitals pick, 78th overall, fourth round.

DALE KRENTZ

Left Wing . . . 5'11" . . . 185 lbs. . . . Born, Steinbach, Man., December 19, 1961 . . . Shoots left . . . (December 27, 1989)—Suspended six AHL games for coming off the bench to fight vs. Rochester.

Year	Team	League	Games	G.	A.	Pts.	Pen.
1982-83—Michigan State Univ.		CCHA	42	11	24	35	50
1983-84—Michigan State Univ.		CCHA	44	12	20	32	34
1984-85—Michigan State Univ. (c)		CCHA	44	24	30	54	26
1985-86—Adirondack Red Wings		AHL	79	19	27	46	27
1986-87—Adirondack Red Wings		AHL	71	32	39	71	68
1986-87—Detroit Red Wings		NHL	8	0	0	0	0
1987-88—Adirondack Red Wings		AHL	67	39	43	82	65
1987-88—Detroit Red Wings		NHL	6	2	0	2	5
1988-89—Adirondack Red Wings		AHL	36	21	20	41	30
1988-89—Detroit Red Wings		NHL	16	3	3	6	4
1989-90—Adirondack Red Wings (d)		AHL	74	38	50	88	36
NHL TOTALS			30	5	3	8	9

(c)—June, 1985—Signed by Detroit Red Wings as a free agent.

(d)—April, 1990—Signed to play in West Germany in 1990-91.

RICHARD KROMM

Left Wing . . . 5'11" . . . 180 lbs. . . . Born, Trail, B.C., March 29, 1964 . . . Shoots left . . . Son of Bobby Kromm (Member of World Champion 1961 Trail Smoke Eaters, and former WHA/NHL coach) . . . (October, 1981)—Broken ankle . . . Brother of David Kromm . . . Also plays Center . . . (February, 1985)—Pinched nerve . . . (December 2, 1986)—Missed seven games with a sprained left knee at Edmonton . . . (March, 1987)—Reinjured knee . . . (February, 1988)—Fractured rib.

Year	Team	League	Games	G.	A.	Pts.	Pen.
1980-81—Windsor Royals		Jr. 'B'	39	22	31	53	40
1981-82—Portland Winter Hawks (c)		WHL	60	16	38	54	30
1982-83—Portland Winter Hawks		WHL	72	35	68	103	64
1983-84—Portland Winter Hawks		WHL	10	10	4	14	13
1983-84—Calgary Flames		NHL	53	11	12	23	27
1984-85—Calgary Flames		NHL	73	20	32	52	32
1985-86—Calgary Flames (d)		NHL	63	12	17	29	31
1985-86—New York Islanders		NHL	14	7	7	14	4
1986-87—New York Islanders		NHL	70	12	17	29	20
1987-88—New York Islanders		NHL	71	5	10	15	20
1988-89—New York Islanders		NHL	20	1	6	7	4
1988-89—Springfield Indians		AHL	48	21	26	47	15
1989-90—Played in Sweden			....	....	....	....	....
1989-90—Springfield Indians		AHL	9	3	4	7	4
NHL TOTALS			364	68	101	169	138

(c)—June, 1982—Drafted as underage junior by Calgary Flames in 1982 NHL entry draft. Second Flames pick, 37th overall, second round.

(d)—March, 1986—Traded by Calgary Flames with Steve Konroyd to New York Islanders for John Tonelli.

ROBERT KRON

Right Wing and Center . . . 5'10" . . . 174 lbs. . . . Born, Brno, Czechoslovakia, February 27, 1967 . . . Shoots right.

Year	Team	League	Games	G.	A.	Pts.	Pen.
1986-87—Zetor Brno (c)		Czech.	28	14	11	25	....
1987-88—Zetor Brno		Czech.	32	12	6	18	....
1988-89—Zetor Brno		Czech.	43	28	19	47	....
1989-90—Dukla Trencin		Czech.	39	22	22	44	....

(c)—June, 1985—Selected by Vancouver Canucks in 1985 NHL entry draft. Fifth Canucks pick, 88th overall, fourth round.

UWE KRUPP

Defense . . . 6'6" . . . 230 lbs. . . . Born, Cologne, West Germany, June 24, 1965 . . . Shoots right . . . (November, 1987)—Bruised hip . . . (April, 1988)—Injured head in playoff game vs. Boston . . . (January 6, 1989)—Broke rib at New Jersey . . . (October, 1989)—Charley horse . . . (April 20, 1990)—Banned from International competition for 18 months by IIHF after failing a random substance test.

Year	Team	League	Games	G.	A.	Pts.	Pen.
1986-87—Rochester Americans (c)		AHL	42	3	19	22	50
1986-87—Buffalo Sabres		NHL	26	1	4	5	23
1987-88—Buffalo Sabres		NHL	75	2	9	11	151
1988-89—Buffalo Sabres		NHL	70	5	13	18	55
1989-90—Buffalo Sabres		NHL	74	3	20	23	85
NHL TOTALS			245	11	46	57	314

(c)—June, 1983—Drafted by Buffalo Sabres in 1983 NHL entry draft. Thirteenth Sabres pick, 214th overall, 11th round.

GORDON KRUPPKE

Defense . . . 6'1" . . . 200 lbs. . . . Born, Edmonton, Alta., April 2, 1969 . . . Shoots right . . . (December, 1986)—Had his spleen removed . . . (October, 1987)—Injured left knee ligaments in WHL game.

Year	Team	League	Games	G.	A.	Pts.	Pen.
1984-85—Calgary Buffaloes		Alta. Midget	36	3	22	25	77
1985-86—Prince Albert Raiders		WHL	62	1	8	9	81
1985-86—Prince Albert Raiders (c)		WHL	49	2	10	12	129
1987-88—Prince Albert Raiders		WHL	54	8	8	16	113
1988-89—Prince Albert Raiders (b)		WHL	62	6	26	32	254
1989-90—Adirondack Red Wings		AHL	59	2	12	14	103

(c)—June, 1987—Drafted as underage junior by Detroit Red Wings in 1987 NHL entry draft. Second Red Wings pick, 32nd overall, second round.

PAUL KRUSE

Left Wing . . . 6'1" . . . 202 lbs. . . . Born, Merritt, B.C., March 15, 1970 . . . Shoots left.

Year	Team	League	Games	G.	A.	Pts.	Pen.
1986-87—Merritt		BCJHL	35	8	15	23	120
1987-88—Merritt		BCJHL	44	12	32	44	227
1987-88—Moose Jaw Warriors		WHL	1	0	0	0	0
1988-89—Kamloops Blazers		WHL	68	8	15	23	209
1989-90—Kamloops Blazers (c)		WHL	67	22	23	45	291

(c)—June 16, 1990—Selected by Calgary Flames in 1990 NHL entry draft. Sixth Flames pick, 83rd overall, fourth round.

MIKE KRUSHELNYSKI

Left Wing and Center . . . 6'2" . . . 200 lbs. . . . Born, Montreal, Que., April 27, 1960 . . . Shoots left . . . Started the 1978-79 season at St. Louis University but left to return to junior hockey . . . (January, 1984)—Separated right shoulder . . . (December 10, 1985)—Sprained right knee at St. Louis and missed 17 games . . . (February 14, 1986)—Twisted knee vs. Quebec and missed nine games . . . (September, 1987)—Suspended by Edmonton Oilers for not reporting to training camp . . . (October 5, 1989)—Fractured left wrist vs. Toronto when checked by Luke Richardson and missed 17 games.

Year	Team	League	Games	G.	A.	Pts.	Pen.
1978-79—Montreal Juniors		QMJHL	46	15	29	44	42
1979-80—Montreal Juniors (c)		QMJHL	72	39	61	100	78
1980-81—Springfield Indians		AHL	80	25	38	53	47
1981-82—Erie Blades		AHL	62	31	52	83	44
1981-82—Boston Bruins		NHL	17	3	3	6	2
1982-83—Boston Bruins		NHL	79	23	42	65	43
1983-84—Boston Bruins (d)		NHL	66	25	20	45	55
1984-85—Edmonton Oilers		NHL	80	43	45	88	60
1985-86—Edmonton Oilers		NHL	54	16	24	40	22
1986-87—Edmonton Oilers		NHL	80	16	35	51	67
1987-88—Edmonton Oilers (e)		NHL	76	20	27	47	64
1988-89—Los Angeles Kings		NHL	78	26	36	62	110
1989-90—Los Angeles Kings		NHL	63	16	25	41	50
NHL TOTALS			593	188	257	445	473

(c)—August, 1979—Drafted by Boston Bruins as an underage junior in 1979 NHL entry draft. Seventh Bruins pick, 120th overall, sixth round.
(d)—June, 1984—Traded by Boston Bruins to Edmonton Oilers for Ken Linseman.
(e)—August, 1988—Traded with Wayne Gretzky and Marty McSorley by Edmonton Oilers to Los Angeles Kings for Jimmy Carson, Martin Gelinas, first-round draft choices in 1989 (traded to New Jersey), '91 and '93, plus $15 million.

VLADIMIR KRUTOV

Left Wing . . . 5'9" . . . 195 lbs. . . . Born, Moscow, Soviet Union, June 1, 1960 . . . Shoots left.

Year	Team	League	Games	G.	A.	Pts.	Pen.
1977-78—CSKA Moscow		USSR	1	0	0	0	0
1978-79—CSKA Moscow		USSR	25	8	3	11	6
1979-80—CSKA Moscow		USSR	40	30	12	42	16
1980-81—CSKA Moscow		USSR	47	25	15	40	20
1981-82—CSKA Moscow (a)		USSR	46	37	29	66	30
1982-83—CSKA Moscow (a)		USSR	44	32	21	53	34
1983-84—CSKA Moscow (a)		USSR	44	37	20	57	20
1984-85—CSKA Moscow (a)		USSR	40	23	30	53	26
1985-86—CSKA Moscow (a-c)		USSR	40	31	17	48	10
1986-87—CSKA Moscow (a)		USSR	39	26	24	50	16
1987-88—CSKA Moscow (a)		USSR	38	19	23	42	20
1988-89—CSKA Moscow		USSR	35	10	21	41	12
1989-90—Vancouver Canucks		NHL	61	11	23	34	20
NHL TOTALS			61	11	23	34	20

(c)—June, 1986—Selected by Vancouver Canucks in 1986 NHL entry draft. Eleventh Canucks pick, 238th overall, 12th round.

TODD KRYGIER

Center . . . 5'11" . . . 180 lbs. . . . Born, Northville, Mich., October 12, 1965 . . . Shoots left . . . First NHL player from University of Connecticut . . . Suffers from asthma . . . (March 13, 1990)—Bruised heel at Calgary.

Year	Team	League	Games	G.	A.	Pts.	Pen.
1984-85—Univ. of Connecticut		ECAC-II	14	14	11	25	12
1985-86—Univ. of Connecticut		ECAC-II	32	29	27	56	46
1986-87—Univ. of Connecticut		ECAC-II	28	24	24	48	44
1987-88—Univ. of Connecticut (c)		ECAC-II	27	32	39	71	38
1987-88—New Haven Nighthawks		AHL	13	1	5	6	34
1988-89—Binghamton Whalers		AHL	76	26	42	68	77
1989-90—Binghamton Whalers		AHL	12	1	9	10	16
1989-90—Hartford Whalers		NHL	58	18	12	30	52
NHL TOTALS			58	18	12	30	52

(c)—June, 1988—Selected by Hartford Whalers in 1988 NHL supplemental draft.

MARK KRYS

Defense . . . 6' . . . 185 lbs. . . . Born, Timmons, Ont., May 29, 1969 . . . Shoots left.

Year	Team	League	Games	G.	A.	Pts.	Pen.
1986-87—St. Mike's Jr. A.		OHA	34	4	22	26	61
1987-88—Boston University (c)		H. East	34	0	6	6	40
1988-89—Boston University		H. East	35	0	7	7	54
1989-90—Boston University		H. East	30	0	4	4	34

(c)—June, 1988—Drafted by Boston Bruins in 1988 NHL entry draft. Sixth Bruins pick, 165th overall, eighth round.

BOB KUDELSKI

Center . . . 6'1" . . . 200 lbs. . . . Born, Springfield, Mass., March 3, 1964 . . . Shoots right . . . (November 22, 1989)—Broke knuckle on left hand during fight with Wayne Van Dorp vs. Chicago and missed 15 games.

Year	Team	League	Games	G.	A.	Pts.	Pen.
1983-84—Yale University		ECAC	21	14	12	26	12
1984-85—Yale University		ECAC	32	21	23	44	38
1985-86—Yale University (c)		ECAC	31	18	23	41	48
1986-87—Yale University		ECAC	30	25	22	47	34
1987-88—New Haven Nighthawks		AHL	50	15	19	34	41
1987-88—Los Angeles Kings		NHL	26	0	1	1	8
1988-89—New Haven Nighthawks		AHL	60	32	19	51	43
1988-89—Los Angeles Kings		NHL	14	1	3	4	17
1989-90—Los Angeles Kings		NHL	62	23	13	36	49
NHL TOTALS			102	24	17	41	74

(c)—October, 1986—Drafted by Los Angeles Kings in 1986 NHL supplemental draft.

STUART KULAK

Right Wing . . . 5'10" . . . 175 lbs. . . . Born, Edmonton, Alta., March 10, 1963 . . . Shoots right . . . Missed entire 1984-85 season with a torn abdominal muscle that required surgery . . . (January 27, 1987)—Separated shoulder at Vancouver . . . (March 14, 1987)—Struck in left eye by a deflected shot at Pittsburgh and required 12 stitches . . . (October, 1987)—Broken left thumb . . . (November, 1989)—Broken hand.

Year	Team	League	Games	G.	A.	Pts.	Pen.
1979-80—Sherwood Park Crusaders		AJHL	53	30	23	53	111
1979-80—Victoria Cougars		WHL	3	0	0	0	0
1980-81—Victoria Cougars (c)		WHL	72	23	24	47	43
1981-82—Victoria Cougars		WHL	71	38	50	88	92
1982-83—Victoria Cougars		WHL	50	29	33	62	130
1982-83—Vancouver Canucks		NHL	4	1	1	2	0
1983-84—Fredericton Express		AHL	52	12	16	28	55
1984-85—Vancouver Canucks		NHL	....	....	....	....	....
1985-86—Kalamazoo Wings		IHL	30	14	8	22	38
1985-86—Fredericton Express		AHL	3	1	0	1	0
1986-87—Vancouver Canucks (d)		NHL	28	1	1	2	37
1986-87—Edmonton Oilers (e)		NHL	23	3	1	4	41
1986-87—New York Rangers		NHL	3	0	0	0	0
1987-88—Moncton Golden Flames		AHL	37	9	12	21	58
1987-88—Quebec Nordiques (f)		NHL	14	1	1	2	28
1988-89—Winnipeg Jets		NHL	18	2	0	2	24
1988-89—Moncton Hawks		AHL	51	30	29	59	98
1989-90—Moncton Hawks		AHL	56	14	23	37	72
NHL TOTALS			90	8	4	12	130

(c)—June, 1981—Drafted as underage junior by Vancouver Canucks in 1981 NHL entry draft. Fifth Canucks pick, 115th overall, sixth round.
(d)—December, 1986—Acquired by Edmonton Oilers on waivers from Vancouver Canucks.
(e)—March, 1987—Sent to New York Rangers by Edmonton Oilers as compensaton for Reijo Ruotsalainen signing with Edmonton. The Rangers also sent a 12th-round 1987 draft pick (Jesper Duus) to the Oilers as part of the deal.
(f)—December, 1987—Traded by Quebec Nordiques to Winnipeg Jets for Bobby Dollas.

AL KUMMU

Defense . . . 6'4" . . . 195 lbs. . . . Born, Kitchener, Ont., January 21, 1969 . . . Shoots right . . . Brother of Ryan Kummu.

Year	Team	League	Games	G.	A.	Pts.	Pen.
1988-89—Humboldt Jr. A (c)		OPJHL	35	7	22	29	115
1989-90—R.P.I. (d)		ECAC	33	9	13	22	50

(c)—June, 1989—Drafted by Philadelphia Flyers in 1989 NHL entry draft. Eighth Flyers pick, 201st overall, 10th round.
(d)—Named to ECAC All-Rookie Team.

MARK KUMPEL

Right Wing . . . 6' . . . 190 lbs. . . . Born, Wakefield, Mass., March 7, 1961 . . . Shoots right . . . Member of 1984 U.S. Olympic team . . . (October, 1980)—Suffered knee ligament damage in first game and missed remainder of season . . . (February 16, 1986)—Separated shoulder at Calgary . . . (March, 1987)—Broken wrist . . . (December, 1987)—Dislocated left thumb . . . (November 6, 1989)—Sprained left ankle and missed eight games . . . (January, 1990)—Separated shoulder.

Year	Team	League	Games	G.	A.	Pts.	Pen.
1979-80—Lowell University (c)		ECAC	30	18	18	36	12
1980-81—Lowell University		ECAC	1	2	0	2	0
1981-82—Lowell University		ECAC	35	17	13	30	23
1982-83—Lowell University		ECAC	7	8	5	13	0
1982-83—U.S. National Team		Int'l	30	14	18	32	6
1983-84—U.S. National Team		Int'l	61	14	19	33	19
1983-84—U.S. Olympic Team		Int'l	6	1	1	2	2
1983-84—Fredericton Express		AHL	16	1	1	2	5
1984-85—Fredericton Express		AHL	18	9	6	15	17
1984-85—Quebec Nordiques		NHL	42	8	7	15	26
1985-86—Fredericton Express		AHL	7	4	2	6	4
1985-86—Quebec Nordiques		NHL	47	10	12	22	17
1986-87—Quebec Nordiques (d)		NHL	40	1	8	9	16
1986-87—Detroit Red Wings		NHL	5	0	1	1	4
1986-87—Adirondack Red Wings		AHL	7	2	5	7	2
1987-88—Adirondack Red Wings		AHL	4	5	0	5	2
1987-88—Detroit Red Wings (e)		NHL	13	0	2	2	4
1987-88—Winnipeg Jets		NHL	32	4	4	8	19
1988-89—Moncton Hawks		AHL	53	22	23	45	25
1989-90—Winnipeg Jets		NHL	56	8	9	17	21
NHL TOTALS			235	31	43	74	103

(c)—June, 1980—Drafted by Quebec Nordiques in NHL entry draft. Fourth Nordiques pick, 108th overall, sixth round.
(d)—January, 1987—Traded with Brent Ashton and Gilbert Delorme by Quebec Nordiques to Detroit Red Wings for John Ogrodnick, Doug Shedden and Basil McRae.
(e)—January, 1988—Traded by Detroit Red Wings to Winnipeg Jets for Jim Nill.

JARI KURRI

Right Wing . . . 6' . . . 183 lbs. . . . Born, Helsinki, Finland, May 18, 1960 . . . Shoots right . . . Played on Finnish Olympic Team in 1980 . . . (November 24, 1981)—Pulled groin during Oilers practice . . . First Finland-born player to have 100-point season in NHL . . . (January, 1984)—Missed 16 games with a pulled groin muscle . . . (May, 1985)—Set NHL playoff record for hat tricks (4) and goals (12) in a single series (vs. Chicago) . . . (May, 1985)—Tied NHL playoff record with 19 goals for a single playoff season . . . (1985-86)—First European to lead NHL in goals in one season . . . (February 12, 1989)—Sprained medial collateral ligament in left knee when checked by Michel Petit at N.Y. Rangers . . . (May 18, 1990)—Set NHL playoff record by scoring his 90th career goal (old record was held by Wayne Gretzky with 89).

Year	Team	League	Games	G.	A.	Pts.	Pen.
1977-78	Jokerit	Fin. Elite	29	2	9	11	12
1978-79	Jokerit	Fin. Elite	33	16	14	30	12
1979-80	Jokerit (c)	Fin. Elite	33	23	16	39	22
1980-81	Edmonton Oilers	NHL	75	32	43	75	40
1981-82	Edmonton Oilers	NHL	71	32	54	86	32
1982-83	Edmonton Oilers	NHL	80	45	59	104	22
1983-84	Edmonton Oilers (b-d)	NHL	64	52	61	113	14
1984-85	Edmonton Oilers (a-e-f)	NHL	73	71	64	135	30
1985-86	Edmonton Oilers (b)	NHL	78	*68	63	131	22
1986-87	Edmonton Oilers (a-g)	NHL	79	54	54	108	41
1987-88	Edmonton Oilers (d)	NHL	80	43	53	96	30
1988-89	Edmonton Oilers	NHL	76	44	58	102	69
1989-90	Edmonton Oilers (h)	NHL	78	33	60	93	48
NHL TOTALS			754	474	569	1043	348

(c)—June, 1980—Drafted by Edmonton Oilers in NHL entry draft. Third Oilers pick, 69th overall, fourth round.
(d)—Led Stanley Cup Playoffs with 14 goals.
(e)—Led Stanley Cup Playoffs with 19 goals.
(f)—Won Lady Byng Memorial Trophy (Combination of Sportsmanship and Quality play).
(g)—Led Stanley Cup Playoffs with 15 goals.
(h)—July 30, 1990—Signed two-year contract to play for Milan Devils in Italian Hockey League.

TOM KURVERS

Defense . . . 6' . . . 190 lbs. . . . Born, Minneapolis, Minn., October 14, 1962 . . . Shoots left . . . Set UMD record with 149 career assists . . . (October 23, 1984)—Missed five games when Mario Marois' shot deflected off Chris Chelios' stick and struck Kurvers in the nose and above the right eye . . . (November, 1987)—Fractured left index finger . . . (February, 1988)—Pulled groin . . . (May, 1988)—Injured right thumb in fight with Moe Lemay vs Boston . . . (November 17, 1988)—Pulled groin vs Calgary . . . (March 8, 1990)—Injured knee at Hartford.

Year	Team	League	Games	G.	A.	Pts.	Pen.
1980-81	Univ. of Minn/Duluth (c)	WCHA	39	6	24	30	48
1981-82	Univ. of Minn/Duluth	WCHA	37	11	31	42	18
1982-83	Univ. of Minn/Duluth	WCHA	45	8	36	44	42
1983-84	Univ. of Minn/Duluth (a-d-e)	WCHA	43	18	58	76	46
1984-85	Montreal Canadiens	NHL	75	10	35	45	30
1985-86	Montreal Canadiens	NHL	62	7	23	30	36
1986-87	Montreal Canadiens (f)	NHL	1	0	0	0	0
1986-87	Buffalo Sabres (g)	NHL	55	6	17	23	24
1987-88	New Jersey Devils	NHL	56	5	29	34	46
1988-89	New Jersey Devils	NHL	74	16	50	66	38
1989-90	New Jersey Devils (h)	NHL	1	0	0	0	0
1989-90	Toronto Maple Leafs	NHL	70	15	37	52	29
NHL TOTALS			394	59	191	250	203

(c)—June, 1981—Drafted as underage player by Montreal Canadiens in 1981 NHL entry draft. Tenth Canadiens pick, 145th overall, seventh round.
(d)—Named to All-America Team (West).
(e)—Won Hobey Baker Award (Top NCAA Hockey Player).
(f)—November, 1986—Traded by Montreal Canadiens to Buffalo Sabres for a second-round 1988 draft pick (Martin St. Amour).
(g)—June, 1987—Traded by Buffalo Sabres to New Jersey Devils for a third-round 1988 draft pick.
(h)—October 16, 1989—Traded by New Jersey Devils to Toronto Maple Leafs for first-round 1991 draft pick.

DALE KUSHNER

Left Wing . . . 6'1" . . . 205 lbs. . . . Born, Terrace, B.C., June 13, 1966 . . . Shoots left . . . (December 30, 1988)—Suspended six games for leaving the penalty box to fight Al Tuer vs. Binghamton . . . (November 24, 1989)—Suspended eight AHL games for leaving the penalty box to enter a fight vs. New Haven.

Year	Team	League	Games	G.	A.	Pts.	Pen.
1983-84	Fort McMurray	AJHL	44	15	6	21	139
1983-84	Prince Albert Raiders	WHL	1	0	0	0	5
1984-85	Prince Albert Raiders	WHL	2	0	0	0	2
1984-85	Moose Jaw Warriors	WHL	17	5	2	7	23
1984-85	Medicine Hat Tigers	WHL	48	23	17	40	173
1985-86	Medicine Hat Tigers	WHL	66	25	19	44	218
1986-87	Medicine Hat Tigers (c)	WHL	65	34	34	68	250
1987-88	Springfield Indians	AHL	68	13	23	36	201
1988-89	Springfield Indians	AHL	45	5	8	13	132
1989-90	New York Islanders	NHL	2	0	0	0	2
1989-90	Springfield Indians	AHL	45	14	11	25	163
NHL TOTALS			2	0	0	0	2

(c)—March, 1987—Signed by New York Islanders as a free agent.

RYAN KUWABARA

Right Wing . . . 6'1" . . . 205 lbs. . . . Born, Hamilton, Ont., March 23, 1972 . . . Shoots right . . . Also plays Defense.

Year	Team	League	Games	G.	A.	Pts.	Pen.
1988-89	Hamilton Kilty Bees	OHL	39	13	23	36	128
1989-90	Ottawa 67's (c)	OHL	66	30	38	68	62

(c)—June 16, 1990—Selected by Montreal Canadiens in 1990 NHL entry draft. Second Canadiens pick, 39th overall, second round.

NICK KYPREOS

Left Wing . . . 6' . . . 190 lbs. . . . Born, Toronto, Ont., June 4, 1966 . . . Shoots left . . . (1988-89)—Missed 52 games following surgery to right knee . . . (February 8, 1990)—Surgery to right knee.

Year	Team	League	Games	G.	A.	Pts.	Pen.
1983-84	North Bay Centennials (c)	OHL	51	12	11	23	36
1984-85	North Bay Centennials	OHL	64	41	36	77	71
1985-86	North Bay Centennials (a)	OHL	64	62	35	97	112
1986-87	North Bay Centennials (b)	OHL	46	49	41	90	54
1986-87	Hershey Bears	AHL	10	0	1	1	4
1987-88	Hershey Bears	AHL	71	24	20	44	101
1988-89	Hershey Bears	AHL	28	12	15	27	19
1989-90	Washington Capitals (d)	NHL	31	5	4	9	82
1989-90	Baltimore Skipjacks	AHL	14	6	5	11	6
NHL TOTALS			31	5	4	9	82

(c)—September, 1984—Signed by Philadelphia Flyers as a free agent.
(d)—October 2, 1989—Selected by Washington Capitals in 1989 NHL waiver draft for the waiver price of $20,000.

JIM KYTE

Defense . . . 6'5" . . . 200 lbs. . . . Born, Ottawa, Ont., March 21, 1964 . . . Shoots left . . . Wears hearing aids when he plays . . . (March, 1980)—Broken left wrist . . . (February, 1988)—Stress fracture in lower back . . . (March, 1989)—Sprained shoulder.

Year	Team	League	Games	G.	A.	Pts.	Pen.
1980-81	Hawksbury Hawks	Tier II	42	2	24	26	133
1981-82	Cornwall Royals (c)	OHL	52	4	13	17	148
1982-83	Cornwall Royals	OHL	65	6	30	36	195
1982-83	Winnipeg Jets	NHL	2	0	0	0	0
1983-84	Winnipeg Jets	NHL	58	1	2	3	55
1984-85	Winnipeg Jets	NHL	71	0	3	3	111
1985-86	Winnipeg Jets	NHL	71	1	3	4	126
1986-87	Winnipeg Jets	NHL	72	5	5	10	162
1987-88	Winnipeg Jets	NHL	51	1	3	4	128
1988-89	Winnipeg Jets (d)	NHL	74	3	9	12	190
1989-90	Pittsburgh Penguins	NHL	56	3	1	4	125
NHL TOTALS			455	14	26	40	897

(c)—June, 1982—Drafted as underage junior by Winnipeg Jets in 1982 NHL entry draft. First Jets pick, 12th overall, first round.
(d)—June 17, 1989—Traded with Andrew McBain and Randy Gilhen by Winnipeg Jets to Pittsburgh Penguins for Randy Cunneyworth, Richard Tabaracci and Dave McLlwain.

NORMAND LACOMBE

Right Wing . . . 5'11" . . . 205 lbs. . . . Born, Pierrefond, Que., October 18, 1964 . . . Shoots right . . . (February 21, 1986)—Fractured jaw vs. N.Y. Islanders . . . (April, 1987)—Surgery for chronic compartment syndrome to both legs (a form of shin splints) . . . (September, 1988)—Injured knee in Edmonton Oilers training camp . . . (December 14, 1988)—Broke two fingers on right hand at Toronto . . . (January, 1989)—Sprained right shoulder . . . (March, 1990)—Recurring shin splint problems . . . (April, 1990)—Additional surgery for compartment syndrome problem on both legs.

Year	Team	League	Games	G.	A.	Pts.	Pen.
1981-82	Univ. New Hampshire	ECAC	35	18	16	34	38
1982-83	Univ. New Hampshire (b-c)	ECAC	35	18	25	43	48
1983-84	Rochester Americans	AHL	44	10	16	26	45
1984-85	Rochester Americans	AHL	33	13	16	29	33
1984-85	Buffalo Sabres	NHL	30	2	4	6	25
1985-86	Rochester Americans	AHL	32	10	13	23	56
1985-86	Buffalo Sabres	NHL	25	6	7	13	13
1986-87	Rochester Americans	AHL	13	6	5	11	4
1986-87	Buffalo Sabres (d)	NHL	39	4	7	11	8
1986-87	Edmonton Oilers	NHL	1	0	0	0	2
1986-87	Nova Scotia Oilers	AHL	10	3	5	8	4
1987-88	Edmonton Oilers	NHL	53	8	9	17	36
1988-89	Edmonton Oilers	NHL	64	17	11	28	57
1989-90	Edmonton Oilers (e)	NHL	15	5	2	7	21
1989-90	Philadelphia Flyers	NHL	18	0	2	2	9
NHL TOTALS			245	42	42	84	169

(c)—June, 1983—Drafted by Buffalo Sabres in 1983 NHL entry draft. Second Sabres pick, 10th overall, first round.
(d)—March, 1987—Traded with Wayne Van Dorp and future considerations by Buffalo Sabres to Edmonton Oilers for Lee Fogolin and Mark Napier.
(e)—January 5, 1990—Traded by Edmonton Oilers to Philadelphia Flyers for a fourth round 1990 draft pick (Joel Blain).

WILLIAM LACOUTURE

Right Wing . . . 6'2" . . . 192 lbs. . . . Born, Framingham, Mass., May 28, 1968 . . . Shoots right . . . Brother of David Lacouture.

Year	Team	League	Games	G.	A.	Pts.	Pen.
1985-86	Natick H.S.	Mass. H.S.		20	18	38	....
1986-87	Natick H.S. (c)	Mass. H.S.	19	15	39	54	....
1987-88	Univ. of New Hampshire	H. East	13	1	3	4	2

Year Team	League	Games	G.	A.	Pts.	Pen.
1988-89—Univ. of New Hampshire	H. East	20	1	0	1	2
1989-90—Univ. of New Hampshire	H. East	2	0	0	0	0

(c)—June, 1987—Drafted by Chicago Black Hawks in 1987 NHL entry draft. Eleventh Black Hawks pick, 218th overall, 11th round.

DANIEL LACROIX

Left Wing . . . 6'2'' . . . 185 lbs. . . . Born, Montreal, Que., March 11, 1969 . . . Shoots left.

Year Team	League	Games	G.	A.	Pts.	Pen.
1985-86—Hull Frontaliers	Que. Midget	37	10	13	23	46
1986-87—Granby Bisons (c)	QMJHL	54	9	16	25	311
1987-88—Granby Bisons	QMJHL	58	24	50	74	468
1988-89—Granby Bisons	QMJHL	70	45	49	94	*320
1988-89—Denver Rangers	IHL	2	0	1	1	0
1989-90—Flint Spirits	IHL	61	12	16	28	128

(c)—June, 1987—Drafted as underage junior by New York Rangers in 1987 NHL entry draft. Second Rangers pick, 31st overall, second round.

RANDY LADOUCEUR

Defense . . . 6'2'' . . . 220 lbs. . . . Born, Brockville, Ont., June 30, 1960 . . . Shoots left . . . (March, 1986)—Back spasms . . . (March, 1990)—Sprained right knee.

Year Team	League	Games	G.	A.	Pts.	Pen.
1978-79—Brantford Alexanders	OMJHL	64	3	17	20	141
1979-80—Brantford Alexanders (c)	OMJHL	37	6	15	21	125
1980-81—Kalamazoo Wings	IHL	80	7	30	37	52
1981-82—Adirondack Red Wings	AHL	78	4	28	32	78
1982-83—Adirondack Red Wings	AHL	48	11	21	32	54
1982-83—Detroit Red Wings	NHL	27	0	4	4	16
1983-84—Adirondack Red Wings	AHL	11	3	5	8	12
1983-84—Detroit Red Wings	NHL	71	3	17	20	58
1984-85—Detroit Red Wings	NHL	80	3	27	30	108
1985-86—Detroit Red Wings	NHL	78	5	13	18	196
1986-87—Detroit Red Wings (d)	NHL	34	3	6	9	70
1986-87—Hartford Whalers	NHL	36	2	3	5	51
1987-88—Hartford Whalers	NHL	68	1	7	8	91
1988-89—Hartford Whalers	NHL	75	2	5	7	95
1989-90—Hartford Whalers	NHL	71	3	12	15	143
NHL TOTALS		540	22	94	116	828

(c)—November, 1979—Signed by Detroit Red Wings as a free agent
(d)—January, 1987—Traded by Detroit Red Wings to Hartford Whalers for Dave Barr.

JUSTIN LAFAYETTE

Left Wing . . . 6'6'' . . . 200 lbs. . . . Born, Vancouver, B.C., January 23, 1970 . . . Shoots left . . . Son of David Lafayette (Played professional football with the B.C. Lions).

Year Team	League	Games	G.	A.	Pts.	Pen.
1986-87—Mississauga Reps. Midget	OHA	42	24	28	52	....
1987-88—Ferris State Univ. (c)	CCHA	36	1	2	3	20
1988-89—Ferris State Univ.	CCHA	36	3	4	7	59
1989-90—Ferris State Univ.	CCHA	34	4	5	9	38

(c)—June, 1988—Drafted by Chicago Black Hawks in 1988 NHL entry draft. Fifth Black Hawks pick, 113th overall, sixth round.

GUY DAMIEN LAFLEUR

Right Wing and Center . . . 6' . . . 175 lbs. . . . Born, Thurso, Que., September 20, 1951 . . . Shoots right . . . Missed part of 1974-75 season with fractured index finger . . . Youngest player to score 400 NHL-career goals (Broken by Wayne Gretzky) . . . Missed conclusion of 1979-80 season and playoffs with knee injury . . . (October 8, 1980)—Pulled right hamstring . . . (November, 1980)—Tonsilitis . . . (December 30, 1980)—Injured his right eye when struck by errant stick . . . (February, 1981)—Nine stitch cut under eye . . . (March 4, 1981)—Collected 1,000th NHL point in his 720th game, faster than any player in NHL history (Broken by Wayne Gretzky) . . . (March, 1981)—Charley horse . . . (March 24, 1981)—Fell asleep at the wheel of his car, hit a fence and a metal sign post sliced off the top part of his right ear after the post went through his windshield . . . (November 10, 1981)—Errant stick entered eye at Los Angeles . . . (March 11, 1982)—Bruised bone of left foot when hit by puck vs. Chicago . . . (October 11, 1982)—Eye injured at Quebec . . . (November 4, 1982)—Broke little toe on right foot at Minnesota . . . Holds Montreal Canadien club career records for most assists and points . . . 1988 Hall-of-Fame Inductee . . . Only second Hall-of-Fame member to play after being inducted (The other was Gordie Howe) . . . (December 10, 1988)—Missed 11 games with fractured left foot when hit by a shot at Boston . . . (November 14, 1989)—Bruised left ankle vs. Winnipeg and missed 16 games . . . (January 30, 1990)—Broke left cheekbone vs. Buffalo when checked from behind by Dean Kennedy and missed 25 games.

Year Team	League	Games	G.	A.	Pts.	Pen.
1966-67—Quebec Jr. Aces	QMJHL	8	1	1	2	0
1967-68—Quebec Jr. Aces	QMJHL	43	30	19	49	....
1968-69—Quebec Jr. Aces	QMJHL	49	50	60	110	83
1969-70—Quebec Remparts	QMJHL	56	*103	67	170	89
1070-71—Quebec Remparts (c)	QMJHL	62	*130	79	*209	135
1971-72—Montreal Canadiens	NHL	73	29	35	64	48
1972-73—Montreal Canadiens	NHL	69	28	27	55	51
1973-74—Montreal Canadiens	NHL	73	21	35	56	29
1974-75—Montreal Canadiens (a-d-e)	NHL	70	53	66	119	37
1975-76—Montreal Canadiens (a-f)	NHL	80	56	69	*125	36
1976-77—Montreal Canadiens (a-f-g-h-i-j)	NHL	80	56	*80	*136	20
1977-78—Montreal Canadiens (a-f-g-h-k)	NHL	78	*60	72	*132	26

Year Team	League	Games	G.	A.	Pts.	Pen.
1978-79—Montreal Canadiens (a-l)	NHL	80	52	77	129	28
1979-80—Montreal Canadiens (a)	NHL	74	50	75	125	12
1980-81—Montreal Canadiens	NHL	51	27	43	70	29
1981-82—Montreal Canadiens	NHL	66	27	57	84	24
1982-83—Montreal Canadiens	NHL	68	27	49	76	12
1983-84—Montreal Canadiens	NHL	80	30	40	70	19
1984-85—Montreal Canadiens (m)	NHL	19	2	3	5	10
1985-86—Did not play		.....	....	...	...	...
1986-87—Did not play		.....	....	...	...	...
1987-88—Did not play (n)		.....	....	...	...	...
1988-89—New York Rangers (o)	NHL	67	18	27	45	12
1989-90—Quebec Nordiques	NHL	39	12	22	34	4
NHL TOTALS		1067	548	777	1325	397

(c)—Drafted from Quebec Remparts by Montreal Canadiens in first round of 1971 amateur draft.
(d)—Led Stanley Cup Playoffs with 12 goals.
(e)—Selected Most Valuable Player in Prince of Wales Conference in poll of players by THE SPORTING NEWS.
(f)—Won Art Ross Memorial Trophy (NHL Leading Scorer).
(g)—Won Hart Memorial Trophy (Most Valuable Player).
(h)—Selected THE SPORTING NEWS' NHL Player-of-the-Year in poll of NHL players.
(i)—Led Stanley Cup Playoffs with 17 assists and 26 points.
(j)—Won Conn Smythe Trophy (MVP in Stanley Cup playoffs).
(k)—Led Stanley Cup Playoffs with 10 goals and tied for lead with 21 points.
(l)—Tied for lead in Stanley Cup Playoffs with 13 assists and 23 points.
(m)—November, 1984—Announced his retirement.
(n)—August, 1988—Signed by New York Rangers as a free agent.
(o)—July 14, 1989—Signed by Quebec Nordiques as a free agent. The Rangers received the Nordiques' fifth-round 1990 draft pick (Sergei Zubov) as compensation.

PAT La FONTAINE

Center . . . 5'9'' . . . 170 lbs. . . . Born, St. Louis, Mo., February 22, 1965 . . . Shoots right . . . Set Quebec Junior League records (1982-83) with points in 43 consecutive games (since broken by Mario Lemieux), and most goals (104), assists (130) and points (234) by a Quebec Junior League Rookie . . . Member of 1984 U.S. Olympic team . . . (August 16, 1984)—Damaged ligaments in left knee when checked by Team Canada's Scott Stevens in pre-Canada Cup game at Bloomington, Minn. . . . (January, 1985)—Mononucleosis . . . (January 25, 1986)—Separated right shoulder vs. Chicago . . . (March, 1988)—Bruised knee . . . (October 7, 1988)—Broke nose in collision with Steve Smith vs. Edmonton and played with the broken nose the entire season . . . (November 5, 1988)—Sprained ligaments in right wrist vs. Washington . . . (May 3, 1989)—Had nose repaired.

Year Team	League	Games	G.	A.	Pts.	Pen.
1981-82—Detroit Compuware	Mich. Midget	79	175	149	324	...
1982-83—Verdun Juniors (a-c-d-e-f-g)	QMJHL	70	*104	*130	*234	10
1983-84—U.S. National Team	Int'l	58	56	55	111	22
1983-84—U.S. Olympic Team	Int'l	6	5	5	10	0
1983-84—New York Islanders	NHL	15	13	6	19	6
1984-85—New York Islanders	NHL	67	19	35	54	32
1985-86—New York Islanders	NHL	65	30	23	53	43
1986-87—New York Islanders	NHL	80	38	32	70	70
1987-88—New York Islanders	NHL	75	47	45	92	52
1988-89—New York Islanders	NHL	79	45	43	88	26
1989-90—New York Islanders	NHL	74	54	51	105	38
NHL TOTALS		455	246	235	481	267

(c)—Won Frank Selke Trophy (Most Gentlemanly Player).
(d)—Won Des Instructeurs Trophy (Top Rookie Forward).
(e)—Won Jean Beliveau Trophy (Leading Scorer).
(f)—Won Guy Lafleur Trophy (Playoff MVP).
(g)—June, 1983—Drafted as underage junior by New York Islanders in 1983 NHL entry draft. First Islanders pick, third overall, first round.

MARC LAFORGE

Defense . . . 6'2'' . . . 200 lbs. . . . Born, Sudbury, Ont., January 3, 1968 . . . Shoots left . . . (October, 1986)—Suspended for nine games by OHL . . . (November 6, 1987)—Given a two-year suspension by OHL for attacking several members of the Guelph Platers in a game-ending fight . . . (November 26, 1988)—Suspended three AHL games for head-butting Lou Crawford vs. Adirondack . . . (December 8, 1988)—Suspended six games after he came off the bench to start a fight with Rob MacInnis . . . (December 28, 1988)—Suspended by Hartford Whalers for refusing to report to Indianapolis . . . (January 19, 1989)—Hartford lifted the suspension when he reported to Indianapolis . . . (November, 1989)—Sore back . . . (February 5, 1990)—Suspended five AHL games for head-butting Serge Roberge vs. Sherbrooke.

Year Team	League	Games	G.	A.	Pts.	Pen.
1984-85—Kingston Canadians	OHL	57	1	5	6	214
1985-86—Kingston Canadians (c)	OHL	60	1	13	14	248
1986-87—Kingston Canadians	OHL	53	2	10	12	224
1986-87—Binghamton Whalers (d)	AHL	..	..	..	..	..
1987-88—Sudbury Wolves	OHL	14	0	2	2	68
1988-89—Indianapolis Ice	IHL	14	0	2	2	138
1988-89—Binghamton Whalers	AHL	38	2	2	4	179
1989-90—Hartford Whalers (e)	NHL	9	0	0	0	43
1989-90—Binghamton Whalers	AHL	25	2	6	8	111
1989-90—Cape Breton Oilers	AHL	3	0	1	1	24
NHL TOTALS		9	0	0	0	43

(c)—June, 1986—Drafted as underage junior by Hartford Whalers in 1986 NHL entry draft. Second Whalers pick, 32nd overall, second round.
(d)—No regular season record. Played four playoff games.
(e)—March 6, 1990—Traded by Hartford Whalers to Edmonton Oilers for NHL rights to Cam Brauer.

JASON LAFRENIERE

Center . . . 6' . . . 185 lbs. . . . Born, St. Catharines, Ont., December 6, 1966 . . . Shoots right . . . Son of Roger Lafreniere (Detroit 1962-63, and St. Louis 1972-73. He played several seasons in the old WHL, AHL and CPHL).

Year	Team	League	Games	G.	A.	Pts.	Pen.
1982-83—Orillia Travelways		OHA	48	17	40	57	9
1983-84—Brantford Alexanders		OHL	70	24	57	81	4
1984-85—Hamilton Steelhawks (c)		OHL	59	26	69	95	10
1985-86—Hamilton Steelhawks (d)		OHL	14	12	10	22	2
1985-86—Belleville Bulls (a-e)		OHL	48	37	73	110	2
1986-87—Fredericton Express		AHL	11	3	11	14	0
1986-87—Quebec Nordiques		NHL	56	13	15	28	8
1987-88—Fredericton Express		AHL	32	12	19	31	38
1987-88—Quebec Nordiques (f)		NHL	40	10	19	29	4
1988-89—New York Rangers		NHL	38	8	16	24	6
1988-89—Denver Rangers		IHL	24	10	19	29	17
1989-90—Flint Spirits		IHL	41	9	25	34	13
1989-90—Phoenix Roadrunners		IHL	14	4	9	13	0
NHL TOTALS			134	31	50	81	18

(c)—June, 1985—Drafted as underage junior by Quebec Nordiques in 1985 NHL entry draft. Second Nordiques pick, 36th overall, second round.
(d)—November, 1985—Traded with Lawrence Hinch and Peter Choma by Hamilton Steelhawks to Belleville Bulls for Sean Doyl, John Purves and Brian Hoard.
(e)—Won William Hanley Trophy (Most Gentlemanly Player).
(f)—August, 1988—Traded with Normand Rochefort by Quebec Nordiques to New York Rangers for Walt Poddubny, Bruce Bell, Jari Gronstrand and fourth-round draft choice in 1989 (Eric DuBois).

TOM LAIDLAW

Defense . . . 6'2" . . . 215 lbs. . . . Born, Brampton, Ont., April 15, 1958 . . . Shoots left . . . (December, 1984)—Spleen surgery . . . (March 12, 1986)—Back spasms . . . (October 8, 1987)—Sprained medial collateral ligament in right knee at Edmonton . . . (October, 1988)—Pulled hamstring . . . (March, 1990)—Missed final eight regular season games, and all 10 playoff games, due to a disc problem.

Year	Team	League	Games	G.	A.	Pts.	Pen.
1978-79—Northern Michigan Univ. (c)		CCHA	29	10	20	30	137
1979-80—Northern Michigan Univ. (a-d)		CCHA	39	8	30	38	83
1979-80—New Haven Nighthawks		AHL	1	0	0	0	0
1980-81—New York Rangers		NHL	80	6	23	29	100
1981-82—New York Rangers		NHL	79	3	18	21	104
1982-83—New York Rangers		NHL	80	0	10	10	75
1983-84—New York Rangers		NHL	79	3	15	18	62
1984-85—New York Rangers		NHL	61	1	11	12	52
1985-86—New York Rangers		NHL	68	6	12	18	103
1986-87—New York Rangers (e)		NHL	63	1	10	11	65
1986-87—Los Angeles Kings		NHL	11	0	3	3	4
1987-88—Los Angeles Kings		NHL	57	1	12	13	47
1988-89—Los Angeles Kings		NHL	70	3	17	20	63
1989-90—Los Angeles Kings		NHL	57	1	8	9	42
NHL TOTALS			705	25	139	164	717

(c)—June, 1978—Drafted by New York Rangers in 1978 NHL amateur draft. Seventh Rangers pick, 93rd overall, sixth round.
(d)—Named to All-NCAA-Tournament team.
(e)—March, 1987—Traded with Bobby Carpenter by New York Rangers to Los Angeles Kings for Marcel Dionne, Jeff Crossman and a third round 1989 draft pick.

BOB LAKSO

Left Wing . . . 6' . . . 180 lbs. . . . Born, Baltimore, Md., April 3, 1962 . . . Shoots left.

Year	Team	League	Games	G.	A.	Pts.	Pen.
1980-81—Univ. of Minnesota/Duluth (c)		WCHA	36	7	6	13	2
1981-82—Univ. of Minnesota/Duluth		WCHA	28	12	11	23	8
1982-83—Univ. of Minnesota/Duluth		WCHA	45	18	25	43	8
1983-84—Univ. of Minnesota/Duluth		WCHA	43	32	34	66	12
1984-85—Indianapolis Checkers		IHL	76	26	32	58	4
1984-85—Springfield Indians		AHL	8	2	1	3	0
1985-86—Indianapolis Checkers		IHL	58	41	35	76	4
1985-86—Springfield Indians		AHL	17	3	6	9	2
1986-87—Indianapolis Checkers		IHL	79	39	55	94	6
1987-88—Milwaukee Admirals		IHL	80	43	28	71	10
1988-89—Indianapolis Ice		IHL	82	38	34	72	10
1989-90—Fort Wayne Komets		IHL	82	42	58	100	6

(c)—June, 1980—Drafted by Minnesota North Stars in NHL entry draft. Ninth North Stars pick, 184th overall, ninth round.

TODD LALONDE

Left Wing . . . 6' . . . 190 lbs. . . . Born, Sudbury, Ont., August 4, 1969 . . . Shoots left . . . (December, 1986)—Sprained knee.

Year	Team	League	Games	G.	A.	Pts.	Pen.
1984-85—Garson Midget		OHA	29	38	38	76	42
1985-86—Sudbury Wolves		OHL	57	17	30	47	43
1986-87—Sudbury Wolves (c)		OHL	29	5	11	16	71
1987-88—Sudbury Wolves		OHL	59	27	43	70	79
1988-89—Sudbury Wolves		OHL	52	32	44	76	57
1989-90—Maine Mariners		AHL	3	2	0	2	6
1989-90—Johnstown Chiefs		ECHL	1	1	0	1	2

(c)—June, 1987—Drafted as underage junior by Boston Bruins in 1987 NHL entry draft. Third Bruins pick, 56th overall, third round.

JOHN MICHAEL (MIKE) LALOR

Defense . . . 6' . . . 190 lbs. . . . Born, Fort Erie, Ont., March 8, 1963 . . . Shoots left . . . (September, 1987)—Bursitis in right ankle during Montreal training camp . . . (November 1, 1988)—Stress fracture of left ankle in fight with Torrie Robertson at Hartford.

Year	Team	League	Games	G.	A.	Pts.	Pen.
1981-82—Brantford Alexanders		OHL	64	3	13	16	114
1982-83—Brantford Alexanders		OHL	65	10	30	40	113
1983-84—Nova Scotia Voyageurs (c)		AHL	67	5	11	16	80
1984-85—Sherbrooke Canadiens		AHL	79	9	23	32	114
1985-86—Montreal Canadiens		NHL	62	3	5	8	56
1986-87—Montreal Canadiens		NHL	57	0	10	10	47
1987-88—Montreal Canadiens		NHL	66	1	10	11	113
1988-89—Montreal Canadiens (d)		NHL	12	1	4	5	15
1988-89—St. Louis Blues		NHL	36	1	14	15	54
1989-90—St. Louis Blues (e)		NHL	78	0	16	16	81
NHL TOTALS			311	6	59	65	366

(c)—September, 1983—Signed by Nova Scotia Voyageurs as a free agent.
(d)—January 16, 1989—Traded by Montreal Canadiens to St. Louis Blues for the option to flip first-round 1990 picks and second or third-round picks in 1991.
(e)—July 13, 1990—Traded with Peter Zezel by St. Louis Blues to Washington Capitals for Geoff Courtnall.

JEFF LAMB

Center . . . 5'11" . . . 170 lbs. . . . Born, Waterloo, Iowa, July 14, 1964 . . . Shoots left.

Year	Team	League	Games	G.	A.	Pts.	Pen.
1983-84—Austin Mavericks		USHL	24	25	21	46	18
1983-84—Univ. of Denver		WCHA	15	0	2	2	8
1984-85—Univ. of Denver		WCHA	39	14	25	39	62
1985-86—Univ. of Denver (c)		WCHA	45	23	31	54	75
1986-87—Univ. of Denver		WCHA	40	10	24	34	58
1987-88—Maine Mariners		AHL	57	7	12	19	96
1988-89—Maine Mariners		AHL	58	11	15	26	64
1989-90—Phoenix Roadrunners (d-e)		IHL	78	20	33	53	152

(c)—June, 1986—Selected by Pittsburgh Penguins in 1986 NHL supplemental draft.
(d)—Sepember, 1989—Signed by Phoenix Roadrunners as a free agent.
(e)—August, 1990—Signed by St. Louis Blues as a free agent.

MARK LAMB

Left Wing . . . 5'9" . . . 170 lbs. . . . Born, Swift Current, Sask., August 3, 1964 . . . Shoots left . . . (December, 1982)—Refused, with team captain Bob Rouse, to dress for a game after Nanaimo (WHL) released coach Les Calder. Both players asked to be traded . . . Also plays Center . . . Brother of Garth Lamb (former player in WHL).

Year	Team	League	Games	G.	A.	Pts.	Pen.
1980-81—Billings Bighorns		WHL	24	1	8	9	12
1981-82—Billings Bighorns (c)		WHL	72	45	56	101	46
1982-83—Nanaimo Islanders (d)		WHL	30	14	37	51	16
1982-83—Medicine Hat Tigers		WHL	46	22	43	65	33
1983-84—Medicine Hat Tigers (a-e)		WHL	72	59	77	136	30
1984-85—Medicine Hat Tigers (f)		WHL	..	..	..	..	..
1984-85—Moncton Golden Flames		AHL	80	23	49	72	53
1985-86—Calgary Flames		NHL	1	0	0	0	0
1985-86—Moncton Golden Flames		AHL	79	26	50	76	51
1986-87—Detroit Red Wings		NHL	22	2	1	3	8
1986-87—Adirondack Red Wings		AHL	49	14	36	50	45
1987-88—Nova Scotia Oilers (g)		AHL	69	27	61	88	45
1987-88—Edmonton Oilers		NHL	2	0	0	0	0
1988-89—Cape Breton Oilers		AHL	54	33	49	82	29
1988-89—Edmonton Oilers		NHL	20	2	8	10	14
1989-90—Edmonton Oilers		NHL	58	12	16	28	42
NHL TOTALS			103	16	25	41	64

(c)—June, 1982—Drafted as underage junior by Calgary Flames in 1982 NHL entry draft. Fifth Flames pick, 72nd overall, fourth round.
(d)—December, 1982—Traded by Nanaimo Islanders to Medicine Hat Tigers for Glen Kulka and Daryl Reaugh.
(e)—Won Frank Boucher Memorial Trophy (Most Gentlemanly Player).
(f)—Played six playoff games.
(g)—October, 1987—Acquired by Edmonton Oilers on waivers from Detroit Red Wings.

DANIEL LAMBERT

Defense . . . 5'8" . . . 180 lbs. . . . Born, St. Boniface, Man., January 12, 1970 . . . Shoots left.

Year	Team	League	Games	G.	A.	Pts.	Pen.
1986-87—Swift Current Broncos		WHL	68	13	53	66	95
1987-88—Swift Current Broncos		WHL	69	20	63	83	120
1988-89—Swift Current Broncos (a-c)		WHL	57	25	77	102	158
1989-90—Swift Current Broncos (a)		WHL	50	17	51	68	119

(c)—June, 1989—Drafted by Quebec Nordiques in 1989 NHL entry draft. Eighth Nordiques pick, 106th overall, sixth round.

LANE LAMBERT

Right Wing . . . 6' . . . 175 lbs. . . . Born, Melfort, Sask., November 18, 1964 . . . Shoots right . . . (September, 1982)—Eye injured vs. Brandon . . . (March, 1985)—Surgery to left knee . . . (October, 1986)—Missed 26 games with an injured hip flexor . . . (December, 1987)—Complex fracture of second finger on left hand.

Year	Team	League	Games	G.	A.	Pts.	Pen.
1980-81—Swift Current Broncos		SJHL	55	43	54	97	63
1981-82—Saskatoon Blades		WHL	72	45	69	114	111
1982-83—Saskatoon Blades (b-c)		WHL	64	59	60	119	126
1983-84—Detroit Red Wings		NHL	73	20	15	35	115
1984-85—Detroit Red Wings		NHL	69	14	11	25	104
1985-86—Adirondack Red Wings		AHL	45	16	25	41	69
1985-86—Detroit Red Wings		NHL	34	2	3	5	130
1986-87—New Haven Nighthawks		AHL	11	3	3	6	19
1986-87—New York Rangers (e)		NHL	18	2	2	4	33
1987-88—Quebec Nordiques		NHL	15	5	11	18	18
1987-88—Quebec Nordiques		NHL	61	13	27	40	98

Year	Team	League	Games	G.	A.	Pts.	Pen.
1988-89—Quebec Nordiques		NHL	13	2	2	4	23
1988-89—Halifax Citadels		AHL	59	25	35	60	162
1989-90—Canadian National Team		Int'l.	54	28	36	64	48
NHL TOTALS			283	58	66	124	521

(c)—June, 1983—Drafted as underage junior by Detroit Red Wings in 1983 NHL entry draft. Second Red Wings pick, 25th overall, second round.

(d)—July, 1986—Traded with Kelly Kisio, Jim Leavins and a fifth-round 1988 draft pick by Detroit Red Wings to New York Rangers for Glen Hanlon, third round 1987 (Dennis Holland) and 1988 draft picks and future considerations.

(e)—March, 1987—Traded by New York Rangers to Quebec Nordiques for Pat Price.

HANK LAMMENS

Defense . . . 6'2'' . . . 196 lbs. . . . Born, Brockville, Ont., February 21, 1966 . . . Shoots left . . . (November, 1984)—Broken wrist and separated shoulder.

Year	Team	League	Games	G.	A.	Pts.	Pen.
1983-84—Brockville Braves		OHA	46	7	11	18	106
1984-85—St. Lawrence Univ. (c)		ECAC	21	1	7	8	16
1985-86—St. Lawrence Univ.		ECAC	30	3	14	17	60
1986-87—St. Lawrence Univ. (b-d)		ECAC	35	6	13	19	92
1987-88—St. Lawrence Univ.		ECAC	36	3	7	10	70
1988-89—Springfield Indians		AHL	69	1	13	14	55
1989-90—Springfield Indians		AHL	43	0	6	6	27

(c)—June, 1985—Drafted by New York Islanders in 1985 NHL entry draft. Tenth Islanders pick, 160th overall, 10th round.

(d)—Named Second team All-America (East).

MITCH LAMOUREUX

Center . . . 5'6'' . . . 185 lbs. . . . Born, Ottawa, Ont., August 22, 1962 . . . Shoots left . . . Set AHL record for most goals by a rookie (57) in 1982-83, and most goals by an AHL player . . . (September, 1988)—Damaged knee playing hockey in Italy and returned to the United States for major surgery . . . (1988-89)—Assistant coach for Hershey Bears while undergoing therapy . . . (September, 1989)—Injured knee while playing in Italy.

Year	Team	League	Games	G.	A.	Pts.	Pen.
1979-80—Oshawa Generals		OMJHL	67	28	48	76	63
1980-81—Oshawa Generals (c)		OMJHL	63	50	69	119	256
1981-82—Oshawa Generals		OHL	66	43	78	121	275
1982-83—Baltimore Skipjacks (b-d)		AHL	80	*57	50	107	107
1983-84—Baltimore Skipjacks		AHL	68	30	38	68	136
1983-84—Pittsburgh Penguins		NHL	8	1	1	2	6
1984-85—Pittsburgh Penguins		NHL	62	11	8	19	53
1984-85—Baltimore Skipjacks		AHL	18	10	14	24	34
1985-86—Baltimore Skipjacks		AHL	75	22	31	53	129
1986-87—Hershey Bears		AHL	78	43	46	89	122
1987-88—Philadelphia Flyers		NHL	3	0	0	0	0
1987-88—Hershey Bears		AHL	78	35	52	87	171
1988-89—..............		Italy	....	...	....	....	....
1988-89—Hershey Bears		AHL	9	9	7	16	14
1989-90—Maine Mariners (e)		AHL	10	4	7	11	10
NHL TOTALS			73	12	9	21	59

(c)—June, 1981—Drafted as underage junior by Pittsburgh Penguins in 1981 NHL entry draft. Sixth Penguins pick, 154th overall, eighth round.

(d)—Won Dudley (Red) Garrett Memorial Trophy (Top AHL Rookie).

(e)—March, 1990—Signed by Maine Mariners after spending most of the season as an assistant coach for the Hershey Bears while undergoing therapy on his knee.

DEREK LANGILLE

Defense . . . 6' . . . 185 lbs. . . . Born, Toronto, Ont., June 25, 1969 . . . Shoots left.

Year	Team	League	Games	G.	A.	Pts.	Pen.
1985-86—Wexford Minor Midget		OHA Midg.	..	18	32	50	185
1986-87—Belleville Bulls		OHL	42	0	2	2	27
1987-88—Belleville Bulls		OHL	36	3	7	10	45
1987-88—Kingston Canadians (c)		OHL	32	4	7	11	66
1988-89—North Bay Centennials (d)		OHL	60	20	38	58	128
1989-90—Newmarket Saints		AHL	64	5	12	17	75

(c)—September, 1988—Traded with John Battice by Kingston Raiders to North Bay Centennials for Greg Capson and Brock Shyiak.

(d)—June, 1989—Drafted by Toronto Maple Leafs in 1989 NHL entry draft. Ninth Maple Leafs pick, 150th overall, eighth round.

ROD CORRY LANGWAY

Defense . . . 6'3'' . . . 215 lbs. . . . Born, Maag, Taiwan, May 3, 1957 . . . Shoots left . . . Attended University of New Hampshire and was member of football and hockey teams . . . Brother of Kim Langway . . . (January 5, 1982)—Bruised left foot vs. Boston . . . (February 9, 1982)—Injured left knee in NHL All-Star game. Examination in March discovered dried blood in the knee which had weakened the muscle in his left leg . . . (October 23, 1985)—Bruised right knee vs. Calgary and missed eight games . . . (November, 1987)—Ruptured disc in back . . . (February, 1988)—Pulled thigh muscle . . . (April, 1988)—Charley Horse . . . Does not wear a helmet . . . (November, 1988)—Bruised left knee . . . (October 7, 1989)—Strained left knee ligaments vs. Chicago and missed six games . . . (December 28, 1989)—Surgery to both knees and missed 10 games.

Year	Team	League	Games	G.	A.	Pts.	Pen.
1975-76—University of New Hampshire		ECAC	..	..	..	..	....
1976-77—Univ. of New Hampshire (c-d)		ECAC	34	10	43	53	52
1977-78—Hampton Gulls		AHL	30	6	16	22	50
1977-78—Birmingham Bulls		WHA	52	3	18	21	52
1978-79—Montreal Canadiens		NHL	45	3	4	7	30
1978-79—Nova Scotia Voyageurs		AHL	18	6	13	19	29
1979-80—Montreal Canadiens		NHL	77	7	29	36	81

Year	Team	League	Games	G.	A.	Pts.	Pen.
1980-81—Montreal Canadiens		NHL	80	11	34	45	120
1981-82—Montreal Canadiens (f)		NHL	66	5	34	39	116
1982-83—Washington Capitals (a-g)		NHL	80	3	29	32	75
1983-84—Washington Capitals (a-g)		NHL	80	9	24	33	61
1984-85—Washington Capitals (b)		NHL	79	4	22	26	54
1985-86—Washington Capitals		NHL	71	1	17	18	61
1986-87—Washington Capitals		NHL	78	2	25	27	53
1987-88—Washington Capitals		NHL	63	3	13	16	28
1988-89—Washington Capitals		NHL	76	2	19	21	67
1989-90—Washington Capitals		NHL	58	0	8	8	39
WHA TOTALS			52	3	18	21	53
NHL TOTALS			853	50	258	308	785

(c)—Drafted from University of New Hampshire by Montreal Canadiens in second round of 1977 amateur draft.

(d)—May, 1977—Selected by Birmingham Bulls in World Hockey Association amateur players' draft.

(e)—October, 1978—Signed by Montreal Canadiens as free agent.

(f)—September, 1982—Traded by Montreal Canadiens with Brian Engblom, Doug Jarvis and Craig Laughlin to Washington Capitals for Ryan Walter and Rick Green.

(g)—Won James Norris Memorial Trophy (Top NHL Defenseman).

MARC LANIEL

Defense . . . 6'1'' . . . 185 lbs. . . . Born, Oshawa, Ont., January 16, 1968 . . . Shoots left.

Year	Team	League	Games	G.	A.	Pts.	Pen.
1984-85—Toronto Red Wings		MTHL	37	15	28	43	68
1985-86—Oshawa Generals (c)		OHL	66	9	25	34	27
1986-87—Oshawa Generals		OHL	63	14	31	45	42
1987-88—Oshawa Generals		OHL	41	8	32	40	56
1987-88—Utica Devils		AHL	2	0	0	0	0
1988-89—Utica Devils		AHL	80	6	28	34	43
1989-90—Utica Devils		AHL	20	0	0	0	25
1989-90—Phoenix Roadrunners		IHL	26	3	15	18	10

(c)—June, 1986—Drafted as underage junior by New Jersey Devils in 1986 NHL entry draft. Fourth Devils pick, 62nd overall, third round.

JEAN-MARC LANTHIER

Right Wing . . . 6'2'' . . . 198 lbs. . . . Born, Montreal, Que., March 27, 1963 . . . Shoots right . . . (October 25, 1989)—Hospitalized with pneumonia.

Year	Team	League	Games	G.	A.	Pts.	Pen.
1979-80—Quebec Remparts		QMJHL	63	14	32	46	4
1980-81—Quebec Remparts		QMJHL	37	13	32	45	18
1980-81—Sorel Black Hawks (d)		QMJHL	35	6	33	39	29
1981-82—Laval Voisins (e)		QMJHL	60	44	34	78	48
1982-83—Laval Voisins		QMJHL	69	39	71	110	54
1983-84—Fredericton Express		AHL	60	25	17	42	29
1983-84—Vancouver Canucks		NHL	11	2	1	3	2
1984-85—Fredericton Express		AHL	50	21	21	42	13
1984-85—Vancouver Canucks		NHL	27	6	4	10	13
1985-86—Fredericton Express		AHL	7	5	5	10	2
1985-86—Vancouver Canucks		NHL	62	7	10	17	12
1986-87—Fredericton Express		AHL	78	15	38	53	24
1987-88—Vancouver Canucks		NHL	5	1	1	2	2
1987-88—Fredericton Express (f)		AHL	74	35	71	106	37
1988-89—Utica Devils (g)		AHL	55	23	26	49	22
1988-89—Maine Mariners		AHL	24	7	16	23	16
1989-90—Fort Wayne Komets		IHL	7	4	7	11	4
1989-90—Utica Devils		AHL	50	13	19	32	32
NHL TOTALS			105	16	16	32	29

(c)—December, 1980—Traded by Quebec Remparts to Sorel Black Hawks for Andre Cote.

(d)—June, 1981—Drafted as underage junior by Vancouver Canucks in 1981 NHL entry draft. Second Canucks pick, 52nd overall, third round.

(e)—August, 1981—Acquired by Laval Voisins in QMJHL dispersal draft of players from defunct Sorel Black Hawks.

(f)—July, 1988—Signed by Boston Bruins as a free agent.

(g)—December 9, 1988—Traded by Boston Bruins to New Jersey Devils for Dan Dorion.

RICK ROMAN LANZ

Defense . . . 6'1'' . . . 195 lbs. . . . Born, Karlouyvary, Czechoslovakia, September 16, 1961 . . . Shoots right . . . (January, 1982)—Surgery to repair torn knee ligaments . . . (December, 1984)—Dislocated disk in neck and missed 23 games . . . (October 16, 1986)—Broke jaw when struck by Derrick Smith at Philadelphia . . . (January, 1988)—Asthma . . . (April, 1988)—Sprained neck . . . (October, 1988)—Sprained shoulder . . . (December, 1988)—Flu . . . (January, 1988)—Injured knee . . . (March, 1989)—Bruised shoulder.

Year	Team	League	Games	G.	A.	Pts.	Pen.
1977-78—Oshawa Generals		OMJHL	65	1	41	42	51
1978-79—Oshawa Generals		OMJHL	65	12	47	59	88
1979-80—Oshawa Generals (b-c)		OMJHL	52	18	38	56	51
1980-81—Vancouver Canucks		NHL	76	7	22	29	40
1981-82—Vancouver Canucks		NHL	39	3	11	14	48
1982-83—Vancouver Canucks		NHL	74	10	38	48	46
1983-84—Vancouver Canucks		NHL	79	18	39	57	45
1984-85—Vancouver Canucks		NHL	57	2	17	19	69
1985-86—Vancouver Canucks		NHL	75	15	38	53	73
1986-87—Vancouver Canucks (d)		NHL	17	1	6	7	10
1986-87—Toronto Maple Leafs		NHL	44	2	19	21	32
1987-88—Toronto Maple Leafs		NHL	75	6	22	28	65
1988-89—Toronto Maple Leafs		NHL	32	1	9	10	18
1989-90—Ambri (e)		Switzerland	....	...	...	....	....
NHL TOTALS			568	65	221	286	446

244

(c)—June, 1980—Drafted as underage junior in 1980 NHL entry draft by Vancouver Canucks. First Canucks pick, seventh overall, first round

(d)—December, 1986—Traded by Vancouver Canucks to Toronto Maple Leafs for Jim Benning and Dan Hodgson.

(e)—August, 1990—Signed by Chicago Black Hawks as a free agent.

DANIEL LAPERRIERE

Defense . . . 6'1" . . . 180 lbs. . . . Born, Laval, Que., March 28, 1969 . . . Shoots left . . . Son of Hall-of-Famer Jacques Laperriere (Played 12 seasons with Montreal). His grandfather played amateur hockey in the 1940's and his mother was a figure skater.

Year	Team	League	Games	G.	A.	Pts.	Pen.
1988-89—St. Lawrence Univ. (c)		ECAC	34	1	11	12	14
1989-90—St. Lawrence Univ.		ECAC	29	6	19	25	16

(c)—June, 1989—Drafted by St. Louis Blues in 1989 NHL entry draft. Fourth Blues pick, 93rd overall, fifth round.

CLAUDE LAPOINTE

Left Wing . . . 5'9" . . . 173 lbs. . . . Born, Ville Emard, Que., October 11, 1968 . . . Shoots left.

Year	Team	League	Games	G.	A.	Pts.	Pen.
1985-86—Trois-Rivieres Draveurs		QMJHL	72	19	38	57	74
1986-87—Trois-Rivieres Draveurs (c)		QMJHL	70	47	57	104	123
1987-88—Laval Titans (d)		QMJHL	69	37	83	120	143
1988-89—Laval Titans		QMJHL	63	32	72	104	158
1989-90—Halifax Citadels		AHL	63	18	19	37	51

(c)—May, 1987—Traded with Alain Dubeau and a third-round draft pick (Patrice Brisbois) by Trois-Rivieres Draveurs to Laval Titans for Raymond Saumier, Mike Gober, Eric Gobeil and a second round draft pick (Eric Charron).

(d)—June, 1988—Drafted by Quebec Nordiques in 1988 NHL entry draft. Twelfth Nordiques pick, 234th overall, 12th round.

PETER LAPPIN

Center . . . 5'11' . . . 180 lbs. . . . Born, St. Charles, Ill., December 31, 1965 . . . Shoots right . . . (January, 1988)—Injured knee . . . Brother of Chris, Mike and Tim Lappin.

Year	Team	League	Games	G.	A.	Pts.	Pen.
1984-85—St. Lawrence Univ.		ECAC	32	10	12	22	22
1985-86—St. Lawrence Univ.		ECAC	30	20	26	46	64
1986-87—St. Lawrence Univ. (b-c)		ECAC	35	34	24	58	32
1987-88—St. Lawrence Univ. (d)		ECAC	34	21	39	60	30
1987-88—Salt Lake Golden Eagles		IHL	3	1	1	2	0
1988-89—Salt Lake Golden Eagles		IHL	81	48	42	90	50
1989-90—Kalamazoo Wings (b)		IHL	74	45	35	80	42
1989-90—Minnesota North Stars (e)		NHL	6	0	0	0	2
NHL TOTALS			6	0	0	0	2

(c)—June, 1987—Selected by Calgary Flames in 1987 NHL supplemental draft.

(d)—Named Second team All-America (East).

(e)—September 4, 1989—Traded by Calgary Flames to Minnesota North Stars for a second round 1990 draft pick (eventually traded to New Jersey).

IGOR LARIONOV

Center . . . 5'11" . . . 165 lbs. . . . Born, Voskresensk, U.S.S.R., December 3, 1960 . . . Shoots left.

Year	Team	League	Games	G.	A.	Pts.	Pen.
1977-78—Khimik Voskresensk		USSR	6	3	0	3	4
1978-79—Khimik Voskresensk		USSR	25	3	4	7	12
1979-80—Khimik Voskresensk		USSR	42	11	7	18	24
1980-81—Khimik Voskresensk		USSR	56	22	23	45	36
1981-82—Central Red Army		USSR	46	31	22	53	6
1982-83—Central Red Army		USSR	44	20	19	39	20
1983-84—Central Red Army		USSR	43	15	26	41	30
1984-85—Central Red Army (c)		USSR	40	18	28	46	20
1985-86—Central Red Army		USSR	40	21	31	52	33
1986-87—Central Red Army		USSR	39	20	26	46	34
1987-88—Central Red Army		USSR	51	25	32	57	54
1988-89—Central Red Army		USSR	31	15	12	27	22
1989-90—Vancouver Canucks		NHL	74	17	27	44	20
NHL TOTALS			74	17	27	44	20

(c)—June, 1985—Drafted by Vancouver Canucks in 1985 NHL entry draft. Eleventh Canucks pick, 214th overall, 11th round.

JAMES LARKIN

Left Wing . . . 6' . . . 170 lbs. . . . Born, South Weymouth, Mass., April 15, 1970 . . . Shoots left.

Year	Team	League	Games	G.	A.	Pts.	Pen.
1986-87—Mt. St. Joseph H.S.		Vt. H.S.	..	30	26	56	..
1987-88—Mt. St. Joseph H.S. (c)		Vt. H.S.	..	44	41	85	..
1988-89—Univ. of Vermont		ECAC	34	16	19	35	8
1989-90—Univ. of Vermont		ECAC	28	20	15	35	14

(c)—June, 1988—Drafted by Los Angeles Kings in 1988 NHL entry draft. Tenth Kings pick, 175th overall, ninth round.

STEVE DONALD LARMER

Right Wing . . . 5'10" . . . 185 lbs. . . . Born, Peterborough, Ont., June 16, 1961 . . . Shoots left . . . Brother of Jeff Larmer . . . (1982-83)—Set Chicago club records for most goals by a right wing (43), most goals by a Chicago rookie (43) and most points by a Chicago rookie (90). He also tied club record for most assists by a Chicago rookie (47) set by Denis Savard in 1980-81 . . . (March 13, 1990)—Moved into fourth on the NHL all-time consecutive played list (613 straight games). Starts the 1990-91 season having played 640 straight games.

Year	Team	League	Games	G.	A.	Pts.	Pen.
1977-78—Peterborough Petes		OMJHL	62	24	17	41	51
1978-79—Niagara Falls Flyers		OMJHL	66	37	47	84	108
1979-80—Niagara Falls Flyers (c)		OMJHL	67	45	69	114	71
1980-81—Niagara Falls Flyers (b)		OHL	61	55	78	133	73
1980-81—Chicago Black Hawks		NHL	4	0	1	1	0
1981-82—New Brunswick Hawks (b)		AHL	74	38	44	82	46
1981-82—Chicago Black Hawks		NHL	3	0	0	0	0
1982-83—Chicago Black Hawks (d-e)		NHL	80	43	47	90	28
1983-84—Chicago Black Hawks		NHL	80	35	40	75	34
1984-85—Chicago Black Hawks		NHL	80	46	40	86	16
1985-86—Chicago Black Hawks		NHL	80	31	45	76	47
1986-87—Chicago Black Hawks		NHL	80	28	56	84	22
1987-88—Chicago Black Hawks		NHL	80	41	48	89	42
1988-89—Chicago Black Hawks		NHL	80	43	44	87	54
1989-90—Chicago Black Hawks		NHL	80	31	59	90	40
NHL TOTALS			647	298	380	678	283

(c)—June, 1980—Drafted as underage junior in 1980 NHL entry draft by Chicago Black Hawks. Eleventh Black Hawks pick, 120th overall, sixth round.

(d)—Selected as NHL Rookie of the Year in vote of players conducted by THE SPORTING NEWS.

(e)—Won Calder Memorial Trophy (Top NHL Rookie).

DENIS LAROCQUE

Defense . . . 6'1" . . . 200 lbs. . . . Born, Hawkesbury, Ont., October 5, 1967 . . . Shoots left . . . (October, 1986)—Suspended eight games by OHL for a stick fight with Gary Callaghan vs. Belleville.

Year	Team	League	Games	G.	A.	Pts.	Pen.
1982-83—Hawkesbury Hawks		CJHL	31	0	13	13	83
1983-84—Guelph Platers		OHL	65	1	5	6	74
1984-85—Guelph Platers		OHL	62	1	15	16	67
1985-86—Guelph Platers (c)		OHL	66	2	16	18	144
1986-87—Guelph Platers		OHL	45	4	10	14	82
1987-88—New Haven Nighthawks		AHL	58	4	10	14	154
1987-88—Los Angeles Kings		NHL	8	0	1	1	18
1988-89—New Haven Nighthawks (d)		AHL	15	2	2	4	51
1988-89—Denver Rangers		IHL	30	2	8	10	39
1989-90—Flint Spirits		IHL	31	1	2	3	66
1989-90—Cape Breton Oilers		AHL	26	2	4	6	39
NHL TOTALS			8	0	1	1	18

(c)—June, 1986—Drafted by Los Angeles Kings in 1986 NHL entry draft. Second Kings pick, 44th overall, third round.

(d)—December 12, 1988—Traded with Dean Kennedy by Los Angeles Kings to New York Rangers for Igor Liba, Todd Elik, Michael Boyce and future considerations.

GUY LAROSE

Center . . . 5'10" . . . 175 lbs. . . . Born, Hull, Que., July 31, 1967 . . . Shoots left . . . Son of Claude Larose (NHL 1960s and 70s, and currently scout with Hartford Whalers) . . . (February 22, 1985)—Fractured third left metacarpal.

Year	Team	League	Games	G.	A.	Pts.	Pen.
1983-84—Ottawa Senators		COJL	54	37	66	103	66
1984-85—Guelph Platers (c)		OHL	58	30	30	60	639
1985-86—Guelph Platers		OHL	37	12	36	48	55
1985-86—Ottawa 67's		OHL	28	19	25	44	63
1986-87—Ottawa 67's		OHL	66	28	49	77	77
1987-88—Moncton Golden Flames		AHL	77	22	31	53	127
1988-89—Winnipeg Jets		NHL	3	0	1	1	6
1988-89—Moncton Hawks		AHL	72	32	27	59	176
1989-90—Moncton Hawks		AHL	79	44	26	70	232
NHL TOTALS			3	0	1	1	6

(c)—June, 1985—Drafted as underage junior by Buffalo Sabres in 1985 NHL entry draft. Eleventh Sabres pick, 224th overall, 11th round.

STEVE LAROUCHE

Center . . . 5'11" . . . 165 lbs. . . . Born, Rouyn, Que., April 14, 1971 . . . Shoots right . . . (October 8, 1989)—Injured shoulder at St. Hyancinthe.

Year	Team	League	Games	G.	A.	Pts.	Pen.
1987-88—Trois-Rivieres Draveurs		QMJHL	66	11	29	40	25
1988-89—Trois-Rivieres Draveurs (c)		QMJHL	70	51	102	153	53
1989-90—Trois-Rivieres Draveurs (d)		QMJHL	60	55	90	145	40

(c)—June, 1989—Drafted by Montreal Canadiens in 1989 NHL entry draft. Third Canadiens pick, 41st overall, second round.

(d)—May 26, 1990—His QMJHL rights traded with Sabastien Parent and a sixth-round 1990 draft pick by Trois-Rivieres Draveurs to Chicoutimi Sagueneens for Paul Brosseau and Jasmin Ouellet.

JON LARSON

Defense . . . 6'1" . . . 190 lbs. . . . Born, Roseau, Minn., April 12, 1971 . . . Shoots left.

Year	Team	League	Games	G.	A.	Pts.	Pen.
1987-88—Roseau H.S.		Minn. H.S.	19	9	11	20	....
1988-89—Roseau H.S. (c)		Minn. H.S.	24	7	23	30	....
1989-90—University of North Dakota		WCHA	18	0	1	1	10

(c)—June, 1989—Drafted by New York Islanders in 1989 NHL entry draft. Eighth Islanders pick, 128th overall, seventh round.

REED DAVID LARSON

Defense . . . 6' . . . 195 lbs. . . . Born, Minneapolis, Minn., July 30, 1956 . . . Shoots right . . . (July, 1981)—Surgery to remove bone chips from right elbow . . . Holds NHL record for defensemen, scoring 20 goals in five straight seasons . . . Holds Detroit club record for most goals (27 in 1980-81), most assists (52 in 1982-83) and

points (74 in 1982-83) by a defenseman in one season . . . (1983-84)—Passed Tommy Williams to become all-time U.S.-born NHL career leader in points (Williams had 430) and assists (Williams had 269) . . . (1984-85)—Passed Tommy Williams to become highest goal scoring U.S. born player ever (Williams had 161 goals) . . . Holds Detroit Red Wings career record for goals, assists and points by a defenseman . . . (October, 1986)—Separated shoulder in Boston training camp . . . (June, 1987)—Crushed artery in his left arm in automobile accident . . . (October 14, 1987)—Injured left arm . . . (April, 1988)—Separated right shoulder.

Year	Team	League	Games	G.	A.	Pts.	Pen.
1974-75	University of Minnesota	WCHA	41	11	17	28	37
1975-76	University of Minnesota (a-c)	WCHA	42	13	29	42	94
1976-77	University of Minnesota	WCHA	21	10	15	25	30
1976-77	Detroit Red Wings	NHL	14	0	1	1	23
1977-78	Detroit Red Wings	NHL	75	19	41	60	95
1978-79	Detroit Red Wings	NHL	79	18	49	67	169
1979-80	Detroit Red Wings	NHL	80	22	44	66	101
1980-81	Detroit Red Wings	NHL	78	27	31	58	153
1981-82	Detroit Red Wings	NHL	80	21	39	60	112
1982-83	Detroit Red Wings	NHL	80	22	52	74	104
1983-84	Detroit Red Wings	NHL	78	23	39	62	122
1984-85	Detroit Red Wings	NHL	77	17	45	62	139
1985-86	Detroit Red Wings (d)	NHL	67	19	41	60	109
1985-86	Boston Bruins	NHL	13	3	4	7	8
1986-87	Boston Bruins	NHL	66	12	24	36	95
1987-88	Boston Bruins	NHL	62	10	24	34	93
1987-88	Maine Mariners	AHL	2	2	0	2	4
1988-89	Edmonton Oilers (e)	NHL	10	2	7	9	15
1988-89	New York Islanders (f)	NHL	33	7	13	20	35
1988-89	Minnesota North Stars (g-h)	NHL	11	0	9	9	18
1989-90	Alleghe	Italy	43	24	50	74	51
1989-90	Buffalo Sabres (i)	NHL	1	0	0	0	0
NHL TOTALS			904	222	463	685	1391

(c)—Drafted from University of Minnesota by Detroit Red Wings in second round of 1976 amateur draft.
(d)—March, 1986—Traded by Detroit Red Wings to Boston Bruins for Mike O'Connell.
(e)—September 30, 1988—Signed tryout agreement with Edmonton Oilers as a free agent and was released after 10 games.
(f)—December 5, 1988—Signed tryout agreement with New York Islanders.
(g)—March 7, 1989—Traded by New York Islanders to Minnesota North Stars for a seventh-round 1989 draft pick (Brett Harkins) and future considerations (Mike Kelfer).
(h)—August, 1989—Agreed to play in Italy for 1989-90 season.
(i)—March 6, 1990—Signed by Buffalo Sabres as free agent.

TYLER LARTER

Center . . . 5'10'' . . . 180 lbs. . . . Born, Charlottetown, P.E.I., March 12, 1968 . . . Shoots left.

Year	Team	League	Games	G.	A.	Pts.	Pen.
1983-84	Charlottetown Tigers	PEIJHL	26	24	32	56	....
1984-85	Sault Ste. Marie Greyhounds	OHL	64	14	26	40	48
1985-86	Sault Ste. Marie Greyhounds	OHL	60	15	40	55	137
1986-87	Sault Ste. Marie Greyhounds (c)	OHL	59	34	59	93	122
1987-88	Sault Ste. Marie Greyhounds	OHL	65	44	65	109	155
1988-89	Baltimore Skipjacks	AHL	71	9	19	28	189
1989-90	Baltimore Skipjacks	AHL	79	31	36	67	124
1989-90	Washington Capitals	NHL	1	0	0	0	0
NHL TOTALS			1	0	0	0	0

(c)—June, 1987—Drafted by Washington Capitals in 1987 NHL entry draft. Third Capitals pick, 78th overall, fourth round.

JIRI LATAL

Defense . . . 6' . . . 190 lbs. . . . Born, Olomouc, Czechoslovakia, February 2, 1967 . . . Shoots left . . . (December 19, 1989)—Fractured rib vs. Washington and missed 13 games . . . (January 25, 1990)—Separated shoulder vs. Winnipeg and missed five games . . . (February 28, 1990)—Bruised shoulder at Vancouver and missed five games . . . Younger brother of Joromir Latal.

Year	Team	League	Games	G.	A.	Pts.	Pen.
1984-85	Sparta Praha (c)	Czechoslovakia	26	2	2	4	10
1985-86	Sparta Praha	Czechoslovakia	27	3	2	5	....
1986-87	Sparta Praha	Czechoslovakia	9	1	0	1	2
1987-88	Dukla Trencin	Czechoslovakia	43	8	12	20	27
1988-89	Dukla Trencin	Czechoslovakia	45	6	17	23	....
1989-90	Philadelphia Flyers (d)	NHL	32	6	13	19	6
1989-90	Hershey Bears	AHL	22	10	18	28	10
NHL TOTALS			32	6	13	19	6

(c)—June, 1985—Selected by Toronto Maple Leafs in 1985 NHL entry draft. Sixth Maple Leafs pick, 106th overall, sixth round.
(d)—August 28, 1989—NHL Rights traded by Toronto Maple Leafs to Philadelphia Flyers for a third-round 1990 draft pick (Al Kinisky).

JAMES LATOS

Right Wing . . . 6'1'' . . . 200 lbs. . . . Born, Wakaw, Sask., January 4, 1966 . . . Shoots right . . . (September, 1988)—Injured right shoulder.

Year	Team	League	Games	G.	A.	Pts.	Pen.
1982-83	Prince Albert Midget	Sask.	28	11	18	29	20
1983-84	Humboldt Broncos	SAJHL	53	12	15	27	131
1984-85	Saskatoon Blades	WHL	62	9	9	18	120
1985-86	Saskatoon Blades	WHL	40	4	7	11	111
1985-86	Portland Winter Hawks	WHL	21	6	13	19	80
1986-87	Portland Winter Hawks	WHL	69	27	18	45	210
1987-88	Colorado Rangers (c)	IHL	38	11	12	23	98
1988-89	Denver Rangers	IHL	37	7	5	12	157

Year	Team	League	Games	G.	A.	Pts.	Pen.
1988-89	New York Rangers	NHL	1	0	0	0	0
1989-90	Flint Spirits	IHL	71	12	15	27	244
NHL TOTALS			1	0	0	0	0

(c)—June 5, 1987—Signed by New York Rangers as a free agent.

DAVE LATTA

Left Wing . . . 6' . . . 185 lbs. . . . Born, Thunder Bay, Ont., January 3, 1967 . . . Shoots left . . . Brother of Ken Latta . . . (December, 1984)—Shoulder injury . . . (October, 1987)—Separated shoulder . . . (May, 1989)—Shoulder surgery . . . (September 22, 1989)—Sprained left knee ligament during training camp.

Year	Team	League	Games	G.	A.	Pts.	Pen.
1982-83	Orillia Travelways	OJHL	43	16	25	41	26
1983-84	Kitchener Rangers	OHL	66	17	26	43	54
1984-85	Kitchener Rangers (c)	OHL	52	38	27	65	26
1985-86	Kitchener Rangers	OHL	55	36	34	70	60
1985-86	Fredericton Express	AHL	3	1	0	1	0
1985-86	Quebec Nordiques	NHL	1	0	0	0	0
1986-87	Kitchener Rangers	OHL	50	32	46	78	46
1987-88	Fredericton Express	AHL	34	11	21	32	28
1987-88	Quebec Nordiques	NHL	10	0	0	0	0
1988-89	Halifax Citadels	AHL	42	20	26	46	36
1988-89	Quebec Nordiques	NHL	24	4	8	12	4
1989-90	Halifax Citadels	AHL	34	11	5	16	45
NHL TOTALS			35	4	8	12	4

(c)—June, 1985—Drafted as underage junior by Quebec Nordiques in 1985 NHL entry draft. First Nordiques pick, 15th overall, first round.

BRAD LAUER

Right Wing . . . 6' . . . 195 lbs. . . . Born, Humbolt, Sask., October 27, 1966 . . . Shoots left . . . (October, 1988)—Fractured left kneecap . . . (March, 1989)—Reinjured left knee . . . (February, 1990)—Abdominal strain . . . (April, 1990)—Bruised right quadricep.

Year	Team	League	Games	G.	A.	Pts.	Pen.
1983-84	Regina Pats	WHL	60	5	7	12	51
1984-85	Regina Pats (c)	WHL	72	33	46	79	57
1985-86	Regina Pats	WHL	57	36	38	74	69
1986-87	New York Islanders	NHL	61	7	14	21	65
1987-88	New York Islanders	NHL	69	17	18	35	67
1988-89	Springfield Indians	AHL	8	1	5	6	0
1988-89	New York Islanders	NHL	14	3	2	5	2
1989-90	New York Islanders	NHL	63	6	18	24	19
1989-90	Springfield Indians	AHL	7	4	2	6	0
NHL TOTALS			207	33	52	85	153

(c)—June, 1985—Drafted as underage junior by New York Islanders in 1985 NHL entry draft. Third Islanders pick, 34th overall, second round.

PAUL LAUS

Defense . . . 6'1'' . . . 205 lbs. . . . Born, Grimsby, Ont., September 26, 1970 . . . Shoots right . . . (September, 1988)—Inflamed knuckles . . . (April 28, 1989)—Suspended three OHL playoff games for spearing Jamie Pegg vs. Peterborough.

Year	Team	League	Games	G.	A.	Pts.	Pen.
1986-87	St. Catherines Falcons	OPJHL	40	1	8	9	56
1987-88	Hamilton Steelhawks	OHL	56	1	9	10	171
1988-89	Niagara Falls Thunder (c)	OHL	49	1	10	11	225
1989-90	Niagara Falls Thunder	OHL	60	13	35	48	231

(c)—June, 1989—Drafted by Pittsburgh Penguins in 1989 NHL entry draft. Second Penguins pick, 37th overall, second round.

PETER LAVIOLETTE

Defense . . . 6'2'' . . . 200 lbs. . . . Born, Franklin, Mass., December 7, 1964 . . . Shoots left.

Year	Team	League	Games	G.	A.	Pts.	Pen.
1986-87	Indianapolis Checkers	IHL	72	10	20	30	146
1987-88	U. S. Olympic Team (c)	Int'l.	56	3	22	25	....
1987-88	Colorado Rangers	IHL	19	2	5	7	27
1988-89	Denver Rangers	IHL	57	6	19	25	120
1988-89	New York Rangers	NHL	12	0	0	0	6
1989-90	Flint Spirits	IHL	62	6	18	24	82
NHL TOTALS			12	0	0	0	6

(c)—June, 1987—Signed by New York Rangers as a free agent.

JAMES LAVISH

Right Wing . . . 5'11'' . . . 175 lbs. . . . Born, Albany, N.Y., October 13, 1970 . . . Shoots right.

Year	Team	League	Games	G.	A.	Pts.	Pen.
1988-89	Dearfield Academy (c)	Mass. H.S.	....	16	18	34	....
1989-90	Yale University	ECAC	27	6	11	17	40

(c)—June, 1989—Drafted by Boston Bruins in 1989 NHL entry draft. Ninth Bruins pick, 185th overall, ninth round.

DOMINIC LAVOIE

Defense . . . 6'2'' . . . 187 lbs. . . . Born, Montreal, Que., November 21, 1967 . . . Shoots right.

Year	Team	League	Games	G.	A.	Pts.	Pen.
1984-85	St. Jean Castors	QMJHL	30	1	1	2	10
1985-86	St. Jean Castors (c)	QMJHL	70	12	37	49	99
1986-87	St. Jean Castors	QMJHL	64	12	42	54	97

Year	Team	League	Games	G.	A.	Pts.	Pen.
1987-88—Peoria Rivermen		IHL	65	7	26	33	54
1988-89—St. Louis Blues		NHL	1	0	0	0	0
1988-89—Peoria Rivermen		IHL	69	11	31	42	98
1989-90—St. Louis Blues		NHL	13	1	1	2	16
1989-90—Peoria Rivermen		IHL	58	19	23	42	32
NHL TOTALS			14	1	1	2	16

(c)—September, 1986—Signed by St. Louis Blues as a free agent.

PAUL LAWLESS

Left Wing . . . 6' . . . 190 lbs. . . . Born, Scarborough, Ont., July 2, 1964 . . . Shoots left . . . (January 7, 1987)—Strained ligaments in left knee and missed 18 games . . . (April 1, 1987)—Broke finger in right hand when slashed by Claude Lemieux at Montreal . . . (November, 1987)—Bruised ribs.

Year	Team	League	Games	G.	A.	Pts.	Pen.
1980-81—Wexford Midgets		MTHL	40	38	40	78	....
1981-82—Windsor Spitfires (c)		OHL	68	24	25	49	47
1982-83—Windsor Spitfires		OHL	33	15	20	35	25
1982-83—Hartford Whalers		NHL	47	6	9	15	4
1983-84—Hartford Whalers		NHL	6	0	3	3	0
1983-84—Windsor Spitfires (b)		OHL	55	31	49	80	26
1984-85—Binghamton Whalers		AHL	8	1	1	2	0
1984-85—Salt Lake Golden Eagles		IHL	72	49	48	97	14
1985-86—Hartford Whalers		NHL	64	17	21	38	20
1986-87—Hartford Whalers		NHL	60	22	32	54	14
1987-88—Hartford Whalers (d)		NHL	27	4	5	9	16
1987-88—Philadelphia Flyers (e)		NHL	8	0	5	5	0
1987-88—Vancouver Canucks		NHL	13	0	1	1	0
1988-89—Milwaukee Admirals (f)		IHL	53	30	35	65	58
1988-89—Toronto Maple Leafs		NHL	7	0	0	0	0
1989-90—Davos		Switzerland	....	....	....	....	....
1989-90—Toronto Maple Leafs		NHL	6	0	1	1	0
1989-90—Newmarket Saints		AHL	3	1	0	1	0
NHL TOTALS			238	49	77	126	54

(c)—June, 1982—Selected by Hartford Whalers in 1982 NHL entry draft. First Whalers pick, 14th overall, first round.

(d)—January, 1988—Traded by Hartford Whalers to Philadelphia Flyers for Lindsay Carson.

(e)—March, 1988—Traded with Vancouver's fifth-round 1989 draft pick by Philadelphia Flyers to Vancouver Canucks for Willie Huber.

(f)—February 25, 1989—Traded by Vancouver Canucks to Toronto Maple Leafs for Peter DeBoer.

BRIAN LAWTON

Center . . . 6' . . . 180 lbs. . . . Born, New Brunswick, N.J., June 29, 1965 . . . Shoots left . . . First American-born player to be a first overall draft choice in the NHL . . . (November, 1983)—Separated shoulder . . . (October, 1984)—Injured shoulder during training camp . . . (October, 1987)—Broken thumb . . . (February, 1988)—Bruised ribs when struck by teammate Frantisek Musil at Toronto . . . (October 8, 1988)—Suspended by Minnesota North Stars for refusing to report to Kalamazoo Wings . . . (January 27, 1989)—Lost 2 teeth and needed 12 stitches to close cut over left eye when struck by stick of Perry Anderson at New Jersey . . . (January 28, 1989)—Broke left wrist when slashed by Robert Picard vs. Quebec . . . (March 25, 1989)—Ran into the boards and sprained an ankle vs. St. Louis . . . (September, 1989)—Cracked bone in left foot.

Year	Team	League	Games	G.	A.	Pts.	Pen.
1981-82—Mount St. Charles H.S.		R.I. H.S.	26	45	43	88	..
1982-83—Mount St. Charles H.S. (c)		R.I. H.S.	23	40	43	83	..
1982-83—U.S. National Team		Int'l	7	3	2	5	6
1983-84—Minnesota North Stars		NHL	58	10	21	31	33
1984-85—Springfield Indians		AHL	42	14	28	42	37
1984-85—Minnesota North Stars		NHL	40	5	6	11	24
1985-86—Minnesota North Stars		NHL	65	18	17	35	36
1986-87—Minnesota North Stars		NHL	66	21	23	44	86
1987-88—Minnesota North Stars		NHL	74	17	24	41	71
1988-89—New York Rangers (d-e)		NHL	30	7	10	17	39
1988-89—Hartford Whalers		NHL	35	10	16	26	28
1989-90—Hartford Whalers (f)		NHL	13	2	1	3	6
1989-90—Quebec Nordiques (g)		NHL	14	5	6	11	10
1989-90—Boston Bruins (h)		NHL	8	0	0	0	14
1989-90—Maine Mariners		AHL	5	0	0	0	14
NHL TOTALS			403	95	124	219	347

(c)—June, 1983—Drafted by Minnesota North Stars in 1983 NHL entry draft. First North Stars pick, first overall, first round.

(d)—October 11, 1988—Traded with Igor Liba and NHL rights to Eric Bennett by Minnesota North Stars to New York Rangers for Mark Tinordi, Paul Jerrard, Mike Sullivan, Bret Barnett and the Los Angeles Kings third-round draft pick (Murray Garbutt).

(e)—December 26, 1988—Traded with Norm Maciver and Don Maloney by New York Rangers to Hartford Whalers for Carey Wilson and a fifth-round 1990 draft pick.

(f)—December 1, 1989—Acquired by Quebec Nordiques on waivers from the Hartford Whalers for $12,500.

(g)—February 1, 1990—Released by Quebec Nordiques.

(h)—February 6, 1990—Signed by Boston Bruins as a free agent.

DEREK LAXDAL

Right Wing . . . 6'1" . . . 180 lbs. . . . Born, St. Boniface, Man., February 21, 1966 . . . Shoots right . . . (January, 1985)—Broken hand . . . (October 22, 1988)—Injured back vs. Calgary . . . (November, 1988)—Bruised knee . . . (January, 1989)—Injured finger . . . (April, 1990)—Hyperextended elbow.

Year	Team	League	Games	G.	A.	Pts.	Pen.
1982-83—Portland Winter Hawks		WHL	39	4	9	13	27
1983-84—Brandon Wheat Kings (c)		WHL	70	23	20	43	86
1984-85—Brandon Wheat Kings		WHL	69	61	41	102	72

Year	Team	League	Games	G.	A.	Pts.	Pen.
1984-85—St. Catharines Saints		AHL	5	3	2	5	2
1984-85—Toronto Maple Leafs		NHL	3	0	0	0	6
1985-86—Brandon Wheat Kings		WHL	42	34	35	69	62
1985-86—New Westminister Bruins		WHL	18	9	6	15	14
1985-86—St. Catharines Saints		AHL	7	0	1	1	15
1986-87—Newmarket Saints		AHL	78	24	20	44	89
1986-87—Toronto Maple Leafs		NHL	2	0	0	0	7
1987-88—Toronto Maple Leafs		NHL	5	0	0	0	0
1987-88—Newmarket Saints		AHL	67	18	25	43	81
1988-89—Toronto Maple Leafs		NHL	41	9	6	15	65
1988-89—Newmarket Saints		AHL	34	22	22	44	53
1989-90—Newmarket Saints (d)		AHL	23	7	8	15	52
1989-90—New York Islanders		NHL	12	3	1	4	4
1989-90—Springfield Indians		AHL	28	13	12	25	42
NHL TOTALS			63	12	7	19	88

(c)—June, 1984—Drafted as an underage junior by Toronto Maple Leafs in 1984 NHL entry draft. Seventh Maple Leafs pick, 151st overall, eighth round.

(d)—December 20, 1989—Traded with Paul Gagne and Jack Capuano by Toronto Maple Leafs to New York Islanders for Gilles Thibaudeau and Mike Stevens.

STEPHEN LEACH

Right Wing . . . 5'11" . . . 180 lbs. . . . Born, Cambridge, Mass., January 16, 1966 . . . Shoots right . . . (February, 1989)—Strained left knee . . . Brother of Jay Leach (assistant coach of Hartford Whalers) . . . (March, 1990)—Injured thumb.

Year	Team	League	Games	G.	A.	Pts.	Pen.
1983-84—Matignon H.S. (c)		Mass. H.S.	21	27	22	49	49
1984-85—Univ. of New Hampshire		H. East	41	12	25	37	53
1985-86—Univ. of New Hampshire		H. East	25	22	6	28	30
1985-86—Washington Capitals		NHL	11	1	1	2	2
1986-87—Binghamton Whalers		AHL	54	18	21	39	39
1986-87—Washington Capitals		NHL	15	1	0	1	6
1987-88—U.S. Olympic Team		Int'l	53	26	20	46	..
1987-88—Washington Capitals		NHL	8	1	1	2	17
1988-89—Washington Capitals		NHL	74	11	19	30	94
1989-90—Washington Capitals		NHL	70	18	14	32	104
NHL TOTALS			178	32	35	67	223

(c)—June, 1984—Drafted by Washington Capitals in 1984 NHL entry draft. Second Capitals pick, 34th overall, second round.

WILLIAM (JAMIE) LEACH

Right Wing . . . 6'1" . . . 190 lbs. . . . Born, Winnipeg, Man., August 25, 1969 . . . Shoots right . . . Son of Reggie Leach (Philadelphia Flyer in 1970s) . . . (February, 1986)—Hip injury.

Year	Team	League	Games	G.	A.	Pts.	Pen.
1984-85—Cherry Hill East H.S.		NJHS	60	48	51	99	68
1985-86—New Westminster Bruins		WHL	58	8	7	15	20
1986-87—Hamilton Steelhawks (c)		OHL	64	12	19	31	67
1987-88—Hamilton Steelhawks		OHL	64	24	19	43	79
1988-89—Niagara Falls Thunder		OHL	58	45	62	107	47
1989-90—Muskegon Lumberjacks		IHL	72	22	36	58	39
1989-90—Pittsburgh Penguins		NHL	10	0	3	3	0
NHL TOTALS			10	0	3	3	0

(c)—June, 1987—Drafted as underage junior by Pittsburgh Penguins in 1987 NHL entry draft. Third Penguins pick, 47th overall, third round.

GREG LEAHY

Center . . . 6'3" . . . 185 lbs. . . . Born, North Bay, Ont., February 19, 1970 . . . Shoots left.

Year	Team	League	Games	G.	A.	Pts.	Pen.
1986-87—Calgary Wranglers		WHL	64	6	16	22	170
1987-88—Lethbridge Hurricanes		WHL	56	18	24	42	161
1988-89—Portland Winter Hawks (c)		WHL	66	28	49	77	128
1989-90—Portland Winter Hawks		WHL	50	20	43	63	131

(c)—June, 1989—Drafted by New York Rangers in 1989 NHL entry draft. Eighth Rangers pick, 139th overall, seventh round.

JAMES T. LEAVINS

Defense . . . 5'11" . . . 185 lbs. . . . Born, Dinsmore, Sask., July 28, 1960 . . . Shoots left . . . (October, 1986)—Lower back spasms.

Year	Team	League	Games	G.	A.	Pts.	Pen.
1980-81—Univ. of Denver		WCHA	40	8	18	26	18
1981-82—Univ. of Denver		WCHA	41	8	34	42	56
1982-83—Univ. of Denver		WCHA	33	16	24	40	20
1983-84—Univ. of Denver		WCHA	39	13	24	37	38
1983-84—Tulsa Oilers		CHL	1	0	0	0	0
1984-85—Fort Wayne Komets		IHL	76	5	50	55	57
1985-86—Adirondack Red Wings		AHL	36	4	21	25	19
1985-86—Detroit Red Wings (c-d)		NHL	37	2	11	13	26
1986-87—New Haven Nighthawks		AHL	54	7	21	28	16
1986-87—New York Rangers		NHL	4	0	1	1	4
1987-88—New Haven Nighthawks		AHL	11	2	5	7	6
1987-88—Salt Lake Golden Eagles (b-e)		IHL	68	12	45	57	45
1988-89—KooKoo		Finland	42	12	11	23	39
1988-89—Salt Lake Golden Eagles		IHL	25	8	13	21	14
1989-90—KooKoo		Finland	44	7	24	31	36
1989-90—Salt Lake Golden Eagles		IHL	11	0	6	6	2
NHL TOTALS			41	2	12	14	30

(c)—November, 1985—Signed by Detroit Red Wings as a free agent.

(d)—July, 1986—Traded with Kelly Kisio, Lane Lambert and a fifth-round 1988 draft pick by Detroit Red Wings to New York Rangers for Glen Hanlon, third-round 1987 (Dennis Holland) and 1988 draft pick and future considerations.

(e)—November, 1987—Traded by New York Rangers to Calgary Flames for Don Mercier.

247

BENOIT LEBEAU

Left Wing . . . 6'1" . . . 185 lbs. . . . Born, Montreal, Que., June 4, 1968 . . . Shoots left.

Year	Team	League	Games	G.	A.	Pts.	Pen.
1987-88—Merrimack College (c)	ECAC	40	35	38	73	52
1988-89—Merrimack College	ECAC	32	18	20	38	46
1989-90—Merrimack College	ECAC	32	9	6	15	46

(c)—June, 1988—Drafted by Winnipeg Jets in 1988 NHL entry draft. Sixth Jets pick, 101st overall, fifth round.

PATRICK LEBEAU

Left Wing . . . 5'10" . . . 175 lbs. . . . Born, St. Jerome, Que., March 17, 1970 . . . Shoots left . . . Brother of Stephane Lebeau.

Year	Team	League	Games	G.	A.	Pts.	Pen.
1986-87—Shawinigan Cataractes	QMJHL	65	77	90	167	60
1987-88—Shawinigan Cataractes	QMJHL	53	43	56	99	116
1988-89—Shaw./St. Jean Castors (c-d)	QMJHL	66	62	87	149	89
1989-90—St. Jean/Vict. Tigres (a-e-f)	QMJHL	72	68	*106	*174	109

(c)—November 5, 1988—Traded with QHL rights to Eric Metivier by Shawinigan Cataractes to St. Jean Castors for Steve Cadieux and Pierre Cote.
(d)—June, 1989—Drafted by Montreal Canadiens in 1989 NHL entry draft. Eighth Canadiens pick, 147th overall, eighth round.
(e)—February 15, 1990—Traded with Francois Leroux and Jean Blouin by St. Jean Lynx to Victoriaville Tigres for Trevor Duhaime and second and third round draft picks and future considerations.
(f)—Won Jean Beliveau Trophy (Leading QMJHL scorer).

STEPHAN LEBEAU

Center . . . 5'10" . . . 180 lbs. . . . Born, Sherbrooke, Que., February 28, 1968 . . . Shoots right . . . (1988-89)—Set AHL single-season goal-scoring and points records . . . Brother of Patrick Lebeau.

Year	Team	League	Games	G.	A.	Pts.	Pen.
1984-85—Shawinigan Cataractes	QMJHL	66	41	38	79	18
1985-86—Shawinigan Cataractes	QMJHL	72	69	77	146	22
1986-87—Shawinigan Cataractes (a-c)	QMJHL	65	77	90	167	60
1987-88—Shawinigan Cataractes (b-d)	QMJHL	67	*94	94	188	66
1988-89—Sherbrooke Canadiens (a-e-f-g)	AHL	78	*70	64	*134	47
1988-89—Montreal Canadiens	NHL	1	0	1	1	2
1989-90—Montreal Canadiens	NHL	57	15	20	35	11
NHL TOTALS		58	15	21	36	13

(c)—September, 1986—Signed as a free agent by Montreal Canadiens.
(d)—Won Frank Selke Trophy (Most Gentlemanly Player).
(e)—Won John B. Sollenberger Trophy (Leading AHL scorer).
(f)—Won Les Cunningham Plaque (AHL MVP).
(g)—Won Dudley (Red) Garrett Memorial Trophy (Top AHL Rookie).

JOHN GLENN LeBLANC

Left Wing . . . 6'1" . . . 190 lbs. . . . Born, Campellton, N.B., January 21, 1964 . . . Shoots left . . . (March, 1989)—Tendinitis in right knee.

Year	Team	League	Games	G.	A.	Pts.	Pen.
1985-86—U. of New Brunswick (c-d)	CIAU	24	38	26	64	32
1986-87—Fredericton Express	AHL	75	40	30	70	27
1986-87—Vancouver Canucks	NHL	2	1	0	1	0
1987-88—Fredericton Express	AHL	35	26	25	51	54
1987-88—Vancouver Canucks	NHL	41	12	10	22	18
1988-89—Milwaukee Admirals (e)	IHL	61	39	31	70	42
1988-89—Edmonton Oilers	NHL	2	1	0	1	0
1988-89—Cape Breton Oilers	AHL	3	4	0	4	0
1989-90—Cape Breton Oilers	AHL	77	54	34	88	50
NHL TOTALS		45	14	10	24	18

(c)—Named winner of the Senator Joseph A. Sullivan Trophy to the top Canadian college player.
(d)—April, 1986—Signed by Vancouver Canucks as a free agent.
(e)—March 7, 1989—Traded with a fifth-round 1989 draft pick (Peter White) by Vancouver Canucks to Edmonton Oilers for Greg Adams and Doug Smith.

SEAN LeBRUN

Left Wing . . . 6'2" . . . 200 lbs. . . . Born, Prince George, B.C., May 2, 1969 . . . Shoots left . . . (March 26, 1989)—Broken wrist in WHL game vs. Portland.

Year	Team	League	Games	G.	A.	Pts.	Pen.
1984-85—Prince George Midget	B.C. Midget	53	61	51	112	46
1985-86—Spokane Chiefs	WHL	70	6	11	17	41
1986-87—Spokane Chiefs	WHL	6	2	5	7	9
1986-87—New Westminster Bruins	WHL	55	21	32	53	47
1987-88—New Westminster Bruins (b-c)	WHL	72	36	53	89	59
1988-89—Tri-City Americans	WHL	71	52	73	125	92
1989-90—Springfield Indians	AHL	63	9	33	42	20

(c)—June, 1988—Drafted by New York Islanders in 1988 NHL entry draft. Third Islanders pick, 37th overall, third round.

JOHN LeCLAIR

Center . . . 6'1" . . . 185 lbs. . . . Born, St. Albans, Vt., July 5, 1969 . . . Shoots left . . . (1988-89)—Missed 16 games with thigh injury . . . (January 20, 1990)—Injured knee at R.P.I., required surgery and out for the season.

Year	Team	League	Games	G.	A.	Pts.	Pen.
1985-86—Bellows Free Acad.	Ver. H.S.	22	41	28	69	14
1986-87—Bellows Free Acad. (c)	Ver. H.S.	23	44	40	84	25
1987-88—University of Vermont	ECAC	31	12	22	34	62
1988-89—University of Vermont	ECAC	19	9	12	21	40
1989-90—University of Vermont	ECAC	10	10	6	16	38

(c)—June, 1987—Drafted by Montreal Canadiens in 1987 NHL entry draft. Second Canadiens pick, 33rd overall, second round.

GRANT LEDYARD

Defense . . . 6'2" . . . 190 lbs. . . . Born, Winnipeg, Man., November 19, 1961 . . . Shoots left . . . (October, 1984)—Hip injury . . . (October, 1987)—Sprained ankle.

Year	Team	League	Games	G.	A.	Pts.	Pen.
1979-80—Fort Garry Blues	MJHL	49	13	24	37	90
1980-81—Saskatoon Blades	WHL	71	9	28	37	148
1981-82—Fort Garry Blues (a-c)	MJHL	63	25	45	70	150
1982-83—Tulsa Oilers (d)	CHL	80	13	29	42	115
1983-84—Tulsa Oilers (e)	CHL	58	9	17	26	71
1984-85—New Haven Nighthawks	AHL	36	6	20	26	18
1984-85—New York Rangers	NHL	42	8	12	20	53
1985-86—New York Rangers (f)	NHL	27	2	9	11	20
1985-86—Los Angeles Kings	NHL	52	7	18	25	78
1986-87—Los Angeles Kings	NHL	67	14	23	37	93
1987-88—New Haven Nighthawks	AHL	3	2	1	3	4
1987-88—Los Angeles Kings (g)	NHL	23	1	7	8	52
1987-88—Washington Capitals	NHL	21	4	3	7	14
1988-89—Washington Capitals (h)	NHL	61	3	11	14	43
1988-89—Buffalo Sabres	NHL	13	1	5	6	8
1989-90—Buffalo Sabres	NHL	67	2	13	15	37
NHL TOTALS		373	42	101	143	398

(c)—Named Manitoba Junior Hockey League Most Valuable Player.
(d)—July, 1982—Signed by New York Rangers as a free agent.
(e)—Won Max McNab Trophy (Playoff MVP).
(f)—December, 1986—Traded by New York Rangers to Los Angeles Kings for Brian MacLellan and a fourth round 1987 draft pick (Michael Sullivan). The Rangers also sent a second round 1986 (Neil Wilkinson) and a fourth round 1987 draft pick (John Weisbrod) to Minnesota and the North Stars sent Roland Melanson to the Kings as part of the same deal.
(g)—February, 1988—Traded by Los Angeles Kings to Washington Capitals for Craig Laughlin.
(h)—March 6, 1989—Traded with Clint Malarchuk and a sixth-round 1991 draft pick by the Washington Capitals to Buffalo Sabres for Calle Johansson and a second-round 1989 draft pick (Bryon Dafoe).

GARY LEEMAN

Right Wing . . . 6' . . . 175 lbs. . . . Born, Toronto, Ont., February 19, 1964 . . . Shoots right . . . (January, 1984)—Broken finger . . . (March, 1984)—Broken wrist . . . (March, 1985)—Shoulder separation . . . (April 14, 1987)—Cracked kneecap at St. Louis . . . (April, 1988)—Cracked bone in right hand . . . (October 22, 1988)—Fractured bone behind left ear when struck by a shot vs. Calgary . . . (January, 1988)—Injured back . . . Has also played Defense.

Year	Team	League	Games	G.	A.	Pts.	Pen.
1980-81—Notre Dame Midgets	SCMHL	24	15	23	38	28
1981-82—Regina Pats (c)	WHL	72	19	41	60	112
1982-83—Regina Pats (a-d)	WHL	63	24	62	86	88
1983-84—Toronto Maple Leafs	NHL	52	4	8	12	31
1984-85—St. Catharines Saints	AHL	7	2	2	4	11
1984-85—Toronto Maple Leafs	NHL	53	5	26	31	72
1985-86—St. Catharines Saints	AHL	25	15	13	28	6
1985-86—Toronto Maple Leafs	NHL	53	9	23	32	20
1986-87—Toronto Maple Leafs	NHL	80	21	31	52	66
1987-88—Toronto Maple Leafs	NHL	80	30	31	61	62
1988-89—Toronto Maple Leafs	NHL	61	32	43	75	66
1989-90—Toronto Maple Leafs	NHL	80	51	44	95	63
NHL TOTALS		459	152	206	358	380

(c)—June, 1982—Drafted by Toronto Maple Leafs as underage junior in 1982 NHL entry draft. Second Maple Leafs pick, 24th overall, second round.
(d)—Won WHL Top Defenseman Trophy.

BRIAN LEETCH

Defense . . . 5'11" . . . 170 lbs. . . . Born, Corpus Christi, Tex., March 3, 1968 . . . Shoots left . . . (July, 1987)—Suffered sprained ligaments in his left knee at U.S. Olympic Sports Festival . . . (December, 1988)—Fractured bone in left foot . . . (March 15, 1989)—Hip pointer vs. Winnipeg . . . Set NHL record for rookie defensemen with 23 goals in 1988-89 . . . (March 14, 1990)—Fractured left ankle at Toronto.

Year	Team	League	Games	G.	A.	Pts.	Pen.
1984-85—Avon Old Farms H.S.	Conn.	26	30	46	76	15
1985-86—Avon Old Farms H.S. (c)	Conn.	28	40	44	84	18
1986-87—Boston College (a-d-e-f)	H. East	37	9	38	47	10
1987-88—U.S. Olympic Team	Int'l	53	13	64	77	..
1987-88—New York Rangers	NHL	17	2	12	14	0
1988-89—New York Rangers (g-h)	NHL	68	23	48	71	50
1989-90—New York Rangers	NHL	72	11	45	56	26
NHL TOTALS		157	36	105	141	76

(c)—June, 1986—Drafted by New York Rangers in 1986 NHL entry draft. First Rangers pick, ninth overall, first round.
(d)—Named Hockey East Rookie-of-the-Year.
(e)—Named Hockey East Player-of-the-Year.
(f)—Named to U.S. College First-Team All-America Team.
(g)—Named THE SPORTING NEWS NHL Rookie of the Year.
(h)—Won Calder Memorial Trophy (NHL Rookie-of-the-Year).

SYLVAIN LEFEBVRE

Defense . . . 6'2" . . . 185 lbs. . . . Born, Richmond, Que., October 14, 1967 . . . Shoots left.

Year	Team	League	Games	G.	A.	Pts.	Pen.
1984-85—Laval Voisins	QMJHL	66	7	5	12	31
1985-86—Laval Voisins (c)	QMJHL	71	8	17	25	48
1986-87—Laval Voisins	QMJHL	70	10	36	46	44

Year	Team	League	Games	G.	A.	Pts.	Pen.
1987-88—Sherbrooke Canadiens		AHL	79	3	24	27	73
1988-89—Sherbrooke Canadiens (b)		AHL	77	15	32	47	119
1989-90—Montreal Canadiens		NHL	68	3	10	13	61
NHL TOTALS			68	3	10	13	61

(c)—September, 1986—Signed by Montreal Canadiens as a free agent.

ALEXANDER LEGAULT

Defense . . . 6'1'' . . . 205 lbs. . . . Born, Chicoutimi, Que., December 27, 1971 . . . Shoots right.

Year	Team	League	Games	G.	A.	Pts.	Pen.
1987-88—Ste. Foy Gouverneurs		Que. Midget	39	15	30	45	....
1988-89—Notre Dame Hounds		SJHL	64	9	31	40	....
1989-90—Boston University (c)		H. East	43	9	21	30	54

(c)—June 16, 1990—Selected by Edmonton Oilers in 1990 NHL entry draft. Second Oilers pick, 38th overall, second round.

JONI LEHTO

Defense . . . 6' . . . 190 lbs. . . . Born, Turku, Finland, July 15, 1970 . . . Shoots left . . . Brother of Petteri Lehto.

Year	Team	League	Games	G.	A.	Pts.	Pen.
1987-88—Turko TPS		Finland	30	9	14	23	42
1988-89—Ottawa 67's		OHL	63	9	25	34	26
1989-90—Ottawa 67's (b-c)		OHL	60	17	55	72	58

(c)—June 16, 1990—Selected by New York Islanders in 1990 NHL entry draft. Fifth Islanders pick, 111th overall, sixth round.

ERIC LeMARQUE

Right Wing . . . 5'10'' . . . 183 lbs. . . . Born, Canoga Park, Calif., July 1, 1969 . . . Shoots right.

Year	Team	League	Games	G.	A.	Pts.	Pen.
1986-87—Northern Michigan Univ. (c)		WCHA	38	5	12	17	49
1987-88—Northern Michigan Univ.		WCHA	39	8	22	30	54
1988-89—Northern Michigan Univ.		WCHA	43	20	17	37	40
1989-90—Northern Michigan Univ.		WCHA	40	17	32	49	45

(c)—June, 1987—Drafted by Boston Bruins in 1987 NHL entry draft. Twelfth Bruins pick, 224th overall, 11th round.

CLAUDE LEMIEUX

Right Wing . . . 6'1'' . . . 215 lbs. . . . Born, Buckingham, Que., July 16, 1965 . . . Shoots right . . . Brother of Jocelyn Lemieux . . . (October, 1987)—Torn ankle ligaments during Canada Cup . . . (January 14, 1988)—Fractured orbital bone above right eye when elbowed by Gord Kluzak vs. Boston . . . (March, 1989)—Pulled groin . . . (November 1, 1989)—Surgery to repair torn stomach muscle and missed 41 games.

Year	Team	League	Games	G.	A.	Pts.	Pen.
1981-82—Richelieu Eclairevrs		Que. Midget	48	24	48	72	96
1982-83—Trois-Rivieres Draveurs (c)		QMJHL	62	28	38	66	187
1983-84—Verdun Juniors (b)		QMJHL	51	41	45	86	225
1983-84—Montreal Canadiens		NHL	8	1	1	2	12
1984-85—Verdun Juniors (a-d)		QMJHL	52	58	66	124	152
1984-85—Montreal Canadiens		NHL	1	0	1	1	7
1985-86—Sherbrooke Canadiens		AHL	58	21	32	53	145
1985-86—Montreal Canadiens		NHL	10	1	2	3	22
1986-87—Montreal Canadiens		NHL	76	27	26	53	156
1987-88—Montreal Canadiens		NHL	80	31	30	61	137
1988-89—Montreal Canadiens		NHL	69	29	22	51	136
1989-90—Montreal Canadiens (e)		NHL	39	8	10	18	106
NHL TOTALS			283	97	92	189	576

(c)—June, 1983—Drafted as underage junior by Montreal Canadiens in 1983 NHL entry draft. Second Canadiens pick, 26th overall, second round.

(d)—Won Guy Lafleur Trophy (Playoff MVP).

(e)—September 4, 1990—Traded by Montreal Canadiens to New Jersey Devils for Sylvain Turgeon.

JOCELYN LEMIEUX

Left Wing . . . 5'11'' . . . 205 lbs. . . . Born, Mont Laurier, Que., November 18, 1967 . . . Shoots left . . . Brother of Claude Lemieux . . . Also plays Right Wing . . . (December, 1986)—Severed tendon in little finger of left hand . . . (January, 1988)—Broke left leg and tore ligaments.

Year	Team	League	Games	G.	A.	Pts.	Pen.
1984-85—Laval Voisins		QMJHL	68	13	19	32	92
1985-86—Laval Titans (a-c)		QMJHL	71	57	68	125	131
1986-87—St. Louis Blues		NHL	53	10	8	18	94
1987-88—Peoria Rivermen		IHL	8	0	5	5	35
1987-88—St. Louis Blues (d)		NHL	23	1	0	1	42
1988-89—Montreal Canadiens		NHL	1	0	1	1	0
1988-89—Sherbrooke Canadiens		AHL	73	25	28	53	134
1989-90—Montreal Canadiens (e)		NHL	34	4	2	6	61
1989-90—Chicago Black Hawks		NHL	39	10	11	21	47
NHL TOTALS			150	25	22	47	244

(c)—June, 1986—Drafted as underage junior by St. Louis Blues in 1986 NHL entry draft. First Blues pick, 10th overall, first round.

(d)—August, 1988—Traded with Darrell May and second-round draft choice in 1989 (Patrice Brisebois) by St. Louis Blues to Montreal Canadiens for Sergio Momesso and Vincent Riendeau.

(e)—January 15, 1990—Traded by Montreal Canadiens to Chicago Black Hawks for a third-round 1990 draft pick (Charles Poulin).

MARIO LEMIEUX

Center . . . 6'4'' . . . 200 lbs. . . . Born, Montreal, Que., October 5, 1965 . . . Shoots right . . . Set single-season record in Quebec Junior League in 1983-84 for goals (133) and points (282) as well as a Quebec League record for most career assists (315) . . . Brother of Alain Lemieux . . . (September, 1984)—Sprained left knee in training camp and fitted with a playing brace. . . . (December 2, 1984)—Resprained knee in collision with Darren Veitch at Washington . . . (December 20, 1986)—Sprained right knee when checked by Ron Sutter vs. Philadelphia . . . (March, 1987)—Fitted for two knee braces . . . (November, 1987)—Bruised right shoulder when checked by Alan Kerr vs. N.Y. Islanders . . . (November 3, 1988)—Sprained right wrist at Quebec . . . (December 15, 1988)—Became Pittsburgh Penguins all-time assist leader, passing Syl Apps (349) . . . Became the first NHL scoring leader to have 100 penalty minutes since Bobby Orr in 1974-75 . . . Set NHL record for most shorthanded goals in a season (13 in 1988-89) . . . Tied single playoff game records for most goals (5 on April 25, 1989) and most points (8 on April 25, 1989) . . . (February, 1990)—Disclosed he was playing with a herniated disk . . . (February 14, 1990)—After collecting points in 45 straight games, he was unable to play vs. N.Y. Rangers due to back pain. He was out until the last game of the season, undergoing physical therapy. (July 11, 1990)—Had surgery to remove part of herniated disk and may miss beginning of season . . . One of only three players (Wayne Gretzky and Peter Stastny) to have 100-point seasons in their first six NHL seasons.

Year	Team	League	Games	G.	A.	Pts.	Pen.
1981-82—Laval Voisins		QMJHL	64	30	66	96	22
1982-83—Laval Voisins (b)		QMJHL	66	84	100	184	76
1983-84—Laval Voisins (a-c)		QMJHL	70	*133	*149	*282	92
1984-85—Pittsburgh Penguins (d-e)		NHL	73	43	57	100	54
1985-86—Pittsburgh Penguins (b-f)		NHL	79	48	93	141	43
1986-87—Pittsburgh Penguins (b)		NHL	63	54	53	107	57
1987-88—Pittsburgh Penguins (a-g-h-i)		NHL	77	*70	98	*168	92
1988-89—Pittsburgh Penguins (a-g-i)		NHL	76	*85	*114	*199	100
1989-90—Pittsburgh Penguins		NHL	59	45	78	123	78
NHL TOTALS			427	345	493	838	424

(c)—June, 1984—Drafted as underage junior by Pittsburgh Penguins in 1984 NHL entry draft. First Penguins pick, first overall, first round.

(d)—Won Calder Memorial Trophy (NHL Top Rookie).

(e)—Named NHL Rookie of the Year in poll of players by THE SPORTING NEWS.

(f)—Won 1986 Lester B. Pearson Award as the NHL's outstanding player. Voting is done by the NHLPA.

(g)—Won Art Ross Memorial Trophy (NHL Leading Scorer).

(h)—Won Hart Memorial Trophy (Most Valuable Player).

(i)—Named NHL Player of the Year in poll of players by THE SPORTING NEWS.

TIM LENARDON

Center . . . 6'2'' . . . 185 lbs. . . . Born, Trail, B.C., May 11, 1962 . . . Shoots left . . . (December, 1986)—Separated shoulder in AHL game.

Year	Team	League	Games	G.	A.	Pts.	Pen.
1981-82—Trail		KIHL	40	48	61	138	....
1982-83—Trail		KIHL	38	86	86	172	....
1983-84—Univ. of Brandon		CWUAA	24	22	21	43	....
1984-85—Univ. of Brandon		CWUAA	24	21	39	60	....
1985-86—Univ. of Brandon (c-d)		CWUAA	26	26	40	66	33
1986-87—New Jersey Devils		NHL	7	1	1	2	0
1986-87—Maine Mariners		AHL	61	28	35	63	30
1987-88—Utica Devils		AHL	79	38	53	91	72
1988-89—Utica Devils (e)		AHL	63	28	27	55	48
1988-89—Milwaukee Admirals		IHL	15	6	5	11	27
1989-90—Vancouver Canucks		NHL	8	1	0	1	4
1989-90—Milwaukee Admirals		IHL	66	32	36	68	134
NHL TOTALS			15	2	1	3	4

(c)—Named Canadian College Player of the Year.

(d)—August, 1986—Signed by New Jersey Devils as a free agent.

(e)—March 7, 1989—Traded by New Jersey Devils to Vancouver Canucks for Claude Vilgrain.

FRANCOIS LEROUX

Defense . . . 6'5'' . . . 217 lbs. . . . Born, St. Adele, Que., April 18, 1970 . . . Shoots left . . . (March 20, 1989)—Separated shoulder vs. Laval when checked by Neil Carnes . . . (March 18, 1990)—Torn left knee ligaments vs. St. Jean when teammate Patrick Cloutier and a St. Jean player fell on his leg . . . (March 22, 1990)—Surgery to left knee.

Year	Team	League	Games	G.	A.	Pts.	Pen.
1986-87—Laval Laurentides Midget		Quebec	42	5	11	16	76
1987-88—St. Jean Casters (c)		QMJHL	58	3	8	11	143
1988-89—Edmonton Oilers		NHL	2	0	0	0	0
1988-89—St. Jean Casters		QMJHL	57	8	34	42	185
1989-90—Edmonton Oilers		NHL	3	0	1	1	0
1989-90—St. Jean/Victoria. Tigres (d)		QHL	54	4	33	37	160
NHL TOTALS			5	0	1	1	0

(c)—June, 1988—Drafted by Edmonton Oilers in 1988 NHL entry draft. First Oilers pick, 19th overall, first round.

(d)—February 15, 1990—Traded with Patrick Lebeau and Jean Blouin by St. Jean Lynx to Victoriaville Tigres for Trevor Duhaime, second and third round draft picks and future considerations.

CURTIS LESCHYSHYN

Defense . . . 6' . . . 205 lbs. . . . Born, Thompson, Manitoba, September 21, 1969 . . . Shoots left . . . (January 10, 1989)—Separated shoulder when checked by Dale Hunter vs. Washington . . . (November, 1989)—Sprained left knee.

Year	Team	League	Games	G.	A.	Pts.	Pen.
1985-86—Saskatoon Blades		WHL	1	0	0	0	0
1986-87—Saskatoon Blades		WHL	70	14	26	40	107

Year	Team	League	Games	G.	A.	Pts.	Pen.
1987-88—Saskatoon Blades (a-c)		WHL	56	14	41	55	86
1988-89—Quebec Nordiques		NHL	71	4	9	13	71
1989-90—Quebec Nordiques		NHL	68	2	6	8	44
NHL TOTALS			139	6	15	21	115

(c)—June, 1988—Drafted by Quebec Nordiques in 1988 NHL entry draft. First Nordiques pick, third overall, first round.

RICHARD LESSARD

Defense . . . 6'2" . . . 200 lbs. . . . Born, Timmons, Ont., January 9, 1968 . . . Shoots left.

Year	Team	League	Games	G.	A.	Pts.	Pen.
1984-85—Ottawa 67's		OHL	60	2	13	15	128
1985-86—Ottawa 67's (c)		OHL	64	1	20	21	231
1986-87—Ottawa 67's		OHL	66	5	36	41	188
1987-88—Ottawa 67's		OHL	58	5	34	39	210
1988-89—Calgary Flames		NHL	6	0	1	1	2
1988-89—Salt Lake Golden Eagles (a)		IHL	76	10	42	52	239
1989-90—Salt Lake Golden Eagles		IHL	66	3	18	21	169
NHL TOTALS			6	0	1	1	2

(c)—June, 1986—Drafted as an underage junior by Calgary Flames in 1986 NHL entry draft. Sixth Flames pick, 142nd overall, seventh round.

SCOTT LEVINS

Right Wing . . . 6'3" . . . 200 lbs. . . . Born, Portland, Ore., January 30, 1970 . . . Shoots right . . . (1986-87)—Broken sternum.

Year	Team	League	Games	G.	A.	Pts.	Pen.
1988-89—Penticton Knights		BCJHL	50	27	58	85	154
1989-90—Tri-City Americans (b-c)		WHL	71	25	37	62	132

(c)—June 16, 1990—Selected by Winnipeg Jets in 1990 NHL entry draft. Fourth Jets pick, 75th overall, fourth round.

DOUG LIDSTER

Defense . . . 6'1" . . . 195 lbs. . . . Born, Kamloops, B.C., October 18, 1960 . . . Shoots right . . . (1982-83)—Tied Colorado College record for most points by a defenseman in a season (56) . . . Member of 1984 Canadian Olympic Team . . . (January, 1988)—Strained left knee vs. Chicago . . . (October, 1988)—Hyperextended elbow . . . (November 13, 1988)—Broke hand vs. Pittsburgh . . . (March, 1989)—Fractured cheekbone.

Year	Team	League	Games	G.	A.	Pts.	Pen.
1979-80—Colorado College (c)		WCHA	39	18	25	43	52
1980-81—Colorado College		WCHA	36	10	30	40	54
1981-82—Colorado College (a)		WCHA	36	13	22	35	32
1982-83—Colorado College		WCHA	34	15	41	56	30
1983-84—Canadian Olympic Team		Int'l	59	6	20	26	28
1983-84—Vancouver Canucks		NHL	8	0	0	0	4
1984-85—Vancouver Canucks		NHL	78	6	24	30	55
1985-86—Vancouver Canucks		NHL	78	12	16	28	56
1986-87—Vancouver Canucks		NHL	80	12	51	63	40
1987-88—Vancouver Canucks		NHL	64	4	32	36	105
1988-89—Vancouver Canucks		NHL	63	5	17	22	78
1989-90—Vancouver Canucks		NHL	80	8	28	36	36
NHL TOTALS			451	47	168	215	374

(c)—June, 1980—Drafted by Vancouver Canucks in 1980 NHL entry draft. Sixth Canucks pick, 133rd overall, seventh round.

TREVOR LINDEN

Center . . . 6'4" . . . 185 lbs. . . . Born, Medicine Hat, Alta., April 11, 1970 . . . Shoots right . . . (October, 1989)—Hyperextended elbow . . . (March 17, 1990)—Separated shoulder when checked by Kevin Hatcher at Washington.

Year	Team	League	Games	G.	A.	Pts.	Pen.
1985-86—Medicine Hat Tigers		WHL	5	2	0	2	0
1986-87—Medicine Hat Tigers		WHL	72	14	22	36	59
1987-88—Medicine Hat Tigers (b-c)		WHL	67	46	64	110	76
1988-89—Vancouver Canucks		NHL	80	30	29	59	41
1989-90—Vancouver Canucks		NHL	73	21	30	51	43
NHL TOTALS			153	51	59	110	84

(c)—June, 1988—Drafted by Vancouver Canucks in 1988 NHL entry draft. First Canucks pick, second overall, first round.

MIKAEL LINDHOLM

Center . . . 6'1" . . . 194 lbs. . . . Born, Gavle, Sweden, December 19, 1964 . . . Shoots left . . . (December 28, 1990)—Injured back vs. Calgary and missed seven games.

Year	Team	League	Games	G.	A.	Pts.	Pen.
1981-82—Gavle GIK		Sweden-II	18	3	3	6	8
1982-83—Gavle GIK		Sweden-II	27	6	7	13	44
1983-84—Stromsbro		Sweden-II	20	9	10	19	4
1984-85—Stromsbro		Sweden-II	30	14	17	31	29
1985-86—Stromsbro		Sweden-II	32	15	20	35	26
1986-87—Brynas IF (c)		Sweden	36	8	9	17	46
1987-88—Brynas IF		Sweden	38	9	8	17	56
1988-89—Brynas IF		Sweden	40	9	17	26	98
1989-90—Los Angeles Kings		NHL	18	2	2	4	2
1989-90—New Haven Nighthawks		AHL	28	4	16	20	24
NHL TOTALS			18	2	2	4	2

(c)—June, 1987—Selected by Los Angeles Kings in 1987 NHL entry draft. Tenth Kings pick, 237th overall, 12th round.

KEN LINSEMAN

Center . . . 5'11" . . . 175 lbs. . . . Born, Kingston, Ont., August 11, 1958 . . . Shoots left . . . (September, 1980)—Broke tibia bone in leg in preseason game vs. N.Y. Rangers . . . Brother of John, Ted and Steve Linseman . . . (February, 1983)—Suspended for four games for fight in stands at Vancouver . . . (November, 1984)—Shoulder injury . . . (November 21, 1985)—Broke right hand vs. N.Y. Islanders and missed 10 games . . . (December 28, 1985)—Injured hand at St. Louis and missed six games . . . (March, 1988)—Sprained right ankle . . . (March 27, 1989)—Tore ligament in left knee in collision with Stephane Richer at Montreal . . . (September 28, 1989)—Surgery to left arm to correct a circulatory problem and missed first 14 games of season.

Year	Team	League	Games	G.	A.	Pts.	Pen.
1974-75—Kingston Canadians		Jr."A" OHA	59	19	28	47	70
1975-76—Kingston Canadians		Jr."A" OHA	65	61	51	112	92
1976-77—Kingston Canadians (b-c)		Jr."A" OHA	63	53	74	127	210
1977-78—Birmingham Bulls (d)		WHA	71	38	38	76	126
1978-79—Maine Mariners		AHL	38	17	23	40	106
1978-79—Philadelphia Flyers		NHL	30	5	20	25	23
1979-80—Philadelphia Flyers (e)		NHL	80	22	57	79	107
1980-81—Philadelphia Flyers		NHL	51	17	30	47	150
1981-82—Philadelphia Flyers (f)		NHL	79	24	68	92	275
1982-83—Edmonton Oilers		NHL	72	33	42	75	181
1983-84—Edmonton Oilers (g)		NHL	72	18	49	67	119
1984-85—Boston Bruins		NHL	74	25	49	74	126
1985-86—Boston Bruins		NHL	64	23	58	81	97
1986-87—Boston Bruins		NHL	64	15	34	49	126
1987-88—Boston Bruins		NHL	77	29	45	74	167
1988-89—Boston Bruins		NHL	78	27	45	72	164
1989-90—Boston Bruins (h)		NHL	32	6	16	22	66
1989-90—Philadelphia Flyers (i)		NHL	29	5	9	14	30
WHA TOTALS			71	38	38	76	126
NHL TOTALS			802	249	522	771	1631

(c)—June, 1977—Selected by Birmingham Bulls in World Hockey Association amateur player draft as underage junior.

(d)—Drafted from Birmingham Bulls by Philadelphia Flyers (with choice obtained from N. Y. Rangers) in first round of 1978 amateur draft.

(e)—Led Stanley Cup Playoffs with 18 assists.

(f)—August, 1982—Traded with Greg Adams and first and third-round 1983 draft picks by Philadelphia Flyers to Hartford Whalers for Mark Howe and Whalers third-round '83 pick. Linseman was then traded with Don Nachbaur by Hartford Whalers to Edmonton Oilers for Risto Siltanen and Brent Loney.

(g)—June, 1984—Traded by Edmonton Oilers to Boston Bruins for Mike Krushelnyski.

(h)—January 16, 1990—Traded by Boston Bruins to Philadelphia Flyers for Dave Poulin.

(i)—August, 1990—Signed by Edmonton Oilers as a free agent.

LONNIE LOACH

Left Wing . . . 5'10" . . . 180 lbs. . . . Born, New Liskeard, Ont., April 14, 1968 . . . Shoots left.

Year	Team	League	Games	G.	A.	Pts.	Pen.
1984-85—St. Mary's Jr. B		OHA	44	26	36	62	113
1985-86—Guelph Platers (c-d)		OHL	65	41	42	83	63
1986-87—Guelph Platers		OHL	56	31	24	55	42
1987-88—Guelph Platers		OHL	66	43	49	92	75
1988-89—Saginaw Hawks		IHL	32	7	6	13	27
1988-89—Flint Spirits		IHL	41	22	26	48	30
1989-90—Indianapolis Ice		IHL	3	0	1	1	0
1989-90—Fort Wayne Komets		IHL	54	15	33	48	40

(c)—Won Emms Family Award (OHL Rookie of the Year).

(d)—June, 1986—Drafted as underage junior by Chicago Black Hawks in 1986 NHL entry draft. Fourth Black Hawks pick, 98th overall, fifth round.

DARCY LOEWEN

Left Wing . . . 5'10" . . . 180 lbs. . . . Born, Calgary, Alta., February 26, 1969 . . . Shoots left.

Year	Team	League	Games	G.	A.	Pts.	Pen.
1985-86—Spokane Chiefs		WHL	8	2	1	3	19
1986-87—Spokane Chiefs		WHL	68	15	25	40	129
1987-88—Spokane Chiefs (c)		WHL	72	30	44	74	231
1988-89—Spokane Chiefs		WHL	60	31	27	58	194
1988-89—Canadian National Team		Int'l.	2	0	0	0	0
1989-90—Rochester Americans		AHL	50	7	11	18	193
1989-90—Buffalo Sabres		NHL	4	0	0	0	4
NHL TOTALS			4	0	0	0	4

(c)—June, 1988—Drafted by Buffalo Sabres in 1988 NHL entry draft. Second Sabres pick, 55th overall, third round.

BOB LOGAN

Right Wing . . . 6' . . . 190 lbs. . . . Born, Montreal, Que., February 22, 1964 . . . Shoots right.

Year	Team	League	Games	G.	A.	Pts.	Pen.
1982-83—Yale University (c)		ECAC	28	13	12	25	8
1983-84—Yale University		ECAC	22	9	13	22	25
1984-85—Yale University		ECAC	32	19	12	31	18
1985-86—Yale University (b)		ECAC	31	21	23	44	24
1986-87—Buffalo Sabres		NHL	22	7	3	10	0
1986-87—Rochester Americans		AHL	56	30	14	44	27
1987-88—Rochester Americans		AHL	45	23	15	38	35
1987-88—Buffalo Sabres		NHL	16	3	2	5	0
1988-89—Rochester Americans (d)		AHL	5	2	2	4	2
1988-89—New Haven Nighthawks		AHL	66	21	32	53	27
1988-89—Los Angeles Kings		NHL	4	0	0	0	0
1989-90—Played in Italy		Italy	....	....	....	....	....
1989-90—New Haven Nighthawks		AHL	11	2	4	6	4
NHL TOTALS			42	10	5	15	0

(c)—June, 1982—Drafted by Buffalo Sabres in 1982 NHL entry draft. Eighth Sabres pick, 100th overall, fifth round.

(d)—October 21, 1988—Traded with ninth-round 1989 draft pick (Jim Giacin) by Buffalo Sabres to Los Angeles Kings for Larry Playfair.

CLAUDE LOISELLE

Center . . . 5'11" . . . 195 lbs. . . . Born, Ottawa, Ont., May 29, 1963 . . . Shoots left . . . (January 7, 1984)—Given six-game suspension by NHL for a stick-swinging incident with Paul Holmgren of Philadelphia . . . (December 17, 1985)—Injured knee at Minnesota and missed 11 games . . . (February, 1988)—Separated right shoulder . . . (February, 1990)—Broke finger on left hand.

Year	Team	League	Games	G.	A.	Pts.	Pen.
1979-80—Gloucester Rangers		OPJHL	50	21	38	59	26
1980-81—Windsor Spitfires (c)		OHL	68	38	56	94	103
1981-82—Windsor Spitfires		OHL	68	36	73	109	192
1981-82—Detroit Red Wings		NHL	4	1	0	1	2
1982-83—Detroit Red Wings		NHL	18	2	0	2	15
1982-83—Windsor Spitfires		OHL	46	39	49	88	75
1982-83—Adirondack Red Wings		AHL	6	1	7	8	0
1983-84—Adirondack Red Wings		AHL	29	13	16	29	59
1983-84—Detroit Red Wings		NHL	28	4	6	10	32
1984-85—Adirondack Red Wings		AHL	47	22	29	51	24
1984-85—Detroit Red Wings		NHL	30	8	1	9	45
1985-86—Adirondack Red Wings		AHL	21	15	11	26	32
1985-86—Detroit Red Wings (d)		NHL	48	7	15	22	142
1986-87—New Jersey Devils		NHL	75	16	24	40	137
1987-88—New Jersey Devils		NHL	68	17	18	35	118
1988-89—New Jersey Devils (e)		NHL	74	7	14	21	209
1989-90—Quebec Nordiques		NHL	72	11	14	25	104
NHL TOTALS			417	73	92	165	804

(c)—June, 1981—Drafted as underage junior by Detroit Red Wings in 1981 NHL entry draft. First Red Wings pick, 23rd overall, second round.

(d)—June, 1986—Traded by Detroit Red Wings to New Jersey Devils for Tim Higgins.

(e)—June 17, 1989—Traded with Joe Cirella by New Jersey Devils to Quebec Nordiques for Walt Poddubny.

BYRON LOMOW

Center . . . 5'11" . . . 180 lbs. . . . Born, Sherwood Park, Alta., April 27, 1965 . . . Shoots right . . . (November 25, 1989)—Fined $300 and suspended one game for fighting with Kevin Evans vs. Kalamazoo.

Year	Team	League	Games	G.	A.	Pts.	Pen.
1982-83—Kamloops Junior Oilers		WHL	40	13	17	30	21
1982-83—Brandon Wheat Kings		WHL	22	6	9	15	9
1983-84—Brandon Wheat Kings		WHL	71	44	57	101	44
1984-85—Brandon Wheat Kings		WHL	71	42	70	112	90
1985-86—Brandon Wheat Kings (c)		WHL	72	52	67	119	77
1985-86—Indianapolis Checkers		IHL	9	8	3	11	10
1986-87—Indianapolis Checkers		IHL	81	28	43	71	225
1987-88—Baltimore Skipjacks (d)		AHL	71	14	26	40	77
1987-88—Colorado Rangers		IHL	10	2	10	12	7
1988-89—Fort Wayne Komets		IHL	81	22	35	57	207
1989-90—Fort Wayne Komets		IHL	79	29	24	53	230

(c)—April, 1986—Signed by Minnesota North Stars as a free agent.

(d)—November, 1987—Traded by Minnesota North Stars to New York Rangers for Curt Giles.

TROY LONEY

Left Wing . . . 6'3" . . . 215 lbs. . . . Born, Bow Island, Alta., September 21, 1963 . . . Shoots left . . . (December, 1986)—Suspended by AHL . . . (January 17, 1987)—Sprained right shoulder at Boston . . . (October, 1987)—Knee surgery . . . (November 13, 1988)—Suspended 10 games by NHL for fighting with Garth Butcher at Vancouver after coming off the bench . . . (November 24, 1989)—Broke right hand at Washington and missed 12 games.

Year	Team	League	Games	G.	A.	Pts.	Pen.
1980-81—Lethbridge Broncos		WHL	71	18	13	31	100
1981-82—Lethbridge Broncos (c)		WHL	71	26	31	57	152
1982-83—Lethbridge Broncos		WHL	72	33	34	67	156
1983-84—Baltimore Skipjacks		AHL	63	18	13	31	147
1983-84—Pittsburgh Penguins		NHL	13	0	0	0	9
1984-85—Baltimore Skipjacks		AHL	15	4	2	6	25
1984-85—Pittsburgh Penguins		NHL	46	10	8	18	59
1985-86—Baltimore Skipjacks		AHL	33	12	11	23	84
1985-86—Pittsburgh Penguins		NHL	47	3	9	12	95
1986-87—Baltimore Skipjacks		AHL	40	13	14	27	134
1986-87—Pittsburgh Penguins		NHL	23	8	7	15	22
1987-88—Pittsburgh Penguins		NHL	65	5	13	18	151
1988-89—Pittsburgh Penguins		NHL	69	10	6	16	165
1989-90—Pittsburgh Penguins		NHL	67	11	16	27	168
NHL TOTALS			330	47	59	106	669

(c)—June, 1982—Drafted as underage junior by Pittsburgh Penguins in 1982 NHL entry draft. Third Penguins pick, 52nd overall, third round.

CHRIS LONGO

Right Wing . . . 5'11" . . . 180 lbs. . . . Born, Belleville, Ont., January 5, 1972 . . . Shoots right.

Year	Team	League	Games	G.	A.	Pts.	Pen.
1987-88—Kingston Voyageurs		OHA	37	15	16	31	....
1988-89—Kingston Voyageurs		OHA	40	28	29	57	54
1989-90—Peterborough Petes (c-d)		OHL	66	33	42	75	48

(c)—Won Emms Family Award (Rookie of the Year).

(d)—June 16, 1990—Selected by Washington Capitals in 1990 NHL entry draft. Third Capitals pick, 51st overall, third round.

DAVE LORENTZ

Left Wing . . . 5'9" . . . 185 lbs. . . . Born, Kitchener, Ont., March 16, 1969 . . . Shoots left.

Year	Team	League	Games	G.	A.	Pts.	Pen.
1987-88—Peterborough Petes		OHL	65	8	25	33	78
1988-89—Peterborough Petes (c)		OHL	65	18	38	56	47
1989-90—Peterborough Petes		OHL	57	22	32	54	55

(c)—June, 1989—Drafted by Washington Capitals in 1989 NHL entry draft. Sixth Capitals pick, 145th overall, seventh round.

KEVIN HUGH LOWE

Defense . . . 6' . . . 185 lbs. . . . Born, Lachute, Que., April 15, 1959 . . . Shoots left . . . Cousin of Mike Lowe (St. Louis 1969 draft pick) . . . (March 7, 1986)—Broke index finger vs. Pittsburgh and missed six games . . . (March 9, 1988)—Broke left wrist vs. Montreal . . . (September, 1988)—Pulled rib muscle during Edmonton Oilers training camp . . . (October 14, 1988)—Concussion when struck by Mark Hunter's stick at Calgary . . . (April 8, 1990)—Back spasms . . . (June 16, 1990)—Married Karen Percy, a Canadian Olympic Bronze medal-winning downhill skier.

Year	Team	League	Games	G.	A.	Pts.	Pen.
1976-77—Quebec Remparts		QMJHL	69	3	19	22	39
1977-78—Quebec Remparts		QMJHL	64	13	52	65	86
1978-79—Quebec Remparts (b-c)		QMJHL	68	26	60	86	120
1979-80—Edmonton Oilers		NHL	64	2	19	21	70
1980-81—Edmonton Oilers		NHL	79	10	24	34	94
1981-82—Edmonton Oilers		NHL	80	9	31	40	63
1982-83—Edmonton Oilers		NHL	80	6	34	40	43
1983-84—Edmonton Oilers		NHL	80	4	42	46	59
1984-85—Edmonton Oilers		NHL	80	4	22	26	104
1985-86—Edmonton Oilers		NHL	74	2	16	18	90
1986-87—Edmonton Oilers		NHL	77	8	29	37	94
1987-88—Edmonton Oilers		NHL	70	9	15	24	89
1988-89—Edmonton Oilers		NHL	76	7	18	25	98
1989-90—Edmonton Oilers		NHL	78	7	26	33	140
NHL TOTALS			838	68	276	344	944

(c)—August, 1979—Drafted by Edmonton Oilers in 1979 entry draft. First Oilers pick, 21st overall, first round.

DAVE LOWRY

Left Wing . . . 6'2" . . . 175 lbs. . . . Born, Sudbury, Ont., January 14, 1965 . . . Shoots left . . . (December, 1982)—Arthroscopic surgery on knee . . . (March, 1990)—Groin injury.

Year	Team	League	Games	G.	A.	Pts.	Pen.
1981-82—Nepean Midgets		Ont. Midget	60	50	64	114	46
1982-83—London Knights (c)		OHL	42	11	16	27	48
1983-84—London Knights		OHL	66	29	47	76	125
1984-85—London Knights (a)		OHL	61	60	60	120	94
1985-86—Vancouver Canucks		NHL	73	10	8	18	143
1986-87—Vancouver Canucks		NHL	70	8	10	18	176
1987-88—Fredericton Express		AHL	46	18	27	45	59
1987-88—Vancouver Canucks		NHL	22	1	3	4	38
1988-89—Peoria Rivermen (d)		IHL	58	31	35	66	45
1988-89—St. Louis Blues		NHL	21	3	3	6	11
1989-90—St. Louis Blues		NHL	78	19	6	25	75
NHL TOTALS			264	41	30	71	443

(c)—June, 1983—Drafted as underage junior by Vancouver Canucks in 1983 NHL entry draft. Fourth Canucks pick, 110th overall, sixth round.

(d)—September 29, 1988—Traded by Vancouver Canucks to St. Louis Blues for Ernie Vargas.

CRAIG LEE LUDWIG

Defense . . . 6'3" . . . 212 lbs. . . . Born, Rhinelander, Wis., March 15, 1961 . . . Shoots left . . . (October, 1984)—Fractured knuckle in left hand in pre-season game . . . (December 2, 1985)—Broke hand vs. Vancouver and missed nine games . . . (January, 1988)—Missed five games with a broken right facial bone in a collision with Mikael Andersson vs. Buffalo . . . (November 19, 1988)—Suspended five games for elbowing Trent Yawney vs. Chicago . . . (March 21, 1990)—Separated right shoulder vs. Winnipeg.

Year	Team	League	Games	G.	A.	Pts.	Pen.
1979-80—University of North Dakota (c)		WCHA	33	1	8	9	32
1980-81—University of North Dakota		WCHA	34	4	8	12	48
1981-82—University of North Dakota (b)		WCHA	47	5	26	31	70
1982-83—Montreal Canadiens		NHL	80	0	25	25	59
1983-84—Montreal Canadiens		NHL	72	4	13	17	45
1984-85—Montreal Canadiens		NHL	72	5	14	19	90
1985-86—Montreal Canadiens		NHL	69	2	4	6	63
1986-87—Montreal Canadiens		NHL	75	4	12	16	105
1987-88—Montreal Canadiens		NHL	74	4	10	14	69
1988-89—Montreal Canadiens		NHL	74	3	13	16	73
1989-90—Montreal Canadiens (d)		NHL	73	1	15	16	108
NHL TOTALS			589	23	106	129	612

(c)—June, 1980—Drafted by Montreal Canadiens in 1980 NHL entry draft. Fifth Canadiens pick, 61st overall, third round.

(d)—September 4, 1990—Traded by Montreal Canadiens to New York Islanders for Gerald Diduck.

STEVE LUDZIK

Center . . . 5'11" . . . 185 lbs. . . . Born, Toronto, Ont., April 3, 1961 . . . Shoots left . . . (October 19, 1985)—Broke left foot at Detroit . . . (January 26, 1987)—Broke collarbone at Montreal . . . (November 12, 1989) Struck in left eye by Shaun Van Allen stick vs. Cape Breton and missed 10 games.

Year	Team	League	Games	G.	A.	Pts.	Pen.
1977-78—Markham Waxers		OPJHL	34	15	24	39	20
1978-79—Niagara Falls Flyers		OMJHL	68	32	65	97	138
1979-80—Niagara Falls Flyers (c)		OMJHL	67	43	76	119	102
1980-81—Niagara Falls Flyers		OHL	58	50	92	142	108
1981-82—Chicago Black Hawks		NHL	8	2	1	3	2
1981-82—New Brunswick Hawks		AHL	75	21	41	62	142
1982-83—Chicago Black Hawks		NHL	66	6	19	25	63
1983-84—Chicago Black Hawks		FHL	80	9	20	29	73
1984-85—Chicago Black Hawks		NHL	79	11	20	31	86
1985-86—Chicago Black Hawks		NHL	49	6	5	11	21
1986-87—Chicago Black Hawks		NHL	52	5	12	17	34
1987-88—Chicago Black Hawks		NHL	73	6	15	21	40
1988-89—Chicago Black Hawks		NHL	6	1	0	1	8
1988-89—Saginaw Hawks		IHL	65	21	57	78	129
1989-90—Rochester Americans		AHL	54	25	29	54	71
1989-90—Buffalo Sabres (d)		NHL	11	0	1	1	6
NHL TOTALS			424	46	93	139	333

(c)—June, 1980—Drafted as underage junior by Chicago Black Hawks in 1980 NHL entry draft. Third Black Hawks pick, 28th overall, second round.

(d)—September 28, 1989—Traded with a sixth round 1990 draft pick (Derek Edgerly) by Chicago Black Hawks to Buffalo Sabres to complete an earlier deal involving Jacques Cloutier.

JAAN LUIK

Defense . . . 6'1'' . . . 210 lbs. . . . Born, Scarborough, Ont., January 15, 1970 . . . Shoots left . . . Twin brother of Scott Luik.

Year	Team	League	Games	G.	A.	Pts.	Pen.
1986-87—Toronto Marlboro Midget		MTHL	66	7	27	34	125
1987-88—Miami Univ. of Ohio (c)		CCHA	35	2	5	7	93
1988-89—Miami Univ. of Ohio		CCHA	35	1	8	9	43
1989-90—Miami Univ. of Ohio		CCHA	35	1	11	12	64

(c)—June, 1988—Drafted by St. Louis Blues in 1988 NHL entry draft. Fourth Blues pick, 72nd overall, fourth round.

SCOTT LUIK

Right Wing . . . 6'1'' . . . 210 lbs. . . . Born, Scarborough, Ont., January 15, 1970 . . . Shoots right . . . Twin brother of Jaan Luik.

Year	Team	League	Games	G.	A.	Pts.	Pen.
1986-87—Toronto Marlboro Midget		MTHL	65	34	37	71	102
1987-88—Miami Univ. of Ohio (c)		CCHA	34	4	10	14	47
1988-89—Miami Univ. of Ohio		CCHA	36	13	13	26	92
1989-90—Miami Univ. of Ohio		CCHA	16	4	7	11	32

(c)—June, 1988—Drafted by New Jersey Devils in 1988 NHL entry draft. Fifth Devils pick, 75th overall, fourth round.

JYRKI LUMME

Defense . . . 6'1'' . . . 190 lbs. . . . Born, Tampere, Finland, July 16, 1967 . . . Shoots left . . . First Finland-born player to play for Montreal Canadiens . . . (December, 1988)—Strained left knee ligaments . . . (February, 21, 1989)—Stretched knee ligaments vs. Moncton . . . (November, 1989)—Bruised right foot.

Year	Team	League	Games	G.	A.	Pts.	Pen.
1984-85—Koo Vee		Finland	30	6	4	10	44
1985-86—Ilves Tampere (c)		Finland	31	1	5	6	4
1986-87—Ilves Tampere		Finland	43	12	12	24	52
1987-88—Ilves Tampere		Finland	43	8	22	30	75
1988-89—Montreal Canadiens		NHL	21	1	3	4	10
1988-89—Sherbrooke Canadiens		AHL	26	4	11	15	10
1989-90—Montreal Canadiens (d)		NHL	54	1	19	20	41
1989-90—Vancouver Canucks		NHL	11	3	7	10	8
NHL TOTALS			86	5	29	34	59

(c)—June, 1986—Drafted by Montreal Canadiens in 1986 NHL entry draft. Third Canadiens pick, 57th overall, third round.

(d)—March 6, 1990—Traded by Montreal Canadiens to Vancouver Canucks for second round 1991 draft pick.

CHRISTOPHER LUONGO

Defense . . . 6' . . . 180 lbs. . . . Born, Detroit, Mich., March 17, 1967 . . . Shoots right.

Year	Team	League	Games	G.	A.	Pts.	Pen.
1984-85—St. Clair Shores Falcons (c)		NAJHL	41	2	25	27	....
1985-86—Michigan State Univ.		CCHA	38	1	5	6	29
1986-87—Michigan State Univ.		CCHA	27	4	16	20	38
1987-88—Michigan State Univ.		CCHA	45	3	15	18	49
1988-89—Michigan State Univ. (b)		CCHA	47	4	21	25	42
1989-90—Adirondack Red Wings		AHL	53	9	14	23	37
1989-90—Phoenix Roadrunners		IHL	23	5	9	14	41

(c)—June, 1985—Drafted by Detroit Red Wings in 1985 NHL entry draft. Fifth Red Wings pick, 92nd overall, fifth round.

COREY LYONS

Right Wing . . . 5'10'' . . . 185 lbs. . . . Born, Calgary, Alta., June 1, 1970 . . . Shoots left.

Year	Team	League	Games	G.	A.	Pts.	Pen.
1987-88—Lethbridge Broncos		WHL	2	0	0	0	0
1988-89—Lethbridge Broncos (c)		WHL	71	53	59	112	6
1989-90—Lethbridge Hurricanes		WHL	72	63	79	142	26

(c)—June, 1989—Drafted by Calgary Flames in 1989 NHL entry draft. Fourth Flames pick, 63rd overall, third round.

KEN MacARTHUR

Defense . . . 6'1'' . . . 185 lbs. . . . Born, Rossland, B.C., March 15, 1968 . . . Shoots left . . . (November, 1986)—Strained knee.

Year	Team	League	Games	G.	A.	Pts.	Pen.
1986-87—Penticton Knights		BCJHL	30	20	23	43	25
1987-88—University of Denver (c)		WCHA	38	6	16	22	69
1988-89—University of Denver		WCHA	42	11	19	30	77
1989-90—University of Denver		WCHA	38	12	29	41	96
1989-90—Canadian National Team		Int'l.	13	2	1	3	14

(c)—June, 1988—Drafted by Minnesota North Stars in 1988 NHL entry draft. Fifth North Stars pick, 148th overall, eighth round.

KEN MacDERMID

Left Wing . . . 6'1'' . . . 195 lbs. . . . Born, Sidney, N.S., May 12, 1970 . . . Shoots left.

Year	Team	League	Games	G.	A.	Pts.	Pen.
1986-87—Hull Olympiques		QMJHL	65	9	18	27	40
1987-88—Hull Olympiques		QMJHL	54	10	10	20	62
1988-89—Hull Olympiques (c)		QMJHL	68	17	20	37	76
1989-90—Hull/St. Jean Lynx		QMJHL	67	28	48	76	139

(c)—June, 1989—Drafted by New York Rangers in 1989 NHL entry draft. Thirteenth Rangers pick, 244th overall, 12th round.

PAUL MacDERMID

Center . . . 6' . . . 188 lbs. . . . Born, Chesley, Ont., April 14, 1963 . . . Shoots right . . . (December, 1982)—Injured knee . . . (December 6, 1988)—Injured neck and shoulder vs. Buffalo . . . (February 4, 1989)—Sprained right knee ligament at N.Y. Islanders.

Year	Team	League	Games	G.	A.	Pts.	Pen.
1979-80—Port Elgin Bears		OHA Jr.'C'	30	23	20	43	87
1980-81—Windsor Spitfires (c)		OHL	68	15	17	32	106
1981-82—Windsor Spitfires		OHL	65	26	45	71	179
1981-82—Hartford Whalers		NHL	3	1	0	1	2
1982-83—Windsor Spitfires		OHL	42	35	45	80	90
1982-83—Hartford Whalers		NHL	7	0	0	0	2
1983-84—Hartford Whalers		NHL	3	0	1	1	0
1983-84—Binghamton Whalers		AHL	70	31	30	61	130
1984-85—Binghamton Whalers		AHL	48	9	31	40	87
1984-85—Hartford Whalers		NHL	31	4	7	11	299
1985-86—Hartford Whalers		NHL	74	13	10	23	160
1986-87—Hartford Whalers		NHL	72	7	11	18	202
1987-88—Hartford Whalers		NHL	80	20	14	34	139
1988-89—Hartford Whalers		NHL	74	17	27	44	141
1989-90—Hartford Whalers (d)		NHL	29	6	12	18	69
1989-90—Winnipeg Jets		NHL	44	7	10	17	100
NHL TOTALS			417	75	92	167	844

(c)—June, 1981—Drafted as underage junior in 1981 NHL entry draft by Hartford Whalers. Second Whalers pick, 61st overall, third round.

(d)—December 13, 1989—Traded by Hartford Whalers to Winnipeg Jets for Randy Cunneyworth.

DOUG MacDONALD

Center . . . 6' . . . 192 lbs. . . . Born, Assiniboia, Sask., February 8, 1969 . . . Shoots left.

Year	Team	League	Games	G.	A.	Pts.	Pen.
1984-85—Burnaby Midgets		BC Midg.	50	53	105	158	..
1985-86—Langley Eagles		BCJHL	42	19	37	56	..
1986-87—Delta Flyers		BCJHL	51	28	49	77	61
1987-88—Delta Flyers		BCJHL	51	50	54	104	70
1988-89—Univ. of Wisconsin (c)		WCHA	44	23	25	48	50
1989-90—Univ. of Wisconsin		WCHA	44	16	35	51	52

(c)—June, 1989—Drafted by Buffalo Sabres in 1989 NHL entry draft. Third Sabres pick, 77th overall, fourth round.

ALLAN MacINNIS

Defense . . . 6'1'' . . . 183 lbs. . . . Born, Inverness, N.S., July 11, 1963 . . . Shoots right . . . (February, 1985)—Twisted knee . . . (March 23, 1986)—Lacerated hand at Winnipeg . . . Set Flames club record for goals (25 in '87-88) by a defenseman in one season . . . (April 8, 1990)—Stretched ligaments of knee after a collision with Tony Granato at Los Angeles . . . Brother of Rob MacInnis.

Year	Team	League	Games	G.	A.	Pts.	Pen.
1979-80—Regina Blues		SJHL	59	20	28	48	110
1980-81—Kitchener Rangers (c)		OHL	47	11	28	39	59
1981-82—Kitchener Rangers (a)		OHL	59	25	50	75	145
1981-82—Calgary Flames		NHL	2	0	0	0	0
1982-83—Kitchener Rangers (a-d)		OHL	51	38	46	84	67
1982-83—Calgary Flames		NHL	14	1	3	4	9
1983-84—Colorado Flames		CHL	19	5	14	19	22
1983-84—Calgary Flames		NHL	51	11	34	45	42
1984-85—Calgary Flames		NHL	67	14	52	66	75
1985-86—Calgary Flames (e)		NHL	77	11	57	68	76
1986-87—Calgary Flames (b)		NHL	79	20	56	76	97
1987-88—Calgary Flames		NHL	80	25	58	83	114
1988-89—Calgary Flames (b-f-g)		NHL	79	16	58	74	126
1989-90—Calgary Flames (a)		NHL	79	28	62	90	82
NHL TOTALS			528	126	380	506	621

(c)—June, 1981—Drafted as underage junior by Calgary Flames in 1981 NHL entry draft. First Flames pick, 15th overall, first round.

(d)—Won Max Kaminsky Trophy (Outstanding Defenseman).

(e)—Led Stanley Cup Playoffs with 15 assists.

(f)—Led Stanley Cup Playoffs with 24 assists and 31 points.

(g)—Won Conn Smythe Trophy (Stanley Cup Playoff MVP).

ROBERT MacINNIS

Defense . . . 5'11" . . . 185 lbs. . . . Born, Port Hood, N.S., September 12, 1965 . . . Shoots left . . . Brother of Al MacInnis.

Year	Team	League	Games	G.	A.	Pts.	Pen.
1981-82—Antigonish Midgets	N.S. Midget	56	23	47	70	96
1982-83—Kitchener Rangers	OHL	41	0	5	5	33
1983-84—Kitchener Rangers	OHL	12	3	3	6	9
1983-84—Guelph Platers	OHL	5	0	3	3	20
1984-85—Toronto Marlboros (c)	OHL	..	..	..	..	..
1985-86—Moncton Golden Flames	AHL	2	0	0	0	0
1986-87—...............		..	..	..	..	..
1987-88—...............		......	..	..	..	..
1988-89—Cape Breton Oilers (d)	AHL	62	8	18	26	170
1989-90—Maine Mariners	AHL	34	3	12	15	48

(c)—No regular season record. Played four playoff games.
(d)—October, 1988—Signed as a free agent by Cape Breton Oilers.

NORM MacIVER

Defense . . . 5'11" . . . 180 lbs. . . . Born, Thunder Bay, Ont., September 8, 1964 . . . Shoots left . . . (March, 1988)—Dislocated right shoulder . . . (November, 1988)—Hip pointer.

Year	Team	League	Games	G.	A.	Pts.	Pen.
1982-83—Univ. of Minn./Duluth	WCHA	45	1	26	27	40
1983-84—Univ. of Minn./Duluth	WCHA	31	13	28	41	28
1984-85—Univ. of Minn./Duluth	WCHA	47	14	47	61	63
1985-86—Univ. of Minn./Duluth	WCHA	42	11	51	62	36
1986-87—New Haven Nighthawks	AHL	71	6	30	36	73
1986-87—New York Rangers (c)	NHL	3	0	1	1	0
1987-88—Colorado Rangers	IHL	27	6	20	26	22
1987-88—New York Rangers	NHL	37	9	15	24	14
1988-89—New York Rangers (d)	NHL	26	0	10	10	14
1988-89—Hartford Whalers	NHL	37	1	22	23	24
1989-90—Binghamton Whalers (e)	AHL	2	0	0	0	0
1989-90—Cape Breton Oilers	AHL	68	13	37	50	77
1989-90—Edmonton Oilers	NHL	1	0	0	0	0
NHL TOTALS		104	10	48	58	52

(c)—September, 1986—Signed by New York Rangers as a free agent.
(d)—December 26, 1988—Traded with Don Maloney and Brian Lawton by New York Rangers to Hartford Whalers for Carey Wilson and a fifth-round 1990 draft pick.
(e)—October 9, 1989—Traded by Hartford Whalers to Edmonton Oilers for Jim Ennis.

DAVID MACKEY

Left Wing . . . 6'3" . . . 190 lbs. . . . Born, New Westminster, B.C., July 24, 1966 . . . Shoots left . . . (November 6, 1989)—Torn right thumb ligaments at Toronto and missed 10 games . . . (December 28, 1989)—Suspended five games for fighting at Chicago and fined $500 . . . (January 24, 1990)—Sprained knee and ankle at Toronto and missed 15 games.

Year	Team	League	Games	G.	A.	Pts.	Pen.
1981-82—Seafair	B.C. Midgets	60	48	62	110	99
1982-83—Victoria Cougars	WHL	69	16	16	32	53
1983-84—Victoria Cougars (c)	WHL	69	15	15	30	97
1984-85—Victoria Cougars	WHL	16	5	6	11	45
1984-85—Portland Winter Hawks	WHL	56	28	32	60	122
1985-86—Kamloops Blazers (d)	WHL	9	3	4	7	13
1985-86—Medicine Hat Tigers	WHL	60	25	32	57	167
1986-87—Saginaw Gears	IHL	81	26	49	75	173
1987-88—Saginaw Hawks	IHL	62	29	22	51	211
1987-88—Chicago Black Hawks	NHL	23	1	3	4	71
1988-89—Chicago Black Hawks	NHL	23	1	2	3	78
1988-89—Saginaw Hawks	IHL	57	22	23	45	223
1989-90—Minnesota North Stars (e)	NHL	16	2	0	2	28
NHL TOTALS		62	4	5	9	177

(c)—June, 1984—Drafted as underage junior by Chicago Black Hawks in NHL entry draft. Twelfth Black Hawks pick, 224th overall, 11th round.
(d)—December, 1986—Traded with Rob Dimaio and Calvin Knibbs by Kamloops Blazers to Medicine Hat Tigers for Doug Pickel and Sean Pass.
(e)—October 2, 1989—Selected by Minnesota North Stars in 1989 NHL waiver draft on waivers for $40,000.

JOHN MacLEAN

Right Wing . . . 6' . . . 200 lbs. . . . Born, Oshawa, Ont., November 20, 1964 . . . Shoots right . . . (November, 1984)—Bruised shoulder vs. N.Y. Rangers . . . (January 25, 1985)—Injured right knee at Edmonton . . . (January 31, 1985)—Reinjured knee and underwent arthroscopic surgery . . . (November 2, 1986)—Bruised ankle vs. N.Y. Rangers . . . (December, 1988)—Sprained right elbow . . . (March 1, 1989)—Bruised ribs when slashed by Jim Johnson at Pittsburgh.

Year	Team	League	Games	G.	A.	Pts.	Pen.
1981-82—Oshawa Generals	OHL	67	17	22	39	197
1982-83—Oshawa Generals (c-d)	OHL	66	47	51	98	138
1983-84—New Jersey Devils	NHL	23	1	0	1	10
1983-84—Oshawa Generals	OHL	30	23	36	59	58
1984-85—New Jersey Devils	NHL	61	13	20	33	44
1985-86—New Jersey Devils	NHL	74	21	37	58	112
1986-87—New Jersey Devils	NHL	80	31	36	67	120
1987-88—New Jersey Devils	NHL	76	23	16	39	145
1988-89—New Jersey Devils	NHL	74	42	45	87	127
1989-90—New Jersey Devils	NHL	80	41	38	79	80
NHL TOTALS		468	172	192	364	638

(c)—Led OHL playoffs with 18 goals and shared OHL playoff point lead with teammate Dave Gans with 38 points.
(d)—June, 1983—Drafted as underage junior by New Jersey Devils in 1983 NHL entry draft. First Devils pick, sixth overall, first round.

PAUL MacLEAN

Right Wing . . . 6' . . . 205 lbs. . . . Born, Grostenquin, France, March 9, 1958 . . . Shoots right . . . Member of 1980 Canadian Olympic team . . . (October, 1985)—Jammed thumb . . . (March 8, 1987)—Stretched knee ligaments in a collision with Mario Lemieux vs. Pittsburgh . . . (October, 1989)—Bruised left ankle.

Year	Team	League	Games	G.	A.	Pts.	Pen.
1977-78—Hull Festivals (c)	QMJHL	66	38	33	71	125
1978-79—Canadian National Team	Int'l	....	....	....	....	....
1979-80—Canadian National Team	Int'l	50	21	11	32	90
1979-80—Canadian Olympic Team	Oly.	6	2	3	5	6
1980-81—Salt Lake City	CHL	80	36	42	78	160
1980-81—St. Louis Blues (d)	NHL	1	0	0	0	0
1981-82—Winnipeg Jets	NHL	74	36	25	61	106
1982-83—Winnipeg Jets	NHL	80	32	44	76	121
1983-84—Winnipeg Jets	NHL	76	40	31	71	155
1984-85—Winnipeg Jets	NHL	79	41	60	101	119
1985-86—Winnipeg Jets	NHL	69	27	29	56	74
1986-87—Winnipeg Jets	NHL	72	32	42	74	75
1987-88—Winnipeg Jets (e)	NHL	77	40	39	79	76
1988-89—Detroit Red Wings (f)	NHL	76	36	35	71	118
1989-90—St. Louis Blues	NHL	78	34	33	67	100
NHL TOTALS		682	318	338	656	944

(c)—June, 1978—Drafted by St. Louis Blues in 1978 NHL amateur draft. Sixth Blues pick, 109th overall, seventh round.
(d)—July, 1981—Traded by St. Louis Blues with Ed Staniowski and Bryan Maxwell to Winnipeg Jets for John Markell and Scott Campbell.
(e)—June, 1988—Traded by Winnipeg Jets to Detroit Red Wings for Brent Ashton.
(f)—June 15, 1989—Traded with Adam Oates by Detroit Red Wings to St. Louis Blues for Bernie Federko and Tony McKegney.

TERRY MacLEAN

Center . . . 6'1" . . . 178 lbs. . . . Born, Montreal, Que., January 14, 1968 . . . Shoots left.

Year	Team	League	Games	G.	A.	Pts.	Pen.
1984-85—Quebec Remparts	QMJHL	69	21	45	66	10
1985-86—Longueuil Chevaliers (c)	QMJHL	70	36	45	81	18
1986-87—Longueuil-Trois-Rivieres	QMJHL	69	41	76	117	20
1987-88—Trois-Rivieres Draveurs	QMJHL	69	52	91	143	44
1987-88—Peoria Rivermen	IHL	5	0	1	1	0
1988-89—Peoria Rivermen	IHL	73	18	30	48	46
1989-90—Peoria Rivermen	IHL	67	9	32	41	15

(c)—June, 1986—Drafted by St. Louis in 1986 NHL entry draft. Eleventh Blues pick, 220th overall, 11th round.

BRIAN MacLELLAN

Left Wing . . . 6'3" . . . 212 lbs. . . . Born, Guelph, Ont., October 27, 1958 . . . Shoots left.

Year	Team	League	Games	G.	A.	Pts.	Pen.
1978-79—Bowling Green University	CCHA	44	34	29	63	94
1979-80—Bowling Green University	CCHA	38	8	15	23	46
1980-81—Bowling Green University	CCHA	37	11	14	25	96
1981-82—Bowling Green University (c)	CCHA	41	11	21	32	109
1982-83—Los Angeles Kings	NHL	8	0	3	3	7
1982-83—New Haven Nighthawks	AHL	71	11	15	26	40
1983-84—New Haven Nighthawks	AHL	2	0	2	2	0
1983-84—Los Angeles Kings	NHL	72	25	29	54	45
1984-85—Los Angeles Kings	NHL	80	31	54	85	53
1985-86—Los Angeles Kings (d)	NHL	27	5	8	13	19
1985-86—New York Rangers	NHL	51	11	21	32	47
1986-87—Minnesota North Stars (e)	NHL	76	32	31	63	69
1987-88—Minnesota North Stars	NHL	75	16	32	48	74
1988-89—Minnesota North Stars (f)	NHL	60	16	23	39	104
1988-89—Calgary Flames	NHL	12	2	3	5	14
1989-90—Calgary Flames	NHL	78	8	27	35	70
NHL TOTALS		539	146	231	377	502

(c)—April, 1982—Signed by Los Angeles Kings as a free agent.
(d)—December, 1985—Traded with a fourth round 1987 draft pick by Los Angeles Kings to New York Rangers for Roland Melanson and Grant Ledyard. The Rangers had earlier traded a second round 1986 pick (Neil Wilkinson) and a fourth round 1987 draft pick to Minnesota for Melanson. Melanson was then traded with Ledyard to Los Angeles.
(e)—September, 1986—Traded by New York Rangers to Minnesota North Stars for a third-round 1987 draft pick (Simon Gagne).
(f)—March 4, 1989—Traded with a fourth-round 1989 draft pick (Robert Reichel) by Minnesota North Stars to Calgary Flames for Shane Churla and Perry Berezan.

PAT MacLEOD

Defense . . . 5'10" . . . 187 lbs. . . . Born, Melfort, Sask., June 15, 1969 . . . Shoots left . . . (March, 1989)—Injured knee vs. Victoria.

Year	Team	League	Games	G.	A.	Pts.	Pen.
1987-88—Kamloops Blazers	WHL	50	13	33	46	27
1988-89—Kamloops Blazers (a-c)	WHL	37	11	34	45	14
1989-90—Kalamazoo Wings	IHL	82	9	38	47	27

(c)—June, 1989—Drafted by Minnesota North Stars in 1989 NHL entry draft. Fifth North Stars pick, 87th overall, fifth round.

JAMIE MACOUN

Defense . . . 6'2" . . . 200 lbs. . . . Born, Newmarket, Ont., August 17, 1961 . . . Shoots left . . . (December 26, 1984)—Cheekbone fractured in altercation with Mark Messier vs. Edmonton . . . (May, 1987)—Nerve damage to left arm in automobile accident . . . (January 23, 1989)—Concussion when his helmet was broken by a

Stephane Richer shot at Montreal . . . Brother of Mike Macoun (Miami/Ohio player, 1983-87).

Year	Team	League	Games	G.	A.	Pts.	Pen.
1980-81—Ohio State University	CCHA	38	9	20	29	83
1981-82—Ohio State University	CCHA	25	2	18	20	89
1982-83—Ohio State University (c)	CCHA	....	....	....	....	....
1982-83—Calgary Flames	NHL	22	1	4	5	25
1983-84—Calgary Flames	NHL	72	9	23	32	97
1984-85—Calgary Flames	NHL	70	9	30	39	67
1985-86—Calgary Flames	NHL	77	11	21	32	81
1986-87—Calgary Flames	NHL	79	7	33	40	111
1987-88—Did not play	....	....	....	....	....	....
1988-89—Calgary Flames	NHL	72	8	19	27	40
1989-90—Calgary Flames	NHL	78	8	27	35	70
NHL TOTALS			470	53	157	210	491

(c)—January, 1983—Left Ohio State University to sign with Calgary Flames as a free agent.

CRAIG MacTAVISH

Center . . . 6'1'' . . . 195 lbs. . . . Born, London, Ont., August 15, 1958 . . . Shoots left . . . Also plays Left Wing . . . (January, 1984)—Involved in automobile accident in which Kim Lea Radley was killed. He was charged with vehicular homicide, driving while under the influence of alcohol and reckless driving. In May he pleaded guilty and was convicted by Essex, Mass., Superior court and sentenced to a year in prison . . . Does not wear a helmet.

Year	Team	League	Games	G.	A.	Pts.	Pen.
1977-78—University of Lowell (b-c-d)	ECAC	....	....	....	....	....
1978-79—University of Lowell (a-e)	ECAC-II	....	36	52	*88	....
1979-80—Binghamton Dusters	AHL	34	17	15	32	20
1979-80—Boston Bruins	NHL	46	11	17	28	8
1980-81—Boston Bruins	NHL	24	3	5	8	13
1980-81—Springfield Indians	AHL	53	19	24	43	89
1981-82—Erie Blades	AHL	72	23	32	55	37
1981-82—Boston Bruins	NHL	2	0	1	1	0
1982-83—Boston Bruins	NHL	75	10	20	30	18
1983-84—Boston Bruins	NHL	70	20	23	43	35
1984-85—Boston Bruins (f)	NHL	....	....	....	....	....
1985-86—Edmonton Oilers	NHL	74	23	24	47	70
1986-87—Edmonton Oilers	NHL	79	20	19	39	55
1987-88—Edmonton Oilers	NHL	80	15	17	32	47
1988-89—Edmonton Oilers	NHL	80	21	31	52	55
1989-90—Edmonton Oilers	NHL	80	21	22	43	89
NHL TOTALS			610	144	179	323	390

(c)—June, 1978—Drafted by Boston Bruins in amateur draft. Ninth Bruins pick, 153rd overall, ninth round.
(d)—Named ECAC Division II Rookie of the Year.
(e)—Named ECAC Division II Player of the Year.
(f)—February, 1984—Signed by Edmonton Oilers as a free agent.

ANDREW MacVICAR

Left Wing . . . 6'1'' . . . 195 lbs. . . . Born, Halifax, N.S., March 12, 1969 . . . Shoots left.

Year	Team	League	Games	G.	A.	Pts.	Pen.
1985-86—Halifax Midget	N.S. Midget	34	29	32	61	77
1986-87—Peterborough Petes (c)	OHL	64	6	13	19	33
1987-88—Peterborough Petes	OHL	62	30	51	81	45
1988-89—Peterborough Petes	OHL	66	25	29	54	56
1989-90—Sudbury Wolves	OHL	41	12	16	28	47
1989-90—Phoenix Roadrunners	IHL	1	0	0	0	0

(c)—June, 1987—Drafted as underage junior by Buffalo Sabres in 1987 NHL entry draft. Third Sabres pick, 53rd overall, third round.

JEFF MADILL

Right Wing . . . 5'11'' . . . 195 lbs. . . . Born, Oshawa, Ont., June 21, 1965 . . . Shoots right . . . Son of former NHL referee Greg Madill . . . (April 11, 1990)—Given three game suspension for abusing an official vs. Rochester.

Year	Team	League	Games	G.	A.	Pts.	Pen.
1984-85—Ohio State Univ.	CCHA	12	5	6	11	18
1985-86—Ohio State Univ.	CCHA	41	32	25	57	65
1986-87—Ohio State Univ. (c)	CCHA	43	38	32	70	139
1987-88—Utica Devils	AHL	58	18	15	33	127
1988-89—Utica Devils	AHL	69	23	25	48	225
1989-90—Utica Devils	AHL	74	43	26	69	233

(c)—June, 1987—Selected by New Jersey Devils in 1987 NHL supplemental draft.

KEVIN MAGUIRE

Right Wing . . . 6'2'' . . . 200 lbs. . . . Born, Toronto, Ont., January 5, 1963 . . . Shoots right . . . (February, 1988)—Fractured ankle vs. Winnipeg . . . (September, 1988) —Bruised ribs in Buffalo training camp . . . (December, 1988)—Sprained ankle . . . (March, 1989)—Cut hand . . . (March 18, 1990)—Sprained right knee vs. Los Angeles.

Year	Team	League	Games	G.	A.	Pts.	Pen.
1983-84—Orillia Travelways	OHA	....	35	42	77	....
1984-85—St. Catharines Saints (c)	AHL	76	10	15	25	112
1985-86—St. Catharines Saints	AHL	61	6	9	15	161
1986-87—Newmarket Saints	AHL	51	4	2	6	131
1986-87—Toronto Maple Leafs	NHL	17	0	0	0	74
1987-88—Buffalo Sabres (d)	NHL	46	4	6	10	162
1988-89—Buffalo Sabres	NHL	60	8	10	18	241
1989-90—Buffalo Sabres (e)	NHL	61	6	9	15	115
1989-90—Philadelphia Flyers (f)	NHL	5	1	0	1	6
NHL TOTALS			189	19	25	44	598

(c)—September, 1984—Signed by Toronto Maple Leafs as a free agent.
(d)—October, 1988—Acquired by Buffalo Sabres in 1987 NHL waiver draft.
(e)—March 5, 1990—Traded with a second-round 1990 draft pick (Mikael Renberg) by Buffalo Sabres to Philadelphia Flyers for Jay Wells and a fourth-round 1991 draft pick.
(f)—June 16, 1990—Traded with an eighth-round 1991 draft pick by Philadelphia Flyers to Toronto Maple Leafs for a third-round 1990 draft pick (Al Kinisky).

JAMES MAHER

Defense . . . 6'1'' . . . 210 lbs. . . . Born, Warren, Mich., June 10, 1970 . . . Shoots left.

Year	Team	League	Games	G.	A.	Pts.	Pen.
1987-88—Detroit Jr. Red Wings	NAJHL	24	6	11	17	26
1988-89—Univ. of Illinois/Chicago (c)	CCHA	41	1	5	6	40
1989-90—Univ. of Illinois/Chicago	CCHA	38	4	12	16	64

(c)—June, 1989—Drafted by Los Angeles Kings in 1989 NHL entry draft. Second Kings pick, 81st overall, fourth round.

SCOTT MAHONEY

Left Wing . . . 6' . . . 188 lbs. . . . Born, Peterborough, Ont., April 19, 1969 . . . Shoots right.

Year	Team	League	Games	G.	A.	Pts.	Pen.
1985-86—Peterborough Minor Midget	OHL	31	18	39	57	89
1986-87—Oshawa Generals (c)	OHL	54	13	9	22	161
1987-88—Oshawa Generals	OHL	60	10	21	31	272
1988-89—Oshawa Generals	OHL	56	14	22	36	207
1989-90—Sudbury Wolves (d)	OHL	54	13	22	35	151

(c)—June, 1987—Drafted by Calgary Flames as an underage junior in 1987 NHL entry draft. Fourth Flames pick, 61st overall, third round.
(d)—September 20, 1989—Traded by Oshawa Generals to Sudbury Wolves for a sixth-round 1991 priority draft pick.

MARK MAJOR

Left Wing . . . 6'3'' . . . 205 lbs. . . . Born, Toronto, Ont., March 20, 1970 . . . Shoots left . . . (September, 1989)—Missed Pittsburgh Penguins training camp due to broken hand.

Year	Team	League	Games	G.	A.	Pts.	Pen.
1986-87—Don Mills Flyers Midget	MTHL	36	12	14	26	81
1987-88—North Bay Centennials (c)	OHL	57	16	17	33	272
1988-89—North Bay Centennials	OHL	11	3	2	5	58
1988-89—Kingston Raiders	OHL	53	22	29	51	193
1989-90—Kingston Frontenacs	OHL	62	29	32	61	168

(c)—June, 1988—Drafted by Pittsburgh Penguins in 1988 NHL entry draft. Second Penguins pick, 25th overall, second round.

SERGEI MAKAROV

Right Wing . . . 5'11'' . . . 185 lbs. . . . Born, Chelyabinsk, U.S.S.R., June 19, 1958 . . . Shoots left.

Year	Team	League	Games	G.	A.	Pts.	Pen.
1976-77—Traktor Chelyabinsk	USSR	11	1	0	1	4
1977-78—Traktor Chelyabinsk	USSR	36	18	13	31	10
1978-79—Central Red Army	USSR	44	18	21	39	12
1979-80—Central Red Army	USSR	44	29	39	68	16
1980-81—Central Red Army	USSR	49	42	37	79	22
1981-82—Central Red Army	USSR	46	32	43	75	18
1982-83—Central Red Army (c)	USSR	30	25	17	42	6
1983-84—Central Red Army	USSR	44	36	37	73	28
1984-85—Central Red Army	USSR	40	26	39	65	28
1985-86—Central Red Army	USSR	40	30	32	62	28
1986-87—Central Red Army	USSR	40	21	32	53	26
1987-88—Central Red Army	USSR	51	23	45	68	50
1988-89—Central Red Army	USSR	44	21	33	54	42
1989-90—Calgary Flames (d)	NHL	80	24	62	86	55
NHL TOTALS			80	24	62	86	55

(c)—June, 1983—Drafted by Calgary Flames in 1983 NHL entry draft. Fourteenth Flames pick, 231st overall, twelfth round.
(d)—Won Calder Memorial Trophy (NHL Rookie of the Year).

MIKKO MAKELA

Right Wing . . . 6'2'' . . . 195 lbs. . . . Born, Tampere, Finland, February 28, 1965 . . . Shoots left . . . Also plays Center . . . (November 1, 1985)—Injured back at Washington and missed 15 games . . . (February, 1988)—Infected elbow . . . (December 13, 1989)—Bruised shoulder at Hartford.

Year	Team	League	Games	G.	A.	Pts.	Pen.
1984-85—Ilves Tampere	Finland	35	17	11	28	....
1984-85—Ilves Tampere (a-c-d)	Finland	36	*34	25	59	24
1985-86—Springfield Indians	AHL	2	1	1	2	0
1985-86—New York Islanders	NHL	58	16	20	36	28
1986-87—New York Islanders	NHL	80	24	33	57	24
1987-88—New York Islanders	NHL	73	36	40	76	22
1988-89—New York Islanders	NHL	76	17	28	45	22
1989-90—New York Islanders (e)	NHL	20	2	3	5	2
1989-90—Los Angeles Kings	NHL	45	7	14	21	16
NHL TOTALS			352	102	138	240	114

(c)—June, 1983—Drafted by New York Islanders in 1983 NHL entry draft. Fifth Islanders pick, 65th overall, fourth round.
(d)—Won Most Gentlemanly Player Trophy.
(e)—November 29, 1989—Traded by New York Islanders to Los Angeles Kings for Ken Baumgartner and Hubie McDonough.

DAVID MALEY

Center . . . 6'3" . . . 200 lbs. . . . Born, Beaver Dam, Wis., April 24, 1963 . . . Shoots left . . . (May, 1987)—Suspended prior to a playoff game with Rochester . . . (December, 1988)—Injured back . . . (January 16, 1990)—Torn right knee cartilage vs. Washington . . . (January 24, 1990)—Surgery to right knee and missed eight games . . . (February 22, 1990)—Injured knee vs. Winnipeg.

Year	Team	League	Games	G.	A.	Pts.	Pen.
1981-82—Edina H.S. (c)	Minn. H.S.	26	22	28	50	26
1982-83—University of Wisconsin	WCHA	47	17	23	40	24
1983-84—University of Wisconsin	WCHA	38	10	28	38	56
1984-85—University of Wisconsin	WCHA	35	19	9	28	86
1985-86—University of Wisconsin	WCHA	42	20	40	60	*135
1985-86—Montreal Canadiens	NHL	3	0	0	0	0
1986-87—Sherbrooke Canadiens	AHL	11	1	5	6	25
1986-87—Montreal Canadiens (d)	NHL	48	6	12	18	55
1987-88—Utica Devils	AHL	9	5	3	8	40
1987-88—New Jersey Devils	NHL	44	4	2	6	65
1988-89—New Jersey Devils	NHL	68	5	6	11	249
1989-90—New Jersey Devils	NHL	67	8	17	25	160
NHL TOTALS			230	23	37	60	529

(c)—June, 1982—Drafted by Montreal Canadiens as underage player in 1982 NHL entry draft. Fourth Canadiens pick, 33rd overall, second round.

(d)—June, 1987—Traded by Montreal Canadiens to New Jersey Devils for a third-round 1987 draft pick (Mathieu Schneider).

STEWART MALGUNAS

Defense . . . 5'11" . . . 190 lbs. . . . Born, Prince George, B.C., April 21, 1970 . . . Shoots left.

Year	Team	League	Games	G.	A.	Pts.	Pen.
1985-86—Prince George Bantam	B.C.	49	10	25	35	85
1986-87—Prince George Midget	B.C.	50	11	31	42	102
1987-88—Prince George Junior	BCJHL	54	12	34	46	99
1987-88—New Westminster Bruins	WHL	6	0	0	0	0
1988-89—Seattle Thunderbirds	WHL	72	11	41	52	51
1989-90—Seattle Thunderbirds (a-c)	WHL	63	15	48	63	116

(c)—June 16, 1990—Selected by Detroit Red Wings in 1990 NHL entry draft. Third Red Wings pick, 66th overall, fourth round.

DEAN MALKOC

Defense . . . 6'2" . . . 202 lbs. . . . Born, Vancouver, B.C., January 26, 1970 . . . Shoots left.

Year	Team	League	Games	G.	A.	Pts.	Pen.
1987-88—Williams Lake	PCJHL	..	6	32	38	215
1988-89—Powell River	BCJHL	55	10	32	42	370
1989-90—Kamloops Blazers (c)	WHL	48	3	18	21	209

(c)—June 16, 1990—Selected by New Jersey Devils in 1990 NHL entry draft. Seventh Devils pick, 95th overall, fifth round.

TROY MALLETTE

Center . . . 6'2" . . . 190 lbs. . . . Born, Sudbury, Ont., February 25, 1970 . . . Shoots left . . . Also plays Left Wing . . . (October 28, 1990)—Fined $500 for attempting to injure Dean Chynoweth vs. N.Y. Islanders . . . (March 19, 1990)—Fined $500 for head-butting Ron Stern vs. Vancouver.

Year	Team	League	Games	G.	A.	Pts.	Pen.
1985-86—Rayside-Belfour Midget	OHA	27	24	26	50	75
1986-87—Sault Ste. Marie Greyhounds	OHL	65	20	25	45	157
1987-88—Sault Ste. Marie Greyhounds (c)	OHL	62	18	30	48	186
1988-89—Sault Ste. Marie Greyhounds	OHL	64	39	37	76	172
1989-90—New York Rangers	NHL	79	13	16	29	305
NHL TOTALS			79	13	16	29	305

(c)—June, 1988—Drafted by New York Rangers in 1988 NHL entry draft. First Rangers pick, 22nd overall, first round.

MATTHEW MALLGRAVE

Right Wing . . . 5'11" . . . 175 lbs. . . . Born, Washington, D.C., May 3, 1970 . . . Shoots right.

Year	Team	League	Games	G.	A.	Pts.	Pen.
1987-88—St. Paul's H.S. (c)	Maryland	..	21	22	43	..
1988-89—St. Paul's H.S.	Maryland	..	24	14	38	..
1989-90—Harvard University	ECAC	26	3	3	6	33

(c)—June, 1988—Selected by Toronto Maple Leafs in 1988 NHL entry draft. Sixth Maple Leafs pick, 132nd overall, seventh round.

DONALD MICHAEL MALONEY

Left Wing . . . 6'1" . . . 190 lbs. . . . Born, Lindsay, Ont., September 5, 1958 . . . Shoots left . . . Brother of Dave Maloney . . . (October, 1980)—Mononucleosis . . . Set record for most points by a rookie in playoffs (20) in 1979 (broken in 1981 by Dino Ciccarelli with 21) . . . (October 24, 1981)—Partial ligament tear in right knee at Toronto, missed 25 games and returned to lineup December 23, 1981 . . . (November 28, 1983)—Broke ring finger of right hand with Vancouver . . . (October, 1984)—Pulled abdominal muscle injury . . . (November 18, 1984)—Broke leg and ankle in collision with Bruce Driver vs. New Jersey, required surgery and a pin was inserted in his leg . . . (October 1, 1985)—Suspended by NHL for first three games of season for fighting vs. Philadelphia . . . (November 20, 1985)—Injured knee vs. Toronto and missed nine games . . . (November, 1987)—Injured left shoulder rotator cuff . . . (December, 1987)—Groin injury . . . (December 31, 1988)—Fractured left collarbone when checked by Joe Kocur at Detroit . . . (March 16, 1989)—Reinjured left shoulder when checked by Mike Ramsey vs. Buffalo.

Year	Team	League	Games	G.	A.	Pts.	Pen.
1974-75—Kitchener Rangers	Jr."A"OHA	5	1	3	4	0
1975-76—Kitchener Rangers	Jr."A"OHA	61	27	41	68	132
1976-77—Kitchener Rangers	Jr."A"OHA	38	22	34	56	126
1977-78—Kitchener Rangers (c)	Jr."A"OHA	62	30	74	104	143
1978-79—New Haven Nighthawks	AHL	38	18	26	44	62
1978-79—New York Rangers (d)	NHL	28	9	17	26	39
1979-80—New York Rangers	NHL	79	25	48	73	97
1980-81—New York Rangers	NHL	61	29	23	52	99
1981-82—New York Rangers	NHL	54	22	36	58	73
1982-83—New York Rangers	NHL	78	29	40	69	88
1983-84—New York Rangers	NHL	79	24	42	66	62
1984-85—New York Rangers	NHL	37	11	16	27	32
1985-86—New York Rangers	NHL	68	11	17	28	56
1986-87—New York Rangers	NHL	72	19	38	57	117
1987-88—New York Rangers	NHL	66	12	21	33	60
1988-89—New York Rangers (e)	NHL	31	4	9	13	16
1988-89—Hartford Whalers (f-g)	NHL	21	3	11	14	23
1989-90—New York Islanders	NHL	79	16	27	43	47
NHL TOTALS			753	214	345	559	809

(c)—Drafted from Kitchener Rangers by New York Rangers in second round of 1978 amateur draft.

(d)—Tied for lead in assists (13) during playoffs.

(e)—December 26, 1988—Traded with Norm Maciver and Brian Lawton by New York Rangers to Hartford Whalers for Carey Wilson and a fifth-round 1990 draft pick.

(f)—July, 1989—Released by Hartford Whalers.

(g)—August, 1989—Signed as a free agent by New York Islanders.

STEVE MALTAIS

Left Wing . . . 6'1" . . . 190 lbs. . . . Born, Ottawa, Ont., January 25, 1969 . . . Shoots left.

Year	Team	League	Games	G.	A.	Pts.	Pen.
1985-86—Wexford Raiders	MTHL	33	35	19	54	38
1986-87—Cornwall Royals (c)	OHL	65	32	12	44	29
1987-88—Cornwall Royals	OHL	59	39	46	85	30
1988-89—Cornwall Royals	OHL	58	53	70	123	67
1988-89—Fort Wayne Komets (d)	IHL	..	..	..	..	..
1989-90—Washington Capitals	NHL	8	0	0	0	2
1989-90—Baltimore Skipjacks	AHL	67	29	37	66	54
NHL TOTALS			8	0	0	0	2

(c)—June, 1987—Drafted as underage junior by Washington Capitals in 1987 NHL entry draft. Second Capitals pick, 57th overall, third round.

(d)—No regular season record. Played four playoff games.

KENT MANDERVILLE

Left Wing . . . 6'3" . . . 195 lbs. . . . Born, Edmonton, Alta., April 12, 1971 . . . Shoots left.

Year	Team	League	Games	G.	A.	Pts.	Pen.
1987-88—Notre Dame Midget	Sask.	32	22	18	40	42
1988-89—Notre Dame Hounds (c)	SJHL	58	39	36	75	165
1989-90—Cornell University (d-e)	ECAC	26	11	15	26	28

(c)—June, 1989—Drafted by Calgary Flames in 1989 NHL entry draft. First Flames pick, 24th overall, second round.

(d)—Named to ECAC All-Rookie team.

(e)—Named ECAC Rookie-of-the-Year.

DAVID MANSON

Defense . . . 6'2" . . . 192 lbs. . . . Born, Prince Albert, Sask., January 27, 1967 . . . Shoots left . . . (October 8, 1989)—Suspended three games for pushing linesman Ron Asselstine during a fight with Chris Nilan vs. N.Y. Rangers . . . (December 8, 1989) —Charley horse in right leg after colliding with John McIntyre vs. Toronto . . . (December 23, 1989)—Suspended 13 games for fighting at Toronto (Three games for abusing linesman Ron Finn and 10 games for returning to the ice to participate in a fight with Gary Leeman) . . . (February 27, 1990)—Suspended three games for biting Scott Stevens vs. Washington.

Year	Team	League	Games	G.	A.	Pts.	Pen.
1983-84—Prince Albert Raiders	WHL	70	2	7	9	233
1984-85—Prince Albert Raiders (c)	WHL	72	8	30	38	247
1985-86—Prince Albert Raiders (b)	WHL	70	14	34	48	177
1986-87—Chicago Black Hawks	NHL	63	1	8	9	146
1987-88—Saginaw Hawks	IHL	6	0	3	3	37
1987-88—Chicago Black Hawks	NHL	54	1	6	7	185
1988-89—Chicago Black Hawks	NHL	79	18	36	54	352
1989-90—Chicago Black Hawks	NHL	59	5	23	28	301
NHL TOTALS			255	25	73	98	984

(c)—June, 1985—Drafted as underage junior by Chicago Black Hawks in 1985 NHL entry draft. First Black Hawks pick, 11th overall, first round.

MAURICE (MOE) WILLIAM MANTHA

Defense . . . 6'2" . . . 197 lbs. . . . Born, Lakewood, O., January 21, 1961 . . . Shoots right . . . Son of Maurice Mantha (AHL early 1960s) . . . Missed 20 games during 1980-81 season with recurring back problems . . . (October, 1981)—Eye injury . . . (October, 1982)—Surgery for injured shoulder . . . (December 7, 1984)—Broke nose when hit by a puck at N.Y. Rangers . . . (February, 1985)—Bruised spine . . . (February 16, 1986)—Sprained knee at New Jersey . . . (November 26, 1986)—Fractured right wrist at N.Y. Islanders . . . (February 26, 1987)—Missed four games with eye injury at N.Y. Islanders . . . (March 24, 1987)—Sprained left knee vs. Philadelphia . . . (February 29, 1988)—Bruised kneecap vs. New Jersey . . . (September, 1988)—Separated left shoulder during Minnesota North Stars training camp . . . (January, 1989)—Pulled groin . . . (March, 1990)—Pulled groin.

Year	Team	League	Games	G.	A.	Pts.	Pen.
1978-79—Toronto Marlboros		OMJHL	68	10	38	48	57
1979-80—Toronto Marlboros (c)		OMJHL	58	8	38	46	86
1980-81—Winnipeg Jets		NHL	58	2	23	25	35
1981-82—Tulsa Oilers		CHL	33	8	15	23	56
1981-82—Winnipeg Jets		NHL	25	0	12	12	28
1982-83—Sherbrooke Jets		AHL	13	1	4	5	13
1982-83—Winnipeg Jets		NHL	21	2	7	9	6
1983-84—Sherbrooke Jets		AHL	7	1	1	2	10
1983-84—Winnipeg Jets (d)		NHL	72	16	38	54	67
1984-85—Pittsburgh Penguins		NHL	71	11	40	51	54
1985-86—Pittsburgh Penguins		NHL	78	15	52	67	102
1986-87—Pittsburgh Penguins		NHL	62	9	31	40	44
1987-88—Pittsburgh Penguins (e)		NHL	21	2	8	10	23
1987-88—Edmonton Oilers (f)		NHL	25	0	6	6	26
1987-88—Minnesota North Stars		NHL	30	9	13	22	4
1988-89—Minnesota North Stars (g)		NHL	16	1	6	7	10
1988-89—Philadelphia Flyers		NHL	30	3	8	11	33
1989-90—Winnipeg Jets (h)		NHL	73	2	26	28	28
NHL TOTALS			582	72	270	342	460

(c)—June, 1980—Drafted as underage junior by Winnipeg Jets in 1980 NHL entry draft. Second Jets pick, 23rd overall, second round.

(d)—May, 1984—Traded by Winnipeg Jets to Pittsburgh Penguins to complete March trade for Randy Carlyle.

(e)—November, 1987—Traded with Craig Simpson, Dave Hannan and Chris Joseph by Pittsburgh Penguins to Edmonton Oilers for Paul Coffey, Dave Hunter and Wayne Van Dorp.

(f)—January, 1988—Traded by Edmonton Oilers to Minnesota North Stars for Keith Acton.

(g)—December 8, 1988—Traded by Minnesota North Stars to Philadelphia Flyers for fifth round pick of 1989 entry draft (Pat MacLeod).

(h)—October 2, 1989—Selected by Winnipeg Jets in 1989 NHL waiver draft for $5,000.

BRYAN MARCHMENT

Defense . . . 6'1'' . . . 195 lbs. . . . Born, Scarborough, Ont., May 1, 1969 . . . Shoots left . . . (October 1, 1986)—Suspended for three games by OHL . . . (December 10, 1989)—Suspended six AHL games for fighting Bobby Babcock vs. Baltimore . . . (March, 1990)—Sprained shoulder.

Year	Team	League	Games	G.	A.	Pts.	Pen.
1984-85—Toronto Nats.		MTHL	....	14	35	49	229
1985-86—Belleville Bulls		OHL	57	5	15	20	225
1986-87—Belleville Bulls (c)		OHL	52	6	38	44	238
1987-88—Belleville Bulls		OHL	56	7	51	58	200
1988-89—Belleville Bulls (b)		OHL	43	14	36	50	198
1988-89—Winnipeg Jets		NHL	2	0	0	0	2
1989-90—Winnipeg Jets		NHL	7	0	2	2	28
1989-90—Moncton Hawks		AHL	56	4	19	23	217
NHL TOTALS			9	0	2	2	30

(c)—June, 1987—Drafted as underage junior by Winnipeg Jets in 1987 NHL entry draft. First Jets pick, 16th overall, first round.

LANCE MARCIANO

Defense . . . 6'2'' . . . 200 lbs. . . . Born, Mt. Vernon, N.Y., September 12, 1969 . . . Shoots right.

Year	Team	League	Games	G.	A.	Pts.	Pen.
1985-86—Choate Prep.		Conn. H.S.	....	....	....	....	....
1986-87—Choate Prep. (c)		Conn. H.S.		8	16	24	....
1987-88—Yale University		ECAC	18	0	2	2	16
1988-89—Yale University		ECAC	24	1	0	1	26
1989-90—Yale University		ECAC	27	0	9	9	34

(c)—June, 1987—Drafted by New York Rangers in 1987 NHL entry draft. Twelfth Rangers pick, 220th overall, 11th round.

DAVID MARCINYSHYN

Defense . . . 6'3'' . . . 195 lbs. . . . Born, Edmonton, Alta., February 4, 1967 . . . Shoots left.

Year	Team	League	Games	G.	A.	Pts.	Pen.
1984-85—Fort Saskatchewan		AJHL	55	11	41	52	311
1985-86—Kamloops Blazers		WHL	57	2	7	9	211
1986-87—Kamloops Blazers (c)		WHL	68	5	27	32	106
1987-88—Utica Devils		AHL	73	2	7	9	179
1987-88—Flint Spirits		IHL	3	0	0	0	4
1988-89—Utica Devils		AHL	74	4	14	18	101
1989-90—Utica Devils		AHL	74	6	18	24	164

(c)—September, 1986—Signed by New Jersey Devils as a free agent.

CHRIS MARINUCCI

Center . . . 6' . . . 175 lbs. . . . Born, Grand Rapids, Minn., December 29, 1971 . . . Shoots left.

Year	Team	League	Games	G.	A.	Pts.	Pen.
1988-89—Grand Rapids H.S.		Minn. H.S.	25	24	18	42	....
1989-90—Grand Rapids H.S. (c)		Minn. H.S.	28	24	39	63	....

(c)—June 16, 1990—Selected by New York Islanders in 1990 NHL entry draft. Fourth Islanders pick, 90th overall, fifth round.

MICHAEL A. MARKOVICH

Defense . . . 6'3'' . . . 200 lbs. . . . Born, Grand Forks, North Dakota, April 25, 1969 . . . (September, 1988)—Subflexation of left shoulder . . . Played Left Wing in high school.

Year	Team	League	Games	G.	A.	Pts.	Pen.
1984-85—Central High School		No. Dak.	23	8	11	19	12
1985-86—Central High School		No. Dak.	23	19	18	37	20
1986-87—Central High School		No. Dak.	23	26	25	51	24

Year	Team	League	Games	G.	A.	Pts.	Pen.
1987-88—Rochester Mustangs		USHL	48	13	41	54	38
1988-89—Univ. of Denver (c)		WCHA	43	5	13	18	38
1989-90—Univ. of Denver		WCHA	42	4	17	21	34

(c)—June, 1989—Drafted by Pittsburgh Penguins in 1989 NHL entry draft. Sixth Penguins pick, 121st overall, sixth round.

NEVIN MARKWART

Left Wing . . . 5'11'' . . . 175 lbs. . . . Born, Toronto, Ont., December 9, 1964 . . . Shoots left . . . (January, 1983)—Shoulder separation . . . (October, 1984)—Bruised hip . . . (December 28, 1985)—Hip-pointer at St. Louis and missed four games . . . (March 22, 1986)—Sprained right knee vs. N.Y. Islanders . . . (October, 1987)—Dislocated left shoulder . . . (April, 1988)—Strained groin . . . (October, 1988)—Strained abdominal muscle kept him out all season . . . (July, 1989)—Abdominal surgery, missed training camp and first three games of season . . . (October 29, 1989)—Dislocated left shoulder at Buffalo . . . (November 13, 1989)—Reinjured left shoulder in team practice . . .(November 18, 1989)—Surgery to dislocated and fractured left shoulder . . . (February 20, 1990)—Additional shoulder surgery.

Year	Team	League	Games	G.	A.	Pts.	Pen.
1981-82—Regina Blues		SJHL	....				
1981-82—Regina Pats		WHL	25	2	12	14	56
1982-83—Regina Pats (c)		WHL	43	27	39	66	91
1983-84—Boston Bruins		NHL	70	14	16	30	121
1984-85—Hershey Bears		AHL	38	13	18	31	79
1984-85—Boston Bruins		NHL	26	0	4	4	36
1985-86—Boston Bruins		NHL	65	7	15	22	207
1986-87—Boston Bruins		NHL	64	10	9	19	225
1986-87—Moncton Golden Flames		AHL	3	3	3	6	11
1987-88—Boston Bruins		NHL	25	1	12	13	85
1988-89—Maine Mariners		AHL	1	0	1	1	0
1989-90—Boston Bruins		NHL	8	1	2	3	15
NHL TOTALS			258	33	58	91	689

(c)—June, 1983—Drafted as underage junior by Boston Bruins in 1983 NHL entry draft. First Bruins pick, 21st overall, first round.

DANIEL MAROIS

Right Wing . . . 6' . . . 180 lbs. . . . Born, Montreal, Que., October 3, 1968 . . . Shoots right . . . (January, 1989)—Flu . . . (April 2, 1989)—Damaged ligaments in right knee and required surgery . . . (November 12, 1989)—Bruised left shoulder at Minnesota and missed 11 games.

Year	Team	League	Games	G.	A.	Pts.	Pen.
1985-86—Verdun Junior Canadiens		QMJHL	58	42	35	77	110
1986-87—Chicoutimi Sagueneens (c)		QMJHL	40	22	26	48	143
1987-88—Verdun Junior Canadiens		QMJHL	67	52	36	88	153
1987-88—Newmarket Saints		AHL	8	4	4	8	4
1988-89—Toronto Maple Leafs		NHL	76	31	23	54	76
1989-90—Toronto Maple Leafs		NHL	68	39	37	76	82
NHL TOTALS			144	70	60	130	158

(c)—June, 1987—Drafted as underage junior by Toronto Maple Leafs in 1987 NHL entry draft. Second Maple Leafs pick, 28th overall, second round.

MARIO JOSEPH MAROIS

Defense . . . 5'11'' . . . 170 lbs. . . . Born, Ancienne Lorette, Que., December 15, 1957 . . . Shoots right . . . Missed part of 1977-78 season with broken ankle . . . (March 27, 1982)—Broke right wrist at Montreal . . . (December 30, 1982)—Broke right leg in exhibition game vs. USSR National Team . . . (October, 1988)—Played first three weeks of season with an undetected stress fracture of his ankle. He had injured it during the Winnipeg Jets training camp . . . (January 28, 1989)—Fractured collarbone at Hartford . . . (November 9, 1989)—Sprained right shoulder at N.Y. Islanders and missed 12 games.

Year	Team	League	Games	G.	A.	Pts.	Pen.
1975-76—Quebec Remparts		QMJHL	67	11	42	53	270
1976-77—Quebec Remparts (b-c)		QMJHL	72	17	67	84	249
1977-78—New Haven Nighthawks		AHL	52	8	23	31	147
1977-78—New York Rangers		NHL	8	1	1	2	15
1978-79—New York Rangers		NHL	71	5	26	31	153
1979-80—New York Rangers		NHL	79	8	23	31	142
1980-81—New York Rangers (d)		NHL	8	1	2	3	46
1980-81—Vancouver Canucks (e)		NHL	50	4	12	16	115
1980-81—Quebec Nordiques		NHL	11	0	7	7	20
1981-82—Quebec Nordiques		NHL	71	11	32	43	161
1982-83—Quebec Nordiques		NHL	36	2	12	14	108
1983-84—Quebec Nordiques		NHL	80	13	36	49	151
1984-85—Quebec Nordiques		NHL	76	6	37	43	91
1985-86—Quebec Nordiques (f)		NHL	20	1	12	13	42
1985-86—Winnipeg Jets		NHL	56	4	28	32	110
1986-87—Winnipeg Jets		NHL	79	4	40	44	106
1987-88—Winnipeg Jets		NHL	79	7	44	51	111
1988-89—Winnipeg Jets (g)		NHL	7	1	1	2	17
1988-89—Quebec Nordiques		NHL	42	2	11	13	101
1989-90—Quebec Nordiques		NHL	67	3	15	18	104
NHL TOTALS			840	73	339	412	1593

(c)—Drafted from Quebec Remparts by New York Rangers in fourth round of 1977 amateur draft.

(d)—November, 1980—Traded by New York Rangers with Jim Mayer to Vancouver Canucks for Jere Gillis and Jeff Bandura.

(e)—March, 1981—Traded by Vancouver Canucks to Quebec Nordiques for Garry Lariviere in a three-way deal that saw Lariviere then go to Edmonton Oilers for Blair MacDonald.

(f)—November, 1985—Traded by Quebec Nordiques to Winnipeg Jets for Robert Picard.

(g)—December 6, 1988—Traded by Winnipeg Jets to Quebec Nordiques for Gord Donnelly.

DALE MARQUETTE

Left Wing . . . 5'11" . . . 190 lbs. . . . Born, Prince George, B.C., March 8, 1968 . . . Shoots left.

Year	Team	League	Games	G.	A.	Pts.	Pen.
1984-85—Lethbridge Broncos		WHL	50	4	4	8	46
1985-86—Lethbridge Broncos		WHL	64	12	14	26	83
1986-87—Brandon Wheat Kings (c)		WHL	68	41	29	70	59
1987-88—Saginaw Hawks (d)		IHL	....	....	....	....	....
1987-88—Brandon Wheat Kings		WHL	62	51	52	103	48
1988-89—Saginaw Hawks		IHL	46	11	8	19	35
1989-90—Indianapolis Ice		IHL	32	3	3	6	13

(c)—June, 1987—Drafted by Chicago Black Hawks in 1987 NHL entry draft. Tenth Black Hawks pick, 197th overall, 10th round.
(d)—No regular season record. Played three playoff games.

CHARLES BRADLEY (BRAD) MARSH

Defense . . . 6'2" . . . 215 lbs. . . . Born, London, Ont., March 31, 1958 . . . Shoots left . . . Brother of Paul Marsh . . . Set NHL record by playing a total of 83 games in 1981-82 . . . (January 2, 1983)—Bruised knee tendon at Chicago . . . (March 24, 1983)—Broken fibula vs. Toronto . . . (December, 1987)—Concussion . . . (February, 1988)—Bruised knee . . . (October 31, 1989)—Injured groin at Minnesota . . . Does not wear a helmet.

Year	Team	League	Games	G.	A.	Pts.	Pen.
1974-75—London Knights		Jr."A"OHA	70	4	17	21	160
1975-76—London Knights		Jr."A"OHA	61	3	26	29	184
1976-77—London Knights		Jr."A"OHA	63	7	33	40	121
1977-78—London Knights (a-c-d)		Jr."A"OHA	62	8	55	63	192
1978-79—Atlanta Flames		NHL	80	0	19	19	101
1979-80—Atlanta Flames		NHL	80	2	9	11	119
1980-81—Calgary Flames		NHL	80	1	12	13	87
1981-82—Calgary Flames (e)		NHL	17	0	1	1	10
1981-82—Philadelphia Flyers		NHL	66	2	22	24	106
1982-83—Philadelphia Flyers		NHL	68	2	11	13	52
1983-84—Philadelphia Flyers		NHL	77	3	14	17	83
1984-85—Philadelphia Flyers		NHL	77	2	18	20	91
1985-86—Philadelphia Flyers		NHL	79	0	13	13	123
1986-87—Philadelphia Flyers		NHL	77	2	9	11	124
1987-88—Philadelphia Flyers		NHL	70	3	9	12	57
1988-89—Toronto Maple Leafs (f)		NHL	80	1	15	16	79
1989-90—Toronto Maple Leafs		NHL	79	1	13	14	95
NHL TOTALS			930	19	165	184	1127

(c)—Drafted from London Knights by Atlanta Flames in first round of 1978 amateur draft.
(d)—Shared Max Kaminsky Memorial Trophy (Outstanding Defenseman) with Rob Ramage.
(e)—November, 1981—Traded by Calgary Flames to Philadelphia Flyers for Mel Bridgman.
(f)—October 3, 1988—Selected by Toronto Maple Leafs in 1988 NHL waiver draft for $2,500.

JASON MARSHALL

Defense . . . 6'2" . . . 185 lbs. . . . Born, Cranbrook, B.C., February 22, 1971 . . . Shoots right.

Year	Team	League	Games	G.	A.	Pts.	Pen.
1987-88—Columbia Valley Rockies		KIJHL	40	4	28	32	150
1988-89—Vernon Lakers (c-d)		BCJHL	48	10	30	40	197
1988-89—Canadian National Team		Int'l.	2	0	1	1	0
1989-90—Canadian National Team		Int'l.	72	1	11	12	57

(c)—August, 1988—WHL rights traded with Kevin Derksen by Regina Pats to Tri-City Americans for Mark Cipriano.
(d)—June, 1989—Drafted by St. Louis Blues in 1989 NHL entry draft. First Blues pick, ninth overall, first round.

CRAIG MARTIN

Right Wing . . . 6'2" . . . 219 lbs. . . . Born, Amherst, Nova Scotia, January 21, 1971 . . . Shoots right . . . (April 14, 1990)—Suspended for opening game of 1990-91 season for fighting in a playoff game vs. Laval.

Year	Team	League	Games	G.	A.	Pts.	Pen.
1986-87—Picton County Midget		Quebec	38	19	15	34	90
1987-88—Hull Olympiques		QMJHL	66	5	5	10	137
1988-89—Hull Olympiques		QMJHL	70	14	29	43	260
1989-90—Hull Olympiques (c)		QMJHL	66	14	31	45	299

(c)—June 16, 1990—Selected by Winnipeg Jets in 1990 NHL entry draft. Sixth Jets pick, 98th overall, fifth round.

TOM MARTIN

Left Wing . . . 6'2" . . . 190 lbs. . . . Born, Kelowna, B.C., May 11, 1964 . . . Shoots left . . . Set University of Denver record for penalty minutes during his freshman year (1982-83) . . . (March 21, 1990)—Broke nose when struck by a Randy Cunneyworth shot during a team practice.

Year	Team	League	Games	G.	A.	Pts.	Pen.
1981-82—Kelowna (c)		BCJHL	51	35	45	80	293
1982-83—University of Denver (d)		WCHA	37	8	18	26	128
1983-84—Victoria Cougars		WHL	60	30	45	75	261
1983-84—Sherbrooke Jets		AHL	5	0	0	0	16
1984-85—Sherbrooke Canadiens		AHL	58	4	15	19	212
1984-85—Winnipeg Jets		NHL	8	1	0	1	42
1985-86—Winnipeg Jets		NHL	5	0	0	0	0
1985-86—Sherbrooke Canadiens		AHL	69	11	18	29	227
1986-87—Adirondack Red Wings		AHL	18	5	6	11	57
1986-87—Winnipeg Jets (e)		NHL	11	1	0	1	49

Year	Team	League	Games	G.	A.	Pts.	Pen.
1987-88—Binghamton Whalers		AHL	71	28	61	89	344
1987-88—Hartford Whalers		NHL	5	1	2	3	14
1988-89—Minnesota North Stars (f-g)		NHL	4	1	1	2	4
1988-89—Hartford Whalers		NHL	38	7	6	13	113
1989-90—Binghamton Whalers		AHL	24	4	10	14	113
1989-90—Hartford Whalers (h)		NHL	21	1	2	3	37
NHL TOTALS			92	12	11	23	259

(c)—June, 1982—Drafted as underage player by Winnipeg Jets in 1982 NHL entry draft. Second Jets pick, 74th overall, fourth round.
(d)—January, 1983—WHL rights traded by Seattle Breakers with cash to Victoria Cougars for used team bus and player to be named later.
(e)—August, 1987—Signed as free agent by Hartford Whalers.
(f)—October 3, 1988—Selected by Minnesota North Stars in 1988 NHL waiver draft for $30,000.
(g)—November 29, 1988—Reclaimed by Hartford Whalers from Minnesota North Stars.
(h)—July 11, 1990—Signed by Los Angeles Kings as a free agent.

DARCY MARTINI

Defense . . . 6'4" . . . 220 lbs. . . . Born, Castlegar, B.C., January 30, 1969 . . . Shoots left.

Year	Team	League	Games	G.	A.	Pts.	Pen.
1984-85—Castlegar Rebels		KIJHL	38	4	17	21	58
1985-86—Castlegar Rebels		KIJHL	38	8	28	36	180
1986-87—Castlegar Rebels		KIJHL	40	12	53	65	260
1987-88—Vernon Lakers		BCJHL	48	9	26	35	193
1988-89—Michigan Tech. Univ. (c)		WCHA	37	1	2	3	107
1989-90—Michigan Tech. Univ.		WCHA	36	3	16	19	150

(c)—June, 1989—Drafted by Edmonton Oilers in 1989 NHL entry draft. Eighth Oilers pick, 162nd overall, eighth round.

STEVE MARTINSON

Left Wing . . . 6'1" . . . 205 lbs. . . . Born, Minnetonka, Minn., June 21, 1957 . . . Shoots left . . . Set AHL single-season penalty minute record in 1985-86 . . . (May, 1986)—Disc operation . . . (March 12, 1988)—Suspended six AHL games for fighting with Mark Ferner vs. Rochester . . . (October 10, 1989)—Back spasms and missed 10 games.

Year	Team	League	Games	G.	A.	Pts.	Pen.
1981-82—Toledo Goaldiggers		IHL	35	12	18	30	128
1982-83—Birmingham Bulls (c)		CHL	43	4	5	9	184
1982-83—Toledo Goaldiggers		IHL	32	9	10	19	111
1983-84—Tulsa Oilers (d)		CHL	42	3	6	9	*240
1984-85—Salt Lake Golden Eagles		IHL	32	4	7	11	140
1984-85—Toledo Goaldiggers (e)		IHL	22	0	3	3	160
1984-85—New Haven Nighthawks		AHL	4	0	0	0	17
1985-86—Hershey Bears (f)		AHL	69	3	6	9	*432
1986-87—Hershey Bears		AHL	17	0	3	3	85
1986-87—Adirondack Red Wings (g)		AHL	14	1	1	2	78
1987-88—Adirondack Red Wings		AHL	32	6	8	14	146
1987-88—Detroit Red Wings		NHL	10	1	1	2	84
1988-89—Sherbrooke Canadiens		AHL	10	5	7	12	61
1988-89—Montreal Canadiens (h)		NHL	25	1	0	1	87
1989-90—Montreal Canadiens		NHL	13	0	0	0	64
1989-90—Sherbrooke Canadiens		AHL	37	6	20	26	111
NHL TOTALS			48	2	1	3	235

(c)—Led CHL playoffs with 80 penalty minutes.
(d)—Led CHL playoffs with 43 penalty minutes.
(e)—February, 1985—Traded with Kurt Kleinendorst by Salt Lake Golden Eagles to Toledo Goaldiggers for Kevin Conway, Blake Stephan, Grant Rezansoff and Steve Harrison.
(f)—September, 1985—Signed by Philadelphia Flyers as a free agent.
(g)—March, 1987—Signed by Adirondack Red Wings as a free agent.
(h)—August, 1988—Signed by Montreal Canadiens as a free agent.

DAVID MARVIN

Defense . . . 6'1" . . . 170 lbs. . . . Born, Warroad, Minn., March 10, 1968 . . . Shoots right . . . Son of Cal Marvin (Former player at North Dakota and a member of the U.S. Hockey Hall-of-Fame).

Year	Team	League	Games	G.	A.	Pts.	Pen.
1986-87—Warroad H.S. (c)		Minn. H.S.	....	....	....	....	....
1987-88—Univ. of North Dakota		WCHA	35	4	17	21	12
1988-89—Univ. of North Dakota		WCHA	38	4	6	10	24
1989-90—Univ. of North Dakota		WCHA	45	3	23	26	70

(c)—June, 1987—Drafted by St. Louis Blues in 1987 NHL entry draft. Tenth Blues pick, 201st overall, 10th round.

JIM MATHIESON

Defense . . . 6'1" . . . 209 lbs. . . . Born, Kindersley, Sask., January 24, 1970 . . . Shoots left.

Year	Team	League	Games	G.	A.	Pts.	Pen.
1986-87—Regina Pats		WHL	40	0	9	9	40
1987-88—Regina Pats		WHL	72	3	12	15	115
1988-89—Regina Pats (c)		WHL	62	5	22	27	151
1989-90—Regina Pats		WHL	67	1	26	27	158
1989-90—Baltimore Skipjacks (d)		AHL	....	....	....	....	....
1989-90—Washington Capitals		NHL	2	0	0	0	4
NHL TOTALS			2	0	0	0	4

(c)—June, 1989—Drafted by Washington Capitals in 1989 NHL entry draft. Third Capitals pick, 59th overall, third round.
(d)—No regular season games. Played three playoff games.

STEPHANE MATTEAU

Left Wing . . . 6'3" . . . 185 lbs. . . . Born, Rouyn, Que., September 2, 1969 . . . Shoots left.

Year	Team	League	Games	G.	A.	Pts.	Pen.
1985-86—Hull Olympiques		QMJHL	60	6	8	14	19
1986-87—Hull Olympiques (c)		QMJHL	69	27	48	75	113
1987-88—Hull Olympiques		QMJHL	57	17	40	57	179
1988-89—Hull Olympiques		QMJHL	59	44	45	89	202
1988-89—Salt Lake Golden Eagles (d)		IHL	....	....	....	....	....
1989-90—Salt Lake Golden Eagles		IHL	81	23	35	58	130

(c)—June, 1987—Drafted as underage junior by Calgary Flames in 1987 NHL entry draft. Second Flames pick, 25th overall, second round.

(d)—No regular season record. Played nine playoff games.

IVAN MATULIK

Left Wing . . . 6' . . . 194 lbs. . . . Born, Nitra, Czechoslovakia, June 17, 1968 . . . Shoots left . . . (September 27, 1988)—Tore medial collateral ligament in right knee during Edmonton Oilers training camp, required surgery and missed most of the season.

Year	Team	League	Games	G.	A.	Pts.	Pen.
1986-87—Slovan Bratislava (c)		Czech.	25	1	3	4	..
1987-88—Nova Scotia Oilers		AHL	46	13	10	23	29
1988-89—Cape Breton Oilers		AHL	1	0	0	0	0
1989-90—Phoenix Roadrunners		IHL	29	3	5	8	46
1989-90—Cape Breton Oilers		AHL	32	2	6	8	44

(c)—June, 1986—Drafted by Edmonton Oilers in 1986 NHL entry draft. Seventh Oilers pick, 147th overall, seventh round.

SCOTT MATUSOVICH

Defense . . . 6'2" . . . 205 lbs. . . . Born, Derby, Conn., January 31, 1969 . . . Shoots left.

Year	Team	League	Games	G.	A.	Pts.	Pen.
1986-87—Canterbury H.S.		Ct. H.S.	..	10	22	32	..
1987-88—Canterbury H.S. (c)		Ct. H.S.	..	20	31	51	..
1988-89—Yale University		ECAC	25	3	11	14	40
1989-90—Yale University		ECAC	28	1	15	16	55

(c)—June, 1988—Drafted by Calgary Flames in 1988 NHL entry draft. Fifth Flames pick, 90th overall, fifth round.

DANIEL MAURICE

Center . . . 6' . . . 175 lbs. . . . Born, Repentigny, Que., April 19, 1969 . . . Shoots left . . . (September, 1989)—Missed Chicoutimi training camp with mononucleosis.

Year	Team	League	Games	G.	A.	Pts.	Pen.
1985-86—Chicoutimi Sagueneens		QMJHL	67	6	22	28	41
1986-87—Chicoutimi Sagueneens		QMJHL	68	31	61	92	151
1987-88—Chicoutimi Sagueneens (c)		QMJHL	69	56	90	146	150
1988-89—Drummondville Voltigeurs		QMJHL	70	46	72	118	150
1989-90—Chicoutimi Sagueneens		QMJHL	62	43	49	92	228

(c)—June, 1988—Drafted by Chicago Black Hawks in 1988 NHL entry draft. Ninth Black Hawks pick, 197th overall, 10th round.

ALAN MAY

Right Wing . . . 6'1" . . . 215 lbs. . . . Born, Barrhead, Alta., January 14, 1965 . . . Shoots right.

Year	Team	League	Games	G.	A.	Pts.	Pen.
1984-85—Estevan		SAJHL	64	51	47	98	409
1985-86—Medicine Hat Tigers		WHL	6	1	0	1	25
1986-87—New Westminster Bruins		WHL	32	8	9	17	81
1986-87—Springfield Indians		AHL	4	0	2	2	11
1986-87—Carolina Thunderbirds		ACHL	42	23	14	37	310
1987-88—Maine Mariners (c)		AHL	61	14	11	25	357
1987-88—Boston Bruins (d)		NHL	3	0	0	0	15
1987-88—Nova Scotia Oilers		AHL	12	4	1	5	54
1988-89—Edmonton Oilers (e-f)		NHL	3	1	0	1	7
1988-89—Cape Breton Oilers		AHL	50	12	13	25	214
1988-89—New Haven Nighthawks		AHL	12	2	8	10	99
1989-90—Washington Capitals		NHL	77	7	10	17	339
NHL TOTALS			83	8	10	18	361

(c)—September, 1987—Signed by Boston Bruins as a free agent.

(d)—March, 1988—Traded by Boston Bruins to Edmonton Oilers for Moe Lemay.

(e)—March 7, 1989—Traded with Jim Wiemer by Edmonton Oilers to Los Angeles Kings for Brian Wilks and John English.

(f)—June 17, 1989—Traded by Los Angeles Kings to Washington Capitals for a fifth-round 1989 draft pick (Tom Newman).

ANDY MAY

Center . . . 6'2" . . . 180 lbs. . . . Born, Mississauga, Ont., May 2, 1968 . . . Shoots left . . . (November 18, 1988)—Suspended one Hockey East game for butt-ending during a fight with Lowell . . . (November 28, 1989)—Given a two-game suspension for fighting at Merrimack.

Year	Team	League	Games	G.	A.	Pts.	Pen.
1985-86—Bramalea Jr. B (c)		OHA	35	21	26	47	41
1986-87—Northeastern Univ.		H. East	36	4	8	12	25
1987-88—Northeastern Univ.		H. East	17	2	5	7	10
1988-89—Northeastern Univ.		H. East	30	12	14	26	43
1989-90—Northeastern Univ.		H. East	35	13	15	28	35

(c)—June, 1986—Drafted by St. Louis Blues in 1986 NHL entry draft. Seventh Blues pick, 136th overall, seventh round.

BRAD MAY

Left Wing . . . 6' . . . 200 lbs. . . . Born, Toronto, Ont., November 29, 1971 . . . Shoots left . . . (August, 1990)—Knee injury and expected to miss first two months of season.

Year	Team	League	Games	G.	A.	Pts.	Pen.
1987-88—Markham		OHA	31	22	37	59	58
1988-89—Niagara Falls Thunder		OHL	65	8	14	22	304
1989-90—Niagara Falls Thunder (b-c)		OHL	61	33	58	91	223

(c)—June 16, 1990—Selected by Buffalo Sabres in 1990 NHL entry draft. First Sabres pick, 14th overall, first round.

DEREK MAYER

Defense . . . 6' . . . 190 lbs. . . . Born, Rossland, B.C., May 21, 1967 . . . Shoots right . . . (January, 1986)—Dislocated shoulder . . . (December, 1987)—Separated shoulder.

Year	Team	League	Games	G.	A.	Pts.	Pen.
1985-86—University of Denver (c)		WCHA	44	2	7	9	42
1986-87—University of Denver		WCHA	38	5	17	22	87
1987-88—University of Denver		WCHA	34	5	16	21	82
1988-89—Canadian National Team		Int'l.	58	3	13	16	81
1989-90—Adirondack Red Wings		AHL	62	4	26	30	56

(c)—June, 1986—Drafted by Detroit Red Wings in 1986 NHL entry draft. Third Red Wings pick, 43rd overall, third round.

JAY MAZUR

Right Wing . . . 6'2" . . . 200 lbs. . . . Born, Hamilton, Ont., January 22, 1965 . . . Shoots right.

Year	Team	League	Games	G.	A.	Pts.	Pen.
1982-83—Breck H.S. (c)		Minn. H.S.					
1983-84—Univ. of Maine		H. East	34	14	9	23	14
1984-85—Univ. of Maine		H. East	31	0	6	6	20
1985-86—Univ. of Maine		H. East	35	5	7	12	18
1986-87—Univ. of Maine		H. East	39	16	10	26	61
1987-88—Flint Spirits		IHL	43	17	11	28	36
1987-88—Fredericton Express		AHL	31	14	6	20	28
1988-89—Milwaukee Admirals		IHL	73	33	31	64	86
1988-89—Vancouver Canucks		NHL	1	0	0	0	0
1989-90—Milwaukee Admirals		IHL	70	20	27	47	63
1989-90—Vancouver Canucks		NHL	5	0	0	0	4
NHL TOTALS			6	0	0	0	4

(c)—June, 1983—Drafted by Vancouver Canucks in 1983 NHL entry draft. Twelfth Canucks pick, 230th overall, 12th round.

ANDREW McBAIN

Right Wing . . . 6'1" . . . 190 lbs. . . . Born, Toronto, Ont., January 18, 1965 . . . Shoots right . . . (November, 1982)—Fractured cheekbone . . . (March, 1983)—Separated sterno clavicular joint . . . Also plays Center . . . (April 25, 1985)—Lost for the playoffs with mononucleosis . . . (September, 1985)—Switched to center . . . (December 8, 1985)—Injured knee vs. Los Angeles . . . (March, 1987)—Suspended four games by NHL for stick-swinging incident . . . (February, 1990)—Sore ribs.

Year	Team	League	Games	G.	A.	Pts.	Pen.
1981-82—Niagara Falls Flyers		OHL	68	19	25	44	35
1982-83—North Bay Centennials (b-c)		OHL	67	33	87	120	61
1983-84—Winnipeg Jets		NHL	78	11	19	30	37
1984-85—Winnipeg Jets		NHL	77	7	15	22	45
1985-86—Winnipeg Jets		NHL	28	3	3	6	17
1986-87—Winnipeg Jets		NHL	71	11	21	32	106
1987-88—Winnipeg Jets		NHL	74	32	31	63	145
1988-89—Winnipeg Jets (d)		NHL	80	37	40	77	71
1989-90—Pittsburgh Penguins (e)		NHL	41	5	9	14	51
1989-90—Vancouver Canucks		NHL	26	4	5	9	22
NHL TOTALS			475	110	143	253	494

(c)—June, 1983—Drafted as underage junior by Winnipeg Jets in 1983 NHL entry draft. First Jets pick, eighth overall, first round.

(d)—June 17, 1989—Traded with Jim Kyte and Randy Gilhen by Winnipeg Jets to Pittsburgh Penguins for Randy Cunneyworth, Richard Tabaracci and Dave McLlwain.

(e)—January 8, 1990—Traded with Dan Quinn and Dave Capuano by Pittsburgh Penguins to Vancouver Canucks for Tony Tanti, Barry Pederson and Rod Buskas.

WAYNE McBEAN

Defense . . . 6'2" . . . 190 lbs. . . . Born, Calgary, Alta., February 21, 1969 . . . Shoots left.

Year	Team	League	Games	G.	A.	Pts.	Pen.
1984-85—Calgary North Stars		Alta. Midget	38	8	34	42	46
1985-86—Medicine Hat Tigers		WHL	67	1	14	15	73
1986-87—Medicine Hat Tigers (a-c-d)		WHL	71	12	41	53	163
1987-88—Los Angeles Kings		NHL	27	0	1	1	26
1987-88—Medicine Hat Tigers		WHL	30	15	30	45	48
1988-89—New Haven Nighthawks		AHL	7	1	1	2	2
1988-89—Los Angeles Kings (e)		NHL	33	0	5	5	23
1988-89—New York Islanders		NHL	19	0	1	1	12
1989-90—Springfield Indians		AHL	68	6	33	39	48
1989-90—New York Islanders		NHL	5	0	1	1	2
NHL TOTALS			84	0	8	8	63

(c)—Named WHL Top Defenseman (East Division).

(d)—June, 1987—Drafted as underage junior by Los Angeles Kings in 1987 NHL entry draft. First Kings pick, fourth overall, first round.

(e)—February 22, 1989—Traded with Mark Fitzpatrick and future considerations (Doug Crossman was sent to the N.Y. Islanders to complete the deal) by Los Angeles Kings to New York Islanders for Kelly Hrudey.

BRIAN McCARTHY

Center . . . 6'2" . . . 190 lbs. . . . Born, Salem, Mass., December 6, 1971 . . . Shoots left . . . Plans to attend Providence College.

Year	Team	League	Games	G.	A.	Pts.	Pen.
1986-87	Pingree School	Mass. H.S.	20	15	16	31	..
1987-88	Pingree School	Mass. H.S.	24	22	36	58	24
1988-89	Pingree School	Mass. H.S.	26	37	43	80	24
1989-90	Pingree School (c)	Mass. H.S.	..	25	40	65	..

(c)—June 16, 1990—Selected by Buffalo Sabres in 1990 NHL entry draft. Second Sabres pick, 82nd overall, fourth round.

KEVIN WILLIAM McCLELLAND

Center . . . 6' . . . 180 lbs. . . . Born, Oshawa, Ont., July 4, 1962 . . . Shoots right . . . (September 21, 1981)—Dislocated shoulder in preseason game . . . (January 24, 1983)—Dislocated shoulder in fight with Paul Higgins at Toronto, required surgery on shoulder and was lost for the season . . . (January, 1985)—Sprained left knee . . . (December 10, 1986)—Suspended for three games by NHL for being the first off the bench during a fight at Winnipeg . . . (November, 1987)—Sprained knee . . . (February, 1988)—Bruised right knee vs. Vancouver.

Year	Team	League	Games	G.	A.	Pts.	Pen.
1979-80	Niagara Falls Flyers (c)	OMJHL	67	14	14	28	71
1980-81	Niagara Falls Flyers (d)	OHL	68	36	72	108	184
1981-82	Niagara Falls Flyers	OHL	46	36	47	83	184
1981-82	Pittsburgh Penguins	NHL	10	1	4	5	4
1982-83	Pittsburgh Penguins	NHL	38	5	4	9	73
1983-84	Baltimore Skipjacks	AHL	3	1	1	2	0
1983-84	Pittsburgh Penguins (e)	NHL	24	2	4	6	62
1983-84	Edmonton Oilers	NHL	52	8	20	28	127
1984-85	Edmonton Oilers	NHL	62	8	15	23	205
1985-86	Edmonton Oilers	NHL	79	11	25	36	266
1986-87	Edmonton Oilers	NHL	72	12	13	25	238
1987-88	Edmonton Oilers	NHL	74	10	6	16	281
1988-89	Edmonton Oilers	NHL	79	6	14	20	161
1989-90	Edmonton Oilers (f)	NHL	10	1	1	2	13
1989-90	Pittsburgh Penguins	NHL	61	4	5	9	183
NHL TOTALS			561	68	111	179	1613

(c)—June, 1980—Drafted as underage junior by Hartford Whalers in 1980 NHL entry draft. Fourth Whalers pick, 71st overall, fourth round.

(d)—July, 1981—Acquired by Pittsburgh Penguins with Pat Boutette as compensation from Hartford Whalers for Hartford signing free agent Greg Millen. Decision required by NHL Arbitrator Judge Joseph Kane when Hartford and Pittsburgh were unable to agree on compensation.

(e)—December, 1983—Traded with sixth round 1984 draft pick (Emanuel Viveiros) by Pittsburgh Penguins to Edmonton Oilers for Tom Roulston.

(f)—Traded with Jimmy Carson and a fifth-round 1991 draft pick by Edmonton Oilers to Detroit Red Wings for Joe Murphy, Adam Graves, Petr Klima and Jeff Sharples.

SHAWN McCOSH

Center . . . 6' . . . 188 lbs. . . . Born, Oshawa, Ont., June 5, 1969 . . . Shoots right . . . Son of Ron McCosh and nephew of Gord McCosh (Minor league players in the 1960's and 70's).

Year	Team	League	Games	G.	A.	Pts.	Pen.
1985-86	Oshawa Midgets	OHA	68	67	81	148	145
1986-87	Hamilton Steelhawks	OHL	50	11	17	28	49
1987-88	Hamilton Steelhawks	OHL	64	17	36	53	96
1988-89	Niagara Falls Thunder (c)	OHL	56	41	62	103	75
1989-90	Niagara Falls Thunder	OHL	9	6	10	16	24
1989-90	Dukes of Hamilton (d)	OHL	39	24	28	52	65

(c)—June, 1989—Drafted by Detroit Red Wings in 1989 NHL entry draft. Fifth Red Wings pick, 95th overall, fifth round.

(d)—August, 1990—Traded by Detroit Red Wings to Los Angeles Kings for 10th round 1992 draft pick.

SCOTT McCRADY

Defense . . . 6'1" . . . 190 lbs. . . . Born, Bassang, Alta., October 10, 1968 . . . Shoots right . . . (October 5, 1987)—Injured left knee ligament during Minnesota North Stars training camp.

Year	Team	League	Games	G.	A.	Pts.	Pen.
1985-86	Medicine Hat Tigers	WHL	65	8	25	33	114
1985-86	Calgary Spurs	AJHL	6	0	4	4	37
1986-87	Medicine Hat Tigers (c)	WHL	70	10	66	76	157
1987-88	Medicine Hat Tigers (a)	WHL	65	7	70	77	132
1988-89	Kalamazoo Wings	IHL	73	8	29	37	169
1989-90	Kalamazoo Wings	IHL	3	0	0	0	11
1989-90	Played in Finland						

(c)—June, 1987—Drafted by Minnesota North Stars as underage junior in 1987 NHL entry draft. Second North Stars pick, 35th overall, second round.

BYRON BRAD McCRIMMON
(Known by middle name.)

Defense . . . 5'11" . . . 193 lbs. . . . Born, Dodsland, Sask., March 29, 1959 . . . Shoots left . . . (February 2, 1985)—Broke bone in right hand and missed 13 games . . . (May 9, 1985)—Separated left shoulder, requiring surgery, during playoff game vs. Quebec when he was checked by Wilf Paiement . . . Missed start of 1986-87 season in contract dispute . . . (February, 1989)—Skin rash . . . (March, 1989)—Fractured ankle . . . Older brother of Kelly McCrimmon (General Manager of Brandon Wheat Kings).

Year	Team	League	Games	G.	A.	Pts.	Pen.
1976-77	Brandon Wheat Kings (b)	WCHL	72	18	66	84	96
1977-78	Brandon Wheat Kings (a-c)	WCHL	65	19	78	97	245
1978-79	Brandon Wheat Kings (a-d)	WHL	66	24	74	98	139

Year	Team	League	Games	G.	A.	Pts.	Pen.
1979-80	Boston Bruins	NHL	72	5	11	16	94
1980-81	Boston Bruins	NHL	78	11	18	29	148
1981-82	Boston Bruins (e)	NHL	78	1	8	9	83
1982-83	Philadelphia Flyers	NHL	79	4	21	25	61
1983-84	Philadelphia Flyers	NHL	71	0	24	24	76
1984-85	Philadelphia Flyers	NHL	66	8	25	33	81
1985-86	Philadelphia Flyers	NHL	80	13	42	55	85
1986-87	Philadelphia Flyers (f)	NHL	71	10	29	39	52
1987-88	Calgary Flames (b)	NHL	80	7	35	42	98
1988-89	Calgary Flames	NHL	72	5	17	22	96
1989-90	Calgary Flames (g)	NHL	79	4	15	19	78
NHL TOTALS			826	68	245	313	952

(c)—Named outstanding defenseman.

(d)—August, 1979—Drafted by Boston Bruins in 1979 entry draft. Second Boston pick, 15th overall, first round.

(e)—June, 1982—Traded by Boston Bruins to Philadelphia Flyers for Pete Peeters.

(f)—August, 1987—Traded by Philadelphia Flyers to Calgary Flames for a first-round draft choice in 1989 and a third-round draft choice in 1988 (Dominic Roussel).

(g)—June 16, 1990—Traded by Calgary Flames to Detroit Red Wings for a second-round 1990 draft pick (which was then traded with a first-round pick by Detroit to New Jersey for the Devils first and second-round picks).

SCOTT McCRORY

Center . . . 5'10" . . . 175 lbs. . . . Born, Sudbury, Ont., February 27, 1967 . . . Shoots right.

Year	Team	League	Games	G.	A.	Pts.	Pen.
1983-84	Sudbury Midget	OHA	65	92	76	168	32
1984-85	Oshawa Generals	OHL	64	9	24	33	28
1985-86	Oshawa Generals (c)	OHL	66	52	80	132	40
1986-87	Oshawa Generals (a-d-e-f-g-h)	OHL	66	51	*99	*150	35
1987-88	Binghamton Whalers	AHL	72	18	33	51	29
1988-89	Baltimore Skipjacks	AHL	80	38	51	89	25
1989-90	Rochester Americans (i)	AHL	51	14	51	55	46

(c)—June, 1986—Drafted as underage junior by Washington Capitals in 1986 NHL entry draft. Thirteenth Capitals pick, 250th overall, 12th round.

(d)—Won Eddie Powers Memorial Trophy (Scoring Champion).

(e)—Won Red Tilson Trophy (Outstanding Player).

(f)—Co-Winner of William Hanley Trophy (Most Gentlemanly) with Keith Gretzky.

(g)—Named OHL Player of the Year.

(h)—Led OHL Playoffs with 22 assists and 37 points.

(i)—June 1, 1989—Traded by Washington Capitals to Buffalo Sabres for Mark Ferner.

HUBIE McDONOUGH

Center . . . 5'9" . . . 180 lbs. . . . Born, Manchester, N.H., July 8, 1963 . . . Shoots left.

Year	Team	League	Games	G.	A.	Pts.	Pen.
1984-85	St. Anselm College	ECAC-II	..	..	..	..	..
1985-86	St. Anselm College	ECAC-II	..	..	..	..	..
1986-87	Flint Spirits	IHL	82	27	52	79	59
1987-88	New Haven Nighthawks (c)	AHL	78	30	29	59	43
1988-89	New Haven Nighthawks	AHL	74	37	55	92	41
1988-89	Los Angeles Kings	NHL	4	0	1	1	0
1989-90	Los Angeles Kings (d)	NHL	22	3	4	7	10
1989-90	New York Islanders	NHL	54	18	11	29	26
NHL TOTALS			80	21	16	37	36

(c)—October, 1987—Signed by Los Angeles Kings as a free agent.

(d)—November 29, 1989—Traded with Ken Baumgartner by Los Angeles Kings to New York Islanders for Mikko Makela.

SHAWN McEARCHERN

Center . . . 6' . . . 170 lbs. . . . Born, Waltham, Mass., February 28, 1969 . . . Shoots left.

Year	Team	League	Games	G.	A.	Pts.	Pen.
1985-86	Matignon H.S.	Mass. H.S.	20	32	20	52	..
1986-87	Matignon H.S. (c)	Mass. H.S.	16	29	28	57	..
1987-88	Matignon H.S.	Mass. H.S.	..	52	40	92	..
1988-89	Boston University	H. East	36	20	28	48	32
1989-90	Boston University (b)	H. East	43	25	31	56	78

(c)—June, 1987—Selected by Pittsburgh Penguins in 1987 NHL entry draft. Sixth Penguins pick, 110th overall, sixth round.

ROBERT PAUL McGILL

Defense . . . 6' . . . 202 lbs. . . . Born, Edmonton, Alta., April 27, 1962 . . . Shoots right . . . (January, 1985)—Given three-game NHL suspension . . . (March 1, 1986)—Suspended by NHL for seven games . . . (October, 1986)—Ankle injury . . . (November 4, 1989)—Broke cheekbone in fight with Shane Churla vs. Minnesota . . . (December 28, 1989)—Fined $500 by NHL for fighting vs. Minnesota . . . (May, 1990)—Bruised left foot.

Year	Team	League	Games	G.	A.	Pts.	Pen.
1978-79	Abbotsford	BCJHL	46	3	20	23	242
1979-80	Victoria Cougars (c)	WHL	70	3	18	21	230
1980-81	Victoria Cougars	WHL	66	5	36	41	295
1981-82	Toronto Maple Leafs	NHL	68	1	10	11	263
1982-83	Toronto Maple Leafs	NHL	30	0	0	0	146
1982-83	St. Catharines Saints	AHL	32	2	5	7	95
1983-84	Toronto Maple Leafs	NHL	11	0	2	2	51
1983-84	St. Catharines Saints	AHL	55	1	15	16	217
1984-85	Toronto Maple Leafs	NHL	72	0	5	5	250
1985-86	Toronto Maple Leafs	NHL	61	1	4	5	141
1986-87	Toronto Maple Leafs (d)	NHL	56	1	4	5	103

Year	Team	League	Games	G.	A.	Pts.	Pen.
1987-88—Chicago Black Hawks		NHL	67	4	7	11	131
1988-89—Chicago Black Hawks		NHL	68	0	4	4	155
1989-90—Chicago Black Hawks		NHL	69	2	10	12	204
NHL TOTALS			502	9	46	55	1444

(c)—June, 1980—Drafted as underage junior by Toronto Maple Leafs in 1980 NHL entry draft. Second Maple Leafs pick, 26th overall, second round.

(d)—September, 1987—Traded with Rick Vaive and Steve Thomas by Toronto Maple Leafs to Chicago Black Hawks for Al Secord and Ed Olczyk.

RYAN McGILL

Defense . . . 6'2" . . . 198 lbs. . . . Born, Prince Albert, Sask., February 28, 1969 . . . Shoots right . . . (January, 1986)—Sprained ankle . . . (July, 1986)—Knee operation.

Year	Team	League	Games	G.	A.	Pts.	Pen.
1985-86—Lethbridge Broncos		WHL	64	5	10	15	171
1986-87—Swift Current Broncos (c)		WHL	71	12	36	48	226
1987-88—Medicine Hat Tigers (d)		WHL	67	5	30	35	224
1988-89—Medicine Hat Tigers		WHL	57	26	45	71	172
1988-89—Saginaw Hawks		IHL	8	2	0	2	12
1989-90—Indianapolis Ice		IHL	77	11	17	28	215

(c)—June, 1987—Drafted as underage junior by Chicago Black Hawks in 1987 NHL entry draft. Second Black Hawks pick, 29th overall, second round.

(d)—September, 1987—Traded by Swift Current Broncos to Medicine Hat Tigers for Kelly Hitching.

CAL McGOWAN

Center . . . 6'1" . . . 182 lbs. . . . Born, Sidney, Neb., June 19, 1970 . . . Shoots left.

Year	Team	League	Games	G.	A.	Pts.	Pen.
1986-87—Merritt Centennials		BCJHL	50	18	30	48	60
1987-88—Merritt Centennials		BCJHL	50	24	62	86	40
1988-89—Kamloops Blazers		WHL	72	21	31	52	44
1989-90—Kamloops Blazers (c)		WHL	71	33	44	77	78

(c)—June 16, 1990—Selected by Minnesota North Stars in 1990 NHL entry draft. Third North Stars pick, 70th overall, fourth round.

MIKE McHUGH

Left Wing . . . 5'10" . . . 190 lbs. . . . Born, Bowdoin, Mass., August 16, 1965 . . . Shoots left.

Year	Team	League	Games	G.	A.	Pts.	Pen.
1984-85—Univ. of Maine		H. East	25	9	8	17	9
1985-86—Univ. of Maine		H. East	38	9	10	19	24
1986-87—Univ. of Maine		H. East	42	21	29	50	40
1987-88—Univ. of Maine (c-d)		H. East	44	29	37	66	90
1988-89—Kalamazoo Wings		IHL	70	17	29	46	89
1988-89—Minnesota North Stars		NHL	3	0	0	0	2
1989-90—Kalamazoo Wings		IHL	73	14	17	31	96
1989-90—Minnesota North Stars		NHL	3	0	0	0	0
NHL TOTALS			6	0	0	0	2

(c)—Named Second team All-America (East).

(d)—June, 1988—Selected by Minnesota North Stars in 1988 NHL supplemental draft.

MARTY McINNIS

Center . . . 5'11" . . . 175 lbs. . . . Born, Weymouth, Mass., June 2, 1970 . . . Shoots right.

Year	Team	League	Games	G.	A.	Pts.	Pen.
1986-87—Milton Academy		Mass. H.S.	....	21	19	40	....
1987-88—Milton Academy (c)		Mass. H.S.	....	26	25	51	....
1988-89—Boston College		H. East	39	13	19	32	8
1989-90—Boston College		H. East	41	24	29	53	43

(c)—June, 1988—Drafted by New York Islanders in 1988 NHL entry draft. Tenth Islanders pick, 163rd overall, eighth round.

JOHN McINTYRE

Center . . . 6'1" . . . 175 lbs. . . . Born, Ravenswood, Ont., April 29, 1969 . . . Shoots left . . . Also plays Left Wing . . . (November, 1985)—Broken ankle . . . (February, 1987)—Severed nerve in right leg at Sault Ste. Marie.

Year	Team	League	Games	G.	A.	Pts.	Pen.
1984-85—Strathroy Jr. B		OHA	48	21	23	44	49
1985-86—Guelph Platers		OHL	30	4	6	10	25
1986-87—Guelph Platers (c)		OHL	47	8	22	30	95
1987-88—Guelph Platers		OHL	39	24	18	42	109
1988-89—Guelph Platers		OHL	52	30	26	56	129
1988-89—Newmarket Saints		AHL	3	0	2	2	7
1989-90—Newmarket Saints		AHL	6	2	2	4	12
1989-90—Toronto Maple Leafs		NHL	59	5	12	17	117
NHL TOTALS			59	5	12	17	117

(c)—June, 1987—Drafted as underage junior by Toronto Maple Leafs in 1987 NHL entry draft. Third Maple Leafs pick, 49th overall, third round.

RANDY McKAY

Right Wing . . . 6'1" . . . 170 lbs. . . . Born, Montreal, Que., January 25, 1967 . . . Shoots right . . . (February, 1989)—Knee injury.

Year	Team	League	Games	G.	A.	Pts.	Pen.
1983-84—Lac. St. Louis Midget		Que. Midget	38	18	28	46	62
1984-85—Michigan Tech. (c)		WCHA	25	4	5	9	32
1985-86—Michigan Tech.		WCHA	40	12	22	34	46

Year	Team	League	Games	G.	A.	Pts.	Pen.
1986-87—Michigan Tech.		WCHA	39	5	11	16	46
1987-88—Michigan Tech.		WCHA	41	17	24	41	70
1987-88—Adirondack Red Wings		AHL	10	0	3	3	12
1988-89—Adirondack Red Wings		AHL	58	29	34	63	170
1988-89—Detroit Red Wings		NHL	3	0	0	0	0
1989-90—Detroit Red Wings		NHL	33	3	6	9	51
1989-90—Adirondack Red Wings		AHL	36	16	23	39	99
NHL TOTALS			36	3	6	9	51

(c)—June, 1985—Drafted by Detroit Red Wings in 1985 NHL entry draft. Sixth Red Wings pick, 113th overall, sixth round.

ANTHONY SYIIYD (TONY) McKEGNEY

Left Wing . . . 6'1" . . . 195 lbs. . . . Born, Montreal, Que., February 15, 1958 . . . Shoots left . . . Brother of Mike (1974 Montreal draft pick) and Ian (Dallas-CHL) McKegney and adopted son of Lawrey McKegney . . . (February, 1985)—Separated shoulder that required surgery . . . (January 16, 1986)—Injured shoulder vs. St. Louis and missed seven games . . . (April, 1989)—Strained right knee . . . (November 11, 1989)—Reinjured groin.

Year	Team	League	Games	G.	A.	Pts.	Pen.
1974-75—Kingston Canadians		Jr. "A" OHA	52	27	48	75	36
1975-76—Kingston Canadians		Jr. "A" OHA	65	24	56	80	20
1976-77—Kingston Canadians (a)		Jr. "A" OHA	66	58	77	135	30
1977-78—Kingston Canadians (b-c)		Jr. "A" OHA	55	43	49	92	19
1978-79—Buffalo Sabres		NHL	52	8	14	22	10
1978-79—Hershey Bears		AHL	24	21	18	39	4
1979-80—Buffalo Sabres		NHL	80	23	29	52	24
1980-81—Buffalo Sabres		NHL	80	37	32	69	24
1981-82—Buffalo Sabres		NHL	73	23	29	52	41
1982-83—Buffalo Sabres (d)		NHL	78	36	37	73	18
1983-84—Quebec Nordiques		NHL	75	24	27	51	23
1984-85—Quebec Nordiques (e)		NHL	30	12	9	21	12
1984-85—Minnesota North Stars		NHL	27	11	13	24	4
1985-86—Minnesota North Stars		NHL	70	15	25	40	48
1986-87—Minnesota North Stars (f)		NHL	11	2	3	5	15
1986-87—New York Rangers (g)		NHL	64	29	17	46	56
1987-88—St. Louis Blues		NHL	80	40	38	78	82
1988-89—St. Louis Blues (h)		NHL	71	25	17	42	58
1989-90—Detroit Red Wings (i)		NHL	14	2	1	3	8
1989-90—Quebec Nordiques		NHL	48	16	11	27	45
NHL TOTALS			853	303	302	605	468

(c)—Drafted from Kingston Canadians by Buffalo Sabres in second round of 1978 amateur draft.

(d)—June, 1983—Traded by Buffalo Sabres with Andre Savard, Jean-Francois Sauve and Buffalo's third-round pick in 1983 (Iiro Jarvi) to Quebec Nordiques for Real Cloutier and Quebec's first-round draft choice in 1983 (Adam Creighton).

(e)—December, 1984—Traded with Bo Berglund by Quebec Nordiques to Minnesota North Stars for Brad Maxwell and Brent Ashton.

(f)—November, 1986—Traded with Curt Giles and a second-round 1988 draft pick by Minnesota North Stars to New York Rangers for Bob Brooke and a fourth-round 1988 draft pick.

(g)—June, 1987—Traded with Rob Whistle by New York Rangers to St. Louis Blues for Bruce Bell, a fourth-round 1988 draft pick and future considerations.

(h)—June 15, 1989—Traded with Bernie Federko by St. Louis Blues to Detroit Red Wings for Adam Oates and Paul MacLean.

(i)—December 3, 1989—Traded by Detroit Red Wings to Quebec Nordiques for Robert Picard and Greg C. Adams.

SEAN MICHAEL McKENNA

Right Wing . . . 6' . . . 186 lbs. . . . Born, Asbestos, Que., March 7, 1962 . . . Shoots right . . . (March, 1987)—Hip pointer . . . (September, 1988)—Torn tendon in right hand during Toronto Maple Leafs training camp.

Year	Team	League	Games	G.	A.	Pts.	Pen.
1978-79—Montreal Juniors		QMJHL	66	9	14	23	14
1979-80—Sherbrooke Beavers (c)		QMJHL	59	20	19	39	24
1980-81—Sherbrooke Beavers (a)		QMJHL	71	57	47	104	122
1981-82—Sherbrooke Beavers (b-d-e)		QMJHL	59	57	33	90	29
1981-82—Buffalo Sabres		NHL	3	0	1	1	2
1982-83—Buffalo Sabres		NHL	46	10	14	24	4
1982-83—Rochester Americans (f)		AHL	26	16	10	26	14
1983-84—Buffalo Sabres		NHL	78	20	10	30	45
1984-85—Buffalo Sabres		NHL	65	20	16	36	41
1985-86—Buffalo Sabres (g)		NHL	45	6	12	18	28
1985-86—Los Angeles Kings		NHL	30	4	0	4	7
1986-87—Los Angeles Kings (h)		NHL	69	14	19	33	10
1987-88—Los Angeles Kings		NHL	30	3	2	5	12
1987-88—Toronto Maple Leafs		NHL	40	5	5	10	12
1988-89—Toronto Maple Leafs		NHL	3	0	1	1	0
1988-89—Newmarket Saints		AHL	61	14	27	41	35
1989-90—Toronto Maple Leafs		NHL	5	0	0	0	20
1989-90—Newmarket Saints (i)		AHL	73	17	17	34	30
NHL TOTALS			414	82	80	162	181

(c)—June, 1980—Drafted as underage junior by Buffalo Sabres in 1980 NHL entry draft. Third Sabres pick, 56th overall, third round.

(d)—Led QMJHL President Cup Playoffs with 26 goals.

(e)—Named MVP of 1982 Memorial Cup Tournament.

(f)—Led AHL playoffs with a record 14 goals.

(g)—January, 1986—Traded with Larry Playfair and Ken Baumgartner by Buffalo Sabres to Los Angeles Kings for Brian Englblom and Doug Smith.

(h)—December, 1987—Traded by Los Angeles Kings to Toronto Maple Leafs for Mike Allison.

(i)—August, 1990—Signed by Chicago Black Hawks as a free agent.

JIM McKENZIE

Left Wing . . . 6'3'' . . . 205 lbs. . . . Born, Gull Lake, Sask., November 3, 1969 . . . Shoots left.

Year	Team	League	Games	G.	A.	Pts.	Pen.
1987-88—Moose Jaw Warriors		WHL	62	1	17	18	134
1988-89—Victoria Cougars (c)		WHL	67	15	27	42	176
1989-90—Binghamton Whalers		AHL	56	4	12	16	149
1989-90—Hartford Whalers		NHL	5	0	0	0	4
NHL TOTALS			5	0	0	0	4

(c)—June, 1989—Drafted by Hartford Whalers in 1989 NHL entry draft. Third Whalers pick, 73rd overall, fourth round.

MICHAEL McLAUGHLIN

Left Wing . . . 6'1'' . . . 185 lbs. . . . Born, Springfield, Mass., March 29, 1970 . . . Shoots left.

Year	Team	League	Games	G.	A.	Pts.	Pen.
1986-87—Choate H.S.		Mass. H.S.	..	19	18	37	..
1987-88—Choate H.S. (c)		Mass. H.S.	..	17	18	35	..
1988-89—University of Vermont		ECAC	32	5	6	11	12
1989-90—University of Vermont		ECAC	29	11	12	23	37

(c)—June, 1988—Drafted by Buffalo Sabres in 1988 NHL entry draft. Seventh Sabres pick, 118th overall, sixth round.

DONALD McLENNAN

Defense . . . 6'4'' . . . 200 lbs. . . . Born, Winnipeg, Man., October 4, 1968 . . . Shoots left.

Year	Team	League	Games	G.	A.	Pts.	Pen.
1985-86—Winnipeg South Blues		MJHL	45	2	10	12	65
1986-87—University of Denver (c)		WCHA	35	2	2	4	38
1987-88—University of Denver		WCHA	29	0	3	3	24
1988-89—University of Denver		WCHA	26	1	3	4	28
1989-90—University of Denver		WCHA	42	0	6	6	41

(c)—June, 1987—Drafted by Winnipeg Jets in 1987 NHL entry draft. Third Jets pick, 79th overall, fourth round.

DAVID McLLWAIN

Right Wing . . . 6' . . . 190 lbs. . . . Born, Seaforth, Ont., January 9, 1967 . . . Shoots right.

Year	Team	League	Games	G.	A.	Pts.	Pen.
1984-85—Kitchener Rangers		OHL	61	13	21	34	29
1985-86—Kitchener Rangers (c)		OHL	13	7	7	14	12
1985-86—North Bay Centennials (d)		OHL	51	30	28	58	25
1986-87—North Bay Centennials (b)		OHL	60	46	73	119	35
1987-88—Muskegon Lumberjacks		IHL	9	4	6	10	23
1987-88—Pittsburgh Penguins		NHL	66	11	8	19	40
1988-89—Muskegon Lumberjacks		IHL	46	37	35	72	51
1988-89—Pittsburgh Penguins (e)		NHL	24	1	2	3	4
1989-90—Winnipeg Jets		NHL	80	25	26	51	60
NHL TOTALS			170	37	36	73	104

(c)—November, 1985—Traded with John Keller and Todd Stromback by Kitchener Rangers to North Bay Centennials for Ron Sanko, Peter Lisy, Richard Hawkins and Brett McDonald.

(d)—June, 1986—Drafted as underage junior by Pittsburgh Penguins in 1986 NHL entry draft. Ninth Penguins pick, 172nd overall, ninth round.

(e)—June 17, 1989—Traded with Randy Cunneyworth and Richard Tabaracci by Pittsburgh Penguins to Winnipeg Jets for Andrew McBain, Jim Kyte and Randy Gilhen.

MIKE McNEIL

Center . . . 6'1'' . . . 175 lbs. . . . Born, Winona, Minn., July 22, 1966 . . . Shoots right.

Year	Team	League	Games	G.	A.	Pts.	Pen.
1984-85—Notre Dame Univ.		NCAA	28	16	26	42	12
1985-86—Notre Dame Univ.		NCAA	34	18	29	47	32
1986-87—Notre Dame Univ.		NCAA	30	21	16	37	24
1987-88—Notre Dame Univ. (c)		NCAA	32	28	44	72	12
1988-89—Fort Wayne Komets		IHL	75	27	35	62	12
1988-89—Moncton Hawks		AHL	1	0	0	0	0
1989-90—Indianapolis Ice (d)		IHL	74	17	24	41	15

(c)—June, 1988—Selected by St. Louis Blues in 1988 NHL supplemental draft.

(d)—Won N.R. Bud Poile Trophy (IHL Playoff MVP).

MICHAEL JOSEPH McPHEE

Left Wing . . . 6'2'' . . . 200 lbs. . . . Born, Sydney, N.S., February 14, 1960 . . . Shoots left . . . (September, 1982)—Broke hand in training camp . . . (January 10, 1986)—Injured ankle at N.Y. Rangers and missed 10 games . . . (February, 1989)—Broke little toe on left foot . . . (April 8, 1989)—Pulled muscle in rib cage vs. Hartford . . . (October 7, 1989)—Torn abdominal muscle vs. Buffalo and missed 13 games.

Year	Team	League	Games	G.	A.	Pts.	Pen.
1978-79—R.P.I.		ECAC	26	14	19	33	16
1979-80—R.P.I. (c)		ECAC	27	15	21	36	22
1980-81—R.P.I.		ECAC	29	28	18	46	22
1981-82—R.P.I.		ECAC	6	0	3	3	4
1982-83—Nova Scotia Voyageurs		AHL	42	10	15	25	29
1983-84—Nova Scotia Voyageurs		AHL	67	22	33	55	101
1983-84—Montreal Canadiens		NHL	14	5	2	7	41
1984-85—Montreal Canadiens		NHL	70	17	22	39	120
1985-86—Montreal Canadiens		NHL	70	19	21	40	69
1986-87—Montreal Canadiens		NHL	79	18	21	39	58
1987-88—Montreal Canadiens		NHL	77	23	20	43	53
1988-89—Montreal Canadiens		NHL	73	19	22	41	74
1989-90—Montreal Canadiens		NHL	56	23	18	41	47
NHL TOTALS			439	124	126	250	462

(c)—June, 1980—Drafted by Montreal Canadiens in 1980 NHL entry draft. Eighth Canadiens pick, 124th overall, sixth round.

DARWIN McPHERSON

Defense . . . 6'1'' . . . 195 lbs. . . . Born, Flin Flon, Man., May 16, 1968 . . . Shoots left.

Year	Team	League	Games	G.	A.	Pts.	Pen.
1984-85—Brandon Wheat Kings		WHL	39	2	0	2	36
1985-86—New Westminster Bruins		WHL	63	2	8	10	149
1986-87—New Westminster Bruins (c)		WHL	65	10	22	32	242
1987-88—New Westminster Bruins		WHL	47	1	17	18	192
1988-89—Saskatoon Blades (d)		WHL	59	4	13	17	266
1989-90—Peoria Rivermen		IHL	18	1	0	1	94

(c)—June, 1987—Drafted by Boston Bruins in 1987 NHL entry draft. Fourth Bruins pick, 67th overall, fourth round.

(d)—July, 1989—Signed by St. Louis Blues as a free agent.

BASIL PAUL McRAE

Left Wing . . . 6'2'' . . . 200 lbs. . . . Born, Orillia, Ont., January 1, 1961 . . . Shoots left . . . Brother of Chris McRae . . . (October 10, 1989)—Strained right knee ligaments vs. St. Louis and missed nine games . . . (December 28, 1989)—Suspended five games for fighting at Chicago and was fined $500.

Year	Team	League	Games	G.	A.	Pts.	Pen.
1977-78—Seneca Nats		OHA Jr. ''B''	36	21	38	59	80
1978-79—London Knights		OMJHL	66	13	28	41	79
1979-80—London Knights (c)		OMJHL	67	23	35	58	116
1980-81—London Knights		OHL	65	29	23	52	266
1981-82—Fredericton Express		AHL	47	11	15	26	175
1981-82—Quebec Nordiques		NHL	20	4	3	7	69
1982-83—Fredericton Express		AHL	53	22	19	41	146
1982-83—Quebec Nordiques		NHL	22	1	1	2	59
1983-84—Toronto Maple Leafs (d)		NHL	3	0	0	0	19
1983-84—St. Catharines Saints		AHL	78	14	25	39	187
1984-85—St. Catharines Saints		AHL	72	30	25	55	186
1984-85—Toronto Maple Leafs		NHL	1	0	0	0	0
1985-86—Detroit Red Wings (e)		NHL	4	0	0	0	5
1985-86—Adirondack Red Wings		AHL	69	22	30	52	259
1986-87—Detroit Red Wings (f)		NHL	36	2	2	4	193
1986-87—Quebec Nordiques (g)		NHL	33	9	5	14	149
1987-88—Minnesota North Stars		NHL	80	5	11	16	378
1988-89—Minnesota North Stars		NHL	78	12	19	31	365
1989-90—Minnesota North Stars		NHL	66	9	17	26	*351
NHL TOTALS			343	42	58	100	1588

(c)—June, 1980—Drafted as underage junior by Quebec Nordiques in 1980 NHL entry draft. Third Nordiques pick, 87th overall, fifth round.

(d)—August, 1983—Traded by Quebec Nordiques to Toronto Maple Leafs for Richard Trumel.

(e)—August, 1985—Signed by Detroit Red Wings as a free agent.

(f)—January, 1987—Traded with John Ogrodnick and Doug Shedden by Detroit Red Wings to Quebec Nordiques for Brent Ashton, Mark Kumpel and Gilbert Delorme.

(g)—July, 1987—Signed by Minnesota North Stars as a free agent.

CHRIS McRAE

Left Wing . . . 6' . . . 180 lbs. . . . Born, Newmarket, Ont., August 26, 1965 . . . Shoots left . . . Brother of Basil McRae . . . (September, 1988)—Cracked knuckle in left hand during fight with Tie Domi in Toronto Maple Leafs training camp . . . (February 28, 1990)—Fractured right eye orbit when struck by Mick Vukota vs. N.Y. Islanders.

Year	Team	League	Games	G.	A.	Pts.	Pen.
1982-83—Newmarket Tier II		OHA	42	11	22	33	207
1983-84—Sudbury Wolves		OHL	53	14	31	45	120
1983-84—Belleville Bulls		OHL	9	0	0	0	19
1984-85—Sudbury Wolves		OHL	6	0	2	2	10
1984-85—Oshawa Generals		OHL	43	8	7	15	118
1984-85—St. Catharines Saints		AHL	6	4	3	7	24
1985-86—St. Catharines Saints (c)		AHL	59	1	1	2	233
1986-87—Newmarket Saints		AHL	51	3	6	9	193
1987-88—Newmarket Saints		AHL	34	7	6	13	165
1987-88—Toronto Maple Leafs		NHL	11	0	0	0	65
1988-89—Toronto Maple Leafs (d)		NHL	3	0	0	0	12
1988-89—Newmarket Saints		AHL	18	3	1	4	85
1988-89—Denver Rangers		IHL	23	1	4	5	121
1989-90—Detroit Red Wings (e)		NHL	7	1	0	1	45
1989-90—Adirondack Red Wings		AHL	46	9	10	19	290
NHL TOTALS			21	1	0	1	122

(c)—October, 1985—Signed by Toronto Maple Leafs as a free agent.

(d)—February 19, 1989—Traded by Toronto Maple Leafs to New York Rangers for Ken Hammond.

(e)—September 7, 1989—Traded with a fifth-round 1990 draft pick by New York Rangers to Detroit Red Wings for Kris King.

KEN McRAE

Center . . . 6'1'' . . . 195 lbs. . . . Born, Finch, Ont., April 23, 1968 . . . Shoots right . . . (December 26, 1989)—Lacerated right elbow vs. Hartford and missed seven games . . . (March 10, 1990)—Bruised shoulder at New Jersey.

Year	Team	League	Games	G.	A.	Pts.	Pen.
1984-85—Hawkesbury Tier II		OHA	51	38	50	88	77
1985-86—Sudbury Wolves (c)		OHL	66	25	40	65	127
1986-87—Sudbury Wolves (d)		OHL	21	12	15	27	40

Year	Team	League	Games	G.	A.	Pts.	Pen.
1986-87—Hamilton Steelhawks		OHL	20	7	12	19	25
1987-88—Quebec Nordiques		NHL	1	0	0	0	0
1987-88—Hamilton Steelhawks		OHL	62	30	55	85	158
1988-89—Halifax Citadels		AHL	41	20	21	41	87
1988-89—Quebec Nordiques		NHL	37	6	11	17	68
1989-90—Quebec Nordiques		NHL	66	7	8	15	191
NHL TOTALS			104	13	19	32	259

(c)—June, 1986—Drafted as underage junior by Quebec Nordiques in 1986 NHL entry draft. First Nordiques pick, 18th overall, first round.

(d)—December, 1986—Traded with Andy Paquette and Ken Alexander by Sudbury Wolves to Hamilton Steelhawks for Dan Hie, Joe Simon, Steve Locke, Shawn Heaphy and Jordan Fois.

BRIAN McREYNOLDS

Center . . . 6'1" . . . 180 lbs. . . . Born, Penetanguishene, Ont., January 5, 1965 . . . Shoots left.

Year	Team	League	Games	G.	A.	Pts.	Pen.
1984-85—Orillia Travelways (c)		OHA	48	40	54	94	....
1985-86—Michigan State Univ.		CCHA	45	14	24	38	78
1986-87—Michigan State Univ.		CCHA	45	16	24	40	68
1987-88—Michigan State Univ.		CCHA	43	10	24	34	50
1988-89—Canadian National Team		Int'l	58	5	25	30	59
1989-90—Winnipeg Jets (d-e)		NHL	9	0	2	2	4
1989-90—Moncton Hawks		AHL	72	18	41	59	87
NHL TOTALS			9	0	2	2	4

(c)—June, 1985—Drafted by New York Rangers in 1985 NHL entry draft. Sixth Rangers pick, 112th overall, sixth round.

(d)—July, 1989—Signed by Winnipeg Jets as a free agent.

(e)—July 10, 1990—Traded by Winnipeg Jets to New York Rangers for Simon Wheeldon.

MARTY McSORLEY

Right Wing and Defense . . . 6'1" . . . 190 lbs. . . . Born, Hamilton, Ont., May 18, 1963 . . . Shoots right . . . (March, 1987)—Suspended by the NHL for an AHL incident . . . (November, 1987)—Sprained knee vs. New Jersey . . . (April 23, 1988)—Suspended three NHL playoff games for spearing Mike Bullard vs. Calgary . . . (December 31, 1988)—Injured shoulder in exhibition game with Dynamo Riga . . . (February, 1989) —Sprained knee . . . (1989-90)—Missed four games from automatic suspensions for game misconduct penalties.

Year	Team	League	Games	G.	A.	Pts.	Pen.
1981-82—Belleville Bulls		OHL	58	6	13	19	234
1982-83—Belleville Bulls		OHL	70	10	41	51	183
1982-83—Baltimore Skipjacks (c)		AHL	2	0	0	0	22
1983-84—Pittsburgh Penguins		NHL	72	2	7	9	224
1984-85—Baltimore Skipjacks		AHL	58	6	24	30	154
1984-85—Pittsburgh Penguins		NHL	15	0	0	0	15
1985-86—Edmonton Oilers (d)		NHL	59	11	12	23	265
1985-86—Nova Scotia Oilers		AHL	9	2	4	6	34
1986-87—Edmonton Oilers		NHL	41	2	4	6	159
1986-87—Nova Scotia Oilers		AHL	7	2	2	4	48
1987-88—Edmonton Oilers (e)		NHL	60	9	17	26	223
1988-89—Los Angeles Kings		NHL	66	10	17	27	350
1989-90—Los Angeles Kings		NHL	75	15	21	36	322
NHL TOTALS			388	49	78	127	1558

(c)—April, 1983—Signed by Pittsburgh Penguins as a free agent.

(d)—August, 1985—Traded with Tim Hrynewich by Pittsburgh Penguins to Edmonton Oilers for Gilles Meloche.

(e)—August, 1988—Traded with Wayne Gretzky and Mike Krushelnyski by Edmonton Oilers to Los Angeles Kings for Jimmy Carson, Martin Gelinas, first-round draft choices in 1989 (traded to New Jersey), '91 and '93, plus $15 million.

DON McSWEEN

Defense . . . 5'10" . . . 190 lbs. . . . Born, Detroit, Mich., June 9, 1964 . . . Shoots left.

Year	Team	League	Games	G.	A.	Pts.	Pen.
1983-84—Michigan State Univ. (c)		CCHA	46	10	26	36	30
1984-85—Michigan State Univ.		CCHA	44	2	23	25	52
1985-86—Michigan State Univ.		CCHA	45	9	29	38	18
1986-87—Michigan State Univ. (a-d)		CCHA	45	7	23	30	34
1987-88—Rochester Americans		AHL	63	9	29	38	108
1987-88—Buffalo Sabres		NHL	5	0	1	1	4
1988-89—Rochester Americans		AHL	66	7	22	29	45
1989-90—Buffalo Sabres		NHL	4	0	0	0	6
1989-90—Rochester Americans (a)		AHL	70	16	43	59	43
NHL TOTALS			9	0	1	1	10

(c)—June, 1983—Drafted by Buffalo Sabres in 1983 NHL entry draft. Tenth Sabres pick, 154th overall, eighth round.

(d)—Named Second team All-America (West).

RICK MEAGHER

Center . . . 5'8" . . . 175 lbs. . . . Born, Belleville, Ont., November 4, 1953 . . . Shoots left . . . Member of Boston University Hall of Fame . . . Named Boston University Athlete of the Decade (1970-79) . . . Elected to ECAC All-Decade Team (1970-79) . . . Brother of Terry Meagher . . . (December, 1981)—Back and knee problems . . . (November, 1982)—Missed eight games with shoulder separation suffered at Montreal . . . (January, 1984)—Fractured rib . . . (October, 1984)—Cut right forearm when run over by a skate vs. Hartford . . . (January, 1985)—Bruised ribs . . . (April 22, 1990)—Torn ligaments in right knee vs. Chicago, required surgery and could miss six months.

Year	Team	League	Games	G.	A.	Pts.	Pen.
1973-74—Boston University		ECAC	30	19	21	40	26
1974-75—Boston University		ECAC	32	25	28	53	80
1975-76—Boston University		ECAC	28	12	25	37	22
1976-77—Boston University (a-c)		ECAC	34	34	46	80	42
1977-78—Nova Scotia Voyageurs		AHL	57	20	27	47	33
1978-79—Nova Scotia Voyageurs		AHL	79	35	46	81	57
1979-80—Nova Scotia Voyageurs		AHL	64	32	44	76	53
1979-80—Montreal Canadiens (d)		NHL	2	0	0	0	0
1980-81—Binghamton Whalers		AHL	50	23	35	58	54
1980-81—Hartford Whalers		NHL	27	7	10	17	19
1981-82—Hartford Whalers		NHL	65	24	19	43	51
1982-83—Hartford Whalers		NHL	4	0	0	0	0
1982-83—New Jersey Devils		NHL	57	15	14	29	11
1983-84—Maine Mariners		AHL	10	6	4	10	2
1983-84—New Jersey Devils		NHL	52	14	14	28	16
1984-85—New Jersey Devils (e)		NHL	71	11	20	31	22
1985-86—St. Louis Blues		NHL	79	11	19	30	28
1986-87—St. Louis Blues		NHL	80	18	21	39	54
1987-88—St. Louis Blues		NHL	76	18	16	34	76
1988-89—St. Louis Blues		NHL	78	15	14	29	53
1989-90—St. Louis Blues (f)		NHL	71	12	10	22	4
NHL TOTALS			662	145	157	302	334

(c)—Named First team All-America (East).

(d)—June, 1980—Traded with third (Paul MacDermid) and fifth (Dan Bourbonnais) round picks in 1981 draft by Montreal Canadiens to Hartford Whalers for third (Dieter Hegen) and fifth (Steve Rooney) round Whalers picks in 1981 draft.

(e)—August, 1985—Traded with 1986 12th round draft choice (Bill Butler) by New Jersey Devils to St. Louis Blues for Perry Anderson.

(f)—Won Frank Selke Trophy (Best Defensive Forward).

GLEN MEARS

Defense . . . 6'3" . . . 215 lbs. . . . Born, Anchorage, Alaska, July 14, 1972 . . . Shoots right.

Year	Team	League	Games	G.	A.	Pts.	Pen.
1987-88—Alaska All-Star Bantams		Alaska	58	27	38	65	80
1988-89—Rochester Mustangs		USHL	39	2	7	9	56
1989-90—Rochester Mustangs (c)		USHL	46	5	20	25	95

(c)—June 16, 1990—Selected by Calgary Flames in 1990 NHL entry draft. Fifth Flames pick, 62nd overall, third round.

SCOTT MELLANBY

Right Wing . . . 6'1" . . . 195 lbs. . . . Born, Montreal, Que., June 11, 1966 . . . Shoots right . . . (October, 1987)—Cut index finger on right hand . . . (August, 1989)— Severed nerve and tendon damage in left forearm and missed first part of season . . . (November, 1989)—Viral infection.

Year	Team	League	Games	G.	A.	Pts.	Pen.
1983-84—Henry Carr H.S. (c)		MTJHL	39	37	37	74	97
1984-85—University of Wisconsin		WCHA	40	14	24	38	60
1985-86—University of Wisconsin		WCHA	32	21	23	44	89
1985-86—Philadelphia Flyers		NHL	2	0	0	0	0
1986-87—Philadelphia Flyers		NHL	71	11	21	32	94
1987-88—Philadelphia Flyers		NHL	75	25	26	51	185
1988-89—Philadelphia Flyers		NHL	76	21	29	50	183
1989-90—Philadelphia Flyers		NHL	57	6	17	23	77
NHL TOTALS			281	63	93	156	539

(c)—June, 1984—Drafted as underage junior by Philadelphia Flyers in NHL entry draft. First Flyers pick, 27th overall, second round.

DOUG MELNYK

Defense . . . 6' . . . 185 lbs. . . . Born, Ottawa, Ont., August 9, 1967 . . . Shoots left . . . (January, 1989)—Injured shoulder.

Year	Team	League	Games	G.	A.	Pts.	Pen.
1985-86—London Diamonds		OPJHL	....	...	....	....	....
1986-87—Western Michigan Univ.		CCHA	43	2	7	9	40
1987-88—Western Michigan Univ. (c)		CCHA	42	2	16	18	22
1988-89—Western Michigan Univ.		CCHA	30	2	4	6	28
1989-90—Western Michigan Univ.		CCHA	33	2	10	12	26

(c)—June, 1988—Selected by New York Islanders in 1988 NHL supplemental draft.

LARRY JOSEPH MELNYK

Defense . . . 6' . . . 180 lbs. . . . Born, New Westminster, B.C., February 21, 1960 . . . Shoots left . . . (January 16, 1985)—Twisted knee vs. N.Y. Islanders . . . (December, 1985)—Separated shoulder . . . (November, 1987)—Cut eye and concussion . . . (April 1, 1988)—Severed tendon in right arm vs. Minnesota . . . (February, 1989) —Twisted knee . . . (April 8, 1989)—Injured knee vs. Calgary.

Year	Team	League	Games	G.	A.	Pts.	Pen.
1977-78—Abbotsford		BCJHL	39	10	9	19	100
1977-78—New Westminster Bruins		WCHL	44	3	22	25	71
1978-79—New Westminster Bruins (c)		WHL	71	7	33	40	142
1979-80—New Westminster Bruins		WHL	67	13	38	51	236
1980-81—Boston Bruins		NHL	26	0	4	4	39
1980-81—Springfield Indians		AHL	47	1	10	11	109
1981-82—Erie Blades		AHL	10	0	3	3	36
1981-82—Boston Bruins		NHL	48	0	8	8	84
1982-83—Baltimore Skipjacks		AHL	72	2	24	26	215
1982-83—Boston Bruins		NHL	1	0	0	0	0
1983-84—Hershey Bears (d)		AHL	51	0	18	18	156
1983-84—Moncton Alpines		AHL	14	0	3	3	17
1983-84—Edmonton Oilers (e)		NHL	...	...	...	...	....
1984-85—Nova Scotia Voyageurs		AHL	37	2	10	12	97
1984-85—Edmonton Oilers		NHL	28	0	11	11	25
1985-86—Nova Scotia Oilers		AHL	19	2	8	10	72

Year	Team	League	Games	G.	A.	Pts.	Pen.
1985-86—Edmonton Oilers (f)		NHL	6	2	3	5	11
1985-86—New York Rangers		NHL	46	1	8	9	65
1986-87—New York Rangers		NHL	73	3	12	15	182
1987-88—New York Rangers (g)		NHL	14	0	1	1	34
1987-88—Vancouver Canucks		NHL	49	2	3	5	73
1988-89—Vancouver Canucks		NHL	74	3	11	14	82
1989-90—Vancouver Canucks		NHL	67	0	2	2	91
NHL TOTALS			432	11	63	74	686

(c)—August, 1979—Drafted as underage junior by Boston Bruins in 1979 NHL entry draft. Fifth Bruins pick, 78th overall, fourth round.
(d)—March, 1983—Traded by Boston Bruins to Edmonton Oilers for John Blum.
(e)—No regular season record. Played six playoff games.
(f)—December, 1985—Traded with Todd Strueby by Edmonton Oilers to New York Rangers for Mike Rogers.
(g)—November, 1987—Traded with Willie Huber by New York Rangers to Vancouver Canucks for Michel Petit.

KEVAN MELROSE

Defense . . . 5'10" . . . 180 lbs. . . . Born, Calgary, Alta., March 28, 1966 . . . Shoots left . . . (Summer, 1984)—Knee surgery.

Year	Team	League	Games	G.	A.	Pts.	Pen.
1983-84—Red Deer Rustlers (c)		AJHL	42	9	26	35	89
1984-85—Penticton		BCJHL	24	15	10	25	42
1985-86—Penticton		BCJHL	22	18	15	33	56
1986-87—Canadian Olympic Team		Int'l	8	1	0	1	4
1987-88—Harvard Univ.		ECAC	31	4	6	10	50
1988-89—Harvard Univ.		ECAC	32	2	13	15	126
1989-90—Harvard Univ.		ECAC	16	1	6	7	124

(c)—June, 1984—Drafted by Calgary Flames in 1984 NHL entry draft. Seventh Flames pick, 138th overall, seventh round.

ROBERT MENDEL

Defense . . . 6'1" . . . 185 lbs. . . . Born, Los Angeles, Calif., September 19, 1968 . . . Shoots left.

Year	Team	League	Games	G.	A.	Pts.	Pen.
1985-86—Edina High School		Minn. H.S.	21	2	27	29	....
1986-87—Univ. of Wisconsin (c)		WCHA	42	1	7	8	26
1987-88—Univ. of Wisconsin		WCHA	40	0	7	7	22
1988-89—Univ. of Wisconsin		WCHA	44	1	14	15	37
1989-90—Univ. of Wisconsin		WCHA	44	1	13	14	30

(c)—June, 1987—Drafted by Quebec Nordiques in 1987 NHL entry draft. Fifth Nordiques pick, 93rd overall, fifth round.

GLENN MERKOSKY

Center . . . 5'10" . . . 175 lbs. . . . Born, Edmonton, Alta., April 8, 1960 . . . Shoots left.

Year	Team	League	Games	G.	A.	Pts.	Pen.
1977-78—Seattle Breakers		WCHL	6	4	3	7	2
1978-79—Michigan Tech		WCHA	38	14	29	43	22
1979-80—Calgary Wranglers		WHL	72	49	40	89	95
1980-81—Binghamton Whalers (c)		AHL	80	26	35	61	61
1981-82—Hartford Whalers		NHL	7	0	0	0	2
1981-82—Binghamton Whalers		AHL	72	29	40	69	83
1982-83—New Jersey Devils (d)		NHL	34	4	10	14	20
1982-83—Wichita Wind		CHL	45	26	23	49	15
1983-84—Maine Mariners		AHL	75	28	28	56	56
1983-84—New Jersey Devils		NHL	5	1	0	1	0
1984-85—Maine Mariners (b)		AHL	80	38	38	76	19
1985-86—Adirondack Red Wings		AHL	59	24	33	57	22
1985-86—Detroit Red Wings (e)		NHL	17	0	2	2	0
1986-87—Adirondack Red Wings (a-f)		AHL	77	*54	31	85	66
1987-88—Rosenheim SB		W. Germany	16	2	3	5	17
1987-88—Adirondack Red Wings		AHL	66	34	42	76	34
1988-89—Adirondack Red Wings		AHL	76	31	46	77	13
1989-90—Detroit Red Wings		NHL	3	0	0	0	0
1989-90—Adirondack Red Wings		AHL	75	33	31	64	29
NHL TOTALS			66	5	12	17	22

(c)—August, 1980—Signed by Hartford Whalers as a free agent.
(d)—September, 1982—Signed by New Jersey Devils as a free agent.
(e)—August, 1985—Signed by Detroit Red Wings as a free agent.
(f)—Won Fred Hunt Trophy (Sportsmanship Trophy).

MIKE MERSH

Defense . . . 6'2" . . . 210 lbs. . . . Born, Skokie, Ill., September 29, 1964 . . . Shoots left . . . (January, 1987)—Missed 32 games with a separated shoulder.

Year	Team	League	Games	G.	A.	Pts.	Pen.
1983-84—Univ. of Illinois/Chicago		CCHA	29	0	5	5	18
1984-85—Univ. of Illinois/Chicago		CCHA	35	1	14	15	36
1985-86—Univ. of Illinois/Chicago (c)		CCHA	36	4	19	23	30
1986-87—Salt Lake Golden Eagles		IHL	43	3	12	15	101
1987-88—Salt Lake Golden Eagles		IHL	1	0	0	0	2
1987-88—Flint Spirits		IHL	58	1	14	15	118
1988-89—Muskegon Lumberjacks		IHL	16	0	2	2	26
1988-89—Flint Spirits		IHL	55	5	20	25	101
1988-89—New Haven Nighthawks		AHL	1	0	0	0	4
1989-90—Muskegon Lumberjacks (d)		IHL	82	10	38	48	161

(c)—April, 1986—Signed by Calgary Flames as a free agent.
(d)—August 3, 1989—Signed by Pittsburgh Penguins as a free agent.

JOBY MESSIER

Defense . . . 6' . . . 193 lbs. . . . Born, Regina, Sask., March 2, 1970 . . . Shoots right . . . Brother of Mitch Messier and cousin of Mark Messier . . . (December, 1984)—Broke right arm . . . (September, 1987)—Broke right arm.

Year	Team	League	Games	G.	A.	Pts.	Pen.
1987-88—Notre Dame Hounds		SJHL	53	9	22	31	208
1988-89—Michigan State Univ. (c)		CCHA	46	2	10	12	70
1989-90—Michigan State Univ.		CCHA	42	1	11	12	58

(c)—June, 1989—Drafted by New York Rangers in 1989 NHL entry draft. Seventh Rangers pick, 118th overall, sixth round.

MARK MESSIER

Center and Left Wing . . . 6' . . . 205 lbs. . . . Born, Edmonton, Alta., January 18, 1961 . . . Shoots left . . . Son of Doug Messier (WHL), brother of Paul Messier and cousin of Mitch and Joby Messier . . . (November 7, 1981)—Injured ankle at Chicago . . . (March, 1983)—Chipped bone in wrist . . . (January 18, 1984)—Given six-game suspension by NHL for hitting Vancouver's Thomas Gradin over the head with his stick . . . Brother-in-law of John Blum . . . (November, 1984)—Sprained knee ligaments . . . (December 26, 1984)—Given 10-game NHL suspension for cracking cheekbone of Jamie Macoun at Calgary . . . (December 3, 1985)—Bruised left foot at Los Angeles and missed 17 games . . . (October, 1987)—Suspended and fined by Edmonton Oilers after refusing to report to training camp. He missed three weeks of camp . . . (October 23, 1988)—Suspended six games after his stick injured Rich Sutter's mouth at Vancouver . . . (January 28, 1989)—Twisted left knee vs. Los Angeles . . . (February 3, 1989)—Strained right knee vs. Detroit . . . (February 12, 1989)—Bruised left knee when checked by Michel Petit at N.Y. Rangers.

Year	Team	League	Games	G.	A.	Pts.	Pen.
1976-77—Spruce Grove Mets		AJHL	57	27	39	66	91
1977-78—St. Albert Saints		AJHL	....	...	....	....	....
1978-79—Indianapolis Racers (c)		WHA	5	0	0	0	0
1978-79—Cincinnati Stingers (d-e)		WHA	47	1	10	11	58
1979-80—Houston Apollos		CHL	4	0	3	3	4
1979-80—Edmonton Oilers		NHL	75	12	21	33	120
1980-81—Edmonton Oilers		NHL	72	23	40	63	102
1981-82—Edmonton Oilers (a)		NHL	78	50	38	88	119
1982-83—Edmonton Oilers (a)		NHL	77	48	58	106	72
1983-84—Edmonton Oilers (b-f)		NHL	73	37	64	101	165
1984-85—Edmonton Oilers		NHL	55	23	31	54	57
1985-86—Edmonton Oilers		NHL	63	35	49	84	68
1986-87—Edmonton Oilers		NHL	77	37	70	107	73
1987-88—Edmonton Oilers		NHL	77	37	74	111	103
1988-89—Edmonton Oilers		NHL	72	33	61	94	130
1989-90—Edmonton Oilers (a-g-h)		NHL	79	45	84	129	79
WHA TOTALS			52	1	10	11	58
NHL TOTALS			798	380	590	970	1088

(c)—November, 1978—Given five-game trial by Indianapolis Racers.
(d)—January, 1979—Signed by Cincinnati Stingers as free agent.
(e)—August, 1979—Drafted by Edmonton Oilers in 1979 NHL entry draft. Second Edmonton pick, 48th overall, third round.
(f)—Won Conn Smythe Trophy (Stanley Cup Playoff MVP).
(g)—Won Hart Memorial Trophy (NHL MVP).
(h)—Named NHL Player of the Year in poll of players by THE SPORTING NEWS.

MITCH MESSIER

Center . . . 6'2" . . . 185 lbs. . . . Born, Regina, Sask., August 21, 1965 . . . Shoots right . . . Cousin of Mark Messier . . . Brother of Joby Messier . . . (November, 1987)—Bruised knee.

Year	Team	League	Games	G.	A.	Pts.	Pen.
1981-82—Notre Dame H.S.		Sask. Midget	26	8	20	28	..
1982-83—Notre Dame H.S. (c)		Sask. Juvenile	60	108	73	181	160
1983-84—Michigan State University		CCHA	37	6	15	21	22
1984-85—Michigan State University		CCHA	42	12	21	33	46
1985-86—Michigan State University		CCHA	38	24	40	64	36
1986-87—Michigan State Univ. (a-d)		CCHA	45	44	48	92	89
1987-88—Kalamazoo Wings		IHL	69	29	37	66	42
1987-88—Minnesota North Stars		NHL	13	0	1	1	11
1988-89—Minnesota North Stars		NHL	3	0	1	1	0
1988-89—Kalamazoo Wings		IHL	67	34	46	80	71
1989-90—Minnesota North Stars		NHL	2	0	0	0	0
1989-90—Kalamazoo Wings		IHL	65	26	58	84	56
NHL TOTALS			18	0	2	2	11

(c)—June, 1983—Drafted by Minnesota North Stars in 1983 NHL entry draft. Fourth North Stars pick, 56th overall, third round.
(d)—Named U.S. College All-America First-Team All-Star.

SCOTT METCALFE

Left Wing . . . 6' . . . 195 lbs. . . . Born, Toronto, Ont., January 6, 1967 . . . Shoots left.

Year	Team	League	Games	G.	A.	Pts.	Pen.
1982-83—Toronto Young Nats		OHA	39	22	43	65	74
1983-84—Kingston Canadians		OHL	68	25	49	74	154
1984-85—Kingston Canadians (c)		OHL	58	27	33	60	100
1985-86—Kingston Canadians		OHL	66	36	43	79	213
1986-87—Kingston Canadians (d)		OHL	39	15	45	60	14
1986-87—Windsor Spitfires		OHL	18	10	12	22	52
1987-88—Nova Scotia Oilers		AHL	43	9	19	28	87
1987-88—Rochester Americans		AHL	22	2	13	15	56
1987-88—Edmonton Oilers (e)		NHL	2	0	0	0	0
1987-88—Buffalo Sabres		NHL	1	0	1	1	0
1988-89—Rochester Americans		AHL	60	20	31	51	241

Year	Team	League	Games	G.	A.	Pts.	Pen.
1988-89—Buffalo Sabres		NHL	9	1	1	2	13
1989-90—Buffalo Sabres		NHL	7	0	0	0	5
1989-90—Rochester Americans		AHL	43	12	17	29	93
NHL TOTALS			19	1	2	3	18

(c)—June, 1985—Drafted as underage junior by Edmonton Oilers in 1985 NHL entry draft. First Oilers pick, 20th overall, first round.

(d)—February, 1987—Traded by Kingston Canadians to Windsor Spitfires for future draft considerations.

(e)—February, 1988—Traded by Edmonton Oilers to Buffalo Sabres for Steve Dykstra.

HAROLD RANDALL (HARRY) MEWS

Center . . . 5'11" . . . 175 lbs. . . . Born, Nepean, Ont., February 9, 1967 . . . Shoots left . . . (November 18, 1988)—Suspended one Hockey East game for fighting vs. Lowell.

Year	Team	League	Games	G.	A.	Pts.	Pen.
1986-87—Northeastern Univ.		H. East	29	10	15	25	70
1987-88—Northeastern Univ. (c)		H. East	37	16	23	39	82
1988-89—Northeastern Univ. (b)		H. East	31	18	24	42	103
1989-90—Northeastern Univ. (b)		H. East	36	20	39	59	82

(c)—June, 1988—Selected by Washington Capitals in 1988 supplemental draft.

DAVID MICHAYLUK

Right Wing . . . 5'10" . . . 175 lbs. . . . Born, Wakaw, Sask., May 18, 1962 . . . Shoots left . . . Also plays Left Wing . . . (May, 1989)—Cut on right arm by skate vs. Salt Lake.

Year	Team	League	Games	G.	A.	Pts.	Pen.
1979-80—Prince Albert Saints		AJHL	60	46	67	113	49
1980-81—Regina Pats (b-c-d)		WHL	72	62	71	133	39
1981-82—Regina Pats (b-e)		WHL	72	62	111	173	128
1981-82—Philadelphia Flyers		NHL	1	0	0	0	0
1982-83—Philadelphia Flyers		NHL	13	2	6	8	8
1982-83—Maine Mariners		AHL	69	32	40	72	16
1983-84—Springfield Indians		AHL	79	18	44	62	37
1984-85—Hershey Bears		AHL	3	0	2	2	2
1984-85—Kalamazoo Wings (b)		IHL	82	*66	33	99	49
1985-86—Nova Scotia Oilers		AHL	3	0	1	1	0
1985-86—Muskegon Lumberjacks		IHL	77	52	52	104	73
1986-87—Muskegon Lumberjacks (b)		IHL	82	47	53	100	69
1987-88—Muskegon Lumberjacks (a)		IHL	81	56	81	137	46
1988-89—Muskegon Lumberjacks (a-f-g-h)		IHL	80	50	72	*122	84
1989-90—Muskegon Lumberjacks (a)		IHL	79	*51	51	102	80
NHL TOTALS			14	2	6	8	8

(c)—Winner of Stewart "Butch" Paul Memorial Trophy (Top Rookie).

(d)—June, 1981—Drafted as underage junior by Philadelphia Flyers in 1981 NHL entry draft. Fifth Flyers pick, 65th overall, fourth round.

(e)—Led WHL playoffs with 40 points.

(f)—Won James Gatschene Memorial Trophy (IHL MVP).

(g)—Won Leo P. Lamoureux Memorial Trophy (IHL Leading scorer).

(h)—Co-leader in IHL playoffs with nine goals (Peter Lappin) and 21 points (Mark Recchi).

TROY MICK

Left Wing . . . 6' . . . 180 lbs. . . . Born, Burnaby, B.C., March 30, 1969 . . . Shoots left . . . (March, 1987)—Left knee surgery.

Year	Team	League	Games	G.	A.	Pts.	Pen.
1985-86—Portland Winter Hawks		WHL	6	2	5	7	2
1986-87—Portland Winter Hawks		WHL	57	30	33	63	60
1987-88—Portland Winter Hawks (a-c)		WHL	72	63	84	147	78
1988-89—Portland Winter Hawks (a)		WHL	66	49	87	136	70
1989-90—Regina Pats (a-d)		WHL	66	60	53	113	67

(c)—June, 1988—Drafted by Pittsburgh Penguins in 1988 NHL entry draft. Sixth Penguins pick, 130th overall, seventh round.

(d)—October 5, 1989—Traded by Portland Winter Hawks to Regina Pats for Jeff Sebastien.

MAX MIDDENDORF

Right Wing . . . 6'4" . . . 195 lbs. . . . Born, Syracuse, N.Y., August 18, 1967 . . . Shoots right . . . (February 1, 1987)—Dislocated thumb . . . (January 26, 1990)—Suspended five AHL games for a stick fight with Larry Bernard at Moncton.

Year	Team	League	Games	G.	A.	Pts.	Pen.
1983-84—New Jersey Rockets		N.J. Midget	58	94	74	168	....
1984-85—Sudbury Wolves (c)		OHL	63	16	28	44	106
1985-86—Sudbury Wolves		OHL	61	40	42	82	71
1986-87—Quebec Nordiques		NHL	6	1	4	5	4
1986-87—Sudbury Wolves		OHL	31	31	29	60	7
1986-87—Kitchener Rangers		OHL	17	7	15	22	6
1987-88—Fredericton Express		AHL	38	11	13	24	57
1987-88—Quebec Nordiques		NHL	1	0	0	0	0
1988-89—Halifax Citadels		AHL	72	41	39	80	85
1989-90—Quebec Nordiques		NHL	3	0	0	0	0
1989-90—Halifax Citadels		AHL	48	20	17	37	60
NHL TOTALS			10	1	4	5	4

(c)—June, 1985—Drafted as underage junior by Quebec Nordiques in 1985 NHL entry draft. Third Nordiques pick, 57th overall, third round.

KEVIN MIEHM

Center . . . 6'2" . . . 190 lbs. . . . Born, Kitchener, Ont., September 10, 1969 . . . Shoots left.

Year	Team	League	Games	G.	A.	Pts.	Pen.
1985-86—Kitchener Greenshirts		OHA	20	20	37	57	65
1986-87—Oshawa Generals (c)		OHL	61	12	27	39	19

Year	Team	League	Games	G.	A.	Pts.	Pen.
1987-88—Oshawa Generals		OHL	52	16	36	52	30
1988-89—Oshawa Generals		OHL	63	43	79	122	19
1988-89—Peoria Rivermen		IHL	3	1	1	2	0
1989-90—Peoria Rivermen		IHL	76	23	38	61	20

(c)—June, 1987—Drafted as underage junior by St. Louis Blues in 1987 NHL entry draft. Second Blues pick, 54th overall, third round.

MIKE MILLAR

Right Wing . . . 5'10" . . . 170 lbs. . . . Born, St. Catharines, Ont., April 28, 1965 . . . Shoots left.

Year	Team	League	Games	G.	A.	Pts.	Pen.
1981-82—St. Catharines Midgets		Ont. Midget	30	32	32	64	24
1982-83—Brantford Alexanders		OHL	53	20	29	49	10
1983-84—Brantford Alexanders (c)		OHL	69	50	45	95	48
1984-85—Hamilton Steelhawks		OHL	63	*66	60	126	54
1985-86—Team Canada		Int'l.	69	50	38	88	74
1986-87—Hartford Whalers		NHL	10	2	2	4	0
1986-87—Binghamton Whalers		AHL	61	45	32	77	38
1987-88—Binghamton Whalers		AHL	31	32	17	49	42
1987-88—Hartford Whalers (d)		NHL	28	7	7	14	6
1988-89—Washington Capitals		NHL	18	6	3	9	4
1988-89—Baltimore Skipjacks (b)		AHL	53	47	35	82	58
1989-90—Boston Bruins (e)		NHL	15	1	4	5	0
1989-90—Maine Mariners		AHL	60	40	33	73	77
NHL TOTALS			71	16	16	32	10

(c)—June, 1984—Drafted as underage junior by Hartford Whalers in 1984 NHL entry draft. Second Whalers pick, 110th overall, sixth round.

(d)—July, 1988—Traded with Neil Sheehy by Hartford Whalers to Washington Capitals for Ed Kastelic and Grant Jennings.

(e)—October 1, 1989—Traded by Washington Capitals to Boston Bruins for Alfie Turcotte.

COREY MILLEN

Center . . . 5'7" . . . 165 lbs. . . . Born, Cloquet, Minn., April 29, 1964 . . . Shoots right . . . (November, 1982)—Injured knee in WCHA game vs. Colorado College, requiring surgery . . . (October, 1984)—Shoulder injury . . . (April, 1989)—Tested positive for a non-anabolic steroid in a random test at World Cup Tournament and was banned from play . . . (September 18, 1989)—Sprained left knee ligaments vs. N.Y. Islanders after colliding with Bryan Trottier, required surgery and missed four months.

Year	Team	League	Games	G.	A.	Pts.	Pen.
1981-82—Cloquet H.S. (c)		Minn. H.S.	18	46	35	81	....
1982-83—University of Minnesota		WCHA	21	14	15	29	18
1983-84—U.S. National Team		Int'l	45	15	11	26	10
1983-84—U.S. Olympic Team		Int'l	6	0	0	0	2
1984-85—University of Minnesota (b)		WCHA	38	28	36	64	60
1985-86—University of Minnesota (b)		WCHA	48	41	42	83	64
1986-87—University of Minnesota (b)		WCHA	42	36	29	65	62
1987-88—U.S. Olympic Team		Int'l	51	46	45	91	..
1988-89—Ambri Piotta		Switzerland	36	32	22	54	..
1989-90—New York Rangers		NHL	4	0	0	0	2
1989-90—Flint Spirits		IHL	11	4	5	9	2
NHL TOTALS			4	0	0	0	2

(c)—June, 1982—Drafted by New York Rangers in 1982 NHL entry draft as underage player. Third Rangers pick, 57th overall, third round.

AARON MILLER

Defense . . . 6'4" . . . 180 lbs. . . . Born, Buffalo, N.Y., August 11, 1971 . . . Shoots right . . . Nephew of Robert Miller (Professional baseball).

Year	Team	League	Games	G.	A.	Pts.	Pen.
1987-88—Niagara Scenic		NAJHL	30	4	9	13	2
1988-89—Niagara Scenic (c)		NAJHL	59	24	38	62	60
1989-90—University of Vermont (d)		ECAC	31	1	15	16	24

(c)—June, 1989—Drafted by New York Rangers in 1989 NHL entry draft. Sixth Rangers pick, 88th overall, fifth round.

(d)—Named to ECAC All-Rookie team.

BRAD MILLER

Defense . . . 6'4" . . . 205 lbs. . . . Born, Edmonton, Alta., July 23, 1969 . . . Shoots left . . . (February 23, 1990)—Given a three game AHL suspension for abuse of an official vs. New Haven . . . (April 11, 1990)—Given a nine game AHL suspension for abuse of AHL officials. He tried to continue a fight with Jeff Madill vs. Utica after he returned to the ice following a game misconduct.

Year	Team	League	Games	G.	A.	Pts.	Pen.
1984-85—Edmonton K. of C.		Alta. Midget	42	7	26	33	154
1985-86—Regina Pats		WHL	71	2	14	16	99
1986-87—Regina Pats (c)		WHL	67	10	38	48	154
1987-88—Regina Pats		WHL	61	9	34	43	148
1987-88—Rochester Americans		AHL	3	0	0	0	4
1988-89—Buffalo Sabres		NHL	7	0	0	0	6
1988-89—Rochester Americans		AHL	3	0	0	0	4
1988-89—Regina Pats		WHL	34	8	18	26	95
1989-90—Buffalo Sabres		NHL	1	0	0	0	0
1989-90—Rochester Americans		AHL	60	2	10	12	273
NHL TOTALS			8	0	0	0	6

(c)—June, 1987—Drafted as underage junior by Buffalo Sabres in 1987 NHL entry draft. Second Sabres pick, 22nd overall, second round.

JASON MILLER

Center . . . 6'1" . . . 184 lbs. . . . Born, Edmonton, Alta., March 1, 1971 . . . Shoots left . . . (May, 1986)—Separated shoulder.

Year	Team	League	Games	G.	A.	Pts.	Pen.
1987-88—Medicine Hat Tigers		WHL	71	11	18	29	28
1988-89—Medicine Hat Tigers (c)		WHL	72	51	55	106	44
1989-90—Medicine Hat Tigers		WHL	66	43	56	99	40

(c)—June, 1989—Drafted by New Jersey Devils in 1989 NHL entry draft. Second Devils pick, 18th overall, first round.

JAY MILLER

Left Wing . . . 6'2" . . . 215 lbs. . . . Born, Wellesley, Mass., July 16, 1960 . . . Shoots left . . . (November, 1984)—Broken bone in right hand . . . Also plays Defense . . . (April, 1988)—Strained right knee ligaments.

Year	Team	League	Games	G.	A.	Pts.	Pen.
1979-80—Univ. of New Hampshire		ECAC	28	7	12	19	53
1981-82—Univ. of New Hampshire		ECAC	10	4	8	12	14
1982-83—Univ. of New Hampshire		ECAC	24	6	4	10	34
1983-84—Toledo Goaldiggers		IHL	2	0	0	0	4
1983-84—Mohawk Valley Comets		ACHL	48	15	36	51	167
1983-84—Maine Mariners		AHL	15	1	1	2	27
1984-85—Muskegon Mohawks		IHL	56	5	29	34	177
1985-86—Moncton Golden Flames		AHL	18	4	6	10	113
1985-86—Boston Bruins (c)		NHL	46	3	0	3	178
1986-87—Boston Bruins		NHL	55	1	4	5	208
1987-88—Boston Bruins		NHL	78	7	12	19	304
1988-89—Boston Bruins (d)		NHL	37	2	4	6	168
1989-89—Los Angeles Kings		NHL	29	5	3	8	133
1989-90—Los Angeles Kings		NHL	68	10	2	12	224
NHL TOTALS			313	28	25	53	1215

(c)—September, 1985—Signed by Boston Bruins as a free agent.
(d)—January 22, 1989—Traded by Boston Bruins to Los Angeles Kings. Two days later the deal was completed when the Bruins sent Steve Kasper to Los Angeles for Bobby Carpenter.

KEITH MILLER

Left Wing . . . 6'2" . . . 212 lbs. . . . Born, Toronto, Ont., March 18, 1967 . . . Shoots left.

Year	Team	League	Games	G.	A.	Pts.	Pen.
1984-85—Guelph Platers		OHL	18	1	3	4	7
1984-85—Aurora Tigers Tier II		OJHL	24	7	11	18	31
1985-86—Guelph Platers (c)		OHL	61	32	17	49	30
1986-87—Guelph Platers		OHL	66	50	31	81	44
1987-88—Baltimore Skipjacks		AHL	21	6	5	11	12
1988-89—Fort Wayne Komets		IHL	54	35	25	60	13
1988-89—Halifax Citadels		AHL	12	6	3	9	6
1989-90—Fort Wayne Komets		IHL	51	26	19	45	10

(c)—June, 1986—Drafted by Quebec Nordiques in 1986 NHL entry draft. Tenth Nordiques pick, 165th overall, eighth round.

KELLY MILLER

Left Wing . . . 5'11" . . . 185 lbs. . . . Born, Lansing, Mich., March 3, 1963 . . . Shoots left . . . (September, 1985)—Injured ankle in training camp . . . (January 27, 1986)—Sprained knee at Quebec and missed five games . . . Brother of Kip and Kevin Miller . . . (November, 1988)—Pulled groin . . . Son of Lyle Miller, part owner of the Lansing (Mich.) Arena.

Year	Team	League	Games	G.	A.	Pts.	Pen.
1981-82—Michigan State Univ. (c)		CCHA	40	11	19	30	21
1982-83—Michigan State Univ.		CCHA	36	16	19	35	12
1983-84—Michigan State Univ.		CCHA	46	28	21	49	12
1984-85—Michigan State Univ. (d)		CCHA	43	27	23	50	21
1984-85—New York Rangers		NHL	5	0	2	2	2
1985-86—New York Rangers		NHL	74	13	20	33	52
1986-87—New York Rangers (e)		NHL	38	6	14	20	22
1986-87—Washington Capitals		NHL	39	10	12	22	26
1987-88—Washington Capitals		NHL	80	9	23	32	35
1988-89—Washington Capitals		NHL	78	19	21	40	45
1989-90—Washington Capitals		NHL	80	18	22	40	49
NHL TOTALS			394	75	114	189	231

(c)—June, 1982—Drafted by New York Rangers in NHL entry draft. Ninth Rangers pick, 183rd overall, ninth round.
(d)—Named First team All-America (West).
(e)—January, 1987—Traded with Mike Ridley and Bobby Crawford by New York Rangers to Washington Capitals for Bobby Carpenter and a second-round 1989 draft pick (Jason Prosofsky).

KEVIN MILLER

Center . . . 5'9" . . . 170 lbs. . . . Born, Lansing, Mich., August 9, 1965 . . . Shoots right . . . Brother of Kip and Kelly Miller . . . Also plays Right Wing . . . Son of Lyle Miller, part owner of the Lansing (Mich.) Arena.

Year	Team	League	Games	G.	A.	Pts.	Pen.
1984-85—Michigan State Univ. (c)		CCHA	44	11	29	40	84
1985-86—Michigan State Univ.		CCHA	45	19	52	71	112
1986-87—Michigan State Univ.		CCHA	42	25	56	81	63
1987-88—Michigan State Univ.		CCHA	9	6	3	9	18
1987-88—U.S. Olympic Team		Int'l	50	32	34	66	..
1988-89—New York Rangers		NHL	24	3	5	8	2
1988-89—Denver Rangers		IHL	55	29	47	76	19
1989-90—New York Rangers		NHL	16	0	5	5	2
1989-90—Flint Spirits		IHL	48	19	23	42	41
NHL TOTALS			40	3	10	13	4

(c)—June, 1984—Drafted by New York Rangers in 1984 NHL entry draft. Tenth Rangers pick, 202nd overall, 10th round.

KIP MILLER

Center . . . 5'10" . . . 160 lbs. . . . Born, Lansing, Mich., June 11, 1969 . . . Shoots left . . . Brother of Kevin Miller and Kelly Miller . . . (November, 1987)—Accidentally put hand and forearm through a storm-door window . . . Son of Lyle Miller, part owner of the Lansing (Mich.) Arena.

Year	Team	League	Games	G.	A.	Pts.	Pen.
1986-87—Michigan State Univ. (c)		CCHA	45	22	19	41	96
1987-88—Michigan State Univ.		CCHA	39	16	25	41	51
1988-89—Michigan State Univ. (a-d)		CCHA	47	32	45	77	94
1989-90—Michigan State Univ. (a-d-e-f)		CCHA	45	*48	53	*101	60

(c)—June, 1987—Drafted by Quebec Nordiques in 1987 NHL entry draft. Fourth Nordiques pick, 72nd overall, fourth round.
(d)—Named First team All-America (West).
(e)—Named CCHA Player of the Year.
(f)—Won Hobey Baker Award (Top U.S. Collegiate Hockey Player).

KRIS MILLER

Defense . . . 6' . . . 185 lbs. . . . Born, Bemidji, Minn., March 30, 1969 . . . Shoots left . . . Brother of Kurtis Miller.

Year	Team	League	Games	G.	A.	Pts.	Pen.
1985-86—Greenway H.S.		Minn. H.S.	20	9	16	25	....
1986-87—Greenway H.S. (c)		Minn. H.S.	26	10	33	43	....
1987-88—Univ. of Minnesota/Duluth		WCHA	30	1	6	7	30
1988-89—Univ. of Minnesota/Duluth		WCHA	39	2	10	12	37
1989-90—Univ. of Minnesota/Duluth		WCHA	39	2	11	13	59

(c)—June, 1987—Drafted by Montreal Canadiens in 1987 NHL entry draft. Sixth Canadiens pick, 80th overall, fourth round.

KURTIS MILLER

Left Wing . . . 5'11" . . . 180 lbs. . . . Born, Bemidji, Minn., June 1, 1970 . . . Shoots left . . . (December, 1986)—Injured back . . . (January, 1989)—Injured back and shoulder . . . (June, 1989)—Hip pointer . . . Brother of Kris Miller.

Year	Team	League	Games	G.	A.	Pts.	Pen.
1988-89—Rochester Mustangs		USHL	48	28	21	49	50
1989-90—Rochester Mustangs (a-c-d-e)		USHL	50	50	39	89	56

(c)—Named USHL MVP.
(d)—Won USHL Best Forward Trophy.
(e)—June 16, 1990—Selected by St. Louis Blues in 1990 NHL entry draft. Fourth Blues pick, 117th overall, sixth round.

JOHN MINER

Defense . . . 5'10" . . . 170 lbs. . . . Born, Moose Jaw, Sask., August 28, 1965 . . . Shoots right . . . (September, 1982)—Eye injury . . . (November, 1986)—Injured foot.

Year	Team	League	Games	G.	A.	Pts.	Pen.
1981-82—Regina Pats		SJHL	..	..	1	1	11
1981-82—Regina Pats		WHL	10	0	1	1	11
1982-83—Regina Pats (c)		WHL	71	11	23	34	126
1983-84—Regina Pats (b)		WHL	70	27	42	69	132
1984-85—Regina Pats (a)		WHL	66	30	54	84	128
1984-85—Nova Scotia Oilers (d)		AHL	....	....	....	....	....
1985-86—Nova Scotia Oilers		AHL	79	10	33	43	90
1986-87—Nova Scotia Oilers		AHL	45	5	28	33	38
1987-88—Nova Scotia Oilers		AHL	61	8	26	34	61
1987-88—Edmonton Oilers (e)		NHL	14	2	3	5	16
1988-89—New Haven Nighthawks		AHL	7	2	3	5	4
1989-90—New Haven Nighthawks		AHL	7	1	6	7	2
NHL TOTALS			14	2	3	5	16

(c)—June, 1983—Drafted as underage junior by Edmonton Oilers in 1983 NHL entry draft. Tenth Oilers pick, 220th overall, 11th round.
(d)—No regular season record. Played three playoff games.
(e)—August, 1988—Traded by Edmonton Oilers to Los Angeles Kings for Craig Redmond.

ROY MITCHELL

Defense . . . 6'1" . . . 196 lbs. . . . Born, Edmonton, Alta., March 14, 1969 . . . Shoots right.

Year	Team	League	Games	G.	A.	Pts.	Pen.
1985-86—St. Albert Saints		AJHL	39	2	18	20	32
1986-87—Portland Winter Hawks		WHL	68	7	32	39	103
1987-88—Portland Winter Hawks		WHL	72	5	42	47	219
1988-89—Portland Winter Hawks (c)		WHL	72	9	34	43	177
1989-90—Sherbrooke Canadiens		AHL	77	5	12	17	98

(c)—June, 1989—Drafted by Montreal Canadiens in 1989 NHL entry draft. Ninth Canadiens pick, 188th overall, ninth round.

MIKE MODANO

Center . . . 6'3" . . . 175 lbs. . . . Born, Detroit, Mich., June 7, 1970 . . . Shoots left . . . (January 24, 1989)—Fractured scaphoid bone in left wrist in collision with Steve Jaques in WHL All-star game . . . (March 4, 1990)—Nose broken when elbowed by Chris Dahlquist vs. Pittsburgh.

Year	Team	League	Games	G.	A.	Pts.	Pen.
1986-87—Prince Albert Raiders		WHL	70	32	30	62	96
1987-88—Prince Albert Raiders (c)		WHL	65	47	80	127	80
1988-89—Prince Albert Raiders (a)		WHL	41	39	66	105	74
1988-89—Minnesota North Stars (d)		NHL	..	..	..	..	..
1989-90—Minnesota North Stars		NHL	80	29	46	75	63
NHL TOTALS			80	29	46	75	63

(c)—June, 1988—Drafted by Minnesota North Stars in 1988 NHL entry draft. First North Stars pick, first overall, first round.
(d)—No regular season record. Played two playoff games.

SANDY MOGER

Defense . . . 6'2" . . . 190 lbs. . . . Born, 100 Mile House, B.C., March 21, 1969 . . . Shoots right . . . (September, 1988)—Broken wrist.

Year	Team	League	Games	G.	A.	Pts.	Pen.
1984-85—Vernon Midgets		B.C. Midget	42	21	22	43	102
1985-86—Vernon Midgets		B.C. Midget	45	33	28	61	89
1986-87—Vernon Midgets		B.C. Midget	45	40	34	74	120
1987-88—Yorkton Terriers		SJHL	60	39	41	80	144
1988-89—Lake Superior State Univ. (c)		CCHA	31	4	6	10	28
1989-90—Lake Superior State Univ.		CCHA	46	17	15	32	76

(c)—June, 1989—Drafted by Vancouver Canucks in 1989 NHL entry draft. Seventh Canucks pick, 176th overall, ninth round.

ALEXANDER MOGILNY

Right Wing . . . 5'11" . . . 186 lbs. . . . Born, Khabarovsk U.S.S.R., February 18, 1969 . . . Shoots left . . . Earliest selected Soviet player ever in the NHL entry draft . . . (November 26, 1989)—Flu . . . (January 22, 1990)—Missed games due to a fear of flying. He spent the remainder of the season traveling on trains and limos.

Year	Team	League	Games	G.	A.	Pts.	Pen.
1986-87—Central Red Army		U.S.S.R.	28	15	1	16	4
1987-88—Central Red Army (c)		U.S.S.R.	39	12	8	20	20
1988-89—Central Red Army		U.S.S.R.	31	11	11	22	24
1989-90—Buffalo Sabres		NHL	65	15	28	43	16
NHL TOTALS			65	15	28	43	16

(c)—June, 1988—Drafted by Buffalo Sabres in 1988 NHL entry draft. Fourth Sabres pick, 89th overall, fifth round.

CARL MOKOSAK

Left Wing . . . 6'1" . . . 181 lbs. . . . Born, Fort Saskatchewan, Alta., September 22, 1962 . . . Shoots left . . . Brother of John Mokosak.

Year	Team	League	Games	G.	A.	Pts.	Pen.
1978-79—Brandon		MJHL	44	12	11	23	146
1979-80—Brandon Wheat Kings		WHL	61	12	21	33	226
1980-81—Brandon Wheat Kings		WHL	70	20	40	60	118
1981-82—Brandon Wheat Kings (c)		WHL	69	46	61	107	363
1981-82—Oklahoma City Stars		CHL	2	1	1	2	2
1981-82—Calgary Flames		NHL	1	0	1	1	0
1982-83—Colorado Flames		CHL	28	10	12	22	106
1982-83—Calgary Flames (d)		NHL	41	7	6	13	87
1983-84—New Haven Nighthawks		AHL	80	18	21	39	206
1984-85—New Haven Nighthawks		AHL	11	6	6	12	26
1984-85—Los Angeles Kings (e)		NHL	30	4	8	12	43
1985-86—Philadelphia Flyers		NHL	1	0	0	0	5
1985-86—Hershey Bears (f)		AHL	79	30	42	72	312
1986-87—Pittsburgh Penguins		NHL	3	0	0	0	4
1986-87—Baltimore Skipjacks		AHL	67	23	27	50	228
1987-88—Muskegon Lumberjacks		IHL	81	29	37	66	308
1988-89—Boston Bruins		NHL	7	0	0	0	31
1988-89—Maine Mariners		AHL	53	20	18	38	337
1989-90—Fort Wayne Komets (g)		IHL	55	12	21	33	315
1989-90—Phoenix Roadrunners		IHL	15	6	6	12	48
NHL TOTALS			83	11	15	26	170

(c)—August, 1981—Signed by Calgary Flames as a free agent.
(d)—June, 1983—Traded by Calgary Flames with Kevin LaVallee to Los Angeles Kings for Steve Bozek.
(e)—June, 1985—Released by Los Angeles Kings and subequently signed by Philadelphia Flyers as a free agent.
(f)—July, 1986—Signed by Pittsburgh Penguins as a free agent.
(g)—August, 1989—Signed multi-year contract with Fort Wayne Komets.

JOHN MOKOSAK

Defense . . . 5'11" . . . 185 lbs. . . . Born, Edmonton, Alta., September 7, 1963 . . . Shoots left . . . Brother of Carl Mokosak.

Year	Team	League	Games	G.	A.	Pts.	Pen.
1979-80—Fort Saskatchewan Traders		SJHL	58	5	13	18	57
1980-81—Victoria Cougars (c)		WHL	71	2	18	20	59
1981-82—Victoria Cougars		WHL	69	6	45	51	102
1982-83—Victoria Cougars		WHL	70	10	33	43	102
1983-84—Binghamton Whalers		AHL	79	3	21	24	80
1984-85—Salt Lake Golden Eagles		CHL	22	1	10	11	41
1984-85—Binghamton Whalers		AHL	54	1	13	14	109
1985-86—Binghamton Whalers		AHL	64	0	9	9	196
1986-87—Binghamton Whalers		AHL	72	2	15	17	187
1987-88—Springfield Indians		AHL	77	1	16	17	178
1988-89—Adirondack Red Wings		AHL	65	4	31	35	195
1988-89—Detroit Red Wings		NHL	8	0	1	1	14
1989-90—Detroit Red Wings		NHL	33	0	1	1	82
1989-90—Adirondack Red Wings		AHL	29	2	6	8	80
NHL TOTALS			41	0	2	2	96

(c)—June, 1981—Drafted as underage junior by Hartford Whalers in 1981 NHL entry draft. Sixth Whalers pick, 130th overall, seventh round.

RANDY MOLLER

Defense . . . 6'2" . . . 205 lbs. . . . Born, Red Deer, Alta., August 23, 1963 . . . Shoots right . . . (December, 1980)—Torn knee ligaments required surgery . . . Brother of Mike Moller . . . (October 28, 1986)—Broken hand when slashed by Morris Lukowich vs. Los Angeles . . . (November, 1987)—Lingering neck problem . . . (January, 1988)—Knee injury . . . (March, 1988)—Back spasms . . . (October 29, 1988)—Separated shoulder vs. N.Y. Islanders . . . (September, 1989)—Broke toe in training camp . . . (December 13, 1989)—Dislocated right shoulder vs. St. Louis and missed 12 games . . . (March 21, 1990)—Back spasms and missed six games.

Year	Team	League	Games	G.	A.	Pts.	Pen.
1979-80—Red Deer Rustlers		AJHL	56	3	34	37	253
1980-81—Lethbridge Broncos (c)		WHL	46	4	21	25	176
1981-82—Lethbridge Broncos (b)		WHL	60	20	55	75	249
1982-83—Quebec Nordiques		NHL	75	2	12	14	145
1983-84—Quebec Nordiques		NHL	74	4	14	18	147
1984-85—Quebec Nordiques		NHL	79	7	22	29	120
1985-86—Quebec Nordiques		NHL	69	5	18	23	141
1986-87—Quebec Nordiques		NHL	71	5	9	14	144
1987-88—Quebec Nordiques		NHL	66	3	22	25	169
1988-89—Quebec Nordiques		NHL	74	7	22	29	136
1989-90—New York Rangers (d)		NHL	60	1	12	13	139
NHL TOTALS			568	34	131	165	1141

(c)—June, 1981—Drafted by Quebec Nordiques in 1981 NHL entry draft. First Nordiques pick, 11th overall, first round.
(d)—October 5, 1989—Traded by Quebec Nordiques to New York Rangers for Michel Petit.

MITCH MOLLOY

Left Wing . . . 6'3" . . . 212 lbs. . . . Born, Red Lake, Ont., October 10, 1966 . . . Shoots left.

Year	Team	League	Games	G.	A.	Pts.	Pen.
1987-88—Virginia Lancers		AAHL	43	26	45	71	196
1988-89—Maine Mariners (c)		AHL	47	1	8	9	177
1989-90—Johnstone Chiefs		ECHL	18	10	10	20	102
1989-90—Rochester Americans (d)		AHL	15	1	1	2	43
1989-90—Buffalo Sabres		NHL	2	0	0	0	10
NHL TOTALS			2	0	0	0	10

(c)—October, 1988—Signed by Boston Bruins as a free agent.
(d)—February, 1990—Signed by Buffalo Sabres as a free agent.

SERGIO MOMESSO

Left Wing . . . 6'3" . . . 205 lbs. . . . Born, Montreal, Que, September 4, 1965 . . . Shoots left . . . Also plays Center . . . (December 5, 1985)—Torn cruciate ligament in left knee, required surgery and missed remainder of season . . . (December 5, 1986)—Tore ligaments, injured cartilage and fractured left knee in a collision with Michael Thelvin vs. Boston . . . (February, 1988)—Cut leg . . . (November 12, 1988)—Fractured right ankle in his home.

Year	Team	League	Games	G.	A.	Pts.	Pen.
1982-83—Shawinigan Cataractes (c)		QMJHL	70	27	42	69	93
1983-84—Shawinigan Cataractes		QMJHL	68	42	88	130	235
1983-84—Montreal Canadiens		NHL	1	0	0	0	0
1984-85—Shawinigan Cataractes (a)		QMJHL	64	56	90	146	216
1985-86—Montreal Canadiens		NHL	24	8	7	15	46
1986-87—Montreal Canadiens		NHL	59	14	17	31	96
1986-87—Sherbrooke Canadiens		AHL	6	1	6	7	10
1987-88—Montreal Canadiens (d)		NHL	53	7	14	21	91
1988-89—St. Louis Blues		NHL	53	9	17	26	139
1989-90—St. Louis Blues		NHL	79	24	32	56	199
NHL TOTALS			269	62	87	149	571

(c)—June, 1983—Drafted as underage junior by Montreal Canadiens in 1983 NHL entry draft. Third Canadiens pick, 27th overall, second round.
(d)—August, 1988—Traded with Vincent Riendeau by Montreal Canadiens to St. Louis Blues for Jocelyn Lemieux, Darrell May and a second-round 1989 draft pick (Patrice Brisebois).

MICHEL MONGEAU

Center . . . 5'9" . . . 180 lbs. . . . Nun's Island, Que., February 9, 1965 . . . Shoots left.

Year	Team	League	Games	G.	A.	Pts.	Pen.
1983-84—Laval Voisons		QMJHL	60	45	49	94	30
1984-85—Laval Titans		QMJHL	67	60	84	144	56
1985-86—Laval Titans		QMJHL	72	71	109	180	45
1986-87—Saginaw Generals (c)		IHL	76	42	53	95	34
1987-88—Played in France		France	30	31	21	52	....
1988-89—Flint Spirits		IHL	82	41	*76	117	57
1989-90—St. Louis Blues (d)		NHL	7	1	5	6	2
1989-90—Peoria Rivermen (a-e-f)		IHL	73	39	*78	*117	53
NHL TOTALS			7	1	5	6	2

(c)—Won Garry F. Longman Memorial Trophy (IHL Rookie of the Year).
(d)—August 21, 1989—Signed by St. Louis Blues as a free agent.
(e)—Won Leo P. Lamoureux Memorial Trophy (Leading Scorer).
(f)—Won James Gatschne Memorial Trophy (MVP).

MARK MONTANARI

Center . . . 5'9" . . . 185 lbs. . . . Born, Toronto, Ont., June 3, 1969 . . . Shoots left.

Year	Team	League	Games	G.	A.	Pts.	Pen.
1985-86—Toronto Marlboro Minor Midget		OHA	36	26	32	58	90
1986-87—Kitchener Rangers		OHL	63	9	7	16	112
1987-88—Kitchener Rangers		OHL	63	25	31	56	146
1988-89—Kitchener Rangers (c)		OHL	64	33	69	102	172
1989-90—Kitchener Rangers		OHL	33	15	36	51	71
1989-90—Maine Mariners		AHL	17	0	7	7	90

(c)—June, 1989—Drafted by Boston Bruins in 1989 NHL entry draft. Fifth Bruins pick, 101st overall, fifth round.

IAN MORAN

Defense . . . 5'11" . . . 170 lbs. . . . Born, Cleveland, Ohio, August 24, 1972 . . . Shoots right . . . (June, 1988)—Knee surgery . . . (March, 1989)—Shoulder separation.

Year	Team	League	Games	G.	A.	Pts.	Pen.
1984-85—Southern Connecticut		Conn. H.S.	80	25	63	88	28
1985-86—Southern Connecticut		Conn. H.S.	85	20	60	80	55

Year	Team	League	Games	G.	A.	Pts.	Pen.
1986-87—Southern Connecticut	Conn. H.S.	91	35	67	102	60
1987-88—Belmont Hill H.S.	Mass. H.S.	25	3	13	16	15
1988-89—Belmont Hill H.S.	Mass. H.S.	23	7	25	32	8
1989-90—Belmont Hill H.S. (c)	Mass. H.S.	..	10	30	40	

(c)—June 16, 1990—Selected by Pittsburgh Penguins in 1990 NHL entry draft. Fifth Penguins pick, 107th overall, sixth round.

JAYSON MORE

Defense . . . 6'1" . . . 191 lbs. . . . Born, Souris, Man., January 12, 1969 . . . Shoots right.

Year	Team	League	Games	G.	A.	Pts.	Pen.
1984-85—Lethbridge Broncos	WHL	71	3	9	12	101
1985-86—Lethbridge Broncos	WHL	61	7	18	25	155
1986-87—New Westminster Bruins (c)	WHL	64	8	29	37	217
1987-88—New Westminster Bruins (a)	WHL	70	13	47	60	270
1988-89—Denver Rangers	IHL	62	7	15	22	138
1988-89—New York Rangers	NHL	1	0	0	0	0
1989-90—Flint Spirits (d)	IHL	9	1	5	6	41
1989-90—Kalamazoo Wings	IHL	64	9	25	34	216
1989-90—Minnesota North Stars	NHL	5	0	0	0	16
NHL TOTALS		6	0	0	0	16

(c)—June, 1987—Drafted as underage junior by New York Rangers in 1987 NHL entry draft. First Rangers pick, 10th overall, first round.

(d)—November 1, 1989—Traded by New York Rangers to Minnesota North Stars for Dave Archibald.

STEPHANE MORIN

Center . . . 6' . . . 174 lbs. . . . Born, Montreal, Que., March 27, 1969 . . . Shoots left.

Year	Team	League	Games	G.	A.	Pts.	Pen.
1986-87—Shawinigan Cataractes	QMJHL	65	9	14	23	28
1987-88—Shawinigan/Chicoutimi (c)	QMJHL	68	38	45	83	18
1988-89—C'timi Sagueneens (a-d-e-f)	QMJHL	70	77	*109	*186	71
1989-90—Quebec Nordiques	NHL	6	0	2	2	2
1989-90—Halifax Citadels	AHL	65	28	32	60	60
NHL TOTALS		6	0	2	2	2

(c)—December, 1987—Traded with second-round draft pick by Shawinigan Cataractes to Chicoutimi Sagueneens for Daniel Bock.

(d)—Won Jean Beliveau (Leading QHL scorer).

(e)—Won Michel Briere Trophy (QMJHL MVP).

(f)—June, 1989—Drafted by Quebec Nordiques in 1989 NHL entry draft. Third Nordiques pick, 43rd overall, third round.

JON MORRIS

Center . . . 6' . . . 165 lbs. . . . Born, Lowell, Mass., May 6, 1966 . . . Shoots right . . . (1988-89)—Missed most of season while attending school.

Year	Team	League	Games	G.	A.	Pts.	Pen.
1983-84—Chelmsford H.S. (c)	Mass. H.S.	24	31	50	81	....
1984-85—University of Lowell	H. East	42	29	31	60	16
1985-86—University of Lowell	H. East	39	25	31	56	52
1986-87—University of Lowell (a-d)	H. East	36	28	33	61	48
1987-88—University of Lowell	H. East	37	15	39	54	39
1988-89—New Jersey Devils	NHL	4	0	2	2	0
1989-90—Utica Devils	AHL	49	27	37	64	6
1989-90—New Jersey Devils	NHL	20	6	7	13	8
NHL TOTALS		24	6	9	15	8

(c)—June, 1984—Drafted by New Jersey Devils in NHL entry draft. Fifth Devils pick, 86th overall, fifth round.

(d)—Named Second team All-America (East).

SCOTT MORROW

Left Wing . . . 6'1" . . . 180 lbs. . . . Born, Chicago, Ill., June 18, 1969 . . . Shoots left . . . Brother and teammate of Steve Morrow . . . (November 18, 1988)—Broke ankle vs. Boston College.

Year	Team	League	Games	G.	A.	Pts.	Pen.
1987-88—Northwood Prep. (c)	Mass. H.S.	24	10	13	23	..
1988-89—Univ. of New Hampshire	H. East	19	6	7	13	14
1989-90—Univ. of New Hampshire	H. East	29	10	11	21	35

(c)—June, 1988—Selected by Hartford Whalers in 1988 NHL entry draft. Fourth Whalers pick, 95th overall, fifth round.

STEVEN MORROW

Defense . . . 6'2" . . . 210 lbs. . . . Born, Plano, Tex., April 3, 1968 . . . Shoots left . . . Brother of Scott Morrow.

Year	Team	League	Games	G.	A.	Pts.	Pen.
1986-87—Westminster H.S. (c)	Mass. H.S.	20	10	18	28	30
1987-88—Northwood Prep.	Mass. H.S.	27	4	20	24	..
1988-89—Univ. of New Hampshire	H. East	30	0	0	0	28
1989-90—Univ. of New Hampshire	H. East	35	2	7	9	40

(c)—June, 1987—Drafted by Philadelphia Flyers in 1987 NHL entry draft. Tenth Flyers pick, 209th overall, 10th round.

DEAN MORTON

Defense . . . 6'1" . . . 195 lbs. . . . Born, Peterborough, Ont., February 27, 1968 . . . Shoots right . . . (October, 1986)—Suspended by OHL for being involved in a bench-clearing incident vs. Peterborough.

Year	Team	League	Games	G.	A.	Pts.	Pen.
1984-85—Peterborough Midgets	OHA	47	9	38	47	158
1985-86—Ottawa 67's (c)	OHL	16	3	1	4	32
1986-87—Oshawa Generals	OHL	62	1	11	12	165

Year	Team	League	Games	G.	A.	Pts.	Pen.
1987-88—Oshawa Generals	OHL	57	6	19	25	187
1988-89—Adirondack Red Wings	AHL	66	2	15	17	186
1989-90—Adirondack Red Wings	AHL	75	1	15	16	183
1989-90—Detroit Red Wings	NHL	1	1	0	1	2
NHL TOTALS		1	1	0	1	2

(c)—June, 1986—Drafted as underage junior by Detroit Red Wings in 1986 NHL entry draft. Eighth Red Wings pick, 148th overall, eighth round.

DAVID MOYLAN

Defense . . . 6'1" . . . 195 lbs. . . . Born, Tillsonburg, Ont., August 13, 1967 . . . Shoots left . . . (November, 1983)—Separated shoulder.

Year	Team	League	Games	G.	A.	Pts.	Pen.
1983-84—St. Mary's Lincolns	OHA	46	7	13	20	143
1984-85—Sudbury Wolves (c)	OHL	66	1	15	16	108
1985-86—Sudbury Wolves	OHL	52	10	25	35	87
1986-87—Sudbury Wolves	OHL	13	5	6	11	41
1986-87—Kitchener Rangers	OHL	38	1	7	8	57
1987-88—Flint Spirits	IHL	9	0	2	2	10
1987-88—Rochester Americans	AHL	16	0	0	0	2
1987-88—Baltimore Skipjacks	AHL	20	4	5	9	35
1988-89—Rochester Americans	AHL	20	0	2	2	15
1988-89—Jokerit	Finland	15	4	4	8	30
1989-90—Jokerit	Finland	42	3	8	11	107

(c)—June, 1985—Drafted as underage junior by Buffalo Sabres in 1985 entry draft. Fourth Sabres pick, 77th overall, fourth round.

BRIAN MULLEN

Left Wing . . . 5'10" . . . 170 lbs. . . . Born, New York, N.Y., March 16, 1962 . . . Shoots left . . . Brother of Joe Mullen . . . (January, 1988)—Bruised left knee.

Year	Team	League	Games	G.	A.	Pts.	Pen.
1977-78—New York Westsiders	NYMJHL	33	21	36	57	38
1978-79—New York Westsiders	NYMJHL	....	....	....	....	....
1979-80—New York Westsiders	NYMJHL	....	....	....	....	....
1980-81—University of Wisconsin (c)	WCHA	38	11	13	24	28
1981-82—University of Wisconsin	WCHA	33	20	17	37	10
1982-83—Winnipeg Jets	NHL	80	24	26	50	14
1983-84—Winnipeg Jets	NHL	75	21	41	62	28
1984-85—Winnipeg Jets	NHL	69	32	39	71	32
1985-86—Winnipeg Jets	NHL	79	28	34	62	38
1986-87—Winnipeg Jets (d)	NHL	69	19	32	51	20
1987-88—New York Rangers	NHL	74	25	29	54	42
1988-89—New York Rangers	NHL	78	29	35	64	60
1989-90—New York Rangers	NHL	76	27	41	68	42
NHL TOTALS		600	205	277	482	276

(c)—June, 1980—Drafted by Winnipeg Jets in 1981 NHL entry draft. Seventh Jets pick, 128th overall, seventh round.

(d)—June, 1987—Traded with 10th round draft choice in 1987 by Winnipeg Jets to New York Rangers for fifth round draft choice in 1988 and third round draft choice in 1989.

JOE MULLEN

Right Wing . . . 5'9" . . . 180 lbs. . . . Born, New York, N.Y., February 26, 1957 . . . Shoots right . . . Brother of Brian Mullen . . . (1981-82)—First player to have 20-goal year in minors and majors in the same season . . . (October 3, 1982)—Leg injury at Minnesota . . . (January 29, 1983)—Tore ligaments in left knee vs. Los Angeles, requiring surgery. He was lost for remainder of season . . . Established record for goals in single season by U.S.-born player in 1983-84 (Broken by Bobby Carpenter) . . . (April, 1988)—Bruised knee in playoff game vs. Los Angeles . . . Set NHL record for most points in a season by American-born player (110), 1988-89 . . . (April, 1989)—Flu during the playoffs. His spot in the lineup was taken by Sergei Priakin, the first Soviet-born player to play in the Stanley Cup Playoffs . . . (January, 1990)—Passed Reed Larson to become the highest scoring U.S. born player in NHL history.

Year	Team	League	Games	G.	A.	Pts.	Pen.
1971-72—New York 14th Precinct	NYMJHL	30	13	11	24	2
1972-73—New York Westsiders	NYMJHL	40	14	28	42	8
1973-74—New York Westsiders	NYMJHL	42	71	49	120	41
1974-75—New York Westsiders (c)	NYMJHL	40	110	72	*182	20
1975-76—Boston College	ECAC	24	16	18	34	4
1976-77—Boston College	ECAC	28	28	26	54	8
1977-78—Boston College (a)	ECAC	34	34	34	68	12
1978-79—Boston College (a-d)	ECAC	25	32	24	56	8
1979-80—Salt Lake Golden Eagles (b-e-g)	CHL	75	40	32	72	21
1979-80—St. Louis Blues (f)	NHL	....	....	....	....	....
1980-81—Salt Lake Golden Eagles (a-h-i)	CHL	80	59	58	*117	8
1981-82—Salt Lake Golden Eagles	CHL	27	21	27	48	12
1981-82—St. Louis Blues	NHL	45	25	34	59	4
1982-83—St. Louis Blues	NHL	49	17	30	47	6
1983-84—St. Louis Blues	NHL	80	41	44	85	19
1984-85—St. Louis Blues	NHL	79	40	52	92	6
1985-86—St. Louis Blues (j)	NHL	48	28	24	52	10
1985-86—Calgary Flames (k)	NHL	29	16	22	38	11
1986-87—Calgary Flames (l)	NHL	79	47	40	87	14
1987-88—Calgary Flames	NHL	80	40	44	84	30
1988-89—Calgary Flames (a-l-m-n)	NHL	79	51	59	110	16
1989-90—Calgary Flames (o)	NHL	78	36	33	69	24
NHL TOTALS		646	341	382	723	140

(c)—Named Most Valuable Player.

(d)—August, 1979—Signed as free agent by St. Louis Blues.

(e)—Co-leader with Red Laurence in goals (9) during CHL playoffs.

(f)—No regular season game. Played one playoff game.

(g)—Won Ken McKenzie Trophy (Top Rookie).

(h)—Winner of Phil Esposito Trophy (Leading Scorer).

(i)—Winner of Tommy Ivan Trophy (MVP).
(j)—February, 1986—Traded with Terry Johnson and Rik Wilson by St. Louis Blues to Calgary Flames for Eddy Beers, Gino Cavallini and Charles Bourgeois.
(k)—Led Stanley Cup Playoffs with 12 goals.
(l)—Won Lady Byng Trophy (Combination of Sportsmanship and Quality play).
(m)—Won Emery Edge Trophy (Top NHL Plus/Minus) with a +51.
(n)—Led Stanley Cup Playoffs with 16 goals.
(o)—June 16, 1990—Traded by Calgary Flames to Pittsburgh Penguins for a second-round 1990 draft pick (Nicolas Perreault).

KIRK MULLER

Center . . . 5'11" . . . 185 lbs. . . . Born, Kingston, Ont., February 8, 1966 . . . Shoots left . . . Member of 1984 Canadian Olympic team . . . (January 13, 1986)—Strained knee . . . (April, 1986)—Fractured ribs at world championships in Soviet Union.

Year	Team	League	Games	G.	A.	Pts.	Pen.
1980-81	Kingston Canadians	OHL	2	0	0	0	0
1981-82	Kingston Canadians	OHL	67	12	39	51	27
1982-83	Guelph Platers (c)	OHL	66	52	60	112	41
1983-84	Canadian Olympic Team	Int'l	15	2	2	4	6
1983-84	Guelph Platers (d)	OHL	49	31	63	94	27
1984-85	New Jersey Devils	NHL	80	17	37	54	69
1985-86	New Jersey Devils	NHL	77	25	42	67	45
1986-87	New Jersey Devils	NHL	79	26	50	76	75
1987-88	New Jersey Devils	NHL	80	37	57	94	114
1988-89	New Jersey Devils	NHL	80	31	43	74	119
1989-90	New Jersey Devils	NHL	80	30	56	86	74
	NHL TOTALS		476	166	285	451	496

(c)—Won William Hanley Trophy (Most Gentlemanly).
(d)—June, 1984—Drafted as underage junior by New Jersey Devils in NHL entry draft. First Devils pick, second overall, first round.

MIKE MULLER

Defense . . . 6'2" . . . 205 lbs. . . . Born, Minneapolis, Minn., September 18, 1971 . . . Shoots left . . . Plans to attend University of Minnesota.

Year	Team	League	Games	G.	A.	Pts.	Pen.
1988-89	Wayzata H.S.	Minn. H.S.	24	10	11	21	56
1989-90	Wayzata H.S. (c)	Minn. H.S.	23	11	15	26	45

(c)—June 16, 1990—Selected by Winnipeg Jets in 1990 NHL entry draft. Second Jets pick, 35th overall, second round.

CRAIG DOUGLAS MUNI

Defense . . . 6'2" . . . 201 lbs. . . . Born, Toronto, Ont., July 19, 1962 . . . Shoots left . . . (September, 1981)—Tore left knee ligaments while skating in Windsor, Ont., prior to the opening of Toronto training camp . . . (January, 1983)—Broken ankle in AHL game at Fredericton . . . (May, 1987)—Bruised kidney in playoffs . . . (January, 1988)—Bruised ankle vs. Calgary . . . (December 17, 1988)—Bruised ankle when he blocked a shot at Hartford . . . (January, 1989)—Strained right shoulder . . . (January 27, 1990)—Broke little finger of right hand when he blocked a Trevor Linden shot vs. Vancouver and missed eight games.

Year	Team	League	Games	G.	A.	Pts.	Pen.
1979-80	Kingston Canadians (c)	OMJHL	66	6	28	34	114
1980-81	Kingston Canadians	OHL	38	2	14	16	65
1980-81	Windsor Spitfires	OHL	25	5	11	16	41
1980-81	New Brunswick Hawks (d)	AHL	....	...	...	...	....
1981-82	Windsor Spitfires	OHL	49	5	32	37	92
1981-82	Cincinnati Tigers (e)	CHL	....	...	...	...	....
1982-83	Toronto Maple Leafs	NHL	2	0	1	1	0
1982-83	St. Catharines Saints	AHL	64	6	32	38	52
1983-84	St. Catharines Saints	AHL	64	4	16	20	79
1984-85	St. Catharines Saints	AHL	68	7	17	24	54
1984-85	Toronto Maple Leafs	NHL	8	0	0	0	0
1985-86	Toronto Maple Leafs	NHL	6	0	1	1	4
1985-86	St. Catharines Saints	AHL	73	3	34	37	91
1986-87	Edmonton Oilers (f)	NHL	79	7	22	29	85
1987-88	Edmonton Oilers	NHL	72	4	15	19	77
1988-89	Edmonton Oilers	NHL	69	5	13	18	71
1989-90	Edmonton Oilers	NHL	71	5	12	17	81
	NHL TOTALS		307	21	64	85	318

(c)—June, 1980—Drafted as underage junior by Toronto Maple Leafs in 1980 NHL entry draft. First Maple Leafs pick, 25th overall, second round.
(d)—No regular season appearance. Played two playoff games.
(e)—No regular season appearance. Played three playoff games.
(f)—August, 1986—Signed by Edmonton Oilers as a free agent.

ERIC A. MURANO

Center . . . 6' . . . 190 lbs. . . . Born, LaSalle, Que., May 4, 1967 . . . Shoots right.

Year	Team	League	Games	G.	A.	Pts.	Pen.
1985-86	Calgary Canucks (c)	AJHL	52	34	47	81	32
1986-87	Univ. of Denver	WCHA	31	5	7	12	12
1987-88	Univ. of Denver	WCHA	37	8	13	21	26
1988-89	Univ. of Denver	WCHA	42	13	16	29	52
1989-90	Univ. of Denver (b)	WCHA	42	33	35	68	52
1989-90	Canadian National Team	Int'l.	6	1	0	1	4

(c)—June, 1986—Drafted by Vancouver Canucks in 1986 NHL entry draft. Fourth Canucks pick, 91st overall, fifth round.

GORDON MURPHY

Defense . . . 6'1" . . . 180 lbs. . . . Born, Willowdale, Ont., February 23, 1967 . . . Shoots right . . . (January, 1985)—Injured clavicle . . . (March 24, 1990)—Chipped point in left foot and hip pointer vs. New Jersey.

Year	Team	League	Games	G.	A.	Pts.	Pen.
1983-84	Don Mills Flyers	MTHL	65	24	42	66	130
1984-85	Oshawa Generals (c)	OHL	59	3	12	15	25
1985-86	Oshawa Generals	OHL	64	7	15	22	56
1986-87	Oshawa Generals	OHL	56	7	30	37	95
1987-88	Hershey Bears	AHL	62	8	20	28	44
1988-89	Philadelphia Flyers	NHL	75	4	31	35	68
1989-90	Philadelphia Flyers	NHL	75	14	27	41	95
	NHL TOTALS		150	18	58	76	163

(c)—June, 1985—Drafted as underage junior by Philadelphia Flyers in 1985 NHL entry draft. Tenth Flyers pick, 189th overall, ninth round.

JOSEPH PATRICK MURPHY

Center . . . 6'1" . . . 185 lbs. . . . Born, London, Ont., October 16, 1967 . . . Shoots left . . . Also plays Left Wing . . . First college player to be taken first-overall in an NHL draft . . . (January, 1988)—Sprained right ankle . . . (March, 1990)—Charley horse in both legs.

Year	Team	League	Games	G.	A.	Pts.	Pen.
1984-85	Penticton Knights (c)	BCJHL	51	68	84	*152	92
1985-86	Michigan State Univ. (d-e)	CCHA	35	24	37	61	50
1985-86	Team Canada	Int'l	8	3	3	6	2
1986-87	Adirondack Red Wings	AHL	71	21	38	59	61
1986-87	Detroit Red Wings	NHL	5	0	1	1	2
1987-88	Adirondack Red Wings	AHL	6	5	6	11	4
1987-88	Detroit Red Wings	NHL	50	10	9	19	37
1988-89	Detroit Red Wings	NHL	26	1	7	8	28
1988-89	Adirondack Red Wings	AHL	47	31	35	66	66
1989-90	Detroit Red Wings (f)	NHL	9	3	1	4	4
1989-90	Edmonton Oilers	NHL	62	7	18	25	56
	NHL TOTALS		152	21	36	57	127

(c)—Named AJHL Rookie of the Year.
(d)—Named CCHA Rookie of the Year.
(e)—June, 1986—Drafted by Detroit Red Wings in 1986 NHL entry draft. First Red Wings pick, first overall, first round.
(f)—November 2, 1989—Traded with Adam Graves, Petr Klima and Jeff Sharples by Detroit Red Wings to Edmonton Oilers for Jimmy Carson, Kevin McClelland and a fifth round 1991 draft pick.

LAWRENCE THOMAS MURPHY

Defense . . . 6'1" . . . 210 lbs. . . . Born, Scarborough, Ont., March 8, 1961 . . . Shoots right . . . Set record for most points by NHL rookie defenseman in 1980-81 (76 points) . . . Holds Los Angeles Kings club record for most goals, assists and points by a defenseman in a career as well as L.A. record for assists by a rookie . . . (1980-81)—Set NHL record for most assists (60) and points (76) by a rookie defenseman . . . (October 29, 1985)—Injured foot . . . (May, 1988)—Broken ankle in swimming pool accident.

Year	Team	League	Games	G.	A.	Pts.	Pen.
1978-79	Peterborough Petes	OMJHL	66	6	21	27	82
1979-80	Peterborough Petes (a-c-d)	OMJHL	68	21	68	89	88
1980-81	Los Angeles Kings	NHL	80	16	60	76	79
1981-82	Los Angeles Kings	NHL	79	22	44	66	95
1982-83	Los Angeles Kings	NHL	77	14	48	62	81
1983-84	Los Angeles Kings	NHL	6	0	3	3	0
1983-84	Washington Capitals (e)	NHL	72	13	33	46	50
1984-85	Washington Capitals	NHL	79	13	42	55	51
1985-86	Washington Capitals	NHL	78	21	44	65	50
1986-87	Washington Capitals (b)	NHL	80	23	58	81	39
1987-88	Washington Capitals	NHL	79	8	53	61	72
1988-89	Washington Capitals (f)	NHL	65	7	29	36	70
1988-89	Minnesota North Stars	NHL	13	4	6	10	12
1989-90	Minnesota North Stars	NHL	77	10	58	68	44
	NHL TOTALS		785	151	478	629	643

(c)—Won Max Kaminsky Memorial Trophy (Outstanding Defenseman).
(d)—June, 1980—Drafted as underage junior by Los Angeles Kings in 1980 NHL entry draft. First Kings pick, fourth overall, first round.
(e)—October, 1983—Traded by Los Angeles Kings to Washington Capitals for Brian Engblom and Ken Houston.
(f)—March 7, 1989—Traded with Mike Gartner by Washington Capitals to Minnesota North Stars for Dino Ciccarelli and Bob Rouse.

ROBERT MURPHY

Center . . . 6'2" . . . 195 lbs. . . . Born, Hull, Que., April 7, 1969 . . . Shoots left . . . (November 13, 1988)—Separated shoulder vs. Pittsburgh.

Year	Team	League	Games	G.	A.	Pts.	Pen.
1985-86	Outaouais Midget	Que. Mdgt.	41	17	33	50	47
1986-87	Laval Titans (c)	QMJHL	70	35	54	89	86
1987-88	Vancouver Canucks	NHL	5	0	0	0	2
1987-88	Drummondville Voltigeurs	QMJHL	59	27	53	80	123
1988-89	Drummondville Voltigeurs	QMJHL	26	13	25	38	16
1988-89	Vancouver Canucks	NHL	8	0	1	1	2
1988-89	Milwaukee Admirals	IHL	8	4	2	6	4
1989-90	Milwaukee Admirals (d)	IHL	64	24	47	71	87
1989-90	Vancouver Canucks	NHL	12	1	1	2	0
	NHL TOTALS		25	1	2	3	4

(c)—June, 1987—Drafted as underage junior by Vancouver Canucks in 1987 NHL entry draft. First Canucks pick, 24th overall, second round.
(d)—Won Garry F. Longman Memorial Trophy (Rookie of the Year.)

PAT MURRAY

Left Wing . . . 6'2'' . . . 180 lbs. . . . Born, Stratford, Ont., August 20, 1969 . . . Shoots left.

Year	Team	League	Games	G.	A.	Pts.	Pen.
1986-87	Stratford Jr. B	OHA	42	34	75	109	38
1987-88	Michigan State Univ. (c)	CCHA	44	14	23	37	26
1988-89	Michigan State Univ.	CCHA	46	21	41	62	65
1989-90	Michigan State Univ. (b)	CCHA	45	24	60	84	36

(c)—June, 1988—Drafted by Philadelphia Flyers in 1988 NHL entry draft. Second Flyers pick, 35th overall, second round.

ROBERT MURRAY

Center . . . 6'1'' . . . 175 lbs. . . . Born, Toronto, Ont., April 4, 1967 . . . Shoots right . . . (November 2, 1986)—Suspended for two games by OHL . . . (December 21, 1989)—Injured right hip at Pittsburgh and missed 10 games.

Year	Team	League	Games	G.	A.	Pts.	Pen.
1983-85	Mississauga Reps	OHA	35	18	36	54	32
1984-85	Peterborough Petes (c)	OHL	63	12	9	21	155
1985-86	Peterborough Petes	OHL	52	14	18	32	125
1986-87	Peterborough Petes	OHL	62	17	37	54	204
1987-88	Fort Wayne Komets	IHL	80	12	21	33	139
1988-89	Baltimore Skipjacks	AHL	80	11	23	34	235
1989-90	Baltimore Skipjacks	AHL	23	5	4	9	63
1989-90	Washington Capitals	NHL	41	2	7	9	58
NHL TOTALS			41	2	7	9	58

(c)—June, 1985—Drafted as underage junior by Washington Capitals in 1985 NHL entry draft. Third Capitals pick, 61st overall, third round.

ROBERT FREDERICK MURRAY

Defense . . . 5'9'' . . . 175 lbs. . . . Born, Kingston, Ont., November 26, 1954 . . . Shoots right . . . (December 20, 1981)—Tore ligaments in left knee vs. Toronto and required surgery . . . (November, 1987)—Twisted left knee.

Year	Team	League	Games	G.	A.	Pts.	Pen.
1971-72	Cornwall Royals	QMJHL	62	14	49	63	88
1972-73	Cornwall Royals	QMJHL	32	9	26	35	34
1973-74	Cornwall Royals (c)	QMJHL	63	23	76	99	88
1974-75	Dallas Black Hawks	CHL	75	14	43	57	130
1975-76	Chicago Black Hawks	NHL	64	1	2	3	44
1976-77	Chicago Black Hawks	NHL	77	10	11	21	71
1977-78	Chicago Black Hawks	NHL	70	14	17	31	41
1978-79	Chicago Black Hawks	NHL	79	19	32	51	38
1979-80	Chicago Black Hawks	NHL	74	16	34	50	60
1980-81	Chicago Black Hawks	NHL	77	13	47	60	93
1981-82	Chicago Black Hawks	NHL	45	8	22	30	48
1982-83	Chicago Black Hawks	NHL	79	7	32	39	73
1983-84	Chicago Black Hawks	NHL	78	11	37	48	78
1984-85	Chicago Black Hawks	NHL	80	5	38	43	56
1985-86	Chicago Black Hawks	NHL	80	9	29	38	75
1986-87	Chicago Black Hawks	NHL	79	6	38	44	80
1987-88	Chicago Black Hawks	NHL	63	6	20	26	44
1988-89	Saginaw Hawks	IHL	18	3	7	10	14
1988-89	Chicago Black Hawks	NHL	15	2	4	6	27
1989-90	Chicago Black Hawks (d)	NHL	49	5	19	24	45
NHL TOTALS			1009	132	382	514	873

(c)—Drafted from Cornwall Royals by Chicago Black Hawks in third round of 1974 amateur draft.
(d)—August, 1990—Announced his retirement.

TROY NORMAN MURRAY

Center . . . 6'1'' . . . 195 lbs. . . . Born, Winnipeg, Man., July 31, 1962 . . . Shoots right . . . (November, 1983)—Knee ligament injury . . . (December, 1988)—Facial lacerations . . . (December 26, 1989)—Injured right elbow at St. Louis, required surgery and missed 11 games . . . (February 8, 1990)—Developed a bursa on right elbow and hospitalized.

Year	Team	League	Games	G.	A.	Pts.	Pen.
1979-80	St. Albert Saints (c)	AJHL	60	53	47	100	101
1980-81	Univ. of North Dakota (b-d)	WCHA	38	33	45	78	28
1981-82	Univ. of North Dakota (b)	WCHA	42	22	29	51	62
1981-82	Chicago Black Hawks	NHL	1	0	0	0	0
1982-83	Chicago Black Hawks	NHL	54	8	8	16	27
1983-84	Chicago Black Hawks	NHL	61	15	15	30	45
1984-85	Chicago Black Hawks	NHL	80	26	40	66	82
1985-86	Chicago Black Hawks (e)	NHL	80	45	54	99	94
1986-87	Chicago Black Hawks	NHL	77	28	43	71	59
1987-88	Chicago Black Hawks	NHL	79	22	36	58	96
1988-89	Chicago Black Hawks	NHL	79	21	30	51	113
1989-90	Chicago Black Hawks	NHL	68	17	38	55	86
NHL TOTALS			579	182	264	446	602

(c)—June, 1980—Drafted by Chicago Black Hawks in 1980 NHL entry draft. Sixth Black Hawks pick, 57th overall, third round.
(d)—Named Outstanding Freshman in WCHA.
(e)—Won Frank Selke Trophy (Best Defensive Forward).

DANA MURZYN

Defense . . . 6'3'' . . . 205 lbs. . . . Born, Regina, Sask., December 9, 1966 . . . Shoots left . . . (March 13, 1989)—Strained knee at N.Y. Rangers . . . (February 4, 1990)—Pulled groin at Winnipeg.

Year	Team	League	Games	G.	A.	Pts.	Pen.
1983-84	Calgary Wranglers	WHL	65	11	20	31	135
1984-85	Calgary Wranglers (a-c)	WHL	72	32	60	92	233
1985-86	Hartford Whalers	NHL	78	3	23	26	125
1986-87	Hartford Whalers	NHL	74	9	19	28	95

Year	Team	League	Games	G.	A.	Pts.	Pen.
1987-88	Hartford Whalers (d)	NHL	33	1	6	7	45
1987-88	Calgary Flames	NHL	41	6	5	11	94
1988-89	Calgary Flames	NHL	63	3	19	22	142
1989-90	Calgary Flames	NHL	78	7	13	20	140
NHL TOTALS			367	29	85	114	641

(c)—June, 1985—Drafted as underage junior by Hartford Whalers in 1985 NHL entry draft. First Whalers pick, fifth overall, first round.
(d)—January, 1988—Traded with Shane Churla by Hartford Whalers to Calgary Flames for Carey Wilson, Neil Sheehy and Lane MacDonald.

FRANTISEK MUSIL

Defense . . . 6'3'' . . . 205 lbs. . . . Born, Pardubice, Czechoslovakia, December 17, 1964 . . . Shoots left . . . (December 9, 1986)—Shoulder separation vs. Edmonton . . . (December 17, 1988)—Fractured foot vs. Los Angeles . . . (February 9, 1989)—Concussion when checked by Daryl Stanley vs. Vancouver . . . (February 18, 1989)—Strained lower back muscles . . . (November 2, 1989)—Missed 10 games with back spasms . . . (April, 1990)—Separated right shoulder.

Year	Team	League	Games	G.	A.	Pts.	Pen.
1985-86	Dukla Jihlava (c)	Czech.	35	3	7	10	85
1986-87	Minnesota North Stars	NHL	72	2	9	11	148
1987-88	Minnesota North Stars	NHL	80	9	8	17	213
1988-89	Minnesota North Stars	NHL	55	1	19	20	54
1989-90	Minnesota North Stars	NHL	56	2	8	10	109
NHL TOTALS			263	14	44	58	524

(c)—June, 1983—Drafted by Minnesota North Stars in 1983 NHL entry draft. Third North Stars pick, 38th overall, second round.

DONALD KENNETH NACHBAUR

Center . . . 6'2'' . . . 200 lbs. . . . Born, Kitimat, B.C., January 30, 1959 . . . Shoots left . . . Also plays Left Wing . . . (October 20, 1984)—Injured forearm at Baltimore and spent remainder of season as assistant coach of Hershey Bears . . . (March, 1988)—Sprained back . . . (October, 1989)—Shoulder surgery.

Year	Team	League	Games	G.	A.	Pts.	Pen.
1976-77	Merritt Luckies	......	54	22	27	49	31
1977-78	Billings Bighorns	WCHL	68	23	27	50	128
1978-79	Billings Bighorns (c)	WHL	69	44	52	96	175
1979-80	Springfield Indians	AHL	70	12	17	29	119
1980-81	Hartford Whalers	NHL	77	16	17	33	139
1981-82	Hartford Whalers (d)	NHL	77	5	21	26	117
1982-83	Edmonton Oilers	NHL	4	0	0	0	17
1982-83	Moncton Alpines	AHL	70	33	33	66	125
1983-84	New Haven Nighthawks (e)	AHL	70	33	32	65	194
1984-85	Hershey Bears	AHL	7	2	3	5	21
1985-86	Philadelphia Flyers (f)	NHL	5	1	1	2	7
1985-86	Hershey Bears	AHL	74	23	24	47	301
1986-87	Philadelphia Flyers	NHL	23	0	2	2	89
1986-87	Hershey Bears	AHL	57	18	17	35	274
1987-88	Philadelphia Flyers	NHL	20	0	4	4	61
1987-88	Hershey Bears	AHL	42	19	21	40	174
1988-89	Philadelphia Flyers	NHL	15	1	0	1	37
1988-89	Hershey Bears	AHL	49	24	31	55	172
1989-90	Philadelphia Flyers	NHL	2	0	1	1	0
1989-90	Hershey Bears	AHL	30	10	9	19	72
NHL TOTALS			223	23	46	69	467

(c)—August, 1979—Drafted by Hartford Whalers in 1979 NHL entry draft. Third Hartford pick, 60th overall, third round.
(d)—August, 1982—Traded with Ken Linseman by Hartford Whalers to Edmonton Oilers for Risto Siltanen and Brent Loney.
(e)—October, 1983—Selected by Los Angeles Kings in NHL waiver draft.
(f)—July, 1985—Signed by Philadelphia Flyers as a free agent.

MARTY NANNE

Right Wing . . . 6' . . . 180 lbs. . . . Born, Edina, Minn., July 21, 1967 . . . Shoots right . . . Son of Lou Nanne (Minnesota North Stars player and General Manager).

Year	Team	League	Games	G.	A.	Pts.	Pen.
1984-85	Edina H.S.	Minn. H.S.	17	10	7	17	....
1985-86	Univ. of Minnesota (c)	WCHA	20	5	5	10	20
1986-87	Univ. of Minnesota	WCHA	31	3	4	7	41
1987-88	Univ. of Minnesota	WCHA	17	1	3	4	16
1988-89	Saginaw Hawks	IHL	36	4	10	14	47
1989-90	Indianapolis Ice	IHL	50	3	3	6	36

(c)—June, 1986—Drafted by Chicago Black Hawks in 1986 NHL entry draft. Seventh Black Hawks pick, 161st overall, eighth round.

MATS NASLUND

Left Wing . . . 5'7'' . . . 158 lbs. . . . Born, Timra, Sweden, October 31, 1959 . . . Shoots left . . . (September 25, 1988)—Injured mouth vs. Pittsburgh . . . (January 31, 1989)—Sprained ankle at Pittsburgh . . . (October 7, 1989)—Bruised shoulder when struck by Doug Bodger vs. Buffalo . . . (March 21, 1990)—Injured groin vs. Winnipeg.

Year	Team	League	Games	G.	A.	Pts.	Pen.
1980-81	Brynas IF (c)	Sweden	....	17	25	42	....
1981-82	Brynas IF	Sweden	....	25	20	45	....
1982-83	Montreal Canadiens	NHL	74	26	45	71	10
1983-84	Montreal Canadiens	NHL	77	29	35	64	4
1984-85	Montreal Canadiens	NHL	80	42	37	79	14
1985-86	Montreal Canadiens	NHL	80	43	67	110	16
1986-87	Montreal Canadiens	NHL	79	25	55	80	16
1987-88	Montreal Canadiens (d)	NHL	78	24	59	83	14
1988-89	Montreal Canadiens	NHL	77	33	51	84	14
1989-90	Montreal Canadiens (e)	NHL	72	21	20	41	19
NHL TOTALS			617	243	369	612	107

(c)—August, 1979—Drafted by Montreal Canadiens in 1979 NHL entry draft. Second Canadiens pick, 37th overall, second round.
(d)—Won Lady Byng Memorial Trophy (Most Gentlemanly Player).
(e)—May 4, 1990—Signed a three-year contract to play for Lugano (Italy).

ERIC RIC NATTRESS
(Known by middle name.)

Defense . . . 6'2" . . . 208 lbs. . . . Born, Hamilton, Ont., May 25, 1962 . . . Shoots right . . . (August, 1983)—Fined $150 in Brantford, Ontario for possession of three grams of marijuana and one gram of hashish . . . (September, 1983)—Given 40-game suspension by NHL following his conviction in Ontario court . . . (March, 1984)—Fractured finger . . . (March 17, 1986)—Injured shoulder at Minnesota . . . (February, 1987)—Strained knee . . . (March, 1988)—Bruised right shoulder . . . (March, 1988)—Knee surgery . . . (November, 1988)—Pulled hamstring . . . (February, 1989)—Injured groin . . . (December 10, 1989)—Bruised hand at Washington and missed six games . . . (February 7, 1990)—Broke right ankle when he slipped on a patch of ice while attending a team banquet. Was in a cast until March 16.

Year	Team	League	Games	G.	A.	Pts.	Pen.
1979-80—Brantford Alexanders (c)	OMJHL	65	3	21	24	94
1980-81—Brantford Alexanders	OHL	51	8	34	42	106
1981-82—Brantford Alexanders	OHL	59	11	50	61	126
1982-83—Nova Scotia Voyageurs	AHL	9	0	4	4	16
1982-83—Montreal Canadiens	NHL	40	1	3	4	19
1983-84—Montreal Canadiens	NHL	34	0	12	12	15
1984-85—Sherbrooke Canadiens	AHL	72	8	40	48	37
1984-85—Montreal Canadiens	NHL	5	0	1	1	2
1985-86—St. Louis Blues (d)	NHL	78	4	20	24	52
1986-87—St. Louis Blues (e)	NHL	73	6	22	28	24
1987-88—Calgary Flames	NHL	63	2	13	15	37
1988-89—Calgary Flames	NHL	38	1	8	9	47
1989-90—Calgary Flames	NHL	49	1	14	15	26
NHL TOTALS		380	15	93	108	222

(c)—June, 1980—Drafted as underage junior by Montreal Canadiens in 1980 NHL entry draft. Second Canadiens pick, 27th overall, second round.
(d)—September, 1985—Traded by Montreal Canadiens to St. Louis Blues to complete June deal for Mark Hunter.
(e)—June, 1987—Traded by St. Louis Blues to Calgary Flames for a fourth-round 1987 draft pick (Andy Rymsha) and a fifth-round 1988 draft pick (Dave Lacouture).

DARREN NAUSS

Right Wing . . . 5'11" . . . 180 lbs. . . . Born, Vancouver, B.C., March 19, 1967 . . . Shoots right.

Year	Team	League	Games	G.	A.	Pts.	Pen.
1986-87—North Battleford (c)	SAJHL	64	58	43	101	....
1987-88—Univ. of Minn./Duluth	WCHA	41	8	13	21	24
1988-89—Univ. of Minn./Duluth	WCHA	40	10	4	14	40
1989-90—Univ. of Minn./Duluth	WCHA	37	21	17	38	24

(c)—June, 1987—Drafted by Quebec Nordiques in 1987 NHL entry draft. Eleventh Nordiques pick, 198th overall, 10th round.

PETR NEDVED

Center . . . 6'3" . . . 180 lbs. . . . Born, Liberec, Czechoslovakia, December 9, 1971 . . . Shoots left . . . (January, 1989)—Defected from Czechoslovakian midget team that was playing in Calgary, Alberta . . . (June, 1989) Granted landed immigrant status by Canadian Government.

Year	Team	League	Games	G.	A.	Pts.	Pen.
1988-89—Litvinov Midgets (c)	Czech.	20	32	19	51	12
1989-90—Seattle Thunderbirds (d-e)	WHL	71	65	80	145	80

(c)—February 3, 1989—WHL rights traded with Brian Ilkuf by Moose Jaw Warriors to Seattle Thunderbirds for Corey Beaulieu.
(d)—Won Jim Piggott Memorial Trophy (Rookie of the Year).
(e)—June 16, 1990—Selected by Vancouver Canucks in 1990 NHL entry draft. First Canucks pick, second overall, first round.

MIKE NEEDHAM

Right Wing . . . 5'10" . . . 198 lbs. . . . Born, Calgary, Alta., April 4, 1970 . . . Shoots right.

Year	Team	League	Games	G.	A.	Pts.	Pen.
1985-86—Ft. Saskatchewan Traders (c)	AJHL	49	19	26	45	97
1986-87—Ft. Saskatchewan Traders	AJHL	..	..	..	..	..
1986-87—Kamloops Blazers	WHL	3	1	2	3	0
1987-88—Kamloops Blazers	WHL	64	31	33	64	93
1988-89—Kamloops Blazers (d)	WHL	49	24	27	51	55
1989-90—Kamloops Blazers (a)	WHL	60	59	66	125	75

(c)—Co-winner of Most Dedicated Player Trophy with Bob Calhoon.
(d)—June, 1989—Drafted by Pittsburgh Penguins in 1989 NHL entry draft. Seventh Penguins pick, 126th overall, sixth round.

CAM NEELY

Right Wing . . . 6'1" . . . 185 lbs. . . . Born, Comox, B.C., June 6, 1965 . . . Shoots right . . . (October, 1984)—Dislocated kneecap . . . (March, 1988)—Slipped right kneecap . . . (December, 1988)—Fractured right thumb and inflammed right knee . . . (March, 1989)—Recurrence of right knee inflammation . . . (October, 1989)—Hyperextended knee . . . (March, 1990)—Pulled groin.

Year	Team	League	Games	G.	A.	Pts.	Pen.
1981-82—Ridge Meadow	B.C. Midget	64	73	68	141	134
1982-83—Portland Winter Hawks (c)	WHL	72	56	64	120	130
1983-84—Portland Winter Hawks	WHL	19	8	18	26	29
1983-84—Vancouver Canucks	NHL	56	16	15	31	57
1984-85—Vancouver Canucks	NHL	72	21	18	39	137

Year	Team	League	Games	G.	A.	Pts.	Pen.
1985-86—Vancouver Canucks (d)	NHL	73	14	20	34	126
1986-87—Boston Bruins	NHL	75	36	36	72	143
1987-88—Boston Bruins (b)	NHL	69	42	27	69	175
1988-89—Boston Bruins	NHL	74	37	38	75	190
1989-90—Boston Bruins (b)	NHL	76	55	37	92	117
NHL TOTALS		495	221	191	412	945

(c)—June, 1983—Drafted as underage junior by Vancouver Canucks in 1983 NHL entry draft. First Canucks pick, ninth overall, first round.
(d)—June, 1986—Traded with first-round draft choice in 1987 (Glen Wesley) by Vancouver Canucks to Boston Bruins for Barry Pederson.

CHRISTOPHER NELSON

Defense . . . 6'2" . . . 190 lbs. . . . Born, Philadelphia, Pa., February 12, 1969 . . . Shoots right.

Year	Team	League	Games	G.	A.	Pts.	Pen.
1987-88—Rochester Mustangs (c)	USHL	48	6	29	35	82
1988-89—Univ. of Wisconsin	WCHA	21	1	4	5	24
1989-90—Univ. of Wisconsin	WCHA	38	1	3	4	48

(c)—June, 1988—Drafted by New Jersey Devils in 1988 NHL entry draft. Sixth Devils pick, 96th overall, fifth round.

TODD NELSON

Defense . . . 6' . . . 195 lbs. . . . Born, Prince Albert, Sask., May 15, 1969 . . . Shoots left . . . (October, 1986)—Dislocated right shoulder . . . (May, 1987)—Dislocated left shoulder.

Year	Team	League	Games	G.	A.	Pts.	Pen.
1984-85—Prince Albert Raiders	SMHL	36	3	18	21	50
1985-86—Prince Albert Raiders	SMHL	36	6	22	28	72
1985-86—Prince Albert Raiders	WHL	4	0	0	0	0
1986-87—Prince Albert Raiders	WHL	35	1	6	7	10
1987-88—Prince Albert Raiders	WHL	72	3	21	24	59
1988-89—Prince Albert Raiders (b-c)	WHL	71	30	57	87	74
1989-90—Prince Albert Raiders (b)	WHL	72	28	69	97	79

(c)—June, 1989—Drafted by Pittsburgh Penguins in 1989 NHL entry draft. Fourth Penguins pick, 79th overall, fourth round.

STEVE NEMETH

Center . . . 5'8" . . . 167 lbs. . . . Born, Calgary, Alta., February 11, 1967 . . . Shoots left . . . (November, 1984)—Dislocated left shoulder . . . (March, 1987)—Given a one-year suspension from international competition by the IIHF for being involved in an on-ice fight between National Junior Canadian and Soviet Teams in Prague, Czechoslovakia.

Year	Team	League	Games	G.	A.	Pts.	Pen.
1983-84—Lethbridge Broncos	WHL	68	22	20	42	33
1984-85—Lethbridge Broncos (c)	WHL	67	39	55	94	39
1985-86—Lethbridge Broncos	WHL	70	42	69	111	47
1986-87—Kamloops Blazers	WHL	10	4	10	14	0
1986-87—Canadian Olympic Team	Int'l.	43	14	7	21	12
1987-88—Colorado Rangers	IHL	57	13	24	37	28
1987-88—New York Rangers	NHL	12	2	0	2	2
1988-89—Denver Rangers (d)	IHL	11	5	2	7	8
1988-89—Canadian National Team	Int'l.	26	6	10	16	10
1989-90—Canadian National Team	Int'l.	73	24	42	66	38
NHL TOTALS		12	2	0	2	2

(c)—June, 1985—Drafted as underage junior by New York Rangers in 1985 NHL entry draft. Tenth Rangers pick, 196th overall, 10th round.
(d)—November 30, 1988—Released by New York Rangers.

JIM NESICH

Right Wing and Center . . . 5'11" . . . 160 lbs. . . . Born, Dearborn, Mich., February 22, 1966 . . . Shoots right . . . (December 10, 1989)—Broke ankle at Springfield.

Year	Team	League	Games	G.	A.	Pts.	Pen.
1983-84—Verdun Juniors (c)	WHL	70	22	24	46	35
1984-85—Verdun Juniors	QMJHL	65	19	33	52	72
1985-86—Verdun Juniors	OHL	71	26	55	81	114
1985-86—Sherbrooke Canadiens	AHL	4	0	1	1	0
1986-87—Verdun Junior Canadiens	QMJHL	62	20	50	70	133
1987-88—Sherbrooke Canadiens	AHL	53	4	10	14	51
1988-89—Sherbrooke Canadiens	AHL	74	12	34	46	112
1989-90—Sherbrooke Canadiens	AHL	62	21	31	52	79

(c)—June, 1984—Drafted by Montreal Canadiens in NHL entry draft. Eighth Canadiens pick, 116th overall, sixth round.

RAY NEUFELD

Right Wing . . . 6'2" . . . 215 lbs. . . . Born, St. Boniface, Man., April 15, 1959 . . . Shoots right . . . (September, 1978)—Broken ribs . . . (January 7, 1985)—Injured shoulder when checked by Gary Leeman at Toronto . . . (April 11, 1987)—Stretched knee ligaments when checked by Craig Muni vs. Edmonton . . . (January 26, 1989)—Tore ligaments in right ankle when checked by Paul Cavallini vs. St. Louis and missed 23 games.

Year	Team	League	Games	G.	A.	Pts.	Pen.
1976-77—Flin Flon Bombers	WCHL	68	13	19	32	63
1977-78—Flin Flon Bombers	WCHL	72	23	46	69	224
1978-79—Edmonton Oil Kings (c)	WCHL	57	54	48	102	138
1979-80—Springfield Indians	AHL	73	23	29	52	51
1979-80—Hartford Whalers	NHL	8	1	0	1	0
1980-81—Binghamton Whalers	AHL	25	7	7	14	43
1980-81—Hartford Whalers	NHL	52	5	10	15	44
1981-82—Binghamton Whalers (d)	AHL	61	28	31	59	81
1981-82—Hartford Whalers	NHL	19	4	3	7	4

Year	Team	League	Games	G.	A.	Pts.	Pen.
1982-83—Hartford Whalers		NHL	80	26	31	57	86
1983-84—Hartford Whalers		NHL	80	27	42	69	97
1984-85—Hartford Whalers		NHL	76	27	35	62	129
1985-86—Hartford Whalers (e)		NHL	16	5	10	15	40
1985-86—Winnipeg Jets		NHL	60	20	28	48	62
1986-87—Winnipeg Jets		NHL	80	18	18	36	105
1987-88—Winnipeg Jets		NHL	78	18	18	36	169
1988-89—Winnipeg Jets (f)		NHL	31	5	2	7	52
1988-89—Boston Bruins		NHL	14	1	3	4	28
1989-90—Maine Mariners		AHL	76	27	29	56	117
1989-90—Boston Bruins		NHL	1	0	0	0	0
NHL TOTALS			595	157	200	357	816

(c)—August, 1979—Drafted by Hartford Whalers in 1979 entry draft. Fourth Whalers pick, 81st overall, fourth round.
(d)—Co-leader (with Florent Robidoux of New Brunswick) during AHL Calder Cup Play-offs with nine goals.
(e)—November, 1985—Traded by Hartford Whalers to Winnipeg Jets for Dave Babych.
(f)—December 30, 1988—Traded by Winnipeg Jets to Boston Bruins for Moe Lemay.

TOM NEZOIL

Left Wing . . . 6'1" . . . 190 lbs. . . . Born, Burlington, Ont., August 7, 1967 . . . Shoots left.

Year	Team	League	Games	G.	A.	Pts.	Pen.
1986-87—Miami of Ohio Univ. (c)		CCHA	39	11	18	29	80
1987-88—Miami of Ohio Univ.		CCHA	34	13	13	26	52
1988-89—Miami of Ohio Univ.		CCHA	12	5	4	9	14
1989-90—Miami of Ohio Univ.		CCHA	31	11	4	15	14

(c)—June, 1987—Drafted by New Jersey Devils in 1987 NHL entry draft. Sixth Devils pick, 128th overall, seventh round.

BERNIE IRVINE NICHOLLS

Center . . . 6' . . . 185 lbs. . . . Born, Haliburton, Ont., June 24, 1961 . . . Shoots right . . . (November 18, 1982)—Partial tear of medial colateral ligament in right knee vs. Detroit when hit by Willie Huber . . . (February, 1984)—Broken jaw, missed only two games but lost 13 pounds before the end of season with jaw wired shut . . . (October 8, 1987)—Fractured left index finger in three places vs. St. Louis.

Year	Team	League	Games	G.	A.	Pts.	Pen.
1978-79—Kingston Canadians		OMJHL	2	0	1	1	0
1979-80—Kingston Canadians (c)		OMJHL	68	36	43	79	85
1980-81—Kingston Canadians		OHL	65	63	89	152	109
1981-82—New Haven Nighthawks		AHL	55	41	30	71	31
1981-82—Los Angeles Kings		NHL	22	14	18	32	27
1982-83—Los Angeles Kings		NHL	71	28	22	50	124
1983-84—Los Angeles Kings		NHL	78	41	54	95	83
1984-85—Los Angeles Kings		NHL	80	46	54	100	76
1985-86—Los Angeles Kings		NHL	80	36	61	97	78
1986-87—Los Angeles Kings		NHL	80	33	48	81	101
1987-88—Los Angeles Kings		NHL	65	32	46	78	114
1988-89—Los Angeles Kings		NHL	79	70	80	150	96
1989-90—Los Angeles Kings (d)		NHL	47	27	48	75	66
1989-90—New York Rangers		NHL	32	12	25	37	20
NHL TOTALS			634	339	456	795	785

(c)—June, 1980—Drafted by Los Angeles Kings as underage junior in 1980 NHL entry draft. Fourth Kings pick, 73rd overall, fourth round.
(d)—January 20, 1990—Traded by Los Angeles Kings to New York Rangers for Tomas Sandstrom and Tony Granato.

ROB NICHOLS

Left Wing . . . 5'11" . . . 172 lbs. . . . Born, Hamilton, Ontario, August 4, 1964 . . . Shoots left.

Year	Team	League	Games	G.	A.	Pts.	Pen.
1982-83—Kitchener Rangers (c)		OHL	54	17	26	43	208
1983-84—Kitchener Rangers		OHL	12	5	8	13	46
1983-84—North Bay Centennials		OHL	46	36	32	68	98
1984-85—North Bay Centennials		OHL	41	27	39	66	72
1984-85—Fredericton Express		AHL	1	0	0	0	2
1984-85—Kalamazoo Wings		IHL	8	2	1	3	0
1985-86—Kalamazoo Wings		IHL	73	38	41	79	406
1986-87—Kalamazoo Wings		IHL	71	29	27	56	357
1987-88—Adirondack Red Wings		AHL	65	21	16	37	256
1988-89—Adirondack Red Wings		AHL	56	8	7	15	154
1989-90—Phoenix Roadrunners		IHL	69	25	25	50	265

(c)—June, 1983—Drafted as underage junior by Philadelphia Flyers in 1983 NHL entry draft. Eighth Flyers pick, 181st overall, ninth round.

JEFFREY NIELSEN

Right Wing . . . 6'0" . . . 170 lbs. . . . Born, Grand Rapids, Minn., September 20, 1971 . . . Shoots right.

Year	Team	League	Games	G.	A.	Pts.	Pen.
1985-86—Grand Rapids "A" Bantams		Minn. H.S.	58	23	52	75	20
1986-87—Grand Rapids "A" Bantams		Minn. H.S.	64	47	95	142	32
1987-88—Grand Rapids H. S.		Minn. H.S.	21	9	11	20	14
1988-89—Grand Rapids H. S.		Minn. H.S.	25	13	17	30	26
1989-90—Grand Rapids H. S. (c)		Minn. H.S.	28	32	25	57	....

(c)—June 16, 1990—Selected by New York Rangers in 1990 NHL entry draft. Fourth Rangers pick, 69th overall, fourth round.

JOE NIEUWENDYK

Center . . . 6'2" . . . 185 lbs. . . . Born, Oshawa, Ont., September 10, 1966 . . . Shoots left . . . Cousin of Jeff, John and Brian Beukeboom . . . (November, 1987)—Concussion vs. N.Y. Rangers . . . Only the third player in NHL history to score 50 goals in each of his first two seasons (Mike Bossy and Wayne Gretzky were others) . . . (May 25, 1989)—Ribs bruised by Craig Ludwig slash . . . (April 17, 1990)—Tore anterior

cruciate ligament of left knee with Team Canada vs. Team USA when he collided with Jim Johnson.

Year	Team	League	Games	G.	A.	Pts.	Pen.
1983-84—Pickering Panthers Jr. B.		MTJHL	38	30	28	58	35
1984-85—Cornell University (c-d)		ECAC	29	21	24	45	30
1985-86—Cornell University (a)		ECAC	29	26	28	54	67
1986-87—Cornell University (a-e-f)		ECAC	23	26	26	52	26
1986-87—Calgary Flames		NHL	9	5	1	6	0
1987-88—Calgary Flames (g-h)		NHL	75	51	41	92	23
1988-89—Calgary Flames		NHL	77	51	31	82	40
1989-90—Calgary Flames		NHL	79	45	50	95	40
NHL TOTALS			240	152	123	275	103

(c)—Won Ivy-League Rookie of the Year Trophy.
(d)—June, 1985—Drafted by Calgary Flames in 1985 NHL entry draft. Second Flames pick, 27th overall, second round.
(e)—Named ECAC Player-of-the-Year.
(f)—Named to U.S. College First-Team All-America Team.
(g)—Won Calder Memorial Trophy (Top NHL Rookie).
(h)—Named NHL Rookie of the Year in poll of players by THE SPORTING NEWS.

CHRIS NILAN

Right Wing . . . 6' . . . 200 lbs. . . . Born, Boston, Mass., February 9, 1958 . . . Shoots right . . . (November 21, 1981)—Threw puck at Paul Baxter of Pittsburgh while sitting in penalty box and given a three-game suspension by NHL . . . (January 22, 1985)—Became all-time Montreal Canadien career penalty-minute leader (previous record held by Maurice Richard with 1285 minutes) . . . (October 13, 1985)—Given eight-game suspension by NHL for intentional injury of Rick Middleton at Boston . . . (November 20, 1986)—Given three-game suspension by NHL after an altercation with Ken Linseman at Boston . . . (February, 1987)—Left knee braced . . . (March, 1987)—Hip injury . . . (February 2, 1988)—Sprained medial colateral ligament in right knee when he collided with Mikko Makela vs. N.Y. Islanders in his first game with Rangers . . . (December, 1988)—Strained abdominal ligament on front pelvic bone . . . (November 4, 1989)—Broke right forearm at Montreal and missed 35 games . . . (February 14, 1990)—Sprained right knee vs. Pittsburgh . . . (April 11, 1990)—Broke ulnar bone in right arm vs. N.Y. Islanders when checked by Ken Baumgartner.

Year	Team	League	Games	G.	A.	Pts.	Pen.
1977-78—Northeastern University (c)		ECAC	....	...	...	...	....
1978-79—Northeastern University		ECAC	32	9	13	22	....
1979-80—Nova Scotia Voyageurs		AHL	49	15	10	25	*304
1979-80—Montreal Canadiens		NHL	15	0	2	2	50
1980-81—Montreal Canadiens		NHL	57	7	8	15	262
1981-82—Montreal Canadiens		NHL	49	7	4	11	204
1982-83—Montreal Canadiens		NHL	66	6	8	14	213
1983-84—Montreal Canadiens (d)		NHL	76	16	10	26	*338
1984-85—Montreal Canadiens		NHL	77	21	16	37	*358
1985-86—Montreal Canadiens (e)		NHL	72	19	15	34	274
1986-87—Montreal Canadiens		NHL	44	4	16	20	266
1987-88—Montreal Canadiens (f)		NHL	50	7	5	12	209
1987-88—New York Rangers		NHL	22	3	5	8	96
1988-89—New York Rangers		NHL	38	7	7	14	177
1989-90—New York Rangers (g)		NHL	25	1	2	3	59
NHL TOTALS			591	98	98	196	2506

(c)—June, 1978—Drafted by Montreal Canadiens in 1978 amateur draft. Twenty-first Canadiens pick, 231st overall, 19th round.
(d)—Led Stanley Cup Playoffs with 81 penalty minutes.
(e)—Led Stanley Cup Playoffs with 141 penalty minutes.
(f)—January 27, 1988—Traded by Montreal Canadiens to New York Rangers for the option to flip first round 1989 draft picks.
(g)—June 28, 1990—Traded by New York Rangers to Boston Bruins for Greg Johnston and future considerations. Johnston was then traded by the Rangers to Toronto for Tie Domi and Mark Laforest.

JIM EDWARD NILL

Right Wing . . . 6' . . . 185 lbs. . . . Born, Hanna, Alta., April 11, 1958 . . . Shoots right . . . (March, 1983)—Concussion . . . (October 10, 1985)—Dislocated shoulder at Edmonton and missed 15 games . . . (October 14, 1986)—Injured knee vs. Boston . . . (October 24, 1989)—Groin injury and missed 24 games . . . (March 20, 1990)—Injured knee and out for the season.

Year	Team	League	Games	G.	A.	Pts.	Pen.
1974-75—Drumheller Falcons		AJHL	59	30	30	60	103
1975-76—Medicine Hat Tigers		WCHL	62	5	11	16	69
1976-77—Medicine Hat Tigers		WCHL	71	23	24	47	140
1977-78—Medicine Hat Tigers (c)		WCHL	72	47	46	93	252
1978-79—Canadian National Team		Int'l	....	...	....	....	....
1979-80—Canadian National Team		Int'l	51	14	21	35	58
1979-80—Canadian Olympic Team		Olympics	6	1	2	3	4
1980-81—Salt Lake Golden Eagles (b)		CHL	79	28	34	62	222
1981-82—St. Louis Blues (d)		NHL	61	9	12	21	127
1981-82—Vancouver Canucks		NHL	8	1	2	3	5
1982-83—Vancouver Canucks		NHL	65	7	15	22	136
1983-84—Vancouver Canucks (e)		NHL	51	9	6	15	78
1983-84—Boston Bruins		NHL	27	3	2	5	81
1984-85—Boston Bruins (f)		NHL	49	1	9	10	62
1984-85—Winnipeg Jets		NHL	20	8	8	16	38
1985-86—Winnipeg Jets		NHL	61	6	8	14	75
1986-87—Winnipeg Jets		NHL	36	3	4	7	52
1987-88—Moncton Golden Flames		AHL	3	0	0	0	6
1987-88—Winnipeg Jets (g)		NHL	24	0	1	1	44
1987-88—Detroit Red Wings		NHL	36	3	11	14	55
1988-89—Detroit Red Wings		NHL	71	8	7	15	83
1989-90—Detroit Red Wings		NHL	15	0	2	2	18
1989-90—Adirondack Red Wings (h)		AHL	20	10	8	18	24
NHL TOTALS			524	58	87	145	854

(c)—June, 1978—Drafted by St. Louis Blues in 1978 NHL amateur draft. Fourth Blues pick, 89th overall, sixth round.
(d)—March, 1982—Traded with Tony Currie and Rick Heinz by St. Louis Blues to Vancouver Canucks for Glen Hanlon and a fourth-round 1982 draft pick (Shawn Kilroy).
(e)—February, 1984—Traded by Vancouver Canucks to Boston Bruins for Peter McNab.
(f)—January, 1985—Traded by Boston Bruins to Winnipeg Jets for Morris Lukowich.
(g)—January, 1988—Traded by Winnipeg Jets to Detroit Red Wings for Mark Kumpel.
(h)—February 7, 1990—Assigned to Adirondack Red Wings and named a player/assistant coach.

OWEN NOLAN

Right Wing . . . 6'1" . . . 195 lbs. . . . Born, Belfast, Ireland, February 12, 1972 . . . Shoots right . . . (February 22, 1990)—Separated shoulder vs. Dukes of Hamilton and missed eight games.

Year	Team	League	Games	G.	A.	Pts.	Pen.
1987-88	Thorold Bantams	OHA	28	53	32	85	24
1988-89	Cornwall Royals (c)	OHL	62	34	25	59	213
1989-90	Cornwall Royals (a-d)	OHL	58	51	59	110	240

(c)—Won Emms Family Award (Rookie of the Year).
(d)—June 16, 1990—Selected by Quebec Nordiques in 1990 NHL entry draft. First Nordiques pick, first overall, first round.

BRIAN NOONAN

Center . . . 6'1" . . . 180 lbs. . . . Born, Boston, Mass., May 29, 1965 . . . Shoots right . . . (April 3, 1988)—Separated shoulder vs. New Jersey.

Year	Team	League	Games	G.	A.	Pts.	Pen.
1982-83	Archbishop Williams H.S. (c)	Mass. H.S.	21	26	17	43	....
1983-84	Archbishop Williams H.S.	Mass. H.S.	17	14	23	37	....
1984-85	New Westminister Bruins	WHL	72	50	66	116	76
1985-86	Saginaw Generals (d)	IHL	76	39	39	78	69
1985-86	Nova Scotia Oilers	AHL	2	0	0	0	0
1986-87	Nova Scotia Oilers	AHL	70	25	26	51	30
1987-88	Chicago Black Hawks	NHL	77	10	20	30	44
1988-89	Chicago Black Hawks	NHL	45	4	12	16	28
1988-89	Saginaw Hawks	IHL	19	18	13	31	36
1989-90	Chicago Black Hawks	NHL	8	0	2	2	6
1989-90	Indianapolis Ice (b)	IHL	56	40	36	76	85
NHL TOTALS			130	14	34	48	78

(c)—June, 1983—Drafted by Chicago Black Hawks in 1983 NHL entry draft. Tenth Black Hawks pick, 179th overall, ninth round.
(d)—Won Ken McKenzie Trophy (Top IHL U.S.-Born player).

ROBERT NORDMARK

Defense . . . 6'1" . . . 190 lbs. . . . Born, Lulea, Sweden, August 20, 1962 . . . Shoots right . . . (September, 1987)—Separated shoulder during St. Louis training camp . . . (November, 1989)—Back spasms and missed seven games.

Year	Team	League	Games	G.	A.	Pts.	Pen.
1986-87	Lulea (c-d)	Sweden	32	7	8	15	42
1987-88	St. Louis Blues	NHL	67	3	18	21	60
1988-89	Vancouver Canucks (e)	NHL	80	6	35	41	97
1989-90	Vancouver Canucks	NHL	44	2	11	13	34
NHL TOTALS			191	11	64	75	191

(c)—June, 1981—Drafted by Detroit Red Wings in 1981 NHL entry draft. Eighth Red Wings pick, 191st overall, 10th round.
(d)—June, 1987—Drafted by St. Louis Blues in 1987 NHL entry draft. Third Blues pick, 59th overall, third round.
(e)—September 7, 1988—Traded with second-round 1990 draft pick by St. Louis Blues to Vancouver Canucks for Dave Richter.

DWAYNE NORRIS

Right Wing . . . 5'10" . . . 175 lbs. . . . Born, St. John's, Newfoundland, January 8, 1970 . . . Shoots right . . . Brother of Ian Norris.

Year	Team	League	Games	G.	A.	Pts.	Pen.
1988-89	Michigan State Univ.	CCHA	47	16	23	39	40
1989-90	Michigan State Univ. (c)	CCHA	36	19	26	45	30

(c)—June 16, 1990—Selected by Quebec Nordiques in 1990 NHL entry draft. Fifth Nordiques pick, 127th overall, seventh round.

CHRIS NORTON

Defense . . . 6'2" . . . 200 lbs. . . . Born, Oakville, Ont., March 11, 1965 . . . Shoots right . . . Holds career point record for Cornell defensemen . . . (July, 1988)—Fractured ankle playing summer hockey . . . (December 6, 1989)—Broke foot at Utica.

Year	Team	League	Games	G.	A.	Pts.	Pen.
1984-85	Cornell Univ. (c)	ECAC	29	4	19	23	34
1985-86	Cornell Univ.	ECAC	21	8	15	23	56
1986-87	Cornell Univ.	ECAC	24	10	21	31	79
1987-88	Cornell Univ.	ECAC	27	9	25	34	53
1988-89	Moncton Hawks	AHL	60	1	21	22	49
1989-90	Moncton Hawks	AHL	62	9	20	29	49

(c)—June, 1985—Drafted by Winnipeg Jets in 1985 NHL entry draft. Eleventh Jets pick, 228th overall, 11th round.

D'ARCY NORTON

Left Wing . . . 6' . . . 175 lbs. . . . Born, Camrose, Alta., May 2, 1967 . . . Shoots left.

Year	Team	League	Games	G.	A.	Pts.	Pen.
1984-85	Lethbridge Broncos	WHL	50	4	11	15	49
1985-86	Lethbridge Broncos	WHL	69	19	25	44	69
1986-87	Kamloops Blazers (c)	WHL	71	45	57	102	66
1987-88	Kamloops Blazers (a)	WHL	68	64	43	107	82
1988-89	Kalamazoo Wings	IHL	75	39	38	77	79
1989-90	Kalamazoo Wings	IHL	66	22	25	47	55

(c)—June, 1987—Drafted by Minnesota North Stars in 1987 NHL entry draft. Sixth North Stars pick, 109th overall, sixth round.

JEFF NORTON

Defense . . . 6'2" . . . 190 lbs. . . . Born, Cambridge, Mass., November 25, 1965 . . . Shoots left . . . (November 16, 1988)—Bruised ribs when slashed by Stephane Richer at Montreal . . . (February, 1990)—Injured groin . . . (March 2, 1990)—Strained groin and abdominal muscles when his skate struck a rut vs. N.Y. Rangers and missed six games . . . (April 9, 1990)—Concussion when checked by Troy Mallette vs. N.Y. Rangers.

Year	Team	League	Games	G.	A.	Pts.	Pen.
1983-84	Cushing Academy (c)	Mass. H.S.	21	22	33	55	..
1984-85	University of Michigan	CCHA	37	8	16	24	103
1985-86	University of Michigan	CCHA	37	15	30	45	99
1986-87	University of Michigan (b)	CCHA	39	12	37	49	92
1987-88	U.S. Olympic Team	Int'l	57	7	25	32	..
1987-88	New York Islanders	NHL	15	1	6	7	14
1988-89	New York Islanders	NHL	69	1	30	31	74
1989-90	New York Islanders	NHL	60	4	49	53	65
NHL TOTALS			144	6	85	91	153

(c)—June, 1984—Drafted by New York Islanders in NHL entry draft. Third Islanders pick, 62nd overall, third round.

LEE CHARLES NORWOOD

Defense . . . 6' . . . 190 lbs. . . . Born, Oakland, Calif., February 2, 1960 . . . Shoots left . . . (February, 1987)—Pulled stomach muscle . . . (October, 1987)—Groin injury . . . (December, 1987)—Knee injury . . . (November, 1988)—Sprained ankle . . . (February, 1989)—Pulled hamstring . . . (November 6, 1989)—Hip pointer and missed six games . . . (March 15, 1990)—Sprained right wrist at Pittsburgh.

Year	Team	League	Games	G.	A.	Pts.	Pen.
1977-78	Hull Olympiques	QMJHL	51	3	17	20	83
1978-79	Oshawa Generals (c)	OMJHL	61	23	38	61	171
1979-80	Oshawa Generals	OMJHL	60	13	39	52	143
1980-81	Hershey Bears	AHL	52	11	32	43	78
1980-81	Quebec Nordiques	NHL	11	1	1	2	9
1981-82	Fredericton Express	AHL	29	6	13	19	74
1981-82	Quebec Nordiques (d)	NHL	2	0	0	0	2
1981-82	Washington Capitals	NHL	26	7	10	17	125
1982-83	Washington Capitals	NHL	8	0	1	1	14
1982-83	Hershey Bears	AHL	67	12	36	48	90
1983-84	St. Catharines Saints	AHL	75	13	46	59	91
1984-85	Peoria Rivermen (a-e)	IHL	80	17	60	77	229
1985-86	St. Louis Blues (f)	NHL	71	5	24	29	134
1986-87	Adirondack Red Wings	AHL	3	0	3	3	0
1986-87	Detroit Red Wings	NHL	57	6	21	27	163
1987-88	Detroit Red Wings	NHL	51	9	22	31	131
1988-89	Detroit Red Wings	NHL	66	10	32	42	100
1989-90	Detroit Red Wings	NHL	64	8	14	22	95
NHL TOTALS			356	46	125	171	773

(c)—August, 1979—Drafted by Quebec Nordiques as underage junior in 1979 NHL entry draft. Third Nordiques pick, 62nd overall, third round.
(d)—January, 1982—Traded by Quebec Nordiques to Washington Capitals for Tim Tookey.
(e)—Won Governor's Trophy (Top Defenseman).
(f)—August, 1986—Traded by St. Louis Blues to Detroit Red Wings for Larry Trader.

TEPPO KALEVI NUMMINEN

Defense . . . 6'1" . . . 190 lbs. . . . Born, Tampere, Finland, July 3, 1968 . . . Shoots right . . . (March 5, 1989)—Separated shoulder when checked by Gary Nylund vs. N.Y. Islanders . . . (April 14, 1990)—Broke thumb vs. Edmonton.

Year	Team	League	Games	G.	A.	Pts.	Pen.
1984-85	Tappara (c)	Finland	30	14	17	31	10
1985-86	Tappara	Finland	39	2	4	6	6
1986-87	Tappara	Finland	44	9	9	18	19
1987-88	Tappara	Finland	44	10	10	20	29
1988-89	Winnipeg Jets	NHL	69	1	14	15	36
1989-90	Winnipeg Jets	NHL	79	11	32	43	20
NHL TOTALS			148	12	46	58	56

(c)—June, 1986—Drafted by Winnipeg Jets in 1986 NHL entry draft. Second Jets pick, 29th overall, second round.

GARY NYLUND

Defense . . . 6'4" . . . 210 lbs. . . . Born, Surrey, B.C., October 28, 1963 . . . Shoots left . . . (September, 1982)—Injury to left knee, requiring surgery . . . (October, 1983)—Knee surgery . . . (November 5, 1984)—Concussion at Minnesota . . . (October, 1987)—Bruised elbow . . . (September, 1988)—Broke bone in right forearm during Chicago Black Hawks training camp . . . (January 11, 1989)—Missed 10 games following arthroscopic surgery to right knee . . . (March, 1989)—Bruised ribs and lung . . . (March 8, 1990)—Irritated right knee ligament at New Jersey.

Year	Team	League	Games	G.	A.	Pts.	Pen.
1978-79	Delta	BCJHL	57	6	29	35	107
1978-79	Portland Winter Hawks	WHL	2	0	0	0	0
1979-80	Portland Winter Hawks	WHL	72	5	21	26	59
1980-81	Portland Winter Hawks (b)	WHL	70	6	40	46	186
1981-82	Portland Winter Hawks (a-c-d)	WHL	65	7	59	66	267
1982-83	Toronto Maple Leafs	NHL	16	0	3	3	16
1983-84	Toronto Maple Leafs	NHL	47	2	14	16	103
1984-85	Toronto Maple Leafs	NHL	76	3	17	20	99
1985-86	Toronto Maple Leafs (e)	NHL	79	2	16	18	180
1986-87	Chicago Black Hawks	NHL	80	7	20	27	190
1987-88	Chicago Black Hawks	NHL	76	4	15	19	208
1988-89	Chicago Black Hawks (f)	NHL	23	3	2	5	63
1988-89	New York Islanders	NHL	46	4	8	12	74
1989-90	New York Islanders	NHL	64	4	21	25	144
NHL TOTALS			507	29	116	145	1077

(c)—Winner of WHL Top Defenseman Trophy.
(d)—June, 1982—Drafted as underage junior by Toronto Maple Leafs in 1982 NHL entry draft. First Maple Leafs pick, third overall, first round.
(e)—August, 1986—Signed by Chicago Black Hawks as a free agent. An NHL arbitrator subsequently ruled that the Black Hawks had to send Ken Yaremchuk, Jerome Dupont and a fourth-round 1987 draft pick (Joe Sacco) to compensate the Maple Leafs.
(f)—January 11, 1989—Traded with Mark Bergevin by Chicago Black Hawks to New York Islanders for Steve Konroyd and Bob Bassen.

ADAM OATES

Center . . . 5'11" . . . 190 lbs. . . . Born, Weston, Ont., August 27, 1962 . . . Shoots right . . . Holds All-time career record for assists at R.P.I. (150) . . . (1984-85)—Set R.P.I. record for assists and points in a single season . . . (October, 1987)—Pulled abdominal muscle . . . (November, 1988)—Chicken pox . . . (December, 1988)—Bruised thigh.

Year	Team	League	Games	G.	A.	Pts.	Pen.
1982-83—R.P.I.		ECAC	22	9	33	42	8
1983-84—R.P.I. (b)		ECAC	38	26	57	83	15
1984-85—R.P.I. (a-c-d)		ECAC	38	31	60	91	29
1985-86—Adirondack Red Wings		AHL	34	18	28	46	4
1985-86—Detroit Red Wings		NHL	38	9	11	20	10
1986-87—Detroit Red Wings		NHL	76	15	32	47	21
1987-88—Detroit Red Wings		NHL	63	14	40	54	20
1988-89—Detroit Red Wings (e)		NHL	69	16	62	78	14
1989-90—St. Louis Blues		NHL	80	23	79	102	30
NHL TOTALS			326	77	224	301	95

(c)—Named to All America Team (East).
(d)—June, 1985—Signed by Detroit Red Wings as a free agent.
(e)—June 15, 1989—Traded with Paul MacLean by Detroit Red Wings to St. Louis Blues for Tony McKegney and Bernie Federko.

DAVID O'BRIEN

Right Wing . . . 6'1" . . . 180 lbs. . . . Born, Brighton, Mass., September 13, 1966 . . . Shoots right.

Year	Team	League	Games	G.	A.	Pts.	Pen.
1984-85—Northeastern Univ.		H. East	30	8	7	15	6
1985-86—Northeastern Univ. (c)		H. East	39	23	16	39	18
1986-87—Northeastern Univ.		H. East	35	16	24	40	12
1987-88—Northeastern Univ.		H. East	37	18	29	47	18
1988-89—Binghamton Whalers (d)		AHL	53	3	12	15	11
1989-90—Peoria Rivermen		IHL	57	9	14	23	21

(c)—June, 1986—Drafted by St. Louis Blues in 1986 NHL entry draft. Thirteenth Blues pick, 241st overall, 12th round.
(d)—October 8, 1988—Loaned to Binghamton Whalers by St. Louis Blues.

MICHAEL THOMAS O'CONNELL

Defense . . . 5'11" . . . 176 lbs. . . . Born, Chicago, Ill., November 25, 1955 . . . Shoots right . . . Son of former Cleveland Browns quarterback Tommy O'Connell . . . Brother of Tim O'Connell . . . Missed part of 1976-77 season with torn muscle in right shoulder . . . First member of the Black Hawks to be born in Chicago . . . (November 27, 1987)—Suspended eight NHL games for high sticking Doug Evans vs. St. Louis . . . (February, 1988)—Broke left index finger.

Year	Team	League	Games	G.	A.	Pts.	Pen.
1973-74—Kingston Canadians		Jr."A"OHA	70	16	43	59	81
1974-75—King. Canadians (a-c-d)		Jr."A"OHA	50	18	55	73	47
1975-76—Dallas Black Hawks (e)		CHL	70	6	37	43	50
1976-77—Dallas Black Hawks (a-f)		CHL	63	15	53	68	30
1977-78—Dallas Black Hawks (g)		CHL	62	6	45	51	75
1977-78—Chicago Black Hawks		NHL	6	1	1	2	2
1978-79—Chicago Black Hawks		NHL	48	4	22	26	20
1978-79—New Brunswick Hawks		AHL	35	5	20	25	21
1979-80—Chicago Black Hawks		NHL	78	8	22	30	52
1980-81—Chicago Black Hawks (h)		NHL	34	5	16	21	32
1980-81—Boston Bruins		NHL	48	10	22	32	42
1981-82—Boston Bruins		NHL	80	5	34	39	75
1982-83—Boston Bruins		NHL	80	14	39	53	42
1983-84—Boston Bruins		NHL	75	18	42	60	42
1984-85—Boston Bruins		NHL	78	15	40	55	64
1985-86—Boston Bruins (i)		NHL	63	8	21	29	47
1985-86—Detroit Red Wings		NHL	13	1	7	8	16
1986-87—Detroit Red Wings		NHL	77	5	26	31	70
1987-88—Detroit Red Wings		NHL	48	6	13	19	38
1988-89—Detroit Red Wings		NHL	66	1	15	16	41
1989-90—Detroit Red Wings (j)		NHL	66	4	14	18	22
NHL TOTALS			860	105	334	439	605

(c)—Drafted from Kingston Canadians by Chicago Black Hawks in third round of 1975 amateur draft.
(d)—Won Max Kaminsky Memorial Trophy (Outstanding Defenseman).
(e)—Tied for lead in assists (5) during playoffs.
(f)—Won CHL Most Valuable Defenseman Award.
(g)—Tied for lead in assists (11) during playoffs.
(h)—December, 1980—Traded by Chicago Black Hawks to Boston Bruins for Al Secord.
(i)—March, 1986—Traded by Detroit Red Wings to Boston Bruins for Reed Larson.
(j)—July, 1990—Released by Detroit Red Wings and will coach at San Diego (IHL).

MYLES O'CONNOR

Defense . . . 5'11" . . . 165 lbs. . . . Born, Calgary, Alta., April 2, 1967 . . . Shoots left.

Year	Team	League	Games	G.	A.	Pts.	Pen.
1984-85—Notre Dame Hounds (c)		MICHL	40	20	35	55	40
1985-86—Univ. of Michigan		CCHA	37	6	19	25	73
1985-86—Team Canada		Int'l	8	0	0	0	0
1986-87—Univ. of Michigan		CCHA	39	15	30	45	111

Year	Team	League	Games	G.	A.	Pts.	Pen.
1987-88—Univ. of Michigan		CCHA	40	9	25	34	78
1988-89—Univ. of Michigan (a-d)		CCHA	40	3	31	34	91
1988-89—Utica Devils		AHL	1	0	0	0	0
1989-90—Utica Devils		AHL	76	14	33	47	124

(c)—June, 1985—Drafted by New Jersey Devils in 1985 NHL entry draft. Fourth Devils pick, 45th overall, third round.
(d)—Named First team All-America (West).

LYLE ODELEIN

Defense . . . 6' . . . 180 lbs. . . . Born, Quill Lake, Sask., July 21, 1968 . . . Shoots right . . . Brother of Selmar Odelein.

Year	Team	League	Games	G.	A.	Pts.	Pen.
1984-85—Regina Pat Canadians		Sask. Midget	26	12	13	25	30
1985-86—Moose Jaw Warriors (c)		WHL	67	9	37	46	117
1986-87—Moose Jaw Warriors		WHL	59	9	50	59	70
1987-88—Moose Jaw Warriors		WHL	63	15	43	58	166
1988-89—Sherbrooke Canadiens		AHL	33	3	4	7	120
1988-89—Peoria Rivermen		IHL	36	2	8	10	116
1989-90—Sherbrooke Canadiens		AHL	68	7	24	31	265
1989-90—Montreal Canadiens		NHL	8	0	2	2	33
NHL TOTALS			8	0	2	2	33

(c)—June, 1986—Drafted as underage junior by Montreal Canadiens in 1986 NHL entry draft. Eighth Canadiens pick, 141st overall, seventh round.

SELMAR ODELEIN

Defense . . . 6' . . . 195 lbs. . . . Born, Quill Lake, Sask., April 11, 1966 . . . Shoots right . . . Brother of Lyle Odelein . . . (October, 1986)—Knee injury.

Year	Team	League	Games	G.	A.	Pts.	Pen.
1982-83—Regina Canadians		Sask.Midget	70	30	84	114	38
1983-84—Regina Pats (c)		WHL	71	9	42	51	45
1984-85—Regina Pats		WHL	64	24	35	59	121
1985-86—Regina Pats		WHL	36	13	28	41	57
1985-86—Edmonton Oilers		NHL	4	0	0	0	0
1986-87—Nova Scotia Oilers		AHL	2	0	1	1	2
1987-88—Nova Scotia Oilers		AHL	43	9	14	23	75
1987-88—Edmonton Oilers		NHL	12	0	2	2	33
1988-89—Edmonton Oilers		NHL	2	0	0	0	2
1988-89—Cape Breton Oilers		AHL	63	8	21	29	150
1989-90—Canadian National Team		Int'l.	72	7	29	36	69
NHL TOTALS			18	0	2	2	35

(c)—June, 1984—Drafted as underage junior by Edmonton Oilers in NHL entry draft. First Oilers pick, 21st overall, first round.

GINO ODJICK

Left Wing . . . 6'2" . . . 220 lbs. . . . Born, Maniwaki, Que., September 7, 1970 . . . Shoots left . . . (May 1, 1989)—Suspended five games for attempting to attack Trevor Duhaime vs. Victoriaville . . . (March 19, 1990)—Suspended one game for fighting vs. Shawinigan . . . (April 14, 1990)—Suspended one game for fighting vs. Hull.

Year	Team	League	Games	G.	A.	Pts.	Pen.
1988-89—Laval Titans		QMJHL	50	9	15	24	278
1989-90—Laval Titans (c)		QMJHL	51	12	26	38	280

(c)—June 16, 1990—Selected by Vancouver Canucks in 1990 NHL entry draft. Fifth Canucks pick, 86th overall, fifth round.

BILL O'DWYER

Center . . . 6' . . . 190 lbs. . . . Born, South Boston, Mass., January 25, 1960 . . . Shoots left . . . (October, 1985)—Injured jaw . . . (October, 1986)—Broken jaw . . . (March, 1988)—Strained right hip . . . (April, 1988)—Injured left knee . . . (December, 1988)—Inflammation of left knee.

Year	Team	League	Games	G.	A.	Pts.	Pen.
1978-79—Boston College		ECAC	30	9	30	39	14
1979-80—Boston College (b-c-d)		ECAC	33	20	22	42	22
1980-81—Boston College (b)		ECAC	31	20	20	40	6
1981-82—Boston College (b)		ECAC	30	15	26	41	10
1982-83—New Haven Nighthawks		AHL	77	24	23	47	29
1983-84—Los Angeles Kings		NHL	5	0	0	0	0
1983-84—New Haven Nighthawks		AHL	58	15	42	57	39
1984-85—New Haven Nighthawks		AHL	46	19	24	43	27
1984-85—Los Angeles Kings (e)		NHL	13	1	0	1	15
1985-86—New Haven Nighthawks		AHL	41	10	15	25	41
1986-87—New Haven Nighthawks		AHL	65	22	42	64	74
1987-88—Boston Bruins (f)		NHL	77	7	10	17	83
1988-89—Boston Bruins		NHL	19	1	2	3	8
1989-90—Maine Mariners		AHL	71	26	45	71	56
1989-90—Boston Bruins (g)		NHL	6	0	1	1	2
NHL TOTALS			120	9	13	22	108

(c)—Named to second team All-New England Team (Division I).
(d)—June, 1980—Drafted by Los Angeles Kings in 1980 NHL entry draft. Ninth Kings pick, 157th overall, eighth round.
(e)—August, 1985—Signed by New York Rangers as a free agent.
(f)—July, 1987—Signed by Boston Bruins as a free agent.
(g)—July 16, 1990—Signed by Los Angeles Kings as a free agent.

JOHN ALEXANDER OGRODNICK

Left Wing . . . 6' . . . 190 lbs. . . . Born, Ottawa, Ont., June 20, 1959 . . . Shoots left . . . (February 26, 1984)—Fractured left wrist at Chicago . . . (October, 1986)—Sprained ankle . . . (December, 1987)—Ligaments damage and cracked bone in left instep . . . (February, 1988)—Bruised ribs.

Year	Team	League	Games	G.	A.	Pts.	Pen.
1976-77—Maple Ridge Bruins		BCJHL	67	54	56	110	63
1976-77—New Westminster Bruins		WCHL	14	2	4	6	0
1977-78—New Westminster Bruins (c)		WCHL	72	59	29	88	47
1978-79—New Westminster Bruins (d)		WHL	72	48	36	84	38
1979-80—Adirondack Red Wings		AHL	39	13	20	33	21
1979-80—Detroit Red Wings		NHL	41	8	24	32	8
1980-81—Detroit Red Wings		NHL	80	35	35	70	14
1981-82—Detroit Red Wings		NHL	80	28	26	54	28
1982-83—Detroit Red Wings		NHL	80	41	44	85	30
1983-84—Detroit Red Wings		NHL	64	42	36	78	14
1984-85—Detroit Red Wings (a)		NHL	79	55	50	105	30
1985-86—Detroit Red Wings		NHL	76	38	32	70	18
1986-87—Detroit Red Wings (e)		NHL	39	12	28	40	6
1986-87—Quebec Nordiques		NHL	32	11	16	27	4
1987-88—New York Rangers (f)		NHL	64	22	32	54	16
1988-89—Denver Rangers		IHL	3	2	0	2	0
1988-89—New York Rangers		NHL	60	13	29	42	14
1989-90—New York Rangers		NHL	80	43	31	74	44
NHL TOTALS			775	348	383	731	226

(c)—Shared Rookie of Year award in WCHL with Keith Brown.
(d)—August, 1979—Drafted by Detroit Red Wings in 1979 entry draft. Fourth Red Wings pick, 66th overall, fourth round.
(e)—January, 1987—Traded with Doug Shedden and Basil McRae by Detroit Red Wings to Quebec Nordiques for Brent Ashton, Mark Kumpel and Gilbert Delorme.
(f)—September, 1987—Traded with David Shaw by Quebec Nordiques to New York Rangers for Jeff Jackson and Terry Carkner.

JANNE OJANEN

Center . . . 6'2'' . . . 190 lbs. . . . Born, Tampere, Finland, April 9, 1968 . . . Shoots left . . . (January 24, 1990)—Bruised ribs vs. Washington.

Year	Team	League	Games	G.	A.	Pts.	Pen.
1985-86—Tappara Jrs.		Finland	14	5	17	22	14
1985-86—Tappara (c)		Finland	3	0	0	0	7
1986-87—Tappara		Finland	40	18	13	31	16
1987-88—Tappara		Finland	44	21	31	52	30
1988-89—Utica Devils		AHL	72	23	37	60	10
1988-89—New Jersey Devils		NHL	3	0	1	1	2
1989-90—New Jersey Devils (d)		NHL	64	17	13	30	12
NHL TOTALS			67	17	14	31	14

(c)—June, 1986—Drafted by New Jersey Devils in 1984 NHL entry draft. Third Devils pick, 45th overall, third round.
(d)—August, 1990—Assigned to Finnish Elite League.

FREDRIK OLAUSSON

Defense . . . 6'2'' . . . 200 lbs. . . . Born, Vaxsjo, Sweden, October 5, 1966 . . . Shoots right . . . (August, 1987)—Dislocated shoulder in training for Canada Cup tournament . . . (November, 1987)—Shoulder surgery.

Year	Team	League	Games	G.	A.	Pts.	Pen.
1983-84—Nybro		Sweden	28	8	14	22	32
1984-85—Farjestad (c)		Sweden	34	6	12	18	24
1985-86—Farjestad		Sweden	33	5	12	17	14
1986-87—Winnipeg Jets		NHL	72	7	29	36	24
1987-88—Winnipeg Jets		NHL	38	5	10	15	18
1988-89—Winnipeg Jets (d)		NHL	75	15	47	62	32
1989-90—Winnipeg Jets		NHL	77	9	46	55	32
NHL TOTALS			262	36	132	168	106

(c)—June, 1985—Drafted by Winnipeg Jets in NHL entry draft. Fourth Jets pick, 81st overall, fourth round.
(d)—June 19, 1989—Signed a five-year contract with Farjestads (Sweden). The two clubs agreed to allow Olausson to remain in Winnipeg.

ED OLCZYK

Center . . . 6'1'' . . . 195 lbs. . . . Born, Chicago, Ill., August 16, 1966 . . . Shoots left . . . (September, 1984)—Hyperextended knee during training camp . . . (December 16, 1984)—Broken bone in left foot when hit by shot of Doug Wilson vs. Minnesota . . . Also plays Right Wing . . . (January 3, 1990)—Pinched nerve in left knee.

Year	Team	League	Games	G.	A.	Pts.	Pen.
1983-84—U.S. National Team		Int'l	56	19	40	59	36
1983-84—U.S. Olympic Team (c)		Int'l	6	2	7	9	0
1984-85—Chicago Black Hawks		NHL	70	20	30	50	67
1985-86—Chicago Black Hawks		NHL	79	29	50	79	47
1986-87—Chicago Black Hawks (d)		NHL	79	16	35	51	119
1987-88—Toronto Maple Leafs		NHL	80	42	33	75	55
1988-89—Toronto Maple Leafs		NHL	80	38	52	90	75
1989-90—Toronto Maple Leafs		NHL	79	32	56	88	78
NHL TOTALS			467	177	256	433	441

(c)—June, 1984—Drafted by Chicago Black Hawks in NHL entry draft. First Black Hawks pick, 3rd overall, first round. (Black Hawks traded Rich Preston and Don Dietrich to New Jersey, who had the second overall pick, not to draft Olczyk. Devils also sent Bob MacMillan to Chicago in the deal.)
(d)—September, 1987—Traded with Al Secord by Chicago Black Hawks to Toronto Maple Leafs for Rick Vaive, Steve Thomas and Bob McGill.

RYAN O'LEARY

Center . . . 6'1'' . . . 205 lbs. . . . Born, Duluth, Minn., June 8, 1971 . . . Shoots left . . . (September, 1988)—Sprained ankle.

Year	Team	League	Games	G.	A.	Pts.	Pen.
1986-87—Hermantown H.S.		Minn. H.S.	23	10	13	23	4
1987-88—Hermantown H.S.		Minn. H.S.	23	16	16	32	14
1988-89—Hermantown H.S. (c)		Minn. H.S.	23	29	20	49	20
1989-90—University of Denver		WCHA	39	4	6	10	30

(c)—June, 1989—Drafted by Calgary Flames in 1987 NHL entry draft. Sixth Flames pick, 84th overall, fourth round.

LARRY OLIMB

Defense . . . 5'10'' . . . 155 lbs. . . . Born, Warroad, Minn., August 11, 1969 . . . Shoots left.

Year	Team	League	Games	G.	A.	Pts.	Pen.
1986-87—Warroad H. S. (c)		Minn. H.S.	26	23	30	53	....
1987-88—Warroad H. S.		Minn. H.S.	27	35	31	66	....
1988-89—Univ. of Minnesota		WCHA	47	10	29	39	50
1989-90—Univ. of Minnesota		WCHA	46	6	36	42	44

(c)—June, 1987—Selected by Minnesota North Stars in 1987 NHL entry draft. Tenth North Stars pick, 193rd overall, 10th round.

DARRYL OLSEN

Defense . . . 6' . . . 180 lbs. . . . Born, Calgary, Alta., October 7, 1966 . . . Shoots left.

Year	Team	League	Games	G.	A.	Pts.	Pen.
1984-85—St. Albert Saints (c)		AJHL	57	19	48	67	77
1985-86—Northern Michigan Univ.		WCHA	37	5	20	25	46
1986-87—Northern Michigan Univ.		WCHA	37	5	20	25	96
1987-88—Northern Michigan Univ.		WCHA	35	11	20	31	59
1988-89—Northern Michigan Univ. (d)		WCHA	45	16	26	42	88
1988-89—Canadian National Team		Int'l.	3	1	0	1	4
1989-90—Salt Lake Golden Eagles		IHL	72	16	50	66	90

(c)—June, 1985—Drafted by Calgary Flames in 1985 NHL entry draft. Tenth Flames pick, 185th overall, ninth round.
(d)—Named Second team All-America (West).

KEITH OSBORNE

Right Wing . . . 6'1'' . . . 181 lbs. . . . Born, Toronto, Ont., April 2, 1969 . . . Shoots right . . . (September, 1987)—Broken wrist . . . (October, 1987)—Broken ankle.

Year	Team	League	Games	G.	A.	Pts.	Pen.
1985-86—Toronto Red Wings Midget		MTHL	42	48	63	111	36
1986-87—North Bay Centennials (c)		OHL	61	34	55	89	31
1987-88—North Bay Centennials		OHL	30	14	22	36	20
1988-89—North Bay Centennials		OHL	15	11	15	26	12
1988-89—Niagara Falls Thunder		OHL	50	34	49	83	45
1989-90—St. Louis Blues		NHL	5	0	2	2	8
1989-90—Peoria Rivermen		IHL	56	23	24	47	58
NHL TOTALS			5	0	2	2	8

(c)—June, 1987—Drafted as underage junior by St. Louis Blues in 1987 NHL entry draft. First Blues pick, 12th overall, first round.

MARK ANATOLE OSBORNE

Left Wing . . . 6'2'' . . . 200 lbs. . . . Born, Toronto, Ont., August 13, 1961 . . . Shoots left . . . (October, 1984)—Hip injury . . . (February 12, 1986)—Sprained ankle vs. Vancouver and missed 12 games . . . (February, 1987)—Skate cut behind left knee . . . (April, 1988)—Separated left shoulder.

Year	Team	League	Games	G.	A.	Pts.	Pen.
1978-79—Niagara Falls Flyers		OMJHL	62	17	25	42	53
1979-80—Niagara Falls Flyers (c)		OMJHL	52	10	33	43	104
1980-81—Niagara Falls Flyers		OHL	54	39	41	80	140
1980-81—Adirondack Red Wings (d)		AHL	....	....	....	....	....
1981-82—Detroit Red Wings		NHL	80	26	41	67	61
1982-83—Detroit Red Wings (e)		NHL	80	19	24	43	83
1983-84—New York Rangers		NHL	73	23	28	51	88
1984-85—New York Rangers		NHL	23	4	4	8	33
1985-86—New York Rangers		NHL	62	16	24	40	80
1986-87—New York Rangers (f)		NHL	58	17	15	32	101
1986-87—Toronto Maple Leafs		NHL	16	5	10	15	12
1987-88—Toronto Maple Leafs		NHL	79	23	37	60	102
1988-89—Toronto Maple Leafs		NHL	75	16	30	46	112
1989-90—Toronto Maple Leafs		NHL	78	23	50	73	91
NHL TOTALS			624	172	263	435	763

(c)—June, 1980—Drafted as underage junior by Detroit Red Wings in 1980 NHL entry draft. Second Red Wings pick, 46th overall, third round.
(d)—No regular season record. Played 13 playoff games.
(e)—June, 1983—Traded by Detroit Red Wings with Willie Huber and Mike Blaisdell to New York Rangers for Ron Duguay, Eddie Mio and Ed Johnstone.
(f)—March, 1987—Traded by New York Rangers to Toronto Maple Leafs for a third-round 1989 draft pick (Rob Zamuner).

KEVIN O'SULLIVAN

Defense . . . 6' . . . 180 lbs. . . . Born, Dorchester, Mass., November 13, 1970 . . . Shoots left.

Year	Team	League	Games	G.	A.	Pts.	Pen.
1987-88—Catholic Mem. H.S.		Mass. H.S.	..	8	24	32	..
1988-89—Catholic Mem. H.S. (c)		Mass. H.S.	19	6	14	20	..
1989-90—Boston University		H. East	43	0	6	6	42

(c)—June, 1989—Drafted by New York Islanders in 1989 NHL entry draft. Seventh Islanders pick, 99th overall, fifth round.

JOEL OTTO

Center . . . 6'4'' . . . 220 lbs. . . . Born, St. Cloud, Minn., October 29, 1961 . . . Shoots right . . . (March 10, 1987)—Torn cartilage in right knee at Washington . . . (October 8, 1987)—Strained right knee ligaments vs. Detroit . . . (November, 1989)—Bruised ribs . . . (January 13, 1990)—Hospitalized in Toronto after being cross-checked from behind.

Year	Team	League	Games	G.	A.	Pts.	Pen.
1980-81—Bemidji State Univ.		NCAA-II	23	5	11	16	10
1981-82—Bemidji State Univ.		NCAA-II	31	19	33	52	24
1982-83—Bemidji State Univ.		NCAA-II	37	33	28	61	68
1983-84—Bemidji State Univ. (c)		NCAA-II	31	32	43	75	32

Year	Team	League	Games	G.	A.	Pts.	Pen.
1984-85—Moncton Golden Flames		AHL	56	27	36	63	89
1984-85—Calgary Flames		NHL	17	4	8	12	20
1985-86—Calgary Flames		NHL	79	25	34	59	188
1986-87—Calgary Flames		NHL	68	19	31	50	185
1987-88—Calgary Flames		NHL	62	13	39	52	194
1988-89—Calgary Flames		NHL	72	23	30	53	213
1989-90—Calgary Flames		NHL	75	13	20	33	116
NHL TOTALS			373	97	162	259	916

(c)—September, 1984—Signed by Calgary Flames as a free agent.

MARK OUIMET

Center ... 5'10'' ... 165 lbs. ... Born, London, Ont., October 2, 1971 ... Shoots left ... (August, 1989)—Pulled groin.

Year	Team	League	Games	G.	A.	Pts.	Pen.
1987-88—Strathroy Blades Jr. B.		OHA	47	28	36	64	12
1988-89—Strathroy Blades Jr. B.		OHA	42	43	50	93	20
1989-90—Univ. of Michigan (c)		CCHA	38	15	32	47	14

(c)—June 16, 1990—Selected by Washington Capitals in 1990 NHL entry draft. Fifth Capitals pick, 94th overall, fifth round.

GORDON PADDOCK

Defense ... 6' ... 180 lbs. ... Born, Hamiota, Man., February 15, 1964 ... Shoots right ... Brother of John Paddock.

Year	Team	League	Games	G.	A.	Pts.	Pen.
1981-82—Saskatoon Jays		SJHL	59	8	21	29	232
1982-83—Saskatoon Blades		WHL	67	4	25	29	158
1983-84—Brandon Wheat Kings		WHL	72	14	37	51	151
1984-85—Indianapolis Checkers		IHL	65	10	21	31	92
1984-85—Springfield Indians		AHL	12	0	2	2	24
1985-86—Indianapolis Checkers (c)		IHL	11	1	1	2	11
1985-86—Muskegon Lumberjacks		IHL	47	1	20	21	87
1985-86—Springfield Indians		AHL	20	1	1	2	52
1986-87—Springfield Indians		AHL	78	6	11	17	127
1987-88—Springfield Indians		AHL	74	8	26	34	127
1988-89—Hershey Bears		AHL	75	6	36	42	105
1989-90—Hershey Bears		AHL	65	4	19	23	60

(c)—November, 1985—Traded by Indianapolis Checkers to Muskegon Lumberjacks for Don Murdoch.

JIM PAEK

Defense ... 6' ... 188 lbs. ... Born, Weston, Ont., April 7, 1967 ... Shoots left ... (November 2, 1986)—Suspended for two games by OHL for being involved in a bench clearing incident vs. Peterborough.

Year	Team	League	Games	G.	A.	Pts.	Pen.
1983-84—St. Michael's Midget		OHA	39	8	26	34	21
1984-85—Oshawa Generals (c)		OHL	54	2	13	15	57
1985-86—Oshawa Generals		OHL	64	5	21	26	122
1986-87—Oshawa Generals		OHL	57	5	17	22	75
1987-88—Muskegon Lumberjacks		IHL	82	7	52	59	141
1988-89—Muskegon Lumberjacks		IHL	80	3	54	57	96
1989-90—Muskegon Lumberjacks		IHL	81	9	41	50	115

(c)—June, 1985—Drafted as underage junior by Pittsburgh Penguins in 1985 NHL entry draft. Ninth Penguins pick, 170th overall, ninth round.

SCOTT PALUCH

Defense ... 6'3'' ... 185 lbs. ... Born, Chicago, Ill., March 9, 1966 ... Shoots left ... Named to second all-star team at 1986 IIHF World Junior Championships as a member of Team USA.

Year	Team	League	Games	G.	A.	Pts.	Pen.
1983-84—Chicago Jets (c)		CJHL	50	44	46	90	42
1984-85—Bowling Green Univ.		CCHA	42	11	25	36	64
1985-86—Bowling Green Univ.		CCHA	34	10	11	21	44
1986-87—Bowling Green Univ.		CCHA	45	13	38	51	88
1987-88—Bowling Green Univ. (d)		CCHA	44	14	47	61	88
1988-89—Peoria Rivermen		IHL	81	10	39	49	92
1989-90—Peoria Rivermen		IHL	79	10	28	38	59

(c)—June, 1984—Drafted by St. Louis Blues in 1984 NHL entry draft. Seventh Blues pick, 92nd overall, fifth round.

(d)—Named First team All-America (West).

RUSSELL L. PARENT

Defense ... 5'9'' ... 180 lbs. ... Born, Winnipeg, Man., May 6, 1968 ... Shoots left ... (November, 1987)—Broken kneecap.

Year	Team	League	Games	G.	A.	Pts.	Pen.
1985-86—South Winnipeg Blues (c)		MJHL	47	16	65	81	106
1986-87—Univ. of North Dakota		WCHA	47	2	17	19	50
1987-88—Univ. of North Dakota		WCHA	30	4	20	24	38
1988-89—Univ. of North Dakota (b)		WCHA	40	9	28	37	51
1989-90—Univ. of North Dakota (a-d-e)		WCHA	45	9	50	59	86

(c)—June, 1986—Drafted by New York Rangers in 1986 NHL entry draft. Eleventh Rangers pick, 219th overall, 11th round.

(d)—June, 1989—NHL rights released by New York Rangers.

(e)—Named first Team NCAA All-America (West).

JEFF PARKER

Right Wing ... 6'3'' ... 198 lbs. ... Born, St. Paul, Minn., September 7, 1964 ... Shoots right ... Brother of John Parker ... (December, 1988)—Missed 28 games with a back injury ... (October, 1988)—Left the Rochester Americans ... (November 13, 1988)—Sprained knee vs. Edmonton ... (December, 1988)—Injured finger ... (March, 1989)—Sprained knee ... (March 16, 1990)—Sprained back vs. Toronto.

Year	Team	League	Games	G.	A.	Pts.	Pen.
1983-84—Michigan State Univ. (c)		CCHA	44	8	13	21	82
1984-85—Michigan State Univ.		CCHA	42	10	12	22	85
1985-86—Michigan State Univ.		CCHA	41	15	20	35	88
1986-87—Rochester Americans		AHL	54	14	8	22	75
1986-87—Buffalo Sabres		NHL	15	3	3	6	7
1987-88—Buffalo Sabres		NHL	4	0	2	2	2
1987-88—Rochester Americans		AHL	34	13	31	44	60
1988-89—Rochester Americans		AHL	6	2	4	6	9
1988-89—Buffalo Sabres		NHL	57	9	9	18	82
1989-90—Buffalo Sabres (d)		NHL	61	4	5	9	70
NHL TOTALS			137	16	19	35	161

(c)—June, 1982—Drafted by Buffalo Sabres in 1982 NHL entry draft. Ninth Sabres pick, 111th overall, sixth round.

(d)—June 16, 1990—Traded with Scott Arniel, Phil Housley and a first-round 1990 draft pick (Keith Tkachuk) by Buffalo Sabres to Winnipeg Jets for Dale Hawerchuk and a first-round 1990 draft pick (Brad May).

JOHN PARKER

Center ... 6'1'' ... 180 lbs. ... Born, St. Paul, Minn., March 5, 1968 ... Shoots right ... Brother of Jeff Parker.

Year	Team	League	Games	G.	A.	Pts.	Pen.
1984-85—White Bear Lake H.S.		Minn. H.S.	23	13	26	39	....
1985-86—White Bear Lake H.S. (c)		Minn. H.S.	24	12	13	25	....
1986-87—Univ. of Wisconsin		WCHA	8	0	1	1	4
1987-88—Univ. of Wisconsin		WCHA	4	0	0	0	6
1988-89—Univ. of Wisconsin		WCHA	20	1	7	8	16
1989-90—Univ. of Wisconsin		WCHA	35	11	9	20	22

(c)—June, 1986—Drafted by Calgary Flames in 1986 NHL entry draft. Fifth Flames pick, 121st overall, sixth round.

JEFF PARROTT

Defense ... 6'1'' ... 195 lbs. ... Born, The Pas, Man., April 6, 1971 ... Shoots right ... (November, 1988)—Strained knee ligaments.

Year	Team	League	Games	G.	A.	Pts.	Pen.
1987-88—Notre Dame Midget		Sask.	42	19	23	42	....
1988-89—Notre Dame Jr. A		SJHL	51	6	18	24	143
1989-90—Univ. of Minnesota/Duluth (c)		WCHA	35	1	6	7	64

(c)—June, 1990—Selected by Quebec Nordiques in 1990 NHL entry draft. Fourth Nordiques pick, 106th overall, sixth round.

BRAD PASCALL

Defense ... 6'2'' ... 192 lbs. ... Born, Coquitlam, B.C., July 29, 1970 ... Shoots left.

Year	Team	League	Games	G.	A.	Pts.	Pen.
1988-89—Univ. of North Dakota		WCHA	3	0	0	0	0
1989-90—Univ. of North Dakota (c)		WCHA	45	1	9	10	98

(c)—June 16, 1990—Selected by Buffalo Sabres in 1990 NHL entry draft. Fifth Sabres pick, 103rd overall, fifth round.

DAVE PASIN

Right Wing ... 6'1'' ... 195 lbs. ... Born, Edmonton, Alta., July 8, 1966 ... Shoots right ... (November, 1987)—Injured eye during Maine Mariners practice when struck by a puck.

Year	Team	League	Games	G.	A.	Pts.	Pen.
1982-83—Prince Albert Raiders		WHL	62	40	42	82	48
1983-84—Prince Albert Raiders (b-c)		WHL	71	68	54	122	68
1984-85—Prince Albert Raiders (b)		WHL	65	64	52	116	88
1985-86—Boston Bruins		NHL	71	18	19	37	50
1986-87—Moncton Golden Flames		AHL	66	27	25	52	47
1987-88—Maine Mariners		AHL	30	8	14	22	39
1988-89—Los Angeles Kings (d)		NHL	5	0	0	0	0
1988-89—Maine Mariners		AHL	11	2	5	7	6
1988-89—New Haven Nighthawks		AHL	48	25	23	48	42
1989-90—New Haven Nighthawks		AHL	7	7	4	11	14
1989-90—Played in Switzerland		Switzerland	....	...	...	....	....
1989-90—Springfield Indians (e)		AHL	11	2	3	5	2
NHL TOTALS			76	18	19	37	50

(c)—June, 1984—Drafted as underage junior by Boston Bruins in 1984 NHL entry draft. First Bruins pick, 19th overall, first round.

(d)—November 3, 1988—Traded by Boston Bruins to Los Angeles Kings for Paul Guay.

(e)—March 6, 1990—Claimed by New York Islanders on waivers from Los Angeles Kings after returning from playing in Switzerland.

GREGORY STEPHEN PASLAWSKI

Right Wing ... 5'11'' ... 195 lbs. ... Born, Kindersley, Sask., August 25, 1961 ... Shoots right ... (February 20, 1986)—Injured knee at N.Y. Rangers ... (December, 1986)—Injured knee ... (October, 1987)—Pinched nerve in left leg ... (November, 1987)—Disc surgery.

Year	Team	League	Games	G.	A.	Pts.	Pen.
1980-81—Prince Albert Raiders		SJHL	59	55	60	115	106
1981-82—Nova Scotia Voyageurs (c)		AHL	43	15	11	26	31
1982-83—Nova Scotia Voyageurs		AHL	75	46	42	88	32
1983-84—Montreal Canadiens (d)		NHL	26	1	4	5	4
1983-84—St. Louis Blues		NHL	34	8	6	14	7
1984-85—St. Louis Blues		NHL	72	22	20	42	21
1985-86—St. Louis Blues		NHL	56	22	11	33	18
1986-87—St. Louis Blues		NHL	76	29	35	64	27
1987-88—St. Louis Blues		NHL	17	1	5	6	4
1988-89—St. Louis Blues (e)		NHL	75	26	26	52	18
1989-90—Winnipeg Jets		NHL	71	18	30	48	14
NHL TOTALS			427	128	133	261	123

(c)—January, 1982—Signed by Montreal Canadiens as a free agent.
(d)—December, 1983—Traded with Doug Wickenheiser and Gilbert Delorme by Montreal Canadiens to St. Louis Blues for Perry Turnbull.
(e)—June 17, 1989—Traded with a third round 1989 draft pick (Kris Draper) by St. Louis Blues to Winnipeg Jets for a second-round 1989 draft pick (Denny Felsner).

ROD PASMA

Defense . . . 6'4" . . . 207 lbs. . . . Born, Hespler, Ont., February 26, 1972 . . . Shoots left.

Year	Team	League	Games	G.	A.	Pts.	Pen.
1988-89—Georgetown Raiders Jr. B	OHA	37	4	14	18	58
1989-90—Cornwall Royals (c)	OHL	64	3	16	19	142

(c)—June 16, 1990—Selected by Washington Capitals in 1990 NHL entry draft. Second Capitals pick, 30th overall, second round.

JOE ANDREW PATERSON

Left Wing and Center . . . 6'1" . . . 208 lbs. . . . Born, Toronto, Ont., June 25, 1960 . . . Shoots left . . . (October, 1982)—Pulled groin muscle . . . (October, 1987)—Pulled groin.

Year	Team	League	Games	G.	A.	Pts.	Pen.
1977-78—London Knights	OMJHL	68	17	16	33	100
1978-79—London Knights (c)	OMJHL	60	22	19	41	158
1979-80—London Knights	OMJHL	65	21	50	71	156
1979-80—Kalamazoo Wings	IHL	4	1	2	3	2
1980-81—Detroit Red Wings	NHL	38	2	5	7	53
1980-81—Adirondack Red Wings	AHL	39	9	16	25	68
1981-82—Adirondack Red Wings	AHL	74	22	28	50	132
1981-82—Detroit Red Wings	NHL	3	0	0	0	0
1982-83—Adirondack Red Wings	AHL	36	11	10	21	85
1982-83—Detroit Red Wings	NHL	33	2	1	3	14
1983-84—Detroit Red Wings	NHL	41	2	5	7	148
1983-84—Adirondack Red Wings (d)	AHL	20	10	15	25	43
1984-85—Hershey Bears	AHL	67	26	27	53	173
1984-85—Philadelphia Flyers	NHL	6	0	0	0	31
1985-86—Hershey Bears	AHL	20	5	10	15	68
1985-86—Philadelphia Flyers (e)	NHL	5	0	0	0	12
1985-86—Los Angeles Kings	NHL	47	9	18	27	153
1986-87—Los Angeles Kings	NHL	45	2	1	3	158
1987-88—Los Angeles Kings (f)	NHL	32	1	3	4	113
1987-88—New York Rangers	NHL	21	1	3	4	63
1988-89—New York Rangers	NHL	20	0	1	1	84
1988-89—Denver Rangers	IHL	9	5	4	9	31
1988-89—New Haven Nighthawks	AHL	7	0	0	0	24
1989-90—Flint Spirits	IHL	69	21	26	47	198
NHL TOTALS		291	19	37	56	829

(c)—August, 1979—Drafted by Detroit Red Wings as underage junior in 1979 NHL entry draft. Fifth Red Wings pick, 87th overall, fifth round.
(d)—October, 1984—Traded with Murray Craven by Detroit Red Wings to Philadelphia Flyers for Darryl Sittler.
(e)—December, 1985—Traded by Philadelphia Flyers to Los Angeles Kings for future considerations.
(f)—January, 1988—Traded by Los Angeles Kings to New York Rangers for Mike Siltala and Gord Walker.

JAMES PATRICK

Defense . . . 6'2" . . . 185 lbs. . . . Born, Winnipeg, Man., June 14, 1963 . . . Shoots right . . . Brother of Steve Patrick . . . (October, 1984)—Groin injury . . . (December 15, 1985)—Pinched nerve vs. Pittsburgh . . . (March, 1988)—Strained left knee ligaments . . . (December, 1988)—Bruised shoulder and chest . . . (March 13, 1989)—Pulled groin vs. Calgary.

Year	Team	League	Games	G.	A.	Pts.	Pen.
1980-81—Prince Albert Raiders (a-c-d)	SJHL	59	21	61	82	162
1981-82—Univ. of North Dakota (b-e)	WCHA	42	5	24	29	26
1982-83—Univ. of North Dakota	WCHA	36	12	36	48	29
1983-84—Canadian Olympic Team	Int'l	63	7	24	31	52
1983-84—New York Rangers	NHL	12	1	7	8	2
1984-85—New York Rangers	NHL	75	8	28	36	71
1985-86—New York Rangers	NHL	75	14	29	43	88
1986-87—New York Rangers	NHL	78	10	45	55	62
1987-88—New York Rangers	NHL	70	17	45	62	52
1988-89—New York Rangers	NHL	68	11	36	47	41
1989-90—New York Rangers	NHL	73	14	43	57	50
NHL TOTALS		451	75	233	308	366

(c)—June, 1981—Drafted by New York Rangers as underage player in 1981 NHL entry draft. First Rangers pick, ninth overall, first round.
(d)—Named Chapstick Player-of-the-Year as top Tier II Canadian Junior Player.
(e)—Named WCHA Rookie-of-the-Year.

COLIN PATTERSON

Right Wing . . . 6'2" . . . 195 lbs. . . . Born, Rexdale, Ont., May 11, 1960 . . . Shoots right . . . (March 14, 1984)—Shoulder injury . . . (January, 1985)—Torn knee ligaments . . . (October, 1987)—Pulled hamstring . . . (December, 1987)—Sprained ankle . . . (November, 1988)—Concussion . . . (January 11, 1989)—Bruised foot when he stopped a shot vs. Winnipeg . . . (April 24, 1989)—Broke nose when elbowed by Mike Allison vs. Los Angeles . . . (March 24, 1990)—Broke right ankle vs. Pittsburgh when he collided with Barry Pederson.

Year	Team	League	Games	G.	A.	Pts.	Pen.
1980-81—Clarkson College	ECAC	34	20	31	51	8
1981-82—Clarkson College	ECAC	35	21	31	52	32
1982-83—Clarkson College (b)	ECAC	31	23	29	52	30
1982-83—Colorado Flames (c)	CHL	7	1	1	2	0
1983-84—Colorado Flames	CHL	6	2	3	5	9

Year	Team	League	Games	G.	A.	Pts.	Pen.
1983-84—Calgary Flames	NHL	56	13	14	27	15
1984-85—Calgary Flames	NHL	57	22	21	43	5
1985-86—Calgary Flames	NHL	61	14	13	27	22
1986-87—Calgary Flames	NHL	68	13	13	26	41
1987-88—Calgary Flames	NHL	39	7	11	18	28
1988-89—Calgary Flames	NHL	74	14	24	38	56
1989-90—Calgary Flames	NHL	61	5	3	8	20
NHL TOTALS		416	88	99	187	187

(c)—March, 1983—Signed by Calgary Flames as a free agent.

DAVIS PAYNE

Left Wing . . . 6'1" . . . 190 lbs. . . . Born, King City, Ont., October 24, 1970 . . . Shoots left . . . (February 9, 1990)—During a stick-swinging incident with Brett Petersen, WCHA linesman Scott Zelkin stepped on his right hand, lacerating tendons in his index and middle fingers, and missed remainder of season.

Year	Team	League	Games	G.	A.	Pts.	Pen.
1988-89—Michigan Tech. Univ. (c)	WCHA	35	5	3	8	39
1989-90—Michigan Tech. Univ.	WCHA	30	11	10	21	81

(c)—June, 1989—Drafted by Edmonton Oilers in 1989 NHL entry draft. Sixth Oilers pick, 140th overall, seventh round.

KENT PAYNTER

Defense . . . 6' . . . 186 lbs. . . . Born, Summerside, P.E.I., April 27, 1965 . . . Shoots left.

Year	Team	League	Games	G.	A.	Pts.	Pen.
1981-82—Western Capitals	P.E.I.JHL	35	7	23	30	66
1982-83—Kitchener Rangers (c)	OHL	65	4	11	15	97
1983-84—Kitchener Rangers	OHL	65	9	27	36	94
1984-85—Kitchener Rangers	OHL	58	7	28	35	93
1985-86—Nova Scotia Oilers	AHL	23	1	2	3	36
1985-86—Saginaw Generals	IHL	4	0	1	1	2
1986-87—Nova Scotia Oilers	AHL	66	2	6	8	57
1987-88—Saginaw Hawks	IHL	74	8	20	28	141
1987-88—Chicago Black Hawks	NHL	2	0	0	0	2
1988-89—Chicago Black Hawks	NHL	1	0	0	0	2
1988-89—Saginaw Hawks (d)	IHL	69	12	14	26	148
1989-90—Washington Capitals	NHL	13	1	2	3	18
1989-90—Baltimore Skipjacks	AHL	60	7	20	27	110
NHL TOTALS		16	1	2	3	22

(c)—June, 1983—Drafted by Chicago Black Hawks as underage junior in 1983 NHL entry draft. Ninth Black Hawks pick, 159th overall, eighth round.
(d)—August, 1989—Signed by Washington Capitals as a free agent.

RANDY PEARCE

Left Wing . . . 5'11" . . . 203 lbs. . . . Born, Kitchener, Ont., February 23, 1970 . . . Shoots left.

Year	Team	League	Games	G.	A.	Pts.	Pen.
1986-87—Elmira Jr. B	OHA	42	22	24	46	28
1987-88—Kitchener Rangers	OHL	66	12	10	22	83
1988-89—Kitchener Rangers	OHL	64	23	21	44	87
1989-90—Kitchener Rangers (c)	OHL	62	31	34	65	139

(c)—June 16, 1990—Selected by Washington Capitals in 1990 NHL entry draft. Fourth Capitals pick, 72nd overall, fourth round.

ROB PEARSON

Right Wing . . . 6'1" . . . 175 lbs. . . . Born, Oshawa, Ont., August 3, 1971 . . . Shoots right . . . (November 13, 1988)—Broken wrist vs. Kingston . . . (August 15, 1989)—Dislocated right knee at Canadian National junior team camp . . . (February 7, 1990)—Suspended five games for checking Dale Craigwell from behind vs. Oshawa.

Year	Team	League	Games	G.	A.	Pts.	Pen.
1987-88—Oshawa Major Midget	OHA	72	68	65	133	188
1988-89—Belleville Bulls (c)	OHL	26	8	12	20	51
1989-90—Belleville Bulls	OHL	58	48	40	88	174

(c)—June, 1989—Drafted by Toronto Maple Leafs in 1989 NHL entry draft. Second Maple Leafs pick, 12th overall, first round.

SCOTT PEARSON

Left Wing . . . 6'1" . . . 205 lbs. . . . Born, Cornwall, Ont., December 19, 1969 . . . Shoots left . . . (May, 1988)—Surgery to left wrist.

Year	Team	League	Games	G.	A.	Pts.	Pen.
1984-85—Cornwall Midgets	OHA	60	40	40	80	60
1985-86—Kingston Canadians	OHL	63	16	23	39	56
1986-87—Kingston Canadians	OHL	62	30	24	54	101
1987-88—Kingston Canadians (c)	OHL	46	26	32	58	118
1988-89—Kingston Raiders	OHL	13	9	8	17	34
1988-89—Niagara Falls Thunder	OHL	32	26	34	60	90
1988-89—Toronto Maple Leafs	NHL	9	0	1	1	2
1989-90—Newmarket Saints	AHL	18	12	11	23	64
1989-90—Toronto Maple Leafs	NHL	41	5	10	15	90
NHL TOTALS		50	5	11	16	92

(c)—June, 1988—Drafted by Toronto Maple Leafs in 1988 NHL entry draft. First Maple Leafs pick, sixth overall, first round.

ALLEN PEDERSEN

Defense . . . 6'3" . . . 180 lbs. . . . Born, Edmonton, Alta., January 13, 1965 . . . Shoots left . . . (November 3, 1988)—Separated right shoulder when checked by Scott Young vs. Hartford . . . (December, 1988)—Pulled abdominal muscle . . . (December, 1989)—Sore back . . . (January, 1990)—Bruised hip.

Year	Team	League	Games	G.	A.	Pts.	Pen.
1982-83—Medicine Hat Tigers (c)	WHL	63	3	10	13	49
1983-84—Medicine Hat Tigers	WHL	44	0	11	11	47
1984-85—Medicine Hat Tigers	WHL	72	6	16	22	66
1985-86—Moncton Golden Flames	AHL	59	1	8	9	39
1986-87—Boston Bruins	NHL	79	1	11	12	71
1987-88—Boston Bruins	NHL	78	0	6	6	90
1988-89—Boston Bruins	NHL	51	0	6	6	69
1989-90—Boston Bruins	NHL	68	1	2	3	71
NHL TOTALS			276	2	25	27	301

(c)—June, 1983—Drafted as underage junior by Boston Bruins in 1983 NHL entry draft. Fifth Bruins pick, 102nd overall, fifth round.

BARRY ALAN PEDERSON

Center . . . 5'11" . . . 171 lbs. . . . Born, Big River, Sask., March 13, 1961 . . . Shoots right . . . (1981-82)—Set Boston Bruin rookie records with 44 goals and 92 points . . . (1982-83)—Became youngest player to ever lead Boston in scoring . . . (October 2, 1984)—Broke knuckle on right hand during fight with Mario Marois at Quebec . . . (January, 1985)—Surgery to remove a benign fibrous tumor from rear shoulder muscle of right arm. Doctors had to cut away parts of the muscle when they removed the growth and he missed remainder of season . . . Cousin of Brian Skrudland . . . (December 12, 1987)—Whiplash injury when he struck the back of a truck on the way to a game in Vancouver . . . (November 18, 1988)—Separated right shoulder vs. Pittsburgh . . . (February 12, 1989)—Broken nose when hit by Benoit Hogue vs. Buffalo . . . (March 5, 1989)—Broken collarbone when checked by Scott Stevens at Washington . . . (October 28, 1989)—Broke thumb vs. Calgary and missed 15 games.

Year	Team	League	Games	G.	A.	Pts.	Pen.
1977-78—Nanaimo	BCJHL	....	...	....	...	....
1977-78—Victoria Cougars	WCHL	3	1	4	5	2
1978-79—Victoria Cougars	WHL	72	31	53	84	41
1979-80—Victoria Cougars (b-c)	WHL	72	52	88	140	50
1980-81—Victoria Cougars (a)	WHL	55	65	82	147	65
1980-81—Boston Bruins	NHL	9	1	4	5	6
1981-82—Boston Bruins	NHL	80	44	48	92	53
1982-83—Boston Bruins	NHL	77	46	61	107	47
1983-84—Boston Bruins	NHL	80	39	77	116	64
1984-85—Boston Bruins	NHL	22	4	8	12	10
1985-86—Boston Bruins (d)	NHL	79	29	47	76	60
1986-87—Vancouver Canucks	NHL	79	24	52	76	50
1987-88—Vancouver Canucks	NHL	76	19	52	71	92
1988-89—Vancouver Canucks	NHL	62	15	26	41	22
1989-90—Vancouver Canucks (e)	NHL	16	2	7	9	10
1989-90—Pittsburgh Penguins	NHL	38	4	18	22	29
NHL TOTALS			618	227	400	627	443

(c)—June, 1980—Drafted as underage junior by Boston Bruins in 1980 NHL entry draft. First Bruins pick, 18th overall, first round.

(d)—June, 1986—Traded by Boston Bruins to Vancouver Canucks for Cam Neely and first round 1987 draft pick (Glen Wesley).

(e)—January 8, 1990—Traded with Tony Tanti annd Rod Buskas by Vancouver Canucks to Pittsburgh Penguins for Dan Quinn, Andrew McBain and Dave Capuano.

MARK PEDERSON

Left Wing . . . 6'1" . . . 195 lbs. . . . Born, Prelate, Sask., January 14, 1968 . . . Shoots left . . . (March, 1985)—Shoulder injury.

Year	Team	League	Games	G.	A.	Pts.	Pen.
1983-84—Cablevision Tigers	Alta. Midget	42	43	47	90	64
1984-85—Medicine Hat Tigers	WHL	71	42	40	82	63
1985-86—Medicine Hat Tigers (c)	WHL	72	46	60	106	46
1986-87—Medicine Hat Tigers (a)	WHL	69	56	46	102	58
1987-88—Medicine Hat Tigers (b)	WHL	62	53	58	111	55
1988-89—Sherbrooke Canadiens	AHL	75	43	38	81	53
1989-90—Montreal Canadiens	NHL	9	0	2	2	2
1989-90—Sherbrooke Canadiens (a)	AHL	72	53	42	95	60
NHL TOTALS			9	0	2	2	2

(c)—June, 1986—Drafted as underage junior by Montreal Canadiens in 1986 NHL entry draft. First Canadiens pick, 15th overall, first round.

TOM PEDERSON

Defense . . . 5'9" . . . 165 lbs. . . . Born, Bloomington, Minn., January 14, 1970 . . . Shoots right.

Year	Team	League	Games	G.	A.	Pts.	Pen.
1987-88—Bloomington Jefferson H.S.	Minn. H.S.	22	16	27	43	....
1988-89—Univ. of Minnesota (c)	WCHA	42	5	24	29	46
1989-90—Univ. of Minnesota	WCHA	43	8	30	38	58

(c)—June, 1989—Drafted by Minnesota North Stars in 1989 NHL entry draft. Twelfth North Stars pick, 217th overall, 11th round.

SCOTT PELLERIN

Left Wing . . . 5'10" . . . 185 lbs. . . . Born, Shediac, N.B., January 9, 1970 . . . Shoots left.

Year	Team	League	Games	G.	A.	Pts.	Pen.
1987-88—Notre Dame Hounds	SJHL	57	37	49	86	139
1988-89—Univ. of Maine (c-d-e)	H. East	45	29	33	62	92
1989-90—Univ. of Maine	H. East	42	22	34	56	68

(c)—Named to Hockey East All-Rookie team.

(d)—Named Hockey East co-Rookie-of-the-Year with Rob Gaudreau.

(e)—June, 1989—Drafted by New Jersey Devils in 1989 NHL entry draft. Fourth Devils pick, 47th overall, third round.

PEKEKA PELTOLA

Center . . . 6'2" . . . 196 lbs. . . . Born, Helsinki, Finland, June 24, 1965 . . . Shoots right.

Year	Team	League	Games	G.	A.	Pts.	Pen.
1988-89—Helsinki HPK (c)	Finland	43	28	30	58	62
1989-90—Helsinki HPK	Finland	44	25	24	49	42

(c)—June, 1989—Selected by Winnipeg Jets in 1989 NHL entry draft. Eighth Jets pick, 130th overall, sixth round.

MIKE PELUSO

Defense . . . 6'4" . . . 200 lbs. . . . Born, Hibbing, Minn., November 8, 1965 . . . Shoots left.

Year	Team	League	Games	G.	A.	Pts.	Pen.
1984-85—Stratford (c)	OPJHL	52	11	45	56	114
1985-86—Univ. of Alaska/Anchorage	GWHC	32	2	11	13	59
1986-87—Univ. of Alaska/Anchorage	GWCH	30	5	21	26	68
1987-88—Univ. of Alaska/Anchorage	GWCH	35	4	33	37	76
1988-89—Univ. of Alaska/Anchorage	GWCH	....	...	...	...	...
1989-90—Indianapolis Ice	IHL	75	7	10	17	279
1989-90—Chicago Black Hawks	NHL	2	0	0	0	15
NHL TOTALS			2	0	0	0	15

(c)—June, 1985—Drafted by New Jersey Devils in 1985 NHL entry draft. Tenth Devils pick, 190th ovrall, 10th round.

JACKSON PENNEY

Center . . . 5'10" . . . 178 lbs. . . . Born, Edmonton, Alta., February 5, 1969 . . . Shoots left.

Year	Team	League	Games	G.	A.	Pts.	Pen.
1987-88—Victoria Cougars	WHL	53	22	36	58	31
1988-89—Victoria Cougars (a-c)	WHL	63	41	49	90	78
1989-90—Victoria Cougars (d)	WHL	3	0	1	1	4
1989-90—Prince Albert Raiders (b)	WHL	55	53	32	85	51

(c)—June, 1989—Drafted by Boston Bruins in 1989 NHL entry draft. Fourth Bruins pick, 80th overall, fourth round.

(d)—October 23, 1989—Traded by Victoria Cougars to Prince Albert Raiders for Terry Bendera. He did not report until November 1.

JIM DESMOND PEPLINSKI

Center . . . 6'2" . . . 201 lbs. . . . Born, Renfrew, Ont., October 24, 1960 . . . Shoots right . . . (September, 1987)—Fractured sinus vs. Winnipeg.

Year	Team	League	Games	G.	A.	Pts.	Pen.
1977-78—Toronto Marlboros	OMJHL	66	13	28	41	44
1978-79—Toronto Marlboros (c)	OMJHL	66	23	32	55	60
1979-80—Toronto Marlboros	OMJHL	67	35	66	101	89
1980-81—Calgary Flames	NHL	80	13	25	38	108
1981-82—Calgary Flames	NHL	74	30	37	67	115
1982-83—Calgary Flames	NHL	80	15	26	41	134
1983-84—Calgary Flames	NHL	74	11	22	33	114
1984-85—Calgary Flames	NHL	80	16	29	45	111
1985-86—Calgary Flames	NHL	77	24	35	59	214
1986-87—Calgary Flames	NHL	80	18	32	50	181
1987-88—Calgary Flames	NHL	75	20	31	51	234
1987-88—Canadian Olympic Team	Olympics	7	0	1	1	6
1988-89—Calgary Flames	NHL	79	13	25	38	241
1989-90—Calgary Flames (d)	NHL	6	1	0	1	4
NHL TOTALS			705	161	262	423	1456

(c)—August, 1979—Drafted by Atlanta Flames as underage junior in 1979 NHL entry draft. Fifth Flames pick, 75th overall, fourth round.

(d)—October 31, 1989—Announced his retirement.

NICOLAS PERREAULT

Defense . . . 6'3" . . . 200 lbs. . . . Born, Lorettville, Que., April 24, 1972 . . . Shoots left . . . (April, 1988)—Separated shoulder.

Year	Team	League	Games	G.	A.	Pts.	Pen.
1986-87—Charlesbourg Elans Bantam	Quebec	30	6	20	26	40
1987-88—Charlesbourg Elans Bantam	Quebec	15	10	15	25	30
1987-88—Ste. Foy Gouveneurs Midget	Quebec	23	1	2	3	24
1988-89—Ste. Foy Gouveneurs Midget	Quebec	38	8	15	23	89
1989-90—Hawksbury Hawks (c)	QMJHL	46	22	34	56	188

(c)—June 16, 1990—Selected by Calgary Flames in 1990 NHL entry draft. Second Flames pick, 26th overall, second round.

BRETT PETERSON

Defense . . . 6'2" . . . 195 lbs. . . . Born, St. Paul, Minn., February 1, 1969 . . . Shoots right.

Year	Team	League	Games	G.	A.	Pts.	Pen.
1986-87—Roseville H.S.	Minn. H.S.	26	7	15	22	....
1987-88—St. Paul Vulcans (c)	USHL	37	2	9	11	68
1988-89—St. Paul Vulcans	USHL	....	...	...	...	...
1988-89—Univ. of Denver	WCHA	19	0	3	3	4
1989-90—Univ. of Denver	WCHA	34	3	6	9	23

(c)—June, 1988—Drafted by Calgary Flames in 1988 NHL entry draft. Ninth Flames pick, 189th overall, ninth round.

MICHEL PETIT

Defense . . . 6'1" . . . 185 lbs. . . . Born, St. Malo, Que., February 12, 1964 . . . Shoots right . . . (March, 1984)—Separated shoulder . . . (February, 1987)—Knee injury . . . (December, 1987)—Pulled groin . . . (December 27, 1988)—Fractured right collarbone when checked by John MacLean at New Jersey and missed 11 games.

Year	Team	League	Games	G.	A.	Pts.	Pen.
1980-81—St. Foy Midget AAA	QAAAMHL	48	10	45	55	84
1981-82—Sherbrooke Beavers (a-c-d-e)	QMJHL	63	10	39	49	106
1982-83—St. Jean Beavers (a)	QMJHL	62	19	67	86	196
1982-83—Vancouver Canucks	NHL	2	0	0	0	0
1983-84—Vancouver Canucks	NHL	44	6	9	15	53
1984-85—Vancouver Canucks	NHL	69	5	26	31	127
1985-86—Fredericton Express	AHL	25	0	13	13	79
1985-86—Vancouver Canucks	NHL	32	1	6	7	27
1986-87—Vancouver Canucks	NHL	69	12	13	25	131
1987-88—Vancouver Canucks (f)	NHL	10	0	3	3	35
1987-88—New York Rangers	NHL	64	9	24	33	223
1988-89—New York Rangers	NHL	69	8	25	33	156
1989-90—Quebec Nordiques (g)	NHL	63	12	24	36	215
NHL TOTALS		422	53	130	183	967

(c)—Winner of Raymond Lagace Trophy (Top Rookie Defenseman).
(d)—Winner of the Association of Journalist of Hockey Trophy (Top Pro Prospect).
(e)—June, 1982—Drafted as underage junior by Vancouver Canucks in 1982 NHL entry draft. First Canucks pick, 11th overall, first round.
(f)—November, 1987—Traded by Vancouver Canucks to New York Rangers for Willie Huber and Larry Melnyk.
(g)—October 5, 1989—Traded by New York Rangers to Quebec Nordiques for Randy Moller.

MICHEL PICARD

Left Wing . . . 5'11" . . . 190 lbs. . . . Born, Beauport, Que., November 7, 1969 . . . Shoots left.

Year	Team	League	Games	G.	A.	Pts.	Pen.
1986-87—Trois-Rivieres Draveurs	QMJHL	66	33	35	68	53
1987-88—Trois-Rivieres Draveurs	QMJHL	69	40	55	95	71
1988-89—Trois-Rivieres Draveurs (c)	QMJHL	66	59	81	140	107
1989-90—Binghamton Whalers	AHL	67	16	24	40	98

(c)—June, 1989—Drafted by Hartford Whalers in 1989 NHL entry draft. Eighth Whalers pick, 178th overall, ninth round.

ROBERT RENE JOSEPH PICARD

Defense . . . 6'2" . . . 203 lbs. . . . Born, Montreal, Que., May 25, 1957 . . . Shoots left . . . Nephew of former NHL defenseman Noel Picard . . . (November 12, 1980)—Strained knee ligaments . . . (January, 1983)—Broken bone in foot . . . (September, 1985)—Concussion in training camp . . . (January 4, 1986)—Cut hand at Detroit . . . (October, 1987)—Injured ligaments in left knee . . . (February 6, 1988)—Crushed lumbar vertebrae at Boston . . . (October, 1988)—Missed two weeks with bruised right shoulder . . . (January 2, 1990)—Sprained right ankle vs. Vancouver . . . (February 19, 1990)—Reinjured ankle vs. Montreal and missed six games.

Year	Team	League	Games	G.	A.	Pts.	Pen.
1973-74—Montreal Red, White and Blue	QMJHL	70	7	46	53	296
1974-75—Montreal Red, White and Blue	QMJHL	70	13	74	87	339
1975-76—Montreal Juniors (b)	QMJHL	72	14	67	81	282
1976-77—Montreal Juniors (a-c-d)	QMJHL	70	32	60	92	267
1977-78—Washington Capitals	NHL	75	10	27	37	101
1978-79—Washington Capitals	NHL	77	21	44	65	85
1979-80—Washington Capitals (e)	NHL	78	11	43	54	122
1980-81—Toronto Maple Leafs (f)	NHL	59	6	19	25	68
1980-81—Montreal Canadiens	NHL	8	2	2	4	6
1981-82—Montreal Canadiens	NHL	62	2	26	28	106
1982-83—Montreal Canadiens	NHL	64	7	31	38	60
1983-84—Montreal Canadiens (g)	NHL	7	0	2	2	0
1983-84—Winnipeg Jets	NHL	62	6	16	22	34
1984-85—Winnipeg Jets	NHL	78	12	22	34	107
1985-86—Winnipeg Jets (h)	NHL	20	2	5	7	17
1985-86—Quebec Nordiques	NHL	48	7	27	34	36
1986-87—Quebec Nordiques	NHL	78	8	20	28	71
1987-88—Quebec Nordiques	NHL	65	3	13	16	103
1988-89—Quebec Nordiques	NHL	74	7	14	21	61
1989-90—Quebec Nordiques (i)	NHL	24	0	5	5	28
1989-90—Detroit Red Wings	NHL	20	0	3	3	20
NHL TOTALS		899	104	319	423	1025

(c)—Outstanding Defenseman in QJHL.
(d)—Drafted from Montreal Juniors by Washington Capitals in first round of 1977 amateur draft.
(e)—June, 1980—Traded with Tim Coulis and second round draft choice in 1980 (Bob McGill) by Washington Capitals to Toronto Maple Leafs for Mike Palmateer and third round draft choice (Torrie Robertson).
(f)—March, 1981—Traded by Toronto Maple Leafs with a future eighth round draft pick to Montreal Canadiens for Michel Larocque.
(g)—November, 1983—Traded by Montreal Canadiens to Winnipeg Jets for third-round 1984 draft pick (Patrick Roy).
(h)—November, 1985—Traded by Winnipeg Jets to Quebec Nordiques for Mario Marois.
(i)—December 3, 1989—Traded with Greg C. Adams by Quebec Nordiques to Detroit Red Wings for Tony McKegney.

DAVE PICHETTE

Defense . . . 6'3" . . . 195 lbs. . . . Born, Grand Falls, N. B., February 4, 1960 . . . Shoots left . . . (January, 1983)—Back injury . . . (January 8, 1986)—Concussion at Chicago and missed eight games.

Year	Team	League	Games	G.	A.	Pts.	Pen.
1978-79—Quebec Remparts	QMJHL	57	10	16	26	134
1979-80—Quebec Remparts	QMJHL	56	8	19	27	129
1980-81—Quebec Nordiques (c)	NHL	46	4	16	20	62
1980-81—Hershey Bears	AHL	20	2	3	5	37
1981-82—Quebec Nordiques	NHL	67	7	30	37	152
1982-83—Fredericton Express	AHL	16	3	11	14	14

Year	Team	League	Games	G.	A.	Pts.	Pen.
1982-83—Quebec Nordiques	NHL	53	3	21	24	49
1983-84—Fredericton Express	AHL	10	2	1	3	13
1983-84—Quebec Nordiques (d)	NHL	23	2	7	9	12
1983-84—St. Louis Blues	NHL	23	0	11	11	6
1984-85—New Jersey Devils (e)	NHL	71	17	40	57	41
1985-86—Maine Mariners	AHL	25	4	15	19	28
1985-86—New Jersey Devils	NHL	33	7	12	19	22
1987-88—New York Rangers	NHL	6	1	3	4	4
1987-88—New Haven Nighthawks	AHL	46	10	21	31	37
1988-89—Cape Breton Oilers (f)	AHL	39	5	21	26	20
1989-90—Halifax Citadels (g-h)	AHL	58	3	18	21	65
NHL TOTALS		322	41	140	181	348

(c)—September, 1980—Signed by Quebec Nordiques as a free agent.
(d)—February, 1984—Traded by Quebec Nordiques to St. Louis Blues for Andre Dore.
(e)—October, 1984—Drafted by New Jersey Devils in NHL waiver draft.
(f)—December, 1988—Claimed on AHL waivers by Cape Breton Oilers from Moncton Hawks after he returned from Europe.
(g)—September 1, 1989—Named player/assistant coach of Halifax Citadels.
(h)—February 4, 1990—Named interim head coach of Halifax Citadels.

RICHARD PILON

Defense . . . 5'11" . . . 197 lbs. . . . Born, Saskatoon, Sask., April 30, 1968 . . . Shoots left . . . (December, 1988)—Swollen right leg . . . (November 4, 1989)—Right eye struck by a Brent Fedyk slapshot vs. Vancouver and was out remainder of season.

Year	Team	League	Games	G.	A.	Pts.	Pen.
1984-85—Prince Albert Midget Raiders	Sask. Midg.	26	3	11	14	41
1985-86—Prince Albert Midget Raiders	Sask. Midg.	35	3	28	31	142
1985-86—Prince Albert Raiders (c)	WHL	6	0	0	0	0
1986-87—Prince Albert Raiders	WHL	68	4	21	25	192
1987-88—Prince Albert Raiders (b)	WHL	65	13	34	47	177
1988-89—New York Islanders	NHL	62	0	14	14	242
1989-90—New York Islanders	NHL	14	0	2	2	31
NHL TOTALS		76	0	16	16	273

(c)—June, 1986—Drafted as underage junior by New York Islanders in 1986 NHL entry draft. Ninth Islanders pick, 143rd overall, seventh round.

LANCE PITLICK

Defense . . . 6' . . . 185 lbs. . . . Born, Fridley, Minn., November 5, 1967 . . . Shoots right . . . (December 1, 1989)—Severely pulled lower abdominal muscles . . . (January 18, 1990)—Surgery to have tendons sewn onto his abdominal muscle for reinforcement.

Year	Team	League	Games	G.	A.	Pts.	Pen.
1984-85—Cooper H.S.	Minn. H.S.	23	8	4	12	....
1985-86—Cooper H.S. (c)	Minn. H.S.	21	17	8	25	....
1986-87—Univ. of Minnesota	WCHA	45	0	9	9	88
1987-88—Univ. of Minnesota	WCHA	38	3	9	12	76
1988-89—Univ. of Minnesota	WCHA	47	4	9	13	95
1989-90—Univ. of Minnesota	WCHA	14	3	2	5	26

(c)—June, 1986—Drafted by Minnesota North Stars in 1986 NHL entry draft. Tenth North Stars pick, 180th overall, ninth round.

MICHAL PIVONKA

Center . . . 6'2" . . . 192 lbs. . . . Born, Kladno, Czechoslovakia, January 28, 1966 . . . Shoots left . . . (March, 1987)—Strained ankle ligaments . . . (October, 1987)—Sprained right wrist . . . (March, 1988)—Sprained left ankle . . . (March 9, 1990)—Sprained left knee vs. Quebec.

Year	Team	League	Games	G.	A.	Pts.	Pen.
1985-86—Dukla Jihlava (c)	Czech.	....	....	....	....	....
1986-87—Washington Capitals	NHL	73	18	25	43	41
1987-88—Washington Capitals	NHL	71	11	23	34	28
1988-89—Baltimore Skipjacks	AHL	31	12	24	36	19
1988-89—Washington Capitals	NHL	52	8	19	27	30
1989-90—Washington Capitals	NHL	77	25	39	64	54
NHL TOTALS		273	62	106	168	153

(c)—June, 1984—Drafted by Washington Capitals in 1984 NHL entry draft. Third Capitals pick, 59th overall, third round.

DAN PLANTE

Right Wing . . . 5'11" . . . 190 lbs. . . . Born, St. Louis, Mo., October 5, 1971 . . . Shoots right . . . Plans to attend University of Wisconsin.

Year	Team	League	Games	G.	A.	Pts.	Pen.
1988-89—Edina H. S.	Minn. H. S.	27	10	26	36	12
1989-90—Edina H. S. (c)	Minn. H. S.	24	8	18	26	....

(c)—June 16, 1990—Selected by New York Islanders in 1990 NHL entry draft. Third Islanders pick, 48th overall, third round.

DEREK PLANTE

Center . . . 5'11" . . . 160 lbs. . . . Born, Cloquet, Minn., January 17, 1971 . . . Shoots left . . . (March, 1988)—Broken arm . . . (December 15, 1989)—Injured collarbone vs. Univ. of Alberta . . . (January 20, 1990)—Reinjured collarbone vs. Univ. of Minnesota.

Year	Team	League	Games	G.	A.	Pts.	Pen.
1987-88—Cloquet H.S.	Minn.	23	16	25	41	..
1988-89—Cloquet H.S. (c)	Minn.	24	30	33	63	..
1989-90—Univ. of Minnesota/Duluth	WCHA	28	10	11	21	12

(c)—June, 1989—Drafted by Buffalo Sabres in 1989 NHL entry draft. Seventh Sabres pick, 161st overall, eighth round.

ADRIEN PLAVSIC

Defense . . . 6' . . . 190 lbs. . . . Born, Montreal, Que., January 13, 1970 . . . Shoots left . . . (September 25, 1989)—Concussion when checked by Shawn Burr vs. Detroit.

Year	Team	League	Games	G.	A.	Pts.	Pen.
1986-87—Lac St. Louis Midget	Que. Midget	42	8	27	35	22
1987-88—Univ. of New Hampshire (c)	H. East	30	5	6	11	456
1988-89—Canadian National Team	Int'l.	62	5	10	15	25
1989-90—Peoria Rivermen	IHL	51	7	14	21	87
1989-90—St. Louis Blues (d)	NHL	4	0	1	1	2
1989-90—Vancouver Canucks	NHL	11	3	2	5	8
1989-90—Milwaukee Admirals	IHL	3	1	2	3	14
NHL TOTALS			15	3	3	6	10

(c)—June, 1988—Drafted by St. Louis Blues in 1988 NHL entry draft. Second Blues pick, 30th overall, second round.

(d)—March 6, 1990—Traded with first-round 1990 draft pick and a second-round 1991 draft pick by St. Louis Blues to Vancouver Canucks for Rich Sutter, Harold Snepsts and the Blues' second-round 1990 draft pick that had been traded to Vancouver in an earlier deal.

JIM PLAYFAIR

Defense . . . 6'3" . . . 200 lbs. . . . Born, Vanderhoof, B.C., May 22, 1964 . . . Shoots left . . . Brother of Larry Playfair . . . (November, 1984)—Severe groin pull . . . (February, 1987)—Bruised liver at Sherbrooke . . . (October 18, 1988)—Bruised left shoulder at Detroit . . . (November, 1988)—Strained back . . . (March, 1990)—Sore back.

Year	Team	League	Games	G.	A.	Pts.	Pen.
1980-81—Fort Saskatchewan	AJHL	31	2	17	19	105
1981-82—Portland Winter Hawks (c)	WHL	70	4	13	17	121
1982-83—Portland Winter Hawks	WHL	63	8	27	35	218
1983-84—Portland Winter Hawks	WHL	16	5	6	11	38
1983-84—Calgary Wranglers	WHL	44	6	9	15	96
1983-84—Edmonton Oilers	NHL	2	1	1	2	2
1984-85—Nova Scotia Oilers	AHL	41	0	4	4	107
1985-86—Nova Scotia Oilers	AHL	73	2	12	14	160
1986-87—Nova Scotia Oilers (d)	AHL	60	1	21	22	82
1987-88—Saginaw Hawks	IHL	50	5	21	26	133
1987-88—Chicago Black Hawks	NHL	12	1	3	4	21
1988-89—Saginaw Hawks	IHL	23	3	6	9	73
1988-89—Chicago Black Hawks	NHL	7	0	0	0	28
1989-90—Indianapolis Ice	IHL	67	7	24	31	137
NHL TOTALS			21	2	4	6	51

(c)—June, 1982—Drafted by Edmonton Oilers in 1982 NHL entry draft. First Oilers pick, 20th overall, first round.

(d)—August, 1987—Signed by Chicago Black Hawks as a free agent.

LARRY WILLIAM PLAYFAIR

Defense . . . 6'4" . . . 215 lbs. . . . Born, Fort St. James, B.C., June 23, 1958 . . . Shoots left . . . (October 9, 1980)—Severely cut right hand kept him out of Sabres lineup for 10 days . . . Brother of Jim Playfair . . . (April, 1983)—Chipped bone in right elbow vs. Boston . . . (January, 1986)—Injured shoulder . . . (March 1, 1986)—Injured left knee . . . (May, 1986)—Shoulder surgery . . . (December 17, 1986)—Injured left knee when he collided with Terry Ruskowski vs. Pittsburgh . . . (January, 1987)—Surgery to left knee . . . (January 31, 1987)—Reinjured knee at Montreal . . . (February 19, 1987)—Reconstructive surgery to left knee . . . (November, 1987)—Reconstructive knee surgery . . . (March, 1988)—Bruised chest . . . (December 1, 1989)—Pulled hamstring at New Jersey . . . (February, 1990)—Strained back.

Year	Team	League	Games	G.	A.	Pts.	Pen.
1975-76—Langley	Jr. "A"BCHL	72	10	20	30	162
1976-77—Portland Winter Hawks	WCHL	65	2	17	19	199
1977-78—Portland Winter Hawks (a-c)	WCHL	71	13	19	32	402
1978-79—Buffalo Sabres	NHL	26	0	3	3	60
1978-79—Hershey Bears	AHL	45	0	12	12	148
1979-80—Buffalo Sabres	NHL	79	2	10	12	145
1980-81—Buffalo Sabres	NHL	75	3	9	12	169
1981-82—Buffalo Sabres	NHL	77	6	10	16	258
1982-83—Buffalo Sabres	NHL	79	4	13	17	180
1983-84—Buffalo Sabres	NHL	76	5	11	16	211
1984-85—Buffalo Sabres	NHL	72	3	14	17	157
1985-86—Buffalo Sabres (d)	NHL	47	1	2	3	100
1985-86—Los Angeles Kings	NHL	14	0	1	1	26
1986-87—Los Angeles Kings	NHL	37	2	7	9	181
1987-88—Los Angeles Kings	NHL	54	0	7	7	197
1988-89—Los Angeles Kings (e)	NHL	6	0	3	3	16
1988-89—Buffalo Sabres	NHL	42	0	3	3	110
1989-90—Buffalo Sabres (f)	NHL	4	0	1	1	2
NHL TOTALS			688	26	94	120	1812

(c)—Drafted from Portland Winter Hawks by Buffalo Sabres in first round of 1978 amateur draft.

(d)—January, 1986—Traded with Sean McKenna and Ken Baumgartner by Buffalo Sabres to Los Angeles Kings for Brian Engblom and Doug Smith.

(e)—October 16, 1988—Traded by Los Angeles Kings to Buffalo Sabres for Bob Logan and ninth-round 1989 draft pick (Jim Giacin).

(f)—August, 1990—Announced his retirement.

TREVOR POCHIPINSKI

Defense . . . 6'2" . . . 190 lbs. . . . Born, Prince Albert, Sask., July 8, 1968 . . . Shoots right.

Year	Team	League	Games	G.	A.	Pts.	Pen.
1986-87—Penticton Knights (c)	BCJHL	..	..	..	..	..
1987-88—Colorado College	WCHA	37	2	6	8	91

Year	Team	League	Games	G.	A.	Pts.	Pen.
1988-89—Colorado College	WCHA	40	4	10	14	74
1989-90—Colorado College	WCHA	40	5	13	18	54

(c)—June, 1986—Drafted by Los Angeles Kings in 1986 NHL entry draft. Ninth Kings pick, 170th overall, ninth round.

WALT MICHAEL PODDUBNY

Center . . . 6'1" . . . 203 lbs. . . . Born, Thunder Bay, Ont. February 14, 1960 . . . Shoots left . . . (October, 1982)—Injured leg . . . Shares Toronto goal scoring record for rookies (28) with Peter Ihnacak . . . (October, 1983)—Broken ankle . . . (February, 1985)—Broke thumb in AHL game . . . (September, 1985)—Infected foot during training camp . . . (December, 1986)—Injured hip . . . (December 21, 1986)—Concussion vs. Hartford . . . (October, 1988)—Sprained left knee . . . (March 23, 1989)—Took 20 stitches and a broken nose when struck by an Ulf Samuelsson shot vs. Hartford . . . (October, 1989)—Recurring back injury and missed 26 games . . . (February 19, 1990)—Tore cruciate ligament of right knee when he fell with Kelly Kisio vs. N.Y. Rangers and missed final 20 games of season.

Year	Team	League	Games	G.	A.	Pts.	Pen.
1978-79—Brandon Wheat Kings	WHL	20	11	11	22	12
1979-80—Kitchener Rangers	OMJHL	19	3	9	12	35
1979-80—Kingston Canadians (c)	OMJHL	43	30	17	47	36
1980-81—Milwaukee Admirals	IHL	5	4	2	6	4
1980-81—Wichita Wind	CHL	70	21	29	50	207
1981-82—Edmonton Oilers (d)	NHL	4	0	0	0	0
1981-82—Wichita Wind	CHL	60	35	46	81	79
1981-82—Toronto Maple Leafs	NHL	11	3	4	7	8
1982-83—Toronto Maple Leafs	NHL	72	28	31	59	71
1983-84—Toronto Maple Leafs	NHL	38	11	14	25	48
1984-85—St. Catharines Saints	AHL	8	5	7	12	10
1984-85—Toronto Maple Leafs	NHL	32	5	15	20	26
1985-86—St. Catharines Saints	AHL	37	28	27	55	52
1985-86—Toronto Maple Leafs (e)	NHL	33	12	22	34	25
1986-87—New York Rangers	NHL	75	40	47	87	49
1987-88—New York Rangers (f)	NHL	77	38	50	88	76
1988-89—Quebec Nordiques (g)	NHL	72	38	37	75	107
1989-90—Utica Devils	AHL	2	1	2	3	0
1989-90—New Jersey Devils	NHL	33	4	10	14	28
NHL TOTALS			447	179	230	409	438

(c)—June, 1980—Drafted by Edmonton Oilers in 1980 NHL entry draft. Fourth Oilers pick, 90th overall, fifth round.

(d)—March, 1982—Traded with NHL rights to Phil Drouillard by Edmonton Oilers to Toronto Maple Leafs for Laurie Boschman.

(e)—August, 1986—Traded by Toronto Maple Leafs to New York Rangers for Mike Allison.

(f)—August, 1988—Traded with Bruce Bell and Jari Gronstrand and a fourth-round draft choice in 1989 by New York Rangers to Quebec Nordiques for Normand Rochefort and Jason Lafreniere.

(g)—June 17, 1989—Traded by Quebec Nordiques to New Jersey Devils for Claude Loiselle and Joe Cirella.

RUDY POESCHEK

Defense . . . 6'2" . . . 205 lbs. . . . Born, Terrace, B.C., September 29, 1966 . . . Shoots right . . . (December, 1984)—Knee injury . . . (November, 1986)—Injured shoulder . . . (December, 1988)—Played 11 games at Right Wing . . . (February, 1989)—Bruised right hand.

Year	Team	League	Games	G.	A.	Pts.	Pen.
1983-84—Kamloops Jr. Oilers	WHL	47	3	9	12	93
1984-85—Kamloops Blazers (c)	WHL	34	6	7	13	100
1985-86—Kamloops Blazers	WHL	32	3	13	16	92
1986-87—Kamloops Blazers	WHL	54	13	18	31	153
1987-88—New York Rangers	NHL	1	0	0	0	2
1987-88—Colorado Rangers	IHL	82	7	31	38	210
1988-89—Denver Rangers	IHL	2	0	0	0	6
1988-89—New York Rangers	NHL	52	0	2	2	199
1989-90—Flint Spirits	IHL	38	8	13	21	109
1989-90—New York Rangers	NHL	15	0	0	0	55
NHL TOTALS			68	0	2	2	256

(c)—June, 1985—Drafted as underage junior by New York Rangers in 1985 NHL entry draft. Twelfth Rangers pick, 238th overall, 12th round.

MICHAEL POSMA

Defense . . . 6'1" . . . 195 lbs. . . . Born, Utica, N.Y., December 16, 1967 . . . Shoots right.

Year	Team	League	Games	G.	A.	Pts.	Pen.
1984-85—Buffalo Junior Sabres	NAJHL	43	4	28	32	....
1985-86—Buffalo Junior Sabres (c)	NAJHL	40	16	47	63	62
1986-87—Western Michigan Univ.	CCHA	35	12	20	32	46
1987-88—Western Michigan Univ.	CCHA	42	16	38	54	30
1988-89—Western Michigan Univ.	CCHA	43	7	34	41	58
1989-90—Western Michigan Univ.	CCHA	39	8	28	36	28

(c)—June, 1986—Drafted by St. Louis Blues in 1986 NHL entry draft. Second Blues pick, 31st overall, second round.

MARC POTVIN

Right Wing . . . 6'1" . . . 185 lbs. . . . Born, Ottawa, Ont., January 29, 1967 . . . Shoots right.

Year	Team	League	Games	G.	A.	Pts.	Pen.
1985-86—Stratford (c)	OPJHL	63	5	6	11	117
1986-87—Bowling Green Univ.	CCHA	43	5	15	20	74
1987-88—Bowling Green Univ.	CCHA	45	15	21	36	80
1988-89—Bowling Green Univ.	CCHA	46	23	12	35	63
1989-90—Bowling Green Univ.	CCHA	40	19	17	36	72
1989-90—Adirondack Red Wings	AHL	5	2	1	3	9

(c)—June, 1986—Drafted by Detroit Red Wings in 1986 NHL entry draft. Ninth Red Wings pick, 169th overall, ninth round.

DAVE POULIN

Center . . . 5'11" . . . 175 lbs. . . . Born, Mississauga, Ont., December 17, 1958 . . . Shoots left . . . (1983-84)—Set Philadelphia record for most points by a rookie . . . (November, 1986)—Pulled hamstring and groin muscle . . . (April 16, 1987)—Cracked rib at N.Y. Rangers . . . (February, 1988)—Pulled groin . . . (November, 1988)—Separated shoulder . . . (December 15, 1988)—Sent home due to irregular heartbeat at Washington . . . (January, 1989)—Bruised right hand . . . (April 8, 1989)—Fractured ring finger of right hand vs. Washington . . . (May, 1989)—suffered a multiple fracture of left thumb . . . (October, 1989)—Abdominal bruise . . . (October 28, 1989)—Broke left thumb at Minnesota . . . (April 21, 1990)—Hit in the side of neck, stretching a nerve that runs down his shoulder and left arm vs. Montreal.

Year	Team	League	Games	G.	A.	Pts.	Pen.
1978-79—University of Notre Dame	WCHA	37	28	31	59	32
1979-80—University of Notre Dame	WCHA	24	19	24	43	46
1980-81—University of Notre Dame	WCHA	35	13	22	35	53
1981-82—University of Notre Dame	CCHA	39	29	30	59	44
1982-83—Rogle	Sweden	33	35	18	53	..
1982-83—Maine Mariners	AHL	16	7	9	16	2
1982-83—Philadelphia Flyers	NHL	2	2	0	2	2
1983-84—Philadelphia Flyers	NHL	73	31	45	76	47
1984-85—Philadelphia Flyers	NHL	73	30	44	74	59
1985-86—Philadelphia Flyers	NHL	79	27	42	69	49
1986-87—Philadelphia Flyers (d)	NHL	75	25	45	70	53
1987-88—Philadelphia Flyers	NHL	68	19	32	51	32
1988-89—Philadelphia Flyers	NHL	69	18	17	35	49
1989-90—Philadelphia Flyers (e)	NHL	28	9	8	17	12
1989-90—Boston Bruins	NHL	32	6	19	25	12
NHL TOTALS			499	167	252	419	315

(c)—February, 1983—Signed by Philadelphia Flyers as a free agent.
(d)—Won Frank J. Selke Trophy (Best Defensive Forward).
(e)—January 16, 1990—Traded by Philadelphia Flyers to Boston Bruins for Ken Linseman.

PETR PRAJSLER

Defense . . . 6'3" . . . 200 lbs. . . . Born, Hradec Kralove, Czechoslovakia, September 21, 1965 . . . Shoots left . . . (October, 1987)—Pulled groin . . . (March, 1990)—Flu.

Year	Team	League	Games	G.	A.	Pts.	Pen.
1985-86—Pardubice (c)	Czech.	27	5	5	10	34
1986-87—Pardubice	Czech.	41	3	4	7	..
1987-88—Los Angeles Kings	NHL	7	0	0	0	2
1987-88—New Haven Nighthawks	AHL	41	3	8	11	58
1988-89—New Haven Nighthawks	AHL	43	4	6	10	96
1988-89—Los Angeles Kings	NHL	2	0	3	3	0
1989-90—Los Angeles Kings	NHL	34	3	7	10	47
1989-90—New Haven Nighthawks	AHL	6	1	7	8	2
NHL TOTALS			43	3	10	13	49

(c)—June, 1985—Drafted by Los Angeles Kings in 1985 NHL entry draft. Fifth Kings pick, 93rd overall, fifth round.

WAYNE PRESLEY

Right Wing . . . 5'11" . . . 175 lbs. . . . Born, Dearborn, Mich., March 23, 1965 . . . Shoots right . . . (November, 1987)—Missed 36 games following surgery to repair ligaments and cartilage in right knee . . . (May 6, 1989)—Dislocated shoulder when crosschecked by Al MacInnis vs. Calgary.

Year	Team	League	Games	G.	A.	Pts.	Pen.
1981-82—Detroit Little Ceasars	Mich. Midget	61	38	56	94	146
1982-83—Kitchener Rangers (c)	OHL	70	39	48	87	99
1983-84—Kitchener Rangers (a-d)	OHL	70	63	76	139	156
1984-85—Kitchener Rangers (e)	OHL	31	25	21	46	77
1984-85—Sault Ste. Marie Greyhounds	OHL	11	5	9	14	14
1984-85—Chicago Black Hawks	NHL	3	0	1	1	0
1985-86—Nova Scotia Oilers	AHL	29	6	9	15	22
1985-86—Chicago Black Hawks	NHL	38	7	8	15	38
1986-87—Chicago Black Hawks	NHL	80	32	29	61	114
1987-88—Chicago Black Hawks	NHL	42	12	10	22	52
1988-89—Chicago Black Hawks	NHL	72	21	19	40	100
1989-90—Chicago Black Hawks	NHL	49	6	7	13	67
NHL TOTALS			284	78	74	152	371

(c)—June, 1983—Drafted as underage junior by Chicago Black Hawks in 1983 NHL entry draft. Second Black Hawks pick, 39th overall, second round.
(d)—Won Jim Mahon Memorial Trophy (Highest scoring right wing).
(e)—January, 1985—Traded by Kitchener Rangers to Sault Ste. Marie Greyhounds for Shawn Tyers.

SERGEI PRIAKIN

Left and Right Wing . . . 6'3" . . . 210 lbs. . . . Born, Moscow, USSR, December 7, 1963 . . . Shoots left . . . First Soviet-born player to play in the Stanley Cup Playoffs.

Year	Team	League	Games	G.	A.	Pts.	Pen.
1987-88—Soviet Wings	USSR	44	10	15	25	16
1988-89—Soviet Wings (c)	USSR	44	11	15	26	23
1988-89—Calgary Flames	NHL	2	0	0	0	2
1989-90—Calgary Flames	NHL	20	2	2	4	0
1989-90—Salt Lake Golden Eagles	IHL	3	1	0	1	0
NHL TOTALS			22	2	2	4	2

(c)—June, 1988—Drafted by Calgary Flames in 1988 NHL entry draft. Twelfth Flames pick, 252nd overall, 12th round.

KEN PRIESTLAY

Center . . . 5'11" . . . 175 lbs. . . . Born, Vancouver, B.C., August 24, 1967 . . . Shoots left . . . (November, 1984)—Shoulder separation.

Year	Team	League	Games	G.	A.	Pts.	Pen.
1983-84—Victoria Cougars	WHL	55	10	18	28	31
1984-85—Victoria Cougars (c)	WHL	50	25	37	62	48
1985-86—Victoria Cougars (b)	WHL	72	73	72	145	45
1985-86—Rochester Americans	AHL	4	0	2	2	0
1986-87—Victoria Cougars (b)	WHL	33	43	39	82	37
1986-87—Buffalo Sabres	NHL	34	11	6	17	8
1986-87—Rochester Americans (d)	AHL	..	..	..	..	..
1987-88—Buffalo Sabres	NHL	33	5	12	17	35
1987-88—Rochester Americans	AHL	43	27	24	51	47
1988-89—Rochester Americans	AHL	64	56	37	93	60
1988-89—Buffalo Sabres	NHL	15	2	0	2	2
1989-90—Rochester Americans	AHL	40	19	39	58	46
1989-90—Buffalo Sabres	NHL	35	7	7	14	14
NHL TOTALS			117	25	25	50	59

(c)—June, 1985—Drafted as underage junior by Buffalo Sabres in 1985 NHL entry draft. Fifth Sabres pick, 98th overall, fifth round.
(d)—No regular season record. Played eight playoff games.

KEITH PRIMEAU

Center . . . 6'4" . . . 217 lbs. . . . Born, Toronto, Ont., November 24, 1971 . . . Shoots left.

Year	Team	League	Games	G.	A.	Pts.	Pen.
1986-87—Whitby Bantams	OHA	65	69	80	149	116
1987-88—Hamilton Steelhawks	OHL	47	6	6	12	69
1988-89—Niagara Falls Thunder	OHL	48	20	35	55	56
1989-90—Niagara Falls Thunder (b-c-d)	OHL	65	*57	70	*127	97

(c)—Won Eddie Powers Memorial Trophy (OHL scoring leader).
(d)—June 16, 1990—Selected by Detroit Red Wings in 1990 NHL entry draft. First Red Wings pick, third overall, first round.

ROBERT PROBERT

Left Wing . . . 6'3" . . . 205 lbs. . . . Born, Windsor, Ont., June 5, 1965 . . . Shoots left . . . (July 22, 1986)—Entered Hazelden Foundation . . . (July, 1986)—Entered Lindstrom, Minn. Hospital to deal with alcohol abuse problem . . . (November 2, 1986)—Not allowed to re-enter U.S. by customs agents. He was on probation for assaulting a police officer and driving while impaired in July . . . (December 19, 1986)—Suspended by the Detroit Red Wings . . . (1987-88)—Suspended six games during the season for game misconduct penalties . . . (September 23, 1988)—Suspended without pay by Detroit for skipping practice, missing team busses, flights and curfews . . . (November 23, 1988)—Reactivated by Detroit . . . (December 10, 1988)—Suspended three games by NHL for hitting Allan Bester vs. Toronto . . . (January 26, 1989)—Removed from team after showing up late for a game vs. Buffalo . . . (February 15, 1989)—Reactivated by Detroit . . . (March 2, 1989)—Charged with smuggling cocaine into the U.S. . . . (March 4, 1989)—Expelled from the NHL . . . (March 14, 1990)—Reinstated by NHL.

Year	Team	League	Games	G.	A.	Pts.	Pen.
1981-82—Windsor Club 240	Ont. Midget	55	60	40	100	40
1982-83—Brantford Alexanders (c)	OHL	51	12	16	28	133
1983-84—Brantford Alexanders	OHL	65	35	38	73	189
1984-85—Hamilton Steelhawks	OHL	4	0	1	1	21
1984-85—Sault Ste. Marie Greyhounds	OHL	44	20	52	72	172
1985-86—Adirondack Red Wings	AHL	32	12	15	27	152
1985-86—Detroit Red Wings	NHL	44	8	13	21	186
1986-87—Detroit Red Wings	NHL	63	13	11	24	221
1986-87—Adirondack Red Wings	AHL	7	1	4	5	15
1987-88—Detroit Red Wings	NHL	74	29	33	62	*398
1988-89—Detroit Red Wings	NHL	25	4	2	6	106
1989-90—Detroit Red Wings	NHL	4	3	0	3	21
NHL TOTALS			210	57	59	116	932

(c)—June, 1983—Drafted as underage junior by Detroit Red Wings in 1983 NHL entry draft. Third Red Wings pick, 46th overall, third round.

BRIAN PROPP

Left Wing . . . 5'9" . . . 185 lbs. . . . Born, Lanigan, Sask., February 15, 1959 . . . Shoots left . . . Was all-time Western Hockey League scoring leader with 511 points (Broken by Rob Brown in 1986-87) . . . Brother of Ron Propp . . . (January, 1985)—Given four-game suspension . . . (March 4, 1986)—Injured eye vs. Buffalo and missed eight games . . . (December 7, 1986)—Fractured left knee vs. Edmonton . . . (December, 1987)—Sprained left knee.

Year	Team	League	Games	G.	A.	Pts.	Pen.
1975-76—Melville Millionaires	SJHL	57	76	92	168	36
1976-77—Brandon Wheat Kings (b-c-d)	WCHL	72	55	80	135	47
1977-78—Brandon Wheat Kings	WCHL	70	70	*112	*182	200
1978-79—Brandon Wheat Kings (a-e)	WHL	71	*94	*100	*194	127
1979-80—Philadelphia Flyers	NHL	80	34	41	75	54
1980-81—Philadelphia Flyers	NHL	79	26	40	66	110
1981-82—Philadelphia Flyers	NHL	80	44	47	91	117
1982-83—Philadelphia Flyers	NHL	80	40	42	82	72
1983-84—Philadelphia Flyers	NHL	79	39	53	92	37
1984-85—Philadelphia Flyers	NHL	76	43	53	96	43
1985-86—Philadelphia Flyers	NHL	72	40	57	97	47
1986-87—Philadelphia Flyers	NHL	53	31	36	67	45
1987-88—Philadelphia Flyers	NHL	74	27	49	76	76
1988-89—Philadelphia Flyers	NHL	77	32	46	78	37
1989-90—Philadelphia Flyers (f)	NHL	40	13	15	28	31
1989-90—Boston Bruins (g)	NHL	14	3	9	12	10
NHL TOTALS			804	372	488	860	679

(c)—Named WCHL Rookie of the Year.
(d)—Shared lead in goals (14) during playoffs.
(e)—August, 1979—Drafted by Philadelphia Flyers in 1979 NHL entry draft. First Flyers pick, 14th overall, first round.
(f)—March 2, 1990—Traded by Philadelphia Flyers to Boston Bruins for a second-round 1990 draft pick (Terran Sandwith).
(g)—July, 1990—Signed by Minnesota North Stars as a free agent.

JASON PROSOFSKY

Right Wing . . . 6'4'' . . . 220 lbs. . . . Born, Medicine Hat, Alta., May 4, 1971 . . . Shoots right.

Year	Team	League	Games	G.	A.	Pts.	Pen.
1986-87	Medicine Hat Tigers	WHL	1	0	0	0	0
1987-88	Medicine Hat Tigers	WHL	47	6	1	7	94
1988-89	Medicine Hat Tigers (c)	WHL	67	7	16	23	170
1989-90	Medicine Hat Tigers	WHL	71	12	13	25	153

(c)—June, 1989—Drafted by New York Rangers in 1989 NHL entry draft. Second Rangers pick, 40th overall, second round.

CHRIS PRYOR

Defense . . . 5'11'' . . . 210 lbs. . . . Born, St. Paul, Minn., January 31, 1961 . . . Shoots right.

Year	Team	League	Games	G.	A.	Pts.	Pen.
1979-80	Univ. of New Hampshire	ECAC	27	9	13	22	27
1980-81	Univ. of New Hampshire	ECAC	33	10	27	37	36
1981-82	Univ. of New Hampshire	ECAC	35	3	16	19	36
1982-83	Univ. of New Hampshire	ECAC	34	4	9	13	23
1983-84	Salt Lake Golden Eagles	CHL	72	7	21	28	215
1984-85	Springfield Indians	AHL	77	3	21	24	158
1984-85	Minnesota North Stars (c)	NHL	4	0	0	0	16
1985-86	Springfield Indians	AHL	55	4	16	20	104
1985-86	Minnesota North Stars	NHL	7	0	1	1	0
1986-87	Minnesota North Stars	NHL	50	1	3	4	49
1986-87	Springfield Indians	AHL	5	0	2	2	17
1987-88	Minnesota North Stars (d)	NHL	3	0	0	0	6
1987-88	New York Islanders	NHL	1	0	0	0	2
1987-88	Kalamazoo Wings	IHL	56	4	16	20	171
1988-89	New York Islanders	NHL	7	0	0	0	25
1988-89	Springfield Indians	AHL	54	3	6	9	205
1989-90	Springfield Indians	AHL	60	3	7	10	105
1989-90	New York Islanders	NHL	10	0	0	0	24
	NHL TOTALS		82	1	4	5	122

(c)—January, 1985—Signed by Minnesota North Stars as a free agent.
(d)—March, 1988—Traded with future considerations by Minnesota North Stars to New York Islanders for Gord Dineen.

JOHN PURVES

Right Wing . . . 6'2'' . . . 185 lbs. . . . Born, Toronto, Ont., February 12, 1968 . . . Shoots right . . . (October, 1986)—Broken wrist.

Year	Team	League	Games	G.	A.	Pts.	Pen.
1984-85	Belleville Bulls	OHL	55	15	14	29	39
1984-85	Belleville Bulls	OHL	16	3	9	12	6
1984-85	Hamilton Steelhawks (c)	OHL	36	13	28	41	36
1986-87	Hamilton Steelhawks	OHL	28	12	11	23	37
1987-88	Hamilton Steelhawks	OHL	64	39	44	83	65
1988-89	Niagara Falls Flyers	OHL	5	5	11	16	2
1988-89	North Bay Centennials (b)	OHL	42	34	52	86	38
1989-90	Baltimore Skipjacks	AHL	75	29	35	64	12

(c)—June, 1986—Drafted as underage junior by Washington Capitals in 1986 NHL entry draft. Sixth Capitals pick, 103rd overall, fifth round.

JOEL NORMAN QUENNEVILLE

Defense . . . 6'1'' . . . 200 lbs. . . . Born, Windsor, Ont., September 15, 1958 . . . Shoots left . . . (March, 1980)—Rib-cage injury . . . (March, 1980)—Surgery to repair torn ligaments in ring finger of left hand . . . (January 4, 1982)—Sprained ankle, twisted knee and suffered facial cuts when he crashed into boards during a Rockies practice . . . (December 18, 1986)—Broke right shoulder at Boston and missed 42 games . . . (January 19, 1989)—Separated left shoulder when checked by Shayne Corson at Montreal and missed nine games.

Year	Team	League	Games	G.	A.	Pts.	Pen.
1975-76	Windsor Spitfires	Jr."A"OHA	66	15	33	48	61
1976-77	Windsor Spitfires	Jr."A"OHA	65	19	59	78	169
1977-78	Windsor Spitfires (b-c)	Jr."A"OHA	66	27	76	103	114
1978-79	Toronto Maple Leafs	NHL	61	2	9	11	60
1978-79	New Brunswick Hawks	AHL	16	1	10	11	10
1979-80	Toronto Maple Leafs (d)	NHL	32	1	4	5	24
1979-80	Colorado Rockies	NHL	35	5	7	12	26
1980-81	Colorado Rockies	NHL	71	10	24	34	86
1981-82	Colorado Rockies	NHL	64	5	10	15	55
1982-83	New Jersey Devils (e-f)	NHL	74	5	12	17	46
1983-84	Hartford Whalers	NHL	80	5	8	13	95
1984-85	Hartford Whalers	NHL	79	6	16	22	96
1985-86	Hartford Whalers	NHL	71	5	20	25	83
1986-87	Hartford Whalers	NHL	37	3	7	10	24
1987-88	Hartford Whalers	NHL	77	1	8	9	44
1988-89	Hartford Whalers	NHL	69	4	7	11	42
1989-90	Hartford Whalers	NHL	44	1	4	5	34
	NHL TOTALS		794	53	136	189	705

(c)—Drafted from Windsor Spitfires by Toronto Maple Leafs in second round of 1978 amateur draft.
(d)—December, 1979—Traded with Lanny McDonald by Toronto Maple Leafs to Colorado Rockies for Wilf Paiement and Pat Hickey.
(e)—July, 1983—Traded by New Jersey Devils with Steve Tambellini to Calgary Flames

for Mel Bridgman and Phil Russell.
(f)—August, 1983—Traded by Calgary Flames with Richie Dunn to Hartford Whalers for Mickey Volcan and third-round draft choice in 1984.

DAN QUINN

Center . . . 5'11'' . . . 175 lbs. . . . Born, Ottawa, Ont., June 1, 1965 . . . Shoots left . . . Son of Peter Quinn (former CFL player with Ottawa) . . . (October, 1987)—Broken left wrist.

Year	Team	League	Games	G.	A.	Pts.	Pen.
1981-82	Belleville Bulls	OHL	67	19	32	51	41
1982-83	Belleville Bulls (c)	OHL	70	59	88	147	27
1983-84	Belleville Bulls	OHL	24	23	36	59	12
1983-84	Calgary Flames	NHL	54	19	33	52	20
1984-85	Calgary Flames	NHL	74	20	38	58	22
1985-86	Calgary Flames	NHL	78	30	42	72	44
1986-87	Calgary Flames (d)	NHL	16	3	6	9	14
1986-87	Pittsburgh Penguins	NHL	64	28	43	71	40
1987-88	Pittsburgh Penguins	NHL	70	40	39	79	50
1988-89	Pittsburgh Penguins	NHL	79	34	60	94	102
1989-90	Pittsburgh Penguins (e)	NHL	41	9	20	29	22
1989-90	Vancouver Canucks	NHL	37	16	18	34	27
	NHL TOTALS		513	199	299	498	341

(c)—June, 1983—Drafted as underage junior by Calgary Flames in 1983 NHL entry draft. First Flames pick, 13th overall, first round.
(d)—November, 1986—Traded by Calgary Flames to Pittsburgh Penguins for Mike Bullard.
(e)—January 8, 1990—Traded with Andrew McBain and Dave Capuano by Pittsburgh Penguins to Vancouver Canucks for Tony Tanti, Barry Pederson and Rod Buskas.

KEN QUINNEY

Right Wing . . . 5'10'' . . . 195 lbs. . . . Born, New Westminster, B.C., May 23, 1965 . . . Shoots right . . . (February, 1986)—Broken wrist.

Year	Team	League	Games	G.	A.	Pts.	Pen.
1981-82	Calgary Wranglers	WHL	63	11	17	28	55
1982-83	Calgary Wranglers	WHL	71	26	25	51	71
1983-84	Calgary Wranglers (c)	WHL	71	64	54	118	38
1984-85	Calgary Wranglers (a)	WHL	56	47	67	114	65
1985-86	Fredericton Express	AHL	61	11	26	37	34
1986-87	Quebec Nordiques	NHL	25	2	7	9	16
1986-87	Fredericton Express	AHL	48	14	27	41	20
1987-88	Fredericton Express	AHL	58	37	39	76	39
1987-88	Quebec Nordiques	NHL	15	2	2	4	5
1988-89	Halifax Citadels	AHL	72	41	49	90	65
1989-90	Halifax Citadels	AHL	44	9	16	25	63
	NHL TOTALS		40	4	9	13	21

(c)—June, 1984—Drafted as underage junior by Quebec Nordiques in NHL entry draft. Ninth Nordiques pick, 203rd overall, 10th round.

STEPHANE QUINTAL

Defense . . . 6'3'' . . . 215 lbs. . . . Born, Boucherville, Que., October 22, 1968 . . . Shoots right . . . (December, 1985)—Broken wrist . . . (October, 1988)—Broken bone near eye . . . (January, 1989)—Injured knee . . . (October 17, 1989)—Sprained right knee and missed eight games.

Year	Team	League	Games	G.	A.	Pts.	Pen.
1985-86	Granby Bisons	QMJHL	67	2	17	19	144
1986-87	Granby Bisons (a-c)	QMJHL	67	13	41	54	178
1987-88	Hull Olympiques	QMJHL	38	13	23	36	138
1988-89	Maine Mariners	AHL	16	4	10	14	28
1988-89	Boston Bruins	NHL	26	0	1	1	29
1989-90	Boston Bruins	NHL	38	2	2	4	22
1989-90	Maine Mariners	AHL	37	4	16	20	27
	NHL TOTALS		64	2	3	5	51

(c)—June, 1987—Drafted as underage junior by Boston Bruins in 1987 NHL entry draft. Second Bruins pick, 14th overall, first round.

JEAN-FRANCOIS QUINTIN

Center . . . 6' . . . 187 lbs. . . . Born, St. Jean, Que., May 28, 1969 . . . Shoots left . . . (October, 1985)—Fractured knee.

Year	Team	League	Games	G.	A.	Pts.	Pen.
1986-87	Shawinigan Cataractes	QMJHL	43	1	9	10	17
1987-88	Shawinigan Cataractes	QMJHL	70	28	70	98	143
1988-89	Shawinigan Cataractes (c)	QMJHL	69	52	100	152	105
1989-90	Kalamazoo Wings	IHL	68	20	18	38	38

(c)—June, 1989—Drafted by Minnesota North Stars in 1989 NHL entry draft. Fourth North Stars pick, 75th overall, fourth round.

YVES RACINE

Defense . . . 6' . . . 183 lbs. . . . Born, Matane, Que., February 7, 1969 . . . Shoots left.

Year	Team	League	Games	G.	A.	Pts.	Pen.
1985-86	Ste. Foy Gouverneurs	Que. Midget	42	4	38	42	66
1986-87	Longueuil Chevaliers (c)	QMJHL	70	7	43	50	50
1987-88	Victoriaville Tigres (a)	QMJHL	69	10	84	94	150
1988-89	Victoriaville Tigres (a-d-e)	QMJHL	63	23	85	108	95
1988-89	Adirondack Red Wings (f)	AHL	....	...	...	...	....
1989-90	Detroit Red Wings	NHL	28	4	9	13	23
1989-90	Adirondack Red Wings	AHL	46	8	27	35	31
	NHL TOTALS		28	4	9	13	23

(c)—June, 1987—Drafted by Detroit Red Wings as underage junior in 1987 NHL entry draft. First Red Wings pick, 11th overall, first round.
(d)—Won Emile 'Butch' Bouchard Trophy (Top QHL Defenseman).
(e)—Led QHL Playoffs with 30 assists and 33 points.
(f)—No regular season games. Played two playoff games.

HERB RAGLAN

Right Wing . . . 6' . . . 200 lbs. . . . Born, Peterborough, Ont., August 5, 1967 . . . Shoots right . . . Son of Clare Raglan (Detroit and Chicago in early '50s) . . . (December, 1985)—Severely sprained ankle . . . (November, 1987)—Strained right knee ligaments . . . (October, 1988)—Sprained right wrist . . . (November, 1988)—Separated left shoulder . . . (February, 1989)—Pulled right groin . . . (November 4, 1989)—Broke right wrist in a collision with Marc Fortier at Quebec and required surgery.

Year	Team	League	Games	G.	A.	Pts.	Pen.
1983-84—Peterborough Midget		OHA	26	39	21	60	60
1984-85—Kingston Canadians (c)		OHL	58	20	22	42	166
1985-86—Kingston Canadians		OHL	28	10	9	19	88
1985-86—St. Louis Blues		NHL	7	0	0	0	5
1986-87—St. Louis Blues		NHL	62	6	10	16	159
1987-88—St. Louis Blues		NHL	73	10	15	25	190
1988-89—St. Louis Blues		NHL	50	7	10	17	144
1989-90—St. Louis Blues		NHL	11	0	1	1	21
NHL TOTALS			203	23	36	59	519

(c)—June, 1985—Drafted as underage junior by St. Louis Blues in 1985 NHL entry draft. First Blues pick, 37th overall, second round.

GEORGE ROBERT (ROB) RAMAGE

Defense . . . 6'2" . . . 210 lbs. . . . Born, Byron, Ont., January 11, 1959 . . . Shoots right . . . (March 22, 1986)—Sprained knee vs. Montreal . . . (November 24, 1986)—Missed 21 games with tendinitis around left kneecap . . . (February 3, 1989)—Suspended eight NHL games for high sticking Doug Bodger.

Year	Team	League	Games	G.	A.	Pts.	Pen.
1975-76—London Knights		Jr."A"OHA	65	12	31	43	113
1976-77—London Knights		Jr."A"OHA	65	15	58	73	177
1977-78—London Knights (a-c-d)		Jr."A"OHA	59	17	47	64	162
1978-79—Birmingham Bulls (a-e)		WHA	80	12	36	48	165
1979-80—Colorado Rockies		NHL	75	8	20	28	135
1980-81—Colorado Rockies		NHL	79	20	42	62	193
1981-82—Colorado Rockies (f)		NHL	80	13	29	42	201
1982-83—St. Louis Blues		NHL	78	16	35	51	193
1983-84—St. Louis Blues		NHL	80	15	45	60	121
1984-85—St. Louis Blues		NHL	80	7	31	38	178
1985-86—St. Louis Blues		NHL	77	10	56	66	171
1986-87—St. Louis Blues		NHL	59	11	28	39	106
1987-88—St. Louis Blues (g)		NHL	67	8	34	42	127
1987-88—Calgary Flames		NHL	12	1	6	7	37
1988-89—Calgary Flames (h)		NHL	68	3	13	16	156
1989-90—Toronto Maple Leafs		NHL	80	8	41	49	202
WHA TOTALS			80	12	36	48	165
NHL TOTALS			835	120	380	500	1820

(c)—July, 1978—Signed by Birmingham Bulls (WHA) as underage junior.
(d)—Shared Max Kaminsky Memorial Trophy (Outstanding Defenseman) with Brad Marsh.
(e)—Drafted by Colorado Rockies in 1979 NHL entry draft. First Rockies pick, first overall, first round.
(f)—June, 1982—Traded by Colorado Rockies to St. Louis Blues for St. Louis' first-round draft choices in 1982 (Rocky Trottier) and 1983 (John MacLean).
(g)—March, 1988—Traded with Rick Wamsley by St. Louis Blues to Calgary Flames for Brett Hull and Steve Bozek.
(h)—June 16, 1989—Traded by Calgary Flames to Toronto Maple Leafs for a second-round 1989 draft pick (Kent Manderville).

MICHAEL ALLEN RAMSEY

Defense . . . 6'2" . . . 185 lbs. . . . Born, Minneapolis, Minn., December 3, 1960 . . . Shoots left . . . Member of 1980 gold-medal U.S. Olympic hockey team . . . (December 4, 1983)—Dislocated thumb vs. Montreal . . . (October, 1987)—Injured groin . . . (January, 1988)—Charlie Horse . . . (November 2, 1988)—Fractured bone in right hand . . . (January 12, 1989)—Pulled groin vs. Chicago.

Year	Team	League	Games	G.	A.	Pts.	Pen.
1978-79—Univ. of Minnesota (c)		WCHA	26	6	11	17	30
1979-80—U.S. Olympic Team		Int'l	63	11	24	35	63
1979-80—Buffalo Sabres		NHL	13	1	6	7	6
1980-81—Buffalo Sabres		NHL	72	3	14	17	56
1981-82—Buffalo Sabres		NHL	80	7	23	30	56
1982-83—Buffalo Sabres		NHL	77	8	30	38	55
1983-84—Buffalo Sabres		NHL	72	9	22	31	82
1984-85—Buffalo Sabres		NHL	79	8	22	30	102
1985-86—Buffalo Sabres		NHL	76	7	21	28	117
1986-87—Buffalo Sabres		NHL	80	8	31	39	109
1987-88—Buffalo Sabres		NHL	63	5	16	21	77
1988-89—Buffalo Sabres		NHL	56	2	14	16	84
1989-90—Buffalo Sabres		NHL	73	4	21	25	47
NHL TOTALS			741	62	220	282	791

(c)—August, 1979—Drafted by Buffalo Sabres in entry draft. First Sabres pick, 11th overall, first round.

PAUL RANHEIM

Left Wing . . . 6' . . . 195 lbs. . . . Born, St. Louis, Mo., January 25, 1966 . . . Shoots right.

Year	Team	League	Games	G.	A.	Pts.	Pen.
1982-83—Edina H.S.		Minn. H.S.	26	12	25	37	4
1983-84—Edina H.S. (c)		Minn. H.S.	26	16	24	40	6
1984-85—Univ. of Wisconsin		WCHA	42	11	11	22	40
1985-86—Univ. of Wisconsin		WCHA	33	17	17	34	34
1986-87—Univ. of Wisconsin		WCHA	42	24	35	59	54
1987-88—Univ. of Wisconsin		WCHA	44	36	26	62	63

Year	Team	League	Games	G.	A.	Pts.	Pen.
1988-89—Calgary Flames		NHL	5	0	0	0	0
1988-89—Salt Lake Golden Eagles (b-d-e)		IHL	75	68	29	97	16
1989-90—Calgary Flames		NHL	80	26	28	54	23
NHL TOTALS			85	26	28	54	23

(c)—June, 1983—Drafted by Calgary Flames in 1983 NHL entry draft. Flames third pick, 38th overall, second round.
(d)—Won Garry F. Longman Memorial Trophy (Top IHL Rookie).
(e)—Won Ken McKenzie Trophy (Top American-born IHL Rookie).

JASON RATHBONE

Right Wing . . . 6' . . . 175 lbs. . . . Born, Syracuse, N.Y., April 13, 1970 . . . Shoots right.

Year	Team	League	Games	G.	A.	Pts.	Pen.
1986-87—Brookline H.S.		Mass. H.S.	....	9	11	20	....
1987-88—Brookline H.S. (c)		Mass. H.S.	....	23	23	46	....
1988-89—Boston College		H. East	21	0	3	3	10
1989-90—Boston College		H. East	37	4	7	11	20

(c)—June, 1988—Drafted by New York Islanders in 1988 NHL entry draft. Eighth Islanders pick, 121st overall, sixth round.

DAN RATUSHNY

Defense . . . 6'1" . . . 185 lbs. . . . Born, Nepean, Ont., October 29, 1970 . . . Shoots right.

Year	Team	League	Games	G.	A.	Pts.	Pen.
1987-88—Napean Jr. A		COJHL	54	8	20	28	116
1988-89—Cornell University (c)		ECAC	28	2	13	15	50
1988-89—Canadian National Team		Int'l	2	0	0	0	2
1989-90—Cornell University		ECAC	26	5	14	19	54

(c)—June, 1989—Drafted by Winnipeg Jets in 1989 NHL entry draft. Second Jets pick, 25th overall, second round.

ROB RAY

Left Wing . . . 6' . . . 200 lbs. . . . Born, Belleville, Ont., June 8, 1968 . . . Shoots left . . . (January, 1987)—Broken jaw . . . (1988-89)—Set AHL record with 446 minutes in penalties.

Year	Team	League	Games	G.	A.	Pts.	Pen.
1984-85—Whitby Lawmen		OPJHL	35	5	10	15	318
1985-86—Cornwall Royals		OHL	53	6	13	19	253
1986-87—Cornwall Royals		OHL	46	17	20	37	158
1987-88—Cornwall Royals (c)		OHL	61	11	41	52	179
1988-89—Rochester Americans		AHL	74	11	18	29	*446
1989-90—Buffalo Sabres		NHL	27	2	1	3	99
1989-90—Rochester Americans		AHL	43	2	13	15	335
NHL TOTALS			27	2	1	3	99

(c)—June, 1988—Drafted by Buffalo Sabres in 1988 NHL entry draft. Fifth Sabres pick, 97th overall, fifth round.

MARK RECCHI

Center . . . 5'10" . . . 185 lbs. . . . Born, Kamloops, B.C., February 1, 1968 . . . Shoots left . . . (January, 1987)—Broken ankle.

Year	Team	League	Games	G.	A.	Pts.	Pen.
1984-85—Langley Eagles		BCJHL	51	26	39	65	39
1985-86—New Westminster Bruins		WHL	72	21	40	61	55
1986-87—Kamloops Blazers		WHL	40	26	50	76	63
1987-88—Kamloops Blazers (c)		WHL	62	61	93	154	75
1988-89—Pittsburgh Penguins		NHL	15	1	1	2	0
1988-89—Muskegon Lumberjacks (b)		IHL	63	50	49	99	86
1989-90—Muskegon Lumberjacks		IHL	4	7	4	11	2
1989-90—Pittsburgh Penguins		NHL	74	30	37	67	44
NHL TOTALS			89	31	38	69	44

(c)—June, 1988—Drafted by Pittsburgh Penguins in 1988 NHL entry draft. Fourth Penguins pick, 67th overall, fourth round.

JACE REED

Defense . . . 6'3" . . . 205 lbs. . . . Born, Grand Rapids, Minn., March 22, 1971 . . . Shoots left.

Year	Team	League	Games	G.	A.	Pts.	Pen.
1987-88—Grand Rapids H.S.		Minn. H.S.	28	8	14	22	..
1988-89—Grand Rapids H.S. (c)		Minn. H.S.	25	4	17	21	10
1989-90—Univ. of North Dakota		WCHA	10	0	0	0	0

(c)—June, 1989—Drafted by New York Islanders in 1989 NHL entry draft. Fifth Islanders pick, 86th overall, fifth round.

JOE JAMES REEKIE

Defense . . . 6'2" . . . 176 lbs. . . . Born, Victoria, B.C., February 22, 1965 . . . Shoots left . . . (March 14, 1987)—Injured ankle at Edmonton . . . (October, 1987)—Injured shoulder . . . (November 15, 1987)—Broken kneecap at Toronto . . . (September, 1988)—Left knee operation . . . (November, 1989)—Sprained right knee . . . (December 7, 1989)—Broke two bones in left hand and suffered facial cuts in automobile accident and required surgery . . . (March 21, 1990)—Broke left middle finger vs. Calgary.

Year	Team	League	Games	G.	A.	Pts.	Pen.
1981-82—Nepean Raiders		CJHL	16	2	5	7	4
1982-83—North Bay Centennials (c)		OHL	59	2	9	11	49
1983-84—North Bay Centennials		OHL	9	1	0	1	18
1983-84—Cornwall Royals		OHL	53	6	27	33	166
1984-85—Cornwall Royals (e)		OHL	65	19	63	82	134
1985-86—Rochester Americans		AHL	77	3	25	28	178

Year	Team	League	Games	G.	A.	Pts.	Pen.
1985-86—Buffalo Sabres		NHL	3	0	0	0	14
1986-87—Buffalo Sabres		NHL	56	1	8	9	82
1986-87—Rochester Americans		AHL	22	0	6	6	52
1987-88—Buffalo Sabres		NHL	30	1	4	5	68
1988-89—Rochester Americans		AHL	21	1	2	3	56
1988-89—Buffalo Sabres (f)		NHL	15	1	3	4	26
1989-90—New York Islanders		NHL	31	1	8	9	43
1989-90—Springfield Indians		AHL	15	1	4	5	24
NHL TOTALS			135	4	23	27	233

(c)—June, 1983—Drafted as underage junior by Hartford Whalers in 1983 NHL entry draft. Eighth Whalers pick, 124th overall, seventh round.

(d)—June, 1984—Released by Hartford Whalers.

(e)—June, 1985—Drafted by Buffalo Sabres in 1985 NHL entry draft. Sixth Sabres pick, 119th overall, sixth round.

(f)—June 17, 1989—Traded by Buffalo Sabres to New York Islanders for a sixth-round 1989 draft pick (Bill Pye).

ROBERT REICHEL

Center . . . 5'10" . . . 180 lbs. . . . Born, Litvinov, Czechoslovakia, June 25, 1971 . . . Shoots right.

Year	Team	League	Games	G.	A.	Pts.	Pen.
1988-89—Litvinov (c)		Czech.	....	20	31	51	....
1989-90—Litvinov		Czech.	52	49	34	83	....

(c)—June, 1989—Selected by Calgary Flames in 1989 NHL entry draft. Fifth Flames pick, 70th overall, fourth round.

DAVID REID

Left Wing . . . 6'1" . . . 205 lbs. . . . Born, Toronto, Ont., May 15, 1964 . . . Shoots left . . . (December, 1986)—Knee surgery . . . (November, 1987)—Missed 10 games with separated shoulder in AHL game.

Year	Team	League	Games	G.	A.	Pts.	Pen.
1980-81—Mississauga Midgets		Ont. Midget	39	21	32	53	....
1981-82—Peterborough Petes (c)		OHL	68	10	32	42	41
1982-83—Peterborough Petes		OHL	70	23	34	57	33
1983-84—Peterborough Petes		OHL	60	33	64	97	12
1983-84—Boston Bruins		NHL	8	1	0	1	2
1984-85—Hershey Bears		AHL	43	10	14	24	6
1984-85—Boston Bruins		NHL	35	14	13	27	27
1985-86—Moncton Golden Flames		AHL	26	14	18	32	4
1985-86—Boston Bruins		NHL	37	10	10	20	10
1986-87—Boston Bruins		NHL	12	3	3	6	0
1986-87—Moncton Golden Flames		AHL	40	12	22	34	23
1987-88—Maine Mariners		AHL	63	21	37	58	40
1987-88—Boston Bruins		NHL	3	0	0	0	0
1988-89—Toronto Maple Leafs (d)		NHL	77	9	21	30	22
1989-90—Toronto Maple Leafs		NHL	70	9	19	28	9
NHL TOTALS			242	46	66	112	70

(c)—June, 1982—Drafted by Boston Bruins as underage junior in 1982 NHL entry draft. Fourth Bruins pick, 60th overall, third round.

(d)—August, 1988—Signed by Toronto Maple Leafs as a free agent.

PAUL REINHART

Defense . . . 5'11" . . . 216 lbs. . . . Born, Kitchener, Ont., January 8, 1960 . . . Shoots left . . . (January 13, 1981)—Strained ligaments . . . (September, 1981)—Injured ligaments in right ankle during Canada Cup . . . Brother of Kevin Reinhart (Toronto '78 draft pick, 132nd overall) . . . (November 24, 1983)—Injured back vs. Winnipeg . . . (April, 1984)—Reinjured back vs. Edmonton . . . (December, 1984)—Recurring back problems . . . (November, 1987)—Deteriorating back disc . . . (November, 1988)—Bruised thigh . . . (November 13, 1988)—Injured back . . . (February 16, 1989)—Cracked rib and bruised spleen when checked by Ken McRae vs. Quebec . . . (November 11, 1989)—Sprained ankle at Quebec.

Year	Team	League	Games	G.	A.	Pts.	Pen.
1975-76—Kitchener Rangers		OMJHL	53	6	33	39	42
1976-77—Kitchener Rangers		OMJHL	51	4	14	18	16
1977-78—Kitchener Rangers		OMJHL	47	17	28	45	15
1978-79—Kitchener Rangers (c)		OMJHL	66	51	78	129	57
1979-80—Atlanta Flames		NHL	79	9	38	47	31
1980-81—Calgary Flames		NHL	74	18	49	67	52
1981-82—Calgary Flames		NHL	62	13	48	61	17
1982-83—Calgary Flames		NHL	78	17	58	75	28
1983-84—Calgary Flames		NHL	27	6	15	21	10
1984-85—Calgary Flames		NHL	75	23	46	69	18
1985-86—Calgary Flames		NHL	32	8	25	33	15
1986-87—Calgary Flames		NHL	76	15	54	69	22
1987-88—Calgary Flames		NHL	14	0	3	3	10
1988-89—Vancouver Canucks (d)		NHL	64	7	50	57	44
1989-90—Vancouver Canucks (e)		NHL	67	17	40	57	30
NHL TOTALS			648	133	426	559	277

(c)—August, 1979—Drafted by Atlanta Flames as underage junior in 1979 NHL entry draft. First Flames pick, 12th overall, first round.

(d)—September 6, 1988—Traded with Steve Bozek by Calgary Flames to Vancouver Canucks for a third-round 1989 draft pick (Veli Pekka Kautonen).

(e)—September 5, 1990—Announced his retirement.

ERIC REISMAN

Defense . . . 6'2" . . . 220 lbs. . . . Born, Manhattan, N.Y., May 19, 1968 . . . Shoots left.

Year	Team	League	Games	G.	A.	Pts.	Pen.
1987-88—Ohio State Univ. (c)		CCHA	29	0	3	3	45
1988-89—Ohio State Univ.		CCHA	38	4	6	10	56
1989-90—Ohio State Univ.		CCHA	39	1	2	3	91

(c)—June, 1988—Drafted by Boston Bruins in 1988 NHL entry draft. Eighth Bruins pick, 228th overall, 11th round.

ROBERT REYNOLDS

Center . . . 5'11" . . . 175 lbs. . . . Born, Flint, Mich., July 14, 1967 . . . Shoots left . . . Also plays Left Wing.

Year	Team	League	Games	G.	A.	Pts.	Pen.
1983-84—St. Clair Shores Falcons		GLJHL	60	25	34	59	....
1984-85—St. Clair Shores Falcons (c)		GLJHL	43	20	30	50	....
1985-86—Michigan State Univ.		CCHA	45	9	10	19	26
1986-87—Michigan State Univ.		CCHA	40	20	13	33	40
1987-88—Michigan State Univ.		CCHA	46	42	25	67	52
1988-89—Michigan State Univ. (b-d)		CCHA	47	36	41	77	78
1989-90—Newmarket Saints		AHL	66	22	28	50	55
1989-90—Toronto Maple Leafs		NHL	7	1	1	2	0
NHL TOTALS			7	1	1	2	0

(c)—June, 1985—Drafted by Toronto Maple Leafs in 1985 NHL entry draft. Tenth Maple Leafs pick, 190th overall, 10th round.

(d)—Named First team All-America (West).

ERIC RICARD

Defense . . . 6'4" . . . 220 lbs. . . . Born, St. Cesaire, Que., February 16, 1969 . . . Shoots left.

Year	Team	League	Games	G.	A.	Pts.	Pen.
1986-87—Granby Bisons		QMJHL	42	2	5	7	69
1987-88—Granby Bisons		QMJHL	65	3	10	13	362
1988-89—Granby Bisons (c)		QMJHL	68	5	31	36	213
1989-90—New Haven Nighthawks		AHL	28	1	1	2	55

(c)—June, 1989—Drafted by Los Angeles Kings in 1989 NHL entry draft. Third Kings pick, 102nd overall, fifth round.

MIKE RICCI

Center . . . 6'1" . . . 191 lbs. . . . Born, Scarborough, Ont., October 27, 1971 . . . Shoots left . . . (December, 1989)—Separated right shoulder.

Year	Team	League	Games	G.	A.	Pts.	Pen.
1986-87—Toronto Marlboro Bantams		OHA	38	29	42	71	27
1987-88—Peterborough Petes		OHL	41	24	37	61	20
1988-89—Peterborough Petes (b)		OHL	60	54	52	106	43
1989-90—Peterborough Petes (a-c-d-e)		OHL	60	52	64	116	39

(c)—Won Red Tilson Trophy (Outstanding OHL Player).

(d)—Won William Hanley Trophy (OHL Most Gentlemanly Player).

(e)—June 16, 1990—Selected by Philadelphia Flyers in 1990 NHL entry draft. First Flyers pick, fourth overall, first round.

STEVEN RICE

Right Wing . . . 6' . . . 210 lbs. . . . Born, Waterloo, Ont., May 26, 1971 . . . Shoots right . . . (October, 1986)—Knee surgery . . . (September 14, 1989)—Back spasms during N.Y. Rangers training camp.

Year	Team	League	Games	G.	A.	Pts.	Pen.
1986-87—Waterloo Midgets		OHA	32	17	16	33	87
1987-88—Kitchener Rangers		OHL	59	11	14	25	43
1988-89—Kitchener Rangers (c)		OHL	64	36	31	67	42
1989-90—Kitchener Rangers		OHL	58	39	37	76	102

(c)—June, 1989—Drafted by New York Rangers in 1989 NHL entry draft. First Rangers pick, 20th overall, first round.

JEAN-MARC RICHARD

Defense . . . 5'11" . . . 170 lbs. . . . Born, St. Raymond, Que., October 8, 1966 . . . Shoots left.

Year	Team	League	Games	G.	A.	Pts.	Pen.
1983-84—Chicoutimi Sagueneens		QMJHL	61	1	20	21	41
1984-85—Chicoutimi Sagueneens		QMJHL	68	10	61	71	57
1985-86—Chicoutimi Sagueneens (a)		QMJHL	72	19	88	107	111
1986-87—Chicoutimi Sagueneens (a-c)		QMJHL	67	21	81	102	105
1987-88—Fredericton Express		AHL	68	14	42	56	52
1987-88—Quebec Nordiques		NHL	4	2	1	3	2
1988-89—Halifax Citadels		AHL	57	8	25	33	38
1989-90—Quebec Nordiques		NHL	1	0	0	0	0
1989-90—Halifax Citadels		AHL	40	1	24	25	38
NHL TOTALS			5	2	1	3	2

(c)—April, 1987—Signed by Quebec Nordiques as a free agent.

MIKE RICHARD

Center . . . 5'9" . . . 175 lbs. . . . Born, Toronto, Ont., July 9, 1966 . . . Shoots left . . . (December, 1987)—Set AHL record with points in 31 straight games between October 18 and December 26, 1987 (25g, 30a) . . . (February, 1990)—Missed 19 games with knee injury.

Year	Team	League	Games	G.	A.	Pts.	Pen.
1982-83—Don Mills Midgets		OHA	40	25	30	55	10
1983-84—Toronto Marlboros		OHL	66	19	17	36	12
1984-85—Toronto Marlboros		OHL	66	31	41	72	15
1985-86—Toronto Marlboros		OHL	63	32	48	80	28
1986-87—Toronto Marlboros (c)		OHL	66	*57	50	107	38
1986-87—Baltimore Skipjacks (d)		AHL	9	5	2	7	2
1987-88—Washington Capitals (e)		NHL	4	0	0	0	0
1987-88—Binghamton Whalers		AHL	72	46	48	94	23
1988-89—Baltimore Skipjacks		AHL	80	44	63	107	51
1989-90—Baltimore Skipjacks (b-f)		AHL	53	41	42	83	14
1989-90—Washington Capitals		NHL	3	0	2	2	2
NHL TOTALS			7	0	2	2	2

(c)—Won Leo Lalonde Memorial Trophy (Top Overage Player).

(d)—April, 1987—Signed by Baltimore Skipjacks as a free agent.

(e)—October, 1988—Signed by Washington Capitals as a free agent.

(f)—May, 1990—Signed to play in Zurich, Switzerland in 1990-91.

TODD RICHARDS

Defense . . . 6' . . . 180 lbs. . . . Born, Robbinsdale, Minn., October 20, 1966 . . . Shoots right . . . (January 8, 1988)—Separated shoulder vs. North Dakota.

Year	Team	League	Games	G.	A.	Pts.	Pen.
1984-85—Armstrong H.S. (c)	Minn. H.S.	24	10	23	33	24
1985-86—Univ. of Minnesota	WCHA	38	6	23	29	38
1986-87—Univ. of Minnesota (b)	WCHA	49	8	43	51	70
1987-88—Univ. of Minnesota	WCHA	34	10	30	40	26
1988-89—Univ. of Minnesota (b-d)	WCHA	46	6	32	38	60
1989-90—Sherbrooke Canadiens	AHL	71	6	18	24	73

(c)—June, 1985—Drafted by Montreal Canadiens in 1985 NHL entry draft. Third Canadiens pick, 33rd overall, second round.
(d)—Named Second team All-America (West).

LUKE RICHARDSON

Defense . . . 6'4" . . . 210 lbs. . . . Born, Ottawa, Ont., March 26, 1969 . . . Shoots left.

Year	Team	League	Games	G.	A.	Pts.	Pen.
1984-85—Ottawa Golden Knights	OHA	35	5	26	31	72
1985-86—Peterborough Petes	OHL	63	6	18	24	57
1986-87—Peterborough Petes (c)	OHL	59	13	32	45	70
1987-88—Toronto Maple Leafs	NHL	78	4	6	10	90
1988-89—Toronto Maple Leafs	NHL	55	2	7	9	106
1989-90—Toronto Maple Leafs	NHL	67	4	14	18	122
NHL TOTALS		200	10	27	37	318

(c)—June, 1987—Drafted as underage junior by Toronto Maple Leafs in 1987 NHL entry draft. First Maple Leafs pick, seventh overall, first round.

STEPHANE (J.G.) RICHER

Defense . . . 5'11" . . . 200 lbs. . . . Born, Hull, Que., April 23, 1966 . . . Shoots right.

Year	Team	League	Games	G.	A.	Pts.	Pen.
1983-84—Hull Olympiques	QMJHL	70	8	38	46	42
1984-85—Hull Olympiques	QMJHL	67	21	56	77	98
1985-86—Hull Olympiques	QMJHL	71	14	52	66	166
1986-87—Hull Olympiques	QMJHL	33	6	22	28	74
1987-88—Baltimore Skipjacks	AHL	22	0	3	3	6
1987-88—Sherbrooke Canadiens (c)	AHL	41	4	7	11	46
1988-89—Sherbrooke Canadiens	AHL	70	7	26	33	158
1989-90—Sherbrooke Canadiens (d)	AHL	60	10	12	22	85

(c)—January 9, 1988—Signed by Montreal Canadiens as a free agent.
(d)—July 11, 1990—Signed by Los Angeles Kings as a free agent.

STEPHANE RICHER

Center . . . 6' . . . 190 lbs. . . . Born, Buckingham, Que., June 7, 1966 . . . Shoots right . . . (November 18, 1985)—Sprained ankle vs. Boston and missed 13 games . . . (March 12, 1988)—Bruised right hand in fight with Kevin Dineen vs. Hartford . . . (April, 1988)—Broke right thumb when slashed by Michael Thelven vs. Boston . . . (September, 1988)—Sprained right thumb in Montreal Canadiens training camp . . . (November 16, 1988)—Suspended 10 games for slashing Jeff Norton vs. N.Y. Islanders . . . (March 15, 1989)—Flu . . . (September, 1989)—Bruised right shoulder vs. Quebec . . . (February, 1990)—Bruised left foot . . . (April 21, 1990)—Injured left ankle at Boston.

Year	Team	League	Games	G.	A.	Pts.	Pen.
1983-84—Granby Bisons (c)	QMJHL	67	39	37	76	58
1984-85—G'y Bisons/Chic. Sags. (b-d)	QMJHL	57	61	59	120	71
1984-85—Montreal Canadiens	NHL	1	0	0	0	0
1984-85—Sherbrooke Canadiens (e)	AHL	....	....	....	....	....
1985-86—Montreal Canadiens	NHL	65	21	16	37	50
1986-87—Sherbrooke Canadiens	AHL	12	10	4	14	11
1986-87—Montreal Canadiens	NHL	57	20	19	39	80
1987-88—Montreal Canadiens	NHL	72	50	28	78	72
1988-89—Montreal Canadiens	NHL	68	25	35	60	61
1989-90—Montreal Canadiens	NHL	75	51	40	91	46
NHL TOTALS		337	167	138	305	309

(c)—June, 1984—Drafted as underage junior by Montreal Canadiens in NHL entry draft. Third Canadiens pick, 29th overall, second round.
(d)—January, 1985—Traded with Greg Choules by Granby Bisons to Chicoutimi Sagueneens for Stephane Roy, Marc Bureau, Lee Duhemee, Sylvain Demers and Rene Lecuyer.
(e)—No regular season record. Played nine playoff games.

STEVE RICHMOND

Defense . . . 6'1" . . . 205 lbs. . . . Born, Chicago, Ill., December 11, 1959 . . . Shoots left . . . (December, 1986)—Three-game NHL suspension . . . (February, 1987)—Strained left knee . . . (September, 1988)—Separated shoulder during Los Angeles Kings training camp.

Year	Team	League	Games	G.	A.	Pts.	Pen.
1978-79—University of Michigan	WCHA	34	2	5	7	38
1979-80—University of Michigan	WCHA	38	10	19	29	26
1980-81—University of Michigan	WCHA	39	22	32	54	46
1981-82—University of Michigan (b-c)	CCHA	38	6	30	36	68
1982-83—Tulsa Oilers	CHL	78	5	13	18	187
1983-84—Tulsa Oilers	CHL	38	1	17	18	114
1983-84—New York Rangers	NHL	26	2	5	7	110
1984-85—New Haven Nighthawks	AHL	37	3	10	13	122
1984-85—New York Rangers	NHL	34	0	5	5	90
1985-86—New Haven Nighthawks	AHL	11	2	6	8	32
1985-86—New York Rangers (d)	NHL	17	0	2	2	63

Year	Team	League	Games	G.	A.	Pts.	Pen.
1985-86—Adirondack Red Wings	AHL	20	1	7	8	23
1985-86—Detroit Red Wings (e)	NHL	29	1	2	3	82
1986-87—New Jersey Devils	NHL	44	1	7	8	143
1987-88—Utica Devils	AHL	79	6	27	33	141
1987-88—Flint Spirits	IHL	2	0	2	2	2
1988-89—New Haven Nighthawks	AHL	49	6	35	41	114
1988-89—Los Angeles Kings (f)	NHL	9	0	2	2	26
1989-90—Flint Spirits	IHL	10	1	3	4	19
NHL TOTALS		159	4	23	27	514

(c)—July, 1982—Signed by New York Rangers as a free agent.
(d)—December, 1985—Traded by New York Rangers to Detroit Red Wings for Mike McEwen.
(e)—August, 1986—Traded by Detroit Red Wings to New Jersey Devils for Sam St. Laurent.
(f)—July, 1988—Signed by Los Angeles Kings as a free agent.

BARRY RICHTER

Defense . . . 6'2" . . . 190 lbs. . . . Born, Madison, Wis., September 11, 1970 . . . Shoots left . . . Also plays Right Wing . . . Father Pat Richter is Athletic Director of University of Wisconsin and former Washington Redskins football player.

Year	Team	League	Games	G.	A.	Pts.	Pen.
1986-87—Culver Academy	Indiana H.S.	35	19	26	45	..
1987-88—Culver Academy (c)	Indiana H.S.	35	24	29	53	18
1988-89—Culver Academy	Indiana H.S.	19	21	29	50	16
1989-90—University of Wisconsin	WCHA	42	13	23	36	26

(c)—June, 1988—Drafted by Hartford Whalers in 1988 NHL entry draft. Second Whalers pick, 32nd overall, second round.

DAVE RICHTER

Defense . . . 6'5" . . . 217 lbs. . . . Born, Winnipeg, Man., April 8, 1960 . . . Shoots right . . . (November, 1982)—Strained knee ligaments . . . (Summer, 1983)—Elbow surgery . . . (October, 1984)—Strained abdominal muscle during training camp . . . (February, 1985)—Shoulder injury . . . (September, 1985)—Missed first seven games of season due to a pulled groin from training camp . . . (January 17, 1986)—Sprained knee vs. N.Y. Islanders and missed six games . . . (November, 1987)—Strained left knee . . . (February, 1988)—Bruised eye . . . (March 9, 1988)—Suspended 10 NHL games . . . (December 11, 1988)—Broke nose in fight with Everett Sanipass at Chicago.

Year	Team	League	Games	G.	A.	Pts.	Pen.
1979-80—University of Michigan	WCHA	34	0	4	4	54
1980-81—University of Michigan	WCHA	36	2	13	15	56
1981-82—University of Michigan	CCHA	36	9	12	21	78
1981-82—Nashville South Stars	CHL	2	0	1	1	0
1981-82—Minnesota North Stars (c)	NHL	3	0	0	0	11
1982-83—Minnesota North Stars	NHL	6	0	0	0	4
1982-83—Birmingham South Stars	CHL	69	6	17	23	211
1983-84—Salt Lake Golden Eagles	CHL	10	1	4	5	39
1983-84—Minnesota North Stars	NHL	42	2	3	5	132
1984-85—Springfield Indians	AHL	3	0	0	0	2
1984-85—Minnesota North Stars	NHL	55	2	8	10	221
1985-86—Minnesota North Stars (d)	NHL	14	0	3	3	29
1985-86—Philadelphia Flyers (e)	NHL	50	0	2	2	138
1986-87—Vancouver Canucks	NHL	78	2	15	17	172
1987-88—Vancouver Canucks	NHL	49	2	4	6	224
1988-89—St. Louis Blues (f)	NHL	66	1	5	6	99
1989-90—St. Louis Blues	NHL	2	0	0	0	0
1989-90—Peoria Rivermen (g)	IHL	12	1	4	5	28
1989-90—Phoenix Roadrunners	IHL	20	0	5	5	49
1989-90—Baltimore Skipjacks	AHL	13	0	1	1	13
NHL TOTALS		365	9	40	49	1030

(c)—June, 1982—Signed by Minnesota North Stars as a free agent.
(d)—November, 1985—Traded with Bo Berglund by Minnesota North Stars to Philadelphia Flyers for Todd Bergen and Ed Hospodar.
(e)—June, 1986—Traded by Philadelphia Flyers with Rich Sutter and a third-round draft choice in 1986 to Vancouver Canucks for J.J. Daigneault, a second-round draft choice (Kent Hawley) in 1986 and a fifth-round pick in 1987.
(f)—September 7, 1988—Traded by Vancouver Canucks to St. Louis Blues for Robert Nordmark and a second-round 1990 draft pick.
(g)—November 21, 1989—Released by St. Louis Blues.

MIKE RIDLEY

Center . . . 6'1" . . . 200 lbs. . . . Born, Winnipeg, Man., July 8, 1963 . . . Shoots left . . . (March 9, 1990)—Hospitalized with collapsed left lung following a collision with Michel Petit at Quebec and missed six games . . . (April 5, 1990)—Bruised ribs when checked by Randy Velischek vs. New Jersey.

Year	Team	League	Games	G.	A.	Pts.	Pen.
1983-84—University of Manitoba (c)	GPAC	46	39	41	80	..
1984-85—University of Manitoba	GPAC	30	29	38	67	..
1985-86—New York Rangers (d)	NHL	80	22	43	65	69
1986-87—New York Rangers (e)	NHL	38	16	20	36	20
1986-87—Washington Capitals	NHL	40	15	19	34	20
1987-88—Washington Capitals	NHL	70	28	31	59	22
1988-89—Washington Capitals	NHL	80	41	48	89	49
1989-90—Washington Capitals	NHL	74	30	43	73	27
NHL TOTALS		382	152	204	356	207

(c)—Won Sen. Joseph Sullivan Award as the top Canadian College hockey player.
(d)—September, 1985—Signed by New York Rangers as a free agent.
(e)—January, 1987—Traded with Kelly Miller and Bobby Crawford by New York Rangers to Washington Capitals for Bobby Carpenter and a second-round 1989 draft pick.

MARIO ROBERGE

Left Wing . . . 5'11" . . . 185 lbs. . . . Born, Quebec City, Que., January 31, 1964 . . . Shoots left . . . Brother of Serge Roberge.

Year	Team	League	Games	G.	A.	Pts.	Pen.
1981-82—Quebec Remparts	QMJHL	8	0	3	3	2
1982-83—Quebec Remparts	QMJHL	69	3	27	30	153
1983-84—Quebec Remparts	QMJHL	60	12	28	40	253
1984-85—...............	......				
1985-86—...............	......				
1986-87—...............	......				
1987-88—Port Aux Basques (c)	Nova Scotia	35	25	64	89	152
1988-89—Sherbrooke Canadiens	AHL	58	4	9	13	249
1989-90—Sherbrooke Canadiens	AHL	73	13	27	40	247

(c)—January, 1988—Signed by Sherbrooke Canadiens as a free agent.

SERGE ROBERGE

Right Wing . . . 6'1" . . . 195 lbs. . . . Born, Quebec City, Que., March 31, 1965 . . . Shoots right . . . Brother of Mario Roberge.

Year	Team	League	Games	G.	A.	Pts.	Pen.
1982-83—Quebec Remparts	QMJHL	9	0	0	0	30
1982-83—Hull Olympiques	QMJHL	22	0	4	4	115
1983-84—Drummondville Voltigeurs	QMJHL	58	1	7	8	287
1984-85—Drummondville Voltigeurs	QMJHL	45	8	19	27	299
1985-86—Out of hockey					
1986-87—Virginia Lancers	ACHL	52	25	43	68	178
1987-88—Sherbrooke Canadiens (c)	AHL	30	0	1	1	130
1988-89—Sherbrooke Canadiens	AHL	65	5	7	12	352
1989-90—Sherbrooke Canadiens	AHL	66	8	5	13	*343

(c)—January 25, 1988—Signed by Montreal Canadiens as a free agent.

DAVID ROBERTS

Left Wing . . . 6' . . . 180 lbs. . . . Born, Alameda, Calif., May 28, 1970 . . . Shoots left . . . Son of Doug Roberts (Former NHL player with Oakland, Detroit, California, Boston; WHA player with New England, and currently head hockey coach at Central Connecticut State College), cousin of Alex Roberts and nephew of Gordie Roberts.

Year	Team	League	Games	G.	A.	Pts.	Pen.
1987-88—Avon Old Farms H.S.	Conn. H.S.	....	18	39	57	....
1988-89—Avon Old Farms H.S. (c)	Conn. H.S.	....	28	48	76	....
1989-90—University of Michigan (d-e)	CCHA	42	21	32	53	46

(c)—June, 1989—Drafted by St. Louis Blues in 1989 NHL entry draft. Fifth Blues pick, 114th overall, sixth round.
(d)—Named to CCHA All-Rookie team.
(e)—Named CCHA Rookie of the Year.

GARY ROBERTS

Left Wing . . . 6'1" . . . 190 lbs. . . . Born, North York, Ont., May 23, 1966 . . . Shoots left . . . (January, 1989)—Injured back.

Year	Team	League	Games	G.	A.	Pts.	Pen.
1981-82—Whitby Midgets	Ont. Midgets	44	55	31	86	133
1982-83—Ottawa 67's	OHL	53	12	8	20	83
1983-84—Ottawa 67's (c-d)	OHL	48	27	30	57	144
1984-85—Ottawa 67's (b)	OHL	59	44	62	106	186
1984-85—Moncton Golden Flames	AHL	7	4	2	6	7
1985-86—Ottawa 67's	OHL	24	26	25	51	83
1985-86—Guelph Platers (b)	OHL	23	18	15	33	65
1986-87—Moncton Golden Flames	AHL	38	20	18	38	72
1986-87—Calgary Flames	NHL	32	5	10	15	85
1987-88—Calgary Flames	NHL	74	13	15	28	282
1988-89—Calgary Flames	NHL	71	22	16	38	250
1989-90—Calgary Flames	NHL	78	39	33	72	222
NHL TOTALS		255	79	74	153	839

(c)—Led OHL playoffs with 62 penalty minutes.
(d)—June, 1984—Drafted as underage junior by Calgary Flames in 1984 NHL entry draft. First Flames pick, 12th overall, first round.

GORDON ROBERTS

Defense . . . 6' . . . 195 lbs. . . . Born, Detroit, Mich., October 2, 1957 . . . Shoots left . . . Brother of former NHLers Dave and Doug Roberts and uncle of David Roberts and Alex Roberts . . . (April, 1984)—Bruised hip vs. Edmonton . . . (November 13, 1985)—Injured foot at Hartford and missed four games . . . (October, 1986)—Dislocated shoulder . . . (January, 1988)—Bruised shoulder.

Year	Team	League	Games	G.	A.	Pts.	Pen.
1973-74—Detroit Jr. Red Wings	SOJHL	70	25	55	80	340
1974-75—Victoria Cougars (c)	WCHL	53	19	45	64	145
1975-76—New England Whalers	WHA	77	3	19	22	102
1976-77—New England Whalers (d)	WHA	77	13	33	46	169
1977-78—New England Whalers	WHA	78	15	46	61	118
1978-79—New England Whalers	WHA	79	11	46	57	113
1979-80—Hartford Whalers	NHL	80	8	28	36	89
1980-81—Hartford Whalers (e)	NHL	27	2	11	13	81
1980-81—Minnesota North Stars	NHL	50	6	31	37	94
1981-82—Minnesota North Stars	NHL	79	4	30	34	119
1982-83—Minnesota North Stars	NHL	80	3	41	44	103
1983-84—Minnesota North Stars	NHL	77	8	45	53	132
1984-85—Minnesota North Stars	NHL	78	6	36	42	112
1985-86—Minnesota North Stars	NHL	76	2	21	23	101
1986-87—Minnesota North Stars	NHL	67	3	10	13	68
1987-88—Minnesota North Stars (f)	NHL	48	1	10	11	103
1987-88—Philadelphia Flyers (g)	NHL	11	1	2	3	15

(Continued in next column)

Year	Team	League	Games	G.	A.	Pts.	Pen.
1987-88—St. Louis Blues	NHL	11	1	3	4	25
1988-89—St. Louis Blues	NHL	77	2	24	26	90
1989-90—St. Louis Blues	NHL	75	3	14	17	140
WHA TOTALS		311	42	144	186	502
NHL TOTALS		836	50	306	356	1272

(c)—September, 1975—Signed by New England Whalers (WHA).
(d)—Drafted from New England Whalers (WHA) by Montreal Canadiens in third round of 1977 amateur draft.
(e)—December, 1980—Traded by Hartford Whalers to Minnesota North Stars for Mike Fidler.
(f)—February, 1988—Traded by Minnesota North Stars to Philadelphia Flyers for a fourth round 1989 draft pick (Jean Francois Quintin).
(g)—March, 1988—Traded by Philadelphia Flyers to St. Louis Blues for a fourth-round 1989 draft pick (Reid Simpson).

TORRIE ANDREW ROBERTSON

Left Wing . . . 5'11" . . . 185 lbs. . . . Born, Victoria, B.C., August 2, 1961 . . . Shoots left . . . Brother of Geordie Robertson . . . (November 29, 1986)—Multiple fracture of left leg at Montreal and missed remainder of season . . . (November 16, 1987)—Returned to Hartford lineup . . . (November 1, 1988)—Broke right leg in fight with Mike Lalor vs. Montreal and missed 29 games.

Year	Team	League	Games	G.	A.	Pts.	Pen.
1978-79—Victoria Cougars	WHL	69	18	23	41	141
1979-80—Victoria Cougars (c)	WHL	72	23	24	47	298
1980-81—Victoria Cougars (b)	WHL	59	45	66	111	274
1980-81—Washington Capitals	NHL	3	0	0	0	0
1981-82—Hershey Bears	AHL	21	5	3	8	60
1981-82—Washington Capitals	NHL	54	8	13	21	204
1982-83—Washington Capitals	NHL	5	2	0	2	4
1982-83—Hershey Bears	AHL	69	21	33	54	187
1983-84—Hartford Whalers (d)	NHL	66	7	13	20	198
1984-85—Hartford Whalers	NHL	74	11	30	41	337
1985-86—Hartford Whalers	NHL	76	13	24	37	358
1986-87—Hartford Whalers	NHL	20	1	0	1	98
1987-88—Hartford Whalers	NHL	63	2	8	10	293
1988-89—Hartford Whalers (e)	NHL	27	2	4	6	84
1988-89—Detroit Red Wings	NHL	12	2	2	4	63
1989-90—Adirondack Red Wings	AHL	27	3	13	16	47
1989-90—Detroit Red Wings	NHL	42	1	5	6	112
NHL TOTALS		442	49	99	148	1751

(c)—June, 1980—Drafted by Washington Capitals as underage junior in 1980 NHL entry draft. Third Capitals pick, 55th overall, third round.
(d)—October, 1983—Traded by Washington Capitals to Hartford Whalers for Greg Adams.
(e)—March 7, 1989—Traded by Hartford Whalers to Detroit Red Wings for Jim Pavese.

LARRY CLARK ROBINSON

Defense . . . 6'3" . . . 210 lbs. . . . Born, Winchester, Ont., June 2, 1951 . . . Shoots left . . . Also plays Left Wing . . . Brother of Moe Robinson . . . Missed part of 1978-79 season with water on the knee . . . (March 6, 1980)—Right shoulder separation vs. Edmonton . . . (October, 1980)—Groin injury . . . (November 14, 1980)—Separated left shoulder . . . (January 8, 1981)—Broken nose . . . (October, 1982)—Sore left shoulder . . . (October, 1983)—Skin infection behind right knee . . . (March, 1985)—Hyperextended left elbow . . . (March 9, 1987)—Strained ligaments in right ankle when checked by Dennis Maruk at Minnesota . . . (August, 1987)—Broke leg in a polo accident . . . (December, 1987)—Sprained right wrist . . . (November 9, 1988)—Sinus problem . . . (May 23, 1989)—Hyperextended knee at Calgary . . . Holds Canadiens career records in goals (197), assists (686) and points (883) by a defenseman . . . (March, 1990)—Missed games with food poisoning and lost 10 pounds.

Year	Team	League	Games	G.	A.	Pts.	Pen.
1968-69—Brockville Braves	Cent. Jr. OHA	....	....	....	....	....
1969-70—Brockville Braves (a)	Cent. Jr. OHA	40	22	29	51	74
1970-71—Kitchener Rangers (c)	Jr."A" OHA	61	12	39	51	65
1971-72—Nova Scotia Voyageurs	AHL	74	10	14	24	54
1972-73—Nova Scotia Voyageurs	AHL	38	6	33	39	33
1972-73—Montreal Canadiens	NHL	36	2	4	6	20
1973-74—Montreal Canadiens	NHL	78	6	20	26	66
1974-75—Montreal Canadiens	NHL	80	14	47	61	76
1975-76—Montreal Canadiens	NHL	80	10	30	40	59
1976-77—Montreal Canadiens	NHL	77	19	66	85	45
1977-78—Montreal Canadiens (b-e-f)	NHL	80	13	52	65	39
1978-79—Montreal Canadiens (a)	NHL	67	16	45	61	33
1979-80—Montreal Canadiens (a-d)	NHL	72	14	61	75	39
1980-81—Montreal Canadiens (b)	NHL	65	12	38	50	37
1981-82—Montreal Canadiens	NHL	71	12	47	59	41
1982-83—Montreal Canadiens	NHL	71	14	49	63	33
1983-84—Montreal Canadiens	NHL	74	9	34	43	39
1984-85—Montreal Canadiens	NHL	76	14	33	47	44
1985-86—Montreal Canadiens (b)	NHL	78	19	63	82	39
1986-87—Montreal Canadiens	NHL	70	13	37	50	44
1987-88—Montreal Canadiens	NHL	53	6	34	40	30
1988-89—Montreal Canadiens (g)	NHL	74	4	26	30	22
1989-90—Los Angeles Kings	NHL	64	7	32	39	34
NHL TOTALS		1266	204	718	922	740

(c)—Drafted from Kitchener Rangers by Montreal Canadiens in second round of 1971 amateur draft.
(d)—Won James Norris Memorial Trophy (Outstanding Defenseman).
(e)—Led in assists (17) and tied for lead in points (21) during playoffs.
(f)—Won Conn Smythe Trophy (MVP in Stanley Cup playoffs).
(g)—July 26, 1989—Signed multi-year contract with Los Angeles Kings as a free agent.

ROB ROBINSON

Defense . . . 6'3'' . . . 210 lbs. . . . Born, St. Catharines, Ont., April 19, 1967 . . . Shoots left . . . Son of Doug Robinson (former NHL defenseman with Chicago, N.Y. Rangers and Los Angeles; and currently chief scout with Montreal).

Year	Team	League	Games	G.	A.	Pts.	Pen.
1985-86—Miami of Ohio Univ.		CCHA	38	1	9	10	24
1986-87—Miami of Ohio Univ. (c)		CCHA	33	3	5	8	32
1987-88—Miami of Ohio Univ.		CCHA	35	1	3	4	56
1988-89—Miami of Ohio Univ.		CCHA	30	3	4	7	42
1988-89—Peoria Rivermen		IHL	11	2	0	2	6
1989-90—Peoria Rivermen		IHL	60	2	11	13	72

(c)—June, 1987—Drafted by St. Louis Blues in 1987 NHL entry draft. Sixth Blues pick, 117th overall, sixth round.

SCOTT ROBINSON

Right Wing . . . 6'2'' . . . 180 lbs. . . . Born, Mile House, B.C., March 29, 1964 . . . Shoots left.

Year	Team	League	Games	G.	A.	Pts.	Pen.
1982-83—Seattle Breakers		WHL	63	14	13	27	151
1983-84—Seattle Breakers		WHL	44	17	18	35	105
1984-85—Seattle Breakers		WHL	64	44	53	97	106
1985-86—University of Calgary		CWUAA	18	3	9	12	61
1986-87—University of Calgary		CWUAA	19	12	14	26	95
1987-88—University of Calgary (c)		CWUAA	21	14	14	28	64
1988-89—Kalamazoo Wings		IHL	49	14	17	31	129
1989-90—Kalamazoo Wings		IHL	48	13	12	25	97
1989-90—Minnesota North Stars		NHL	1	0	0	0	2
NHL TOTALS			1	0	0	0	2

(c)—September 27, 1988—Signed by Minnesota North Stars as a free agent.

JEFFREY ROBISON

Defense . . . 6'1'' . . . 180 lbs. . . . Born, Norwood, Mass., June 3, 1970 . . . Shoots left . . . (January, 1988)—Broken wrist.

Year	Team	League	Games	G.	A.	Pts.	Pen.
1986-87—Mt. St. Charles		R.I. H.S.	24	11	14	25	..
1987-88—Mt. St. Charles (c)		R.I. H.S.	..	5	30	35	..
1988-89—Providence College		H. East	41	0	5	5	36
1989-90—Providence College		H. East	35	2	8	10	16

(c)—June, 1988—Drafted by Los Angeles Kings in 1988 NHL entry draft. Fifth Kings pick, 91st overall, fifth round.

LUC ROBITAILLE

Left Wing . . . 6' . . . 180 lbs. . . . Born, Montreal, Que., February 17, 1966 . . . Shoots left.

Year	Team	League	Games	G.	A.	Pts.	Pen.
1983-84—Hull Olympiques (c)		QMJHL	70	32	53	85	48
1984-85—Hull Olympiques		QMJHL	64	55	94	148	115
1985-86—Hull Olympiques (a-d-e)		QMJHL	63	68	*123	*191	93
1986-87—Los Angeles Kings (b-f)		NHL	79	45	39	84	28
1987-88—Los Angeles Kings (a)		NHL	80	53	58	111	82
1988-89—Los Angeles Kings (a)		NHL	78	46	52	98	65
1989-90—Los Angeles Kings (a)		NHL	80	52	49	101	38
NHL TOTALS			317	196	198	394	213

(c)—June, 1984—Drafted as underage junior by Los Angeles Kings in 1984 NHL entry draft. Ninth Kings pick, 171st overall, ninth round.
(d)—Named Canadian Major Junior Hockey League Player of the Year.
(e)—Shared Guy Lafleur Trophy (Playoff MVP) with Sylvain Cote.
(f)—Won Calder Memorial Trophy (NHL Rookie of the Year).

NORMAND ROCHEFORT

Defense . . . 6'1'' . . . 200 lbs. . . . Born, Trois-Rivieres, Que., January 28, 1961 . . . Shoots left . . . (November, 1980)—Neck injury . . . Missed parts of 1982-83 season with injured knee . . . Nephew of Leon Rochefort (NHL, 1961-1976) . . . (October 19, 1985)—Sprained ankle vs. Pittsburgh . . . (February 8, 1986)—Separated shoulder vs. Chicago . . . (October, 1987)—Injured neck and upper back . . . (January, 1988)—Bruised left foot . . . (February, 1988)—Sprained right foot . . . (October, 1988)—Sprained right knee . . . (November 9, 1988)—Reinjured knee and had surgery . . . (February 5, 1989)—Reinjured knee vs. Minnesota and had major reconstructive surgery . . . (October, 1990)—Returned after missing 347 days.

Year	Team	League	Games	G.	A.	Pts.	Pen.
1977-78—Trois-Rivieres Draveurs		QMJHL	72	9	37	46	36
1978-79—Trois-Rivieres Draveurs		QMJHL	72	17	57	74	80
1979-80—Trois-Rivieres Draveurs		QMJHL	20	5	25	30	22
1979-80—Quebec Remparts (b-c)		QMJHL	52	8	39	47	68
1980-81—Quebec Remparts		QMJHL	9	2	6	8	14
1980-81—Quebec Nordiques		NHL	56	3	7	10	51
1981-82—Quebec Nordiques		NHL	72	4	14	18	115
1982-83—Quebec Nordiques		NHL	62	6	17	23	40
1983-84—Quebec Nordiques		NHL	75	2	22	24	47
1984-85—Quebec Nordiques		NHL	73	3	21	24	74
1985-86—Quebec Nordiques		NHL	26	5	4	9	30
1986-87—Quebec Nordiques		NHL	70	6	9	15	46
1987-88—Quebec Nordiques (d)		NHL	46	3	10	13	49
1988-89—New York Rangers		NHL	11	1	5	6	18
1989-90—Flint Spirits		IHL	7	3	2	5	4
1989-90—New York Rangers		NHL	31	3	1	4	24
NHL TOTALS			522	36	110	146	494

(c)—June, 1980—Drafted by Quebec Nordiques as underage junior in 1980 NHL entry draft. First Nordiques pick, 24th overall, second round.
(d)—August, 1988—Traded with Jason Lafreniere by Quebec Nordiques to New York Rangers for Walt Poddubny, Bruce Bell, Jari Gronstrand and a fourth-round draft choice in 1989.

JEREMY ROENICK

Center . . . 5'11'' . . . 170 lbs. . . . Born, Boston, Mass., January 17, 1970 . . . Shoots right . . . (December, 1988)—The first U.S.-born player to lead the world junior hockey championships in scoring (8 goals, 8 assists) . . . (January 9, 1989)—Missed a month with sprained knee ligaments.

Year	Team	League	Games	G.	A.	Pts.	Pen.
1986-87—Thayer Academy		Mass. H.S.	24	31	34	65	..
1987-88—Thayer Academy (c)		Mass. H.S.	..	34	50	84	..
1988-89—Chicago Black Hawks		NHL	20	9	9	18	4
1988-89—Hull Olympiques		QMJHL	28	34	36	70	14
1989-90—Chicago Black Hawks (d)		NHL	78	26	40	66	54
NHL TOTALS			98	35	49	84	58

(c)—June, 1988—Drafted by Chicago Black Hawks in 1988 NHL entry draft. First Black Hawks pick, eighth overall, first round.
(d)—Named THE SPORTING NEWS NHL Rookie of the Year.

JEFF ROHLICEK

Left Wing . . . 6' . . . 180 lbs. . . . Born, Park Ridge, Ill., January 27, 1966 . . . Shoots left.

Year	Team	League	Games	G.	A.	Pts.	Pen.
1982-83—Chicago Jets Midget		Ill. H.S.	35	57	73	130	....
1982-83—Main West H.S.		Ill. H.S.	25	60	60	120	....
1983-84—Portland Winter Hawks (b-c)		WHL	71	44	53	97	22
1984-85—Portland Winter Hawks		WHL	16	5	13	18	2
1984-85—Kelowna Wings (b)		WHL	49	34	39	73	24
1985-86—Spokane Chiefs		WHL	57	50	52	102	39
1986-87—Fredericton Express		AHL	70	19	37	56	22
1987-88—Vancouver Canucks		NHL	7	0	0	0	4
1987-88—Fredericton Express		AHL	65	26	31	57	50
1988-89—Vancouver Canucks		NHL	2	0	0	0	4
1988-89—Milwaukee Admirals (a)		IHL	78	47	63	110	106
1989-90—Springfield Indians		AHL	12	1	2	3	4
1989-90—Milwaukee Admirals (d)		IHL	53	22	26	48	37
NHL TOTALS			9	0	0	0	8

(c)—June, 1984—Drafted as underage junior by Vancouver Canucks in 1984 NHL entry draft. Second Canucks pick, 31st overall, second round.
(d)—March 6, 1990—Traded by Vancouver Canucks to New York Islanders for Jack Capuano.

STEVE ROHLIK

Left Wing . . . 6' . . . 180 lbs. . . . Born, St. Paul, Minn., May 15, 1968 . . . Shoots left.

Year	Team	League	Games	G.	A.	Pts.	Pen.
1984-85—Hill Murray H.S.		Minn. H.S.	25	16	24	40	....
1985-86—Hill Murray H.S. (c)		Minn. H.S.	27	26	33	59	....
1986-87—Univ. of Wisconsin		WCHA	31	3	0	3	34
1987-88—Univ. of Wisconsin		WCHA	44	3	10	13	59
1988-89—Univ. of Wisconsin		WCHA	45	11	14	25	44
1989-90—Univ. of Wisconsin (d)		WCHA	46	17	23	40	52

(c)—June, 1986—Drafted by Pittsburgh Penguins in 1986 NHL entry draft. Eighth Penguins pick, 151st overall, eighth round.
(d)—Named MVP of WCHA playoffs.

JON ROHLOFF

Defense . . . 6' . . . 200 lbs. . . . Born, Mankato, Minn., October 3, 1969 . . . Shoots right.

Year	Team	League	Games	G.	A.	Pts.	Pen.
1986-87—Grand Rapids H.S.		Minn. H.S.	21	12	23	35	16
1987-88—Grand Rapids H.S. (c)		Minn. H.S.	23	10	13	23	..
1988-89—Univ. of Minn./Duluth		WCHA	39	1	2	3	44
1989-90—Univ. of Minn./Duluth		WCHA	5	0	1	1	6

(c)—June, 1988—Drafted by Boston Bruins in 1988 NHL entry draft. Seventh Bruins pick, 186th overall, ninth round.

DANIEL ROLFE

Defense . . . 6'4'' . . . 200 lbs. . . . Born, Inglewood, Calif., December 25, 1967 . . . Shoots left . . . Son of Dale Rolfe, former NHL defenseman with Boston, Los Angeles, Detroit and N.Y. Rangers.

Year	Team	League	Games	G.	A.	Pts.	Pen.
1986-87—Brockville (c)		OPJHL	41	14	23	37	....
1987-88—Ferris State Univ.		CCHA	13	1	1	2	36
1988-89—Ferris State Univ.		CCHA	26	0	2	2	54
1989-90—Ferris State Univ.		CCHA	31	0	6	6	48

(c)—June, 1987—Drafted by St. Louis Blues in 1987 NHL entry draft. Twelfth Blues pick, 222nd overall, 11th round.

RUSSELL ROMANIUK

Left Wing . . . 6'1'' . . . 186 lbs. . . . Born, Winnipeg, Man., June 9, 1970 . . . Shoots left . . . (December, 1987)—Chip fracture of left knee . . . (February, 1988)—Sprained right shoulder.

Year	Team	League	Games	G.	A.	Pts.	Pen.
1987-88—St. Boniface Saints (c)		MJHL	...	...	...	...	...
1988-89—Univ. of North Dakota		WCHA	39	17	14	31	32
1989-90—Canadian National Team		Int'l.	3	1	0	1	0
1989-90—Univ. of North Dakota (d)		WCHA	45	36	15	51	54

(c)—June, 1988—Drafted by Winnipeg Jets in 1988 NHL entry draft. Second Jets pick, 31st overall, second round.
(d)—Named to WCHA All-Tournament team.

ED RONAN

Right Wing . . . 5'11" . . . 170 lbs. . . . Born, Quincy, Mass., March 21, 1968 . . . Shoots right.

Year	Team	League	Games	G.	A.	Pts.	Pen.
1986-87—Andover H.S. (c)	Mass. H.S.	22	12	20	32	10
1987-88—Boston Univ.	H. East	31	2	5	7	20
1988-89—Boston Univ.	H. East	36	4	11	15	34
1989-90—Boston Univ.	H. East	44	17	23	40	50

(c)—June, 1987—Drafted by Montreal Canadiens in 1987 NHL entry draft. Thirteenth Canadiens pick, 227th overall, 11th round.

CLIFF RONNING

Center . . . 5'8" . . . 160 lbs. . . . Born, Vancouver, B.C., October 1, 1965 . . . Shoots left . . . (1984-85)—Set WHL record with goals in 18 straight games . . . (1984-85)—Set WHL single season record with 197 points (Broken by Rob Brown in 1986-87) . . . (November, 1988)—Injured groin.

Year	Team	League	Games	G.	A.	Pts.	Pen.
1982-83—New Westm'ter Royals	BCJHL	52	82	68	150	42
1983-84—New Westm'ter Bruins (b-c-d)	WHL	71	69	67	136	10
1984-85—New Westm'ter Bruins (a-e-f-g)	WHL	70	*89	108	*197	20
1985-86—Team Canada	Int'l	71	55	63	118	53
1985-86—St. Louis Blues (h)	NHL	...	...	...	...	...
1986-87—Canadian National Team	Int'l	...	...	...	...	...
1986-87—Canadian Olympic Team	Int'l	71	55	63	118	53
1986-87—St. Louis Blues	NHL	42	11	14	25	6
1987-88—Canadian Olympic Team	Int'l	...	...	...	...	...
1987-88—St. Louis Blues	NHL	26	5	8	13	12
1988-89—St. Louis Blues	NHL	64	24	31	55	18
1988-89—Peoria Rivermen (i)	IHL	12	11	20	31	8
1989-90—Played in Italy	Italy	42	76	60	136	....
NHL TOTALS		132	40	53	93	36

(c)—Won Stewart Paul Memorial Trophy (Top Rookie).
(d)—June, 1984—Drafted by St. Louis Blues as underage junior in 1984 NHL entry draft. Ninth Blues pick, 134th overall, seventh round.
(e)—Won Bob Brownridge Memorial Trophy (Scoring Leader).
(f)—Won Frank Boucher Memorial Trophy (Most Gentlemanly).
(g)—Won MVP Trophy.
(h)—No regular season record. Played five playoff games.
(i)—August, 1989—Agreed to play in Italy for 1989-90 season.

LARRY ROONEY

Left Wing . . . 5'11" . . . 165 lbs. . . . Born, Boston, Mass., January 30, 1968 . . . Shoots left.

Year	Team	League	Games	G.	A.	Pts.	Pen.
1985-86—Thayer H.S. (c)	Mass. H.S.	24	20	35	55	....
1986-87—Thayer H.S.	Mass. H.S.	26	15	26	41	....
1987-88—Providence College	H. East	33	1	9	10	34
1988-89—Providence College	H. East	10	0	4	4	18
1989-90—Providence College	H. East	33	7	12	19	24

(c)—June, 1986—Drafted by Buffalo Sabres in 1986 NHL entry draft. Sixth Sabres pick, 89th overall, fifth round.

STEVEN PAUL ROONEY

Left Wing . . . 6'2" . . . 195 lbs. . . . Born, Canton, Mass., June 28, 1962 . . . Shoots left . . . (November 26, 1985)—Shoulder surgery . . . (November 1, 1987)—Broken ankle . . . (February, 1988)—Fractured rib . . . (September, 1988)—Injured left shoulder when checked by Joe Peterson vs. N.Y. Rangers . . . (October, 1988)—Injured right shoulder and required surgery . . . (April 7, 1989)—Had post-season surgery to tighten ligaments in right shoulder.

Year	Team	League	Games	G.	A.	Pts.	Pen.
1981-82—Providence College (c)	ECAC	31	7	10	17	41
1982-83—Providence College	ECAC	42	10	20	30	31
1983-84—Providence College	ECAC	33	11	16	27	46
1984-85—Providence College	H. East	42	28	22	50	63
1984-85—Montreal Canadiens	NHL	3	1	0	1	7
1985-86—Montreal Canadiens	NHL	38	2	3	5	114
1986-87—Sherbrooke Canadiens	AHL	22	4	11	15	66
1986-87—Montreal Canadiens (d)	NHL	2	0	0	0	22
1986-87—Winnipeg Jets	NHL	30	2	3	5	57
1987-88—Winnipeg Jets (e)	NHL	56	7	6	13	217
1988-89—New Jersey Devils	NHL	25	3	1	4	79
1989-90—Utica Devils	AHL	57	9	16	25	134
NHL TOTALS		154	15	13	28	496

(c)—June, 1981—Drafted by Montreal Canadiens in 1981 NHL entry draft. Eighth Canadiens pick, 88th overall, fifth round.
(d)—January, 1987—Traded by Montreal Canadiens to Winnipeg Jets for a third-round 1987 draft pick (Francois Gravel).
(e)—July, 1988—Traded with fourth-round draft choice in 1989 by Winnipeg Jets to New Jersey Devils for Alain Chevrier and seventh-round draft choice in 1989 (Doug Evans).

WILLIAM JOHN ROOT

Defense . . . 6' . . . 210 lbs. . . . Born, Toronto, Ont., September 6, 1959 . . . Shoots right . . . (March, 1985)—Broken finger . . . (October, 1985)—Broke foot when struck by a puck vs. Winnipeg . . . (February, 1988)—Pulled groin.

Year	Team	League	Games	G.	A.	Pts.	Pen.
1976-77—Niagara Falls Flyers	OMJHL	66	3	19	22	114
1977-78—Niagara Falls Flyers	OMJHL	67	6	11	17	61
1978-79—Niagara Falls Flyers (c)	OMJHL	67	4	31	35	119
1979-80—Nova Scotia Voyageurs	AHL	55	4	15	19	57

Year	Team	League	Games	G.	A.	Pts.	Pen.
1980-81—Nova Scotia Voyageurs	AHL	63	3	12	15	76
1981-82—Nova Scotia Voyageurs	AHL	77	6	25	31	105
1982-83—Montreal Canadiens	NHL	46	2	3	5	24
1982-83—Nova Scotia Voyageurs	AHL	24	0	7	7	29
1983-84—Montreal Canadiens (d)	NHL	72	4	13	17	45
1984-85—St. Catharines Saints	AHL	28	5	9	14	10
1984-85—Toronto Maple Leafs	NHL	35	1	1	2	23
1985-86—Toronto Maple Leafs	NHL	27	0	1	1	29
1985-86—St. Catharines Saints	AHL	14	7	4	11	11
1986-87—Toronto Maple Leafs	NHL	34	3	3	6	37
1986-87—Newmarket Saints	AHL	32	4	11	15	23
1987-88—St. Louis Blues (e-f)	NHL	9	0	0	0	6
1987-88—Philadelphia Flyers (g)	NHL	24	1	2	3	16
1988-89—Newmarket Saints	AHL	66	10	22	32	39
1989-90—Newmarket Saints	AHL	47	8	7	15	20
NHL TOTALS		247	11	23	34	180

(c)—October, 1979—Signed by Montreal Canadiens as a free agent.
(d)—August, 1984—Traded by Montreal Canadiens to Toronto Maple Leafs for future considerations.
(e)—October, 1987—Selected by St. Louis Blues in 1987 NHL waiver draft.
(f)—November, 1987—Claimed on waivers by Philadelphia Flyers from St. Louis Blues for $7,500.
(g)—June, 1988—Traded by Philadelphia Flyers to Toronto Maple Leafs for Mike Stothers.

BOB ROUSE

Defense . . . 6'1" . . . 210 lbs. . . . Born, Surrey, B.C., June 18, 1964 . . . Shoots right . . . (January, 1988)—Hip contusions vs. Toronto . . . (December 12, 1989)—Sprained right knee vs. Khimik in an exhibition game and missed eight games.

Year	Team	League	Games	G.	A.	Pts.	Pen.
1980-81—Billings Bighorns	WHL	70	0	13	13	116
1981-82—Billings Bighorns (c)	WHL	71	7	22	29	209
1982-83—Nanaimo Islanders	WHL	29	7	20	27	86
1982-83—Lethbridge Broncos	WHL	71	15	50	65	168
1983-84—Lethbridge Broncos (a-d)	WHL	71	18	42	60	101
1983-84—Minnesota North Stars	NHL	1	0	0	0	0
1984-85—Springfield Indians	AHL	8	0	3	3	6
1984-85—Minnesota North Stars	NHL	63	2	9	11	113
1985-86—Minnesota North Stars	NHL	75	1	14	15	151
1986-87—Minnesota North Stars	NHL	72	2	10	12	179
1987-88—Minnesota North Stars	NHL	74	0	12	12	168
1988-89—Minnesota North Stars (e)	NHL	66	4	13	17	124
1988-89—Washington Capitals	NHL	13	0	2	2	36
1989-90—Washington Capitals	NHL	70	4	16	20	123
NHL TOTALS		434	13	76	89	894

(c)—June, 1982—Drafted as underage junior by Minnesota North Stars in 1982 NHL entry draft. Third North Stars pick, 80th overall, fourth round.
(d)—Won WHL Top Defenseman Trophy.
(e)—March 7, 1989—Traded with Dino Ciccarelli by Minnesota North Stars to Washington Capitals for Mike Gartner and Larry Murphy.

MARC ROUSSEAU

Defense . . . 6' . . . 185 lbs. . . . Born, North Vancouver, B.C., May 17, 1968 . . . Shoots left . . . (August, 1984)—Torn knee ligaments.

Year	Team	League	Games	G.	A.	Pts.	Pen.
1985-86—Penticton Knights	BCJHL	42	7	23	30	176
1986-87—Univ. of Denver (c)	WCHA	39	3	18	21	70
1987-88—Univ. of Denver	WCHA	38	6	22	28	92
1988-89—Univ. of Denver	WCHA	43	10	18	28	68
1989-90—Univ. of Denver	WCHA	42	6	26	32	62

(c)—June, 1987—Drafted by Hartford Whalers in 1987 NHL entry draft. Fourth Whalers pick, 102nd overall, fifth round.

JEAN-MARC ROUTHIER

Right Wing . . . 6'2" . . . 180 lbs. . . . Born, Quebec City, Que., February 2, 1968 . . . Shoots right.

Year	Team	League	Games	G.	A.	Pts.	Pen.
1984-85—Ste. Foy Midgets	Quebec	41	13	22	35	68
1985-86—Hull Olympiques (c)	QMJHL	71	18	16	34	111
1986-87—Hull Olympiques	QMJHL	59	17	18	35	98
1987-88—Victoriaville Tigres (d)	QMJHL	57	16	28	44	267
1988-89—Halifax Citadels	AHL	52	13	13	26	189
1989-90—Quebec Nordiques	NHL	8	0	0	0	9
1989-90—Halifax Citadels (e)	AHL	17	4	8	12	29
NHL TOTALS		8	0	0	0	9

(c)—June, 1986—Drafted as underage junior by Quebec Nordiques in 1986 NHL entry draft. Second Nordiques pick, 39th overall, second round.
(d)—July, 1987—Traded by Hull Olympiques to Victoriaville Tigres for Marc Saumier.
(e)—December 11, 1989—Quit the Halifax Citadels to return to school.

MATTHEW RUCHTY

Left Wing . . . 6'1" . . . 205 lbs. . . . Born, Kitchener, Ont., November 27, 1969 . . . Shoots left.

Year	Team	League	Games	G.	A.	Pts.	Pen.
1986-87—Kitchener Greenshirts Midget	OHA	75	58	44	102	...
1987-88—Bowling Green Univ. (c)	CCHA	41	6	15	21	78
1988-89—Bowling Green Univ.	CCHA	43	11	21	32	110
1989-90—Bowling Green Univ.	CCHA	42	28	21	49	135

(c)—June, 1988—Drafted by New Jersey Devils in 1988 NHL entry draft. Fourth Devils pick, 65th overall, fourth round.

MIKE RUCINSKI

Center . . . 6' . . . 193 lbs. . . . Born, Chicago, Ill., December 12, 1963 . . . Shoots right . . . Also plays Right Wing . . . (February, 1985)—Broke arm vs. Bowling Green University.

Year	Team	League	Games	G.	A.	Pts.	Pen.
1983-84	Univ. Illinois/Chicago	CCHA	33	17	26	43	12
1984-85	Univ. Illinois/Chicago	CCHA	40	29	32	61	28
1985-86	Univ. Illinois/Chicago	CCHA	37	16	31	47	18
1986-87	Salt Lake Golden Eagles (c)	IHL	28	16	25	41	19
1986-87	Moncton Golden Flames (d)	AHL	42	5	9	14	14
1987-88	Saginaw Hawks	IHL	44	19	31	50	32
1988-89	Chicago Black Hawks	NHL	1	0	0	0	0
1988-89	Saginaw Hawks	IHL	81	35	72	107	40
1989-90	Indianapolis Ice	IHL	80	28	41	69	27
	NHL TOTALS		1	0	0	0	0

(c)—August, 1986—Signed by Calgary Flames as a free agent.
(d)—August, 1987—Signed by Chicago Black Hawks as a free agent.

JASON RUFF

Left Wing . . . 6'2" . . . 192 lbs. . . . Born, Kelowna, B.C., February 27, 1970 . . . Shoots left . . . (May, 1988)—Heel surgery.

Year	Team	League	Games	G.	A.	Pts.	Pen.
1986-87	Kelowna Packers	BCJHL	45	25	20	45	70
1987-88	Lethbridge Hurricanes	WHL	69	25	22	47	109
1988-89	Lethbridge Hurricanes	WHL	69	42	38	80	127
1989-90	Lethbridge Hurricanes (c)	WHL	72	55	64	119	114

(c)—June 16, 1990—Selected by St. Louis Blues in 1990 NHL entry draft. Third Blues pick, 96th overall, fifth round.

LINDY CAMERON RUFF

Defense . . . 6'2" . . . 190 lbs. . . . Born, Warburg, Alta., February 17, 1960 . . . Shoots left . . . (December, 1980)—Fractured ankle . . . Also plays Left Wing . . . Brother of Marty Ruff and brother of Brent Ruff, one of four junior hockey players who died in December, 1986 when the team bus of the Swift Current Broncos overturned . . . (March, 1983)—Broken hand . . . (January 14, 1984)—Injured shoulder at Detroit . . . (October 26, 1984)—Separated shoulder at Detroit . . . (March 5, 1986)—Broke left clavicle at Hartford . . . (November, 1988)—Sprained shoulder . . . (January 23, 1990)—Fractured rib at Edmonton and missed seven games . . . (March 21, 1990)—Broke nose when checked by Lou Franceschetti vs. Toronto . . . (April, 1990)—Bruised left thigh.

Year	Team	League	Games	G.	A.	Pts.	Pen.
1976-77	Taber Golden Suns	AJHL	60	13	33	46	112
1976-77	Lethbridge Broncos	WCHL	2	0	2	2	0
1977-78	Lethbridge Broncos	WCHL	66	9	24	33	219
1978-79	Lethbridge Broncos (c)	WHL	24	9	18	27	108
1979-80	Buffalo Sabres	NHL	63	5	14	19	38
1980-81	Buffalo Sabres	NHL	65	8	18	26	121
1981-82	Buffalo Sabres	NHL	79	16	32	48	194
1982-83	Buffalo Sabres	NHL	60	12	17	29	130
1983-84	Buffalo Sabres	NHL	58	14	31	45	101
1984-85	Buffalo Sabres	NHL	39	13	11	24	45
1985-86	Buffalo Sabres	NHL	54	20	12	32	158
1986-87	Buffalo Sabres	NHL	50	6	14	20	74
1987-88	Buffalo Sabres	NHL	77	2	23	25	179
1988-89	Buffalo Sabres (d)	NHL	63	6	11	17	86
1988-89	New York Rangers	NHL	13	0	5	5	31
1989-90	New York Rangers	NHL	56	3	6	9	77
	NHL TOTALS		677	105	194	299	1234

(c)—August, 1979—Drafted by Buffalo Sabres as underage junior in entry draft. Second Buffalo pick, 32nd overall, second round.
(d)—March 7, 1989—Traded by Buffalo Sabres to New York Rangers for a fifth-round 1990 draft pick.

DARREN RUMBLE

Defense . . . 6'1" . . . 185 lbs. . . . Born, Barrie, Ont., January 23, 1969 . . . Shoots left . . . (November 27, 1988)—Stretched knee ligaments when checked by Craig Booker vs. London.

Year	Team	League	Games	G.	A.	Pts.	Pen.
1985-86	Barrie Jr. B	OHA	46	14	32	46	91
1986-87	Kitchener Rangers (c)	OHL	64	11	32	43	44
1987-88	Kitchener Rangers	OHL	55	15	50	65	64
1988-89	Kitchener Rangers	OHL	46	11	29	40	25
1989-90	Hershey Bears	AHL	57	2	13	15	31

(c)—June, 1987—Drafted as underage junior by Philadelphia Flyers in 1987 NHL entry draft. First Flyers pick, 20th overall, first round.

REIJO RUOTSALAINEN

Defense . . . 5'8" . . . 170 lbs. . . . Born, Kaakkuri, Finland, April 1, 1960 . . . Shoots right . . . (October 22, 1983)—Hip pointer at N.Y. Islanders.

Year	Team	League	Games	G.	A.	Pts.	Pen.
1976-77	Oulu Karpat	Finland-II	36	23	35	58	14
1977-78	Oulu Karpat	Finland	30	9	14	23	4
1978-79	Oulu Karpat	Finland	36	14	8	22	47
1979-80	Oulu Karpat (c)	Finland	30	15	13	28	31
1980-81	Oulu Karpat	Finland	36	28	23	51	28
1981-82	New York Rangers	NHL	78	18	38	56	27
1982-83	New York Rangers	NHL	77	16	53	69	22
1983-84	New York Rangers	NHL	74	20	39	59	26

Year	Team	League	Games	G.	A.	Pts.	Pen.
1984-85	New York Rangers	NHL	80	28	45	73	32
1985-86	New York Rangers	NHL	80	17	42	59	47
1986-87	Edmonton Oilers (d-e-f)	NHL	16	5	8	13	6
1986-87	Bern	Switzerland	36	26	28	54	....
1987-88	HV-71 (g)	Sweden	39	10	22	32	26
1988-89	Bern	Switzerland	36	17	30	47	....
1989-90	New Jersey Devils (h)	NHL	31	2	5	7	14
1989-90	Edmonton Oilers (i)	NHL	10	1	7	8	6
	NHL TOTALS		446	107	237	344	180

(c)—June, 1980—Selected by New York Rangers in 1980 NHL entry draft. Fifth Rangers pick, 119th overall, sixth round.
(d)—July, 1986—Signed to play with Bern, Switzerland.
(e)—October, 1986—Traded with NHL rights to Ville Horava, Clark Donatelli and Jim Wiemer by New York Rangers to Edmonton Oilers to complete an earlier deal that saw the Rangers acquire Don Jackson and Mike Golden.
(f)—March, 1987—Signed with Edmonton Oilers. Stu Kulak was then sent to the Rangers as additional compensation.
(g)—October 5, 1987—Selected by New Jersey in the 1987 NHL waiver draft.
(h)—March 6, 1990—Traded by New Jersey Devils to Edmonton Oilers for Jeff Sharples.
(i)—June 6, 1990—Announced he had signed to play 1990-91 with a European team.

CAM RUSSELL

Defense . . . 6'3" . . . 180 lbs. . . . Born, Halifax, N.S., January 12, 1969 . . . Shoots left.

Year	Team	League	Games	G.	A.	Pts.	Pen.
1985-86	Hull Olympiques	QMJHL	56	3	4	7	24
1986-87	Hull Olympiques (c)	QMJHL	66	3	16	19	119
1987-88	Hull Olympiques	QMJHL	53	9	18	27	141
1988-89	Hull Olympiques	QMJHL	66	8	32	40	109
1989-90	Indianapolis Ice	IHL	46	3	15	18	114
1989-90	Chicago Black Hawks	NHL	19	0	1	1	27
	NHL TOTALS		19	0	1	1	27

(c)—June, 1987—Drafted as underage junior by Chicago Black Hawks in 1987 NHL entry draft. Third Black Hawks pick, 50th overall, third round.

KERRY RUSSELL

Right Wing . . . 5'11" . . . 165 lbs. . . . Born, Kamloops, B.C., June 23, 1969 . . . Shoots right.

Year	Team	League	Games	G.	A.	Pts.	Pen.
1987-88	Michigan State Univ. (c)	CCHA	46	16	23	39	50
1988-89	Michigan State Univ.	CCHA	46	5	23	28	50
1989-90	Michigan State Univ.	CCHA	45	15	12	27	62

(c)—June, 1988—Drafted by Hartford Whalers in 1988 NHL entry draft. Sixth Whalers pick, 137th overall, seventh round.

PAUL RUTHERFORD

Center . . . 6' . . . 190 lbs. . . . Born, Sudbury, Ont., January 1, 1969 . . . Shoots left.

Year	Team	League	Games	G.	A.	Pts.	Pen.
1986-87	Richmond Sockeyes	BCJHL	40	22	17	39	33
1987-88	Ohio State Univ. (c)	CCHA	40	18	23	41	40
1988-89	Ohio State Univ.	CCHA	39	16	27	43	52
1989-90	Ohio State Univ.	CCHA	40	15	16	31	40

(c)—June, 1988—Drafted by New York Islanders in 1988 NHL entry draft. Fifth Islanders pick, 100th overall, fifth round.

CHRISTIAN RUUTTU

Center . . . 5'11" . . . 180 lbs. . . . Born, Lappeenranta, Finland, February 20, 1964 . . . Shoots left . . . (February, 1988)—Knee injury . . . (September, 1988)—Sprained knee in Buffalo training camp . . . (October 22, 1988)—Torn pectoral muscle at Montreal . . . (April 5, 1989)—Separated left shoulder when checked by Bobby Carpenter vs. Boston.

Year	Team	League	Games	G.	A.	Pts.	Pen.
1982-83	Assat Pori (c)	Finland	36	15	18	33	34
1983-84	Assat Pori	Finland	37	18	42	60	72
1984-85	Assat Pori	Finland	32	14	32	46	34
1985-86	Helsinki IFK	Sweden	36	14	42	56	41
1986-87	Buffalo Sabres	NHL	76	22	43	65	62
1987-88	Buffalo Sabres	NHL	73	26	45	71	85
1988-89	Buffalo Sabres	NHL	67	14	46	60	98
1989-90	Buffalo Sabres	NHL	75	19	41	60	66
	NHL TOTALS		291	81	175	256	311

(c)—June, 1983—Drafted by Buffalo Sabres in 1983 entry draft. Ninth Sabres pick, 134th overall, seventh round.

VLADIMIR RUZICKA

Center . . . 6'1" . . . 175 lbs. . . . Born, Most, Czechoslovakia, June 6, 1963 . . . Shoots left.

Year	Team	League	Games	G.	A.	Pts.	Pen.
1986-87	CHZ Litvinov (c)	Czech.	32	24	15	39	....
1987-88	Dukla Trencin	Czech.	34	32	21	53	....
1988-89	Dukla Trencin	Czech.	45	46	38	84	....
1989-90	CHZ Litvinov (d)	Czech.	32	21	23	44	....
1989-90	Edmonton Oilers	NHL	25	11	6	17	10
	NHL TOTALS		25	11	6	17	10

(c)—June, 1982—Selected by Toronto Maple Leafs in 1982 NHL entry draft. Fifth Maple Leafs pick, 73rd overall, fourth round.
(d)—December, 1989—NHL rights traded by Toronto Maple Leafs to Edmonton Oilers for fourth-round draft choice (Greg Walters) in 1990.

WARREN RYCHEL

Left Wing . . . 6' . . . 190 lbs. . . . Born, Tecumseh, Ont., May 12, 1967 . . . Shoots left . . . (February, 1989)—Hyperextended left knee.

Year	Team	League	Games	G.	A.	Pts.	Pen.
1983-84—Essex Jr. "C"		OHA	24	11	16	27	86
1984-85—Sudbury Wolves		OHL	35	5	8	13	74
1984-85—Guelph Platers		OHL	29	1	3	4	48
1985-86—Guelph Platers		OHL	38	14	5	19	119
1985-86—Ottawa 67's		OHL	29	11	18	29	54
1986-87—Ottawa 67's (c)		OHL	28	11	7	18	57
1986-87—Kitchener Rangers		OHL	21	5	5	10	39
1987-88—Saginaw Hawks		IHL	51	2	7	9	113
1987-88—Peoria Rivermen		IHL	7	2	1	3	7
1988-89—Saginaw Hawks		IHL	50	15	14	29	226
1988-89—Chicago Black Hawks		NHL	2	0	0	0	17
1989-90—Indianapolis Ice		IHL	77	23	16	39	374
NHL TOTALS			2	0	0	0	17

(c)—September, 1986—Signed by Chicago Black Hawks as a free agent.

ANDY RYMSHA

Left Wing . . . 6'1" . . . 203 lbs. . . . Born, St. Catharines, Ont., December 10, 1968 . . . Shoots left.

Year	Team	League	Games	G.	A.	Pts.	Pen.
1985-86—St. Catharines Falcons		OHA	39	6	13	19	170
1986-87—Western Michigan Univ. (c)		CCHA	42	7	10	17	122
1987-88—Western Michigan Univ.		CCHA	42	5	6	11	114
1988-89—Western Michigan Univ.		CCHA	35	3	4	7	139
1989-90—Western Michigan Univ.		CCHA	37	1	10	11	108

(c)—June, 1987—Drafted by St. Louis Blues in 1987 NHL entry draft. Fifth Blues pick, 82nd overall, fourth round.

SHAWN SABOL

Defense . . . 6'3" . . . 215 lbs. . . . Born, Fargo, N.D., July 13, 1966 . . . Shoots left.

Year	Team	League	Games	G.	A.	Pts.	Pen.
1983-84—St. Paul Volcans		USHL	47	6	10	16	32
1984-85—St. Paul Volcans		USHL	47	4	13	17	137
1985-86—St. Paul Volcans (c)		USHL	46	10	19	29	129
1986-87—Univ. of Wisconsin		WCHA	40	7	16	23	98
1987-88—Univ. of Wisconsin		WCHA	8	4	3	7	10
1987-88—Hershey Bears		AHL	51	1	9	10	66
1988-89—Hershey Bears		AHL	58	7	11	18	134
1989-90—Hershey Bears		AHL	46	6	16	22	49
1989-90—Philadelphia Flyers		NHL	2	0	0	0	0
NHL TOTALS			2	0	0	0	0

(c)—June, 1986—Drafted by Philadelphia Flyers in 1986 NHL entry draft. Ninth Flyers pick, 209th overall, 10th round.

KEN SABOURIN

Defense . . . 6'4" . . . 200 lbs. . . . Born, Scarborough, Ont., April 28, 1966 . . . Shoots left.

Year	Team	League	Games	G.	A.	Pts.	Pen.
1981-82—Don Mills Midgets		MTHL	40	10	20	30	..
1982-83—Sault Ste. Marie Greyhounds		OHL	58	0	8	8	90
1983-84—Sault Ste. Marie Greyhounds (c)		OHL	63	7	13	20	157
1984-85—Sault Ste. Marie Greyhounds		OHL	63	5	19	24	139
1985-86—Sault Ste. Marie Greyhounds (d)		OHL	25	1	5	6	77
1985-86—Cornwall Royals		OHL	37	3	12	15	94
1985-86—Moncton Golden Flames		AHL	3	0	0	0	0
1986-87—Moncton Golden Flames		AHL	75	1	10	11	166
1987-88—Salt Lake Golden Eagles		IHL	71	2	8	10	186
1988-89—Calgary Flames		NHL	6	0	1	1	26
1988-89—Salt Lake Golden Eagles		IHL	74	2	18	20	197
1989-90—Calgary Flames		NHL	5	0	0	0	10
1989-90—Salt Lake Golden Eagles		IHL	76	5	19	24	336
NHL TOTALS			11	0	1	1	36

(c)—June, 1984—Drafted as underage junior by Washington Capitals in NHL entry draft. Second Capitals pick, 34th overall, second round.

(d)—March, 1986—Traded by Sault Ste. Marie Greyhounds to Cornwall Royals for Kent Trolley and a fifth round 1986 OHL priority draft pick.

DAVID SACCO

Defense . . . 6'1" . . . 180 lbs. . . . Born, Medford, Mass., July 31, 1970 . . . Shoots right . . . Brother of Joe Sacco.

Year	Team	League	Games	G.	A.	Pts.	Pen.
1988-89—Boston University (c)		H. East	35	14	29	43	40
1989-90—Boston University		H. East	3	0	4	4	2

(c)—June, 1988—Selected by Toronto Maple Leafs in 1988 NHL entry draft. Ninth Maple Leafs pick, 195th overall, 10th round.

JOSEPH SACCO

Left Wing . . . 6'1" . . . 180 lbs. . . . Born, Medford, Mass., February 4, 1969 . . . Shoots left . . . Brother of David Sacco.

Year	Team	League	Games	G.	A.	Pts.	Pen.
1985-86—Medford H.S.		Mass. H.S.	20	30	30	60	..
1986-87—Medford H.S. (c)		Mass. H.S.	21	22	32	54	..
1987-88—Boston University		H. East	34	14	22	36	38
1988-89—Boston University		H. East	33	21	19	40	66
1989-90—Boston University		H. East	44	28	24	52	70

(c)—June, 1987—Drafted by Toronto Maple Leafs in 1987 NHL entry draft. Fourth Maple Leafs pick, 71st overall, fourth round.

THOMAS SAGISSOR

Center . . . 5'11" . . . 180 lbs. . . . Born, Hastings, Minn., September 12, 1967 . . . Shoots left.

Year	Team	League	Games	G.	A.	Pts.	Pen.
1985-86—Hastings H.S. (c)		Minn. H.S.	25	26	38	64	28
1986-87—Univ. of Wisconsin		WCHA	41	1	4	5	32
1987-88—Univ. of Wisconsin		WCHA	38	4	5	9	65
1988-89—Univ. of Wisconsin		WCHA	40	7	11	18	119
1989-90—Univ. of Wisconsin		WCHA	43	19	28	47	*122

(c)—June, 1985—Drafted by Montreal Canadiens in 1985 NHL entry draft. Seventh Canadiens pick, 96th overall, fifth round.

BRIAN SAKIC

Center . . . 5'10" . . . 179 lbs. . . . Born, Burnaby, B.C., April 9, 1971 . . . Shoots left . . . Also plays Left Wing . . . Brother of Joe Sakic . . . (March 15, 1990)—Broke jaw in team practice when checked by Steve Rennie. Had a metal plate inserted into the right side of his face.

Year	Team	League	Games	G.	A.	Pts.	Pen.
1986-87—Burnaby, Bantam		British Col.	56	89	117	206	64
1987-88—Swift Current Broncos		WHL	65	12	37	49	12
1988-89—Swift Current Broncos		WHL	71	36	64	100	28
1989-90—Swift Current Broncos (c)		WHL	8	6	7	13	4
1989-90—Tri-City Americans (b-d)		WHL	58	47	92	139	8

(c)—October 18, 1989—Traded with Wade Smith by Swift Current Broncos to Tri-City Americans for Murray Duval and Jason Smith.

(d)—June 16, 1990—Selected by Washington Capitals in 1990 NHL entry draft. Fifth Capitals pick, 93rd overall, fifth round.

JOE SAKIC

Center . . . 5'11" . . . 185 lbs. . . . Born, Vancouver, B.C. July 7, 1969 . . . Shoots left . . . Brother of Brian Sakic . . . (November 28, 1988)—Sprained right ankle when he fell with Esa Tikkanen vs. Edmonton . . . (1989-90)—First player from a last place overall team to collect 100 points.

Year	Team	League	Games	G.	A.	Pts.	Pen.
1985-86—Burnaby Hawks		BC Midgets	60	83	73	156	96
1986-87—Swift Current Broncos (b-c-d-e)		WHL	72	60	73	133	31
1987-88—Swift Current Broncos (a-e-f-g)		WHL	64	*78	82	*160	64
1988-89—Quebec Nordiques		NHL	70	23	39	62	24
1989-90—Quebec Nordiques		NHL	80	39	63	102	27
NHL TOTALS			150	62	102	164	51

(c)—June, 1987—Drafted as underage junior by Quebec Nordiques in 1987 NHL entry draft. Second Nordiques pick, 15th overall, first round.

(d)—Named WHL East Division Rookie-of-the-Year.

(e)—Named WHL East Division MVP.

(f)—Named WHL Player of the Year.

(g)—Shared WHL scoring title with Theo Fleury.

ANDERS BORJE SALMING
(Known by middle name.)

Defense . . . 6'1" . . . 185 lbs. . . . Born, Kiruna, Sweden, April 17, 1951 . . . Shoots left . . . Missed part of 1974-75 season with cracked bone in heel and part of the 1978 playoffs with facial injuries . . . (January, 1980)—Surgery to clear sinus problem . . . (March, 1981)—Separated shoulder . . . (December 2, 1981)—Separated shoulder vs. Hartford . . . (December, 1982)—Suffered Charley horse and missed eight games . . . (January 17, 1983)—Cut by skate on knee at St. Louis . . . (March 12, 1984)—Broke kneecap vs. Winnipeg and out for the season . . . (October, 1984)—Eye infection . . . (January 19, 1985)—Injured sinus vs. Boston . . . (November 8, 1985)—Injured back at Detroit and missed 38 games . . . (September 4, 1986)—Suspended for first eight games of season for cocaine use . . . (November 5, 1986)—Cracked orbital bone above left eye when struck by Bernie Federko vs. St. Louis . . . (November 26, 1986)—Cut by Gerard Gallant's skate during a goal-mouth pile-up at Detroit, requiring 250 facial stitches . . . (December, 1987)—Sprained back . . . (November, 1988)—Missed 10 games with the flu . . . (January, 1989)—Charley horse . . . (January 31, 1990)—Fractured bone in left hand vs. Edmonton and missed 10 games.

Year	Team	League	Games	G.	A.	Pts.	Pen.
1971-72—Swedish National Team			12	0	....	....	....
1972-73—Swedish National Team (c)			23	4	....	....	....
1973-74—Toronto Maple Leafs	NHL		76	5	34	39	48
1974-75—Toronto Maple Leafs (b)	NHL		60	12	25	37	34
1975-76—Toronto Maple Leafs (b-d)	NHL		78	16	41	57	70
1976-77—Toronto Maple Leafs (a-d)	NHL		76	12	66	78	46
1977-78—Toronto Maple Leafs (b)	NHL		80	16	60	76	70
1978-79—Toronto Maple Leafs (b-d)	NHL		78	17	56	73	76
1979-80—Toronto Maple Leafs (b)	NHL		74	19	52	71	94
1980-81—Toronto Maple Leafs	NHL		72	5	61	66	154
1981-82—Toronto Maple Leafs	NHL		69	12	44	56	170
1982-83—Toronto Maple Leafs	NHL		69	7	38	45	104
1983-84—Toronto Maple Leafs	NHL		68	5	38	43	92
1984-85—Toronto Maple Leafs	NHL		73	6	33	39	76
1985-86—Toronto Maple Leafs	NHL		41	7	15	22	48
1986-87—Toronto Maple Leafs	NHL		56	4	16	20	42
1987-88—Toronto Maple Leafs	NHL		66	2	24	26	82
1988-89—Toronto Maple Leafs (e)	NHL		63	3	17	20	86
1989-90—Detroit Red Wings (f-g)	NHL		49	2	17	19	52
NHL TOTALS			1148	150	637	787	1345

(c)—Selected most valuable player in Sweden.

(d)—Named winner of Viking Award (Top Swedish player in NHL/WHA as selected by poll of Swedish players).

(e)—June 12, 1989—Signed by Detroit Red Wings as a free agent.

(f)—April 26, 1990—Released by Detroit Red Wings.

(g)—May 28, 1990—Signed two-year contract with Stockholm AIK (Sweden).

KJELL SAMUELSSON

Defense . . . 6'6" . . . 227 lbs. . . . Born, Tingsryd, Sweden, October 18, 1956 . . . Shoots right . . . (February, 1988)—Pulled groin . . . (October, 1988)—Herniated disc . . . (March, 1989)—Bruised hand . . . (November 22, 1989)—Bruised right shoulder vs. Montreal and missed 13 games . . . (March, 1990)—Played last two months of season with a separated shoulder. He had post-season surgery.

Year	Team	League	Games	G.	A.	Pts.	Pen.
1983-84—Leksand (c)	Sweden	36	6	7	13	59
1984-85—Leksand	Sweden	35	9	5	14	34
1985-86—New York Rangers	NHL	9	0	0	0	10
1985-86—New Haven Nighthawks	AHL	56	6	21	27	87
1986-87—New York Rangers (d)	NHL	30	2	6	8	50
1986-87—Philadelphia Flyers	NHL	46	1	6	7	86
1987-88—Philadelphia Flyers	NHL	74	6	24	30	184
1988-89—Philadelphia Flyers	NHL	69	3	14	17	140
1989-90—Philadelphia Flyers	NHL	66	5	17	22	91
NHL TOTALS		294	17	67	84	561

(c)—June, 1984—Drafted by New York Rangers in 1984 NHL entry draft. Fifth Rangers pick, 119th overall, sixth round.

(d)—December, 1986—Traded with second-round 1989 draft pick (Patrik Juhlin) by New York Rangers to Philadelphia Flyers for Bob Froese.

ULF SAMUELSSON

Defense . . . 6'1" . . . 195 lbs. . . . Born, Leksand, Sweden, March 26, 1964 . . . Shoots left . . . (December, 1988)—Missed nine games with the flu . . . (August, 1989)—Tore ligaments in right knee while doing off-ice training in Sweden, required surgery and missed some of 1989-90 season.

Year	Team	League	Games	G.	A.	Pts.	Pen.
1983-84—Leksands (c)	Sweden	36	5	10	15	53
1984-85—Binghamton Whalers	AHL	36	5	11	16	92
1984-85—Hartford Whalers	NHL	41	2	6	8	83
1985-86—Hartford Whalers	NHL	80	5	19	24	174
1986-87—Hartford Whalers	NHL	78	2	31	33	162
1987-88—Hartford Whalers	NHL	76	8	33	41	159
1988-89—Hartford Whalers	NHL	71	9	26	35	181
1989-90—Hartford Whalers	NHL	55	2	11	13	167
NHL TOTALS		401	28	126	154	926

(c)—June, 1982—Drafted by Hartford Whalers in 1982 NHL entry draft. Fourth Whalers pick, 67th overall, fourth round.

SCOTT SANDELIN

Defense . . . 6' . . . 190 lbs. . . . Born, Hibbing, Minn., August 8, 1964 . . . Shoots right . . . (October, 1984)—Stretched knee ligaments.

Year	Team	League	Games	G.	A.	Pts.	Pen.
1981-82—Hibbing H.S. (c)	Minn. H.S.	20	5	15	20	30
1982-83—Univ. of North Dakota	WCHA	30	1	6	7	10
1983-84—Univ. of North Dakota	WCHA	41	4	23	27	24
1984-85—Univ. of North Dakota	WCHA	38	4	17	21	30
1985-86—Univ. of North Dakota (a)	WCHA	40	7	31	38	38
1985-86—Sherbrooke Canadiens	AHL	6	0	2	2	2
1986-87—Montreal Canadiens	NHL	1	0	0	0	0
1986-87—Sherbrooke Canadiens	AHL	74	7	22	29	35
1987-88—Montreal Canadiens	NHL	8	0	1	1	2
1987-88—Sherbrooke Canadiens	AHL	58	8	14	22	35
1988-89—Sherbrooke Canadiens (d)	AHL	12	0	9	9	8
1988-89—Hershey Bears	AHL	39	6	9	15	38
1989-90—Hershey Bears	AHL	70	4	27	31	38
NHL TOTALS		9	0	1	1	2

(c)—June, 1982—Drafted as underage player by Montreal Canadiens in 1982 NHL entry draft. Fifth Canadiens pick, 40th overall, second round.

(d)—November, 1988—Traded by Montreal Canadiens to Philadelphia Flyers for J.J. Daigneault.

GEOFF SANDERSON

Center . . . 6' . . . 185 lbs. . . . Born, Hay River, Northwest Territories, February 1, 1972 . . . Shoots left.

Year	Team	League	Games	G.	A.	Pts.	Pen.
1987-88—St. Albert Bantams	Alta.	45	65	55	120	200
1988-89—Swift Current Broncos	WHL	58	17	11	28	16
1989-90—Swift Current Broncos (c)	WHL	70	32	62	94	56

(c)—June 16, 1990—Selected by Hartford Whalers in 1990 NHL entry draft. Second Whalers pick, 36th overall, second round.

JAMES SANDLAK JR.

Right Wing . . . 6'3" . . . 205 lbs. . . . Born, Kitchener, Ont., December 12, 1966 . . . Shoots right . . . Named to All-Tournament team at 1986 World Junior Championships as well as being named top forward . . . (January, 1986)—Ruptured ligaments in right thumb . . . (October, 1988)—Bruised shoulder.

Year	Team	League	Games	G.	A.	Pts.	Pen.
1982-83—Kitchener Rangers	OHA	38	26	25	51	100
1983-84—London Knights	OHL	68	23	18	41	143
1984-85—London Knights (c)	OHL	58	40	24	64	128
1985-86—London Knights	OHL	16	7	13	20	36
1985-86—Vancouver Canucks	NHL	23	1	3	4	10
1986-87—Vancouver Canucks	NHL	78	15	21	36	66
1987-88—Vancouver Canucks	NHL	49	16	15	31	81
1987-88—Fredericton Express	AHL	24	10	15	25	47
1988-89—Vancouver Canucks	NHL	72	20	20	40	99
1989-90—Vancouver Canucks	NHL	70	15	8	23	104
NHL TOTALS		292	67	67	134	360

(c)—June, 1985—Drafted as underage junior by Vancouver Canucks in 1985 NHL entry draft. First Canucks pick, fourth overall, first round.

TOMAS SANDSTROM

Right Wing . . . 6'2" . . . 200 lbs. . . . Born, Fagersta, Sweden, September 4, 1964 . . . Shoots left . . . (February 24, 1986)—Concussion at Minnesota . . . (February 11, 1987)—Fractured right ankle vs. Soviet National Team when checked by Andrei Khomutov at Rendez-Vous '87 . . . (November, 1987)—Fractured right index finger.

Year	Team	League	Games	G.	A.	Pts.	Pen.
1983-84—Brynas (c)	Sweden	....	20	10	30	....
1984-85—New York Rangers	NHL	74	29	29	58	51
1985-86—New York Rangers	NHL	73	25	29	54	109
1986-87—New York Rangers	NHL	64	40	34	74	60
1987-88—New York Rangers	NHL	69	28	40	68	95
1988-89—New York Rangers	NHL	79	32	56	88	148
1989-90—New York Rangers (d)	NHL	48	19	19	38	100
1989-90—Los Angeles Kings	NHL	28	13	20	33	28
NHL TOTALS		435	186	227	413	591

(c)—June, 1982—Drafted by New York Rangers in 1982 NHL entry draft. Second Rangers pick, 36th overall, second round.

(d)—January 20, 1990—Traded with Tony Granato by New York Rangers to Los Angeles Kings for Bernie Nicholls.

TERRAN SANDWITH

Defense . . . 6'4" . . . 210 lbs. . . . Born, Edmonton, Alta., April 17, 1972 . . . Shoots left.

Year	Team	League	Games	G.	A.	Pts.	Pen.
1987-88—Hobbema Hawks	AJHL	58	5	8	13	106
1988-89—Tri-City Americans	WHL	31	0	0	0	29
1989-90—Tri-City Americans (c)	WHL	70	4	14	18	92

(c)—June 16, 1990—Selected by Philadelphia Flyers in 1990 NHL entry draft. Fourth Flyers pick, 42nd overall, second round.

ROB SANGSTER

Left Wing . . . 5'11" . . . 190 lbs. . . . Born, Kitchener, Ont., May 2, 1969 . . . Shoots left.

Year	Team	League	Games	G.	A.	Pts.	Pen.
1986-87—Kitchener Midgets	OHA	50	19	19	38	236
1987-88—Kitchener Rangers	OHL	58	2	7	9	196
1988-89—Kitchener Rangers (c)	OHL	64	10	25	35	337
1989-90—Kitchener Rangers	OHL	24	6	18	24	151
1989-90—Ottawa 67's	OHL	21	2	8	10	100
1989-90—Milwaukee Admirals	IHL	1	0	0	0	4

(c)—June, 1989—Drafted by Vancouver Canucks in 1989 NHL entry draft. Sixth Canucks pick, 155th overall, eighth round.

EVERETT SANIPASS

Left Wing . . . 6'2" . . . 190 lbs. . . . Born, Big Cove, New Brunswick, February 13, 1968 . . . Shoots left . . . Micmac Indian descendant . . . (December, 1987)—Back spasms . . . (January 17, 1988)—Back spasms and concussion vs. Washington . . . (March, 1988)—Broken hand . . . (August, 1988)—Broke right ankle in eight places playing a softball game . . . (September 5, 1989)—Broken jaw . . . (October 17, 1989)—Fractured right foot when he blocked a shot at N.Y. Rangers . . . (March 17, 1990)—Struck on left ankle by a shot vs. Philadelphia.

Year	Team	League	Games	G.	A.	Pts.	Pen.
1984-85—Verdun Junior Canadiens	QMJHL	38	8	11	19	84
1985-86—Verdun Junior Canadiens (c)	QMJHL	67	28	66	94	320
1986-87—Granby Bisons (a)	QMJHL	35	34	48	82	220
1986-87—Chicago Black Hawks	NHL	7	1	3	4	2
1987-88—Chicago Black Hawks	NHL	57	8	12	20	126
1988-89—Chicago Black Hawks	NHL	50	6	9	15	164
1988-89—Saginaw Hawks	IHL	23	9	12	21	76
1989-90—Indianapolis Ice	IHL	33	15	13	28	121
1989-90—Chicago Black Hawks (d)	NHL	12	2	2	4	17
1989-90—Quebec Nordiques	NHL	9	3	3	6	8
NHL TOTALS		135	20	29	49	317

(c)—June, 1986—Drafted as underage junior by Chicago Black Hawks in 1986 NHL entry draft. First Black Hawks pick, 14th overall, first round.

(d)—March 5, 1990—Traded with Dan Vincelette and Mario Doyon by Chicago Black Hawks to Quebec Nordiques for Michel Goulet, Greg Millen and a sixth-round 1991 draft pick.

BRENT SAPERGIA

Right Wing . . . 5'10" . . . 195 lbs. . . . Born, Moose Jaw, Sask., November 16, 1962 . . . Shoots right . . . (March 12, 1989)—Suspended seven IHL games for his fifth high-sticking infraction of the season.

Year	Team	League	Games	G.	A.	Pts.	Pen.
1979-80—Saskatoon Blades	WHL	50	17	18	35	72
1981-82—Saskatoon Blades	WHL	10	6	3	9	8
1981-82—Medicine Hat Tigers	WHL	19	4	4	8	45
1982-83—	......	..	..	..	..
1983-84—Erie Golden Blades	ACHL	4	2	4	6	0
1984-85—Salt Lake Golden Eagles (b)	IHL	76	47	47	94	36
1985-86—Salt Lake Golden Eagles (a)	IHL	80	*58	65	123	127
1986-87—New Haven Nighthawks (c)	AHL	2	0	1	1	0
1986-87—Kalpa	Finland	33	25	13	38	117
1987-88—Salt Lake Golden Eagles	IHL	22	10	6	16	22
1988-89—Indianapolis Ice	IHL	52	43	33	76	246
1989-90—Phoenix Roadrunners (d)	IHL	43	19	13	32	159

(c)—March 6, 1987—Signed by New York Rangers as a free agent.

(d)—March 31, 1989—Released by Phoenix Roadrunners.

RAYMOND SAUMIER

Right Wing . . . 6' . . . 189 lbs. . . . Born, Hull, Que., February 27, 1969 . . . Shoots right . . . (November, 1986)—Suspended indefinitely by QMJHL (his second suspension of the season).

Year	Team	League	Games	G.	A.	Pts.	Pen.
1986-87—Laval Titans (c)		QMJHL	57	13	37	50	301
1987-88—Trois-Rivieres Draveurs		QMJHL	62	30	58	88	356
1988-89—Trois-Rivieres Draveurs (d)		QMJHL	65	30	62	92	307
1989-90—Binghamton Whalers		AHL	56	9	11	20	171

(c)—May, 1987—Traded with Mike Gober, Eric Gobiel and a second-round draft pick (Eric Charron) by Laval Titans to Trois-Rivieres Draveurs for Claude LaPointe, Alain Dubeau and a third-round draft pick (Patrice Brisbois).
(d)—June, 1989—Drafted by Hartford Whalers in 1989 NHL entry draft. Seventh Whalers pick, 157th overall, eighth round.

MATTHEW SAUNDERS

Left Wing . . . 6' . . . 180 lbs. . . . Born, Ottawa, Ont., July 17, 1970 . . . Shoots left . . . Brother of David Saunders . . . (November 28, 1989)—Given a two game suspension for fighting.

Year	Team	League	Games	G.	A.	Pts.	Pen.
1986-87—Nepean Raiders		OCJHL	55	15	23	38	....
1987-88—Nepean Raiders		OCJHL	49	30	27	57	122
1988-89—Northeastern Univ. (c)		H. East	27	8	8	16	17
1989-90—Northeastern Univ.		H. East	35	19	21	40	51

(c)—June, 1989—Drafted by Chicago Black Hawks in 1989 NHL entry draft. Eighth Black Hawks pick, 195th overall, 10th round.

JOEL SAVAGE

Right Wing . . . 5'11' . . . 195 lbs. . . . Born, Surrey, B.C., December 25, 1969 . . . Shoots right . . . (October, 1985)—Concussion.

Year	Team	League	Games	G.	A.	Pts.	Pen.
1986-87—Victoria Cougars		WHL	68	14	13	27	48
1987-88—Victoria Cougars (b-c)		WHL	69	37	32	69	73
1988-89—Victoria Cougars		WHL	60	17	30	47	95
1989-90—Rochester Americans		AHL	43	6	7	13	39

(c)—June, 1988—Drafted by Buffalo Sabres in 1988 NHL entry draft. First Sabres pick, 13th overall, first round.

REGINALD SAVAGE

Center . . . 5'10" . . . 177 lbs. . . . Born, Montreal, Que., May 1, 1970 . . . Shoots left . . . (February 19, 1989)—Suspended six QHL games for stick-swinging incident vs. Trois-Rivieres.

Year	Team	League	Games	G.	A.	Pts.	Pen.
1986-87—Richelieu Midget AAA		Quebec	42	82	57	139	44
1987-88—Victoriaville Tigres (c)		QMJHL	68	68	54	122	77
1988-89—Victoriaville Tigres		QMJHL	54	58	55	113	178
1989-90—Victoriaville Tigres		QMJHL	63	51	43	94	79

(c)—June, 1988—Drafted by Washington Capitals in 1988 NHL entry draft. First Capitals pick, 15th overall, first round.

DENIS SAVARD

Center . . . 5'9" . . . 157 lbs. . . . Born, Pointe Gatineau, Que., February 4, 1961 . . . Shoots right . . . Cousin of Jean Savard . . . Set Chicago rookie record with 75 points in 1980-81 (broken by Steve Larmer) . . . (October 15, 1980)—Strained knee vs. Vancouver . . . Set Chicago records for assists (87) and points (119) in one season in 1981-82 . . . Broke his own points record with 131 in 1987-88 . . . (January 7, 1984)—Broke nose at N.Y. Islanders . . . (October 13, 1984)—Injured ankle when he blocked a shot at N.Y. Islanders . . . (March 22, 1987)—Bruised ribs when checked by Jeff Jackson at N.Y. Rangers . . . (January 21, 1989)—Missed 19 games with a broken right ankle vs. St. Louis . . . (January 17, 1990)—Sprained left ankle vs. Minnesota . . . (January 26, 1990)—Broke left index finger at Buffalo and missed 17 games.

Year	Team	League	Games	G.	A.	Pts.	Pen.
1977-78—Montreal Juniors		QMJHL	72	37	79	116	22
1978-79—Montreal Juniors		QMJHL	70	46	*112	158	88
1979-80—Montreal Juniors (a-c-d)		QMJHL	72	63	118	181	93
1980-81—Chicago Black Hawks		NHL	76	28	47	75	47
1981-82—Chicago Black Hawks		NHL	80	32	87	119	82
1982-83—Chicago Black Hawks (b)		NHL	78	35	86	121	99
1983-84—Chicago Black Hawks		NHL	75	37	57	94	71
1984-85—Chicago Black Hawks		NHL	79	38	67	105	56
1985-86—Chicago Black Hawks		NHL	80	47	69	116	111
1986-87—Chicago Black Hawks		NHL	70	40	50	90	108
1987-88—Chicago Black Hawks		NHL	80	44	87	131	95
1988-89—Chicago Black Hawks		NHL	58	23	59	82	110
1989-90—Chicago Black Hawks (e)		NHL	60	27	53	80	56
NHL TOTALS			736	351	662	1013	835

(c)—Won Michel Briere Trophy (MVP).
(d)—June, 1980—Drafted as underage junior by Chicago Black Hawks in 1980 NHL entry draft. First Black Hawks pick, third overall, first round.
(e)—June 29, 1990—Traded by Chicago Black Hawks to Montreal Canadiens for Chris Chelios and a second-round 1991 draft pick.

PATRICK SCHAFHAUSER

Defense . . . 6'1" . . . 195 lbs. . . . Born, St. Paul, Minn., July 27, 1971 . . . Shoots left . . . (July, 1988)—Fractured fibula.

Year	Team	League	Games	G.	A.	Pts.	Pen.
1984-85—Roseville Bantams		Minn. H.S.	60	22	30	52	42
1985-86—Hill Murray H.S.		Minn. H.S.	21	4	8	12	16
1986-87—Hill Murray H.S.		Minn. H.S.	28	5	10	15	24
1987-88—Hill Murray H.S.		Minn. H.S.	28	8	11	19	30
1988-89—Hill Murray H.S. (c)		Minn. H.S.	25	2	29	31	....
1989-90—Boston College		H. East	39	1	6	7	30

(c)—June, 1989—Drafted by Pittsburgh Penguins in 1989 NHL entry draft. Eighth Penguins pick, 142nd overall, seventh round.

STEVE SCHEIFELE

Right Wing . . . 6' . . . 175 lbs. . . . Born, Alexandria, Va., April 18, 1968 . . . Shoots right.

Year	Team	League	Games	G.	A.	Pts.	Pen.
1985-86—Stratford (c)		OPJHL	40	41	39	80	84
1986-87—Boston College		H. East	38	13	13	26	28
1987-88—Boston College		H. East	30	11	16	27	22
1988-89—Boston College		H. East	40	24	14	38	30
1989-90—Boston College		H. East	12	7	0	7	2
1989-90—Hershey Bears		AHL	35	2	3	5	6

(c)—June, 1986—Drafted by Philadelphia Flyers in 1986 NHL entry draft. Fifth Flyers pick, 125th overall, sixth round.

ROB SCHENA

Defense . . . 6'1" . . . 190 lbs. . . . Born, Saugus, Mass., February 6, 1967 . . . Shoots left . . . (December 8, 1989)—Throat pierced by a piece of his broken stick in exhibition game vs. Sokol Kiev and missed a month.

Year	Team	League	Games	G.	A.	Pts.	Pen.
1985-86—R.P.I. (c)		ECAC	32	0	6	6	63
1986-87—R.P.I.		ECAC	32	1	9	10	34
1987-88—R.P.I.		ECAC	30	5	9	14	56
1988-89—R.P.I.		ECAC	32	7	5	12	64
1988-89—Adirondack Red Wings		AHL	9	1	1	2	2
1989-90—Adirondack Red Wings		AHL	43	5	8	13	36
1989-90—Phoenix Roadrunners		IHL	2	0	0	0	0
1989-90—Hampton Roads Admirals		ECHL	5	3	2	5	0

(c)—June, 1985—Drafted by Detroit Red Wings in 1985 NHL entry draft. Ninth Red Wings pick, 197th overall, 10th round.

BRAD SCHLEGAL

Defense . . . 5'10" . . . 180 lbs. . . . Born, Kitchener, Ont., July 22, 1968 . . . Shoots right.

Year	Team	League	Games	G.	A.	Pts.	Pen.
1984-85—Kitchener Midget		OHA	40	30	50	80	70
1985-86—London Knights		OHA	62	2	13	15	35
1986-87—London Knights		OHA	65	4	23	27	24
1987-88—London Knights (b-c)		OHA	66	13	63	76	49
1988-89—Canadian National Team		Int'l.	60	2	22	24	30
1989-90—Canadian National Team		Int'l.	72	7	25	32	44

(c)—June, 1988—Drafted by Washington Capitals in 1988 NHL entry draft. Eighth Capitals pick, 144th overall, seventh round.

MATHIEU SCHNEIDER

Defense . . . 5'11" . . . 180 lbs. . . . Born, New York, N.Y., June 12, 1969 . . . Shoots left . . . (February, 1990)—Bruised left shoulder.

Year	Team	League	Games	G.	A.	Pts.	Pen.
1985-86—Mt. St. Charles H.S.		RIHS	19	3	27	30	....
1986-87—Cornwall Royals (c)		OHL	63	7	29	36	75
1987-88—Montreal Canadiens		NHL	4	0	0	0	2
1987-88—Cornwall Royals (a)		OHL	48	21	40	61	85
1988-89—Cornwall Royals (a)		OHL	59	16	57	73	96
1989-90—Sherbrooke Canadiens		AHL	28	6	13	19	20
1989-90—Montreal Canadiens		NHL	44	7	14	21	25
NHL TOTALS			48	7	14	21	25

(c)—June, 1987—Drafted by Montreal Canadiens in 1987 NHL entry draft. Fourth Canadiens pick, 44th overall, third round.

SCOTT SCHNEIDER

Center . . . 6'1" . . . 174 lbs. . . . Born, Rochester, Minn., May 18, 1965 . . . Shoots right . . . (November, 1989)—Broke thumb and missed 11 games . . . (December 10, 1989)—Reinjured thumb in fight with Baltimore's Kent Paynter.

Year	Team	League	Games	G.	A.	Pts.	Pen.
1983-84—Colorado College (c)		WCHA	35	19	14	33	24
1984-85—Colorado College		WCHA	33	16	13	29	60
1985-86—Colorado College		WCHA	40	16	22	38	32
1986-87—Colorado College		WCHA	42	21	22	43	36
1987-88—Moncton Golden Flames		AHL	68	12	23	35	28
1988-89—Moncton Hawks		AHL	64	29	36	65	51
1989-90—Moncton Hawks		AHL	61	17	23	40	57

(c)—June, 1984—Drafted by Winnipeg Jets in NHL entry draft. Fourth Jets pick, 93rd overall, fifth round.

SCOTT SCISSONS

Center . . . 6'1" . . . 201 lbs. . . . Born, Saskatoon, Sask., October 29, 1971 . . . Shoots left.

Year	Team	League	Games	G.	A.	Pts.	Pen.
1985-86—Saskatoon Flyers Bantam		Sask.	65	45	55	100	45
1986-87—Saskatoon Flyers Bantam		Sask.	62	55	65	120	50
1987-88—Saskatoon Contacts Midget		Sask.	29	25	16	41	51
1988-89—Saskatoon Blades		WHL	71	30	56	86	65
1989-90—Saskatoon Blades (c)		WHL	61	40	47	87	81

(c)—June 16, 1990—Selected by New York Islanders in 1990 NHL entry draft. First Islanders pick, sixth overall, first round.

KEVIN SCOTT

Center . . . 5'10" . . . 180 lbs. . . . Born, Kimberly, B.C., March 11, 1967 . . . Shoots left.

Year	Team	League	Games	G.	A.	Pts.	Pen.
1986-87—Vernon Lakers (c)	BCJHL	52	56	72	128	50
1987-88—Northern Michigan Univ.	WCHA	36	9	12	21	42
1988-89—Northern Michigan Univ.	WCHA	40	11	14	25	36
1989-90—Northern Michigan Univ.	WCHA	34	20	14	34	46

(c)—June, 1987—Drafted by Detroit Red Wings in 1987 NHL entry draft. Ninth Red Wings pick, 158th overall, eighth round.

GLEN SEABROOKE

Left Wing . . . 6'1" . . . 175 lbs. . . . Born, Peterborough, Ont., September 11, 1967 . . . Shoots left . . . Also plays Center . . . (July, 1983)—Broken collarbone . . . (February, 1985)—Groin injury . . . (September, 1985)—Summer long injury, thought to be a pulled groin muscle, turned out to be a dislocated pelvis and he missed most of the 1985-86 season following surgery . . . (October, 1989)—Shoulder surgery.

Year	Team	League	Games	G.	A.	Pts.	Pen.
1983-84—Peterborough Midget	OHA	29	36	31	67	31
1984-85—Peterborough Petes (c)	OHL	45	21	13	34	59
1985-86—Peterborough Petes	OHL	19	8	12	20	33
1986-87—Peterborough Petes	OHL	48	30	39	69	29
1986-87—Philadelphia Flyers	NHL	10	1	4	5	2
1987-88—Hershey Bears	AHL	73	32	46	78	39
1987-88—Philadelphia Flyers	NHL	6	0	1	1	2
1988-89—Hershey Bears	AHL	51	23	15	38	19
1988-89—Philadelphia Flyers	NHL	3	0	1	1	0
1989-90—Did not play.		....	....	....	....	....
NHL TOTALS		19	1	6	7	4

(c)—June, 1985—Drafted as underage junior by Philadelphia Flyers in 1985 NHL entry draft. First Flyers pick, 21st overall, first round.

SVERRE SEARS

Defense . . . 6'2" . . . 185 lbs. . . . Born, Boston, Mass., October 17, 1970 . . . Shoots left.

Year	Team	League	Games	G.	A.	Pts.	Pen.
1987-88—Belmont Hill H.S.	Mass. H.S.	..	2	8	10	..
1988-89—Belmont Hill H.S. (c)	Mass. H.S.	23	5	19	24	34
1989-90—Princeton University	ECAC	18	0	1	1	14

(c)—June, 1989—Drafted by Philadelphia Flyers in 1989 NHL entry draft. Sixth Flyers pick, 159th overall, eighth round.

ALAN WILLIAM SECORD

Left Wing . . . 6'1" . . . 210 lbs. . . . Born, Sudbury, Ont., March 3, 1958 . . . Shoots left . . . (October, 1980)—Bruised right knee . . . (March, 1981)—Ankle injury . . . (April, 1983)—Suspended for one game in playoffs for abusive language to an official . . . (October, 1983)—Tore abdominal muscles . . . (December 12, 1984)—Pulled abductor muscles in thigh during a team practice . . . (October, 1987)—Separated ribs and torn rib cartilage . . . (November, 1988)—Injured knee . . . Does not wear a helmet . . . (February 5, 1990)—Stretched right knee ligament, underwent surgery and missed 17 games.

Year	Team	League	Games	G.	A.	Pts.	Pen.
1974-75—Wexford Raiders	OPJHL	41	5	13	18	104
1975-76—Hamilton Fincups	Jr."A" OHA	63	9	13	22	117
1976-77—St. Catharines Fincups	Jr."A" OHA	57	32	34	66	343
1977-78—Hamilton Fincups (c)	Jr."A" OHA	59	28	22	50	185
1978-79—Rochester Americans	AHL	4	4	2	6	40
1978-79—Boston Bruins	NHL	71	16	7	23	125
1979-80—Boston Bruins	NHL	77	23	16	39	170
1980-81—Springfield Indians	AHL	8	3	5	8	21
1980-81—Boston Bruins (d)	NHL	18	0	3	3	42
1980-81—Chicago Black Hawks	NHL	41	13	9	22	145
1981-82—Chicago Black Hawks	NHL	80	44	31	75	303
1982-83—Chicago Black Hawks	NHL	80	54	32	86	180
1983-84—Chicago Black Hawks	NHL	14	4	4	8	77
1984-85—Chicago Black Hawks	NHL	51	15	11	26	193
1985-86—Chicago Black Hawks	NHL	80	40	36	76	201
1986-87—Chicago Black Hawks (e)	NHL	77	29	29	58	196
1987-88—Toronto Maple Leafs (f)	NHL	74	15	27	42	221
1988-89—Toronto Maple Leafs	NHL	40	5	10	15	71
1988-89—Philadelphia Flyers (g)	NHL	20	1	0	1	38
1989-90—Chicago Black Hawks (h)	NHL	43	14	7	21	131
NHL TOTALS		766	273	222	495	2093

(c)—Drafted from Hamilton Fincups by Boston Bruins in first round of 1978 amateur draft.

(d)—December, 1980—Traded by Boston Bruins to Chicago Black Hawks for Mike O'Connell.

(e)—September, 1987—Traded with Ed Olczyk by Chicago Black Hawks to Toronto Maple Leafs for Rick Vaive, Steve Thomas and Bob McGill.

(f)—February 7, 1989—Traded by Toronto Maple Leafs to Philadelphia Flyers for a fifth-round 1989 draft pick (Keith Carney).

(g)—August 7, 1989—Signed by Chicago Black Hawks as a free agent.

(h)—August, 1990—Announced his retirement.

STEVEN SEFTEL

Left Wing . . . 6'1" . . . 185 lbs. . . . Born, Kitchener, Ont., May 14, 1968 . . . Shoots left . . . (September, 1985)—Broken ankle.

Year	Team	League	Games	G.	A.	Pts.	Pen.
1984-85—Kitchener Greenshirts	OHA Midget	69	58	52	110	176
1985-86—Kingston Canadians (c)	OHL	42	11	16	27	53
1986-87—Kingston Canadians	OHL	54	21	43	64	55
1987-88—Kingston Canadians	OHL	66	32	43	75	51

Year	Team	League	Games	G.	A.	Pts.	Pen.
1987-88—Binghamton Whalers	AHL	3	0	0	0	2
1988-89—Baltimore Skipjacks	AHL	58	12	15	27	70
1989-90—Baltimore Skipjacks	AHL	74	10	19	29	52

(c)—June, 1986—Drafted as underage junior by Washington Capitals in 1986 NHL entry draft. Second Capitals pick, 40th overall, second round.

TEEMU SELANNE

Right Wing . . . 6' . . . 176 lbs. . . . Born, Helsinki, Finland, March 7, 1970 . . . Shoots right . . . (October 19, 1989)—Broke left leg in collison with Vesa Kulha vs. JYP Jyvaskyla when shin bone and calf bone snapped.

Year	Team	League	Games	G.	A.	Pts.	Pen.
1987-88—Jokerit (c)	Finland	33	42	23	65	18
1988-89—Jokerit	Finland	34	35	33	68	12
1989-90—Jokerit	Finland	11	4	8	12	0

(c)—June, 1988—Drafted by Winnipeg Jets in 1988 NHL entry draft. First Jets pick, 10th overall, first round.

THOMAS SEMCHUK

Right Wing . . . 6'1" . . . 185 lbs. . . . Born, Calgary, Alta., September 22, 1971 . . . Shoots right . . . Also plays Left Wing . . . (December, 1989)—Charley horse . . . (March, 1990)—Strained hip flexor.

Year	Team	League	Games	G.	A.	Pts.	Pen.
1985-86—Calgary Royals Bantam	Alta.	65	55	50	105	90
1986-87—Calgary Royals Bantam	Alta.	70	52	55	107	100
1987-88—Calgary Canucks	AJHL	90	44	42	86	120
1988-89—Canadian National Team	Int'l.	42	11	11	22	60
1989-90—Canadian National Team (c)	Int'l.	60	9	14	23	14

(c)—June 16, 1990—Selected by Los Angeles Kings in 1990 NHL entry draft. Second Kings pick, 28th overall, second round.

ANATOLI SEMENOV

Center . . . 6'2" . . . 190 lbs. . . . Born, Moscow, USSR, March 5, 1962 . . . Shoots left.

Year	Team	League	Games	G.	A.	Pts.	Pen.
1979-80—Moscow Dynamo	USSR	8	3	0	3	2
1980-81—Moscow Dynamo	USSR	47	18	14	32	18
1981-82—Moscow Dynamo	USSR	44	12	14	26	28
1982-83—Moscow Dynamo	USSR	44	22	18	40	26
1983-84—Moscow Dynamo	USSR	19	10	5	15	14
1984-85—Moscow Dynamo	USSR	30	17	12	29	32
1985-86—Moscow Dynamo	USSR	32	18	17	35	19
1986-87—Moscow Dynamo	USSR	40	15	29	44	32
1987-88—Moscow Dynamo	USSR	32	17	8	25	22
1988-89—Moscow Dynamo (c)	USSR	31	9	12	21	24
1989-90—Moscow Dynamo	USSR	48	13	20	33	16

(c)—June, 1989—Selected by Edmonton Oilers in 1989 NHL entry draft. Fifth Oilers pick, 120th overall, sixth round.

JEFF SEROWIK

Defense . . . 6' . . . 190 lbs. . . . Born, Manchester, N.H., October 1, 1967 . . . Shoots right . . . (April, 1982)—Broken left ankle . . . (March, 1983)—Broken right ankle.

Year	Team	League	Games	G.	A.	Pts.	Pen.
1983-84—Manchester West H.S.	N. Hamp.	21	12	12	24	....
1984-85—Lawrence Academy (c)	N. Hamp.	24	8	25	33	....
1985-86—Lawrence Academy	N. Hamp.	....	....	....	....	....
1986-87—Providence College	H. East	33	3	8	11	22
1987-88—Providence College	H. East	33	3	9	12	44
1988-89—Providence College	H. East	35	3	14	17	48
1989-90—Providence College (b)	H. East	35	6	19	25	34

(c)—June, 1985—Drafted by Toronto Maple Leafs in 1985 NHL entry draft. Fifth Maple Leafs pick, 85th overall, fifth round.

JAROSLAV SEVCIK

Left Wing . . . 5'8" . . . 170 lbs. . . . Born, Brno, Czech., May 15, 1965 . . . Shoots left.

Year	Team	League	Games	G.	A.	Pts.	Pen.
1986-87—Zetor Brno (c)	Czech.	34	12	5	17	....
1987-88—Fredericton Express	AHL	32	9	7	16	8
1988-89—Halifax Citadels	AHL	78	17	41	58	17
1989-90—Halifax Citadels	AHL	50	17	17	34	36
1989-90—Quebec Nordiques	NHL	13	0	2	2	2
NHL TOTALS		13	0	2	2	2

(c)—June, 1987—Drafted by Quebec Nordiques in 1987 NHL entry draft. Ninth Nordiques pick, 177th overall, ninth round.

BRENT SEVERYN

Defense . . . 6'2" . . . 210 lbs. . . . Born, Vegreville, Alta., February 22, 1966 . . . Shoots left . . . (October, 1985)—Knee injury.

Year	Team	League	Games	G.	A.	Pts.	Pen.
1982-83—Vegreville Rangers	CAJHL	21	20	22	42	10
1983-84—Seattle Breakers (c)	WHL	72	14	22	36	49
1984-85—Seattle Breakers	WHL	38	8	32	40	54
1984-85—Brandon Wheat Kings	WHL	26	7	16	23	57
1985-86—Seattle Thunderbirds	WHL	33	11	20	31	164
1985-86—Saskatoon Blades	WHL	9	1	4	5	38
1986-87—Univ. of Alberta	CWUAA	....	....	....	....	....
1987-88—Univ. of Alberta	CWUAA	46	21	29	50	178
1988-89—Halifax Citadels (d)	AHL	47	2	12	14	141
1989-90—Quebec Nordiques	NHL	35	0	2	2	42
1989-90—Halifax Citadels	AHL	43	6	9	15	105
NHL TOTALS		35	0	2	2	42

(c)—June, 1984—Selected by Winnipeg Jets in 1984 NHL entry draft. Fifth Jets pick, 99th overall, fifth round.

(d)—July 15, 1988—Signed by Quebec Nordiques as a free agent.

PIERRE SEVIGNY

Left Wing . . . 5'11" . . . 180 lbs. . . . Born, Trois-Rivieres, Que., September 8, 1971 . . . Shoots left.

Year	Team	League	Games	G.	A.	Pts.	Pen.
1987-88—Magog Cantenniers Midget		Que.	40	43	78	121	72
1988-89—Verdun Jr. Canadiens (c)		QMJHL	67	27	43	70	88
1989-90—St. Hyacinthe Lasers (b)		QMJHL	67	47	72	119	205

(c)—June, 1989—Drafted by Montreal Canadiens in 1989 NHL entry draft. Fourth Canadiens pick, 51st overall, third round.

BRENDAN SHANAHAN

Center . . . 6'3" . . . 200 lbs. . . . Born, Mimico, Ont., January 23, 1969 . . . Shoots right . . . (January, 1987)—Bruised tendons in shoulder . . . (December, 1987)—Broken nose . . . (March, 1989)—Back spasms . . . (January 13, 1990)—Suspended five games for a stick fight with Michel Petit at Quebec . . . (February, 1990)—Lower abdominal strain.

Year	Team	League	Games	G.	A.	Pts.	Pen.
1984-85—Mississauga Reps		MTHL	36	20	21	41	26
1985-86—London Knights		OHL	59	28	34	62	70
1986-87—London Knights (c)		OHL	56	39	53	92	128
1987-88—New Jersey Devils		NHL	65	7	19	26	131
1988-89—New Jersey Devils		NHL	68	22	28	50	115
1989-90—New Jersey Devils		NHL	73	30	42	72	137
NHL TOTALS			206	59	89	148	383

(c)—June, 1987—Drafted as underage junior by New Jersey Devils in 1987 NHL entry draft. First Devils pick, second overall, first round.

DANIEL SHANK

Right Wing . . . 5'10" . . . 190 lbs. . . . Born, Montreal, Que., May 12, 1967 . . . Shoots right.

Year	Team	League	Games	G.	A.	Pts.	Pen.
1985-86—Shawinigan Cataracts		QMJHL	51	34	38	72	184
1986-87—Hull Olympiques		QMJHL	46	26	43	69	325
1987-88—Hull Olympiques		QMJHL	42	23	34	57	274
1988-89—Adirondack Red Wings (c)		AHL	42	5	20	25	113
1989-90—Detroit Red Wings		NHL	57	11	13	24	143
1989-90—Adirondack Red Wings		AHL	14	8	8	16	36
NHL TOTALS			57	11	13	24	143

(c)—October, 1988—Signed by Detroit Red Wings as a free agent.

DARRIN SHANNON

Left Wing . . . 6'2" . . . 190 lbs. . . . Born, Barrie, Ont., December 8, 1969 . . . Shoots left . . . (November, 1986)—Separated right shoulder . . . (November, 1987)—Dislocated left elbow vs. Toronto Marlboros . . . (January, 1988)—Separated left shoulder . . . Brother of Darryl Shannon . . . (May, 1990)—Strained knee ligaments vs. Springfield.

Year	Team	League	Games	G.	A.	Pts.	Pen.
1985-86—Barrie Colts Jr. B		OHA	40	13	22	35	21
1986-87—Windsor Spitfires (c)		OHL	60	16	67	83	116
1987-88—Windsor Spitfires (a-d)		OHL	43	33	41	74	49
1988-89—Windsor Spitfires		OHL	54	33	48	81	47
1988-89—Buffalo Sabres (e)		NHL	3	0	0	0	0
1989-90—Buffalo Sabres		NHL	17	2	7	9	4
1989-90—Rochester Americans		AHL	50	20	23	43	25
NHL TOTALS			20	2	7	9	4

(c)—Named to OHL All-Scholastic team.
(d)—June, 1988—Drafted by Pittsburgh Penguins in 1988 NHL entry draft. First Penguins pick, fourth overall, first round.
(e)—November 12, 1988—Traded with Doug Bodger by Pittsburgh Penguins to Buffalo Sabres for Tom Barrasso and a third-round 1990 draft pick (Joe Dziedzic).

DARRYL SHANNON

Defense . . . 6'2" . . . 190 lbs. . . . Born, Barrie, Ont., June 21, 1968 . . . Shoots left . . . Brother of Darrin Shannon.

Year	Team	League	Games	G.	A.	Pts.	Pen.
1984-85—Barrie Jr. 'B'		OHA	39	5	23	28	50
1985-86—Windsor Spitfires (c)		OHL	57	6	21	27	52
1986-87—Windsor Spitfires (b)		OHL	64	23	27	50	83
1987-88—Windsor Spitfires		OHL	60	16	70	86	116
1988-89—Toronto Maple Leafs		NHL	14	1	3	4	6
1988-89—Newmarket Saints		AHL	61	5	24	29	37
1989-90—Newmarket Saints		AHL	47	4	15	19	58
1989-90—Toronto Maple Leafs		NHL	10	0	1	1	12
NHL TOTALS			24	1	4	5	18

(c)—June, 1986—Drafted by Toronto Maple Leafs in 1986 NHL entry draft. Second Maple Leafs pick, 36th overall, second round.

JEFF SHARPLES

Defense . . . 6' . . . 190 lbs. . . . Born, Terrace, B.C., July 28, 1967 . . . Shoots left . . . (February, 1989)—Injured ankle . . . (October 20, 1989)—Separated shoulder vs. Cape Breton.

Year	Team	League	Games	G.	A.	Pts.	Pen.
1983-84—Kelowna Wings		WHL	72	9	24	33	51
1984-85—Kelowna Wings (b-c)		WHL	72	12	41	53	90
1985-86—Portland Winter Hawks		WHL	19	2	6	8	44
1985-86—Spokane Chiefs		WHL	3	0	0	0	4
1986-87—Portland Winter Hawks		WHL	44	25	35	60	92
1986-87—Detroit Red Wings		NHL	3	0	1	1	2
1987-88—Detroit Red Wings		NHL	56	10	25	35	42
1987-88—Adirondack Red Wings		AHL	4	2	1	3	4
1988-89—Adirondack Red Wings		AHL	10	0	4	4	8

SCOTT SHAUNESSY

Defense . . . 6'4" . . . 220 lbs. . . . Born, Newport, R.I., January 22, 1964 . . . Shoots left . . . (November 20, 1987)—Given a six-game AHL suspension for returning to fight after going to the dressing room vs. Fredericton.

Year	Team	League	Games	G.	A.	Pts.	Pen.
1982-83—St. John's Prep. (c)		R.I. H.S.	23	7	32	39	....
1983-84—Boston University		ECAC	40	6	22	28	48
1984-85—Boston University (b)		H. East	42	7	15	22	87
1985-86—Boston University (a)		H. East	38	4	22	26	60
1986-87—Boston University		H. East	32	2	13	15	71
1986-87—Quebec Nordiques		NHL	3	0	0	0	7
1987-88—Fredericton Express		AHL	60	0	9	9	257
1988-89—Quebec Nordiques		NHL	4	0	0	0	16
1988-89—Halifax Citadels		AHL	41	3	10	13	106
1989-90—Halifax Citadels		AHL	27	3	5	8	105
1989-90—Fort Wayne Komets		IHL	45	3	9	12	267
NHL TOTALS			7	0	0	0	23

(c)—June, 1983—Drafted by Quebec Nordiques in 1983 NHL entry draft. Ninth Nordiques pick, 192nd overall, 10th round.

BRAD SHAW

Defense . . . 5'11" . . . 163 lbs. . . . Born, Cambridge, Ont., April 28, 1964 . . . Shoots right . . . (February, 1988)—Fractured finger on left hand . . . (October 21, 1989)—Broke nose when struck by stick of Joe Kocur vs. Detroit . . . (November 12, 1989)—Back spasms . . . (February 28, 1990)—Bruised right foot when struck by a Petr Svoboda slapshot vs. Montreal.

Year	Team	League	Games	G.	A.	Pts.	Pen.
1980-81—Kitchener Greenshirts		Ont. Midgets	62	14	58	72	14
1981-82—Ottawa 67's (c)		OHL	68	13	59	72	24
1982-83—Ottawa 67's		OHL	63	12	66	78	24
1983-84—Ottawa 67's (a-d-e-f)		OHL	68	11	71	82	75
1984-85—Salt Lake Golden Eagles		IHL	44	3	29	32	25
1984-85—Binghamton Whalers		AHL	24	1	10	11	4
1985-86—Hartford Whalers		NHL	8	0	2	2	4
1985-86—Binghamton Whalers		AHL	64	10	44	54	33
1986-87—Hartford Whalers		NHL	2	0	0	0	0
1986-87—Binghamton Whalers (a-g)		AHL	77	9	30	39	43
1987-88—Binghamton Whalers		AHL	73	12	50	62	50
1987-88—Hartford Whalers		NHL	1	0	0	0	0
1988-89—Verice		Italy	....	....	....	....	....
1988-89—Hartford Whalers (h)		NHL	3	1	0	1	0
1988-89—Canadian National Team		Int'l.	4	1	0	1	2
1989-90—Hartford Whalers		NHL	64	3	32	35	40
NHL TOTALS			78	4	34	38	44

(c)—June, 1982—Drafted as underage junior by Detroit Red Wings in 1982 NHL entry draft. Fifth Red Wings pick, 86th overall, fifth round.
(d)—Won Max Kaminsky Trophy (Top Defenseman).
(e)—Led OHL playoffs with 27 assists.
(f)—May, 1984—Traded by Detroit Red Wings to Hartford Whalers for eighth-round 1984 draft pick (Lars Karlsson).
(g)—Won Eddie Shore Award (Top Defenseman).
(h)—May 2, 1989—Signed multi-year contract with Hartford Whalers.

DAVE SHAW

Defense . . . 6'2" . . . 190 lbs. . . . Born, St. Thomas, Ont., May 25, 1964 . . . Shoots right . . . (December 18, 1985)—Sprained wrist at Montreal . . . (October, 1987)—Separated shoulder . . . (October 27, 1988)—Given 12-game suspension for slashing Mario Lemieux at Pittsburgh . . . (March 15, 1989)—Bruised shoulder vs. Winnipeg . . . (November 2, 1989)—Dislocated right shoulder when checked by Marc Fortier vs. Quebec . . . (November 22, 1989)—Reinjured right shoulder at Buffalo and missed 10 games . . . (February 7, 1990)—Surgery to right shoulder.

Year	Team	League	Games	G.	A.	Pts.	Pen.
1980-81—Stratford Jr. B		OPJHL	41	12	19	31	30
1981-82—Kitchener Rangers (c)		OHL	68	6	25	31	99
1982-83—Kitchener Rangers		OHL	57	18	56	74	78
1982-83—Quebec Nordiques		NHL	2	0	0	0	0
1983-84—Kitchener Rangers (a)		OHL	58	14	34	48	73
1983-84—Quebec Nordiques		NHL	3	0	0	0	0
1984-85—Guelph Platers		OHL	2	0	0	0	0
1984-85—Fredericton Express		AHL	48	7	6	13	73
1984-85—Quebec Nordiques		NHL	14	0	0	0	11
1985-86—Quebec Nordiques		NHL	73	7	19	26	78
1986-87—Quebec Nordiques		NHL	75	0	19	19	69
1987-88—New York Rangers (d)		NHL	68	7	25	32	100
1988-89—New York Rangers		NHL	63	6	11	17	88
1989-90—New York Rangers		NHL	22	2	10	12	22
NHL TOTALS			320	22	84	106	368

(c)—June, 1982—Drafted as underage junior by Quebec Nordiques in 1982 NHL entry draft. First Nordiques pick, 13th overall, first round.
(d)—September, 1987—Traded with John Ogrodnick by Quebec Nordiques to New York Rangers for Jeff Jackson and Terry Carkner.

Continued from top of second column:

Year	Team	League	Games	G.	A.	Pts.	Pen.
1988-89—Detroit Red Wings		NHL	46	4	9	13	26
1989-90—Adirondack Red Wings (d)		AHL	9	2	5	7	6
1989-90—Cape Breton Oilers (e)		AHL	38	4	13	17	28
1989-90—Utica Devils		AHL	13	2	5	7	19
NHL TOTALS			105	14	35	49	70

(c)—June, 1985—Drafted as underage junior by Detroit Red Wings in 1985 NHL entry draft. Second Red Wings pick, 29th overall, second round.
(d)—November 2, 1989—Traded with Joe Murphy, Adam Graves and Petr Klima by Detroit Red Wings to Edmonton Oilers for Jimmy Carson, Kevin McClelland and a fifth-round 1991 draft pick.
(e)—March 6, 1990—Traded by Edmonton Oilers to New Jersey Devils for Reijo Ruotsalainen.

DOUGLAS ARTHUR SHEDDEN

Right Wing . . . 6' . . . 184 lbs. . . . Born, Wallaceburg, Ont., April 29, 1961 . . . Shoots right . . . (October 25, 1981)—Suffered a broken finger and leg and ankle injuries during a team practice . . . Also plays Center . . . (March 24, 1986)—Kidney infection . . . (December, 1988)—Torn knee ligaments vs. Calgary . . . (January 16, 1990)—Knee injury.

Year	Team	League	Games	G.	A.	Pts.	Pen.
1977-78—Hamilton Fincups		OMJHL	32	1	9	10	32
1977-78—Kitchener Rangers		OMJHL	18	5	7	12	14
1978-79—Kitchener Rangers		OMJHL	66	16	42	58	29
1979-80—Kitchener Rangers		OMJHL	16	10	16	26	26
1979-80—Sault Ste. Marie Greyhounds (c)		OMJHL	45	30	44	74	59
1980-81—Sault Ste. Marie Greyhounds		OHL	66	51	72	123	78
1981-82—Erie Blades		AHL	17	4	6	10	14
1981-82—Pittsburgh Penguins		NHL	38	10	15	25	12
1982-83—Pittsburgh Penguins		NHL	80	24	43	67	54
1983-84—Pittsburgh Penguins		NHL	67	22	35	57	20
1984-85—Pittsburgh Penguins		NHL	80	35	32	67	30
1985-86—Pittsburgh Penguins (d)		NHL	67	32	34	66	32
1985-86—Detroit Red Wings		NHL	11	2	3	5	2
1986-87—Adirondack Red Wings		AHL	5	2	2	4	4
1986-87—Detroit Red Wings (e)		NHL	33	6	12	18	6
1986-87—Fredericton Express		AHL	15	12	6	18	0
1986-87—Quebec Nordiques		NHL	16	0	2	2	8
1987-88—Baltimore Skipjacks (f)		AHL	80	37	51	88	32
1988-89—Toronto Maple Leafs		NHL	1	0	0	0	2
1988-89—Newmarket Saints		AHL	29	14	26	40	6
1989-90—Newmarket Saints		AHL	47	26	33	59	12
NHL TOTALS			393	131	176	307	166

(c)—June, 1980—Drafted as underage junior by Pittsburgh Penguins in 1980 NHL entry draft. Fourth Penguins pick, 93rd overall, sixth round.

(d)—March, 1986—Traded by Pittsburgh Penguins to Detroit Red Wings for Ron Duguay.

(e)—January, 1987—Traded with John Ogrodnick and Basil McRae by Detroit Red Wings to Quebec Nordiques for Brent Ashton, Mark Kumpel and Gilbert Delorme.

(f)—August, 1988—Signed by Toronto Maple Leafs as a free agent.

NEIL SHEEHY

Defense . . . 6'2" . . . 210 lbs. . . . Born, International Falls, Minn., February 9, 1960 . . . Shoots right . . . Brother of Shawn and Tim Sheehy (hockey players) and nephew of Bronko Nagurski (football star for University of Minnesota and Hall-of-Famer with Chicago Bears) . . . (October, 1986)—Dislocated shoulder . . . (December, 1986)—Missed games due to recurring shoulder problems . . . (March 10, 1987)—Deep thigh bruise when kneed by Lou Franceschetti at Washington . . . (January, 1988)—Injured hip . . . (March 9, 1990)—Bruised left shin vs. Quebec.

Year	Team	League	Games	G.	A.	Pts.	Pen.
1979-80—Harvard University		ECAC	13	0	0	0	10
1980-81—Harvard University		ECAC	26	4	8	12	22
1981-82—Harvard University		ECAC	30	7	11	18	46
1982-83—Harvard University		ECAC	34	5	13	18	48
1983-84—Colorado Flames (c)		CHL	74	5	18	23	151
1983-84—Calgary Flames		NHL	1	1	0	1	2
1984-85—Moncton Golden Flames		AHL	34	6	9	15	101
1984-85—Calgary Flames		NHL	31	3	4	7	109
1985-86—Moncton Golden Flames		AHL	4	1	1	2	21
1985-86—Calgary Flames		NHL	65	2	16	18	271
1986-87—Calgary Flames		NHL	54	4	6	10	151
1987-88—Calgary Flames (d)		NHL	36	2	6	8	73
1987-88—Hartford Whalers (e)		NHL	26	1	4	5	116
1988-89—Washington Capitals		NHL	72	3	4	7	179
1989-90—Washington Capitals		NHL	59	1	5	6	291
NHL TOTALS			344	17	45	62	1192

(c)—August, 1983—Signed by Calgary Flames as a free agent.

(d)—January, 1988—Traded with Carey Wilson and Lane MacDonald by Calgary Flames to Hartford Whalers for Dana Murzyn and Shane Churla.

(e)—July, 1988—Traded with Mike Millar by Hartford Whalers to Washington Capitals for Ed Kastelic and Grant Jennings.

RAY SHEPPARD

Right Wing . . . 6'1" . . . 180 lbs. . . . Born, Pembroke, Ont., May 27, 1966 . . . Shoots right . . . (September, 1986)—Missed Buffalo training camp with a left knee injury . . . (September, 1988)—Bruised back during Buffalo Sabres training camp . . . (November 25, 1988)—Face cut by stick of Troy Murray vs. Chicago . . . (November 27, 1988)—Face cut by stick of Mark Howe vs. Philadelphia . . . (December, 1988)—Flu . . . (January 30, 1989)—Sprained ankle . . . (March 16, 1990)—Injured left knee vs. Newmarket.

Year	Team	League	Games	G.	A.	Pts.	Pen.
1982-83—Brockville		OPHL	48	27	36	63	81
1983-84—Cornwall Royals (c)		OHL	68	44	36	80	69
1984-85—Cornwall Royals		OHL	49	25	33	58	51
1985-86—Cornwall Royals (a-d-e-f)		OHL	63	*81	61	*142	25
1986-87—Rochester Americans		AHL	55	18	13	31	11
1987-88—Buffalo Sabres		NHL	74	38	27	65	14
1988-89—Buffalo Sabres		NHL	67	22	21	43	15
1989-90—Buffalo Sabres (g)		NHL	18	4	2	6	0
1989-90—Rochester Americans		AHL	5	3	5	8	2
NHL TOTALS			159	64	50	114	29

(c)—June, 1984—Drafted as underage junior by Buffalo Sabres in 1984 NHL entry draft. Third Sabres pick, 60th overall, third round.

(d)—Won Eddie Powers Memorial Trophy (Scoring Champion).

(e)—Won Jim Mahon Memorial Trophy (Top Scoring Right Winger).

(f)—Won Red Tilson Trophy (Outstanding Player).

(g)—July 10, 1990—Traded by Buffalo Sabres to New York Rangers for future considerations and cash.

DAVE SHIELDS

Center . . . 5'9" . . . 170 lbs. . . . Born, Calgary, Alta., April 24, 1967 . . . Shoots left . . . (January, 1988)—Major reconstructive surgery to his right shoulder. He had arthroscopic surgery to same shoulder after 1986-87 season.

Year	Team	League	Games	G.	A.	Pts.	Pen.
1986-87—Univ. of Denver (c-d)		WCHA	40	18	30	48	8
1987-88—Univ. of Denver		WCHA	21	10	7	17	2
1988-89—Univ. of Denver		WCHA	43	12	28	40	12
1989-90—Univ. of Denver (a-e)		WCHA	42	31	43	74	24

(c)—June, 1987—Drafted by Minnesota North Stars in 1987 NHL entry draft. Twelfth North Stars pick, 235th overall, 12th round.

(d)—Named WCHA Rookie-of-the-Year.

(e)—Named second team NCAA All-America (West).

BRUCE SHOEBOTTOM

Defense . . . 6'2" . . . 200 lbs. . . . Born, Windsor, Ont., August 20, 1965 . . . Shoots left . . . (December, 1982)—Broken leg . . . (January 24, 1987)—IHL suspension for going into the stands at Salt Lake City . . . (April, 1988)—Broken collarbone . . . (November 29, 1989)—Required 60 stitches on right side of his face when caught by the blade of Tom Martin's skate vs. Binghamton.

Year	Team	League	Games	G.	A.	Pts.	Pen.
1981-82—Peterborough Petes		OHL	51	0	4	4	67
1982-83—Peterborough Petes (c)		OHL	34	2	10	12	106
1983-84—Peterborough Petes		OHL	16	0	5	5	73
1984-85—Peterborough Petes		OHL	60	2	15	17	143
1985-86—New Haven Nighthawks (d)		AHL	6	2	0	2	12
1985-86—Binghamton Whalers		AHL	62	7	5	12	249
1986-87—Fort Wayne Komets		IHL	75	2	10	12	309
1987-88—Maine Mariners		AHL	70	2	12	14	138
1987-88—Boston Bruins		NHL	3	0	1	1	0
1988-89—Maine Mariners		AHL	44	0	8	8	265
1988-89—Boston Bruins		NHL	29	1	3	4	44
1989-90—Maine Mariners		AHL	66	3	11	14	228
1989-90—Boston Bruins		NHL	2	0	0	0	4
NHL TOTALS			34	1	4	5	48

(c)—June, 1983—Drafted as underage junior by Los Angeles Kings in 1983 NHL entry draft. First Kings pick, 47th overall, third round.

(d)—October, 1985—Traded by Los Angeles Kings to Washington Capitals for Bryan Erickson.

GARY SHUCHUK

Center . . . 5'10" . . . 185 lbs. . . . Born, Edmonton, Alta., February 17, 1967 . . . Shoots right.

Year	Team	League	Games	G.	A.	Pts.	Pen.
1986-87—Univ. of Wisconsin		WCHA	42	19	11	30	72
1987-88—Univ. of Wisconsin (c)		WCHA	44	7	22	29	70
1988-89—Univ. of Wisconsin		WCHA	46	18	19	37	102
1989-90—Univ. of Wisconsin (a-d-e)		WCHA	45	*41	39	*80	70

(c)—June, 1988—Selected by Detroit Red Wings in 1988 NHL supplemental draft.

(d)—Named WCHA MVP.

(e)—Named first-team NCAA All-America (West).

RONALD SHUDRA

Defense . . . 6'1" . . . 180 lbs. . . . Born, Winnipeg, Man., November 28, 1967 . . . Shoots left . . . Also plays Left Wing.

Year	Team	League	Games	G.	A.	Pts.	Pen.
1984-85—Red Deer Rustlers		AJHL	57	14	57	71	70
1985-86—Kamloops Blazers (b-c-d)		WHL	72	10	40	50	81
1986-87—Kamloops Blazers (b)		WHL	71	49	70	119	68
1987-88—Nova Scotia Oilers		AHL	49	7	15	22	21
1987-88—Edmonton Oilers		NHL	10	0	5	5	6
1988-89—Cape Breton Oilers (e)		AHL	5	0	0	0	0
1988-89—Denver Rangers		IHL	64	11	14	25	44
1989-90—Fort Wayne Komets		IHL	67	11	16	27	48
NHL TOTALS			10	0	5	5	6

(c)—Co-winner of WHL Rookie-of-the-Year Trophy with Dave Waldie.

(d)—June, 1986—Drafted as underage junior by Edmonton Oilers in 1986 NHL entry draft. Third Oilers pick, 63rd overall, third round.

(e)—October 27, 1988—Traded by Edmonton Oilers to New York Rangers for Jeff Crossman.

DAVE SHUTE

Center . . . 5'11" . . . 175 lbs. . . . Born, Carlyle, Penn., February 10, 1971 . . . Shoots left . . . (February, 1987)—Dislocated shoulder.

Year	Team	League	Games	G.	A.	Pts.	Pen.
1984-85—Richfield Bantams		Minn. H.S.	50	47	51	98	60
1985-86—Richfield Bantams		Minn. H.S.	35	45	50	95	75
1986-87—Richfield H.S.		Minn. H.S.	23	17	15	32	26
1987-88—Richfield H.S.		Minn. H.S.	13	7	9	16	38
1988-89—Victoria Cougars (c)		WHL	69	5	11	16	26
1989-90—Victoria Cougars		WHL	14	4	5	9	25
1989-90—Medicine Hat Tigers		WHL	48	13	15	28	56

(c)—June, 1989—Drafted by Pittsburgh Penguins in 1989 NHL entry draft. Ninth Penguins pick, 163rd overall, eighth round.

MIKE SILLINGER

Center . . . 5'10" . . . 190 lbs. . . . Born, Regina, Sask., June 29, 1971 . . . Shoots right.

Year	Team	League	Games	G.	A.	Pts.	Pen.
1986-87—Regina Kings Bantam		Regina	31	83	51	134	....
1987-88—Regina Pats		WHL	67	18	25	43	17
1988-89—Regina Pats (c)		WHL	72	53	78	131	52
1989-90—Regina Pats (b)		WHL	70	57	72	129	41

(c)—June, 1989—Drafted by Detroit Red Wings in 1989 NHL entry draft. First Red Wings pick, 11th overall, first round.

TREVOR SIM

Center . . . 6'2'' . . . 180 lbs. . . . Born, Calgary, Alta., June 9, 1970 . . . Shoots right.

Year	Team	League	Games	G.	A.	Pts.	Pen.
1986-87—Calgary Spurs		AJHL	57	38	50	88	48
1987-88—Seattle Thunderbirds (c)		WHL	67	17	18	35	87
1988-89—Regina Pats (d)		WHL	21	4	8	12	48
1988-89—Swift Current Broncos		WHL	42	16	19	35	69
1989-90—Swift Current Broncos		WHL	6	3	2	5	21
1989-90—Kamloops Blazers		WHL	43	27	35	62	53
1989-90—Edmonton Oilers		NHL	3	0	1	1	2
NHL TOTALS			3	0	1	1	2

(c)—June, 1988—Drafted by Edmonton Oilers in 1988 NHL entry draft. Third Oilers pick, 53rd overall, third round.

(d)—September 26, 1988—Traded by Seattle Thunderbirds to Regina Pats for Bart Cole.

MARTIN SIMARD

Right Wing . . . 6'3'' . . . 215 lbs. . . . Born, June 25, 1966, Montreal, Que., . . . Shoots right . . . (September 26, 1988)—Surgery to right knee . . . (December 11, 1988)—Suspended 10 IHL games for fighting with Mark Janssens vs. Denver when Janssens suffered a fractured skull . . . (November 28, 1989)—Appendectomy.

Year	Team	League	Games	G.	A.	Pts.	Pen.
1983-84—Quebec Remparts		QMJHL	59	6	10	16	26
1984-85—Granby Bisons		QMJHL	58	22	31	53	78
1985-86—Hull Olympiques		QMJHL	68	40	36	76	184
1986-87—Granby Bisons (c)		QMJHL	41	30	47	77	105
1987-88—Salt Lake Golden Eagles		IHL	82	8	23	31	281
1988-89—Salt Lake Golden Eagles		IHL	71	13	15	28	221
1989-90—Salt Lake Golden Eagles		IHL	59	22	23	45	151

(c)—May, 1987—Signed by Calgary Flames as a free agent.

CHRIS SIMON

Left Wing . . . 6'3'' . . . 220 lbs. . . . Born, Wawa, Ont., January 30, 1972 . . . Shoots left . . . (January 20, 1990)—Suspended six OHL games for shooting the puck in frustration, and striking Chris Taylor in the face vs. London.

Year	Team	League	Games	G.	A.	Pts.	Pen.
1986-87—Wawa Midget		OHA	36	12	20	32	108
1987-88—Sault Ste. Marie Thunderbirds		OHL	55	42	36	78	172
1988-89—Ottawa 67's		OHL	36	4	2	6	31
1989-90—Ottawa 67's (c)		OHL	57	36	38	74	146

(c)—June 16, 1990—Selected by Philadelphia Flyers in 1990 NHL entry draft. Second Flyers pick, 25th overall, second round.

JASON SIMON

Left Wing . . . 6'1'' . . . 190 lbs. . . . Born, Sarnia, Ont., March 21, 1969 . . . Shoots left.

Year	Team	League	Games	G.	A.	Pts.	Pen.
1985-86—Chatham Jr. B		OHA	32	5	19	24	118
1986-87—London Knights		OHL	33	1	2	3	33
1986-87—Sudbury Wolves		OHL	26	2	3	5	50
1987-88—Sudbury Wolves		OHL	26	5	7	12	35
1987-88—Hamilton Steelhawks (c)		OHL	29	5	13	18	124
1988-89—Kingston Raiders		OHL	17	7	12	19	58
1988-89—Windsor Spitfires (d)		OHL	45	16	27	43	135
1989-90—Utica Devils		AHL	16	3	4	7	28
1989-90—Nashville Knights		ECHL	13	4	3	7	81

(c)—August, 1988—Traded with Garth Joy, Kevin Lune and a fourth-round 1989 draft pick by Niagara Falls Thunder to Kingston Raiders for Brian Fogarty.

(d)—June, 1989—Drafted by New Jersey Devils in 1989 NHL entry draft. Ninth Devils pick, 215th overall, 11th round.

CRAIG SIMPSON

Left Wing . . . 6'2'' . . . 185 lbs. . . . Born, London, Ont., February 15, 1967 . . . Shoots right . . . Brother of Dave Simpson . . . Son of Marion Simpson (Member of 1952 Canadian Women's Olympic Track Team) . . . (March, 1987)—Pulled muscle in right hip . . . (March 14, 1987)—Sprained right wrist vs. Philadelphia . . . (December 4, 1988)—Broke right ankle when he blocked a Brian Leetch shot vs. N.Y. Rangers . . . Also plays center.

Year	Team	League	Games	G.	A.	Pts.	Pen.
1982-83—London Diamonds Jr. B.		OHA	....	48	63	*111	....
1983-84—Michigan State		CCHA	30	8	28	36	22
1984-85—Michigan State (a-c-d)		CCHA	42	31	53	84	33
1985-86—Pittsburgh Penguins		NHL	76	11	17	28	49
1986-87—Pittsburgh Penguins		NHL	72	26	25	51	57
1987-88—Pittsburgh Penguins (e)		NHL	21	13	13	26	34
1987-88—Edmonton Oilers		NHL	59	43	21	64	43
1988-89—Edmonton Oilers		NHL	66	35	41	76	80
1989-90—Edmonton Oilers		NHL	80	29	32	61	180
NHL TOTALS			374	157	149	306	443

(c)—First Team All-America (West).

(d)—June, 1985—Drafted by Pittsburgh Penguins in 1985 NHL entry draft. First Penguins pick, second overall, first round.

(e)—November, 1987—Traded with Dave Hannan, Chris Joseph and Moe Mantha by Pittsburgh Penguins to Edmonton Oilers for Paul Coffey, Dave Hunter and Wayne Van Dorp.

GEOFF SIMPSON

Defense . . . 6'1'' . . . 180 lbs. . . . Born, Victoria, B.C., March 6, 1969 . . . Shoots right . . . (February, 1988)—Broken ankle.

Year	Team	League	Games	G.	A.	Pts.	Pen.
1984-85—Port Alberni Midget		B.C. Midg.	40	17	29	46	65
1985-86—Parksville Midget		B.C. Midg.	30	10	14	24	52

Year	Team	League	Games	G.	A.	Pts.	Pen.
1986-87—Estevan Bruins		SJHL	62	5	16	21	145
1987-88—Estevan Bruins		SJHL	58	9	28	37	151
1988-89—Estevan Bruins (c)		SJHL	63	20	53	73	57
1989-90—Northern Michigan Univ.		WCHA	39	4	9	13	40

(c)—June, 1989—Drafted by Boston Bruins in 1989 NHL entry draft. Tenth Bruins pick, 206th overall, 10th round.

REID SIMPSON

Left Wing . . . 6'1'' . . . 210 lbs. . . . Born, Flin Flon, Man., May 21, 1969 . . . Shoots left.

Year	Team	League	Games	G.	A.	Pts.	Pen.
1984-85—Flin Flon Midget Bombers		Man.	50	60	70	130	100
1985-86—Flin Flon Bombers		MJHL	40	20	21	41	200
1985-86—New Westminster Bruins		WHL	2	0	0	0	0
1986-87—Prince Albert Raiders		WHL	47	3	8	11	105
1987-88—Prince Albert Raiders		WHL	72	13	14	27	164
1988-89—Prince Albert Raiders (c)		WHL	59	26	29	55	264
1989-90—Prince Albert Raiders		WHL	29	15	17	32	121
1989-90—Hershey Bears		AHL	28	2	2	4	175

(c)—June, 1989—Drafted by Philadelphia Flyers in 1989 NHL entry draft. Third Flyers pick, 72nd overall, fourth round.

ILKKA SINISALO

Left Wing . . . 6'1'' . . . 190 lbs. . . . Born, Valeskoski, Finland, July 10, 1958 . . . Shoots left . . . (September, 1982)—Broke collarbone . . . (December, 1984)—Missed 10 games with back spasms . . . (December, 1986)—Strained left knee and required surgery . . . (December, 1987)—Back spasms . . . (February, 1988)—Bruised knee . . . (March, 1988)—Twisted left knee . . . (November, 1988)—Sprained right ankle . . . (January 17, 1989)—Fractured left wrist in three places when he crashed into the boards at Vancouver . . . (February, 1989)—Reinjured left wrist in a fall . . . (December 27, 1989)—Sprained right knee at Edmonton and missed 10 games . . . (March 17, 1990)—Bruised collarbone at Quebec.

Year	Team	League	Games	G.	A.	Pts.	Pen.
1979-80—Helsinki IFK		Finland	35	16	9	25	16
1980-81—Helsinki IFK		Finland	36	27	17	44	14
1981-82—Philadelphia Flyers (c)		NHL	66	15	22	37	22
1982-83—Philadelphia Flyers		NHL	61	21	29	50	16
1983-84—Philadelphia Flyers		NHL	73	29	17	46	29
1984-85—Philadelphia Flyers		NHL	70	36	37	73	16
1985-86—Philadelphia Flyers		NHL	74	39	37	76	31
1986-87—Philadelphia Flyers		NHL	42	10	21	31	8
1987-88—Philadelphia Flyers		NHL	68	25	17	42	30
1988-89—Philadelphia Flyers		NHL	13	1	6	7	2
1989-90—Philadelphia Flyers (d)		NHL	59	23	23	46	26
NHL TOTALS			526	199	209	408	180

(c)—February, 1981—Signed by Philadelphia Flyers as a free agent.

(d)—July 3, 1990—Signed by Minnesota North Stars as a free agent.

VILLE SIREN

Defense . . . 6'2'' . . . 185 lbs. . . . Born, Helsinki, Finland, November 2, 1964 . . . Shoots left . . . (October 16, 1985)—Fractured right ankle at Chicago and missed 19 games . . . (March 10, 1987)—Sprained ligaments in left knee vs. N.Y. Islanders . . . (October, 1987)—Sore shoulder . . . (December, 1987)—Missed 17 games with broken foot . . . (November 16, 1988)—Sprained ankle at Toronto . . . (February, 1989)—Flu . . . (March, 1990)—Sore back.

Year	Team	League	Games	G.	A.	Pts.	Pen.
1984-85—Ilves (c-d)		Finland	36	11	3	24	..
1985-86—Pittsburgh Penguins		NHL	60	4	8	12	32
1986-87—Pittsburgh Penguins		NHL	69	5	17	22	50
1987-88—Pittsburgh Penguins		NHL	58	1	20	21	62
1988-89—Pittsburgh Penguins (e)		NHL	12	1	0	1	14
1988-89—Minnesota North Stars		NHL	38	2	10	12	58
1989-90—Minnesota North Stars		NHL	53	1	13	14	60
NHL TOTALS			290	14	68	82	276

(c)—June, 1983—Drafted by Hartford Whalers in 1983 NHL entry draft. Third Whalers pick, 23rd overall, second round.

(d)—November, 1984—Traded by Hartford Whalers to Pittsburgh Penguins for Pat Boutette.

(e)—December 17, 1988—Traded with Steve Gotaas by Pittsburgh Penguins to Minnesota North Stars for Scott Bjugstad and Gord Dineen.

JEFF SIRKKA

Defense . . . 6'1'' . . . 204 lbs. . . . Born, Copper Cliff, Ont., June 17, 1968 . . . Shoots left.

Year	Team	League	Games	G.	A.	Pts.	Pen.
1984-85—Sudbury Midget		OHA	78	8	27	35	211
1985-86—Kingston Canadians		OHL	34	1	6	7	51
1986-87—Kingston Canadians		OHL	64	0	5	5	156
1987-88—Kingston Canadians		OHL	59	1	16	17	114
1988-89—North Bay Centennials (c)		OHL	12	0	3	3	66
1988-89—Toronto Marlboros		OHL	29	1	14	15	71
1989-90—Maine Mariners (d-e)		AHL	56	0	9	9	110
1989-90—Binghamton Whalers		AHL	16	0	1	1	38

(c)—November 28, 1988—Traded by North Bay Centennials to Toronto Marlboros for a sixth-round 1989 draft pick (Michael Murray).

(d)—September, 1989—Signed by Boston Bruins as a free agent.

(e)—March 3, 1990—Traded by Boston Bruins to Hartford Whalers for Steve Dykstra.

JARROD SKALDE

Center . . . 6' . . . 178 lbs. . . . Born, Niagara Falls, Ont., February 26, 1971 . . . Shoots left.

Year	Team	League	Games	G.	A.	Pts.	Pen.
1986-87—Fort Erie Meteors		OHA	41	27	34	61	36
1987-88—Oshawa Generals		OHL	60	12	16	28	24
1988-89—Oshawa Generals (c)		OHL	65	38	38	76	36
1989-90—Oshawa Generals		OHL	62	40	52	92	66

(c)—June, 1989—Drafted by New Jersey Devils in 1989 NHL entry draft. Third Devils pick, 26th overall, second round.

RANDALL SKARDA

Defense . . . 6'1" . . . 195 lbs. . . . Born, St. Paul, Minn., May 5, 1968 . . . Shoots right.

Year	Team	League	Games	G.	A.	Pts.	Pen.
1984-85—St. Thomas Academy		Minn. H.S.	23	14	42	56	....
1985-86—St. Thomas Academy (c)		Minn. H.S.	23	15	27	42	....
1986-87—Univ. of Minnesota		WCHA	43	3	10	13	77
1987-88—Univ. of Minnesota (d)		WCHA	42	19	26	45	102
1988-89—Univ. of Minnesota		WCHA	43	6	24	30	91
1989-90—St. Louis Blues		NHL	25	0	5	5	11
1989-90—Peoria Rivermen		IHL	38	7	17	24	40
NHL TOTALS			25	0	5	5	11

(c)—June, 1986—Drafted by St. Louis Blues in 1986 NHL entry draft. Eighth Blues pick, 157th overall, eighth round.
(d)—Named Second team All-America (West).

PETRI SKRIKO

Right Wing . . . 5'10" . . . 172 lbs. . . . Born, Laapeenranta, Finland, March 12, 1962 . . . Shoots left . . . (October, 1984)—Broken thumb . . . (October, 1987)—Bruised knee . . . (January, 1988)—Sprained ankle . . . (December, 1988)—Strained knee . . . (February 12, 1989)—Twisted knee vs. Buffalo . . . (March, 1990)—Flu.

Year	Team	League	Games	G.	A.	Pts.	Pen.
1980-81—Saipa		Finland	36	20	13	33	14
1981-82—Saipa		Finland	33	19	27	46	24
1982-83—Saipa		Finland	36	23	12	35	12
1983-84—Saipa (c)		Finland	32	25	26	51	13
1984-85—Vancouver Canucks		NHL	72	21	14	35	10
1985-86—Vancouver Canucks		NHL	80	38	40	78	34
1986-87—Vancouver Canucks		NHL	76	33	41	74	44
1987-88—Vancouver Canucks		NHL	73	30	34	64	32
1988-89—Vancouver Canucks		NHL	74	30	36	66	57
1989-90—Vancouver Canucks		NHL	77	15	33	48	36
NHL TOTALS			452	167	198	365	213

(c)—June, 1981—Drafted by Vancouver Canucks in 1981 NHL entry draft. Seventh Canucks pick, 157th overall, seventh round.

BRIAN SKRUDLAND

Center . . . 6' . . . 180 lbs. . . . Born, Peace River, Alta, July 31, 1963 . . . Shoots left . . . Cousin of Barry Pederson . . . (February, 1988)—Groin injury . . . (December 27, 1988)—Strained left knee ligaments at Los Angeles . . . (January, 1989)—Bruised right foot . . . (October 7, 1989)—Sprained right ankle vs. Buffalo and missed 21 games.

Year	Team	League	Games	G.	A.	Pts.	Pen.
1980-81—Saskatoon Blades		WHL	66	15	27	42	97
1981-82—Saskatoon Blades		WHL	71	27	29	56	135
1982-83—Saskatoon Blades (c)		WHL	71	35	59	94	42
1983-84—Nova Scotia Voyageurs		AHL	56	13	12	25	55
1984-85—Sherbrooke Canadiens		AHL	70	22	28	50	109
1985-86—Montreal Canadiens		NHL	65	9	13	22	57
1986-87—Montreal Canadiens		NHL	79	11	17	28	107
1987-88—Montreal Canadiens		NHL	79	12	24	36	112
1988-89—Montreal Canadiens		NHL	71	12	29	41	84
1989-90—Montreal Canadiens		NHL	59	11	31	42	56
NHL TOTALS			353	55	114	169	416

(c)—August, 1983—Signed as free agent by Montreal Canadiens.

JOHN SLANEY

Defense . . . 5'11" . . . 186 lbs. . . . Born, St. John's, Newfoundland, February 7, 1972 . . . Shoots left.

Year	Team	League	Games	G.	A.	Pts.	Pen.
1987-88—St. John's Capitals Midget		Nova Scotia	65	41	69	110	70
1988-89—Cornwall Royals		OHL	66	16	43	59	23
1989-90—Cornwall Royals (a-c-d)		OHL	64	38	59	97	60

(c)—Won Max Kaminsky Trophy (Outstanding OHL defenseman).
(d)—June 16, 1990—Selected by Washington Capitals in 1990 NHL entry draft. First Capitals pick, ninth overall, first round.

DOUG SMAIL

Left Wing . . . 5'10" . . . 175 lbs. . . . Born, Moose Jaw, Sask., September 2, 1957 . . . Shoots left . . . (January 10, 1981)—Suffered fractured jaw and also broke jaw in a November 1980 practice . . . (December 20, 1981)—Set NHL record for fastest goal at start of game (5 seconds) vs. St. Louis . . . (December, 1983)—Stretched knee ligaments . . . (October 25, 1985)—Pulled leg muscle vs. Washington and missed seven games . . . (September, 1987)—Arthroscopic knee surgery . . . (December, 1988)—Lacerated left calf . . . (February 13, 1989)—Fractured orbital bone near eye when struck by Fredrik Olausson shot at Detroit.

Year	Team	League	Games	G.	A.	Pts.	Pen.
1977-78—Univ. of North Dakota		WCHA	38	22	28	50	52
1978-79—Univ. of North Dakota		WCHA	35	24	34	58	46
1979-80—Univ. of North Dakota (b-c-d)		WCHA	40	43	44	87	70

Year	Team	League	Games	G.	A.	Pts.	Pen.
1980-81—Winnipeg Jets		NHL	30	10	8	18	45
1981-82—Winnipeg Jets		NHL	72	17	18	35	55
1982-83—Winnipeg Jets		NHL	80	15	29	44	32
1983-84—Winnipeg Jets		NHL	66	20	17	37	62
1984-85—Winnipeg Jets		NHL	80	31	35	66	45
1985-86—Winnipeg Jets		NHL	73	16	26	42	32
1986-87—Winnipeg Jets		NHL	78	25	18	43	36
1987-88—Winnipeg Jets		NHL	71	15	16	31	34
1988-89—Winnipeg Jets		NHL	47	14	15	29	52
1989-90—Winnipeg Jets		NHL	79	25	24	49	63
NHL TOTALS			676	188	206	394	456

(c)—Named to NCAA Tournament All-Star team and Tournament's Most Valuable Player.
(d)—May, 1980—Signed by Winnipeg Jets as a free agent.

JASON SMART

Center . . . 6'3" . . . 212 lbs. . . . Born, Prince George, B.C., January 23, 1970 . . . Shoots left . . . (November, 1986)—Missed 10 days due to injured shoulder . . . (May, 1987)—Shoulder surgery.

Year	Team	League	Games	G.	A.	Pts.	Pen.
1986-87—Prince Albert Raiders		WHL	57	9	22	31	62
1987-88—Prince Albert Raiders		WHL	72	16	29	45	79
1988-89—Prince Albert Raiders (c)		WHL	12	1	3	4	31
1988-89—Saskatoon Blades (d)		WHL	36	6	17	23	33
1989-90—Saskatoon Blades		WHL	66	27	48	75	187

(c)—December 1, 1988—Traded by Prince Albert Raiders to Brandon Wheat Kings for Graham Garden. Smart refused to report to Brandon and was later dealt to Saskatoon Blades.
(d)—June, 1989—Drafted by Pittsburgh Penguins in 1989 NHL entry draft. Thirteenth Penguins pick, 247th overall, 12th round.

DARIN SMITH

Left Wing . . . 6'2" . . . 200 lbs. . . . Born, St. Catharines, Ont., February 20, 1967 . . . Shoots left . . . (November, 1986)—Broken wrist.

Year	Team	League	Games	G.	A.	Pts.	Pen.
1984-85—London Knights		OHL	52	1	9	10	98
1985-86—London Knights (c)		OHL	9	2	5	7	23
1985-86—North Bay Centennials		OHL	45	7	24	31	131
1986-87—North Bay Centennials (d)		OHL	59	22	25	47	142
1987-88—Peoria Rivermen		IHL	81	21	23	44	144
1988-89—Peoria Rivermen		IHL	62	13	17	30	127
1989-90—Peoria Rivermen		IHL	76	16	13	29	147

(c)—November, 1985—Claimed by North Bay Centennials from London Knights to complete an earlier trade.
(d)—June, 1987—Drafted by St. Louis Blues in 1987 NHL entry draft. Fourth Blues pick, 75th overall, fourth round.

DENNIS SMITH

Defense . . . 5'11" . . . 192 lbs. . . . Born, Livonia, Mich., July 27, 1964 . . . Shoots left.

Year	Team	League	Games	G.	A.	Pts.	Pen.
1981-82—Kingston Canadians		OHL	48	2	23	25	83
1982-83—Kingston Canadians		OHL	65	6	24	30	90
1983-84—Kingston Canadians		OHL	62	10	40	50	136
1984-85—Erie Blades		ACHL	19	5	20	25	67
1985-86—Peoria Rivermen		IHL	70	5	15	20	102
1986-87—Adirondack Red Wings (c)		AHL	64	4	24	28	120
1987-88—Adirondack Red Wings		AHL	75	6	24	30	213
1988-89—Adirondack Red Wings (d)		AHL	75	5	35	40	176
1989-90—Baltimore Skipjacks (b)		AHL	74	8	25	33	103
1989-90—Washington Capitals (e)		NHL	4	0	0	0	0
NHL TOTALS			4	0	0	0	0

(c)—September, 1986—Signed by Detroit Red Wings as a free agent.
(d)—June 29, 1989—Signed by Washington Capitals as a free agent.
(e)—July 11, 1990—Signed by Los Angeles Kings as a free agent.

DERRICK SMITH

Left Wing . . . 6'1" . . . 185 lbs. . . . Born, Scarborough, Ont., January 22, 1965 . . . Shoots left . . . (November, 1987)—Bruised back . . . (February, 1989)—Bruised left shoulder . . . (September, 1989)—Fractured left foot during training camp . . . (October 30, 1989)—Sprained right ankle at N.Y. Islanders and developed an infected toe . . . (February 20, 1990)—Injured ribs at Pittsburgh and missed six games.

Year	Team	League	Games	G.	A.	Pts.	Pen.
1981-82—Wexford Midgets		Ont. Midgets	45	35	47	82	40
1982-83—Peterborough Petes (c)		OHL	70	16	19	35	47
1983-84—Peterborough Petes		OHL	70	30	36	66	31
1984-85—Philadelphia Flyers		NHL	77	17	22	39	31
1985-86—Philadelphia Flyers		NHL	69	6	6	12	57
1986-87—Philadelphia Flyers		NHL	71	11	21	32	34
1987-88—Philadelphia Flyers		NHL	76	16	8	24	104
1988-89—Philadelphia Flyers		NHL	74	16	14	30	43
1989-90—Philadelphia Flyers		NHL	55	3	6	9	32
NHL TOTALS			422	69	77	146	301

(c)—June, 1983—Drafted as underage junior by Philadelphia Flyers in 1983 NHL entry draft. Second Flyers pick, 44th overall, third round.

DOUG SMITH

Center . . . 6' . . . 185 lbs. . . . Born, Ottawa, Ont., May 17, 1963 . . . Shoots right . . . (October, 1980)—Knee injury . . . (October 27, 1982)—Broke left wrist and missed 34 games . . . Also plays Right Wing . . . (January 16, 1985)—Partially tore medial collateral ligament in right knee vs. Toronto . . . (September, 1988)—Suspended by Buffalo Sabres after he failed a team physical (he injured his left shoulder and collar-

bone in an off-season automobile accident) . . . (October 31, 1989)—Tore groin muscle vs. New Jersey and missed nine games . . . (February 28, 1990)—Separated left shoulder vs. New Jersey and missed six games.

Year	Team	League	Games	G.	A.	Pts.	Pen.
1979-80—Ottawa 67s	OJHL	64	23	34	57	45
1980-81—Ottawa 67s (c)	OHL	54	45	56	101	61
1981-82—Ottawa 67's	OHL	1	1	2	3	17
1981-82—Los Angeles Kings	NHL	80	16	14	30	64
1982-83—Los Angeles Kings	NHL	42	11	11	22	12
1983-84—Los Angeles Kings	NHL	72	16	20	36	28
1984-85—Los Angeles Kings	NHL	62	21	20	41	58
1985-86—Los Angeles Kings (d)	NHL	48	8	9	17	56
1985-86—Buffalo Sabres	NHL	30	10	11	21	73
1986-87—Buffalo Sabres	NHL	62	16	24	40	106
1986-87—Rochester Americans	AHL	15	5	6	11	35
1987-88—Buffalo Sabres	NHL	70	9	19	28	117
1988-89—Edmonton Oilers (e-f)	NHL	19	1	1	2	9
1988-89—Vancouver Canucks	NHL	10	3	4	7	4
1988-89—Cape Breton Oilers	AHL	24	11	11	22	69
1989-90—Vancouver Canucks (g)	NHL	30	3	4	7	72
1989-90—Pittsburgh Penguins	NHL	10	1	1	2	25
1989-90—Jamestown Chiefs	ECHL	3	0	0	0	29
NHL TOTALS		535	115	138	253	624

(c)—June, 1981—Drafted by Los Angeles Kings in 1981 NHL entry draft. First Kings pick, second overall, first round.

(d)—January, 1986—Traded with Brian Engblom by Los Angeles Kings to Buffalo Sabres for Larry Playfair, Sean McKenna and Ken Baumgartner.

(e)—October 3, 1988—Selected by Edmonton Oilers in 1988 NHL waiver draft for $10,000.

(f)—March 7, 1989—Traded with Greg C. Adams by Edmonton Oilers to Vancouver Canucks for Jean LeBlanc and a fifth-round 1989 draft pick (Peter White).

(g)—February 26, 1990—Sold by Vancouver Canucks to Pittsburgh Penguins.

GEOFF SMITH

Defense . . . 6'1" . . . 180 lbs. . . . Born, Edmonton, Alta., March 7, 1969 . . . Shoots left . . . (October, 1988)—Missed the first 10 games at Univ. of North Dakota due to a fractured ankle . . . (March, 1989)—Broke jaw vs. Victoria.

Year	Team	League	Games	G.	A.	Pts.	Pen.
1985-86—Carnwood Wireline	Cgy. Midget	41	9	21	30	58
1986-87—St. Albert Saints (c)	AJHL	57	7	28	35	101
1987-88—Univ. of North Dakota	WCHA	42	4	12	16	34
1988-89—Kamloops Blazers (a-d)	WHL	32	4	31	35	29
1989-90—Edmonton Oilers	NHL	74	4	11	15	52
NHL TOTALS		74	4	11	15	52

(c)—June, 1987—Drafted by Edmonton Oilers in 1987 NHL entry draft. Third Oilers pick, 63rd overall, third round.

(d)—January, 1989—Left University of North Dakota and signed to play with Kamloops Blazers.

RANDY SMITH

Center . . . 6'4" . . . 200 lbs. . . . Born, Saskatoon, Sask., July 7, 1965 . . . Shoots left.

Year	Team	League	Games	G.	A.	Pts.	Pen.
1982-83—Battleford Barons	SAJHL	64	25	20	45	141
1983-84—Saskatoon Blades	WHL	69	19	21	40	53
1984-85—Saskatoon Blades	WHL	25	6	16	22	9
1984-85—Calgary Wranglers	WHL	46	28	35	63	17
1985-86—Saskatoon Blades (b)	WHL	70	60	86	146	44
1985-86—Minnesota North Stars (c)	NHL	1	0	0	0	0
1986-87—Springfield Indians	AHL	75	20	44	64	24
1986-87—Minnesota North Stars	NHL	2	0	0	0	0
1987-88—Kalamazoo Wings	IHL	77	13	43	56	54
1988-89—Kalamazoo Wings	IHL	23	4	9	13	2
1988-89—Maine Mariners	AHL	33	9	16	25	34
1989-90—Kalamazoo Wings	IHL	9	1	2	3	12
1989-90—Salt Lake Golden Eagles	IHL	30	5	6	11	10
NHL TOTALS		3	0	0	0	0

(c)—March, 1986—Signed by Minnesota North Stars as a free agent.

ROBERT DAVID SMITH

Center . . . 6'4" . . . 210 lbs. . . . Born, N. Sydney, N.S., February 12, 1958 . . . Shoots left . . . Missed part of 1979-80 season with fractured ankle . . . (December, 1984)—Broken jaw . . . (December 1, 1988)—Lost a tooth when caught flush in the face by a Chris Chelios shot at Philadelphia . . . (January 6, 1990)—Separated right shoulder vs. Los Angeles and missed seven games . . . (February 4, 1990)—Struck in cheek by a shot vs. Hartford, broke his jaw and missed 18 games.

Year	Team	League	Games	G.	A.	Pts.	Pen.
1975-76—Ottawa 67's	Jr."A"OHA	62	24	34	58	21
1976-77—Ottawa 67's (b)	Jr."A"OHA	64	*65	70	135	52
1977-78—Ottawa 67's (a-c-d)	Jr."A"OHA	61	69	*123	*192	44
1978-79—Minnesota North Stars (e-f)	NHL	80	30	44	74	39
1979-80—Minnesota North Stars	NHL	61	27	56	83	24
1980-81—Minnesota North Stars	NHL	78	29	64	93	73
1981-82—Minnesota North Stars	NHL	80	43	71	114	82
1982-83—Minnesota North Stars	NHL	77	24	53	77	81
1983-84—Minnesota North Stars (g)	NHL	10	3	6	9	9
1983-84—Montreal Canadiens	NHL	70	26	37	63	62
1984-85—Montreal Canadiens	NHL	65	16	40	56	59
1985-86—Montreal Canadiens	NHL	79	31	55	86	55
1986-87—Montreal Canadiens	NHL	80	28	47	75	72
1987-88—Montreal Canadiens	NHL	78	27	66	93	78
1988-89—Montreal Canadiens	NHL	80	32	51	83	69
1989-90—Montreal Canadiens (h)	NHL	53	12	14	26	35
NHL TOTALS		891	328	604	932	738

(c)—Won Eddie Powers Memorial Trophy (Leading Scorer) and Albert "Red" Tilson Memorial Trophy (MVP).

(d)—Drafted from Ottawa 67's by Minnesota North Stars in first round of 1978 amateur draft.

(e)—Won Calder Memorial Trophy (NHL Rookie of the Year).

(f)—Named THE SPORTING NEWS NHL Rookie of the Year in poll of players.

(g)—October, 1983—Traded by Minnesota North Stars to Montreal Canadiens for Mark Napier, Keith Acton and third-round draft pick (Kenneth Hodge).

(h)—August 7, 1990—Traded by Montreal Canadiens to Minnesota North Stars for 1992 fourth-round draft pick.

SANDY SMITH

Center . . . 5'11" . . . 185 lbs. . . . Born, Brainerd, Minn., October 23, 1967 . . . Shoots right . . . (September, 1985)—Torn knee ligaments.

Year	Team	League	Games	G.	A.	Pts.	Pen.
1984-85—Brainerd H.S.	Minn. H.S.	21	30	20	50	..
1985-86—Brainerd H.S. (c)	Minn. H.S.	17	28	22	50	..
1986-87—Univ. of Minnesota/Duluth	WCHA	35	3	3	6	26
1987-88—Univ. of Minnesota/Duluth	WCHA	41	22	9	31	47
1988-89—Univ. of Minnesota/Duluth	WCHA	40	6	16	22	75
1989-90—Univ. of Minnesota/Duluth	WCHA	39	15	16	31	53
1989-90—Muskegon Lumberjacks	IHL	3	1	0	1	0

(c)—June, 1986—Drafted by Pittsburgh Penguins in 1986 NHL entry draft. Fifth Penguins pick, 88th overall, fifth round.

JAMES STEPHEN (STEVE) SMITH

Defense . . . 6'4" . . . 215 lbs. . . . Born, Glasgow, Scotland, April 30, 1963 . . . Shoots left . . . Also plays Right Wing . . . (November 1, 1985)—Strained right shoulder in fight vs. Buffalo . . . (February, 1986)—Pulled stomach muscle . . . (September 20, 1988)—Separated left shoulder vs. N.Y. Rangers at Denver after stepping on Lucien DeBlois' stick and falling to the ice . . . (October, 1988)—Aggravated shoulder injury . . . (January 2, 1989)—Dislocated left shoulder and tore cartilage when he wound-up for a slap shot at Minnesota . . . (January 23, 1989)—Missed 45 games following surgery to left shoulder.

Year	Team	League	Games	G.	A.	Pts.	Pen.
1980-81—London Knights (c)	OMJHL	62	4	12	16	141
1981-82—London Knights	OHL	58	10	36	46	207
1982-83—London Knights	OHL	50	6	35	41	133
1982-83—Moncton Alpines	AHL	2	0	0	0	0
1983-84—Moncton Alpines	AHL	64	1	8	9	176
1984-85—Nova Scotia Oilers	AHL	68	2	28	30	161
1984-85—Edmonton Oilers	NHL	2	0	0	0	2
1985-86—Nova Scotia Oilers	AHL	4	0	2	2	11
1985-86—Edmonton Oilers	NHL	55	4	20	24	166
1986-87—Edmonton Oilers	NHL	62	7	15	22	165
1987-88—Edmonton Oilers	NHL	79	12	43	55	286
1988-89—Edmonton Oilers	NHL	35	3	19	22	97
1989-90—Edmonton Oilers	NHL	75	7	34	41	171
NHL TOTALS		308	33	131	164	887

(c)—June, 1981—Drafted as underage junior by Edmonton Oilers in 1981 NHL entry draft. Fifth Oilers pick, 111th overall, sixth round.

STEVE SMITH

Defense . . . 5'9" . . . 202 lbs. . . . Born, Trenton, Ont., April 4, 1963 . . . Shoots left . . . (February, 1987)—Hip flexor injury.

Year	Team	League	Games	G.	A.	Pts.	Pen.
1979-80—Belleville Tier 2	OHL	41	8	25	33	105
1980-81—S.S. Marie Greyhounds (b-c-d)	OHL	61	3	37	40	143
1981-82—Sault Ste. Marie Greyhounds (b)	OHL	50	7	20	27	179
1981-82—Philadelphia Flyers	NHL	8	0	1	1	0
1982-83—Sault Ste. Marie Greyhounds (b)	OHL	55	11	33	44	139
1983-84—Springfield Indians	AHL	70	4	25	29	77
1984-85—Philadelphia Flyers	NHL	2	0	0	0	7
1984-85—Hershey Bears	AHL	65	10	20	30	83
1985-86—Hershey Bears	AHL	49	1	11	12	96
1985-86—Philadelphia Flyers	NHL	2	0	0	0	2
1986-87—Hershey Bears	AHL	66	11	26	37	191
1986-87—Philadelphia Flyers	NHL	2	0	0	0	6
1987-88—Hershey Bears	AHL	66	10	19	29	132
1987-88—Philadelphia Flyers (e)	NHL	1	0	0	0	0
1988-89—Buffalo Sabres (f)	NHL	3	0	0	0	0
1988-89—Rochester Americans	AHL	48	2	12	14	79
1989-90—Rochester Americans	AHL	42	3	15	18	107
NHL TOTALS		18	0	1	1	15

(c)—Won Max Kaminsky Award (Outstanding Defenseman).

(d)—June, 1981—Drafted by Philadelphia Flyers in 1981 NHL entry draft. First Flyers pick, 16th overall, first round.

(e)—July, 1988—Signed by Calgary Flames as a free agent.

(f)—October 3, 1988—Selected by Buffalo Sabres in 1988 NHL waiver draft for $10,000.

VERN SMITH

Defense . . . 6'1" . . . 190 lbs. . . . Born, Winnipeg, Man., May 30, 1964 . . . Shoots left . . . (February 10, 1988)—Torn knee ligaments vs. Utica.

Year	Team	League	Games	G.	A.	Pts.	Pen.
1981-82—Lethbridge Broncos (c)	WHL	72	5	38	43	73
1982-83—Lethbridge Broncos	WHL	30	2	10	12	54
1982-83—Nanaimo Islanders	WHL	42	6	21	27	62
1983-84—New Westminster Bruins	WHL	69	13	44	57	94
1984-85—Springfield Indians	AHL	76	6	20	26	115
1984-85—New York Islanders	NHL	1	0	0	0	0
1985-86—Springfield Indians	AHL	55	3	11	14	83
1986-87—Springfield Indians	AHL	41	1	10	11	58

Year	Team	League	Games	G.	A.	Pts.	Pen.
1987-88—Springfield Indians		AHL	64	5	22	27	78
1988-89—Springfield Indians		AHL	80	3	26	29	121
1989-90—Binghamton Whalers (d)		AHL	17	3	2	5	15
1989-90—Phoenix Roadrunners		IHL	48	4	19	23	37
NHL TOTALS			1	0	0	0	0

(c)—June, 1982—Drafted as underage junior by New York Islanders in 1982 NHL entry draft. Second Islanders pick, 42nd overall, second round.

(d)—September, 1989—Signed by Hartford Whalers as a free agent.

BRYAN SMOLINSKI

Center . . . 6' . . . 185 lbs. . . . Born, Toledo, Ohio, December 27, 1971 . . . Shoots right.

Year	Team	League	Games	G.	A.	Pts.	Pen.
1987-88—Detroit Little Caesars		MNHL	80	43	77	120	....
1988-89—Stratford Cullitons		OHA	46	32	62	94	132
1989-90—Michigan State Univ. (c-d)		CCHA	39	10	17	27	45

(c)—Named to CCHA All-Rookie team.

(d)—June 16, 1990—Selected by Boston Bruins in 1990 NHL entry draft. First Bruins pick, 21st overall, first round.

STAN SMYL

Right Wing . . . 5'8" . . . 200 lbs. . . . Born, Glendon, Alta., January 28, 1958 . . . Shoots right . . . Set Vancouver record for points in a season in 1982-83 (Broken by Patrik Sundstrom with 91 in '83-84) . . . Only player to ever play in four Memorial Cup Tournaments . . . (March 26, 1986)—Twisted knee vs. Quebec that required surgery . . . (February 11, 1988)—Pulled groin . . . (November 29, 1989)—Strained knee ligaments vs. Toronto and missed 24 games . . . (March 13, 1990)—Bruised lower back in collision with goalpost vs. Hartford and missed six games with back spasms.

Year	Team	League	Games	G.	A.	Pts.	Pen.
1974-75—Bellingham Blazers	Jr. "A" BCHL	....	...	...	....	....
1974-75—New Westminster Bruins (c)		WCHL	...	...	...	....	....
1975-76—New Westminster Bruins		WCHL	72	32	42	74	169
1976-77—New Westminster Bruins		WCHL	72	35	31	66	200
1977-78—New Westminster Bruins (d)		WCHL	53	29	47	76	211
1978-79—Vancouver Canucks		NHL	62	14	24	38	89
1978-79—Dallas Black Hawks		CHL	3	1	1	2	9
1979-80—Vancouver Canucks		NHL	77	31	47	78	204
1980-81—Vancouver Canucks		NHL	80	25	38	63	171
1981-82—Vancouver Canucks		NHL	80	34	44	78	144
1982-83—Vancouver Canucks		NHL	74	38	50	88	114
1983-84—Vancouver Canucks		NHL	80	24	43	67	136
1984-85—Vancouver Canucks		NHL	80	27	37	64	100
1985-86—Vancouver Canucks		NHL	73	27	35	62	144
1986-87—Vancouver Canucks		NHL	66	20	23	43	84
1987-88—Vancouver Canucks		NHL	57	12	25	37	110
1988-89—Vancouver Canucks		NHL	75	7	18	25	102
1989-90—Vancouver Canucks		NHL	47	1	15	16	71
NHL TOTALS			851	260	399	659	1469

(c)—No regular season record. Played three playoff games.

(d)—Drafted from New Westminster Bruins by Vancouver Canucks in third round of 1978 amateur draft.

GREG SMYTH

Defense . . . 6'3" . . . 195 lbs. . . . Born, Oakville, Ont., April 23, 1966 . . . Shoots right . . . (December, 1984)—Given 10-game OHL suspension for fight with fans in Hamilton . . . (October, 1985)—Suspended by London Knights . . . (November 7, 1985)—Given eight-game suspension by OHL . . . (September, 1988)—Broke two bones in right hand during Quebec Nordiques training camp . . . (December 17, 1988)—Suspended eight AHL games for fighting at Moncton . . . (February 15, 1990)—Injured back at St. Louis.

Year	Team	League	Games	G.	A.	Pts.	Pen.
1983-84—London Knights (c)		OHL	64	4	21	25	*252
1984-85—London Knights		OHL	47	7	16	23	188
1985-86—London Knights (b)		OHL	46	12	42	54	197
1985-86—Hershey Bears		AHL	2	0	1	1	5
1986-87—Hershey Bears		AHL	35	0	2	2	158
1986-87—Philadelphia Flyers		NHL	1	0	0	0	0
1987-88—Hershey Bears		AHL	21	0	10	10	102
1987-88—Philadelphia Flyers (d)		NHL	48	1	6	7	192
1988-89—Halifax Citadels		AHL	43	3	9	12	310
1988-89—Quebec Nordiques		NHL	10	0	1	1	70
1989-90—Quebec Nordiques		NHL	13	0	0	0	57
1989-90—Halifax Citadels		AHL	49	5	14	19	235
NHL TOTALS			72	1	7	8	319

(c)—June, 1984—Drafted as underage junior by Philadelphia Flyers in 1984 NHL entry draft. First Flyers pick, 22nd overall, second round.

(d)—July, 1988—Traded with third-round 1989 draft choice (John Tanner) by Philadelphia Flyers to Quebec Nordiques for Terry Carkner.

HAROLD JOHN SNEPSTS

Defense . . . 6'3" . . . 215 lbs. . . . Born, Edmonton, Alta., October 24, 1954 . . . Shoots left . . . (October, 1981)—Knee injury . . . (November, 1982)—Fractured orbit bone of right eye . . . (January 12, 1983)—Five-game suspension for fight with Doug Risebrough outside Calgary lockerroom . . . Holds Vancouver club record for most career games (683) and penalty minutes (1351) . . . (October 12, 1985)—Strained left knee ligaments in Boston and missed 13 games . . . (November 16, 1985)—Injured knee at Minnesota and missed 19 games . . . (February, 1987)—Separated right shoulder against N.Y. Rangers. Injured same shoulder in playoffs and had arthroscopic surgery in July . . . (October, 1987)—Shoulder surgery . . . Does

not wear a helmet . . . (October, 1988)—Pulled abdominal muscle . . . (February 1, 1989)—Hospitalized with a viral infection in Edmonton . . . (February 26, 1990)—Jammed right wrist vs. Toronto . . . (March 15, 1990)—Concussion when he collided with teammate Mike Lalor.

Year	Team	League	Games	G.	A.	Pts.	Pen.
1972-73—Edmonton Oil Kings		WCHL	68	2	24	26	155
1973-74—Edmonton Oil Kings (c)		WCHL	68	8	41	49	239
1974-75—Seattle Totems		CHL	19	1	6	7	58
1974-75—Vancouver Canucks		NHL	27	1	2	3	30
1975-76—Vancouver Canucks		NHL	78	3	15	18	125
1976-77—Vancouver Canucks		NHL	79	4	18	22	149
1977-78—Vancouver Canucks		NHL	75	4	16	20	118
1978-79—Vancouver Canucks		NHL	76	7	24	31	130
1979-80—Vancouver Canucks		NHL	79	3	20	23	202
1980-81—Vancouver Canucks		NHL	76	3	16	19	212
1981-82—Vancouver Canucks		NHL	68	3	14	17	153
1982-83—Vancouver Canucks		NHL	46	2	8	10	80
1983-84—Vancouver Canucks (d)		NHL	79	4	16	20	152
1984-85—Minnesota North Stars (e)		NHL	71	0	7	7	232
1985-86—Detroit Red Wings		NHL	35	0	6	6	75
1986-87—Detroit Red Wings		NHL	54	1	13	14	129
1987-88—Adirondack Red Wings		AHL	3	0	2	2	14
1987-88—Detroit Red Wings		NHL	31	1	4	5	67
1988-89—Vancouver Canucks (f)		NHL	59	0	8	8	69
1989-90—Vancouver Canucks (g)		NHL	39	1	3	4	26
1989-90—St. Louis Blues		NHL	7	0	1	1	10
NHL TOTALS			979	37	191	228	1959

(c)—Drafted from Edmonton Oil Kings by Vancouver Canucks in fourth round of 1974 amateur draft.

(d)—June, 1984—Traded by Vancouver Canucks to Minnesota North Stars for Al Mac-Adam.

(e)—August, 1985—Signed by Detroit Red Wings as a free agent.

(f)—September 7, 1988—Signed by Vancouver Canucks as a free agent.

(g)—March 6, 1990—Traded with Rich Sutter and a second-round 1990 draft pick by Vancouver Canucks to St. Louis Blues for Adrien Plavsic, a first-round 1990 and a second-round 1991 draft pick. The second-round 1990 pick was the one acquired by the Canucks from the Blues in an earlier deal. The first-round 1990 pick was later traded to Montreal.

DAVE SNUGGERUD

Left Wing . . . 6' . . . 170 lbs. . . . Born, Minnetonka, Minn., June 20, 1966 . . . Shoots left.

Year	Team	League	Games	G.	A.	Pts.	Pen.
1984-85—Minneapolis Junior Stars (b)		USHL	48	38	35	73	26
1985-86—Univ. of Minnesota		WCHA	42	14	18	32	47
1986-87—Univ. of Minnesota (c)		WCHA	39	30	29	59	38
1987-88—U.S. Olympic Team		Int'l	54	16	22	38	....
1988-89—Univ. of Minnesota (b-d)		WCHA	45	29	20	49	39
1989-90—Buffalo Sabres		NHL	80	14	16	30	41
NHL TOTALS			80	14	16	30	41

(c)—June, 1987—Selected by Buffalo Sabres in 1987 NHL supplemental draft.

(d)—Named Second team All-America (West).

PETER SOBERLAK

Left Wing . . . 6'2" . . . 185 lbs. . . . Born, Trail, B.C., May 12, 1969 . . . Shoots left . . . (March 18, 1987)—Fractured right ankle.

Year	Team	League	Games	G.	A.	Pts.	Pen.
1985-86—Kamloops Blazers		WHL	55	10	11	21	46
1986-87—Swift Current Broncos (c)		WHL	68	33	42	75	45
1987-88—Swift Current Broncos		WHL	67	43	56	99	47
1988-89—Swift Current Broncos		WHL	37	25	33	58	21
1989-90—Cape Breton Oilers		AHL	60	15	8	23	22

(c)—June, 1987—Drafted as underage junior by Edmonton Oilers in 1987 NHL entry draft. First Oilers pick, 21st overall, first round.

JIM SOLLY

Center . . . 6' . . . 177 lbs. . . . Born, Hamilton, Ont., March 19, 1970 . . . Shoots left.

Year	Team	League	Games	G.	A.	Pts.	Pen.
1987-88—St. Catharines Jr. B		OHA	41	23	39	62	71
1988-89—Bowling Green Univ. (c)		CCHA	40	4	9	13	14
1989-90—Bowling Green Univ.		CCHA	44	9	11	20	14

(c)—June, 1989—Drafted by Winnipeg Jets in 1989 NHL entry draft. Tenth Jets pick, 151st overall, eighth round.

JASON SOULES

Defense . . . 6'2" . . . 212 lbs. . . . Born, Hamilton, Ont., March 14, 1971 . . . Shoots left . . . (July, 1987)—Broken clavicle.

Year	Team	League	Games	G.	A.	Pts.	Pen.
1987-88—Hamilton Kilty B's		OHA	27	3	10	13	99
1987-88—Hamilton Steelhawks		OHL	19	1	1	2	56
1988-89—Niagara Falls Thunder (c)		OHL	57	3	8	11	187
1989-90—Niagara Falls Thunder		OHL	9	2	8	10	20
1989-90—Dukes of Hamilton		OHL	18	0	2	2	42

(c)—June, 1989—Drafted by Edmonton Oilers in 1989 NHL entry draft. First Oilers pick, 15th overall, first round.

KENNETH W. SPANGLER

Defense . . . 5'11" . . . 190 lbs. . . . Born, Edmonton, Alta., May 2, 1967 . . . Shoots left.

Year	Team	League	Games	G.	A.	Pts.	Pen.
1983-84—Calgary Wranglers		WHL	71	1	12	13	119
1984-85—Calgary Wranglers (c)		WHL	71	5	30	35	251
1985-86—Calgary Wranglers (a)		WHL	66	19	36	55	237

Year	Team	League	Games	G.	A.	Pts.	Pen.
1985-86—St. Catharines Saints		AHL	7	0	0	0	16
1986-87—Calgary Wranglers		WHL	49	12	24	36	185
1987-88—Newmarket Saints		AHL	64	3	6	9	128
1988-89—Flint Spirits		IHL	37	4	15	19	97
1988-89—Baltimore Skipjacks		AHL	12	0	3	3	33
1989-90—Phoenix Roadrunners		IHL	58	3	16	19	156

(c)—June, 1985—Drafted as underage junior by Toronto Maple Leafs in 1985 NHL entry draft. Second Maple Leafs pick, 22nd overall, second round.

MICHAEL SPEER

Defense . . . 6'2" . . . 200 lbs. . . . Born, Toronto, Ont., March 26, 1971 . . . Shoots left.

Year	Team	League	Games	G.	A.	Pts.	Pen.
1986-87—Toronto Marlboro Midget		MTHL	69	16	28	44	71
1987-88—Guelph Platers		OHL	53	4	10	14	60
1988-89—Guelph Platers (c)		OHL	65	9	31	40	185
1989-90—Owen Sound Platers		OHL	61	18	39	57	176

(c)—June, 1989—Drafted by Chicago Black Hawks in 1989 NHL entry draft. Second Black Hawks pick, 27th overall, second round.

GREG SPENRATH

Left Wing . . . 6'1" . . . 212 lbs. . . . Born, Edmonton, Alta., September 27, 1969 . . . Shoots left.

Year	Team	League	Games	G.	A.	Pts.	Pen.
1987-88—New Westminster Bruins		WHL	72	18	24	42	201
1988-89—Tri-City Americans (c)		WHL	64	26	35	61	213
1989-90—Tri-City Americans		WHL	67	36	32	68	256

(c)—June, 1989—Drafted by New York Rangers in 1989 NHL entry draft. Ninth Rangers pick, 160th overall, eighth round.

JIM SPROTT

Defense . . . 6'1" . . . 185 lbs. . . . Born, Hanover, Ont., April 11, 1969 . . . Shoots left.

Year	Team	League	Games	G.	A.	Pts.	Pen.
1985-86—Oakville Blades Jr.B		OHA	26	2	7	9	47
1986-87—London Knights (c)		OHL	66	8	30	38	153
1987-88—London Knights		OHL	65	8	23	31	216
1988-89—London Knights (b)		OHL	64	15	42	57	236
1989-90—Halifax Citadels		AHL	22	2	1	3	103

(c)—June, 1987—Drafted as underage junior by Quebec Nordiques in 1987 NHL entry draft. Third Nordiques pick, 51st overall, third round.

MARTIN ST. AMOUR

Left Wing . . . 6'2" . . . 195 lbs. . . . Born, Montreal, Que., January 30, 1970 . . . Shoots left.

Year	Team	League	Games	G.	A.	Pts.	Pen.
1986-87—Laval Laurentides Midget		Quebec	52	55	95	150	58
1987-88—Verdun Junior Canadiens (c)		QMJHL	61	20	50	70	111
1988-89—Trois-Rivieres Draveurs		QMJHL	54	27	38	65	156
1989-90—Trois-Rivieres Draveurs		QMJHL	60	57	79	136	162

(c)—June, 1988—Drafted by Montreal Canadiens in 1988 NHL entry draft. Second Canadiens pick, 34th overall, second round.

DARYL STANLEY

Defense . . . 6'2" . . . 200 lbs. . . . Born, Winnipeg, Man., December 2, 1962 . . . Shoots left . . . (January 21, 1985)—Dislocated neck vertebrae and bruised kidney in automobile accident and missed several games at start of 1985-86 season . . . (February, 1987)—Missed six games with injured left ankle . . . (March, 1987)—Reinjured left ankle ligaments . . . (October, 1987)—Sprained left ankle . . . (December, 1987)—Bruised shoulder . . . (January, 1988)—Back spasms . . . (March 6, 1988)—Separated shoulder vs. Washington . . . (September, 1988)—Sprained ankle during Vancouver Canucks training camp . . . (October 6, 1988)—Canucks suspended him for three games . . . (October 18, 1988)—Announced his retirement . . . (January 24, 1989)—Returned to Canucks . . . (March, 1989)—Twisted knee . . . (January 13, 1990)—Surgery to repair tendon damage in finger.

Year	Team	League	Games	G.	A.	Pts.	Pen.
1979-80—New Westminster Bruins		WHL	64	2	12	14	110
1980-81—New Westminster Bruins		WHL	66	7	27	34	127
1981-82—Saskatoon Blades (c-d)		WHL	65	7	25	32	175
1981-82—Maine Mariners (e)		AHL	....	....	....	....	....
1982-83—Toledo Goaldiggers		IHL	5	0	2	2	2
1982-83—Maine Mariners		AHL	44	2	5	7	95
1983-84—Springfield Indians		AHL	52	4	10	14	122
1983-84—Philadelphia Flyers		NHL	23	1	4	5	71
1984-85—Hershey Bears		AHL	24	0	7	7	13
1985-86—Philadelphia Flyers		NHL	33	0	2	2	69
1985-86—Hershey Flyers		AHL	27	0	4	4	88
1986-87—Philadelphia Flyers (f)		NHL	33	1	2	3	76
1987-88—Vancouver Canucks		NHL	57	2	7	9	151
1988-89—Vancouver Canucks		NHL	20	3	1	4	14
1989-90—Vancouver Canucks (g)		NHL	23	1	1	2	27
NHL TOTALS			189	8	17	25	408

(c)—October, 1981—Signed by Philadelphia Flyers as a free agent.
(d)—September, 1981—Traded by Kamloops Junior Oilers to Saskatoon Blades for Brian Propp and Mike Spencer.
(e)—No regular season record. Played two playoff games.
(f)—August, 1987—Traded by Philadelphia Flyers with Darren Jensen to Vancouver Canucks for Wendell Young and a 1991 third-round draft choice.
(g)—August, 1990—Signed by Winnipeg Jets as a free agent.

PAUL STANTON

Defense . . . 6' . . . 175 lbs. . . . Born, Boston, Mass., June 22, 1967 . . . Shoots right.

Year	Team	League	Games	G.	A.	Pts.	Pen.
1983-84—Catholic Memorial H.S.		Mass.H.S.	....	15	20	35	....
1984-85—Catholic Memorial H.S. (c)		Mass.H.S.	20	16	21	37	17
1985-86—Univ. of Wisconsin		WCHA	36	4	6	10	16
1986-87—Univ. of Wisconsin		WCHA	41	5	17	22	70
1987-88—Univ. of Wisconsin (d)		WCHA	45	9	38	47	98
1988-89—Univ. of Wisconsin (a)		WCHA	45	7	29	36	126
1989-90—Muskegon Lumberjacks		IHL	77	5	27	32	61

(c)—June, 1985—Drafted by Pittsburgh Penguins in 1985 NHL entry draft. Eighth Penguins pick, 149th overall, eighth round.
(d)—Named First team All-America (West).

SERGEI STARIKOV

Defense . . . 5'10" . . . 215 lbs. . . . Born, Chelyabinsk, U.S.S.R., December 4, 1958 . . . Shoots left.

Year	Team	League	Games	G.	A.	Pts.	Pen.
1976-77—Traktor Chelyabinsk		USSR	35	2	4	6	28
1977-78—Traktor Chelyabinsk		USSR	36	3	5	8	26
1978-79—Traktor Chelyabinsk		USSR	44	6	8	14	34
1979-80—Central Red Army		USSR	39	10	8	18	14
1980-81—Central Red Army		USSR	49	4	8	12	26
1981-82—Central Red Army		USSR	40	1	4	5	14
1982-83—Central Red Army		USSR	44	6	14	20	14
1983-84—Central Red Army		USSR	44	11	7	18	20
1984-85—Central Red Army		USSR	40	3	10	13	12
1985-86—Central Red Army		USSR	37	3	2	5	6
1986-87—Central Red Army		USSR	34	4	2	6	8
1987-88—Central Red Army		USSR	38	2	11	13	12
1988-89—Central Red Army (c)		USSR	30	3	3	6	4
1989-90—Utica Devils		AHL	43	8	11	19	14
1989-90—New Jersey Devils		NHL	16	0	1	1	8
NHL TOTALS			16	0	1	1	8

(c)—June, 1989—Drafted by New Jersey Devils in 1989 NHL entry draft. Seventh Devils pick, 152nd overall, eighth round.

PETER STASTNY

Center . . . 6'1" . . . 200 lbs. . . . Born, Bratislava, Czechoslovakia, September 18, 1956 . . . Shoots left . . . Brother of Anton, Marion and Bohuslav Stastny . . . (December 18, 1982)—Knee injury at Buffalo . . . One of only four players to break in NHL with three straight 100-point seasons (Wayne Gretzky, Mario Lemieux and Mike Rogers being the others) . . . (1980-81)—Set NHL records for most assists and points by a rookie . . . One of only three players (Wayne Gretzky and Mario Lemieux) to have 100-point seasons in their first six NHL seasons . . . (October, 1984)—Served five-game suspension . . . (May 2 and 5, 1985)—Scored overtime goals in consecutive playoff games to tie record by Mel Hill and Maurice Richard . . . (November, 1987)—Injured lower back . . . (December, 1988)—Sprained left shoulder . . . (December, 1989)—Sore left knee.

Year	Team	League	Games	G.	A.	Pts.	Pen.
1977-78—Slovan Bratislava (b)		Czech.	44	29	24	53	....
1977-78—Czechoslovakia Nat's.		Int'l.	16	5	2	7	....
1978-79—Slovan Bratislava (a)		Czech.	44	32	23	55	....
1978-79—Czechoslovakia Nat's.		Int'l.	18	12	9	21	....
1979-80—Slovan Bratislava		Czech.	40	28	30	58	....
1979-80—Czech. Olympic Team (c)		Oly.	6	7	7	14	6
1980-81—Quebec Nordiques (d-e)		NHL	77	39	70	109	37
1981-82—Quebec Nordiques		NHL	80	46	93	139	91
1982-83—Quebec Nordiques		NHL	75	47	77	124	78
1983-84—Quebec Nordiques		NHL	80	46	73	119	73
1984-85—Quebec Nordiques		NHL	75	32	68	100	95
1985-86—Quebec Nordiques		NHL	76	41	81	122	60
1986-87—Quebec Nordiques		NHL	64	24	53	77	43
1987-88—Quebec Nordiques		NHL	76	46	65	111	69
1988-89—Quebec Nordiques		NHL	72	35	50	85	117
1989-90—Quebec Nordiques (f)		NHL	62	24	38	62	24
1989-90—New Jersey Devils		NHL	12	5	6	11	16
NHL TOTALS			749	385	674	1059	703

(c)—August, 1980—Signed by Quebec Nordiques as a free agent.
(d)—Winner of Calder Trophy (NHL Rookie of the Year).
(e)—Selected THE SPORTING NEWS NHL Rookie of the Year in a vote of the players.
(f)—March 6, 1990—Traded by Quebec Nordiques to New Jersey Devils for Craig Wolanin and future considerations (Randy Velischek was sent to Quebec in August, 1990).

PETER STAUBER

Left Wing . . . 5'11" . . . 185 lbs. . . . Born, Duluth, Minn., May 10, 1966 . . . Shoots left . . . Brother of Robb Stauber.

Year	Team	League	Games	G.	A.	Pts.	Pen.
1986-87—Lake Superior State Univ.		CCHA	40	22	13	35	80
1987-88—Lake Superior State Univ.		CCHA	45	25	33	58	103
1988-89—Lake Superior State Univ.		CCHA	46	25	13	38	115
1989-90—Lake Superior State Univ. (c)		CCHA	46	25	31	56	90

(c)—June 21, 1990—Signed by Detroit Red Wings as a free agent.

THOMAS STEEN

Center . . . 5'10" . . . 195 lbs. . . . Born, Tocksmark, Sweden, June 8, 1960 . . . Shoots left . . . (September, 1981)—Lacerated elbow during Canada Cup as a member of Team Sweden . . . (October, 1981)—Injured knee in training camp . . . (December, 1989)—Protruding disk and missed 22 games.

Year	Team	League	Games	G.	A.	Pts.	Pen.
1978-79—Leksands IF		Sweden	25	13	4	17	35
1979-80—Leksands IF (c)		Sweden	18	7	7	14	14
1980-81—Farjestads BK (d)		Sweden	32	16	23	39	30
1981-82—Winnipeg Jets		NHL	73	15	29	44	42
1982-83—Winnipeg Jets		NHL	75	26	33	59	60
1983-84—Winnipeg Jets		NHL	78	20	45	65	69
1984-85—Winnipeg Jets		NHL	79	30	54	84	80
1985-86—Winnipeg Jets		NHL	78	17	47	64	76
1986-87—Winnipeg Jets		NHL	75	17	33	50	59
1987-88—Winnipeg Jets		NHL	76	16	38	54	53
1988-89—Winnipeg Jets		NHL	80	27	61	88	80
1989-90—Winnipeg Jets		NHL	53	18	48	66	35
NHL TOTALS			667	186	388	574	554

(c)—June, 1980—Drafted by Winnipeg Jets in 1980 NHL entry draft. Fifth Jets pick, 103rd overall, fifth round.

(d)—Named Player of the Year in Swedish National League.

RONALD STERN

Right Wing . . . 6'1" . . . 195 lbs. . . . Born, Ste. Agatha Des Mont, Que., January 11, 1967 . . . Shoots right . . . (April, 1989)—Bruised shoulder vs. Calgary . . . (March 19, 1990)—Cut near eye when head-butted by Troy Mallette at Rangers and dislocated his shoulder.

Year	Team	League	Games	G.	A.	Pts.	Pen.
1984-85—Longueuil Chevaliers		QMJHL	67	6	14	20	176
1985-86—Longueuil Chevaliers (c)		QMJHL	70	39	33	72	317
1986-87—Longueuil Chevaliers		QMJHL	56	32	39	71	266
1987-88—Fredericton Express		AHL	2	1	0	1	4
1987-88—Flint Spirits		IHL	55	14	19	33	294
1987-88—Vancouver Canucks		NHL	15	0	0	0	52
1988-89—Milwaukee Admirals		IHL	45	19	23	42	280
1988-89—Vancouver Canucks		NHL	17	1	0	1	49
1989-90—Milwaukee Admirals		IHL	26	8	9	17	165
1989-90—Vancouver Canucks		NHL	34	2	3	5	208
NHL TOTALS			66	3	3	6	309

(c)—June, 1986—Drafted as underage junior by Vancouver Canucks in 1986 NHL entry draft. Third Canucks pick, 70th overall, fourth round.

JOHN STEVENS

Defense . . . 6'1" . . . 180 lbs. . . . Born, Completon, N.B., May 4, 1966 . . . Shoots left . . . (September, 1984)—Knee surgery.

Year	Team	League	Games	G.	A.	Pts.	Pen.
1982-83—Newmarket Flyers		OJHL	48	2	9	11	111
1983-84—Oshawa Generals (c)		OHL	70	1	10	11	71
1984-85—Oshawa Generals		OHL	45	2	10	12	61
1984-85—Hershey Bears		AHL	3	0	0	0	2
1985-86—Oshawa Generals		OHL	65	1	7	8	146
1985-86—Kalamazoo Wings		IHL	6	0	1	1	8
1986-87—Hershey Bears (d)		AHL	63	1	15	16	131
1986-87—Philadelphia Flyers		NHL	6	0	2	2	14
1987-88—Philadelphia Flyers		NHL	3	0	0	0	0
1987-88—Hershey Bears		AHL	59	1	15	16	108
1988-89—Hershey Bears		AHL	78	3	13	16	129
1989-90—Hershey Bears (e)		AHL	79	3	10	13	193
NHL TOTALS			9	0	2	2	14

(c)—June, 1984—Drafted as underage junior by Chicago Black Hawks in NHL entry draft. Second Black Hawks pick, 45th overall, third round.

(d)—September, 1987—Signed by Philadelphia Flyers as a free agent.

(e)—July 16, 1990—Signed by Hartford Whalers as a free agent.

KEVIN STEVENS

Center . . . 6'3" . . . 207 lbs. . . . Born, Brockton, Mass., April 15, 1965 . . . Shoots left . . . Also plays Left Wing . . . Son of Arthur Stevens who played baseball in the Cincinnati Reds minor league system.

Year	Team	League	Games	G.	A.	Pts.	Pen.
1982-83—Silver Lake H.S. (c)		Minn. H.S.	18	24	27	51	..
1983-84—Boston College (d)		ECAC	37	6	14	20	36
1984-85—Boston College		H. East	40	13	23	36	36
1985-86—Boston College		H. East	42	17	27	44	56
1986-87—Boston College (a-e)		H. East	39	*35	35	70	54
1987-88—U.S. Olympic Team		Int'l	....	....	....	....	....
1987-88—Pittsburgh Penguins		NHL	16	5	2	7	8
1988-89—Pittsburgh Penguins		NHL	24	12	3	15	19
1988-89—Muskegon Lumberjacks		IHL	45	24	41	65	113
1989-90—Pittsburgh Penguins		NHL	76	29	41	70	171
NHL TOTALS			116	46	46	92	198

(c)—June, 1983—Drafted by Los Angeles Kings in 1983 NHL entry draft. Sixth Kings pick, 108th overall, sixth round.

(d)—September, 1983—Traded by Los Angeles Kings to Pittsburgh Penguins for Anders Hakansson.

(e)—Named Second team All-America (East).

MIKE STEVENS

Center . . . 5'11" . . . 195 lbs. . . . Born, Kitchener, Ont., December 30, 1965 . . . Shoots left . . . (October, 1984)—Arthroscopic knee surgery . . . Brother of Scott Stevens . . . Also plays Left Wing.

Year	Team	League	Games	G.	A.	Pts.	Pen.
1982-83—Kitchener Ranger B's		MWOJBHL	29	5	18	23	86
1983-84—Kitchener Rangers (c)		OHL	66	19	21	40	109
1984-85—Kitchener Rangers		OHL	37	17	18	35	121
1984-85—Vancouver Canucks		NHL	6	0	3	3	6
1985-86—Fredericton Express		AHL	79	12	19	31	208

Year	Team	League	Games	G.	A.	Pts.	Pen.
1986-87—Fredericton Express		AHL	71	7	18	25	258
1987-88—Maine Mariners (d)		AHL	63	30	25	55	265
1987-88—Boston Bruins (e)		NHL	7	0	1	1	9
1988-89—Springfield Indians		AHL	42	17	13	30	120
1988-89—New York Islanders		NHL	9	1	0	1	14
1989-90—Springfield Indians (f)		AHL	28	12	10	22	75
1989-90—Toronto Maple Leafs		NHL	1	0	0	0	0
1989-90—Newmarket Saints		AHL	46	16	28	44	86
NHL TOTALS			23	1	4	5	29

(c)—June, 1984—Drafted as underage junior by Vancouver Canucks in 1984 NHL entry draft. Fourth Canucks pick, 58th overall, third round.

(d)—October, 1987—Traded by Vancouver Canucks to Boston Bruins for future considerations.

(e)—August, 1988—Signed by New York Islanders as a free agent.

(f)—December 20, 1989—Traded with Gilles Thibaudeau by New York Islanders to Toronto Maple Leafs for Paul Gagne, Derek Laxdal and Jack Capuano.

SCOTT STEVENS

Defense . . . 6'1" . . . 215 lbs. . . . Born, Kitchener, Ont., April 1, 1964 . . . Shoots left . . . Brother of Mike Stevens . . . (November 6, 1985)—Bruised right knee at Pittsburgh and missed seven games . . . (December 14, 1986)—Broke right index finger vs. N.Y. Islanders . . . (April, 1988)—Bruised shoulder vs. Philadelphia in playoffs . . . (November, 1988)—Picked up poison oak . . . (April 21, 1989)—Needed 88 stitches to close a facial cut caused by Borje Salming who was playing for Team Sweden at the World Cup . . . (December 29, 1989)—Broken left foot at Detroit and missed 17 games . . . (February 27, 1990)—Suspended three games for scratching David Manson at Chicago . . . (March 27, 1990)—Bruised left shoulder vs. New Jersey . . . (May 3, 1990)—Dislocated left shoulder at Boston.

Year	Team	League	Games	G.	A.	Pts.	Pen.
1980-81—Kitchener Jr. B.		OPJHL	39	7	33	40	82
1981-82—Kitchener Rangers (c)		OHL	68	6	36	42	158
1982-83—Washington Capitals		NHL	77	9	16	25	195
1983-84—Washington Capitals		NHL	78	13	32	45	201
1984-85—Washington Capitals		NHL	80	21	44	65	221
1985-86—Washington Capitals		NHL	73	15	38	53	165
1986-87—Washington Capitals		NHL	77	10	51	61	283
1987-88—Washington Capitals (a)		NHL	80	12	60	72	184
1988-89—Washington Capitals		NHL	80	7	61	68	225
1989-90—Washington Capitals (d)		NHL	56	11	29	40	154
NHL TOTALS			601	98	331	429	1628

(c)—June, 1982—Drafted as underage junior by Washington Capitals in 1982 NHL entry draft. First Capitals pick, fifth overall, first round.

(d)—July 9, 1990—Signed by St. Louis Blues as a free agent with compensation. The Blues will owe Washington two first round draft picks among the top seven over the next two years, as well as $100,000 cash. If the Blues fail to obtain the two picks in the top seven, they will owe Washington a total of five first-round picks over the next five seasons.

SHAYNE STEVENSON

Right Wing . . . 6'1" . . . 190 lbs. . . . Born, London, Ont., October 26, 1970 . . . Shoots right.

Year	Team	League	Games	G.	A.	Pts.	Pen.
1985-86—Barrie Jr. B		OHA	38	14	23	37	75
1986-87—London Knights		OHL	61	7	15	22	56
1987-88—London Knights		OHL	36	14	25	39	56
1987-88—Kitchener Rangers		OHL	30	10	25	35	48
1988-89—Kitchener Rangers (c)		OHL	56	25	51	76	86
1989-90—Kitchener Rangers (d)		OHL	56	28	62	90	115

(c)—June, 1989—Drafted by Boston Bruins in 1989 NHL entry draft. First Bruins pick, 17th overall, first round.

(d)—Led Memorial Cup tournament with 11 points.

TURNER STEVENSON

Right Wing . . . 6'3" . . . 200 lbs. . . . Born, Port Alberni, B.C., May 18, 1972 . . . Shoots right . . . (August, 1987)—Surgery to remove a growth in his chest . . . (December, 1987)—Injured shoulder.

Year	Team	League	Games	G.	A.	Pts.	Pen.
1987-88—Prince George Bantam		B.C.	53	45	46	91	127
1988-89—Seattle Thunderbirds		WHL	69	15	12	27	84
1989-90—Seattle Thunderbirds (c)		WHL	62	29	32	61	276

(c)—June 16, 1990—Selected by Montreal Canadiens in 1990 NHL entry draft. First Canadiens pick, 12th overall, first round.

ALLAN STEWART

Left Wing . . . 5'11" . . . 173 lbs. . . . Born, Fort St. John, B.C., January 31, 1964 . . . Shoots left . . . (1983-84)—Set WHL record with 14 shorthanded goals . . . (October, 1987)—Missed two months following hernia surgery . . . (September 21, 1989)—Broke left leg in four places trying to avoid a collision with teammate Kirk Muller during a team practice and out until the last game of season.

Year	Team	League	Games	G.	A.	Pts.	Pen.
1981-82—Prince Albert Raiders		SJHL	46	9	25	34	53
1982-83—Prince Albert Raiders (c)		WHL	70	25	34	59	272
1983-84—Prince Albert Raiders		WHL	67	44	39	83	216
1984-85—Maine Mariners		AHL	75	8	11	19	241
1985-86—Maine Mariners		AHL	58	7	12	19	181
1985-86—New Jersey Devils		NHL	4	0	0	0	21
1986-87—Maine Mariners		AHL	74	14	24	38	143
1986-87—New Jersey Devils		NHL	7	1	0	1	26
1987-88—New Jersey Devils		NHL	1	0	0	0	0
1987-88—Utica Devils		AHL	49	8	17	25	129

Year	Team	League	Games	G.	A.	Pts.	Pen.
1988-89—New Jersey Devils	NHL	6	0	2	2	15
1988-89—Utica Devils	AHL	72	9	23	32	110
1989-90—Utica Devils	AHL	1	0	0	0	0
NHL TOTALS			18	1	2	3	62

(c)—June, 1983—Drafted as underage junior by New Jersey Devils in 1983 NHL entry draft. Ninth Devils pick, 205th overall, 11th round.

CAMERON STEWART

Center . . . 5'10'' . . . 188 lbs. . . . Born, Kitchener, Ont., September 18, 1971 . . . Shoots left . . . (June, 1989)—Strained knee ligaments.

Year	Team	League	Games	G.	A.	Pts.	Pen.
1987-88—Woolrich Midget	OHA	21	25	32	57	65
1988-89—Elmira Sugar Kings Jr. B	OHA	43	38	50	88	138
1989-90—Elmira Sugar Kings Jr. B (c)	OHA	46	44	95	139	172

(c)—June 16, 1990—Selected by Boston Bruins in 1990 NHL entry draft. Second Bruins pick, 63rd overall, third round.

MICHAEL STEWART

Defense . . . 6'2'' . . . 197 lbs. . . . Born, Calgary, Alta., March 30, 1972 . . . Shoots left.

Year	Team	League	Games	G.	A.	Pts.	Pen.
1988-89—Calgary Buffalos Midget	Alta.	77	16	88	104	163
1989-90—Michigan State Univ. (c-d)	CCHA	45	2	6	8	45

(c)—Named to CCHA All-Rookie team.
(d)—June 16, 1990—Selected by New York Rangers in 1990 NHL entry draft. First Rangers pick, 13th overall, first round.

BRETT STICKNEY

Left Wing . . . 6'5'' . . . 220 lbs. . . . Born, Hanover, N.H., May 26, 1972 . . . Shoots left.

Year	Team	League	Games	G.	A.	Pts.	Pen.
1988-89—St. Paul's H.S.	N.H. H.S.	20	11	20	31	....
1989-90—St. Paul's H.S. (c)	N.H. H.S.	19	12	16	28	....

(c)—June 16, 1990—Selected by Chicago Black Hawks in 1990 NHL entry draft. Fourth Black Hawks pick, 121st overall, sixth round.

TREVOR STIENBURG

Right Wing . . . 6'1'' . . . 180 lbs. . . . Born, Kingston, Ont., May 13, 1966 . . . Shoots right . . . (September, 1985)—Torn knee ligaments in Quebec training camp . . . (October, 1988)—Sprained left ankle . . . (November, 1988)—Sprained right shoulder.

Year	Team	League	Games	G.	A.	Pts.	Pen.
1982-83—Brockville Braves	COJHL	47	39	30	69	182
1983-84—Guelph Platers (c)	OHL	65	33	18	51	104
1984-85—Guelph Platers (d)	OHL	18	7	12	19	38
1984-85—London Knights	OHL	22	9	11	20	45
1984-85—Fredericton Express (e)	AHL	....	....	....	....	....
1985-86—Quebec Nordiques	NHL	2	1	0	1	0
1985-86—London Knights	OHL	31	12	18	30	88
1986-87—Fredericton Express	AHL	48	14	12	26	123
1986-87—Quebec Nordiques	NHL	6	1	0	1	12
1987-88—Quebec Nordiques	NHL	8	0	1	1	24
1987-88—Fredericton Express	AHL	55	12	24	36	279
1988-89—Quebec Nordiques	NHL	55	6	3	9	125
1989-90—Halifax Citadels	AHL	11	3	3	6	36
NHL TOTALS			71	8	4	12	161

(c)—June, 1984—Drafted as underage junior by Quebec Nordiques in 1984 NHL entry draft. First Nordiques pick, 15th overall, first round.
(d)—January, 1985—Traded by Guelph Platers to London Knights for Mike Murray and Ron Coutts.
(e)—No regular season record. Played two playoff games.

MICHAEL PATRICK STOTHERS

Defense . . . 6'4'' . . . 210 lbs. . . . Born, Toronto, Ont., February 22, 1962 . . . Shoots left . . . (December, 1984)—Ankle injury . . . (October, 1989)—Injured hand.

Year	Team	League	Games	G.	A.	Pts.	Pen.
1979-80—Kingston Canadians (c)	OMJHL	66	4	23	27	137
1980-81—Kingston Canadians	OHL	65	4	22	26	237
1981-82—Kingston Canadians	OHL	61	1	20	21	203
1981-82—Maine Mariners	AHL	5	0	0	0	4
1982-83—Maine Mariners	AHL	80	2	16	18	139
1983-84—Maine Mariners	AHL	61	2	10	12	109
1984-85—Philadelphia Flyers	NHL	1	0	0	0	0
1984-85—Hershey Bears	AHL	59	8	18	26	142
1985-86—Hershey Bears	AHL	66	4	9	13	221
1985-86—Philadelphia Flyers	NHL	6	0	1	1	6
1986-87—Philadelphia Flyers	NHL	2	0	0	0	4
1986-87—Hershey Bears	AHL	75	5	11	16	283
1987-88—Philadelphia Flyers (d)	NHL	3	0	0	0	13
1987-88—Toronto Maple Leafs	NHL	18	0	1	1	42
1987-88—Hershey Bears	AHL	13	3	2	5	55
1987-88—Newmarket Saints	AHL	38	1	9	10	69
1988-89—Hershey Bears (e)	AHL	76	4	11	15	262
1989-90—Hershey Bears	AHL	56	1	6	7	170
NHL TOTALS			30	0	2	2	65

(c)—June, 1980—Drafted as underage junior by Philadelphia Flyers in 1980 NHL entry draft. First Flyers pick, 21st overall, first round.
(d)—November, 1987—Traded by Philadelphia Flyers to Toronto Maple Leafs for future considerations. Returned to Flyers in June of 1988.
(e)—June 21, 1988—Traded by Philadelphia Flyers to Toronto Maple Leafs for a fifth-round 1989 draft pick. The Flyers traded the pick to Minnesota in December, 1988 for Moe Mantha and the North Stars used the pick to choose Pat MacLeod.

ANDY SUHY

Defense . . . 6'1'' . . . 195 lbs. . . . Born, Detroit, Mich., March 9, 1970 . . . Shoots left . . . (October, 1986)—Separated left shoulder . . . (January, 1987)—Dislocated right shoulder . . . Has broken his thumbs five times.

Year	Team	League	Games	G.	A.	Pts.	Pen.
1987-88—Little Caesar Midget	Mich.	24	4	9	13	52
1988-89—Western Mich. Univ. (c)	CCHA	42	0	4	4	74
1989-90—Western Mich. Univ.	CCHA	34	3	5	8	52

(c)—June, 1989—Drafted by Detroit Red Wings in 1989 NHL entry draft. Eighth Red Wings pick, 158th overall, eighth round.

SIMON DOUGLAS SULLIMAN
(Known by middle name.)

Left Wing . . . 5'9'' . . . 195 lbs. . . . Born, Glace Bay, Nova Scotia, August 29, 1959 . . . Shoots left . . . Missed part of 1979-80 season with injury to right knee . . . Also plays Right Wing . . . (November, 1983)—Groin pull . . . (December 14, 1985)—Bruised tailbone at Quebec . . . (December, 1987)—Bruised left shoulder . . . (March, 1988)—Strained left knee.

Year	Team	League	Games	G.	A.	Pts.	Pen.
1976-77—Kitchener Rangers	OMJHL	65	30	41	71	123
1977-78—Kitchener Rangers	OMJHL	68	50	39	89	87
1978-79—Kitchener Rangers (c)	OMJHL	68	38	77	115	88
1979-80—New York Rangers	NHL	31	4	7	11	2
1979-80—New Haven Nighthawks	AHL	31	9	7	16	9
1980-81—New Haven Nighthawks	AHL	45	10	16	26	18
1980-81—New York Rangers	NHL	32	4	1	5	32
1981-82—Hartford Whalers (d)	NHL	77	29	40	69	39
1982-83—Hartford Whalers	NHL	77	22	19	41	14
1983-84—Hartford Whalers (e)	NHL	67	6	13	19	20
1984-85—New Jersey Devils	NHL	57	22	16	38	4
1985-86—New Jersey Devils	NHL	73	21	22	43	20
1986-87—New Jersey Devils	NHL	78	27	26	53	14
1987-88—New Jersey Devils	NHL	59	16	14	30	22
1988-89—Philadelphia Flyers (f)	NHL	52	6	6	12	8
1989-90—Philadelphia Flyers (g)	NHL	28	3	4	7	0
NHL TOTALS			631	160	168	328	175

(c)—August, 1979—Drafted by New York Rangers in 1979 NHL entry draft. First Rangers pick, 13th overall, first round.
(d)—October, 1981—Traded with Chris Kotsopoulos and Gerry McDonald by New York Rangers to Hartford Whalers for Mike Rogers and a 10th-round 1982 entry draft pick (Simo Saarinen).
(e)—July, 1984—Released by Hartford Whalers and signed by New Jersey Devils as a free agent.
(f)—October 3, 1988—Selected by Philadelphia Flyers in 1988 NHL waiver draft for $5,000.
(g)—August, 1990—Named by New Jersey Devils as an assistant coach.

BRIAN SULLIVAN

Right Wing . . . 6'4'' . . . 195 lbs. . . . Born, South Windsor, Conn., April 23, 1969 . . . Shoots right . . . Brother of Kevin Sullivan . . . (February, 1988)—Set Northeastern Univ. record for goals by a freshman . . . (November, 1989)—Bruised shoulder vs. St. Lawrence Univ.

Year	Team	League	Games	G.	A.	Pts.	Pen.
1985-86—South Windsor H.S.	Conn. H.S.	....	39	50	89	....
1986-87—Springfield Olympics (c)	NEJHL		30	35	65	....
1987-88—Northeastern Univ.	H. East	37	20	12	32	18
1988-89—Northeastern Univ.	H. East	34	13	14	27	65
1989-90—Northeastern Univ.	H. East	34	24	21	45	72

(c)—June, 1987—Drafted by New Jersey Devils in 1987 NHL entry draft. Third Devils pick, 65th overall, fourth round.

KEVIN SULLIVAN

Center . . . 6'2'' . . . 180 lbs. . . . Born, South Windsor, Conn., May 16, 1968 . . . Shoots right . . . Brother of Brian Sullivan.

Year	Team	League	Games	G.	A.	Pts.	Pen.
1986-87—Princeton Univ. (c)	ECAC	25	1	0	1	10
1987-88—Princeton Univ.	ECAC	22	0	3	3	8
1988-89—Princeton Univ.	ECAC	26	7	7	14	58
1989-90—Princeton Univ. (d)	ECAC	27	12	13	25	28

(c)—June, 1987—Selected by Hartford Whalers in 1987 NHL entry draft. Ninth Whalers pick, 228th overall, 11th round.
(d)—October 7, 1989—Traded by Hartford Whalers to Minnesota North Stars for Mike Berger.

MICHAEL SULLIVAN

Center . . . 6'2'' . . . 185 lbs. . . . Born, Marshfield, Mass., February 28, 1968 . . . Shoots left.

Year	Team	League	Games	G.	A.	Pts.	Pen.
1985-86—Boston College H.S.	Mass. H.S.	22	26	33	59	....
1986-87—Boston University (c)	H. East	37	13	18	31	18
1987-88—Boston University	H. East	30	18	22	40	30
1988-89—Boston University (d)	H. East	36	19	17	36	30
1988-89—Virginia Lancers	ECHL	2	0	0	0	0
1989-90—Boston University	H. East	38	11	20	31	26

(c)—June, 1987—Drafted by New York Rangers in 1987 NHL entry draft. Fourth Rangers pick, 69th overall, fourth round.
(d)—October 11, 1988—Traded with Mark Tinordi, Paul Jerrard, Bret Barnett and Los Angeles Kings third-round 1989 draft pick (Murray Garbutt) by New York Rangers to Minnesota North Stars for Igor Liba, Brian Lawton and NHL rights to Eric Bennett.

PATRIK SUNDSTROM

Center . . . 6' . . . 195 lbs. . . . Born Skellefteaa, Sweden, December 14, 1961 . . . Shoots left . . . (November, 1982)—Shoulder separation . . . (1983-84)—Set Vancouver club records for most points in a season and most goals by a center . . . Twin brother of Peter Sundstrom . . . (September, 1985)—Broke left wrist in final game of Canada Cup Tournament . . . (January, 1987)—Missed six games with torn rotator cuff . . . (April 22, 1988)—Set NHL record for most points in playoff game (8—Later tied by Mario Lemieux) . . . (March, 1988)—Abdominal strain . . . (October, 1988)—Strained lower back . . . (December, 1988)—Bruised right thigh . . . (March, 1989)—Bruised left knee.

Year	Team	League	Games	G.	A.	Pts.	Pen.
1979-80—Umea Bjorkloven IF (c)	Sweden	26	5	7	12	20
1980-81—Umea Bjorkloven IF	Sweden	36	10	18	28	30
1981-82—Umea Bjorkloven IF	Sweden	36	22	13	35	38
1982-83—Vancouver Canucks	NHL	74	23	23	46	30
1983-84—Vancouver Canucks (d)	NHL	78	38	53	91	37
1984-85—Vancouver Canucks	NHL	71	25	43	68	46
1985-86—Vancouver Canucks	NHL	79	18	48	66	28
1986-87—Vancouver Canucks	NHL	72	29	42	71	40
1987-88—New Jersey Devils (e)	NHL	78	15	36	51	42
1988-89—New Jersey Devils	NHL	65	28	41	69	36
1989-90—New Jersey Devils	NHL	74	27	49	76	34
NHL TOTALS			591	203	335	538	293

(c)—June, 1980—Drafted by Vancouver Canucks in 1980 NHL entry draft. Eighth Canucks pick, 175th overall, ninth round.

(d)—Won Viking Award (Outstanding Swedish-born player in NHL as voted on by fellow Swedish-born players).

(e)—September, 1987—Traded with a fourth-round 1988 NHL entry draft (Matt Ruchty) by Vancouver Canucks to New Jersey Devils for Kirk McLean and Greg Adams.

PETER SUNDSTROM

Left Wing . . . 6' . . . 180 lbs. . . . Born, Skelleftea, Sweden, December 14, 1961 . . . Shoots left . . . Twin brother of Patrik Sundstrom . . . (November, 1987)—Bruised right shoulder when checked by Brian MacLellan vs. Minnesota . . . (January, 1989)—Twisted back . . . (February, 1989)—Hyperextended right knee.

Year	Team	League	Games	G.	A.	Pts.	Pen.
1979-80—Umea Bjorkloven IF	Sweden	8	0	0	0	2
1980-81—Umea Bjorkloven IF (c)	Sweden	29	7	2	9	8
1981-82—Umea Bjorkloven IF	Sweden	35	10	14	24	18
1982-83—Umea Bjorkloven IF	Sweden	36	17	10	27	....
1983-84—New York Rangers	NHL	77	22	22	44	24
1984-85—New York Rangers	NHL	76	18	25	43	34
1985-86—New Haven Nighthawks	AHL	8	3	6	9	4
1985-86—New York Rangers	NHL	53	8	15	23	12
1986-87—Bjorkloven (d)	Sweden	36	22	16	38	44
1987-88—Washington Capitals	NHL	76	8	17	25	34
1988-89—Washington Capitals (e)	NHL	35	4	2	6	12
1989-90—New Jersey Devils	NHL	21	1	2	3	4
1989-90—Utica Devils	AHL	31	11	28	39	6
NHL TOTALS			338	61	83	144	120

(c)—June, 1981—Drafted by New York Rangers in 1981 NHL entry draft. Third Rangers pick, 50th overall, third round.

(d)—July, 1987—Signed as free agent by Washington Capitals with Capitals sending a fifth-round draft choice in 1988 (Martin Bergeron) to New York Rangers as compensation.

(e)—June 19, 1989—Traded by Washington Capitals to New Jersey Devils for a 10th-round 1991 draft pick.

GARY SUTER

Defense . . . 6' . . . 190 lbs. . . . Born, Madison, Wis., June 24, 1964 . . . Shoots left . . . (December, 1986)—Stretched ligament in knee vs. Chicago . . . (September 4, 1987)—High-sticked Andrei Lomakin in a USA/Soviet game at Hartford during Canada Cup. Suter was suspended for the first four NHL games as well as the next six international games in which the NHL is a participant . . . (February, 1988)—Injured left knee vs. Winnipeg . . . Set Flames club records for assists (70 in '87-88) and points (91 in '87-88) by a defenseman in one season . . . (February, 1989)—Pulled hamstring . . . (February 22, 1989)—Missed 16 games due to ruptured appendix vs. Toronto . . . (April 11, 1989)—Broken jaw vs. Vancouver.

Year	Team	League	Games	G.	A.	Pts.	Pen.
1981-82—Dubuque Fighting Saints	USHL	18	3	4	7	32
1982-83—Dubuque Fighting Saints (a-c)	USHL	41	9	10	39	112
1983-84—Univ. of Wisconsin (d)	WCHA	35	4	18	22	68
1984-85—Univ. of Wisconsin	WCHA	39	12	39	51	110
1985-86—Calgary Flames (e)	NHL	80	18	50	68	141
1986-87—Calgary Flames	NHL	68	9	40	49	70
1987-88—Calgary Flames (b)	NHL	75	21	70	91	126
1988-89—Calgary Flames	NHL	63	13	49	62	78
1989-90—Calgary Flames	NHL	76	16	60	76	97
NHL TOTALS			362	77	269	346	512

(c)—Named USHL Top Defenseman.

(d)—June, 1984—Drafted by Calgary Flames in 1984 NHL entry draft. Ninth Flames pick, 180th overall, ninth round.

(e)—Won Calder Memorial Trophy (NHL Rookie of the Year).

BRENT COLIN SUTTER

Center . . . 5'11" . . . 175 lbs. . . . Born, Viking, Alta., June 10, 1962 . . . Shoots right . . . Brother of Brian, Darryl, Ron, Gary, Rich and Duane Sutter . . . (January, 1984)—Missed 11 games with damaged tendon and infection in right hand . . . (March, 1985)—Separated shoulder . . . (October 19, 1985)—Bruised left shoulder

vs. N.Y. Rangers and missed 12 games . . . (December 21, 1985)—Bruised shoulder vs. N.Y. Rangers and missed seven games . . . (March, 1987)—Strained abductor muscle in right leg . . . (December, 1987)—Non-displaced fracture of right thumb . . . (January 19, 1990)—Right leg cut just above the ankle by a skate blade at Winnipeg . . . (January 28, 1990) Hospitalized when an infection developed in right leg after stitches were removed and missed seven games.

Year	Team	League	Games	G.	A.	Pts.	Pen.
1977-78—Red Deer Rustlers	AJHL	60	12	18	30	33
1978-79—Red Deer Rustlers	AJHL	60	42	42	84	79
1979-80—Red Deer Rustlers (c)	AJHL	59	70	101	171	131
1980-81—New York Islanders	NHL	3	2	2	4	0
1980-81—Lethbridge Broncos	WHL	68	54	54	108	116
1981-82—Lethbridge Broncos	WHL	34	46	34	80	162
1981-82—New York Islanders	NHL	43	21	22	43	114
1982-83—New York Islanders	NHL	80	21	19	40	128
1983-84—New York Islanders	NHL	69	34	15	49	69
1984-85—New York Islanders	NHL	72	42	60	102	51
1985-86—New York Islanders	NHL	61	24	31	55	74
1986-87—New York Islanders	NHL	69	27	36	63	73
1987-88—New York Islanders	NHL	70	29	31	60	55
1988-89—New York Islanders	NHL	77	29	34	63	77
1989-90—New York Islanders	NHL	67	33	35	68	65
NHL TOTALS			611	262	285	547	706

(c)—June, 1980—Drafted by New York Islanders as underage junior in 1980 NHL entry draft. First Islanders pick, 17th overall, first round.

DUANE CALVIN SUTTER

Right Wing . . . 6'1" . . . 185 lbs. . . . Born, Viking, Alta., March 16, 1960 . . . Shoots right . . . Brother of Brian, Brent, Ron, Rich, Gary and Darryl Sutter . . . (November 11, 1980)—Damaged ligaments in right knee requiring surgery . . . (April 2, 1981)—Two weeks after coming back from knee surgery he dislocated right shoulder . . . (November, 1983)—Strained ligaments in left knee vs. Quebec . . . (May, 1986)—Surgery to left shoulder . . . (October, 1987)—Damaged right knee cartilage . . . (February 15, 1989)—Suspended five NHL games following a stick incident with Neil Sheehy vs. Washington . . . (December 28, 1989)—Fined $500 for fighting vs. Minnesota.

Year	Team	League	Games	G.	A.	Pts.	Pen.
1976-77—Red Deer Rustlers	AJHL	60	9	26	35	76
1977-78—Red Deer Rustlers	AJHL	59	47	53	100	218
1977-78—Lethbridge Broncos	WCHL	5	1	5	6	19
1978-79—Lethbridge Broncos (c)	WHL	71	50	75	125	212
1979-80—Lethbridge Broncos	WHL	21	18	16	34	74
1979-80—New York Islanders	NHL	56	15	9	24	55
1980-81—New York Islanders	NHL	23	7	11	18	26
1981-82—New York Islanders	NHL	77	18	35	53	100
1982-83—New York Islanders	NHL	75	13	19	32	118
1983-84—New York Islanders	NHL	78	17	23	40	94
1984-85—New York Islanders	NHL	78	17	24	41	174
1985-86—New York Islanders	NHL	80	20	33	53	157
1986-87—New York Islanders	NHL	80	14	17	31	169
1987-88—Chicago Black Hawks (d)	NHL	37	7	9	16	70
1988-89—Chicago Black Hawks	NHL	75	7	9	16	214
1989-90—Chicago Black Hawks (e)	NHL	72	4	14	18	156
NHL TOTALS			731	139	203	342	1333

(c)—August, 1979—Drafted by New York Islanders as underage junior in 1979 NHL entry draft. First Islanders pick, 17th overall, first round.

(d)—September, 1987—Traded by New York Islanders to Chicago Black Hawks for a second-round 1988 draft pick (Wayne Doucet).

(e)—July 5, 1990—Announced his retirement and named a scout by Chicago Black Hawks.

RICHARD SUTTER

Right Wing . . . 5'11" . . . 190 lbs. . . . Born, Viking, Alta., December 2, 1963 . . . Shoots right . . . Brother of Brian, Brent, Darryl, Duane, Gary and twin brother of Ron Sutter . . . (October 23, 1988)—Had four teeth broken by stick of Mark Messier . . . (January 17, 1989)—Injured lower back when checked by Craig Berube vs. Philadelphia . . . (March 24, 1989)—Broken nose when checked by Larry Playfair at Buffalo . . . (January 27, 1990)—Suspended five games for slashing Glenn Anderson vs. Edmonton.

Year	Team	League	Games	G.	A.	Pts.	Pen.
1979-80—Red Deer Rustlers	AJHL	60	13	19	32	157
1980-81—Lethbridge Broncos	WHL	72	23	18	41	255
1981-82—Lethbridge Broncos (c)	WHL	57	38	31	69	263
1982-83—Lethbridge Broncos	WHL	64	37	30	67	200
1982-83—Pittsburgh Penguins	NHL	4	0	0	0	0
1983-84—Baltimore Skipjacks	AHL	2	0	1	1	0
1983-84—Pittsburgh Penguins (d)	NHL	5	0	0	0	0
1983-84—Philadelphia Flyers	NHL	70	16	12	28	93
1984-85—Hershey Bears	AHL	13	3	7	10	14
1984-85—Philadelphia Flyers	NHL	56	6	10	16	89
1985-86—Philadelphia Flyers (e)	NHL	78	14	25	39	199
1986-87—Vancouver Canucks	NHL	74	20	22	42	113
1987-88—Vancouver Canucks	NHL	80	15	15	30	165
1988-89—Vancouver Canucks	NHL	75	17	15	32	122
1989-90—Vancouver Canucks (f)	NHL	62	9	9	18	133
1989-90—St. Louis Blues	NHL	12	2	0	2	22
NHL TOTALS			516	99	108	207	936

(c)—June, 1982—Drafted as underage junior by Pittsburgh Penguins in 1982 NHL entry draft. First Penguins pick, 10th overall, first round.

(d)—October, 1983—Traded with second (Greg Smyth) and third (David McLay) round 1984 draft picks by Pittsburgh Penguins to Philadelphia Flyers for Ron Flockhart, Mark Taylor, Andy Brickley, first (Roger Belanger) and third-round 1984 draft picks.

(e)—June, 1986—Traded by Philadelphia Flyers with Dave Richter and a third-round draft choice in 1986 to Vancouver Canucks for J.J. Daigneault, a second-round draft choice (Kent Hawley) in 1986 and a fifth-round pick in 1987.

(f)—March 6, 1990—Traded with Harold Snepsts and a second-round 1990 draft pick by Vancouver Canucks to St. Louis Blues for Adrien Plavsic and a first-round 1990 and second-round 1991 draft pick. The second-round 1990 pick was acquired by Vancouver from St. Louis in an earlier deal. The first-round 1990 pick was later traded to Montreal.

RONALD SUTTER

Center . . . 6′ . . . 180 lbs. . . . Born, Viking, Alta., December 2, 1963 . . . Shoots right . . . Brother of Brian, Brent, Darryl, Duane, Gary and twin brother of Rich Sutter . . . (November 27, 1981)—Broke ankle vs. Medicine Hat . . . (March, 1985)—Bruised ribs . . . (January, 1987)—Lower back stress fracture . . . (March, 1988)—Torn rib cartilage . . . (October 29, 1988)—Jaw broken by a James Patrick crosscheck vs. N.Y. Rangers . . . (March, 1989)—Pulled groin.

Year	Team	League	Games	G.	A.	Pts.	Pen.
1979-80—Red Deer Rustlers		AJHL	60	12	33	35	44
1980-81—Lethbridge Broncos		WHL	72	13	32	45	152
1981-82—Lethbridge Broncos (c)		WHL	59	38	54	92	207
1982-83—Lethbridge Broncos		WHL	58	35	48	83	98
1982-83—Philadelphia Flyers		NHL	10	1	1	2	9
1983-84—Philadelphia Flyers		NHL	79	19	32	51	101
1984-85—Philadelphia Flyers		NHL	73	16	29	45	94
1985-86—Philadelphia Flyers		NHL	75	18	42	60	159
1986-87—Philadelphia Flyers		NHL	39	10	17	27	69
1987-88—Philadelphia Flyers		NHL	69	8	25	33	146
1988-89—Philadelphia Flyers		NHL	55	26	22	48	80
1989-90—Philadelphia Flyers		NHL	75	22	26	48	104
NHL TOTALS			475	120	193	313	762

(c)—June, 1982—Drafted as underage junior by Philadelphia Flyers in 1982 NHL entry draft. First Flyers pick, fourth overall, first round.

BOYD SUTTON

Center . . . 5′10″ . . . 175 lbs. . . . Born, Anchorage, Alaska, December 6, 1966 . . . Shoots left.

Year	Team	League	Games	G.	A.	Pts.	Pen.
1985-86—Miami Univ. of Ohio (c)		CCHA	33	8	12	20	24
1986-87—Miami Univ. of Ohio		CCHA	39	19	18	37	44
1987-88—Miami Univ. of Ohio		CCHA	37	17	16	33	34
1988-89—Miami Univ. of Ohio		CCHA	37	16	23	39	24
1989-90—Greensboro Monarchs		ECHL	60	32	26	58	25

(c)—June, 1985—Drafted by Buffalo Sabres in 1985 NHL entry draft. Tenth Sabres pick, 203rd overall, 10th round.

KEN SUTTON

Defense . . . 6′ . . . 185 lbs. . . . Born, Edmonton, Alta., May 11, 1969 . . . Shoots left.

Year	Team	League	Games	G.	A.	Pts.	Pen.
1987-88—Calgary Canucks		AJHL	53	13	43	56	228
1988-89—Saskatoon Blades (c)		WHL	71	22	31	53	104
1989-90—Rochester Americans		AHL	57	5	14	19	83

(c)—June, 1989—Drafted by Buffalo Sabres in 1989 NHL entry draft. Fourth Sabres pick, 98th overall, fifth round.

PETR SVOBODA

Defense . . . 6′1″ . . . 160 lbs. . . . Born, Most, Czechoslovakia, February 14, 1966 . . . Shoots left . . . (January, 1988)—Back spasms . . . (March, 1988)—Hip pointer . . . (November 21, 1988)—Missed five games with a sprained right wrist vs. N.Y. Rangers . . . (March, 1989)—Injured back . . . (November, 1989)—Separated shoulder . . . (November 22, 1989)—Pulled groin vs. Philadelphia . . . (December 11, 1989)—Aggravated groin injury vs. Los Angeles and missed 15 games . . . (March 11, 1990)—Bruised left foot vs. Detroit.

Year	Team	League	Games	G.	A.	Pts.	Pen.
1983-84—Czechoslovakia Jr. (c)		Czech.	40	15	21	36	14
1984-85—Montreal Canadiens		NHL	73	4	27	31	65
1985-86—Montreal Canadiens		NHL	73	1	18	19	93
1986-87—Montreal Canadiens		NHL	70	5	17	22	63
1987-88—Montreal Canadiens		NHL	69	7	22	29	149
1988-89—Montreal Canadiens		NHL	71	8	37	45	147
1989-90—Montreal Canadiens		NHL	60	5	31	36	98
NHL TOTALS			416	30	152	182	615

(c)—June, 1984—Drafted by Montreal Canadiens in 1984 NHL entry draft. First Canadiens pick, fifth overall, first round.

DON SWEENEY

Defense . . . 5′11″ . . . 170 lbs. . . . Born, St. Stephen, N.B., August 17, 1966 . . . Shoots left . . . (February 22, 1990)—Bruised left heel at Chicago.

Year	Team	League	Games	G.	A.	Pts.	Pen.
1983-84—St. Paul N.B. H.S. (c)		N.B.H.S.	22	33	26	59	....
1984-85—Harvard University		ECAC	29	3	7	10	30
1985-86—Harvard University		ECAC	31	4	5	9	29
1986-87—Harvard University		ECAC	34	7	14	21	22
1987-88—Harvard University (d)		ECAC	30	6	23	29	37
1987-88—Maine Mariners (e)		AHL	..	..	..	..	..
1988-89—Maine Mariners		AHL	42	8	17	25	24
1988-89—Boston Bruins		NHL	36	3	5	8	20
1989-90—Boston Bruins		NHL	58	3	5	8	58
1989-90—Maine Mariners		AHL	11	0	8	8	8
NHL TOTALS			94	6	10	16	78

(c)—June, 1984—Drafted by Boston Bruins in 1984 NHL entry draft. Eighth Bruins pick, 166th overall, eighth round.

(d)—Named Second team All-America (East).

(e)—No regular season record. Played six playoff games.

ROBERT SWEENEY

Center . . . 6′3″ . . . 200 lbs. . . . Born, Boxborough, Mass., January 25, 1964 . . . Shoots right . . . Brother of Timothy Sweeney . . . (November, 1989)—Pulled rib muscle and missed six games.

Year	Team	League	Games	G.	A.	Pts.	Pen.
1982-83—Boston College (c)		ECAC	30	17	11	28	10
1983-84—Boston College		ECAC	23	14	7	21	10
1984-85—Boston College		H. East	44	32	32	64	43
1985-86—Boston College		H. East	41	15	24	39	52
1986-87—Boston Bruins		NHL	14	2	4	6	21
1986-87—Moncton Golden Flames		AHL	58	29	26	55	81
1987-88—Boston Bruins		NHL	80	22	23	45	73
1988-89—Boston Bruins		NHL	75	14	14	28	99
1989-90—Boston Bruins		NHL	70	22	24	46	93
NHL TOTALS			239	60	65	125	286

(c)—June, 1982—Drafted by Boston Bruins in 1982 NHL entry draft. Sixth Bruins pick, 123rd overall, sixth round.

TIMOTHY SWEENEY

Center . . . 5′11″ . . . 180 lbs. . . . Born, Boston, Mass., April 12, 1967 . . . Shoots left . . . Brother of Bob Sweeney . . . (January 26, 1988)—Fractured index finger vs. Northeastern Univ. . . . (May, 1990)—Bruised ankle.

Year	Team	League	Games	G.	A.	Pts.	Pen.
1983-84—Weymouth North H.S.		Mass. H.S.	23	33	26	59	....
1984-85—Weymouth North H.S. (c)		Mass. H.S.	22	32	56	88	....
1985-86—Boston College		H. East	32	8	4	12	8
1986-87—Boston College		H. East	38	31	16	47	28
1987-88—Boston College		H. East	18	9	11	20	18
1988-89—Boston College (a-d)		H. East	39	29	44	73	26
1989-90—Salt Lake Golden Eagles (b-e)		IHL	81	46	51	97	32

(c)—June, 1985—Drafted by Calgary Flames in 1985 NHL entry draft. Seventh Flames pick, 122nd overall, sixth round.

(d)—Named Second team All-America (East).

(e)—Won Ken McKenzie Trophy (Top US-born IHL rookie).

DARRYL SYDOR

Defense . . . 6′ . . . 205 lbs. . . . Born, Edmonton, Alta., March 13, 1972 . . . Shoots left.

Year	Team	League	Games	G.	A.	Pts.	Pen.
1985-86—Genstar Cement Bantam		Alta.	34	20	17	37	60
1986-87—Genstar Cement Bantam		Alta.	36	15	20	35	60
1987-88—Edmonton Vets Midget		Alta.	38	10	11	21	54
1988-89—Kamloops Blazers		WHL	65	12	14	26	86
1989-90—Kamloops Blazers (a-c)		WHL	67	29	66	95	129

(c)—June 16, 1990—Selected by Los Angeles Kings in 1990 NHL entry draft. First Kings pick, seventh overall, first round.

PHIL SYKES

Left Wing . . . 6′ . . . 185 lbs. . . . Born, Dawson Creek, B.C., May 18, 1959 . . . Shoots left . . . (May, 1986)—Injured left wrist during world championships in Moscow and required surgery in September, 1986 . . . (March, 1987)—Sprained knee . . . (May, 1987)—Injured left wrist during World Championships in Moscow that required surgery . . . (October, 1987)—Partially torn groin muscle . . . (March, 1988)—Strained knee . . . (October 4, 1988)—Left Los Angeles Kings for two weeks . . . (March, 1989)—Pulled groin.

Year	Team	League	Games	G.	A.	Pts.	Pen.
1978-79—North Dakota University		WCHA	41	9	5	14	16
1979-80—North Dakota University		WCHA	37	22	27	49	34
1980-81—North Dakota University		WCHA	38	28	34	62	22
1981-82—North Dakota University (c-d)		WCHA	45	39	24	63	20
1982-83—Los Angeles Kings		NHL	7	2	0	2	2
1982-83—New Haven Nighthawks		AHL	71	19	26	45	111
1983-84—New Haven Nighthawks		AHL	77	29	37	66	101
1983-84—Los Angeles Kings		NHL	3	0	0	0	2
1984-85—Los Angeles Kings		NHL	79	17	15	32	38
1985-86—Los Angeles Kings		NHL	76	20	24	44	97
1986-87—Los Angeles Kings		NHL	58	6	15	21	133
1987-88—Los Angeles Kings		NHL	40	9	12	21	82
1988-89—New Haven Nighthawks		AHL	34	9	17	26	23
1988-89—Los Angeles Kings		NHL	23	0	1	1	8
1989-90—New Haven Nighthawks (e)		AHL	25	3	12	15	32
1989-90—Winnipeg Jets		NHL	48	9	6	15	26
1989-90—Moncton Hawks		AHL	5	0	1	1	20
NHL TOTALS			334	63	73	136	388

(c)—Named to Western All-America Team.

(d)—April, 1982—Signed by Los Angeles Kings as a free agent.

(e)—November 30, 1989—Traded by Los Angeles Kings to Winnipeg Jets for Brad Jones.

PETER TAGLIANETTI

Defense . . . 6′2″ . . . 200 lbs. . . . Born, Framingham, Mass., August 15, 1963 . . . Shoots left . . . (October, 1985)—Dislocated shoulder in fight with Perry Turnbull during Winnipeg Jets training camp . . . (February 20, 1986)—Dislocated shoulder . . . (March, 1986)—Surgery to correct recurring shoulder dislocations . . . (September, 1988)—Damaged right knee cartilage during Winnipeg Jets training camp and required surgery . . . (October 6, 1989)—Injured knee vs. N.Y. Rangers and required surgery . . . (February 20, 1990)—Suspended five games for trying to injure Christian Ruuttu vs. Buffalo . . . (April, 1990)—Bruised ribs.

Year	Team	League	Games	G.	A.	Pts.	Pen.
1981-82—Providence College		ECAC	2	0	0	0	2
1982-83—Providence College (c)		ECAC	43	4	17	21	68
1983-84—Providence College		ECAC	30	4	25	29	68
1984-85—Providence College (a)		H. East	43	8	21	29	114
1984-85—Winnipeg Jets		NHL	1	0	0	0	0
1985-86—Sherbrooke Canadiens		AHL	24	1	8	9	75
1985-86—Winnipeg Jets		NHL	18	0	0	0	48
1986-87—Winnipeg Jets		NHL	3	0	0	0	12
1986-87—Sherbrooke Canadiens		AHL	54	5	14	19	104
1987-88—Winnipeg Jets		NHL	70	6	17	23	182
1988-89—Winnipeg Jets		NHL	66	1	14	15	226
1989-90—Moncton Hawks		AHL	3	0	2	2	2
1989-90—Winnipeg Jets		NHL	49	3	6	9	136
NHL TOTALS			207	10	37	47	604

(c)—June, 1983—Drafted by Winnipeg Jets in 1983 NHL entry draft. Fourth Jets pick, 43rd overall, third round.

CHRIS TAMER

Defense . . . 6'2" . . . 185 lbs. . . . Born, Dearborn, Mich., November 17, 1970 . . . Shoots left.

Year	Team	League	Games	G.	A.	Pts.	Pen.
1987-88—Redford Royals Jr. A		OHA	40	10	20	30	217
1988-89—Redford Royals Jr. A		OHA	31	6	13	19	79
1989-90—Univ. of Michigan (c)		CCHA	42	2	7	9	147

(c)—June 16, 1990—Selected by Pittsburgh Penguins in 1990 NHL entry draft. Third Penguins pick, 68th overall, fourth round.

TONY TANTI

Right Wing . . . 5'9" . . . 181 lbs. . . . Born, Toronto, Ont., September 7, 1963 . . . Shoots left . . . Broke Wayne Gretzky's record for most goals in rookie OHL season . . . (November, 1981)—Separated shoulder . . . (December, 1981)—Sore hip . . . (1983-84)—Set Vancouver club records for most goals (45) and most power-play goals (19) . . . (November, 1984)—Strained knee . . . Also plays Left Wing . . . (December 8, 1987)—Broken foot when struck by puck vs. Minnesota . . . (March 24, 1989)—Twisted knee at Buffalo . . . (March, 1990)—Charley horse.

Year	Team	League	Games	G.	A.	Pts.	Pen.
1979-80—St. Michaels Jr. B		OHL	37	31	27	58	67
1980-81—Oshawa Generals (a-c-d)		OHL	67	81	69	150	197
1981-82—Oshawa Generals (b-e)		OHL	57	62	64	126	138
1981-82—Chicago Black Hawks		NHL	2	0	0	0	0
1982-83—Oshawa Generals		OHL	30	34	28	62	35
1982-83—Chicago Black Hawks (f)		NHL	1	1	0	1	0
1982-83—Vancouver Canucks		NHL	39	8	8	16	16
1983-84—Vancouver Canucks		NHL	79	45	41	86	50
1984-85—Vancouver Canucks		NHL	68	39	20	59	45
1985-86—Vancouver Canucks		NHL	77	39	33	72	85
1986-87—Vancouver Canucks		NHL	77	41	38	79	84
1987-88—Vancouver Canucks		NHL	73	40	37	77	90
1988-89—Vancouver Canucks		NHL	77	24	25	49	69
1989-90—Vancouver Canucks (g)		NHL	41	14	18	32	50
1989-90—Pittsburgh Penguins		NHL	37	14	18	32	22
NHL TOTALS			571	265	238	503	511

(c)—Won Hap Emms OHL Rookie Award.
(d)—June, 1981—Drafted by Chicago Black Hawks in 1981 NHL entry draft. First Black Hawks pick, 12th overall, first round.
(e)—Won Jim Mahon Memorial Trophy (Top Scoring Right Wing).
(f)—January, 1983—Traded by Chicago Black Hawks to Vancouver Canucks for Curt Fraser.
(g)—January 8, 1990—Traded with Barry Pederson and Rod Buskas by Vancouver Canucks to Pittsburgh Penguins for Dan Quinn, Andrew McBain and Dave Capuano.

PATRICE TARDIF

Center . . . 6'2" . . . 175 lbs. . . . Born, Thetford Mines, Que., October 30, 1970 . . . Shoots left.

Year	Team	League	Games	G.	A.	Pts.	Pen.
1989-90—Champlain Jr. Coll. (c)		Can. Coll.	27	58	36	94	36

(c)—June 16, 1990—Selected by St. Louis Blues in 1990 NHL entry draft. Second Blues pick, 54th overall, third round.

JERRY TARRANT

Defense . . . 6'2" . . . 190 lbs. . . . Born, Burlington, Vt., April 3, 1966 . . . Shoots left.

Year	Team	League	Games	G.	A.	Pts.	Pen.
1985-86—Univ. of Vermont		ECAC	23	0	4	4	22
1986-87—Univ. of Vermont		ECAC	32	3	9	12	34
1987-88—Univ. of Vermont (c)		ECAC	31	2	8	10	28
1988-89—Univ. of Vermont		ECAC	34	3	19	22	54
1989-90—Salt Lake Golden Eagles		IHL	8	0	0	0	12
1989-90—Flint Spirits		IHL	23	0	0	0	27
1989-90—Erie Panthers		ECHL	10	1	16	17	36

(c)—June, 1988—Selected by Calgary Flames in 1988 NHL supplemental draft.

CHRIS TAYLOR

Center . . . 5'11" . . . 186 lbs. . . . Born, Stratford, Ont., March 6, 1972 . . . Shoots left . . . Brother of Tim Taylor . . . (March, 1989)—Torn knee ligaments when checked by Scott Pearson vs. Niagara Falls.

Year	Team	League	Games	G.	A.	Pts.	Pen.
1987-88—Stratford Midget		OHA	52	28	37	65	112
1988-89—London Knights		OHL	62	7	16	23	52
1989-90—London Knights (c)		OHL	66	45	60	105	60

(c)—June 16, 1990—Selected by New York Islanders in 1990 NHL entry draft. Second Islanders pick, 27th overall, second round.

DAVID ANDREW TAYLOR

Right Wing . . . 6' . . . 200 lbs. . . . Born, Levack, Ont., December 4, 1955 . . . Shoots right . . . Set ECAC record and tied NCAA record with 108 points in 1976-77 . . . Missed parts of 1979-80 season with pulled back muscle and sprained left knee . . . (November 5, 1980)—Sprained shoulder . . . (October 29, 1982)—Broke right wrist in collision with Kevin Lowe at Edmonton and missed 33 games . . . (January, 1983)—Right knee injury . . . (May 28, 1983)—Operation on right wrist he broke for second time in World Championships at West Germany . . . Holds single season record for most goals, assists and points by a former college player . . . Holds Los Angeles club records for goals, assists and points by a right wing . . . (November 10, 1983)—Returned from broken wrist vs. St. Louis . . . (November, 1986)—Sprained knee . . . (December, 1987)—Groin injury . . . (January, 1989)—Torn knee cartilage . . . (December 13, 1989)—Pulled groin at Hartford and missed 15 games . . . (January, 1990)—Inflamed knee . . . (April, 1990)—Strained shoulder.

Year	Team	League	Games	G.	A.	Pts.	Pen.
1974-75—Clarkson College (c)		ECAC	....	20	34	54	....
1975-76—Clarkson College		ECAC	....	26	33	59	....
1976-77—Clarkson College (d-e)		ECAC	34	41	67	108	....
1976-77—Fort Worth Texans		CHL	7	2	4	6	6
1977-78—Los Angeles Kings		NHL	64	22	21	43	47
1978-79—Los Angeles Kings		NHL	78	43	48	91	124
1979-80—Los Angeles Kings		NHL	61	37	53	90	72
1980-81—Los Angeles Kings (b)		NHL	72	47	65	112	130
1981-82—Los Angeles Kings		NHL	78	39	67	106	130
1982-83—Los Angeles Kings		NHL	46	21	37	58	76
1983-84—Los Angeles Kings		NHL	63	20	49	69	91
1984-85—Los Angeles Kings		NHL	79	41	51	92	132
1985-86—Los Angeles Kings		NHL	76	33	38	71	110
1986-87—Los Angeles Kings		NHL	67	18	44	62	84
1987-88—Los Angeles Kings		NHL	68	26	41	67	129
1988-89—Los Angeles Kings		NHL	70	26	37	63	80
1989-90—Los Angeles Kings		NHL	58	15	26	41	96
NHL TOTALS			880	388	577	965	1301

(c)—Drafted by Los Angeles Kings in 15th round of 1975 amateur draft.
(d)—Named ECAC Player of the Year.
(e)—Named to All-America team (East).

RANDY TAYLOR

Defense . . . 6'2" . . . 195 lbs. . . . Born, Cornwall, Ont., July 30, 1965 . . . Shoots right.

Year	Team	League	Games	G.	A.	Pts.	Pen.
1983-84—Harvard Univ.		ECAC	23	0	3	3	4
1984-85—Harvard Univ.		ECAC	30	6	30	36	12
1985-86—Harvard Univ. (b-c)		ECAC	33	5	20	25	30
1986-87—Harvard Univ. (a)		ECAC	34	3	35	38	30
1987-88—Peoria Rivermen		IHL	27	1	7	8	22
1987-88—Muskegon Lumberjacks		IHL	37	0	14	14	14
1988-89—Indianapolis Ice (d)		IHL	44	2	15	17	31
1988-89—Flint Spirits		IHL	31	2	6	8	11
1989-90—Muskegon Lumberjacks		IHL	63	2	22	24	29
1989-90—Virginia Lancers		ECHL	7	0	8	8	4

(c)—June, 1986—Selected by Pittsburgh Penguins in 1986 NHL supplemental draft.
(d)—February 14, 1989—Traded with Rick Boyd and Graeme Bonar by Indianapolis Ice to Flint Spirits for Tom Karalis.

TIM TAYLOR

Center . . . 5'11" . . . 170 lbs. . . . Born, Stratford, Ont., February 6, 1969 . . . Shoots left . . . (October, 1986)—Mononucleosis . . . Brother of Chris Taylor.

Year	Team	League	Games	G.	A.	Pts.	Pen.
1986-87—London Knights		OHL	34	7	9	16	11
1987-88—London Knights (c)		OHL	64	46	50	96	66
1988-89—London Knights		OHL	61	34	80	114	93
1989-90—Baltimore Skipjacks		AHL	74	22	21	43	63

(c)—June, 1988—Drafted by Washington Capitals in 1988 NHL entry draft. Second Capitals pick, 36th overall, second round.

STEPHEN TEPPER

Right Wing . . . 6'5" . . . 225 lbs. . . . Born, Santa Ana, Calif., March 10, 1969 . . . Shoots right . . . Attended Maine on a four-year football scholarship . . . (1989-90) —Renounced his football scholarship.

Year	Team	League	Games	G.	A.	Pts.	Pen.
1985-86—Westboro H.S.		Mass. H.S.	..	18	26	44	..
1986-87—Westboro H.S. (c)		Mass. H.S.	..	34	18	52	..
1987-88—Westboro H.S.		Mass. H.S.	24	39	24	63	..
1988-89—Univ. of Maine		H. East	26	3	9	12	32
1989-90—Univ. of Maine		H. East	41	10	6	16	68

(c)—June, 1987—Selected by Chicago Black Hawks in 1987 NHL entry draft. Seventh Black Hawks pick, 134th overall, seventh round.

MICHAEL THELVEN

Defense . . . 5'11" . . . 180 lbs. . . . Born, Stockholm, Sweden, January 7, 1961 . . . Shoots right . . . (February 6, 1986)—Injured groin vs. Buffalo . . . (February 18, 1986)—Dislocated shoulder at Calgary . . . (September, 1986)—Dislocated left shoulder in Boston Bruins training camp and required surgery . . . (January, 1988)—Sprained neck . . . (March, 1988)—Groin strain . . . (April, 1988)—Strained right shoulder vs. Montreal during playoffs . . . (October, 1988)—Charley horse . . . (November, 1988)—Groin strain . . . (December 26, 1988)—Missed 31 games with tendinitis in right knee . . . (April 25, 1989)—Aggravated knee injury when he was checked by Mike McPhee vs. Montreal . . . (May 1, 1989)—Surgery to right knee and will require four to six months of therapy . . . (1989-90)—Missed first 19 games of season . . . (December 20, 1989)—Surgery to remove an inch of damaged cartilage on the underside of the right kneecap.

TOM TILLEY

Defense . . . 6' . . . 180 lbs. . . . Born, Trenton, Ont., March 28, 1965 . . . Shoots right . . . (January 28, 1989)—Collapsed on the St. Louis bench during a game vs. Washington due to the flu . . . (March, 1989)—Bruised left shoulder . . . (October 14, 1989)—Strained lower back after being checked by Steve Thomas and Troy Murray vs. Chicago and missed eight games.

Year	Team	League	Games	G.	A.	Pts.	Pen.
1983-84	Orillia Travelways (c)	OJHL	38	16	35	51	113
1984-85	Michigan State Univ.	CCHA	37	1	5	6	58
1985-86	Michigan State Univ.	CCHA	42	9	25	34	48
1986-87	Michigan State Univ.	CCHA	42	7	14	21	46
1987-88	Michigan State Univ.	CCHA	46	8	18	26	44
1988-89	St. Louis Blues	NHL	70	1	22	23	47
1989-90	St. Louis Blues	NHL	34	0	5	5	6
1989-90	Salt Lake Golden Eagles	IHL	22	1	8	9	13
	NHL TOTALS		104	1	27	28	53

(c)—June, 1984—Drafted as underage junior by St. Louis Blues in 1984 NHL entry draft. Thirteenth Blues pick, 196th overall, 10th round.

MARK TINORDI

Defense . . . 6'4" . . . 205 lbs. . . . Born, Reed Deer, Alta., May 9, 1965 . . . Shoots left . . . (January, 1988)—Abdominal pains . . . (October 6, 1988)—Left knee surgery . . . (December, 1988)—Bruised ribs . . . (April, 1989)—Knee surgery . . . (September 27, 1989)—Suspended for regular season games for crosschecking Al Secord in a pre-season game vs. Chicago . . . (December, 1989)—Bruised shoulder . . . (December 28, 1989)—Fined $500 for fighting at Chicago . . . (January 17, 1990)—Concussion at Chicago and missed six games.

Year	Team	League	Games	G.	A.	Pts.	Pen.
1982-83	Lethbridge Broncos	WHL	64	0	4	4	50
1983-84	Lethbridge Broncos	WHL	72	5	14	19	53
1984-85	Lethbridge Broncos	WHL	58	10	15	25	134
1985-86	Lethbridge Broncos	WHL	58	8	30	37	139
1986-87	Calgary Wranglers (a)	WHL	61	29	37	66	148
1986-87	New Haven Nighthawks (c)	AHL	2	0	0	0	2
1987-88	New York Rangers	NHL	24	1	2	3	50
1987-88	Colorado Rangers	IHL	41	8	19	27	150
1988-89	Minnesota North Stars (d)	NHL	47	2	3	5	107
1988-89	Kalamazoo Wings	IHL	10	0	0	0	35
1989-90	Minnesota North Stars	NHL	66	3	7	10	240
	NHL TOTALS		137	6	12	18	397

(c)—January, 1987—Signed by New York Rangers as a free agent.
(d)—October 11, 1988—Traded with Paul Jerrard, Mike Sullivan, Bret Barnett and Los Angeles Kings third-round 1989 draft pick (Murray Garbutt) by New York Rangers to Minnesota North Stars for Igor Liba, Brian Lawton and NHL rights to Eric Bennett.

DAVE TIPPETT

Center . . . 5'10" . . . 175 lbs. . . . Born, Moosomin, Sask., August 25, 1961 . . . Shoots left . . . Brother of Brad Tippett (Coach of Regina Pats) . . . (October 8, 1989)—Games played streak ended at 419 games after injuring right thumb tendons vs. Montreal.

Year	Team	League	Games	G.	A.	Pts.	Pen.
1979-80	Prince Albert Raiders	SAJHL	85	72	95	177	..
1980-81	Prince Albert Raiders	SAJHL	84	62	93	155	..
1981-82	University of North Dakota	WCHA	43	13	28	41	24
1982-83	University of North Dakota	WCHA	36	15	31	46	44
1983-84	Canadian Olympic Team	Int'l	66	14	19	33	24
1983-84	Hartford Whalers (c)	NHL	17	4	2	6	2
1984-85	Hartford Whalers	NHL	80	7	12	19	12
1985-86	Hartford Whalers	NHL	80	14	20	34	18
1986-87	Hartford Whalers	NHL	80	9	22	31	42
1987-88	Hartford Whalers	NHL	80	16	21	37	32
1988-89	Hartford Whalers	NHL	80	17	24	41	45
1989-90	Hartford Whalers	NHL	66	8	19	27	32
	NHL TOTALS		483	75	120	195	183

(c)—February, 1984—Signed by Hartford Whalers as a free agent.

TIM TISDALE

Center . . . 6'1" . . . 186 lbs. . . . Born, Shaunavon, Sask., May 28, 1968 . . . Shoots right.

Year	Team	League	Games	G.	A.	Pts.	Pen.
1986-87	Swift Current Broncos	WHL	66	20	29	49	25
1987-88	Swift Current Broncos (c)	WHL	32	11	15	26	15
1988-89	Swift Current Broncos (b)	WHL	68	57	82	139	89
1989-90	Cape Breton Oilers	AHL	66	15	21	36	24

(c)—June, 1988—Drafted by Edmonton Oilers in 1988 NHL entry draft. Thirteenth Oilers pick, 250th overall, 12th round.

GRANT TKACHUK

Left Wing . . . 5'9" . . . 175 lbs. . . . Born, Lac La Bichi, Alta., September 24, 1968 . . . Shoots left . . . (September, 1988)—Injured left eye when struck by a puck during Buffalo Sabres training camp.

Year	Team	League	Games	G.	A.	Pts.	Pen.
1983-84	Lac La Bichi	Alta. Midgt.	40	31	35	66	40
1984-85	Saskatoon Blades	WHL	71	8	16	24	55
1985-86	Saskatoon Blades	WHL	52	18	27	45	82
1986-87	Saskatoon Blades (c)	WHL	71	46	36	82	108
1987-88	Saskatoon Blades (a)	WHL	70	51	46	97	126
1988-89	Rochester Americans	AHL	64	12	13	25	26
1989-90	Phoenix Roadrunners	IHL	72	17	23	40	66

(c)—June, 1987—Drafted by Buffalo Sabres in 1987 NHL entry draft. Tenth Sabres pick, 169th overall, ninth round.

KEITH TKACHUK

Center . . . 6'1" . . . 220 lbs. . . . Born, Melrose, Mass., March 28, 1972 . . . Shoots left . . . (May, 1990)—Signed letter of intent to attend Boston University.

Year	Team	League	Games	G.	A.	Pts.	Pen.
1988-89	Malden Catholic H.S.	Mass. H.S.	21	30	16	46	....
1989-90	Malden Catholic H.S. (c)	Mass. H.S.	6	12	14	26	....

(c)—June 16, 1990—Selected by Winnipeg Jets in 1990 NHL entry draft. First Jets pick, 19th overall, first round.

RICK TOCCHET

Right Wing . . . 6' . . . 195 lbs. . . . Born, Scarborough, Ont., April 9, 1964 . . . Shoots right . . . (November 23, 1985)—Bruised right knee at Philadelphia and missed seven games . . . (February, 1988)—Separated left shoulder . . . (October 27, 1988)—Given a 10-game suspension for injuring the eye of Dean Chynoweth during a fight vs. N.Y. Islanders . . . (April 21, 1989)—Hyperextended right knee vs. Pittsburgh . . . (November, 1989)—Viral infection.

Year	Team	League	Games	G.	A.	Pts.	Pen.
1981-82	Sault Ste. Marie Greyhounds	OHL	59	7	15	22	184
1982-83	Sault Ste. M. Greyhounds (c-d-e)	OHL	66	32	34	66	146
1983-84	Sault Ste. Marie Greyhounds (f)	OHL	64	44	64	108	209
1984-85	Philadelphia Flyers	NHL	75	14	25	39	181
1985-86	Philadelphia Flyers	NHL	69	14	21	35	284
1986-87	Philadelphia Flyers	NHL	69	21	26	47	288
1987-88	Philadelphia Flyers	NHL	65	31	33	64	301
1988-89	Philadelphia Flyers	NHL	66	45	36	81	183
1989-90	Philadelphia Flyers	NHL	75	37	59	96	196
	NHL TOTALS		419	162	200	362	1433

(c)—Led OHL playoffs with 67 penalty minutes.
(d)—June, 1983—Drafted as underage junior by Philadelphia Flyers in 1983 NHL entry draft. Fifth Flyers pick, 121st overall, sixth round.
(e)—Led OHL playoffs with 62 penalty minutes.
(f)—Led OHL playoffs witth 22 goals and co-leader (with teammate Wayne Groulx) with 36 points.

KEVIN TODD

Center . . . 5'11" . . . 180 lbs. . . . Born, Winnipeg, Man., May 4, 1968 . . . Shoots left . . . (December, 1985)—Stretched knee ligaments.

Year	Team	League	Games	G.	A.	Pts.	Pen.
1984-85	Winnipeg Stars	Man. Midget	60	66	100	166	....
1985-86	Prince Albert Raiders (c)	WHL	55	14	25	39	19
1986-87	Prince Albert Raiders	WHL	71	39	46	85	92
1987-88	Prince Albert Raiders	WHL	72	49	72	121	83
1988-89	New Jersey Devils	NHL	1	0	0	0	0
1988-89	Utica Devils	AHL	78	26	45	71	62
1989-90	Utica Devils	AHL	71	18	36	54	72
	NHL TOTALS		1	0	0	0	0

(c)—June, 1986—Drafted as underage junior by New Jersey Devils in 1986 NHL entry draft. Seventh Devils pick, 129th overall, seventh round.

MIKE TOMLAK

Left Wing and Center . . . 6'3" . . . 205 lbs. . . . Born, Thunder Bay, Ont., October 17, 1964 . . . Shoots left . . . (February 9, 1990)—Sprained right wrist vs. Vancouver.

Year	Team	League	Games	G.	A.	Pts.	Pen.
1981-82	Thunder Bay Burger Kings	TBJHL	25	19	26	45	30
1982-83	Cornwall Royals (c)	OHL	70	18	49	67	26
1983-84	Cornwall Royals	OHL	64	24	64	88	21
1984-85	Cornwall Royals	OHL	66	30	70	100	9
1985-86	Univ. of Western Ontario	OUAA	....	...	...	....	....
1986-87	Univ. of Western Ontario (d)	OUAA	....	...	...	....	....
1987-88	Univ. of Western Ontario	OUAA	39	24	52	76	....
1988-89	Univ. of Western Ontario (a-e)	OUAA	35	16	34	50	....
1989-90	Hartford Whalers	NHL	70	7	14	21	48
	NHL TOTALS		70	7	14	21	48

(c)—June, 1983—Selected by Toronto Maple Leafs in 1983 NHL entry draft. Tenth Maple Leafs pick, 208th overall, 11th round.
(d)—Named to CIAU All-Canada team.
(e)—May 28, 1989—Signed two-year contract with Hartford Whalers as a free agent.

JOHN TONELLI

Left Wing and Center . . . 6'1" . . . 190 lbs. . . . Born, Hamilton, Ont., March 23, 1957 . . . Shoots left . . . Did not take part in 1975 playoffs after signing pro contract . . . Brother of Ray Tonelli . . . (February, 1981)—Shoulder injury . . . Set N.Y. Islanders club record for left wings with 93 points in 1981-82 . . . (December, 1983)—Knee injury . . . (Fall, 1985)—Sat out 22 days of N.Y. Islanders training camp in contract dispute . . . (April, 1988)—Missed first four playoff games vs. Edmonton due to flu . . . (April, 1989)—Strained knee . . . (March, 1990)—Sinus infection.

Year	Team	League	Games	G.	A.	Pts.	Pen.
1973-74	Toronto Marlboros	Jr."A" OHA	69	18	37	55	62
1974-75	Toronto Marlboros (a-c)	Jr."A" OHA	70	49	86	135	85
1975-76	Houston Aeros	WHA	79	17	14	31	66
1976-77	Houston Aeros (d)	WHA	80	24	31	55	109
1977-78	Houston Aeros (e)	WHA	65	23	41	64	103
1978-79	New York Islanders	NHL	73	17	39	56	44
1979-80	New York Islanders	NHL	77	14	30	44	49
1980-81	New York Islanders	NHL	70	20	32	52	57
1981-82	New York Islanders (b)	NHL	80	35	58	93	57
1982-83	New York Islanders	NHL	76	31	40	71	55
1983-84	New York Islanders	NHL	73	27	40	67	66
1984-85	New York Islanders (b)	NHL	80	42	58	100	95
1985-86	New York Islanders (f)	NHL	65	20	41	61	50

Year	Team	League	Games	G.	A.	Pts.	Pen.
1979-80—Djurgardens		Sweden	10	0	1	1	8
1980-81—Djurgardens (c)		Sweden	28	2	4	6	38
1981-82—Djurgardens		Sweden	34	5	3	8	53
1982-83—Djurgardens		Sweden	30	3	14	17	50
1983-84—Djurgardens		Sweden	27	6	8	14	51
1984-85—Djurgardens		Sweden	33	8	13	21	54
1985-86—Boston Bruins		NHL	60	6	20	26	48
1986-87—Boston Bruins		NHL	34	5	15	20	18
1987-88—Boston Bruins		NHL	67	6	25	31	57
1988-89—Boston Bruins		NHL	40	3	18	21	71
1989-90—Boston Bruins		NHL	6	0	2	2	23
NHL TOTALS			207	20	80	100	217

(c)—June, 1980—Drafted by Boston Bruins in 1980 NHL entry draft. Eighth Bruins pick, 186th overall, ninth round.

GILLES THIBAUDEAU

Center . . . 5'10'' . . . 165 lbs. . . . Born, Montreal, Que., March 4, 1963 . . . Shoots left . . . (September, 1984)—Quit his job as a forklift driver to try out for the Montreal Canadiens . . . (April, 1987)—Injured shoulder . . . (October, 1988)—Sprained left ankle . . . (March 8, 1990)—Tore ligaments in left knee at Hartford.

Year	Team	League	Games	G.	A.	Pts.	Pen.
1984-85—Flint Generals (b-c)		IHL	71	52	45	97	91
1984-85—Sherbrooke Canadiens		AHL	7	2	4	6	2
1985-86—Sherbrooke Canadiens (d)		AHL	61	15	21	36	20
1986-87—Sherbrooke Canadiens		AHL	62	27	40	67	26
1986-87—Montreal Canadiens		NHL	9	1	3	4	0
1987-88—Montreal Canadiens		NHL	17	5	6	11	0
1987-88—Sherbrooke Canadiens		AHL	59	39	57	96	45
1988-89—Montreal Canadiens		NHL	32	6	6	12	6
1989-90—New York Islanders (e-f)		NHL	20	4	4	8	17
1989-90—Springfield Indians		AHL	6	5	8	13	0
1989-90—Newmarket Saints		AHL	10	7	13	20	4
1989-90—Toronto Maple Leafs		NHL	21	7	11	18	13
NHL TOTALS			99	23	30	53	36

(c)—Won Harry F. Longman Memorial Trophy (Rookie-of-the-Year).
(d)—September, 1985—Signed by Montreal Canadiens as a free agent.
(e)—September, 1989—Released by Montreal Canadiens and signed by New York Islanders as a free agent.
(f)—December 20, 1989—Traded with Mike Stevens by New York Islanders to Toronto Maple Leafs for Paul Gagne, Derek Laxdal and Jack Capuano.

JOHN SCOTT THOMAS
(Known by middle name.)

Right Wing . . . 6'2'' . . . 195 lbs. . . . Born, Buffalo, N.Y., January 18, 1970 . . . Shoots right.

Year	Team	League	Games	G.	A.	Pts.	Pen.
1987-88—Nichols H.S.		N.Y. H.S.	16	23	39	62	82
1988-89—Nichols H.S. (c)		N.Y. H.S.	..	38	52	90	..
1989-90—Clarkson University (d)		ECAC	34	19	13	32	95

(c)—June, 1989—Drafted by Buffalo Sabres in 1989 NHL entry draft. Second Sabres pick, 56th overall, third round.
(d)—Named to ECAC All-Rookie team.

STEVE THOMAS

Left Wing . . . 5'10'' . . . 180 lbs. . . . Born, Markham, Ont., July 15, 1963 . . . Shoots left . . . (September, 1984)—Broke wrist on second day of training camp . . . Also plays Right Wing . . . (October, 1987)—Pulled stomach muscle . . . (February 20, 1988)—Separated left shoulder at Detroit and required surgery in May . . . (October 18, 1988)—Pulled back muscle at Detroit . . . (December 21, 1988)—Separated right shoulder in fight with Scott Stevens vs. Washington . . . (January 25, 1989)—Surgery to repair chronic shoulder separation problem.

Year	Team	League	Games	G.	A.	Pts.	Pen.
1981-82—Markham Tier-II		OHA	48	68	57	125	113
1982-83—Toronto Marlboros		OHL	61	18	20	38	42
1983-84—Toronto Marlboros		OHL	70	51	54	105	77
1984-85—Toronto Maple Leafs (c)		NHL	18	1	1	2	2
1984-85—St. Catharines Saints (a-d)		AHL	64	42	48	90	56
1985-86—St. Catharines Saints		AHL	19	18	14	32	35
1985-86—Toronto Maple Leafs		NHL	65	20	37	57	36
1986-87—Toronto Maple Leafs (e)		NHL	78	35	27	62	114
1987-88—Chicago Black Hawks		NHL	30	13	13	26	40
1988-89—Chicago Black Hawks		NHL	45	21	19	40	69
1989-90—Chicago Black Hawks		NHL	76	40	30	70	91
NHL TOTALS			312	130	127	257	352

(c)—June, 1984—Signed by Toronto Maple Leafs as a free agent.
(d)—Won Dudley Red Garrett Memorial Trophy (Top Rookie).
(e)—September, 1987—Traded with Rick Vaive and Bob McGill by Toronto Maple Leafs to Chicago Black Hawks for Al Secord and Ed Olczyk.

DAVE THOMLINSON

Left Wing . . . 6'1'' . . . 185 lbs. . . . Born, Edmonton, Alta., October 22, 1966 . . . Shoots left . . . (November, 1983)—Separated shoulder . . . (November, 1984)—Separated shoulder . . . (February, 1990)—Bruised foot when struck by a shot.

Year	Team	League	Games	G.	A.	Pts.	Pen.
1983-84—Brandon Wheat Kings		WHL	41	17	12	29	62
1984-85—Brandon Wheat Kings (c)		WHL	26	13	14	27	70
1985-86—Brandon Wheat Kings		WHL	53	25	20	45	116
1986-87—Moose Jaw Warriors (d)		WHL	71	44	37	81	126
1987-88—Peoria Rivermen		IHL	74	27	30	57	56
1988-89—Peoria Rivermen		IHL	64	27	29	56	154
1989-90—St. Louis Blues		NHL	19	1	2	3	12
1989-90—Peoria Rivermen		IHL	59	27	40	67	87
NHL TOTALS			19	1	2	3	12

(c)—June, 1985—Drafted as underage junior by Toronto Maple Leafs in the 1985 NHL entry draft. Third Maple Leafs pick, 43rd overall, third round.
(d)—July, 1987—Signed by St. Louis Blues as a free agent.

BRENT THOMPSON

Defense . . . 6'2'' . . . 175 lbs. . . . Born, Calgary, Alta., January 9, 1971 . . . Shoots left . . . (September, 1987)—Stretched knee ligaments and separated shoulder.

Year	Team	League	Games	G.	A.	Pts.	Pen.
1987-88—Calgary North Stars		Alta. Midg.	25	0	13	13	33
1988-89—Medicine Hat Tigers (c)		WHL	72	3	10	13	160
1989-90—Medicine Hat Tigers		WHL	68	10	35	45	167

(c)—June, 1989—Drafted by Los Angeles Kings in 1989 NHL entry draft. First Kings pick, 39th overall, second round.

JIM THOMSON

Right Wing . . . 6'2'' . . . 205 lbs. . . . Born, Edmonton, Alta., December 30, 1965 . . . Shoots right.

Year	Team	League	Games	G.	A.	Pts.	Pen.
1982-83—Markham Waxers		OJHL	35	6	7	13	81
1983-84—Toronto Marlboros (c)		OHL	60	10	18	28	68
1984-85—Toronto Marlboros		OHL	63	23	28	51	122
1984-85—Binghamton Whalers		AHL	4	0	0	0	2
1985-86—Binghamton Whalers		AHL	59	15	9	24	195
1986-87—Binghamton Whalers		AHL	57	13	10	23	*360
1986-87—Washington Capitals		NHL	10	0	0	0	35
1987-88—Binghamton Whalers		AHL	25	8	9	17	64
1988-89—Baltimore Skipjacks		AHL	41	25	16	41	129
1988-89—Washington Capitals (d)		NHL	14	2	0	2	53
1988-89—Hartford Whalers		NHL	5	0	0	0	14
1989-90—Binghamton Whalers (e)		AHL	8	1	2	3	30
1989-90—Utica Devils		AHL	60	20	23	43	124
1989-90—New Jersey Devils (f)		NHL	3	0	0	0	31
NHL TOTALS			32	2	0	2	133

(c)—June, 1984—Drafted as underage junior by Washington Capitals in 1984 NHL entry draft. Eighth Capitals pick, 185th overall, ninth round.
(d)—March 6, 1989—Traded by Washington Capitals to Hartford Whalers for Scot Kleinendorst.
(e)—October 31, 1989—Traded by Hartford Whalers to New Jersey Devils for Chris Cichocki.
(f)—July 11, 1990—Signed contract with Los Angeles Kings as a free agent.

SCOTT C. THORNTON

Center . . . 6'2'' . . . 200 lbs. . . . Born, London, Ont., January 9, 1971 . . . Shoots left . . . (February 7, 1990)—Given 12 game OHL suspension for refusing to leave the ice following a penalty.

Year	Team	League	Games	G.	A.	Pts.	Pen.
1986-87—London Diamonds		OPJHL	31	10	7	17	10
1987-88—Belleville Bulls		OHL	62	11	19	30	54
1988-89—Belleville Bulls (c)		OHL	59	28	34	62	103
1989-90—Belleville Bulls		OHL	47	21	28	49	91

(c)—June, 1989—Drafted by Toronto Maple Leafs in 1989 NHL entry draft. First Maple Leafs pick, third overall, first round.

MARIO THYER

Center . . . 5'11'' . . . 170 lbs. . . . Born, Montreal, Que., September 29, 1966 . . . Shoots left . . . (November, 1988)—Broke leg.

Year	Team	League	Games	G.	A.	Pts.	Pen.
1986-87—St. Laurent College		QCAAA	....	..	....	....	....
1987-88—Univ. of Maine		H. East	44	24	42	66	4
1988-89—Univ. of Maine (c)		H. East	9	9	7	16	0
1989-90—Minnesota North Stars		NHL	5	0	0	0	0
1989-90—Kalamazoo Wings		IHL	68	19	42	61	12
NHL TOTALS			5	0	0	0	0

(c)—July 12, 1989—Signed by Minnesota North Stars as a free agent.

ESA TIKKANEN

Left Wing . . . 6' . . . 200 lbs. . . . Born, Helsinki, Finland, January 25, 1965 . . . Shoots left . . . (December 10, 1985)—Broke foot at St. Louis . . . (December 9, 1986)—Cut on elbow developed into bursitis that required surgery . . . (January, 1989)—Fractured left wrist . . . (October 28, 1989)—Injured right knee at Quebec.

Year	Team	League	Games	G.	A.	Pts.	Pen.
1981-82—Regina Pats		WHL	2	0	0	0	0
1982-83—Helsinki Jr. IFK		Finland	30	34	31	65	104
1983-84—Helsinki Jr. IFK		Finland	6	5	9	14	13
1983-84—Helsinki IFK		Finland	36	19	11	30	30
1984-85—Helsinki IFK (c)		Finland	36	21	33	54	42
1984-85—Edmonton Oilers (d)		NHL	...	...	...	...	...
1985-86—Nova Scotia Oilers		AHL	15	4	8	12	17
1985-86—Edmonton Oilers		NHL	35	7	6	13	28
1986-87—Edmonton Oilers		NHL	76	34	44	78	120
1987-88—Edmonton Oilers		NHL	80	23	51	74	153
1988-89—Edmonton Oilers		NHL	67	31	47	78	92
1989-90—Edmonton Oilers		NHL	79	30	33	63	161
NHL TOTALS			337	125	181	306	554

(c)—August, 1983—Drafted by Edmonton Oilers in 1983 NHL entry draft. Fourth Oilers pick, 82nd overall, fourth round.
(d)—No regular season record. Played three playoff games.

Year	Team	League	Games	G.	A.	Pts.	Pen.
1985-86—Calgary Flames		NHL	9	3	4	7	10
1986-87—Calgary Flames		NHL	78	20	31	51	72
1987-88—Calgary Flames (g)		NHL	74	17	41	58	84
1988-89—Los Angeles Kings		NHL	77	31	33	64	110
1989-90—Los Angeles Kings		NHL	73	31	37	68	62
WHA TOTALS			224	64	86	150	278
NHL TOTALS			905	308	484	792	811

(c)—March, 1975—Signed by Houston Aeros (WHA).

(d)—Drafted from Houston Aeros by New York Islanders in second round of 1977 amateur draft.

(e)—July, 1978—Signed to multi year contract by New York Islanders.

(f)—March, 1986—Traded by New York Islanders to Calgary Flames for Richard Kromm and Steve Konroyd.

(g)—July, 1988—Signed by Los Angeles Kings as a free agent.

TIMOTHY RAYMOND TOOKEY

Center . . . 5'11" . . . 180 lbs. . . . Born, Edmonton, Alta., August 29, 1960 . . . Shoots left . . . (December 30, 1981)—Sprained left ankle at Pittsburgh . . . (February, 1983)—Concussion . . . (April, 1983)—Injured shoulder during AHL playoffs . . . (December, 1987)—Knee surgery . . . (October, 1989)—Knee surgery.

Year	Team	League	Games	G.	A.	Pts.	Pen.
1977-78—Portland Winter Hawks		WCHL	72	16	15	31	55
1978-79—Portland Winter Hawks (c)		WHL	56	33	47	80	55
1979-80—Portland Winter Hawks		WHL	70	58	83	141	55
1980-81—Hershey Bears		AHL	47	20	38	58	129
1980-81—Washington Capitals		NHL	29	10	13	23	18
1981-82—Washington Capitals (d)		NHL	28	8	8	16	35
1981-82—Hershey Bears		AHL	14	4	9	13	10
1981-82—Fredericton Express		AHL	16	6	10	16	16
1982-83—Quebec Nordiques		NHL	12	1	6	7	4
1982-83—Fredericton Express		AHL	53	24	43	67	24
1983-84—Pittsburgh Penguins (e)		NHL	8	0	2	2	2
1983-84—Baltimore Skipjacks		AHL	58	16	28	44	25
1984-85—Baltimore Skipjacks (f)		AHL	74	25	43	68	74
1985-86—Hershey Bears (a-g-h)		AHL	69	35	*62	97	66
1986-87—Hershey Bears (a-i-j)		AHL	80	51	*73	*124	45
1986-87—Philadelphia Flyers		NHL	2	0	0	0	0
1987-88—Los Angeles Kings (k)		NHL	20	1	6	7	8
1987-88—New Haven Nighthawks		AHL	11	6	7	13	2
1988-89—Muskegon Lumberjacks		IHL	18	7	14	21	7
1988-89—New Haven Nighthawks (l-m)		AHL	33	11	18	29	30
1988-89—Los Angeles Kings		NHL	7	2	1	3	4
1989-90—Hershey Bears		AHL	42	18	22	40	28
NHL TOTALS			106	22	36	58	71

(c)—August, 1979—Drafted by Washington Capitals as underage junior in 1979 NHL entry draft. Fourth Capitals pick, 88th overall, fifth round.

(d)—January, 1982—Traded by Washington Capitals to Quebec Nordiques for Lee Norwood.

(e)—August, 1983—Signed by Pittsburgh Penguins as a free agent.

(f)—August, 1985—Signed by Philadelphia Flyers as a free agent.

(g)—Led AHL Calder Cup Playoffs with 11 goals.

(h)—Won Jack Butterfield Trophy (Playoff MVP).

(i)—Winner of Les Cunningham Award (MVP).

(j)—Won John Sollenberger Trophy (Leading Scorer).

(k)—October, 1987—Selected by Los Angeles Kings in 1987 NHL waiver draft. The Kings put him on recallable waivers in an attempt to assign him to New Haven. Philadelphia claimed him. The Kings then recalled him from the waiver wire and assigned him to New Haven.

(l)—March 7, 1989—Traded by Los Angeles Kings to Pittsburgh Penguins for Patrick Mayer.

(m)—July 12, 1989—Signed by Philadelphia Flyers as a free agent.

JARI TORKKI

Left Wing . . . 5'11" . . . 167 lbs. . . . Born, Rauma, Finland, August 11, 1965 . . . Shoots left . . . Also plays Right Wing.

Year	Team	League	Games	G.	A.	Pts.	Pen.
1981-82—Lukko		Finland	8	15	10	25	8
1982-83—Lukko (c)		Finland	34	13	17	30	34
1983-84—Lukko		Finland	36	41	25	66	70
1984-85—Lukko		Finland	36	26	20	46	40
1984-85—Finland National Team		Int'l	7	5	4	9	8
1985-86—Finland National Team		Int'l	..	..	..	..	..
1986-87—Lukko		Finland	44	27	8	35	42
1987-88—Lukko		Finland	43	23	24	47	54
1988-89—Chicago Black Hawks		NHL	4	1	0	1	0
1988-89—Saginaw Hawks		IHL	72	30	42	72	22
1989-90—Indianapolis Ice		IHL	66	25	29	54	50
NHL TOTALS			4	1	0	1	0

(c)—June, 1983—Drafted by Chicago Black Hawks in 1983 NHL entry draft. Sixth Black Hawks pick, 115th overall, sixth round.

DOUGLAS TORREL

Center . . . 6'2" . . . 180 lbs. . . . Born, Hibbing, Minn., April 29, 1969 . . . Shoots right . . . Brother of Steve Torrel (Hartford Whalers 1986 draft pick) . . . (January, 1987)—Broke hand.

Year	Team	League	Games	G.	A.	Pts.	Pen.
1985-86—Hibbing H.S.		Minn. H.S.	26	13	18	31	....
1986-87—Hibbing H.S. (c)		Minn. H.S.	20	22	21	43	....
1987-88—Hibbing H.S.		Minn. H.S.	20	22	16	38	38
1988-89—Univ. of Minnesota/Duluth		WCHA	40	4	6	10	36
1989-90—Univ. of Minnesota/Duluth		WCHA	39	11	11	22	48

(c)—June, 1987—Drafted by Vancouver Canucks in 1987 NHL entry draft. Third Canucks pick, 66th overall, fourth round.

GRAEME TOWNSHEND

Right Wing . . . 6'2" . . . 225 lbs. . . . Born, Kingston, Jamaica, October 2, 1965 . . . Shoots right . . . Also plays Defense.

Year	Team	League	Games	G.	A.	Pts.	Pen.
1985-86—R.P.I.		ECAC	29	1	7	8	52
1986-87—R.P.I.		ECAC	31	7	1	8	56
1987-88—R.P.I.		ECAC	32	6	14	20	64
1988-89—R.P.I. (c)		ECAC	31	6	16	22	50
1988-89—Maine Mariners		AHL	5	2	1	3	11
1989-90—Boston Bruins		NHL	4	0	0	0	7
1989-90—Maine Mariners		AHL	64	15	13	28	162
NHL TOTALS			4	0	0	0	7

(c)—May 12, 1989—Signed by Boston Bruins as a free agent.

LADISLAV TRESL

Center . . . 6'1" . . . 180 lbs. . . . Born, Brno, Czechoslovakia, July 30, 1961 . . . Shoots left.

Year	Team	League	Games	G.	A.	Pts.	Pen.
1986-87—Zetor Brno (c)		Czech.	33	13	11	24	..
1987-88—Fredericton Express		AHL	30	6	16	22	16
1988-89—Halifax Citadels		AHL	67	24	35	59	28
1989-90—Halifax Citadels		AHL	66	35	39	74	64

(c)—June, 1987—Drafted by Quebec Nordiques in 1987 NHL entry draft. Tenth Nordiques pick, 183rd overall, ninth round.

DAVE TRETOWICZ

Defense . . . 5'11" . . . 186 lbs. . . . Born, Pittsfield, Mass., March 15, 1969 . . . Shoots left . . . Brother of Mark Tretowicz.

Year	Team	League	Games	G.	A.	Pts.	Pen.
1987-88—Clarkson Univ. (c)		ECAC	35	8	14	22	28
1988-89—Clarkson Univ.		ECAC	32	6	17	23	22
1989-90—Clarkson Univ. (b-d)		ECAC	35	2	27	29	12

(c)—June, 1988—Drafted by Calgary Flames in 1988 NHL entry draft. Eleventh Flames pick, 231st overall, 11th round.

(d)—Named to NCAA All-Tournament team.

BRYAN JOHN TROTTIER

Center . . . 5'10" . . . 205 lbs. . . . Born, Val Marie, Sask., July 17, 1956 . . . Shoots left . . . (1975-76)—Set NHL records for most assists and points in rookie season (broken by Peter Stastny, 1980-81) . . . Set Stanley Cup Playoff record with 29 points during 1980 playoffs (broken by Mike Bossy's 35 points in 1981) . . . Set NHL record for consecutive playoff games with points (25) covering more than one season . . . Set NHL record for consecutive playoff games with points one season (18) . . . Brother of Monty and Rocky Trottier . . . (April, 1983)—Sprained left knee vs. N.Y. Rangers . . . (January, 1984)—Injured left knee . . . (July, 1984)—Became U.S. citizen and played with Team USA in 1984 Canada Cup Tournament . . . (October, 1984)—Knee injury . . . (March, 1987)—Fined $1,000 by NHL for being critical of NHL officiating . . . (March, 1989)—Missed seven games with back spasms . . . (September 23, 1989)—Broke little toe on left foot vs. Boston . . . (December 13, 1989)—Broke rib at New Jersey and missed 12 games.

Year	Team	League	Games	G.	A.	Pts.	Pen.
1972-73—Swift Current Broncos		WCHL	67	16	29	45	10
1973-74—Swift Current Broncos (c)		WCHL	68	41	71	112	76
1974-75—Lethbridge Broncos (a)		WCHL	67	46	*98	144	103
1975-76—New York Islanders (d-e)		NHL	80	32	63	95	21
1976-77—New York Islanders		NHL	76	30	42	72	34
1977-78—New York Islanders (a)		NHL	77	46	*77	123	46
1978-79—New York Islanders (a-f-g-h)		NHL	76	47	*87	*134	50
1979-80—New York Islanders (i-j)		NHL	78	42	62	104	68
1980-81—New York Islanders (k)		NHL	73	31	72	103	74
1981-82—New York Islanders (b-l)		NHL	80	50	79	129	88
1982-83—New York Islanders		NHL	80	34	55	89	68
1983-84—New York Islanders (b)		NHL	68	40	71	111	59
1984-85—New York Islanders		NHL	68	28	31	59	47
1985-86—New York Islanders		NHL	78	37	59	96	72
1986-87—New York Islanders		NHL	80	23	64	87	50
1987-88—New York Islanders		NHL	77	30	52	82	48
1988-89—New York Islanders (m)		NHL	73	17	28	45	44
1989-90—New York Islanders (n-o)		NHL	59	13	11	24	29
NHL TOTALS			1123	500	853	1353	798

(c)—Drafted from Swift Current Broncos by New York Islanders in second round of 1974 amateur draft.

(d)—Won Calder Memorial Trophy (NHL Rookie of the Year).

(e)—Selected NHL Rookie of the Year in poll of players by THE SPORTING NEWS.

(f)—Won Hart Memorial Trophy (NHL MVP).

(g)—Won Art Ross Trophy (NHL Top Scorer).

(h)—Named THE SPORTING NEWS NHL Player of the Year in poll of players.

(i)—Led Stanley Cup Playoffs in points (29) and co-leader, with Bill Barber, in goals (12).

(j)—Won Conn Smythe Trophy (NHL Playoff MVP).

(k)—Tied for Stanley Cup Playoffs assist lead (18 assists) with teammate Mike Bossy.

(l)—Led Stanley Cup Playoffs with 23 assists and 29 points.

(m)—Won King Clancy Trophy (Humanitarian Contribution).

(n)—July 3, 1990—Released by New York Islanders.

(o)—July 20, 1990—Signed by Pittsburgh Penguins as a free agent.

CHRIS TUCKER

Center . . . 6'1" . . . 181 lbs. . . . Born, White Plains, N.Y., February 9, 1972 . . . Shoots left.

Year	Team	League	Games	G.	A.	Pts.	Pen.
1988-89—Bloomington Jefferson H.S.		Minn. H.S.	25	41	23	64	....
1989-90—Bloom. Jefferson H.S. (c)		Minn. H.S.	24	24	24	48	....

(c)—June 16, 1990—Selected by Chicago Black Hawks in 1990 NHL entry draft. Third Black Hawks pick, 79th overall, fourth round.

JOHN TUCKER

Center . . . 6' . . . 197 lbs. . . . Born, Windsor, Ont., September 29, 1964 . . . Shoots right . . . (November 7, 1984)—Broke bone in foot at Minnesota . . . (January 28, 1987)—Injured disc in back vs. Philadelphia and required off-season surgery . . . (November 7, 1987)—Torn knee ligaments at Edmonton . . . (December, 1987)—Shoulder injury . . . (February 25, 1988)—Injured shoulder vs. St. Louis . . . (January, 1989)—Missed 16 games with a back injury.

Year	Team	League	Games	G.	A.	Pts.	Pen.
1981-82—Kitchener Rangers		OHL	67	16	32	48	32
1982-83—Kitchener Rangers (c)		OHL	70	60	80	140	33
1983-84—Kitchener Rangers (a-d)		OHL	39	40	60	100	25
1983-84—Buffalo Sabres		NHL	21	12	4	16	4
1984-85—Buffalo Sabres		NHL	64	22	27	49	21
1985-86—Buffalo Sabres		NHL	75	31	34	65	39
1986-87—Buffalo Sabres		NHL	54	17	34	51	21
1987-88—Buffalo Sabres		NHL	45	19	19	38	20
1988-89—Buffalo Sabres		NHL	60	13	31	44	31
1989-90—Buffalo Sabres (e)		NHL	8	1	2	3	2
1989-90—Washington Capitals (f)		NHL	38	9	19	28	10
NHL TOTALS			365	124	170	294	148

(c)—June, 1983—Drafted as underage junior by Buffalo Sabres in 1983 NHL entry draft. Fourth Sabres pick, 31st overall, second round.
(d)—Won Red Tilson Trophy (Most Outstanding player).
(e)—January 4, 1990—Traded by Buffalo Sabres to Washington Capitals for a conditional 1990 draft pick.
(f)—July 3, 1990—Sold by Washington Capitals to Buffalo Sabres.

ALLAN TUER

Defense . . . 6' . . . 190 lbs. . . . Born, North Battleford, Sask., July 19, 1963 . . . Shoots left . . . (March 11, 1989)—Suspended five AHL games for returning from dressing room to enter an on-ice fight vs. Rochester.

Year	Team	League	Games	G.	A.	Pts.	Pen.
1980-81—Regina Pats (c)		WHL	31	0	7	7	58
1981-82—Regina Pats		WHL	63	2	18	20	*486
1982-83—Regina Pats		WHL	71	3	27	30	229
1983-84—New Haven Nighthawks		AHL	78	0	20	20	195
1984-85—New Haven Nighthawks		AHL	56	0	7	7	241
1985-86—New Haven Nighthawks		AHL	8	1	0	1	53
1985-86—Los Angeles Kings (d)		NHL	45	0	1	1	150
1986-87—Nova Scotia Oilers		AHL	31	0	1	1	4
1987-88—Minnesota North Stars		NHL	6	1	0	1	29
1987-88—Kalamazoo Wings (e-f)		IHL	68	2	15	17	303
1988-89—Hartford Whalers		NHL	4	0	0	0	23
1988-89—Binghamton Whalers		AHL	43	1	7	8	234
1989-90—Hartford Whalers		NHL	2	0	0	0	6
1989-90—Binghamton Whalers		AHL	58	3	7	10	176
NHL TOTALS			57	1	1	2	208

(c)—June, 1980—Drafted as underage junior by Los Angeles Kings in 1980 NHL entry draft. Eighth Kings pick, 186th overall, ninth round.
(d)—August, 1986—Signed by Edmonton Oilers as a free agent.
(e)—October, 1987—Selected by Minnesota North Stars in 1987 NHL waiver draft.
(f)—August, 1988—Signed by Hartford Whalers as a free agent.

ALFIE TURCOTTE

Center . . . 5'10" . . . 175 lbs. . . . Born, Gary, Ind., June 5, 1965 . . . Shoots left . . . Son of Real Turcotte (Former Coach and General Manager of Nanaimo Islanders of WHL) . . . (November 5, 1988)—Cut below right eye, scratched cornea and a cut eyelid when struck by Larry Robinson's stick at Montreal.

Year	Team	League	Games	G.	A.	Pts.	Pen.
1981-82—Detroit Compuware		Mich. Midget	93	131	152	283	40
1982-83—Nanaimo Islanders		WHL	36	23	27	50	22
1982-83—Portland Winter Hawks (c)		WHL	39	26	51	77	26
1983-84—Portland Winter Hawks		WHL	32	22	41	63	39
1983-84—Montreal Canadiens		NHL	30	7	7	14	10
1984-85—Montreal Canadiens		NHL	53	8	16	24	35
1985-86—Sherbrooke Canadiens		AHL	75	29	36	65	60
1985-86—Montreal Canadiens (d)		NHL	2	0	0	0	2
1986-87—Nova Scotia Oilers (e)		AHL	70	27	41	68	37
1987-88—Winnipeg Jets (f)		NHL	3	0	0	0	0
1987-88—Baltimore Skipjacks		AHL	33	21	33	54	42
1987-88—Moncton Golden Flames		AHL	25	12	25	37	18
1987-88—Sherbrooke Canadiens		AHL	8	3	8	11	4
1988-89—Winnipeg Jets		NHL	14	1	3	4	2
1988-89—Moncton Hawks		AHL	54	27	39	66	74
1989-90—Baltimore Skipjacks		AHL	65	26	40	66	42
1989-90—Washington Capitals		NHL	4	0	2	2	0
NHL TOTALS			106	16	28	44	49

(c)—June, 1983—Drafted as underage junior by Montreal Canadiens in 1983 NHL entry draft. First Canadiens pick, 17th overall, first round.
(d)—July, 1986—Traded by Montreal Canadiens to Edmonton Oilers for future considerations.
(e)—May, 1987—Sold by Edmonton Oilers to Montreal Canadiens.
(f)—January, 1988—Traded by Montreal Canadiens to Winnipeg Jets for future considerations.

DARREN TURCOTTE

Center . . . 6' . . . 170 lbs. . . . Born, Boston, Mass., March 2, 1968 . . . Shoots left . . . (October, 1987)—Missed 34 games due to shoulder separation . . . (March, 1989)—Concussion . . . (October, 1989)—Sprained left ankle . . . (April 11, 1990)—Injured knee when checked by Randy Wood vs. N.Y. Rangers . . . (April 27, 1990)—Broke left foot when hit by a Kevin Hatcher shot vs. Washington.

Year	Team	League	Games	G.	A.	Pts.	Pen.
1984-85—North Bay Centennials		OHL	62	33	32	65	28
1985-86—North Bay Centennials (c)		OHL	62	35	37	72	35
1986-87—North Bay Centennials		OHL	55	30	48	78	20
1987-88—Colorado Rangers		IHL	8	4	3	7	9
1987-88—North Bay Centennials		OHL	32	30	33	63	16
1988-89—Denver Rangers		IHL	40	21	28	49	32
1988-89—New York Rangers		NHL	20	7	3	10	4
1989-90—New York Rangers		NHL	76	32	34	66	32
NHL TOTALS			96	39	37	76	36

(c)—June, 1986—Drafted as underage junior by New York Rangers in 1986 NHL entry draft. Sixth Rangers pick, 114th overall, sixth round.

PIERRE TURGEON

Center . . . 6'1" . . . 200 lbs. . . . Born, Noranda, Que., August 29, 1969 . . . Shoots left . . . Brother of Sylvain Turgeon . . . (June, 1985)—Knee surgery.

Year	Team	League	Games	G.	A.	Pts.	Pen.
1985-86—Granby Bisons		QMJHL	69	47	67	114	31
1986-87—Granby Bisons (c)		QMJHL	58	69	85	154	8
1987-88—Buffalo Sabres		NHL	76	14	28	42	34
1988-89—Buffalo Sabres		NHL	80	34	54	88	26
1989-90—Buffalo Sabres		NHL	80	40	66	106	29
NHL TOTALS			236	88	148	236	89

(c)—June, 1987—Drafted as underage junior by Buffalo Sabres in 1987 NHL entry draft. First Sabres pick, first overall, first round.

SYLVAIN TURGEON

Left Wing . . . 6' . . . 190 lbs. . . . Born, Noranda, Que., January 17, 1965 . . . Shoots left . . . Also plays center . . . Set Hartford club record for goals and points by an NHL rookie in 1983-84 . . . (October, 1984)—Pulled abdominal muscles . . . Brother of Pierre Turgeon . . . (November 14, 1986)—Abdominal surgery to repair torn stomach muscle and missed 39 games . . . (August 11, 1987)—Broken left arm when slashed by Ron Hextall during a Team Canada practice . . . (September, 1988)—Sprained right knee during Hartford Whalers training camp . . . (December 21, 1988)—Missed 36 games after separating his left shoulder vs. Boston . . . (February 28, 1989)—Burned both eyes from ultra-violet light produced by welder's torch while working on his car . . . (March 20, 1990)—Aggravated a groin injury vs. Philadelphia.

Year	Team	League	Games	G.	A.	Pts.	Pen.
1981-82—Hull Olympics (c)		QMJHL	57	33	40	73	78
1982-83—Hull Olympics (a-d-e)		QMJHL	67	54	109	163	103
1983-84—Hartford Whalers		NHL	76	40	32	72	55
1984-85—Hartford Whalers		NHL	64	31	31	62	67
1985-86—Hartford Whalers		NHL	76	45	34	79	88
1986-87—Hartford Whalers		NHL	41	23	13	36	45
1987-88—Hartford Whalers		NHL	71	23	26	49	71
1988-89—Hartford Whalers (f)		NHL	42	16	14	30	40
1989-90—New Jersey Devils (g)		NHL	72	30	17	47	81
NHL TOTALS			442	208	167	375	447

(c)—Won Des Instructeurs Trophy (Top Rookie Forward).
(d)—Won The Association of Journalist of Hockey Trophy (Top Pro Prospect).
(e)—June, 1983—Drafted as underage junior by Hartford Whalers in 1983 NHL entry draft. First Whalers pick, second overall, first round.
(f)—June 17, 1989—Traded by Hartford Whalers to New Jersey Devils for Pat Verbeek.
(g)—September 4, 1990—Traded by New Jersey Devils to Montreal Canadiens for Claude Lemieux.

BRAD TURNER

Defense . . . 6'2" . . . 200 lbs. . . . Born, Winnipeg, Man., May 25, 1968 . . . Shoots right.

Year	Team	League	Games	G.	A.	Pts.	Pen.
1984-85—Darien H.S.		Conn.	24	32	34	66	....
1985-86—Calgary Canucks (c)		AJHL	52	14	21	35	109
1986-87—Univ. of Michigan		CCHA	40	3	10	13	40
1987-88—Univ. of Michigan		CCHA	39	3	11	14	52
1988-89—Univ. of Michigan		CCHA	33	3	8	11	38
1989-90—Univ. of Michigan		CCHA	32	8	9	17	34

(c)—June, 1986—Drafted by Minnesota North Stars in 1986 NHL entry draft. Sixth North Stars pick, 58th overall, third round.

BRIAN TUTT

Defense . . . 6'1" . . . 195 lbs. . . . Born, Swallwell, Alta., June 9, 1962 . . . Shoots left . . . (September, 1981)—Broke leg while attending Philadelphia Flyers training camp.

Year	Team	League	Games	G.	A.	Pts.	Pen.
1979-80—Calgary Canucks		AJHL	59	6	14	20	55
1979-80—Calgary Wranglers (c)		WHL	2	0	0	0	2
1980-81—Calgary Wranglers		WHL	72	10	41	51	111
1981-82—Calgary Wranglers		WHL	40	2	16	18	85
1982-83—Toledo Goaldiggers		IHL	42	7	13	20	56
1982-83—Maine Mariners		AHL	31	0	0	0	28
1983-84—Toledo Goaldiggers (b)		IHL	82	7	44	51	79
1983-84—Springfield Indians		AHL	1	0	0	0	2
1984-85—Hershey Bears		AHL	3	0	0	0	4
1984-85—Kalamazoo Wings (b)		IHL	80	8	45	53	62
1985-86—Kalamazoo Wings		IHL	82	11	39	50	129
1986-87—Maine Mariners		AHL	41	6	15	21	19
1986-87—Kalamazoo Wings		IHL	19	2	7	9	10
1987-88—New Haven Nighthawks		AHL	32	1	12	13	33
1988-89—Canadian National Team		Int'l.	63	0	19	19	87
1988-89—Baltimore Skipjacks (d)		AHL	6	1	5	6	6
1989-90—Baltimore Skipjacks		AHL	67	2	13	15	80
1989-90—Washington Capitals		NHL	7	1	0	1	2
NHL TOTALS			7	1	0	1	2

(c)—June, 1980—Drafted as underage junior by Philadelphia Flyers in 1980 NHL entry draft. Sixth Flyers pick, 126th overall, sixth round.
(d)—February 21, 1989—Signed AHL contract with Washington Capitals as a free agent.

STEVE TUTTLE

Right Wing . . . 6'1" . . . 180 lbs. . . . Born, Vancouver, B.C., January 5, 1966 . . . Shoots right . . . (December, 1988)—Missed 15 games with sprained left knee . . . (February, 1989)—Sprained shoulder.

Year	Team	League	Games	G.	A.	Pts.	Pen.
1983-84—Richmond (c)	BCJHL	46	46	34	80	22
1984-85—Univ. of Wisconsin	WCHA	28	3	4	7	0
1985-86—Univ. of Wisconsin	WCHA	32	2	10	12	2
1986-87—Univ. of Wisconsin	WCHA	42	31	21	52	14
1987-88—Univ. of Wisconsin (d)	WCHA	45	27	39	66	18
1988-89—St. Louis Blues	NHL	53	13	12	25	6
1989-90—St. Louis Blues	NHL	71	12	10	22	4
NHL TOTALS		124	25	22	47	10

(c)—June, 1984—Drafted by St. Louis Blues in 1984 NHL entry draft. Eighth Blues pick, 113th overall, sixth round.
(d)—Named Second team All-America (West).

TONY TWIST

Defense . . . 6' . . . 210 lbs. . . . Born, Sherwood Park, Alta., May 9, 1968 . . . Shoots left . . . (January 28, 1988)—Suspended three WHL games and fined $250 for leaving the penalty box to fight.

Year	Team	League	Games	G.	A.	Pts.	Pen.
1986-87—Saskatoon Blades	WHL	64	0	8	8	181
1987-88—Saskatoon Blades (c)	WHL	55	1	8	9	226
1988-89—Peoria Rivermen	IHL	67	3	8	11	312
1989-90—St. Louis Blues	NHL	28	0	0	0	124
1989-90—Peoria Rivermen	IHL	36	1	5	6	200
NHL TOTALS		28	0	0	0	124

(c)—June, 1988—Drafted by St. Louis Blues in 1988 NHL entry draft. Ninth Blues pick, 177th overall, ninth round.

RICK VAIVE

Right Wing . . . 6' . . . 180 lbs. . . . Born, Ottawa, Ont., May 14, 1959 . . . Shoots right . . . (February, 1981)—Slight groin pull . . . First Toronto Maple Leafs player to have a 50-goal season when he set a club record with 54 goals in 1981-82 . . . (February 25, 1984)—Injured ankle at Edmonton . . . (December, 1984)—Knee injury . . . (December 23, 1985)—Injured hand and missed 12 games . . . (October, 1986)—Pinched nerve in neck . . . (January 27, 1989)—Injured stomach muscle when speared by Chris Chelios and Steve Martinson vs. Montreal . . . (February 19, 1989)—Pinched nerve in neck vs. Detroit . . . (November 22, 1989)—Pulled groin vs. N.Y. Rangers.

Year	Team	League	Games	G.	A.	Pts.	Pen.
1976-77—Sherbrooke Beavers (c)	QMJHL	68	51	59	110	91
1977-78—Sherbrooke Beavers (d)	QMJHL	68	76	79	155	199
1978-79—Birmingham Bulls (e)	WHA	75	26	33	59	*248
1979-80—Vancouver Canucks (f)	NHL	47	13	8	21	111
1979-80—Toronto Maple Leafs	NHL	22	9	7	16	77
1980-81—Toronto Maple Leafs	NHL	75	33	29	62	229
1981-82—Toronto Maple Leafs	NHL	77	54	35	89	157
1982-83—Toronto Maple Leafs	NHL	78	51	28	79	105
1983-84—Toronto Maple Leafs	NHL	76	52	41	93	114
1984-85—Toronto Maple Leafs	NHL	72	35	33	68	112
1985-86—Toronto Maple Leafs	NHL	61	33	31	64	85
1986-87—Toronto Maple Leafs (g)	NHL	73	32	34	66	61
1987-88—Chicago Black Hawks	NHL	76	43	26	69	108
1988-89—Chicago Black Hawks (h)	NHL	30	12	13	25	60
1988-89—Buffalo Sabres	NHL	28	19	13	32	64
1989-90—Buffalo Sabres	NHL	70	29	19	48	74
WHA TOTALS		75	26	33	59	248
NHL TOTALS		785	415	317	732	1357

(c)—Won Rookie of the Year Award.
(d)—July, 1978—Signed by Birmingham Bulls (WHA) as underage junior.
(e)—June, 1979—Drafted by Vancouver Canucks in 1979 NHL entry draft. First Vancouver pick, fifth overall, first round.
(f)—February, 1980—Traded with Bill Derlago by Vancouver Canucks to Toronto Maple Leafs for Dave Williams and Jerry Butler.
(g)—September, 1987—Traded with Steve Thomas and Bob McGill by Toronto Maple Leafs to Chicago Black Hawks for Al Secord and Ed Olczyk.
(h)—December 26, 1988—Traded by Chicago Black Hawks to Buffalo Sabres for Adam Creighton.

CARL VALIMONT

Defense . . . 6'1" . . . 180 lbs. . . . Born, Southington, Conn., March 1, 1966 . . . Shoots left.

Year	Team	League	Games	G.	A.	Pts.	Pen.
1984-85—University of Lowell (c)	H. East	40	4	11	15	24
1985-86—University of Lowell	H. East	26	1	9	10	12
1986-87—University of Lowell	H. East	36	8	9	17	36
1987-88—University of Lowell	H. East	38	6	26	32	59
1988-89—Milwaukee Admirals	IHL	79	4	33	37	56
1989-90—Milwaukee Admirals	IHL	78	13	28	41	48

(c)—June, 1985—Drafted by Vancouver Canucks in 1985 NHL entry draft. Tenth Canucks pick, 193rd overall, 10th round.

GARRY VALK

Left Wing . . . 6'1" . . . 190 lbs. . . . Born, Edmonton, Alta., November 27, 1967 . . . Shoots left . . . Also plays Right Wing.

Year	Team	League	Games	G.	A.	Pts.	Pen.
1985-86—Sherwood Park Crusaders	AJHL	40	20	26	46	116
1986-87—Sherwood Park Crusaders (c)	AJHL	59	42	44	86	204

Year	Team	League	Games	G.	A.	Pts.	Pen.
1987-88—Univ. of North Dakota	WCHA	38	23	12	35	64
1988-89—Univ. of North Dakota	WCHA	40	14	17	31	71
1989-90—Univ. of North Dakota	WCHA	43	22	17	39	92

(c)—June, 1987—Drafted by Vancouver Canucks in 1987 NHL entry draft. Fifth Canucks pick, 108th overall, sixth round.

LINDSAY VALLIS

Right Wing . . . 6'2" . . . 205 lbs. . . . Born, Winnipeg, Man., January 12, 1971 . . . Shoots right.

Year	Team	League	Games	G.	A.	Pts.	Pen.
1987-88—Seattle Thunderbirds	WHL	68	31	45	76	65
1988-89—Seattle Thunderbirds (c)	WHL	63	21	32	53	48
1989-90—Seattle Thunderbirds	WHL	65	34	43	77	68

(c)—June, 1989—Drafted by Montreal Canadiens in 1989 NHL entry draft. First Canadiens pick, 13th overall, first round.

SHAUN VAN ALLEN

Center . . . 6'1" . . . 200 lbs. . . . Born, Shaunavon, Sask., August 29, 1967 . . . Shoots left.

Year	Team	League	Games	G.	A.	Pts.	Pen.
1984-85—Swift Current	SAJHL	61	12	20	32	136
1985-86—Saskatoon Blades	WHL	55	12	11	23	43
1986-87—Saskatoon Blades (c)	WHL	72	38	59	97	116
1987-88—Nova Scotia Oilers	AHL	19	4	10	14	17
1987-88—Milwaukee Admirals	IHL	40	14	28	42	34
1988-89—Cape Breton Oilers	AHL	76	32	42	74	81
1989-90—Cape Breton Oilers	AHL	61	25	44	69	83

(c)—June, 1987—Drafted by Edmonton Oilers in 1987 NHL entry draft. Fifth Oilers pick, 105th overall, fifth round.

WAYNE VAN DORP

Right Wing . . . 6'5" . . . 230 lbs. . . . Born, Vancouver, B.C., May 19, 1961 . . . Shoots right . . . (February, 1988)—Injured right knee in collision with Bryan Erickson during a team practice . . . (December 2, 1988)—Suspended two AHL games . . . (December 28, 1989)—Suspended 10 games for fighting vs. Minnesota and fined $500.

Year	Team	League	Games	G.	A.	Pts.	Pen.
1978-79—Billington	BCJHL	61	18	30	48	66
1979-80—Seattle Breakers	WHL	68	8	13	21	195
1980-81—Seattle Breakers	WHL	63	22	30	52	242
1981-82—..................	......	....	....	....	....	....
1982-83—..................	......	....	....	....	....	....
1983-84—Erie Blades	ACHL	45	19	18	37	131
1984-85—Erie Blades	ACHL	7	9	8	17	21
1985-86—..................	Holland	29	27	32	59	69
1986-87—Rochester Americans (c)	AHL	47	7	3	10	192
1986-87—Nova Scotia Oilers	AHL	11	2	3	5	37
1986-87—Edmonton Oilers	NHL	3	0	0	0	25
1987-88—Pittsburgh Penguins (d)	NHL	25	1	3	4	75
1987-88—Nova Scotia Oilers	AHL	12	2	2	4	87
1988-89—Rochester Americans (e-f)	AHL	28	3	6	9	202
1988-89—Chicago Black Hawks	NHL	8	0	0	0	23
1988-89—Saginaw Hawks	IHL	11	4	3	7	60
1989-90—Chicago Black Hawks	NHL	61	7	4	11	303
NHL TOTALS		97	8	7	15	426

(c)—March, 1987—Traded with Norm Lacombe and future considerations by Buffalo Sabres to Edmonton Oilers for Lee Fogolin and Mark Napier.
(d)—November, 1987—Traded with Paul Coffey and Dave Hunter by Edmonton Oilers to Pittsburgh Penguins for Chris Joseph, Craig Simpson, Dave Hannan and Moe Mantha.
(e)—October 3, 1988—Traded by Pittsburgh Penguins to Buffalo Sabres for future considerations.
(f)—February 16, 1989—Traded by Buffalo Sabres to Chicago Black Hawks for future considerations.

JOHN VanKESSEL

Right Wing . . . 6'4" . . . 180 lbs. . . . Born, Bridgewater, Ont., December 19, 1969 . . . Shoots right.

Year	Team	League	Games	G.	A.	Pts.	Pen.
1985-86—Antigosh Midget	N. Scotia	83	52	65	117	40
1986-87—Belleville Bulls	OHL	61	1	10	11	58
1987-88—North Bay Centennials (c)	OHL	50	13	16	29	214
1988-89—North Bay Centennials	OHL	50	7	13	20	218
1989-90—North Bay Centennials	OHL	40	7	21	28	127
1989-90—New Haven Nighthawks	AHL	6	1	1	2	9

(c)—June, 1988—Drafted by Los Angeles Kings in 1988 NHL entry draft. Third Kings pick, 49th overall, third round.

ERNESTO VARGAS

Center . . . 6'2" . . . 205 lbs. . . . Born, St. Paul, Minn., January 3, 1964 . . . Shoots left . . . Also plays Left Wing . . . (December 13, 1987)—Injured ankle in AHL game at Baltimore . . . (December 28, 1988)—Fined $100 and suspended three games for fighting vs. Kalamazoo.

Year	Team	League	Games	G.	A.	Pts.	Pen.
1981-82—Coon Rapids H.S. (c)	Minn. H.S.	24	28	28	56	22
1982-83—University of Wisconsin	WCHA	37	2	4	6	32
1983-84—University of Wisconsin	WCHA	36	5	15	20	32
1984-85—University of Wisconsin	WCHA	42	8	16	24	68
1985-86—University of Wisconsin	WCHA	41	20	23	43	67
1986-87—Sherbrooke Canadiens	AHL	69	22	32	54	52
1987-88—Baltimore Skipjacks	AHL	5	1	0	1	2
1987-88—Sherbrooke Canadiens	AHL	31	6	21	27	48

Year	Team	League	Games	G.	A.	Pts.	Pen.
1987-88—Peoria Rivermen (d)		IHL	31	9	13	22	26
1988-89—Milwaukee Admirals (e)		IHL	61	16	35	51	89
1989-90—Milwaukee Admirals		IHL	63	15	15	30	79

(c)—June, 1982—Drafted as underage player by Montreal Canadiens in 1982 NHL entry draft. Ninth Canadiens pick, 117th overall, sixth round.

(d)—February, 1988—Traded by Montreal Canadiens to St. Louis Blues for a conditional 1989 draft pick.

(e)—September 29, 1988—Traded by St. Louis Blues to Vancouver Canucks for Dave Lowry.

JOHN VARY

Defense . . . 6'1" . . . 207 lbs. . . . Born, Owen Sound, Ont., February 11, 1972 . . . Shoots right . . . (1988-89)—Injured knee.

Year	Team	League	Games	G.	A.	Pts.	Pen.
1987-88—Owen Sound Jr. B		OHA	43	16	25	41	171
1988-89—North Bay Centennials		OHL	45	2	7	9	38
1989-90—North Bay Centennials (c)		OHL	59	7	39	46	79

(c)—June 16, 1990—Selected by New York Rangers in 1990 NHL entry draft. Third Rangers pick, 55th overall, third round.

DENNIS VASKE

Defense . . . 6'2" . . . 210 lbs. . . . Born, Rockford, Ill., October 11, 1967 . . . Shoots left.

Year	Team	League	Games	G.	A.	Pts.	Pen.
1984-85—Armstrong H.S.		Minn. H.S.	22	5	18	23	..
1985-86—Armstrong H.S. (c)		Minn. H.S.	20	9	13	22	..
1986-87—Univ. of Minn./Duluth		WCHA	33	0	2	2	40
1987-88—Univ. of Minn./Duluth		WCHA	39	1	6	7	90
1988-89—Univ. of Minn./Duluth		WCHA	37	9	19	28	86
1989-90—Univ. of Minn./Duluth		WCHA	37	5	24	29	72

(c)—June, 1986—Drafted by New York Islanders in 1986 NHL entry draft. Second Islanders pick, 38th overall, second round.

STEVE VEILLEUX

Defense . . . 6' . . . 190 lbs. . . . Born, Montreal, Que., March 9, 1969 . . . Shoots right . . . Cousin of Corrado Micalef.

Year	Team	League	Games	G.	A.	Pts.	Pen.
1985-86—Trois-Rivieres Draveurs		QMJHL	67	1	20	21	132
1986-87—Trois-Rivieres Draveurs (c)		QMJHL	62	6	22	28	227
1987-88—Trois-Rivieres Draveurs (b)		QMJHL	63	7	25	32	150
1988-89—Trois-Rivieres Draveurs		QMJHL	49	5	28	33	149
1988-89—Milwaukee Admirals		IHL	1	0	0	0	0
1989-90—Milwaukee Admirals		IHL	76	4	12	16	195

(c)—June, 1987—Drafted as underage junior by Vancouver Canucks in 1987 NHL entry draft. Second Canucks pick, 45th overall, third round.

DARREN WILLIAM VEITCH

Defense . . . 5'11" . . . 188 lbs. . . . Born, Saskatoon, Sask., April 24, 1960 . . . Shoots right . . . (October 27, 1982)—Fractured collarbone in three places at Pittsburgh . . . (February 19, 1983)—Broke collarbone again at Los Angeles . . . (February 11, 1984)—Suffered broken ribs vs. Philadelphia . . . (January, 1985)—Bruised ribs . . . (March, 1988)—Injured ankle.

Year	Team	League	Games	G.	A.	Pts.	Pen.
1976-77—Regina Blues		SJHL	60	15	21	36	121
1976-77—Regina Pats		WCHL	1	0	0	0	0
1977-78—Regina Pats		WCHL	71	13	32	45	135
1978-79—Regina Pats		WHL	51	11	36	47	80
1979-80—Regina Pats (a-c)		WHL	71	29	*93	122	118
1980-81—Hershey Bears		AHL	26	6	22	28	12
1980-81—Washington Capitals		NHL	59	4	21	25	46
1981-82—Hershey Bears		AHL	10	5	10	15	16
1981-82—Washington Capitals		NHL	67	9	44	53	54
1982-83—Hershey Bears		AHL	5	0	1	1	2
1982-83—Washington Capitals		NHL	10	0	8	8	0
1983-84—Washington Capitals		NHL	46	6	18	24	17
1983-84—Hershey Bears		AHL	11	1	6	7	4
1984-85—Washington Capitals		NHL	75	3	18	21	37
1985-86—Washington Capitals (d)		NHL	62	3	9	12	27
1985-86—Detroit Red Wings		NHL	13	0	5	5	2
1986-87—Detroit Red Wings		NHL	77	13	45	58	52
1987-88—Detroit Red Wings (e)		NHL	63	7	33	40	45
1988-89—Newmarket Saints		AHL	33	5	19	24	29
1988-89—Toronto Maple Leafs		NHL	37	3	7	10	16
1989-90—Newmarket Saints (b)		AHL	78	13	54	67	30
NHL TOTALS			509	48	208	256	296

(c)—June, 1980—Drafted by Washington Capitals in 1980 NHL entry draft. First Capitals pick, fifth overall, first round.

(d)—March, 1986—Traded by Washington Capitals to Detroit Red Wings for John Barrett and Greg Smith.

(e)—June, 1988—Traded by Detroit Red Wings to Toronto Maple Leafs for Miroslav Frycer.

RANDY VELISCHEK

Defense . . . 6' . . . 200 lbs. . . . Born, Montreal, Que., February 10, 1962 . . . Shoots left . . . (September, 1988)—Sprained left knee during New Jersey Devils training camp . . . (March 20, 1990—Concussion when checked by Ron Sutter vs. Philadelphia.

Year	Team	League	Games	G.	A.	Pts.	Pen.
1979-80—Providence College (c)		ECAC	31	5	5	10	20
1980-81—Providence College		ECAC	33	3	12	15	26
1981-82—Providence College (b)		ECAC	33	1	14	15	34

Year	Team	League	Games	G.	A.	Pts.	Pen.
1982-83—Providence College (a-d-e)		ECAC	41	18	34	52	50
1982-83—Minnesota North Stars		NHL	3	0	0	0	2
1983-84—Salt Lake Golden Eagles		CHL	43	7	21	28	54
1983-84—Minnesota North Stars		NHL	33	2	2	4	10
1984-85—Springfield Indians		AHL	26	2	7	9	22
1984-85—Minnesota North Stars		NHL	52	4	9	13	26
1985-86—New Jersey Devils (f)		NHL	47	2	7	9	39
1985-86—Maine Mariners		AHL	21	0	4	4	4
1986-87—New Jersey Devils		NHL	64	2	16	18	52
1987-88—New Jersey Devils		NHL	51	3	9	12	66
1988-89—New Jersey Devils		NHL	80	4	14	18	70
1989-90—New Jersey Devils (g)		NHL	62	0	6	6	72
NHL TOTALS			392	17	63	80	337

(c)—June, 1980—Drafted by Minnesota North Stars as underage player in 1980 NHL entry draft. Third North Stars pick, 53rd overall, third round.

(d)—ECAC Player of the Year.

(e)—NCAA All-America Team (East).

(f)—Acquired by New Jersey Devils in 1985 NHL waiver draft.

(g)—August, 1990—Traded by New Jersey Devils to Quebec Nordiques to complete trade of Peter Stastny from Quebec to New Jersey for Craig Wolanin and future considerations, March 6, 1990.

MIKE VELLUCCI

Defense . . . 6'1" . . . 180 lbs. . . . Born, Farmington, Mich., August 11, 1966 . . . Shoots left . . . (August, 1984)—Missed season with fractured vertebrae in automobile accident . . . (March, 1987)—Injured collarbone.

Year	Team	League	Games	G.	A.	Pts.	Pen.
1982-83—Detroit Compuware		Mich. Midget	70	23	20	43	98
1983-84—Belleville Bulls (c)		OHL	67	2	20	22	83
1984-85—Belleville Bulls		OHL	..	..	..	..	....
1985-86—Belleville Bulls		OHL	64	11	32	43	154
1986-87—Salt Lake Golden Eagles		IHL	60	5	30	35	94
1987-88—Hartford Whalers		NHL	2	0	0	0	11
1987-88—Binghamton Whalers		AHL	3	0	0	0	2
1987-88—Milwaukee Admirals		IHL	66	7	18	25	202
1988-89—Binghamton Whalers		AHL	37	9	9	18	59
1988-89—Indianapolis Ice		IHL	12	1	2	3	43
1989-90—Phoenix Roadrunners		IHL	4	0	0	0	5
1989-90—Winston Salem Thunderbirds		ECHL	10	2	7	9	21
1989-90—Erie Blades		ECHL	22	7	20	27	57
NHL TOTALS			2	0	0	0	11

(c)—June, 1984—Drafted as underage junior by Hartford Whalers in 1984 NHL entry draft. Third Whalers pick, 131st overall, seventh round.

STEPHANE VENNE

Defense . . . 6'3" . . . 210 lbs. . . . Born, Montreal, Que., April 29, 1969 . . . Shoots right.

Year	Team	League	Games	G.	A.	Pts.	Pen.
1987-88—Univ. of Vermont (c)		ECAC	31	9	12	21	64
1988-89—Univ. of Vermont		ECAC	19	4	5	9	35
1989-90—Univ. of Vermont		ECAC	31	6	9	15	62

(c)—June, 1988—Drafted by Quebec Nordiques in 1988 NHL entry draft. Sixth Nordiques pick, 87th overall, fifth round.

PAT VERBEEK

Right Wing . . . 5'9" . . . 195 lbs. . . . Born, Sarnia, Ont., May 24, 1964 . . . Shoots right . . . (May 15, 1985)—Left thumb severed between knuckles in a corn-planting machine on his farm near Forest, Ontario. Doctors reconnected the thumb surgically . . . Brother of Brian Verbeek . . . (March, 1987)—Pulled side muscle . . . (October 28, 1988)—Bruised chest when checked by Paul MacDermid vs. Hartford.

Year	Team	League	Games	G.	A.	Pts.	Pen.
1980-81—Petrolia Jr. B.		OPJHL	42	44	44	88	155
1981-82—Sudbury Wolves (c-d)		OHL	66	37	51	88	180
1982-83—Sudbury Wolves		OHL	61	40	67	107	184
1982-83—New Jersey Devils		NHL	6	3	2	5	8
1983-84—New Jersey Devils		NHL	79	20	27	47	158
1984-85—New Jersey Devils		NHL	78	15	18	33	162
1985-86—New Jersey Devils		NHL	76	25	28	53	79
1986-87—New Jersey Devils		NHL	74	35	24	59	120
1987-88—New Jersey Devils		NHL	73	46	31	77	227
1988-89—New Jersey Devils (e)		NHL	77	26	21	47	189
1989-90—Hartford Whalers		NHL	80	44	45	89	228
NHL TOTALS			543	214	196	410	1171

(c)—Winner of Emms Family Award (Rookie of the Year).

(d)—June, 1982—Drafted as underage junior by New Jersey Devils in 1982 NHL entry draft. Third Devils pick, 43rd overall, third round.

(e)—June 17, 1989—Traded by New Jersey Devils to Hartford Whalers for Sylvain Turgeon.

MARK VERMETTE

Right Wing . . . 6'1" . . . 203 lbs. . . . Born, Cochenour, Ont., October 3, 1967 . . . Shoots right.

Year	Team	League	Games	G.	A.	Pts.	Pen.
1985-86—Lake Superior State Univ. (c)		CCHA	32	1	4	5	7
1986-87—Lake Superior State Univ.		CCHA	38	19	17	36	59
1907-00—Lake Superior State Univ.		CCHA	46	45	29	74	154
1988-89—Quebec Nordiques		NHL	12	0	4	4	7
1988-89—Halifax Citadels		AHL	52	12	16	28	30
1989-90—Quebec Nordiques		NHL	11	1	5	6	8
1989-90—Halifax Citadels		AHL	47	20	17	37	44
NHL TOTALS			23	1	9	10	15

(c)—June, 1986—Drafted by Quebec Nordiques in 1986 NHL entry draft. Eighth Nordiques pick, 134th overall, seventh round.

JIM VESEY

Center . . . 6'1" . . . 200 lbs. . . . Born, Charlestown, Mass., September 29, 1965 . . . Shoots right . . . (April 20, 1990)—Broke two bones above right wrist vs. Indianapolis.

Year	Team	League	Games	G.	A.	Pts.	Pen.
1984-85—Merrimack College (c)	ECAC-II	33	19	11	30	28
1985-86—Merrimack College	ECAC-II	32	29	32	61	67
1986-87—Merrimack College	ECAC	35	22	36	58	57
1987-88—Merrimack College	ECAC	40	40	55	95	95
1988-89—St. Louis Blues	NHL	5	1	1	2	7
1988-89—Peoria Rivermen (a)	IHL	76	47	46	93	137
1989-90—St. Louis Blues	NHL	6	0	1	1	0
1989-90—Peoria Rivermen	IHL	60	47	44	91	75
NHL TOTALS		11	1	2	3	7

(c)—June, 1984—Drafted by St. Louis Blues in 1984 NHL entry draft. Eleventh Blues pick, 155th overall, eighth round.

DENNIS VIAL

Defense . . . 6'1" . . . 195 lbs. . . . Born, Sault Ste. Marie, Ont., April 10, 1969 . . . Shoots left . . . (October, 1986)—Suspended three OHL games for spearing. (March 23, 1989)—Suspended indefinitely by OHL for leaving the bench to fight Jim Revenberg vs. Windsor.

Year	Team	League	Games	G.	A.	Pts.	Pen.
1984-85—Sault Ste. Marie Legion Midgets	OHA	31	4	19	23	40
1985-86—Hamilton Steelhawks	OHL	31	1	1	2	66
1986-87—Hamilton Steelhawks	OHL	53	1	8	9	194
1987-88—Hamilton Steelhawks (c)	OHL	52	3	17	20	229
1988-89—Niagara Falls Thunder	OHL	50	10	27	37	230
1989-90—Flint Spirits	IHL	79	6	29	35	351

(c)—June, 1988—Drafted by New York Rangers in 1988 NHL entry draft. Fifth Rangers pick, 110th overall, sixth round.

MARK VICHOREK

Defense . . . 6'3" . . . 207 lbs. . . . Born, Moose Lake, Minn., August 11, 1966 . . . Shoots right.

Year	Team	League	Games	G.	A.	Pts.	Pen.
1981-82—Sioux City Musketeers (c)	USHL	48	11	27	38	111
1982-83—Lake Superior State Univ.	CCHA	36	2	13	15	24
1983-84—Lake Superior State Univ.	CCHA	40	3	8	11	14
1984-85—Lake Superior State Univ.	CCHA	44	4	11	15	36
1985-86—Lake Superior State Univ.	CCHA	41	9	11	20	40
1986-87—Binghamton Whalers (d)	AHL	64	1	12	13	63
1986-87—Salt Lake Golden Eagles	IHL	16	1	0	1	32
1987-88—Binghamton Whalers	AHL	26	0	4	4	48
1987-88—Milwaukee Admirals	IHL	49	4	5	9	67
1988-89—New Haven Nighthawks	AHL	23	1	5	6	26
1988-89—Flint Spirits	IHL	44	4	9	13	47
1989-90—Fort Wayne Komets	IHL	31	2	4	6	30
1989-90—Phoenix Roadrunners	IHL	29	2	8	10	57

(c)—June, 1982—Drafted by Philadelphia Flyers in 1982 NHL entry draft. Twelfth Flyers pick, 245th overall, 12th round.

(d)—August, 1986—Signed by Hartford Whalers as a free agent.

CLAUDE VILGRAIN

Right Wing . . . 6'1" . . . 195 lbs. . . . Born, Port-au-Prince, Haiti, March 1, 1963 . . . Shoots right . . . First Haitian-born player in the NHL.

Year	Team	League	Games	G.	A.	Pts.	Pen.
1980-81—Laval Voisons	QMJHL	72	20	31	51	65
1981-82—Laval Voisons (c)	QMJHL	58	26	29	55	64
1982-83—Laval Voisons	QMJHL	69	46	80	126	72
1983-84—Univ. of Moncton (c)	AUAA	20	11	20	31	8
1984-85—Univ. of Moncton	AUAA	24	35	28	63	20
1985-86—Univ. of Moncton	AUAA	19	17	20	37	25
1986-87—Canadian Olympic Team	Int'l	78	28	42	70	38
1987-88—Canadian Olympic Team (d)	Int'l	67	21	20	41	41
1987-88—Vancouver Canucks	NHL	6	1	1	2	0
1988-89—Milwaukee Admirals (e)	IHL	23	9	13	22	26
1988-89—Utica Devils	AHL	55	23	30	53	41
1989-90—New Jersey Devils	NHL	6	1	2	3	4
1989-90—Utica Devils	AHL	73	37	52	89	32
NHL TOTALS		12	2	3	5	4

(c)—June, 1982—Drafted by Detroit Red Wings in 1982 NHL entry draft. Sixth Red Wings pick, 107th overall, sixth round.

(d)—June, 1987—Signed by Vancouver Canucks as a free agent.

(e)—March 7, 1989—Traded by Vancouver Canucks to New Jersey Devils for Tim Lenardon.

DANIEL VINCELETTE

Left Wing . . . 6'1" . . . 202 lbs. . . . Born, Verdun, Que., August 1, 1967 . . . Shoots left . . . (December, 1983)—Knee surgery . . . (February, 1988)—Bruised ribs.

Year	Team	League	Games	G.	A.	Pts.	Pen.
1983-84—Magog Cantonniers	Que. Midget	40	9	13	22	43
1984-85—Drummondville Voltigeurs (c)	QMJHL	64	11	24	35	124
1985-86—Drummondville Voltigeurs	QMJHL	70	37	47	84	234
1986-87—Drummondville Voltigeurs	QMJHL	50	34	35	69	288
1986-87—Chicago Black Hawks (d)	NHL	....	....	....	....	....
1987-88—Chicago Black Hawks	NHL	69	6	11	17	109
1988-89—Chicago Black Hawks	NHL	66	11	4	15	119
1988-89—Saginaw Hawks	IHL	2	0	0	0	14
1989-90—Indianapolis Ice	IHL	49	16	13	29	262
1989-90—Chicago Black Hawks (e)	NHL	2	0	0	0	4
1989-90—Quebec Nordiques	NHL	11	0	1	1	25
1989-90—Halifax Citadels (f)	AHL	....	....	....	....	....
NHL TOTALS		148	17	16	33	257

(c)—June, 1985—Drafted as underage junior by Chicago Black Hawks in 1985 NHL entry draft. Third Black Hawks pick, 74th overall, fourth round.

(d)—No regular season record. Played three playoff games.

(e)—March 5, 1990—Traded with Everett Sanipass and Mario Doyon by Chicago Black Hawks to Quebec Nordiques for Michel Goulet, Greg Millen and a sixth-round 1991 draft pick.

(f)—No regular season record. Played two playoff games.

EMANUEL VIVEIROS

Defense . . . 5'11" . . . 160 lbs. . . . Born, St. Albert, Alta., January 8, 1966 . . . Shoots left . . . (January, 1990)—Sprained right shoulder while playing for a West German club and out for season.

Year	Team	League	Games	G.	A.	Pts.	Pen.
1982-83—Prince Albert Raiders	WHL	59	6	26	32	55
1983-84—Prince Albert Raiders (b-c)	WHL	67	15	94	109	48
1984-85—Prince Albert Raiders (b)	WHL	68	17	71	88	94
1985-86—Prince Albert Raiders (a-d-e-f)	WHL	57	22	70	92	30
1985-86—Minnesota North Stars	NHL	4	0	1	1	0
1986-87—Minnesota North Stars	NHL	1	0	1	1	0
1986-87—Springfield Indians	AHL	76	7	35	42	38
1987-88—Kalamazoo Wings	IHL	57	15	48	63	41
1987-88—Minnesota North Stars	NHL	24	1	9	10	6
1988-89—Kalamazoo Wings	IHL	54	11	29	40	37
1989-90—Kaufbeuren ESV (g)	W. Germany	8	2	7	9	8
NHL TOTALS		29	1	11	12	6

(c)—June, 1984—Drafted as underage junior by Edmonton Oilers in 1984 NHL entry draft. Sixth Oilers pick, 106th overall, sixth round.

(d)—Named best WHL Defenseman (East).

(e)—Named WHL MVP (East).

(f)—December, 1985—Traded by Edmonton Oilers with Marc Habscheid and Don Barber to Minnesota North Stars for Gord Sherven and Don Biggs.

(g)—Signed by Hartford Whalers as a free agent.

DAVID VOLEK

Right Wing . . . 6' . . . 183 lbs. . . . Born, Czechoslovakia, June 18, 1966 . . . Shoots right . . . (August, 1988)—Suspended six months by the International Ice Hockey Federation for steroid use . . . (October, 1988)—Separated right shoulder.

Year	Team	League	Games	G.	A.	Pts.	Pen.
1986-87—Sparta Praha (c)	Czech.	39	27	25	52	....
1987-88—Sparta Praha	Czech.	30	18	12	30	....
1988-89—New York Islanders	NHL	77	25	34	59	24
1989-90—New York Islanders	NHL	80	17	22	39	41
NHL TOTALS		157	42	56	98	65

(c)—June, 1984—Drafted by New York Islanders in 1984 NHL entry draft. Eleventh Islanders pick, 208th overall, 10th round.

PHIL Von STEFENELLI

Defense . . . 6'1" . . . 185 lbs. . . . Born, Vancouver, B.C., April 10, 1969 . . . Shoots left.

Year	Team	League	Games	G.	A.	Pts.	Pen.
1986-87—Richmond Jr. A	BCJHL	35	5	19	24	14
1987-88—Boston Univ. (c)	H. East	34	3	13	16	38
1988-89—Boston Univ.	H. East	33	2	6	8	34
1989-90—Boston University	H. East	44	8	20	28	40

(c)—June, 1988—Drafted by Vancouver Canucks in 1988 NHL entry draft. Fifth Canucks pick, 122nd overall, sixth round.

MICHAEL VUKONICH

Center . . . 6'1" . . . 190 lbs. . . . Born, Duluth, Minn., November 5, 1968 . . . Shoots left . . . Coached by his father at Duluth Denfeld H.S. . . . (November, 1988)—Mononucleosis.

Year	Team	League	Games	G.	A.	Pts.	Pen.
1985-86—Duluth Denfeld Hunters	Minn. H.S.	24	14	20	34	....
1986-87—Duluth Denfeld Hunters (c)	Minn. H.S.	22	30	23	53	....
1987-88—Harvard University	ECAC	32	9	14	23	24
1988-89—Harvard University	ECAC	27	11	8	19	12
1989-90—Harvard University (a)	ECAC	27	22	29	51	18

(c)—June, 1987—Drafted by Los Angeles Kings in 1987 NHL entry draft. Fourth Kings pick, 90th overall, fifth round.

MICK VUKOTA

Right Wing . . . 6'2" . . . 195 lbs. . . . Born, Saskatoon, Sask., September 14, 1966 . . . Shoots right . . . (November 20, 1987)—Given a six-game AHL suspension for returning to fight after being sent to the dressing room vs. Fredericton . . . (February, 1990)—Sore back . . . (March 18, 1990)—Separated left shoulder vs. Pittsburgh . . . (April 5, 1990)—Suspended 10 games for fighting vs. N.Y. Rangers. He served four games. The remaining six games will be served at the beginning of the 1990-91 season.

Year	Team	League	Games	G.	A.	Pts.	Pen.
1983-84—Winnipeg Warriors	WHL	3	1	1	2	10
1984-85—Kelowna Wings	WHL	66	10	6	16	247
1985-86—Spokane Chiefs	WHL	64	19	14	33	369
1986-87—Spokane Chiefs	WHL	61	25	28	53	*337
1987-88—New York Islanders (c)	NHL	17	1	0	1	82
1987-88—Springfield Indians	AHL	52	7	9	16	372
1988-89—Springfield Indians	AHL	3	1	0	1	33
1988-89—New York Islanders	NHL	48	2	6	8	237
1989-90—New York Islanders	NHL	76	4	8	12	290
NHL TOTALS		141	7	10	17	609

(c)—September, 1987—Signed by New York Islanders as a free agent.

GORDON WALKER

Left Wing . . . 6' . . . 178 lbs. . . . Born, Castlegar, B.C., August 12, 1965 . . . Shoots left . . . Also plays Center.

Year	Team	League	Games	G.	A.	Pts.	Pen.
1981-82—Drumheller Miners		AJHL	60	35	44	79	90
1982-83—Portland Winter Hawks (c)		WHL	66	24	30	54	95
1983-84—Portland Winter Hawks		WHL	58	28	41	69	65
1984-85—Kamloops Blazers (a-d-e)		WHL	66	67	67	134	76
1985-86—New Haven Nighthawks		AHL	46	11	28	39	66
1986-87—New York Rangers		NHL	1	1	0	1	4
1986-87—New Haven Nighthawks		AHL	59	24	20	44	58
1987-88—New York Rangers (f)		NHL	18	1	4	5	17
1987-88—Colorado Rangers		IHL	16	4	9	13	4
1987-88—New Haven Nighthawks		AHL	14	10	9	19	17
1988-89—Los Angeles Kings		NHL	11	1	0	1	2
1988-89—New Haven Nighthawks		AHL	60	21	25	46	50
1989-90—Los Angeles Kings		NHL	1	0	0	0	0
1989-90—New Haven Nighthawks		AHL	24	14	7	21	8
NHL TOTALS			31	3	4	7	23

(c)—June, 1983—Drafted as underage junior by New York Rangers in 1983 NHL entry draft. Fifth Rangers pick, 53rd overall, third round.

(d)—September, 1984—Traded with Craig Benning by Portland Winter Hawks to Kamloops Blazers for Brad Werenka.

(e)—Led WHL Playoffs with 13 goals.

(f)—January, 1988—Traded with Mike Siltala by New York Rangers to Los Angeles Kings for Joe Paterson.

ROBERT WALLWORK

Center . . . 5'11" . . . 180 lbs. . . . Born, Boston, Mass., March 15, 1968 . . . Shoots right . . . Also plays Defense.

Year	Team	League	Games	G.	A.	Pts.	Pen.
1986-87—New Hampton H.S.		Mass. H.S.	35	25	27	52	48
1987-88—Miami Univ. of Ohio (c)		CCHA	36	6	24	30	59
1988-89—Miami Univ. of Ohio		CCHA	19	1	8	9	30
1989-90—Miami Univ. of Ohio		CCHA	40	12	30	42	60

(c)—June, 1988—Drafted by Buffalo Sabres in 1988 NHL entry draft. Twelfth Sabres pick, 244th overall, 12th round.

MICHAEL WALSH

Left Wing . . . 6'2" . . . 195 lbs. . . . Born, New York, N.Y., April 3, 1962 . . . Shoots left.

Year	Team	League	Games	G.	A.	Pts.	Pen.
1985-86—Springfield Indians		AHL	2	1	0	1	0
1986-87—Springfield Indians (c)		AHL	67	20	26	46	32
1987-88—New York Islanders		NHL	1	0	0	0	0
1987-88—Springfield Indians		AHL	77	27	23	50	48
1988-89—Springfield Indians		AHL	68	31	34	65	73
1988-89—New York Islanders		NHL	13	2	0	2	4
1989-90—Springfield Indians		AHL	69	34	20	54	43
NHL TOTALS			69	34	20	54	43

(c)—August, 1986—Signed by New York Islanders as a free agent.

BRET WALTER

Center . . . 6'1" . . . 195 lbs. . . . Born, Calgary, Alta., April 28, 1968 . . . Shoots right . . . (October, 1985)—Injured shoulder.

Year	Team	League	Games	G.	A.	Pts.	Pen.
1984-85—Fort Saskatchewan Manville		Alta. Midg.	32	38	39	77	44
1985-86—Univ. of Alberta (c)		CWUAA	18	3	11	14	6
1986-87—Univ. of Alberta		CWUAA	43	17	17	34	24
1986-87—Canadian Olympic Team		Olympics	2	0	0	0	0
1987-88—Univ. of Alberta		CWUAA	21	7	10	17	18
1988-89—Denver Rangers		IHL	47	12	10	22	41
1989-90—Flint Spirits		IHL	6	1	1	2	4
1989-90—Fort Wayne Komets		IHL	24	5	5	10	47

(c)—June, 1986—Drafted by New York Rangers in 1986 NHL entry draft. Second Rangers pick, 51st overall, third round.

RYAN WILLIAM WALTER

Left Wing . . . 6' . . . 195 lbs. . . . Born, New Westminster, B. C., April 23, 1958 . . . Shoots left . . . Brother of George Walter . . . (November, 1983)—Injured groin muscle . . . (October 27, 1984)—Concussion and twisted knee when checked by Andy Brickley at Pittsburgh . . . (March 8, 1986)—Back spasms . . . (March, 1986)—Broke ankle and missed remainder of regular season and all of playoffs except for Stanley Cup finals . . . (October, 1987)—Bruised ribs . . . (November, 1987)—Back spasms . . . (December 9, 1989)—Concussion at Toronto.

Year	Team	League	Games	G.	A.	Pts.	Pen.
1973-74—Langley Lords		Jr."A"BCHL	....	...	....	....	....
1973-74—Kamloops Chiefs		WCHL	2	0	0	0	0
1974-75—Langley Lords		Jr."A"BCHL	....	...	....	....	....
1974-75—Kamloops Chiefs		WCHL	9	8	4	12	2
1975-76—Kamloops Chiefs		WCHL	72	35	49	84	96
1976-77—Kamloops Chiefs		WCHL	71	41	58	99	100
1977-78—Seattle Breakers (a-c)		WCHL	62	54	71	125	148
1978-79—Washington Capitals		NHL	69	28	28	56	70
1979-80—Washington Capitals		NHL	80	24	42	66	106
1980-81—Washington Capitals		NHL	80	24	44	68	150
1981-82—Washington Capitals (d)		NHL	78	38	49	87	142
1982-83—Montreal Canadiens		NHL	80	29	46	75	40
1983-84—Montreal Canadiens		NHL	73	20	29	49	83
1984-85—Montreal Canadiens		NHL	72	19	19	38	59
1985-86—Montreal Canadiens		NHL	69	15	34	49	45
1986-87—Montreal Canadiens		NHL	76	23	23	46	34
1987-88—Montreal Canadiens		NHL	61	13	23	36	39
1988-89—Montreal Canadiens		NHL	78	14	17	31	48
1989-90—Montreal Canadiens		NHL	70	8	16	24	59
NHL TOTALS			886	255	370	625	875

(c)—Drafted from Seattle Breakers by Washington Capitals in first round of 1978 amateur draft.

(d)—September, 1982—Traded by Washington Capitals with Rick Green to Montreal Canadiens for Rod Langway, Brian Engblom, Doug Jarvis and Craig Laughlin.

GREG WALTERS

Center . . . 6'1" . . . 195 lbs. . . . Born, Calgary, Alta., August 8, 1970 . . . Shoots left . . . (December, 1989)—Broke leg.

Year	Team	League	Games	G.	A.	Pts.	Pen.
1986-87—North York Midget		OHA	37	21	28	49	72
1987-88—Ottawa 67's		OHL	63	11	25	36	52
1988-89—Ottawa 67's		OHL	28	17	21	38	20
1989-90—Ottawa 67's (c)		OHL	63	36	54	90	57

(c)—June, 1990—Selected by Toronto Maple Leafs in 1990 NHL entry draft. Third Maple Leafs pick, 80th overall, fourth round.

WES WALZ

Center . . . 5'10" . . . 181 lbs. . . . Born, Calgary, Alta., May 15, 1970 . . . Shoots right.

Year	Team	League	Games	G.	A.	Pts.	Pen.
1987-88—Prince Albert Raiders		WHL	1	1	1	2	0
1988-89—Lethbridge Broncos (c)		WHL	63	29	75	104	32
1989-90—Boston Bruins		NHL	2	1	1	2	0
1989-90—Lethbridge Broncos (a-d)		WHL	56	54	86	140	69
NHL TOTALS			2	1	1	2	0

(c)—June, 1989—Drafted by Boston Bruins in 1989 NHL entry draft. Third Bruins pick, 57th overall, third round.

(d)—Named WHL Player of the Year.

ED WARD

Right Wing . . . 6'3" . . . 190 lbs. . . . Born, Edmonton, Alta., November 10, 1969 . . . Shoots right . . . (August, 1987)—Torn knee cartilage.

Year	Team	League	Games	G.	A.	Pts.	Pen.
1986-87—Sherwood Park Crusaders		AJHL	60	18	28	46	272
1987-88—Northern Michigan Univ. (c)		WCHA	25	0	2	2	40
1988-89—Northern Michigan Univ.		WCHA	42	5	15	20	36
1989-90—Northern Michigan Univ.		WCHA	39	5	11	16	77

(c)—June, 1988—Drafted by Quebec Nordiques in 1988 NHL entry draft. Seventh Nordiques pick, 108th overall, sixth round.

DIXON WARD JR.

Right Wing . . . 6'1" . . . 195 lbs. . . . Born, Edmonton, Alta., September 23, 1968 . . . Shoots right.

Year	Team	League	Games	G.	A.	Pts.	Pen.
1986-87—Red Deer Rustlers		AJHL	59	46	40	86	153
1987-88—Red Deer Rustlers (c)		AJHL	51	60	71	131	167
1988-89—Univ. of North Dakota		WCHA	37	8	9	17	26
1989-90—Univ. of North Dakota		WCHA	45	35	34	69	44

(c)—June, 1988—Drafted by Vancouver Canucks in 1988 NHL entry draft. Sixth Canucks pick, 128th overall, seventh round.

MICHAEL WARE

Right Wing . . . 6'5" . . . 225 lbs. . . . Born, York, Ont., March 22, 1967 . . . Shoots right . . . Also plays Defense . . . (October, 1985)—Broke collarbone . . . (December 8, 1988)—Suspended six games for leaving bench to fight Mark Laforge vs. Binghamton . . . (February 18, 1989)—Suspended 20 games for throwing his stick at referee Kevin Muench and linesmen Pierre Champoux and John Pierre from the penalty box vs. Moncton.

Year	Team	League	Games	G.	A.	Pts.	Pen.
1983-84—Mississauga Reps		OHA	30	14	20	34	50
1984-85—Hamilton Steelhawks (c)		OHL	57	4	14	18	225
1985-86—Hamilton Steelhawks		OHL	44	8	11	19	155
1986-87—Cornwall Royals		OHL	50	5	19	24	173
1987-88—Nova Scotia Oilers		AHL	52	0	8	8	253
1988-89—Edmonton Oilers		NHL	2	0	1	1	11
1988-89—Cape Breton Oilers		AHL	48	1	11	12	317
1989-90—Cape Breton Oilers		AHL	54	6	13	19	191
1989-90—Edmonton Oilers		NHL	3	0	0	0	4
NHL TOTALS			5	0	1	1	15

(c)—June, 1985—Drafted as underage junior by Edmonton Oilers in 1985 NHL entry draft. Third Oilers pick, 62nd overall, third round.

TIM WATTERS

Defense . . . 5'11" . . . 180 lbs. . . . Born, Kamloops, B.C., July 25, 1959 . . . Shoots left . . . Set record for assists and points by a defenseman at Michigan Tech in 1980-81 . . . (October, 1983)—Pulled hamstring . . . (December, 1984)—Broken wrist . . . (February, 1986)—Back spasms . . . (December, 1987)—Strained knee in collision with Kevin Lowe vs. Edmonton . . . (March, 1989)—Bruised calf . . . (December 23, 1989)—Bruised ankle vs. Vancouver and missed nine games . . . (April, 1990)—Bruised ankle.

Year	Team	League	Games	G.	A.	Pts.	Pen.
1977-78—Michigan Tech		WCHA	37	1	15	16	47
1978-79—Michigan Tech (c)		WCHA	31	6	21	27	48
1979-80—Canadian Olympic Team		Int'l.	56	8	21	29	43

Year	Team	League	Games	G.	A.	Pts.	Pen.
1979-80—Canadian Olympic Team		Int'l.	6	1	1	2	0
1980-81—Michigan Tech (a-d)		WCHA	43	12	38	50	36
1981-82—Tulsa Oilers		CHL	5	1	2	3	0
1981-82—Winnipeg Jets		NHL	69	2	22	24	97
1982-83—Winnipeg Jets		NHL	77	5	18	23	98
1983-84—Winnipeg Jets		NHL	74	3	20	23	169
1984-85—Winnipeg Jets		NHL	63	2	20	22	74
1985-86—Winnipeg Jets		NHL	56	6	8	14	97
1986-87—Winnipeg Jets		NHL	63	3	13	16	119
1987-88—Winnipeg Jets		NHL	36	0	0	0	106
1987-88—Canadian Olympic Team (e)		Int'l.	10	0	3	3	2
1988-89—Los Angeles Kings		NHL	76	3	18	21	168
1989-90—Los Angeles Kings		NHL	62	1	10	11	92
NHL TOTALS			576	25	129	154	1020

(c)—August, 1979—Drafted by Winnipeg Jets in NHL draft. Sixth Jets pick, 124th overall, sixth round.
(d)—Named to All-America Team (West).
(e)—July, 1988—Signed by Los Angeles Kings as a free agent.

DOUGLAS WEIGHT

Center . . . 5'11" . . . 185 lbs. . . . Born, Warren, Mich., January 21, 1971 . . . Shoots left.

Year	Team	League	Games	G.	A.	Pts.	Pen.
1988-89—Bloomfield Jets		NAJHL	34	26	53	79	105
1989-90—Lake Superior St. Univ. (c-d)		CCHA	46	21	48	69	44

(c)—Named to CCHA All-Rookie team.
(d)—June 16, 1990—Selected by New York Rangers in 1990 NHL entry draft. Second Rangers pick, 34th overall, second round.

ERIC WEINRICH

Defense . . . 6'1" . . . 205 lbs. . . . Born, Roanoke, Vir., December 19, 1966 . . . Shoots left . . . (December, 1984)—Dislocated shoulder . . . Brother of Alex and Jason Weinrich.

Year	Team	League	Games	G.	A.	Pts.	Pen.
1983-84—North Yarmouth Acad.		Mass. H.S.	17	23	33	56	..
1984-85—North Yarmouth Acad. (c)		Mass. H.S.	20	6	21	27	..
1985-86—Univ. of Maine		H. East	34	0	15	15	26
1986-87—Univ. of Maine (a-d)		H. East	41	12	32	44	59
1987-88—U.S. Olympic Team		Int'l	39	3	9	12	24
1987-88—Univ. of Maine		H. East	8	4	7	11	22
1988-89—Utica Devils		AHL	80	17	27	44	70
1988-89—New Jersey Devils		NHL	2	0	0	0	0
1989-90—Utica Devils (a-e)		AHL	57	12	48	60	38
1989-90—New Jersey Devils		NHL	19	2	7	9	11
NHL TOTALS			21	2	7	9	11

(c)—June, 1985—Drafted by New Jersey Devils in 1985 NHL entry draft. Third Devils pick, 32nd overall, second round.
(d)—Named Second team All-America (East).
(e)—Won Eddie Shore Plaque (Best AHL Defenseman).

JASON WEINRICH

Defense . . . 6'2" . . . 189 lbs. . . . Born, Lewiston, Maine, February 13, 1972 . . . Shoots right . . . Brother of Alex and Eric Weinrich . . . (May, 1990)—Signed letter of intent to attend University of Maine . . . (April, 1989)—Separated shoulder.

Year	Team	League	Games	G.	A.	Pts.	Pen.
1988-89—North Yarmouth H.S.		Maine	35	12	30	42	22
1989-90—Springfield Olympics (c)		NEJHL	30	7	35	42	....

(c)—June 16, 1990—Selected by New York Rangers in 1990 NHL entry draft. Eighth Rangers pick, 118th overall, sixth round.

JOHN WEISBROD

Center . . . 6'1" . . . 185 lbs. . . . Born, Syosset, N.Y., October 8, 1968 . . . Shoots right.

Year	Team	League	Games	G.	A.	Pts.	Pen.
1985-86—Choate Academy		Conn.	26	21	25	46	..
1986-87—Choate Academy (c)		Conn.	23	13	14	27	..
1987-88—Harvard Univ.		ECAC	22	8	11	19	16
1988-89—Harvard Univ.		ECAC	31	22	13	35	61
1989-90—Harvard Univ.		ECAC	27	11	21	32	62

(c)—June, 1987—Drafted by Minnesota North Stars in 1987 NHL entry draft. Fourth North Stars pick, 73rd overall, fourth round.

GORDON JAY WELLS
(Known by middle name.)

Defense . . . 6'1" . . . 205 lbs. . . . Born, Paris, Ont., May 18, 1959 . . . Shoots left . . . (October 16, 1981)—Broke right hand in team practice when hit by a puck . . . (December 14, 1982)—Tore medial collateral ligament in right knee at Washington . . . (December, 1983)—Sprained ankle . . . (February, 1987)—Struck in eye by a puck during a team practice . . . (November, 1987)—Strained lower back . . . (October, 1988)—Bruised right shoulder . . . (January, 1989)—Broke knuckle on right hand . . . (November, 1989)—Broke toe . . . (March 6, 1990)—Fractured right ankle at Boston.

Year	Team	League	Games	G.	A.	Pts.	Pen.
1976-77—Kingston Canadians		OMJHL	59	4	7	11	90
1977-78—Kingston Canadians		OMJHL	68	9	13	22	195
1978-79—Kingston Canadians (a-c)		OMJHL	48	6	21	27	100
1979-80—Los Angeles Kings		NHL	43	0	0	0	113
1979-80—Binghamton Dusters		AHL	28	0	6	6	48
1980-81—Los Angeles Kings		NHL	72	5	13	18	155
1981-82—Los Angeles Kings		NHL	60	1	8	9	145

Year	Team	League	Games	G.	A.	Pts.	Pen.
1982-83—Los Angeles Kings		NHL	69	3	12	15	167
1983-84—Los Angeles Kings		NHL	69	3	18	21	141
1984-85—Los Angeles Kings		NHL	77	2	9	11	185
1985-86—Los Angeles Kings		NHL	79	11	31	42	226
1986-87—Los Angeles Kings		NHL	77	7	29	36	155
1987-88—Los Angeles Kings		NHL	58	2	23	25	159
1988-89—Philadelphia Flyers (d)		NHL	67	2	19	21	184
1989-90—Philadelphia Flyers (e)		NHL	59	3	16	19	129
1989-90—Buffalo Sabres		NHL	1	0	1	1	0
NHL TOTALS			731	39	179	218	1759

(c)—August, 1979—Drafted by Los Angeles Kings in 1979 NHL entry draft. First Kings pick, 16th overall, first round.
(d)—September 29, 1988—Traded by Los Angeles Kings to Philadelphia Flyers for Doug Crossman.
(e)—March 5, 1990—Traded with a fourth-round 1991 draft pick by Philadelphia Flyers to Buffalo Sabres for Kevin Maguire and a second-round 1990 draft pick (Mike Renberg).

JEFF WENAAS

Center . . . 5'11" . . . 185 lbs. . . . Born, Eastend, Sask., September 1, 1967 . . . Shoots left . . . Brother of Stu Wenaas (Pittsburgh 10th round 1982 draft pick).

Year	Team	League	Games	G.	A.	Pts.	Pen.
1983-84—Medicine Hat Midget Tigers		AHA	38	16	22	38	77
1984-85—Medicine Hat Tigers (c)		WHL	70	27	27	54	70
1985-86—Medicine Hat Tigers		WHL	65	20	26	46	57
1986-87—Medicine Hat Tigers		WHL	70	42	29	71	68
1987-88—Salt Lake Golden Eagles		IHL	80	23	39	62	109
1988-89—Salt Lake Golden Eagles		IHL	17	2	8	10	6
1988-89—Canadian National Team		Int'l.	21	2	3	5	17
1989-90—Salt Lake Golden Eagles		IHL	38	4	4	8	29

(c)—June, 1985—Drafted as underage junior by Calgary Flames in 1985 NHL entry draft. Third Flames pick, 38th overall, second round.

BRAD WERENKA

Defense . . . 6'2" . . . 205 lbs. . . . Born, Two Hills, Alta., February 12, 1969 . . . Shoots left . . . (October, 1988)—Torn stomach muscles . . . (November 3, 1989)—Sprained right knee at Colorado College.

Year	Team	League	Games	G.	A.	Pts.	Pen.
1985-86—Fort Saskatchewan Traders		SJHL	29	12	23	35	24
1986-87—Northern Michigan Univ. (c)		WCHA	30	4	4	8	35
1987-88—Northern Michigan Univ.		WCHA	34	7	23	30	26
1988-89—Northern Michigan Univ.		WCHA	28	7	13	20	16
1989-90—Northern Michigan Univ.		WCHA	8	2	5	7	8

(c)—June, 1987—Drafted as underage junior by Edmonton Oilers in 1987 NHL entry draft. Second Oilers pick, 42nd overall, second round.

GLEN WESLEY

Defense . . . 6'1" . . . 195 lbs. . . . Born, Red Deer, Alta., October 2, 1968 . . . Shoots left . . . Brother of Blake Wesley . . . (October, 1988)—Sprained left knee.

Year	Team	League	Games	G.	A.	Pts.	Pen.
1983-84—Red Deer Rustlers		AJHL	57	9	20	29	40
1984-85—Portland Winterhawks		WHL	67	16	52	68	76
1985-86—Portland Winterhawks (a-c)		WHL	69	16	75	91	96
1986-87—Portland Winterhawks (a-d)		WHL	63	16	46	62	72
1987-88—Boston Bruins		NHL	79	7	30	37	69
1988-89—Boston Bruins		NHL	77	19	35	54	61
1989-90—Boston Bruins		NHL	78	9	27	36	48
NHL TOTALS			234	35	92	127	178

(c)—Named Best WHL Defenseman (West).
(d)—June, 1987—Drafted as underage junior by Boston Bruins in 1987 NHL entry draft. First Bruins pick, third overall, first round.

SIMON WHEELDON

Center . . . 5'11" . . . 170 lbs. . . . Born, Vancouver, B.C., August 30, 1966 . . . Shoots left.

Year	Team	League	Games	G.	A.	Pts.	Pen.
1982-83—Kelowna Bucks		BCJHL	60	...	....	86	....
1983-84—Victoria Cougars (c)		WHL	56	14	24	38	43
1984-85—Victoria Cougars (b)		WHL	67	50	76	126	78
1984-85—Nova Scotia Oilers		AHL	4	0	1	1	0
1985-86—Victoria Cougars (b)		WHL	70	61	96	157	85
1986-87—Flint Spirits		IHL	41	17	53	70	67
1986-87—New Haven Nighthawks (d)		AHL	38	11	28	39	39
1987-88—New York Rangers		NHL	5	0	1	1	4
1987-88—Colorado Rangers		IHL	69	45	54	99	80
1988-89—New York Rangers		NHL	6	0	1	1	2
1988-89—Denver Rangers (b)		IHL	74	50	56	106	77
1989-90—Flint Spirits (e)		IHL	76	34	49	83	61
NHL TOTALS			11	0	2	2	6

(c)—June, 1984—Drafted as underage junior by Edmonton Oilers in 1984 NHL entry draft. Eleventh Oilers pick, 229th overall, 11th round.
(d)—August, 1987—Signed by New York Rangers as a free agent.
(e)—July 10, 1990—Traded by New York Rangers to Winnipeg Jets for Brian McReynolds.

PETER WHITE

Left Wing . . . 5'11" . . . 201 lbs. . . . Born, Montreal, Que., March 15, 1969 . . . Shoots left.

Year	Team	League	Games	G.	A.	Pts.	Pen.
1987-88—Pembrook Jr. A		OHA	56	90	136	226	32
1988-89—Michigan State Univ. (c-d)		CCHA	46	20	33	53	17
1989-90—Michigan State Univ. (e-f)		CCHA	45	22	40	62	6

(c)—Named to CCHA All-Rookie Team.
(d)—June, 1989—Drafted by Edmonton Oilers in 1989 NHL entry draft. Fourth Oilers pick, 92nd overall, fifth round.
(e)—Named CCHA All-Tournament team.
(f)—Named CCHA Tournament MVP.

SCOTT WHITE

Defense . . . 6' . . . 190 lbs. . . . Born, Ormstown, Que., April 21, 1968 . . . Shoots right.

Year	Team	League	Games	G.	A.	Pts.	Pen.
1985-86	Michigan Tech. Univ. (c)	WCHA	40	3	15	18	58
1986-87	Michigan Tech. Univ.	WCHA	36	4	15	19	58
1987-88	Michigan Tech. Univ.	WCHA	40	7	25	32	32
1988-89	Michigan Tech. Univ.	WCHA	38	6	18	24	38
1989-90	Greensboro Monarchs	ECHL	30	9	13	22	67

(c)—June, 1986—Drafted by Quebec Nordiques in 1986 NHL entry draft. Sixth Nordiques pick, 117th overall, sixth round.

SEAN WHYTE

Right Wing . . . 6' . . . 198 lbs. . . . Born, Sudbury, Ont., May 4, 1970 . . . Shoots right . . . (October 2, 1988)—Stretched left knee ligaments vs. Oshawa.

Year	Team	League	Games	G.	A.	Pts.	Pen.
1985-86	Gloucester Bantams	OHA	34	23	15	38	45
1986-87	Guelph Platers	OHL	41	1	3	4	13
1987-88	Guelph Platers	OHL	62	6	22	28	71
1988-89	Guelph Platers (c)	OHL	53	20	44	64	57
1989-90	Owen Sound Platers	OHL	54	23	30	53	90

(c)—June, 1989—Drafted by Los Angeles Kings in 1989 NHL entry draft. Seventh Kings pick, 165th overall, eighth round.

DOUGLAS PETER WICKENHEISER

Center . . . 6' . . . 199 lbs. . . . Born, Regina, Sask., March 30, 1961 . . . Shoots left . . . Brother of Kurt Wickenheiser . . . (March 30, 1983)—Broke rib at Pittsburgh . . . (March 13, 1985)—Suffered complete tears of the entire medial complex and both cruciate ligaments in his left knee . . . (January 21, 1986)—Returned to St. Louis lineup after missing 56 games (12 in '84-85 and 44 in '85-86).

Year	Team	League	Games	G.	A.	Pts.	Pen.
1976-77	Regina Blues	SJHL	59	42	46	88	63
1977-78	Regina Pats	WCHL	68	37	51	88	49
1978-79	Regina Pats	WHL	68	32	62	94	141
1979-80	Regina Pats (a-c-d-e)	WHL	71	*89	81	*170	99
1980-81	Montreal Canadiens	NHL	41	7	8	15	20
1981-82	Montreal Canadiens	NHL	56	12	23	35	43
1982-83	Montreal Canadiens	NHL	78	25	30	55	49
1983-84	Montreal Canadiens (f)	NHL	27	5	5	10	6
1983-84	St. Louis Blues	NHL	46	7	21	28	19
1984-85	St. Louis Blues	NHL	68	23	20	43	36
1985-86	St. Louis Blues	NHL	36	8	11	19	16
1986-87	St. Louis Blues	NHL	80	13	15	28	37
1987-88	Vancouver Canucks (g-h)	NHL	80	7	19	26	36
1988-89	Flint Spirits	IHL	21	9	7	16	18
1988-89	Canadian National Team	Int'l.	26	7	15	22	40
1988-89	Baltimore Skipjacks	AHL	2	0	5	5	0
1988-89	New York Rangers (i)	NHL	1	1	0	1	0
1988-89	Washington Capitals (j)	NHL	16	2	5	7	4
1989-90	Washington Capitals	NHL	27	1	8	9	20
1989-90	Baltimore Skipjacks	AHL	35	9	19	28	22
NHL TOTALS			556	111	165	276	286

(c)—Won Bob Brownridge Memorial Trophy (Leading Scorer).
(d)—Named WHL Most Valuable Player.
(e)—June, 1980—Drafted as underage junior by Montreal Canadiens in 1980 NHL entry draft. First Canadiens pick, first overall, first round.
(f)—December, 1983—Traded by Montreal Canadiens with Gilbert Delorme and Greg Paslawski to St. Louis Blues for Perry Turnbull.
(g)—October, 1987—Acquired by Hartford Whalers in 1987 NHL waiver draft as compensation for St. Louis Blues drafting Bill Root from Whalers. He was then selected by Vancouver Canucks from the Whalers unprotected list with the Whalers taking Brent Peterson from Vancouver as compensation.
(h)—July, 1988—Signed by New York Rangers as a free agent.
(i)—November 30, 1988—Released by New York Rangers.
(j)—February 24, 1989—Signed by Washington Capitals as a free agent.

JAMES DUNCAN WIEMER

Defense . . . 6'4" . . . 197 lbs. . . . Born, Sudbury, Ont., January 9, 1961 . . . Shoots left . . . (November, 1989)—Bruised right leg.

Year	Team	League	Games	G.	A.	Pts.	Pen.
1978-79	Peterborough Petes	OMJHL	63	15	12	27	50
1979-80	Peterborough Petes (c)	OMJHL	53	17	32	49	63
1980-81	Peterborough Petes	OHL	65	41	54	95	102
1981-82	Rochester Americans	AHL	74	19	26	45	57
1982-83	Rochester Americans	AHL	74	15	44	59	43
1982-83	Buffalo Sabres (d)	NHL		..	..	..	..
1983-84	Buffalo Sabres	NHL	64	5	15	20	48
1983-84	Rochester Americans	AHL	12	4	11	15	11
1984-85	Rochester Americans	AHL	13	1	9	10	24
1984-85	New Haven Nighthawks	AHL	33	9	27	36	39
1984-85	Buffalo Sabres (e)	NHL	10	3	2	5	4
1984-85	New York Rangers	NHL	22	4	3	7	30
1985-86	New Haven Nighthawks (a-f)	AHL	73	24	49	73	108
1985-86	New York Rangers	NHL	7	3	0	3	2
1986-87	New Haven Nighthawks (g)	AHL	6	0	7	7	6

Year	Team	League	Games	G.	A.	Pts.	Pen.
1986-87	Nova Scotia Oilers	AHL	59	9	25	34	72
1987-88	Nova Scotia Oilers	AHL	57	11	32	43	99
1987-88	Edmonton Oilers	NHL	12	1	2	3	15
1988-89	Cape Breton Oilers (h)	AHL	51	12	29	41	80
1988-89	Los Angeles Kings	NHL	9	2	3	5	20
1988-89	New Haven Nighthawks (i)	AHL	3	1	1	2	2
1989-90	Maine Mariners	AHL	6	3	4	7	27
1989-90	Boston Bruins	NHL	61	5	14	19	63
NHL TOTALS			185	23	39	62	182

(c)—June, 1980—Drafted by Buffalo Sabres as underage junior in 1980 NHL entry draft. Fifth Sabres pick, 83rd overall, fourth round.
(d)—No regular season record. Played one playoff game.
(e)—December, 1984—Traded with Steve Patrick by Buffalo Sabres to New York Rangers for Chris Renaud and Dave Maloney.
(f)—Won Eddie Shore Plaque (Top Defenseman).
(g)—October, 1986—Traded with NHL rights to Reijo Ruotsalainen, Ville Horava and Clark Donatelli by New York Rangers to Edmonton Oilers to complete an earlier deal that saw the Rangers acquire Don Jackson and Mike Golden.
(h)—March 7, 1989—Traded with Alan May by Edmonton Oilers to Los Angeles Kings for Brian Wilks and John English.
(i)—July, 1989—Signed by Boston Bruins as a free agent.

BOB WILKIE

Defense . . . 6'2" . . . 200 lbs. . . . Born, Calgary, Alta., February 11, 1969 . . . Shoots right . . . (January, 1990)—Fractured kneecap.

Year	Team	League	Games	G.	A.	Pts.	Pen.
1984-85	Calgary Buffaloes	Atla. Midget	37	20	33	53	116
1985-86	Calgary Wranglers	WHL	63	8	19	27	56
1986-87	Swift Current Broncos (c)	WHL	65	12	38	50	50
1987-88	Swift Current Broncos	WHL	67	12	68	80	124
1988-89	Swift Current Broncos	WHL	62	18	67	85	89
1989-90	Adirondack Red Wings	AHL	58	5	33	38	64

(c)—June, 1987—Drafted as underage junior by Detroit Red Wings in 1987 NHL entry draft. Third Red Wings pick, 41st overall, second round.

NEIL WILKINSON

Defense . . . 6'3" . . . 190 lbs. . . . Born, Selkirk, Manitoba, August 15, 1967 . . . Shoots right . . . (January, 1986)—Broken nose and concussion . . . (September, 1988)—Twisted knee ligaments during Minnesota North Stars training camp . . . (November 9, 1989)—Bruised left instep . . . (January, 1990)—Strained back.

Year	Team	League	Games	G.	A.	Pts.	Pen.
1985-86	Selkirk Steelers (c)	MJHL	42	14	35	49	91
1986-87	Michigan State Univ.	CCHA	19	3	4	7	18
1987-88	Medicine Hat Tigers	WHL	55	11	21	32	157
1988-89	Kalamazoo Wings	IHL	39	5	15	20	96
1989-90	Kalamazoo Wings	IHL	20	6	7	13	62
1989-90	Minnesota North Stars	NHL	36	0	5	5	100
NHL TOTALS			36	0	5	5	100

(c)—June, 1986—Drafted by Minnesota North Stars in 1986 NHL entry draft. Second North Stars pick, 30th overall, second round.

BRIAN WILKS

Center . . . 5'11" . . . 175 lbs. . . . Born, Toronto, Ont., February 22, 1966 . . . Shoots right.

Year	Team	League	Games	G.	A.	Pts.	Pen.
1981-82	Toronto Marlboro Midgets	MTMHL	36	40	48	88	22
1982-83	Kitchener Rangers	OHL	69	6	17	23	25
1983-84	Kitchener Rangers (c)	OHL	64	21	54	75	36
1984-85	Kitchener Rangers	OHL	58	30	63	93	52
1984-85	Los Angeles Kings	NHL	2	0	0	0	0
1985-86	Los Angeles Kings	NHL	43	4	8	12	25
1986-87	Los Angeles Kings	NHL	1	0	0	0	0
1986-87	New Haven Nighthawks	AHL	43	16	20	36	23
1987-88	New Haven Nighthawks	AHL	18	4	8	12	26
1988-89	New Haven Nighthawks	AHL	44	15	19	34	48
1988-89	Los Angeles Kings (d)	NHL	2	0	0	0	2
1988-89	Cape Breton Oilers	AHL	12	4	11	15	27
1989-90	Cape Breton Oilers (e)	AHL	53	13	20	33	85
1989-90	Muskegon Lumberjacks	IHL	15	6	11	17	10
NHL TOTALS			48	4	8	12	27

(c)—June, 1984—Drafted as underage junior by Los Angeles Kings in 1984 NHL entry draft. Second Kings pick, 24th overall, second round.
(d)—March 7, 1989—Traded with John English by Los Angeles Kings to Edmonton Oilers for Jim Wiemer and Alan May.
(e)—March 6, 1990—Traded by Edmonton Oilers to Pittsburgh Penguins for future considerations.

SEAN WILLIAMS

Center . . . 6'2" . . . 180 lbs. . . . Born, Oshawa, Ont., January 28, 1968 . . . Shoots left.

Year	Team	League	Games	G.	A.	Pts.	Pen.
1984-85	Oshawa Generals	OHL	40	6	7	13	28
1985-86	Oshawa Generals (c)	OHL	55	15	23	38	23
1986-87	Oshawa Generals	OHL	62	21	23	44	32
1987-88	Oshawa Generals	OHL	65	58	65	123	38
1988-89	Saginaw Hawks	IHL	77	32	27	59	75
1989-90	Indianapolis Ice	IHL	78	27	31	58	25

(c)—June, 1986—Drafted as underage junior by Minnesota North Stars in 1986 NHL entry draft. Eleventh North Stars pick, 245th overall, 12th round.

RICK WILLIS JR.

Left Wing . . . 6' . . . 185 lbs. . . . Born, Lynn, Mass., January 9, 1972 . . . Shoots left.

Year	Team	League	Games	G.	A.	Pts.	Pen.
1986-87—Pingree H.S.		Mass. H.S.	22	14	17	31	..
1987-88—Pingree H.S.		Mass. H.S.	22	25	30	55	..
1988-89—Pingree H.S.		Mass. H.S.	24	23	30	53	..
1989-90—Pingree H.S. (c)		Mass. H.S.		17	30	47	..

(c)—June 16, 1990—Selected by New York Rangers in 1990 NHL entry draft. Fifth Rangers pick, 76th overall, fourth round.

CAREY WILSON

Center . . . 6'2" . . . 205 lbs. . . . Born, Winnipeg, Man., May 19, 1962 . . . Shoots right . . . Son of Dr. Gerry Wilson, former vice-president and team doctor of Winnipeg Jets (WHA) . . . (April 28, 1986)—Suffered ruptured spleen and missed remainder of playoffs . . . (October, 1987)—Strained shoulder . . . (February, 1989)—Bruised wrist . . . (October 28, 1989)—Sprained left knee ligaments at N.Y. Islanders and missed 26 games . . . (March 3, 1990)—Sprained right knee at Hartford and missed eight games.

Year	Team	League	Games	G.	A.	Pts.	Pen.
1978-79—Calgary Chinooks		AJHL	60	30	34	64	....
1979-80—Dartmouth College (c)		ECAC	31	16	22	38	20
1980-81—Dartmouth College		ECAC	21	9	13	22	52
1981-82—Helsinki IFK		Finland	39	15	17	32	58
1982-83—Helsinki IFK (d)		Finland	36	18	22	40	...
1983-84—Canadian Olympic Team		Int'l	59	21	24	45	34
1983-84—Calgary Flames		NHL	15	2	5	7	2
1984-85—Calgary Flames		NHL	74	24	48	72	27
1985-86—Calgary Flames		NHL	76	29	29	58	24
1986-87—Calgary Flames		NHL	80	20	36	56	42
1987-88—Calgary Flames (e)		NHL	34	9	21	30	18
1987-88—Hartford Whalers		NHL	36	18	20	38	22
1988-89—Hartford Whalers (f)		NHL	34	11	11	22	14
1988-89—New York Rangers		NHL	41	21	34	55	45
1989-90—New York Rangers (g)		NHL	41	9	17	26	57
NHL TOTALS			431	143	221	364	251

(c)—June, 1980—Drafted by Chicago Black Hawks in 1980 NHL entry draft. Eighth Black Hawks pick, 67th overall, fourth round.

(d)—November, 1982—Traded by Chicago Black Hawks to Calgary Flames for Denis Cyr.

(e)—January, 1987—Traded with Neil Sheehy and the NHL rights to Lane MacDonald by Calgary Flames to Hartford Whalers for Shane Churla and Dana Murzyn.

(f)—December 26, 1988—Traded with a fifth-round 1990 draft pick by Hartford Whalers to New York Rangers for Brian Lawton, Don Maloney and Norm Maciver.

(g)—July 9, 1990—Traded with future considerations by New York Rangers to Hartford Whalers for Jody Hull.

DOUGLAS WILSON

Defense . . . 6'1" . . . 187 lbs. . . . Born, Ottawa, Ont., July 5, 1957 . . . Shoots left . . . Missed part of 1976-77 season with knee surgery . . . Brother of Murray Wilson . . . Missed part of 1978-79 season with shoulder injury that required surgery . . . (November 25, 1981)—Broken jaw at Vancouver. Had his jaw wired shut, lost 25 pounds and has his vision restricted by special protective mask he had to wear . . . Set Chicago Black Hawks record for defensemen in 1981-82 with 39 goals and 85 points . . . Set Chicago record of 54 assists by a defenseman in 1984-85 (broke own record of 51 set in 1982-83) . . . (November, 1983)—Ankle injury . . . (February 3, 1984)—Broke nose at Winnipeg . . . (March 4, 1984)—Played his first game without a facemask after recovering from broken nose. He was accidently hit by the stick of Walt Poddubny of Toronto, suffered a fractured skull and missed remainder of the season . . . (March 8, 1987)—Sprained right knee vs. N.Y. Islanders . . . Holds Chicago Black Hawks career record for goals, assists and points by a defenseman . . . (December, 1987)—Shoulder surgery . . . (January 25, 1989)—Fractured right hand in fight with Craig Simpson at Edmonton . . . (March 4, 1989)—Bruised left shoulder when checked by Todd Gill at Toronto . . . (April 9, 1989)—Pulled left groin when his skate got caught in a rut in fourth playoff game vs. Detroit . . . Does not wear a helmet . . . (January, 1990)—Bruised toe . . . (March, 1990)—Pulled groin . . . (April, 1990)—Bruised forearm.

Year	Team	League	Games	G.	A.	Pts.	Pen.
1974-75—Ottawa 67's		Jr."A"OHA	55	29	58	87	75
1975-76—Ottawa 67's (b)		Jr."A"OHA	58	26	62	88	142
1976-77—Ottawa 67's (a-c)		Jr."A"OHA	43	25	54	79	85
1977-78—Chicago Black Hawks		NHL	77	14	20	34	72
1978-79—Chicago Black Hawks		NHL	56	5	21	26	37
1979-80—Chicago Black Hawks		NHL	73	12	49	61	70
1980-81—Chicago Black Hawks		NHL	76	12	39	51	80
1981-82—Chicago Black Hawks (a-d)		NHL	76	39	46	85	54
1982-83—Chicago Black Hawks		NHL	74	18	51	69	58
1983-84—Chicago Black Hawks		NHL	66	13	45	58	64
1984-85—Chicago Black Hawks (b)		NHL	78	22	54	76	44
1985-86—Chicago Black Hawks		NHL	79	17	47	64	80
1986-87—Chicago Black Hawks		NHL	69	16	32	48	36
1987-88—Chicago Black Hawks		NHL	27	8	24	32	28
1988-89—Chicago Black Hawks		NHL	66	15	47	62	69
1989-90—Chicago Black Hawks (b)		NHL	70	23	50	73	40
NHL TOTALS			887	214	525	739	732

(c)—Drafted from Ottawa 67's by Chicago Black Hawks in first round of 1977 amateur draft.

(d)—Won James Norris Memorial Trophy (Top NHL Defenseman).

MITCH WILSON

Right Wing . . . 5'8" . . . 185 lbs. . . . Born, Kelowna, B.C., February 15, 1962 . . . Shoots right . . . (May, 1989)—Separated right shoulder vs. Salt Lake.

Year	Team	League	Games	G.	A.	Pts.	Pen.
1980-81—Seattle Breakers		WHL	64	8	23	31	253
1981-82—Seattle Breakers		WHL	60	18	17	35	436
1982-83—Wichita Wind (c)		CHL	55	4	6	10	186
1983-84—Maine Mariners		AHL	71	6	8	14	*349
1984-85—Maine Mariners		AHL	51	6	3	9	220
1984-85—New Jersey Devils		NHL	9	0	2	2	21
1985-86—Maine Mariners		AHL	64	4	3	7	217
1986-87—Baltimore Skipjacks		AHL	58	8	9	17	353
1986-87—Pittsburgh Penguins		NHL	17	2	1	3	83
1987-88—Muskegon Lumberjacks		IHL	68	27	25	52	400
1988-89—Muskegon Lumberjacks		IHL	61	16	34	50	382
1989-90—Muskegon Lumberjacks		IHL	63	13	24	37	283
NHL TOTALS			26	2	3	5	104

(c)—October, 1982—Signed by New Jersey Devils as a free agent.

RONALD LEE WILSON

Center . . . 5'9" . . . 170 lbs. . . . Born, Toronto, Ont., May 13, 1956 . . . Shoots left.

Year	Team	League	Games	G.	A.	Pts.	Pen.
1974-75—Markham Waxers		OPJHL	43	26	28	54	24
1974-75—Toronto Marlboros		Jr."A"OHA	16	6	12	18	6
1975-76—St. Cath. Black Hawks		Jr."A"OHA	64	37	62	99	44
1976-77—Nova Scotia Voyageurs		AHL	67	15	21	36	18
1977-78—Nova Scotia Voyageurs		AHL	59	15	25	40	17
1978-79—Nova Scotia Voyageurs (d)		AHL	77	33	42	75	91
1979-80—Winnipeg Jets		NHL	79	21	36	57	28
1980-81—Winnipeg Jets		NHL	77	18	33	51	55
1981-82—Tulsa Oilers		CHL	41	20	38	58	22
1981-82—Winnipeg Jets		NHL	39	3	13	16	49
1982-83—Sherbrooke Jets		AHL	65	30	55	85	71
1982-83—Winnipeg Jets		NHL	12	6	3	9	4
1983-84—Winnipeg Jets		NHL	51	3	12	15	12
1983-84—Sherbrooke Jets		AHL	22	10	30	40	16
1984-85—Winnipeg Jets		NHL	75	10	9	19	31
1985-86—Winnipeg Jets		NHL	54	6	7	13	16
1985-86—Sherbrooke Canadiens		AHL	10	9	8	17	9
1986-87—Winnipeg Jets		NHL	80	3	13	16	13
1987-88—Winnipeg Jets (e)		NHL	69	5	8	13	28
1988-89—Moncton Hawks (b-f)		AHL	80	31	61	92	110
1989-90—Moncton Hawks (g)		AHL	47	16	37	53	64
1989-90—St. Louis Blues		NHL	33	3	17	20	23
NHL TOTALS			569	78	151	229	259

(c)—Drafted from St. Catharines Black Hawks by Montreal Canadiens in 15th round of 1976 amateur draft.

(d)—June, 1979—Sold by Montreal Canadiens to Winnipeg Jets.

(e)—May, 1988—Named playing/assistant coach of Moncton Golden Flames.

(f)—May, 1988—Named player/assistant coach of Moncton Flames by Winnipeg Jets.

(g)—January 22, 1990—Traded by Winnipeg Jets to St. Louis Blues for Doug Evans.

ROSS WILSON

Right Wing . . . 6'3" . . . 200 lbs. . . . Born, The Pas, Man., June 26, 1969 . . . Shoots right.

Year	Team	League	Games	G.	A.	Pts.	Pen.
1985-86—Sudbury Burgess Midget		SMHA	71	53	64	117	52
1986-87—Peterborough Petes (c)		OHL	66	28	11	39	91
1987-88—Peterborough Petes		OHL	66	29	30	59	114
1988-89—Peterborough Petes		OHL	64	48	41	89	90
1989-90—New Haven Nighthawks		AHL	61	19	14	33	39

(c)—June, 1987—Drafted as underage junior by Los Angeles Kings in 1987 NHL entry draft. Third Kings pick, 43rd overall, third round.

CHRISTOPHER WINNES

Right Wing . . . 6' . . . 180 lbs. . . . Born, Columbus, Ohio, February 12, 1968 . . . Shoots right.

Year	Team	League	Games	G.	A.	Pts.	Pen.
1985-86—Ridgefield H.S.		Conn. H.S.	24	40	30	70	..
1986-87—Northwood Prep. (c)		Mass. H.S.	27	25	25	50	..
1987-88—Univ. of New Hampshire		H. East	30	17	19	36	28
1988-89—Univ. of New Hampshire		H. East	30	11	20	31	22
1989-90—Univ. of New Hampshire		H. East	24	10	13	23	12

(c)—June, 1987—Drafted by Boston Bruins in 1987 NHL entry draft. Ninth Bruins pick, 161st overall, eighth round.

MICHAEL LAWRENCE WOLAK

Center . . . 5'11" . . . 170 lbs. . . . Born, Utica, Mich., April 29, 1968 . . . Shoots left.

Year	Team	League	Games	G.	A.	Pts.	Pen.
1984-85—Detroit Compuware Midget		Mich.	75	85	95	180	80
1985-86—Kitchener Rangers (c)		OHL	62	24	44	68	48
1986-87—Kitchener Rangers		OHL	9	3	6	9	6
1986-87—Belleville Bulls		OHL	25	20	16	36	18
1986-87—Windsor Spitfires		OHL	26	7	14	21	26
1987-88—Windsor Spitfires		OHL	63	42	72	114	86
1988-89—Windsor Spitfires		OHL	35	19	38	57	56
1988-89—Flint Spirits		IHL	2	0	1	1	4
1988-89—Peoria Rivermen		IHL	8	2	4	6	16
1989-90—Peoria Rivermen		IHL	50	7	16	23	31

(c)—June, 1986—Drafted as underage junior by St. Louis Blues in 1986 NHL entry draft. Fifth Blues pick, 87th overall, fifth round.

CHRIS WOLANIN

Defense . . . 6'2'' . . . 205 lbs. . . . Born, Detroit, Mich., October 21, 1969 . . . Shoots right . . . Brother of Craig Wolanin.

Year	Team	League	Games	G.	A.	Pts.	Pen.
1986-87—St. Mikes Jr. B		MTHL	25	4	9	13	50
1987-88—Univ. of Illinois/Chicago (c)		CCHA	37	1	6	7	38
1988-89—Univ. of Illinois/Chicago		CCHA	30	1	9	10	33
1989-90—Univ. of Illinois/Chicago		CCHA	34	1	6	7	116

(c)—June, 1988—Drafted by Vancouver Canucks in 1988 NHL entry draft. Tenth Canucks pick, 212th overall, 11th round.

CRAIG WOLANIN

Defense . . . 6'3'' . . . 205 lbs. . . . Born, Grosse Point, Mich., July 27, 1967 . . . Shoots left . . . (October 31, 1985)—Bruised left shoulder vs. Detroit . . . (February 1, 1986)—Broke ring finger on left hand at Washington . . . (February 19, 1986)—Surgery to finger . . . (December, 1987)—Sore left hip . . . Brother of Chris Wolanin . . . (November 15, 1988)—Fitted with knee brace for a sprained right knee . . . (December, 1988)—Surgery to right knee . . . (November 22, 1989)—Injured finger at Pittsburgh . . . (April 1, 1990)—Injured knee at Boston.

Year	Team	League	Games	G.	A.	Pts.	Pen.
1983-84—Detroit Compuware		Mich. Midget	69	8	42	50	86
1984-85—Kitchener Rangers (c)		OHL	60	5	16	21	95
1985-86—New Jersey Devils		NHL	44	2	16	18	74
1986-87—New Jersey Devils		NHL	68	4	6	10	109
1987-88—New Jersey Devils		NHL	78	6	25	31	170
1988-89—New Jersey Devils		NHL	56	3	8	11	69
1989-90—Utica Devils		AHL	6	2	4	6	2
1989-90—New Jersey Devils (d)		NHL	37	1	7	8	47
1989-90—Quebec Nordiques		NHL	13	0	3	3	10
NHL TOTALS			296	16	65	81	479

(c)—June, 1985—Drafted as underage junior by New Jersey Devils in 1985 NHL entry draft. First Devils pick, third overall, first round.

(d)—March 6, 1990—Traded with future considerations by New Jersey Devils to Quebec Nordiques for Peter Stastny. Randy Velischek was sent to Quebec in August, 1990, to complete deal.

ANDREW WOLF

Defense . . . 5'11'' . . . 196 lbs. . . . Born, Richmond, B.C., May 29, 1969 . . . Shoots right . . . (March, 1989)—Separated shoulder vs. Kamloops.

Year	Team	League	Games	G.	A.	Pts.	Pen.
1986-87—Victoria Cougars		WHL	65	5	25	30	167
1987-88—Victoria Cougars		WHL	65	11	29	40	143
1988-89—Victoria Cougars (c)		WHL	36	4	12	16	74
1989-90—Victoria Cougars		WHL	4	1	2	3	7

(c)—June, 1989—Drafted by Pittsburgh Penguins in 1989 NHL entry draft. Tenth Penguins pick, 184th overall, ninth round.

RANDY WOOD

Right Wing . . . 6' . . . 190 lbs. . . . Born, Manchester, Mass., October 12, 1963 . . . Shoots left . . . (October 17, 1989)—Suspended four games for swinging his stick at Curt Giles vs. Minnesota . . . (March 17, 1990)—Strained right shoulder vs. N.Y. Rangers.

Year	Team	League	Games	G.	A.	Pts.	Pen.
1982-83—Yale University		ECAC	26	5	14	19	10
1983-84—Yale University		ECAC	18	7	7	14	10
1984-85—Yale University		ECAC	32	25	28	53	23
1985-86—Yale University		ECAC	31	25	30	55	26
1986-87—Springfield Indians		AHL	75	23	24	47	57
1986-87—New York Islanders (c)		NHL	6	1	0	1	4
1987-88—New York Islanders		NHL	75	22	16	38	80
1987-88—Springfield Indians		AHL	1	0	1	1	0
1988-89—Springfield Indians		AHL	1	1	1	2	0
1988-89—New York Islanders		NHL	77	15	13	28	44
1989-90—New York Islanders		NHL	74	24	24	48	39
NHL TOTALS			232	62	53	115	167

(c)—August, 1986—Signed by New York Islanders as a free agent.

CRAIG WOODCROFT

Left Wing . . . 6'1'' . . . 185 lbs. . . . Born, Toronto, Ont., December 3, 1969 . . . Shoots left.

Year	Team	League	Games	G.	A.	Pts.	Pen.
1986-87—Pickering Jr. B		OHA	37	21	21	42	42
1987-88—Colgate Univ. (c)		ECAC	29	7	10	17	28
1988-89—Colgate Univ.		ECAC	29	20	29	49	62
1988-89—Canadian National Team		Int'l.	2	0	0	0	4
1989-90—Colgate Univ. (d-e)		ECAC	37	20	26	46	108

(c)—June, 1988—Drafted by Chicago Black Hawks in 1988 NHL entry draft. Sixth Black Hawks pick, 134th overall, seventh round.

(d)—Named to ECAC All-Tournament team.

(e)—Named ECAC Tournament MVP.

DAN WOODLEY

Center . . . 5'11'' . . . 190 lbs. . . . Born, Oklahoma City, Okla., December 29, 1967 . . . Shoots right . . . Also plays either Wing . . . (February 1985)—Torn cartilage in right knee . . . (October, 1986)—Surgery to repair torn abdominal muscle.

Year	Team	League	Games	G.	A.	Pts.	Pen.
1983-84—Summerland Buckeroos		BCJHL	53	17	34	51	100
1984-85—Portland Winter Hawks		WHL	63	21	36	57	108
1985-86—Portland Winter Hawks (c)		WHL	62	45	47	92	100
1986-87—Portland Winter Hawks		WHL	47	30	50	80	81
1987-88—Vancouver Canucks		NHL	5	2	0	2	17
1987-88—Flint Spirits (d)		IHL	69	29	37	66	104

Year	Team	League	Games	G.	A.	Pts.	Pen.
1988-89—Milwaukee Admirals (e)		IHL	30	9	12	21	48
1988-89—Sherbrooke Canadiens		AHL	30	9	16	25	69
1989-90—Sherbrooke Canadiens		AHL	65	18	40	58	144
NHL TOTALS			5	2	0	2	17

(c)—June, 1986—Drafted as underage junior by Vancouver Canucks in 1986 NHL entry draft. First Canucks pick, seventh overall, first round.

(d)—Winner of Ken McKenzie Trophy (Outstanding American-born Rookie).

(e)—January 24, 1989—Traded by Vancouver Canucks to Montreal Canadiens for Jose Charbonneau.

BOB WOODS

Defense . . . 6' . . . 175 lbs. . . . Born, Chilliwack, B.C., January 24, 1968 . . . Shoots left . . . (January 24, 1989)—Bruised shoulder in WHL All-star game when checked by Darcy Loewen.

Year	Team	League	Games	G.	A.	Pts.	Pen.
1987-88—Brandon Wheat Kings (c)		WHL	72	21	56	77	84
1988-89—Brandon Wheat Kings (b)		WHL	63	26	50	76	100
1988-89—Utica Devils		AHL	11	0	1	1	2
1989-90—Utica Devils		AHL	58	2	12	14	30

(c)—June, 1988—Drafted by New Jersey Devils in 1988 NHL entry draft. Eleventh Devils pick, 201st overall, 10th round.

ROBERT WOODWARD

Left Wing . . . 6'4'' . . . 225 lbs. . . . Born, Evanston, Ill., January 15, 1971 . . . Shoots left . . . (October, 1987)—Bruised kidney playing football.

Year	Team	League	Games	G.	A.	Pts.	Pen.
1987-88—Deerfield H.S.		Ill.	25	36	55	91	..
1988-89—Deerfield H.S. (c)		Ill.	29	46	71	117	12
1989-90—Michigan State Univ.		CCHA	44	17	9	26	8

(c)—June, 1989—Drafted by Vancouver Canucks in 1989 NHL entry draft. Second Canucks pick, 29th overall, second round.

JASON WOOLLEY

Defense . . . 6' . . . 186 lbs. . . . Born, Toronto, Ont., July 27, 1969 . . . Shoots left.

Year	Team	League	Games	G.	A.	Pts.	Pen.
1987-88—St. Michael's Jr. B		OHA	31	19	37	56	22
1988-89—Michigan State Univ. (c-d)		CCHA	47	12	25	37	26
1989-90—Michigan State Univ.		CCHA	45	10	38	48	26

(c)—Named to CCHA All-Rookie Team.

(d)—June, 1989—Drafted by Washington Capitals in 1989 NHL entry draft. Fourth Capitals pick, 61st overall, third round.

TERRY YAKE

Center . . . 5'11'' . . . 175 lbs. . . . Born, New Westminister, B.C., October 22, 1968 . . . Shoots right.

Year	Team	League	Games	G.	A.	Pts.	Pen.
1984-85—Brandon Wheat Kings		WHL	11	1	1	2	0
1985-86—Brandon Wheat Kings		WHL	72	26	26	52	49
1986-87—Brandon Wheat Kings (c)		WHL	71	44	58	102	64
1987-88—Brandon Wheat Kings		WHL	72	55	85	140	59
1988-89—Hartford Whalers		NHL	2	0	0	0	0
1988-89—Binghamton Whalers		AHL	75	39	56	95	57
1989-90—Hartford Whalers		NHL	2	0	1	1	0
1989-90—Binghamton Whalers		AHL	77	13	42	55	37
NHL TOTALS			4	0	1	1	0

(c)—June, 1987—Drafted by Hartford Whalers in 1987 NHL entry draft. Third Whalers pick, 81st overall, fourth round.

TRENT YAWNEY

Defense . . . 6'3'' . . . 185 lbs. . . . Born, Hudson Bay, Sask., September 29, 1965 . . . Shoots left . . . (March, 1989)—Bruised left shoulder . . . (April 24, 1989)—Strained left shoulder when checked by Doug Evans vs. St. Louis . . . (November 11, 1989)—Bruised kidney at N.Y. Islanders . . . (January, 1990)—Charley horse.

Year	Team	League	Games	G.	A.	Pts.	Pen.
1981-82—Saskatoon Blades		WHL	6	1	0	1	0
1982-83—Saskatoon Blades		WHL	59	6	31	37	44
1983-84—Saskatoon Blades (c)		WHL	72	13	46	59	81
1984-85—Saskatoon Blades		WHL	72	16	51	67	158
1985-86—Team Canada		Int'l.	73	6	15	21	60
1986-87—Team Canada		Int'l.	51	4	15	19	37
1987-88—Canadian Olympic Team		Int'l.	68	5	13	18	87
1987-88—Chicago Black Hawks		NHL	15	2	8	10	15
1988-89—Chicago Black Hawks		NHL	69	5	19	24	116
1989-90—Chicago Black Hawks		NHL	70	5	15	20	82
NHL TOTALS			154	12	42	54	213

(c)—June, 1984—Drafted as underage junior by Chicago Black Hawks in 1984 NHL entry draft. Second Black Hawks pick, 45th overall, third round.

C. J. YOUNG

Right Wing . . . 5'10'' . . . 180 lbs. . . . Born, Waban, Mass., January 1, 1968 . . . Shoots right . . . (December 18, 1988)—Set ECAC record with three shorthanded goals in 49 seconds against Dartmouth. He also set a record for fastest three goals.

Year	Team	League	Games	G.	A.	Pts.	Pen.
1986-87—Harvard Univ.		ECAC	34	17	12	29	30
1987-88—Harvard Univ.		ECAC	28	13	16	29	40
1988-89—Harvard Univ. (b-c)		ECAC	34	33	22	55	24
1989-90—Harvard Univ. (a-d)		ECAC	28	21	28	49	32

(c)—June, 1989—Selected by New Jersey Devils in 1989 NHL supplemental draft.

(d)—Named to NCAA second-team All-America team (East).

SCOTT YOUNG

Right Wing . . . 6' . . . 185 lbs. . . . Born, Clinton, Mass., October 1, 1967 . . . Shoots right . . . (October 8, 1988)—Took 22 stitches to close a facial cut vs. Boston when Garry Galley's aluminum stick shattered and a sliver caught him just above the right eye . . . (February 18, 1990)—Required 19 stitches to close cuts on his face after being hit by Mike Foligno.

Year	Team	League	Games	G.	A.	Pts.	Pen.
1984-85—St. Marks H.S.		Mass.	23	28	41	69	....
1985-86—Boston University (c)		H. East	38	16	13	29	31
1986-87—Boston University		H. East	33	15	21	36	24
1987-88—U.S. Olympic Team		Int'l	59	13	53	66	..
1987-88—Hartford Whalers		NHL	7	0	0	0	2
1988-89—Hartford Whalers		NHL	76	19	40	59	27
1989-90—Hartford Whalers		NHL	80	24	40	64	47
NHL TOTALS			163	43	80	123	76

(c)—June, 1986—Drafted by Hartford Whalers in 1986 NHL entry draft. First Whalers pick, 11th overall, first round.

STEVE YOUNG

Right Wing . . . 6'3'' . . . 200 lbs. . . . Born, Calgary, Alta., May 17, 1969 . . . Shoots right.

Year	Team	League	Games	G.	A.	Pts.	Pen.
1986-87—Calgary Wranglers		WHL	4	1	0	1	0
1987-88—New Westminster Bruins		WHL	35	5	6	11	35
1987-88—Lethbridge Broncos		WHL	36	7	10	17	50
1988-89—Moose Jaw Warriors (c)		WHL	72	20	17	37	224
1989-90—Moose Jaw Warriors		WHL	1	1	0	1	11
1989-90—Prince Albert Raiders		WHL	45	15	17	32	169
1989-90—Portland Winter Hawks		WHL	42	15	17	32	169

(c)—June, 1989—Drafted by New York Islanders in 1989 NHL entry draft. Sixth Islanders pick, 90th overall, fifth round.

PAUL YSEBAERT

Center . . . 6'1'' . . . 170 lbs. . . . Born, Sarnia, Ont., May 15, 1966 . . . Shoots left . . . (December, 1988)—Pulled stomach and groin muscles . . . (March, 1989)—Left thigh contusion.

Year	Team	League	Games	G.	A.	Pts.	Pen.
1983-84—Petrolia Jets (c)		WOJBHL	33	35	42	77	20
1984-85—Bowling Green Univ.		CCHA	42	23	32	55	54
1985-86—Bowling Green Univ. (b)		CCHA	42	23	45	68	50
1986-87—Bowling Green Univ. (b)		CCHA	45	27	58	85	44
1986-87—Canadian Olympic Team		Int'l	5	1	0	1	4
1987-88—Utica Devils		AHL	78	30	49	79	60
1988-89—Utica Devils		AHL	56	36	44	80	22
1988-89—New Jersey Devils		NHL	5	0	4	4	0
1989-90—New Jersey Devils		NHL	5	1	2	3	0
1989-90—Utica Devils (a-d-e)		AHL	74	53	52	*105	61
NHL TOTALS			10	1	6	7	0

(c)—June, 1984—Drafted by New Jersey Devils in 1984 NHL entry draft. Fourth Devils pick, 74th overall, fourth round.
(d)—Won John B. Sollenberger Trophy (AHL Leading Scorer).
(e)—Won Les Cunningham Award (AHL MVP).

STEVE YZERMAN

Center . . . 5'11'' . . . 185 lbs. . . . Born, Cranbrook, B.C., May 9, 1965 . . . Shoots right . . . (January 31, 1984)—Became youngest person to ever play in NHL All-Star Game . . . (January 31, 1986)—Broke collarbone vs. St. Louis . . . (March 1, 1988)—Fell into a goalpost vs. Buffalo moments after scoring his 50th goal of the season. He required surgery to his right knee to repair damaged ligaments.

Year	Team	League	Games	G.	A.	Pts.	Pen.
1981-82—Peterborough Petes		OHL	58	21	43	64	65
1982-83—Peterborough Petes (c)		OHL	56	42	49	91	33
1983-84—Detroit Red Wings (d)		NHL	80	39	48	87	33
1984-85—Detroit Red Wings		NHL	80	30	59	89	58
1985-86—Detroit Red Wings		NHL	51	14	28	42	16
1986-87—Detroit Red Wings		NHL	80	31	59	90	43
1987-88—Detroit Red Wings		NHL	64	50	52	102	44
1988-89—Detroit Red Wings		NHL	80	65	90	155	61
1989-90—Detroit Red Wings		NHL	79	62	65	127	79
NHL TOTALS			514	291	401	692	334

(c)—June, 1983—Drafted as underage junior by Detroit Red Wings in 1983 NHL entry draft. First Red Wings pick, fourth overall, first round.
(d)—Named NHL Rookie of the Year in poll of players by THE SPORTING NEWS.

ZARLEY ZALAPSKI

Defense . . . 6'1'' . . . 195 lbs. . . . Born, Edmonton, Alta., April 22, 1968 . . . Shoots left . . . (October, 1987)—Spondylothesis (Deterioration of the bony structure of the spine) . . . (December 29, 1988)—Tore ligaments in right knee vs. Philadelphia . . . (October 25, 1989)—Broke right collarbone vs. Toronto . . . (February 24, 1990)—Sprained right knee at Montreal and missed 13 games.

Year	Team	League	Games	G.	A.	Pts.	Pen.
1984-85—Fort Saskatchewan Traders		AJHL	23	17	30	47	14
1985-86—Fort Saskatchewan Traders		AJHL	27	20	33	53	46
1985-86—Team Canada (c)		Int'l	32	2	4	6	10
1986-87—Team Canada		Int'l	74	11	29	40	28
1987-88—Canadian Olympic Team		Int'l	55	4	16	20	34
1987-88—Pittsburgh Penguins		NHL	15	3	8	11	7
1988-89—Pittsburgh Penguins		NHL	58	12	33	45	57
1989-90—Pittsburgh Penguins		NHL	51	6	25	31	37
NHL TOTALS			124	21	66	87	101

(c)—June, 1986—Drafted by Pittsburgh Penguins in 1986 NHL entry draft. First Penguins pick, fourth overall, first round.

ROB ZAMUNER

Center . . . 6'2'' . . . 202 lbs. . . . Born, Oakville, Ont., September 17, 1969 . . . Shoots left.

Year	Team	League	Games	G.	A.	Pts.	Pen.
1985-86—Oakville Midgets		OHA	48	43	50	93	66
1986-87—Guelph Platers		OHL	62	6	15	21	8
1987-88—Guelph Platers		OHL	58	20	41	61	18
1988-89—Guelph Platers (c)		OHL	66	46	65	111	38
1989-90—Flint Spirits		IHL	77	44	35	79	32

(c)—June, 1989—Drafted by New York Rangers in 1989 NHL entry draft. Third Rangers pick, 45th overall, third round.

BRAD ZAVISHA

Left Wing . . . 6'1'' . . . 195 lbs. . . . Born, Hines Creek, Alta., January 4, 1972 . . . Shoots left . . . Also plays Center.

Year	Team	League	Games	G.	A.	Pts.	Pen.
1987-88—St. Albert Midget		Alta.	35	10	20	30	84
1988-89—Seattle Thunderbirds		WHL	52	8	13	21	43
1989-90—Seattle Thunderbirds (c)		WHL	69	22	38	60	124

(c)—June 16, 1990—Selected by Quebec Nordiques in 1990 NHL entry draft. Third Nordiques pick, 43rd overall, third round.

RICHARD ANDREW ZEMLAK

Center . . . 6'2'' . . . 190 lbs. . . . Born, Wynard, Sask., March 3, 1963 . . . Shoots right . . . (November, 1988)—Sprained right knee . . . (February, 1989)—Injured shoulder.

Year	Team	League	Games	G.	A.	Pts.	Pen.
1979-80—Regina Pat Blues		SJHL	30	4	7	11	80
1980-81—Spokane Flyers (c)		WHL	72	19	19	38	132
1981-82—Spokane Flyers (d)		WHL	28	10	22	32	113
1981-82—Medicine Hat Tigers		WHL	41	11	20	31	70
1981-82—Salt Lake Golden Eagles		CHL	6	0	0	0	2
1982-83—Medicine Hat Tigers		WHL	51	20	17	37	119
1982-83—Nanaimo Islanders		WHL	18	2	8	10	50
1983-84—Montana Magic		CHL	14	2	2	4	17
1983-84—Toledo Goaldiggers (e)		IHL	45	8	19	27	101
1984-85—Fredericton Express		AHL	16	3	4	7	59
1984-85—Muskegon Lumberjacks		IHL	64	19	18	37	221
1985-86—Muskegon Lumberjacks		IHL	3	1	2	3	36
1985-86—Fredericton Express		AHL	58	6	5	11	305
1986-87—Fredericton Express		AHL	28	9	6	15	201
1986-87—Quebec Nordiques		NHL	20	0	2	2	47
1987-88—Minnesota North Stars (f)		NHL	54	1	4	5	307
1988-89—Kalamazoo Wings		IHL	2	1	3	4	22
1988-89—Minnesota North Stars (g)		NHL	3	0	0	0	13
1988-89—Pittsburgh Penguins		NHL	31	0	0	0	135
1988-89—Muskegon Lumberjacks		IHL	18	5	4	9	55
1989-90—Muskegon Lumberjacks		IHL	61	17	39	56	263
1989-90—Pittsburgh Penguins		NHL	19	1	5	6	43
NHL TOTALS			127	2	11	13	545

(c)—June, 1981—Drafted as underage junior by St. Louis Blues in 1981 NHL entry draft. Ninth Blues pick, 209th overall, 10th round.
(d)—December, 1981—Selected by Medicine Hat Tigers in special WHL draft of players from defunct Spokane Flyers.
(e)—August, 1984—Sold by St. Louis Blues to Quebec Nordiques.
(f)—October, 1987—Acquired by the New York Rangers in the 1987 NHL waiver draft as compensation for the Quebec Nordiques drafting of Stu Kulak. The Minnesota North Stars then selected him from the New York Rangers list.
(g)—November 1, 1988—Traded by Minnesota North Stars to Pittsburgh Penguins for Rob Gaudreau.

JASON ZENT

Left Wing . . . 5'11'' . . . 180 lbs. . . . Born, Buffalo, N.Y., April 15, 1971 . . . Shoots left.

Year	Team	League	Games	G.	A.	Pts.	Pen.
1984-85—Depew Saints Bantams		N.Y.	48	40	30	70	26
1985-86—Depew Saints Bantams		N.Y.	55	50	33	83	34
1986-87—Depew Saints Bantams		N.Y.	40	44	38	82	56
1987-88—Nichols H.S.		N.Y.	21	20	16	36	28
1988-89—Nichols H.S. (c)		N.Y.	29	49	32	81	26
1989-90—Nichols H.S.		N.Y.	....	...	...	....	....

(c)—June, 1989—Drafted by New York Islanders in 1989 NHL entry draft. Third Islanders pick, 44th overall, third round.

ROB ZETTLER

Defense . . . 6'2'' . . . 180 lbs. . . . Born, Sept Illes, Que., March 8, 1968 . . . Shoots left.

Year	Team	League	Games	G.	A.	Pts.	Pen.
1984-85—Sault Ste. Marie Greyhounds		OHL	60	2	14	16	37
1985-86—Sault Ste. Marie Greyhounds (c)		OHL	57	5	23	28	92
1986-87—Sault Ste. Marie Greyhounds		OHL	64	13	22	35	89
1987-88—Sault Ste. Marie Greyhounds		OHL	64	7	41	48	77
1987-88—Kalamazoo Wings		IHL	2	0	1	1	0
1988-89—Minnesota North Stars		NHL	2	0	0	0	0
1988-89—Kalamazoo Wings		IHL	80	5	21	26	79
1989-90—Minnesota North Stars		NHL	31	0	8	8	45
1989-90—Kalamazoo Wings		IHL	41	6	10	16	64
NHL TOTALS			33	0	8	8	45

(c)—June, 1986—Drafted as underage junior by Minnesota North Stars in 1986 NHL entry draft. Fifth North Stars pick, 55th overall, fifth round.

PETER ZEZEL

Center . . . 5'9" . . . 200 lbs. . . . Born, Toronto, Ont., April 22, 1965 . . . Shoots left. . . (November, 1984)—Broken hand . . . (March, 1987)—Torn medial cartilage in left knee . . . (November, 1987)—Sprained right ankle . . . (March, 1988)—Separated left shoulder . . . (December, 1988)—Pulled groin . . . (January, 1989)—Bruised sternum . . . (March 5, 1989)—Sprained right knee when he became entangled with Dirk Graham's stick at Chicago . . . (March 11, 1990)—Bruised right hip when checked by Duane Sutter and Jocelyn Lemieux vs. Chicago . . . (1982)—Played three games as a striker for Toronto Blizzard in the North American Soccer League.

Year	Team	League	Games	G.	A.	Pts.	Pen.
1981-82—Don Mills Flyers		MTHL	40	43	51	94	36
1982-83—Toronto Marlboros (c)		OHL	66	35	39	74	28
1983-84—Toronto Marlboros		OHL	68	47	86	133	31
1984-85—Philadelphia Flyers		NHL	65	15	46	61	26
1985-86—Philadelphia Flyers		NHL	79	17	37	54	76
1986-87—Philadelphia Flyers		NHL	71	33	39	72	71
1987-88—Philadelphia Flyers		NHL	69	22	35	57	42
1988-89—Philadelphia Flyers (d)		NHL	26	4	13	17	15
1988-89—St. Louis Blues		NHL	52	17	36	53	27
1989-90—St. Louis Blues (e)		NHL	73	25	47	72	30
NHL TOTALS			435	133	253	386	287

(c)—June, 1983—Drafted as underage junior by Philadelphia Flyers in 1983 NHL entry draft. First Flyers pick, 41st overall, second round.

(d)—November 29, 1988—Traded by Philadelphia Flyers to St. Louis Blues for Mike Bullard.

(e)—July 13, 1990—Traded with Mike Lalor by St. Louis Blues to Washington Capitals for Geoff Courtnall.

DOUG ZMOLEK

Defense . . . 6'1" . . . 195 lbs. . . . Born, Rochester, Minn., November 3, 1970 . . . Shoots left.

Year	Team	League	Games	G.	A.	Pts.	Pen.
1987-88—Rochester John Marshall H.S.		Minn.	27	4	32	36	..
1988-89—Rochester John Marshall H.S. (c)		Minn.	29	17	41	58	..
1989-90—Univ. of Minnesota		WCHA	40	1	10	11	52

(c)—June, 1989—Drafted by Minnesota North Stars in 1989 NHL entry draft. First North Stars pick, seventh overall, first round.

RICK ZOMBO

Defense . . . 6'1" . . . 190 lbs. . . . Born, Des Plaines, Ill., May 8, 1963 . . . Shoots right . . . (December, 1984)—Injured knee . . . (December, 1987)—Injured shoulder . . . (December, 1988)—Strained knee . . . (December 27, 1989)—Suspended three games for high sticking Al Iafrate.

Year	Team	League	Games	G.	A.	Pts.	Pen.
1980-81—Austin Mavericks (a-c-d)		USHL	43	10	26	36	73
1981-82—Univ. of North Dakota		WCHA	45	1	15	16	31
1982-83—Univ. of North Dakota		WCHA	33	5	11	16	41
1983-84—Univ. of North Dakota		WCHA	34	7	24	31	40
1984-85—Adirondack Red Wings		AHL	56	3	32	35	70
1984-85—Detroit Red Wings		NHL	1	0	0	0	0
1985-86—Adirondack Red Wings		AHL	69	7	34	41	94
1985-86—Detroit Red Wings		NHL	14	0	1	1	16
1986-87—Adirondack Red Wings		AHL	25	0	6	6	22
1986-87—Detroit Red Wings		NHL	44	1	4	5	59
1987-88—Detroit Red Wings		NHL	62	3	14	17	96
1988-89—Detroit Red Wings		NHL	75	1	20	21	106
1989-90—Detroit Red Wings		NHL	77	5	20	25	95
NHL TOTALS			273	10	59	69	372

(c)—Named USHL Best Defenseman.

(d)—June, 1981—Drafted by Detroit Red Wings in 1981 NHL entry draft. Sixth Red Wings pick, 149th overall, eighth round.

SCOTT ZYGULSKI

Defense . . . 6'1" . . . 190 lbs. . . . Born, South Bend, Ind., April 11, 1970 . . . Shoots right.

Year	Team	League	Games	G.	A.	Pts.	Pen.
1984-85—South Bend Major Bantam		Ind.	60	22	46	68	40
1985-86—South Bend Major Bantam		Ind.	60	31	44	75	38
1986-87—St. Joseph's H.S.		Ind.	53	21	50	71	46
1987-88—St. Joseph's H.S.		Ind.	57	18	44	62	32
1988-89—Culver Military Acad. (c)		Ind.	29	11	16	27	16
1989-90—Boston College		H. East	14	0	1	1	6

(c)—June, 1989—Drafted by Detroit Red Wings in 1989 NHL entry draft. Seventh Red Wings pick, 137th overall, seventh round.

GOALTENDERS

DEAN ANDERSON

Goaltender . . . 5'10" . . . 175 lbs. . . . Born, Oshawa, Ont., July 14, 1966 . . . Shoots left.

Year	Team	League	Games	Mins.	Goals	SO.	Avg.	A.	Pen.
1984-85—Univ. of Wisconsin		WCHA	36	2072	148	0	4.29	1	21
1985-86—Univ. of Wisconsin		WCHA	20	1128	80	0	4.26	1	4
1986-87—Univ. of Wisconsin		WCHA	9	409	27	0	3.96	0	0
1987-88—Univ. of Wisconsin (c)		WCHA	45	2718	148	2	3.27	1	31
1988-89—Newmarket Saints		AHL	2	38	4	0	6.32	0	0
1988-89—Flint Spirits		IHL	16	770	82	1	6.39	0	6
1989-90—Knoxville Cherokees		ECHL	17	997	73	...	4.39	1	10

(c)—June, 1988—Selected by Toronto Maple Leafs in 1988 NHL supplemental draft.

MIKE BALES

Goaltender . . . 6'1" . . . 180 lbs. . . . Born, Saskatoon, Sask., August 6, 1971 . . . Shoots left.

Year	Team	League	Games	Mins.	Goals	SO.	Avg.	A.	Pen.
1988-89—Estevan Bruins		SJHL	44	2412	197	1	4.90	..	....
1989-90—Ohio State Univ. (c)		CCHA	21	1117	95	0	5.10	1	2

(c)—June 16, 1990—Selected by Boston Bruins in 1990 NHL entry draft. Fourth Bruins pick, 105th overall, fifth round.

THOMAS BARRASSO

Goaltender . . . 6'3" . . . 195 lbs. . . . Born, Boston, Mass., March 31, 1965 . . . Shoots right . . . Member of 1983 U.S. National Junior Team . . . Left 1984 U.S. Olympic team to sign with Buffalo Sabres . . . First U.S.-born player to win Calder Trophy (top NHL rookie) since Frank Brimsek (Boston goalie) in 1939 . . . First goaltender to win Calder Trophy since Ken Dryden in 1972 . . . (June, 1985)—Twisted knee during Molson Softball Tournament in Niagara Falls, Ont. . . . (November, 1987)—Chip fracture of ankle . . . (April 9, 1988)—Pulled groin vs. Boston . . . (January 17, 1989)—Pulled groin muscle at N.Y. Islanders . . . (March, 1989)—Injured shoulder . . . (October 30, 1989)—Surgery to right wrist and missed 21 games . . . (February, 1990)—Pulled groin . . . (February 9, 1990)—Granted a leave of absence to be with his daughter as she underwent cancer treatment in Los Angeles . . . (March 19, 1990)—Rejoined the Penguins.

Year	Team	League	Games	Mins.	Goals	SO.	Avg.	A.	Pen.
1981-82—Acton Boxboro H.S.		Mass. H.S.	23	1035	32	7	1.86	..	....
1982-83—Acton Boxboro H.S. (c)		Mass. H.S.	23	1035	17	10	0.99	..	....
1983-84—Buffalo Sabres (a-d-e)		NHL	42	2475	117	2	2.84	2	20

Year	Team	League	Games	Mins.	Goals	SO.	Avg.	A.	Pen.
1984-85—Rochester Americans		AHL	5	267	6	1	1.35	0	2
1984-85—Buffalo Sabres (b)		NHL	54	3248	144	5	2.66	6	41
1985-86—Buffalo Sabres		NHL	60	3561	214	2	3.61	4	28
1986-87—Buffalo Sabres		NHL	46	2501	152	2	3.65	1	22
1987-88—Buffalo Sabres		NHL	54	3133	173	2	3.31	1	50
1988-89—Buffalo Sabres (f)		NHL	10	545	45	0	4.95	3	21
1988-89—Pittsburgh Penguins		NHL	44	2406	162	0	4.04	5	49
1989-90—Pittsburgh Penguins		NHL	24	1294	101	0	4.68	0	8
NHL TOTALS			334	19163	1108	13	3.47	22	239

(c)—June, 1983—Drafted by Buffalo Sabres in 1983 NHL entry draft. First Sabres pick, fifth overall, first round.

(d)—Won Calder Memorial Trophy (Top NHL Rookie).

(e)—Won Vezina Trophy (Outstanding NHL Goaltender).

(f)—November 12, 1988—Traded with a third-round 1990 draft pick by Buffalo Sabres to Pittsburgh Penguins for Doug Bodger and Darrin Shannon.

DON BEAUPRE

Goaltender . . . 5'9" . . . 195 lbs. . . . Born, Kitchener, Ont., September 19, 1961 . . . Shoots left . . . (October, 1981)—Bruised ribs . . . (February, 1985)—Sprained knee . . . (December, 1987)—Pulled groin muscle . . . (January 31, 1990)—Injured ligaments in right thumb at Minnesota and missed nine games.

Year	Team	League	Games	Mins.	Goals	SO.	Avg.	A.	Pen.
1978-79—Sudbury Wolves		OMJHL	54	3248	259	2	4.78	0	0
1979-80—Sudbury Wolves (a-c)		OMJHL	59	3447	248	0	4.32	4	18
1980-81—Minnesota North Stars		NHL	44	2585	138	0	3.20	0	20
1981-82—Nashville South Stars		CHL	5	299	25	0	5.02	0	4
1981-82—Minnesota North Stars		NHL	29	1634	101	0	3.71	0	19
1982-83—Birmingham South Stars		CHL	10	599	31	0	3.11	0	6
1982-83—Minnesota North Stars		NHL	36	2011	120	0	3.58	2	10
1983-84—Salt Lake Golden Eagles		CHL	7	419	30	0	4.30	0	0
1983-84—Minnesota North Stars		NHL	33	1791	123	0	4.12	0	17
1984-85—Minnesota North Stars		NHL	21	1770	109	1	3.69	0	4
1985-86—Minnesota North Stars		NHL	52	3073	182	1	3.55	0	34
1986-87—Minnesota North Stars		NHL	47	2622	174	1	3.98	0	16
1987-88—Minnesota North Stars		NHL	43	2288	161	0	4.22	0	8
1988-89—Minnesota North Stars (d)		NHL	1	59	3	0	3.05	0	0
1988-89—Washington Capitals		NHL	11	578	28	1	2.91	0	6
1988-89—Baltimore Skipjacks		AHL	30	1715	102	0	3.57	0	9
1988-89—Kalamazoo Wings		IHL	3	179	9	0	3.02	0	0
1989-90—Washington Capitals		NHL	48	2793	150	2	3.22	1	24
NHL TOTALS			365	21204	1289	6	3.65	4	158

(c)—June, 1980—Drafted by Minnesota North Stars as underage junior in 1980 NHL entry draft. Second North Stars pick, 37th overall, second round.

(d)—November 1, 1988—Traded by Minnesota North Stars to Washington Capitals for NHL rights to Claudio Scremin.

STEPHANE BEAUREGARD

Goaltender . . . 5'11" . . . 185 lbs. . . . Born, Cowansville, Que., January 10, 1968 . . . Shoots right.

Year	Team	League	Games	Mins.	Goals	SO.	Avg.	A.	Pen.
1986-87	St. Jean Castors	QMJHL	13	785	58	0	4.43	0	0
1987-88	St. Jean Castors (a-c-d-e)	QMJHL	66	3766	229	2	3.65	1	12
1988-89	Moncton Hawks	AHL	15	824	62	0	4.51	0	2
1988-89	Fort Wayne Komets	IHL	16	830	43	0	3.10	0	0
1989-90	Fort Wayne Komets	IHL	33	1949	115	1	3.54	0	16
1989-90	Winnipeg Jets	NHL	19	1079	59	0	3.28	0	4
NHL TOTALS			19	1079	59	0	3.28	0	4

(c)—June, 1988—Drafted by Winnipeg Jets in 1988 NHL entry draft. Third Jets pick, 52nd overall, third round.
(d)—Won Raymond Lagace Trophy (Top Rookie Defenseman or Goaltender).
(e)—Won Jacques Plante Trophy (Best Goalie).

ED BELFOUR

Goaltender . . . 6' . . . 175 lbs. . . . Born, Carman, Man., April 21, 1965 . . . Shoots left.

Year	Team	League	Games	Mins.	Goals	SO.	Avg.	A.	Pen.
1985-86	Winkler Flyers (c)	MJHL	....	.....	....	..	.....	..	....
1986-87	Univ. of North Dakota (a-d-e)	WCHA	34	2049	81	3	2.37	2	6
1987-88	Saginaw Gears (a-f)	IHL	61	3446	183	3	3.19	2	23
1988-89	Chicago Black Hawks	NHL	23	1148	74	0	3.87	1	6
1988-89	Saginaw Hawks	IHL	29	1760	92	0	3.10	1	47
1989-90	Canadian National Team	Int'l.	33	1808	93	...	3.09	..	....
1989-90	Chicago Black Hawks (g)	NHL	....	.....	....	..	.....	..	....
NHL TOTALS			23	1148	74	0	3.87	1	6

(c)—Named top goaltender in Manitoba Junior Hockey League.
(d)—Named Second team All-America (West).
(e)—June, 1987—Signed by Chicago Black Hawks as a free agent.
(f)—Shared Garry F. Longham Memorial Trophy (Outstanding Rookie) with John Cullen.
(g)—No regular-season record. Played nine playoff games.

JEAN-CLAUDE BERGERON

Goaltender . . . 6'2" . . . 180 lbs. . . . Born, Havreziue, Que., October 14, 1968 . . . Shoots left.

Year	Team	League	Games	Mins.	Goals	SO.	Avg.	A.	Pen.
1985-86	Shawinigan Cataractes	QMJHL	33	1796	156	0	5.21	2	17
1986-87	Verdun Junior Canadiens	QMJHL	52	2991	*306	0	6.14	1	0
1987-88	Verdun Junior Canadiens (c)	QMJHL	49	2715	265	0	5.86	2	4
1988-89	Verdun Junior Canadiens	QMJHL	44	2417	199	0	4.94	..	2
1988-89	Sherbrooke Canadiens	AHL	5	302	18	0	3.58	0	2
1989-90	Sherbrooke Canadiens (a-d-e)	AHL	40	2254	103	2	*2.74	0	0

(c)—June, 1988—Drafted by Montreal Canadiens in 1988 NHL entry draft. Sixth Canadiens pick, 104th overall, fifth round.
(d)—Shared Harry Hap Holmes Award (Lowest team GAA) with teammate Andre Racicot.
(e)—Won Baz Bastien Award (Best AHL Goaltender).

TIMOTHY JOHN BERNHARDT

Goaltender . . . 5'9" . . . 160 lbs. . . . Born, Sarnia, Ont., January 17, 1958 . . . Shoots left . . . (October, 1980)—Surgery to remove abscess at base of spine . . . (November 18, 1989)—Groin injury.

Year	Team	League	Games	Mins.	Goals	SO.	Avg.	A.	Pen.
1975-76	Cornwall Royals	QMJHL	51	2985	195	2	3.92	..	....
1976-77	Cornwall Royals (a-c)	QMJHL	44	2497	151	0	*3.63	1	2
1977-78	Cornwall Royals (a-d)	QMJHL	54	3165	179	2	3.39	..	....
1978-79	Tulsa Oilers	CHL	46	2705	191	0	4.24	1	4
1979-80	Birmingham Bulls	CHL	34	1933	122	1	3.79	0	0
1980-81	Birmingham Bulls	CHL	29	1598	106	1	3.98	1	0
1981-82	Oklahoma City Stars	CHL	10	526	45	0	5.13	0	0
1981-82	Rochester Americans	AHL	29	1586	95	0	3.59	2	0
1982-83	Calgary Flames	NHL	6	280	21	0	4.50	0	0
1982-83	Colorado Flames	CHL	34	1896	122	0	3.86	0	4
1983-84	St. Catharines Saints (b)	AHL	42	2501	154	0	3.69	0	0
1984-85	St. Catharines Saints (e)	AHL	14	801	55	0	4.12	0	2
1984-85	Toronto Maple Leafs	NHL	37	2182	136	0	3.74	2	4
1985-86	St. Catharines Saints	AHL	14	776	38	1	2.94	1	2
1985-86	Toronto Maple Leafs	NHL	23	1266	107	0	5.07	1	0
1986-87	Newmarket Saints	AHL	31	1705	117	1	4.12	2	0
1986-87	Toronto Maple Leafs	NHL	1	20	3	0	9.00	0	0
1987-88	Newmarket Saints	AHL	49	2704	166	0	3.68	1	2
1988-89	Newmarket Saints	AHL	37	2004	145	1	4.34	2	0
1989-90	Newmarket Saints	AHL	14	755	51	0	4.05	0	0
NHL TOTALS			104	5752	412	1	4.30	5	4

(c)—Won leading goalie award.
(d)—Drafted from Cornwall Royals by Atlanta Flames in third round of 1978 amateur draft.
(e)—September, 1984—Signed by Toronto Maple Leafs as a free agent.

DANIEL BERTHIAUME

Goaltender . . . 5'9" . . . 151 lbs. . . . Born, Longueuil, Que., January 26, 1966 . . . Shoots left . . . (March 1, 1988)—Pulled chest muscle . . . (October 4, 1988)—Suspended by Winnipeg Jets for failing to report to Moncton (lifted on October 11) . . . (November 4, 1988)—Suspended by Moncton (lifted on November 29) . . . (December 17, 1988)—Injured shoulder and drew an eight-game AHL suspension in incident with Greg Smyth of Halifax . . . (February 13, 1990)—Injured knee vs. St. Louis, required surgery and missed 13 games.

Year	Team	League	Games	Mins.	Goals	SO.	Avg.	A.	Pen.
1983-84	Drummondville Voltigeurs	QMJHL	28	1562	131	0	5.03	1	0
1984-85	Drum'dville/Chicoutimi (c-d)	QMJHL	59	3347	215	*2	*3.85	3	16
1985-86	Chicoutimi Sagueneens	QMJHL	*66	*3718	*286	1	4.62	2	12
1985-86	Winnipeg Jets (e)	NHL	....	.....	....	..	....	..	....
1986-87	Sherbrooke Canadiens	AHL	7	420	23	0	3.29	0	2
1986-87	Winnipeg Jets	NHL	31	1758	93	1	3.17	0	2
1987-88	Winnipeg Jets	NHL	56	3010	176	2	3.51	2	12
1988-89	Winnipeg Jets	NHL	9	443	44	0	5.96	0	0
1988-89	Moncton Hawks	AHL	21	1083	76	0	4.21	0	27
1989-90	Winnipeg Jets (f)	NHL	24	1387	86	1	3.72	1	6
1989-90	Minnesota North Stars (g)	NHL	5	240	14	0	3.50	0	2
NHL TOTALS			125	6838	413	4	3.62	3	22

(c)—October, 1984—Traded by Drummondville Voltigeurs to Chicoutimi Saguenees for Simon Masse.
(d)—June, 1985—Drafted as underage junior by Winnipeg Jets in 1985 NHL entry draft. Third Jets pick, 60th overall, third round.
(e)—No regular season record. Played one playoff game.
(f)—January 22, 1990—Traded by Winnipeg Jets to Minnesota North Stars for future considerations.
(g)—September 6, 1990—Traded by Minnesota North Stars to Los Angeles Kings for Craig Duncanson.

ALLAN J. BESTER

Goaltender . . . 5'7" . . . 152 lbs. . . . Born, Hamilton, Ont., March 26, 1964 . . . Shoots left . . . (February, 1988)—Missed 14 games with sprained left knee ligaments . . . (January, 1989)—Phlebitis in right leg . . . (April, 1989)—Stretched knee ligaments in pre-tournament game for Team Canada . . . (October, 1989)—Bone spurs in right heel.

Year	Team	League	Games	Mins.	Goals	SO.	Avg.	A.	Pen.
1981-82	Brantford Alexanders	OHL	19	970	68	0	4.21	1	4
1982-83	Brantford Alexanders (a-c-d)	OHL	56	3210	188	0	3.51	0	16
1983-84	Brantford Alexanders	OHL	23	1271	71	1	3.35	1	4
1983-84	Toronto Maple Leafs	NHL	32	1848	134	0	4.35	0	6
1984-85	St. Catharines Saints	AHL	30	1669	133	0	4.78	0	2
1984-85	Toronto Maple Leafs	NHL	15	767	54	1	4.22	1	4
1985-86	St. Catharines Saints	AHL	50	2855	173	1	3.64	1	6
1985-86	Toronto Maple Leafs	NHL	1	20	2	0	6.00	0	0
1986-87	Newmarket Saints	AHL	3	190	6	0	1.89	0	0
1986-87	Toronto Maple Leafs	NHL	36	1808	110	2	3.65	0	8
1987-88	Toronto Maple Leafs	NHL	30	1607	102	2	3.81	3	6
1988-89	Toronto Maple Leafs	NHL	43	2460	156	2	3.80	2	2
1989-90	Newmarket Saints	AHL	5	264	18	0	4.09	0	0
1989-90	Toronto Maple Leafs	NHL	42	2206	165	0	4.49	2	4
NHL TOTALS			199	10716	723	7	4.05	8	30

(c)—Led OHL playoffs with a 2.50 average and one shutout.
(d)—June, 1983—Drafted as underage junior by Toronto Maple Leafs in 1983 NHL entry draft. Third Maple Leafs pick, 48th overall, third round.

CRAIG BILLINGTON

Goaltender . . . 5'10" . . . 150 lbs. . . . Born, London, Ont., September 11, 1966 . . . Shoots left . . . (July, 1984)—Mononucleosis.

Year	Team	League	Games	Mins.	Goals	SO.	Avg.	A.	Pen.
1982-83	London Diamonds	WOJBHL	23	1338	76	0	3.39	..	..
1983-84	Belleville Bulls (c)	OHL	44	2335	162	1	4.16	2	7
1984-85	Belleville Bulls (a)	OHL	47	2544	180	1	4.25	0	2
1985-86	Belleville Bulls	OHL	3	180	11	0	3.67	0	0
1985-86	New Jersey Devils	NHL	18	902	77	0	5.12	1	0
1986-87	Maine Mariners	AHL	20	1151	70	0	3.65	1	4
1986-87	New Jersey Devils	NHL	22	1114	89	0	4.79	0	12
1987-88	Utica Devils	AHL	59	3404	208	1	3.67	2	19
1988-89	New Jersey Devils	NHL	3	140	11	0	4.71	0	0
1988-89	Utica Devils	AHL	41	2432	150	2	3.70	0	10
1989-90	Utica Devils	AHL	38	2087	138	0	3.97	5	6
NHL TOTALS			43	2156	177	0	4.93	1	12

(c)—June, 1984—Drafted as underage junior by New Jersey Devils in 1984 NHL entry draft. Second Devils pick, 23rd overall, second round.

JOHN BLUE

Goaltender . . . 5'10" . . . 185 lbs. . . . Born, Huntington Beach, Calif., February 9, 1966 . . . Shoots left.

Year	Team	League	Games	Mins.	Goals	SO.	Avg.	A.	Pen.
1983-84	Des Moines Buccaneers	USHL	15	753	63	..	5.02	0	4
1984-85	Univ. of Minnesota (b)	WCHA	34	1964	111	2	3.39	1	7
1985-86	Univ. of Minnesota (a-c)	WCHA	29	1588	80	3	3.02	1	4
1986-87	Univ. of Minnesota	WCHA	33	1889	99	3	3.14	6	6
1987-88	Kalamazoo Wings (d)	IHL	15	847	65	0	4.60	0	4
1987-88	U.S. Olympic Team	Int'l	8	....	..	..	3.37	..	..
1988-89	Kalamazoo Wings	IHL	17	970	69	0	4.27	1	4
1988-89	Virginia Lancers	ECHL	10	570	38	0	4.00	2	9
1989-90	Kalamazoo Wings	IHL	4	232	18	0	4.66	1	0
1989-90	Phoenix Roadrunners	IHL	19	986	93	0	5.66	1	10
1989-90	Knoxville Cherokees	ECHL	19	1000	85	...	5.10	0	0

(c)—June, 1986—Drafted by Winnipeg Jets in 1986 NHL entry draft. Ninth Jets pick, 197th overall, 10th round.
(d)—March, 1988—Traded by Winnipeg Jets to Minnesota North Stars for a seventh-round 1988 draft pick (Markus Akerbloom).

TODD BOJCUN

Goaltender . . . 5'9" . . . 151 lbs. . . . Born, Toronto, Ont., April 13, 1970 . . . Shoots right.

Year	Team	League	Games	Mins.	Goals	SO.	Avg.	A.	Pen.
1986-87	Mississauga Reps Midget	OHA	32	1920	115	4	3.59	..	....
1987-88	Peterborough Petes	OHL	42	2500	122	*3	2.93	2	6
1988-89	Peterborough Petes	OHL	35	2054	123	1	3.59	1	10
1989-90	Peterborough Petes (b-c)	OHL	41	2345	125	1	*3.20	2	14

(c)—June 16, 1990—Selected by Buffalo Sabres in 1990 NHL entry draft. Fourth Sabres pick, 100th overall, fifth round.

JOHN BRADLEY

Goaltender . . . 6' . . . 165 lbs. . . . Born, Pawtucket, R.I., February 6, 1968 . . . Shoots left.

Year	Team	League	Games	Mins.	Goals	SO.	Avg.	A.	Pen.
1986-87	New Hampton H.S. (c)	R.I. H.S.	34	2040	96	4	2.82	..	....
1987-88	Boston University	H. East	9	523	40	0	4.59	0	2
1988-89	Boston University	H. East	11	583	53	0	5.45	0	4
1989-90	Boston University	H. East	7	377	20	1	3.18	0	0

(c)—June, 1987—Drafted by Buffalo Sabres in 1987 NHL entry draft. Fourth Sabres pick, 84th overall, fourth round.

MARTIN BRODEUR

Goaltender . . . 6' . . . 189 lbs. . . . Born, Montreal, Que., May 6, 1972 . . . Shoots left . . . (March 9, 1990)—Pinched nerve in elbow and slight concussion vs. Trois-Rivieres.

Year	Team	League	Games	Mins.	Goals	SO.	Avg.	A.	Pen.
1988-89	Montreal Bourassa Midget	Que.	27	1580	98	0	3.72	..	....
1989-90	St. Hyacinthe Lasers (c)	QMJHL	42	2333	156	0	4.01	..	....

(c)—June 16, 1990—Selected by New Jersey Devils in 1990 NHL entry draft. First Devils pick, 20th overall, first round.

SCOTT BROWER

Goaltender . . . 6' . . . 185 lbs. . . . Born, Viking, Alta., September 26, 1964 . . . Shoots left.

Year	Team	League	Games	Mins.	Goals	SO.	Avg.	A.	Pen.
1983-84	Lloydminster (c)	SJHL	43	2566	173	2	4.04	..	....
1984-85	University of North Dakota	WCHA	31	1808	99	2	3.29	1	0
1985-86	University of North Dakota	WCHA	20	1096	67	1	3.67	0	0
1986-87	University of North Dakota	WCHA	15	803	44	0	3.29	1	4
1987-88	University of North Dakota	WCHA	24	1450	88	1	3.64	0	2
1988-89	Flint Spirits	IHL	5	235	22	0	5.62	0	0
1988-89	Denver Rangers	IHL	20	938	82	0	5.25	1	0
1989-90	Flint Spirits	IHL	21	1078	79	0	4.40	0	2
1989-90	Phoenix Roadrunners	IHL	1	20	1	0	3.00	0	0
1989-90	Erie Panthers	ECHL	5	243	20	...	4.94	0	0

(c)—June, 1984—Drafted by New York Rangers in NHL entry draft. Twelfth Rangers pick, 243rd overall, 12th round.

MARIO BRUNETTA

Goaltender . . . 6'3" . . . 180 lbs. . . . Born, St. Fidele, Que., January 25, 1967 . . . Shoots left . . . (February, 1990)—Broken finger.

Year	Team	League	Games	Mins.	Goals	SO.	Avg.	A.	Pen.
1983-84	Ste. Foy Midget	Que. Midget	39	2169	162	0	4.48	..	..
1984-85	Quebec Remparts (c)	QMJHL	45	2255	192	0	5.11	1	16
1985-86	Laval Titans	QMJHL	63	3383	279	0	4.95	3	34
1986-87	Laval Titans	QMJHL	59	3469	261	1	4.51	0	23
1987-88	Fredericton Express	AHL	5	300	24	0	4.80	0	4
1987-88	Quebec Nordiques	NHL	29	1550	96	0	3.72	0	16
1988-89	Quebec Nordiques	NHL	5	226	19	0	5.04	0	0
1988-89	Halifax Citadels	AHL	36	1898	124	0	3.92	0	14
1989-90	Quebec Nordiques (d)	NHL	6	191	13	0	4.08	0	0
1989-90	Halifax Citadels	AHL	24	1444	99	0	4.11	0	16
NHL TOTALS			40	1967	128	0	3.90	0	16

(c)—June, 1985—Drafted as underage junior by Quebec Nordiques in 1985 NHL entry draft. Ninth Nordiques pick, 162nd overall, eighth round.
(d)—May 4, 1990—Signed contract with Asiago (Italy).

SEAN BURKE

Goaltender . . . 6'3" . . . 205 lbs. . . . Born, Windsor, Ont., January 29, 1967 . . . Shoots left . . . (December, 1988)—Injured groin . . . (September 5, 1989)—Exploratory arthroscopic surgery to right knee.

Year	Team	League	Games	Mins.	Goals	SO.	Avg.	A.	Pen.
1983-84	St. Michael's H.S.	MTHL	25	1482	120	0	4.85	..	..
1984-85	Toronto Marlboros (c)	OHL	49	2987	211	0	4.24	2	6
1985-86	Toronto Marlboros	OHL	47	2840	*233	0	4.92	5	32
1985-86	Team Canada	Int'l	5	284	22	0	4.65	..	..
1986-87	Team Canada	Int'l	46	2670	138	0	3.10	..	..
1987-88	Canadian Olympic Team	Int'l	41	2200	104	1	2.84	..	..
1987-88	New Jersey Devils (d)	NHL	13	689	35	1	3.05	1	6
1988-89	New Jersey Devils	NHL	62	3590	230	3	3.84	3	54
1989-90	New Jersey Devils	NHL	52	2914	175	0	3.60	1	38
NHL TOTALS			127	7193	440	4	3.67	5	98

(c)—June, 1985—Drafted as underage junior by New Jersey Devils in 1985 NHL entry draft. Second Devils pick, 24th overall, second round.
(d)—Tied for lead in NHL Playoffs with one shutout.

FRANK CAPRICE

Goaltender . . . 5'9" . . . 160 lbs. . . . Born, Hamilton, Ont., May 2, 1962 . . . Shoots left . . . (December, 1985)—Injured knee . . . (September, 1989)—Fractured left hand vs. Boston.

Year	Team	League	Games	Mins.	Goals	SO.	Avg.	A.	Pen.
1979-80	London Knights	OHL	18	919	74	1	4.84	0	2
1980-81	London Knights (c)	OHL	42	2171	190	0	5.25	1	9
1981-82	London Knights	OHL	45	2614	196	0	4.50	3	6
1981-82	Dallas Black Hawks	CHL	3	178	19	0	6.40	0	0
1982-83	Vancouver Canucks	NHL	1	20	3	0	9.00	0	0
1982-83	Fredericton Express	AHL	14	819	50	0	3.67	3	0
1983-84	Vancouver Canucks	NHL	19	1099	62	1	3.38	0	2
1983-84	Fredericton Express	AHL	18	1089	49	2	2.70	0	2
1984-85	Vancouver Canucks	NHL	28	1523	122	0	4.81	2	0
1985-86	Fredericton Express	AHL	26	1526	109	0	4.29	0	4
1985-86	Vancouver Canucks	NHL	7	308	28	0	5.45	1	0
1986-87	Fredericton Express	AHL	12	686	47	0	4.11	0	2
1986-87	Vancouver Canucks	NHL	25	1390	89	0	3.84	0	9
1987-88	Vancouver Canucks	NHL	22	1250	87	0	4.18	0	6
1988-89	Milwaukee Admirals (d)	IHL	39	2204	143	2	3.89	0	2
1989-90	Maine Mariners	AHL	10	550	46	0	5.02	0	0
1989-90	Milwaukee Admirals	IHL	20	1098	79	0	4.32	0	0
NHL TOTALS			111	5590	391	1	4.20	3	17

(c)—June, 1981—Drafted as underage junior by Vancouver Canucks in NHL entry draft. Eighth Canucks pick, 178th overall, ninth round.
(d)—June 17, 1989—Traded by Vancouver Canucks to Boston Bruins for a twelfth-round 1989 draft pick (Jan Bergman).

JON CASEY

Goaltender . . . 5'10" . . . 155 lbs. . . . Born, Grand Rapids, Minn., August 29, 1962 . . . Shoots left.

Year	Team	League	Games	Mins.	Goals	SO.	Avg.	A.	Pen.
1980-81	Univ. of North Dakota	WCHA	6	300	19	0	3.80	..	....
1981-82	Univ. of North Dakota	WCHA	18	1038	48	1	2.77	0	0
1982-83	Univ. of North Dakota	WCHA	17	1021	42	0	2.47	1	4
1983-84	Univ. of North Dakota (c)	WCHA	37	2180	115	...	3.17	1	20
1983-84	Minnesota North Stars	NHL	2	84	6	0	4.29	0	0
1984-85	Baltimore Skipjacks (a-d)	AHL	46	2646	116	*4	*2.63	2	2
1985-86	Springfield Indians	AHL	9	464	30	0	3.88	0	6
1985-86	Minnesota North Stars	NHL	26	1402	91	0	3.89	0	6
1986-87	Indianapolis Checkers	IHL	31	1794	133	0	4.45	2	28
1986-87	Springfield Indians	AHL	13	770	56	0	4.36	1	8
1987-88	Kalamazoo Wings	IHL	42	2541	154	2	3.64	1	23
1987-88	Minnesota North Stars	NHL	14	663	41	0	3.71	0	2
1988-89	Minnesota North Stars	NHL	55	2961	151	1	3.06	1	10
1989-90	Minnesota North Stars	NHL	61	3407	183	3	3.22	3	18
NHL TOTALS			158	8517	472	4	3.33	4	36

(c)—March, 1984—Signed by Minnesota North Stars as a free agent.
(d)—Won Baz Bastien Award (Coaches pick as Top Goaltender).

FREDERIC CHABOT

Goaltender . . . 5'10" . . . 160 lbs. . . . Born, Hebertville, Que., February 12, 1968 . . . Shoots right.

Year	Team	League	Games	Mins.	Goals	SO.	Avg.	A.	Pen.
1986-87	Drummondville Voltigeurs (c)	QMJHL	*62	*3508	293	1	5.01	2	14
1987-88	Drummondville Voltigeurs	QMJHL	58	3276	237	1	4.34	3	20
1988-89	Moose Jaw Warriors	WHL	26	1385	114	1	4.94	3	22
1988-89	Prince Albert Raiders (a)	WHL	28	1572	88	1	3.36	0	6
1989-90	Fort Wayne Komets	IHL	23	1208	87	1	4.32	0	26
1989-90	Sherbrooke Canadiens	AHL	2	119	8	0	4.03	0	0

(c)—June, 1986—Drafted by New Jersey Devils in 1986 NHL entry draft. Tenth Devils pick, 192nd overall, 10th round.

TIM CHEVELDAE

Goaltender . . . 5'11" . . . 175 lbs. . . . Born, Melville, Sask., February 15, 1968 . . . Shoots left.

Year	Team	League	Games	Mins.	Goals	SO.	Avg.	A.	Pen.
1984-85	Melville Millionaires	SAJHL	23	1167	98	0	5.04	..	..
1985-86	Saskatoon Blades (c)	WHL	37	1862	143	0	4.61	3	0
1986-87	Saskatoon Blades	WHL	33	1909	133	2	4.18	4	2
1987-88	Saskatoon Blades (a)	WHL	66	3798	235	1	3.71	7	10
1988-89	Detroit Red Wings	NHL	2	122	9	0	4.43	0	0
1988-89	Adirondack Red Wings	AHL	30	1694	98	1	3.47	0	4
1989-90	Adirondack Red Wings	AHL	31	1848	116	0	3.77	3	2
1989-90	Detroit Red Wings	NHL	28	1600	101	0	3.79	1	2
NHL TOTALS			30	1722	110	0	3.83	1	2

(c)—June, 1986—Drafted as underage junior by Detroit Red Wings in 1986 NHL entry draft. Fourth Red Wings pick, 64th overall, fourth round.

ALAIN CHEVRIER

Goaltender . . . 5'8" . . . 180 lbs. . . . Born, Cornwall, Ont., April 23, 1961 . . . Shoots left . . . (February 22, 1989)—Strained left knee ligaments vs. Minnesota.

Year	Team	League	Games	Mins.	Goals	SO.	Avg.	A.	Pen.
1980-81	Miami of Ohio Univ.	Ind.	16	778	44	0	4.01	..	..
1981-82	Miami of Ohio Univ.	CCHA	19	1053	73	..	4.16	..	..
1982-83	Miami of Ohio Univ.	CCHA	33	1894	125	..	3.96	1	..
1983-84	Miami of Ohio Univ.	CCHA	32	1509	123	..	4.89	1	0
1984-85	Fort Wayne Komets (c)	IHL	56	3219	194	0	3.62	1	8
1985-86	New Jersey Devils	NHL	37	1862	143	0	4.61	3	0
1986-87	New Jersey Devils	NHL	58	3153	227	0	4.32	0	17
1987-88	New Jersey Devils (d)	NHL	45	2354	148	1	3.77	1	8
1988-89	Winnipeg Jets (e)	NHL	22	1092	78	1	4.29	4	2
1988-89	Chicago Black Hawks	NHL	27	1573	92	0	3.51	0	0
1989-90	Chicago Black Hawks (f)	NHL	39	1894	132	0	4.18	2	6
1989-90	Pittsburgh Penguins (g)	NHL	3	166	14	0	5.06	1	2
NHL TOTALS			231	12094	834	2	4.14	11	35

(c)—May, 1985—Signed by New Jersey Devils as a free agent.
(d)—July 19, 1988—Traded with seventh-round 1989 draft pick (Doug Evans) by New Jersey Devils to Winnipeg Jets for Steve Rooney and the return of the Devil's fourth-round 1989 draft pick.
(e)—January 19, 1989—Traded by Winnipeg Jets to Chicago Black Hawks for a fourth-round 1989 draft pick (Allain Roy).
(f)—March 6, 1990—Traded by Chicago Black Hawks to Pittsburgh Penguins for future considerations.
(g)—July 5, 1990—Signed by Detroit Red Wings as a free agent.

CHRIS CLIFFORD

Goaltender . . . 5'9" . . . 150 lbs. . . . Born, Kingston, Ont., May 26, 1966 . . . Shoots left . . . First OHL goalie to score a goal (1985-86).

Year	Team	League	Games	Mins.	Goals	SO.	Avg.	A.	Pen.
1982-83	Brockville Braves	COJHL	32	1746	126	1	4.33	..	....
1983-84	Kingston Canadians (c)	OHL	50	2808	229	2	4.89	3	6
1984-85	Kingston Canadians	OHL	52	2768	241	0	5.22	2	6
1984-85	Chicago Black Hawks	NHL	1	20	0	0	0.00	0	0
1985-86	Kingston Canadians	OHL	50	2988	178	1	3.57	7	16
1986-87	Kingston Canadians	OHL	44	2576	188	1	4.38	2	24
1987-88	Saginaw Hawks	IHL	22	1146	80	0	4.19	0	4
1988-89	Chicago Black Hawks	NHL	1	4	0	0	0.00	0	0
1988-89	Saginaw Hawks	IHL	7	321	23	0	4.30	0	0
1989-90	Muskegon Lumberjacks	IHL	23	1352	77	0	3.42	0	12
1989-90	Virginia Lancers	ECHL	10	547	16	..	1.76	0	2
	NHL TOTALS		2	24	0	0	0.00	0	0

(c)—June, 1984—Drafted as underage junior by Chicago Black Hawks in NHL entry draft. Sixth Black Hawks pick, 111th overall, sixth round.

JACQUES CLOUTIER

Goaltender . . . 5'7" . . . 154 lbs. . . . Born, Noranda, Que., January 3, 1960 . . . Shoots left . . . (January, 1982)—Broken collarbone when hit by a slap shot in practice . . . (December, 1984)—Tore ligaments in knee and was lost for the season. He spent the year as an assistant coach with Rochester . . . (December 11, 1989)—Pulled groin at team practice and missed six games . . . (March 25, 1990)—Strained left knee vs. Detroit.

Year	Team	League	Games	Mins.	Goals	SO.	Avg.	A.	Pen.
1976-77	Trois-Rivieres Draveurs	QMJHL	24	1109	93	0	5.03	0	0
1977-78	Trois-Rivieres Draveurs	QMJHL	71	4134	240	*4	3.48	..	....
1978-79	Trois-Rivieres Draveurs (a-c)	QMJHL	72	4168	218	*3	*3.14	..	....
1979-80	Trois-Rivieres Draveurs	QMJHL	55	3222	231	*2	4.30	0	0
1980-81	Rochester Americans	AHL	61	3478	209	1	3.61	3	9
1981-82	Rochester Americans	AHL	23	1366	64	0	2.81	2	0
1981-82	Buffalo Sabres	NHL	7	311	13	0	2.51	0	0
1982-83	Buffalo Sabres	NHL	25	1390	81	0	3.50	0	0
1982-83	Rochester Americans	AHL	13	634	42	0	3.97	0	4
1983-84	Rochester Americans	AHL	*51	*2841	172	1	3.63	2	10
1984-85	Rochester Americans	AHL	14	803	36	0	2.69	0	6
1984-85	Buffalo Sabres	NHL	1	65	4	0	3.69	1	0
1985-86	Rochester Americans	AHL	14	835	38	1	2.73	0	4
1985-86	Buffalo Sabres	NHL	15	872	49	1	3.36	2	2
1986-87	Buffalo Sabres	NHL	40	2167	137	0	3.79	2	10
1987-88	Buffalo Sabres	NHL	20	851	67	0	4.72	0	0
1988-89	Buffalo Sabres	NHL	36	1786	108	0	3.63	2	6
1988-89	Rochester Americans	AHL	11	527	41	0	4.67	1	2
1989-90	Chicago Black Hawks (d)	NHL	43	2178	112	2	3.09	0	8
	NHL TOTALS		187	9620	571	3	3.56	7	26

(c)—August, 1979—Drafted by Buffalo Sabres as underage junior in 1979 entry draft. Fourth Sabres pick, 55th overall, third round.

(d)—September, 1989—Traded by Buffalo Sabres to Chicago Black Hawks for future considerations (Steve Ludzik and a draft pick).

PAUL CONNELL

Goaltender . . . 5'8" . . . 160 lbs. . . . Born, Cranston, R. I., March 19, 1967 . . . Shoots left.

Year	Team	League	Games	Mins.	Goals	SO.	Avg.	A.	Pen.
1986-87	Bowling Green Univ.	CCHA	7	324	23	0	4.26	0	0
1987-88	Bowling Green Univ. (c)	CCHA	39	2322	155	0	4.00	3	10
1988-89	Bowling Green Univ.	CCHA	41	2439	140	...	3.44	3	14
1989-90	Bowling Green Univ.	CCHA	18	943	79	0	5.03	1	2

(c)—June, 1988—Selected by Philadelphia Flyers in 1988 NHL supplemental draft.

JEFF COOPER

Goaltender . . . 5'10" . . . 170 lbs. . . . Born, Nepean, Ont., June 12, 1962 . . . Shoots left.

Year	Team	League	Games	Mins.	Goals	SO.	Avg.	A.	Pen.
1981-82	Colgate University	ECAC	10	....	36	..	3.71	1	2
1982-83	Colgate University	ECAC	26	1486	100	..	4.03	..	..
1983-84	Colgate University	ECAC	32	1874	121	..	3.88	..	..
1984-85	Colgate University (c)	ECAC	31	1778	110	..	3.71	1	2
1985-86	Baltimore Skipjacks	AHL	23	1099	77	2	4.20	0	4
1986-87	Muskegon Lumberjacks (a)	IHL	45	2673	147	2	*3.30	3	4
1987-88	Muskegon Lumberjacks	IHL	21	1195	80	0	4.02	0	0
1987-88	New Haven Nighthawks	AHL	9	485	37	0	4.58	0	0
1988-89	Saginaw Hawks	IHL	4	226	16	0	4.25	0	0
1988-89	Muskegon Lumberjacks	IHL	7	428	31	0	4.35	0	0
1988-89	Indianapolis Ice	IHL	9	491	32	0	3.91	0	2
1989-90	Indianapolis Ice	IHL	1	40	4	0	6.00	0	0

(c)—May, 1985—Signed by Pittsburgh Penguins as a free agent.

WAYNE COWLEY

Goaltender . . . 6' . . . 185 lbs. . . . Born, Scarborough, Ont., December 4, 1964 . . . Shoots left . . . (December 19, 1987)—Dislocated left shoulder in automobile accident.

Year	Team	League	Games	Mins.	Goals	SO.	Avg.	A.	Pen.
1985-86	Colgate University	ECAC	7	313	23	1	4.42	0	2
1986-87	Colgate University	ECAC	31	1805	106	0	3.52	2	6
1987-88	Colgate University (c)	ECAC	20	1162	58	1	2.99	3	10
1988-89	Salt Lake Golden Eagles	IHL	29	1423	94	0	3.96	1	12
1989-90	Salt Lake Golden Eagles	IHL	36	2009	124	1	3.70	1	12

(c)—May 1, 1988—Signed by Calgary Flames as a free agent.

BYRON DAFOE

Goaltender . . . . 5'11" . . . 175 lbs. . . . Born, Duncan, B.C., February 25, 1971 . . . Shoots left . . . (December, 1989)—Emergency appendectomy.

Year	Team	League	Games	Mins.	Goals	SO.	Avg.	A.	Pen.
1987-88	Juan de Fuca	BCJHL	32	1716	129	0	4.51	..	..
1988-89	Portland Winter Hawks (c)	WHL	59	3279	291	1	5.32	6	18
1989-90	Portland Winter Hawks	WHL	40	2265	193	0	5.11	3	10

(c)—June, 1989—Drafted by Washington Capitals in 1989 NHL entry draft. Second Capitals pick, 35th overall, second round.

CORRIE D'ALESSIO

Goaltender . . . 5'11" . . . 155 lbs. . . . Born, September 9, 1969, Cornwall, Ont., . . . Shoots left.

Year	Team	League	Games	Mins.	Goals	SO.	Avg.	A.	Pen.
1986-87	Pembroke Jr. A	BCJHL	25	1327	95	0	4.29	..	....
1987-88	Cornell University (c)	ECAC	25	1457	67	0	2.76	1	0
1988-89	Cornell University	ECAC	29	1684	96	1	3.42	0	0
1989-90	Cornell University	ECAC	16	887	50	0	3.38	1	0

(c)—June, 1988—Drafted by Vancouver Canucks in 1988 NHL entry draft. Fourth Canucks pick, 107th overall, sixth round.

MARC D'AMOUR

Goaltender . . . 5'9" . . . 185 lbs. . . . Born, Sudbury, Ont., April 29, 1961 . . . Shoots left . . . (January 28, 1986)—Pulled groin.

Year	Team	League	Games	Mins.	Goals	SO.	Avg.	A.	Pen.
1978-79	Sault Ste. Marie Greyhounds	OHL	30	1501	149	0	5.96	0	15
1979-80	Sault Ste. Marie Greyhounds	OHL	33	1429	117	0	4.91	2	31
1980-81	Sault Ste. Marie Greyhounds	OHL	16	653	38	0	3.49	0	0
1981-82	S.S. Marie Greyhounds (a-c-d)	OHL	46	2384	130	1	*3.27	1	29
1982-83	Colorado Flames	CHL	42	2373	153	1	3.87	1	23
1983-84	Colorado Flames	CHL	36	1917	131	0	4.10	2	6
1984-85	Salt Lake Golden Eagles	IHL	12	694	33	0	2.85	0	4
1984-85	Moncton Golden Flames	AHL	37	2051	115	0	3.36	0	59
1985-86	Moncton Golden Flames	AHL	21	1129	72	0	3.83	0	10
1985-86	Calgary Flames	NHL	15	560	32	0	3.43	0	22
1986-87	Binghamton Whalers	AHL	8	461	30	0	3.90	0	2
1986-87	Salt Lake Golden Eagles	IHL	10	523	37	0	4.24	0	0
1987-88	Salt Lake Golden Eagles	IHL	62	3245	177	0	3.27	2	99
1988-89	Philadelphia Flyers	NHL	1	19	0	0	0.00	0	0
1988-89	Hershey Bears	AHL	39	2174	127	0	3.51	0	14
1988-89	Indianapolis Ice	IHL	6	324	20	0	3.70	0	0
1989-90	Hershey Bears	AHL	43	2505	148	2	3.54	1	16
	NHL TOTALS		16	579	32	0	3.32	0	22

(c)—Co-winner, with teammate John Vanbiesbrouck, of Dave Pinkey Trophy (Top Team Goaltending).

(d)—April, 1982—Signed by Calgary Flames as a free agent.

DUANE DERKSEN

Goaltender . . . 6'1" . . . 180 lbs. . . . Born, St. Boniface, Man., July 7, 1968 . . . Shoots left.

Year	Team	League	Games	Mins.	Goals	SO.	Avg.	A.	Pen.
1986-87	Winkler	SOJHL	48	2140	171	1	4.80	..	....
1987-88	Winkler (c)	SOJHL	38	2294	198	0	5.20	..	....
1988-89	Univ. of Wisconsin	WCHA	11	560	37	0	3.96	0	4
1989-90	Univ. of Wisconsin	WCHA	41	2345	133	2	3.40	3	4

(c)—June, 1988—Drafted by Washington Capitals in 1988 NHL entry draft. Fourth Capitals choice, 57th overall, third round.

TOM DRAPER

Goaltender . . . 5'11" . . . 180 lbs. . . . Born, Outremont, Que., November 20, 1966 . . . Shoots left.

Year	Team	League	Games	Mins.	Goals	SO.	Avg.	A.	Pen.
1983-84	Univ. of Vermont	ECAC	20	1205	82	0	4.08	..	..
1984-85	Univ. of Vermont (c)	ECAC	24	1316	90	0	4.11	..	..
1985-86	Univ. of Vermont	ECAC	29	1697	87	1	3.08	1	0
1986-87	Univ. of Vermont (a)	ECAC	29	1662	96	2	3.47	..	..
1987-88	Tappara	Finland	28	1619	87	0	3.22	..	..
1988-89	Moncton Hawks (b)	AHL	54	2962	171	2	3.46	1	23
1988-89	Winnipeg Jets	NHL	2	120	12	0	6.00	0	0
1989-90	Moncton Hawks	AHL	51	2844	167	1	3.52	3	4
1989-90	Winnipeg Jets	NHL	6	359	26	0	4.35	0	0
	NHL TOTALS		8	479	38	0	4.76	0	0

(c)—June, 1985—Drafted by Winnipeg Jets in 1985 NHL entry draft. Eighth Jets pick, 165th overall, eighth round.

MIKE DUNHAM

Goaltender . . . 6'2" . . . 170 lbs. . . . Born, Johnson City, N.Y., June 1, 1972 . . . Shoots left . . . (May, 1990)—Signed letter of intent to attend University of Maine.

Year	Team	League	Games	Mins.	Goals	SO.	Avg.	A.	Pen.
1988-89	Canterbury Prep.	Conn. H.S.	25	.....	63	2	2.52	..	....
1989-90	Canterbury Prep. (c)	Conn. H.S.	32	1558	55	...	2.12	..	....

(c)—June 16, 1990—Drafted by New Jersey Devils in 1990 NHL entry draft. Fourth Devils pick, 53rd overall, third round.

LARRY DYCK

Goaltender . . . 5'11" . . . 170 lbs. . . . Born, Winkler, Man., December 15, 1965 . . . Shoots left.

Year	Team	League	Games	Mins.	Goals	SO.	Avg.	A.	Pen.
1986-87	Univ. of Manitoba (a-c)	CWUAA	18	1019	61	*3	3.59	..	..
1987-88	Univ. of Manitoba (b)	CWUAA	*19	*1118	87	0	4.78	..	..
1988-89	Kalamazoo Wings (d)	IHL	42	2308	168	0	4.37	4	18

Year	Team	League	Games	Mins.	Goals	SO.	Avg.	A.	Pen.
1989-90—Kalamazoo Wings		IHL	36	1959	116	0	3.55	2	4
1989-90—Knoxville Cherokees		ECHL	3	184	12	...	3.91	0	0

(c)—CWUAA Freshman of the Year.

(d)—August, 1988—Signed by Minnesota North Stars as a free agent.

CHAD ERICKSON

Goaltender . . . 5'9'' . . . 175 lbs. . . . Born, Minneapolis, Minn., August 21, 1970 . . . Shoots right.

Year	Team	League	Games	Mins.	Goals	SO.	Avg.	A.	Pen.
1986-87—Warroad H.S.		Minn. H.S.	21	945	36	1	2.29	..	..
1987-88—Warroad H.S. (c)		Minn. H.S.	24	1080	33	7	1.83	..	..
1988-89—Univ. of Minn./Duluth		WCHA	15	821	49	...	3.58	0	4
1989-90—Univ. of Minn./Duluth (a-d)		WCHA	39	2301	141	...	3.68	0	0

(c)—June, 1988—Drafted by New Jersey Devils in 1988 NHL entry draft. Eighth Devils pick, 138th overall, seventh round.

(d)—Named to NCAA All-America team (West).

BOB ESSENSA

Goaltender . . . 6' . . . 160 lbs. . . . Born, Toronto, Ont., January 14, 1965 . . . Shoots left . . . (February, 1985)—Severe lacerations to both hands and wrist from broken window.

Year	Team	League	Games	Mins.	Goals	SO.	Avg.	A.	Pen.
1981-82—Henry Carr H.S.		MJBHL	17	948	79	..	5.00	..	..
1982-83—Henry Carr H.S. (c)		MJBHL	31	1840	98	2	3.20	..	..
1983-84—Michigan State University		CCHA	17	947	44	...	2.79	2	0
1984-85—Michigan State University (a)		CCHA	18	1059	29	2	1.64	1	0
1985-86—Michigan State University (b)		CCHA	23	1333	74	0	3.33	1	2
1986-87—Michigan State University		CCHA	25	1383	64	*2	*2.78	1	0
1987-88—Moncton Golden Flames		AHL	27	1287	100	1	4.66	1	4
1988-89—Winnipeg Jets		NHL	20	1102	68	1	3.70	0	2
1988-89—Fort Wayne Komets		IHL	22	1287	70	0	3.26	0	0
1989-90—Moncton Hawks		AHL	6	358	15	0	2.51	0	0
1989-90—Winnipeg Jets		NHL	36	2035	107	1	3.15	2	0
NHL TOTALS			56	3137	175	2	3.35	2	2

(c)—June, 1983—Drafted by Winnipeg Jets in 1983 NHL entry draft. Fifth Jets pick, 69th overall, fourth round.

RANDY EXELBY

Goaltender . . . 5'9'' . . . 170 lbs. . . . Born, Toronto, Ont., August 13, 1965 . . . Shoots left.

Year	Team	League	Games	Mins.	Goals	SO.	Avg.	A.	Pen.
1983-84—Lake Superior State		CCHA	21	905	75	0	4.97	..	..
1984-85—Lake Superior State		CCHA	36	1999	112	..	3.36	..	..
1985-86—Lake Superior State (c)		CCHA	28	1626	98	0	3.62	3	2
1986-87—Lake Superior State		CCHA	27	1358	91	0	4.02	0	4
1987-88—Sherbrooke Canadiens		AHL	19	1050	49	0	2.80	1	27
1988-89—Montreal Canadiens		NHL	1	3	0	0	0.00	0	0
1988-89—Sherbrooke Canadiens (a-d)		AHL	52	2935	146	*6	2.98	3	46
1989-90—Edmonton Oilers (e)		NHL	1	60	5	0	5.00	0	0
1989-90—Phoenix Roadrunners		IHL	41	2146	163	0	4.56	4	24
NHL TOTALS			2	63	5	0	4.76	0	0

(c)—June, 1986—Selected by Montreal Canadiens in 1986 NHL supplemental draft.

(d)—Won Baz Bastien Award (Top AHL Goaltender).

(e)—September 29, 1989—Traded by Montreal Canadiens to Edmonton Oilers for future considerations.

MARC FELICO

Goaltender . . . 5'7'' . . . 170 lbs. . . . Born, Woonsocket, R.I., December 1, 1968 . . . Shoots left.

Year	Team	League	Games	Mins.	Goals	SO.	Avg.	A.	Pen.
1986-87—Northwood Prep. (c)		Mass. H.S.	....	.....	....	..	.....	..	..
1987-88—Ferris State Univ.		CCHA	18	807	74	0	5.50	0	2
1988-89—Ferris State Univ.		CCHA	19	1045	85	..	4.88	1	2
1989-90—Ferris State Univ.		CCHA	17	738	59	..	4.80	0	2

(c)—June, 1987—Drafted by Minnesota North Stars in 1987 NHL entry draft. Eleventh North Stars pick, 214th overall, 11th round.

STEPHANE FISET

Goaltender . . . 6' . . . 175 lbs. . . . Born, Montreal, Que., June 17, 1970 . . . Shoots left . . . (May, 1989)—Shoulder surgery.

Year	Team	League	Games	Mins.	Goals	SO.	Avg.	A.	Pen.
1986-87—Montreal Midget		Quebec	29	1445	142	0	5.90	..	..
1987-88—Victoriaville Tigres (c)		QMJHL	40	2221	146	1	3.94	3	6
1988-89—Victoriaville Tigres (d)		QMJHL	43	2401	138	1	3.45	..	18
1989-90—Victoriaville Tigres		QMJHL	24	1383	63	1	*2.73	0	6
1989-90—Quebec Nordiques		NHL	6	342	34	0	5.96	0	0
NHL TOTALS			6	342	34	0	5.96	0	0

(c)—June, 1987—Drafted by Quebec Nordiques in 1988 NHL entry draft. Third Nordiques pick, 24th overall, second round.

(d)—Named Canadian Major Junior League goaltender of the Year (combination of QHL, OHL and WHL).

MARK FITZPATRICK

Goaltender . . . 6'2'' . . . 190 lbs. . . . Born, Toronto, Ont., November 13, 1968 . . . Shoots left . . . (February, 1987)—Injured knee.

Year	Team	League	Games	Mins.	Goals	SO.	Avg.	A.	Pen.
1983-84—Medicine Hat Tigers		AJHL	....	.....	....	..	.....	..	..
1983-84—Revelstoke Rockets		BCJHL	21	1019	90	0	5.30	..	....
1984-85—Medicine Hat Tigers		WHL	3	180	9	0	3.00	0	0

Year	Team	League	Games	Mins.	Goals	SO.	Avg.	A.	Pen.
1985-86—Medicine Hat Tigers (b)		WHL	41	2074	99	1	*2.86	1	6
1986-87—Medicine Hat Tigers (c)		WHL	50	2844	159	*4	*3.35	8	16
1987-88—Medicine Hat Tigers (b)		WHL	63	3600	194	*2	*3.23	9	29
1988-89—New Haven Nighthawks		AHL	18	980	54	1	3.31	1	10
1988-89—Los Angeles Kings (d)		NHL	17	957	64	0	4.01	1	2
1988-89—New York Islanders		NHL	11	627	41	0	3.92	1	2
1989-90—New York Islanders		NHL	47	2653	150	3	3.39	2	18
NHL TOTALS			75	4237	255	3	3.61	4	22

(c)—June, 1987—Drafted as underage junior by Los Angeles Kings in 1987 NHL entry draft. Second Kings pick, 27th overall, second round.

(d)—February 22, 1989—Traded with Wayne McBean and future considerations (Doug Crossman sent to the Islanders on May 23 to complete the trade) by Los Angeles Kings to New York Islanders for Kelly Hrudey.

WADE FLAHERTY

Goaltender . . . 5'11'' . . . 160 lbs. . . . Born, Terreace, B.C., January 11, 1968 . . . Shoots right.

Year	Team	League	Games	Mins.	Goals	SO.	Avg.	A.	Pen.
1986-87—Nanaimo Clippers		BCJHL	15	830	53	0	3.83	..	..
1986-87—Victoria Cougars		WHL	3	127	16	0	7.56	1	0
1987-88—Victoria Cougars (b-c)		WHL	36	2052	135	0	3.95	3	10
1988-89—Victoria Cougars		WHL	42	2408	180	0	4.49	3	14
1989-90—Kalamazoo Wings		IHL	1	13	0	0	0.00	0	0
1989-90—Greensboro Monarchs (d)		ECHL	27	1308	96	0	4.40	0	0

(c)—June, 1988—Drafted by Buffalo Sabres in 1988 NHL Entry draft. Tenth Sabres pick, 181st overall, ninth round.

(d)—Named ECHL Playoff MVP.

JOHN FLETCHER

Goaltender . . . 5'7'' . . . 163 lbs. . . . Born, Newton, Mass., October 14, 1967 . . . Shoots left.

Year	Team	League	Games	Mins.	Goals	SO.	Avg.	A.	Pen.
1986-87—Clarkson Univ. (c)		ECAC	23	1240	62	4	3.00	0	....
1987-88—Clarkson Univ. (d)		ECAC	33	1820	97	1	3.20	0	0
1988-89—Clarkson Univ.		ECAC	23	1147	79	0	4.13	2	0
1989-90—Clarkson Univ.		ECAC	34	1900	99	0	3.13	1	16

(c)—June, 1987—Drafted by Vancouver Canucks in 1987 NHL entry draft. Ninth Canucks pick, 166th overall, eighth round.

(d)—Named Second team All-America (East).

BRIAN FORD

Goaltender . . . 5'10'' . . . 170 lbs. . . . Born, Edmonton, Alta., September 22, 1961 . . . Shoots left.

Year	Team	League	Games	Mins.	Goals	SO.	Avg.	A.	Pen.
1980-81—Billings Bighorns		WHL	44	2435	204	0	5.03	2	52
1981-82—Billings Bighorns		WHL	53	2791	256	0	5.50	0	0
1982-83—Fredericton Express (c-d)		AHL	27	1444	84	0	3.49	2	0
1982-83—Carolina Thunderbirds		ACHL	4	204	7	0	2.07	0	0
1983-84—Fredericton Express (a-e-f)		AHL	36	2142	105	2	*2.94	4	8
1983-84—Quebec Nordiques		NHL	3	123	13	0	6.34	0	0
1984-85—Pittsburgh Penguins (g)		NHL	8	457	48	0	6.30	0	0
1984-85—Baltimore Skipjacks		AHL	6	363	21	0	3.47	0	0
1984-85—Muskegon Lumberjacks		IHL	22	1321	59	1	2.68	3	4
1985-86—Baltimore Skipjacks		AHL	39	2230	136	1	3.66	1	8
1985-86—Muskegon Lumberjacks (h)		IHL	9	513	33	0	3.86	2	2
1986-87—Baltimore Skipjacks		AHL	32	1541	99	0	3.85	1	2
1987-88—Springfield Indians		AHL	35	1898	118	0	3.73	2	10
1988-89—Rochester Americans (i)		AHL	19	1075	60	2	3.35	1	0
1989-90—Rochester Americans (j)		AHL	19	1076	69	0	3.85	1	0
NHL TOTALS			11	580	61	0	6.31	0	0

(c)—August, 1982—Signed by Quebec Nordiques as a free agent.

(d)—Co-winner of Harry (Hap) Holmes Memorial Trophy (Top Goaltenders) with teammate Ken Ellacott.

(e)—Won Harry (Hap) Holmes Memorial Trophy (Top Goaltender).

(f)—Won Baz Bastien Trophy (Coaches pick as top goalie; first time awarded).

(g)—December, 1984—Traded by Quebec Nordiques to Pittsburgh Penguins for Tom Thornbury.

(h)—Led IHL playoff goaltenders with 13 games, 793 minutes, 41 goals against and a 3.10 average.

(i)—January 30, 1989—Signed AHL contract with Buffalo Sabres as a free agent. He had been playing in a Newfoundland senior league.

(j)—January 16, 1990—Announced his retirement.

NORM FOSTER

Goaltender . . . 5'9'' . . . 175 lbs. . . . Born, Vancouver, B.C., February 10, 1965 . . . Shoots left.

Year	Team	League	Games	Mins.	Goals	SO.	Avg.	A.	Pen.
1981-82—Penticton Knights		BCJHL	21	1187	58	..	2.93	..	..
1982-83—Penticton Knights (c)		BCJHL	33	1999	156	0	4.68	..	..
1983-84—Michigan State University		CCHA	32	1814	83	...	2.75	0	2
1984-85—Michigan State University		CCHA	26	1531	67	1	2.63	1	0
1985-86—Michigan State University (d)		CCHA	24	1414	87	1	3.69	1	0
1986-87—Michigan State University		CCHA	24	1384	90	1	3.90	2	4
1987-88—Milwaukee Admirals		IHL	38	2001	170	0	5.10	2	0
1988-89—Maine Mariners		AHL	47	2411	156	1	3.88	1	4
1989-90—Maine Mariners		AHL	*64	*3664	*217	3	3.55	4	6

(c)—June, 1983—Drafted by Boston Bruins in 1983 NHL entry draft. Eleventh Bruins pick, 222nd overall, 11th round.

(d)—Named to NCAA All-Tournament team.

ROB FOURNIER

Goaltender . . . 6' . . . 185 lbs. . . . Born, Sudbury, Ont., April 8, 1969 . . . Shoots left . . . (May, 1987)—Broken ankle.

Year Team	League	Games	Mins.	Goals	SO.	Avg.	A.	Pen.
1985-86—Valley East Midget	OHA	35	1575	84	6	3.20	..	..
1986-87—North Bay Centennials	OHL	25	1281	72	2	3.37	0	12
1987-88—North Bay Centennials (b-c)	OHL	61	3601	210	1	3.50	1	48
1988-89—North Bay Centennials	OHL	9	502	49	0	5.86	1	6
1988-89—Niagara Falls Thunder	OHL	32	1293	104	0	4.83	1	12
1989-90—Niagara Thunder	OHL	1	60	7	0	7.00	0	0
1989-90—North Bay Centennials	OHL	24	1342	92	0	4.11	0	10

(c)—June, 1988—Drafted by St. Louis Blues in 1988 NHL entry draft. Third Blues pick, 51st overall, third round.

BOB FROESE

Goaltender . . . 5'11" . . . 178 lbs. . . . Born, St. Catharines, Ont., June 30, 1958 . . . Shoots left . . . (October, 1980)—Pulled hamstring . . . Set NHL record for most consecutive games without a loss from the start of an NHL career (13 games, 12-0-1) in 1982-83 . . . (December 8, 1984)—Strained left knee ligaments vs. N.Y. Rangers . . . (March 10, 1985)—Pulled groin vs. Pittsburgh . . . (November 13, 1985)—Pulled groin . . . (November, 1987)—Dislocated right shoulder . . . (November 15, 1988)—Bruised left hip in a collision with Doug Sulliman at Philadelphia.

Year Team	League	Games	Mins.	Goals	SO.	Avg.	A.	Pen.
1974-75—St. Cath. Black Hawks	OMJHL	15	871	71	0	4.89	0	2
1975-76—St. Cath. Black Hawks	OMJHL	39	1976	193	0	5.86	0	10
1976-77—Oshawa Generals	OMJHL	39	2063	161	*2	4.68	2	40
1977-78—Niagara Falls Flyers (c)	OMJHL	53	3128	246	0	4.72	1	39
1978-79—Saginaw Gears	IHL	21	1050	58	0	3.31	0	56
1978-79—Milwaukee Admirals	IHL	14	715	42	1	3.52	..	....
1979-80—Maine Mariners (d)	AHL	1	60	5	...	5.00	0	0
1979-80—Saginaw Gears	IHL	52	2827	178	0	3.78	7	45
1980-81—Saginaw Gears (e)	IHL	43	2298	114	3	2.98	2	22
1981-82—Maine Mariners	AHL	33	1900	104	2	3.28	0	2
1982-83—Maine Mariners	AHL	33	1966	110	2	3.36	1	11
1982-83—Philadelphia Flyers	NHL	25	1407	59	4	2.52	2	2
1983-84—Philadelphia Flyers	NHL	48	2863	150	2	3.14	2	10
1984-85—Hershey Bears	AHL	4	245	15	0	3.67	0	0
1984-85—Philadelphia Flyers	NHL	17	923	37	1	2.41	1	2
1985-86—Philadelphia Flyers (b-f)	NHL	51	2728	116	5	2.55	1	8
1986-87—Philadelphia Flyers (g)	NHL	3	180	8	0	2.67	0	0
1986-87—New York Rangers	NHL	28	1474	92	0	3.74	2	56
1987-88—New York Rangers	NHL	25	1443	85	0	3.53	1	6
1988-89—New York Rangers	NHL	30	1621	102	1	3.78	1	6
1989-90—New York Rangers	NHL	15	812	45	0	3.33	0	0
NHL TOTALS		242	13451	694	13	3.10	10	90

(c)—June, 1978—Drafted by St. Louis Blues in amateur draft. Eleventh St. Louis pick, 160th overall, 10th round.
(d)—September, 1979—Signed by Philadelphia Flyers as a free agent.
(e)—Led IHL playoffs in goals-against average (2.15) and shutouts (2).
(f)—Shared Bill Jennings Trophy with teammate Darren Jensen (team that allows the fewest goals).
(g)—December, 1986—Traded by Philadelphia Flyers to New York Rangers for Kjell Samuelsson and a second-round 1989 draft pick.

GRANT FUHR

Goaltender . . . 5'10" . . . 181 lbs. . . . Born, Spruce Grove, Alta., September 28, 1962 . . . Shoots right . . . (December, 1981)—Partial separation of right shoulder . . . (December 13, 1983)—Strained left knee ligaments vs. Hartford and required surgery . . . (January 27, 1984)—Collected ninth assist of season to set NHL record for goaltenders. He ended the season with 14 . . . First black player to be on Stanley Cup-winning team . . . (February, 1985)—Separated shoulder . . . (November 3, 1985)—Bruised left shoulder vs. Toronto and missed 10 games . . . (November, 1987)—Bruised left shoulder at N.Y. Rangers . . . (March 1988)—Set NHL record for appearances in a single season . . . (September, 1988)—Wrenched right knee during Edmonton Oilers training camp . . . (January 18, 1989)—Cervical neck strain when struck by shoulder of Andrew McBain at Winnipeg . . . (September 14, 1989)—Appendectomy and missed first six games of season . . . (December 27, 1989)—Reconstructive surgery to his left shoulder . . . (March 13, 1990)—Torn adhesions in his left shoulder at Quebec.

Year Team	League	Games	Mins.	Goals	SO.	Avg.	A.	Pen.
1979-80—Victoria Cougars (a-c)	WHL	43	2488	130	2	3.14	1	2
1980-81—Victoria Cougars (a-d-e)	WHL	59	*3448	160	*4	*2.78	2	6
1981-82—Edmonton Oilers (b)	NHL	48	2847	157	0	3.31	6	6
1982-83—Moncton Alpines	AHL	10	604	40	0	3.98	0	0
1982-83—Edmonton Oilers	NHL	32	1803	129	0	4.29	0	6
1983-84—Edmonton Oilers	NHL	45	2625	171	1	3.91	14	6
1984-85—Edmonton Oilers	NHL	46	2559	165	1	3.87	3	6
1985-86—Edmonton Oilers	NHL	40	2184	143	0	3.93	2	0
1986-87—Edmonton Oilers	NHL	44	2388	137	0	3.44	2	6
1987-88—Edmonton Oilers (a-f)	NHL	*75	*4304	246	*4	3.43	8	16
1988-89—Edmonton Oilers	NHL	59	3341	213	1	3.83	1	6
1989-90—Cape Breton Oilers	AHL	2	120	6	0	3.00	0	0
1989-90—Edmonton Oilers	NHL	21	1081	70	1	3.89	0	2
NHL TOTALS		410	23132	1431	8	3.71	36	54

(c)—Won Stewart Paul Memorial Trophy (WHL Rookie of the Year).
(d)—Named outstanding goalie in WHL.
(e)—June, 1981—Drafted by Edmonton Oilers in 1981 NHL entry draft. First Oilers pick, eighth overall, first round.
(f)—Won Vezina Trophy (Top NHL Goalie).

FRANK FURLAN

Goaltender . . . 5'9" . . . 175 lbs. . . . Born, Nanaimo, B.C., March 8, 1968 . . . Shoots left.

Year Team	League	Games	Mins.	Goals	SO.	Avg.	A.	Pen.
1985-86—Sherwood Park Crusaders (c)	AJHL	23	1290	91	0	4.23	0	12
1986-87—Michigan Tech. Univ.	WCHA	11	623	66	0	6.36	1	2
1987-88—Michigan Tech. Univ.	WCHA	16	854	77	0	5.41	1	7
1988-89—Tri-City Americans	WHL	46	2662	191	0	4.31	1	12
1989-90—Moncton Hawks	AHL	2	29	7	0	14.48	0	0
1989-90—Fort Wayne Komets	IHL	1	40	6	0	9.00	0	0
1989-90—Hampton Roads Admirals	ECHL	7	380	24	0	3.79	0	4

(c)—June, 1986—Drafted by Winnipeg Jets in 1986 NHL entry draft. Seventh Jets pick, 155th overall, eighth round.

DAVE GAGNON

Goaltender . . . 6' . . . 190 lbs. . . . Born, Essex, Ont., October 31, 1967 . . . Shoots left.

Year Team	League	Games	Mins.	Goals	SO.	Avg.	A.	Pen.
1987-88—Colgate University	ECAC	13	743	43	..	3.47	2	6
1988-89—Colgate University	ECAC	28	1622	102	..	3.77	4	24
1989-90—Colgate Univ. (a-c-d-e-f)	ECAC	33	1986	93	2	2.81	6	2

(c)—Named ECAC Player of the Year.
(d)—Named to ECAC All-Tournament team.
(e)—Named to NCAA First All-American team (East).
(f)—June 11, 1990—Signed by Detroit Red Wings as a free agent.

TROY GAMBLE

Goaltender . . . 5'11" . . . 190 lbs. . . . Born, Toronto, Ont., April 7, 1967 . . . Shoots left.

Year Team	League	Games	Mins.	Goals	SO.	Avg.	A.	Pen.
1983-84—Hobbema Hawks	AJHL	22	1102	90	0	4.90	..	....
1984-85—Medicine Hat Tigers (a-c-d)	WHL	37	2095	100	*3	*2.86	2	4
1985-86—Medicine Hat Tigers	WHL	45	2264	142	0	3.76	3	29
1986-87—Medicine Hat Tigers (e)	WHL	11	646	46	0	4.27	1	0
1986-87—Spokane Chiefs	WHL	38	2157	163	0	4.53	2	23
1986-87—Vancouver Canucks	NHL	1	60	4	0	4.00	0	0
1987-88—Spokane Chiefs (a-c)	WHL	67	3824	235	0	3.69	3	47
1988-89—Vancouver Canucks	NHL	5	302	12	0	2.38	0	0
1988-89—Milwaukee Admirals	IHL	42	2198	138	0	3.77	2	27
1989-90—Milwaukee Admirals	IHL	56	3033	213	2	4.21	4	38
NHL TOTALS		6	362	16	0	2.65	0	0

(c)—Won WHL Top Goaltender Trophy.
(d)—June, 1985—Drafted as underage junior by Vancouver Canucks in 1985 NHL entry draft. Second Canucks pick, 25th overall, second round.
(e)—December, 1986—Traded with Kevin Ekdahl by Medicine Hat Tigers to Spokane Flyers for Keith Van Rooyen, Kirby Lindal and Rocky Dundas.

DARRYL GILMOUR

Goaltender . . . 5'11" . . . 155 lbs. . . . Born, Winnipeg, Manitoba, February 13, 1967 . . . Shoots left.

Year Team	League	Games	Mins.	Goals	SO.	Avg.	A.	Pen.
1983-84—St. James Canadiens	MJHL	15	900	45	...	3.00	..	....
1984-85—Moose Jaw Warriors (c)	WHL	58	3004	297	0	5.93	6	4
1985-86—Moose Jaw Warriors (a)	WHL	*62	*3482	*276	1	4.76	2	4
1986-87—Moose Jaw Warriors	WHL	31	1776	123	2	4.16	1	4
1986-87—Portland Winter Hawks	WHL	24	1460	111	0	4.56	2	0
1987-88—Hershey Bears	AHL	25	1273	78	1	3.68	1	2
1988-89—Hershey Bears	AHL	38	2093	144	0	4.13	0	8
1989-90—New Haven Nighthawks	AHL	23	1356	85	0	3.76	0	4
1989-90—Nashville Knights	ECHL	10	529	43	..	4.88	1	0

(c)—June, 1985—Drafted as underage junior by Philadelphia Flyers in 1985 NHL entry draft. Third Flyers pick, 48th overall, third round.

JASON GLICKMAN

Goaltender . . . 5'9" . . . 179 lbs. . . . Born, Chicago, Ill., March 25, 1969 . . . Shoots left.

Year Team	League	Games	Mins.	Goals	SO.	Avg.	A.	Pen.
1986-87—Hull Olympiques	QMJHL	49	2696	170	1	3.78	..	..
1987-88—Hull Olympiques (b)	QMJHL	54	3065	196	0	3.84	..	18
1988-89—Hull Olympiques (c)	QMJHL	40	2116	131	1	3.71	..	39
1989-90—Regina Pats (d)	WHL	52	2836	195	0	4.13	0	13

(c)—June, 1989—Drafted by Detroit Red Wings in 1989 NHL entry draft. Fourteenth Red Wings pick, 246th overall, 12th round.
(d)—October 5, 1989—WHL rights traded by Seattle Thunderbirds to Regina Pats for Cam Brauer.

SCOTT GORDON

Goaltender . . . 5'10" . . . 175 lbs. . . . Born, South Easton, Mass., February 6, 1963 . . . Shoots left.

Year Team	League	Games	Mins.	Goals	SO.	Avg.	A.	Pen.
1982-83—Boston College	ECAC	9	371	15	...	2.43	0	0
1983-84—Boston College	ECAC	35	2034	127	...	3.75	0	6
1984-85—Boston College	H. East	36	2179	131	1	3.61	1	4
1985-86—Boston College (a)	H. East	32	1851	112	2	3.63	1	14
1986-87—Fredericton Express (c)	AHL	31	1599	119	0	4.47	2	12
1987-88—Baltimore Skipjacks	AHL	34	1638	145	0	5.31	0	10
1988-89—Halifax Citadels	AHL	2	116	10	0	5.17	0	0
1988-89—Johnstown Chiefs	ECHL	31	1839	117	2	3.82	2	8
1989-90—Quebec Nordiques	NHL	10	597	53	0	5.33	0	0
1989-90—Halifax Citadels	AHL	48	2851	158	0	3.33	1	8
NHL TOTALS		10	597	53	0	5.33	0	0

(c)—October, 1986—Signed by Quebec Nordiques as a free agent.

MARIO GOSSELIN

Goaltender . . . 5'8'' . . . 160 lbs. . . . Born, Thetford Mines, Que., June 15, 1963 . . . Shoots left . . . Member of 1984 Canadian Olympic team . . . (February 25, 1984)—First NHL game was 5-0 shutout of St. Louis Blues . . . (March 8, 1984)—Injured knee vs. Pittsburgh and out for the season . . . (January 16, 1986)—Missed one game with the flu . . . (October, 1989)—Flu.

Year	Team	League	Games	Mins.	Goals	SO.	Avg.	A.	Pen.
1980-81—Shawinigan Cataractes		QMJHL	21	907	75	0	4.96	1	0
1981-82—Shawinigan Cataractes (b-c)		QMJHL	*60	*3404	230	0	4.50	3	10
1982-83—Shawinigan Cataractes (a-d)		QMJHL	46	2556	133	*3	*3.12	4	18
1983-84—Canadian Olympic Team		Int'l.	36	2007	126	0	3.77	..	....
1983-84—Quebec Nordiques		NHL	3	148	3	1	1.22	0	2
1984-85—Quebec Nordiques		NHL	35	1960	109	1	3.34	0	2
1985-86—Fredericton Express		AHL	5	304	15	0	2.96	0	0
1985-86—Quebec Nordiques		NHL	31	1726	111	2	3.86	3	2
1986-87—Quebec Nordiques		NHL	30	1625	86	0	3.18	3	20
1987-88—Quebec Nordiques		NHL	54	3002	189	2	3.78	0	8
1988-89—Quebec Nordiques (e)		NHL	39	2064	146	0	4.24	2	6
1988-89—Halifax Citadels		AHL	3	183	9	0	2.95	1	0
1989-90—Los Angeles Kings		NHL	26	1226	79	0	3.87	0	0
NHL TOTALS			218	11751	723	6	3.69	8	40

(c)—June, 1982—Drafted as underage junior by Quebec Nordiques in 1982 NHL entry draft. Third Nordiques pick, 55th overall, third round.
(d)—Won Jacques Plante Trophy (Top Goalie).
(e)—June, 1989—Signed by Los Angeles Kings as a free agent.

DAVID GOVERDE

Goaltender . . . 6' . . . 210 lbs. . . . Born, Toronto, Ont., April 9, 1970 . . . Shoots left.

Year	Team	League	Games	Mins.	Goals	SO.	Avg.	A.	Pen.
1986-87—North Toronto Midgets		OHA	21	1259	47	3	2.24	..	..
1987-88—Windsor Spitfires		OHL	10	471	28	0	3.57	0	0
1988-89—Windsor Spitfires		OHL	5	221	24	0	6.52	0	2
1988-89—Sudbury Wolves		OHL	39	2189	156	0	4.28	1	25
1989-90—Sudbury Wolves (c)		OHL	52	2941	182	0	3.71	1	32

(c)—June 16, 1990—Selected by Los Angeles Kings in 1990 NHL entry draft. Fifth Kings pick, 91st overall, fifth round.

FRANCOIS GRAVEL

Goaltender . . . 6'2'' . . . 185 lbs. . . . Born, Ste. Foy, Que., October 21, 1968 . . . Shoots left.

Year	Team	League	Games	Mins.	Goals	SO.	Avg.	A.	Pen.
1985-86—St. Jean Castors (c)		QMJHL	42	2450	212	0	5.19	2	8
1986-87—Shawinigan Cataractes (d)		QMJHL	40	2415	194	0	4.82	0	0
1987-88—Shawinigan Cataractes		QMJHL	44	2499	200	1	4.80	2	30
1988-89—Sherbrooke Canadiens		AHL	33	1625	95	2	3.51	1	12
1989-90—Sherbrooke Canadiens (e)		AHL	12	545	38	0	4.18	1	4
1989-90—Halifax Citadels (f)		AHL	2	125	10	0	4.80	0	0

(c)—November, 1986—Traded by St. Jean Castors to Shawinigan Cataracts for Miguel Baldris.
(d)—June, 1987—Selected by Montreal Canadiens in 1987 NHL entry draft. Fifth Canadiens pick, 58th overall, third round.
(e)—January, 1990—Released by Sherbrooke Canadiens.
(f)—February 6, 1990—Signed pro-tryout with Halifax Citadels.

MIKE GREENLAY

Goaltender . . . 6'3'' . . . 200 lbs. . . . Born, Calgary, Alta., September 15, 1968 . . . Shoots left.

Year	Team	League	Games	Mins.	Goals	SO.	Avg.	A.	Pen.
1986-87—Lake Superior State (c)		CCHA	17	744	44	..	3.55	0	0
1987-88—Lake Superior State		CCHA	19	1023	57	..	3.34	0	2
1988-89—Lake Superior State		CCHA	2	85	6	0	4.24	0	0
1988-89—Saskatoon Blades		WHL	20	1128	86	0	4.57	1	8
1989-90—Cape Breton Oilers		AHL	46	2595	146	2	3.38	2	14
1989-90—Edmonton Oilers		NHL	2	20	4	0	12.00	1	0
NHL TOTALS			2	20	4	0	12.00	1	0

(c)—June, 1986—Drafted by Edmonton Oilers in 1986 NHL entry draft. Ninth Oilers pick, 189th overall, ninth round.

STEVE GUENETTE

Goaltender . . . 5'9'' . . . 170 lbs. . . . Born, Montreal, Que., November 13, 1965 . . . Shoots left.

Year	Team	League	Games	Mins.	Goals	SO.	Avg.	A.	Pen.
1984-85—Guelph Platers		OHL	47	2593	200	1	4.63	1	2
1985-86—Guelph Platers (b-c)		OHL	50	2910	165	3	3.40	2	16
1986-87—Baltimore Skipjacks		AHL	54	3035	157	*5	3.10	2	13
1986-87—Pittsburgh Penguins		NHL	2	113	8	0	4.25	0	0
1987-88—Pittsburgh Penguins		NHL	19	1092	61	1	3.35	0	2
1987-88—Muskegon Lumberjacks (b-d)		IHL	33	1943	91	*4	2.81	0	22
1988-89—Pittsburgh Penguins (e)		NHL	11	574	41	0	4.29	1	0
1988-89—Salt Lake Golden Eagles (a)		IHL	30	1810	82	2	2.72	1	26
1988-89—Muskegon Lumberjacks		IHL	10	597	39	0	3.92	0	2
1989-90—Calgary Flames		NHL	2	119	8	0	4.03	0	2
1989-90—Salt Lake Golden Eagles		IHL	47	2779	160	0	3.45	0	53
NHL TOTALS			34	1898	118	1	3.73	1	4

(c)—June, 1985—Signed by Pittsburgh Penguins as a free agent.
(d)—Won James Norris Memorial Trophy (Top Goaltender).
(e)—January 9, 1989—Traded by Pittsburgh Penguins to Calgary Flames for sixth-round 1989 draft pick (Mike Needham).

JEFF HACKETT

Goaltender . . . 6'1'' . . . 175 lbs. . . . Born, London, Ont., June 1, 1968 . . . Shoots left . . . (May 13, 1990)—Strained groin at Rochester.

Year	Team	League	Games	Mins.	Goals	SO.	Avg.	A.	Pen.
1985-86—London Diamonds Jr. B		OHA	19	1150	66	0	3.44	..	..
1986-87—Oshawa Generals (c-d-e)		OHA	31	1672	85	2	3.05	2	0
1987-88—Oshawa Generals		OHL	53	3165	205	0	3.89	4	39
1988-89—New York Islanders		NHL	13	662	39	0	3.53	1	2
1988-89—Springfield Indians		AHL	29	1677	116	0	4.15	2	26
1989-90—Springfield Indians		AHL	54	3045	187	1	3.68	1	16
NHL TOTALS			13	662	39	0	3.53	1	2

(c)—Won F. W. Dinty Moore Trophy (Lowest average among rookie goaltenders).
(d)—Co-Winner of Dave Pinkney Trophy with teammate Sean Evoy (Lowest team goals-against average).
(e)—June, 1987—Drafted as underage junior by New York Islanders in 1987 NHL entry draft. Second Islanders pick, 34th overall, second round.

GLEN HANLON

Goaltender . . . 6' . . . 185 lbs. . . . Born, Brandon, Man., February 20, 1957 . . . Shoots right . . . Missed part of 1977-78 season with torn ankle ligaments . . . Missed part of 1979-80 season with shoulder injury . . . (October 18, 1980)—Stretched knee ligaments . . . (March, 1981)—Shoulder separation . . . (October 16, 1987)—Cut finger . . . (January, 1988)—Broken left index finger . . . (March, 1989)—Injured hip.

Year	Team	League	Games	Mins.	Goals	SO.	Avg.	A.	Pen.
1973-74—Brandon Travellers		MJHL	20	1059	64	*1	3.63	0	5
1974-75—Brandon Wheat Kings		WCHL	43	2498	176	0	4.22	1	6
1975-76—Brandon Wheat Kings (a)		WCHL	64	3523	234	4	3.99	2	35
1976-77—Brandon Wheat K. (a-c-d)		WCHL	65	3784	195	*4	*3.09	5	8
1977-78—Tulsa Oilers (a-e)		CHL	53	3123	160	*3	3.07	4	30
1977-78—Vancouver Canucks		NHL	4	200	9	0	2.70	0	0
1978-79—Vancouver Canucks		NHL	31	1821	94	3	3.10	1	30
1979-80—Vancouver Canucks		NHL	57	3341	193	0	3.47	1	43
1980-81—Dallas Black Hawks		CHL	4	239	8	1	2.01	0	0
1980-81—Vancouver Canucks		NHL	17	798	59	1	4.44	1	10
1981-82—Vancouver Canucks (f)		NHL	28	1610	106	1	3.95	0	22
1981-82—St. Louis Blues		NHL	2	76	8	0	6.32	0	0
1982-83—St. Louis Blues (g)		NHL	14	671	50	0	4.47	0	0
1982-83—New York Rangers		NHL	21	1173	67	0	3.43	0	2
1983-84—New York Rangers		NHL	50	2837	166	1	3.51	2	30
1984-85—New York Rangers		NHL	44	2510	175	0	4.18	0	4
1985-86—Adirondack Red Wings		AHL	10	605	33	0	3.27	0	2
1985-86—New Haven Nighthawks		AHL	5	279	22	0	4.73	1	4
1985-86—New York Rangers (h)		NHL	23	1170	65	0	3.33	1	4
1986-87—Detroit Red Wings		NHL	36	1963	104	1	3.18	0	20
1987-88—Detroit Red Wings (i)		NHL	47	2623	141	*4	3.23	1	30
1988-89—Detroit Red Wings		NHL	39	2092	124	1	3.56	1	12
1989-90—Detroit Red Wings		NHL	45	2290	154	1	4.03	3	24
NHL TOTALS			458	25175	1515	13	3.61	11	233

(c)—Won WCHL Leading Goalie Award.
(d)—Drafted from Brandon Wheat Kings by Vancouver Canucks in third round of 1977 amateur draft.
(e)—Won CHL Rookie-of-the-Year Award.
(f)—March, 1982—Traded by Vancouver Canucks to St. Louis Blues for Tony Currie, Jim Nill, Rick Heinz and fourth-round 1982 entry draft pick (Shawn Kilroy).
(g)—January, 1983—Traded by St. Louis Blues with Vaclav Nedomansky to New York Rangers for Andre Dore and future considerations.
(h)—August, 1986—Traded by New York Rangers with third-round draft choices in 1987 (Dennis Holland) and 1988 (Guy Dupuis) and future considerations to Detroit Red Wings for Kelly Kisio, Lane Lambert and Jim Leavins and a fifth round 1988 draft pick.
(i)—Tied for lead in NHL Playoffs with one shutout.

CHRIS HARVEY

Goaltender . . . 6'1'' . . . 180 lbs. . . . Born, Cambridge, Mass., December 8, 1967 . . . Shoots left.

Year	Team	League	Games	Mins.	Goals	SO.	Avg.	A.	Pen.
1986-87—Brown University		ECAC	22	1241	88	0	4.26	..	....
1987-88—Brown University (c)		ECAC	21	1235	104	0	5.05	0	12
1988-89—Brown University		ECAC	23	1327	131	0	5.92	0	34
1989-90—Brown University (b-d)		ECAC	28	1646	107	1	3.90	2	6

(c)—June, 1988—Selected by Boston Bruins in 1988 NHL supplemental draft.
(d)—Named to second-team NCAA All-America Team (East).

DOMINIK HASEK

Goaltender . . . 5'11'' . . . 165 lbs. . . . Born, Pardubice, Czechoslovakia, January 29, 1965.

Year	Team	League	Games	Mins.	Goals	SO.	Avg.	A.	Pen.
1981-82—Pardubice		Czech.	12	661	34	0	3.09	..	....
1982-83—Pardubice (c)		Czech.	42	2358	105	0	2.67	..	....
1983-84—Pardubice		Czech.	40	2304	108	0	2.81	..	....
1984-85—Pardubice		Czech.	42	2419	131	0	3.25	..	....
1985-86—Pardubice		Czech.	45	2689	138	0	3.08	..	....
1986-87—Pardubice		Czech.	23	2515	103	0	2.46	..	....
1987-88—Pardubice		Czech.	31	2265	98	0	2.60	..	....
1988-89—Pardubice		Czech.	42	2507	114	0	2.73	..	....
1989-90—Dukla Jihlava		Czech.	40	2251	80	0	2.13	..	....

(c)—June, 1983—Selected by Chicago Black Hawks in 1983 NHL entry draft. Eleventh Black Hawks pick, 211th overall, 11th round.

BRIAN HAYWARD

Goaltender . . . 5'10" . . . 175 lbs. . . . Born, Georgetown, Ont., June 25, 1960 . . . Shoots left . . . (November, 1987)—Back spasms . . . (December 26, 1987)—Pulled thigh muscle at Toronto . . . (February 23, 1988)—Injured back when checked into boards by Gord Donnelly . . . (November, 1988)—Back spasms . . . (February, 1990)—Sprained left wrist vs. Boston.

Year	Team	League	Games	Mins.	Goals	SO.	Avg.	A.	Pen.
1978-79	Cornell University	ECAC	25	1469	95	0	3.88	..	....
1979-80	Cornell University	ECAC	12	508	52	0	6.02	..	....
1980-81	Cornell University	ECAC	19	967	58	1	3.54	..	....
1981-82	Cornell University	ECAC	....	1320	68	0	3.09	..	....
1982-83	Sherbrooke Jets (c)	AHL	22	1208	89	1	4.42	0	0
1982-83	Winnipeg Jets	NHL	24	1440	89	1	3.71	1	0
1983-84	Sherbrooke Jets	AHL	15	781	69	0	5.30	1	2
1983-84	Winnipeg Jets	NHL	28	1530	124	0	4.86	1	2
1984-85	Winnipeg Jets	NHL	61	3416	220	0	3.84	4	10
1985-86	Sherbrooke Canadiens	AHL	3	185	5	0	1.62	1	0
1985-86	Winnipeg Jets (d)	NHL	52	2721	217	0	4.79	2	25
1986-87	Montreal Canadiens	NHL	37	2178	102	1	2.81	2	2
1987-88	Montreal Canadiens (e)	NHL	39	2247	107	2	2.86	2	24
1988-89	Montreal Canadiens (e)	NHL	36	2091	101	1	2.90	0	10
1989-90	Montreal Canadiens	NHL	29	1674	94	1	3.37	0	4
NHL TOTALS			306	17297	1054	6	3.66	12	77

(c)—September, 1982—Signed by Winnipeg Jets as a free agent.
(d)—August, 1986—Traded by Winnipeg Jets to Montreal Canadiens for Steve Penney and Jan Ingman.
(e)—Co-winner (with teammate Patrick Roy) of Bill Jennings Trophy (Top NHL Goaltending tandem).

GLEN HEALY

Goaltender . . . 5'10" . . . 185 lbs. . . . Born, Pickering, Ont., August 23, 1962 . . . Shoots left.

Year	Team	League	Games	Mins.	Goals	SO.	Avg.	A.	Pen.
1981-82	Western Mich. Univ.	CCHA	27	1569	116	0	4.44	2	2
1982-83	Western Mich. Univ.	CCHA	30	1733	116	0	4.02	3	4
1983-84	Western Mich. Univ.	CCHA	38	2242	146	..	3.91	1	13
1984-85	Western Mich. Univ. (b-c-d)	CCHA	37	2172	118	..	3.26	2	8
1985-86	Toledo Goaldiggers	IHL	7	402	28	0	4.18	0	0
1985-86	New Haven Nighthawks	AHL	43	2410	160	0	3.98	2	18
1985-86	Los Angeles Kings	NHL	1	51	6	0	7.06	0	0
1986-87	New Haven Nighthawks	AHL	47	2828	173	1	3.67	2	24
1987-88	Los Angeles Kings	NHL	34	1869	135	1	4.33	2	6
1988-89	Los Angeles Kings (e)	NHL	48	2699	192	0	4.27	1	28
1989-90	New York Islanders	NHL	39	2197	128	2	3.50	1	7
NHL TOTALS			122	6816	461	3	4.06	4	41

(c)—Second team All-America Goaltender.
(d)—June, 1985—Signed by Los Angeles Kings as a free agent.
(e)—August, 1989—Signed by New York Islanders as a free agent with Los Angeles Kings receiving fourth-round 1990 draft choice (pick traded to Minnesota).

GUY HEBERT

Goaltender . . . 5'11" . . . 180 lbs. . . . Born, Troy, N.Y., January 7, 1967 . . . Shoots left.

Year	Team	League	Games	Mins.	Goals	SO.	Avg.	A.	Pen.
1986-87	Hamilton College (c)	Div. II	18	1070	40	...	2.19	..	....
1987-88	Hamilton College	Div. II	8	450	19	...	2.53	..	....
1988-89	Hamilton College	Div. II	25	1453	62	...	2.56	..	....
1989-90	Peoria Rivermen	IHL	30	1706	124	1	4.36	0	0

(c)—June, 1987—Selected by St. Louis Blues in NHL entry draft. Eighth Blues choice, 159th overall, eighth round.

RON HEXTALL

Goaltender . . . 6'3" . . . 192 lbs. . . . Born, Winnipeg, Manitoba, May 3, 1964 . . . Shoots left . . . (May, 1987)—Given eight-game suspension by the NHL for slashing Kent Nilsson during playoff series vs. Edmonton. The suspension to take affect for the first eight games of the 1987-88 season . . . (1988-89)—Set NHL record for penalty minutes by a goaltender . . . (December 2, 1987)—Scored a goal into an empty Boston Bruins net . . . (March 7, 1989)—Pulled hamstring vs. Edmonton . . . (April 11, 1989)—Scored a goal into a Washington empty net with 1:02 to play, becoming the first goalie to score a goal in Stanley Cup play . . . (May 11, 1989)—Suspended for first 12 games of 1989-90 season for an attack on Chris Chelios in the final minute of the final playoff game vs. Montreal . . . (September, 1989)—Did not attend training camp due to a contract dispute. He reported October 19 . . . (November 4, 1989)—Pulled groin at Toronto . . . (November 15, 1989)—Pulled hamstring . . . (December 13, 1989)—Tore right groin muscle at New Haven and missed 29 games . . . (March 8, 1990)—Injured left groin vs. N.Y. Rangers.

Year	Team	League	Games	Mins.	Goals	SO.	Avg.	A.	Pen.
1980-81	Melville	SJHL	42	2127	254	0	7.17	..	....
1981-82	Brandon Wheat Kings (c)	WHL	30	1398	133	0	5.71	0	0
1982-83	Brandon Wheat Kings	WHL	44	2589	249	0	5.77	4	66
1983-84	Brandon Wheat Kings	WHL	46	2670	190	0	4.27	8	117
1984-85	Kalamazoo Wings	IHL	19	1103	80	0	4.35	2	18
1984-85	Hershey Bears	AHL	11	555	34	0	3.68	2	4
1985-86	Hershey Bears (a-d)	AHL	*53	*3061	*174	*5	3.41	2	54
1986-87	Philadelphia Flyers (a-e-f)	NHL	66	3799	190	1	3.00	6	104
1987-88	Philadelphia Flyers	NHL	62	3561	208	0	3.51	6	104
1988-89	Philadelphia Flyers	NHL	64	3756	202	0	3.23	8	113
1989-90	Philadelphia Flyers	NHL	8	419	29	0	4.15	0	14
1989-90	Hershey Bears	AHL	1	49	3	0	3.67	0	2
NHL TOTALS			200	11535	629	1	3.27	20	335

(c)—June, 1982—Drafted as underage junior by Philadelphia Flyers in 1982 NHL entry draft. Sixth Flyers pick, 119th overall, sixth round.
(d)—Won Dudley (Red) Garrett Memorial Trophy (Top Rookie).
(e)—Won Vezina Trophy (Top NHL Goaltender).
(f)—Won Conn Smythe Trophy (Stanley Cup Playoff MVP).

BRUCE HOFFORT

Goaltender . . . 5'10" . . . 185 lbs. . . . Born, North Battleford, Sask., July 30, 1966 . . . Shoots left.

Year	Team	League	Games	Mins.	Goals	SO.	Avg.	A.	Pen.
1987-88	Lake Superior St.	CCHA	31	1787	79	3	2.65	2	2
1988-89	Lake Superior St. (c-d-e)	CCHA	44	2595	117	3	2.71	2	6
1989-90	Philadelphia Flyers	NHL	7	329	20	0	3.65	0	2
1989-90	Hershey Bears	AHL	40	2284	139	1	3.65	1	6
NHL TOTALS			7	329	20	0	3.65	0	2

(c)—Named First team All-America (West).
(d)—Named CCHA Player of the Year.
(e)—August, 1989—Signed by Philadelphia Flyers as a free agent.

JIM HRIVNAK

Goaltender . . . 6'2" . . . 185 lbs. . . . Born, Montreal, Que., May 28, 1968 . . . Shoots left.

Year	Team	League	Games	Mins.	Goals	SO.	Avg.	A.	Pen.
1984-85	Montreal Concordia Midgets	Que.	34	1822	182	0	5.99	..	..
1985-86	Merrimack College (c)	ECAC-II	21	1230	75	0	3.66	..	..
1986-87	Merrimack College	ECAC-II	34	1618	58	3	2.14	..	..
1987-88	Merrimack College	ECAC-II	37	2119	84	4	2.38	2	12
1988-89	Merrimack College	ECAC-II	22	1295	52	4	2.41	1	0
1988-89	Baltimore Skipjacks	AHL	10	502	55	0	6.57	0	0
1989-90	Washington Capitals	NHL	11	609	36	0	3.55	1	0
1989-90	Baltimore Skipjacks	AHL	47	2722	139	*4	3.06	4	2
NHL TOTALS			11	609	36	0	3.55	1	0

(c)—June, 1986—Drafted by Washington Capitals in 1986 NHL entry draft. Fourth Capitals pick, 61st overall, third round.

KELLY HRUDEY

Goaltender . . . 5'10" . . . 183 lbs. . . . Born, Edmonton, Alta., January 13, 1961 . . . Shoots left . . . (April, 1989)—Flu . . . (February, 1990)—Missed 14 games with Cytomegalo Virus, a form of mononucleosis . . . (April 20, 1990)—Bruised ribs when checked into goalpost by Joe Nieuwendyk vs. Calgary.

Year	Team	League	Games	Mins.	Goals	SO.	Avg.	A.	Pen.
1978-79	Medicine Hat Tigers	WHL	57	3093	*318	0	6.17	2	43
1979-80	Medicine Hat Tigers (c)	WHL	57	3049	212	1	4.17	6	12
1980-81	Medicine Hat Tigers (b)	WHL	55	3023	200	*4	3.97	0	21
1980-81	Indianapolis Checkers (d)	CHL	....	.....	....	...	.....	..	....
1981-82	Indianapolis Checkers (a-e-f-g)	CHL	51	3033	149	1	*2.95	0	6
1982-83	Indianapolis Checkers (a-e-h-i)	CHL	47	2744	139	2	3.04	0	28
1983-84	Indianapolis Checkers	CHL	6	370	21	0	3.41	1	0
1983-84	New York Islanders	NHL	12	535	28	0	3.14	0	0
1984-85	New York Islanders	NHL	41	2335	141	2	3.62	1	17
1985-86	New York Islanders	NHL	45	2563	137	1	3.21	3	14
1986-87	New York Islanders	NHL	46	2634	145	0	3.30	1	37
1987-88	New York Islanders	NHL	47	2751	153	3	3.34	2	20
1988-89	New York Islanders (j)	NHL	50	2800	183	0	3.92	1	17
1988-89	Los Angeles Kings	NHL	16	974	47	1	2.90	2	2
1989-90	Los Angeles Kings	NHL	52	2860	194	2	4.07	0	18
NHL TOTALS			309	17452	1028	9	3.53	10	125

(c)—June, 1980—Drafted by New York Islanders as underage junior in 1980 NHL entry draft. Second Islanders pick, 38th overall, second round.
(d)—No regular season games. Played two playoff games.
(e)—Co-winner of Terry Sawchuk Trophy (Top Goaltenders) with teammate Robert Holland.
(f)—Winner of Max McNab Trophy (Playoff MVP).
(g)—Led CHL Playoffs with 2.42 goals-against-average and one shutout.
(h)—Won Tommy Ivan Trophy (MVP).
(i)—Led CHL playoffs with 2.64 average.
(j)—February 27, 1989—Traded by N.Y. Islanders to Los Angeles Kings for Wayne McBean, Mark Fitzpatrick and future considerations (Doug Crossman was sent to the Islanders on May 23 to complete the deal).

PETER ING

Goaltender . . . 6'2" . . . 165 lbs. . . . Born, Toronto, Ont., April 28, 1969 . . . Shoots left.

Year	Team	League	Games	Mins.	Goals	SO.	Avg.	A.	Pen.
1985-86	Toronto Marlboros Midget	OHA	35	1800	91	4	3.03	..	..
1986-87	Windsor Spitfires	OHL	28	1615	105	0	3.90	1	9
1987-88	Windsor Spitfires (c)	OHL	43	2422	125	2	3.10	3	6
1988-89	Windsor Spitfires	OHL	19	1043	76	1	4.37	1	4
1988-89	London Knights	OHL	32	1848	104	2	3.38	1	11
1989-90	Toronto Maple Leafs	NHL	3	182	18	0	5.93	0	0
1989-90	Newmarket Saints	AHL	48	2829	184	1	3.90	2	4
NHL TOTALS			3	182	18	0	5.93	0	0

(c)—June, 1988—Drafted by Toronto Maple Leafs in 1988 NHL entry draft. Third Maple Leafs pick, 48th overall, third round.

PAT JABLONSKI

Goaltender . . . 6' . . . 170 lbs. . . . Born, Toledo, O., June 20, 1967 . . . Shoots right.

Year	Team	League	Games	Mins.	Goals	SO.	Avg.	A.	Pen.
1984-85	Detroit Compuware Jr. A. (c)	NASHL	29	1483	95	0	3.84	..	....
1985-86	Windsor Spitfires	OHL	29	1600	119	1	4.46	3	4
1986-87	Windsor Spitfires	OHL	41	2328	128	*3	3.30	1	16

Year	Team	League	Games	Mins.	Goals	SO.	Avg.	A.	Pen.
1987-88	Windsor Spitfires	OHL	18	994	48	2	2.90	0	2
1987-88	Peoria Rivermen	IHL	5	285	17	0	3.58	0	2
1988-89	Peoria Rivermen	IHL	35	2051	163	1	4.77	0	10
1989-90	St. Louis Blues	NHL	4	208	17	0	4.90	0	0
1989-90	Peoria Rivermen	IHL	36	2043	165	0	4.85	1	2
	NHL TOTALS		4	208	17	0	4.90	0	0

(c)—June, 1985—Drafted by St. Louis Blues in 1985 NHL entry draft. Sixth Blues pick, 138th overall, seventh round.

MIKE JEFFERY

Goaltender . . . 6'3'' . . . 195 lbs. . . . Born, Kamloops, B.C., April 6, 1965 . . . Shoots right.

Year	Team	League	Games	Mins.	Goals	SO.	Avg.	A.	Pen.
1984-85	Northern Michigan Univ.	WCHA	12	573	44	0	4.61	2	0
1985-86	Northern Michigan Univ.	WCHA	15	743	58	0	4.68	0	2
1986-87	Northern Michigan Univ. (c)	WCHA	28	1601	102	0	3.82	0	0
1987-88	Northern Michigan Univ.	WCHA	30	1801	107	0	3.56	4	0
1988-89	Maine Mariners	AHL	44	2368	148	1	3.75	0	19
1989-90	Maine Mariners	AHL	13	633	46	0	4.36	0	0
1989-90	Johnstown Chiefs	ECHL	14	755	49		3.89	1	12

(c)—June, 1987—Selected by Boston Bruins in 1987 NHL supplemental draft.

CURTIS JOSEPH

Goaltender . . . 5'10'' . . . 170 lbs. . . . Born, Keswick, Ont., April 29, 1967 . . . Shoots left . . . (April 11, 1990)—Dislocated left shoulder when checked and slashed by Dave Hannan vs. Toronto . . . (May 10, 1990)—Surgery to left shoulder.

Year	Team	League	Games	Mins.	Goals	SO.	Avg.	A.	Pen.
1986-87	Richmond Hill Dynes (c)	OHA	....	....	....	..	....	..	....
1987-88	Notre Dame Hounds	SJHL	36	2174	94	1	2.59	..	....
1988-89	Univ. of Wis. (a-d-e-f-g)	WCHA	38	2267	94	1	2.49	1	15
1989-90	Peoria Rivermen	IHL	23	1241	80	0	3.87	0	0
1989-90	St. Louis Blues	NHL	15	852	48	0	3.38	1	0
	NHL TOTALS		15	852	48	0	3.38	1	0

(c)—Named League MVP.
(d)—Named WCHA Rookie-of-the-Year.
(e)—Named WCHA MVP.
(f)—Named Second team All-America (West).
(g)—June 16, 1989—Signed with St. Louis Blues as a free agent.

TREVOR KIDD

Goaltender . . . 6'2'' . . . 176 lbs. . . . Born, St. Boniface, Man., March 26, 1972 . . . Shoots left . . . (December, 1987)—Broken finger.

Year	Team	League	Games	Mins.	Goals	SO.	Avg.	A.	Pen.
1987-88	Eastman Selects Midget	Manitoba	14	840	66	0	4.71	..	....
1988-89	Brandon Wheat Kings	WHL	32	1509	102	0	4.06	1	2
1989-90	Brandon Wheat Kings (a-c-d)	WHL	63	3676	254	2	4.15	0	0

(c)—Won Del Wilson Trophy (WHL goaltending trophy).
(d)—June 16, 1990—Selected by Calgary Flames in 1990 NHL entry draft. First Flames pick, 11th overall, first round.

SCOTT KING

Goaltender . . . 6'1'' . . . 170 lbs. . . . Born, Thunder Bay, Ont., June 25, 1967 . . . Shoots left.

Year	Team	League	Games	Mins.	Goals	SO.	Avg.	A.	Pen.
1985-86	Vernon (c)	BCJHL	29	1718	134	0	4.68	..	....
1986-87	University of Maine	H. East	21	1111	58	0	3.13	1	0
1987-88	University of Maine (a)	H. East	33	1762	91	0	3.10	1	4
1988-89	University of Maine (b)	H. East	27	1394	83	...	3.57	0	14
1989-90	University of Maine (a)	H. East	29	1526	67	1	2.63	1	2

(c)—June, 1986—Drafted by Detroit Red Wings in 1986 NHL entry draft. Tenth Red Wings pick, 190th overall, 10th round.

RICK KNICKLE

Goaltender . . . 5'10'' . . . 155 lbs. . . . Born, Chatham, N.B., February 26, 1960 . . . Shoots left . . . (February, 1981)—Sprained thumb.

Year	Team	League	Games	Mins.	Goals	SO.	Avg.	A.	Pen.
1977-78	Brandon Wheat Kings	WCHL	49	2806	182	0	3.89	5	27
1978-79	Brandon Wheat Kings (a-c-d)	WHL	38	2240	118	0	*3.16	3	15
1979-80	Muskegon Mohawks	IHL	16	829	51	0	3.69	0	25
1980-81	Erie Blades (a-e)	EHL	43	2347	125	1	*3.20	0	12
1981-82	Rochester Americans	AHL	31	1753	108	1	3.70	1	0
1982-83	Flint Generals	IHL	27	1638	92	2	3.37	2	6
1982-83	Rochester Americans	AHL	4	143	11	0	4.64	0	0
1983-84	Flint Generals (b-f)	IHL	60	3518	203	3	3.46	6	16
1984-85	Sherbrooke Canadiens	AHL	14	780	53	0	4.08	0	6
1984-85	Flint Generals	IHL	36	2018	115	2	3.42	3	8
1985-86	Saginaw Gears	IHL	39	2235	135	2	3.62	0	6
1986-87	Saginaw Generals	IHL	26	1413	113	0	4.80	0	23
1987-88	Flint Spirits	IHL	1	60	4	0	4.00	0	0
1987-88	Peoria Rivermen	IHL	13	705	58	0	4.94	1	0
1988-89	Fort Wayne Komets (a)	IHL	47	2719	141	3	3.11	1	2
1989-90	Flint Spirits	IHL	55	2998	210	1	4.20	5	6

(c)—Named top Goaltender in WHL.
(d)—August, 1979—Drafted by Buffalo Sabres as underage junior in 1979 NHL entry draft. Seventh Buffalo pick, 116th overall, sixth round.
(e)—Led EHL playoffs with 1.88 goals-against average.
(f)—Led IHL playoffs with 3.00 average.

OLAF KOLZIG

Goaltender . . . 6'3'' . . . 207 lbs. . . . Born, Johannesburg, South Africa, April 6, 1970 . . . Shoots left . . . (November, 1988)—Right knee surgery . . . (November 29, 1989)—First WHL goalie to score a goal. He fired the puck into an empty net in 5-2 win vs. Seattle.

Year	Team	League	Games	Mins.	Goals	SO.	Avg.	A.	Pen.
1987-88	New Westminster Bruins	WHL	15	650	48	1	4.43	1	13
1988-89	Tri-City Americans (c)	WHL	30	1671	97	1	3.48	2	24
1989-90	Washington Capitals	NHL	2	120	12	0	6.00	0	0
1989-90	Tri-City Americans	WHL	48	2504	187	1	4.48	5	36
	NHL TOTALS		2	120	12	0	6.00	0	0

(c)—June, 1989—Drafted by Washington Capitals in 1989 NHL entry draft. First Capitals pick, 19th overall, first round.

LES KUNTAR

Goaltender . . . 6'2'' . . . 194 lbs. . . . Born, Buffalo, N.Y., July 28, 1969 . . . Shoots left.

Year	Team	League	Games	Mins.	Goals	SO.	Avg.	A.	Pen.
1986-87	Nicholls H.S. (c)	N.Y.	22	1585	56	3	2.12	..	....
1987-88	St. Lawrence Univ.	ECAC	10	488	27	0	3.32	3	0
1988-89	St. Lawrence Univ.	ECAC	14	786	31	0	2.37	0	4
1989-90	St. Lawrence Univ.	ECAC	19	1076	76	1	4.24	0	0

(c)—June, 1987—Drafted by Montreal Canadiens in 1987 NHL entry draft. Sixth Canadiens pick, 122nd overall, sixth round.

MARK LAFOREST

Goaltender . . . 5'11'' . . . 190 lbs. . . . Born, Welland, Ont., July 10, 1962 . . . Shoots left . . . (March 16, 1989)—Sprained knee vs. St. Louis . . . (January 11, 1990)—Slipped on a patch of ice while walking on the street, twisted his left ankle and missed five weeks.

Year	Team	League	Games	Mins.	Goals	SO.	Avg.	A.	Pen.
1981-82	Niagara Falls Flyers	OHL	24	1365	105	1	4.62	1	14
1982-83	North Bay Centennials	OHL	54	3140	195	0	3.73	4	20
1983-84	Adirondack Red Wings (c)	AHL	7	351	29	0	4.96	0	2
1983-84	Kalamazoo Wings	IHL	13	718	48	1	4.01	0	11
1984-85	Mohawk Valley Stars	ACHL	8	420	60	0	8.57	1	15
1984-85	Adirondack Red Wings	AHL	11	430	35	0	4.88	0	0
1985-86	Adirondack Red Wings	AHL	19	1142	57	0	2.29	1	14
1985-86	Detroit Red Wings	NHL	28	1383	114	1	4.95	0	23
1986-87	Adirondack Red Wings (d)	AHL	37	2229	105	3	2.83	0	10
1986-87	Detroit Red Wings (e)	NHL	5	219	12	0	3.29	0	10
1987-88	Hershey Bears	AHL	5	309	13	0	2.52	0	2
1987-88	Philadelphia Flyers	NHL	21	972	60	1	3.70	0	8
1988-89	Philadelphia Flyers	NHL	17	933	64	0	4.12	4	4
1988-89	Hershey Bears	AHL	3	185	9	0	2.92	0	0
1989-90	Toronto Maple Leafs (f-g)	NHL	27	1343	87	0	3.89	1	23
1989-90	Newmarket Saints	AHL	10	604	33	1	3.28	1	10
	NHL TOTALS		98	4850	337	2	4.17	5	68

(c)—September, 1983—Signed by Detroit Red Wings as a free agent.
(d)—Won Baz Bastien Trophy (Coaches pick as top Goalie).
(e)—June, 1987—Traded by Detroit Red Wings to Philadelphia Flyers for second-round 1987 draft pick (Bob Wilkie).
(f)—September 8, 1989—Traded by Philadelphia Flyers to Toronto Maple Leafs for sixth and seventh round 1991 draft picks.
(g)—June 18, 1990—Traded with Tie Domi by Toronto Maple Leafs to New York Rangers for Greg Johnston.

SCOTT LaGRAND

Goaltender . . . 6' . . . 155 lbs. . . . Born, Potsdam, N.Y., February 11, 1970 . . . Shoots right.

Year	Team	League	Games	Mins.	Goals	SO.	Avg.	A.	Pen.
1986-87	Hotchkiss	N.Y. H.S.	17	1020	36	0	2.77	..	..
1987-88	Hotchkiss (c)	N.Y. H.S.	...	...	...	..	2.50	..	..
1988-89	Hotchkiss	N.Y. H.S.	...	...	...	..	...	..	..
1989-90	Boston College	H. East	24	1268	57	0	2.70	0	0

(c)—June, 1988—Selected by Philadelphia Flyers in NHL entry draft. Fifth Flyers pick, 77th overall, fourth round.

RAY LeBLANC

Goaltender . . . 5'10'' . . . 170 lbs. . . . Born, Whitby, Ont., October 24, 1964 . . . Shoots left.

Year	Team	League	Games	Mins.	Goals	SO.	Avg.	A.	Pen.
1982-83	Dixie Flyers Jr. A	OHA	30	1705	111	0	3.91	..	..
1983-84	Kitchener Rangers	OHL	*54	2965	185	1	3.74	1	7
1984-85	Pinebridge Bucks (b)	ACHL	40	2178	150	0	4.13	3	2
1985-86	Carolina Thunderbirds	ACHL	42	2505	133	3	3.19	5	4
1986-87	Flint Spirits (b-c)	IHL	64	3417	222	1	3.90	3	20
1987-88	Flint Spirits	IHL	60	3269	*239	1	4.39	3	12
1988-89	Saginaw Hawks	IHL	29	1655	99	0	3.59	1	6
1988-89	New Haven Nighthawks	AHL	1	20	3	0	9.00	0	0
1989-90	Fort Wayne Komets	IHL	15	680	44	0	3.88	1	4
1989-90	Indianapolis Ice	IHL	23	1334	71	2	3.19	0	6

(c)—Won Ken McKenzie Trophy (Top U.S. Born IHL Rookie).

REJEAN LEMELIN

Goaltender . . . 5'11'' . . . 170 lbs. . . . Born, Sherbrooke, Que., November 19, 1954 . . . Shoots left . . . (February 8, 1981)—Broke thumb on right hand at Edmonton . . . (January, 1984)—Back injury.

Year	Team	League	Games	Mins.	Goals	SO.	Avg.	A.	Pen.
1972-73	Sherbrooke Beavers	QMJHL	27	1117	146	0	5.21	2	4
1973-74	Sherbrooke Beavers (c)	QMJHL	35		158	0	4.60	1	2
1974-75	Philadelphia Firebirds	NAHL	43	2277	131	3	3.45	3	16

Year Team	League	Games	Mins.	Goals	SO.	Avg.	A.	Pen.
1975-76—Richmond Robins	AHL	7	402	30	0	4.48	0	0
1975-76—Philadelphia Firebirds	NAHL	29	1601	97	1	3.63	1	6
1976-77—Philadelphia Firebirds	NAHL	51	2763	170	1	3.61	2	0
1976-77—Springfield Indians	AHL	3	180	10	0	3.33	0	0
1977-78—Philadelphia Firebirds (a)	AHL	60	3585	177	4	2.96	1	22
1978-79—Atlanta Flames (d)	NHL	18	994	55	0	3.32	0	4
1978-79—Philadelphia Firebirds	AHL	13	780	36	0	2.77	1	12
1979-80—Birmingham Bulls	CHL	38	2188	137	0	3.76	2	14
1979-80—Atlanta Flames	NHL	3	150	15	0	6.00	0	0
1980-81—Birmingham Bulls	CHL	13	757	56	0	4.44	0	4
1980-81—Calgary Flames	NHL	29	1629	88	2	3.24	1	2
1981-82—Calgary Flames	NHL	34	1866	135	0	4.34	1	0
1982-83—Calgary Flames	NHL	39	2211	133	0	3.61	5	7
1983-84—Calgary Flames	NHL	51	2568	150	0	3.50	3	6
1984-85—Calgary Flames	NHL	56	3176	183	1	3.46	0	4
1985-86—Calgary Flames	NHL	60	3369	229	1	4.08	4	10
1986-87—Calgary Flames (e)	NHL	34	1735	94	2	3.25	0	20
1987-88—Boston Bruins (f)	NHL	49	2828	138	3	2.93	0	2
1988-89—Boston Bruins	NHL	40	2392	120	0	3.01	1	6
1989-90—Boston Bruins (g)	NHL	43	2310	108	2	2.81	0	32
NHL TOTALS		456	25228	1448	11	3.44	15	93

(c)—Drafted from Sherbrooke Beavers by Philadelphia Flyers in sixth round of 1974 amateur draft.
(d)—August, 1978—Signed by Atlanta Flames as free agent.
(e)—August, 1987—Signed by Boston Bruins as a free agent.
(f)—Led NHL Playoffs with a 2.63 average and tied for lead with one shutout.
(g)—Shared William M. Jennings Trophy (with teammate Andy Moog) for playing on the NHL team that allowed the fewest goals.

MIKE LENARDUZZI

Goaltender . . . 6' . . . 165 lbs. . . . Born, Mississauga, Ont., September 14, 1972 . . . Shoots left.

Year Team	League	Games	Mins.	Goals	SO.	Avg.	A.	Pen.
1988-89—Markham Waxers Jr. B	OHA	20	1149	111	0	5.80	..	..
1988-89—Oshawa 67's	OHL	6	166	9	0	3.25	0	0
1989-90—Oshawa 67's (c)	OHL	12	444	32	0	4.32	0	0
1989-90—S.S. Marie Greyhounds (d)	OHL	20	1117	66	0	3.55	0	0

(c)—December 17, 1989—Traded with Mike DeCoff, Jason Denomme, second round 1990 (Drew Banister) and 1991 draft picks and $80,000 cash by Oshawa 67's to Sault Ste. Marie Greyhounds for Eric Lindros.
(d)—June 16, 1990—Selected by Hartford Whalers in 1990 NHL entry draft. Third Whalers pick, 57th overall, third round.

DAVID LITTMAN

Goaltender . . . 6' . . . 175 lbs. . . . Born, Cranston, R.I., June 13, 1967 . . . Shoots left . . . (December, 1989)—Separated shoulder and missed six games.

Year Team	League	Games	Mins.	Goals	SO.	Avg.	A.	Pen.
1985-86—Boston College	H. East	9	442	22	1	2.99	1	0
1986-87—Boston College (c)	H. East	21	1182	68	0	3.45	0	....
1987-88—Boston College	H. East	30	1726	116	0	4.03	2	10
1988-89—Boston College (a-d)	H. East	32	1945	107	0	3.30	2	4
1989-90—Rochester Americans	AHL	14	681	37	0	3.26	2	0
1989-90—Phoenix Roadrunners	IHL	18	1047	64	0	3.67	1	11

(c)—June, 1987—Drafted by Buffalo Sabres in 1987 NHL entry draft. Twelfth Sabres pick, 211th overall, 11th round.
(d)—Named Second team All-America (East).

MICHAEL LIUT

Goaltender . . . 6'2" . . . 195 lbs. . . . Born, Weston, Ont., January 7, 1956 . . . Shoots left . . . Missed part of 1977-78 season with torn cartilage in left knee . . . (January 10, 1981)—Groin injury vs. Los Angeles . . . (March, 1984)—Strained knee ligaments . . . (October, 1987)—Missed 13 days with muscle spasms in lower back . . . (March, 1988)—Twisted knee . . . (April, 1988)—Sprained shoulder vs. Montreal . . . (November, 1988)—Missed two weeks with inflamed rotator cuff in right shoulder . . . (March, 1989)—Twisted knee . . . (December 20, 1989)—Left knee surgery and missed 16 games . . . (1989-90)—Led the NHL with a GAA of 2.527.

Year Team	League	Games	Mins.	Goals	SO.	Avg.	A.	Pen.
1973-74—Bowling Green State U.	CCHA	24	1272	88	0	4.00	0	4
1974-75—Bowling Green State U. (a)	CCHA	20	1174	78	0	3.99	0	10
1975-76—Bowling Green St. U. (b-c-d)	CCHA	21	1171	50	2	2.56	0	0
1976-77—Bowling Green St. U. (a-e-f)	CCHA	24	1346	61	2	2.72	2	4
1977-78—Cincinnati Stingers	WHA	27	1215	86	0	4.25	1	0
1978-79—Cincinnati Stingers (g)	WHA	54	3181	184	*3	3.47	2	9
1979-80—St. Louis Blues	NHL	64	3661	194	2	3.18	0	2
1980-81—St. Louis Blues (a)	NHL	61	3570	199	1	3.34	0	0
1981-82—St. Louis Blues	NHL	64	3691	250	2	4.06	2	2
1982-83—St. Louis Blues	NHL	68	3794	235	1	3.72	0	2
1983-84—St. Louis Blues	NHL	58	3425	197	3	3.45	4	0
1984-85—St. Louis Blues (h)	NHL	32	1869	119	1	3.82	1	4
1984-85—Hartford Whalers	NHL	12	731	36	1	3.04	0	2
1985-86—Hartford Whalers (i)	NHL	57	3282	197	2	3.60	2	0
1986-87—Hartford Whalers (b)	NHL	59	3476	187	*4	3.23	2	4
1987-88—Hartford Whalers	NHL	60	3532	187	2	3.18	1	4
1988-89—Hartford Whalers	NHL	35	2006	142	1	4.25	0	0
1989-90—Hartford Whalers (j)	NHL	29	1683	74	3	2.64	0	0
1989-90—Washington Capitals	NHL	8	478	17	1	2.13	0	0
WHA TOTALS		81	4396	270	3	3.69	3	9
NHL TOTALS		607	35198	2034	24	3.47	12	20

(c)—Drafted from Bowling Green State University by St. Louis Blues in fourth round of 1976 amateur draft.
(d)—May, 1976—Selected by New England Whalers in World Hockey Association amateur player draft.
(e)—May, 1977—WHA rights traded to Cincinnati Stingers by New England Whalers with second-round 1979 draft choice for Greg Carroll and Bryan Maxwell.
(f)—Named CCHA Player-of-the-Year.
(g)—June, 1979—Selected by St. Louis Blues in reclaim draft.
(h)—February, 1985—Traded with future considerations (Jorgen Pettersson) by St. Louis Blues to Hartford Whalers for Greg Millen and Mark Johnson.
(i)—Led Stanley Cup Playoffs with a 1.90 average and tied for lead with one shutout.
(j)—March 5, 1990—Traded by Hartford Whalers to Washington Capitals for Yvon Corriveau.

DANNY LORENZ

Goaltender . . . 5'10" . . . 170 lbs. . . . Born, Murrayville, B.C., December 12, 1969 . . . Shoots left.

Year Team	League	Games	Mins.	Goals	SO.	Avg.	A.	Pen.
1986-87—Seattle Thunderbirds	WHL	38	2103	199	0	5.68	2	6
1987-88—Seattle Thunderbirds (c)	WHL	62	3302	314	0	5.71	1	9
1988-89—Seattle Thunderbirds (a)	WHL	68	4003	240	3	3.60	5	23
1988-89—Springfield Indians	AHL	4	210	12	0	3.43	0	2
1989-90—Seattle Thunderbirds	WHL	56	3226	221	0	4.11	4	23

(c)—June, 1988—Drafted by New York Islanders in 1988 NHL entry draft. Fourth Islanders pick, 58th overall, third round.

CLINT MALARCHUK

Goaltender . . . 6' . . . 190 lbs. . . . Born, Grande, Alta., May 1, 1961 . . . Shoots left . . . (March 22, 1989)—Jugular vein opened when throat was cut by skate of Steve Tuttle vs. St. Louis.

Year Team	League	Games	Mins.	Goals	SO.	Avg.	A.	Pen.
1978-79—Portland Winter Hawks	WHL	2	120	4	0	2.00	..	....
1979-80—Portland Winter Hawks (c)	WHL	37	1948	147	0	4.53	2	10
1980-81—Portland Winter Hawks	WHL	38	2235	142	3	3.81	7	22
1981-82—Quebec Nordiques	NHL	2	120	14	0	7.00	0	0
1981-82—Fredericton Express	AHL	51	2962	*253	0	5.12	4	22
1982-83—Quebec Nordiques	NHL	15	900	71	0	4.73	0	0
1982-83—Fredericton Express	AHL	25	1506	78	1	*3.11	1	2
1983-84—Fredericton Express	AHL	11	663	40	0	3.62	1	5
1983-84—Quebec Nordiques	NHL	23	1215	80	0	3.95	1	9
1984-85—Fredericton Express	AHL	*56	*3347	*198	2	3.55	1	14
1985-86—Quebec Nordiques	NHL	46	2657	142	4	3.21	2	21
1986-87—Quebec Nordiques (d)	NHL	54	3092	175	1	3.40	2	37
1987-88—Washington Capitals	NHL	54	2926	154	*4	3.16	2	10
1988-89—Washington Capitals (e)	NHL	42	2428	141	1	3.48	1	16
1988-89—Buffalo Sabres	NHL	7	326	13	1	2.39	0	2
1989-90—Buffalo Sabres	NHL	29	1596	89	0	3.35	2	14
NHL TOTALS		272	15260	879	11	3.46	10	109

(c)—October, 1980—Signed by Quebec Nordiques as a free agent.
(d)—June, 1987—Traded with Dale Hunter by Quebec Nordiques to Washington Capitals for Alan Haworth, Gaeten Duchesne and a first-round 1987 draft pick (Joe Sakic).
(e)—March 6, 1989—Traded with Grant Ledyard and a sixth-round 1991 draft pick by Washington Capitals to Buffalo Sabres for Calle Johansson and a second-round 1989 draft pick (Byron Dafoe).

GEORGE MANELUK

Goaltender . . . 6' . . . 190 lbs. . . . Born, Winnipeg, Man., July 25, 1967 . . . Shoots left . . . Attended University of Manitoba in 1985-86.

Year Team	League	Games	Mins.	Goals	SO.	Avg.	A.	Pen.
1986-87—Brandon Wheat Kings (c)	WHL	58	3258	315	0	5.80	4	19
1987-88—Brandon Wheat Kings	WHL	64	3651	297	0	4.88	9	14
1987-88—Springfield Indians	AHL	2	125	9	0	4.32	0	0
1987-88—Peoria Rivermen	IHL	3	148	14	0	5.68	0	0
1988-89—Springfield Indians	AHL	24	1202	84	0	4.19	0	6
1989-90—Springfield Indians	AHL	27	1382	94	1	4.08	0	4

(c)—June, 1987—Drafted by New York Islanders in 1987 NHL entry draft. Fourth Islanders pick, 57th overall, fourth round.

BOB MASON

Goaltender . . . 6'1" . . . 180 lbs. . . . Born, International Falls, Minn., April 22, 1961 . . . Shoots right.

Year Team	League	Games	Mins.	Goals	SO.	Avg.	A.	Pen.
1981-82—Univ. of Minnesota/Duluth	WCHA	26	1521	115	..	4.54	..	..
1982-83—Univ. of Minnesota/Duluth	WCHA	43	2594	151	..	3.49	1	4
1983-84—U.S. National Team	Int'l	33	1895	89	..	2.82	..	..
1983-84—U.S. Olympic Team	Int'l	3	160	10	0	3.75	0	0
1983-84—Washington Capitals (c)	NHL	2	120	3	0	1.50	0	0
1983-84—Hershey Bears	AHL	5	282	26	0	5.53	0	0
1984-85—Washington Capitals	NHL	12	661	31	1	2.81	1	0
1984-85—Binghamton Whalers	AHL	20	1052	58	1	3.31	1	0
1985-86—Binghamton Whalers	AHL	34	1940	126	0	3.90	3	6
1985-86—Washington Capitals	NHL	1	16	0	0	0.00	0	0
1986-87—Binghamton Whalers	AHL	2	119	4	0	2.02	0	2
1986-87—Washington Capitals (d)	NHL	45	2536	137	0	3.24	0	0
1987-88—Chicago Black Hawks (e)	NHL	41	2312	160	0	4.15	2	0
1988-89—Quebec Nordiques (f)	NHL	22	1168	92	0	4.73	1	2
1988-89—Halifax Citadels	AHL	23	1278	73	1	3.43	1	0
1989-90—Washington Capitals	NHL	16	822	48	0	3.50	0	4
1989-90—Baltimore Skipjacks	AHL	13	770	44	0	3.43	1	2
NHL TOTALS		139	7635	471	1	3.70	4	6

(c)—February, 1984—Signed by Washington Capitals as a free agent.
(d)—June, 1987—Signed by Chicago Black Hawks as a free agent.
(e)—July, 1988—Traded by Chicago Black Hawks to Quebec Nordiques for Mike Eagles.
(f)—June 17, 1989—Traded by Quebec Nordiques to Washington Capitals for future considerations.

STEVE McKICHAN

Goaltender . . . 5'11" . . . 180 lbs. . . . Born, Strathroy, Ont., May 29, 1967 . . . Shoots left . . . (October, 1987)—Pulled groin.

Year — Team	League	Games	Mins.	Goals	SO.	Avg.	A.	Pen.
1986-87—Miami Univ. of Ohio	CCHA	28	1351	130	0	5.77	0	4
1987-88—Miami Univ. of Ohio (c)	CCHA	34	1767	140	1	4.75	3	27
1988-89—Miami Univ. of Ohio	CCHA	21	1241	105	..	5.08	0	2
1989-90—Milwaukee Admirals	IHL	1	40	2	0	3.00	0	0
1989-90—Virginia Lancers	ECHL	28	1445	97	...	4.03	1	48

(c)—June, 1988—Selected by Vancouver Canucks in 1988 NHL supplemental draft.

KIRK McLEAN

Goaltender . . . 6' . . . 177 lbs. . . . Born, Willowdale, Ont., June 26, 1966 . . . Shoots left.

Year — Team	League	Games	Mins.	Goals	SO.	Avg.	A.	Pen.
1983-84—Oshawa Generals (c)	OHL	17	940	67	0	4.28	0	11
1984-85—Oshawa Generals	OHL	47	2581	143	1	*3.32	1	6
1985-86—Oshawa Generals	OHL	51	2830	169	1	3.58	0	8
1985-86—New Jersey Devils	NHL	2	111	11	0	5.95	0	0
1986-87—New Jersey Devils	NHL	4	160	10	0	3.75	0	0
1986-87—Maine Mariners (d)	AHL	45	2606	140	1	3.22	1	6
1987-88—Vancouver Canucks	NHL	41	2380	147	1	3.71	2	8
1988-89—Vancouver Canucks	NHL	42	2477	127	4	3.08	1	6
1989-90—Vancouver Canucks	NHL	63	3739	216	0	3.47	3	6
NHL TOTALS		152	8867	511	5	3.46	6	20

(c)—June, 1984—Drafted as underage junior by New Jersey Devils in 1984 NHL entry draft. Sixth Devils pick, 10th overall, sixth round.

(d)—September, 1987—Traded with Greg Adams by New Jersey Devils to Vancouver Canucks for Patrik Sundstrom and a fourth-round 1988 draft pick (Matt Ruchty).

ROLAND MELANSON

Goaltender . . . 5'10" . . . 178 lbs. . . . Born, Moncton, N.B., June 28, 1960 . . . Shoots left . . . Led OMJHL in games played by goaltenders in 1978-79 and co-leader in 1979-80 (with Bruce Dowie) . . . (November 19, 1985)—Pulled groin at Calgary. After missing 30 days with the injury he was traded to Los Angeles . . . (January 15, 1986)—Injured groin vs. N.Y. Rangers and missed 13 games . . . (October 6, 1988)—Sprained left knee vs. Detroit.

Year — Team	League	Games	Mins.	Goals	SO.	Avg.	A.	Pen.
1977-78—Windsor Spitfires	OMJHL	44	2592	195	1	4.51	2	12
1978-79—Windsor Spitfires (b-c)	OMJHL	*62	*3461	254	1	4.40	7	16
1979-80—Windsor Spitfires	OMJHL	22	1099	90	0	4.91	0	8
1979-80—Oshawa Generals	OMJHL	38	2240	136	*3	3.64	2	14
1980-81—Indianapolis Checkers (a-d)	CHL	*52	*3056	131	2	*2.57	1	16
1980-81—New York Islanders	NHL	11	620	32	0	3.10	0	4
1981-82—New York Islanders	NHL	36	2115	114	0	3.23	0	14
1982-83—New York Islanders (e)	NHL	44	2460	109	1	2.66	3	22
1983-84—New York Islanders	NHL	37	2019	110	0	3.27	2	10
1984-85—New York Islanders (f)	NHL	8	425	35	0	4.94	0	0
1984-85—Minnesota North Stars	NHL	20	1142	78	0	4.10	0	9
1985-86—New Haven Nighthawks	AHL	3	179	13	0	4.36	0	0
1985-86—Minnesota North Stars (g)	NHL	6	325	24	0	4.43	0	0
1985-86—Los Angeles Kings	NHL	22	1246	87	0	4.19	1	8
1986-87—Los Angeles Kings	NHL	46	2734	168	1	3.69	6	22
1987-88—Los Angeles Kings	NHL	47	2676	195	2	4.37	0	16
1988-89—Los Angeles Kings	NHL	4	178	19	0	6.40	0	4
1988-89—New Haven Nighthawks (h)	AHL	29	1734	106	1	3.67	2	22
1989-90—Utica Devils	AHL	48	2737	167	1	3.66	4	18
NHL TOTALS		281	15940	971	4	3.65	12	109

(c)—August, 1979—Drafted by New York Islanders as underage junior in 1979 NHL entry draft. Fourth Islanders pick, 59th overall, third round.

(d)—Winner of Ken McKenzie Trophy (Top Rookie).

(e)—Shared William Jennings Trophy with Billy Smith for NHL's best team goaltending average.

(f)—November, 1984—Traded by New York Islanders to Minnesota North Stars for first round 1985 draft pick (Brad Dalgarno).

(g)—December, 1985—Traded by Minnesota North Stars to N.Y. Rangers for second round 1986 (Neil Wilkinson) and fourth round 1987 (John Weisbrod) draft picks. He was then traded with Grant Ledyard by the Rangers to Los Angeles Kings for Brian MacLellan and a fourth round 1987 draft pick (Michael Sullivan).

(h)—August, 1989—Signed by New Jersey Devils as a free agent.

MATT MERTEN

Goaltender . . . 6'3" . . . 190 lbs. . . . Born, Milford, Mass., June 29, 1967 . . . Shoots left.

Year — Team	League	Games	Mins.	Goals	SO.	Avg.	A.	Pen.
1986-87—Providence College (c)	H. East	24	1455	104	0	4.29	1	4
1987-88—Providence College	H. East	25	1328	100	1	4.52	1	8
1988-89—Providence College	H. East	20	1047	69	0	3.95	0	0
1989-90—Providence College	H. East	16	908	38	0	*2.51	0	6

(c)—June, 1986—Drafted by Vancouver Canucks in 1986 NHL entry draft. Sixth Canucks pick, 175th overall, ninth round.

GREG MILLEN

Goaltender . . . 5'9" . . . 160 lbs. . . . Born, Toronto, Ont., June 25, 1957 . . . Shoots right . . . (October, 1979)—Pulled hamstring muscle and missed 18 games.

Year — Team	League	Games	Mins.	Goals	SO.	Avg.	A.	Pen.
1974-75—Peterborough TPT's	OMJHL	27	1584	90	2	*3.41	..	....
1975-76—Peterborough Petes	OMJHL	58	3282	233	0	4.26	0	6
1976-77—Peterborough Petes (c)	OMJHL	59	3457	244	0	4.23	2	14
1977-78—S. Ste. Marie Greyhounds	OMJHL	25	1469	105	1	4.29	2	0
1977-78—Kalamazoo Wings	IHL	3	180	14	0	4.67	0	0
1978-79—Pittsburgh Penguins	NHL	28	1532	86	2	3.37	0	0
1979-80—Pittsburgh Penguins	NHL	44	2586	157	2	3.64	3	14
1980-81—Pittsburgh Penguins (d)	NHL	63	3721	258	0	4.16	2	6
1981-82—Hartford Whalers	NHL	55	3201	229	0	4.29	5	2
1982-83—Hartford Whalers	NHL	60	3520	282	1	4.81	2	8
1983-84—Hartford Whalers	NHL	*60	*3583	*221	2	3.70	3	10
1984-85—Hartford Whalers (e)	NHL	44	2659	187	1	4.22	0	4
1984-85—St. Louis Blues	NHL	10	607	35	0	3.47	0	0
1985-86—St. Louis Blues	NHL	36	2168	129	1	3.57	1	8
1986-87—St. Louis Blues	NHL	42	2482	146	0	3.53	2	12
1987-88—St. Louis Blues	NHL	48	2854	167	1	3.51	0	4
1988-89—St. Louis Blues	NHL	52	3019	170	*6	3.38	0	4
1989-90—St. Louis Blues (f)	NHL	21	1245	61	1	2.94	0	0
1989-90—Quebec Nordiques (g)	NHL	18	1080	95	0	5.28	0	0
1989-90—Chicago Black Hawks	NHL	10	575	32	0	3.34	1	0
NHL TOTALS		591	34832	2255	17	3.88	19	72

(c)—June, 1977—Drafted by Pittsburgh Penguins in 1977 NHL amateur draft. Fourth Penguins pick, 102nd overall, sixth round.

(d)—June, 1981—Signed by Hartford Whalers as a free agent. Pat Boutette and Kevin McLelland sent to Pittsburgh as compensation by NHL arbitrator in July.

(e)—February, 1985—Traded with Mark Johnson by Hartford Whalers to St. Louis Blues for Mike Liut and future considerations (Jorgen Pettersson).

(f)—December 13, 1989—Traded with Tony Hrkac by St. Louis Blues to Quebec Nordiques for Jeff Brown. He did not report to Quebec until December 26.

(g)—March 5, 1990—Traded with Michel Goulet and a sixth-round 1991 draft pick by Quebec Nordiques to Chicago Black Hawks for Everett Sanipass, Dan Vincelette and Mario Doyon.

DONALD ANDREW (ANDY) MOOG

Goaltender . . . 5'8" . . . 165 lbs. . . . Born, Penticton, B.C., February 18, 1960 . . . Shoots left . . . (December, 1983)—While visiting a ward of sick children at a local hospital, he entered a quarantined area, caught a viral infection and lost six pounds . . . (March 1, 1985)—Injured ligaments in both knees vs. Los Angeles.

Year — Team	League	Games	Mins.	Goals	SO.	Avg.	A.	Pen.
1976-77—Kamloops Chiefs	WCHL	1	35	6	0	10.29	..	....
1977-78—Penticton	BCJHL	....	.....	....	..	.....	..	....
1978-79—Billings Bighorns	WHL	26	1306	90	*3	4.13	0	6
1979-80—Billings Bighorns (b-c)	WHL	46	2435	149	1	3.67	1	17
1980-81—Wichita Wind	CHL	29	1602	89	0	3.33	0	4
1980-81—Edmonton Oilers	NHL	7	313	20	0	3.83	1	0
1981-82—Edmonton Oilers	NHL	8	399	32	0	4.81	1	2
1981-82—Wichita Wind (b)	CHL	40	2391	119	1	2.99	5	8
1982-83—Edmonton Oilers	NHL	50	2833	167	1	3.54	4	16
1983-84—Edmonton Oilers	NHL	38	2212	139	1	3.77	1	4
1984-85—Edmonton Oilers	NHL	39	2019	111	1	3.30	0	8
1985-86—Edmonton Oilers	NHL	47	2664	164	1	3.69	2	8
1986-87—Edmonton Oilers	NHL	46	2461	144	0	3.51	2	8
1987-88—Canadian Olympic Team	Int'l.	31	1678	95	0	3.40	..	..
1987-88—Boston Bruins (d)	NHL	6	360	17	1	2.83	0	0
1988-89—Boston Bruins	NHL	41	2482	133	1	3.22	1	6
1989-90—Boston Bruins (e)	NHL	46	2536	122	3	2.89	3	18
NHL TOTALS		328	18279	1049	9	3.44	15	70

(c)—June, 1980—Drafted by Edmonton Oilers in 1980 NHL entry draft. Sixth Oilers pick, 132nd overall, seventh round.

(d)—March, 1988—Traded by Edmonton Oilers to Boston Bruins for Geoff Courtnall and Bill Ranford.

(e)—Shared William M. Jennings Trophy with teammate Rejean Lemelin (goaltenders on the NHL team that allows the fewest goals).

GUS MORCHAUSER

Goaltender . . . 5'9" . . . 155 lbs. . . . Born, Kitchener, Ont., March 26, 1969 . . . Shoots left.

Year — Team	League	Games	Mins.	Goals	SO.	Avg.	A.	Pen.
1986-87—Kitchener Midgets	OHA	39	1832	64	0	2.10	..	..
1987-88—Kitchener Rangers	OHL	36	1880	144	0	4.60	2	2
1988-89—Kitchener Rangers (a-c)	OHL	41	2311	132	2	3.43	1	6
1989-90—Kitchener Rangers (d)	OHL	6	345	22	0	3.83	0	6
1989-90—Hamilton Dukes	OHL	38	2110	184	0	5.23	1	26
1989-90—Milwaukee Admirals	IHL	3	119	12	0	6.05	0	0

(c)—June, 1989—Drafted by Vancouver Canucks in 1989 NHL entry draft. Eighth Canucks pick, 197th overall, 10th round.

(d)—October, 1989—Traded by Kitchener Rangers to Dukes of Hamilton for David Schill.

JASON MUZZATTI

Goaltender . . . 6'1" . . . 185 lbs. . . . Born, Toronto, Ont., February 3, 1970 . . . Shoots left.

Year — Team	League	Games	Mins.	Goals	SO.	Avg.	A.	Pen.
1986-87—St. Mikes Jr. B	MTHL	20	1054	69	1	3.93	..	..
1987-88—Michigan State Univ. (c)	CCHA	33	1916	109	1	3.41	4	13
1988-89—Michigan State Univ.	CCHA	42	2515	127	3	3.03	3	35
1989-90—Michigan State Univ. (a-d-e)	CCHA	33	1976	99	0	3.01	9	31

(c)—June, 1988—Drafted by Calgary Flames in 1988 NHL entry draft. First Flames pick, 21st overall, first round.

(d)—Named to CCHA All-Tournament team.

(e)—Named to Second-Team NCAA All-America team (West).

JARMO MYLLYS

Goaltender . . . 5'8" . . . 150 lbs. . . . Born, Sovanlinna, Finland, May 29, 1965 . . . Shoots right . . . (April 22, 1990)—Injured knee vs. Muskegon.

Year — Team	League	Games	Mins.	Goals	SO.	Avg.	A.	Pen.
1987-88—Lukko	Finland	43	2580	160	...	3.72	..	....
1988-89—Kalamazoo Wings (c)	IHL	28	1523	93	0	3.66	1	4
1988-89—Minnesota North Stars	NHL	6	238	22	0	5.55	0	0

Year—Team	League	Games	Mins.	Goals	SO.	Avg.	A.	Pen.
1989-90—Minnesota North Stars	NHL	4	156	16	0	6.15	0	0
1989-90—Kalamazoo Wings (b)	IHL	49	2715	159	1	3.51	8	39
NHL TOTALS		10	394	38	0	5.79	0	0

(c)—June, 1987—Drafted by Minnesota North Stars in 1987 NHL entry draft. Ninth North Stars pick, 172nd overall, ninth round.

SERGEI MYLNIKOV

Goaltender . . . 5'10" . . . 176 lbs. . . . Born, Chelyabinsk, U.S.S.R., October 6, 1958 . . . Shoots left.

Year—Team	League	Games	Mins.	Goals	SO.	Avg.	A.	Pen.
1976-77—Traktor Chelyabinsk	USSR	2	120	2	..	1.00	..	..
1977-78—Traktor Chelyabinsk	USSR	22	1320	71	..	3.22	..	..
1978-79—Traktor Chelyabinsk	USSR	32	1862	90	..	2.90	..	..
1979-80—Traktor Chelyabinsk	USSR	17	1023	58	..	3.40	..	..
1980-81—SKA Leningrad	USSR	40	2415	157	..	3.90	..	..
1981-82—SKA Leningrad	USSR	42	2310	132	..	3.42	..	..
1982-83—Traktor Chelyabinsk	USSR	37	1954	124	..	3.80	..	..
1983-84—Traktor Chelyabinsk	USSR	37	2173	91	..	2.51	..	..
1984-85—Traktor Chelyabinsk	USSR	28	1360	74	..	3.26	..	..
1985-86—Traktor Chelyabinsk	USSR	37	2126	96	..	2.70	..	..
1986-87—Traktor Chelyabinsk	USSR	36	2059	103	..	3.00	..	..
1987-88—Traktor Chelyabinsk	USSR	28	1557	69	..	2.65	..	..
1988-89—Traktor Chelyabinsk (c)	USSR	33	...	85	..	...	..	..
1989-90—Quebec Nordiques	NHL	10	568	47	0	4.96	0	0
NHL TOTALS		10	568	47	0	4.96	0	0

(c)—June, 1989—Drafted by Quebec Nordiques in 1989 NHL entry draft. Ninth Nordiques pick, 127th overall, seventh round.

THOMAS NEWMAN

Goaltender . . . 6'1" . . . 190 lbs. . . . Born, Golden Valley, Minn., February 23, 1971 . . . Shoots left . . . (April, 1987)—Broken foot.

Year—Team	League	Games	Mins.	Goals	SO.	Avg.	A.	Pen.
1987-88—Blaine H.S.	Minn.	16	960	32	..	2.00	..	..
1988-89—Blaine H.S. (c)	Minn.	18	810	43	3	3.19	..	..
1989-90—Univ. of Minnesota	WCHA	35	1982	127	0	3.84	2	2

(c)—June, 1989—Drafted by Los Angeles Kings in 1989 NHL entry draft. Fourth Kings pick, 103rd overall, fifth round.

MICHAEL O'NEILL

Goaltender . . . 5'7" . . . 160 lbs. . . . Born, Montreal, Que., November 3, 1967 . . . Shoots left.

Year—Team	League	Games	Mins.	Goals	SO.	Avg.	A.	Pen.
1986-87—Yale University (a)	ECAC	16	964	55	2	3.42	0	0
1987-88—Yale University (c)	ECAC	24	1385	101	0	4.37	0	2
1988-89—Yale University (a-d)	ECAC	25	1490	93	..	3.74	0	4
1989-90—Tappara	Finland	41	2369	127	2	3.22	0	2

(c)—June, 1988—Selected by Winnipeg Jets in 1988 NHL supplemental draft.
(d)—Named First team All-America (East).

DARREN PANG

Goaltender . . . 5'5" . . . 155 lbs. . . . Born, Medford, Ont., February 17, 1964 . . . Shoots left . . . (January 2, 1989)—Missed two months after pulling a hamstring at Toronto . . . (September 11, 1989)—Reconstructive left knee surgery. A ligament was replaced by a tendon from his kneecap.

Year—Team	League	Games	Mins.	Goals	SO.	Avg.	A.	Pen.
1982-83—Belleville Bulls	OHL	12	570	44	0	4.63	1	0
1982-83—Ottawa 67's	OHL	47	2729	166	1	3.65	1	0
1983-84—Ottawa 67's	OHL	43	2313	117	2	3.03	2	8
1984-85—Milwaukee Admirals (c)	IHL	53	3129	226	0	4.33	1	16
1984-85—Chicago Black Hawks	NHL	1	60	4	0	4.00	0	0
1985-86—Saginaw Generals	IHL	44	2638	148	2	3.37	2	4
1986-87—Nova Scotia Oilers	AHL	7	389	21	0	3.24	0	0
1986-87—Saginaw Generals	IHL	44	2500	151	2	3.62	2	12
1987-88—Chicago Black Hawks	NHL	45	2548	163	0	3.84	6	2
1988-89—Chicago Black Hawks	NHL	35	1644	120	0	4.38	3	4
1988-89—Saginaw Hawks	IHL	2	89	6	0	4.04	0	0
1989-90—Indianapolis Ice	IHL	7	401	17	1	2.54	0	2
NHL TOTALS		81	4252	287	0	4.05	9	6

(c)—September, 1984—Signed by Chicago Black Hawks as a free agent.

MIKE PARSON

Goaltender . . . 6' . . . 169 lbs. . . . Born, Listowel, Ont., March 3, 1970 . . . Shoots left.

Year—Team	League	Games	Mins.	Goals	SO.	Avg.	A.	Pen.
1986-87—Elmira Jr. B	OHA	24	1380	72	2	3.13	..	..
1987-88—Guelph Platers	OHL	31	1703	135	0	4.76	0	6
1988-89—Guelph Platers (c)	OHL	53	3047	194	0	3.82	7	8
1989-90—Owen Sound Platers	OHL	49	2735	200	1	4.39	1	10

(c)—June, 1989—Drafted by Boston Bruins in 1989 NHL entry draft. Second Bruins pick, 38th overall, second round.

PETER PEETERS

Goaltender . . . 6' . . . 195 lbs. . . . Born, Edmonton, Alta., August 1, 1957 . . . Shoots left . . . (November 3, 1983)—Suffered concussion when his head struck crossbar during third period goalmouth pileup vs. St. Louis . . . (September 17, 1984)—Sprained left ankle during Team Canada practice in Canada Cup Tournament . . . (January 28, 1986)—Pulled stomach muscle at Detroit . . . (November 28, 1987)—Strained knee ligaments at Pittsburgh . . . (February, 1988)—Bruised left foot when struck by a Kelly Miller shot during a team practice . . . (October 27, 1988)—Missed

six weeks after pulling a groin . . . (February 18, 1989)—Missed 18 days with a strained hip flexor.

Year—Team	League	Games	Mins.	Goals	SO.	Avg.	A.	Pen.
1975-76—Medicine Hat Tigers	WCHL	37	2074	147	0	4.25	2	29
1976-77—Medicine Hat Tigers (c)	WCHL	62	3423	232	1	4.07	2	30
1977-78—Maine Mariners	AHL	17	855	40	1	2.80	2	6
1977-78—Milwaukee Admirals	IHL	32	1698	93	1	3.29	4	14
1978-79—Philadelphia Flyers	NHL	5	280	16	0	3.43	0	6
1978-79—Maine Mariners (b-d)	AHL	35	2067	100	*2	*2.90	1	8
1979-80—Philadelphia Flyers	NHL	40	2373	108	1	2.73	0	28
1980-81—Philadelphia Flyers	NHL	40	2333	115	2	2.96	1	8
1981-82—Philadelphia Flyers (e)	NHL	44	2591	160	0	3.71	1	19
1982-83—Boston Bruins (a-f)	NHL	62	*3611	142	*8	*2.36	2	33
1983-84—Boston Bruins	NHL	50	2868	151	0	3.16	0	36
1984-85—Boston Bruins	NHL	51	2975	172	1	3.47	0	20
1985-86—Boston Bruins (g)	NHL	8	485	31	0	3.84	2	4
1985-86—Washington Capitals	NHL	34	2021	113	1	3.35	0	8
1986-87—Binghamton Whalers	AHL	4	245	4	1	0.98	0	2
1986-87—Washington Capitals	NHL	37	2002	107	0	3.21	4	16
1987-88—Washington Capitals	NHL	35	1896	88	2	2.78	1	10
1988-89—Washington Capitals (h)	NHL	33	1854	88	4	2.85	1	8
1989-90—Philadelphia Flyers (i-j)	NHL	24	1140	71	1	3.74	1	2
NHL TOTALS		463	26429	1362	20	3.09	13	198

(c)—Drafted from Medicine Hat Tigers by Philadelphia Flyers in eighth round of 1977 amateur draft.
(d)—Shared Harry (Hap) Holmes Memorial Trophy (Top AHL goaltending) with Robbie Moore.
(e)—June, 1982—Traded by Philadelphia Flyers to Boston Bruins for Brad McCrimmon.
(f)—Won Vezina Trophy (Top Goaltender in NHL).
(g)—November, 1985—Traded by Boston Bruins to Washington Capitals for Pat Riggin.
(h)—June 16, 1989—Signed by Philadelphia Flyers as a free agent.
(i)—September 28, 1989—Traded with Keith Acton by Philadelphia Flyers to Winnipeg Jets for future considerations.
(j)—October 3, 1989—Traded with Keith Acton by Winnipeg Jets to Philadelphia Flyers for a fifth or sixth round 1990 draft pick. Also the Jets do not have to surrender future considerations from a previous deal for Shawn Cronin.

JOCELYN PERREAULT

Goaltender . . . 6'4" . . . 210 lbs. . . . Born, Montreal, Que., January 8, 1966 . . . Shoots right.

Year—Team	League	Games	Mins.	Goals	SO.	Avg.	A.	Pen.
1985-86—St. Laurent College (c)	CEGEP	11	582	30	0	3.09	..	..
1986-87—Sherbrooke Canadiens	AHL	13	722	40	0	3.32	0	0
1986-87—Saginaw Generals	IHL	7	286	21	0	4.41	0	0
1987-88—Sherbrooke Canadiens	AHL	25	1244	77	0	3.71	0	4
1988-89—Hershey Bears (d)	AHL	8	394	22	0	3.35	0	0
1988-89—Indianapolis Ice	IHL	5	214	22	0	6.17	0	4
1989-90—Greensboro Monarchs (e)	ECHL	6	294	24	...	4.90	0	14

(c)—September, 1986—Signed by Montreal Canadiens as a free agent.
(d)—September, 1988—Signed by Philadelphia Flyers as a free agent.
(e)—September, 1989—Contract bought out by Philadelphia Flyers and released.

FRANK PIETRANGELO

Goaltender . . . 5'10" . . . 182 lbs. . . . Born, Niagara Falls, Ont., December 17, 1964 . . . Shoots left . . . (February, 1989)—Pulled groin.

Year—Team	League	Games	Mins.	Goals	SO.	Avg.	A.	Pen.
1982-83—Univ. of Minnesota (c)	WCHA	25	1348	80	1	3.56	0	4
1983-84—Univ. of Minnesota	WCHA	20	1141	66	..	3.47	2	0
1984-85—Univ. of Minnesota	WCHA	17	912	52	0	3.42	0	0
1985-86—Univ. of Minnesota	WCHA	23	1284	76	0	3.55	1	0
1986-87—Muskegon Lumberjacks	IHL	35	2090	119	2	3.42	4	2
1987-88—Pittsburgh Penguins	NHL	21	1207	80	1	3.98	2	2
1987-88—Muskegon Lumberjacks	IHL	15	868	43	2	2.97	0	2
1988-89—Pittsburgh Penguins	NHL	15	669	45	0	4.04	0	2
1988-89—Muskegon Lumberjacks	IHL	13	760	38	1	3.00	1	2
1989-90—Muskegon Lumberjacks	IHL	12	691	38	0	3.30	0	6
1989-90—Pittsburgh Penguins	NHL	21	1066	77	0	4.33	0	2
NHL TOTALS		57	2942	202	1	4.12	2	6

(c)—June, 1983—Drafted by Pittsburgh Penguins in 1983 NHL entry draft. Fourth Penguins pick, 63rd overall, fourth round.

FELIX POTVIN

Goaltender . . . 6'1" . . . 181 lbs. . . . Born, Anjou, Que., June 23, 1971 . . . Shoots left.

Year—Team	League	Games	Mins.	Goals	SO.	Avg.	A.	Pen.
1988-89—Chicoutimi Sagueneens	QMJHL	*65	*3489	*271	*2	4.66	..	42
1989-90—Chicoutimi Sagueneens (b-c)	QMJHL	*62	*3478	231	*2	3.99	..	8

(c)—June 16, 1990—Selected by Toronto Maple Leafs in 1990 NHL entry draft. Second Maple Leafs pick, 31st overall, second round.

DAREN PUPPA

Goaltender . . . 6'3" . . . 195 lbs. . . . Born, Kirkland Lake, Ont., March 23, 1965 . . . Shoots right . . . (November 1, 1985)—First NHL game was a 2-0 shutout at Edmonton . . . (February, 1986)—Injured knee in AHL game . . . (October, 1987)—Fractured left index finger . . . (January 14, 1989)—Sprained right wrist at Quebec . . . (January 27, 1989)—Broke right arm vs. Montreal.

Year—Team	League	Games	Mins.	Goals	SO.	Avg.	A.	Pen.
1983-84—Rensselaer Poly. Inst. (c)	ECAC	32	1816	89	..	2.94	0	....
1984-85—Rensselaer Poly. Inst.	ECAC	32	1830	78	..	2.56	0	2
1985-86—Buffalo Sabres	NHL	7	401	21	1	3.14	0	0
1985-86—Rochester Americans	AHL	20	1092	79	0	4.34	1	0
1986-87—Buffalo Sabres	NHL	3	185	13	0	4.22	0	2

Year Team	League	Games	Mins.	Goals	SO.	Avg.	A.	Pen.
1986-87—Rochester Americans (a)	AHL	57	3129	146	1	*2.80	1	12
1987-88—Rochester Americans	AHL	26	1415	65	2	2.76	2	8
1987-88—Buffalo Sabres	NHL	17	874	61	0	4.19	1	4
1988-89—Buffalo Sabres	NHL	37	1908	107	1	3.36	4	12
1989-90—Buffalo Sabres (b)	NHL	56	3241	156	1	2.89	4	4
NHL TOTALS		120	6609	358	3	3.25	9	22

(c)—June, 1983—Drafted by Buffalo Sabres in 1983 NHL entry draft. Sixth Sabres pick, 74th overall, fourth round.

WILLIAM PYE

Goaltender . . . 5'9" . . . 170 lbs. . . . Born, Royal Oak, Mich., April 4, 1969 . . . Shoots right.

Year Team	League	Games	Mins.	Goals	SO.	Avg.	A.	Pen.
1987-88—Northern Michigan Univ.	WCHA	13	654	49	0	4.49	0	0
1988-89—Northern Michigan Univ. (c)	WCHA	43	2533	133	1	3.15	2	8
1989-90—Northern Michigan Univ.	WCHA	36	2035	149	1	4.39	3	4

(c)—June, 1989—Drafted by Buffalo Sabres in 1989 NHL entry draft. Fifth Sabres pick, 107th overall, sixth round.

ANDRE RACICOT

Goaltender . . . 5'11" . . . 155 lbs. . . . Born, Rouyn-Noranda, Que., June 9, 1969 . . . Shoots left.

Year Team	League	Games	Mins.	Goals	SO.	Avg.	A.	Pen.
1986-87—Longueuil Chevaliers	QMJHL	3	180	19	0	6.33	..	....
1987-88—Hull Oly./Granby Bisons	QMJHL	30	1547	105	1	4.07	1	2
1988-89—Granby Bisons (c)	QMJHL	54	2944	198	9	4.04	..	47
1989-90—Sherbrooke Canadiens (d)	AHL	33	1948	97	1	2.99	1	2
1989-90—Montreal Canadiens	NHL	1	13	3	0	13.85	0	0
NHL TOTALS		1	13	3	0	13.85	0	0

(c)—June, 1989—Drafted by Montreal Canadiens in 1989 NHL entry draft. Fifth Canadiens pick, 83rd overall, fourth round.

(d)—Shared Harry (Hap) Holmes Memorial Trophy with teammates Jean-Claude Bergeron (AHL team that allows the fewest goals).

BRUCE M. RACINE

Goaltender . . . 6'1" . . . 180 lbs. . . . Born, Cornwall, Ont., August 9, 1966 . . . Shoots left . . . Son of Maurice Racine (17 years in CFL).

Year Team	League	Games	Mins.	Goals	SO.	Avg.	A.	Pen.
1984-85—Northeastern Univ. (b-c)	H. East	26	1615	103	0	3.83	1	12
1985-86—Northeastern Univ.	H. East	37	2212	171	0	4.64	3	0
1986-87—Northeastern Univ. (a-d)	H. East	33	1966	133	0	4.06	2	0
1987-88—Northeastern Univ. (d)	H. East	30	1809	108	1	3.58	2	0
1988-89—Muskegon Lumberjacks	IHL	51	*3039	184	*3	3.63	5	2
1989-90—Muskegon Lumberjacks	IHL	49	2911	182	1	3.75	2	0

(c)—June, 1985—Drafted by Pittsburgh Penguins in 1985 NHL entry draft. Third Penguins pick, 58th overall, third round.

(d)—Named First team All-America (East).

BILL RANFORD

Goaltender . . . 5'11" . . . 165 lbs. . . . Born, Brandon, Man., December 14, 1966 . . . Shoots left . . . (February 14, 1990)—Sprained ankle vs. Washington and missed six games.

Year Team	League	Games	Mins.	Goals	SO.	Avg.	A.	Pen.
1983-84—New Westminster Bruins	WHL	27	1450	130	0	5.38	2	0
1984-85—New Westminster Bruins (c)	WHL	38	2034	142	0	4.19	0	4
1985-86—New Westminster Bruins (b)	WHL	53	2791	225	1	4.84	1	23
1985-86—Boston Bruins	NHL	4	240	10	0	2.50	0	0
1986-87—Moncton Golden Flames	AHL	3	180	6	0	2.00	0	0
1986-87—Boston Bruins	NHL	41	2234	124	3	3.33	1	8
1987-88—Maine Mariners	AHL	51	1856	165	1	3.47	1	4
1987-88—Edmonton Oilers (d)	NHL	6	325	16	0	2.95	2	0
1988-89—Edmonton Oilers	NHL	29	1509	88	1	3.50	0	2
1989-90—Edmonton Oilers (e)	NHL	56	3107	165	1	3.19	2	18
NHL TOTALS		136	7415	403	5	3.26	5	28

(c)—June, 1985—Drafted as underage junior by Boston Bruins in 1985 NHL entry draft. Second Bruins pick, 52nd overall, third round.

(d)—March, 1988—Traded with Geoff Courtnall and second-round 1988 draft choice (Petro Koivunen) by Boston Bruins to Edmonton Oilers for Andy Moog.

(e)—Won Conn Smythe Trophy (NHL Playoff MVP).

ALAIN RAYMOND

Goaltender . . . 5'10" . . . 177 lbs. . . . Born, Rimouski, Que., June 24, 1965 . . . Shoots left.

Year Team	League	Games	Mins.	Goals	SO.	Avg.	A.	Pen.
1981-82—Cantons de L'Est	Que. Midget	27	1505	128	...	5.10	..	....
1982-83—Hull Olympiques	QMJHL	17	809	80	0	5.93	0	4
1982-83—Trois-Rivieres Draveurs (c)	QMJHL	22	1176	124	0	6.33	0	4
1983-84—Trois-Rivieres Draveurs (a)	QMJHL	53	2725	223	*2	4.91	0	6
1984-85—Trois-Rivieres Draveurs	QMJHL	58	3295	220	*2	4.01	3	2
1985-86—Team Canada	Int'l	46	2571	151	4	3.52	..	..
1986-87—Fort Wayne Komets (d)	IHL	45	2433	134	1	*3.30	0	27
1987-88—Fort Wayne Komets	IHL	40	2271	142	2	3.75	0	8
1987-88—Washington Capitals	NHL	1	40	2	0	3.00	0	0
1988-89—Baltimore Skipjacks	AHL	41	2301	162	0	4.22	1	2
1989-90—Baltimore Skipjacks	AHL	11	612	34	0	3.33	0	0
1989-90—Hampton Roads Admirals (a)	ECHL	31	2048	123	...	3.60	5	18
NHL TOTALS		1	40	2	0	3.00	0	0

(c)—June, 1983—Drafted as underage junior by Washington Capitals in 1983 NHL entry draft. Seventh Capitals pick, 215th overall, 11th round.

(d)—Co-winner of James Norris Memorial Trophy with teammate Michel Dufour (Top Goaltender).

DARYL REAUGH

Goaltender . . . 6'4" . . . 200 lbs. . . . Born, Prince George, B.C., February 13, 1965 . . . Shoots left.

Year Team	League	Games	Mins.	Goals	SO.	Avg.	A.	Pen.
1983-84—Kamloops Junior Oilers (b-c-d)	WHL	55	2748	199	1	4.34	5	18
1984-85—Kamloops Blazers (a)	WHL	49	2749	170	2	3.71	3	19
1984-85—Edmonton Oilers	NHL	1	60	5	0	5.00	0	0
1985-86—Nova Scotia Oilers	AHL	38	2205	156	0	4.24	2	4
1986-87—Nova Scotia Oilers	AHL	46	2637	163	1	3.71	2	8
1987-88—Edmonton Oilers	NHL	6	176	14	0	4.77	0	0
1987-88—Nova Scotia Oilers	AHL	8	443	33	0	4.47	0	0
1987-88—Milwaukee Admirals	IHL	9	493	44	0	5.35	1	0
1988-89—Cape Breton Oilers	AHL	13	778	72	0	5.55	0	4
1988-89—Karpat	Finland	13	756	46	2	3.65	..	....
1989-90—Binghamton Whalers (e)	AHL	52	2735	192	0	4.21	1	4
NHL TOTALS		7	236	19	0	4.83	0	0

(c)—Led WHL playoffs with 3.52 average.

(d)—June, 1984—Drafted as underage junior by Edmonton Oilers in 1984 NHL entry draft. Second Oilers pick, 42nd overall, second round.

(e)—September, 1989—Signed by Hartford Whalers as a free agent.

ELDON (POKEY) REDDICK

Goaltender . . . 5'8" . . . 175 lbs. . . . Born, Halifax, N.S., October 6, 1964 . . . Shoots left . . . Older brother of Stan (Smokey) Reddick (WHL Goaltender).

Year Team	League	Games	Mins.	Goals	SO.	Avg.	A.	Pen.
1981-82—Billings Bighorns	WHL	1	60	7	0	7.00	0	0
1982-83—Nanaimo Islanders	WHL	*66	*3549	*383	0	6.48	5	6
1983-84—New Westminster Bruins (b)	WHL	50	2930	215	0	4.40	1	6
1984-85—Brandon Wheat Kings (c)	WHL	47	2585	243	0	5.64	4	2
1984-85—Fort Wayne Komets	IHL	10	491	32	2	3.91	0	0
1985-86—Fort Wayne Komets (d-e)	IHL	32	1811	92	*3	*3.05	0	6
1986-87—Winnipeg Jets	NHL	48	2762	149	0	3.24	0	8
1987-88—Winnipeg Jets	NHL	28	1487	102	0	4.12	0	6
1987-88—Moncton Golden Flames	AHL	9	545	26	0	2.86	0	2
1988-89—Winnipeg Jets	NHL	41	2109	144	0	4.10	1	6
1989-90—Edmonton Oilers (f)	NHL	11	604	31	0	3.08	0	0
1989-90—Cape Breton Oilers	AHL	15	821	54	0	3.95	3	4
1989-90—Phoenix Roadrunners	IHL	3	185	7	0	2.27	0	0
NHL TOTALS		128	6962	426	0	3.67	1	20

(c)—October, 1984—Traded by New Westminster Bruins to Brandon Wheat Kings for Jayson Meyer and Lee Trimm.

(d)—September, 1985—Signed by Winnipeg Jets as a free agent.

(e)—Co-winner of James Norris Memorial Trophy (Top Goaltender) with teammate Rick St. Croix.

(f)—September 28, 1989—Traded by Winnipeg Jets to Edmonton Oilers for future considerations.

JEFF REESE

Goaltender . . . 5'9" . . . 155 lbs. . . . Born, Brantford, Ont., March 24, 1966 . . . Shoots left . . . (October 23, 1989)—Broke left kneecap at Newmarket and missed two months . . . (April 12, 1990)—Contusion to left kneecap when kicked by Dave Lowry at St. Louis.

Year Team	League	Games	Mins.	Goals	SO.	Avg.	A.	Pen.
1982-83—Hamilton A's	OJHL	40	2380	176	0	4.43	..	....
1983-84—London Knights (c)	OHL	43	2308	173	0	4.50	1	4
1984-85—London Knights (d)	OHL	50	2878	186	1	3.88	1	4
1985-86—London Knights	OHL	*57	*3281	215	0	3.93	1	25
1986-87—Newmarket Saints	AHL	50	2822	193	1	4.10	2	24
1987-88—Newmarket Saints	AHL	28	1587	103	0	3.89	1	14
1987-88—Toronto Maple Leafs	NHL	5	249	17	0	4.10	0	0
1988-89—Toronto Maple Leafs	NHL	10	486	40	0	4.94	0	4
1988-89—Newmarket Saints	AHL	37	2072	132	0	3.82	3	16
1989-90—Newmarket Saints	AHL	7	431	29	0	4.04	0	4
1989-90—Toronto Maple Leafs	NHL	21	1101	81	0	4.41	1	10
NHL TOTALS		36	1836	138	0	4.51	1	14

(c)—June, 1984—Drafted as underage junior by Toronto Maple Leafs in 1984 NHL entry draft. Third Maple Leafs pick, 67th overall, fourth round.

(d)—Led OHL playoffs with one shutout and a 2.73 average.

JOHN REID

Goaltender . . . 5'11" . . . 202 lbs. . . . Born, Windsor, Ont., February 18, 1967. . . Shoots right . . . (January, 1989)—Broke bone in hand.

Year Team	League	Games	Mins.	Goals	SO.	Avg.	A.	Pen.
1983-84—Brantford Knights	OHA	30	1350	59	3	1.95	..	..
1984-85—Belleville Bulls (c)	OHL	31	1443	92	0	3.83	1	8
1985-86—Belleville Bulls	OHL	24	1309	100	0	4.58	0	5
1985-86—North Bay Centennials	OHL	23	1318	64	1	2.91	0	6
1986-87—North Bay Centennials	OHL	47	2737	142	1	3.11	1	39
1987-88—Saginaw Wings	IHL	5	260	11	0	2.54	0	2
1987-88—Colorado Rangers	IHL	32	1673	117	0	4.20	0	18
1988-89—Saginaw Hawks	IHL	12	633	37	0	3.51	0	17
1988-89—Indianapolis Ice	IHL	5	244	16	0	3.93	0	12
1989-90—Nashville Knights	ECHL	36	2004	149	...	4.46	3	66

(c)—June, 1985—Drafted as underage junior by Chicago Black Hawks in 1985 NHL entry draft. Eighth Black Hawks pick, 158th overall, eighth round.

MARK REIMER

Goaltender . . . 5'11" . . . 170 lbs. . . . Born, Calgary, Alta., March 23, 1967 . . . Shoots left.

Year Team	League	Games	Mins.	Goals	SO.	Avg.	A.	Pen.
1984-85—Saskatoon Blades	WHL	2	120	7	0	3.50	1	0
1984-85—Calgary Canucks	AJHL	29	1559	132	1	5.08	..	..
1985-86—Saskatoon Blades	WHL	41	2362	192	0	4.88	4	31

Year	Team	League	Games	Mins.	Goals	SO.	Avg.	A.	Pen.
1986-87—Saskatoon Blades (b-c)	WHL	42	2442	141	1	3.46	6	4
1987-88—Portland Winter Hawks	WHL	38	2268	208	0	5.50	4	31
1987-88—Flint Spirits	IHL	5	169	22	0	7.86	0	0
1987-88—Adirondack Red Wings	AHL	8	459	24	0	3.14	1	0
1988-89—Adirondack Red Wings	AHL	18	900	64	0	4.27	0	2
1988-89—Flint Spirits	IHL	17	1022	83	0	4.87	0	0
1989-90—Adirondack Red Wings	AHL	36	2092	131	0	3.76	1	8

(c)—June, 1987—Drafted by Detroit Red Wings in 1987 NHL entry draft. Fifth Red Wings pick, 74th overall, fourth round.

KENTON REIN

Goaltender . . . 6' . . . 195 lbs. . . . Born, Toronto, Ont., September 12, 1967 . . . Shoots left . . . (September, 1987)—Missed first four months of season after being struck in the mask by a shot during training camp.

Year	Team	League	Games	Mins.	Goals	SO.	Avg.	A.	Pen.
1985-86—Prince Albert Raiders (c-d)	WHL	23	1302	71	0	3.27	3	4
1986-87—Prince Albert Raiders (a-e)	WHL	51	2996	159	0	*3.18	3	29
1987-88—Flint Spirits	IHL	1	20	3	0	9.00	0	0
1988-89—Rochester Americans	AHL	15	676	39	2	3.46	1	34
1988-89—Flint Spirits	IHL	8	439	29	0	3.96	0	5
1988-89—Carolina Thunderbirds	ECHL	4	222	15	0	4.05	1	2
1989-90—Winston-Salem Thunderbirds	ECHL	24	1353	88	...	3.90	3	18

(c)—October, 1984—WHL rights traded with Brent Bobyck by Moose Jaw Warriors to Prince Albert Raiders for Bob Schmidtke, Blaine Gusdal, Dave German and Dale Kushner.

(d)—June, 1986—Drafted as underage junior by Buffalo Sabres in 1986 NHL entry draft. Eleventh Sabres pick, 194th overall, 10th round.

(e)—Named Top Goaltender (East Division).

DAMIAN RHODES

Goaltender . . . 6' . . . 165 lbs. . . . Born, St. Paul, Minn., May 28, 1969 . . . Shoots right . . . (January 21, 1989)—Scored a goal into an empty net vs. Colorado College.

Year	Team	League	Games	Mins.	Goals	SO.	Avg.	A.	Pen.
1985-86—Richfield H.S.	Minn. H.S.	16	720	56	0	4.67	..	..
1986-87—Richfield H.S. (c)	Minn. H.S.	19	673	51	1	4.55	..	..
1987-88—Michigan Tech.	WCHA	29	1623	114	0	4.21	3	4
1988-89—Michigan Tech.	WCHA	37	2216	163	0	4.41	3	0
1989-90—Michigan Tech.	WCHA	25	1358	119	0	5.26	0	16

(c)—June, 1987—Drafted by Toronto Maple Leafs in 1987 NHL entry draft. Sixth Maple Leafs pick, 112th overall, sixth round.

MIKE RICHTER

Goaltender . . . 5'11" . . . 170 lbs. . . . Born, Philadelphia, Pa., September 22, 1966 . . . Shoots left.

Year	Team	League	Games	Mins.	Goals	SO.	Avg.	A.	Pen.
1984-85—Northwood Prep. (c)	Mass. H.S.	24		52	2	2.27	..	..
1985-86—Univ. of Wisconsin (b-d)	WCHA	24	1394	92	1	3.96	0	0
1986-87—Univ. of Wisconsin (b)	WCHA	36	2136	126	0	3.54	1	0
1987-88—U.S. Olympic Team	Int'l.	33	1789	101	0	3.39	..	....
1987-88—Colorado Rangers	IHL	22	1298	68	1	3.14	0	5
1988-89—Denver Rangers	IHL	*57	3031	217	1	4.30	5	8
1989-90—New York Rangers	NHL	23	1320	66	0	3.00	3	0
1989-90—Flint Spirits	IHL	13	782	49	0	3.76	1	0
NHL TOTALS		23	1320	66	0	3.00	3	0

(c)—June, 1985—Drafted by New York Rangers in 1985 NHL entry draft. Second Rangers pick, 28th overall, second round.

(d)—Named WCHA Freshman-of-the-Year.

VINCENT RIENDEAU

Goaltender . . . 5'10" . . . 185 lbs. . . . Born, St. Hyacinthe, Que., April 20, 1966 . . . Shoots left . . . (November, 1987)—Skin rash . . . (April 10, 1988)—Broke leg . . . (October 4, 1989)—Compound fracture of little finger of left hand in team practice the day before the start of the season and missed 10 games.

Year	Team	League	Games	Mins.	Goals	SO.	Avg.	A.	Pen.
1983-84—Verdun Juniors	QMJHL	41	2133	147	2	4.14	1	8
1984-85—Univ. of Sherbrooke (c)	Can. Col.	..	..	..	..	..	..	..
1985-86—Drummondville Voltigeurs (b)	QMJHL	57	3336	215	2	3.87	3	40
1986-87—Sherbrooke Canadiens	AHL	41	2363	114	2	2.89	0	23
1987-88—Sherbrooke Canadiens	AHL	44	2521	112	*4	*2.67	1	22
1987-88—Montreal Canadiens (d)	NHL	1	36	5	0	8.33	0	0
1988-89—St. Louis Blues	NHL	32	1842	108	0	3.52	1	4
1989-90—St. Louis Blues	NHL	43	2551	149	1	3.50	0	6
NHL TOTALS		76	4429	262	1	3.55	1	10

(c)—October, 1985—Signed by Montreal Canadiens as a free agent.

(d)—August, 1988—Traded with Sergio Momesso by Montreal Canadiens to St. Louis Blues for Jocelyn Lemieux, Darrell May and 1989 second-round draft pick (Patrice Brisebois).

MARK ROMAINE

Goaltender . . . 5'9" . . . 160 lbs. . . . Born, Sharon, Mass., October 25, 1968 . . . Shoots left.

Year	Team	League	Games	Mins.	Goals	SO.	Avg.	A.	Pen.
1986-87—Providence College	H. East	5	289	25	0	5.19	..	....
1987-88—Providence College	H. East	19	883	60	0	4.08	..	..
1988-89—Providence College (c)	H. East	29	1536	95	1	3.71	1	2
1989-90—Providence College	H. East	19	1023	52	1	3.05	1	0

(c)—June, 1989—Selected by New Jersey Devils in 1989 supplemental draft.

MIKE ROSATI

Goaltender . . . 5'10" . . . 170 lbs. . . . Born, Toronto, Ont., January 7, 1968 . . . Shoots left.

Year	Team	League	Games	Mins.	Goals	SO.	Avg.	A.	Pen.
1985-86—St. Mikes Jr. B.	MTHL	20	1100	95	0	5.18	..	..
1986-87—Hamilton Steelhawks	OHL	26	1334	85	1	3.82	2	12
1987-88—Hamilton Steelhawks (c)	OHL	62	3468	233	1	4.03	2	18
1988-89—Niagara Falls Thunder	OHL	52	2339	174	1	4.46	2	32
1989-90—Erie Panthers	ECHL	18	1056	73	...	4.15	2	8

(c)—June, 1988—Drafted by New York Rangers in 1988 NHL entry draft. Sixth Rangers pick, 131st overall, seventh round.

DOMINIC ROUSSEL

Goaltender . . . 6'1" . . . 185 lbs. . . . Born, Hull, Quebec, February 22, 1970 . . . Shoots left.

Year	Team	League	Games	Mins.	Goals	SO.	Avg.	A.	Pen.
1986-87—Lac St. Louis Mid. AAA	Que. Midget	24	1334	85	1	3.82	..	..
1987-88—Trois-Rivieres Draveurs (c)	QMJHL	51	2905	251	0	5.18	1	14
1988-89—Shawinigan Cataractes	QMJHL	46	2555	171	0	4.02	0	62
1989-90—Shawinigan Cataractes	QMJHL	37	1985	133	0	4.02	..	59

(c)—June, 1988—Drafted as underage junior by Philadelphia Flyers in 1988 NHL entry draft. Fourth Flyers pick, 63rd overall, third round.

ALLAIN ROY

Goaltender . . . 5'10" . . . 165 lbs. . . . Born, Campbellton, N.B., February 6, 1970 . . . Shoots left.

Year	Team	League	Games	Mins.	Goals	SO.	Avg.	A.	Pen.
1988-89—Harvard Univ. (c-d)	ECAC	16	952	40	0	2.52	1	0
1989-90—Harvard Univ.	ECAC	15	867	54	1	3.74	0	0
1989-90—Canadian National Team	Int'l.	3	180	11	...	3.67	..	....

(c)—June, 1989—Drafted by Winnipeg Jets in 1989 NHL entry draft. Sixth Jets pick, 69th overall, fourth round.

(d)—Named to NCAA All-Tournament team.

PATRICK ROY

Goaltender . . . 6' . . . 174 lbs. . . . Born, Quebec City, Que., October 5, 1965 . . . Shoots left . . . (October 19, 1987)—Suspended eight NHL games for slashing Warren Babe vs. Minnesota . . . (October 16, 1989)—Lost to Washington, ending a 35-game regular season home-ice unbeaten string (an NHL record.)

Year	Team	League	Games	Mins.	Goals	SO.	Avg.	A.	Pen.
1982-83—Granby Bisons	QMJHL	54	2808	293	0	6.26	0	14
1983-84—Granby Bisons (c)	QMJHL	61	3585	265	0	4.44	6	15
1984-85—Granby Bisons	QMJHL	44	2463	228	0	5.55	2	74
1984-85—Montreal Canadiens	NHL	1	20	0	0	0.00	0	0
1984-85—Sherbrooke Canadiens (d)	AHL	1	60	4	0	4.00	0	0
1985-86—Montreal Canadiens (e)	NHL	47	2651	150	1	3.39	3	4
1986-87—Montreal Canadiens	NHL	46	2686	131	1	2.93	1	8
1987-88—Montreal Canadiens (b-f)	NHL	45	2586	125	3	2.90	2	14
1988-89—Montreal Canadiens (a-f-g-h)	NHL	48	2744	113	4	*2.47	6	2
1989-90—Montreal Canadiens (a-g)	NHL	54	3173	134	3	2.53	5	0
NHL TOTALS		241	13860	653	12	2.83	17	28

(c)—June, 1984—Drafted as underage junior by Montreal Canadiens in 1984 NHL entry draft. Fourth Canadiens pick, 51st overall, third round.

(d)—Led AHL playoffs with 2.89 average.

(e)—Won Conn Smythe Trophy (Playoff MVP) and tied for lead in NHL Playoffs with one shutout.

(f)—Shared Bill Jennings Trophy with teammate Brian Hayward (Top NHL Goaltending tandem).

(g)—Winner of Georges Vezina Trophy (Top NHL Goalie).

(h)—Led NHL Playoffs with a 2.09 average.

BRYAN SCHOEN

Goaltender . . . 6'2" . . . 180 lbs. . . . Born, St. Paul, Minn., September 9, 1971 . . . Shoots left.

Year	Team	League	Games	Mins.	Goals	SO.	Avg.	A.	Pen.
1988-89—Minnetonka H.S. (c)	Minn.	17	765	23	2	1.80	..	..
1989-90—Univ. of Denver	WCHA	18	1040	81	0	4.67	4	10

(c)—June, 1989—Drafted by Minnesota North Stars in 1989 NHL entry draft. Sixth North Stars pick, 91st overall, fifth round.

RON SCOTT

Goaltender . . . 5'8" . . . 155 lbs. . . . Born, Guelph, Ont., July 21, 1960 . . . Shoots left . . . (November, 1984)—Severe groin injury and missed three weeks . . . (March, 1990)—Sore back.

Year	Team	League	Games	Mins.	Goals	SO.	Avg.	A.	Pen.
1980-81—Michigan State Univ. (a)	WCHA	33	1899	123	0	3.89	1	4
1981-82—Michigan State Univ. (a-c)	CCHA	39	2298	109	2	2.85	2	2
1982-83—Michigan State Univ. (a-c-d)	CCHA	40	2273	100	...	2.64	5	10
1983-84—Tulsa Oilers	CHL	20	1717	109	0	3.81	0	2
1983-84—New York Rangers	NHL	9	485	29	0	3.59	0	0
1984-85—New Haven Nighthawks	AHL	37	2047	130	0	3.81	1	2
1985-86—New York Rangers	NHL	4	156	11	0	4.23	0	0
1985-86—New Haven Nighthawks	AHL	19	1069	66	1	3.70	2	4
1986-87—New Haven Nighthawks	AHL	29	1744	107	1	3.68	2	4
1986-87—New York Rangers	NHL	1	65	5	0	4.62	0	0
1987-88—New York Rangers	NHL	2	90	6	0	4.00	0	0
1987-88—New Haven Nighthawks	AHL	17	963	49	0	3.05	0	2
1987-88—Colorado Rangers	IHL	8	395	33	0	5.01	0	0
1988-89—Denver Rangers	IHL	20	990	79	0	4.79	0	0
1989-90—Los Angeles Kings (e)	NHL	12	654	40	0	3.67	0	2
1989-90—New Haven Nighthawks	AHL	22	1224	79	1	3.87	0	4
NHL TOTALS		28	1450	91	0	3.77	0	2

(c)—Named to All-America Team (West).
(d)—May, 1983—Signed by New York Rangers as a free agent.
(e)—September, 1989—Released by New York Rangers and signed by Los Angeles Kings as a free agent.

WARREN SHARPLES

Goaltender . . . 6' . . . 170 lbs. . . . Born, Calgary, Alta., March 1, 1968 . . . Shoots left.

Year	Team	League	Games	Mins.	Goals	SO.	Avg.	A.	Pen.
1985-86—Penticton Knights (c)	BCJHL	....	....	....	..	....	..	..	
1986-87—Univ. of Michigan	CCHA	32	1728	148	1	5.14	3	10	
1987-88—Univ. of Michigan	CCHA	33	1930	132	...	4.10	0	12	
1988-89—Univ. of Michigan	CCHA	33	1887	116	...	3.69	1	4	
1989-90—Univ. of Michigan	CCHA	39	2165	117	...	3.24	1	2	
1989-90—Salt Lake Golden Eagles	IHL	3	178	13	0	4.38	0	0	

(c)—June, 1986—Drafted by Calgary Flames in 1986 NHL entry draft. Eighth Flames pick, 184th overall, ninth round.

PETER SIDORKIEWICZ

Goaltender . . . 5'9" . . . 165 lbs. . . . Born, Dabrown Bialostocka, Poland, June 29, 1963 . . . Shoots left.

Year	Team	League	Games	Mins.	Goals	SO.	Avg.	A.	Pen.
1980-81—Oshawa Generals (c)	OHL	7	308	24	0	4.68	0	0
1981-82—Oshawa Generals	OHL	29	1553	123	*2	4.75	1	6
1982-83—Oshawa Generals (d)	OHL	60	3536	213	0	3.61	4	2
1983-84—Oshawa Generals (e)	OHL	52	2966	205	1	4.15	4	16
1984-85—Fort Wayne Komets	IHL	10	590	43	0	4.37	0	0
1984-85—Binghamton Whalers (f)	AHL	45	2691	137	3	3.05	1	14
1985-86—Binghamton Whalers	AHL	49	2819	150	2	*3.19	0	7
1986-87—Binghamton Whalers (b)	AHL	57	3304	161	4	2.92	1	10
1987-88—Hartford Whalers	NHL	1	60	6	0	6.00	0	0
1987-88—Binghamton Whalers	AHL	42	2346	144	0	3.68	0	17
1988-89—Hartford Whalers	NHL	44	2635	133	4	3.03	3	0
1989-90—Hartford Whalers	NHL	46	2703	161	1	3.57	1	4
NHL TOTALS		91	5398	300	5	3.33	4	4

(c)—June, 1981—Drafted as underage junior by Washington Capitals in 1981 NHL entry draft. Fifth Capitals pick, 91st overall, fifth round.
(d)—Co-winner of Dave Pinkney Trophy (Top Goaltenders) with teammate Jeff Hogg.
(e)—Shared OHL playoff lead with one shutout with Darren Pang of Ottawa.
(f)—March, 1985—Traded with Dean Evason by Washington Capitals to Hartford Whalers for David A. Jensen.

SHAWN SIMPSON

Goaltender . . . 5'11" . . . 180 lbs. . . . Born, Gloucester, Ont., August 10, 1968 . . . Shoots left.

Year	Team	League	Games	Mins.	Goals	SO.	Avg.	A.	Pen.
1984-85—Gloucester Midgets	OHA	22	900	36	8	2.40	..	....
1985-86—Sault Ste. Marie Greyhounds (c)	OHL	42	2213	217	1	5.88	0	6
1986-87—Sault Ste. Marie Greyhounds	OHL	46	2673	184	0	4.13	2	15
1987-88—Sault Ste. Marie Greyhounds	OHL	57	3214	234	2	4.37	2	20
1988-89—Oshawa Generals	OHL	33	1818	131	0	4.32	1	10
1988-89—Baltimore Skipjacks	AHL	1	60	7	0	7.00	0	0
1989-90—Baltimore Skipjacks	AHL	15	733	45	0	3.68	1	2

(c)—June, 1986—Drafted by Washington Capitals in 1986 NHL entry draft. Third Capitals pick, 60th overall, third round.

ROBB STAUBER

Goaltender . . . 5'10" . . . 165 lbs. . . . Born, Duluth, Minn., November 25, 1967 . . . Shoots left . . . First Goalie to win the Hobey Baker Award . . . (December 3, 1988)—Twisted left knee and ankle vs. Minnesota/Duluth and missed 14 games . . . (October, 1989)—Injured groin and back . . . Brother of Peter Stauber.

Year	Team	League	Games	Mins.	Goals	SO.	Avg.	A.	Pen.
1985-86—Duluth Denfield H.S. (c)	Minn. H.S.	..	..	..	..	..	..	..
1986-87—Univ. of Minnesota	WCHA	20	1072	63	0	3.53	1	2
1987-88—Univ. of Minnesota (d-e)	WCHA	44	2621	119	5	2.72	5	18
1988-89—Univ. of Minnesota (b-f)	WCHA	34	2024	82	0	2.43	7	10
1989-90—New Haven Nighthawks	AHL	14	851	43	0	3.03	0	8
1989-90—Los Angeles Kings	NHL	2	83	11	0	7.95	0	0
NHL TOTALS		2	83	11	0	7.95	0	0

(c)—June, 1986—Drafted by Los Angeles Kings in 1986 NHL entry draft. Fifth Kings pick, 107th overall, fifth round.
(d)—Named First team All-America (West).
(e)—Won Hobey Baker Award (Top U.S. Collegiate player).
(f)—Named WCHA Goaltender of the Year.

GREG STEFAN

Goaltender . . . 6' . . . 178 lbs. . . . Born, Brantford, Ont., February 11, 1961 . . . Shoots left . . . (March, 1981)—Given six-game suspension by OHL for breaking his goalie stick over shoulder of Bart Wilson of Toronto Marlboros . . . (January, 1985)—Strained left shoulder . . . (April, 1985)—Suspended for first eight games of 1985-86 season for swinging his stick at Al Secord vs. Chicago on April 13 . . . (December 14, 1985)—Suspended for six games for high-sticking incident vs. Pittsburgh . . . (January 7, 1986)—Injured back at Washington and missed 17 games . . . (March 20, 1986)—Dislocated thumb vs. St. Louis when he jammed it against the goalpost . . . (January, 1988)—Left knee ligament injury . . . (May, 1988)—Strained neck when struck by Craig Simpson vs. Edmonton . . . (December, 1988)—Injured back . . . (October 6, 1989)—Back spasms . . . (November 27, 1989)—Injured right knee ligaments vs. Edmonton . . . (January 25, 1990)—Injured knee vs. Pittsburgh . . . (March 6, 1990)—Surgery to right knee ligament.

Year	Team	League	Games	Mins.	Goals	SO.	Avg.	A.	Pen.
1978-79—Oshawa Generals	OMJHL	33	1635	133	0	4.88	1	27
1979-80—Oshawa Generals	OMJHL	17	897	58	0	3.88	2	11
1980-81—Oshawa Generals (c)	OHL	46	2407	174	0	4.34	2	92
1981-82—Detroit Red Wings	NHL	2	120	10	0	5.00	0	0
1981-82—Adirondack Red Wings	AHL	29	1571	99	2	3.78	0	36
1982-83—Detroit Red Wings	NHL	35	1847	139	0	4.52	0	35
1983-84—Detroit Red Wings	NHL	50	2600	152	2	3.51	3	14
1984-85—Detroit Red Wings	NHL	46	2635	190	0	4.33	2	23
1985-86—Detroit Red Wings	NHL	37	2068	155	1	4.50	2	23
1986-87—Detroit Red Wings	NHL	43	2351	135	1	3.45	4	24
1987-88—Detroit Red Wings (d)	NHL	33	1854	96	1	3.11	0	36
1988-89—Detroit Red Wings	NHL	46	2499	167	0	4.01	2	41
1989-90—Detroit Red Wings	NHL	7	359	24	0	4.01	1	4
1989-90—Adirondack Red Wings	AHL	2	128	7	0	3.28	0	0
NHL TOTALS		299	16333	1068	5	3.92	15	210

(c)—June, 1981—Drafted by Detroit Red Wings in 1981 NHL entry draft. Fifth Red Wings pick, 128th overall, seventh round.
(d)—Tied for lead in NHL Playoffs with one shutout.

SAM ST. LAURENT

Goaltender . . . 5'10" . . . 190 lbs. . . . Born, Arvida, Que., February 16, 1959 . . . Shoots left . . . (January, 1989)—Missed 30 days with pulled muscle in leg.

Year	Team	League	Games	Mins.	Goals	SO.	Avg.	A.	Pen.
1975-76—Chicoutimi Sagueneens	QMJHL	17	889	81	0	5.47	..	....
1976-77—Chicoutimi Sagueneens	QMJHL	21	901	81	0	5.39	0	30
1977-78—Chicoutimi Sagueneens	QMJHL	60	3251	*351	0	6.46	..	....
1978-79—Chicoutimi Sagueneens	QMJHL	70	3806	290	0	4.57	1	0
1979-80—Toledo Goaldiggers (c)	IHL	38	2145	138	2	3.86	1	6
1979-80—Maine Mariners	AHL	4	201	15	0	4.48	0	0
1980-81—Maine Mariners	AHL	7	363	28	0	4.63	0	2
1980-81—Toledo Goaldiggers	IHL	30	1614	113	1	4.20	2	0
1981-82—Maine Mariners	AHL	25	1396	76	0	3.27	0	0
1981-82—Toledo Goaldiggers	IHL	4	248	11	0	2.66	0	0
1982-83—Toledo Goaldiggers	IHL	13	785	52	0	3.97	0	0
1982-83—Maine Mariners	AHL	30	1739	109	0	3.76	0	2
1983-84—Maine Mariners (d)	AHL	38	2158	145	0	4.03	0	0
1984-85—Maine Mariners (b)	AHL	55	3245	168	*4	3.11	1	8
1985-86—New Jersey Devils	NHL	4	188	13	1	4.15	0	0
1985-86—Maine Mariners (b-e-f-g)	AHL	50	2862	161	1	3.38	1	8
1986-87—Adirondack Red Wings	AHL	25	1397	98	1	4.21	1	4
1986-87—Detroit Red Wings	NHL	6	342	16	0	2.81	0	0
1987-88—Adirondack Red Wings	AHL	32	1826	104	2	3.42	1	8
1987-88—Detroit Red Wings	NHL	6	294	16	0	3.27	0	2
1988-89—Detroit Red Wings	NHL	4	141	9	0	3.83	0	0
1988-89—Adirondack Red Wings	AHL	34	2054	113	2	3.30	2	10
1989-90—Detroit Red Wings (h)	NHL	14	607	38	0	3.76	0	2
1989-90—Adirondack Red Wings	AHL	13	785	40	0	3.06	0	6
NHL TOTALS		34	1572	92	1	3.51	0	4

(c)—September, 1979—Signed by Philadelphia Flyers as a free agent.
(d)—August, 1984—Traded by Philadelphia Flyers to New Jersey Devils for future considerations.
(e)—Shared Harry (Hap) Holmes Memorial Trophy with teammate Karl Friesen (Top Goalies).
(f)—Won Baz Bastien Trophy (Coaches pick as top Goalie).
(g)—August, 1986—Traded by New Jersey Devils to Detroit Red Wings for Steve Richmond.
(h)—June 26, 1990—Sold by Detroit Red Wings to New York Rangers for $1.

JEFFERY STOLP

Goaltender . . . 6' . . . 175 lbs. . . . Born, Grand Rapids, Minn., June 20, 1970 . . . Shoots left.

Year	Team	League	Games	Mins.	Goals	SO.	Avg.	A.	Pen.
1986-87—Greenway H.S.	Minn. H.S.	24	1080	39	1	2.17	..	..
1987-88—Greenway H.S. (c)	Minn. H.S.	23	1035	57	1	3.30	..	..
1988-89—Univ. of Minnesota	WCHA	16	742	45	0	3.64	1	0
1989-90—Univ. of Minnesota	WCHA	10	417	33	1	4.75	0	4

(c)—June, 1988—Drafted by Minnesota North Stars in 1988 NHL entry draft. Fourth North Stars pick, 64th overall, fourth round.

RICHARD TABARACCI

Goaltender . . . 5'10" . . . 185 lbs. . . . Born, Toronto, Ont., January 2, 1969 . . . Shoots left.

Year	Team	League	Games	Mins.	Goals	SO.	Avg.	A.	Pen.
1985-86—Markha Waxers	OHA	40	2176	188	1	5.18	..	..
1986-87—Cornwall Royals (c)	OHL	59	3347	290	1	5.20	1	30
1987-88—Cornwall Royals (a)	OHL	58	3448	200	2	3.48	2	44
1987-88—Muskegon Lumberjacks (d)	IHL	..	..	..	..	..	..	..
1988-89—Cornwall Royals (b)	OHL	50	2974	210	1	4.24	6	69
1988-89—Pittsburgh Penguins (e)	NHL	1	33	4	0	7.27	0	0
1989-90—Moncton Hawks	AHL	27	1580	107	2	4.06	0	38
1989-90—Fort Wayne Komets	IHL	22	1064	73	0	4.12	2	66
NHL TOTALS		1	33	4	0	7.27	0	0

(c)—June, 1987—Drafted as underage junior by Pittsburgh Penguins in 1987 NHL entry draft. Second Penguins pick, 26th overall, second round.
(d)—No regular season record. Played one playoff game.
(e)—June 17, 1989—Traded with Randy Cunneyworth and Dave McLlwain by Pittsburgh Penguins to Winnipeg Jets for Andrew McBain, Jim Kyte and Randy Gilhen.

KARI TAKKO

Goaltender . . . 6'2" . . . 182 lbs. . . . Born, Kaupunki, Finland, June 23, 1963 . . . Shoots left . . . (December, 1988)—Missed five weeks due to shingles of the ear . . . (August 31, 1989)—Broke right ankle . . . (April, 1990)—Surgery to knee.

Year Team	League	Games	Mins.	Goals	SO.	Avg.	A.	Pen.
1985-86—Springfield Indians (c)	AHL	43	2386	161	1	4.05	0	6
1985-86—Minnesota North Stars (d)	NHL	1	60	3	0	3.00	0	0
1986-87—Springfield Indians	AHL	5	300	16	1	3.20	0	0
1986-87—Minnesota North Stars	NHL	38	2075	119	0	3.44	0	14
1987-88—Minnesota North Stars	NHL	37	1919	143	1	4.47	0	8
1988-89—Minnesota North Stars	NHL	32	1603	93	0	3.48	0	6
1989-90—Minnesota North Stars	NHL	21	1012	68	0	4.03	1	2
1989-90—Kalamazoo Wings	IHL	1	59	5	0	5.08	0	0
NHL TOTALS		129	6669	426	1	3.83	1	30

(c)—June, 1981—Drafted by Quebec Nordiques in 1981 NHL entry draft. Eighth Nordiques pick, 200th overall, 10th round.
(d)—June, 1984—Drafted by Minnesota North Stars in 1984 NHL entry draft. Fifth North Stars pick, 97th overall, fifth round.

JOHN TANNER

Goaltender . . . 6'3" . . . 182 lbs. . . . Born, Cambridge, Ont., March 17, 1971 . . . Shoots left.

Year Team	League	Games	Mins.	Goals	SO.	Avg.	A.	Pen.
1986-87—New Hamburg Jr. C	OHA	15	889	83	0	5.60	..	..
1987-88—Peterborough Petes	OHL	26	1532	88	0	3.45	1	8
1988-89—Peterborough Petes (c)	OHL	34	1923	107	2	3.34	1	32
1989-90—Quebec Nordiques	NHL	1	60	3	0	3.00	0	0
1989-90—Peterborough Petes (d)	OHL	18	1037	70	0	4.05	1	37
1989-90—London Knights	OHL	19	1097	53	1	2.90	5	24
NHL TOTALS		1	60	3	0	3.00	0	0

(c)—June, 1989—Drafted by Quebec Nordiques in 1989 NHL entry draft. Fourth Nordiques pick, 54th overall, third round.
(d)—January, 1990—Traded by Peterborough Petes to London Knights for a second-round 1990 draft pick they had acquired earlier from Windsor, and second and third-round 1991 draft picks.

CHRISTOPHER ARNOLD TERRERI

Goaltender . . . 5'9" . . . 155 lbs. . . . Born, Warwick, R.I., November 15, 1964 . . . Shoots left . . . (October, 1986)—Strained knee.

Year Team	League	Games	Mins.	Goals	SO.	Avg.	A.	Pen.
1982-83—Providence College (c)	ECAC	11	529	17	..	1.93	..	..
1983-84—Providence College	ECAC	10	391	20	..	3.07	0	2
1984-85—Providence College (d-e)	H. East	41	2515	131	..	3.12	0	10
1985-86—Providence College	H. East	27	1540	96	0	3.74	0	4
1986-87—Maine Mariners	AHL	14	765	57	0	4.47	0	0
1986-87—New Jersey Devils	NHL	7	286	21	0	4.41	0	0
1987-88—Utica Devils	AHL	7	399	18	0	2.71	0	0
1987-88—U.S. Olympic Team	Int'l	29	1558	95	0	3.66	..	..
1988-89—New Jersey Devils	NHL	8	402	18	0	2.69	0	2
1988-89—Utica Devils	AHL	39	2314	132	0	3.42	4	6
1989-90—New Jersey Devils	NHL	35	1931	110	0	3.42	0	0
NHL TOTALS		50	2619	149	0	3.41	0	2

(c)—June, 1983—Drafted by New Jersey Devils in 1983 NHL entry draft. Third Devils pick, 87th overall, fifth round.
(d)—Named First team All-America (East).
(e)—Hockey East MVP.

RON TUGNUTT

Goaltender . . . 5'11" . . . 155 lbs. . . . Born, Scarborough, Ont., October 22, 1967 . . . Shoots left . . . (March, 1989)—Sprained ankle . . . (January 13, 1990)—Sprained knee vs. New Jersey.

Year Team	League	Games	Mins.	Goals	SO.	Avg.	A.	Pen.
1984-85—Peterborough Petes (c)	OHL	18	938	59	0	3.77	1	4
1985-86—Peterborough Petes (d-e)	OHL	26	1543	74	1	2.88	0	4
1986-87—Peterborough Petes	OHL	31	1891	88	2	*2.79	1	4
1987-88—Quebec Nordiques	NHL	6	284	16	0	3.38	1	0
1987-88—Fredericton Express	AHL	34	1962	118	1	3.61	1	13
1988-89—Quebec Nordiques	NHL	26	1367	82	0	3.60	3	2
1988-89—Halifax Citadels	AHL	24	1368	79	1	3.46	0	4
1989-90—Quebec Nordiques	NHL	35	1978	152	0	4.61	0	2
1989-90—Halifax Citadels	AHL	6	366	23	0	3.77	1	0
NHL TOTALS		67	3629	250	0	4.13	4	4

(c)—Won F.W. Dinty Moore Trophy (Lowest average by a rookie goalie).
(d)—Shared Dave Pinkney Trophy with teammate Kay Whitmore (Top Goalies).
(e)—June, 1986—Drafted as underage junior by Quebec Nordiques in 1986 NHL entry draft. Fourth Nordiques pick, 81st overall, fourth round.

JOHN VANBIESBROUCK

Goaltender . . . 5'7" . . . 175 lbs. . . . Born, Detroit, Mich., September 4, 1963 . . . Shoots left . . . (October, 1987)—Fractured jaw when struck by shot of teammate Tomas Sandstrom during practice . . . (June, 1988)—Severely cut wrist in accident at home, requiring micro surgery . . . (May 11, 1990)—Knee surgery.

Year Team	League	Games	Mins.	Goals	SO.	Avg.	A.	Pen.
1980-81—S.S. Marie Greyhounds (c-d)	OHL	56	2941	203	0	4.14	2	10
1981-82—S.S. Marie Greyhounds	OHL	31	1686	102	0	3.63	0	23
1981-82—New York Rangers	NHL	1	60	1	0	1.00	0	0
1982-83—S.S. Marie Greyhounds	OHL	*62	3471	209	0	3.61	2	10
1983-84—New York Rangers	NHL	3	180	10	0	3.33	0	2
1983-84—Tulsa Oilers	CHL	37	2153	124	*3	3.46	0	6
1984-85—New York Rangers	NHL	42	2358	166	1	4.22	5	17
1985-86—New Rangers (a-e)	NHL	61	3326	184	3	3.32	3	16
1986-87—New York Rangers	NHL	50	2656	161	0	3.64	1	18
1987-88—New York Rangers	NHL	56	3319	187	2	3.38	5	46
1988-89—New York Rangers	NHL	56	3207	197	0	3.69	2	30
1989-90—New York Rangers	NHL	47	2734	154	1	3.38	2	24
NHL TOTALS		316	17840	1060	7	3.57	18	153

(c)—Winner of Dinty Moore Trophy (Lowest Individual Goalie average in a rookie season).
(d)—June, 1981—Drafted by New York Rangers in 1981 NHL entry draft. Fifth Rangers pick, 72nd overall, fourth round.
(e)—Won Vezina Trophy (Top NHL Goaltender).

MIKE VERNON

Goaltender . . . 5'7" . . . 150 lbs. . . . Born, Calgary, Alta., February 24, 1963 . . . Shoots left . . . Set NHL record in 1986 playoffs for most minutes played (1229) . . . (March 2, 1988)—Injured hip in team practice . . . (February, 1989)—Back spasms . . . (October, 1989)—Back spasms . . . (March, 1990)—Back spasms and missed 10 games.

Year Team	League	Games	Mins.	Goals	SO.	Avg.	A.	Pen.
1980-81—Calgary Wranglers (c)	WHL	59	3154	198	1	3.77	3	21
1981-82—Calgary Wranglers	WHL	42	2329	143	*3	*3.68	0	0
1982-83—Calgary Wranglers	WHL	50	2856	155	*3	*3.26	2	6
1982-83—Calgary Flames (a-d-e)	NHL	2	100	11	0	6.59	0	0
1983-84—Calgary Flames	NHL	1	11	4	0	21.82	0	0
1983-84—Colorado Flames (b)	CHL	*46	*2648	148	1	*3.35	3	4
1984-85—Moncton Golden Flames	AHL	41	2050	134	0	3.92	1	8
1985-86—Salt Lake Golden Eagles	IHL	10	601	34	1	3.39	2	2
1985-86—Moncton Golden Flames	AHL	6	374	21	0	3.37	0	0
1985-86—Calgary Flames (f)	NHL	18	921	52	1	3.39	1	4
1986-87—Calgary Flames	NHL	54	2957	178	1	3.61	2	14
1987-88—Calgary Flames	NHL	64	3565	210	1	3.53	7	47
1988-89—Calgary Flames (b-g)	NHL	52	2938	130	0	2.65	4	18
1989-90—Calgary Flames	NHL	47	2795	146	0	3.13	3	21
NHL TOTALS		238	13287	731	3	3.30	17	104

(c)—June, 1981—Drafted by Calgary Flames in 1981 NHL entry draft. Second Flames pick, 56th overall, third round.
(d)—Named WHL MVP.
(e)—Won WHL goaltending trophy.
(f)—Led NHL playoffs in games played (21), minutes (1229) and goals allowed (60).
(g)—Led NHL playoffs with three shutouts.

JIMMY WAITE

Goaltender . . . 6' . . . 165 lbs. . . . Born, Sherbrooke, Que., April 15, 1969 . . . Shoots right . . . (December 6, 1988)—Broken collarbone at Pittsburgh.

Year Team	League	Games	Mins.	Goals	SO.	Avg.	A.	Pen.
1985-86—Cantonniers de l'est	Que. Midget	29	1643	143	0	5.22	..	....
1986-87—Chicoutimi Sagueneens (c)	QMJHL	50	2569	209	*2	4.88	2	12
1987-88—Chicoutimi Sagueneens	QMJHL	36	200	150	0	4.50	0	14
1988-89—Chicago Black Hawks	NHL	11	494	43	0	5.22	0	0
1988-89—Saginaw Hawks	IHL	5	304	10	0	1.97	0	0
1989-90—Indianapolis Ice (a-d)	IHL	54	3207	135	5	*2.53	2	21
1989-90—Chicago Black Hawks	NHL	4	183	14	0	4.59	0	0
NHL TOTALS		15	677	57	0	5.05	0	0

(c)—June, 1987—Drafted as underage junior by Chicago Black Hawks in 1987 NHL entry draft. First Black Hawks pick, eighth overall, first round.
(d)—Won James Norris Memorial Trophy (Top IHL Goaltender).

DARCY WAKALUK

Goaltender . . . 5'11" . . . 180 lbs. . . . Born, Pincher Creek, Alta., March 14, 1966 . . . Shoots left . . . (December 5, 1987)—Scored a goal into an empty Maine Mariners net . . . (January 10, 1988)—Played Left Wing vs. Nova Scotia.

Year Team	League	Games	Mins.	Goals	SO.	Avg.	A.	Pen.
1982-83—Pincher Creek Oilers	BC Midget	38	2282	116	0	3.05	..	....
1983-84—Kelowna Wings (c)	WHL	31	1555	163	0	6.29	0	16
1985-86—Kelowna Wings	WHL	54	3094	244	0	4.73	1	46
1985-86—Spokane Chiefs	WHL	47	2562	224	1	5.25	8	18
1986-87—Rochester Americans	AHL	11	545	26	0	2.86	1	12
1987-88—Rochester Americans	AHL	55	2763	159	0	3.45	6	36
1988-89—Buffalo Sabres	NHL	6	214	15	0	4.21	0	0
1988-89—Rochester Americans	AHL	33	1566	97	1	3.72	2	10
1989-90—Rochester Americans	AHL	56	3095	173	2	3.35	7	38
NHL TOTALS		6	214	15	0	4.21	0	0

(c)—June, 1984—Drafted as underage junior by Buffalo Sabres in 1984 NHL entry draft. Seventh Sabres pick, 144th overall, seventh round.

RICK WAMSLEY

Goaltender . . . 5'11" . . . 185 lbs. . . . Born, Simcoe, Ont., May 25, 1959 . . . Shoots left . . . (October 16, 1985)—Bruised right hand at Calgary, required surgery and missed nine games . . . (March, 1988)—Pulled groin vs. Hartford.

Year Team	League	Games	Mins.	Goals	SO.	Avg.	A.	Pen.
1976-77—St. Catharines Fincups	OMJHL	12	647	36	0	3.34	0	0
1977-78—Hamilton Fincups (c)	OMJHL	25	1495	74	2	*2.97	1	12
1978-79—Brantford Alexanders (d)	OMJHL	24	1444	128	0	5.32	0	2
1979-80—Nova Scotia Voyageurs	AHL	40	2305	125	2	3.25	3	12
1980-81—Nova Scotia Voyageurs (e)	AHL	43	2372	155	0	3.92	5	10
1980-81—Montreal Canadiens	NHL	5	253	8	1	1.90	0	0
1981-82—Montreal Canadiens (f-g)	NHL	38	2206	101	2	2.75	2	4
1982-83—Montreal Canadiens	NHL	46	2583	151	0	3.51	1	4
1983-84—Montreal Canadiens (h)	NHL	42	2333	144	2	3.70	3	6
1984-85—St. Louis Blues	NHL	40	2319	126	0	3.26	1	0
1985-86—St. Louis Blues	NHL	42	2517	144	1	3.43	0	2
1986-87—St. Louis Blues	NHL	41	2410	142	0	3.54	0	10

Year	Team	League	Games	Mins.	Goals	SO.	Avg.	A.	Pen.
1987-88—St. Louis Blues (i)		NHL	31	1818	103	2	3.40	0	14
1987-88—Calgary Flames		NHL	2	73	5	0	4.11	0	0
1988-89—Calgary Flames		NHL	35	1927	95	2	2.96	1	8
1989-90—Calgary Flames		NHL	36	1969	107	2	3.26	0	4
NHL TOTALS			358	20408	1126	12	3.31	8	52

(c)—Shared Dave Pinkney Trophy (Leading Goalies) with Al Jensen.

(d)—August, 1979—Drafted by Montreal Canadiens in 1979 NHL entry draft. Fifth Canadiens pick, 58th overall, third round.

(e)—Led AHL playoffs with a 1.81 goals-against average.

(f)—Co-winner of Bill Jennings Trophy (Lowest team goaltending average) with teammate Denis Herron.

(g)—Led NHL Playoffs with 2.20 goals-against average.

(h)—June, 1984—Traded with second-round (Brian Benning) and third-round (Robert Dirk) 1984 draft picks by Montreal Canadiens to St. Louis Blues for first-round (Shayne Corson) and second-round (Stephane Richer) 1984 draft picks.

(i)—March, 1988—Traded with Rob Ramage by St. Louis Blues to Calgary Flames for Brett Hull and Steve Bozek.

STEVE WEEKS

Goaltender . . . 5'11" . . . 165 lbs. . . . Born, Scarborough, Ont., June 30, 1958 . . . Shoots left.

Year	Team	League	Games	Mins.	Goals	SO.	Avg.	A.	Pen.
1975-76—Toronto Marlboros		OMJHL	18	873	73	0	4.95	0	0
1976-77—Northern Michigan Univ.		CCHA	16	811	58	0	4.29	..	....
1977-78—Northern Michigan Univ. (c)		CCHA	19	1015	56	1	3.31	..	....
1978-79—Northern Michigan Univ.		CCHA	....	....	....	..	......	..	....
1979-80—North. Mich. U. (a-d-e)		CCHA	36	2133	105	0	*2.95	1	2
1980-81—New Haven Nighthawks		AHL	36	2065	142	1	4.13	0	4
1980-81—New York Rangers		NHL	1	60	2	0	2.00	0	0
1981-82—New York Rangers		NHL	49	2852	179	1	3.77	3	0
1982-83—Tulsa Oilers		CHL	19	1116	60	0	3.23	1	0
1982-83—New York Rangers		NHL	18	1040	68	0	3.92	2	0
1983-84—New York Rangers		NHL	26	1361	90	0	3.97	0	4
1983-84—Tulsa Oilers (f)		CHL	3	180	7	0	2.33	0	0
1984-85—Binghamton Whalers		AHL	5	303	13	0	2.57	0	0
1984-85—Hartford Whalers		NHL	24	1457	93	2	3.79	0	0
1985-86—Hartford Whalers		NHL	27	1544	99	1	3.85	1	9
1986-87—Hartford Whalers		NHL	25	1367	78	1	3.42	0	0
1987-88—Hartford Whalers (g)		NHL	18	918	55	0	3.59	0	2
1987-88—Vancouver Canucks		NHL	9	550	31	0	3.38	0	0
1988-89—Vancouver Canucks		NHL	35	2056	102	0	2.98	0	4
1989-90—Vancouver Canucks		NHL	21	1142	79	0	4.15	0	0
NHL TOTALS			253	14347	876	5	3.66	6	19

(c)—June, 1978—Drafted by New York Rangers in 1978 NHL entry draft. Twelfth Rangers pick, 176th overall, 11th round.

(d)—Named as Most Valuable Player of the CCHA.

(e)—Named to NCAA Tournament All-Star team.

(f)—September, 1984—Traded by New York Rangers to Hartford Whalers for future considerations.

(g)—March, 1988—Traded by Hartford Whalers to Vancouver Canucks for Richard Brodeur.

KAY WHITMORE

Goaltender . . . 6' . . . 170 lbs. . . . Born, Sudbury, Ont., April 10, 1967 . . . Shoots left.

Year	Team	League	Games	Mins.	Goals	SO.	Avg.	A.	Pen.
1982-83—Sudbury Major Midgets		OHA	43	2580	108	4	2.51	..	....
1983-84—Peterborough Petes		OHL	29	1471	110	0	4.49	2	2
1984-85—Peterborough Petes (c)		OHL	53	3077	172	*2	3.35	5	33
1985-86—Peterborough Petes (a-d)		OHL	41	2467	114	*3	*2.77	3	14
1986-87—Peterborough Petes		OHL	36	2159	118	1	3.28	4	13
1987-88—Binghamton Whalers		AHL	38	2137	121	3	3.40	1	20

Year	Team	League	Games	Mins.	Goals	SO.	Avg.	A.	Pen.
1988-89—Binghamton Whalers		AHL	56	3200	241	1	4.52	6	50
1988-89—Hartford Whalers		NHL	3	180	10	0	3.33	2	0
1989-90—Binghamton Whalers		AHL	24	1386	109	0	4.72	0	16
1989-90—Hartford Whalers		NHL	9	442	26	0	3.53	1	4
NHL TOTALS			12	622	36	0	3.47	3	4

(c)—June, 1985—Drafted as underage junior by Hartford Whalers in 1985 NHL entry draft. Second Whalers pick, 26th overall, second round.

(d)—Shared Dave Pinkney Trophy with teammate Ron Tugnutt (Top Goalies).

KEN WREGGET

Goaltender . . . 6'1" . . . 180 lbs. . . . Born, Brandon, Man., March 25, 1964 . . . Shoots left . . . (December 26, 1985)—Injured knee at Hartford . . . (November 1, 1989)—Torn hamstring at Detroit and missed seven games . . . (March 24, 1990)—Pulled hamstring vs. New Jersey.

Year	Team	League	Games	Mins.	Goals	SO.	Avg.	A.	Pen.
1981-82—Lethbridge Broncos (c)		WHL	36	1713	118	1	4.13	0	0
1982-83—Lethbridge Broncos (d)		WHL	48	2696	157	1	3.49	1	18
1983-84—Lethbridge Broncos (a)		WHL	53	3052	161	0	*3.16	1	26
1983-84—Toronto Maple Leafs		NHL	3	165	14	0	5.09	0	0
1984-85—Toronto Maple Leafs		NHL	23	1278	103	0	4.84	1	10
1984-85—St. Catharines Saints		AHL	12	688	48	0	4.19	1	0
1985-86—St. Catharines Saints		AHL	18	1058	78	1	4.42	2	8
1985-86—Toronto Maple Leafs		NHL	30	1566	113	0	4.33	0	16
1986-87—Toronto Maple Leafs		NHL	56	3026	200	0	3.97	4	20
1987-88—Toronto Maple Leafs		NHL	56	3000	222	2	4.44	5	40
1988-89—Toronto Maple Leafs (e)		NHL	32	1888	139	0	4.42	3	20
1988-89—Philadelphia Flyers		NHL	3	130	13	0	6.00	0	0
1989-90—Philadelphia Flyers		NHL	51	2961	169	0	3.42	2	12
NHL TOTALS			254	14014	973	2	4.17	15	118

(c)—June, 1982—Drafted as underage junior by Toronto Maple Leafs in 1982 NHL entry draft. Fourth Maple Leafs pick, 45th overall, third round.

(d)—Led WHL playoffs with 3.02 average and one shutout.

(e)—March 6, 1989—Traded by Toronto Maple Leafs to Philadelphia Flyers for two first-round 1989 draft picks. (Rob Pearson and Steve Bancroft).

WENDELL YOUNG

Goaltender . . . 5'8" . . . 185 lbs. . . . Born, Halifax, N.S., August 1, 1963 . . . Shoots left . . . (October, 1988)—Strained ankle.

Year	Team	League	Games	Mins.	Goals	SO.	Avg.	A.	Pen.
1979-80—Cole Harbour		NSJHL	..	1446	94	0	3.90	..	..
1980-81—Kitchener Rangers (c)		OHL	42	2215	164	1	4.44	2	29
1981-82—Kitchener Rangers		OHL	*60	*3470	195	1	3.37	1	4
1982-83—Kitchener Rangers		OHL	61	*3611	231	1	3.84	7	22
1983-84—Salt Lake Golden Eagles		CHL	20	1094	80	0	4.39	1	2
1983-84—Fredericton Express		AHL	11	569	39	1	4.11	2	4
1983-84—Milwaukee Admirals		IHL	6	339	17	0	3.01	0	0
1984-85—Fredericton Express		AHL	22	1242	83	0	4.01	0	0
1985-86—Fredericton Express		AHL	24	1457	78	0	3.21	0	2
1985-86—Vancouver Canucks		NHL	22	1023	61	0	3.58	0	0
1986-87—Fredericton Express		AHL	30	1676	118	0	4.22	4	8
1986-87—Vancouver Canucks (d)		NHL	8	420	35	0	5.00	1	0
1987-88—Philadelphia Flyers		NHL	6	320	20	0	3.75	0	0
1987-88—Hershey Bears		AHL	51	2922	135	1	2.77	2	8
1988-89—Pittsburgh Penguins		NHL	22	1150	92	0	4.80	2	4
1988-89—Muskegon Lumberjacks		IHL	2	125	7	0	3.36	0	0
1989-90—Pittsburgh Penguins		NHL	43	2318	161	1	4.17	4	8
NHL TOTALS			101	5231	369	1	4.23	7	12

(c)—June, 1981—Drafted as underage junior by Vancouver Canucks in 1981 NHL entry draft. Third Canucks pick, 73rd overall, fourth round.

(d)—August, 1987—Traded with a 1990 third-round draft choice by Vancouver Canucks to Philadelphia Flyers for Daryl Stanley and Darren Jensen.